CURRENT TRENDS IN LINGUISTICS

VOLUME I

# CURRENT TRENDS IN LINGUISTICS

*Edited by*

THOMAS A. SEBEOK

VOLUME I

## *Soviet and East European Linguistics*

*Associate Editors:*

PAUL L. GARVIN · HORACE LUNT

EDWARD STANKIEWICZ

*Assistant Editor:* JOHN R. KRUEGER

*Assistant to the Editor:* ROSE NASH

MOUTON PUBLISHERS · THE HAGUE · PARIS · NEW YORK

*First edition: 1963*
*Second edition: 1980*

ISBN: 90 279 1242 4



Printed in Great Britain

# EDITOR'S INTRODUCTION

A symposium "to develop, and make recommendations concerning, a national program for systematic evaluation, selection, possible abstracting and/or translation, republication, and dissemination of Russian and East European linguistic literature – with special emphasis on research materials in mathematical linguistics and information processing – for use of the American scholarly community" was held under the auspices of the Indiana University Research Center in Anthropology, Folklore, and Linguistics, on December 2–3, 1960, under a grant from the National Science Foundation. This meeting resulted in a number of formal recommendations which were then referred for further discussion and detailed planning to members of a standing committee established by the conference as a whole. Since 1960, this committee has undergone several alterations both in name and in composition, reflecting a series of changes from a regionally circumscribed approach to one less concerned with specific applications than refashioned to explore implications of the problems of information flow – including storage, retrieval, dissemination, in brief, systems design – in the field of general linguistics. The group is now called the Committee on Linguistic Information. International in membership, it currently functions under the auspices of the Center for Applied Linguistics of the Modern Language Association of America (Charles A. Ferguson succeeded Thomas A. Sebeok as its Chairman, beginning 1963).

The Committee, at its initial meeting, March 6, 1961, discussed a range of agenda including the following recommendation of the original conferees: "... that a series of annual volumes be commissioned to assess the current state of linguistic activity in all fields and all countries in the area with which we are concerned". The undersigned was selected to serve as over-all Editor of the series, which came to be entitled *Current Trends in Linguistics*, and which will continue to be published under the imprint of Mouton & Co.

It was further agreed that the first volume should be devoted to Soviet and East European linguistics. It is intended that future volumes appear at intervals of approximately two years. The second volume, to be published in 1965, will cover East Asian linguistics; it is already in preparation. The third volume – to be consolidated on the basis of twenty-eight lectures which will be delivered in connection with the 1964 Linguistic Institute, at Indiana University – will feature seven topics in general linguistics, each representing an important recent development in linguistic theory or practice. The fourth and subsequent volumes will revert to the pattern exemplified in the first two, that is, they will assemble parallel materials concerning current trends in linguistics relating to South and South East Asia, the Middle East and Africa, Central and South America, Oceania, and the like.

The present work was designed in consultation with members of our Committee on Linguistic Information and, of course, the three Associate Editors of Vol. I. The Assistant Editor assumed particular responsibility for technical considerations of style (although it must be emphasized that we did not seek absolute uniformity: on the contrary, we encouraged our contributors to write their respective chapters to suit their individual taste on the one hand, and the requirements of their topic on the other). Several manuscripts in need of restatement in English were also assigned to the Assistant Editor, who accomplished this difficult task much to the benefit of the articles in question.

In addition to her other duties, involving extensive correspondence and proofreading, the Assistant to the Editor compiled the Biographical Notes, Linguistic Index, and the Index of Names.

It was originally intended that a further section be included supplying biographical details concerning Soviet and East European linguists, but it was later decided to incorporate the information we were able to gather in the Roster of Linguists being compiled by the Center for Applied Linguistics. Pertinent inquiries may be addressed there.

Part Two was also to have included a chapter on linguistics in Rumania. Regrettably, the colleague invited to furnish this was forced to withdraw at a juncture when it proved too late for us to secure the collaboration of another specialist.

The project was financed by a grant (G19468) from the National Science Foundation to the Indiana University Research Center in Anthropology, Folklore, and Linguistics. This assistance is acknowledged with pleasure. The Editor also wishes to express his gratitude to the twenty-two contributors, his editorial associates, and the staff of Mouton & Co., for their splendid cooperation.

Vienna, July 1, 1963 Thomas A. Sebeok

# CONTENTS

## PART TWO: LINGUISTICS IN EASTERN EUROPE

# MASTER LIST OF ABBREVIATIONS

| | |
|---|---|
| ALH | *Acta Linguistica Academiae Scientiarum Hungaricae*. Budapest. |
| AN | Akademija Nauk/Navuk. |
| AnnIFiES | *Annuaire de l'Institut Finlandais d'Études Sovietiques*. Helsinki. |
| AO | *Archiv Orientální*. Prague. |
| AOH | *Acta Orientalia Academiae Scientiarum Hungaricae*. Budapest. |
| ASEER | *The American Slavic and East European Review*. New York. |
| AUC-Ph | *Acta Universitatis Carolinae, Filologica*. Prague. |
| BDU | *Dasledavanni pa belaruskaj i ruskaj movax*. Belaruski dzjaržawny universitet imja Ul. I. Lenina, kafedry belaruskaj i ruskaj movaw (Minsk, 1958 & 1960). |
| BOPMP | *Bjulleten' ob''edinenija po problemam mašinnogo perevoda*. Moscow. |
| BPTJ | *Biuletyn polskiego towarzystwa językoznawczego*. Bulletin de la Société polonaise de Linguistique. Wrocław-Kraków. |
| BSL | *Bulletin de la Société de Linguistique de Paris*. |
| BəlEz | *Bəlgarski ezik*. Sofia. |
| ČČM | *Časopis Českého nusea*. Prague. |
| ČMF | *Časopis pro moderní filologii*. Prague. |
| ČSAV | Československá akademie věd. |
| DAN | *Doklady Akademii Nauk SSSR*. Moscow-Leningrad. |
| DB | *Dialektolohičnyj bjuleten'*, AN UkRSR, Instytut movoznavstva im. O. Potebni. Kiev. |
| DLM | *Doslidžennja z literaturoznavstva ta movoznavstva. Zbirnyk*. Č. II, Doslidžennja z movoznavstva. Kyjivs'kyj derzavnyj universytet im. T. Ševčenka. Kiev. |
| DML | *Doslidzennja z movy ta literatury = Naukovi zapysky Instytutu suspil'nyx nauk AN UkRSR*, AN UkRSR, L'vivs'kyj filial. Kiev. |
| DMUM | *Doslidžennja i materialy z ukrajins'koji movy*, Vols. 1-3 (1959-61). AN UkRSR Instytut suspil'nyx nauk. Kiev. |
| DokK | *Doklady na Konferencii po obrabotke informacii, mašinnomu perevodu i avtomatičeskomu čteniju teksta* (Moscow, 1961). |
| Doslidžennja | *Doslidžennja z movoznavstva v Ukrajins'kij RSR za sorok rokiv*, AN UkRSR, Instytut movoznavstva im. O. Potebni (Kiev, 1959). |
| DSIJa | *Doklady i soobščenija Instituta jazykoznanija*. AN SSSR. Moscow. |
| DSIRJa | *Doklady i soobščenija Instituta russkogo jazyka*. Moscow-Leningrad. |
| DSMU | *Doklady i soobščenija Moskovskogo gosudarstvennogo Universiteta*. |
| DSUM | *Doslidžennja z syntaksysu ukrajins'koji movy*. AN UkRSR, Instytut movoznavstva im. O. Potebni (Kiev, 1958). |
| DUM | *Doslidžennja z ukrajins'koji movy (Zbirnyk statej aspirantiv ta dysertantiv)*. AN UkRSR, Instytut movoznavstva im. O. Potebni (Kiev, 1958). |
| EMNyF | *Egyetemi Magyar Nyelvészeti Füzetek*. Budapest. |
| ESA | *Emakeele seltsi aastaraamat*. Tallinn. |
| ETAT | *Eestu NSV Teaduste Akadeemia Toimetised, Ühiskonnateaduste seeria/Izvestija AN Estonskoj. SSR, Serija obščestvennyx nauk*. Tallinn. |
| EzLit | *Ezik i literatura*. Sofia. |
| FUF | *Finnisch-Ugrische Forschungen*. Helsinki. |
| FZ | *Filolohičnyj zbirnyk*. AN UkRSR, Ukrajins'kyj komitet slavistiv (Kiev, 1958). |

| | |
|---|---|
| GodSU | *Godišnik na Sofijskija Universitet*. Sofia. |
| IAN | *Izvestija AN SSSR*. Moscow-Leningrad. |
| IJa AN SSSR | Institut jazykoznanija AN SSSR. Moscow. |
| IJaŠ | *Inostrannye jazyki v škole*. Moscow. |
| IJSLP | *International Journal of Slavic Linguistics and Poetics*. The Hague. |
| IKJa | *Iberijsko-kavkazskoe jazykoznanie*. Tbilisi. |
| ISl | Institut slavjanovedenija, AN SSSR. Moscow. |
| ISN | *Naukovi zapysky Instytutu suspil'nyx nauk*. AN UkRSR. (Kiev, 1961). |
| IzvSS | *Izvestija na Seminara po slavjanska filologija pri Universiteta v Sofija*. Sofia. |
| IzvAN | *Izvestija AN SSSR, Otdelenie literatury i jazyka*. Moscow-Leningrad. |
| IzvIBE | *Izvestija na Instituta za bəlgarski ezik pri Bəlgarskata akademija na naukite*. Sofia. |
| JaD | *Jazyki Dagestana*. Maxačkala. |
| JaSKD | *Jazyki Severnogo Kavkaza i Dagestana*. Moscow-Leningrad. |
| Jęz. Ros. | *Język rosyjski*. Warsaw. |
| JP | *Język polski*. Cracow. |
| JSS | *Journal of Semitic Studies*. Manchester. |
| KDU | *Naukovi zapysky*, Kyjivs'kyj deržavnyj universytet im. T. Ševčenka. Kiev. |
| KK | *Keel ja kirjandus*. Tallinn. |
| KKIU | *Keele ja kirjanduse instituudi uurimused*. Tallinn. |
| Konferencja Pomorska | Konferencja pomorska, 1954. *Prace językoznawcze*, 1956. Warsaw. |
| KSISl | *Kratkie soobščenie AN SSSR, Institut Slavjanovedenia*. Moscow. |
| LB | *Leksykohrafičnyj bjuleten'*, AN UkRSR, Instytut movoznavstva im. O. Potebni. Kiev. |
| LGU | Leningradskij gosudarstvennyj universitet im. A. Ždanova. |
| LK | *Literatūra ir kalba*. Vilna. |
| LKK | *Lietuvių kalbotyros klausimai*. Vilna. |
| LL | *Language Learning*. Ann Arbor, Michigan. |
| LMAD | *Lietuvos TSR Mokslu akademijos Darbai, Serija A*. Vilna. |
| LOIKFN | Leningradskoe obščestvo issledovatelej kul'tury finnougorskix narodnostej. |
| LPI | *Naukovi zapysku*. L'vivs'kyj deržavnyj pedahohičnyj instytut. Lviv. |
| LPos | *Lingua posnaniensis*. Poznan. |
| ŁTN | Łodzkie Towarzystwo Naukowe. |
| LUZR | *Pētera Stučkas Latvijas Valsts universitātes zinātniskie raksti*. Riga. |
| LZAV | *Latvijas PSR Zinātņu Akadēmijas Vēstis*. Riga. |
| M | *Movoznavstvo, Naukovi zapysky*, AN UkRSR. Instytut movoznavstva im. O. Potebni. Kiev. |
| MakPr | *Makedonski pregled*. Sofia. |
| MGU | Moskovskij gosudarstvennyj universitet im. Ul. I. Lenina. |
| MJ | *Makedonski Jazik*. Skopje. |
| MKV | *XXV Meždunarodnyj kongress vostokovedov. Doklady delegacii SSSR*. Moscow 1960. |
| MLJ | *Modern Language Journal*. Ann Arbor, Michigan. |
| MMP | *Materialy po mašinnomu perevodu*. Leningrad. |
| MMZ | *Matėryjaly da IV mižnarodnaha zjezda slavistaw AN BelSSR*, Belaruski kamitėt slavistaw (Minsk, 1958). |
| MPPL | *Mašinnyj perevod i prikladnaja lingvistika*. Moscow. |
| NDVŠ-FN | *Naučnye doklady vyššej školy, Filologičeskie nauki*. |
| NIJaLI | Naučno-issledovatel'skij institut jazyka, literatury i istorii. |
| NIIIÈLJa | Naučno-issledovadel'skij institut istorii, ekonomiki, literatury i jazyka. |
| NIJaLIE | Naučno-issledovatel'skij institut jazyka, literatury, istorii i èkonomiki pri Sovete ministrov… |
| NÈF | *Načal'nyj ètap formirovanija russkogo nacional'nogo jazyke*. LGU. (Leningrad, 1961). |
| ODU | *Zbirnyk filolohičnoho fakul'tetu*, and *Praci*. Odes'kyj deržavnyj universytet im. I. Mečnikova. Odessa. |
| OLZ | *Orientalistische Literaturzeitung*. Berlin. |

| | |
|---|---|
| Onom. | *Onomastica.* Wrocław. |
| Pam. Lit. | *Pamiętnik literacki.* Warsaw. |
| PAN | Polska Akademia Nauk. |
| PhP | *Philologica Pragensia.* Prague. |
| PID | *Pytannja istoriji i dialektolohiji sxidnoslovjans'kyx mov = Naukovi zapysky,* Vol. 31 (1958). Černivec'kyj deržavnyj universytet. Černivci. |
| PIM | *Pracy Instytuta movaznavstva,* AN BelSSR, Instytut movaznawstva imja J. Kolasa. Minsk. |
| PK | *Problemy kibernetiki.* Moscow. |
| PKD | *Poltavs'ko-kyjivs'kyj dialekt – osnova ukrajins'koji nacional'noji movy. Zbirnyk.* AN UkRSR, Instytut movoznavstva im. O. Potebni (Kiev, 1954). |
| PMLA | *Publications of the Modern Language Association of America.* New York. |
| Por. Jęz. | *Poradnik Językowy.* Warsaw. |
| Prace Pol. | *Prace Polonistyczne.* Lodz. |
| Przeg. zach. | *Przegląd zachodni.* Poznan. |
| PSb | *Palestinskij Sbornik.* Moscow-Leningrad. |
| PSF | *Pytannja slovjans'koji filolohiji.* L'vivs'kyj deržavnyj universytet im. I. Franka. Lviv. |
| PSM | *Pytannja slovjans'koho movoznavstva,* L'vivs'kyj deržavnyj universytet im. I. Franka (Vols. 1-4 published as VSJa). |
| PUM | *Pytannja ukrajins'koho movoznavstva,* L'vivs'kyj deržavnyj universytet im. I. Franka. Lviv. |
| PV | *Problemy vostokovedenija.* Moscow (since 1959; previously SovV). |
| RES | *Revue des Études Slaves.* Paris. |
| RJaŠ | *Russkij jazyk v škole.* Moscow. |
| Rocz. Orient. | *Rocznik orientalistyczny.* |
| Rocz. Slaw. | *Rocznik slawistyczny.* Cracow. |
| Rozp. | Rozprawy. |
| RRPI | *Rīgas Pedagoģiskā institūta raksti.* Riga. |
| RVLI | *Latvijas PSR Zinātņu akadēmijas Valodas un literatūras institūta raksti.* Riga. |
| RWF | *Rozprawy wydziału filologicznego Akademii Umiejetności.* Kracow. |
| SANG | *Soobščenija AN Gruzinskoj, SSR.* Tbilisi. |
| SaS | *Slovo a slovesnost.* Prague. |
| SAU | *Sprawozdania z czynnósci i posiedzeń Polskiej Akademii Umiejętnosci.* Cracow. |
| SbBAN | *Sbornik na Bəlgarskata akademija na naukite.* Sofia. |
| SEEJ | *Slavic and East European Journal.* Bloomington, Indiana (Madison, Wisc. since 1961). |
| SFFB | *Sbornik prací Filosofické fakulty Brněnské university.* Brno. |
| SFPSł | *Studia z filologii polskiej i słowiańskiej.* Warsaw. |
| SH | *Seredn'onaddniprjans'ki hovory. Zbirnyk statej.* AN UkRSR, Instytut movoznavstva im. O. Potebni (Kiev, 1960). |
| SIJUJ | *Sprawozdania z posiedzeń naukowych Instytutu jezyko – znawstwa Uniwersytetu Jagiellonskiego za g. 1952-1953* (Kracow, 1953). |
| SJa | *Sovetskoe jazykoznanie.* Moscow. |
| SKJWar. | *Sprawozdania z posiedzeń Komisji językowej towarzystwa naukowego warszawskiego.* Warsaw. |
| Słownik Star. Słow. | Słownik Starożytności Słowiańskich. |
| SM | *Slovjans'ke movoznavstvo,* AN UkRSR. Instytut movoznavstva im. O. Potebni. Kiev. |
| SMBD | *Stat'i i materialy po bolgarskoj dialektologii.* Moscow. |
| SO | *Slavia Occidentalis.* Poznań. |
| SovÈtn | *Sovetskaja ètnografija.* Moscow-Leningrad. |
| SovF | *Sovetskoe Finnougrovedenie.* |
| SovV | *Sovetskoe vostokovedenie.* Moscow. |
| SPAN | *Sprawozdania z prac naukowych wydziału nauk społecmnych PAN.* Warsaw. |
| SpBAN | *Spisanie na Bəlgarskata akademija na naukite.* Sofia. |

| | |
|---|---|
| SSlav | *Studia Slavica Academiae Scientiarum Hungaricae.* Budapest. |
| StSer | *Studia historico-philologica serdicensia.* Sofia. |
| TAI | *Trudy Abxazskogo instituta jazyka, literatury i istorii.* Suxumi. |
| TezSML59 | *Tezisy soveščanija po matematičeskoj lingvistike (15-12 aprelja 1959 goda)* (Leningrad, 1959). |
| TIJa | *Trudy Instituta Jazykoznanija, AN SSSR.* Moscow. |
| TIV | *Trudy Instituta vostokovedenija, AN SSSR.* Moscow-Leningrad. |
| TRÜ | *Tartu riiklik ülikool.* |
| TRÜT | *Tartu riikliku ülikooli toimetised.* |
| TTGU | *Trudy Tbilisskogo gosudarstvennogo universiteta.* |
| UMŠ | *Ukrajins'ka mova v školi.* Kiev. |
| UZ | Učenye zapiski. |
| UZIC | *UZ Instituta istorii, jazyka i literatury im. G. Cadasy.* Maxačkala. |
| UZISl | *UZ Instituta slavjanovedenija.* Moscow. |
| UZIV | *UZ Instituta vostokovedenija, AN SSSR.* Moscow. |
| UZKI | *UZ Kabardino-balkarskogo n.-i. instituta.* Nal'čik. |
| UZLPedI | *UZ Leningradskogo pedagogičeskogo instituta imeni A. I. Gercena.* Leningrad. |
| UZLU | *UZ Leningradskogo ordena Lenina gosudarstwennogo Universiteta im. A. A. Zdanova.* Leningrad. |
| UZMPedI | *UZ Moskovskogo gosudarstvennogo pedagogičeskogo instituta.* Moscow. |
| UZMU | *UZ Moskovskogo gosudarstvennogo Universiteta.* Moscow. |
| V | *Vesci AN BelSSR, Seryja hramadskix navuk.* Minsk. |
| VDI | *Vestnik drevnej istorii.* Moscow. |
| VIIKJa | *Voprosy izučenija iberijsko-kavkazskix jazykov* (Moscow 1961). |
| VJa | *Voprosy jazykoznanija.* Moscow. |
| VKR | *Voprosy kultury reči.* Moscow. |
| VLU | *Vestnik Leningradskogo gosudarstvennogo Universiteta.* |
| VMU | *Vestnik Moskovskogo gosudarstvennogo Universiteta.* |
| VRJa | *Voprosy russkogo jazykoznanija,* L'vovskij gosudarstvennyj universitet im. I. Franko, Kafedra russkogo jazyka i obščego jazykoznanija. |
| VSJa | *Voprosy slavjanskogo jazykoznanija,* L'vovskij gosudarstvennyj universitet im. I. Franko. Lvov. (Continued as PSM.) |
| VSKJa | *Voprosy struktury kartvel'skix jazykov.* Tbilisi. |
| VSlJa(M) | *Voprosy slavjanskogo jazykoznanija.* Institut slavjanovedenija. Moscow. |
| VSR | *Voprosy statistiki reči* (Leningrad 1958). |
| WSP | Wyźsza Szkoła Pedagogiczna. |
| WSl | *Die Welt der Slaven.* Wiesbaden. |
| WTN | Wrocławskie Towarzystwo Naukowe. |
| WZKM | *Wiener Zeitschrift für die Kunde des Morgenlandes.* Vienna. |
| XDU | *Trudy filolohičnoho fakul'tetu,* Vol. 6 (1958). Xarkivs'kyj deržavnyj universytet im. M. Hor'koho. |
| ZIV | *Zapiski Instituta Vostokovedenija AN SSSR.* Moscow. |
| ZNUW | Zeszyty Naukowe Uniwersytetu Wrocławskiego. |
| ZPhon | *Zeitschrift für Phonetik und allgemeine Sprachwissenschaft.* Berlin. |
| ZPNK | *Zbirnyk prac' naukovoji ševčenkivs'koji konferenciji.* AN UkRSR, Instytut literatury im. T. Ševčenka. Kiev. |
| ZSl | *Zeitschrift fur Slawistik.* Berlin. |
| ZUJFil | *Zeszyty naukowe Uniwersytetu Jagiellońskiego, Filologia.* Cracow. |

# PART ONE

## *SELECTED TOPICS IN SOVIET LINGUISTICS*

*GENERAL*

Phonemics, *by* Morris Halle
Morphemics, *by* Cornelis H. Van Schooneveld
Syntax, *by* Dean Worth
Lexicology, *by* Uriel Weinreich
Comparative and Historical Slavistics, *by* Valentin Kiparsky

# PHONEMICS*

MORRIS HALLE

## I. INTRODUCTION

Soviet phonology has been dominated by three major schools. They are the Leningrad school, whose theories and practice bear considerable resemblance to American post-Bloomfieldian linguistics; the Moscow school, which in many ways parallels Sapir's approach to phonology; and the school based on the phonological theories of R. I. Avanesov, which are an attempt to bridge the gap that separates the Moscow and Leningrad schools. In spite of its many striking resemblances to Western phonology, the roots of Russian phonology are indigenous rather than imported. In fact, it might even be argued that Western and Russian phonology are two parallel developments of ideas originated by the Polish linguist Jan Baudouin de Courtenay during his long tenure as professor in various Russian universities.[1]

In his earlier, Kazań period Baudouin de Courtenay was primarily interested in morphophonemic alternations, which he regarded as the central mechanism of sound change; and morphophonemic alternations have remained the primary concern of the Moscow school, though unlike Baudouin the Moscow school focuses mainly on the synchronic, rather than the diachronic manifestations of these alternations.

While psychological and epistemological problems did not play a particularly important role in Baudouin's early work, they occupy the center of the stage in his later studies. In these studies, he tried to answer the question of the reality of the phoneme by developing the well-known theory of the "psycho-phoneme", which became the cornerstone of the work of Baudouin's student, L. Ščerba, the actual founder of the Leningrad school. For Ščerba and his present-day followers, as for Baudouin in his St. Petersburg period, the phonemes of a language are a small subset of the infinite variety of speech sounds that are emitted in speaking; they are those specific varieties of sound of which speakers and hearers are consciously aware. In

* The major portion of this essay was written in the fall of 1960 when I was a fellow at the Center for Advanced Study in the Behavioral Sciences, Stanford, California. During that period I also held a fellowship from the J. S. Guggenheim Memorial Foundation. I am grateful to both institutions for their generous support.

[1] Cf. R. Jakobson, "Kazánska szkoła polskiej lingwistyki i jej miesce w swiatowym rozwoju fonologii", *Bulletin de la Société polonaise de la linguistique* 19.1-34 (1960).

essence, then, this is the theory of the "broad" transcription, and the study of phonetic detail has been one of the primary concerns of the Leningrad school, as it has been the main interest of Daniel Jones in London and of much of post-Bloomfieldian linguistics in the United States.

In an attempt to neutralize the contradictions between the antithetical positions of the Moscow and Leningrad schools, R. I. Avanesov, originally an adherent of the Moscow school, has in recent years outlined a new position on phonology. His views owe a great deal to proposals discussed at length in the early days of the Prague circle. These proposals are combined by Avanesov in an original manner into a coherent theory which contains a number of new and interesting departures. I regard as especially important the fact that in Avanesov's theory considerations of economy or descriptive simplicity play a significant role in selecting one solution from among possible alternatives.

Since my interest is scientific rather than sociological or historical, I have omitted from consideration phonological doctrines, no matter how well publicized, that lack scientific merit or that have not been developed to a point where a judgment as to their scientific merit can be made. I do not discuss, therefore, such episodes as the Marr school or Stalin's extraordinary intervention in the discussion on linguistics, in spite of their fateful importance for the social history of linguistics in the Soviet Union.

I have made a conscious effort to present the various positions in the best possible light and to support them with what seemed to me the strongest, most convincing arguments. I see little use in concentrating on unessential flaws or outright errors in the writings of the proponents of the views to be surveyed, for I regard my task as understanding the theories of Soviet phonologists rather than scoring points in a debate. In line with this, I have chosen to base my survey on the most clearly formulated, unexceptionable statements that I could discover in the literature. Quite often this has made me forego quoting the works of the major figures in favor of less widely known scholars. Thus, in discussing the views of the Leningrad school I follow Gvozdev more often than I do Ščerba, while my survey of the Moscow school is almost wholly based on a fairly recent paper by Reformatskij, rather than on the historically more important writings of Jakovlev, Avanesov, and Sidorov.

The order in which the various schools are discussed below is governed by considerations for ease of presentation and in no way reflects the historical or scientific priorities of the schools. The survey begins with the Leningrad school since it approaches the classical problems of phonology in the most straightforward fashion. The views of Avanesov are considered next, for these were advanced specifically in order to show the connections between the concerns of the Leningrad and Moscow schools. The views of the Moscow school are then surveyed in the concluding chapter.

No serious attempt was made to discuss in detail the manner in which Soviet developments are related to analogous developments elsewhere. In spite of the relative isolation of Soviet linguistics during most of the past half century, outside developments have had a considerable influence in Russia, as have Soviet developments in the West. It is to be hoped that a serious study of this intricate and difficult question will be undertaken by a competent scholar in the not too distant future.

## II. THE ŠČERBA OR LENINGRAD SCHOOL

The problem which is central for the Leningrad school is to account for the fact that though sounds emitted in speaking are of an infinite variety, speakers and listeners are normally conscious of only a small number of individual sound types. It is the latter that the Leningrad school proposes to call phonemes.

Since according to the Leningrad school the purpose of speech is communication, transfer of information, the school postulates that the listener listens not for all acoustical properties present in the utterance, but rather concentrates his attention primarily on the acoustical properties which distinguish the utterance in question from all other utterances. The phoneme is that sound entity which serves to distinguish otherwise identical utterances; i.e., it is the smallest sound entity which if wrongly perceived would cause a misunderstanding. Note that it is the listener rather than the speaker for whom the phoneme thus defined is of maximal importance, because if a distinction is omitted it will be he – rather than the speaker – who will fail to understand correctly. "This fact puts into the forefront of interest the acoustical properties of phonemes, which thus become the most important realia of phonetics..." (Gvozdev, 1949, p. 5).

In view of this, the discovery of minimal pairs – i.e., of utterances where every distinctive property of a phoneme must be perceived correctly for complete understanding – is the most important device for determining whether or not two sounds belong to one phoneme. It is, however, not realistic to believe that the listener is acquainted with all possible utterances in his language, for the number of different utterances is patently too great for that. Since one can reasonably be expected to know all words, it is words which must be used in the minimal pairs, and Ščerba describes phonemes as "the sound types capable of differentiating words and their forms" (Ščerba, 1937, p. 17 – as quoted by Gvozdev, 1949, p. 5).

This, however, raises a problem, for as Gvozdev notes, "even in cases where the speaker pronounces a single word clearly, there is no guarantee that the listener will perceive it as a single word. Quite to the contrary, in a whole series of instances its phonetic composition may be interpreted by the listener as a sequence of two words. In this category belong all cases where an independent word is homonymous (i.e., homophonous – M.H.) with a sequence of an independent word and a form word (preposition, copula, particle); e.g., 1) *sdači* ("change" gen. sg.) vs. *s dači* ("from the summer cottage")... It is, therefore, necessary to modify somewhat the concept of the word. In the communication process it is the "big word" that figures in isolation;

i.e., the independent word as well as the independent word together with the various words (prepositions, particles) that adjoin it" (Gvozdev, 1949, p. 9).

Gvozdev's "big word" is essentially identical with Bloomfield's "minimum free form", i.e., the shortest utterance capable of occurring between two successive pauses. In the transcription of longer utterances such forms are obligatorily delimited by a space symbol, which functions thus as a boundary marker or juncture. It is characteristic of the Leningrad approach, as of almost all Soviet work in phonology, that junctures are admitted only at places where they can be directly associated with actual or potential silence; so-called "internal" juncture is all but unknown.

The decision to restrict the use of juncture in this way leads immediately to the following consequence. In Russian, [ˈe] and [ˈɛ] are usually said to be in complementary distribution, with the former appearing only before palatalized consonants, and the latter elsewhere including before word boundary. Since the Ščerba school insists on using the space – its analog of the word boundary – exclusively to delimit minimally free forms, rather than words as traditionally defined, it must write [gar,'ɛl,i], "to the mountain?", without a space before the question particle *li*, for the particle cannot be separated by a pause from the preceding word. (Gvozdev insists on this fact specifically with regard to the question particle; cf. Gvozdev, 1949, p. 15.) Hence, [gar,ˈɛl,i] constitutes a minimal pair with the minimal free form [gar,ˈel,i] "(they) burned" and [ˈe] must be recognized as phonemically distinct from [ˈɛ]. To my knowledge no one has seen this difficulty. It was overlooked even by Gvozdev, who usually discusses such crucial examples with great care and ingenuity. In the present instance, however, he seems unaware of any problem and specifically cites [ˈe] and [ˈɛ] as variants of a single phoneme (cf. Gvozdev, 1949, pp. 6, 19, 54).

For the Leningrad school phonemes are the sound types of which the speaker and listener are consciously aware. This statement is understood quite literally in the sense that speaker and listener are imagined to have stored in their minds certain typical sounds, of which the individual sounds occurring in utterances are contextually modified tokens. Ščerba notes that "we normally are not conscious of (the contextual variants of phonemes) as distinct from that typical variant, and we require special training of the ear in order to learn to hear them" (Ščerba, 1937, p. 17 as quoted by Gvozdev, 1949, p. 11). To which Gvozdev adds that "one may regard as an indication that a given concrete sound is a contextual variant of a phoneme, the fact that it is not pronounced in isolation but is replaced by a different sound in isolated pronunciation. The sound pronounced in its stead (in isolation – M.H.) is then the fundamental variant of (the phoneme – M.H.); at the same time this (procedure – M.H.) also shows to which phoneme the given contextual variant belongs" (Gvozdev, 1949, p. 11).

The doctrine of the "fundamental variant" has important consequences for the solution of several imperical problems. For instance, it is used to justify the insistence of the Leningrad school that the high unrounded back vowel ("yery") is phonemically distinct from the high unrounded front vowel [i]. In his *Sovremennyj russkij literaturnyj jazyk* (Moscow, 1958), Gvozdev specifically notes that "the representatives of the second direction (Academician L. V. Ščerba, M. I. Matusevič) regard *i* and *y* as separate phonemes, first of all because of our awareness (osoznanost') of the sounds *i* and *y*: the ability to distinguish and pronounce them independently is achieved without difficulty already at the time of learning to read and write, whereas dependent (contextual) variants are not so readily learned (p. 12)". It is significant that in one of his last essays "Teorija russkogo pis'ma" (1944) Ščerba still insists on regarding the two sounds as separate phonemes, albeit with a great deal of misgivings. After reviewing the distribution of the two sounds he continues: "Thus, it would appear that "y" and "i" are to be regarded as variants of a single phoneme, of which the main variant must be "i", since "y" never occurs in an independent (i.e., contextually undetermined – M.H.) position... However, intuitively there is something which prevents us from considering "i" and "y" a single phoneme. And, in fact, although in concrete words "y" does not occur in independent position, nonetheless we have no difficulty in isolating it (i.e., pronouncing it in isolation – M.H.) and, moreover, on the analogy with the verbs *akat'*, *okat'*, *èkat'* and *ikat'* ("to pronounce the sounds [a] [o] [e] [i]" respectively – M.H.) we can produce the verb *ykat'* ("to pronounce the sound [ɨ]" – M.H.)" (p. 178). In sum, since the sound can be produced in isolation and since the speaker is quite conscious of its occurrence in his speech, [ɨ] is an independent phoneme, for if it had been a contextual variant of the phoneme /i/, this could not have been the case.[2]

The doctrine of the fundamental variant plays a decisive role also in the solution of certain problems that arise in connection with the phenomenon of neutralization. The relevant facts are as follows: In Russian we must distinguish in accented position at least five vowels, two high vowels: /i/ and /u/, and three nonhigh vowels: /e/, /o/, and /a/. In unstressed syllable after hard consonants – i.e., after nonpalatalized and nonpalatal consonants, where, by the way, stressed /ˈe/ does not occur – we have only a single nonhigh vowel, which in pretonic position is actualized as [a] and in all other positions as [ə]. Since [ə] is in complementary distribution with [a] and [o], and yet phonetically distinct from both, the question arises as to which phoneme it belongs. Ščerba assigns it to the phoneme /a/ "since in distinct pronunciation it is frequently replaced by *a*" (Gvozdev, 1949, p. 31).[3]

This assignment follows directly from the assumption that the phoneme is an entity present in the mind of the speaker. In order to discover it we must, therefore, only instruct the speaker to behave in such a fashion as to remove all contextual influences that are obscuring the clear manifestation of this entity. There seems to be no doubt that this is regarded by Ščerba and his followers as a perfectly feasible procedure for discovering the proper assignment of each allophone.

[2] It should be noted that the Academy Grammar of Russian (1952) considers [ɨ] a separate phoneme.
[3] In 1912 Ščerba had assigned it to the phoneme /i/. (Gvozdev, 1949, p. 31n.) This, however, is not important here for we are interested primarily in the justification, which is identical in both casee, i.e., that under appropriate circumstances, native speakers will identify [ə] with the accented vowls in question.

The doctrine of the fundamental variant in Ščerba's theory replaces the requirement of phonetic similarity in other phonemic theories. In the most recent work of the Ščerba school, L. R. Zinder's *Obščaja fonetika* (Leningrad, 1960), however, the emphasis is shifted from the discovery of concrete instances where a positional variant is replaced by its fundamental variant, to the utilization of phonetic similarity as a criterion for assigning a sound to a particular phoneme (Zinder, p. 52). Zinder specifically point out that phonetic similarity requires that the segments in question share a number of phonetic features, which apparently must belong to the canonical set of properties utilized in the IPA scheme.

In the light of the essential data-consciousness that characterizes the Leningrad approach it is not surprising that the school insists on the bi-uniqueness condition. Every sound must be assigned unambiguously to a given phoneme and a transcription which allows a sound sequence to represent more than one phoneme string is declared to be of no concern to phonology. Gvozdev (1949, pp. 13-14) is almost incapable of conceiving of phonemes that do not satisfy the bi-uniqueness condition. He sees little practical value in a transcription utilizing such entities, for it "glosses over the most significant socio-phonetic fact that in the communication process (certain pairs of forms – M.H.) are clearly distinguished while (others – M.H.) are phonetically identical and indistinguishable and that for their differentiation only nonphonetic means are used".

Nor are morphemes phonological entities, for in actual utterances they do not appear as delimited phonetic entities. They figure only in words, but the word does not reveal in anything its segmentation into morphemes. Thus, hearing the word [prastˈoj], the listener does not receive signals telling him whether it is to be segmented as [prast-ˈoj] ("simple") or as [pra-stˈoj] ("standing idle") (Gvozdev, 1949, pp. 10-11).

It is not that a morphophonemic transcription is useless – though at times it would appear that Ščerba's followers are implying even this – rather, a morphophonemic transcription has a different aim than a phonemic transcription. The phonemic transcription is designed to account for the fact that speakers and listeners are normally conscious of but a small variety of sound types as constituting the utterances in a language, although the variety of sounds in actual utterances is all but infinite. The morphophonemic transcription, on the other hand, is designed to account for a totally different psychological fact, namely that speakers unite into single entities called morphemes, sound sequences which are only partly alike. "The morphological aspect of the study of sounds is, therefore, opposed to its phonetic aspect. If in the solution of questions regarding the phoneme, the sounds appear as differentiators of meaningful elements, then in the question of the phonic aspect of morphemes, paramount importance attaches to the limits within which they (the morphemes – M.H.) overcome differences in their phonic composition that are produced by the phonetic system (of the language – M.H.) and remain thereby for the speaker single meaningful entities" (Gvozdev, 1949, p. 50). According to the Leningrad school this question, however, is not within the purview of phonology.

## III. THE PHONOLOGICAL THEORY OF R. I. AVANESOV

In his most recent work[4] R. I. Avanesov accepts as legitimate the distinction between morphophonemic and phonemic, but unlike Ščerba and his school he does not regard morphophonemic problems as outside the scope of phonology. He is, moreover, critical of the Ščerba school for attaching too much weight to nonlinguistic factors; e.g., for determining by acoustical, psychological, and physiological criteria exclusively the assignment of individual sounds to phonemes. He sees phonology not as an attempt at providing a rational explanation of the fact that man hears and produces an infinite variety of speech sounds, though being conscious of only a very restricted number, but rather as a "scientific discipline whose object is the sounds of speech as structural elements of language" (1956a, p. 17). In Avanesov's descriptions, internal, linguistic considerations are given great importance. Although he never speaks of it explicitly he uses a notion of simplicity to justify the specific solutions that he proposes. I consider this the most important feature distinguishing Avanesov's approach from that of Ščerba, for in the latter, considerations of descriptive elegance or simplicity have no natural place: every problem has a unique solution forced upon us by acoustical, physiological or behavioral facts – i.e., by facts essentially external to the description.[5]

For Avanesov phonology is focused around three transcriptions, which represent utterances in an increasingly abstract manner. The most concrete of the three – i.e., most directly related to physical properties of the utterance – is the phonetic transcription. Yet even this transcription is not a simple record of the acoustical event, for it segments the quasi-continuous utterance into discrete elements, which Avanesov calls the "shortest phonic units". He characterizes these as "such articulatory-auditory elements as stand out in the word in its sequential ... linear segmentation as the simplest, minimal, further indivisible units occupying a minimal slice of time (i.e., not divisible further with respect to the phonic elements of the given language)" (1956a, p. 18).

It is to be noted that Avanesov makes no attempt to give a procedure for discovering how such a segmentation is to be performed. This may well be due to his unawareness of the fact that there is a problem here. It is, however, conceivable that segmentation procedures are not discussed because Avanesov believes some sort of segmentation to be built into man's perception of speech; i.e., that man is constructed in such a way as to perceive acoustical stimuli as a sequence of segments. If this is the case, the fact that speech is perceived as segmented can then be taken as given, just as linguistics

[4] The position discussed here differs from that embraced by Avanesov some fifteen years ago, when he was an orthodox member of the Moscow school and saw the distinction between phonemic and morphophonemic as neither necessary nor illuminating. See, e.g., Avanesov and Sidorov, *Očerk grammatiki russkogo literaturnogo jazyka*, I (Moscow, 1945) and the criticism by Gvozdev (from the position of the Ščerba school) in his *O fonologičeskix sredstvax russkogo jazyka* (Moscow, 1949), pp. 51-83.

[5] As exemplified, e.g., in their treatment of unaccented nonhigh vowels, cf. above.

now takes as given the fact that man is sensitive to acoustic energy only within a particular frequency range.

The physical actualization of speech sounds is to a greater or lesser extent influenced by the context in which they occur. In the phonetic transcription no distinction is made between attributes of speech sounds that are contextually determined and those not so determined. In the phonemic transcription, on the other hand, this distinction is of paramount importance, since a phonemic transcription must *not* reflect "those aspects (of the sound – M.H.) that are contextually determined" (Avanesov, 1956a, p. 217). For Avanesov, therefore, the phonemic transcription is not a representation of the ideal sound types, of which the speaker and hearer are normally conscious; it is rather a representation in which redundant information about properties determined by general rules of the language has been consistently eliminated.

It is a trivial matter to devise a nonredundant transcription in cases where contextually determined attributes of phonemes are sharply separated from distinctive attributes; e.g., aspiration in English stops. Considerably more difficult and also more interesting is the case where a given phonetic attribute is distinctive in some positions and contextually determined in others. The problem is neatly illustrated by the unaccented nondiffuse (nonhigh) vowels of Russian, which was discussed above. As was noted there, after hard consonants in unaccented position we find only a single nondiffuse vowel; which is actualized as [a] in pretonic position, and as [ə] elsewhere. In this position, therefore, the distinction between [a] and [o] is not phonemic, for [o] does not occur here.[6]

As we have seen above the Ščerba school assigns the unaccented [a] to the phoneme /a/ on phonetic grounds. For Avanesov this solution is unacceptable, for it "fails to take into account the fundamental difference in the functioning of sound units in strong position, on the one hand, and in weak position, on the other. The distinctive role (of sound units), however, is not identical in the two positions: it is weakened in the case of sound units distinguished in weak positions, since each such unit is equivalent to two or more sound units distinguished in strong position" (Avanesov, 1955, p. 136). In other words, if we write the symbol /a/ both in weak and in strong position we are including redundant information in our transcription, for since /a/ is distinct from /o/ in strong position, we are implying that the same distinction holds also in weak position. Avanesov proposes, therefore, that phonemes in strong position be distinguished from phonemes in weak position: he speaks of strong and weak phonemes and uses different symbols in his transcription for the two types of phoneme. For instance, he represents the unaccented non-diffuse vowel in position after hard consonants by the symbol /α/, which is designed to reflect graphically the fact that in this position the distinction between [a] and [o] is not operative, is neutralized. Avanesov's solution to the problem of neutralization is thus similar to that of

[6] In Russian phonology it is customary to refer to positions where certain otherwise phonemic distinctions are not operative, as "weak" positions, in opposition to "strong" positions where all phonemic distinctions are fully operative.

the Prague circle, who proposed to set up a new class of phonemes called *archiphonemes* which differ from regular phonemes in that they have less distinctive power than the latter.

Since in Russian we must recognize a great number of weak positions the number of weak phonemes is correspondingly large. At first sight, Avanesov's proposal appears to make phonemic transcription less redundant at the cost of a considerable increase in the size of the phoneme inventory. Avanesov, however, argues that this is not the case, for "weak phonemes occupy in the phonetic system a subordinate role with respect to the strong phonemes. Hence they can never be considered on the same level as the strong phonemes. It follows, therefore, that if in the phonetic system of some language there are both strong and weak phonemes, then the inventory ... of phonemes ... must be established on the basis of the units that are distinguished in strong position ... The list of phonemes (in cases where there are both strong and weak phonemes) is equal to the list of strong phonemes, and not to the sum of strong and weak phonemes" (Avanesov, 1955, p. 129). In sum, weak phonemes are degenerate instances of strong phonemes and cannot be taken into consideration when establishing the list of phonemes of a language.

The phonemic transcription "starts from the concrete linguistic fact (the word, or some grammatical form of the word) and, by abstracting from it everything that is positionally determined and functionally unessential, isolates that which is independent and functionally significant" (Avanesov, 1956a, p. 217). The morphophonemic transcription, on the other hand, "by abstracting everything that is positionally determined and functionally unessential in the morpheme, isolates that which is independent and functionally significant in the morpheme" (*ibid.*). For Avanesov, therefore, the difference between the two types of transcription is determined by the context that is taken as basic: in the case of phonemics, it is the word, which Avanesov somewhat inaccurately indentifies with the minimal free form, whereas in morphophonemics it is a much more abstract entity, the morpheme.

The morphophonemic transcription must be designed so that a given morpheme (with certain exceptions that will be discussed below) is always represented by the same sequence of symbols. For instance, the Russian morpheme meaning "water" must be represented by the same symbols in the forms [vˈot] (gen. pl.); [vˈodɨ] (nom. pl.); [vadˈa] (nom. sg.); [vad,ˈɛ] (dat. sg.); [vədavˈos] "water carrier"; [vad,inˈoj] "watery," etc. Avanesov proposes the term "phoneme series" (*fonemnyj rjad*) to designate the different sets of morphophonemically alternating phonemes and devises special symbols to represent the different "series". Thus, in the above mentioned morpheme *vod* "water", the stem vowel is to be represented by a symbol standing for: /ˈo/ /a/ /ə/; the final consonant of the stem by a symbol standing for /d/ /d,/ /t/, whereas the initial consonant is represented by a phoneme series consisting of the single strong phoneme /v/.

As the alphabetical symbol to designate the different "phoneme series" Avanesov suggests the symbol representing the strong phoneme; e.g., the morpheme just discussed would be presented by the symbols {vˈo d} (1956b, p. 357). This suggestion is somewhat unfortunate since it immediately has to be amended to take care of cases where no strong phoneme is included in the alternations: e.g., the first vowel in [barˈan] "sheep". In such cases, Avanesov writes: "one must be satisfied with designation by the weak phoneme" (*ibid.*). This difficulty, however, is not very serious as long as it is clear that each letter used in a morphophonemic transcription stands for a specific set of alternating sounds.

The introduction of the "phoneme series" allows Avanesov to claim that a given morpheme is always represented by the same entities ("phoneme series"), and that "different morphemes are distinguished from each other by the fact that at least one of the minimal discrete units constituting their sound envelopes belongs to a different phoneme series" (Avanesov, 1955, p. 134). Thus, the ambiguous utterance [valˈɨ] has two morphophonemic representations: $\left\{ \mathrm{v} \begin{bmatrix} \alpha \\ \mathrm{a} \end{bmatrix} \begin{bmatrix} \mathrm{l,} \\ \mathrm{l} \end{bmatrix} {}^{\shortmid}\mathrm{i} \right\}$ meaning "billows", and $\left\{ \mathrm{v} \begin{bmatrix} \alpha \\ \mathrm{o} \end{bmatrix} \begin{bmatrix} \mathrm{l,} \\ \mathrm{l} \end{bmatrix} {}^{\shortmid}\mathrm{i} \right\}$ meaning "oxen".

The "phoneme series" of Avanesov bears a close resemblance to Trubetzkoy's "morphoneme".[7] There is, however, an essential difference between the two. Whereas Trubetzkoy would incorporate in his "morphoneme" several "strong" phonemes, Avanesov apparently admits at most a single "strong" phoneme in a given "phoneme series" though he does not restrict the number of "weak" phonemes.[8] This makes for a substantive difference in the type of phenomena treated within "morphophonemics" by the two scholars. For Avanesov alternation like k/č in [p,ikˈu] [p,ičˈom] "bake" (l. sg./pl. pres.) are examples of "nonidentical" though variant forms of one and the same morpheme (cf. Avanesov, 1955, p. 133n) and are, therefore, outside the scope of morphophonemics. For Trubetzkoy, on the other hand, the cited forms are examples of a single morpheme and must both, therefore, be represented as containing the same "morphoneme" $\begin{bmatrix} \check{\mathrm{c}} \\ \bar{\mathrm{k}} \end{bmatrix}$. Trubetzkoy's suggestion has the obvious advantage of requiring the postulation of fewer morphemes in the lexicon. To realize this advantage, however, Avanesov would have to give up the distinction between alternations that are conditioned by morphological context and those that are purely phonological. This is a step which he is evidently not ready to take. (Cf. previous discussion.)

The morphophonemic transcription proposed by Avanesov presupposes fairly elaborate rules to indicate which alternant of the "phoneme series" is to be utilized in a particular context. For instance, implicit in the transcription are the following three rules for selecting the appropriate "strong" or "weak" phoneme in the "phoneme

[7] Cf. N. S. Trubetzkoy, "Sur la morphonologie", *Travaux du Cercle linguistique de Prague* 1.85-87 (1929).

[8] I have been unable to find an explicit statement to this effect in Avanesov's writings. None of the examples given by Avanesov, however, contradicts the proposed restriction.

series" $\begin{bmatrix}\text{ə}\\ \alpha\\ \text{o}\end{bmatrix}$ and $\begin{bmatrix}\text{ə}\\ \alpha\\ \text{a}\end{bmatrix}$:

a) Under the accent, select /o/ or /a/, respectively.
b) In immediately pretonic position, select /α/.
c) In post-tonic and in antepretonic positions, select /ə/.

It is to be regretted that Avanesov has not stated these rules explicitly but has rather left them to be inferred by the reader. Had the rules been stated, it would have avoided misunderstandings like that in one of Gvozdev's last papers (1958b, pp. 84-85) where the question is raised whether the four "phoneme series" $\begin{bmatrix}\text{ə}\\ \alpha\\ \text{o}\end{bmatrix}$ (as, e.g., in the first vowel of *voda* "water"), $\begin{bmatrix}\text{ə}\\ \text{o}\end{bmatrix}$ (as in the first vowel of *doktor* "doctor"), $\begin{bmatrix}\text{ə}\\ \alpha\end{bmatrix}$ (as in the first vowel of *topor* "axe") and [α] (as in the first vowel of *saraj* "barn") constitute four distinct morphophonemic entities or not. This question is due to Gvozdev's paying excessive attention to the symbols Avanesov uses to represent the "phoneme series" and not enough attention to the manner in which these symbols are used by Avanesov. Thus, Avanesov has fewer "phonemes" in the "phoneme series" representing the first vowel of *saraj* than in that of *voda* because the former vowel can occur only in pretonic position (the morpheme *saraj* having a fixed accent), whereas the first vowel in *voda* can appear in each of the three positions with respect to the accent that were mentioned in the rules above. Given these rules, however, no matter how many phoneme symbols are included in the "phoneme series" for the vowel in *saraj*, the morphophonemic rules would invariably select the "weak" phoneme /α/, since the vowel in question occurs only in pretonic position. Gvozdev's question becomes thus technically meaningless since it makes no difference whether or not the given four "phoneme series" are distinct; the morphophonemic rules, which Avanesov must include with his transcription in any case, will always select the appropriate phoneme regardless of what other symbols are added to those already included in the brackets.

The phonemic transcription can, therefore, be deduced from the morphophonemic transcription with the help of the morphophonemic rules. The phonemic transcription would thus appear to be redundant and hence strictly speaking unnecessary. There is no discussion of this problem in Avanesov's writings. It has, however, been discussed by other Soviet linguists, for the view that a phonemic transcription is superfluous is a central tenet of the Moscow school, the theoretical position of which we now examine.[9]

[9] I have dealt with other aspects of Avanesov's work in *Word* 16.140-152 (1960).

## IV. THE MOSCOW SCHOOL AS SEEN BY REFORMATSKIJ

Ščerba and his followers as well as Avanesov insist that phonetics must not and cannot be divorced from other linguistic levels, but must form an integral part of a complete description of a language. This axiom, however, seems to be only of marginal relevance for their practice: they somehow do not encounter crucial problems where a particular decision is forced on them as a consequence of their having adopted this view. In this they differ radically from their colleague A. A. Reformatskij, who derives many important consequences from the assumption that phonetics forms an integral part of linguistics.

According to Reformatskij "the whole point of the phonological approach to phonetics is to avoid turning phonetics over to the natural sciences and to conceive of sounds, which are physical phenomena, as obligatory entities of language ..." (1955, p. 93). He regards the bi-unique phonemic transcription as an unnecessary complication which was introduced into linguistics only because phonetics had summarily and incorrectly been read out of linguistics. Reviewing the three level analysis of phonic phenomena which was proposed by the Polish linguist Ułaszyn (and was utilized by G. L. Trager in an analysis of Russian that is quite similar to Avanesov's three transcriptions) Reformatiskij writes:[10] "We get, therefore, a "three level" structure: Laut-Phonema-Morphonema, in accordance with Ułaszyn and in violation of common sense. For instance, if in the nominative plural *voly* ("oxen" – M.H.) and *valy* ("billows" – M.H.) coincide phonetically in [valɨ], then according to Trager (and also to Ułaszyn) we have here the two morphonemes [o] and [a], and of these [o] is "replaced by the phoneme" [a]. How is it possible that one and the same (sound – M.H.) should turn out in the case of (the morphoneme – M.H.) [o] to be the phoneme [a], while in the case of (the morphoneme – M.H.) [a] it is [a] itself? And what are all these [ü] [ö] [ä] etc., which are given without explanation? They are neither "morphonemes" nor "phonemes". And where then is the "Laut"? Perhaps in these very [ü] [ö] [ä]? Would it not be better to remove these artificially erected steps so that everything would appear closer to reality and simpler: there are phonemes (in the Russian vowel system these number 5; according to Trager these are "morphonemes", of which Trager also enumerates 5); there are changes of the type [ü] [ö] [ä]; i.e., variations of the given phonemes without coincidence in sound with other phonemes; and there are the phoneme variants [a] [ə] where different phonemes coincide in a single sound. And a simple conclusion follows from this: for the connection with morphology and for morphology as such, importance attaches only to the elementary entities of phonetics, to the variable constants [i e a o u] and not to the different variatives (regardless of whether they belong to the type [ɨ e ä ö ü]

[10] Although in his critical remarks Reformatskij mentions by name only Western scholars, his criticism applies in equal measure to Soviet linguists. Observe that he effectively cuts the ground out from under Ščerba's program and rejects as useless Avanesov's proposal for a distinction between a phonemic and a morphophonemic transcription.

or to the type [a] [ə] etc.)" (*ibid.* pp. 97-98). In sum, Reformatskij proposes that bi-unique phonemes are superfluous entities in a linguistic description and suggests that the term "phoneme" be applied to what others have called "morpho(pho)-nemes".[11]

Reformatskij is equally critical of the morphophonemic transcription proposed by Trubetzkoy, which except for the name has little in common with the transcription employed by Ułaszyn and others. As will be recalled Trubetzkoy felt that on some level each morpheme of a language should be transcribed by a single sequence of symbols. In a language like Russian, in which there is a wealth of morphologically conditioned alternations among stems, this can be handled in two ways. On the one hand, each stem may be transcribed by a single sequence of phonemes and the derivation of alternant stems may be stated in rules, which on occasion may have to be of fair complexity. On the other hand, it may be possible to lighten the burden on the rules by including in the transcription information about the nature of the alternations. For this purpose, however, special complex symbols will have to be used. It is the latter alternative that was preferred by Trubetzkoy, who would, e.g., transcribe the Russian morpheme meaning "hand, arm" with the symbol $\overset{\bullet}{\begin{bmatrix} \check{c} \\ \bar{k} \end{bmatrix}}$ in order to reflect the fact that both the noun [ruk'a] and the adjective [ručn'oj] derive from that stem.[12] Trubetzkoy suggests the term "morpho(pho)neme" for these complex symbols, which according to him represent "complex concepts (idées complexes), that as a consequence of the morphological structure of the word can replace one another inside the same morpheme".

Reformatskij will have no part of this. He notes that the symbols represent sets of entities undergoing common morphological alternation such as (the Russian) [k/č] [g/ž] [p/pl,] [o or e /zero]. "Trubetzkoy's idea to raise such facts to the level of "complex concepts" is peculiar. What common concept can be shared by [k] and [č]; or by [g] and [ž] (perhaps "voicelessness" in the first, and "voicing" in the second?). Then what do we have in the case of *beregu/bereč'* "save" (l. sg. pres. / infinitive) surely an example of the same type, that yet belongs neither here nor there .... And one would be especially curious to know what common property the "fugitive" vowels share with zero (for after all this is exactly the same type of alternation as that of k/č or g/ž). ... In his search for a straightforward systematization N. S. Trubetzkoy has invented a nonexisting and unnecessary entity which has no correspondences in the objective reality of language. There we find correspondences, relationships or alternations of morpheme variants...; but [k/č], [g/ž] and particularly [o/zero] do not constitute realistic entities of the structure of language" (*ibid.*, p. 99).

11 It might be noted parenthetically that the proposed usage accords with that of Sapir, cf., e.g., "The Psychological Reality of Phonemes".

12 The close relationship between these complex symbols and the "phoneme series" of Avanesov has already been noted, cf. above.

Reformatskij thus opts for the first of the two alternatives outlined above. Rather than include in the transcription some of the information about morphologically conditioned alternations he prefers to concentrate this information entirely in a separate chapter of the description. The essential difference between him and Trubetzkoy, therefore, concerns the need for postulating morpho(pho)nemes, and not the necessity of a separate chapter describing the alternations, on which both are agreed.

There is, however, a subsidiary difference between Reformatskij and Trubetzkoy regarding the scope of this chapter, which both propose to entitle "morphonology". Unlike Trubetzkoy, Reformatskij suggests that alternations which are concomitant with specific morphemes (e.g., the k/č alternation in [p,ik'u] / [p,ič'om] "bake" (l. sg./pl. pres)) and which may, therefore, be considered redundant, should be treated separately from alternations that are the sole signal of the morphological category in question (e.g., the k/č alternation in [d,'ik] "wild" / [d,'ič] "wilderness, game"). For in the former instance "the alternations are not immediately directed towards the production of forms, do not attain the rank of grammatical devices. Whereas here (i.e., in the second instance – M.H.) the alternations directly produce (meaningful – M.H.) forms (flectional as well as derivational); they constitute internal flection, they cannot be removed by analogy (for that would result in a loss of distinctions in morphology); these alternations are already morphology proper, where different variants of a morpheme are at the same time also different (in meaning – M.H.) forms" (Reformatskij, p. 109).

Reformatskij's position is quite consistent with his view, concurred in by almost all of his Soviet colleagues, that a sharp distinction must be drawn between those devices and processes in language which convey meaning directly and those which do so indirectly. Morphology, syntax, lexicology treat only of devices and processes of the former types, while phonology in the broad sense – i.e., including morphonology – deals with those of the second type. Thus, in the Russian conjugation the alternation k/č is subsidiary to the choice of suffix, for there are stems where the l. pl. pres. is added without causing alternation in the final consonant; e.g., [p,j'u]/[p,j'om] "drink" (l. sg./pl. pres.) and hence the meaning of the l. pl. pres. is conveyed by the suffix ['om] alone. The alternation k/č here cannot belong to morphology, for it does not convey meaning directly. Since it is, however, morphologically conditioned it cannot belong to phonology, either, for phonology deals only with devices and processes that are conditioned phonologically and not morphologically (i.e., by semantic factors). The alternation is, therefore, treated in a special chapter "morphonology" which describes processes and devices that do not convey meaning directly, but are conditioned by processes or devices that do.

The k/č alternation in the [d,'ik] [d,'ič] example is quite different. The meaning of the abstract noun [d,'ič] "wilderness, game" can presumably be analyzed into the two semantic components, "wild" and "entity possessing the quality expressed by the corresponding adjective". It is the second component which is directly conveyed by the process of replacing the velar by the palatal stop. Reformatskij must, therefore, include the description of this process in his morphology.

The nature of the argument just advanced is a good illustration of an important aspect of Reformatskij's method. In cases where several alternative solutions are consonant with the data, Reformatskij appeals to formal conditions which he has imposed on his description. Thus, the decision to establish morphology as a separate level from "morphonology" follows from the a priori requirement that in a linguistic description semantic entities cannot be treated together with entities which by themselves do not possess meaning. It is significant, that simplicity, elegance, or conceptual economy is not included among the criteria that are to be used in choosing among possible alternative solutions. This seems to me a serious gap, for the appeal to simplicity has been one of the most powerful tools for the discovery of truths in other areas of human knowledge, and I know of no reason – nor is any given by Reformatskij – why linguistics should refrain from making full use of it. This criticism, however, does not apply to Reformatskij alone, for the use of simplicity is still quite rare in linguistics.

## REFERENCES

Avanesov, R. I., "Kratčajšaja zvukovaja edinica v sostave slova i morfemy", *Voprosy grammatičesko stroja* (Moscow, 1955), pp. 113-139.

——, *Fonetika sovremennogo russkogo literaturnogo jazyka* (Moscow, 1956). (a)

——, "O trex tipax naučno-lingvističeskix transcripcij", *Slavia* 25.347-371 (1956). (b)

——, and V. N. Sidorov, *Očerk grammatiki russkogo literaturnogo jazyka*, I (Moscow, 1945).

Gvozdev, A. N., *O fonologičeskix sredstvax russkogo jazyka* (Moscow-Leningrad, 1949).

——, *Sovremennyj russkij literaturnyj jazyk* (Moscow, 1958). (a)

——, "Voprosy fonetiki: Čto dajut tri tipa transcripcij?", *VJa* 7/6.76-86 (1958). (b)

Reformatskij, A. A., "O sootnošenii fonetiki i grammatiki", *Voprosy grammatičeskogo stroja* (1955), pp. 92-112.

Ščerba, L. V., *Fonetika francuzskogo jazyka* (Moscow, 1937), 2nd ed. 1955. (This book was not available to me.)

——, "Teorija russkogo pis'ma", in *Izbrannye raboty po russkomu jazyku* (Moscow, 1957), pp. 144-179.

Zinder, L. R., *Obščaja fonetika* (Leningrad, 1960).

## SELECTED BIBLIOGRAPHY ON SOVIET PHONOLOGY 1945-1960 PREPARED BY R. P. V. KIPARSKY

Alekberli, B. B., "Problema fonemy v svete marksistsko-leninskoj teorii poznanija", *IzvAN* 12.378-383 (1953).

Avanesov, R. I., "Voprosy fonetičeskoj sistemy russkix govorov i literaturnogo jazyka", *IzvAN* 6.210-228 (1947).

——, "K voprosu o foneme", *IzvAN* 11.463-468 (1952).

——, "Kratčajšaja zvukovaja edinica v sostave slova i morfemy", *Voprosy grammaticeskogo stroja* (Moscow, 1955), pp. 113-139.

——, *Fonetika sovremennogo russkogo literaturnogo jazyka* (Moscow, 1956).

——, "O trex tipax naučno-lingvističeskix transkripcij (v svjazi s voprosami teorij fonem)", *Slavia* 25.347-371 (1956).

——, and Sidorov, V. N., *Očerk grammatiki russkogo literaturnogo jazyka* (Moscow, 1945).

Axmanova, O. S., *Fonologija. Materialy k kursam jazykoznanija*. Izdatel'stvo Moskovskogo Universiteta (Moscow, 1954).

——, "Über die Grundbegriffe der Phonologie", *ZPhon* 10.359-365 (1957).

Bernšteijn, S., "Protiv idealizma v fonetike", *IzvAN* 11.543-559 (1952).

Gvozdev, A. N., *O fonologičeskix sredstvax russkogo jazyka. Sbornik statej* (Moscow-Leningrad, 1949).

——, "O fonologii 'smešannyx' fonem", *IzvAN* 12.49-61 (1953).

——, "Obladajut li pozicii različitel'noj funkciej?", *VJa* 7/6.59-63 (1957).

——, *Sovremennyj russkij literaturnyj jazyk*, I (Moscow, 1958).

——, "Voprosy fonetiki: Čto dajut tri tipa transcripcij?", *VJa* 7/6.76-86 (1958).

Ivanov, V. V., "O priemlemosti fonologičeskix modelej", *Trudy Instituta točnoj mexaniki i vyčislitel'noj texniki AN SSSR*, Vyp. 2 (1961).

Kuznecov, P. S., "Ob opredelenii fonemy", *Bjulleten' ob"edinenija po problemam mašinnogo perevoda* No. 5 (1957).

——, "O differencial'nyx priznakax fonem", *VJa* 7/1.55-61 (1958).

——, "Ob osnovnyx položenijax fonologii", *VJa* 8/2.28-35 (1959).

Lomtev, T. P., "Problema fonemy v svete novogo učenija o jazyke", *IzvAN* 8.321-336 (1949).

Lytkin, V. I., "V kakoj jazykovoj edinice nuždaetsja fonetika", *IzvAN* 12.40-49 (1953).

Matusevic, M., *Voprosy fonetiki. UZLU* 237, Serija filologičeskix nauk, 40.

——, *Vvedenie v obščuju fonetiku* (Moscow, 1959).

"Otkliki na stat'ju S. K. Šaumjana 'Problema fonemy'" (comments by Makaev, Sljusareva, Kirchner, Luknickij, Bertagaev, Panov), *IzvAN* 12.364-377 (1953).

"Ot redakcij" (comment on the discussion raised by Šaumjan), *IzvA N*11.324-333 (1952), *IzvAN* 12.549-554 (1953).

Peter, M., "K teorii 'moskovskoj fonologičeskoj školy'", *SSlav* 3.327-348 (1957).

Piotrovskij, R. G., "Ešče raz o differencial'nyx priznakax fonemy", *VJa* 9/6.24-38 (1960).

Reformatskij, A. A., "K probleme fonemy i fonologii", *IzvAN* 11.469-473 (1952).

——, "O sootnošenii fonetiki i grammatiki (morfologii)", *Voprosy grammatičeskogo stroja*, pp. 92-112 (Moscow, 1955).

——, "Soglasnye, protivopostavlennye po sposobu i mestu obrazovanija, i ix var'irovanie v sovremennom russkom literaturnom jazyke", *DIJa* VIII (Moscow, 1955).

——, "Fonologičeskie zametki", *VJa* 8/2.101-102 (1959).

——, "Možet li byt' matematičeskaja lingvistika?", *VMGU* Serija VII, 5.57-66 1960).

Šaumjan, S. K., "Protiv agnosticizma v fonologii", *UZMU* 150.311-323 (1952).
——, "Problema fonemy", *IzvAN* 11.324-343 (1952).
——, "O nekotoryx voprosax fonologii", *IzvAN* 7.529-548 (1953).
——, "O suščnosti strukturnoj lingvistiki", *VJa* 5/5.38-54 (1956).
——, "Der Gegenstand der Phonologie", *ZPhon* 10.193-203 (1957).
——, *Istorija sistemy differencial'nyx elementov v pol'skom jazyke* (Moscow, 1958).
——, "Dvuxstupenčataja teorija fonemy i differencial'nyx elementov", *VJa* 9/5.18-34 (1960).
——, *Problemy teoretičeskoj fonologii* (Moscow, 1962).
Ščerba, L. V., *Izbrannye raboty po jazykoznaniju i fonetike*, Tom I (Leningrad, 1958).
Smirnickij, A. I., "Fonetičeskaja transkripcija i zvukovye tipy", *VMGU* 7 (1959).
Sokolova, V. S., "O variantax fonemy", *Jazyk i myšlenie* 11.278-282 (1948).
Spirkin, A. G., "Problema fonemy i Leninskaja teorija otraženija", *IzvAN* 11.474-479 (1952).
Toporov, V. N., "I. A. Boduen de Kurtene i razvitie fonologii", in *I. A. Boduen de Kurtene* (Moscow, 1960).
Zareckij, A. I., "Fonema", *UZ Stalinabadskogo pedagogičeskogo instituta* 3.3-33 (1948).
Zinder, L. R., "Suščestvujut li zvuki reči?" *IzvAN* 7.293-302 (1948).
——, *Voprosy fonetiki* (Leningrad, 1948).
——, *Obščaja fonetika* (Leningrad, 1960).

# MORPHEMICS

CORNELIS H. VAN SCHOONEVELD

The picture presented by the development of Russian linguistics, after Stalin's personal interference of 1950, is one of progressing deprovincialization. This characteristic is also apparent in Russian morphology. It must be stated, however, that Russian morphology has been a relatively immovable discipline. Morphologic theory, which itself is still in its infancy, has to account for a great variety of relationships between morphemes, among which the morphology of an inflected language such as Russian presents but one type. In view of the relative primitiveness of the theoretical foundations it is the material itself, the morphemic relationships extant in the Russian language, which to a great extent determine the method of analysis, rather than the other way around, thus creating a good deal of methodological rigidity. On the other hand, when we do notice, in the course of the years, certain changes in the Soviet approach to morphemic problems, they are due, on the whole, to new general views of Soviet linguists, rather than to internal developments within morphology itself. It is not my task to discuss the highly interesting recent Soviet research work on the morphology of the non-Indo-European languages of the Soviet Union.

V. V. Vinogradov, whose publications are of particular importance for the fifties sees, in a statement made in 1954, the year 1952 as an important dividing point in the history of post-1950 Soviet linguistics.[1] Before 1952 there was a theoretical stock-taking, while after that year the main interest was in practical work. With slight emendations to this statement, it would be possible to say that immediately after 1950 the Soviet discussions of general problems consisted largely in the confrontation of existing linguistic theories with Marxian doctrine as interpreted by the given scholar; whereas after 1952 a new type of discussion emerges limiting itself rather to the technical aspects of morphology, without giving, however, essentially new theoretical insights; the problems discussed and the solutions proposed run, on the whole, parallel to statements made at various times in Western Europe and America. After 1960 there appear forceful new ideas which constitute a contributing factor to world linguistics. It has to be borne in mind, to be sure, that this rough classification is like a periodization of *belles lettres*: the first period was to linger on

* Thanks are due to Miss Mary E. Patzer for her kind assistance.

[1] *VJa*, 3/3.151 (1954).

for several years; some scholars, while bearing the imprint of the period in which they worked, cannot be characterized adequately by merely assigning them to the prevailing school. Forerunners of the third period have been active for a long time.

If one were to characterize by one word official Soviet linguistic doctrine as formulated by Stalin in 1950, I would be inclined to term it neogrammarian. Besides the confrontation of linguistic theory with Marxism a neogrammarian spirit permeates Russian linguistics, morphologic discussions included, of the first post-Stalin period.

Of the former type of discussion I mention, by way of example, M. M. Guxman's views on Sapir as set forth in an article of 1954.[2] The author criticizes Bloomfield's and Sapir's exclusion of the lexicon from linguistic structure but endorses Sapir's separation of language and thinking against Whorf, according to whom thinking patterns parallel morphologic patterning. However, according to both Whorf and Sapir, says Guxman, morphologic patterning is autonomous and its development is independent and given *a priori*, which implies a denial of the objective reality of the world perceived by us. This is at variance with Marxian materialism and hence, according to Guxman, to be rejected.

The second, purely linguistic, variety of argument of the beginning period of post-Stalin linguistics is most clearly exemplified in the publications of V. V. Vinogradov and N. S. Pospelov. Language, according to these scholars, forms a system; however, the step to which this statement compels, namely, to determine recurrent identities in various categories, is not taken. The neogrammarian view that the system reveals itself in its diachronic development runs, naturally, aground in that it fails to establish for a later period recurring identities between the members of the system. The diachronic approach to language is apparent in Vinogradov's article on Word Formation,[3] in which Stalin's view of language as the product of a succession of stages has a prominent place. A diachronic conception of linguistic structure underlies also Vinogradov's theory of lexical meaning.[4] The classification of lexical meanings presented in this article is actually one of semantic positional variants: "nominative", "direct" or "free" meaning contains the direct reference to external reality, whereas some types of meaning are contextually conditioned: 1) those that occur in "strictly determined phraseological contexts", e.g. *otvratit' opasnost'*, "to avert a danger"; 2) "functionally-syntactically conditioned", e.g. the lexical meaning of *molodec*, "attaboy", used as a predicate; 3) "constructionally organized" lexical meaning, i.e. such types as occur only in the framework of larger phrases, e.g. the reflexive *plakat'sja* occurs only connected with the preposition *na*. The terms "structure" and "system" are used to denote the relationships of these types of meaning within one lexical morpheme as well as the linguistic system in general, which can hardly mean anything else than the relationships between morphemes. The nature of the latter is not established. Indicative of the style of thinking underlying the investigation is the

[2] Guxman, "È. Sèpir i 'ètnografičeskaja lingvistika'".
[3] Vinogradov, "Slovoobrazovanie i ego otnošenie k grammatike i leksikologii", p. 1, 29 and *passim*.
[4] Vinogradov, "Osnovnye tipy leksičeskix značenij slova".

remark that "the meaning of a word is not only *determined*[5] by its correspondence to the [extralinguistic] concept expressed by this word", but also "depends ... on the concrete lexical connections [of the word] with other words, as conditioned by the laws of word combination operative in the given language...", besides its paradigmatic relationships. Whereas code-style structural linguistics would operate essentially with the latter, and the distributionalist brand of structuralism would view the syntagmatic relations a given word can enter into as an arbitrary appendix to the operational unit, the word, itself, we find here the neogrammarian view that the context is an *influencing* factor contributing to the *nature* of the "Gesamtbedeutung" of the word, a striking parallel to the decisive rôle attributed by the neogrammarians to the phenomenon of assimilation in phonology.

A position very close to Vinogradov's is represented by N. S. Pospelov, in his articles on "the category of tense in grammatical structure", and "the correlation between grammatical categories and the parts of speech".[6] The argumentation is less openly diachronic but does occasionally draw material indiscriminately from various periods and various languages, although Modern Russian is under discussion. Neither exact relationships specific for the given linguistic system of the given period, nor the diachronic relationships between these relationships, are established.

Special attention was paid in the first years after Stalin's intervention in linguistics to the lexicon, centering around Stalin's theory of the so-called "*osnovnoj slovarnyj fond*", "basic lexical stock". By this Stalin meant that part of the vocabulary of the language which a) remains relatively unchanged through the history of the language, b) forms the basis for word formative derivation, c) denotes indispensable concepts for everyday life.[7] The application of his theory, on the other hand, poses problems. It is not easy to establish a criterion for indispensable concepts; some basic words, for instance some pronouns in Russian, are not able to form derivatives; as to the relative stability of words, it turns out to be different for different words, that is, words meaning different concepts, in different languages.[8] More intricate problems are whether morphemes and suffixes also belong to the basic lexical stock and how to treat words with more than one meaning or with various usages.[9] The only way to establish the basic lexical stock is, then, to select those words which in the history of the language remained stable.[10] This method, however, yields, as Guryčeva and Serebrennikov noted,[11] results which are different for each language, so that one wonders whether it can yield any predictability. The conception of the problem as well as the procedures applied to it are, obviously, deeply influenced by neogram-

[5] Italics mine.

[6] Pospelov, "Kategorija vremeni v grammatičeskom stroe" and "Grammatičeskie kategorii i časti reči".

[7] Guryčeva & Serebrennikov, "Zadači izučenija osnovnogo slovarnogo fonda jazyka", pp. 1-2.

[8] *Ibid.*, pp. 7-8.

[9] *VJa*, 2/6.129-130 (1953).

[10] Janko-Trinickaja, "O granicax slovarnogo fonda v slovarnom sostave jazyka", pp. 138-139.

[11] Guryčeva-Serebrennikov, *op. cit.*, pp. 14-15.

marian linguistic theory and find a parallel in the neogrammarian sound laws, which are only valid for a given language at a specific time.

After 1954, another style of morphologic discussion begins to make its influence felt. Its participants do not necessarily hold another view of language than the one prominent in the period I just discussed; but they are less anxious to set forth these views on their own and to support them by adducing random examples. The emphasis is shifting; it is rather the assumptions themselves – which may figure less prominently or even not at all – that are tested on a given body of material. The result is that grammatical theory becomes at the same time less onesided and more technical.

The most enlightening discussion of the period on morphology is the one on case theory. Naturally, the cardinal problem in morphology is to unite a collection of meaningful word elements into a class, whether this class is called a morpheme with its allomorphs, or a grammatical category such as case. In Russian grammatical tradition, until recently, some kind of correlation was always constructed between a given form and meaning. In the nineteenth century there were two traditions. One is represented by K. Aksakov and N. P. Nekrasov, virtually precursors of Prague. To them each different signal [unless in complementary distribution with another signal] represents a different case; [to be sure, the principle of complementary distribution is applied intuitively]. The result is a matching [with the application of certain distributional criteria] between a given form and a meaning – later on developed by the Prague School. E. D. Panfilov[12] characterizes the idea of case in this theory as the MEDIUM to express concepts of relations between objects and between a process and an object, whereas in the other school of thinking "these concepts themselves constitute the contents of the case category". In the nineteenth century scholars like A. A. Potebnja and A. I. Sobolevskij took the initial steps towards this view. They do not operate with complementary and/or parallel distribution. This causes homophonous case morphemes to be allocated into one case, e.g. *dvéri* which, according to the classical interpretation, represents gen. sg., dat. sg., loc. sg., nom. pl., and acc. pl. This leads us, Sobolevskij says, to the existence of more cases for one word than for another in which this homonymy does not exist, and the number of cases is, according to him, undeterminable. If we would, on the other hand, take "grammatical meaning" as our criterion, then one "form *xléba* in various sentences represents three cases: partitivus, ablativus and possessivus". Actually, the three occurences of *xléba* are always in complementary distribution, as is, in fact, each occurence of *xléba* in every single different environment. A. A. Potebnja's statement: "... each special use of the instrumental constitutes a new case..." goes a long way towards the replacement of the investigation of the grammatical category of case by the study of meanings apart from their formal indices. If one applies this approach consistently one could consider each occurence of *xléba* in every single different

[12] Panfilov, "K voprosu o tak nazyvaemom analitičeskom sklonenii".

context a different case. Sobolevskij, who confesses not to be able to give an answer to the question of how many cases there are in Russian, stops, however, at an arbitrary categorization borrowed from Latin grammar. Even more characteristic is the method of the late Leiden Romanist, often quoted on this subject by Soviet scholars, C. de Boer, who sets up even for uninflected languages like French a totally arbitrary system of case meanings which categorizes syntactic phrasecontexts, including prepositional constructions, as cases. Case, says E. A. Bokarev,[13] ceases here to be a morphologic category and becomes a synthetic or semantic category, whereas actually "every formal indicator is an element of a system correlative with other elements" and "every language has its own case system",[14] since case is "a category factually given in the language, based upon the unity of content and form".[15]

Adherents of the first school consider a phraseological combination AS WELL AS A FORM to constitute the category of case. The categorization of contextual meaning is in that case aprioristic. E. V. Češko and V. V. Borodič,[16] as exemplified in their description of the Bulgarian substantive, derive the aprioristic criterion not from Latin or an original categorization but from the existence of cases in the Bulgarian personal pronoun. They feel to have the right to do so since they surmise – wrongly, according to E. D. Panfilov – that the pronoun has the same distribution as the substantives, and case is, in their terminology, "a grammatical category, not only a morphological category". In this recent application, the "concept of the relations themselves" originates again in an arbitrary classification of syntagmatic relations. E. D. Panfilov, although he obviously operates with a general meaning and does not differ in this respect from the Saussurian-Prague tradition, reserves the term "semantic" for the contextual meanings due to syntagmatic combinations.

The principles underlying various approaches to the problem of meaning in morphology are discussed by O. S. Axmanova and others. In modern linguistic theory, there are two important problems: the problem of the semantic categorization underlying the given language, and the related problem of the relation between the *signans* and the *signatum*. The existence of different semantic categorization in various languages is explained through the influence by [diachronically] earlier cognitive processes, and thus the Marxian order of precedence: reality – cognition – form of reflection is defended as contrasted to a hierarchy usual in non-Soviet linguistics: form of reflection – cognition – reality.[17] This earlier cognitive process which leads, in Axmanova's characterization, to "a generalization, a feat of creative imagination", specific "in each language as a result of the peculiarities of its historical development,[18] results in a particular system of external differences, which produces an individual, unique system of linguistic meanings". Thus synchronic differentiations have their

[13] Bokarev, "O kategorii padeža", p. 37.
[14] *Ibid.*, p. 37, 46.
[15] *Ibid.*, p. 33.
[16] Quoted by Panfilov, *op. cit.*, pp. 49-50.
[17] Axmanova, *Očerki po obščej i russkoj leksikologii*, pp. 52-53.
[18] *Ibid.*, p. 44, 51.

diachronic motivation. The same problem is approached in a similar vein by M. N. Alekseev and G. V. Kol'šanskij: while Marxists believe in the unity of the logical structure of thinking and grammatical structure because of the Marxist belief in the unity of language and thinking, logical and grammatical categories differ because they originate in different sources. The relationship between logic and language is brought even more into the linguistic plane by Axmanova: There is a correlation between logical concepts and the meanings of linguistic units whereby the logical concepts are conditioned by three factors: 1) they are based upon the cognition of reality; 2) there has to be a difference in sound (phonological shape) of the corresponding morphemes in order that separate concepts may exist; this creates conversely a dependence of thinking upon language; 3) concepts are not only modified by the given system of phonological differentiations, but they are also modified by the fact that they fit into a conceptual structure.[19] Although especially Axmanova creates very aptly a bridge towards the synchronic plane, diachronic reasoning plays a pronounced rôle in both argumentations. B. A. Serebrennikov states the existence of a principle of selectivity: in both grammar and lexicon the phenomena of external reality are denoted by only certain of their perceivable characteristics. The choice of these characteristics is dependent on the structure of the language, this structure being, in turn, evident from these selections. No attempt, however, is made at establishing interrelations between these characteristics and thus at arranging them into a linguistic structure.[20] Morphology contains more abstract meanings than the lexicon does. Since only more concrete meanings are liable to be borrowed interlinguistically, the morphologic system of a language is more stable than the lexicon.[21]

As to the distinction between lexicon and morphology, V. A. Zvegincev defines lexical meaning on the synchronic plane, as referring to logical classes of phenomena which are objects, and grammatical meanings as referring to classes of phenomena which are not objects. Thus the lexicon is characterized by its correlation to objects.[22] Axmanova follows Smirnickij's characterization: as a lexical entity the word is comparable to a concrete arithmetical number: 2, 3, 7, etc.; from a grammatical point of view, the word is comparable to an algebraic unit, *a* or *x*, which although not being a concrete number can still represent a given number and not another.[23] Thus, she calls grammatical meaning an additional, non-basic meaning denoting a relationship which accompanies the lexical meaning of the word.[24] As to the difference between lexical meaning and concepts ("ponjatija"), according to L. S. Kovtun lexical meaning is the realization of a concept by means of a given linguistic system. The coordinated concepts may be scientific or grown in general human or national everyday life.

[19] *Ibid.*, pp. 28-29.
[20] Serebrennikov, "K probleme tipov abstrakcii", pp. 56, 63, 66-68.
[21] Serebrennikov, "Ob ustojčivosti morfologičeskoj sistemy jazyka", p. 206 sqq.
[22] Zvegincev, *Semasiologija*, p. 110.
[23] Smirnickij, "Leksičeskoe i grammatičeskoe v slove", p. 15.
[24] Axmanova, *op. cit.*, p. 65.

Considering concepts reflections of reality would move us into the realm of logic or psychology.[25]

While the vocabulary of a language constitutes a system which is separate from the morphologic system, it forms, because of the fact that concepts are interrelated, a structure.[26] The phonological structure of a language can comparatively easily be established, because in all the manifestations of a phoneme acoustic invariants create a continuity of the sound phenomena between the allophones; this is due to the fact that phonemes are basically sound signals without a specific meaning. In morphology, this "linearity" between the meanings of the allomorphs is much harder to determine;[27] however, some scholars assume a parallelism between phonemic structure and the linguistic structure in morphology, the so-called isomorphism.[28] In lexical structure, isomorphism seems to be non-existent.[29] Practically nothing has been achieved[30] in determining the structure of the lexicon, probably just because its nature is different.[31] The semantic relationship between the allomorphs of a lexical morpheme is unclarified; therefore, terms like "basic meaning", "direct meaning", and "figurative meaning" are of no use;[32] lexical meaning is nothing but the sum-total of its variants.[33] All Soviet authors recognize polysemy in lexical meaning; the most we can say is that there is a more general meaning (naibolee obščee značenie).[34]

Two morphologists working in the fifties deserve a separate discussion, since they created, dealing with some aspect of morphology, their own coherent theories with special concepts and terminology of their own. A. S. Smirnickij,[35] who clearly shows the influence of F. F. Fortunatov, distinguishes *word* (slovo) from *word form* (slovoforma). *Slovoforma* is the concretization either of the *grammatical form of the word* (grammatičeskaja forma slova) and/or of the *grammatical shaping of the word* (grammatičeskaja oformlennost' slova). The grammatical forms of the word are simply the abstract inflectional forms. The grammatical shaping is always present and equals the presence or absence of grammatical form plus the distributional properties of the word; thus, in inflected forms it is present along with the grammatical form; in non-inflected words, only the grammatical shaping exists. The *slovoforma* is the concrete word, that is, the combination of grammatical form with a lexical morpheme, e.g. *górod*, the nom. sg. of the word *gorod*, that is, of a given masculine word of a certain declension. The *tipoforma* of the same word is constituted by all

25 Kovtun, "O značenii slova", p. 77.
26 Axmanova, Vinogradov & Ivanov, "O nekotoryx voprosax i zadačax leksikologii", p. 5.
27 Axmanova, "O ponjatii 'izomorfizma' lingvističeskix kategorii", p. 87.
28 Axmanova et al., "O nekotoryx voprosax i zadačax", p. 4.
29 Axmanova, *Očerki*, p. 84.
30 Axmanova, "O ponjatii 'izomorfizma'", p. 89; *eadem et al.*, "O nekotoryx voprosax i zadačax", p. 4.
31 Axmanova, "O ponjatii 'izomorfizma'", p. 90.
32 Zvegincev, *op. cit.*, p. 222.
33 *Ibid.*, p. 223.
34 Axmanova, *Očerki*, p. 90.
35 Smirnickij, "Leksičeskoe i grammatičeskoe v slove".

the formal properties except the lexical morpheme; that is, by the nom. sg. of any word of the masculine declension which is bisyllabic and has a stressed initial syllable. The *grammatical form*, finally, equals the nom. sg. The progression of abstraction, then, runs from *slovoforma* via *tipoforma* to *grammatical form*.

Although A. N. Gvozdev's morpheme theory[36] does not essentially differ from Western morpheme theories, it is necessary to mention a few special terms introduced by him. *Synonymous morphemes* are morphemes which "have a common meaning but a different phonemic composition... 1) roots: ... *toska – skorb'* (both words for sorrow); 2) suffixes: *pek-ar' – stekol'-ščik* (nomina agentis); 3) preverbs: *s-prjatat' – po-sejat'* (both merely perfectivizing); 4) inflections: (dative singular) *sel-u – sten-e*...;' It depends, of course, on semantic criteria whether one wishes to posit here synonymousness; Hockett even went so far as to arrange English *I, me, my* and *mine* into one morpheme. *Homonymy of morphemes* is more obvious: 1) roots: *vin-o* (wine) – *vin-a* (guilt); 2) suffixes, e.g. *-k-*: *gor-k-a* (little mountain: deminution) – *cygan-k-a* (female sex); 3) endings: *vod-a* (nom. sg. fem.) – *stol-a* (gen. sg. masc.). There are many morphemes with allomorphs which vary by one or a few phonemes. Gvozdev proceeds with a discussion of morphophonemic alternations. One such alternation is the alternation between stressed and unstressed vowels, called by Gvozdev "sounds in strong and weak position"; however, whereas from the phonetic point of view the allomorph with "a sound in strong position" is the basic variant since it is more differentiated, the basic variant from a morphologic point of view is the variant occuring in the most frequent forms, in basic forms from which other formations are made. Gvozdev concentrates most of his attention, actually, upon a classification of morphophonemic alternations.

In the last few years, Soviet linguistics has initiated a third trend. The testing being done especially since 1960 is often not the testing of material against traditional theories but involves often the testing of evidence against original theories. Original theoretical statements have been made in phonology by S. K. Šaumjan,[37] actually a precursor of this newest period, who also, in morphology, emphasized the distinction between semiotic and semantic: semiotic refers to the relativized meaning in a given linguistic system, whereas semantic refers to the contextual meaning of a form as it is perceived at a given moment.

A new criterium for morphemic identity was created by machine translation theory.[38] From a linguistic point of view the identity relationships on the paradigmatic axis, expressed in set-theoretical terminology, are first of all interesting. Forms are united in one *family*, if they commute without disturbing the formal environment, and provided the new sentence is grammatical. The final criterion for the latter condition is intuitive. The latter condition is the only semantic criterion posed. Homonymous

[36] Gvozdev, "O zvukovom sostave morfem".
[37] Šaumjan, "O suščnosti strukturnoj lingvistiki", p. 41.
[38] Kulagina, "Ob odnom sposobe opredelenija grammatičeskix ponjatij na baze teorii množestv"; Revzin, *Modeli jazyka*; Andreyev, "Models as a Tool in the Development of Linguistic Theory".

cases are considered to belong to one operational unit. Thus the dat. sg. msc. *stolu* and the dat. sg. neuter *oknu* are in one family, since their substitution does not disturb the rection of the adjective, which is in this case for both genders identical. On the other hand, the nominatives of the same words, i.e. *stol* (table) and *okno* (window), belong to two different families because commutation would cause a simultaneous substitution of the coordinated adjectives. But again, *stol* belongs to different family than *slon* (elephant) although they are both masculine words, because *stol* denotes homonymously the nominative and accusative singular cases, whereas *slon* is only nominative singular; therefore, *stol* has not the same range of commutability as *slon*. By the same token, the feminine genitives plural *korov* and *lamp* belong to different families, since the former is also a feminine accusative plural; on the other hand, the feminine genitive plural *lamp* and the masculine genitive plural *domov* are in one family, since there is no gender distinction in the plural, so that the coordinated adjective never changes by a mere gender commutation. Since the adjective must be replaced when the modified noun changes number, the two numbers of the same noun obviously belong to two different families. It is easy to see that the criteria for arranging inflectional forms into a set are quite mechanical and put a minimal reliance upon semantic judgment. While "family" in the noun is comparable to case more than anything else, the *neighborhood* is the category that comes closest to paradigm. Neighborhood is the set of morphologic changes of one and the same word, that is, the inflectional paradigm and, depending on which criteria one wishes to apply, possibly a smaller or larger set of word-formational derivations. Other categories are either derived from traditional linguistics or from "family" and "neighborhood". It is as yet a matter of speculation what morphologic predictabilities can be culled from this approach.

As I mentioned above, there has been in Soviet linguistics since 1960 a strong original trend. This concerns especially structural linguistics, and there is no doubt that many new developments will be forthcoming also in the structural treatment of Russian morphology.

## BIBLIOGRAPHY

Admoni, V. G., "O mnogoaspektno-dominantnom podxode k grammatičeskomu stroju", *VJa*, 10/2.42-52 (1961).

Andreyev, N. D., "Models as a Tool in the Development of Linguistic Theory", *Word*, 18.186-197 (1962).

Arutjunova, N. D., "Nekotorye voprosy obrazovanija i morfologii osnov slova", *NDVŠ-FN*, 1.125-137 (1958).

—, and E. S. Kubrjakova, "Problemy morfologii v trudax amerikanskix deskriptivistov", *Voprosy teorii jazyka v sovremennoj zarubežnoj lingvistike* (Moscow, 1961).

Avanesov, R. I., "Kratšaja zvukovaja edinica v sostave slova i morfemy", *Voprosy grammatičeskogo stroja*, pp. 113-139 (Moscow, 1955).
—, "O trex tipax naučnolingvističeskix transkripcij", *Slavia*, 3.347-371 (1956).
Avilova, N. S., "K voprosu o suffiksal'nom obrazovanii russkogo glagola XVIII v.", *Materialy i issledovanija po istorii russkogo literaturnogo jazyka*, Vol. 2 (Moscow, 1951).
Axmanova, O. S., "Glossematika Lui El'msleva kak projavlenie upadka sovremennogo buržuaznogo jazykoznanija", *VJa*, 2/3.25-47 (1953).
—, "K voprosu ob osnovnyx ponjatijax metajazyka lingvistiki", *VJa*, 10/5.115-121 (1961).
—, *Očerki po obščej i russkoj leksikologii* (Moscow, 1957).
—, "O metode lingvističeskogo issledovanija u amerikanskix strukturalistov", *VJa*, 1/5.92-105 (1952).
—, "O ponjatii 'izomorfizma' lingvističeskix kategorij", *VJa*, 5/3.82-95 (1955).
—, *Osnovnye napravlenija lingvističeskogo strukturalizma* (Moscow, 1955).
—, I. A. Mel'čuk, E. V. Padučeva, and R. M. Frumkina, "*O točnyx metodax issledovanija jazyka*" (Moscow, 1961).
—, V. V. Vinogradov, and V. V. Ivanov, "O nekotoryx voprosax i zadačax leksikologii", *VJa*, 5/3.1-24 (1956).
Belokrinickaja, S. S. *et al.*, "Različnye tipy omonimii i sposoby ix različenija pri mašinnom perevode", *VJa*, 9/2.97-101 (1960).
Bernštejn, S. B., "Očerk sravnitel'noj grammatiki slavjanskix jazykov", *KSISl*, 18.3-26 (1956).
—, "Osnovnye zadači, metody i principy sravnitel'noj grammatiki slavjanskix jazykov", *Voprosy slavjanskogo jazykoznanija*, 1.5-23 (1954).
Boguslavskij, A. S., "Obrazovanija tipa *belet'sja* i otymennye glagoly", *VJa*, 11/1.77-80 (1962).
Bokarev, E. A., "O kategorii padeža", *VJa*, 3/1.30-46 (1954).
Bondarko, A. V., "Sistema glagol'nyx vremen v sovremennom russkom jazyke", *VJa*, 11/3.27-37 (1962).
Bulaxovskij, L. N., "Grammatičeskaja indukcija v slavjanskom sklonenii", *VJa*, 5/4.14-30 (1956).
—, "Ob odnom častnom uslovii grammatičeskoj indukcii", *IzvAN*, 2.129-131 (1960).
Češko, E. V., "K voprosu o padežnyx korreljacijax", *VJa*, 9/2.50-56 (1960).
Čikobava, A. S., "Stalinskij ètap v razvitii sovetskogo jazykoznanija", *Literaturnaja gazeta*, 14 November 1950.
—, *Vvedenie v jazykoznanije*, Vol. I (Moscow, 1952).
Dobromyslova, A. N., "K interpretacii odnogo javlenija padežnogo sinkretizma v drevnem novgorodskom govore", *VJa*, 10/6.83-89 (1961).
Fal'kovič, M. M., "K voprosu ob omonimii i polisemii", *VJa*, 9/5.85-88 (1960).
Gal'kina-Fedoruk, E. M., K. V Gorškova, and N. M. Šanskij, *Sovremennyj russkij jazyk: leksikologija, fonetika, morfologija*, (Moscow, 1958).

Golovin, B. N., "K voprosu o suščnosti grammatičeskoj kategorii", *VJa*, 4/1.117-124 (1955).
—, "Zametki o grammatičeskom značenii", *VJa*, 11/2.29-37 (1962).
Gornung, B. V., "O xaraktere jazykovoj struktury", *VJa*, 8/1.34-38 (1959).
*Grammatika russkogo jazyka*, Vol. I: *Fonetika i morfologija* (Moscow, 1952).
Grigor'ev, V. I., "Neskol'ko zamečanij o strukturalizme i semantike", *VJa*, 7/4.24-36 (1958).
Grigor'ev, V. P., "O granicax meždu slovosloženiem i affiksaciej", *VJa*, 5/4.38-52 (1956).
—, "O vzaimodejstvii slovosloženija i affiksacii", *VJa*, 10/5.71-77 (1961).
Guryčeva, M. S., and B. A. Serebrennikov, "Zadači izučenija osnovnogo slovarnogo fonda jazyka", *VJa*, 2/6.1-20 (1953).
Guxman, M. M., "È. Sèpir i 'ètnografičeskaja lingvistika'", *VJa*, 3/1.110-127 (1954).
Gvozdev, A. N., "O zvukovom sostave morfem", *VJa*, 9/3.28-39 (1960).
—, "K voprosu ob otnošenii fonetiki k morfologii", *Voprosy grammatičeskogo stroja* (Moscow, 1955).
—, *Ob osnovax russkogo pravopisanija* (Moscow, 1960).
—, *Osnovy russkoj orfografii* (Moscow, 1954).
—, *Sovremennyj russkij literaturnyj jazyk: fonetika i morfologija* (Moscow, 1958-61).
—, *Formirovanie u rebenka grammatičeskogo stroja russkogo jazyka* (Moscow, 1949).
Havránek, B., "Dva roky po Stalinově genialním zásahu do vývoje jazykovědy", *Slovo a slovesnost*, 1952, pp. 109-117.
Isačenko, A. V., *Grammatičeskoj stroj russkogo jazyka: morfologija*, 2 vols. (Bratislava, 1954, 1960).
Janko-Trinickaja, N. A., "O granicax slovarnogo fonda v slovarnom sostave jazyka", *VJa*, 2/6.129-140 (1953).
Knabe, G. S., "Slovarnye zaimstvovanija i ètnogenez", *VJa*, 11/1.65-76 (1962).
Kovtun, L. S., "O značenii slova", *VJa*, 4/5.65-77 (1955).
Kržižkova, E., "Nekotorye problemy izučenija kategorii vremeni v sovremennom russkom jazyke", *VJa*, 11/3.17-26 (1962).
Kulagina, O. S., "Ob odnom sposobe opredelenija grammatičeskix ponjatij na baze teorii množestv", *PK*, 1.203-214 (1954).
Kuznecov, P. S., *Istoričeskaja grammatika russkogo jazyka: morfologija* (Moscow, 1953).
—, *Morfologičeskaja klassifikacija jazykov* (Moscow, 1954).
—, *Očerki istoričeskoj morfologii russkogo jazyka* (Moscow, 1959).
—, "O vozniknovenii i razvitii zvukovyx čeredovanij v russkom jazyke", *IzvAN*, 1.61-75 (1952).
—, *Russkaja dialektologija: učebnik dlja učitel'skix institutov* (Moscow, 1954).
Lekov, I., "Otklonenija ot flektivnogo stroja v slavjanskix jazykax", *VJa*, 5/2.18-26 (1956).
Leška, O., "K voprosu o strukturalizme (Dve koncepcii grammatiki v Pražskom

lingvističeskom kružke)", *VJa*, 2/5.88-102 (1953).
Makaev, È. A., "K voprosu ob izomorfizme", *VJa*, 10/5.50-56 (1961).
Mareš, V. F., "Rannij period morfologičeskogo razvitija slavjanskogo sklonenija", *VJa*, 11/6.13-21 (1962).
Mološnaja, T. N., "Voprosy različenija omonimov pro mašinnom perevode s anglijskogo na russkij", *PK*, 1.215ff. (1958).
Muxin, A. M., "Funkcional'nye lingvističeskie edinicy i metody strukturnogo analiza jazyka", *VJa*, 10/1.83-93 (1961).
—, "Ponjatie nejtralizacii i funkcional'nye lingvističeskie edinicy", *VJa*, 11/5.53-61 (1962).
Nikolaeva, T. M., "Čto takoe transformacionnyj analiz?", *VJa*, 9/1.111-115 (1960).
"O nekotoryx aktual'nyx zadačax sovremennogo sovetskogo jazykoznanija", *VJa*, 5/4.3-13 (1956).
Obnorskij, S. P., *Očerki po morfologii russkogo glagola* (Moscow, 1953).
—, "Zamečanija na 'grammatiku russkogo jazyka', tom I", *DSIJa*, 6.143-150 (1954).
Panfilov, E. D., "K voprosu o tak nazyvaemom analitičeskom sklonenii", *VJa*, 3/1.47-54 (1954).
Panov, M. V., "O razgraničitel'nyx signalax v jazyke", *VJa*, 10/1.1-19 (1061).
Perebejnos, V. I., "Ob izpol'zovanii strukturnyx metodov dlja razgraničenija značenij mnogoznačnogo glagola", *VJa*, 11/3.56-61 (1962).
Peterson, M. M., "O častjax reči v russkom jazyke", *Voprosy grammatičeskogo stroja*, pp. 175-187 (Moscow, 1955).
Pospelov, N. S., "Kategorija vremeni v grammatičeskom stroe russkogo glagola", *Voprosy teorii i istorii jazyka v svete trudov I. V. Stalina po jazykoznaniju*, pp. 286-305 (Moscow, 1952).
—, "Sootnošenie meždu grammatičeskimi kategorijami i častjami reči", *Voprosy grammatičeskogo stroja*, pp. 74-91 (Moscow, 1955).
Reformatskij, A. A., "O sootnošenii fonetiki i grammatiki (morfologii)", *Voprosy grammatičeskogo stroja*, pp. 92-112 (Moscow, 1955).
—, *Vvedenie v jazykoznanije* (Moscow, 1960).
Revzin, I. I., *Modeli jazyka* (Moscow, 1962).
—, "Struktural'naja lingvistika i problemy izučenija slova", *VJa*, 6/2.31-41 (1957).
—, and V. Ju. Rozencvejg, "K obosnovaniju lingvističeskoj teorii perevoda", *VJa*, 11/1.51-59 (1962).
Šanskij, N. M., "Izmenenija v morfologičeskoj strukture slova", *RJaŠ*, 4.6-12 (1959).
Šaumjan, S. K., "O ponjatijax lingvističeskoj sistemy i lingvističeskogo znaka", *KSISl*, 1961, pp. 3-13.
—, "O suščnosti strukturnoj lingvistiki", *VJa*, 5/5.38-54 (1956).
Šendel's, E. I., "O grammatičeskom polisemii", *VJa*, 11/3.47-55 (1962).
Serebrennikov, B. A., "Ob ustojčivosti morfologičeskoj sistemy jazyka", *Voprosy ... I. V. Stalina*, pp. 204-224 (Moscow, 1952).
—, "K probleme tipov leksičeskoj i grammatičeskoj abstrakcii", *Voprosy grammati-*

*českogo stroja*, pp. 54-73 (Moscow, 1955).
Sidorov, V. N., "Neproduktivnye klassy glagola v sovremennom russkom literaturnom jazyke", *RJaŠ*, 5.22-23 (1951).
Smirnickij, A. I., "Fonetičeskaja transkripcija i zvukovye tipy", *VMU*, No. 7 (1949).
—, "Leksičeskoe i grammatičeskoe v slove", *Voprosy grammatičeskogo stroja*, pp. 11-53) (Moscow, 1955).
—, "K voprosu o slove", *Voprosy ... I. V. Stalina*, pp. 182-203 (Moscow, 1952).
—, "K voprosu o sravnitel'no-istoričeskom metode v jazykoznanii", *VJa*, 1/4.3-19 (1952).
—, "Značenie v slove", *VJa*, 4/2.79-89 (1955).
*Sovremennyj russkij jazyk: morfologija* (Moscow, 1952).
Steblin-Kamenskij, M. I., "Neskol'ko zamečanij o strukturalizme", *VJa*, 6/1.35-40 (1957).
Sunik, O. P., "O proisxoždenii morfologičeskoj struktury slova", *VJa*, 8/5.43-51 (1959).
Trofimov, V. A., *Sovremennyj russkij literaturnyj jazyk; morfologija* (Leningrad, 1957).
Tyšler, I. S., "K voprosu o sud'be omonimov", *VJa*, 9/5.80-84 (1960).
Ufimceva, A. A., "K voprosu o leksiko-semantičeskoj sisteme jazyka", *VJa*, 11/4.36-46 (1962).
Uspenskij, B. A., "Tipologičeskaja klassifikacija jazykov", *VJa*, 10/6.51-64 (1961).
Uxanov, G. P., *Morfologičeskoe stroenie slova v sovremennom russkom jazyke* (Xarbin, 1955).
Venediktov, G. K., "O morfologičeskix sredstvax imperfektivacii v russkom jazyke", *VJa*, 10/2.88-96 (1961).
Vinogradov, V. V., "Ob omonimii i smežnyx javlenijax", *VJa*, 9/5.3-17 (1960).
—, "Ob osnovnom slovarnom fonde i ego slovoobrazujuščej roli v istorii jazyka", *IzvAN*, 1951, pp. 218-239.
—, "Osnovnye tipy leksičeskix značenij slova", *VJa*, 2/5.1-29 (1953).
—, "Slovoobrazovanie i ego otnošenie k grammatike i leksikologii (na materiale russkogo i rodstvennyx jazykov)", *Voprosy ... I. V. Stalina* ([Moscow], 1952), 99-153.
—, *Sovremennyj russkyj jazyk: morfologija* ([Moscow], 1952).
—, "Voprosy izučenija slovosočetanij (na materiale russkogo jazyka)", *VJa*, 3/3.3-24 (1954).
—, „Voprosy sovremennogo russkogo slovoobrazovanija v svete trudov I. V. Stalina po jazykoznaniju", *RJaŠ*, 2.1-10 (1951).
Volockaja, Z. M., "Ustanovlenie otnošenija proizvodnosti meždu slovami", *VJa*, 9/3.100-107 (1960).
Zemskaja, E. A., "Ob osnovnyx processax slovoobrazovanija prilagatel'nyx v russkom literaturnom jazyke XIX v.", *VJa*, 11/2.46-55 (1962).
Žirmunskij, V. M., "O granicax slova", *VJa*, 10/3.3-21 (1961).
Zvegincev, V. A., *Semasiologija* (Moscow, 1957).

# SYNTAX

DEAN S. WORTH

The post-war period in Soviet linguistics has been one of stock-taking and critical reevaluation, both of the national heritage and of Western structuralism, discussion of which had been forbidden for so long under Stalin. This new period opened with the toppling of old idols of the Marr school, particularly the then dean of Soviet linguists, I. I. Meščaninov. Meščaninov's original but tendentious book *Členy predloženija i časti reči* [Parts of the sentence and parts of speech] (Moscow-Leningrad, 1945), was subjected to a bitingly negative review by V. V. Vinogradov in *VJa*, 1/1 (1952), 142-149, as well as to an extended attack by several linguists during an open session of the Scholarly Council of the Linguistic Institute of the Soviet Academy of Sciences, which took place in November, 1951 and was reported in *VJa*, 1/1 (1952), 170-177. These attacks were a prelude to the seven-year silence imposed on Meščaninov. At the same time, Soviet scholars were rereading and rehabilitating the works of some of their predecessors, as in V. V. Vinogradov's extensive discussion of Šaxmatov's voluminous and penetrating syntactic study "*Sintaksis russkogo jazyka* Akad. A. A. Šaxmatova", in the collective volume *Voprosy sintaksisa sovremennogo russkogo jazyka* [Problems of modern Russian syntax] (Moscow, 1950), pp. 75-126. Not all the reevaluations were positive, however, as was witnessed by the same author's attack on A. M. Peškovskij in the same volume ("Idealističeskie osnovy sintaksičeskoj sistemy Prof. A. M. Peškovskogo, ee èklektizm i vnutrennie protivorečija [The idealistic bases of Prof. A. M. Peškovskij's syntactic system, its eclecticism and internal contradictions]", *ibid.*, pp. 36-74). New material from the Soviet archives was published by È. I. Karataeva, which made available for the first time some of Šaxmatov's views of problems of classifying the compound sentence and certain utterance-length units in which sentences themselves stand in coordinate and subordinate relations to each other, "Akademik A. A. Šaxmatov o predloženii s odnorodnymi členami i o složnom predloženii [Academician A. A. Šaxmatov's views of sentences with homogenous members and of compound sentences]", *DSIRJa*, 1 (1948), 66-80. The views of another great scholar, L. V. Ščerba, were summed up several years later by S. G. Barxudarov in the Vinogradov Festschrift, "L. V. Ščerba o russkom sintaksise", *Akademiku Viktoru Vladimiroviču Vinogradovu k ego šestidesjatiletiju, sbornik statej* (Moscow, 1956), pp. 60-70. The most important work on the history of Russian syntactic studies to appear in the post-war period, however, was V. V. Vinogradov's fundamental book, *Iz istorii izučenija russkogo sintaksisa (ot Lomonosova do Potebni i Fortunatova)* [From the history of Russian syntactic studies (from Lomonosov to Potebnja and Fortunatov)] (Moscow, MGU, 1958), pp. 400. The excellence of this work was recognized in a review by N. S. Pospelov in *VJa*, 8/3 (1959), 102-110, although Pospelov did feel one might quarrel with Vinogradov's periodization of the development of syntactic thought.

Soviet attitutes toward Western syntactic works, and especially toward structural studies, underwent a gradual reorientation. Structural linguistics had of course been a tabu subject for years, so it is not surprising that the first discussions of structuralism were cloaked in a cautious outer garment of political diatribe, as in O. S. Axmanova's "O metode lingvističeskogo issledovanija u amerikanskix strukturalistov [On the linguistic research method of American structuralists]", *VJa*, 1/5 (1952), 92-105. At the time, it often seemed that political views were more important than scientific accuracy, but in retrospect, one wonders whether in fact the often vituperative tone of such articles was not produced by tongue in cheek, with the express purpose of bringing structural linguistics out of the limbo of total inattention in which it had been languishing. During the fifties, the tone of such review and discussion articles grew less political and more scholarly. Western views were often criticized, but this criticism came to be based largely on genuine scholarly differences of opinion, rather than on the narrow preconceptions of political prejudice. Cf., for example, V. G. Admoni's "Razvitie sintaksičeskoj teorii na Zapade v XX v. i strukturalizm [The development of Western syntactic theory in the 20th century and structuralism]", *VJa*, 5/6 (1956), 48-64, or G. B. Mikaèljan, "Voprosy sintaksisa v amerikanskoj 'deskriptivnoj' lingvistike [Syntactic problems in American 'descriptive' linguistics]", *NDVŠ-FN*, 3 (1958), 156-165.

The transformational approach to syntax, both within and independent of the theory of generative grammar, was first officially noticed in the USSR in 1960, when T. M. Nikolaeva published a brief survey, "Čto takoe transformacionnyj analiz [What is transformational analysis]?", *VJa*, 9/1 (1960), 111-115. Nikolaeva outlined the difference between the expansion of constituents in an IC model and the transformation of strings, with examples from several American works in this field, but did not distinguish very clearly between the Harris and Chomsky conceptions of transformations, as was pointed out a year later in the same journal by R. B. Lees, "Čto takoe transformacija [What is a transformation]?", *VJa*, 10/3 (1961), 69-77. Chomsky's work evoked great interest in the Soviet Union, as evidenced by the decision of the journal *Voprosy jazykoznanija* to print translations of A. Hill's article "Grammaticality", *Word*, XVII, 1 (1961) (A. Xill, "O grammatičeskoj otmečennosti predloženija", *VJa*, 11/4, 1962, 104-110) and Chomsky's "Some methodological remarks on generative grammar", *Word*, XVII, 2 (1961) (N. Xomskij, "Neskol'ko metodologičeskix zamečanij o poroždajuščej grammatike", *VJa*, 11/4, 1962, 110-122). In the same year, Chomsky's *Syntactic Structures* was very positively reviewed by T. N. Mološnaja in the extremely interesting collective volume *Strukturno-tipologi-*

*českie issledovanija* [Structural-typological studies] (Moscow, 1962), pp. 214-216, and the second volume of the informative *Novoe v lingvistike* [New trends in linguistics] (Moscow, 1962) contained Russian translations of Chomsky's *Syntactic Structures* (pp. 412-527), Harris's "Co-occurrence and transformation in linguistic structure", *Language*, 33 (1957), 283-340 (528-636), and the present reviewer's "Transform analysis of Russian instrumental constructions", *Word*, 14 (1958), 247-290 (637-683), preceded by a survey of the principles of generative grammar written by S. K. Šaumjan, "Teoretičeskie osnovy transformacionnoj grammatiki [The theoretical bases of transformational grammar]", pp. 391-411. A second article by Lees, "O pereformulirovanii transformacionnyx grammatik [On the reformulation of transformational grammars]", *VJa*, 10/6 (1961), 41-50, took up the cudgels against Householder and Hockett, maintaining that IC grammars cannot be broadened sufficiently to handle the facts covered by transformational models.

The general concept of transformational relations among linguistic units has proved very stimulating, although perhaps not always just as its originators would have wished, in work in several areas of linguistics. One might name, for example, Z. M. Volockaja's study "Ustanovlenie otnošenija proizvodnosti meždu slovami (Opyt primenenija transformacionnogo metoda) [The determination of derivative relations among words (An attempt to apply the transformational method)]", *VJa*, 9/3 (1960), 100-107, in the field of derivational morphology, D. N. Šmelev's discussion of the distinctions between transformationally related phrases and fixed syntactic patterns "O 'svjazannyx' sintaksičeskix konstrukcijax v russkom jazyke [On 'bound' syntactic constructions in Russian]", *VJa*, 9/5 (1960), 47-60, or S. E. Nikitina's work on the Russian passive "Formal'nyj analiz stradatel'nyx konstrukcij v russkom jazyke [The formal analysis of passive constructions in Russian]", in the collective work on machine translation *Mašinnyj perevod i prikladnaja lingvistika* [Machine translation and applied linguistics], 6 (1961), 89-100, which although not formally based on transformational theory, makes use of the same sort of material. The transformation potential of word-combinations is used in an attempt to construct a structural lexicology by Ju. D. Apresjan in "K voprosu o strukturnoj leksikologii [Towards a structural lexicology]", *VJa*, 11/3 (1962), 38-46, and with the more restricted goal of classifying the word-combinations themselves semantically by S. I. Kalabina in "Ispol'zovanie metoda transformacionnogo analiza pri issledovanii semantičeskix svojstv slovosočetanij [The transformational method used to investigate the semantic qualities of word-combinations]", *NDVŠ-FN*, 3 (1962), 63-72. Finally, transformations are used as one of the means of establishing typological relations among language systems by I. I. Rezvin in his article, "O ponjatijax odnorodnogo jazyka i jazyka s polnoj transformaciej (JaPT) i vozmožnosti ix primenenija dlja strukturnoj tipologii [On the concept of a homogenous language and a language with complete transformation, and the possibility of using them for structural typology]", *Strukturno-tipologičeskie issledovanija* (1962), pp. 19-24.

## SYNTAX AND LOGIC

The relations between logical and syntactic categories had been discussed at some length by P. S. Popov in 1950, "Suždenie i predloženie [Judgment and sentence]", *Voprosy sintaksisa* (1950), pp. 5-35, and was continued by such articles as M. N. Alekseev and G. V. Kolšanskij's "O sootnošenii logičeskix i grammatičeskix kategorii [On the correlations of logical and grammatical categories]", *VJa*, 4/5 (1955), 3-19, and K. G. Krušel'nickaja's "K voprosu o smyslovom členenii predloženija [On the semantic segmentation of the sentence]", *VJa*, 5/5 (1956), 55-67. The Marxist view of judgment and sentence was dealt with by P. S. Popov, "Dialektika suždenija [Dialectic of the judgment]", *Akad. V. V. Vinogradovu* (1958), pp. 195-203, and on a more casual level by M. A. Pustynnikova in "K voprosu o dialektičeskoj suščnosti predloženija [On the dialectical essence of the sentence]", *RJaŠ*, 5 (1956), 6-11. There were some attempts to popularize this subject, as for example the brochures by E. M. Galkina-Fedoruk, *Slovo i ponjatie* [Word and concept] and *Suždenie i predloženie* [Judgment and sentence], which both appeared in the series *Voprosy sovetskogo jazykoznanija* [Problems of Soviet linguistics] in 1956, cf. the review by P. S. Popov in *RJaŠ*, 5 (1956), 107-111. The distinction between logical subject and grammatical subject ("sub"ekt" and "podležaščee" in Russian) is discussed by T. A. Bertagaev in "Sub"ekt i podležaščee", *VJa*, 7/5 (1958), 65-69; Bertagaev's conclusions are of general interest although most of his examples are from Mongol rather than Russian. The relations between linguistic systems and thought processes was the subject of an inquiry undertaken by *Voprosy jazykoznanija* in 1958, reported in the anonymous "Problema sootnošenija jazyka i myšlenija (Obzor statej, postupivšix v redakciju) [The problem of the correlation of language and thought (Survey of articles received by the editors)]", *VJa*, 5 (1958), 105-111. Logical emphasis was considered, primarily from the stylistic point of view, by I. P. Raspopov, "Smyslovye i stilističeskie funkcii logičeskogo udarenija [Semantic and stylistic functions of logical stress]", *RJaŠ*, 4 (1957), 18-22, cf. also his "Variantnost' sintaksičeskix konstrukcij i kommunikativnyx edinic jazyka [Variability of syntactic constructions and communicative units of language]", *NDVŠ-FN*, 4 (1962), 198-202, and with more depth by P. S. Popov, "O logičeskom udarenii [On logical stress]", a few years later in *VJa*, 10/3 (1961), 87-97; Popov points out among other facts that logical stress can separate out not only words, but morphemes within words, e.g. "ne *pjat'*desjat, a *šest'*desjat" "not *fif*ty, but *six*ty". Finally, the subject of synaesthesia was approached by N. F. Pelevina in her "O sootnošenii jazyka i dejstvitel'nosti (oboznačenie krasnogo i sinego cvetov) [On the interrelation of language and reality (designations of red and blue colors)]", *NDVŠ-FN*, 2 (1962), 149-152.

## THEORY AND METHODS OF SYNTAX

Interest in general problems of syntactic theory and methodology was apparently dormant during the first years of the fifties, but revived toward the end of that decade. T. P. Lomtev was one of the first to raise general problems of syntactic theory, primarily in his original but somewhat disorganized book *Osnovy sintaksisa sovremennogo russkogo jazyka* [The bases of modern Russian syntax] (Moscow, 1958), pp. 166; cf. the very negative review by A. B. Šapiro, *VJa*, 8/6 (1959), 136-142, and the more friendly comments of E. A. Sedel'nikov, *NDVŠ-FN*, 2 (1958), 127-134, and of S. Karolak, *NDVŠ-FN*, 3 (1960), 155-162. Lomtev replied to Šapiro in *VJa*, 9/6 (1960), 136-142, and also in the journal of which he is editor, the *Naučnye doklady vysšej školy, Filologičeskie nauki*, in the articles "O vvodnyx i odnorodnyx pozicijax slovesnyx form v sovremennom russkom jazyke [On introductory and homogenous word-form positions in modern Russian]", 1 (1958), 114-124, and "O spornyx voprosax teorii sintaksisa [On moot issues of syntactic theory]", 4 (1958), 3-19. The late fifties also saw several articles of general theoretical interest in academic journals, e.g. the discussion by V. G. Admoni of "Zaveršennost' konstrukcii kak javlenie sintaksičeskoj formy [The closed character of a construction as an item of syntactic form]", *VJa*, 7/1 (1958), 111-117. Academician I. I. Meščaninov, who was again permitted to publish after years of exile from the Soviet scholarly journals, dealt with general features of syntactically organized units in his critical discussion of Bally's theories, "Sintaksičeskie gruppy [Syntactic groups]", *VJa*, 7/3 (1958), 24-37, as well as in the more specialized "Osnovnye vidy sintaksičeskix gruppirovok [Basic forms of syntactic groupings]", *IzvAN*, 6 (1959), 490-499. Discussion of syntactic theory grew in scope and vigor in the first years of the following decade. O. S. Axmanova criticized K. Pike's theories in "K voprosu ob osnovnyx ponjatijax metajazyka lingvistiki [On the basic concepts of a linguistic metalanguage]", *VJa*, 10/5 (1961), 115-121, while the discussion in the *Naučnye doklady vysšej školy, Filologičeskie nauki* was continued by A. B. Šapiro, "O predmete sintaksisa [On the subject of syntax]", 3 (1961), 78-85, and A. B. Bondarko, replying to the question, "V čem zaključaetsja predmet sintaksisa i kakova dolžna byt' ego struktura [What does syntax consist of and what should its structure be like]", 1, (1962), 214-215, among others. D. N. Šmelev printed his views of syntactic theory in the same journal in 1961, "Neskol'ko zamečanij k postroeniju sintaksičeskoj teorii [A few remarks on the construction of a syntactic theory]", 3 (1961), 86-94, while T. P. Lomtev continued to defend and expand his own views in "Ob absoljutnyx i reljacionnyx svojstvax sintaksičeskix edinic [On absolute and relative features of syntactic units]", *NDVŠ-FN*, 4 (1960), 15-28, and "Priroda sintaksičeskix javlenij (k voprosu o predmete sintaksisa) [The nature of syntactic phenomena (on the subject of syntax)]", *NDVŠ-FN*, 3 (1961), 26-37. Lomtev had touched upon the idea of paradigmatic structures on the syntactic level, and the same idea was developed by A. M. Muxin in his article, "Sintaksema kak funkcional'naja sintaksičeskaja edinica (o metoda strukturnogo analiza sintaksičeskix èlementov) [The syntaxeme as a functional syntactic unit (on the method of structural analysis of syntactic elements)]", *NDVŠ-FN*, 3 (1961), 53-65. Finally, I. I. Rezvin analyzes the basic syntactic units in a morpheme-to-utterance procedure in "Osnovnye edinicy sintaksičeskogo analiza i ustanovlenie otnošenij meždu nimi [The basic units of syntactic analysis and the establishment of relations among them]", *Strukturno-tipologičeskie issledovanija* (1962), pp. 119-123.

The nature of the syntagma had been the subject of several articles during the Marr period, e.g., Ja. V. Loj, "Sintagmy", *RJaŠ*, 3 (1940); E. V. Krotevič, "K voprosu o sintagmatičeskom členenii rečevogo potoka [On the syntagmatic segmentation of the flow of speech]", *Naukovy zapysky* of Lvov University, 2 (1946); E. V. Krotevič, "Obosoblennye sintagmy [Detached syntagmas]", *VSlJa*, 1 (1948); and G. R. Tukumčev, "Ponjatie o sintagme", *RJaŠ*, 1 (1948), but the first really erudite survey of both Western and Russian views of the syntagma was presented by V. V. Vinogradov in his lengthy article, "Ponjatie sintagmy v sintaksise russkogo jazyka (kritičeskij obzor teorii i zadači sintagmatičeskogo izučenija russkogo jazyka) [The concept of the syntagma in Russian syntax (critical survey of the theory and goal of syntagmatic study of Russian)]", *Voprosy sintaksisa* (1950), pp. 183-256; Vinogradov sums up the opinions of Baudouin de Courtenay, Ščerba, de Saussure, Karcevskij, Reformackij, Bally, Sechehaye, Fortunatov, and many others, and comes to the conclusion that the syntagma is both intonational and semantic in nature, and can be discovered only in concrete sentences; he sees syntagmas in neither the word-combination nor the sentence as such, but rather as an independent but related syntactic form.

A lengthy if not very enlightening discussion on syntagmatic theory was opened in 1957 by F. Mikuš' article, "Obsuždenie voprosov strukturalizma i sintagmatičeskaja teorija [The discussion of questions of structuralism and syntagmatic theory]", *VJa*, 6/1 (1957), 27-34, in which Mikuš expands upon the well-known Geneva view of the syntagma, considering his own views of syntagmatics the only tenable ones. This article evoked a discussion by E. A. Sedel'nikov somewhat over a year later, "Neskol'ko slov o sintagmatičeskoj teorii [A few words about syntagmatic theory]", *VJa*, 8/4 (1958), 51-54, in which the author points out that Mikuš fails to distinguish between predicative and non predicative syntagmatic word-combinations. Mikuš replied in a letter to the editor of *Voprosy jazykoznanija* the following year, *VJa*, 5 (1959), 129-130, denying that he had neglected the semasiological side of syntagmatics, and appealing to the authority of Sapir to demonstrate the identical syntagmatic structure of the English words "reformers" and "unthinkingly". Mikuš, becoming an inveterate contributor to *Voprosy jazykoznanija*, objects to the views both of his Soviet colleagues and of Marcel Cohen, "Zamečanija po povodu nekotoryx statej, opublikovannyx v žurnale *Voprosy jazykoznanija* [Remarks on certain articles published in the journal *Problems of linguistics*]", *VJa*, 8/1 (1959), 49-50, and subjects the structural syntax of Tesnière, *Éléments de syntaxe structurale* (Paris, 1959) to criticism, emphasizing somewhat apodictically the superiority of his own views. Sedel'nikov took up the challenge again in the article, "Ešče o sintagmatičeskoj teorii [More on syntagmatic theory]", *VJa*, 10/1 (1961), 73-82, noting that Mikuš theories, while containing much of interest, also contain a number of debatable points; Sedel'nikov does share Mikuš' view that all syntagmas are binary. Mikuš again replied in a second letter to the editor, *VJa*, 11/2 (1962), 117-121, pointing out that he does not include Bally's phonological syntagmas into his own system. The arguments in this discussion have been rather tendentious, and one thinks back with some pleasure to the relatively simple polemics, say, of Pospelov with Belić, N. S. Pospelov, "Učenie Akademika A. Beliča o sintaksičeskom indikative i sintaksičeskom reljative", *Doklady i soobščenija filologičeskogo fakul'teta MGU*, 3 (1947). In the meantime, a quite original view of syntagmatic structure had been developed by a team of scholars working primarily on machine translation: E. V. Padučeva and A. L. Šumilina, "Opisanie sintagm russkogo jazyka (V svjazi s postroeniem algoritma mašinnogo perevoda) [A description of Russian syntagmas (In connection with the construction of an MT algorhythm)]", *VJa*, 10/4 (1961), 105-115; the validity of these authors' results is only partially vitiated by the fact that their material consists entirely of texts in the field of mathematics. During that same year, O. I. Dikušina published her views of the syntagma, "Kakoj edinicej javljaetsja sintagma [What kind of unit is the syntagma]?", in the collective volume *Voprosy teorii jazyka* (= *UZLU* 283) (1961), 53-59, coming to the conclusion that the syntagma is both intonational and syntactic in nature. Finally, the syntagma is regarded from the point of view of T. P. Lomtev's theory of positions by S. Karolak in "Problema sintagmatičeskoj pozicii èlementov jazyka [The problem of the syntagmatic position of linguistic elements]", *NDVŠ-FN*, 2 (1962), 16-30.

## PARTS OF THE SENTENCE AND PARTS OF SPEECH

The harsh attacks on I. I. Meščaninov's *Členy predloženija i časti reči* (cf. above, p. 35) did not mean that all discussion of the relation of sentence elements to parts of speech was forbidden. Particularly in the last few years of the decade with which we are concerned, there appeared a number of papers on this topic, e.g. V. N. Migirin's general discussion "Otnošenija meždu častjami reči i členami predloženija [The relation between parts of speech and parts of the sentence]", *NDVŠ-FN*, 1 (1959), 130-140; cf. also his "Principy izučenija členov predloženija [Principles of sentence-part study]", *NDVŠ-FN*, 3 (1961), 38-52, or E. V. Krotevič' article "Slovo, čast' reči, člen predloženija [Word, part of speech, sentence part]", *VRJa*, 4 (1960), 3-27.

Meščaninov himself returned to the problem of sentence parts in relation to the categories of subject and object in his article, "Različnye postroenija členov predloženija v svjazi s otnošenijami sub"ekta i ob"ekta [Different structures of the sentence parts in connection with subject-object relations]", *NDVŠ-FN*, 1 (1961), 3-12, whereas the article of G. A. Zolotova, "K voprosu o sposobax vyraženija členov predloženija [On the means of expression of the sentence parts]", *RJaŠ*, 1 (1958), 23-28, was restricted to a brief survey of the principal formal devices by which the sentence parts can be represented in modern Russian. The opposite point of view, namely that of enumerating the various sentence parts which can be expressed by a given morphologically defined class, was apparent in the work of I. A. Kanšin, "Pričastnye i deepričastnye konstrukcii v roli členov predloženija [Participial and gerundive constructions as sentence parts]", *RJaŠ*, 2 (1956), 31-35. Various detailed questions of sentence parts were treated in these journals during the same period, e.g. M. G. Šatux, "Utočnjajuščie členy predloženija kak osobaja sintaksičeskaja kategorija [Delimiting sentence parts as a special syntactic category]", *RJaŠ*, 2 (1959), 31-35, and there appeared also several articles dealing with the so-called secondary sentence parts, e.g. A. A. Xolodovič, "O vtorostepennyx členax predloženija (iz istorii i teorii voprosa) [On the secondary sentence parts (from the history and theory of the problem)]", *NDVŠ-FN*, 4 (1959), 18-31, I. A. Figurovskij, "V zaščitu vtorostepennyx členov predloženija [In defense of the secondary sentence parts]", *RJaŠ*, 2 (1959), 19-27, in which the author objects to A. B. Šapiro's previous attack on the concept of secondary sentence parts, "K učeniju o vtorostepennyx členax predloženija v russkom jazyke [On the study of secondary sentence parts in Russian]", *VJa*, 6/2 (1957), 71-85 and T. P. Lomtev, "O vtorostepennyx členax predloženija [On secondary parts of the sentence]", *RJaŠ*, 4 (1960), 7-13.

The problem of isolated ("obosoblennye") sentence parts was itself the subject of several papers during the decade (and for that matter had been studied in some detail even before the war, cf. E. V. Krotevič' *K voprosu ob obosoblenii vtorostepennyx členov predloženija*, Alma-Ata, 1939, unavailable to me but referred to by V. V. Vinogradov in the collection *Voprosy sintaksisa*, 1950, p. 238 fn.), e.g. G. P. Firsov's brochure for schools, *Obosoblennye vtorostepennye členy predloženija* of 1955 or G. V. Kolšanskij's article, "Grammatičeskaja funkcija obosoblenija členov predloženija [The grammatical function of the isolation of sentence parts]", *NDVŠ-FN*, 1 (1962), 31-41.

The parts of speech themselves were discussed somewhat less often during this period, although one thinks of such articles as N. S. Pospelov's "Sootnošenie meždu grammatičeskimi kategorijami i častjami reči [The interrelation of grammatical categories and parts of speech]", *VJa*, 2/6 (1953), 53-67, and with the same title in the collective volume *Voprosy grammatičeskogo stroja* (Moscow, 1955), pp. 74-91. A general discussion of the parts of speech is reported by N. Z. Gadžieva and E. A. Ivančikova in *VJa*, 4/1 (1955), 162-166, and the subject is further pursued by M. V. Panov, "O častjax reči v russkom jazyke [On the parts of speech in Russian]", *NDVŠ-FN*, 4 (1960), 3-14. The relative merits of morphological and syntactic criteria for the classification of parts of speech in Russian, one concludes, have still not been weighed with finality.

One special problem within the area of parts of speech which attracted the attention of several scholars was that of the shift of class membership, general problems of which were touched upon briefly by N. A. Kalamova in "K voprosu o perexodnosti odnix častej reči v drugie [On the transferability of some parts of speech to others]", *RJaŠ*, 5 (1961), 56-59. The participles were singled out for particularly frequent attention during the late fifties: V. N. Kretova, "Perexod pričastij v drugie časti reči [The shift of participles to other parts of speech]", *RJaŠ*, 4 (1955), 7-10; I. A. Krasnov,

"Puti perexoda pričastij v prilagatel'nye [Routes of transfer of participles to adjectives]", *RJaŠ*, 6 (1957), 20-25; M. F. Lukin, "Perexod pričastij v suščestvitel'nye [The shift of participles to substantives]", *RJaŠ*, 4 (1957), 43-46; cf. also his "O stepenjax sravnenija pričastij, perešedšix v prilagatel'nye [On the degrees of comparison of participles transferred into the adjective class]", *RJaŠ*, 4 (1958), 20-24. Transfers from the adjective class were the subject of two articles in the same journal, I. F. Protčenko's "O substantivirovannyx prilagatel'nyx i pričastijax so značeniem lica [On substantivized adjectives and participles with the meaning of persons]", *RJaŠ*, 4 (1958), 7-11, and N. P. Korženevskaja's "O stilističeskix funkcijax substantivirovannyx prilagatel'nyx", *RJaŠ*, 1 (1961), 6-10. One notes with regret that nearly all these articles in *Russkij jazyk v škole* tend to be overly short and not very profound.

## RUSSIAN SYNTAX, GENERAL

The major event in Russian syntax during the decade 1952-1962 was the appearance in 1953 and 1954 of the syntactic sections of the new grammar of the Soviet Academy of Sciences (AN SSSR, Institut jazykoznanija, *Grammatika russkogo jazyka*, Tom II, Sintaksis, parts 1, 2, Moscow, 1953, 1954, 703, 444 pp.). This work deals with Russian syntax from two viewpoints, first that of morphologically defined word-combinations, and then that of sentence types and parts. Many general problems of syntactic theory, particularly as applied to Russian, are discussed in the "Introduction" (part 1, pp. 5-110) by the principal editor, V. V. Vinogradov, who also described the basic principles of the Academic syntax in a short article in *IzvAN*, 6 (1954), 497-505, entitled "Osnovnye principy russkogo sintaksisa v *Grammatike russkogo jazyka* Akademii Nauk SSSR [The basic principles of Russian syntax in the *Russian Grammar* of the USSR Academy of Sciences]". The volumes were reviewed extensively by N. M. Nikitina and V. P. Suxotin, *VJa*, 4/3 (1955), 110-121, and were the subject of public scholarly discussion, as reported by V. P. Ivanova in the same journal, *VJa*, 4/4 (1955), 145-151. Other general courses of Russian syntax, e.g. the *Sovremennyj russkij jazyk, Sintaksis* [Grammar of modern Russian, Syntax] edited by E. M. Galkina-Fedoruk (Moscow, 1957), or A. N. Gvozdev's *Sovremennyj russkij literaturnij jazyk, čast' II, Sintaksis* [Modern literary Russian, part II, Syntax] (Moscow, 1958), cf. Galkina-Fedoruk's review in *RJaŠ*, 5 (1959), 114-117, were of handier size but offered little that was new in content. The same period saw a new printing of A. M. Peškovskij's valuable *Russkij sintaksis v naučnom osveščenii* [Russian syntax in the light of scholarship], 7th ed., edited by A. B. Šapiro (Moscow, 1956), 511 pp., and two works devoted to the syntactic structure of particular types of Russian: that of conversational Russian in N. Ju. Švedova's *Očerki po sintaksisu russkoj razgovornoj reči* [An outline of the syntax of conversational Russian] (Moscow, 1960), and of Russian dialects in A. B. Šapiro's study of compound sentence structure, *Očerki po sintaksisu russkix narodnyx govorov* [An outline of the syntax of Russian dialects] (Moscow, 1952).

## SENTENCE STRUCTURE

General problems of the study of sentence structure were discussed in detail in V. V. Vinogradov's article, "Osnovnye voprosy sintaksisa predloženija (Na [materiale] russkogo jazyka) [Basic problems of sentence structure (On Russian material)]", *Voprosy grammatičeskogo stroja* (1955), pp. 389-435, an article which partially duplicates the same author's introduction to the Academic syntax mentioned above. A different and less masterly presentation of problems is found in T. P. Lomtev's "O nekotoryx voprosax struktury predloženija [On certain problems of sentence structure]", *NDVŠ-FN*, 4 (1959), 3-17, while the relation of form to content is touched upon by S. G. Il'enko in a later issue of the same journal ("Kakovo sootnošenie meždu strukturoj predloženija i ego soderžaniem [What is the relation of sentence structure to its content]?", *NDVŠ-FN*, 1 (1962), 216-220.

The simple sentence and theoretical problems posed by the study thereof were discussed by V. V. Vinogradov in another article not unconnected with his work as editor of the Academy *Grammar*, "Nekotorye zadači izučenija sintaksisa prostogo predloženija [Some problems of the study of the syntax of simple sentences]", *VJa*, 3/1 (1954), 3-29; Vinogradov's mastery of both theory and material is particularly evident in comparing such an article to the sketchy remarks appearing under a similar title, by L. K. Kuznecova and G. P. Firsov, "Izučenie sintaksisa prostogo predloženija [Syntactic study of the simple sentence]", *RJaŠ*, 3 (1959), 110-113. More interesting was V. N. Jarceva's "O formax razvitija prostogo predloženija [On the forms of expansion of the simple sentence]", *Voprosy grammatiki. Sbornik statej k 75-iletiju I. I. Meščaninova*, (Moscow-Leningrad, 1960), pp. 454-469; Jarceva makes a valuable distinction between expansions within syntactic units (On spit "He sleeps" → On krepko spit "He sleeps soundly") and expansions which create new syntactic connections (On spit "he sleeps" → On spit odetyj "He sleeps [fully] clothed"). More specialized problems of the simple sentence were treated by A. F. Prjatkina, "Konstrukcii s sojuzom *kak* v prostom predloženii sovremennogo russkogo jazyka [Constructions with the conjunction *kak* in the simple sentence of modern Russian]", *RJaŠ*, 6 (1957), 47-52, E. M. Galkina-Fedoruk, "O dvusostavnyx i odnosostavnyx predloženijax v sovremennom russkom jazyke", *NDVŠ-FN*, 2 (1959), 102-112, and V. F. Kiprijanov, "Nečlenimoe predloženie a russkom jazyke kak osobyj strukturnyj tip prostogo predloženija [The indivisible sentence in modern Russian as a special structural type of simple sentence]", *RJaŠ*, 5 (1961), 60-63, whereas E. A. Sedel'nikov makes some use of transformational techniques in his discussion of "Struktura prostogo predloženija s točki zrenija sintagmatičeskix i paradigmatičeskix otnošenij [The structure of the simple sentence from the point of view of syntagmatic and paradigmatic relations]", *NDVŠ-FN*, 3 (1961), 66-77.

## SUBJECT AND PREDICATE

The form of the grammatical subject (noun phrase) was only dealt with once, in the brief note of N. A. Janko-Trinickaja, "O pridatočnyx podležaščix v sovremennom russkom jazyke [On adjoined subjects in modern Russian]", *RJaŠ*, 4 (1955), 11-16, whereas the form of the predicate was the subject of some dozen articles during the same period, only two of which dealt with the relations between subject and predicate, both by E. S. Skoblikova, "Forma skazuemogo pri podležaščem, vyražennom količestvenno-imennym sočetaniem [The form of the predicate with subject expressed by numeral-nominal combinations]", *VKR*, 2 (1959), 91-116; "Upotreblenie skazuemogo pri razdelitel'nyx otnošenijax meždu odnorodnymi podležaščimi [Predicative usage in the case of partitive relations among homogenous subjects]", *NDVŠ-FN*, 2 (1959), 199-205. One of the more interesting general discussions of predicativity and its relation to binary and non-binary sentence types was I. P. Raspopov's article, "K voprosu o predikativnosti [On predicativity]", *VJa*, 7/5 (1958), 70-77, which also discussed the "given" and the "new" (< Mathesius), i.e. Hockett's "topic" and "comment". Particular types of predicate are treated in N. Ju. Švedova, "Nekotorye vidy značenij skazuemogo v sovremennom russkom jazyke [Certain types of meaning of the predicate in modern Russian]", in the collective volume *Issledovanija po grammatike russkogo literaturnogo jazyka* (Moscow, 1955), and A. N. Šramm, "Tipy skazuemogo v dvusostavnom predloženii [Types of predicate in the binary sentence]", *RJaŠ*, 2 (1961), 26-31. The compound predicate was the subject of articles by G. N. Grudneva, "Sostavnoe i složnoe skazuemoe v sovremennom russkom jazyke [Compound and complex predicate in modern Russian]", *VRJa*, 3 (1958), 159-180, and S. A. Xavronina, "Trexčlennoe imennoe skazuemoe v sovremennom russkom jazyke [The three-unit nominal predicate in modern Russian]", *RJaŠ*, 1 (1958), 16-22. Predicate adjective usage was discussed briefly by G. F. Mjasnikov in "Stilističeskoe ispol'zovanie kratkix i polnyx prilagatel'nyx v sostave skazuemogo [Stylistic use of short and full adjectives in the predicate]", *RJaŠ*, 1 (1958), 12-15, and the same journal printed several notes on different types of verbal predicate: E. N. Xlebnikova-Prokopovič, "Osobye formy glagol'nogo skazuemogo v sovremennom russkom jazyke [Special forms of verbal predicate in modern Russian]", *RJaŠ*, 1 (1958), 7-11; E. N. Prokopovič, "Osobye formy prošedšego vremeni v roli skazuemogo [Special past-tense forms as predicates]", *RJaŠ*, 4 (1960), 14-17; and T. Dolin, "Nesoglasuemye glagol'nye skazuemye i ix stilističeskaja funkcija v sovremennom russkom jazyke [Non-agreeing verbal predicates and their stylistic function in modern Russian]", *RJaŠ*, 2 (1962), 22-25. In general, one might still say that the bulk of this material on the simple sentence had not yet been touched by the influence of structural methodology.

## COMPOUND AND COMPLEX SENTENCES

More effort was expended on the analysis and description of the various types of compound and complex sentence in Russian than on any other single subject during the period which interests us in this survey. The discussions, although not the terminology, sometimes remind one of the transformational studies in the West, even as early as 1950, when N. S. Pospelov published his paper, "O grammatičeskoj prirode složnogo predloženija [On the grammatical nature of the compound sentence]", *Voprosy sintaksisa* (1950), pp. 321-337, pointing out that complex sentences can be formed either by "expansion" of some member of a simple sentence or by "joining" two simple sentences into one complex sentence. Briefer discussions of the compound sentence and its parts were printed by V. A. Belošapkova, "Stroenie složnogo predloženija v sovremennom russkom jazyke [The structure of the compound sentence in modern Russian]", *RJaŠ*, 4 (1959), 18-25; S. A. Fessalonickij and M. G. Leščinskaja, "Složnoe predloženie [The compound sentence]", *RJaŠ*, 6 (1962), 99-100; and I. A. Fedosov, "O termine 'časti složnogo predloženija' [On the term 'parts of the compound sentence]", *RJaŠ*, 4 (1959), 26-27. A questionnaire published by the journal *Naučnye doklady vysšej školy, Filologičeskie nauki* asked, "Možno li sčitat' predloženiem časti složnogo predloženija [Can one consider the parts of the compound sentence a sentence]?" and evoked both positive (È. I. Korotaeva, *NDVŠ-FN*, 4, 1961, 164-173) and negative answers (V. V. Ščeulin, *NDVŠ-FN*, 4, 1961, 173-175). A few pages were devoted to an outline of the means of combining sentences in connected speech by N. V. Kirpičnikova, "O sposobax ob''edinenija predloženij v svjaznoj reči", *RJaŠ*, 5 (1960), 34-38, although the same subject had been treated with much more depth over a decade earlier by N. S. Pospelov, "Složnoe sintaksičeskoe celoe i osnovnye osobennosti ego struktury [The complex syntactic whole and the particularities of its structure]", *DSIRJa*, 2 (1948), 43-68.

The interrelations of the halves of compound sentences (složnosočinennye predloženija) and the formal types of such sentences were described by I. A. Popova, "Složno-sočinennoe predloženie v sovremennom russkom jazyke [The compound sentence in modern Russian]", *Voprosy sintaksisa* (1950), pp. 355-396, and various specific types of compound sentence were the subjects of articles, usually brief in nature, by several scholars: V. A. Šitov, "Složnye predloženija s posledovatel'nym podčineniem [Complex sentences with consecutive subordination]", *RJaŠ*, 1 (1955), 13-15; I. A. Vasilenko, "Složnye predloženija s odnorodnym sopodčineniem [Complex sentences with homogenous con-subordination]", *RJaŠ*, 1 (1955), 8-12; V. K. Pokusaenko, "O granicax odnorodnogo sopodčinenija [On the limits of homogenous con-subordination]", *NDVŠ-FN*, 3 (1962), 105-112; and A. N. Surovcev, "Složnoe predloženie s mnogočlennym podčineniem pridatočnogo [The complex sentence with multi-membered subordinate clause]", *Issledovanija po grammatike russkogo jazyka* (=*UZLU*, 235) (1958), 114-130. Gerundive subordinate clauses were glanced at by V. S. Belova, "O vyraženii obstojatel'stvennogo značenija celi v predloženijax s deepričastnymi oborotami [The expression of circumstantial meaning of goal in sentences with gerundive expressions]", *RJaŠ*, 2 (1958), 29-31, as were adverbial constructions by Ju. G. Usiščeva, "Pojasnitel'nye konstrukcii s ukazatel'nymi narečijami [Explicative constructions with demonstrative adverbs]", *RJaŠ*, 1 (1961), 30-33. Two books on complex sentences appeared during the period which concerns us, N. A. Andramonova's *Složnoe predloženie s pridatočnym otnositel'nym v sovremennom russkom jazyke* [The complex sentence with relative subordinate clause in modern Russian] (Kazan', 1959), unavailable to me, and A. G. Rudnev's *Sintaksis osložnennogo predloženija* [Syntax of the complex sentence] (Moscow, 1959), pp. 198, dealing with isolated sentence parts, introductory structures (in Puškin's works only), homogeneous sentence parts, and forms of address, and bearing as much a pedagogical as a scholarly stamp. The general problems inherent in classification of complex sentences, which had been discussed for decades, cf., e.g., A. B. Šapiro, "O principax klassifikacii podčinennyx predloženij [On the principles of classification of subordinate clauses]", *RJaŠ*, 2 (1937), were further discussed by N. S. Pospelov, "Složnopodčinennoe predloženie i ego strukturnye tipy [The complex sentence and its structural types]", *VJa*, 8/2 (1959), 19-27, and in less detail by two later articles, E. V. Gulyga's "Mesto složnopodčinennogo predloženija v sisteme sintaksisa [The place of the complex sentence in the syntactic system]", *NDVŠ-FN*, 3 (1961), 16-25, and I. A. Figurovskij's "K voprosu o klassifikacii složnopodčinennyx predloženij [On the classification of complex sentences]", *RJaŠ*, 6 (1961), 31-34. More restricted topics were treated in the brief notes of I. A. Vasilenko, "Složno-podčinennye predloženija s neodnorodnym sopodčineniem [Complex sentences with non-homogenous consubordination]", *RJaŠ*, 5 (1953), 18-22, and V. V. Babajceva, "Leksiko-grammatičeskie funkcii ukazatel'nyx slov v složnopodčinennyx predloženijax [The lexico-grammatical functions of demonstrative words in complex sentences]", *RJaŠ*, 6 (1962), 3-7, in more detail and with greater penetration by N. S. Pospelov, "O različijax v strukture složnopodčinennogo predloženija (Na materiale složnopodčinennyx predloženij s pridatočnymi vremennymi i opredelitel'nymi) [On differences in the structure of the complex sentence (on material of complex sentences with temporal and determinative subordinate clauses)]", *Issledovanija po sintaksisu russkogo literaturnogo jazyka* (Moscow, 1956), pp. 48-77, and from a different point of view, polemicizing with some of Pospelov's earlier works, by S. E. Krjučkov and L. Ju. Maksimov, "Tipy složnopodčinennyx predloženij s pridatočnoj čast'ju, otnosjaščejsja k odnomu slovu ili slovosočetaniju glavnoj časti [Types of complex sentence with subordinate clauses related to one word or word-combination of the main clause]", *VJa*, 9/1 (1960), 12-21. Conditional sentences were the subject of a special article by R. P. Rogožnikova, "K voprosu o strukture uslovnogo predloženija [On the structure of the conditional sentence]", in the collection *Issledovanija po sintaksisu* (1956), pp. 177-187.

Subordinate clauses themselves were the subject of several articles, ranging from general discussions of the nature of subordination such as G. P. Uxamov, "O grammatičeskoj prirode 'pridatočnogo predloženija' [On the grammatical nature of subordinate clauses]", *VJa*, 10/2 (1961), 74-87, to surveys of various types of subordinate clause, e.g., adnominal clauses, I. G. Čeredničenko, "K izučeniju prisubstantivnyx pridatočnyx v sovremennom russkom jazyke [On the study of adnominal subordinate clauses in Russian]", *RJaŠ*, 6 (1957), 34-40, comparative clauses, L. A. Kiseleva, "Nepolnye pridatočnye predloženija s sravnitel'nymi sojuzami v sovremennom russkom literaturnom jazyke [Incomplete subordinate clauses with comparative conjunctions in modern literary Russian]", *Vestnik LGU*, 14 (1957), 143-155; and I. K. Kučerenko, "O tipax pridatočnyx predloženij, vyražennyx posredstvom sravnenij [On the types of subordinate clause expressed by comparatives]", *RJaŠ*, 6 (1961), 35-38; cf. also L. A. Kiseleva's complementary study to that just mentioned, "Polnye pridatočnye predloženija s sravnitel'nymi sojuzami v sovremennom russkom jazyke [Complete subordinate clauses with comparative conjunctions in modern Russian]", *Issledovanija po grammatike russkogo jazyka* (= *UZLU* 235) (1958), 103-113, or resultative clauses, A. M. Davidovskij, "Pridatočnye predloženija sledstvija [Subordinate clauses of result]", *RJaŠ*, 6 (1955), 20-25.

The syntactic connections between main and subordinate clauses were discussed from several points of view. The various possible types of such connection were outlined very briefly by V. K. Pokusaenko, "Sintaksičeskie svjazi pridatočnoj časti složnopodčinennogo predloženija [The syntactic connections of the subordinate clause of complex sentences]", *RJaŠ*, 1 (1962), 22-27. General and theoretical problems of subordinate clauses connected paratactically rather than by conjunction were weighed by N. S. Pospelov in "O grammatičeskoj prirode i principax klassifikacii bessojuznyx složnyx predloženij [On the grammatical nature and principles of classification of conjunctionless complex sentences]", *Voprosy sintaksisa* (1950), pp. 338-354, and less thoroughly by D. Ja. Val'ter in "O bessojuznyx složnyx predloženijax [On conjunctionless complex sentences]", *RJaŠ*, 1 (1961), 18-25. One of the more interesting items to appear in this field was the posthumously published material of S. O. Karcevskij on conjunctionless subordination presented by N. S. Pospelov and translated by E. A. Ivančikova, "Bessojuzie i podčinenie v russkom jazyke", *VJa*, 10/2 (1961), 125-131, in which Karcevskij divides subordinate structures into open or analytic and closed or synthetic (in the first case, the subordinate clause is added to the head as a type of appendix, whereas in the second case the subordinate clause itself contains the main predication, serving as a conclusion to the main clause); the article was originally written in Geneva in September, 1942, and bore the title, "Asyndète et subordination en russe". More narrow problems of conjunctionless subordination were dealt with in the articles of L. S. Drotvinas, "Bessojuznye uslovnye predloženija v russkom jazyke [Conjunctionless conditional sentences in Russian]", *RJaŠ*, 6 (1959), 17-21; N. V. Kirpičnikova, "Bessojuznye složnye predloženija, v kotoryx vtoraja čast' pojasnjaet odno iz slov pervoj časti [Conjunctionless complex sentences, in which the subordinate clause explains one of the words of the main clause]", *RJaŠ*, 6 (1956), 30-35; and E. A. Ivančikova in a long and solid article, "Sootnositel'noe upotreblenie form buduščego vremeni glagola v sostave častej bessojuznogo složnogo predloženija [The correlative use of the verbal future tense within the parts of the conjunctionless complex sentence]", *Issledovanija po sintaksisu* (1956), pp. 78-130.

The role of coordinating and subordinating conjunctions was discussed in general terms by S. E. Krjučkov, "O prisoedinitel'nyx svjazjax v sovremennom russkom jazyke [On the role of conjoining connections in modern Russian]", *Voprosy sintaksisa* (1950), pp. 397-411, and resumed briefly by A. F. Prijatkina in "Konstrukcii s pojasnitel'nymi sojuzami [Constructions with explicatory conjunctions]", *RJaŠ*, 5 (1956), 19-24. Individual conjunctions and the structures they enter were the subject of several articles of varying length and depth: M. M. Mixajlov, "Složnye predloženija s vremenným sojuzom *kogda* v sovremennom russkom jazyke [Complex sentences with the temporal conjunction *kogda* in modern Russian]", *TIJa*, 3 (1954), 130-142; R. P. Rogožnikova, "Predloženija s sojuzami *esli* i *esli by* v sovremennom russkom jazyke [Sentences with the conjunctions *esli* and *esli by* in modern Russian]", *RJaŠ*, 6 (1957), 41-46; A. K. Fedorov, "Upotreblenie podčinitel'nogo sojuza *čto* v sovremennom russkom jazyke [The use of the subordinating conjunction *čto* in modern Russian]", *Učenye zapiski Kalininskogo gos. ped. Instituta*, XIX, 2 (1957) (unavailable to me); G. P. Uxanov, "Pojasnitel'nye konstrukcii s sojuzom *to est'* i pridatočnym predloženiem vo vtoroj časti [Explicatory constructions with the conjunction *to est'* and a subordinate clause]", *RJaŠ*, 2 (1961), 32-36; V. A. Belošapkova, "Predloženija s sojuzom *kak vdrug* v sovremennom russkom jazyke [Sentences with the conjunction *kak vdrug* in modern Russian]", *RJaŠ*, 6 (1961), 39-43; N. M. Karpenok, "Složnye predloženija frazeologičeskogo tipa s sojuzom *čtoby* [Complex sentences of the phraseological type with the conjunction *čtoby*]", *RJaŠ*, 2 (1962), 26-29.

Connected in one way or another with problems of the compound and complex sentence were several other articles which appeared during this decade, e.g. the studies of word order by G. G. Počepcov, "O meste v predloženii narečij, opredeljajuščix glagol [On the place in the sentence of adverbs determining verbs]", *RJaŠ*, 1 (1957), 25-28, Z. D. Popova, "O principax raspoloženija slov v povestvovatel'nyx predloženijax russkogo literaturnogo jazyka [On the principles of word order in descriptive sentences of modern literary Russian]", *Trudy VGU*, vol. 59, Voronez, (1957) (unavailable to me), and the same author's brief study, "Porjadok slov v sintaksičeskix edinstvax, oborotax i gruppax, naxodjaščixsja v sostave predloženija [Word order in syntactic units, phrases and groups in the composition of the sentence]", *RJaŠ*, 1 (1958), 38-41. Appositive modification and inserted segments were the subjects of articles by M. G. Ovanova, "Neobosoblennye priloženija v sovremennom russkom literaturnom jazyke [Unisolated apposition in modern literary Russian]", *RJaŠ*, 2 (1957), 36-40, cf. also her "Obosoblennye priloženija v sovremennom russkom jazyke [Isolated apposition in modern Russian]", *RJaŠ*, 6 (1959), 13-16; A. K. Vlasov, "Deepričastnyj oborot, ne otnesennyj k podležaščemu [A gerundive structure not related to the subject]", *RJaŠ*, 2 (1958), 35-38; N. S. Valgina, "Bessojuznye prisoedinitel'nye konstrukcii v sovremennom russkom jazyke [Conjunctionless conjoining constructions in modern Russian]", *RJaŠ*, 5 (1958), 40-46; and E. P. Sedun's interesting "O tak nazyvaemyx 'vvodnyx' i 'vstavnyx' konstrukcijax [On the so-called 'introductory' and 'inserted' constructions]", *Slavjanskoe jazykoznanie, sbornik statej* (Moscow, 1959), pp. 186-194.

## MINOR SENTENCE TYPES

The "minor" sentence types, namely mononuclear, incomplete, impersonal, nominal, etc. sentences, which play a larger role in Russian than in English syntax, were discussed at some length during the decade with which this survey is concerned. The mononuclear sentence was discussed only in three rather short articles in *Russkij jazyk v škole*: T. G. Počtennaja, "K voprosu ob odnosostavnyx predloženijax [On mononuclear sentences]", 2 (1956), 17-20, and "Nabljudenija nad upotrebleniem odnosostavnyx predloženij [Observations on the use of mononuclear sentences]", 2 (1957), 41-44; and E. M. Galkina-Fedoruk, "Odnosostavnye predloženija v sovremennom russkom jazyke [The mononuclear sentence in modern Russian]", 2 (1959), 11-18. The incomplete sentence was subjected to detailed scrutiny in I. A. Popova's long paper, "Nepolnye predloženija v sovremennom russkom jazyke [The incomplete sentence in modern Russian]", *TIJa*, 2 (1953), 3-136, and reexamined briefly by A. S. Popov in "K voprosu o nepolnyx predloženijax v sovremennom russkom jazyke [On the incomplete sentence in modern Russian]", *NDVŠ-FN*, 3 (1959), 25-36.

Impersonal sentences have been the particular province of Professor E. M. Galkina-Fedoruk, who already in the late forties had published a series of articles on this subject in Moscow University publications unavailable to me for detailed examination: "Bezličnye predloženija so skazuemym iz bezličnyx glagolov na *-sja* [Impersonal sentences with predicate formed by impersonal verbs in *-sja*]", *Vestnik Moskovskogo Universiteta* 3 (1947), cf. also *Doklady i soobščenija filologiceskogo fakul'teta* 2 (1947); "Bezličnye predloženija, obrazovannye iz sočetanija imeni suščestvitel'nogo i infinitiva, vyražajuščie modal'no-ètičeskuju ocenku dejstvija [Impersonal sentences formed by combinations of noun and infinitive and expressing modal-evaluative estimates of an action]", *Doklady i soobščenija filologičeskogo fakul'teta*, 3 (1947); "Bezličnye predloženija s bezlično-predikativnymi slovami na *-o* [Impersonal sentences with impersonal-predicative words in *-o*]", *Učenye zapiski MGU*, *Trudy kafedry russkogo jazyka*, 1 (1948); "K voprosu ob infinitivnyx konstrukcijax s prepozitivnym i postpozitivnym upotrebleniem bezlično-predikativnogo člena [On infinitive constructions with pre- and postpositive use of impersonal-predicative members]", *Doklady i soobščenija filologičeskogo fakul'teta*, 6 (1948); "Bezličnye infinitivnye predloženija v sovremennom russkom jazyke [Impersonal infinitive sentences in modern Russian]", *Učenye zapiski MGU*, *Trudy kafedry russkogo jazyka*, 2 (1948). Galkina-Fedoruk continued working through the various types of impersonal sentence in Russian, and printed a summary classification of the types thereof in 1950, "Bezličnye predloženija v sovremennom russkom jazyke [Impersonal sentences in modern Russian]", *Voprosy sintaksisa* (1950), pp. 302-320. Finally, all the threads were gathered up in Galkina-Fedoruk's book, *Bezličnye predloženija v sovremennom russkom jazyke* (Moscow, 1958), pp. 332, which presented under one cover most of the previously published individual studies. Only one other author appears to have ventured onto Galkina-Fedoruk's territory: A. E. Vygorbina, in "Predloženija so skazuemym, vyražennym 'sobstvenno-bezličnym' glagolom [Sentences with the predicate expressed by 'properly-impersonal' verbs]", *NDVŠ-FN*, 2 (1960), 57-64.

The nominal sentence was examined in two short articles, by B. P. Ardentov, "O stilističeskom upotreblenii nominativnyx predloženij [On the stylistic use of the nominal sentence]", *RJaŠ*, 1 (1958), 29-33, and by I. P. Cirkina, "O razgraničenii nominativnyx i dvusostavnyx predloženij [On the distinction between nominal and binary sentence]", *RJaŠ*, 5 (1961), 64-68, while two other authors considered the structure of the infinitive sentence, in some detail in the case of K. A. Timofeev, "Ob osnovnyx tipax infinitivnyx predloženij v sovremennom russkom literaturnom jazyke [On the basic types of infinitive sentence in modern literary Russian]", *Voprosy sintaksisa* (1950), pp. 257-301, and more briefly in relation to the impersonal sentence in that of E. I. Voinova, "O sootnošenii infinitivnyx i bezličnyx predloženij [On the interrelation of infinitive and impersonal sentences]", *RJaŠ*, 2 (1958), 12-15. Finally, sentences with numerals in subject and predicate were passed briefly in review by A. A. Kamynina, "K voprosu o predloženijax s količestvennymi slovami v sostave glavnyx členov [On sentences with quantitative words as principal parts]", *RJaŠ*, 2 (1961), 20-25.

I. Stepanjan printed a short discussion of sentences in which the emotive factor plays a major role, "Sintaksičeskie nerasčlenennye predloženija, vyražajuščie èmocii [Syntactically indivisible sentences expressing emotion]", *RJaŠ*, 4 (1957), 47-50, and the same subject was treated the following year in V. V. Babajceva's article, "Èmocional'no-ocenočnye predloženija v sovremennom russkom jazyke [Emotional-evaluative sentences in modern Russian]", *RJaŠ*, 2 (1958), 16-22. Hortatory sentences were the subject of a work unavailable to me, M. K. Milyx's "Pobuditel'nye predloženija v russkom jazyke [Hortatory sentences in Russian]", *Učenye zapiski* of Rostov University, XXII (= *Trudy ist.-filol. fakul'teta, Kafedra russkogo jazyka*, vyp. 4) (1953), and of a later sketch by A. S. Popov, "Obraščenija-predloženija v sovremennom russkom jazyke [Salutation-sentences in modern Russian]", *RJaŠ*, 5 (1958), 36-39. N. I. Žinkin subjected interrogative structures to scrutiny from the viewpoints of content and style in "Vopros i voprositel'noe predloženie [Interrogation and the interrogative sentence]", *VJa*, 4/3 (1955), 22-34, and the same subject was introduced on a more popular level by I. P. Raspopov in "Voprositel'noe predloženie [The interrogative sentence]", *RJaŠ*, 1 (1958), 34-37.

## THE "CATEGORY OF STATE"

The existence of a group of words usually called "category of state" (kategorija sostojanija) as a separate part of speech, which goes back to L. V. Ščerba's "O častjax reči v russkom jazyke [On parts of speech in Russian]" in *Russkaja reč'* (1928) and was most fully developed in V. V. Vinogradov's magistral *Russkij jazyk* (1947), was questioned in an original contribution by A. B. Šapiro, "Est' li v russkom jazyke kategorija sostojanija kak čast' reči [Does the category of state exist in Russian as a part of speech]?", *VJa*, 4/2 (1955), 42-54. The orthodox were quick to take up the defense, e.g. N. S. Pospelov's "V zaščitu kategorii sostojanija [In defense of the category of state]", *VJa*, 4/2 (1955), 55-65, cf. also his "Iz nabljudenij nad upotrebleniem v sovremennom russkom jazyke slov kategorii sostojanija, vosxodjaščix k imenam suščestvitel'nym [From observations on the use of words from the category of state which originate in substantives]", *Akad. V. V. Vinogradovu* (1956), pp. 204-213, and were joined by the ubiquitous A. V. Isačenko in an interesting contribution, "O vozniknovenii i razvitii 'kategorii sostojanija' v slavjanskix jazykax [On the rise and development of the 'category of state' in the Slavic languages]", *VJa*, 4/6 (1955), 48-65. Another non-Soviet scholar, F. Trávníček, criticized the oversimplified view of this category manifested in a recent university course in morphology (*Sovremennyj russkij jazyk. Morfologija* (*Kurs lekcij*) (Moscow, 1952), pp. 394-404, in his article, "Zametki o 'kategorii sostojanija' [Notes on the 'category of state']", *VJa*, 5/3 (1956), 46-53. E. M. Galkina-Fedoruk presented a simplified version of the standard theory to readers of *Russkij jazyk v škole*, "O kategorii sostojanija v russkom jazyke [On the category of state in Russian]", *RJaŠ*, 4 (1957), 6-17, whereas V. P. Timofeev gave a more penetrating analysis of the various morphosyntactic features of some of the items usually considered to belong to this category in his article, "O perexode nekotoryx kratkix prilagatel'nyx v kategoriju sostojanija [On the shift of certain short adjectives to the category of state]", *VJa*, 7/5 (1958), 93-98. The entire discussion was summed up by L. A. Korobčinskaja, "K diskussii o kategorii sostojanija [On the discussion of the category of state]", *VRJa*, 4 (1960), 28-43; Korobčinskaja proposes to substitute the term "predicative" for "category of state", but does not deny the existence of the category as such.

## SYNTACTIC SYNONYMS

The study of syntactic synonyms, i.e. constructions related in form and identical or close to identical in meaning, was by no means new in the decade concerning us here, cf. for example, G. I. Rixter, "Sintaksičeskaja sinonimika v sovremennom russkom jazyke [Syntactic synonyms in modern Russian]", *RJaŠ*, 3 (1937), 14-33; M. K. Milyx, "Voprosy grammatičeskoj stilistiki. K sinonimike častej reči [Problems of grammatical stylistics. The synonymy of parts of speech]", *Russkoe jazykovedenie*, 1 (Rostov-na-Donu, 1945), 31-96 and X. M. Sajkiev, "K voprosu o sintaksičeskoj sinonimike v sovremennom russkom jazyke [On syntactic synonyms in modern Russian]", *Učenye zapiski* of the Kazax University, XIV, 1, Alma-Ata, 1952 (unavailable here). A number of interesting problems in this field were discussed by I. I. Kovtunova, "O sintaksičeskoj sinonimike [On syntactic synonyms]", *VKR*, 1 (1955), 115-142, and V. P. Suxotin, both in his article "Iz materialov po sintaksičeskoj sinonimike v russkom jazyke [From materials on syntactic synonyms in Russian]", *Issledo-*

*vanija po sintaksisu* (1956), pp. 5-47 and in his later book, *Sintaksičeskaja sinonimika v sovremennom russkom literaturnom jazyke. Glagol'nye slovosočetanija* [Syntactic synonyms in modern literary Russian. Verbal combinations] (Moscow, 1960), 160 pp., but there has still been no structural definition of the concept of such synonymy, a situation unchanged by such briefer treatments as E. P. Šendel's' article "Ponjatie grammatičeskoj sinonimii [The concept of grammatical synonymy]", *NDVŠ-FN*, 1 (1959), 68-81, cf. also his "Sintaksičeskie varianty [Syntactic variants]", *NDVŠ-FN*, 1 (1962), 8-18. Particular types of synonymous or homonymous syntactic units were discussed in the articles of T. A. Bertagaev and V. I. Zimin, "O sinonimii frazeologičeskix slovosočetanij v sovremennom russkom jazyke [On the synonymy of phraseological word-combinations in modern Russian]", *RJaŠ*, 3 (1960), 4-9; L. A. Deribas, "O zamene deepričastnyx oborotov sinonimičnymi konstrukcijami [On the replacement of gerundive expressions by synonymous constructions]", *RJaŠ*, 5 (1962), 18-22; and A. L. Šumilina, "Sinonimika v krugu glagol'no-imennyx prostranstvennyx slovosočetanij s predlogami *u*, *pri*, *pod*, *okolo*, *podle*, *bliz*, *vblizi* [Synonymity among verb-noun combinations of spatial relation with the prepositions *u*, *pri*, *pod*, *okolo*, *podle*, *bliz*, *vblizi*]", *RJaŠ*, 6 (1961), 25-30. Syntactic homonymy was the subject of two brief notes in the same journal during this period: N. P. Kolesnikov, "O sintaksičeskoj omonimii v russkom jazyke [On syntactic homonymy in Russian]", *RJaŠ*, 3 (1960), 20-22, and M. F. Palevskaja, "Omonimija kak sledstvie leksikalizacii otdel'nyx grammatičeskix form i perexoda slov iz odnoj časti reči v druguju [Homonymy as a result of the lexicalization of individual grammatical forms and of the shift of words from one part of speech to another]", *RJaŠ*, 3 (1960), 15-19.

Since synonymy and homonymy are as closely linked with the word-combination as with the sentence part, it appears natural to pass now to a survey of Soviet works dealing with the theory and description of word-combinations.

## WORD-COMBINATIONS

Most works on Russian syntax divide their attention between two areas, that of the sentence and its parts on the one hand, and that of the various types of word-combinations on the other. There are numerous theoretical and practical problems involved in the study of the word-combination, in spite of the apparently more evident morphological nature of the classificatory scheme. These general problems have been the subject of several interesting studies in the past decade, attracting the attention of some of the Soviet Union's best syntactic specialists. The first lengthy discussion of the nature of the word-combination to appear in the period with which we are concerned was V. P. Suxotin's article, "Problema slovosočetanija v sovremennom russkom jazyke [The problem of the word-combination in modern Russian]", in the collective volume *Voprosy sintaksisa* (1950), pp. 127-182. Shorter but more succinct, and disagreeing with Suxotin on some points (e.g. on Suxotin's division of word-combinations into predicative and non-predicative) was V. V. Vinogradov's study, "Voprosy izučenija slovosočetanija (Na materiale russkogo jazyka) [Problems of the study of the word-combination (On Russian material)]", *VJa*, 3/3 (1954), 3-24. Another valuable contribution to the discussion was O. S. Axmanova's "Slovosočetanie [The word-combination]", *Voprosy grammatičeskogo stroja* (1955), pp. 452-460, and the debate was pursued by another outstanding scholar, A. B. Šapiro, in an article entitled "Slovosočetanie v russkom jazyke [The word-combination in Russian]", in the collection edited by V. V. Vinogradov, *Slavjanskoe jazykoznanie, sbornik statej* (Moscow, 1959), pp. 195-216. One notes also V. V. Belyj's article, "K voprosu o slovosočetanii [On the word-combination]", *NDVŠ-FN*, 4 (1960), 108-116. The difference between simple and complex word-combinations, which had already been discussed in Vinogradov's article mentioned above, was further treated in N. N. Prokopovič, "K voprosu o prostyx i složnyx slovosočetanijax [On simple and complex word-combinations]", *VJa*, 8/5 (1959), 21-31, where one finds much bibliographical information from both the USSR and the West, in addition to Prokopovič's own views. A particular problem of the word-combination, rection (government), was outlined by E. V. Krotevič in "Upravlenie kak sposob vyraženija sintaksičeskix otnošenij [Government as a means of expressing syntactic relations]", *VRJa*, 3 (1958), 3-11.

The word-combination is related to but distinguished from units on both sides, as it were, that is from the purely syntactic units of the sentence and its parts on the one hand, and the purely morphological units of word-compounding on the other. Both of these distinctions were emphasized in the literature of our period. The relations of word-combination to sentence were the subject of articles by V. N. Jarceva, "Predloženie i slovosočetanie [Sentence and word-combination]", *Voprosy grammatičeskogo stroja* (1955), pp. 436-451; N. Šumilov, "Razgraničenie opredeljaemogo slova i odinočnogo priloženija [The boundary between word modification and isolated adjunction]", *RJaŠ*, 2 (1958), 32-34; E. V. Krotevič "O svjazjax slov v slovosočetanii i v predloženii [On word connections in the word-combination and in the sentence]", *RJaŠ*, 6 (1958), cf. his earlier and more extensive "Slovosočetanie kak stroitel'nyj material predloženija [The word-combination as the building material of the sentence]", *VSJa*, 4 (1955), 46-80; and A. A. Xolodovič, "K voprosu o gruppirovkax slov v predloženii [On the word-groupings within the sentence]", in the Meščaninov Festschrift *Problemy jazykoznanija* (= *UZLU*, 301) (1961), 233-243.

The interrelations, complicated at times, of derivational morphology and word-combination syntax, were explored in an interesting study by N. N. Prokopovič, "O vlijanii slovoobrazovatel'nyx svjazej častej reči na postroenie slovosočetanij [On the influence of the derivational connections of the parts of speech on the structure of word-combinations]", *VJa*, 2/6 (1953), 37-52. M. I. Privalova took up the problems of the limits between compound words and word-combinations in "Složnye slova ili slovosočetanija [Compound words or word-combinations]?", *Očerki po leksikologii, frazeologii i stilistike* (= *UZLU*, 243) (1958), 53-68, a subject that was touched upon briefly by N. N. Prokopovič in "O razgraničenii slovosočetanij i složnyx prilagatel'nyx [On the delimitation of word-combinations from compound adjectives]", *RJaŠ*, 4 (1961), 6-11. Finally, the distinctions between word-combinations and compound abbreviations were emphasized in G. P. Uxanov's article "Ob otnošenij složnosokraščennyx slov k slovosočetanijam s toj že predmetnoj otnesennost'ju [On the relations of compound abbreviations to word-combinations with the same referential meaning]", *NDVŠ-FN*, 1 (1962), 187-196.

## TYPES OF WORD-COMBINATION

Much of the literature devoted to the word-combination was restricted to descriptions of particular types of word-combination, rather than discussing problems of general interest. Such, for example, were the articles dealing with aspects of the nominal combination by A. A. Kamynina, "Upotreblenie vtorogo imenitel'nogo imen suščestvitel'nyx v sovremennom russkom jazyke [Use of the second nominative of nouns in modern Russian]", *RJaŠ*, 2 (1958), 23-28, L. Ju. Maksimov, "Obosoblenija prisubstantivnyx kosvennyx padežej suščestvitel'nyx [The isolation of adnominal oblique-case substantives]", *RJaŠ*, 5 (1962), 23-29, T. A. Tulina, "Grammatičeskij analiz imennyx slovosočetanij s roditel'nym časti i sovokupnosti [Grammatical analysis of nominal word-combinations with the genitive of part and collectivity]", *RJaŠ*, 5 (1962), 7-10. Instrumental case combinations were discussed on a somewhat higher level than the nominals just mentioned, in A. M. Finkel', "Tvoritel'nyj pričiny v sovremennom russkom literaturnom jazyke [The instrumental of cause in modern literary Russian]", *Trudy filolohičnoho fakul'tetu* (of Xar'kov Univ.) 6 (= Xar'kov Univ., *Učeni zapysky* 99) (1958), 43-76, and by V. P. Suxotin in "O nekotoryx funkcijax sočetanij s tvoritel'nym v sovremennom russkom jazyke [On certain functions of combinations with the instrumental in modern Russian]", *Akad. V. V. Vinogradovu* (1956), pp. 241-249. In this context, one cannot help mentioning the historically oriented but very impressive collective volume edited by S. B. Bernštejn, *Tvoritel'nyj padež v slavjanskix jazykax* (Moscow, 1958), 376 pp. The journal *Russkij jazyk v škole* continued to publish miscellaneous articles more or less tangentially related to word-combinations with substantives, e.g. T. A. Bertagaev, "Otgraničenie sočetanij s priloženiem ot sxodnyx sočetanij [The delimitation of combinations with adjunction from similar combinations]", 1 (1957), 15-18; N. G. Kovinina, "Nesoglasovannoe opredelenie kak osobaja forma vyraženija grammatičeskogo attributa [Non-agreeing determination as a special means of expressing the grammatical attribute]", 2 (1956), 26-30; and G. M. Makarov, "Nesoglasovannoe imennoe opredelenie s prostranstvennym značeniem [Non-agreeing substantival determination with spatial meaning]", 2 (1955), 19-22.

Pronominal and numeral word-combinations were the subject of studies by M. M. Mixajlov, "Značenie i upotreblenie mestoimenij *samyj* i *sam* [The meaning and use of the pronouns *samyj* and *sam*]", *RJaŠ*, 2 (1957), 22-26; Ištvan Pete, "Upotreblenie neopredelennyx mestoimenij v sovremennom russkom jazyke [The use of indefinite pronouns in modern Russian]", *RJaŠ*, 2 (1957), 18-21; Ju. V. Bol'šova, "K voprosu o pronominalizacii v sovremennom russkom jazyke [On pronominalization in modern Russian]", *VRJa*, 4 (1960), 50-59; and B. M. Grinšpun, "O sintaksičeskoj roli imen čislitel'nyx v sočetanii s imenami suščestvitel'nymi [On the syntactic role of numerals in combination with substantives]", *RJaŠ*, 2 (1960), 14-16.

Only a few articles were devoted to adjectival and adverbal combinations. A. I. Molotkov, in "Est' li v russkom jazyke kategorija neizmenjaemyx prilagatel'nyx [Does there exist the category of indeclinable adjectives in Russian]?", *VJa*, 9/6 (1960), 68-73, polemicizes with the opinion of E. I. Mel'nikov, "Neizmenjaemye prilagatel'nye v russkom jazyke [Indeclinable adjectives in Russian]", *Slavia*, XXIII, 4 (1954) that these words (*bordo*, *minimum*, *aplike*, etc.) form a separate part of speech. V. A. Trofimov investigates the formation of adverbs from short-form adjectives and other cases of adverbialization in his article, "O nekotoryx slovosočetanijax narečnogo tipa v sovremennom russkom jazyke [On certain adverbial-type word-combinations in modern Russian]", *VJa*, 9/4 (1960), 81-84, whereas N. N. Prokopovič devotes an entire booklet to adverbial combinations: *Sočetanija narečij s imenami prilagatel'nymi v sovremennom russkom jazyke* (Moscow, 1962), 76 pp.; Prokopovič' classification is semantically oriented, as is usual in Soviet works on this subject (Prokopovič divides adverbs into qualitative, quantitative, qualitative-circumstantial, and circumstantial).

Verbal word-combinations attracted the attention of a number of scholars, writing primarily but not exclusively in the pedagogically-oriented *Russkij jazyk v škole*. Verb-noun combinations were discussed by V. P. Suxotin, "O glagol'no-imennyx sočetanijax v russkom jazyke [On verb-noun combinations in Russian]", *RJaŠ*, 2 (1962), 17-21, while I. F. Protčenko compared verbs with adjectives in "Formy glagola i prilagatel'nogo v sočetanii s nazvanijami lic ženskogo pola [Forms of verb and adjective in combination with feminine names]", *VKR*, 3 (1961), 116-126. The syntactic connections of negated verbs were touched upon briefly in two articles, L. A. Deribas' "Prjamoe dopolnenie pri perexodnom glagole s otricaniem [The direct object after negated transitive verb]", *RJaŠ*, 2 (1956), 21-25, and I. Kout's later "Prjamoe dopolnenie v otricatel'nyx predloženijax v russkom jazyke [The direct object in negative sentences in Russian]", *RJaŠ*, 2 (1960), 27-32. The combinatory features of the negative copula *net* were discussed with equal brevity by A. I. Molotkov, "Grammatičeskaja xarakteristika slova *net* [The grammatical characteristics of the word *net*]", *RJaŠ*, 6 (1956), 22-29.

The syntactic particularities of the Russian infinitive were treated only in the short note of A. I. Moiseev, "Sintaksičeskie osobennosti infinitiva v sovremennom russkom jazyke [The syntactic particularities of the infinitive in modern Russian]", *RJaŠ*, 6 (1957), 15-19, cf. however, the discussions of infinitive sentences noted on p. 50 above, whereas the same journal printed two articles dealing with imperative forms, first in more general terms by A. V. Isačenko, "K voprosu ob imperative v russkom jazyke [On the imperative in Russian]", *RJaŠ*, 6 (1957), 7-14, and in transferred functions by D. N. Šmelev, "Vneimperativnoe upotreblenie formy povelitel'nogo naklonenija v sovremennom russkom jazyke [Non-imperative use of the imperative forms in modern Russian]", *RJaŠ*, 5 (1961), 50-55. L. A. Deribas had discussed gerundive modifiers in "Deepričastnye konstrukcii v roli obstojatel'stva [Gerundive constructions in the role of circumstantial modifiers]", *RJaŠ*, 4 (1953), 41-48, and S. I. Gruzdeva provided a rather detailed comparison of Russian and Lithuanian participal usage in the article, "Attributivnye i predikativnye funkcii pričastija na *-es* v litovskom jazyke v sravnenii s russkimi konstrukcijami [Attributive and predicative functions of the *-es* participle in Lithuanian compared to Russian constructions]", *Issledovanija po grammatike* (= *UZLU*, 235) (1958), 222-245.

Prepositions in Russian were the subject of a popular brochure by V. S. Bondarenko, *Predlogi v sovremennom russkom jazyke* [Prepositions in modern Russian] (Moscow, 1961), 75 pp., as well as of several summary discussions in the journal *Russkij jazyk v škole*, e.g. V. P. Malaščenko's article "K voprosu o predložnom upravlenii [On the government of prepositions]", 4 (1961), 30-33; the three-page, two-author summary by V. V. Veselickij and V. S. Bondarenko "Predlogi v sovremennom russkom jazyke [Prepositions in modern Russian]", 4 (1962), 110-112, and G. I. Rixter's survey of primary prepositions, "Nabljudenija nad pervoobraznymi predlogami i predložnymi konstrukcijami v sovremennom russkom literaturnom jazyke [Observations on the primary prepositions and prepositional constructions in modern literary Russian]", 6 (1955), 20-25. A more systematic approach was demonstrated by L. N. Zasorina in her article, "Opyt sistemnogo analiza predlogov sovremennogo russkogo jazyka (Predlogi so značeniem pričiny) [An essay of systemic analysis of the prepositions of modern Russian (Prepositions with causal meaning)]", *Problemy jazykoznanija* (= *UZLU*, 301) (1961), 64-84, and the same problems were treated by L. N. Popova, "Pričinnye ottenki nekotoryx predlogov v russkom jazyke [Causal nuances of certain prepositions in Russian]", *NDVŠ-FN*, 3 (1958), 32-42. The meaning and combinatory possibilities of individual prepositions were outlined in two short studies by A. M. Finkel', "O značenii i upotreblenii predloga *blagodarja* [The meaning and use of the preposition *blagodarja*]", *RJaŠ*, 6 (1956), 13-16, and "Značenie i upotreblenie predloga *vvidu* [The meaning and use of the preposition *vvidu*]", *RJaŠ*, 1 (1962), 19-21, while other authors treated similar problems in much greater detail, e.g. V. D. Levin, "O značenijax predloga *krome* v sovremennom russkom literaturnom jazyke [On the meanings of the preposition *krome* in modern literary Russian]", *Akad. V. V. Vinogradovu* (1956), pp. 147-164, or L. N. Popova, "O značenii predloga v sovremennom russkom jazyke (Predlog *ot* + roditel'nyj padež v značenii pričiny) [On the meaning of the preposition in modern Russian (The preposition *ot* + the genitive in causal meaning)]", *Issledovanija po grammatike* (= *UZLU*, 235) (1958), 190-208.

During this same period, conjunctions were treated in only a few articles (cf., however, the discussions of subordinate clauses in complex sentences, p. 46 ff.above):

V. P. Semenixin's brief "O sojuzax [On conjunctions]", *RJaŠ*, 6 (1956), 17-21; A. P. Sazonov's more specialized "Sojuz *kak esli by* v russkom jazyke [The conjunction *kak esli by* in Russian]", *RJaŠ*, 6 (1962), 8-19, and E. I. Korotaeva's more solid investigation of "Sojuzy, vyražajuščie otnošenija pričiny, celi i sledstvija [Conjunctions expressing relations of cause, of goal and of consequence]", *Issledovanija po grammatike* (= *UZLU*, 235) (1958), 50-78. Another "minor" part of speech, the interjection, was discussed briefly by A. I. Germanovič in "Sintaksičeskie svojstva meždometij [The syntactic features of the interjection]", *RJaŠ*, 6 (1957), 29-33, in more detail by N. Ju. Švedova in "Meždometie kak grammatičeski značimyj èlement predloženija v russkoj razgovornoj reči [The interjection as a grammatically significant element of the sentence in conversational Russian]", *VJa*, 6/1 (1957), 85-95, and as a secondary, derivative category by D. N. Šmelev's study, "K voprosu o 'proizvodnyx' služebnyx častjax reči i meždometijax [On 'derivative' secondary parts of speech and interjections]", *IzvAN*, 6 (1961), 498-505.

The negative particles *ne* and *ni* were touched upon in articles by L. Ju. Maksimov, "Častica *ne* i pristavka *ne* s kratkimi prilagatel'nymi [The particle *ne* and the prefix *ne* with short-form adjectives]", *RJaŠ*, 2 (1957), 7-17, A. F. Kulagin, "O častice *ne* i pristavke *ne*- [On the particle *ne* and the prefix *ne*-]", *RJaŠ*, 6 (1957), 26-28, and S. A. Vasil'eva, "K voprosu o semantike otricatel'nyx častic [On the semantics of negative particles]", *NDVŠ-FN*, 3 (1959), 78-85. Interrogative and limiting particles were passed briefly in review by I. P. Raspopov, "K voprosu o časticax v sovremennom russkom jazyke (častica *li*) [On the particles of modern Russian (The particle *li*)]", *RJaŠ*, 6 (1955), 17-19, and Ju. I. Levin, "O grammatičeskoj roli slov *tol'ko* i *liš'* v sovremennom russkom literaturnom jazyke [On the grammatical role of the words *tol'ko* and *liš'* in modern literary Russian]", *RJaŠ*, 1 (1961), 14-17. Finally, introductory particles and word-combinations were outlined with equal brevity by A. I. Anikin in "Osnovnye grammatičeskie i semantičeskie svojstva vvodnyx slov i slovosočetanij [The basic grammatical and semantic qualities of introductory words and word-combinations]", *RJaŠ*, 4 (1956), 22-27.

Certain word-combinations, often repeated, tend to shift from the status of free combinations to that of phraseological units. Intermediate between free combination and phraseological unit are the so-called fixed word-combinations (ustojčivye slovosočetanija), the nature and features of which were dealt with in articles by O. A. Lapteva, "Raspoloženie komponentov ustojčivogo slovosočetanija kak èlement ego struktury [The distribution of components within the fixed word-combination as an element of its structure]", *VJa*, 8/3 (1959), 73-85, O. I. Moskal'skaja, "Ustojčivye slovosočetanija s grammatičeskoj napravlennost'ju [Fixed word-combinations with grammatical orientation]", *VJa*, 10/5 (1961), 87-93; A. P. Mordvilko, "Glagol'no-imennye opisatel'nye vyraženija kak osobyj tip ustojčivyx slovosočetanij [Verb-noun descriptive expressions as a particular type of fixed word-combination]", *RJaŠ*, 4 (1961), 24-29, and V. L. Arxangel'skij, "O postojannyx i peremennyx v strukture ustojčivoj frazy [On constants and variables within the structure of the fixed phrase]",

*NDVŠ-FN*, 1 (1962), 210-213. The syntactic structure of those combinations which have already passed into the sphere of phraseology was illuminated from various points of view by the works of G. Selivanov, "Tavtologičeskie slovosočetanija kak samobytnye russkie frazeologizmy [Tautological word-combinations as original Russian phraseologisms]", *RJaŠ*, 3 (1955), 24-27; N. Ju. Švedova, "O nekotoryx tipax frazeologizirovannyx konstrukcij v stroe russkoj razgovornoj reči [On certain types of phraseologized construction in the pattern of conversational Russian]", *VJa*, 7/2 (1958), 93-100; P. N. Popov, "Leksičeskie arxaizmy v ustojčivyx slovosočetanijax sovremennogo russkogo jazyka [Lexical archaisms in the fixed word-combinations of modern Russian]", *NDVŠ-FN*, 3 (1959), 46-54; N. N. Amosova, "O sintaksičeskoj organizacii frazeologičeskix edinic [On the syntactic organization of phraseological units]", *Problemy jazykoznanija* (= *UZLU* 301) (1961), 7-14; and V. P. Žukov, "Sootnošenie frazeologičeskoj edinicy i ee komponentov so slovami svobodnogo upotreblenija [The relation of the phraseological unit and its components to words of free occurrence]", *NDVŠ-FN*, 3 (1962), 82-93.

In summing up the accomplishments of Soviet linguists in the field of Russian and general syntactic studies during the past decade or so, one must first of all note the great wealth and variety of individual studies of minor problems, treated in the many articles, short and long, which appeared during this period, and which have been noted in the present survey. The few capital works to appear in the field of Russian syntax, such as the Academic Grammar, Vol. II, have been noteworthy accomplishments, although their value has lain more in the conscientious accumulation of material than in bold new attempts at classification. The structural approach to syntactic analysis (and syntactic synthesis) which has proved to be so stimulating in the West during the past half-dozen years, has been noted and partially digested within the Soviet Union, but has with few exceptions not yet had time to result in really new techniques. There is no doubt that the quality of Soviet linguistic research in general, and of syntactic work in particular, has made enormous strides since the dark days of the Marr hegemony; the work now done in the USSR is on the level of real international competence, and one looks forward to even greater strides in the coming decade, as the many stimulating structuralists now approaching syntax from the directions of phonology (e.g., S. K. Šaumjan) or mathematical typology (I. I. Rezvin, B. A. Uspenskij), as well as the many extremely interesting workers in the field of machine translation, bring their new and special insights to bear on the basic principles of syntactic description.

# LEXICOLOGY

URIEL WEINREICH

## 1. INTRODUCTION

1.1. To an American observer, the strangest thing about Soviet lexicology is that it exists. No corresponding discipline is officially distinguished in Western European or American linguistics; in such American textbooks as H. A. Gleason, Jr.'s *Introduction to Descriptive Linguistics* (New York, 1955) or C. F. Hockett's *Course in Modern Linguistics* (New York, 1958) there is no mention of "lexicology", and what these books have to say about the study of vocabulary bears the marks of half-hearted improvisation. By contrast, Soviet textbooks assign to lexicology a prominence comparable to that enjoyed by phonology and grammar.[1] A sizable literature of articles, dissertations, book-length monographs, specialized collections, and a lively stream of conferences on various lexicological subjects,[2] reflect the relative importance of lexicology in the economy of Soviet scholarship.

1.2. It is instructive to consider some of the reasons for this discrepancy between the scope of Soviet and American linguistics. The most obvious explanation is that Soviet linguistics was never infected with the paralysis of semantic interest which caused most scholars during the Bloomfieldian period of linguistics in the United States to abdicate all semantic investigation to other (ineffectual) sciences. Perhaps Pavlovian psychology did not hold out to linguists the seductive promises which

[1] The entire second volume of *Vvedenie v jazykoznanie* (Bulaxovskij & Čikobava) is devoted to semasiology, lexicology, lexicography, and etymology. In Reformatskij's *Vvedenie v jazykoznanie*, pp. 36-120 deal with lexicology. Mučnik's workbook integrated with these courses (*Vvedenie v jazykoznanie; sbornik zadač i upražnenij*...) provides a matching section of problems and exercises in lexicology on pp. 8-39. In Agajan's *Vvedenie v jazykoznanie* lexicology again receives extended consideration, pp. 193-272. On the inclusion of lexicology in the curriculum of linguistics, see *VJa* 4.77 (1952), 4.77 ff. (1953), and 5.84 (1953). — It is my pleasant duty to thank Professor Ol′ga Sergeevna Axmanova of the University of Moscow for her help in locating some of the source materials for this chapter; needless to say, the responsibility for all errors of fact or of judgment are my own. Some of the articles have been referred to at second hand.

[2] E.g. a conference on lexicography, Moscow, 1952; on homonymy, Leningrad, December 1957; on problems of compiling reference dictionaries, Kiev, May 1958; on phraseology, Samarkand, 1959; on problems of applied linguistics, Černivcy, 1960; on the contemporary problems of lexicology and semasiology, Moscow, 1960; on the application of structural and statistical methods in the study of the vocabulary, Moscow, 1961; on historical lexicology, lexicography, and the language of writers, Leningrad, 1961; on comparative and historical lexicology, Moscow, 1961; and several others, usually summarized in the "Xronikal′nye zametki" of the journal *Voprosy jazykoznanija*.

Bloomfield and his disciples discerned in rigorous American behaviorism;[3] at any rate, Soviet linguists as a group do not seem ever to have fallen prey to the hope that psychology (or neurology, or sociology, as the case may be) would resolve for them the difficult theoretical and methodological problems of semantic analysis. In Soviet lexicology, it seems, neither the traditionalists, who have been content to work with the categories of classical rhetoric and 19th-century historical semantics, nor the critical lexicologists in search of better conceptual tools, have ever found reason to doubt that linguistics alone is centrally responsible for the investigation of the vocabulary of languages. (On the distinction between lexicology and semantics, see § 2 below.)

A second reason for the remarkable vigor of lexicological research in the Soviet Union, in contrast to its feebleness in America, might be sought in the fact that the USSR has managed to escape that pernicious form of specialization under which the philologists have the facts and linguists have the ideas. At least until the very recent trend toward "structural" linguistics, the boldest conceptual experimenters on the Soviet scene have by and large been men and women of deep learning in the history of particular languages. Under a university system stressing the teaching of languages in their full historical and literary perspective, problems of vocabulary have been respected rather than shunned.

A major stimulus to Soviet lexicology, too, has been the prodigious lexicographic activity of the USSR. For cultural reasons, and out of considerations of internal and foreign policy which need not be entered into here, foreign-language study and translation have enjoyed an importance in the Soviet Union unmatched by anything in the United States; dictionaries of all sizes and specialties for scores of languages have been required. Although planning and quality control have not always corresponded to the ambitions of the central scholarly authorities, the scale of lexicographic work in the USSR is certainly unique, and its average quality enviable.[4] The

[3] Cf. Tixomirov's review of B. F. Skinner's *Verbal Behavior* (New York, 1957) in *Word* 15.362-367 (1959). Concerning certain important semantic discoveries of Soviet psychology, see footnote 29 below.

[4] The history of Soviet Russian lexicography is surveyed by Barxudarov, "Russkaja sovetskaja leksikografija za 40 let". But this, of course, is only part of the story; a full and objective history of Soviet lexicography in all languages would be an important and fascinating task. Pending the publication of the fifth volume of *Bibliografičeskij ukazatel' literatury po jazykoznaniju izdannoj v SSSR s 1918 po 1957 god* (cf. vol. I, p. 18), one must rely, for a bibliographic listing of dictionaries, on Section 25 (Linguistics) of the annual *Knižnaja letopis'*. Many dictionaries of the Soviet minority languages are mentioned in Bokarev & Dešeriev (eds.), *Mladopis'mennye jazyki narodov SSSR*. For a view of lexicographic planning in the 1950's, see Kogotkova, "O koordinacionnoj rabote po leksikografii"; Ševeleva, "O koordinacionnoj rabote po leksikografii"; Sumnikova, "Koordinacionnoe regional'noe soveščanie po voprosu sostavlenija tolkovyx slovarej". On planning in Turkic lexicography, cf. Orudžev, "Koordinacionnoe regional'noe soveščanie"; and see Borovkov, "Iz opyta sostavlenija russko-nacional'nyx slovarej" for an interesting multiple review of several dictionaries covering Soviet minority languages. Coordination in the preparation of regional dictionaries is the topic of the articles by Ossoveckij, "O sostavlenii regional'nyx slovarej" and Kačalkin, "O nekotoryx principax sostavlenija regional'nyx istoričeskoj slovarej". Planning activities connected with phraseological dictionaries of Russian and other languages are covered in the publications mentioned in § 3.3 below.

sheer number of qualified lexicographic workers and concerned institutions has produced a need and an opportunity for sharing experiences and criticisms, and in favorable cases such exchanges have yielded valuable results for general, theoretical lexicology as well as for the practical problems of dictionary making. Thus, for example, the system for classifying phraseological units (see § 3.3) devised by V. V. Vinogradov after decades of research in the history of Russian vocabulary has in turn been widely adopted by lexicographers working on other languages.[5] A discussion of problems of homonymy organized by the Leningrad division of the Institute of Linguistics of the Academy of Sciences in December, 1957, in response to a controversial article[6] attracted a score of scholars with theoretical sophistication, factual command of the histories of various languages, and personal lexicographic experience.[7] A similar gathering in the United States would be difficult to imagine.[8] The series *Leksikografičeskij sbornik* (1957ff.), already in its fifth volume, annually exemplifies the lexicological fruits of confronting theory-minded dictionary makers from various fields. In sum, when practicing Soviet lexicographers are taken to task for failing to consider general lexicological principles or preliminary investigations, the critics have clear standards to which they can refer.[9]

The fourth reason, and certainly not the least, for the difference in the state of lexicological research in the two countries, is the fact that Russian linguistics, like its counterpart in most countries, is committed to the cultivation of the standard language, whereas American linguistics has intimately associated itself with anarchic attitudes toward the maintenance and development of norms of English usage. Americans do not, on the whole, pay homage to a writer for the quality of his language, compile multi-volume dictionaries of the works of important authors, or embark on doctoral dissertations dealing with, say, idiomatic phrases in a particular classic novel. What would be the American equivalent of the Russian academic series, *Kul'tura reči*? A "Journal of Cultivated English", enjoying the participation of the best specialists in English linguistics in the United States, stretches our imagination more than science fiction. Yet all these phenomena are familiar features of the Russian

[5] Galkina-Fedoruk et al., *Sovremennyj russkij jazyk*, p. 86, note 2. In the words of Axmanova (*Očerki po obščej i russkoj leksikologii*, p. 3), "it is important for the lexicologist not only to 'reap the fruits' of the lexicographic works of others, but also to take a personal part in such work, for it is the immediate and constant contact with countless and variegated facts of vocabulary, as demanded by lexicography, which provides scientific generalizations with their most solid ground". See also Palamarčuk, "Leksykografy obminjujutsja dosvidom".

[6] Abaev, "O podače omonimov v slovare".

[7] See the brief report by Grigor'ev, "Obsuždenie problemy omonimii", and the full proceedings of the conference in *Leksikografičeskij sbornik* 4.35-92 (1960).

[8] The only similar American undertaking – a conference on lexicography at Indiana University in 1961 – displayed the expected gap between fact-centered practitioners and improvising theoreticians. See Fred W. Householder and Sol Saporta (eds.), *Problems in Lexicography* (= *International Journal of American Linguistics* 28, no. 2, part IV) (1962).

[9] Vinogradov, "O nekotoryx voprosax teorii russkoj leksikografii", and "Osnovnye tipy leksičeskix značenij slova", p. 11; Babkin, "Po voprosam russkoj leksikologii i leksikografii", pp. 11, 14 ff. To be sure, the strictures in many cases concern lack of attention to studies in the history of specific words.

intellectual landscape. The USSR, too, had an episode of wanting to "leave its language alone", but that early post-Revolutionary trend was squashed, in the name of cultural continuity, as a vulgarization of Marxism; it was reversed before the end of the 1920's – i.e. before analogous strivings in the United States had even begun. The normative spirit, bolstered by the full moral and factual support of linguistic scholarship, not only results in the standardization of specific lexical variables,[10] but also creates an atmosphere for teaching the native language in which lexicological investigation can flourish, while in America, by contrast, the field has hardly been sown.

1.3. When one turns from quantity of output and ambitiousness of aim to the quality of Soviet lexicological research, the rosy picture assumes more variegated hues. For if lexicology is to be a discipline within linguistics, masses of observations on words of numerous languages are not enough. To qualify as a "discipline" at all, lexicology must comprise a system of related and researchable questions which can be answered for every language in a repeatable way. The solutions to lexicological problems, if they cannot be unique, must at least vary over a controlled range of possibilities. According to their form, lexicological questions must be applicable to the most varied languages. A study of the types and distribution of homonyms in Russian, for example, can be said to contribute to a discipline of lexicology insofar as the criteria for distinguishing homonymy from related phenomena (polysemy) are explicitly stated and insofar as incidence of homonymy is considered in relation to the grammatical structure of the language under study. A statement about the synonymic resources of the French in a given topical domain qualifies as lexicologically valid only insofar as it is independent of the writer's introspection or the uncriticized evidence of an arbitrary synonym dictionary.

From this rigorous point of view, the achievements of Soviet lexicology are still extremely modest. One still finds putatively lexicological works dealing with specific languages in which material from the given language is used merely as a source of examples of universal categories (e.g. broadening and narrowing of meaning), in which no specific characterization of the language supposedly under investigation is even approached. For example, in a book on French lexicology, the ways in which French words change their meanings are summarized as follows:

In some cases, [the meaning of a word] is broadened. ... In other cases, a word which useg to designate a general concept ... acquires a special meaning (*couver*, *traire*). The meanind of a word may change in a positive direction (*jambe*, *manger*) or, on the contrary, may

[10] "Lexicology as a section in a course on modern Standard Russian not only gives a systematic description of the present make-up of the vocabulary, but also helps [students] to master the literary norms of word usage. [Without such mastery] their speech will contain errors which lower its expressiveness and effectiveness" (Šanskij, *Očerki po russkomu slovoobrazovaniju i leksikologii*, p. 148). Cf. also Ožegov, "Očerednye voprosy kul'tury reči", p. 27: "A particularly essential link in the high cultivation of speech is the correct use of words, in the broad sense...."

acquire a negative coloring (*rosse*, *imbecile*). ... Word meanings also change through transfer ... according to continuity (metonymy) or similarity (metaphor). ...[11]

To be sure, not all lexicological work, even in the "traditional" vein, is equally pedestrian; authors differ in talent and preparation.[12] But the new, critical direction in lexicology is still quite young, not having gone into full swing until the middle 1950's. Even the limited results obtained in the relatively short period are therefore impressive, and numerous promising developments may be afoot.

1.4. It is fashionable in present-day Soviet linguistics on the one hand to glorify the progressiveness of Russian scholarship in the 19th century and, on the other hand, to denigrate everything done during the period when Marrism was in the saddle.[13] The outside observer, however, can discern little connection between contemporary Soviet lexicology and its 19th-century forerunners, and though there was no dearth of occult madness in the Marrist "new doctrine of language", the specific criticisms of Marrist lexicology seem to stem from differences of Marxist dogma rather than from specific Marrist sins of omission or commission.[14] The Marrist period may indeed have been lexicologically barren,[15] but pre-Marrist Soviet lexicology was not distinguished for its fertility, either.[16] It is, in fact, a minor irony that the very event which freed Soviet linguists from Marrism – Stalin's intervention in the *Pravda* debate of 1950 – settled linguistics in the USSR with a new, more

[11] Andreeva, *Leksikologija francuzskogo jazyka*, p. 124. The defects of this approach are, of course, perfectly obvious to the more critical scholars within the Soviet Union; cf. Axmanova, et al., "O nekotoryx voprosax i zadačax opisatel′noj, istoričeskoj i sravnitel′no-istoričeskoj leksikologii", p. 5.

[12] The just cited book by Andreeva, for example, makes no reference to any French literature on the subject of French vocabulary, such as the stimulating and thought-provoking works of Charles Bally. French lexicological problems have fared much better at other hands; cf. the more recent, more critical and imaginative paper by Gak, "Nekotorye obščie semantičeskie osobennosti francuzskogo slova v sravnenii s russkim". Levkovskaja's book on German vocabulary, *Leksikologija nemeckogo jazyka*, in a way a companion volume to Andreeva's treatment of French, is of considerably higher quality. Similarly, Smirnickij's *Leksikologija anglijskogo jazyka* is a critical investigation, full of original suggestions, in comparison with which Andreeva's book is a relic of a previous age. Xajdakov's volume on Lak vocabulary, *Očerki po leksike lakskogo jazyka*, though a basically traditional book published in a period already tending to critical reexamination of lexicological fundamentals, unmistakably reflects abilities not in evidence in such books as Andreeva's on French.

[13] See Vinogradov, "Iz istorii leksikologii", and Ufimceva, *Opyt izučenija leksiki kak sistemy*, pp. 59-64.

[14] Vinogradov, *ibid.*; see also Levkovskaja, "O podxode N. Ja. Marra k slovarnomu sostavu jazyka", and Čerkasova, "Voprosy russkoj leksikologii v rabotax èpigonov 'novogo učenija' o jazyke". Since Marrists regarded language, and its entire vocabulary, as part of the superstructure (in the Marxist sense), there was no doctrinal obstacle to their study of vocabulary and of lexical reflections of social change.

[15] Among the very few papers that I have come across are Dondua, "Metafora v širokom smysle i metafora poetičeskaja", and Gitlic, "Problemy onominov".

[16] The main lexicological topic of interest in the 1920's seems to have been the effect of the Revolution on Russian vocabulary; Seliščev, Polivanov, and several other linguists of major stature devoted papers to the problem. This topic eventually came to be espoused as a privileged area of research for Marxist linguistics by the aggressive "Jazykfront" movement which struggled with the Marrists for the title of true Marxian fundamentalism until it was purged in the 1930's; cf. Danilov, "Programma i priemy issledovanija leksiki". It may also be appropriate to cite A. M. Peškovskij, whose articles on the word make him a significant forerunner of the theoretical developments of the 1940's.

specifically lexicological mystery: the doctrine of the "basic lexical stock". Overnight, this exemplar of vagueness became the subject of servile exegesis by the best scholars.[17] Nothing attests more eloquently to its emptiness than the abruptness with which it disappeared from the pages of Soviet linguistic literature with the abolition of the "cult of personality" in 1955.[18]

Actually the beginnings of Soviet lexicology in its characteristic present form lie in the 1940's. The published outcroppings of the preparatory work are extremely few, but the main guidelines for the brisk development of the 1950's seem to have been laid down by four people – one outstanding student of Russian grammatical structure and vocabulary, V. V. Vinogradov,[19] and three accomplished theoretician-lexicographers: L. V. Ščerba (French),[20] A. I. Smirnickij (English),[21] and O. S. Axmanova (English).[22] From a survey of Soviet lexicological literature, it appears that these scholars, more than any others, are responsible for defining the specific subject-matter of lexicology and for setting the direction of further analysis of concepts and of factual descriptive, historical, and comparative investigation of languages in their lexical aspect.

[17] We may cite, e.g., Vinogradov's early paper, "Ob osnovnom slovarnom fonde i ego slovoobrazujuščej roli v istorii jazyka"; Mel'cer, "Ob osnovnom slovarnom fonde v slovarnom sostave jazyka"; Budagov's pamphlet, *Ob osnovnom slovarnom fonde i slovarnom sostave jazyka*; Černyx, "Učenie I. V. Stalina o slovarnom sostave i osnovnom slovarnom fonde jazyka"; Grigor'eva, *Ob osnovnom fonde i slovarnom sostave russkogo jazyka*; Guryčeva & Serebrennikov, "Zadači izučenija osnovnogo slovarnogo fonda jazyka"; Kissen, "Problems slovarja-minimuma v svete stalinskogo učenija"; and the numerous articles applying the new doctrine to specific languages: Romance (Budagov, "Osnovnoj slovarnyj fond romanskix jazykov"), French (Šaxova, "Nekotorye voprosy izučenija ... francuzskogo jazyka"), German (Stroeva, "K voprosu ob ustojčivosti osnovnogo slovarnogo fonda v nemeckom jazyke"), Swedish (Maslova-Lašanskaja, "K voprosu ob ustojčivosti ... švedskogo jazyka"), and the mountain languages of Dagestan (Žirkov, "Ob osnovnom slovarnom fonde gorskix jazykov Dagestana").

[18] The first edition of Galkina-Fedoruk's *Sovremennyj russkij jazyk: leksika* contained a chapter on the matter (pp. 79-89) which was duly omitted from the revised edition of 1958. In connection with a language like Moldavian, whose Romanceness was contested by the Marrists, the problem of basic vocabulary retains a ligitimate importance and continues to be discussed even in the post-Stalin period (cf. Korlètjanu, "Problema istoričeskogo proisxoždenija ... moldavskogo jazyka"). For an expression of uncertainty regarding the legitimacy of the problem, cf. the remarks by Axmanova et al., "O nekotoryx voprosax i zadačax ... leksikologii".

[19] Especially his papers "O formax slova", "Osnovnye ponjatija russkoj frazeologii kak lingvističeskoj discipliny", and "Ob osnovnyx tipax frazeologičeskix edinic", followed by numerous articles in the 1950's, cited below.

[20] Ščerba, "Opyt obščej teorii leksikografii (I)". See also Ljus'en Ten'er (Lucien Tesnière), "O russko-francuzskom Slovare Ščerby", and Istrina, "L. V. Ščerba kak leksikograf i leksikolog".

[21] E.g. "Nekotorye zamečanija po anglijskoj omonimike". Some of his important later papers are cited in other footnotes below. Smirnickij's excellent Russian-English dictionary and his climactic (posthumous) book on English lexicology date from the 1950's.

[22] E.g. Axmanova, "K voprosu o slove v jazyke i reči". The majority of her fundamental papers, as well as her culminating book-length treatment of Russian and general lexicology, also appeared in the 1950's. The major organazational turn in the recent history of Soviet lexicography (and, indirectly, of lexicology) was the conference on problems of lexicography in Moscow on April 15-16, 1952 (see Il'inskaja, "Soveščanie po voprosam leksikografii"). In that conference, Vinogradov's influence seems again to have been as effective and inspiring as in the general process of de-Marrization.

## 2. THE SCOPE OF LEXICOLOGY

In the considerable body of Soviet literature on lexicology, it is surprisingly difficult to find a comprehensive statement of the theoretical foundations and research goals of this linguistic discipline.[23] The cumulative picture that emerges from a study of available works appears approximately as follows:

The basic object of lexicological study is the word, as a unit of a vocabulary. A word is an invariant relation between a sound complex and a meaning. However, the manifestations of a word are variable, both phonologically (e.g. English /dirékt – dajrékt/) and grammatically (e.g. *writes – write – wrote*; *dependence – dependency*) as well as semantically (e.g. "white" in *white flower*, *white wine*, *white race*, *white lie*, *White Paper*). The task of lexicology, accordingly, is to study the nature of the variations of words against the background of their invariance.

The notion of phonological variants of a word appears to have been formulated first by V. V. Vinogradov; A. I. Smirnickij and O. S. Axmanova attempted to give it a more solid theoretical foundation and to exemplify the phenomenon from their rich experience as practical lexicographers.[24] However, if it was the intent of these scholars to delimit a topic not adequately treated by phonology or grammar, their attempt has so far not been convincing.

That the "grammatical variants" of a word should constitute a problem in themselves can perhaps be understood in terms of the word-paradigm (WP) model of grammatical description[25] to which Soviet linguistics as a whole adheres. Each word, according to this model, has a lexical and a grammatical meaning. The lexical meaning of *wrote*, for example is that which is shared by *write* and *writes*; its grammatical meaning is that which is shared by *worked* and *broke*.[26] Regarding "analytic" forms like *worked*, it might be relevant to object that the "lexical meaning of the word" is simply *the* meaning of the stem morpheme, while its "grammatical meaning" is *the* meaning of the affix. But as soon as one passes to more synthetic forms, such as (*they*) *write* or *wrote*, the "grammatical" meaning cannot be attributed to any isolable segmental constituents. The existence of zero morphs, syncretism, and of syntactic restrictions on distribution of simplex words thus gives considerable advantage to a model in which the word is the basic unit and the morpheme a derivative of the word, rather than vice versa.

[23] For characteristic statements, all of them too elementary or fragmentary to deserve citation in full, cf. Levkovskaja, *Leksikologija nemeckogo jazyka*, pp. 3-10; Axmanova, Vinogradov, and Ivanov, "O nekotoryx voprosax i zadačax ... leksikologii"; Smirnickij, *Leksikologija anglijskogo jazyka*, pp. 5-11; Axmanova, *Očerki po obščej i russkoj leksikologii*, pp. 3-8; Levkovskaja, "O principax strukturno-semantičeskogo analiza jazykovyx edinic". Unfortunately, A. A. Beleckij, *Leksikologija* (Kiev, 1955), was not available to me.

[24] Vinogradov, "O formax slova"; Smirnickij, *Leksikologija anglijskogo jazyka*, pp. 138-143; Axmanova, "Fonologičeskie i grammatičeskie varianty slova" and *Očerki...*, pp. 192-212 (with references to Smirnickij's earlier work on the subject).

[25] C. F. Hockett, "Two Models of Grammatical Description", *Word* 10.210-235 (1954), p. 210.

[26] For details, see e.g. Smirnickij, "Leksičeskoe i grammatičeskoe v slove".

Grammatical "variants" of a word are, admittedly, of two kinds: inflectional, which are treated by grammar (and will not be considered further in this article), and word-formative, which occupy an autonomous area intermediate between grammar and lexicology.[27] (See also § 3.4 below.)

By far the most interesting aspect of variation of words is the semantic one, and it is on this topic that the most original contributions of Soviet lexicology have been made. The notion of semantic variation depends on a conception of "lexical meaning" distinct from that simple relation between a sign-vehicle and a class of phenomena which is studied by a generalized semantics. A simple naming relation is characterized by the monosemy of the sign and by the stable content of the sign vis-à-vis the context in which it occurs. The typical linguistic sign, on the other hand, is polysemous, and furthermore, the submeanings of a polysemous word are subject to thoroughgoing specialization according to the grammatical and phraseological context in which they occur (cf. the example of *white* above). If a meaning can (in part) be specified by the participation of a sign in synonymic series, then it is clear that a polysemous word which has specialized contextual meanings will participate in different synonym series depending on the submeaning under consideration.[28] Thus, whereas for a generalized semantics polysemy and contextual specialization represent special deviations from the naming relation, they are, for lexicology, the principal subject of study. On the contrary, from the lexicological point of view it is the grammatically unrestricted, monosemous, and literally applicable word that is the degenerate and linguistically atypical case.[29] (On theoretical studies of "terminologized" vocabulary, in which this limiting condition is approached, see § 3.6 below.)

[27] Šanskij (*Očerki*..., pp. 145f.) operates with a tripartite division. Cf. also Vinogradov, "Voprosy ... slovoobrazovanija..." and "Slovoobrazovanie..."; Sevortjan, "K sootnošeniju grammatiki i leksiki v tjurkskix jazykax"; Gepner, *Očerki po obščemu i russkomi jazykoznaniju*, pp. 70-123. The isolation of the word from the continuous utterance, its delimitation from lower units (morphemes) and higher ones (phrases), has been one of the main interests of Smirnickij; see "K voprosu o slove (problema otdel'nosti slova)", "K voprosu o slove (problema toždestva slova)", and "Zvučanie slova i ego semantika." It has also interested Axmanova, e.g. her *Očerki*..., pp. 57ff. and earlier papers cited in footnote p. 5, as well as "Ešče k voprosu o slove" and "K voprosu ob otlicii složnyx slov ot frazeologičeskix edinic". To this reader, the attempts of these scholars to define the work partly by semantic criteria seems just as unsuccessful as the efforts in American descriptive linguistics to define it without recourse to semantic considerations.

[28] The development of this theory was influenced by the important paper of Kurilovič (Kuryłowicz), "Zametki o značenii slova". In Šaumjan's formulation ("Strukturnye metody izučenija značenij"), words may have semantic variants of three types. (1) "Denotative" variants pertain to the relation between a word and its referents. (2) The "primary distributional parameters" of words are the invariants of their meaning, i.e. the context-free submeanings of a polysemous word. Typical of language, however, is the existence of (3) "secondary distributional parameters" as well ("connotative variants"), i.e. the relative invariants of a word's meaning within a specific (verbal) context. Polysemy can thus be defined as the aggregate of secondary SDP's (semantic distributional parameters) of a word in their relation to the primary SDP. Synonymy results from the neutralization of lexical oppositions; in conditions of synonymy the secondary SDP's of word A enter a relation of substitution with the primary SDP of word B. Cf. also Apresjan, "K voprosy o strukturnoj leksikologii".

[29] On the distinction between lexical meaning and concept, see Amosova, "O leksičeskom značenii slova"; Zvegincev, *Očerki po obščemu jazykoznaniju*; Axmanova, *Očerki po obščej i russkoj leksiko-*

The general program of lexicological study accordingly includes the following components:

(a) With respect to the (special case of) *monosemous* word, explore its relations to synonymous words (including antonyms), the syntactic functions of the word which contribute to its individuality, the phraseological (collocational) restrictions on its use, and the word-formative potential of the item (i.e. the types of words which may be derived from it).

(b) With respect to the (typical case of) *polysemous* word, explore the same properties as enumerated in (a) separately for each of its meanings; then systematize the several meanings of a word according to the manner of their semiotic functioning[30] (cf. § 3.5 below).

(c) With respect to an entire vocabulary at a given stage of its development: systematize the findings obtained under (b) to show the typical patterns of phraseological and syntactic specialization of meaning, of synonym patterning (word fields), of polysemy structure that prevail in the language. This is the task of *descriptive lexicology* (§ 4).

(d) With respect to a vocabulary over time: compare the findings of descriptive lexicology applied to several historical stages of a language, so as to display the rise, abondonment, and change of typical lexicological patterns, as well as the evolution of specific synonym groups (word fields). This is the task of *historical lexicology* (§ 5).

(e) With respect to the vocabularies of a set of genetically related languages: from the results of historical lexicology, reconstruct the typical lexicological patterns of the proto-language. This is the task of *comparative lexicology* (§ 5).

(f) With respect to language in general: from the results of descriptive lexicology, derive conclusions about universal lexicological patterns and the possibilities of variation in particular languages; from the results of historical lexicology, enumerate all possible regularities in the manner in which lexicological patterns of a language change. These are the tasks of *general lexicology* (§ 6).

Since the very aims of lexicology are still in the process of being defined (cf. footnote 23), not every work referred to in the following survey can be assigned a precise place in the envisioned edifice. Most studies, however, have a clearly specified goal.

*logii*, pp. 31-34; Zvegincev, *Očerki po obščemu jazykoznaniju*, pp. 340-355; Ufimceva, *Opyt izučenija leksiki kak sistemy*, pp. 83-92 (with strong cricism of Zvegincev's position as formulated in his *Semasiologija*), and "K voprosu o leksiko-semantičeskoj sisteme jazyka". The problem of concepts was a frequent subject in the literature of the period immediately following the Linguistic Debate; cf. the references in Axmanova et al., "O nekotoryx voprosax i zadačax ... leksikologii," p. 9, fn. 2, and in Zvegincev, *Očerki*..., p. 340 n.; also Reznikov, *Ponjatie i slovo* and Beljaev, "O slove i ponjatii". These discussions, however, have been almost entirely doctrinal, and are of scant scientific or philosophical interest. By contrast, the psychological investigations of vocabulary in relation to color perception by Šemjakin and his associates (*Myšlenie i reč'*) and of the psychophysics of synonymy by Luria and his students (cf. his and Vinogradova's "An Objective Investigation of the Dynamics of Semantic Systems") are of extraordinary importance.

[30] Vinogradov, "Osnovnye tipy leksičeskix značenij slova". As a fundamental contribution to linguistic theory, this paper is astonishingly rambling and opaque. For a readable reprise, cf. Ufimceva, "Principy istoričeskogo izučenija leksiko-semantičeskix grupp".

The lion's share of research, it will be observed, has been concerned with the basic lexicological phenomena and not with broad analysis of vocabularies. But this is only natural, for although it is the "higher" goals of lexicology that provide motivation for the lowly spadework, each "higher" stage depends for its raw material on the results of the preceding phase.

## 3. THE LEXICOLOGICAL PHENOMENA

### 3.1. *Determination of Word Meanings*

For the sake of brevity, the term "word meaning" will here be used as an abbreviation for "meaning of a monosemous word or submeaning of a polysemous word".

The two conventional ways of specifying a word meaning are (1) lexicographic definition and (2) location of the item in a synonym system. A third way, based on the syntactic properties of words, is also now being explored (see § 3.2). For a time, O. S. Axmanova toyed with the applications of C. E. Osgood's "semantic differential" to the problems of meaning specification (see her *Očerki po obščej i russkoj leksikologii*, Moscow, 1957, pp. 71–103), but no concrete research seems to have resulted.

3.1.1. *Lexicographic Definition.* – Although there are scattered criticisms of the definitory practices of dictionaries in the programmatic articles (cf. footnote 9) and in critical reviews, little systematic study has been devoted to this topic. The fundamental paper remains L. V. Ščerba's "Essay of a General Theory of Lexicography" (see footnote 20). L. S. Kovtun has studied the defining practices of the Academy Dictionary of Contemporary Standard Russian (1950ff.), while L. V. Malaxovskij has analyzed parallel problems in the Oxford English Dictionary. A special paper by E. E. Biržskova is devoted to the definition of words designating animals. The paper by È. F. Skoroxod'ko, of which so far only a brief abstract has become available, is also concerned with this subject. Indirectly, Soviet interest in the topic is evidenced by the translation, in 1958, of Julio Casares' *Introducción a la lexicografía moderna* (Madrid, 1950), although the first major review did not appear until the end of 1962.[31]

3.1.2. *Synonymy.* – Already the "traditionalist" works on lexicology found it necessary to discuss the synonymic resources of a language.[32] However, the criteria for grouping words as synonyms, and the classification of synonym types, were as eclectic and ill-considered in Soviet as in non-Soviet works. For example, E. V. Galkina-Fedoruk et al. (*Sovremennyj russkij jazyk*, Moscow, 1958, pp. 22f.) distinguish these types of synonym: (1) words designat ingthe same thing, but with

[31] Kovtun, "O postroenii slovarnoj stat'i..."; Malaxovskij, "K voprosu o principax smyslovoj xarakteristiki slova v tolkovom slovare"; Biržskova, "Ob opredelenijax ... oboznačajuščix životnyx"; Skoroxod'ko, "Ob opredelenijax slov"; Raxmanova, Review of Casares.

[32] E. G. Levkovskaja, *Leksikologija nemeckogo jazyka*, pp. 136-144; Andreeva, *Leksikologija sovremennogo francuzskogo jazyka*, pp. 162-172. Cf. also Fridman, "O meste sinonimiki...".

a different stylistic coloring; (2) words of Russian origin in a relation of synonymy with words of foreign origin; (3) words with a stronger emotional coloring in a relation of synonymy with others; (4) synonyms resulting from the substitution of a literary word for a dialectal one; (5) synonyms resulting from euphemistic substitution. The concept of synonym which emerges is obviously far too weak to serve as a criterion for dividing the complex meaning of a word into submeanings by the ability of the submeanings to enter into separate synonym series (see § 2 (b) above), and such classifications are therefore of marginal use to lexicology as a discipline.[33]

An awakening to the unresolved theoretical problems of synonymy came with the subtle and thought-provoking essay by A. B. Šapiro and the forthright explanation of the dilemma by Ju. D. Apresjan.[34] At about the same time, discussions of antonyms as a special variety of synonyms served to sharpen the new critical spirit.[35]

In comparison with Western European languages, the number of synonym dictionaries published in Russia has been small. V. N. Kljueva's *Kratkij slovar' sinonimov russkogo jazyka* (Moscow, 1956) was the first book-length synonym dictionary of Russian in nearly a century;[36] the discussion of it led to a number of recommendations for the compilation of fuller, theoretically better founded synonym dictionaries.[37] The freshly stimulated interest in this subject has also been manifested in various papers on synonym lexicography in other languages.[38] A special focus of attention has been the nature of systematic synonymy in languages that have undergone particularly extensive influence by others, such as English, Hindi-Urdu, and Moldavian.[39]

An important place in the discussion of synonym theory has been occupied by the critique of word-field theory as practiced by Trier and other West Europeans. In line with the doctrine of lexical meaning which underlies Soviet vocabulary analysis, it has not been difficult to argue that the semantic study of words as simple designators, without due regard to their polysemy and their contextual specialization, misses the point of linguistic lexicology.[40]

33 Similar criticisms are voiced by Sirotina (pp. 10-16). On different occasions, Galkina-Fedoruk has used at least two other classifications of Russian synonyms (see Sirotina, pp. 13f.).

34 "Nekotorye voprosy teorii sinonimov" and Apresjan, "Problema sinonima". For a rather elementary logician's approach, see Uemov, "Problema sinonimov i sovremennaja logika".

35 Kireev, "Ob antonimax"; Kljueva, "Problema antonimov"; and Komissarov, "Problema opredelenija antonima".

36 Briefer treatments were given by Kljueva in an earlier journal article, "Sinonimy v russkom jazyke", and by Favorin in pamphlet form, *Sinonimy*.

37 Cf. the discussions of Kljueva's dictionary by Gomon, *RJaŠ* 3 (1955); by Šanskij, *RJaŠ* 4 (1957); and especially by Gorbačevic in *Leksikografičeskij sbornik*. Cf. also Levčenko, "Do pytannja pro pryncypy ukladannja slovnyka synonimiv ukrajins'koji movy" (followed by instructions for the compilation of a Ukranian synonym dictionary); Derkač, *Korotkyj slovnyk synonimiv*; Galkina-Fedoruk, "Sinonimy"; and the forthcoming paper by Aleksandrov, "O principax sostavlenija slovarja sinonimov".

38 E. G. Apresjan, "O slovare sinonimov Vebstera".

39 Barxudarov, Beskrovnyj, and Zograf, *Xindi i urdu*; Barannikov, "Leksičeskaja sinonimika jazyka xindi..."; Korlètjanu, "O sinonimax... v sovremennom moldavskom jazyke".

40 Axmanova et al., "O nekotoryx voprosax i zadačax... leksikologii", pp. 7-9; Axmanova, *Očerki* ..., pp. 78-81; Ufimceva, "Principy istoričeskogo izučenija leksiko-semantičeskix grupp";

A radically new approach to the problems of synonymy has been initiated by the new group of "structuralists" seeking a syntactic path to semantics. This trend is dealt with in § 3.2 below.

Since the critical study of synonymy in a disciplined lexicological framework is thus still in its beginnings, the investigation of specialized synonym relationships of the submeanings of a polysemous word cannot be expected to be far advanced. V. V. Vinogradov has given a number of instructive examples of this phenonmenon: he has shown, for example, that *obleč'* in its literal meaning, 'to clothe', is a bookish-solemn synonym of *odet'*, whereas in its derivative meanings (e.g. the phraseologically bound *obleč' tajnoj* 'to envelop in mystery', *obleč' doveriem* 'to bestow confidence on', etc.) it has no synonymic relations with *odet'*. A. D. Grigor'eva has devoted some attention to cases of synonymy among derived word meanings where the basic, designative meanings of the corresponding words are not synonymous (e.g. *gluxaja tišina* 'deaf silence' = *nemaja tišina* 'mute silence') and has considered the phraseological specialization of words which, free of context, appear synonymous.[41] But all these comments are programmatic and anecdotal.

## 3.2 *Syntactic Characterization of Words*

The fundamental papers in Soviet lexicology (cf. footnotes 19 and 20) already called attention to the fact that a polysemous word may have differential syntactic properties depending on the submeaning in which it is used. V. V. Vinogradov, for example, showed that animal names when used as expressive terms for character traits (*gus'* 'goose', *lisa* 'vixen', etc.), unlike the same nouns in their plain designative function, are virtually restricted to the predicate. In another set of illustrations, *igrat'* 'to play (at...)' was shown to govern the preposition *v* plus accusative, while *igrat'* 'to play (on...)' governs *na* plus locative. Similarly, *otozvat' sja* 'to respond (to)' takes *na* + acc., while *otozvat'sja* 'to affect' takes *na* + locative.[42] The discussion of this thought-provoking problem has progressed through detailed investigations;[43] some light has also been shed on the matter by considerations of the obverse problem – the specialization of syntactic patterns according to the lexical material to which they

---

and, in greatest detail, her *Opyt izučenija leksiki kak sistemy*, pp. 17-58 (with additional references). Ufimceva also criticizes, for its excessive vagueness, the recent paper by a Soviet scholar, Filin, "O leksiko-semantičeskix gruppax".

[41] Vinogradov, "Osnovnye tipy leksičeskix značenij slova"; Grigor'eva, "Zametki o leksičeskoj sinonimii"; and the dissertation of Xazanovič, *Sinonimija v frazeologii sovremennogo nemeckogo jazyka*, which has unfortunately not been accessible to me.

[42] Vinogradov, "Osnovnye tipy...", pp. 24, 27f.

[43] Cf. Kotelova, "Ukazanija na sintaksičeskie svjazi slov"; Moskal'skaja, "Strukturno-semantičeskie razrjady slov" and "Ustojčivye slovosočetanija s grammatičeskoj napravlennost'ju"; Amosova, "O sintaksičeskom kontekste"; Staniševa, "Voprosy frazeologii ...".

are applicable.[44] In the theory of lexicography, considerable attention has been devoted to the special problems of rendering the more "grammaticized" parts of speech (prepositions and the like) in dictionaries,[45] and to questions of reflecting profound differences of grammatical structure of two languages in a bilingual translation dictionary.[46]

In this trend of thought, the meaning of a word is taken as already specified in some non-syntactic way, so that the syntactic properties of the word can be correlated with its semantic ones. In the past few years, a fresh approach to this matter has been advocated by the adherents of Soviet "structuralism". From their point of view, the detailed syntactic properties of a word *are* its meaning (in a structural, rather than extraneous, "substantive", sense).[47] Thus Ju. D. Apresjan has been investigating, with significant success, the possibility of factoring out common semantic features among classes of words arrived at by grammatical methods of subclassifying parts-of-speech (with heavy reliance on the criterion of transformational potential). For example, a subclass of Russian verbs, numbered (in a binary code) 0011, contains such elements as *dumat'* 'to think', *skučat'* 'to be bored', *mečtat'* 'to (day)dream', etc. The major class in this case, 0, is syntactically defined as that class of verbs which is incapable of undergoing the "reflexive-passive" transformation; the subclass of the next level, 00, is defined by the further inability of the verbs to take on a complement of direction and a "complementary" infinitive; the subclass on the next level, 001, is defined by the possibility of deleting the accusative object of these verbs; the next subclass, 0011, is defined by the optional nature of locative phrases attached to its members. The same method could presumably be continued to yield even finer syntactic differentiations with even better semantic correlations.[48]

On the basis of this approach to synonymy, Apresjan in another study[49] has proposed a radically "structuralist" revision of the notion of word-field. He envisages an analysis the raw material of which includes an enumeration of the constructional patterns (roughly, phrase types) of the language (as revealed by its syntactic analysis); an indication of the frequency of each constructional pattern; and an enumeration of the word-meanings (already known, no matter how discovered) that occur in each pattern. Preliminary study of fifteen English constructional patterns in which a verb

[44] Especially Šmelev, "O 'svjazannyx' sintaksičeskix konstrukcijax"; Švedova, "O nekotoryx tipax frazeologizirovannyx konstrukcij" and "Problema leksičeskix ograničenij...".

[45] Cf. Babkin, "Predlogi kak ob"ekt leksikografii"; Rogožnikova, "Narečnye i meždometnye značenija nekotoryx suščestvitel'nyx"; Veselitskij, "Priemy podači predlogov v russko-francuzskom slovare".

[46] Majtinskaja, "Otraženie različij grammatičeskogo stroja v dvujazyčnyx slovarjax"; Orudžev, "K voprosu ob otraženii ... leksiko-grammatičeskix osobennostej russkogo jazyka".

[47] Cf. Šaumjan, "Strukturnye metody izučenija značenij".

[48] Apresjan, "Distributivnyj analiz značenij i strukturnye semantičeskie polja". Cf. also Glejbman, "Semantičeskie modeli i spektry slov". The outlines of an approach to synonymy and word fields in terms of set-theory are given by Martynov in a paper so far available only as an abstract, "Opyt postroenija obščej teorii značenija".

[49] Apresjan, "K voprosu o struktornoj leksikologii".

is a constituent has yielded corresponding sets of verbs with some semantic feature in common. A semantic field can therefore be described on the basis of the construction potential of its members. Since a correlation has been found between the frequency of a constructional pattern and the number of word-meanings which may appear in it, Apresjan proposes that a hierarchy of increasingly comprehensive word fields be constructed by considering increasingly frequent constructional patterns.

### 3.3. *Phraseology*

This was one of the most productive foci of interest in Soviet lexicology even before the recent turn to "structuralist" methods. The groundwork was laid by V. V. Vinogradov,[50] who undertook a classification of phraseological units under three main headings: (a) concretions (*sraščenija*) – inseparable and unanalyzable collocations in the meaning of which it is impossible to discern a connection with the meanings of the component elements. Examples: *zagovarivat' zuby* 'to divert', *tak sebe* 'so-so', etc.

(b) Phraseological unities (*edinstva*): these are semantically inseparable, but the connection of the components with the same words in free use is not arbitrary. Examples: *sem' pjatnic na nedele* 'seven Fridays in a week' (i.e. 'to keep changing one's mind'), *plyt' po tečeniju* 'to swim with the current', *kormit' zavtrakami* 'to feed breakfasts to' (i.e. 'to feed hopes to'), etc.

(c) Phraseological collocations (*sočetanija*): closed series of word collocations of which only one is basic and restricted, while the others are used freely: *zatronut' čuvstvo, gordost', interesy* 'to touch [i.e. involve] the feelings, the pride, the interests (of...)'.

Vinogradov's papers gave rise to a lively and still continuing discussion concerned not only with the theoretical issues, but with the design of a phraseological dictionary of Russian. A thorough and constructive critical article was contributed by S. N. Ožegov,[51] who reconsidered the structural properties of phraseological units from another viewpoint and offered a clearer separation than Vinogradov's of two criteria – semantic non-autonomy of the components of a phrase and fixedness of a given word-combination.[52] At about the same time there appeared Smirnickij's brief analysis of English phraseology (on principles similar to Ožegov's) and the rich

[50] Vinogradov, "Osnovny ponjatija russkoj frazeologii kak lingvističeskoj discipliny" and "Obsnovnyx tipax frazeologiceskix edinic".

[51] "O strukture frazeologii (v svjazi s proektom frazeologičeskogo slovarja)". A different classification, supposedly on historical principles, has been suggested by Larin, "Očerki po frazeologii"; cf. also Amosova, "O sintaksičeskoj organizacii frazeologičeskix edinic".

[52] An attempt to formalize these concepts has been made by Mel'čuk, "O terminax *ustojčivost'* i *idiomatičnost'*". For slightly different approaches, cf. Toropcev, "Nekotorye priemy leksikologičeskogo issledovanija" and Kameneckajte, "K voprosu o variantnyx i invariantnyx frazeologičeskix sredstvax vyraženija".

chapters on Russian phraseology in Axmanova's book of essays.[53] There followed a series of articles in the publications of various universities,[54] and two fruitful conferences. The First Inter-Republic Conference on Problems of Phraseology, convened in Samarkand in September, 1959, concentrated on specific phraseological problems of Turkic languages (especially Uzbek, but also Azerbaijani, Turkmen, and Uigur). It also considered a number of details of Russian, English, and French phraseology in the light of the theories of Vinogradov and Axmanova.[55] Of even greater interest is the conference on Problems of Phraseology and the Problems of Compiling a Russian Phraseological Dictionary, held in Leningrad in 1961. The proceedings have not yet been published, but a pamphlet of abstracts[56] contains the following papers, the titles of which (given below in English translation) give an idea of the level of the enterprise:

A. M. Babkin, "Phraseologisms of Russian and the Tasks of an Academic Dictionary of Russian Phraseology"; O. S. Axmanova, "The Content and Tasks of Phraseology in Application to Lexicography"; V. L. Arxangel' skij, "On the Concept of a Stable Phrase and on Types of Phrase"; V. P. Žukov, "On the Semantic Center of Phraseologisms"; P. A. Kirsanova, "On Certain Semantic Features of Phraseological Units (On the Problem of Polysemy and Synonymy in the Sphere of Phraseology)"; E. A. Guzunova, "On the Problem of the Essence of Phraseological Units"; N. N. Amosova, "On English Phraseological Dictionaries".

The rise of new phraseological units has recently been considered by A. P. Xazanovič.[57]

### 3.4 *Word-Formative Potential*

Whether derivational morphology is treated together with inflection in the grammar, or under lexicology, as is the Soviet custom,[58] is largely a matter of convention that raises no significant theoretical issues. More relevant to the present discussion is the use of word-formative criteria for the specifications of submeanings of a polysemous word (cf. § 2(c) above). For example, *klass* in Russian means 1. 'school class' and 2. 'social class', but the derived adjective of $klass_1$ is *klassnyj*, while $klass_2$ yields *klassovyj*[59] (cf. English $authority_1$ → *authoritative*, $authority_2$ → *authoritarian*).

[53] Smirnickij, *Leksikologija anglijskogo jazyka*, pp. 203-230; Axmanova, *Očerki*..., pp. 166-191. To be noted also is the excellent *Anglo-russkij frazeologičeskij slovar'* by Kunin.

[54] Arxangel'skij, "Nekotorye voprosy frazeologii"; Anisimov, "K voprosu o sootnošenii..."; Brovko, "K voprosu o semantiko-strukturnoj klassifikacii..."; Rudov, "K voprosu o suščnosti frazeologičeskix vyraženij". None of these articles were accessible to me.

[55] *Voprosy frazeologii.*

[56] *Problemy frazeologii i zadači sostavlenija frazeologičeskogo slovarja russkogo jazyka (tezisy)*, pp. 3-7 (Leningrad, 1961).

[57] Xazanovič, "K voprosu o vozniknovenii frazeologičeskix edinic".

[58] Cf. footnote 27 above. The cited studies of Russian lexicology by Galkina-Fedoruk, of English by Smirnickij, French by Andreeva, German by Levkovskaja, and Lak by Xajdakov, all contain detailed treatments of compounding and derivation.

[59] Axmanova, *Očerki*..., p. 215.

The strongest stand on this point has been taken by M. M. Fal′ kovič, who believes that differences in submeanings are necessarily manifested in word-formative potential.[60] In this strong form, the claim has subsequently been shown to be false.[61]

Among the scholars who have given attention to the problems of separating affixation from word compounding are V. P. Grigor′ev and M. D. Stepanova (see the Bibliography for the relevant works). Levkovskaja's book, *Imennoe obrazovanie*..., explores word-formation in one specific stratum of modern German terminology.

## 3.5 *Structure of Polysemy*

The existence of polysemy – i. e. a multiplicity of *submeanings* of a word, but not to be confused with the still more numerous and fluid *applications* of the word – has been a postulate of all Soviet lexicological work.[62] Discussions of polysemy have centered around two main points: the types of submeaning and their interrelation, and the distinction between polysemy and homonymy.

3.5.1. *Types of Submeaning and Their Interrelation.* – The traditional approach, based on the standard categories of 19th-century historical semasiology and classical rhetoric, is exemplified by E. V. Galkina-Fedoruk, who arranged the types of polysemy according to the kind of meaning *transfer* involved.[63] This classification (transfer according to similarity; according to contiguity; according to common function; and transfer from proper to appellative function) can, of course, easily be given a synchronic interpretation, but there is little hope that the linguistic relevance of the categories will thereby be increased. Considerably more original is the classification offered by V. V. Vinogradov,[64] who distinguishes, on the one hand, directly designative from transferred (roughly, figurative) submeanings, and, on the other hand, seeks out the primary submeaning among the several designative submeanings of a word. For example, *pit′* 'to drink', whether collocated with *vodu* 'water', *kvas* 'cider', *vino* 'wine', etc., manifests only a single designative meaning; whereas *šapka* 'hat, cap' and *šapka* 'banner headline' are instances of two designative submeanings, the former being primary, the latter secondary. In a case like *otvratit′*, on the other hand, we may distinguish between the designative meaning, 'to turn away (e.g. eyes)', and the abstract, transferred meaning, 'to fend off (danger, threats, misfortune, etc.)'. Similarly, in the case of *bezvyxodnyj*, it is possible to discern the

60 Fal′kovic, "K voprosu ob omonimii i polisemii".

61 Eugene Kleiner, "The Discrimination of Multiple Meaning in English", unpublished seminar report, Columbia University, 1961. The papers by Zvereva, "Razryv semantičeskoj svjazi meždu isxodnym i proizvodnym slovami" and Šaxova, "K voprosu o značenii složnyx slov" are also pertinent to this problem.

62 Cf., e.g. Amosova, "O leksičeskom značenii slova".

63 Galkina-Fedoruk, et al., *Sovremennyj russkij jazyk*, pp. 17-20.

64 Vinogradov, "Osnovnye tipy leksičeskix značenij slova". The problem of the internal structure of polysemy is also considered by Zvegincev, *Semasiologija*, pp. 92-137, 187-214, and especially 215-252.

splitting-off of an abstract-transferred submeaning, 'hopeless', from the designative meaning, 'without exit'. So far, however, the vagueness of the criteria in this suggestive scheme have prevented it from being applied in systematic fashion to any body of lexical material.

The types of word-meaning which have been called "expressive" and "figurative" have been the subject of special studies. These include a number of "psycholinguistic" investigations of metaphor[65] and several factual analyses by linguists.[66]

The first published instance of employing syntactic criteria for the differentiation of submeanings of a polysemous word (as part of the trend toward a "structural" semantics; cf. § 3.2 above) is the study by V. I. Perebejnos.[67] Classifying the syntactic constructions in which the English verb *make* partakes, Perebejnos has obtained a fairly satisfactory approximation of intuitive semantic notions.

A number of interesting suggestions for the use of the concepts "marked" and "unmarked" in the analysis of polysemy have recently been made by O. S. Axmanova.[68]

3.5.2. *Homonymy*. – The distinction between polysemy and homonymy has evoked heated and lengthy discussion in Soviet linguistics, mainly perhaps because the attainment of a synchronic criterion for this distinction is a crucial test of the possibility of a rigorous synchronicism in the science of language. The article by V. I. Abaev (cf. footnote 6 above) was the occasion of a special conference on problems of homonymy in Leningrad in 1957.[69] In addition, a number of articles sent in to *Voprosy jazykoznanija* were reviewed by the editors in number 2 for 1959. In the following years, several additional articles on the problem of homonymy appeared in the journals.[70] On the whole, these contributions have been characterized by a feeling of responsibility for large bodies of data: articles have been devoted to homonymy in particular languages[71] or even to homonymy in particular parts of speech. Particularly impressive is O. S. Axmanova's survey of homonymy in Russian, in which the facts are systematically grouped according to part of speech, with a

[65] Nikiforova, "Vosprijatie metafory"; Litvinenko, "Termin i metafora"; Bel′skij, "Metaforičeskoe upotreblenie suščestvitel′nyx".

[66] Zvegincev, "Èkspressivno-modal′nye èlementy i značenie slova"; Galkina-Fedoruk, "Ob èkspressivnosti i èmocional′nosti v jazyke"; Efremov, "Mnogoznačnost′ slova". Cf. also Fel′dman's paper on polysemy in bilingual dictionaries "Ob analize smyslovoj struktury slova...".

[67] Perebejnos, "Ob ispol′zovanii strukturnyx metodov...". This paper also cites some older, more traditional studies, including the dissertations of Ginzburg, *K voprosu o polisemantizme anglijskogo glagola* and Artemjuk, *Razvitie glagolov "do" i "make" v anglijskom jazyka, "tun" i "machen" v nemeckom jazyke*.

[68] Axmanova, "Ausgedrücktes und Nichtausgedrücktes...".

[69] "Diskussija po voprosam omonimii".

[70] "K obsuždeniju voprosa ob omonimax"; Švedova, "Izučenie omonimov"; Novikov, "K probleme omonimii"; Tyšler, "K voprosu o sud′be omonimov"; and Vinogradov, "Ob omonimii i smežnyx javlenijax".

[71] Skiba, "K voprosu o t.n. antonimičeskoj omonimii v slavjanskix jazykax"; Kutina, "Omonimy ..."; Prorokova, "Nekotorye osobennosti omonimii v nemeckom jazyke". It may also be appropriate to cite here Bulaxovskij's early study, "De l'homonymie dans les langues slaves".

final review of homonymy due to the occasional non-differentiation of grammatical categories.[72]

### 3.6. *Terminology*

In the recurrent discussions of the differences between concepts and lexical meanings, it has been generally recognized that the meaning of a "term" (in the sense of "a unit in a terminology") resembles a concept more than does the meaning of an average word. R. A. Budagov has explicitly discussed this very point.[73]

A separate paper on the essence of terms and terminologies has recently been published by A. A. Reformatskij.[74] Among the features of terms distinguished by Reformatskij are their tendency to monosemy; their extraneousness to the modalities, to expressivity, and to the esthetic functions of language; their stylistic neutrality; and their tendency to systematicity. (A different view of the stylistic function of terms had previously been expressed by R. G. Piotrovskij.[75])

## 4. LEXICOLOGICAL DESCRIPTION OF A LANGUAGE

In § 3 we have surveyed the gradual evolution of a critical lexicology interested in its own theoretical foundations. By the standards of this evolving discipline, the book-length treatments of the vocabulary of Russian, French, English, German, and other languages published in the 1950's are antiquated. No full, or even substantial partial, answers to the types of question enumerated in § 2(c) above have been given. The closest approximation to the execution of a lexicological task in the disciplined sense is probably O. S. Axmanova's analysis of Russian phraseology.[76]

Two topics which belong under the heading of descriptive lexicology and which *have* been discussed on a language-wide basis are the question of passive vocabulary and the stylistic differentiation of language.

The distinction between active and passive vocabulary appears to be due to N. M. Šanskij. The passive vocabulary, in his view, includes words which are not in daily use, i.e. everything which has not yet become or has already ceased to be ordinary: obsolete words and neologisms. The active vocabulary is the rest. Obsolete words are classified according to the degree of their obsoleteness, the causes of their archaization, and the possibilities and character of their continued utilization. Neologisms, in turn, invite classification on the basis of the semantic mechanisms and the stylistic

[72] Axmanova, *Očerki...*, pp. 104-165. Cf. also Prorokova, "K voprosu o častičnoj semantičeskoj omonimii".

[73] Budagov, *Vvedenie v nauku o jazyke*, pp. 23-29.

[74] Reformatskij, "Čto takoe termin i terminologija?". The volume in which this article appears constitutes the proceedings of an interesting conference on terminology in 1959; the remaining materials in it, however, are of only marginal interest to lexicological theory.

[75] Piotrovskij, "K voprosu ob izučenii termina". Note also the study by Danilenko, "O slovoobrazovanii v oblasti proizvodstvenno-texničeskoj terminologii".

[76] Axmanova, *Očerki...*, pp. 166-191.

motivations which characterize them. An entire word as well as one of its contextual variants may, of course, belong to the passive portion of the vocabulary.[77]

The stylistic stratification of language has been studied, with considerable sophistication, but mostly on the basis of Russian facts;[78] no comparative or general theoretical conclusions have therefore been arrived at. A fairly representative approach is again that taken by N. M. Šanskij.[79] The two principal stylistic strata found in Russian are workaday-conversational (*razgovorno-bytovaja*) and bookish (*knižnaja*). But there is, in addition, an important interstylistic (*mežstilevaja*) component of the vocabulary which is neutral with respect to the division just named. The distinction between expressively-emotionally marked words and neutral ones lies along a separate dimension and intersects the other classification.[80] The workaday-conversational vocabulary is in turn either common to the whole nation (*obščenarodnaja*) or is socially or geographically restricted.[81]

Of interest in this connection is the attempt by V. K. Žuravlev to study exhaustively the vocabulary of a rural Bulgarian dialect.[82]

## 5. HISTORICAL AND COMPARATIVE LEXICOLOGY

The basic programmatic papers in this field are the article by O. S. Axmanova, V. V. Vinogradov, and V. V. Ivanov, and a separate paper by V. V. Vinogradov;[83] the outstanding substantive achievement is the book-length study by A. A. Ufimceva of the development of the synonym group *land*, *ground*, *earth*, etc. from Old English to Modern English.[84] A considerable number of apparently more pedestrian dis-

[77] Šanskij, *Očerki*..., pp. 228-244. This material was incorporated in Galkina-Fedoruk et al., *Sovremennyj russkij jazyk*.

[78] See, e.g., the discussion on stylistics in *Voprosy jazykoznanija*, which included papers by Sorokin, "K voprosu ob osnovnyx voprosax stilistiki"; Gal′perin, "Rečevye stili i stilističeskie sredstva jazyka", Stepanov, "O xudožestvennom i naučnom stiljax reči"; Fedorov, "V zaščitu nekotoryx ponjatij stilistiki"; Admoni & Stil′man, "Otbor jazykovyx sredstv i voprosy stilja"; Levin, "O nekotoryx voprosax stilistiki"; Il′inskaja, "O jazykovyx i nejazykovyx stilističeskix sredstvax"; and a number of briefer notes reviewed by the editors in *VJa* 6.80-87 (1954). The discussion was summarized by Vinogradov, "Itogi obsuždenija voprosov stilistiki". Cf. also Efimov, *Stilistika xudožestvennoj reči* and Murat, *Ob osnovnyx problemax stilistiki*.

[79] *Op. cit.*, pp. 217-227, based largely on Gvozdev, *Očerki po stilistike russkogo jazyka*, pp. 73-99, and incorporated into the standard textbook of Galkina-Fedoruk et al.

[80] On expressive vocabulary, see the references in footnote 66.

[81] For slightly divergent approaches, cf. Budagov, "K voprosu o jazykovyx stiljax" (restated in his *Vvedenie*..., pp. 396-481), and Axmanova, "O stilističeskoj differenciacii slov" (restated in her *Očerki*..., pp. 234-279). On the stylistic strata of English and Japanese vocabulary, cf. also Amosova, "K probleme jazykovyx stilej v anglijskom jazyke" and Šemenaev, "K voprosu o stiljax japonskogo literaturnogo jazyka".

[82] Žuravlev, "Opyt issledovanija leksiki mikrodialekta".

[83] Axmanova, Vinogradov, and Ivanov, "O nekotoryx voprosax i zadačax... leksikologii"; Vinogradov, "O nekotoryx voprosax russkoj istoričeskoj leksikologii".

[84] Ufimceva, *Opyt*...; partly summarized in her paper, "Principy istoričeskogo izučenija leksiko-semantičeskix grupp".

sertations have dealt with the evolution of specific word groups in Russian, German, English, and French, and have been published either in abstract or article form.[85]

On the history of Russian vocabulary, the book by P. Ja. Černyx represents an effort in descriptive lexicology applied to an earlier period of a language.[86] More challenging in conception is the recent article by Ju. S. Sorokin, who attempts explicitly to discover regularities in the lexical changes of 19th-century Russian in the context of the changing stylistic system of the language.[87]

In the Germanic field, A. I. Smirnickij has dealt with the structure of Old English vocabulary, while the more recent first-volume of a five-volume comparative Germanic grammar contains a characterization of the common lexicon of this language family by Čemodanov.[88]

There are some signs of a revived interest in the impact of the Bolshevik Revolution on the Russian language and on the languages of various national minorities – a favorite topic of the 1920's which for some decades had been out of fashion.[89]

The classification of vocabularies on etymological principles is a standard topic in lexicology and is pursued along entirely conventional lines. As far as lexical borrowing is concerned, there is a new and forthright interest in the influence of Russian on the languages of national minorities, but the theoretical foundations for such studies remain the traditional ones.[90]

Before the lexical reconstruction of proto-languages could be undertaken, Soviet linguistics has had to recuperate from several decades' sterility caused by the Marrists' rejection of the comparative method. But drawing strength from their renewed work in Slavic etymology, a number of scholars are now proceeding to a confrontation with problems of considerable generality. At the 1961 Conference on Comparative and Historical Lexicology, for example, B. V. Gornung read a paper on "Principles and Tasks of Comparative-Historical Lexicology and the Problem of the 'Lexical System of a Language'"; O. N. Trubačev discussed "The Problem of Reconstructing

[85] E. g. Ivanova, "Semantičeskoe razvitie mnogoznačnyx glagolov v anglijskom jazyke" and "O nekotoryx jazykovyx faktorax, vlijajuščix na semantičeskoe razvitie glagola"; Gorbačevič, *Iz istorii razvitija leksičeskoj gruppy glagolov* ...; Bel'skaja, *Istoriko-semasiologičeskoe issledovanie gruppy slov, svjazannyx s vyraženiem ponjatija 'čelovek'*"; Černyševa, "Izmenenie značenija slova kak put' razvitija slovarnogo sostava"; also numerous dissertations listed in the bibliography to Ufimceva's book (see footnote 84) and in *VJa* 5.136-143 (1959).

[86] Černyx, *Očerk russkoj istoričeskoj leksikologii (drevnerusskij period)*.

[87] Sorokin, "Ob obščix zakonomernostjax razvitija ... jazyka XIX v."; Zvegincev (*Semasiologija*, pp. 253-290) analyzes the classic notion of "semantic laws" (universals of meaning change).

[88] Smirnickij, *Drevneanglijskij jazyk*, pp. 155-206; Čemodanov, "Mesto germanskix jazykov...", pp. 48-113.

[89] Ožegov, "K voprosu ob izmenenii ... jazyka v sovetskuju èpoxu". Cf. also the relevant chapter in Galkina-Fedoruk et al., *Sovremennyj russkij jazyk*, pp. 92-96; Dešeriev, *Razvitie mladopismennyx jazykov narodov SSSR* and *Voprosy terminologii*; and Juldašev, "Voprosy formirovanija edinix norm baškirskogo nacional'nogo jazyka".

[90] *Mladopismennye jazyki* ... (cf. footnote 4), passim; Šanskij, "Leksičeskie i frazeologičeskie kal'ki"; Šaxraj, "K probleme klassifikacii zaimstvovannoj leksiki". No attempt is made here to present a bibliography of Soviet studies in the field of bilingualism and language contact.

Lexical Systems"; and V. N. Toporov spoke on "The Justification of Comparative Lexicology".[91]

With respect to glottochronology, Soviet linguists appear to have remained judiciously aloof.[92]

## 6. GENERAL LEXICOLOGY

Every article or book chapter that has been devoted to a critical examination of a lexicological problem may be thought of as contributing to the future discussion of lexicological universals. But a great deal of additional factual material will have to be accumulated before this problem can be grappled with directly.

Two recent papers, however, bear immediately on this question of the future. A. A. Ufimceva has discussed the systematicity of vocabulary, with special emphasis on the imcomplete nature of this systematicity and the differences between lexical systems and other subsystems in language.[93] A. B. Dolgopol′ skij has proposed to consider the presence or absence of wordmeanings (or "semes") in a language according to a universal inventory derived from the comparison of languages by pairs.[94]

## 7. THEORY AND CRITIQUE OF LEXICOGRAPHY

Apart from works already mentioned in other connections (especially L. V. Ščerba's paper cited in footnote 20 and V. V. Vinogradov's article mentioned in footnote 19), the following deal with lexicographic matters in a way sufficiently general to make them of lexicological interest:

Axmanova & Veselitskij, "O slovarjax pravil'noj reči".
Baskakov, "O nekotoryx tipax tureckix slovarej".
Beskrovnyj, "Sovremennaja leksikografija xindi".
Cejtlin, *Kratkij očerk istorii russkoj leksikografii.*
Čikobava, "O vzaimootnošenii ètimologičeskogo i istoričeskogo slovarja".
——, "O principax sostavlenija tolkovogo slovarja gruzinskogo jazyka".
Fel′dman, "O granicax perevoda v inojazyčno-russkix slovarjax".
——, "Okkazional′nye slova i leksikografija".
Istrina, "Zametki po dvuxjazyčnym slovarjam".

[91] Cited according to *VJa* 6.140 (1961). Toporov's paper is mentioned in a footnote in *VJa* 4.36 (1962). Trubačev's paper is scheduled for publication in *Leksikografičeskij sbornik* 6 (1963). Cf. also Tolstoj, "Iz opytov tipologičeskogo issledovanija slavjanskogo slovarnogo sostava", and, on abstract models for etymology, Toporov, "O nekotoryx teoretičeskix osnovanijax ètimologičeskogo analiza".

[92] Cf. Zvegincev, "Lingvističeskoe datirovanie metodom glottoxronologii (leksikostatistiki)".

[93] Ufimceva, "K voprosu o leksiko-semantičeskoj sisteme jazyka".

[94] Dolgopol′skij, "Izučenie leksiki s točki zrenija transformacionno-perevodnogo analiza plana soderžanija v jazyke". Cf. also Zvegincev's discussion of historical-lexicological universals referred to in footnote 87.

——, "A. A. Šaxmatov kak redaktor Slovarja russkogo jazyka".
Kankava, *V. I. Dal'kak leksikograf.*
Kovtun, "O novyx principax istoričeskoj leksikografii".
*Materialy diskussii po voprosu o slovarjax-minimumax.*
Perebejnos, Blindus, & Čumak, "K voprosu o slovare učebnogo tipa".
Šanskij, "Principy postroenija russkogo ètimologiceškogo slovarja slovoobrazovatel'no-istoričeskogo xaraktera".
Trubačev, "Ob ètimologičeskom slovare russkogo jazyka".

BIBLIOGRAPHY


Abaev, V. I., "O podače omonimov v slovare", *VJa* 6/3.31–43 (1957).
Admoni, V. G., and Sil'man, T. I., "Otbor jazykovyx sredstv i voprosy stilja", *VJa* 3/3.93–101 (1954).
Agajan, E. B., *Vvedenie v jazykoznanie* (Erevan, 1959).
Aleksandrov, A., "O principax sostavlenija slovarja sinonimov russkogo jazyka", *Leksikografičeskij sbornik*, 6 (to appear in 1963).
Amosova, N. N., "K probleme jazykovyx stilej v anglijskom jazyke", *VLU* 5.38ff. (1951).
——, "O leksičeskom značenii slova", *VLU* 2 (1957).
——, "Ob anglijskix frazeologičeskix slovarjax", *Problemy frazeologii i zadači sostavlenija frazeologičeskogo slovarja russkogo jazyka (tezisy)*, pp. 10–11 Leningrad, 1961).
——, "O sintaksičeskoj organizacii frazeologičeskix edinic", *Problemy jazykoznanija; sbornik v čest' akad. I. I. Meščaninova* (UZLU 301 – Serija filologičeskix nauk 60), pp. 7–14 (Leningrad, 1961).
——, "O sintaksičeskom kontekste", *Leksikografičeskij sbornik* 5.36–45 (1962).
——, *Osnovy anglijskoj frazeologii* (to appear in 1963).
Andreeva, V. N., *Leksikologija sovremennogo francuzskogo jazyka* (Moscow, 1955).
Ansimov, "K voprosu o sootnošenii obščego značenija frazeologičeskoj edinicy so značeniem ee komponentov", *UZMPedI* 9 (1956).
Apresjan, Ju. D., "Problema sinonima", *VJa* 6/6.84–88 (1957).
——, "O slovare sinonimov Vebstera", *Naučnye doklady vysšej školy, filologičeskie nauki* 3.159–164 (1959).
——, "K voprosu o strukturnoj leksikologii", *VJa* 11/3.38–46 (1962); revised version in *Problemy strukturnoj lingvistiki*, pp. 141–162 (Moscow, 1962).
——, "Distributivnyj analiz značenij i strukturnye semantičeskie polja", *Leksikografičeskij sbornik* 5.52–72 (1962).
Artemjuk, N. D., *Razvitie glagolov* do *i* make *v anglijskom jazyka*, tun *i* machen *v nemeckom jazyke*. Dissertation (Moscow, 1954).
Arxangel'skij, V. A., "Nekotorye vorprosy russkoj frazeologii v svjazi s istoriej ee

izučenija", *Učenye zapiski Rostovskogo-na-Donu pedinstituta, kafedra russkogo jazyka* 4 (1955).

——, "O ponjatii ustojčivoj frazy i tipax fraz", in *Problemy frazeologii i zadači sostavlenija frazeologičeskogo slovarja russkogo jazyka (tezisy)*, pp. 11–15 (Leningrad, 1961).

Axmanova, O. S., "K voprosu o slove v jazyke i reči", *DSMU* 5.27–32 (1948).

——, "K voprosu ob otličii složnyx slov ot frazeologičeskix edinic", *TIV* 4.50–73 (1954).

——, "Ešče k voprosu o slove kak osnovnoj edinice jazyka", *VMU* 1 (1955).

——, *Očerki po obščej i russkoj leksikologii* (Moscow, 1957).

——, "Fonologičeskie i grammatičeskie varianty slova", in *Akademiku V. V. Vinogradovu...*, pp. 42–59 (Moscow, 1957).

——, "O stilističeskoj differenciacii slov", *Sbornik statej po jazykoznaniju... V. V. Vinogradovu*, pp. 24–39 (Moscow, 1958).

——, "Soderžanie i zadači frazeologii primentel'no k leksikografii", in *Problemy frazeologii i zadači sostavlenija frazeologičeskogo slovarja russkogo jazyka (tezisy)*, pp. 8–10 (Leningrad, 1961).

——, "Ausgedrücktes und Nichtausgedrücktes in der zusammenfassenden Semantik des Wortes", *ZSl* 6.565–573 (1961).

——, and Veselitskij, V. V., "O 'slovarjax pravil'noj reči' (dictionaries of usage)", *Leksikografičeskij sbornik* 4.125–131 (1960).

——, Vinogradov, V. V. and Ivanov, V. V., "O nektoryx voprosax i zadačax opisatel'nej, istoričeskoj i sravnitel'no-istoričeskoj leksikologii", *VJa* 5/3.3–24 (1956).

Babkin, A. M., "Predlogi kak ob"ekt leksikografii", *Leksikografičeskij sbornik* 3.69–76 (1958).

——, "Po voprosam russkoj leksikologii i leksikografii", *Leksikografičeskij sbornik* 4.3–14 (1960).

——, "Frazeologizmy russkogo jazyka i zadači akademičeskogo slovarja russkoj frazeologii", in *Problemy frazeologii i zadači sostavlenija frazeologičeskogo slovarja russkogo jazyka (tezisy)*, pp. 3–7 (Leningrad, 1961).

Barannikov, P. A., "Leksičeskaja sinonimika jazyka xindi v osveščenii indijskix lingvistov", *VJa* 11/2.102–107 (1962).

Barxudarov, S. G., "Russkaja sovetskaja leksikografija za 40 let", *VJa* 6/5.31–45 (1957).

——, Beskrovnyj, V. M., and Zograf, G. A., *Xindi i urdu; voprosy leksikologii i slovoobrazovanija* (Moscow, 1960).

Baskakov, A. N., "O nekotoryx tipax tureckix slovarej", *Leksikografičeskij sbornik* 3.145–153 (1958).

Beleckij, A. A., *Leksikologija—ee soderžanie, zadači, osnovnye terminy i metody issledovanija (tezisy)* (Kiev, 1955) (published as a manuscript).

Beljaev, B. V., "O slove i ponjatii; k voprosu o psixologičeskix predposylkax metodiki

obučenija leksike inostrannogo jazyka", *UZMPedI* 8.201–216 (1954).
Bel'skaja, I. K., *Istoriko-semasiologičeskoe issledovanie gruppy slov, svjazannyx s vyraženiem ponjatija "čelovek" v anglijskom jazyke*, Dissertation (Moscow, 1955).
Bel'skij, A. B., "Metaforičeskoe upotreblenie suščestvitel'nyx", *UZMPedI* 8.279–298 (1954).
Beskrovnyj, V. M., "Sovremennaja leksikografija xindi", *VJa* 8/1.104–109 (1959).
*Bibliografičeskij ukazatel' literatury po jazykoznaniju izdannoj vs SSSR s* 1918 *po* 1957 *god*, I (Moscow, 1958).
Biržskova, E. È., "Ob opredelenijax v tolkovom slovare slov, oboznačajuščix životnyx", *Leksikografičeskij sbornik* 2.74–80 (1957).
Bokarev, E. A., and Dešeriev, Ju. D. (eds.), *Mladopis'mennye jazyki narodov SSSR* (Moscow–Leningrad, 1959).
Borovkov, A. K., "Iz opyta sostavlenija russko-nacional'nyx slovarej", *Leksikografičeskij sbornik* 1.135–159 (1957).
Brovko, A. S., "K voprosu o semantiko-strukturnoj klassifikacii frazeologičeskix edinic russkogo jazyka", *Zaporiz'kyj deržavnyj institut, Naukovy zapysky* 4 (1957).
Budagov, R. A., *Ob osnovnom slovarnom fonde i slovarnom sostave jazyka* (Leningrad, 1952).
——, "Osnovnoj slovarnyj fond romanskix jazykov i zadači ego izučenija", *VJa* 2/2.28–46 (1953).
——, "K voprosu o jazykovyx stiljax", *VJa* 3/3.54–67 (1954).
——, "Mnogoznačnost' slova", *Naučnye doklady vysšej školy, filologičeskie nauki* 1 (1958).
——, *Vvedenie v nauku o jazyke* (Moscow, 1958).
Bulaxovskij, L. A., "De l'homonymie dans les langues slaves", *RESl* 8.68–81 (1928).
Cejtlin, R. M., *Kratkij očerk istorii russkoj leksikografii (slovari russkogo jazyka)* (Moscow, 1958).
Čemodanov, N. S., "Mesto germanskix jazykov sredi drugix indoevropejskix jazykov", chap. I in M. M. Guxman (ed.), *Sravitel'naja grammatika germanskix jazykov*, vol. I, pp. 19–113 (Moscow, 1962).
Čerkasova, E. T., "Voprosy russkoj leksikologii v rabotax èpigonov 'novogo učenija' o jazyke", in *Protiv vul'garizacii i izvraščenija marksizma v jazykoznanii*, I, pp. 331–350 (Moscow, 1951).
Černyševa, I. I., "Izmenenie značenija slova kak put' razvitija slovarnogo sostava", in *Problemy obščego i častnogo jazykoznanija*, ed. T. A. Degtereva, pp. 86–116 (Moscow, 1960).
Černyx, P. Ja., "Učenie I. V. Stalina o slovarnom sostave i osnovnom slovarnom fonde jazyka", in *Voprosy jazykoznanija v svete trudov I. V. Stalina*, 2nd rev. ed., pp. 126–150 (Moscow, 1952).
——, *Očerk russkoj istoričeskoj leksikologii (drevnerusskij period)* (Moscow, 1956).
Čikobava, A. S., "O principax sostavlenija tolkovogo slovarja gruzinskogo jazyka", *Leksikografičeskij sbornik* 1.58–67 (1957).

——, "O vzaimootnošenii ètimologičeskogo i istoričeskogo slovarja", *Leksikografičeskij sbornik* 6 (to appear in 1963).
——, and Bulaxovskij, L. A., *Vvedenie v jazykoznanie*, 2 vols., (Moscow, 1952/3).
Danilenko, V. P., "O slovoobrazovanii v oblasti proizvodstvenno-texničeskoj terminologii", *Voprosy kul'tury reči* 2.31–48 (1959).
Danilov, G. K., "Programma i priemy issledovanija leksiki", *UZ Instituta jazyka i literatury RANIION*, 4.1ff.(1931).
Derkač, P. M., *Korotkyj slovnyk synonimiv ukrajinskoji movy* (Kiev, 1960).
Dešeriev, J. D., *Razvitie mladopis'mennyx jazykov narodov SSSR* (Moscow, 1958).
"Diskussija po voprosam omonimii", *Leksikografičeskij sbornik* 4.35–92 (1960).
Dolgopol'skij, A. B., "Izučenie leksiki a točki zrenija transformacionno-perevodnogo analiza plana soderžanija v jazyke", *Leksikografičeskij sbornik* 5.73–83 (1962).
Dondua, K., "Metafora v širokom smysle i metafora poètičeskaja", *Jazyk i myšlenie* 9.57–64 (1940).
Efimov, A. I., *Stilistika xudožestvennoj reči* (Moscow, 1957).
——, "Mnogoznačnost' slova", *RJaŠ* 3 (1957).
Fal'kovič, M. M., "K voprosu ob omonimii i polisemii", *VJa* 10/5.85–88 (1960).
Favorin, V. K., *Sinonimy* (Sverdlovsk, 1953).
Fedorov, A. V., "V zaščitu nekotoryx ponjatij stilistiki", *VJa* 3/5.65–73 (1954).
Fel'dman, N. I., "Ob analize smyslovoj struktury slova v dvujazyčnyx slovarjax", *Leksikografičeskij sbornik* 1.9–35 (1957).
——, "O granicax perevoda v inojazyčno-russkix slovarjax", *Leksikografičeskij sbornik* 2.81–109 (1957).
——, "Okkazional'nye slova i leksikografija", *VJa* 6/4.64–73 (1957).
Filin, F. P., "O leksiko-semantičeskix gruppax", in *Ezikovedski izsledovanija v čest na akademik Stefan Mladenov*, pp. 523–538 (Sofia, 1957).
Fridman, M. V., "O meste sinonimiki v processe prepodavanija russkogo jazyka inostrancam", in *Principy naučnogo analiza jazyka*, pp. 128–153 (Moscow, 1959).
Gak, V. G., "Nekotorye obščie semantičeskie osobennosti francuzskogo slova v sravnenii s russkim i voprosy leksikografii", *Leksikografičeskij sbornik* 4.15–28 (1960).
Galkina-Fedoruk, E. M., *Sovremennyj russkij jazyk: leksika* (Moscow, 1954).
——, Gorškova, K. V., and Šanskij, N. M., *Sovremennyj russkij jazyk: leksikologija, fonetika, morfologija*, 2nd rev. ed. (Moscow, 1958). (First ed., 1954.)
——, "Ob èkspressivnosti i èmocional'nosti v jazyke", in *Sbornik statej po jazykoznaniju… V. V. Vinogradovu*, pp. 103–124 (Moscow, 1958).
——, "Sinonimy v russkom jazyke", *RJaŠ* 3 (1959).
Gal'perin, I. R., "Rečevye stili i stilističeskie sredstva jazyka", *VJa* 3/4.76–86 (1954).
Gepner, Ju. R., *Očerki po obščemu i russkomu jazykoznaniju* (Kharkov, 1959).
Ginzburg, R. S., *K voprosu o polisemantizme anglijskogo glagola*. Dissertation (Moscow, 1948).
Gitlic, M., "Problemy omonimov", *Akademija Nauk SSSR Akademiku N. Ja. Marru*,

*XLV*, pp. 199–205 (Moscow, 1935).

Glejbman, E. V., "Semantičeskie modeli i spektry slov", in *Pytannja prikladnoji lingvistyky*, pp. 25–27 (Černivcy, 1960).

Gomon, N. M., "Pervyj opyt russkogo slovarja sinonimov", *RJaŠ* 3 (1955).

Gorbačevič, A. A., *Iz iztorii razvitija leksičeskoj gruppy glagolov znanija i proizvodnyx ot nix imen suščestvitel'nyx v anglijskom jazyke*, Dissertation. (Leningrad, 1955).

Gorbačevič, K. S., review of V. N. Kljueva, *Kratkij slovar' sinonimov russkogo jazyka* (Moscow, 1956) in *Leksikografičeskij sbornik* 4.166–171 (1960).

Gigor'eva, A. D., *Ob osnovnom slovarnom fonde i slovarnom sostave russkogo jazyka* (Moscow, 1953).

——, "Zametki o leksičeskoj sinonimii", *Voprosy kul'tury reči* 2.7–30 (1959).

Grigor'ev, V. P., "O granicax meždu slovosloženiem i affiksaciej", *VJa* 5/4 (1956).

——, "Obsuždenie problemy omonimii", *VJa* 7/2.162f. (1958).

——, "O vzaimodejstvii slovosloženija i affiksacii", *VJa* 10/5.71–77 (1961).

Guryčeva, M. S., and Serebrennikov, B. A., "Zadači izučenija osnovnogo slovarnogo fonda jazyka," *VJa* 2/6.3–20 (1953).

Guzunova, E. A., "K voprosu o suščnosti frazeologičeskoj edinicy", in *Problemy frazeologii i zadači sostavlenija frazeologičskogo slovarja russkogo jazyka (tezisy)*, pp. 21–23 (Leningrad, 1961).

Gvozdev A. N., *Očerki po stilistike russkogo jazyka* (Moscow, 1955).

Il'inskaja, S. I., "Soveščanie po voprosam leksikografii", *VJa* 1/4.114–120 (1952).

Il'inskaja, I. S., "O jazykovyx i nejazykovyx stilističeskix sredstvax", *VJa* 3/5.84–89 (1954).

Istrina, E. S., "Zametki po dvujazyčnym slovarjam", *IzvAN* 3/2–3.78–97 (1944).

——, "A. A. Šaxmatov kak redaktor slovarja russkogo jazyka", *IzvAN* 5/5.405–417 (1946).

——, "L. V. Ščerba kak leksikograf i leksikolog", in *Pamjati akademika L'va Vladimiroviča Ščerby (1880–1944)*, pp. 82–87 (Leningrad, 1951).

Ivanova, K. A., *Semantičeskoe razvitie mnogoznačnyx glagolov v anglijskom jazyke* (dissertation, cited in *VJa* 8/3.155 (1959)) (Leningrad, 1958).

——, "O nekotoryx jazykovyx faktorax, vlijajuščix na semantičeskoe razvitie glagola", *Romano-germanskaja filologija* 4.5–32 (1962).

Juldašev, A. A. "Voprosy formirovanija edinix norm baškirskogo nacional'nogo jazyka", in *Voprosy formirovanija i razvitija nacional'nyx jazykov*, pp. 274–294 (Moscow, 1960).

Kačalkin, A. N., "O nekotoryx principax sostavlenija regional'nyx istoričeskix slovarej", *Mežvuzovskaja konferencija po istoričeskoj leksikologii, leksikografii i jazyku pisatelja (tezisy dokladov)*, pp. 22–25 (Leningrad, 1961).

Kameneckaite, N. L., "K voprosu o variantnyx i invariantnyx frazeologičeskix sredstvax vyraženija", *Tezisy dokladov mežvuzovskoj konferencii po primeneniju strukturnyx i statističeskix metodov issledovanija slovarnogo sostava jazyka*, pp. 55–57 (Moscow, 1961).

Kankava, M. V., *V. I. Dal' kak leksikograf* (Tbilisi, 1958).

Kireev, A. A., "Ob antonimax", *RJaŠ* 3 (1954).

Kirsanova, P. A., "O nekotoryx semantičeskix priznakax frazeologičeskix edinic (k voprosu o mnogoznaňnosti i sinonimike v sfere frazeologii)", *Problemy frazeologii i zadači sostavlenija frazeologičeskogo slovarja russkogo jazyka (tezisy)*, pp. 18–21 (Leningrad, 1961).

Kissen, I. A., "Problema slovarja-minimuma v svete stalinskogo učenija ob osnovom slovarnom fonde i slovarnom sostave jazyka", *Materialy diskussii po voprosu o slovarjax-minimumax* (Trudy Sredneaz. Gos. Univ., new series 47 = Filolog. nauki 3), pp. 5–31 (Taškent, 1953).

Kljueva, V. N., "Sinonimy v russkom jazyke", *RJaŠ* 3 (1954).

——, "Problema antonimov", *UZMPedI* 9 (1956).

"K obsuždeniju voprosa ob omonimax (obzor statej, postupivšix v redakciju)", *VJa* 8/2.45–50 (1959).

Kogotkova, T. S., "O koordinacionnoj rabote po leksikografii", *Leksikografičeskij sbornik* 1.172–177 (1957).

Komissarov, V. N., "Problema opredelenija antonima", *VJa* 6/2.49–58 (1957).

Korlètjanu, N. G., "O sinonimax i ix stilističeskoj roli v sovremennom moldavskom jazyke", *Voprosy kul'tury reči* 1.100–114 (1955).

——, "Problema istoričeskogo proisxoždenija osnovnogo slovarnogo fonda moldavskogo jazyka", in *Sbornik statej po jazykoznaniju pamjati ... M. S. Sergievskogo*, pp. 137–154 (Moscow, 1961).

Kotelova, N. Z., "Ukazanija na sintaksičeskie svjazi slov v tolkovom slovare kak sredstvo razgraničenija smyslovyx različij", *Leksikografičeskij sbornik* 1.98–120 (1957).

Kovtun, L. S., "O novyx principax istoričeskoj leksikografii", *Naučnaja sessija molodyx učenyx, posvjaščennaja pamjati N. Ja. Marra (tezisy dokladov)*, pp. 15–18 (Moscow-Leningrad, 1949).

——, "O postroenii slovarnoj stat'i v slovare sovremmenogo russkogo literaturnogo jazyka AN SSSR", *Leksikografičeskij sbornik* 1.68–97 (1957).

Kunin, A. V., *Anglo-russkij frazeologičeskij slovar'* (Moscow, 1955).

Kurilovič, E. (Kuryłowicz), "Zametki o značenii slova", *VJa* 4/3.73–81 (1955).

Kutina, L. L., "Omonimy v tolkovyx slovarjax russkogo jazyka (akademičeskaja leksikografija dorevoljucionnoj pory)", *Leksikografičeskij sbornik* 2.54–63 (1957).

Larin, B. A., "Očerki po frazeologii", *UZLU* 198.200–226 (1956).

Lekomcev, Ju. K., "K voprosu o sistemnosti glagolov reči v anglijskom jazyke", in *Problemy strukturnoj lingvistiki*, pp. 190–197 (Moscow, 1962).

Levčenko, S. P., "Do pytannja pro pryncypy ukladannja slovnyka synonimiv ukrajins'koji movy", *Leksykografičnyj bjuleten'*, no. 5 (Kiev, 1955).

Levin, V. D., "O nekotoryx voprosax stilistiki", *VJa* 3/5.74–83 (1954).

Levkovskaja, K. A., "O podxode N. Ja. Marra k slovarnomu sostavu jazyka",

in *Protiv vulgarizacii i izvraščenija marksizma v jazykoznanii*, vol. I, pp. 384–403 (Moscow, 1951).
——, *Leksikologija nemeckogo jazyka* (Moscow, 1956).
——, "O principax strukturno-semantičeskogo analiza jazykovyx edinic", *VJa* 6/1.41–55 (1957).
——, *Imennoe slovoobrazovanie v sovremennoj nemeckoj obščestvenno-političeskoj terminologii i primykajuščej k nej leksiki* (Moscow, 1960).
——, *Teorija slova, principy ee postroenija i aspekty izučenija leksičeskogo materiala* (Moscow, 1962).
Litvinenko, A. S., "Termin i metafora", *UZMPedI* 8.253–278.
Luria, A. R., and Vinogradova, O. S. "An Objective Investigation of the Dynamics of Semantic Systems", *British Journal of Psychology* 50.89–105 (1959).
Majtinskaja, K. E., "Otraženie različij grammatičeskogo stroja v dvujazyčnyx slovarjax", *Leksikografičeskij sbornik* 1.160–171 (1957).
Malaxovskij. L. V., "K voprosu o principax smyslovoj xarakteristiki slova v tolkovom slovare (analiz priemov tolkovanija slov v 'Oksfordskom slovare anglijskogo jazyka')", *Leksikografičeskij sbornik* 3.84–96 (1958).
Martynov, V. V., "Opyt postroenija obščej teorii značenija", in *Pytannja prykladnoji lingvistyky* (*tezy dopovidej...*), pp. 11–13 (Černivcy, 1960).
Maslova-Lašanskaja, S. S., "K voprosu ob ustojčivosti slovarnogo sostava i osnovnogo slovarnogo fonda švedskogo jazyka", in *Voprosy grammatičeskogo stroja i slovarnogo sostava jazyka*, pp. 200–222 (*UZLU* 161), 1952.
*Materialy diskussii po voprosu o slovarjax-minimumax* (= *Trudy Sredneaz. gos. universiteta*, new series 47 = Filolog. nauki 3) (Taškent, 1953).
Mel'cer, E. M., "Ob osnovnom slovarnom fonde v slovarnom sostave jazyka", *IJaŠ* 6 (1951).
Mel'čuk, I. A., "O terminax 'ustojčivost'' i 'idiomatičnost''", *VJa* 4.73–80(1960).
Moskal'skaja, O. I., "Ustojčivye slovosočetanija s grammatičeskoj napravlennost'ju", *VJa* 10/5.87–93 (1961).
——, "Strukturno-semantičeskie razrjady slov v sostave časti reči", in *Voprosy germanskogo jazykoznanija*, pp. 251–261 (German summary, p. 293) (Leningrad, 1961).
Mučnik, I. P., *Vvedenie v jazykoznanie: sbornik zadač i upražnenij*, 2nd ed. (Moscow, 1961).
Murat, V. P., *Ob osnovnyx problemax stilistiki* (Moscow, 1957).
Nikiforova, O. I., "Vosprijatie metafory", *UZMPedI* 8.299–318 (1954).
Novikov, L. A., "K probleme omonimii", *Leksikografičeskij sbornik* 4.93–102 (1960).
"Obzor polučennyx statej", *VJa* 3/6.80–87 (1954).
Orudžev, A. G., "Koordinacionnoe regional'noe soveščanie po voprosu sostavlenija tolkovyx slovarej tjurkskix jazykov", *Leksikografičeskij sbornik* 2.207–212 (1957).
——, "K voprosu ob otraženii v russko-tjurkskix slovarjax leksiko-grammatičeskix osobennostej russkogo jazyka", *Leksikografičeskij sbornik* 6 (to appear in 1963).

Ossoveckij, I. A., "O sostavlenii regional'nyx slovarej (nekotorye voprosy russkoj dialektnoj leksikografii)", *VJa* 10/4.74–85 (1961).

Ožegov, S. I., "K voprosu ob izmenenii slovarnogo sostava russkogo jazyka v sovetskuju èpoxu", *VJa* 2/2.71–81 (1953).

——, "Očerednye voprosy kul'tury reči", *Voprosy kul'tury reči* 1.5–33 (1955).

——, "O strukture frazeologii (v svjazi s proektom frazeologičeskogo slovarja russkogo jazyka)", *Leksikografičeskij sbornik* 2.31–53 (1957).

Palamarčuk. L. S., "Leksykografy obminjujut'sja dosvidom", *Leksykografičnyj bjuleten'* 8.111–113 (1961).

Perebejnos, V. I., "Ob ispol'zovanii strukturnyx metodov dlja razgraničenija značenij mnogoznačnogo glagola", *VJa* 11/3.38–46 (1962); revised version in *Problemy strukturnoj lingvistiki*, pp. 163–174 (Moscow, 1962).

——, Blindus, E. S., and Čumak, A. V. "K voprosu o slovare učebnogo tipa", *Leksikografičeskij sbornik* 2.110–118 (1957).

Peškovskij, A. M., "Leksema" and "Slovo" in *Literaturnaja enciklopedija* (Moscow-Leningrad, 1925); reprinted as "Ponjatie otdel'nogo slova" in his *Sbornik statej*, pp. 122–140 (Leningrad, 1925).

Piotrovskij, R. G., "K voprosu ob izučenii termina", in *Voprosy grammatičeskogo stroja i slovarnogo sostava jazyka*, pp. 21–36 (*UZLU* 161), 1952.

Prorokova, V. M., "K voprosu o častičnoj semantičeskoj omonimii (na materiale imen suščestvitel'nyx sovremennogo nemeckogo jazyka)", *Naučnye doklady vysšej školy, filologičeskie nauki* 2.157–168 (1959).

——, "Nekotorye osobennosti omonimii v nemeckom jazyke", *VJa* 10/5.76–79 (1960).

*Pytannja prikladnoji lingvistyky: tezisy dopovidej mižvuzovs'koj naukovoji konferenciji* 9.22–28 1960 (Černivcy, 1960).

Raxmanova, L. I., review of Casares' *Vvedenie v sovremennuju leksikografiju* (Moscow, 1958), in *Leksikografičeskij sbornik* 5.183–187 (1962).

Reformatskij, A. A., *Vvedenie v jazykoznanie*, 2nd ed. (Moscow, 1955).

——, "Čto takoe termin i terminologija", in *Voprosy terminologii (materialy Vsesojuznogo terminologičeskogo soveščanija)*, pp. 46–54 (Moscow, 1961).

Reznikov, L. O., *Ponjatie i slovo* (Leningrad, 1958); English translation (mimeographed): Washington, 1961 (Foreign Developments in Machine Translation and Information Processing 18 – U. S. Joint Publications Research Service no. 6678).

Rogožnikova, R. P., "Narečnye i meždometnye značenija nekotoryx suščestvitel'nyx i pokaz ix v slovare", *Leksikografičeskij sbornik* 2.66–73 (1957).

Rudov, V. F., "K voprosu o suščnosti frazeologičeskix vyraženij", *Učenye zapiski Taganrogskogo pedinistituta*, 5 (1958).

Serebrennikov, B. A., "K probleme tipov leksičeskoj i grammatičeskoj abstrakcii", in *Voprosy grammatičeskogo stroja*, pp. 54–73 (Moscow, 1955).

Sevortjan, È. V., "K sootnošeniju grammatiki i leksiki v tjurskix jazykax", in *Voprosy*

*teorii i istorii jazyka v svete trudov I. V. Stalina po jazykoznaniju*, pp. 306–367 (Moscow, 1952).
Sirotina, V. A., *Leksičeskaja sinonimika v russkom jazyke* (L'vov, 1960).
Skiba, Ju. G., "K voprosu o t. n. antonimičeskoj omonimii v slavjanskix jazykax", *Naukovy zapysky Černivec'kogo derž. universyteta* 31 (1958).
Skoroxod'ko, È. F., "Ob opredelenijax slov v tolkovyx slovarjax", *Mežvuzovskaja konferencija po istoričeskoj leksikologii, leksikografii i jazyku pisatelja (tezisy dokladov)*, pp. 19–21 (Leningrad, 1961).
Smirnickij, A. I., "Nekotorye zamečanija po anglijskoj omonimike", *IJaŠ* 5 (1948).
——, "K voprosu o slove (problema "otdel'nosti slova")", in *Voprosy teorii i istorii jazyka*, pp. 182–203 (Moscow, 1952).
——, "K voprosu o slove (problema"toždestva slova")", *TIJa* 4.3–49 (1954).
——, "Leksičeskoe i grammatičeskoe v slove", in *Voprosy grammatičeskogo stroja*, 11–53 (Moscow, 1955).
——, *Drevneanglijskij jazyk* (Moscow, 1955).
——, *Leksikologija anglijskogo jazyka* (Moscow, 1956).
——, "Zvučanie slova i ego semantika", *VJa* 5 (1960), 112–116.
Soboleva, P. A., "Komponentnyj analiz značenij glagola nao snove slovoobrazovatel'-nogo priznaka", in *Problemy strukturnoj lingvistiki*, pp. 175–189 (Moscow, 1962).
Sorokin, Ju. S., "K voprosu ob osnovnyx voprosax stilistiki", *VJa* 2.68–82 (1954).
——, "Ob obščix zakonomernostjax razvitija slovarnogo sostava russkogo literaturnogo jazyka XIX v.", *VJa* 10/3.22–36 (1961).
Stalin, I. V., *Marksizm i voprosy jazykoznanija* (Moscow, 1950); translated in *The Soviet Linguistic Controversy* (New York, 1951).
Staniževa, D. S., "Voprosy frazeologii v issledovnijax po sintaksisu padežej", *KSISI* 28.40–50 (1960).
Stepanova, G. V., "O stile xudožestvennoj literatury", *VJa* 1/5 (1952).
Stepanova, M. D., "Voprosy morfologičeskogo analiza slova", *IJaŠ* 1 (1961).
Stroeva, T. V., "K voprosu ob ustojčivosti osnovnogo slovarnogo fonda v nemeckom jazyke", in *Voprosy grammatičeskogo stroja i slovarnogo sostava jazyka* (= *UZLU* 161), pp. 187–199 (1952).
Sumnikova, T. A., "Koordinacionnoe regional'noe soveščanie po voprosu sostavlenija tolkovyx slovarej", *Leksikografičeskij sbornik* 4.204–206 (1960).
Šanskij, N. M., "Leksičeskie i frazeologičeskie kal'ki v russkom jazyke", *RJaŠ* 3 (1955).
——, Review of V. N. Kljueva, *Kratkij slovar' sinonimov russkogo jazyka*, in *RJaŠ* 4 (1957).
——, *Očerki po russkomu slovoobrazovaniju i leksikologii* (Moscow, 1959).
——, "Principy postroenija russkogo ètimologičeskogo slovarja slovoobrazovatel'no-istoričeskogo xaraktera", *VJa* 8/5.32–42 (1959).
Šapiro, A. B., "Nekotorye voprosy teorii sinonimov", *DSIJa* 8.69–87 (1955).

Šaumjan, S. K., "Strukturnye metody inzučenija značenij", *Leksikografičeskij sbornik* 5.21–25 (1962).
Šaxova, I. N., "Nekotorye voprosy izučenija osnovnogo slovarnogo fonda i slovarnogo sostava francuzskogo jazyka", in *Voprosy grammatiki i leksikologii*, pp. 90–98 (Leningrad, 1955).
——, "K voprosu o značenii složnyx slov", *Romano-germanskaja filologija* 4.33–57 (1962).
Šaxraj, O. B., "K probleme klassifikacii zaimstvovannoj leksiki", *VJa* 10/2.53–58 (1961).
Ščerba, L. V., "Opyt obščej teorii leksikografii (I)", *IzvAN* 3.89–117 (1940).
Šemenaev, P. I., "K voprosu o stiljax japonskogo literaturnogo jazyka", *Trudy voennogo instituta inostrannyx jazykov* 5 (1954).
Šemjakin, F. N. (ed), *Myšlenie i reč (= Izvestija Akademii pedagogičeskix nauk RSFSR*, 113*)* (Moscow, 1960).
Ševeleva, M. S., "O koordinacionnoj rabote po leksikografii", *Leksikografičeskij sbornik* 2.198–205 (1957).
Šmelev, D. N., "O 'svjazannyx' sintaksičeskix konstrukcijax v russkom jazyke", *VJa* 9/5.47–60 (1960).
Švedova, N. Ju., "Izučenie omonimov", *Doklady i soobščenija filologičeskogo fakul'teta MGU* 6 (1948).
——, "O nekotoryx tipax frazeologizirovannyx konstrukcij v stroe russkoj razgovornoj reči", *VJa* 7/2.93–100 (1958).
——, "Problema leksičeskix ograničenij kak odna iz problem izučenija sintaksisa russkogo literaturnogo jazyka XVIII–XIX vv.", *VJa* 6.17–23 (1960).
Ten'er, Ljus'en (Lucien Tesnière), "O russko-francuzskom slovare L. V. Ščerby", *VJa* 7/6.41–43 (1958).
*Tezisy dokladov mežvuzovskoj konferencii po primeneniju strukturnyx metodov i statističeskix issledovanija slovarnogo sostava jazyka* (21–25.11.1961) (Moscow, 1961).
Tolstoj, N. I., "Iz opytov tipologičeskogo issledovanija slavjanskogo slovarnogo sostava", *VJa* 12/1.29–45 (1963).
Toporev, I. S., "Nekotorye priemy leksikologičeskogo issledovanija", *Tezisy dokladov mežvuzovskoj konferencii po primeneniju strukturnyx i statističeskix metodov issledovanija slovarnogo sostava jazyka*, pp. 50–54 (Moscow, 1961).
Toporov, V. N., "O nekotoryx teoretičeskix osnovanijax ètimologičeskogo analiza", *VJa* 9/3.44–59 (1960).
——, "O pravnomernosti sravnitel'noj leksikologii", paper at the 1961 Conference on Problems of Comparative-Historical Lexicology, cf. *VJa* 11/4.36 (1962), fn. 3.
Trubačev, O. N., "Ob ètimologičeskom slovare russkogo jazyka", *VJa* 9/3.60–69 (1960).
——, "K voprosu o rekonstrukcii leksičeskix sistem", *Leksikografičeskij sbornik* 6 (to appear in 1963).

Tyšler, I. S., "K voprosu o sud'be omonimov", *VJa* 9/5.80–84 (1960).
Uemov, A. I., "Problema sinonimov i sovremennaja logika", in *Logiko-grammatičeskie očerki*, pp. 26–48 (Moscow, 1961).
Ufimceva, A. A., "Principy istoričeskogo izučenija leksikosemantičeskix grupp", in *Voprosy germanskogo jazykoznanija*, pp. 160–193 (Leningrad, 1961). (English summary, pp. 287ff.)
——, "K voprosu o leksiko-semantičeskoj sisteme jazyka", *VJa* 11/4.36–46 (1962).
——, *Opyt izučenija leksiki kak sistemy (na materiale anglijskogo jazyka)* (Moscow, 1962).
Veselitskij, V. V., "Priemy podači predlogov v russko-francuzskom slovare pod red. L. V. Ščerby i v russko-anglijskom slovare pod red. A. I. Smirnickogo", *Leksikografičeskij sbornik* 5.112–120 (1962).
Vinogradov, V. V., "O formax slova", *IzvAN* 3.31–44 (1944).
——, "Osnovnye ponjatija russkoj frazeologii kak lingvističeskoj discipliny", *Trudy jubilejnoj naučnoj sessii Leningradskogo Gosudarstvennogo Universiteta*, 1946, pp. 45–69.
——, "Ob osnovnyx tipax frazeologičeskix edinic v russkom jazyka", *Sb. A. A. Šaxmatov (1864–1920)*, pp. 339–364. (Trudy Kommissii po istorii Akademii nauk SSSR, 3). Moscow-Leningrad, 1947.
——, "Ob osnovnom slovarnom fonde i ego slovoobrazujuščej roli v istorii jazyka", *IzvAN* 10.218–239 (1951).
——, "Voprosy sovremennogo russkogo slovoobrazovanija v svete trudov I. V. Stalina po jazykoznaniju", *RJaŠ* 2 (1951).
——, "Ob osnovnom slovarnom fonde i ego slovoobrazujuščej roli v istorii jazyka", pp. 151–182. *Voprosy jazykoznanija v svete trudov I. V. Stalina po jazykoznaniju.* Moscow, 2nd rev. ed., 1952.
——, "Slovoobrazovanie i ego otnošenie k grammatike i leksikologii (na materiale russkogo i rodstvennyx jazykov)", in *Voprosy teorii i istorii jazyka*, pp. 99–152. (Moscow, 1952).
——, "Osnovnye tipy leksičeskix značenij slova", *VJa* 1/5.3–29 (1953).
——, "O nekotoryx voprosax russkoj istoričeskoj leksikologii", *IzvAN* 12.185–210 (1953).
——, "Itogi obsuždenija voprosov stilistiki", *VJa* 4/1.60–89 (1955).
——, "Iz istorii leksikologii", *DSIJa* 10.3–28 (1956).
——, "O nekotoryx voprosax teorii russkoj leksikografii", *VJa* 5/5.80–94 (1956).
——, "Ob omonimii i smežnyx javlenijax", *VJa* 9/5.3–17 (1960).
*Voprosy frazeologii* (Trudy Samarkandskogo Gos. Univ. im.Ališera Navoi, new series 106) (Samarkand, 1961).
Xajdakov, S, M., *Očerki po leksike lakskogo jazyka* (Moscow, 1961).
Xazanovič, A. P., *Sinonimija v frazeologii sovremennogo nemeckogo jazyka.* Dissertation (Leningrad, 1958). Cited in *VJa* 8/3.156 (1959).

——, "K voprosu o vozniknovenii frazeologičeskix edinic", *UZLU* 318.131–146 (1962).

Zvegincev, V. A., "Ekspressivno-modal'nye èlementy i značenie slova", *VMU* 1.69–82 (1955).

——, *Semasiologija* (Moscow, 1957).

——, "Lingvističeskoe datirovanie metodom glottoxronologii (leksikostatistiki)", in *Novoe v lingvistike*, vol. I, pp. 9–22 (Moscow, 1960).

——, *Očerki po obščemu jazykoznaniju* (Moscow, 1962).

Zvereva, E. A., "Razryv semantičeskoj svjazi meždu isxodnym slovami (suffiksal'noe obrazovanie)", *Romano-germanskaja filologija* 4.58–78 (1962).

Žirkov, L. I., "Ob osnovnom slovarnom fonde gorskix jazykov Dagestana", *VJa* 2/3.69–80 (1953).

——, "O smyslovom centre frazeologizmov", in *Problemy frazeologii i zadači sostavlenija frazeologičeskogo slovarja russkogo jazyka (tezisy)*, pp. 15–18 (Leningrad, 1951).

Žuravlev, V. K., "Opyt issledovaniaj leksiki mikrodialekta", *Mežvuzovskaja konferencija po istoričeskoj leksikologii, leksikografii i jazyku pisatelja (tezisy dokladov)*, pp. 25f. (Leningrad, 1961).

## ADDENDUM

Since the completion of this paper two books appeared which deserve comment in the present survey.

Levkovskaja's *Teorija slova* bears the subtitle: "Principles of Constructing a Theory of the Word and Aspects of Investigating Lexical Material". The chief divisions are: (1) "Specifities of Lexicology as a Scientific Discipline"; (2) "The Word as the Basic Unit of Language"; (3) "Bases for a Structural-Semantic Classification of Lexical Units". Although six years have passed since Levkovskaja's first book on German vocabulary, and although Soviet lexicology, both in its more conventional forms (à la Vinogradov) and in its "structuralist" versions, has continued to develop in the interval, Levkovskaja seems to have remained true to the most old-fashioned traditions of Russian vocabulary study. The approach is on some points even more pedestrian than that of the handbook by Galkina-Fedoruk et al., referred to earlier in this paper.

The collective volume *Problemy strukturnoj lingvistiki* encompasses revised, slightly expanded versions of previously published papers by Apresjan, and Perebejnos, as well as two new papers in the same vein of an aggressive "structural" lexicology by Soboleva and by Lekomcev (see Bibliography for the full citation). It is not possible in the present context to subject this work to the detailed criticism which it deserves; the author plans to do so on another occasion in the near future. Briefly, the following points are notable:

(1) The cluster of studies, utilizing mostly English and Russian data, attempts to extend the methods of subclassifying parts of speech, familiar from syntax, to a point where lexical items (mostly verbs) will fall into groupings that intuitively seem to have a common semantic feature;

(2) By combining transform potential with purely distributional properties of verbs, these studies have succeeded in breaking down the verb vocabulary into much finer divisions than are available in ordinary grammars, whether traditional or descriptive;

(3) At the same time, the grammatical apparatus utilized is extremely crude: for the parts of speech of English, they make use of Friesian classes ("simplifying" even those!), and for transformations they indiscriminately mix notions derived from Z. S. Harris and D. S. Worth with those of N. Chomsky, thus losing all advantages of generative grammar;

(4) The "semantic" groupings are accepted without consideration of counter-examples, which do exist, and which will considerably weaken the results so far obtained;

(5) Great liberties are taken with the limits of grammaticality: not only does a strange Moscow dialect of English emerge, but even the idiomaticity of Russian is violated for the sake of the theory;

(6) No argument is offered that this investigation is anything except purely syntactic, and the problem of the autonomy of lexicology vis-à-vis syntax is hardly even raised.

# COMPARATIVE AND HISTORICAL SLAVISTICS

VALENTIN KIPARSKY

From 1925 to World War II, when the only officially accepted linguistic school in Soviet Russia was Nikolaj Marr's "Japhetology", later simply called "Marrism", there was no interest whatever in Slavic languages. The reasons were obvious. First, according to Marr, all languages of the world were of the same origin, issuing from his famous four elements *sal*, *ber*, *yon*, and *rosh*, so that, for instance, English was as well related to German or Swedish as to Russian, Finnish, or Etruscan. Thus, there was no point for a Russian linguist to study a *Slavic* idiom. Moreover, Marr taught that different languages did not develop out of an "Ursprache" (Protoglossa) as was accepted by most of the Western scholars of his time, but by different ways of "hybridation", "crossbreeding" and "dialectical jumps" (*dialectical* is here used in the philosophical, Hegelian sense). Second, the political relations of the Soviet Union to Piłsudski's Poland, Masaryk's Czechoslovakia, and the Kingdom of Yugoslavia were either very bad or simply non-existent, so that there was no point in studying Slavic languages for the sake of politics either. The main interest was centered on the "wild" Finno-Ugric, Turkic, Caucasian, and other languages of the Soviet Union which had to be provided with grammars and literature. Comparative Slavistics were so despised, that G. A. Il'inskij's "Comparative Grammar of the Slavic Languages" which was composed and ready for print about 1930, had to be turned into printer's metal again.[1] Russian itself was so neglected that not even the Great Academic Dictionary, started in 1891, could be finished. The work was many times interrupted, resumed again, and stopped definitely in 1937.[2]

About that year, however, a new, nationally inspired tendency began to appear in the writings of Soviet linguists. The non-Slavic languages, especially those which are or were spoken inside or in the close vicinity of the Soviet Union were "atomized", divided into as many units as possible. New literary languages were standardized out of local dialects for Finns in Ingermanland and Eastern Carelia, for Rumanians in Moldavia, for every little Turkic tribe who could just as well have used some of the great existent Turkic languages. On the contrary, the evident togetherness of the Slavic languages was emphasized and the splitting apart of the Ukrainian and Belorussian literary languages from Russian was opposed by a very ingenious method:

[1] Attested by Vinogradov in his programmatic paper (see footnote 38) in *VJa* 6/6 (1959).
[2] See Unbegaun, *A Bibliographical Guide to the Russian Language*, pp. 124-128.

by and by, from one school textbook to another, the intellectual vocabulary of these languages, which was mainly of Polish origin, became replaced by a Russian one.[3] The role of the Cyrillic alphabet was enhanced by ordering, in 1937, all the small Finno-Ugric, Turkic, and Caucasian tribes, who had accepted, in 1925, Arabic or Latin alphabets for their new languages, to change them to Cyrillic ones.

A few weeks before the Soviet Union entered World War II, the well-known Slavist A. M. Seliščev published an interesting textbook dealing with West Slavic languages which had previously been completely neglected.[4] The great interest in the Slavs, however, began a little later. During the German advance towards Moscow, propaganda leaflets, signed by representatives of all Slavic peoples, were distributed among the Soviet troops. A monthly review "Slavjane" was founded in 1942; its aim was to stress cooperation and close affinity of all Slavic peoples. In 1943, Moscow University got a special "Slavic Department". Comparative Slavistics at once became fashionable and even true Marrists had to pay tribute to it. Of course, there was not much opportunity for serious research work during the war, but the change of attitude is clearly reflected by the following statement in the fully "Marristic" "Introduction to Linguistics" by R. O. Šor and N. S. Čemodanov: "The possibility that closely related languages develop from an old unity through splitting of the latter is not excluded. In that way there developed, for example, the East Slavic or the Romance languages".[5] As I mentioned above, Marr and his followers did not recognize a "Protoglossa", an "old unity" from which "closely related" languages might develop.

Notwithstanding that trend the Marrists, who still seemed to have powerful friends "upstairs", strongly opposed any earnest studies of Comparative Slavistics or Comparative Linguistics in the then current Western meaning. A good illustration is furnished by the following. In 1947, the outstanding student of Russian, V. V. Vinogradov, published an excellent work, his famous monograph *Russkij jazyk* where he quoted not only Soviet and older Russian but also Western authors who had something to say on the subject. There was, of course, no "Marrism" whatever in the book. The work became immediately the subject of furious attacks. Beside his "ignorance of the true Marxist, i.e., Marrist, linguistics", Vinogradov was accused of a much more dangerous crime: *nizkopoklonstvo pered zapadom* "subservient attitude towards the West".[6] But the big change was already on the way and Vinogradov's defense was successful: he had only to present a few perfunctory apologies for his "mistakes" and remained professor in Moscow.

The abrupt change in the linguistic policy of the Soviet Union on June 20, 1950, is well known. It was then celebrated as the great achievement of Stalin's genius, which it undoubtedly was, though not exactly in the way in which it was then described.

[3] A few good examples are given by Akulenko in *VJa* 10/3.63-67 (1961).
[4] Seliščev, *Slavjanskoe jazykoznanie*, I.
[5] Šor & Čemodanov, *Vvedenie v jazykovedenie*, pp. 207-208.
[6] E.g. Agapov & Zelinskij, "Net, èto ne russkij jazyk/ O knige prof. V. Vinogradova", *Literaturnaja Gazeta* 59 (2374), Saturday, November 29, 1947, p. 3.

The real originator of the famous "linguistic discussion" in *Pravda* from May to July, 1950, was not Stalin himself, but A. S. Čikobava, a Caucasian philologist, who happened to quarrel with powerful Marrists and saw his career threatened. Being a good specialist in Caucasian languages, Čikobava was able to uncover the nonsensical character of the Marrist "etymologies" and to prove it to his great fellow-Georgian. Stalin had written a pamphlet about national minorities in his youth and was better acquainted with linguistic problems than politicians usually are. He saw the big opportunity at once and acted thereafter, rehabilitating the 19th century Comparative linguistics with special stress on Comparative studies in Slavic. The main aim was, of course, to switch minds from international Marrism to nationally important Slavistics.

Never has more been published about language problems in Russia than in the 1950's. The Russian is a born debating man who can discuss abstract problems endlessly, and the Soviet intelligentsia has been indoctrinated in dialectal materialism. Moreover, the average Russian values linguistic knowledge as such, not like Western people in general, only as a step to business or technical success. Therefore an abstract science is much more popular in Russia than any engineering or chemistry. As far as I know the so-called "linguistic discussion" of 1950 was far more popular in the Soviet Union than the simultaneous Lysenko-"dispute". In Western Europe and America the opposite was true.

The results of Stalin's decision to reintroduce the neogrammarian methods were, to start with, good. The chief Marrists were fired from their key positions and the formerly persecuted non-Marrists rehabilitated, some of them, like D. V. Bubrix, posthumously. Vinogradov became the head of all Soviet linguistics and of the newly founded Institut Russkogo Jazyka, and the editor-in-chief of practically all linguistic periodicals of the Soviet Union. A new periodical, *Voprosy Jazykoznanija*, was founded, replacing some Marrist periodicals, like *Jazyk i Myšlenie*, which were simply abolished by order. With the "destalinisation", which began slowly in 1956 and seems to be continuing, the merits of the Generalissimo in linguistic matters fell into the memory hole. In a recent work about the history of linguistics by a Soviet Latvian professor, published in September, 1961, there is not even a mention of Stalin's name, though Marr's theory and the "linguistic discussion" of 1950 are amply discussed for eight pages.[7]

One of the main points of Stalin's numerous programmatic papers during the years 1950 and 1951 was the importance of Slavistics. But as the field of Slavic philology, except for Russian and, in some measure, Ukrainian and Belorussian, lay completely fallow for a whole generation, there were practically no young scholars with sufficient training in West Slavic or South Slavic languages. The older ones, such as the well-known Macedonist A. M. Seliščev (1886-1942), the phonetician and specialist in Lusatian L. V. Ščerba (1880-1944), the Bulgarist N. S. Deržavin (1877-1953), and

[7] See Loja, *Valodniecības vēsture*, pp. 231-238.

some minor figures, were slowly withering away. Some of their best works were published posthumously,[8] but having been completely isolated from the West during the 1930's and 1940's those authors were not able to take the general progress of their field into consideration and therefore their books make an "old-fashioned" impression. The only comparatist of prerevolutionary formation who remained active through the whole Marrist period was L. A. Bulaxovskij (1888-1961). Being professor first in Xarkov, later in Kiev, he was less exposed to persecutions than people in Moscow and Leningrad and thus he was able to publish serious works as early as the 1930's.[9] Even during the worst attacks on Vinogradov, Bulaxovskij managed to publish an interesting study in comparative etymology about Slavic bird names[10] without arousing any hullaballoo. After the "linguistic discussion" he published a whole series of "accentological comments" on different Slavic languages.[11] Even in these interesting works the pernicious influence of isolation is recognizable. For example the "comments" on the East Slavic word stress often duplicates the results of my historical investigation on that subject which appeared five years earlier in Helsinki,[12] though it was then generously distributed to Soviet libraries and other institutions.

The best specialist in Russian proper, V. V. Vinogradov, and his close collaborators R. I. Avanesov and V. I. Borkovskij, as well as the outstanding Leningrad scholars S. P. Obnorskij and B. A. Larin, wisely restrained themselves to the field of Russian proper. There were, however, some Soviet scholars who believed that they could cope with Comparative Slavistics though they were trained in only Russian. They recognized at once the implication of Stalin's decisions. "It is not by a pure chance that when speaking about kindred languages I. V. Stalin gives the Slavic ones as example. During the long centuries of their history, the Slavic tribes, later peoples, have often worked together, fought together against common enemies; the cultural ties which united them were very close and of long duration", says P. S. Kuznecov.[13] He concludes that the historical-comparative method should be used and then the reconstruction of the Proto-Slavic might be comparatively easy. However when Kuznecov published his "Historical Grammar of the Russian Language",[14] a year later it was sharply criticized by his colleague T. I. Lomtev who pointed out that Kuznecov even "presents the Ukrainian and Belorussian facts incorrectly".[15]

Almost simultaneously a similar work was published by another Soviet specialist in Russian proper, P. Ja. Černyx.[16] This book was also severely criticized by Bulaxov-

[8] E.g. Seliščev, *Staroslavjanskij jazyk*, I, II; Jakubinskij, *Istorija drevnerusskogo jazyka.*

[9] E. g. his well-known textbook *Istoričeskij kommentarij k russkomu jazyku*, I, II (1938), which still remains the best "historical grammar" of Russian for the 18th-20th centuries.

[10] *Obščeslavjanskie nazvanija ptic.*

[11] *Akcentologičeskij kommentarij k pol'skomu jazyku*; *Akcentologičeskij kommentarij k češskomu jazyku*, I, II; *Sravnitel'no-istoričeskie kommentarii k vostočno-slavjanskomu udareniju.*

[12] Kiparskij, *O kolebanijax udarenija v russkom literaturnom jazyke*, I.

[13] Kuznecov, "Voprosy sravnitel'no-istoričeskogo izučenija slavjanskix jazykov".

[14] Kuznecov, *Istoričeskaja grammatika russkogo jazyka*, *Morfologija.*

[15] See *VJa* 3/5.137-144 (1954), especially, p. 138.

[16] Černyx, *Istoričeskaja grammatika russkogo jazyka.* This grammar was apparently judged to be

skij, who said that "there are very few quotations from other Slavic languages" and that "one half of the ... quoted Slavic [non-Russian] words are misspelled".[17]

In 1954 *Voprosy Jazykoznanija* again carried a programmatic paper, this time by S. B. Bernštejn, dealing with the creation of a new Comparative Slavic Grammar.[18] Bernštejn is undoubtedly right in considering this a very difficult task and asking for collaboration with Czech, Polish, and Bulgarian scholars. Yugoslav scholars were not mentioned. Bernštejn zigzags astutely between the Stalin fashioned criticism of the "antihistorical", "fruitless" bourgeois structuralism which "has brought us into a cul-de-sac" and the cautious statement that "in some [Western] works ... we find valuable and important observations". This is, as far as I know, the first favorable opinion about Western structuralism expressed by a Soviet linguist. Other Soviet scholars continued to write in the pure neogrammarian spirit and there were even some violently antistructuralist books, like A. V. Desnickaja's "Problems of Kinship among the Indo-European languages".[19] This lady, who was strongly "Marristic" in the forties, now became an avowed enemy of Marr. But she calls neolinguists (for example, Vossler, Bartoli, Bonfante) and the Danish school of Louis Hjelmslev, "modern scholasts", "antimarxists", and "pseudoscientific idealists", while some German linguists (Hermann Hirt, Helmut Arntz) are called "racists". Another lady, O. S. Axmanova, launched an attack against the American structuralists.[20]

On the other hand, works of famous West European neogrammarians began to be available to Russian students in translations. The stress was on Comparative Indo-European linguistics, as is seen from the following list of translations:

1952: André Vaillant, *Manuel du vieux slave* (Paris, 1948).
E. Bourciez, *Eléments de linguistique romane* (Paris, 1946).
J. Friedrich, *Kurzgefasste Grammatik des Hettitischen* (Heidelberg, 1940).
1954: H. Pedersen and G. Lewis, *A concise comparative Celtic grammar* (Göttingen, 1937).
Antoine Meillet, *La méthode comparative en linguistique historique* (Oslo, 1925).
1955: Ch. Bally, *Linguistique générale et linguistique française* (Berne, 1944).
E. Benveniste, *Origines de la formation des mots en indo-européen* (Paris, 1935).
1960: Hermann Paul, *Prinzipien der Sprachgeschichte*, fifth edition (1937).

In comparative Slavistics the results were however still minute. Worth mentioning are two monograph collections (*sbornik statej*), *Slavjanskaja Filologija*, I (Moscow, 1951) and II (Moscow, 1954), which contained original Soviet contributions on Czech,

better than Kuznecov's, because it appeared in a second, revised edition in 1954 and was later even translated into German in East Berlin.

[17] See *VJa* 1/1.132 sq. (1953).

[18] Bernštejn, "Osnovnye zadači, metody i principy 'Sravnitel'noj grammatiki slavjanskix jazykov'". See also entry in general bibliography.

[19] Desnickaja, *Voprosy izučenija rodstva indoevropejskix jazykov*.

[20] Axmanova, "O metode lingvističeskogo issledovanija u amerikanskix strukturalistov". See also Axmanova, *Fonologija*.

Slovak, and Bulgarian philology.[21] One of the contributors, N. A. Kondrašov, also published a little book about Slavic languages, primarily meant as a textbook for students.[22] It is a clear, up-to-date presentation of the main features of the 12 Slavic languages, Serbian and Croatian as well as both Upper and Lower Lusatian being considered as linguistic unities, which is controversial. The author is still completely under the impact of Stalin and stresses the close linguistic and racial kinship of all Slavs. He goes out of his way to demonstrate that a Russian is able to understand "at the price of a certain effort" the speech of a Pole, Czech, Bulgarian, or Serbian. Even if a certain understanding is possible with the two latter, the possibility of recognizing the meaning of a normal Czech or Polish sentence is even for a cultivated Russian hardly greater than for an American to understand Swedish or Norwegian. Kondrašov himself seems not to be very firm in some of the languages treated by him; his Polish forms are often misspelled or simply wrong. His main interest seems to be in Slovakian.

Much more important was the fact that in 1954 the Soviet Academy started a new periodical *Voprosy Slavjanskogo Jazykoznanija* which was intended to cover only Comparative and Historical Slavistics. It opened with the editor's (S. B. Bernštejn) programmatic paper which differed little from his above mentioned paper (see footnote 18). The first two volumes contained several original contributions to Comparative and Historical Slavistics by Soviet scholars. Especially to be noted is Ju. S. Maslov's article on the imperfect tense of Slavic perfective verbs,[23] which deals with *all* Slavic languages. Maslov advanced a very interesting theory that the Old Russian Imperfect tense was not, as had been commonly supposed, a Church Slavic intruder, but a really living form of the Russian perfective verbs. It indicated, according to Maslov, a repeated perfective action, just as it still does in Modern Bulgarian. For example, Old Russian (*egda*) *rečaše* 3. Sg. Imperf. from *reči* "to speak" (perfective) could be translated by "(every time when) he spoke".

From the third volume on (1958) the scope of this periodical seems to be enlarged by engulfing Baltic and Romance philology and the contributors come mainly from Lithuania, Poland, Yugoslavia, and Rumania. From the viewpoint of Comparative Slavistics, the most interesting is the reconstruction of Proto-Slavic *u*-stems by R. Ekkert.[24]

At the International Congress of Slavists in Belgrade, September, 1955, a Soviet Slavist delegation, headed by Vinogradov, appeared for the first time. Outside of the field of Modern Russian style and Russian history the Soviet scholars did not have

[21] Širokova, "K voprosu o različii meždu češskim literaturnym jazykom i narodno-razgovornoj reč'ju", pp. 3-37; Kondrašov, "Kategorija ličnosti imën suščestvitel'nyx v slovackom jazyke", pp. 38-67; Bernštejn, "Zametki po bolgarskoj dialektologii", pp. 68-75; Borodič, "Ob odnoj osobennosti bolgarskogo glagola", pp. 76-96. All these articles are in the second volume of 1954.
[22] Kondrašov, *Slavjanskie jazyki*.
[23] Maslov, "Imperfekt glagolov soveršennogo vida v slavjanskix jazykax".
[24] Ekkert, "K voprosu o sostave gruppy imën susčestvitel'nyx s osnovoj na -ŭ v praslavjanskom jazyke".

much to contribute, so that the superiority of Western Slavistics (included the Poles and Czechs) was obvious. As the next International Congress of Slavists was scheduled for 1958, in Moscow, one would expect the Soviet scholars to concentrate on Comparative Slavistics. But that was not the case. Just the opposite, the programmatic article of S. K. Šaumjan in 1956[25] stresses the necessity of studying *structural* linguistics in their Prague, Copenhagen, and American varieties, because they represent "a new stage in the history of linguistics". By 1957, discussions of structural linguistics, machine translation, etc., dominate *Voprosy Jazykoznanija.* The interest in the narrow Slavic field goes back and the more remote Indo-European languages (Baltic, Germanic, Hittite) are put forward. This is the time of the great interest in etymology which hitherto has been the weakest point of the Soviet philologists. One may ask whether the fact that the beginning of that trend coincides with the beginning of the famous cultural "thaw" is just a coincidence.

To begin with, foreign linguists were invited to discuss problems of their field in Soviet learned journals and even allowed to criticize the works of Soviet scholars. In 1957, for instance, a former Russian emigré from Czechoslovakia, Trubetzkoy's pupil and former son-in-law, A. V. Isačenko, simply demolished a book on Russian lexicology by Černyx.[26] Being an eminent specialist in Slovakian and Slovenian, Isačenko paid special attention to the innumerable misspellings and grave mistakes made by Černyx in quoting non-Russian Slavic forms.

A discussion on creating a Russian etymological dictionary was held in Moscow in December, 1957, and a Finnish specialist was invited to participate.[27] During that discussion a Russian scholar made the ominous proposal that the planned dictionary be constructed as a Romance one, i.e., the comparisons with kindred languages should go no further than to Proto-Slavic or, at most, to Balto-Slavic, just as Italian, French, Rumanian, etc., do not go further back than Vulgar or Classical Latin. This proposal was rightly rejected by Vinogradov who presided over the panel. He pointed out that the Slavic languages being very close to each other such a "restricted" Dictionary would become "boring" by repeating twelve times approximately the same forms of a word.

At the time of the Moscow Congress, in September, 1958, there were nevertheless some young Soviet Slavists with considerable practical and theoretical knowledge of different Slavic and Baltic languages, and some of them presented papers of value. Bernštejn, leading a whole team of young Slavists, published an outstanding work on the use of the instrumental case in different Slavic languages[28] – a model for such an investigation. V. V. Ivanov and V. N. Toporov, working mostly together, tackled the complicated question of the Balto-Slavic Protoglossa, and O. N. Trubačëv proved to

[25] Šaumjan, "O suščnosti strukturnoj lingvistiki".

[26] In *VJa* 6/3.119-127 (1957). The demolished book's title: *Očerki po russkoj istoričeskoj leksikologii. Drevnerusskij period.*

[27] See *VJa* 7/2.168 (1958).

[28] Bernštejn, *Tvoritel'nyj padež v slavjanskix jazykax.*

be the first Soviet etymologist to be taken seriously. Of course, we owe a lot of good etymologies to Vinogradov, but they were mainly explanations of recent figurative expressions or late loanwords or neologisms, based on Vinogradov's unique knowledge of modern Russian, not really on Comparative Slavistics. But Trubačëv started by giving a good Slavic etymology to the controversial Russian word *sobaka* "dog", generally believed to be an Old Iranian loanword.[29] He compared it, in my opinion very convincingly, to the similarly isolated Czech word *sob* "reindeer", the name *sobaka* being thus primarily that of a special "reindeer-dog", perhaps a kind of Malemute.[30] The Czech word being already attested in Old Czech,[31] there is no possibility of it being invented or borrowed by the Czech language innovators of the 19th century. The only difficulty is the suffix *-aka* which generally joins only verbal, not nominal stems. Very ingenious, though not strictly proved, is also Trubačëv's etymology of Slavic *pěti* "to sing", 1. Sg. Indic. *pojǫ*, which he simply identifies with 1. Sg. Indic. *pojǫ* from *poiti* "to give or to make somebody drink". The infinitive *poiti* is, according to Trubačëv, a secondary formation, and the original meaning of the verb *pěti* was "to perform a rite with singing and libations". A year later Trubačëv offered an interesting and original investigation about the Slavic words for kinship and social relations, based on the comparative historical method. These words have, of course, been thoroughly investigated before, but Trubačëv still succeeded in offering some new viewpoints.[32] In 1960 he published another comparative-historical study about the Slavic names of domestic animals.[33] Trubačëv's studies joined the general trend of "Words and Things" which was revived in Europe after World War II as a reaction against structuralism and especially glossematics which completely ignored etymology.

The complete isolation of Stalin's time did not return even after the end of the cultural "thaw" in 1959. Soviet scholars still closely follow foreign periodicals, publish articles there, and invite foreigners even from "capitalistic" countries to publish reviews and articles in Soviet journals. *Voprosy Jazykoznanija* introduced a special column about "Works in progress" (*nad čem rabotajut učënye*), sent out questionnaires and published some exhaustive answers from famous Western Slavists. The main interest of the younger generation seems however to be in the more remote Indo-European languages and in General Linguistics. It began by translating in 1957 S. Goldman's *Information Theory*; H. A. Gleason's *An Introduction to Descriptive Linguistics* (1955) followed in 1959, prefaced by one of the ablest young Soviet theoretical linguists, V. A. Zvegincev.[34]

It has been said that it took American linguists 20 years to cover the ground which

[29] E.g. Vasmer, *Russisches etymologisches Wörterbuch*, II, p. 684.

[30] Trubačëv, "K ètimologii slova 'sobaka'".

[31] See Machek, *Slovník etymologický jazyka českého a slovenského*, p. 426.

[32] Trubačëv, *Istorija slavjanskix terminov rodstva i nekotoryx drevnejšix terminov obščestvennogo stroja*. There is a favorable review in *VJa* 9/5.140-144 (1960).

[33] Trubačëv, *Proisxoždenie nazvanij domašnix životnyx v slavjanskix jazykax*.

[34] Goldman, *Teorija informacii*; Glison, *Vvedenie v deskriptivnuju lingvistiku*.

the Europeans covered in 200 years. Well, the Soviets took hardly more than two years to catch up with the Americans. They threw themselves onto the exciting new American linguistic works just as little children in a new playground in spring. In 1959, even a large discussion of structural linguistics by a certain Hsü Ho-chan of Peking was translated from Chinese into Russian and published in *Voprosy Jazykoznanija*.[35] O. S. Axmanova who in 1952 had written an all-out attack on structuralists, wrote in 1959 quite a favorable review of Bloomfield's work on Ojibwa.[36]

All that alienated young and gifted Soviet linguists from Comparative Slavistics. The older students of Russian restricted themselves to the narrow area of Russian proper. The field of Comparative and Historical Slavistics seemed to become fallow again.

In that connection two programmatic papers published in 1959 by *Voprosy Jazykoznanija* deserve attention. The first was anonymous.[37] It stressed that Russian was "the language of one of the most numerous and historically influential Slavic people" which after the October revolution "becomes more and more internationally important" so that it even gives international terms to science (for example *sputnik*). But it still doesn't occupy the place which belongs to it. General linguistics, cybernetics, machine translation, etc., use too little Russian material. There is still no general investigation of Russian on a Marxist basis, no good dictionaries, no good editions of certain Old Russian texts. These latter reproaches were undoubtedly reasonable and often expressed by Western Slavists. The anonymous author stressed that though Max Vasmer recently published in West Berlin an etymological dictionary of Russian it did not free the Russian scholars from the duty of constructing a new one, with more references to the semantic changes. Furthermore a Comparative Slavic Grammar should be created and published. Slavistics should be treated according to "the Marxist theory of linguistics" and bourgeois linguistics should be criticized. The article ends with a quotation from a speech of Xruščëv: "The seven year plan opens ... the widest field of action. There is plenty of place to apply one's knowledge and energy".

The other paper was signed by Vinogradov himself and dealt with Slavistics in general.[38] Vinogradov started by mentioning the age-old consciousness of the Slavs of the genetic kinship of their languages and the different projects of creating a common literary language for all Slavic peoples. In their struggle against Turkic and Germanic peoples the Slavs have always looked upon Russia as the great protector, and the idea of a Slavic Unity operated with Russia as basis. The reason why before World War I Slavistics was "studied" mainly in Austria-Hungary and Germany is to be found in the "specific political edge of the projects of those countries". However,

[35] Sjuj Go-Čžan, "Obzor struktural'nogo napravlenija v lingvistike".
[36] *VJa* 8/3.125-127 (1959).
[37] "XXI s"ezd kommunističeskoj partii Sovetskogo Sojuza i nekotorye zadači russkogo jazykoznanija", *VJa* 8/3.3-10 (1959).
[38] Vinogradov, "Sostojanie i perspektivy razvitija sovetskogo slavjanovedenija".

says Vinogradov, "the alliance between Panslavism and Slavistics was not organic". After World War I, Slavistics was developed with political motives in Italy, England, Scandinavia, Finland. The present-day Slavistics in West Germany and the United States are often specifically politically biased and sometimes led by emigrés – Lednicki, Jakobson, Vernadskij, partly Čiževskyj. After this preamble Vinogradov delineates the assignments of future Soviet Slavists. These are: 1) The Palaeography of the Glagolitic Alphabet, 2) The Vocabulary of Old Church Slavic, 3) The Russian Variety of Old Church Slavic, 4) The Church Slavic Elements in Old Russian, 5) Phonology and Syntax of Old Church Slavic (in that connection Vinogradov emphasizes the importance of a book by the young Swedish Slavist Henrik Birnbaum), 6) Publication of the still unpublished Old Russian manuscripts. Moreover, Soviet Slavists should study Hungarian, Rumanian, Albanian, and other languages which are "inseparably connected with the Slavs and form together with them one cultural-historical world". It is interesting that Vinogradov didn't mention Comparative Slavistics among the assignments at all. The reason might be that the first "Comparative Grammar of Slavic Languages", written by a Soviet scholar, S. B. Bernštejn, was already at the printers.

Bernštejn's book[39] appeared during the late summer of 1961 quite unexpectedly for Western Slavists. The author was known as specialist in Bulgarian and Rumanian, he had written several articles on general subjects, and published an excellent team work on the instrumental case (see footnote 28), but nobody had expected him to write a synthetic survey of that kind. His programmatic article of 1954 (see footnote 18) had been forgotten by most Slavists and the little note in *Voprosy Jazykoznanija*, 1959, 2, p. 61, indicating that his "Comparative Grammar" was in preparation seems not to have been observed. Anyhow, he kept his promise. Bernštejn's work is based on the modern principles of structural linguistics and differs substantially from all older Comparative Slavic Grammars and even from the most recent ones, like André Vaillant's and Herbert Bräuer's.[40] The part now published contains only the Introduction and Phonology, but will be followed by a volume containing Morphology. The main innovation of Bernštejn is the abandonment of the traditional division into Part I "Vowels" and Part II "Consonants". He treats the phonemic system as a whole and tries to make "cross-sections" of it in order to illustrate not the change of individual sounds, but of the whole system. This is very sound as a principle, but extremely difficult in practice and I personally must disagree with Bernštejn in the timing of different phonetic changes. He likes to operate with extremely remote times, so that the oldest Germanic loanwords (according to general opinion, about 1700 years old), for example Old Church Slavic *šlěmъ* "helmet" < **šelmъ* < Germanic **χelmaz* would have entered the Proto-Slavic *after* the change $\chi > \check{s}$ had taken place. In these loanwords, according to Bernštejn, there would have taken place only a substitution of sounds, not the real phonetic change, which would have put the latter

39 Bernštejn, *Očerk sravnitel'noj grammatiki slavjanskix jazykov.*
40 Vaillant, *Grammaire comparée des langues slaves*, I, II; Bräuer, *Slavische Sprachwissenschaft*, I.

into a time B. C. Similar "substitutions" Bernštejn seems to presume in order to explain the rendering of both "strong" and "weak" ъ and ь by /u/ and /i/ in Finnish. In that case it is easy to prove and it has been proved already[41] that there is no question of "substitution", but of real "phonetic correspondence", because Finnish had every possible choice (/æ/, /e/, /y/, /ø/, /Λ/, /i/, /ɔ/) for representing the Slavic /ъ/ and /ь/. On page 177 Bernštejn says himself that Finnish /u/ and /i/ were "the closest" correspondences to /ъ/ and /ь/.

Eliminating in that way the evidence of the loanwords Bernštejn puts most of the well known phonetic changes of Proto-Slavic, like the 1st palatalization, into a very remote past. But when he discusses the phonetic changes of the historical period, for example the vocalization of the "strong" ъ and ь, the development of Ukrainian /i/ from /o/ and /e/ in a syllable which became closed through the disappearance of a "weak" ъ or ь, or the change /e/ > /o/ in Russian, Belorussian, Polish, and Lusatian, his timing differs little from the generally accepted one.

Defining the original abode of the Proto-Slavs about 200 B. C. as lying between Pripjat' in the North, Dnepr in the East, the Carpatians in the South, and the Upper Vistula in the West (map 3, page 65), Bernštejn fully agrees with most of his colleagues. The later movements of the Slavs are however described by him in a quite different way. Most strange is his theory about a special affinity between Polish and Bulgarian which should repose on "an old vicinity of those languages" (page 72). As every Slavist knows there are no two Slavic languages as remote from each other and mutually less understandable than Polish and Bulgarian.

The tendency to underestimate the importance of the Germanic influence on the Slavs, which was very pronounced in Soviet works during the 1940's and 1950's, has obviously not yet been eradicated. On p. 77 Bernštejn says that the present-day Bohemia and Moravia had been occupied by the Celtic tribes of *Volcos*, *Volcae*, which is, of course, true. Immediately afterwards he says, however, that the ancestors of Czechs occupied these provinces and, perhaps, have been influenced by the Celtic substratum, which is, according to Bernštejn, proved by the ethnic name *Valach* (so are called, in Czech, the mountain shepherds in North-Eastern Moravia). The well-known and very important fact that Bohemia and Moravia were occupied in between by the Germanic tribes *Marcomanni* and *Quadi* and that the Slavs got their ethnic names *Vlaxъ*, *Włoch*, *Volox*, *Lah*, etc. for Italians and Rumanians *not* directly from the Celtic but through Germanic intermediation is simply left out.[42]

Approximately at the same time when Bernštejn's book was in press, a young scholar from Odessa, V. V. Martynov published an article with the very outspoken intention to prove that the original abode of the Proto-Slavs included the controversial territories between the Vistula and the Oder, now occupied by Poland.[43] It is well

[41] See Kiparsky, "Chronologie des relations slavobaltiques et slavofinnoises", *Revue des Etudes Slaves* 24.43 (1948).

[42] See Kiparsky, *Die gemeinslavischen Lehnwörter aus dem Germanischen*, p. 90, and Vasmer, *Russisches etymologisches Wörterbuch*, I, p. 222.

[43] Martynov, "K lingvističeskomu obosnovaniju gipotezy o vislooderskoj prarodine slavjan".

known that the best proof for that thesis would be a Proto-Slavic loanword (even better several loanwords!) in Old English, because it would mean that the Proto-Slavs were in contact with the West Germanic tribes before 500 A.D., when the Angles and the Saxons left the Continent. The lack of such loanwords is generally considered as proof of the contrary. Martynov quotes six examples: Proto-Germanic **tila* (Gothic *gatils* "convenient", English *till, until*) < Proto-Slav. **tьlo*; Proto-Germanic **skattaz* (Swedish *skatt* "tax", German *Schatz* "treasure", Old English *sceatt* "money") < Proto-Slav. **skotъ*; Proto-Germanic **tūn-* (English *town*, German *Zaun* "fence") < Proto-Slav. **tynъ*; Proto-Germanic **snēd-* (Old English *snǣdan*, Old Icelandic *snæða* "to eat") < Proto-Slavic **sъnědь*; West Germanic **vapel* (Old English *wapul* "foam", Middle High German *wapel* "swamp") < Proto-Slavic **vapь*; West Germanic **denn* (English *den*) < Proto-Slavic **dъno*. Only one of those items (**skattaz*) has been discussed before and convincingly proved to be borrowed in the opposite direction.[44] The other ones cannot even be considered seriously.

More important is the article by V. M. Illič-Svityč on the origin of the very controversial initial *x-* in Proto-Slavic.[45] He gives a convincing supplement to "Siebs' law" explaining why for example to Lettish *skarbs* "sharp" corresponds Proto-Slavic **xorbrъ*, but to Lettish *skurbt* "to faint", Proto-Slavic **skъrb-*.

A new etymological dictionary of Russian, asked for by the discussion panel in 1957 (see footnote 27), and then again by the anonymous programmatic paper in 1959 (see footnote 37), was at last published in 1961 by three authors.[46] It is a small volume of about 400 pages, intended primarily as a handbook for schoolteachers. Though its makers were serious linguists and it was edited by the well known student of Old Russian, S. G. Barxudarov, it proved to be a complete failure. In his review O. N. Trubačëv states that on each page of this work "an extremely low level of etymological analysis", a "general backwardness" and a "conscienceless treatment of the material" are to be found.[47] This severe criticism provoked, of course, an unusually violent reply from the authors and the editor, but the final statement by the editorial staff of *Voprosy Jazykoznanija* made it sufficiently clear that Trubačëv was on the whole right.[48]

Neither a success nor a failure is Kuznecov's recent study in Proto-Slavic morphology.[49] He discusses in detail most of the controversial points without, however, giving any new solutions. His reconstruction of Proto-Slavic is based mostly on Russian and Old Church Slavic, and he seems not to be very well informed about the neighboring fields. For example, while discussing the partitive meaning of the genitive case (page 42) Kuznecov does not even mention the well-known parallels from the Finnic languages which obviously are in some way connected with the

[44] Vasmer, *Russisches etymologisches Wörterbuch II*, p. 649.
[45] Illič-Svityč, "Odin iz istočnikov načal'nogo *x-*".
[46] Šanskij, Ivanov, & Šanskaja, *Kratkij ètimologičeskij slovar'*.
[47] See *VJa* 10/5.129-135 (1961).
[48] See *VJa* 11/1.133-146 (1962).
[49] Kuznecov, *Očerki po morfologii praslavjanskogo jazyka*.

Slavic facts. It is interesting that Kuznecov still continues the argument against Roman Jakobson's "five-, four-, three-, and two-case-systems" which started at the Moscow Congress of 1958. According to Kuznecov and some minor Soviet scholars, there are only "five-, four-, three-, and two-*form*-systems".

The tentative proposal of a new theory on the Old Church Slavic as a common literary language of South and East Slavs, made by Nikita Tolstoj, a great-grand-son of the famous writer, in a short article[50] is worth mentioning. Instead of restraining themselves to the generally accepted "canon" of Old Church Slavic writing, previous to the 11th century, scholars should, according to N. Tolstoj, consider the later Serbian, Bulgarian, Russian varieties of Church Slavic as specimens of one and the same Old Church Slavic Literary Language, a kind of "Slavic Latin". That would mean extending the "Old Church Slavic" period until the 18th century which was actually done for example by Fr. Miklosich in his *Lexicon Palaeoslovenico-Graeco-Latinum* (Vienna, 1852), but which was later rejected by more sober investigators like August Leskien and Erich Berneker.[51] The later Church Slavic languages, called now by the French scholar André Vaillant "les slavons" as opposed to the "vieux slave" (Old Church Slavic),[52] are very important especially from the point of view of the vocabulary. Their relation to the "canon" texts is approximately the same as that of Late Medieval Latin to the language of Caesar and Cicero.

Of all works on Comparative and Historical Slavistics which were published during the Soviet period Bernštejn's "Comparative Grammar" is undoubtedly the most remarkable. Though offering many points open for criticism, it has the great advantage of being an up-to-date work combining the achievements of the old neogrammarian with the new structuralist point of view. It has obviously been done in a great hurry and will certainly gain much by a second edition, but even in its present state it is superior to many Western works on the same subject. It is a brilliant proof of the almost unlimited adaptability of Russian scholars. Ten years of "freedom from Marr" and five years of "freedom to use foreign literature" were sufficient to lift Soviet Slavistics from below-zero-ignorance and nonsensical humbug-making to the West European level of etymology (Trubačëv) and American level of structural grammar (Bernštejn).

## BIBLIOGRAPHY

Axmanova, O. S., *Fonologija* (Moscow, 1954).

——, "O methode lingvističeskogo issledovanija u amerikanskix strukturalistov", *VJa* 1/5.92-105 (1952).

[50] Tolstoj, "K voprosu o drevneslavjanskom jazyke".

[51] Leskien, A., *Handbuch der altbulgarischen (altkirchenslavischen) Sprache* (Heidelberg, 1871). Berneker, *Slavisches etymologisches Wörterbuch*, I (Heidelberg, 1909-14).

[52] See Vaillant, *Manuel du vieux slave*, I, § 5.

Bernštejn, S. B., *Očerk sravnitel'noj grammatiki slavjanskix jazykov*, ISl. (Moscow, 1961).
——, "Osnovnye zadači, metody i principy 'Sravnitel'noj grammatiki slavjanskix jazykov'", *VJa* 3/2.49-67 (1954). Republished almost without changes under the same title in *VSlJa(M)* 1.5-23 (1954).
—— (ed.) *Slavjanskaja filologija*, Sbornik statej, Vypusk 2. 188 pages + 1 map. (Moscow, 1954).
—— (ed.), *Tvoritel'nyj padež v slavjanskix jazykax* (Moscow, 1958).
Bräuer, Herbert, *Slavische Sprachwissenschaft*, I (= *Sammlung Göschen*, B. 1191/1191a) (Berlin, 1961).
Bulaxovskij, L. A., *Akcentologičeskij kommentarij k češskomu jazyku I*, II (Kiev, 1953-56).
——, *Akcentologičeskij kommentarij k pol'skomu jazyku* (Kiev, 1950).
——, "Obščeslavjanskie nazvanija ptič", *IzvAN*, VII, vypusk 2 (1948).
——, "Sravnitel'no-istoričeskie kommentarii k vostočno-slavjanskomu udareniju", *VSlJa*, kniga 4 (L'vov, 1955).
Bulygina, A. M., *Jazyk 'Seti very' Petra Xel'čickogo* (*iz istorii češskogo jazyka XV v*). Dissertation for M. A. (Moscow, 1952).
Černyx, P. Ja., *Istoričeskaja grammatika russkogo jazyka* (Moscow, 1952).
Desnickaja, A. V., *Voprosy izučenija rodstva indoevropejskix jazykov* (Moscow, 1955).
Ekkert, R., "K voprosu o sostave gruppy imën susčestvitel'nyx s osnovoj na -ŭ v proslavjanskom jazyke", *VSlJa(M)* 4.100-125 (1959).
Glison, G., *Vvedenie v deskriptivnuju lingvistiku* (Moscow, 1959).
Goldman, S., *Teorija informacii* (Moscow, 1957).
Illič-Svityč, V. M., "Odin iz istočnikov načal'nogo 'x-' v praslavjanskom 'Popravka k zakonu Zibsa'", *VJa* 10/4.95-98 (1961).
Jakubinskij, L. P., *Istorija drevnerusskogo jazyka* (Moscow, 1952).
Kiparskij, V., *O kolebanijax udarenija v russkom literaturnom jazyke I* (= *AnnIFiES*, Supplement 1) (Helsinki, 1950).
——, *Die gemeinslavischen Lehnwörter aus dem Germanischen* (Helsinki, 1934).
Kolomiec, V. T., *Porjakok slov v češskoj proze pervoj poloviny XIX st.* Dissertation for M. A. (Kiev, 1950).
Kondrašov, N. A., *Slavjanskie jazyki*. 200 pages + 2 maps in color (Moscow, 1956).
Kuznecov, P. S., *Istoričeskaja grammatika russkogo jazyka, Morfologia* (Moscow, 1953).
——, "Voprosy sravnitel'no-istoričeskogo izučenija slavjanskix jazykov", *VJa* 1/5.38-55 (1952).
——, *Očerki po morfologii praslavjanskogo jazyka* (Moscow, 1961).
Loja, Jānis, *Valodniecības vēsture* (Riga, 1961).
Machek, Vaclav, *Slovník etymologický jazyka českého a slovenského* (Prague, 1957).
Macjusovič, Ja. M., *Složno-podčinënnoe predloženie v pol'skom literaturnom jazyke XIV-XVI vekov*. Dissertation for M. A. (Leningrad, 1953).

——, "Osnovnye osobennosti složno-podčinënnogo predloženija sovremennogo pol'skogo literaturnogo jazyka sravnitel'no s russkim jazykom", *UZLU*, vypusk 15, I.

Martynov, V. V., "K lingvističeskomu obosnovaniju gipotezy o vislooderskoj prarodine slavjan", *VJa* 10/3.51-59 (1961).

Maslov, Ju. S., "Imperfekt glagolov soveršennogo vida v slavjanskix jazykax", *VJa* 3/1.68-138 (1954).

Nemčenko, E. V., *Iz istorii kratkix pričastij dejstvitel'nogo zaloga v češskom jazyke*. Dissertation for M. A. (Moscow, 1951).

Pavljuk, N. V., *Kategorija mestoimenija v staropol'skom jazyke*. Dissertation for M. A. (Odessa, 1952).

Šanskij, N. M., Ivanov, V. V., and Šanskaja, T. V., *Kratkij etimologičeskij slovar' russkogo jazyka, Posobie dlja učitelja* (Moscow, 1961).

Šaumjan, S. K., "O suščnosti strukturnoj lingvistiki", *VJa* 5/5.38-54 (1956).

Seliščev, A. M., *Slavjanskoe jazykoznanie*, I (Moscow, 1941).

——, *Staroslavjanskij jazyk*, I, II (Moscow, 1951-52).

Sjuj Go-Čžan, "Obzor struktural'nogo napravlenija v lingvistike", *VJa* 8/3.40-60 (1959).

Šor, R. O., and Čemodanov, N. S., *Vvedenie v jazykovedenie* (Moscow, 1945).

Tkačenko, O., *Očerk istorii iz"jasnitel'nyx sojuzov v pol'skom literaturnom jazyke (na materiale proizvedenij vtoroj poloviny XVI v.)*. Dissertation for M. A. (Kiev, 1954).

Tolstoj, N. I., "K voprosu o drevneslavjanskom jazyke kak obščem literaturnom jazyke južnyx i vostočnyx slavjan", *VJa* 10/1.52-66 (1961).

Trubačëv, O. N., *Istorija slavjanskix terminov rodstva i nekotoryx drevnejšix terminov obščestvennogo stroja* (Moscow, 1959).

——, *Proisxoždenie nazvanij domašnix životnyx v slavjanskix jazykax* (Moscow, 1960).

——, "K ètimologii slova 'sobaka'", *KSISl* 15.48-55 (1955).

Unbegaun, B. O., *A Bibliographical Guide to the Russian Language* (Oxford, 1953).

Vaillant, André, *Grammaire comparée des langues slaves*, I, II (Paris, 1950-58).

——, *Manuel du vieux slave* (Paris, 1948).

Vasmer, M., *Russisches etymologisches Wörterbuch*, 2 vols. (Heidelberg, 1950-58).

Vinogradov, V. V., "Sostojanie i perspektivy razvitija sovetskogo slavjanovedenija", *VJa* 8/6.3-17 (1959).

## ADDENDUM

Since the above text was left with the printers in June, 1962, a flow of books and articles on Comparative and Historical Slavistics has begun to appear in the USSR. This increased activity is obviously connected with the preparations for the Vth International Congress of Slavists which is scheduled for September, 1963, in Sofia

(Bulgaria). Only the most important of the recent works can be commented on here.

V. N. Toporov published a solid investigation about the locative case in the Slavic languages[53] which may be compared to the work of Bernštejn on the instrumental case (see fn. 28).

In collaboration with the etymologist O. N. Trubačëv (see fns. 30, 32, 33) Toporov analysed the river names of the Upper Dniepr area.[54] The authors accept mostly the old etymologies, given by Max Vasmer or by still older scholars, but they try to outdo Vasmer in finding river names of both Baltic and Iranian origin in the Desna area. If all those etymologies were correct, they would have proved direct contacts between Balts and Iranians in that area for a time B.C. However, out of more than 2000 river names quoted by Toporov and Trubačëv, only a few hundred are probably of Baltic and only a few dozen of Iranian origin, while all the other remain controversial. A detailed review of this interesting work will appear in the next volume of *Zeitschrift für slavische Philologie*.

The most important of all recent contributions to Comparative Slavistics is undoubtedly the book on the formation of the East Slavic[55] by F. P. Filin, which appeared at Christmas, 1962. It is the first of its kind in the USSR, but reminds one of famous Czech, German, and Polish works on the "Urheimat" problem. Though taking into consideration archeology, history, toponymy, etc., Filin is still mainly interested in the vocabulary. He has a critical and very sensible approach to the loanword problem, which basically is the same as that of the Scandinavian (Thomsenian) school. Most laudable is Filin's strong criticism of Martynov's unfortunate hypothesis (see fn. 43).

Toporov, Trubačëv, and Filin, who work with problems of vocabulary (etymologies), have evidently observed that the structural method alone (which has been by now adopted by practically all Soviet linguists) is not sufficient. They seem to have worked out an interesting synthesis of the structural approach to purely phonematic questions and of the purely neogrammarian approach to the lexical ones. Moreover, Filin, who in the 1940s was one of the faithful Marrists, succeeded in finding some useful viewpoints in his old master's works on Caucasian languages.

The investigation of Old Church Slavic vocabulary by A. S. L'vov[56] is a painstaking work which would have been better if the author had observed also the results of recent Western works on the same subject.

*Voprosy slavjanskogo jazykoznanija* 6 (published in October, 1962) contains remarks

[53] V. N. Toporov, *Lokativ v slavjanskix jazykax*, AN SSSR, Institut slavjanovedenija (Moscow, 1961), 380 pp.

[54] V. N. Toporov and O. N. Trubačëv, *Lingvističeskij analiz gidronimov Verxnego Podneprov'ja*, AN SSSR, Institut slavjanovedenija (Moscow, 1962), 271 pp. + 13 maps in a special envelope.

[55] F. P. Filin, *Obrazovanija jazyka vostočnyx slavjan*, AN SSSR, Institut russkogo jazyka (Moscow-Leningrad, 1962), 296 pp.

[56] A. S. L'vov, "Očerki po leksike pamjatnikov staroslavjanskou pis'mennosti", *Issledovanija po leksikologii i grammatike russkogo jazyka*, AN SSSR (Moscow, 1961), pp. 45-131.

on the stress of Proto-Slavic verbs by V. A. Dybo,[57] and a substantial and useful survey of Slavo-Iranian linguistic contacts by A. A. Zaliznjak.[58] The former follows mainly the Norwegian Chr. S. Stang's well-known *Slavonic Accentuation* (Oslo, 1957), the latter relies mostly on Max Vasmer's works. In the same issue, M. I. Burlakova gives a "prehistory" of Slavic velars and tries a structuralistic approach to that age-old problem, which has been more or less unsuccessfully tackled by almost every Neogrammarian.[59]

April, 1963

[57] V. A. Dybo, "O rekonstrukcii udarenija v praslavjanskom glagole", *VSlJa*(*M*) 6.3-27 (1962).
[58] A. A. Zaliznjak, "Problemy slavjano-iranskix jazykovyx otnošenij drevejšego perioda", *VSlJa* (*M*) 6.28-45 (1962).
[59] M. I. Burlakova, "Predystorija slavjanskix zadnenëbnyx", *VSlJa*(*M*) 6.46-65 (1962).

APPLIED

# MATHEMATICAL LINGUISTICS

ROBERT ABERNATHY

## 1. CHRONOLOGICAL SKETCH

The emergence of mathematical linguistics as a specialized field is in the USSR, as elsewhere in the world, quite a recent development. The following brief chronology of events, spanning eight years, may serve to highlight the stages in this process.

1955: First machine translation experiments in the Soviet Union.

1956: Opening of discussion on structuralism in the pages of *Voprosy jazykoznanija*.[1] Inauguration of a seminar in mathematical linguistics at the Moscow State University.

1957: Publication of O. S. Kulagina's set-theoretic language model.[2] Conference on speech statistics in Leningrad, 1-4 October.[3]

1958: Moscow conference on machine translation. Participation of workers in this field in the Fourth International Congress of Slavists (Moscow, 1-10 September). Publication of Volume 51 of the *Bol'šaja sovetskaja ènciklopedija*, containing an article on "Mathematical linguistics" (by V. V. Ivanov).

1959: Conference on mathematical linguistics held in Leningrad, 15-21 April, attended by almost five hundred linguists, mathematicians and others from various parts of the Soviet Union and from Eastern Europe and China: 58 papers, on a wide range of topics in both theory and applications.[4]

1960: Resolution of the Presidium of the Academy of Sciences "on the development of structural and mathematical methods of linguistic research", with corresponding organizational changes in a number of the Academy's institutes.[5] Inclusion of "structural and mathematical methods" in the problematics of the Fifth International Congress of Slavists, to be held 1963.

1961: A series of well-attended conferences touching various aspects of formalized linguistic investigation (machine translation and data processing, lexicography, trans-

[1] Editorial, *VJa* 5/4 (1956), and various articles in this and succeeding numbers.

[2] Kulagina, "Ob odnom sposobe opredelenija lingvističeskix ponjatij".

[3] All but one of the papers delivered published in the collection *Voprosy statistiki reči*, edited by L. R. Zinder.

[4] More or less extensive summaries of papers in: *Tezisy soveščanija po matematičeskoj lingvistike (15-21 aprelja 1959 goda)* (Leningrad, 1959). (Abbreviated in the bibliography as *TezSML59*).

[5] Grigor'ev, "O razvitii strukturnyx i matematičeskix metodov issledovanija jazyka".

formational methods, stylistics). Papers and discussions on linguistic problems figured in the program of the Fourth All-Union Mathematical Congress (Leningrad, 3-12 July), although no special section of the congress was set aside for the purpose.

1962: Publication of books by I. I. Revzin[6] and S. K. Šaumjan[7] seeking to provide, respectively, a general survey of a large part of the subject of mathematical models in linguistics and a detailed mathematical-logical treatment of the particular problems of phonology. Widespread interest in Soviet work in the field was indicated by the fact that one plenary session of the Ninth International Congress of Linguists (Cambridge, Massachusetts, 27-31 August) was devoted to the reading and discussion of N. D. Andreev's paper, "Linguistic theory of translation", reflecting the work of the Leningrad machine translation laboratory and of the recently formed Mathematical Linguistics Group of the Leningrad division of the Academy of Sciences' Linguistic Institute.

## 2. DELIMITATION OF THE SUBJECT

The foregoing catalog is at least sufficient to show that something called "mathematical linguistics" leads a recognized and even a thriving existence in the Soviet academic world. It does not, however, thereby become easy to determine just what recent works by linguists or others are properly "in" the field. A superficial and popular view would assign this label to anything dealing with natural-language material and making use of numbers (in the popular sense, viz. real-number arithmetic). A more sophisticated version would recognize as mathematical also such apparatus as that of abstract algebra or formal logic (cf. the enumeration of methods in the cited article of the Soviet Encyclopedia). Both views are inadequate in that they allow everything to hinge on the "mathematical" part of the label, and neglect (or assume away as obvious) the difficult problem of deciding what makes a study "linguistic". This, which is surely one of the most crucial problems confronting our science today, is one on which satisfactory clarity does not seem to exist anywhere; it remains a subject for cloudy metaphysical profundities or for the dogmatism of schools.

One cannot (especially in a survey of the present kind, which must take cognizance of its place in an overall scheme) simply follow Soviet practice on this point, as reflected say in the editorial policies of various journals.[8] For one thing the guidelines obtained in this way are neither clear nor congruent, and for another, so far as they go, they would lead to much too broad a delimitation of the field for present purposes. One difficulty of this nature is already apparent from the cursory chronolo-

[6] Revzin, *Modeli jazyka*.

[7] Šaumjan, *Problemy teoretičeskoj fonologii*.

[8] Compare – or contrast – the character of articles appearing in the journal *Voprosy jazykoznanija* (*VJa*) and in the series *Problemy kibernetiki* (PK), under the Readings, respectively, of "Prikladnoe i matematičeskoe jazykoznanie" and "Voprosy matematičeskoj lingvistiki".

gy given above: for historical reasons to be touched on later, the link between modern Soviet linguistic research and work on such "applications" as machine translation (and others less publicized, such as coded transmission of messages, information storage and retrieval, voice-directed mechanisms, etc.) is especially close. Yet it seems plain that many of the problems which loom large in such connections are no more essentially concerned with linguistic subject matter *per se* than are, say, the metallurgical problems of typecasting. Engineering solutions in dealing with human language or surrogates for it may certainly be productive of important insights for a science of language, but do not thus become the substance of the science.

On the other hand, in a theoretical direction, linguistics cannot become – some enthusiasms notwithstanding – a branch of mathematics; there is no such branch, and if there were it would mean merely that we needed another name for the study of language in a state of nature. For such a study, abstract properties of formally constructed "languages" are of interest not for their own sake but for their possible usefulness as models which in one way or another serve to increase our understanding of natural languages. This aim may be furthered by the employment of diverse types of usual or unusual mathematical apparatus; it is in any case incorrect to "define" linguistics in terms of some circumscribed class of admissible models.

On this view of the matter (which will certainly not command universal assent, but I do not know of any that does) one can seek to identify those strands in recent Soviet work which properly belong to the subject under consideration. Special comment is perhaps called for with regard to the physical-acoustic investigation of speech sounds, which, like that of non-speech sounds, makes long-established use of special mathematical techniques (Fourier analysis, in particular). For the purposes of the present survey, research in this area and the problem of its relations to linguistic phonology are left out of account.

## 3. GENERAL FEATURES OF THE SOVIET DEVELOPMENT

As was remarked above, although the evolution of mathematical linguistics in the USSR has much in common with that in other countries, certain historical circumstances have tended to shape its course and emphases. In the early 1950's, Soviet linguistics was just emerging from a long period of virtual dormancy (at least so far as serious thinking about basic problems was concerned) imposed by the Marr régime. The Marrist doctrine held in effect that linguistics really has no subject matter of its own, but only the function of a species of marginal commentary on non-linguistic sociological facts. Consequently, in the words of a recent retrospect (1960), "The period of domination by the 'new theory of language' was distinguished by extreme neglect of problems of internal linguistics and of 'speech mechanisms'. Just for this reason, in Soviet linguistics, which strives to draw on everything valuable and fruitful in the world arsenal of linguistic science, a very prominent place should be occupied at the present time by research on basic questions of semiotic, of information theory, and of applied linguistics . . ."[9]

During the period alluded to, it was of course precisely the question of "internal" or "immanent" features of language which was under intensive cultivation in Western Europe and America, in large part and increasingly under the banner of structuralism. By the 1950's this tendency, characterized throughout by the search for logical rigor, had evolved naturally to a stage of explicit rapprochement with the abstract methods of formal logic and mathematics. Another factor (reflected in the foregoing quotation) was, from 1948 on, the development in communications work of the powerful new apparatus of information theory, which quickly captured the imagination of a number of linguists and led to a search for ways of bringing its concepts to bear on linguistic problems.

By virtue of the historical circumstances noted, the impact of these novelties on Soviet linguistic thinking was more abrupt and more nearly simultaneous than it was elsewhere. (It should be remarked that the assimilation of Shannon's information-theory concept was immediate so far as mathematicians were concerned; it is well known that Soviet mathematicians [e.g. Xinčin] made early and important contributions to the development of this theory and in particular to its rigorous axiomatization. But for linguists this and other new ideas seem to form part and parcel of the "structural" reorientation from 1956 on.) One broad effect of this may have been to cause the liberated imagination of workers in the field to soar on occasion to remarkable heights; for an accessible example, cf. the previously mentioned paper by N. D. Andreev for the Ninth International Congress of Linguists, with its sweeping vision of a world-wide network of interconnected "national computers", employing an intermediary language (of the sort being experimented with in Leningrad) to conduct a continuous and instantaneous exchange of scientific information – and waiting to be linked, eventually, into a vaster system for communication with hypothetical extraterrestrial intelligent beings! And other examples could be cited to show that the atmosphere of novel theoretical and technical possibilities has provided a strong stimulus to conjecture and even quite fanciful speculation.[10]

As the quotation above suggests, one feature of the recent period has been the energetic assimilation of both earlier and contemporary work done outside the USSR. Numerous articles, lectures, etc. have been devoted to such matters as: glossematics (at least terminologically quite influential), glottochronology, Harary and Paper's set-theoretic treatment of phoneme distribution, Prague phonology (again very influential, especially via interest in Jakobson's distinctive-feature concept), structural typology, the syntactic connexity investigations of Bar-Hillel, transformation grammar (a subject of lively interest, witness the holding of a conference on "transformational

[9] Editorial, "O perspektivnom plane našix jazykovedčeskix issledovanij na bližajšie gody", *VJa* 9/2 (1960).

[10] Cf. also, e.g., Mel'nikov, "Jazyk mašiny i plan soderžanija", and "O vozmožnosti avtomatizacii lingvističeskix issledovanij".

method" in December 1961 under the auspices of the Academy's Russian language Institute), Yngve's gap analysis and his more recent depth hypothesis, and Zipfian statistics. Translation activity includes not only textbooks (e.g. Gleason's, which devotes considerable attention to mathematical methodology) but also a number of important shorter articles from Western sources.[11]

The programmatic statement of 1960 declares that

> The leading place in the aforementioned scientific trend [toward compensating for earlier neglect of "internal" approaches to language] is occupied by the application of mathematical methods in linguistics, which may permit the exactitude of linguistic analysis and of conclusions from it to be elevated to a new level. Here such problems as the following are important: application of probability analysis, set theory and mathematical statistics, investigation of all "levels" of language structure in connection with the general theory of semiotic and "information theory" – work should be carried on not only on the theoretical plane, but also on every practical one (machine translation, determination of phonological variation and phonetic combinations, systematization of grammatical rules of combinability of morphemes and words into certain possible wholes and determination of classes of these wholes, and also rational rules of planning and composition of various kinds of dictionaries).[12]

One notes the stress on "applications" which was remarked on earlier, in connection with the fact that the radical reshaping of linguistic theory seems to have coincided closely with (or been somewhat anticipated by) the demand for such applications arising from the promise held forth by cybernetics and computer technology. "Mathematical and applied" or "structural and applied" linguistics are commonly mentioned in one breath, so notably and officially (in the second version) in the designation, from 1960, of the relevant section of the Linguistic Institute of the Academy of Sciences; references to the stimulating role of technological developments generally figure even in highly theoretical discussions. It seems not unreasonable to suppose that this ascription of importance to technological factors is really more nearly accurate with respect to the Soviet evolution than it is elsewhere (contrast Chomsky's strictures on this "strange and factually quite incorrect view" of motivations for generative grammar, with particular reference to expression of such an opinion by I. A. Mel'čuk).[13] It is also true that the philosophy of science prevailing in the USSR is insistent on the close interrelationship of theory and practice, whence an emphasis on "engineering" attitudes becomes the more intelligible. One can perhaps detect, however, a tendency to recognize an increasing measure of autonomy for the purely linguistic aspects of such problems.

A symptomatic effect of the comparatively abrupt onset of a new phase might be seen in the disposition of some authors to use the terms "structural" and "mathematical" as virtually interchangeable synonyms in application to linguistic methods and models. Another effect would seem to be that of making the contrast or conflict between the modern and the traditional ("structural" vs. "classical", or the like)

[11] Cf. in particular the series *Novoe v lingvistike*, edited by V. A. Zvegincev (Moscow, 1960, 1962).
[12] Cf. footnote 9.
[13] Chomsky, "The logical basis of linguistic theory", p. 513.

appear sharper than it may for linguists elsewhere in the world, with a consequent tendency for adherents of either sort of view to overstate the differences and to overlook the ways in which modern theories, odd and even outlandish as their symbolic garb may appear, can often be taken just as the formalization of notions already contained or applied in traditional treatments. The progress of innovating tendencies in the Soviet Union has not been without its sharp critics, e.g. B. V. Gornung, who has posed (in order to answer it negatively) the question as to whether structural and traditional linguistics can "coexist",[14] and who, while granting the legitimacy of using mathematical methods, has insisted strongly on their "limited problems and limited scope" as ancillary to linguistic methods properly speaking.[15] Such criticism and that of some of the foregoing lines of thought whose influence was noted above[16] seems to be framed largely in terms of assertions about the philosophical unacceptability of certain ideas, rather than on refutation of specific results, and in the existing intellectual climate it does not appear to be very effective.

## 4. PARTICULAR TRENDS IN SOVIET MATHEMATICAL LINGUISTICS

Mathematical methods and models invite schematic classification, but the grounds adopted for such classifications vary and are not always clear; also, of course, the work of particular individuals may range over a variety of topics. A favored *principium divisionis* with Soviet writers, as with others,[17] is that distinguishing "structural" and "statistical" approaches. So far as this represents a really basic distinction, it would seems to be rather a mathematical than a linguistic one, and comparable say to the distinction between "elementary" and "analytic" methods in number theory, or between "discrete" and "continuous" in topology.[18] In terms of this dichotomy, in the USSR as elsewhere more successful effort has been devoted in the last few years to elaborating the former type of concepts. There is evident moreover a certain differentiation of interests in this respect between the "center" (i.e. primarily Moscow and Leningrad) and the "periphery" of the Soviet academic world (cf. especially the Černovcy conference of September, 1960);[19] this is probably correlated with the "center's" commitment to machine-translation research and for the most part to the attack on

[14] Criticism of a paper by Šaumjan on structural study of meaning, at the 6th plenary session of the committee on problems of lexicology and semasiology of the Academy of Sciences, Literature, and Language Division, October 1960. Cf. "Naučnaja žizn' ", *VJa* 10(1).163 (1961).

[15] Gornung, "Mesto lingvistiki v sisteme nauk i ispol'zovanie v nej metodov drugix nauk", p. 32.

[16] Cf. Zvegincev, "Neopozitivizm i novejšie lingvističeskie napravlenija".

[17] This basis is adopted by Warren Plath, "Mathematical linguistics", in *Trends in European and American linguistics* (Utrecht, 1961).

[18] Cf. on this point, in particular: Andreyev, "Models as a tool in the development of linguistic theory"; Revzin, "Ob otnošenii meždu strukturnymi i statističeskimi metodami"; Zinov'ev, "O matematičeskoj lingvistike".

[19] *Pytannja prykladnoki lingvistyky. Tezy dopovidej mižvuzivs'koji naukovoji konferenciji 22-28 veresnja 1960 roku* (Černivci, 1960).

its problems via the formalization of grammar, which, traditional or modern, offers mostly non-quantitative explicanda and/or explicata. Some interest in statistical methods arises from the same source in connection with the compilation of dictionaries, particularly various specialized lexica aimed at mechanical exploitation.

Another, increasingly popular, principle of classification is the division into "analytic" and "synthetic" models or methods.[20] Intuitively, an analytic scheme, given a language (or, realistically, a sample of the language) produces a systematic description of it, "deciphers" it in some sense, while a synthetic one produces (a sample of) the language from some axiomatically given starting point; it is further frequently proposed that these two kinds of systems should be paired as inverses to one another, a requirement which can easily encounter grave logical difficulties. For all its intuitive plausibility, this distinction tends to become elusive in theoretical contexts, when the difference between "models" and "interpretations" is made to hinge on a sometimes vague notion of degree of abstraction.[21] Recent Soviet investigations show a tendency to focus on the problems of analysis, while regarding those of synthesis as solved at least in principle by the concept of a generative grammar.

A third distinction sometimes stressed is that between "paradigmatic" and "syntagmatic" properties of language models.[22] That the difference intended involves the kinds of classes which play a part in the model is evident, but that it does so in any really significant way is not always clear. Possibly what is felt to be essential here is a division between descriptions constructed respectively with and without reference to classes of elements not obtainable by operations on the linear ordering of such elements (e.g. the "neighborhoods" of the Kulagina set-theoretic model). At all events it is difficult to escape the impression that a preference for paradigmatic models and a feeling that a purely "syntagmatic" treatment leaves essential things unsaid may reflect, even at the level of abstract discussion, native experience with a highly inflected language and perhaps habituation to its traditional grammar, and correspond to the preference which Russian linguists using more traditional terms frequently express for words over morphemes.

The set-theoretic model of language published by O. S. Kulagina in 1957[23] excited a great deal of interest from its first appearance, and has since served as a starting point for numerous elaborations and variants. It assumes as given a finite or countable set of "marked phrases" (finite strings in a finite alphabet, or vocabulary, since the elements are supposed to be interpreted as words), and allows replacement of element-occurrences by other elements or by subsets of the whole alphabet, the definition of "markedness" of the phrase being extended to embrace the latter possibility. Replacement preserving markedness is used to induce an equivalence ("B-equivalence")

[20] Cf. Fitialov, "Formal'no-matematičeskie modeli jazykov i struktura algoritmov perevoda"; Revzin, *Modeli jazyka*.
[21] On the general notion of "models" cf. Zinov'ev & Revzin, "Logičeskaja model' kak sredstvo naučnogo poznanija".
[22] Revzin, *op. cit.*, p. 16.
[23] Cf. footnote 2.

and this to define the "derived partition" based on any arbitrarily given partition of the underlying set. The principal objective of the original formulation was the explication of the troublesomely vague traditional concept of part of speech in terms of "type", defined as the derived partition of the partition into "neighborhoods", understood to answer to the assignment of word-forms to paradigms.

On this basis Kulagina and others have built up various additional concepts, such as those of "uniformity" and "simplicity" as properties of languages (of those with respectively at least and at most one element occupying each cell of a cross-cutting classification). V. A. Uspenskij pointed out that the definition of "type" fails of its aim (in terms of its intended interpretation) for some theoretically possible relationships between given and derived partitions, and proposed to define a "regular" language as one for which the definition does not fail in this way.[24] The original scheme made no provision for homonymy, although this is a problem which looms large in Russian grammar (e.g. homonymy of noun case-forms);[25] proposals for incorporating such a possibility, by defining "elementary grammatical category" in such a way as to determine in general overlapping classes, were made by R. L. Dobrušin,[26] and more recent suggestions for refining the treatment of classes by A. A. Xolodovič.[27] It its original version the relation of Kulagina's model to the "analytic-synthetic" dichotomy is not clear, though it owes a great deal to the schemes of distributional analysis developed by structural linguists. In more recent writings it tends to be regarded as of interest mostly from the analytic standpoint (whence problems arise out of questions left open to begin with, e.g. that of finite or transfinite character of the "set of marked phrases")[28] and efforts are made to work it into analytic counterparts of various types of synthetic or generative grammar. Extending the replacement operation to sequences of more than one element gives rise to the notion of "configuration", similar to that of constituent,[29] and I. I. Revzin has made an (admittedly tentative and inadequate) attempt to elaborate this further into a system of "transformational analysis".[30]

In connection with the "analytic-synthetic" distinction, notice should be taken of the influential part played in Soviet thinking by the idea of an "intermediary language" (*jazyk-posrednik*); this, like much of the model-building activity mentioned above, is closely connected with machine-translation work, and some of its popularity stems from a rather excessively simple argument about economy of translation systems: given $n$ languages, $n(n-1)$ binary algorithms of translation would be needed, but by going through an intermediary this can be reduced to $2n$; one suspects, however, that if it were a question of translating between say Russian and Bulgarian by means of an

[24] Uspenskij, "K opredeleniju časti reči v teoretiko-množestvennoj sisteme jazyka".
[25] On this question, and suggestions for exploiting case-form homonymy for simplifying description of the language, cf. Padučeva, "Nekotorye zamečanija o padežnoj sisteme suščestvitel'nogo".
[26] Dobrušin, "Èlementarnaja grammatičeskaja kategorija".
[27] Xolodovič, "Opyt teorii podklassov slov".
[28] Revzin, "O nekotoryx ponjatijax teoretiko-množestvennoj koncepcii jazyka".
[29] Kulagina, "Ob odnom sposobe opredelenija grammatičeskix ponjatij".
[30] Revzin, *Modeli jazyka*, pp. 145-152, 166f.

intermediary language equally appropriate for Chinese, it would be necessary to recognize something like a "triangular inequality" as relevant to the problem, and it has been justly pointed out that human languages, with all their quaint features, probably resemble one another more than any of them do the constructed languages of logic or computer programming (to which kinds the "intermediary language" is usually supposed to belong, though it assumes somewhat Protean forms in various discussions).[31] At all events, the concept is surely of linguistic interest if only for its bearing on the vexed question of meaning.

The developments considered above are overwhelmingly of the "structural" kind; clearly much of their interest resides in discovering that natural languages are a great deal more complicated than one or another simple model, i.e. such languages generally fail to live up to the austere requirements of "uniformity", "simplicity", etc. It is sometimes suggested[32] that actual languages can be significantly characterized by the extent to which they deviate from such ideal schemes, and if such suggestions were worked out in detail – as so far as I know they have not been – this would seems to call for quantitative or measure-theoretic methods, hence for the model's sharing essential properties with the "statistical" kind; this latter label is really unsatisfactory, but owes its popularity to the fact that probability is the only part of measure theory commonly considered in connection with linguistic problems.

With respect to the aforementioned dichotomy, an effort at an eclectic synthesis of both approaches, with practical ends in view, exists in the shape of N. D. Andreev's "statistical-combinatorial algorithm"[33] for language analysis. As the name implies, this is intended to use both probabilistic and algebraic methods to produce a (primarily algebraic) description from a text sample, assumed given with a segmentation into words, or in an alphabet including a "blank". The procedure which Andreev describes involves investigating the material statistically, partitioning the sample space and singling out maximally probable elements, and forming new sample spaces on the basis of the results of preceding operations, in such a way as to identify certain especially frequent and redundant portions of words as "affixes" and their remainders as "bases", this process to be carried on until it is no longer efficacious according to some fixed criterion. (The criterion is supposed to be such that, for a language in which word equals morpheme, the procedure will apply vacuously.) This is coupled with classifying operations similar to those of the Kulagina scheme, on the material thus placed in an appropriate form for such handling, and eventual further procedures are envisaged to elicit syntactic relationships. The whole is designed to be realized automatically, and it is reported that practical results have been obtained in particular in identifying Russian adjective endings (which would appear to be an especially

[31] For a survey of six types of "intermediary language" concepts, cf. Andreev & Fitialov, "Jazyk-posrednik mašinnogo perevoda i principy ego postroenija".

[32] E. g. by Revzin, *op. cit.*, pp. 85-90.

[33] Cf. especially Andreev, "Modelirovanie jazyka na baze ego statističeskoj i teoretiko-množestvennoj struktury", also other writings of the same author.

favorable case by virtue of their unusually distinctive shapes). Since the scheme is meant to be justified by practical results, it is perhaps beside the point to observe that it involves strong assumptions about the nature of the given material and has a number of features that appear quite *ad hoc* (e.g., why divide a set of probabilities into upper and lower subsets at one point rather than another? – but even a small displacement of this point could radically affect the further course of the analysis). However, such features tend to diminish its strictly linguistic interest.

Andreev has also proposed, though not in any detail, probabilistic approaches to some other problems: transformation grammar[34] and semantics, the latter in terms of six-dimensional vectors to be determined from a rather heterogeneous array of data.[35]

Linguistic statistics of one kind or another are of course no novelty, though relatively little such work has been done by linguists (an exception is the work of Zipf, whose "law" and its refinements continue to be an object of interest also in the Soviet Union),[36] and most of it has dealt with written material[37] – a famous example is A. A. Markov's use of Russian letter-frequency data as illustration for the mathematical theory which bears his name. Whatever philosophical arguments may exist for and against the relevance of quantitative data to various problems, this situation does no credit to the courage of linguists' convictions; apparently everyone believes strongly enough in letters, printed words, etc. to count them, but the linguist to whom, say, phonemes or past participles are "realer" than print is likely to be nonetheless seized with misgivings at the idea of placing these entities in correspondence with the inexorable series 1, 2, . . . . The misgivings may be justified; if so, they ought to be investigated, and, if possible, removed.

I am not convinced that this long-standing situation has changed fundamentally in the USSR in the recent period, even though a large number of research projects of a statistical nature are reported (languages on which frequency investigations of various kind and scope have been made include Russian, Belorussian, Ukrainian, English, French, Rumanian, and Vietnamese, in addition to the widely publicized work on deciphering Maya inscriptions),[38] and though some of the few which have been published in accessible form show a markedly improved level of linguistic sophistication over what used to be the rule. Soviet writers on linguistic theory commonly assign an important place to its statistical aspects[39] and to the illuminating possibilities of new

[34] Andreyev, "Models as a tool in the development of linguistic theory".

[35] Andreyev, "Linguistic aspects of translation", p.7f.

[36] Cf. Frumkina, "K voprosu o tak nazyvaemom zakone 'Cipfa'"; Segal, "Nekotorye utočnenija verojatnostnoj modeli Cipfa".

[37] It is interesting to note in this connection that one of the byproducts of work on machine handling of (usually written) language material has been a recrudescence of interest in graphic representations for their own sake. Among Soviet authors this tendency is shown by T. M. Nikolaeva (well-known otherwise in machine-translation research); cf. her articles: "Pis'mennaja reč' i specifika ee izučenija" and "Klassifikacija russkix grafem".

[38] Cf. Knorozov, "Mašinnaja dešifrovka pis'ma majja", and the counter-polemic Letter to the Editors by S. L. Sobolev, *VJa* 11(3).147 (1962).

[39] Cf. note 18 and: Ivanov, "Matematičeskaja lingvistika"; Frumkina, "Primenenie statistističeskix metodov v jazykoznanii;" Toporov, "Vvedenie verojatnosti v jazykoznanie i ego posledstvija".

developments in cybernetics and information theory, but it is not clear that sufficiently well-defined research goals exist or that new mathematical apparatus has been effectively integrated into the conceptual framework of linguistics. Consequently much of the concrete work done is open to criticism on grounds of "insufficient mathematical exactitude, excessive preoccupation with mathematical terminology and, most important, a not-always-clear conception of the ultimate purpose of research".[40]

A large amount of statistical investigation has been motivated by an interest in literary style, particularly in the group centering around the mathematician A. N. Kolmogorov.[41] Here, in a sometimes disputed border zone of linguistics, an effort is made (along lines similar to those adopted by some workers in Western Europe and in Poland) to use methods of mathematical statistics and communication theory to resolve elusive problems of artistic value, individual stylistic traits of authors, etc. This is one of the cases in which it is difficult to draw a line between what properly belongs to the subject matter of linguistics and what does not, For all the outward differences, the question here is remarkably similar to that which arises in connection with machine-translation research: both lines of thought involve forms of language and both, though in different ways, have a bearing on the knot of concepts commonly lumped together as "meaning" – which (as a problem, not as a *deus ex machina* providing pseudo-solutions) can scarcely be exorcized from linguistics and leave much of interest. As to the apparatus of information theory, after all due warnings have been voiced about the inadvisability of confusing such notions as "information" and "redundancy" with their everyday homonyms, it most surely be recognized that this constitutes an explication of part of what is meant by meaning, though one which has some disconcerting properties when compared with intuition.

Information-theory concepts have been stressed by a number of Soviet linguists, notably by E. V. Padučeva, R. G. Piotrovskij, and V. V. Ivanov.[42] The writings of the last-mentioned, in particular, range over a wide variety of subjects; he has advanced interesting ideas in connection with the possible use of mathematical-linguistic methods in the comparative-historical field. The problems which arise here have considerable points of contact with those which invite algebraic solutions in translation,[43] and, on the other hand, the idea naturally arises of defining "linguistic time" in relation to communication-theory entropy in somewhat the same fashion in which physical time and entropy are related.[44] (The "linguistic time" concept suggests glottochronologic methods, but Ivanov reports dissatisfaction with the results of his experimentation

[40] Remark ascribed to Frumkina at conference on structural and mathematical linguistics in Černivci, September 1960 (cf. "Naučnaja žizn'", *VJa* 10(1).157 (1961).

[42] Cf. Ryčkova, "Lingvistika i matematika".

[42] Cf. Padučeva, "Statističeskoe issledovanie slogovoj struktury" and "Vozmožnosti izučenija jazyka metodami teorii informacii"; Piotrovskij, "Problema mesta v slove u elementov, nesuščix informaciju"; Grigor'ev, "O kode i jazyka"; Jaglom, Dobrušin, & Jaglom, "Teorija informacii i lingvistika".

[43] Ivanov, "Teorija otnošenij meždu jazykovymi sistemami i osnovanija sravnitel'no-istoričeskogo jazykoznanija".

[44] Ivanov, "Verojatnostnoe opredelenie lingvističeskogo vremeni".

with these). Proposals for formalizing the vague appeal to probabilistic factors which often figures in discussions of linguistic evolution have also been made by A. B. Dolgopol'skij,[45] and M. I. Steblin-Kamenskij has contributed some interesting views on synchrony and diachrony.[46] It might be remarked that comparative-historical linguistics is renascent in the USSR, after having suffered almost total eclipse during the Marr period.

Notice should be taken here of some other quantitatively oriented work: V. M. Zolotarev's proposal of a stochastic-process model for the sentence,[47] Ju. K. Lekomcev's investigation of Vietnamese constructions along lines similar to those incorporated in the Andreev algorithm,[48] and I. A. Mel'čuk's examination of the problem of "idioms" in terms of numbers of permitted combinations;[49] also of the publication of descriptive statistical studies dealing e.g. with frequencies of phonemes,[50] of lexical items,[51] of grammatical forms,[52] and sentence lengths.[53]

As some of the topics noted above already illustrate, classifications by the properties of models or methods tend to cut across the long-standing division of linguistic subject matter into phonology, morphology, and syntax, and modern theories perhaps to deny that such levels have any significant degree of autonomy. An exception to this tendency can be seen in the writings of S. K. Šaumjan, focusing closely on problems of phonology and the endeavor to complete the logical formalization of phonological theory begun by the Prague School.[54] Šaumjan holds that attempts to construct phonology on a single level inevitably lead to certain "antinomies", and that to avoid these it is necessary to use a "two-level theory of phonology", in which observational facts and "constructs" are connected by correspondence rules: some of the properties usually ascribed to phonemes, say, belong to the former kind of entities, some to the latter. In working out and defending this view, the author makes increasing use of formal apparatus of mathematical logic (set-theory and relation-theory concepts, mostly), so that his treatment has points of contact with those of some Western investigators (e.g. Ungeheuer, Halle), especially since a prominent role is assigned to the Jakobsonian scheme of binary distinctive features, which of course lends itself readily to algebraic representation. (Šaumjan is far from being the only Soviet linguist to be strongly interested in the last-mentioned scheme; but much of this interest translates

45 Dolgopol'skij, "Faktory razvitija jazyka i častotnost' jazykovyx znakov".
46 Steblin-Kamenskij, "Struktural'naja točka zrenija v istorii jazyka".
47 Zolotarev, "Verojatnostnaja model' predloženija".
48 Lekomcev, "Struktura v'etnamskoj glagol'noj sintagmy".
49 Mel'čuk, "O terminax 'ustojčivost' ' i 'idiomatičnost' ' ".
50 Cf. Zinder. "O lingvističeskoj verojatnosti".
51 Cf. Frumkina, "Statističeskaja struktura leksiki Puškina"; Belonogov, "O nekotoryx statističeskix zakonomernostjax v russkoj pis'mennoj reči".
52 Cf. Nikonov, "Bor'ba padežej".
53 Cf. Lesskis, "O razmerax predloženij v russkoj naučnoj i xudožestvennoj proze 60-x godov XIX v."
54 Šaumjan, "O suščnosti strukturnoj lingvistiki", "Der Gegenstand der Phonologie", "Generalizacija i postulirovanie konstruktov v izučenii struktury jazyka", "Operacionnye opredelenija i ix primenenie v fonologii", "Dvuxstupenčataja teorija fonemy i differencial'nyx èlementov", "Concerning the logical basis of linguistic theory", and *Problemy teoretičeskoj fonologii.*

itself into research in acoustic phonetics, outside the purview of the present summary.[55])

In another border area, viz. psychology, mention should be made of the work of N. I. Žinkin, in view of the conspicuous interest in formal-logical modelling of phenomena (influenced particularly, it seems, by the ideas of Church) expressed already in this author's 1958 book[56] and still more in some of his recent papers. Žinkin has treated in this fashion, among other things, his experimental study of the vocalizations of baboons – surely one of the most exotic "languages" to have been so dealt with.[57]

## 5. CONCLUSIONS

Within less than a decade, mathematical linguistics in the Soviet Union has developed into a recognized discipline, though, naturally enough, its precise outlines and content are still uncertain in many respects (and this could be said also of much older fields). The suddenness of this development and the resulting break with traditional approaches has perhaps been sharper here than in other parts of the world, and the effect of this and possibly some other localized factors can be traced on work done to date; but, by and large, the international communicability of results in this area is probably greater than in linguistics otherwise. The closeness of the tie between theory and "applications" (especially machine translation) is emphasized in the USSR, and this, in conjunction with other factors (such as the general absence among linguists of long-standing commitments to theories of a formal or semi-formal kind) leads to a certain eclecticism in choice of methods.

It must be noted that, in the USSR as elsewhere, the growth of this trend has not proceeded without producing its excesses and aberrations; Soviet publications are by no means free of the sort of thing which betrays a naive belief that just adopting mathematical terminology or literal symbolism somehow automatically confers rigor on an argument. There is just enough truth in this to make it dangerous (it has been remarked that in mathematics a good notation is half the battle), but in some instances the terminology degenerates into jargon, and it is perfectly possible to write nonsense in an impeccable notation. One trusts that such instances will in the course of time become fewer and disappear.

That speculation at present frequently ranges ahead of concrete research should not, however, be counted as a defect. In the present stage it would be rash to predict which of today's proposals will eventually be included among the solid gains of linguistic science and which will be rejected as *hubristikà kaì geloîa* (as Socrates calls his own linguistic theorizing). A certain *hubris* is natural to young and rapidly developing fields of knowledge, and portends well for their survival into a healthy and balanced maturity.

[55] Cf. for a most recent example at present writing: Kibrik, "K voprosu o metode opredelenija differencial'nyx priznakov pri spektral'nom analize (na materiale glasnyx novogrečeskogo jazyka)".
[56] Žinkin, *Mexanizmy reči.*
[57] Žinkin, "Zvukovaja kommunikativnaja sistema obez'jan" and "Four communicative systems and four languages".

## BIBLIOGRAPHY


Andreev, N. D., "Mašinnyj perevod i problema jazyka-posrednika," *VJa* 6/5 (1957).

—, "Modelirovanie jazyka na baze ego statističeskoj i teoretiko-množestvennoj struktury", in *Tezisy soveščanija po matematičeskoj lingvistike* (*15-21 aprelja 1959 goda*) (Leningrad, 1959). [Hereafter *TezSML59*.]

—, and Fitialov, S. Ja., "Jazyk-posrednik mašinnogo perevoda i principy ego postroenija", in *TezSML59* (Leningrad, 1959).

—, and Zinder, L. R., "Osnovnye problemy prikladnoj lingvistiki", *VJa* 8/4 (1959).

Andreyev, N. D., "Linguistic aspects of translation", *Preprints of papers for the Ninth International Congress of Linguists* (*August 27-31, 1962*) (Cambridge, Mass., 1962). (Addition).

—, "Models as a tool in the development of linguistic theory", *Word* 18.186-197 (1962).

Apresjan, Ju. D., "Ispol'zovanie strukturnyx metodov dlja sostavlenija slovarja semantičeskix polej", *Tezisy dokladov na VI plenarnom zasedanii komissii, posvjaščennom sovremennoj problematike leksikologii i semasiologii* (Moscow, 1960).

—, "K voprosu o strukturnoj leksikologii", *VJa* 11/3 (1962).

Artemov, V. A., "Primenenie statističeskix metodov v èksperimental'no-fonetičeskom i psixologičeskom izučenii reči", in *Voprosy statistiki reči* (Leningrad, 1958).

Bagrinovskaja, G. M., Kulagina, O. S., Lyapunov, A. A., Mel'čuk, I. A., and Mološnaja, T. N., "Nekotorye voprosy matematičeskoj lingvistiki, voznikajuščie na počve mašinnogo perevoda", *MPPL* 6 (1961).

Belokrinickaja, S. S. et al., "Različnye tipy omonimii i sposoby ix različenija pri mašinnom perevode (na materiale anglijskogo, nemeckogo, russkogo, kitajskogo i japonskogo jazykov)", *VJa* 9/2 (1960).

Belonogov, G. G., "Nekotorye statističeskie xarakteristiki russkix pečatnyx tekstov", in *Pytannja prykladnoji lingvistyky* (Černivci, 1960).

—, "O nekotoryx statističeskix zakonomernostjax v russkoj pis'mennoj reči", *VJa* 11/1 (1962).

—, Grigor'ev, V. I., and Kotov, R. G. "Avtomatičeskoe leksičeskoe kodirovanie soobščenij", *VJa* 9/4 (1960).

Berkov, V. P., "Grammatičeskaja informacija i informacionnyj jazyk", in *TezSML59* (Leningrad, 1959).

—, and Ermov, V. A., "O popytkax mašinnogo perevoda", *VJa* 4/6 (1955).

—, and Gurov, N. V., "Principy postroenija slovarja jazyka-posrednika", in *TezSML 59* (Leningrad, 1959).

Borodin, V. V., "K modeli opisanija jazyka", in *Doklady na Konferencii po obrabotke informacii, mašinnomu perevodu i avtomatičeskomu čteniju teksta* (Moscow, 1961). [Hereafter *DokK*].

Brudnyj, A. A., "K primeneniju metodov prikladnoj lingvistiki v issledovanii semasiologičeskoj korreljacii", in *Pytannja prykladnoji lingvistyky* (Černivci, 1960).

Cejtin, G. A., "K voprosu o postroenii matematičeskix modelej jazyka", in *DokK*, 3 (Moscow, 1961).
—, "O promežutočnom ètape pri perevode s estestvennogo jazyka na jazyk isčislenija predikatov", in *DokK* (Moscow, 1961).
Chomsky, N., "The logical basis of linguistic theory", *Preprints of papers for the Ninth International Congress of Linguists* (Cambridge, Mass., 1962).
Dobrušin, R. L., "Èlementarnaja grammatičeskaja kategorija", *Bjulleten' ob"edinenija po problemam mašinnogo perevoda*, 5 (1957). [Hereafter *BOPMP*].
—, "Matematičeskie metody v lingvistike" (priloženie), *Matematičeskoe prosveščenie* 6 (1961).
Dolgopol'skij, A. B., "Faktory razvitija jazyka i častotnost' jazykovyx znakov", in *TezSML59* (Leningrad, 1959).
Evreinov, E. V., Kosarev, Ju. G., and Ustinov, V. A., *Issledovanie rukopisej drevnix maj ja s pomošč'ju elektronnoj vyčislitel'noj mašiny. Predvaritel'nye rezul'taty* (Novosibirsk, 1961).
Fitialov, S. Ja., "Formal'no-matematičeskie modeli jazykov i struktura algoritmov perevoda", in *TezSML59* (Leningrad, 1959).
—, "O postroenii formal'noj morfologii v svjazi s mašinnym perevodom", in *DokK* (Moscow, 1961).
Frumkina, R. M., "K voprosu o tak nazyvaemom 'zakone Cipfa'", *VJa* 10/2 (1961).
—, "Metodika sostavlenija statističeskix slovarej", in *TezSML59* (Leningrad, 1959).
—, "Primenenie statističeskix metodov v jazykoznanii", *VJa* 9/4 (1960).
—, "Statističeskaja struktura leksiki Puškina", *VJa* 9/3 (1960).
—, "Statističeskie zakonomernosti v jazyke i reči", in *Pytannja prykladnoji lingvistyky* (Cernivci, 1960).
—, and Zolotarev, V. M., "K verojatnostnoj modeli predloženija", in *TezSML59* (Leningrad, 1959).
Gačečiladze, T. G., Cercvadze, G. N., and Čikoidze, G. B., "Nekotorye zamečanija k metodu analiza probelov", in *TezSML59* (Leningrad, 1959).
Golovin, B. N., "O vošmožnostjax količestvennoj xarakteristiki rečevyx stilej", in *Tezisy dokladov Mežvuzovskoj konferencii po stilistike xudožestvennoj literatury* (Moscow, 1961).
Gornung, B. V., "Mesto lingvistiki v sisteme nauk i ispol'zovanie v nej metodov drugix nauk", *VJa* 9/4 (1960).
Grigor'ev, V. I., "O kode i jazyke", *VJa* 8/6 (1959).
—, Review of M. Halle, *The sound pattern of Russian* in *VJa* 10/1 (1961).
Grigor'ev, V. P., "O razvitii strukturnyx i matematičeskix metodov issledovanija", *VJa* 9/4 (1960).
Ivanov, Vjač. Vs., "Jazyk v sopostavlenii s drugimi sredstvami peredači i xranenija informacii", in *DokK* (Moscow, 1961).
—,"Lingvističeskie voprosy sozdanija mašinnogo jazyka dlja informacionnoj mašiny", in *Materialy po mašinnomu perevodu*, 1 (Leningrad, 1958). [Hereafter *MMP*].

—, "Matematičeskaja lingvistika", *Bol'šaja sovetskaja ènciklopedija*, 2-oe izd., 51 (1958).

—, "O postroenii informacionnogo jazyka dlja tekstov po deskriptivnoj lingvistike", in *DokK*, 7 (Moscow, 1961).

—, "Ponjatie nejtralizacii v morfologii i leksike", *BOPMP* 5 (1957).

—, "Teorija otnošenij meždu jazykovymi sistemami i osnovanija sravnitel'no-istoričeskogo jazykoznanija", in *TezSML59* (Leningrad, 1959).

—, "Tipologija i sravnitel'no-istoričeskoe jazykoznanie", *VJa* 7/5 (1958).

—, "Verojatnostnoe opredelenie lingvističeskogo vremeni", in *Voprosy statistiki reči* (Leningrad, 1958).

—, "Lingvističeskie voprosy stixotvornogo perevoda", in *Mašinnyj perevod.* Trudy Instituta točnoj mexaniki i vyčislitel'noj texniki SSSR, 2 (1961).

—, "O priemlemosti fonologičeskix modelej", *Trudy Instituta točnoj mexaniki i vyčislitel'noj texniki SSSR*, 2 (1961).

Jaglom, A. M., and Jaglom, I. M. *Verojatnost' i informacija* (Moscow, 1960).

Jaglom, I. M., Dobrušin, R. L., and Jaglom, A. M., "Teorija informacii i lingvistika", *VJa* 9/1 (1960).

Kaufman, S. I., "Ob imennom xaraktere texničeskogo stilja (na materiale amerikanskoj literatury)", *VJa* 10/5 (1961).

Kibrik, A. E., "K voprosu o metode opredelenija differencial'nyx priznakov pri spektral'nom analize (na materiale glasnyx novogrečeskogo jazyka)", *VJa* 11/5 (1962).

Knorozov, Ju. V., "Mašinnaja dešifrovka pis'majja", *VJa* 11/1 (1962).

Kolmogorov, A. N., and Kondratov, A. M., "Ritmika poèm Majakovskogo", *VJa* 11/3 (1962).

Kolšanskij, G. V., "V čem različie znakovyx sistem?", *Voprosy filosofii* 14/5 (1960).

Kondratov, A. M., "Èvoljucija ritmiki V. V. Majakovskogo", *VJa* 11/5 (1962).

Koptilov, V. V., "Opyt primenenija statistiki k izučeniju zakonomernostej ukrainskogo udarenija", in *Pytannja prykladnoji lingvistyky* (Černivci, 1960).

Kulagina, O. S., "Ob odnom sposobe opredelenija grammatičeskix ponjatij na baze teorii množestv", *Problemy kibernetiki*, 1 (1958).

—, "Ob odnom sposobe opredelenija lingvističeskix ponjatij", *BOPMP* 3 (1957).

—, and Mel'čuk, I. A., "Mašinnyj perevod s francuzskogo jazyka na russkij", *VJa* 5/5 (1956).

Kuznecov, P. S., "Ob opredelenii fonemy", *BOPMP* 5 (1957).

—, "O differencial'nyx priznakax fonem", *VJa* 7/1 (1958).

—, Ljapunov, A. A., and Reformatskij, A. A., "Osnovnye problemy mašinnogo perevoda", *VJa* 5/5 (1956).

Lejkina, B. M., "Dva tipa grammatičeskoj informacii v ix otnošenii k jazyku posredniku", in *TezSML59* (Leningrad, 1959).

Lekomcev, Ju. K., "Ob odnom sposobe opisanija sočetaemosti fonem v sloge (na

materiale klassičeskogo tibetskogo jazyka)", in *Sbornik pamjati Ju. N. Rerixa* (= *Kratkie soobščenija Instituta narodov Azii*, 57) (Moscow, 1961).
—, "Osnovnye položenija glossematiki", *VJa* 11/4 (1962).
—, "Struktura v'etnamskoj glagol'noj sintagmy", in *Voprosy statistiki reči* (Leningrad, 1958).
—, "Zamečanija k voprosu o dvustoronnem jazykovom znake", *VJa* 10/2 (1961).
Lesskis, G. A., "O razmerax predloženij v russkoj naučnoj i xudožestvennoj proze 60-x godov XIX v.", *VJa* 11/2 (1962).
Mel'cuk, I. A. "K vopro su o 'grammatičeskom' v jazyke-posrednike", in *TezSML59* (Leningrad, 1959).
—, "O terminax 'ustojčivost'' i 'idiomatičnost''", *VJa* 9/4 (1960).
—, "Statistika i zavisimost' roda francuzskix suščestvitel'nyx ot okončanija", in *Voprosy statistiki reči* (Leningrad, 1958).
Mel'nikov, G. P., "Jazyk mašiny i plan soderžanija (o putjax sozdanija samoobučajuščejsja mašiny-perevodčika)," in *TezSML59* (Leningrad, 1959).
—, "O vozmožnosti avtomatizacii lingvističeskix issledovanij", in *TezSML59* (Leningrad, 1959).
Mološnaja, T. N., "Transformacionnyj analiz kak metod izučenija sintaksisa jazyka", in *Pytannja prykladnoji lingvistyky* (Černivci, 1960).
Nikolaeva, T. M., "Klassifikacija russkix grafem", in *DokK*, 6 (Moscow, 1961).
—, "Pis'mennaja reč' i specifika ee izučenija", *VJa* 10/3 (1961).
—, "Vybor vida glagola pri pomošči konteksta", *MPPL* 2 (1959).
Nikonov, V. A., "Bor'ba padežej", *International journal of Slavic linguistics and poetics* 4 (1961).
"O perspektivnom plane našix jazykovedčeskix issledovanij na bližajšie gody", Editorial, *VJa* 9/2 (1960).
Padučeva, E. V., "Klassifikacija složnyx predloženij v svjazi s postroeniem pravil obrazovanija dlja standartizovannogo russkogo jazyka", in *DokK* (Moscow 1961).
—, "Nekotorye zamečanija o padežnoj sisteme suščestvitel'nogo v russkom jazyke", in *TezSML59* (Leningrad, 1959).
—, "Opisanie sintagm russkogo jazyka (v svjazi s postroeniem algoritma mašinnogo perevoda)", *VJa* 10/4 (1961).
—, Review of N. Chomsky, *Syntactic structures* in *VJa* 8/1 (1959).
—, "Statističeskoe issledovanie slogovoj struktury", in *Voprosy statistiki reči* (Leningrad, 1958).
—, "Vozmožnosti izučenija jazyka metodami teorii informacii", in *DokK* (Moscow, 1961).
Pazuxin, R. V., "Rečevaja informacija i uslovija obščenija", in *Pytannja prykladnoji lingvistiky* (Černivci, 1960).
Pelevina, N. F., "Ustanovlenie ètimologičeskogo toždestva s pomošč'ju umnoženija verojatnostej", in *Pytannja prykladnoji lingvistyky* (Černivci, 1960).
Perebejnos, V. I., "Ob ispol'zovanii strukturnyx metodov dlja razgraničenija značenij

mnogoznačnogo glagola (na materiale glagola *make*)", *VJa* 11/3 (1962).
Piotrovskij, R. G., "Nekotorye voprosy statističeskix issledovanij leksičeskix grupp", in *Voprosy statistiki reči* (Leningrad, 1958).
—, "Problema mesta v slove u èlementov, nesuščix informaciju", in *TezSML59* (Leningrad,1959).
—, "Zagadnienia językoznawcze przekładu maszynowego", *Kwartalnik neofilologiczny* 8/1 (1961).
*Pytannja prykladnoji lingvistyky. Tezy dopovidej mižvuzivs'koji naukovoji konferenciji 22-28 veresnja 1960 roku* (Černivci, 1960).
Reformatskij, A. A., "Čto takoe strukturalizm?", *VJa* 6/6 (1957).
—, "Dixotomičeskaja klassifikacija differencial'nyx priznakov i fonematičeskaja model' jazyka", in *Voprosy teorii jazyka v sovremennom zarubežnom jazykoznanii* (Moscow, 1961).
Revzin, I. I., *Modeli jazyka* (Moscow, 1962).
—, "Ob otnošenii meždu strukturnymi i statističeskimi metodami v sovremennoj lingvistike", in *Voprosy statistiki reči* (Leningrad, 1958).
—, "O logičeskoj forme lingvističeskix opredelenij", in *Primenenie logiki v nauke i texnike* (Moscow, 1961).
—, "O nekotoryx ponjatijax teoretiko-množestvennoj koncepcii jazyka", *VJa* 9/6 (1960).
—, "O ponjatii 'množestva otmečennyx fraz' v teoretiko-množestvennoj koncepcii O. S. Kulaginoj", in *TezSML59* (Leningrad, 1959).
—, "Struktural'naja lingvistika, semantika i problemy izučenija slova", *VJa* 6/2 (1957).
—, "Ustanovlenie sintaksičeskix svjazej v mašinnom perevode metodom Ajdukeviča-Bar-Xillela i v terminax konfiguracionnogo analiza", in *DokK*, 2 (Moscow, 1961).
—, and Rozencvejg, V. Ju., "K obosnavaniju lingvističeskoj teorii perevoda", *VJa* 11/1 (1961).
—, and Toporov, V. N., "Novoe issledovanie po stixovedeniju", *VJa* 11/3 (1962).
Rozencvejg, V. Ju., "Obščaja lingvističeskaja teorija perevoda i matematičeskaja lingvistika", in *TezSML59* (Leningrad, 1959).
Ryčkova, N. G., "Lingvistika i matematika", *Nauka i žizn'* 28.76-77 (1961).
Šaumjan, S. K., "Concerning the logical basis of linguistic theory", in *Preprints of papers for the Ninth International Congress of Linguists* (*August 27-31, 1962*), pp. 93-95 (Cambridge, Mass., 1962).
—, "Der Gegenstand der Phonologie", *ZPhon* 10.193-203 (1957).
—, "Dvuxstupenčataja teorija fonemy i differencial'nyx èlementov", *VJa* 9/5 (1960).
—, "Generalizacija i postulirovanie konstruktov v izučenii struktury jazyka", in *TezSML59* (Leningrad, 1959).
—, "O nekotoryx voprosax fonologii',' *IzvAN* 12/6 (1953).
—, "Operacionnye opredelenija i ix primenenie v fonologii", in *Primenenie logiki v nauke i texnike* (Moscow, 1960).

—, "O suščnosti struktornoj lingvistiki", *VJa* 5/5 (1956).

—, "Panxroničeskaja sistema differencial'nyx èlementov i dvuxstupenčataja teorija fonologii", in *Pytannja prykladnoji lingvistyky* (Černivci, 1960).

—, "Preobrazovanie informacii v processe poznanija i dvuxstupenčataja teorija strukturnoj lingvistiki", in *DokK* (Moscow, 1961).

—, "Problema fonemy", *IzvAN* 11/4 (1952).

—, *Problemy teoretičeskoj fonologii* (Moscow, 1962).

—, *Strukturnaja lingvistika kak immanentnaja teorija jazyka* (Moscow, 1958).

—, "Strukturnye metody izučenija značenij", in *Tezisy dokladov na VI plenarnom zasedanii komissii, posvjaščennom sovremennoj problematike leksikologii i semasiologii* (Moscow, 1960).

Segal, D. M., "Nekotorye utočnenija verojatnostnoj modeli Cipfa", *MMPL* 5 (1961).

Steblin-Kamenskij, M. I., "Neskol'ko zamečanij o strukturalizme", *VJa* 6/1 (1957).

—, " Struktural'naja točka zrenija v istorii jazyka", in *Pytannja prykladnoji lingvistyky* (Černivci, 1960).

Suprun, A. E., "O nekotoryx funkcijax i posledstvijax izbytočnosti jazykovoj informacii", in *Pytannja prykladnoji lingvistyky* (Černivci, 1960).

Teplovaja, I. M., Potjavin, V. M., and Agraev, V. A., "O primenenii bystrodejstvujuščix vyčislitel'nyx mašin dlja rešenija nekotoryx zadač fol'kloristiki", in *Pytannja prykladnoji lingvistyky* (Černivci, 1960).

*Tezisy soveščanija po matematičeskoj lingvistike (15-21 aprelja 1959 goda)* (Leningrad, 1959).

Toporov, V. N., "Vvedenie verojatnosti v jazykoznanie i ego posledstvija", in *TezSML59* (Leningrad, 1959).

Uspenskij, B. A., "Lingvističeskaja žizn' Kopengagena", *VJa* 11/3 (1962).

—, Review of H. Spang-Hanssen, *Probability and stuctural classification in language description* in *VJa* 11/2 (1962).

—, "Tipologičeskaja klassifikacija jazykov kak osnova jazykovyx sootvetstvij (struktura jazyka-ètalona pri tipologičeskoj klassifikacii jazykov)", *VJa* 10/6 (1961).

Uspenskij, V. A., "K opredeleniju časti reči v teoretiko-množestvennoj sisteme jazyka", *BOPMP* 5 (1957).

—, "K opredeleniju padeža po Kolmogorovu", *BOPMP* 5 (1957).

Volockaja, Z. M., "Opyt primenenija transformacionnogo metoda", in *Pytannja prykladnoji lingvistyky* (Černivci, 1960).

Xolodovič, A. A., "Opyt teorii podklassov slov", *VJa* 9/1 (1960).

Zaliznjak, A. A., "Opyt obučenija anglo-russkomu perevodu s pomošč'ju algoritma", in *Pytannja prykladnoji lingvistyky* (Černivci, 1960).

Zinder, L. R., "O lingvističeskoj verojatnosti", in *Voprosy statistiki reči* (Leningrad, 1958).

— (ed.), *Voprosy statistiki reči* (Leningrad, 1958).

Žinkin, N. I., "Four communicative systems and four languages", *Word* 18.143-172 (1962).

—, *Mexanizmy reči* (Moscow, 1958).
—, "Zvukovaja kommunikativnaja sistema obez'jan", *Izvestija Akademii pedagogičeskix nauk RSFSR*, 113 (1960).
Zinov'ev, A. A., "O matematičeskoj lingvistike", *Voprosy filosofii* 13/9 (1959).
—, and Revzin, I. I., "Logičeskaja model' kak sredstvo naučnogo poznanija", *Voprosy filosofii* 14/1 (1960).
Žirkov, L.I., "Granicy primenimosti mašinnogo perevoda", *VJa* 5/5 (1956).
Zolotarev, V. M., "Verojatnostnaja model' predloženija", in *TezSML59* (Leningrad, 1959).
Zvegincev, V. A., "Neopozitivizm i novejšie lingvističeskie napravlenija", *Voprosy filosofii* 15/12 (1961).
— (ed.), *Novoe v lingvistike* (Moscow, 1960-62).

# MACHINE TRANSLATION

KENNETH E. HARPER

## 1. INTRODUCTION

Machine translation (MT) has been an active area of research in the Soviet Union for the past decade. (In other East European countries these studies are only now beginning.) This activity may be divided into two periods (1). The first period was characterized by intensive efforts to construct sets of rules (algorithms) by which electronic computers could effect a translation between given language pairs. Translation algorithms were drawn up in varying degrees of depth and complexity for at least twenty language pairs (Russian-English, English-Russian, Hungarian-Russian, etc.). These programs were based on school-grammars of the languages in question; ambiguities in syntax and meaning-transfer were solved by *ad hoc* rules primarily derived from the examination of small text samples. It was assumed that additional ambiguities in new texts would be solved by additional rules. The chief goal appears to have been the demonstration of the feasibility of MT by example; the main shortcomings devolved from an overestimation of the powers of computers (the fascination with a new toy), equally, from an overestimation of the state of linguistic knowledge.

The second period, beginning roughly in 1959, and still continuing, is characterized by a far greater emphasis on linguistic research as a prerequisite to MT. The inadequacy of the algorithm approach was clearly indicated in 1959 by three leading MT researchers (2). This paper, and a later paper by V. V. Ivanov, set forth the following strategic principles: (i) too much attention has been given to detailization of isolated language facts, and no effort has been made to relate these facts to broader principles – "One cannot see the forest for the trees." (2); (ii) "The practical tasks of machine translation can only be solved in the future, after the preliminary study of languages is completed." (3); (iii) "The facts of language must be collected by the machine itself so that linguists will be able then to process them for inclusion in a general system." (2); (iv) "The importance of machine translation is now determined by its stimulating part in the development of linguistics." (3).

The necessity of fitting together fact and theory has been an important motivation for the recent interest in structural linguistics. In this connection, we may note the formation in 1960 of a Sector of Structural and Applied Linguistics in the Institute of Linguistics, AN SSSR. In describing the orientation of this Sector, A. A. Reformatskij emphasized the importance of theory to applied linguistics, and set forth the case for structural linguistics as follows: "The structural aspect presupposes the examination of a language as a whole and each level of its structure as an interconnected system of levels of significance given in a hierarchical gradation of symbols and their combinations, organized in contrast with each other, paradigmatically connected, and linearly distributed in speech." (4) It is not at all clear that this "examination" of a language has yet yielded important results; it is clear, however, that the current emphasis is upon organization of language data, with a view towards generalization. The day of the pair-wise translation algorithm, with its limited objectives, is now past. (It may be added that the reasons for the abandonment of these schemes were not all theoretical: the Soviets did not possess, or did not want to spare, the machines, time, and talent necessary to test and develop these programs.)

In summary, recent MT research in the Soviet Union is proceeding along two main paths: a more detailed analysis of specific language phenomena and the construction of linguistic theory. On the first point, it is interesting to note the large number of studies devoted to a description of the Russian language. (In earlier years, Russian was taken for granted; the challenge lay in transforming Russian into exotic languages, say, Burmese.) Generally, these studies have been based on the examination of small text samples, and apparently without the aid of data processing equipment. The shortage of equipment may, in fact, be taken as the chief reason for the heavy investment in theoretical work. Here, one may note the introduction of concepts from mathematics and symbolic logic, and the lively interest in interlanguage models (the Intermediary Language). In a word, although the computer has not yet been a partner in linguistic research, it has been the stimulus for critical re-examination of linguistic theory.

## 2. RESEARCH CENTERS IN MT

Soviet researchers in MT number in the hundreds. The 1958 MT Conference was attended by 340 representatives of 79 institutions. During the past ten years, however, the most important work has been done at four institutions: the Institute of Precise Mechanics and Computer Technique (ITMVT), the Electromodeling Laboratory of the Institute of Scientific Information, Leningrad State University, and the Steklov Institute of Mathematics. Two additional groups have been active in recent years: the First Moscow State Pedagogical Institute of Foreign Languages, and the Institute of Linguistics. These groups have contributed a major portion of MT literature. Research work at other institutions has been on a smaller scale, and often appears to lack continuity (for example, the studies by individuals at the state universities of Gorky, Kiev, Kharkov, Erevan, Tbilisi, and Petrozavodsk, and at a number of scientific-research institutes).

## 3. PUBLICATIONS IN MT

The sources of publication for MT studies are exceedingly diverse. No regular avenues of publication exist. Because of the relative newness and "newsworthiness" of the subject, many purely promotional and popular articles have been printed, in a wide variety of periodicals (the popular press, semipopular journals, and in scholarly journals ranging from philosophy to computer technology). The recent National Bureau of Standards *Bibliography* (5) cites some 69 different sources for these publications. The more serious papers have also appeared in a number of different source documents, sporadically and in a rather haphazard fashion; papers frequently appear, perhaps in revised form, in more than one periodical. When individual researchers or groups publish their own papers, the quality of editing is often low, and the distribution is limited. Copies are generally available outside the Soviet Union only on an individual exchange basis.

By content, three types of MT publications may be distinguished: *generally informative* (promotional articles, surveys, and articles introducing such concepts as transformational grammar, information theory), *theoretical* (efforts to develop speculatively a given linguistic concept), and *substantive* (results of specific grammatical or lexical studies, routines, programs). All these publications clearly reflect the newness of the subject. In exploratory or projective papers, the line of investigation is rarely pursued to satisfactory lengths. When specific results are reported, the effect is usually unconvincing because of the smallness of the data base. Work completed in a given year may be completely ignored two years later, either because of reassignment of personnel or because of the overall deficiency in planning. Papers written in the first few years of MT research are by now quite dated. (These characteristics, it should be added, are not peculiar to Soviet MT literature.)

To the knowledge of the writer, the only good bibliography of Soviet MT publications is that issued by the National Bureau of Standards (5). Actually, this is a bibliography of translations made by the U.S. Joint Publications Research Service; the translations themselves are inferior, but the coverage of Soviet literature is excellent. A total of 519 items (including abstracts) are contained in the author index of this report. In many instances, the JPRS translation is the only version of the original paper available in this country.

Three main avenues of publication are open to Soviet MT researchers: (i) Scholarly meetings. The abstracts or complete texts of papers presented at large MT conferences are, with one exception, available. To date, four such conferences have been held: the 1958 All-Union Conference on Machine Translation (Moscow), the 1959 All-Union Conference on Mathematical Linguistics (Leningrad), the 1960 Inter-VUZ Conference on Applied Linguistics (Chernovtsy), and the 1961 Conference on Information Processing, Machine Translation, and Automatic Text Reading (Moscow). Translations of papers given at three of these meetings have been made (6, 7, 8); titles and brief summaries of papers presented at the Chernovtsy conference are available (9, 10). In addition, there have been several smaller meetings and seminars, for which papers are apparently not printed, *e.g.*, the 1961 inter-VUZ conference on the application of structural and statistical methods in studying the vocabulary of a language, and the 1961 meeting on structural linguistics (transformational method) held by the Sector on Structural Linguistics, Russian Language Institute, AN SSSR (11).

(ii) Collections (*sborniki*). Two of these collections are of a semiserial nature. *Mašinnyj perevod i prikladnaja lingvistika* (12), once entitled the "Bulletin" of the Society (*Ob"edinenie*) for Machine Translation, has published substantive papers by workers of a number of different groups since 1959, as has *Problemy kibernetiki* (13), since 1958. In addition, various research groups have irregularly issued collected papers by their staff members. Three such collections have been issued by the Leningrad University group (14, 15, 16), two by the Institute of Scientific Information (17, 18), and two by the Institute of Precise Mechanics and Computer Technique (19, 20). Moscow State University has issued the collection, *Exact Methods in Linguistic Research* (21), and the Institute of Linguistics has published separate studies (22, 23). I. S. Muxin is the author of a book surveying MT problems (24).

(iii) Scholarly journals. Papers appearing in these journals tend to be addressed to non-specialists, and rarely deal with problems in a detailed way. *Voprosy lingvistiki* has carried the greatest number of these general articles. Most of the papers referred to below belong to the first two categories mentioned.

## 4. A SAMPLING OF MT STUDIES

The NBS *Bibliography* (5) contains a twelve-page subject index. For present purposes, it seems appropriate to cite representative papers in the traditional areas of linguistic research. Most of the following are concerned with the grammar of Russian.

The *generally informative* papers include I. A. Mel'čuk's objective and rather complete survey of MT studies in the U.S. and Western Europe (25, 26), and the two surveys and critiques of the Soviet MT effort cited above (2, 3). Several papers have introduced MT researchers to non-linguistic concepts and techniques: information theory (27), statistical methods (28), probability theory (29), information processing techniques as applied, for example, in automatic abstracting (30), etc. The importation of linguistic theory from the West is well known (see, *e.g.*, item 31). The most interesting applications of extra-linguistic ideas to linguistic theory have been suggested in the area of mathematical linguistics, rather than in the area of MT research *per se*.

MT studies in *morphology* have centered on problems of automatic recognition, *i.e.*, decomposition of text forms into constituents that can be used in dictionary lookup and in syntactic analysis (of the input language) and synthesis (of the output language). Except as they illustrate the enormously complex mechanism of language, these studies have no great theoretical interest. A number of schemes for achieving machine recognition of grammatical morphemes have been devised. To the knowledge of the writer, none are founded on a rigorous definition of the morpheme or on a systematic processing of text or word lists. Most MT programs are built on the assumption that the computer dictionary will be composed of stems or roots of words, rather than canonical forms or paradigmatic forms. (The purpose here is conserve storage space in the computer). How shall the machine be programmed so as to detach derivational and inflectional affixes from forms encountered in text, so that text stems can be matched automatically with dictionary stems? The most elaborate algorithm for this purpose is that proposed by Mel'čuk, (32); this method is Russian-oriented, but is intended for application to other languages. The problems of stem-homography arising from automatic segmentation are dealt with in several papers, *e.g.*, for Russian (33, 34), for English (35, 36), and for Swedish (37). Other programs describe the means of utilizing the morphological information obtained from these segmentation routines, both in analysis and in synthesis, but in particular with Russian as the output language. (38). One program (French-Russian) has been tested on a computer, and may be considered operational (39).

Distributional characteristics of Russian inflectional affixes have been studied (although not by automatic procedures), as an aid in morphological coding. Thus the frequency of case forms in nouns has been counted in scientific prose (40, 41). Certain coding schemes have taken advantage of the redundancy in Russian declension patterns; *e.g.*, the dative and prepositional cases are coalesced (22, 42).

In *syntax*, as in morphology, MT research has contributed little to theoretical understanding. The chief concern of the algorithm-builders was to solve individual problems as they arose at a given stage in the translation process. The solutions were usually effected in terms of "how to translate" a given construction; there was a minimum of interest in explaining or typifying the construction. An example is the complex set of rules in one scheme for resolving homography in French-Russian MT (39). The rules, as in all Russian algorithms of sentence analysis, are embedded in a kind of flow chart that, for each ambiguous word, asks yes/no questions about the presence or absence of specific words or word-classes in context. (The operational limitations of the flow chart seem not to have been understood by Soviet MT workers.) Absent is any motivation to describe the various syntactic functions of the French homographic words except as they can be fitted into the Russian syntactic and lexical pattern. In effect, this procedure is geared to the solution of isolated problems, rather than to the description of larger syntactic units (the clause or the sentence), in which the isolated problem words or constructions may fit unambiguously.

Recently, the desirability of automatic parsing as a part of the MT process has aroused a certain interest in sentence structure theory. MT researchers have been busy with routines designed to establish in Russian the syntactic connections between pairs of text occurrences. These "governor-dependent" pairs, or "configurations", are of course the building blocks for complete sentence structure description. Two of the most detailed programs are a routine for testing adjective-noun agreement (22), and a routine for testing verb complementation (23). The latter, derived from syntactic information in Daum and Schenk, *Die Russischen Verben*, presents as a first model more than 130 patterns of verb complementation of the type: čto; čto/čemu; čto/čem (čerez čto); čemu/na čto/čem. Criteria of equivalence/non-equivalence and compatibility/incompatibility are employed in the classification. Another system of classification for Russian words (not only verbs), according to their governing capabilities, is given in (43). Other studies have been made of these grammatical configurations in Russian (44), and in English (45). Routines for determining the syntactic governors of prepositional phrases have been written, for Russian (46), and for English (47). Studies have been made on the syntactic role of formulas in Russian mathematical texts (48) and on the function of punctuation marks in Russian (49).

Only in the past year or two have Soviet MT workers come to realize the enormous difficulties of describing syntactic behavior with the required degree of specificity. A native command of the language does not suffice, the best traditional treatments of syntax are notoriously inadequate, and the "brute force" attack on isolated problems through analysis of the microcontext has not proved satisfactory. The alternative source of information is written text, and it is to this source that students are now turning. In this connection, one of the most significant developments in Soviet MT work is a recent paper on the use of machine aids for the collection of syntactic information (50). Here is described a program for automatic parsing of text that will make the computer a full-fledged partner in research: the program is designed to provide the researcher with facts about parsing, or configuration-building, which he originally had not known, or which he had been unable to encode in the grammar. Such a program is indeed a powerful tool, leading to a more complete understanding of the syntactic function and the meaning of word combinations (*slovosočetanija*). The implications of this development to grammar and lexicography are tremendous, so that the achievements of the past decade, as set forth in the present literature, will seem to represent a first stumbling step unaccountably long in the taking.

## SUMMARY

Within the past four years, Soviet linguists have perforce been introduced to a striking variety of new concepts. There has been a veritable onslaught of ideas, from the West, from the symbolic logicians, from engineers, and particularly from mathematicians. The impact of mathematics has perhaps been less dismaying to Soviet linguists than to their confreres in the West. In this initial period, research is almost certain to be suggestive, but non-productive. Linguists flourish mathematical weapons that they are ill-equipped to handle; mathematicians and engineers attack language problems with a depressing degree of self-confidence and a surprising lack of finesse. The literature is often difficult to understand, and even more difficult to evaluate. Nonetheless, it is evident that many of the theoretical constructs presented in MT literature are of doubtful validity, and that some are essentially trivial. This is not to underestimate the potential of cross-fertilization. Here, it would appear that Russian linguists have shown greater responsiveness to this challenge than have linguists in the West. The analogy with computer sciences is perhaps instructive: the best Soviet mathematicians are deeply involved in problems of computer design and programming, and it can well be argued that they benefit from this involvement in both "pure" and "applied" science. The older, established Soviet linguists have made no great contribution to applied linguistics, but they exhibit a remarkable willingness to "be shown". They are likely to foresee and to encourage the rapid change in linguistics that will become evident in the next generation.

## REFERENCES

With few exceptions, the papers listed below are to be found in the National Bureau of Standards *Bibliography* (5). Since a great majority of these papers are available only in the English translation distributed by the U.S. Joint Publications Research Service, the titles have been given as translated by the JPRS. Russian titles are given for the few items not contained in the NBS *Bibliography*.

1. K. E. Harper, "Soviet Research in Machine Translation", *Proceedings of the National Symposium on Machine Translation.* Ed. H.P. Edmundson (Prentice-Hall, Inc., 1961).
2. N. D. Andreev, V. V. Ivanov, and I. A. Mel'čuk, "Some Remarks and Suggestions Relative to Work on Machine Translation in the USSR", JPRS:8026, pp. 1-14; *Mašinnyj Perevod i Prikladnaja Lingvistika* 4.3-24 (1960).
3. V. V. Ivanov, "Some Problems of Machine Translation in the USSR", JPRS: 13439, 49 pp.; *Doklady na Konferencii po Obrabotke Informacii, Mašinnomu Perevodu i Avtomatičeskomu Čteniju Teksta* 10.1-29 (1961).
4. A. A. Reformatskij, "In Place of a Preface" (see Ref. 22, below).
5. J. L. Walkowicz, "A Bibliography of Foreign Developments in Machine Translation and Information Processing", *National Bureau of Standards Report* 7721, Sept. 1, 1962.
6. *Abstracts of the Conference on Machine Translation* (*May 15-21, 1958*), Ministry of Higher Education, USSR, First Moscow State Pedagogical Institute of Foreign Languages (Moscow, 1958). (JPRS:DC-241).
7. *Tezisy Soveščanija po matematičeskoj Lingvistike*, Ministry of Higher Education, USSR (Leningrad, 1959). (JPRS:893-D).
8. *Doklady na Konferencii po Obrabotke Informacii, Mašinnomu Perevodu, i Avto-*

*maticeskomu Čteniju Teksta*, Institute of Scientific Information, AN SSSR (Moscow, 1961).

9. O. S. Širokov, "Conference on Structural and Mathematical Linguistics", JPRS:8132, pp. 1-8; *VJa* 10/1.155-159 (1961).
10. D. M. Segal, "Intervuz Scientific Conference on Applied Linguistics", JPRS: 13761, pp. 118-123; *Mašinnyj Perevod i Prikladnaja Lingvistika* 5.93-99 (1961).
11. S. K. Šaumjan, "Urgent Problems of Structural Linguistics", JPRS:14252, 15 pp.; *IzvAN* 21/2.103-111 (1962).
12. *Mašinnyj Perevod i Prikladnaya Lingvistika*, Association for Machine Translation, First Moscow State Pedagogical Institute of Foreign Languages (Moscow).
13. *Problemy Kibernetiki*, State Publishing House of Physico-Mathematical Literature (Moscow).
14. (See Ref. 7, above).
15. *Materialy po Mašinnomu Perevodu, Sbornik I* (Leningrad, 1958). (JPRS:2150-N).
16. *Voprosy Statistiki Reči*, Edited by L. R. Zinder (Leningrad, 1958), 148 pp. (JPRS:6543).
17. *Soobščenija Laboratorii Elektromodelirovanija*, Institute of Scientific Information of the Academy of Sciences USSR, Moscow, 1.1-250(1960).
18. *Lingvističeskie Issledovanija po Mašinnomu Perevodu*, All-Union Institute of Scientific and Technical Information Publishing House, Issue No. 2 (Moscow, 1961) (JPRS:13173).
19. *Sbornik Statej po Mašinnomu Perevodu*, Institute of Precise Mechanics and Computer Technique AN SSSR (Moscow, 1958). (JPRS:925-D).
20. *Trudy Instituta Točnoj Mexaniki i Vyčislitel'noj Texniki Akademii Nauk SSSR*, No. 2 (Moscow, 1961). (JPRS:13543).
21. O. S. Axmanova, I. A. Mel'čuk, E. V. Padučeva, and R. M. Frumkina, *O Točnyx Metodax Issledovanija Jazyka*, Izdatel'stvo Moskovskogo Universiteta (Moscow, 1961).
22. I. A. Mel'čuk, "Two Operators for Establishing Correspondence (for Automatic Syntactical Analysis)", JPRS:13444, 71 pp. Preliminary Publications of the Sector of Structural and Applied Linguistics, Institute of Linguistics, AN SSSR, 1961, pp. 1-38.
23. L. N. Iordanskaja, "Two Operators for Processing Word Combinations with 'Strong Government' (for Automatic Syntactic Analysis)", JPRS:12441, 41 pp. Preliminary Publications of the Sector of Structural and Applied Linguistics, Institute of Linguistics, AN SSSR (Moscow, 1961), pp. 3-33.
24. D. Ju. Panov, *Avtomatičeskij perevod*, Izdatel'stvo AN SSSR (Moscow, 1958).
25. I. A. Mel'čuk, "Some Problems of Machine Translation Abroad", JPRS:13135, 75 pp. (see Ref. 8, above).
26. I. A. Mel'čuk, "Mašinnyj perevod i lingvistika" (see Ref. 21, above).
27. E. V. Padučeva, "Vozmožnost' izučenija jazyka metodami teorii informacii"

(see Ref. 21, above).

28. R. M. Frumkina, "Primenenie statističeskix metodov v izučenii jazykov" (see Ref. 21, above).
29. R. M. Frumkina, and V. M. Zolatarev, "Toward a Probability Model of a Sentence" JPRS:893-D, p. 27 (see Ref. 7, above).
30. V. A. Purto, "Automatic Abstracting Based on a Statistical Analysis of the Text", JPRS:13196, 15 pp. (see Ref. 8, above).
31. T. M. Nikolaeva, "What is Transform Analysis?" JPRS:3796, pp. 32-41; *VJa* 9/1.111-115 (1960).
32. I. A. Mel'čuk, "Morphological Analysis in Machine Translation", JPRS:13514, pp. 129-302; *Voprosy Kibernetiki* 6.207-276 (1961).
33. L. N. Iordanskaja, "The Morphological Types of Stems in the Russian Language (For Distinction of Homonymy of Morphemes During Analysis in Machine Translation)", JPRS:13514, pp. 313-329; *Voprosy Kibernetiki* 6.281-287 (1961).
34. L. N. Zasorina, N. B. Karačan, S. N. Med'vedeva, and G. S. Cejtin, "A Project of Programs for Morphological Analysis of the Russian Language in Machine Translation", JPRS:2150-N, pp. 99-148 (see Ref. 15, above).
35. M. M. Langleben and E. V. Padučeva, "Elimination of Morphological and Syntactic Homonymy in Analyzing English Texts", JPRS:DC-241, pp. 69-70 (see Ref. 6, above).
36. T. N. Mološnaja, "Problems in Distinguishing Homonyms in Machine Translation from English into Russian", JPRS:646-D, pp. 19-27; *Problemy Kibernetiki* 1.216-221 (1958).
37. S. S. Belokrinickaja and T. N. Mološnaja, "On an Algorithm for Independent Morphological Analysis of the Swedish Language", JPRS:13543, pp. 338-354 (see Ref. 20, above).
38. T. M. Nikolaeva, "Synthesis of Forms of Russian Words During Machine Translation into Russian", JPRS:12047, 19pp.; *Problemy Kibernetiki* 5.263-269 (1961).
39. O. S. Kulagina, "French-to-Russian Machine Translation. French-to-Russian Translation Algorithm", JPRS:6494, pp. 14-86; *Problemy Kibernetiki* 4.207-257 (1960).
40. V. A. Nikonov, "Statistics on Russian Cases", JPRS:3758, pp. 31-51; *Mašinnyj Perevod i Prikladnaja Lingvistika* 3(10).45-65 (1959).
41. Z. M. Volockaja, I. N. Šelimova, and A. L. Šumilina, "Some Numerical Data Pertaining to Forms of Nouns and Verbs of the Russian Language", JPRS:13173, pp. 339-347 (see Ref. 18, above).
42. E. V. Padučeva, "Description of the Case System of the Russian Noun (Certain Problems of Homonyms in Machine Translation)", JPRS:6588, pp. 1-13; *VJa* 9/5.104-111 (1960).
43. E. V. Padučeva and A. L. Šumilina, "Syntagmas of the Russian Language", JPRS:13173, pp. 120-150 (see Ref. 18, above).

44. B. M. Lejkina, "Program for the Analysis of Phraseological Complexes", JPRS: 13134, 11 pp. (see Ref. 8, above).
45. T. N. Mološnaja, "Statistical Investigation of Grammatical Configurations in English Mathematical Text", JPRS:8026, pp. 4050; *Mašinnyj Perevod i Prikladnaya Lingvistika* 4.64-81 (1960).
46. I. N. Šelimova, "Establishment of Syntactic Cues for Prepositional Phrases", JPRS:DC-241, pp. 80-82 (see Ref. 6, above).
47. M. M. Langleben, "Syntactic Analysis of Prepositional Groups in the English language", JPRS:13173, pp. 314-324 (see Ref. 18, above).
48. M. M. Langleben, "Determination of Syntactic Connections for Formulas in Russian Mathematical Texts", JPRS:DC-241, pp. 68-69 (see Ref. 6, above).
49. T. M. Nikolaeva, "Analysis of Punctuation Marks During Machine Translation from Russian", JPRS:DC-241, pp. 73-75 (see Ref. 6, above).
50. O. S. Kulagina, "Ob ispol'zovanii mašiny pri sostavlenii algoritmov analiza teksta", *Problemy Kibernetiki* 7.209-223 (1962).

# FOREIGN LANGUAGE TEACHING

JACOB ORNSTEIN

## PART I

In recent years, particularly since Sputnik I, the Soviet language teaching effort has drawn attention in the Western world. Many exaggerations have, however, appeared about the achievements of the U.S.S.R. in this area. In John W. Gardner's foreword to *The American High School Today*, the well-known work by James B. Conant, ex-president of Harvard, it is noted that: "The surge of publicity about Soviet schools has aroused more false impressions and foolish conclusions than almost any other element in current discussions of education".[1]

The fact remains, nevertheless, that both before and after the Bolshevik Revolution, the value of language study was never questioned. In Czarist days, control of at least one foreign language was an integral part of the preparation of any educated person. After the Revolution, Lenin, his wife N. K. Krupskaja, and other early Soviet leaders often came out for language study and its importance to the U.S.S.R. in the building of Communism. As was to be expected, also, educators have been fond of quoting Karl Marx's statement that "A foreign language is a weapon".

During the early days of the Soviet regime, due to other preoccupations, language training was not very well developed. Up to 1923 and even afterwards, the study remained optional in many educational institutions of all types. Dissatisfied with this state of affairs, the government took steps aimed at improving language teaching and other sectors of instruction. Beginning in 1927 a series of decrees was issued intended to raise classroom accomplishments. Among the most important of these was the Central Committee's decree of September 5, 1931, "Concerning the Elementary and Secondary Schools", as well as one issued August 25, 1932, entitled "Concerning the Instructional Programs and the Regime of the Elementary and Middle School". The 1932 decree stated that it "Recognizes the necessity of providing every secondary school graduate with the knowledge of a foreign language". From then on, the development of language offerings has followed an upward course.

In the following pages of the first part of this study the main facts regarding Soviet language teaching facilities will be noted, while in the second part there will be discussion of the reforms which the field has been undergoing.

[1] Conant, *The American High School Today*, p. xi.

### *Primary and Secondary Levels*

The Khrushchev 1958 school reform provides for the conversion of all ten-year schools into eight- and three-year schools with production training. The latter segment is often referred to by education writers as the "upper secondary". Only a part of the schools have completed the change-over thus far. Despite this, however, foreign language training normally begins in the fifth grade at about age 11 or 12, and continues until completion of secondary school, for a total of six or seven years.

According to Nicholas De Witt, an authority on Russian education, Soviet data indicate that in 1955-56 about two-thirds of the primary and secondary school pupils attended Russian language schools where all subjects were taught in Russian, and the remainder received instruction through the predominant local language in the primary grades.[2] All in all, primary instruction is conducted in about sixty national languages aside from Russian. In such cases, Russian, which is not considered a foreign language any more than is the non-Russian tongue, is usually introduced in the second or third grade. When in the fifth grade English, French, or German (in rare cases, Spanish) is undertaken, it is taught through the medium of Russian, which some youngsters as yet handle imperfectly. This phenomenon is the subject of complaints from time to time in Soviet educational literature. Special conferences have been held and measures taken to improve the teaching of Russian in non-Russian areas. One of these was the founding of a journal entitled *Russkij jazyk v ne-russkoj škole.*[3]

The languages ordinarily studied by Soviet youngsters are German, English, and French, in that order of popularity. Spanish has also apparently been added in a few places. During the past few years, however, the Western press and education writers have frequently repeated a statistic furnished originally by Minister of Education Afanasenko that 45 percent of Soviet secondary youngsters were enrolled in English, 35 percent in German, and 20 percent in French. This is, however, definitely contradicted by Soviet official figures elsewhere. According to the latest available statistics, the following are the enrollments as of 1960-61 in all regular secondary schools, excepting the workers' schools, schools for rural youth, and adult education schools:

| | Number of schools | Enrollments |
|---|---|---|
| German . . . . . . | 64,400 | 8,249,000 |
| English . . . . . . | 22,800 | 4,530,000 |
| French . . . . . . | 7,500 | 1,049,000 |
| Other languages . . | 500 | 8,000 |
| Total . . . . . . . | 95,200 (courses) | 13,836,000 |

[2] De Witt, *Education and Professional Employment in the USSR*, p. 114. The reader is urged to consult the section titled "Soviet Primary and Secondary Education: Foreign Language Instruction," pp. 114-117. This source has provided valuable data, utilized at various points of this study.

[3] On August 21-25, 1956, there was held the first Inter-republic Conference on the Improvement

The above figures represent some 79,000 schools, of pre-reform and post-reform type. It should be noted that an absolute count of the column on the left results in 95,200 courses, but the difference is explainable by the fact that some schools teach several tongues. Altogether our source indicates that the 13,836,000 enrollees constitute about 94 percent of the total number enrolled in grades 5 through 11.[4] A recent report of the House of Representatives Committee on Education and Labor states that about 50 languages are taught in various secondary schools including Chinese, Hindi, and Arabic, but "mass teaching" is offered in only three – English, German, French.[5]

While the latter part of the statement is correct, the figure of 50 languages, unless one includes regional "national" tongues, is erroneous. As will be seen, certain experimental schools do offer Chinese, Hindi-Urdu, Arabic, and Persian, while others teach English, German, and French.

De Witt predicts that English "... is not likely to replace German as the first-ranking foreign language in Soviet schools for another decade".[6] According to him, the reason why French lags far behind English and German in popularity is that it is still associated in many minds with the Czarist bourgeoisie and intelligentsia, which often spoke this language as fluently as Russian.

Foreign language is compulsory in all schools where it is taught and, as we have noted, at least 94 percent of the youngsters are enrolled in the subject. This contrasts with the approximately 27 percent of American public high school pupils, or 2,200,000, so enrolled as of autumn 1959. The distribution in U.S. schools (grades 9-12) was: Spanish 36.2%, Latin 29.2%, French 27.4%, German 5.6%, Italian 1%, Russian .3%, and others .3%.[7] From all indications, in the U.S.S.R. those who fail to take a foreign tongue do so simply because they live in remote areas where no language specialist is available in the schools.

During the seven years of the 11-year school, each student is exposed to a total of 726 hours of foreign language, or about 6 percent of his total instructional time. This represents 66 hours more than in the 10-year school curriculum.[8]

De Witt points out that as a result of the emphasis on polytechnic education brought about by the 1958 reform, the total number of hours devoted to foreign language study has actually declined by about 40 hours. But curricula planned for 1959-63 have

---

of the Teaching of Russian in Non-Russian Areas. At this meeting none other than N. A. Muxtidinov, former member of the Presidium of the Central Committee of the Communist Party, complained that poor control of Russian was a handicap for many non-Russians when they enter the labor force. See *Pravda Vostoka*, August 25, 1956. Also consult Ornstein, "Soviet Language Policy: Theory and Practice," pp. 10-12.

4 *Narodnoe Xozjajstvo SSSR v 1960-m godu*, p. 775.

5 U.S. House of Representatives, *Higher Education in the Soviet Union*, p. 11. This report, consisting of 20 pages, was made by the Special Subcommittee on Education.

6 De Witt, *Education and Professional Employment*, pp. 114-115.

7 Childers, "Foreign Language Offerings and Enrollments in Public Secondary Schools, Fall 1959," p. 15.

8 For a discussion of the new program, see Kreusler, "The New Soviet Foreign Language Curriculum."

TABLE I

*Curriculum Plan for Eight-year School in 1959-1960**

| No. | Subject | Number of hours a week for grades | | | | | | | | Total hours | | Number of hours in 7-year school | |
|---|---|---|---|---|---|---|---|---|---|---|---|---|---|
| | | I | II | III | IV | V | VI | VII | VIII | By the week | By the year | By the week | By the year |
| 1 | Russian language | 12 | 12 | 12 | 10 | 6 | 5 | 3 | 2 | 62 | 2,230 | 71 | 2,436 |
| 2 | Literature | — | — | — | — | 2 | 3 | 2 | 3 | 10 | 357 | — | — |
| 3 | Mathematics | 6 | 6 | 6 | 6 | 6 | 6 | 6 | 5 | 47 | 1,687 | 42 | 1,452 |
| 4 | USSR history and constitution | — | — | — | 2 | 2 | 2 | 2 | 3 | 11 | 393 | 8 | 280 |
| 5 | Natural history | — | — | — | 3 | — | — | — | — | 3 | 108 | — | — |
| 6 | Geography | — | — | — | — | 2 | 2 | 2 | 2 | 8 | 286 | 9 | 315 |
| 7 | Biology | — | — | — | — | 2 | 2 | 2 | 2 | 8 | 286 | 9 | 315 |
| 8 | Physics | — | — | — | — | — | 2 | 2 | 3 | 7 | 249 | 5 | 175 |
| 9 | Chemistry | — | — | — | — | — | — | 2 | 2 | 4 | 142 | 2 | 70 |
| 10 | Drawing | — | — | — | — | — | — | 1 | 1 | 2 | 71 | 1 | 35 |
| 11 | Foreign language | — | — | — | — | 4 | 3 | 3 | 3 | 13 | 465 | 11 | 385 |
| | Total, subjects 1-11 | 18 | 18 | 18 | 21 | 24 | 25 | 25 | 26 | 175 | 6,274 | | |
| 12 | Design drawing | 1 | 1 | 1 | 1 | 1 | 1 | 1 | — | 7 | 252 | 6 | 207 |
| 13 | Music and singing | 1 | 1 | 1 | 1 | 1 | 1 | 1 | 1 | 8 | 287 | 6 | 207 |
| 14 | Physical training | 2 | 2 | 2 | 2 | 2 | 2 | 2 | 2 | 16 | 574 | 14 | 484 |
| | Total, subjects 12-14 | 4 | 4 | 4 | 4 | 4 | 4 | 4 | 3 | 31 | 1,113 | | |
| 15 | Labor training | 2 | 2 | 2 | 2 | 3 | 3 | 3 | 3 | 20 | 717 | | |
| 16 | Socially useful labor | — | — | 2 | 2 | 2 | 2 | 2 | 2 | 12 | 430 | | |
| 17 | Social production practice in grades V-VIII | Two weeks at the end of the academic year | | | | | | | | | | | |
| | Total, subjects 15-17 | 2 | 2 | 4 | 4 | 5 | 5 | 5 | 5 | 32 | 1,147 | | |
| | Total, all subjects | 24 | 24 | 26 | 29 | 33 | 34 | 34 | 34 | 238 | 8,534 | | |

* From Seymour M. Rosen, "Report on Soviet Educational Reform Source Book", U.S. Dept. of Health, Education and Welfare, Office of Education, International Educational Relations (OE-14034-47), Oct. 1960, p. 5. The chart is taken from N. K. Goncharov and F. F. Korolev, eds., *Novaja sistema narodnogo obrazovanija SSSR* (Moscow, Acad. of Pedagogic Sciences, 1960), pp. 213-214.

TABLE II

*Curriculum Plan for Secondary General Education Labor Polytechnical School in 1951-1960**

| No. | Subject | Number of hours a week for grades | | | Total hours | |
|---|---|---|---|---|---|---|
| | | IX | X | XI | By the week | By the year |
| 1 | Literature . . . . . . . . . . . . . . | 3 | 3 | 3 | 9 | 339 |
| 2 | Mathematics . . . . . . . . . . . . . | 4 | 4 | 4 | 12 | 452 |
| 3 | History . . . . . . . . . . . . . . . | 2 | 3 | 4 | 9 | 335 |
| 4 | USSR constitution . . . . . . . . . | — | — | 2 | 2 | 70 |
| 5 | Economic geography . . . . . . . . | — | 2 | 2 | 4 | 148 |
| 6 | Physics . . . . . . . . . . . . . . . | 4 | 4 | 2 | 10 | 382 |
| 7 | Astronomy . . . . . . . . . . . . . . | — | 1 | — | 1 | 39 |
| 8 | Chemistry . . . . . . . . . . . . . . | 2 | 3 | 2 | 7 | 265 |
| 9 | Biology . . . . . . . . . . . . . . . | 3 | — | — | 3 | 117 |
| 10 | Drawing . . . . . . . . . . . . . . . | 2 | — | — | 2 | 78 |
| 11 | Foreign language . . . . . . . . . . | 2 | 2 | 3 | 7 | 261 |
| 12 | Physical training . . . . . . . . . . | 2 | 2 | 2 | 6 | 226 |
| | Total . . . . . . . . . . . . . . . . | 24 | 24 | 24 | 72 | 2,712 |
| 13 | General technical subjects, production (theoretical and practical) training and production work . . . . . . . . . | 12 | 12 | 12 | 36 | 1,356 |
| | Total . . . . . . . . . . . . . . . . | 36 | 36 | 36 | 108 | 4,068 |
| 14 | Electives . . . . . . . . . . . . . . | 2 | 2 | 2 | 6 | 226 |

* From Seymour M. Rosen, "Report on Soviet Educational Reform Source Book", U.S. Dept. of Health, Education and Welfare, Office of Education, International Educational Relations (OE-14034-47), Oct. 1960. The chart is also taken from N. K. Goncharov and F. F. Korolev, eds., *Novaja sistema narodnogo obrazovanija SSSR* (Moscow, Acad. of Pedagogic Sciences, 1960), pp. 213-214.

increased the time allotted by 40 hours, which, nevertheless, still represents a reduction in hours. À propos, Abraham Kreusler gives convincing proof in a recent article that the amount of time devoted to foreign language in Soviet secondary schools is considerably less than it was before the Bolshevik Revolution. In the new curricula, as we have noted, about 6 percent of the total hours are devoted to language training, as contrasted with from 20 to 25 percent in Czarist secondary schools.[9] In addition, it was customary to study two modern tongues plus Latin and sometimes Greek. Of course, this formal instruction was greatly reinforced by the system among the élite of having French, German, and English-speaking governesses and much residence abroad. This in turn gave rise to the persistent legends which have circulated about the formidable "natural-born" prowess of the Russians in mastering foreign languages.

[9] See Kreusler, *op. cit.*, and his article entitled "Foreign Language Teaching in Pre-Revolutionary Russia."

In the new curriculum the lexical minimum for the 8-year school is 800 words, and in the upper secondary school the student is expected to acquire 700 new words, with emphasis on speaking and understanding rather than merely reading and grammar. Tables I and II show the new official curricula for both types of school, which with small modifications also serve as the pattern for evening (*smennye*) schools.

### *The Experimental Schools*

Desiring to intensify their language effort and to expose youngsters to foreign tongues at an earlier age, the Soviets in 1955 undertook a novel experiment, as part of the trend to set up "boarding schools" or "školy internaty".[10] They have designated a number of secondary schools to specialize in certain tongues, calling them "special'nye školy s prepodavaniem rjada disciplin na inostrannyx jazykax" or more briefly "specškoly". These are of two types, one of them being the "škola internat" or boarding school, the other being ordinary day-schools "commissioned" to teach modern foreign languages. Ordinarily the language is begun in the second grade, and by grade 7 or 8 some subjects are taught in it. According to Fan Parker, who in 1956 visited School No. 1 in Moscow, from grades 2 through 5, seven hours of foreign language instruction were given weekly, with six hours per week in grade 7. Of the 11,045 total of instructional hours for the ten-years, 1,848 were devoted to foreign language – about a thousand more than in the regular ten-year schools.[11]

The network of the experimental schools is being constantly enlarged. For English, French, and/or German, at least two schools exist in Moscow, two in Leningrad, and one each in Volgograd, Gor'kij, Jaroslavl', Perm', Kazan', and Ufa.

In Moscow, Boarding School No. 14 of Frunze Rayon is devoted to Chinese, while at Boarding School No. 23 Hindi-Urdu is taught. In Leningrad, two schools teach Chinese and Hindi, respectively. At Boarding School No. 5, the pupils learn Chinese with the assistance of experienced Orientalists and of students from Red China pursuing studies in Moscow. Boarding School No. 4 has introduced Hindi. In two or three Tatar schools in Kazan', Arabic instruction has been added.

From all indications, Central Asia has become a sort of "pilot area" for teaching Eastern tongues in the experimental schools. Five schools in Tashkent are offering Hindi, Chinese, and/or Arabic. Three schools in Bukhara and Samarkand are specializing in Persian and Arabic. Two schools in Dušanbe (formerly Stalinabad)

[10] For a thorough discussion of the *internaty* and their place in Soviet society, see Ambler, "The Soviet Boarding School." She observes: "Khrushchev has chosen his polytechnical boarding school as the educational instrument which will transform the coming generation into the Communist society better than any other type of educational institution. The boarding school provides ideal conditions for the growth of polytechnical education and for the formation of the collective body." (p. 252).

[11] Parker, "The Teaching of English in a Soviet Middle School."

in the Tadžik S.S.R. are giving Persian and Arabic. One school in Baku, and one in Ašxabad, are specializing in Persian.

Altogether upwards of 56,000 youngsters are enrolled in the experimental schools, and from virtually every indication available, the regime considers them to be quite successful. The Council of Ministers decree "Regarding the Improvement of Foreign Language Teaching", issued 4 June 1961, among other things called for the expansion of the experimental schools with teaching in foreign languages by at least 700 during the 1961-65 period. Accordingly, the following were to be organized after September 1959:

| | |
|---|---|
| Kazan' | – one German school |
| | one English school |
| Perm' | – one English school |
| Voronež | – one English school |
| Arzamas | – one English school |
| Rostov-na-Donu | – one English school |
| Tambov | – one English school |
| | – one French school |
| Sverdlovsk | – one German school |
| Tagil' | – one German school |
| Volgograd | – three English schools |
| Rjazan' | – one German school |
| | – one French school |
| | – one English school |
| Čita | – one German school[12] |

One is struck by the high proportion of English-language schools. Indeed, aside from the newly expressed interest in Asian and African languages, the Soviet language teaching effort ever since World War II has been stressing English over all other foreign tongues.

Most of the references which the Soviets make regarding the experimental schools are quite favorable. The only extensive first-hand observations by an American linguist are those recorded by Gordon H. Fairbanks of Cornell University. The latter, together with Kenneth Mildenberger and Marjorie Johnston visited the Soviet Union in 1960 and published a joint article, to be cited later. The Cornell professor himself prepared a report on his visits to a number of schools which taught foreign languages at various levels. In the six experimental schools visited by him, he found performance of differing quality.[13] In common with most American visitors he commented very favorably on Moscow's School No. 1, which is apparently a "show-

[12] See "Rasširenie seti škol s prepodovaniem rjada disciplin na inostrannom jazyke."

[13] Fairbanks, "Foreign Language Teaching in the U.S.S.R." I am grateful both to Dr. Fairbanks and to the U.S. Office of Education, under whose auspices he made this trip, for allowing me to utilize this manuscript, consisting of 20 pages.

piece" for tourists. English there was begun in grade 2 and taught at the rate of 4 hours per week for the first three grades and 6 hours weekly in the succeeding grades. The experience with teaching geography in the eighth grade was considered successful enough for them to decide to add other subjects. He concluded that "This was obviously a high-powered school with experienced teachers and probably select students, a school that the Soviets were proud of".[14]

By contrast, in School No. 23, also in Moscow, where Hindi-Urdu was taught, he found competent teachers but their work appeared disorganized.[15] In School No. 55 in Tbilisi, the first-year English teacher seemed fairly well qualified, although a second-year English teacher spoke so poorly that he was "just barely intelligible and this was naturally reflected in the speech of the students".[16] Visits by Fairbanks to ordinary secondary school language classes revealed sharp variations in performance, with some instructors handling English well, and others very poorly.

### *Kindergartens*

In general language teaching in kindergartens is far less developed in the U.S.S.R. than it is in Western Europe and even in the United States. We are, of course, speaking relatively since in both Western Europe and America this is still an infrequent phenomenon, largely confined to some private schools, although its proportions are growing.

The writer has no exact count of the number of Soviet kindergartens offering foreign languages, but their number is as yet very small. Among others about eight kindergartens (detskie sady) in Leningrad and one in Novosibirsk are teaching Western languages to children 4-5 years of age. Apparently the Herzen Pedagogic Institute in Leningrad is developing a program for the oral training of youngsters at this level.[17] The professional literature generally expresses satisfaction with the results achieved, and the 1961 Council of Ministers decree "Concerning the Improvement of Foreign Language Study" urges the expansion of kindergarten teaching of foreign tongues, without spelling out the number to be thus involved, as it does with experimental schools.

More will be said about foreign language teaching at the pre-*vuz* level in the second part of this study.

14 *Op. cit.*, pp. 5-6.
15 *Op. cit.*, pp. 7-8.
16 *Ibid.*
17 Appreciation must once more be expressed to the U.S. Office of Education, and to Mrs. Julia Petrov in particular, for making available notes compiled by Dr. Marianne Poltoratzky of Vassar College on language teaching in the Soviet Union. These have been utilized in this section.

### *Secondary Semi-Professional Education (Texnikums)*

A large number of these schools, which are of 2-4 years duration, and which prepare youngsters in such specialties as drafting, laboratory work, surveying, and domestic science, require a foreign tongue. In the curriculum, as revised in 1960, about 180 hours is required of a foreign language, usually German, English, or French, in all schools with instruction in Russian. While the subject is an elective in non-Russian schools, the figure of 180 hours is about what the requirement was before the curriculum revision. How many of the students enrolled in the *Texnikums* are actually taking foreign language is not known.

From all indications, instruction at this level is largely non-intensive and follows the grammar-translation approach.

### *Higher Education (Vuz'es)*

Normally, applicants to Soviet higher educational institutions, or *vuz'es*, are expected to take an entrance examination in English, German, or French, with greatest stress laid on the first two. What they are expected to know is spelled out in detail each year in the *Spravočnik dlja postupajuščix v vysšie učebnye zavedenija*[18] (Guide for Those Entering Higher Educational Institutions). Those excused from the requirements are: Applicants to agricultural schools; animal husbandry, veterinary and physical culture curricula; the fine arts; two year teachers' institutes (in other than foreign language specialties);[19] and those applying for admission to certain accelerated engineering and agricultural courses of training.[20]

Altogether De Witt estimates that of Russia's approximately one million students enrolled in *vuz'es* at present, about a fifth or some 200,000 are currently taking a modern language.[21] Ordinarily the requirement is fulfilled during the first two years of the 4-5 year curricula, so that only a part of them are language learners at any given time. In the United States there were, as of fall 1959, a total of 483,720 or 18.7 percent of the 2,555,380 students in our 1,041 institutions of higher education so enrolled. The French language led, with 37.1 percent of the total; Spanish was second with 28.5 percent; followed by German with 25.2 percent, Russian with 5.2 percent, and Italian fifth with 2.1 percent.[22]

An examination of *vuz* curricula reveals that in general about four hours weekly is required in science during the first two years for a total of 240 to 270 hours for majors, with some 65 percent of the students taking English, and most of the remainder taking German, and a smaller proportion, French. In most other curricula, students

[18] See *Spravočnik dlja postupajuščix v vysšie učebnye zavedenija, 1962*, pp. 28-30.

[19] Apparently only one or two such two-year institutions now remain, the rest having been expanded to four or five-year curricula.

[20] Korol, *Soviet Education for Science and Technology*, pp. 239-241; 261-266.

[21] From a conversation with Nicholas De Witt on August 3, 1962.

[22] Vamos, Margulis, and White, "Modern Foreign Language Enrollments in Four-Year Accredited Colleges and Universities," p. 49.

must usually take a minimum of two hours weekly, or a total of 140 hours, during the first two years. Normally, evening and correspondence *vuz'es* prescribe parallel requirements.

Ordinarily teaching of language at the *vuz* level has consisted of three stages. In the first, a review of basic structure and vocabulary is offered. The second stage mostly concentrates on practice in reading in the student's major subject. During the third stage the student for the most part works on his own, occasionally meeting with his instructor to review progress and discuss difficulties.

Candidates for advanced degrees are required to demonstrate reading ability in several foreign tongues. To be admitted to the *aspirantura*, which is a three-year course for prospective science faculty and research personnel at research establishments, the candidate must pass a reading test in one foreign tongue. Before the conclusion of the second year he must pass tests in two foreign languages, proving his ability to translate foreign scientific and technical literature. Those who complete the training and successfully defend their thesis receive the degree of *kandidat nauk*.

As for the *doktorantura*, the highest degree, which is granted after four years of advanced work, no formal entrance examinations exist for it. By the end of this program, nevertheless, students must demonstrate their ability to read scientific literature in three foreign tongues. Since in both the *aspirantura* and *doktorantura*, reading of specialized literature is the main objective, a considerable part of the language training consists, particularly in the later stages, of guided study, with periodic check-ups with instructors.

In addition to the above, there are a considerable number of workers' night schools and correspondence (zaočnye) courses taught under *vuz* auspices. In these the exposure to language is about the same as in regular daytime *vuz* training, with the reading objective predominant. The scope and methods followed by language training in adult education programs is a topic which has received little attention from Western scholars.

### *Training for Language Specialists in State Universities and Pedagogic Institutes*

What has been said above applies to students pursuing specialties other than foreign languages. For the latter, training exists at both regular state universities and certain pedagogic institutes. According to Kreusler, 96 institutions are preparing teachers and specialists for the foreign language field.[23] Ordinarily the course of study for language majors is 5 years in both types of institutions, with 6 years for those aspiring to become interpreters.

While the writer has thus far not been able to compile a complete list of foreign languages offered at Soviet *vuz'es* and the institutions where they are taught, from all

[23] Kreusler, "Soviet Foreign Language Teacher Training Schools," p. 22.

indications, these are, for the most part, German, English, and French, plus certain national tongues in non-Russian areas. However, the languages and literatures available as "special'nosti" or majors at state universities are listed in the already cited *Spravočnik dlja postupajuščix v vysšie učebnye zavedenija SSSR*. In all cases, they are listed as language and literature, although they are administratively under either a "filologičeskij fakul'tet, "istoriko-filologičeskij fakul'tet", or "fakul'tet inostrannyx jazykov". In a number of instances, English, French, and German (and in several cases Spanish and Italian) come under the heading of departments of "romano-germanskie jazyki".

At the L'vov State University, English, French, and German languages and literature come under the "fakul'tet inostrannyx jazykov", while Slavic languages, including Polish, Czech, Ukrainian, Greek, and Latin, are part of the "filologičeskij fakul'tet".

Table III sums up the languages as listed in the *Spravočnik*, and the places where they are taught as *special'nosti* or majors:

TABLE III

*Languages Offered as Majors (Special'nosti) in State Universities and Pedagogic Institutes*[24]

| Language | State University (S.U.) | Pedagogic Institute (P.I.) |
|---|---|---|
| Abxazian (2) . . . . | — | Karačaevo-Čerkes (Karačaevsk, Karačaevo-Cerkes Aut. Ob., (RSFSR)<br>Suxumi (Georgian S.S.R.) P.I. |
| Adygej (1) . . . . . | — | Adygej P.I., Majkop |
| Albanian (1) . . . . | Leningrad S.U. | — |
| Altaj (1) . . . . . . | — | Altajsk (Altaj Kraj, RSFSR) P.I. |
| Amharic (2) . . . . | Leningrad S.U.<br>Moscow S.U. (Institute of Languages) | — |
| Arabic (5) . . . . . | Azerbajdžani S.U.<br>Tashkent S.U.<br>Leningrad S.U.<br>Moscow S.U. (Institute of Languages)<br>Kazan S.U. | — |
| Armenian (4) . . . | Erevan S.U. | Armenian P.I., Erevan<br>Armenian Correspondence (Zaočnyj) P.I., Erevan<br>Tashkent P.I. |
| Avar (1) . . . . . . | Dagestan S.U. | — |
| Azerbajdžani (3) . . | Azerbajdžan S.U. | Azerbajdžani P.I. of Foreign Languages<br>Tashkent P.I. |

[24] The following is largely taken from the *Spravočnik dlja postupajuščix v vysšie učebnye zavedenija* (Moscow, Gosizdat "Vysšaja Skola", 1962), pp. 31-40 and pp. 108-241. In the list "state university" is abbreviated to "S.U." and "pedagogic institute" to P.I.

*Table III (Continued)*

| Language | State University (S.U.) | Pedagogic Institute (P.I.) |
|---|---|---|
| Balkar (1) . . . . . | Kabardino-Balkar S.U. | — |
| Bantu languages (1) . | Leningrad S.U. | — |
| Baškir (1) . . . . . | Baškir S.U. | — |
| Bengali (2) . . . . . | Leningrad S.U. | |
| | Tashkent S.U. | |
| Bulgarian (1) . . . . | Leningrad S.U. | — |
| Burjat Mongolian (2) | Irkutsk S.U. | Burjat P.I., Ulan Ude |
| Burmese (1) . . . . | Leningrad S.U. | — |
| Belorussian (6) . . | Belorussian S.U. | Brest P.I. |
| | | Grodno (Byelorussian S.S.R.) P.I. |
| | | Minsk P.I. |
| | | Mogil'ev P.I. |
| | | Gomel' P.I. |
| Čečen (1) . . . . . | — | Čečeno-Inguš (Grozny, RSFSR) P.I. |
| Chinese (4) . . . . | Leningrad S.U. | Čita (RSFSR) P.I. |
| | Moscow S.U. (Institute of Languages) | |
| | Tashkent S.U. | |
| Circassian (1) . . . | — | Karačaevo-Čerkes P.I. |
| Čuvaš (1) . . . . . | — | Čuvaš P.I. |
| Czech (2) . . . . . | L'vov S.U. | — |
| | Leningrad S.U. | |
| Dagestanian (1) . . | — | Dagestan P.I. |
| Danish (1) . . . . . | Moscow S.U. (Institute of Languages) | — |
| Darginian (1) . . . | Dagestan S.U. | — |
| English[25] | | |
| Estonian (1) . . . . | Tartu S.U. | — |
| Finnish (1) . . . . . | Leningrad S.U. (and Finno-Ugric Philology) | — |
| French[25] | | |
| Georgian (7) . . . . | Tbilisi S.U. | Batumi P.I. |
| German[25] | | Kutajsi (Georgian S.S.R.) P.I. |
| | | Gori (Georgian S.S.R.) P.I. |
| | | Suxumi (Georgian S.S.R.) P.I. |
| | | Tbilisi P.I. |
| | | Telavi (Georgian S.S.R.) P.I. |
| Classical Greek (1) . | L'vov S.U. | — |
| Hausa (2) . . . . . | Leningrad S.U. | — |
| | Moscow S.U. | |
| Hungarian (1) . . . | Leningrad S.U. | — |
| Indic Languages and Literature (3). . . | Moscow S.U. (Institute of Languages) | — |
| | Leningrad S.U. | |
| | Tashkent S.U. | |
| Indonesian (1) . . . | Leningrad S.U. | — |
| Inguš (1) . . . . . | — | Čečeno-Inguš (Grozny, RSFSR) P.I. |

[25] English, French, and German are on a special list, following the present one.

*Table III (Continued)*

| Language | State University (S.U.) | Pedagogic Institute (P.I.) |
|---|---|---|
| Irano-Afghan[26] (3) . | Tashkent S.U., Pashto<br>Leningrad S.U.<br>Tashkent S.U. | — |
| Italian (1) . . . . . | Leningrad S.U. | — |
| Japanese (1) . . . . | Moscow S.U.<br>(Institute of Languages) | — |
| Kabardin (1) . . . . | Kabardino-Balkar S.U. | — |
| Karačaj (1) . . . . | — | Karačaevo-Čerkes (Karačaevsk, Karačaevo-Čerkes Aut. Ob., RSFSR) |
| Kalmyk (1) . . . . | — | Stavropol' (RSFSR) P.I. |
| Kazax (8) . . . . . | Kazax S.U. | Gur'ev (Kazax S.S.R.)<br>Kazax Women's P.I.<br>Karaganda (Kazax S.S.R.) P.I.<br>Kzyl-Orda (Kazax S.S.R.) P.I.<br>Semipalatinsk (Kazax S.S.R.) P.I.<br>Ural'sk (Kazax S.S.R.) P.I.<br>Čimkent (Kazax S.S.R.) P.I. |
| Kirgiz (2) . . . . . | Kirgiz S.U. | Oš (Kirgiz S.S.R.) P.I. |
| Komi (1) . . . . . | — | Komi (Sytyvkar, RSFSR) P.I. |
| Korean (1) . . . . . | Leningrad S.U. | — |
| Kumyk (1) . . . . . | Dagestan S.U. | — |
| Latin (3)[27] . . . . . | L'vov S.U.<br>Leningrad S.U.<br>Moscow S.U.<br>(Institute of Languages) | — |
| Latvian (1) . . . . . | Latvian S.U. | — |
| Lezginian (1) . . . . | Dagestan S.U. | — |
| Lithuanian (3) . . . | Vil'nius S.U. | Vil'nius P.I.<br>Šauljaj (Lithuanian S.S.R.) P.I. |
| Malayan (1) . . . . | Moscow S.U.<br>(Institute of Languages) | — |
| Mari (Cheremis) (1) . | — | Mari (Ioskar-Ola RSFSR) P.I. |
| Marathi (1) . . . . | Leningrad S.U. | — |
| Moldavian (2) . . . | Černovcy Kišinev S.U. | Bel'cy-(Moldavian S.S.R.) P.I. |
| Mongolian (1) . . . | Leningrad S.U. | — |
| Mordvinian (1) . . . | Mordvinian S.U. | — |
| Nogaj (1) . . . . . | — | Karačaevo-Čerkes (RSFSR) |
| Norwegian (1) . . . | Leningrad S.U. | — |
| Ossetian (2) . . . . | — | North Ossetian (Ordžonokidze (RSFSR) P.I.<br>Cxivali (Georgian S.S.R.) P.I. |
| Panjabi (1) . . . . . | Leningrad S.U. | — |
| Pashto (1) . . . . . | Tashkent S.U. | — |

[26] According to N. DeRochefort, in a letter to the editor of the Oct. 1962, *Washington Post*, an Institute of Kurdish Studies has just been created by the Armenian (S.S.R.) Academy of Sciences. It is likely that Kurdish is also taught there.

[27] Actually Latin is studied as a compulsory subject (not as a special'nost') at all the pedagogic institutes. Please examine the sample curriculum which follows.

*Table III (Continued)*

| Language | State University (S.U.) | Pedagogic Institute (P.I.) |
|---|---|---|
| Persian (3) . . . . . | Leningrad S.U. | — |
| | Azerbajdžani S.U. | |
| | Tashkent S.U. | |
| Polish (4) . . . . . | L'vov S.U. | Vil'nius P.I. |
| | Leningrad S.U. | Novaja Vil'nja (Lithuanian SSR) P.I.[28] |
| Rumanian (1) . . . | Leningrad S.U. | — |
| Spanish (4) . . . . | Leningrad S.U. | Irkutsk P.I. of Foreign Languages |
| | Kiev S.U. | Leningrad P.I. imeni Gercen |
| Swahili (1) . . . . . | Leningrad S.U. | — |
| Swedish (1) . . . . | Leningrad S.U. | — |
| Tadžik (4) . . . . . | Tadžik S.U. | Dušanbe (Tadžik S.S.R.) P.I. |
| | | Kuljab (Tadžik S.S.R.) P.I. |
| | | Leninabad (Tadžik S.S.R.) P.I. |
| Tamil (1) . . . . . | Leningrad S.U. | — |
| Tatar (2) . . . . . | Kazan' S.U. | — |
| | Baškir S.U. | |
| Tibetan (2). . . . . | Leningrad S.U. | — |
| | Moscow S.U. (Institute of Languages) | |
| Turkish (2) . . . . | Leningrad S.U. | — |
| | Azerbajdžan S.U. | |
| Turkmen (2) . . . . | Turkmen S.U. | Turkmen State P.I., Čardžou, Turkmen S.S.R. |
| Tuvinian (1) . . . . | — | Kyzyl (Tuva A.S.S.R.) P.I. |
| Udmurt (1) . . . . | — | Udmurt (Udmurt A.S.S.R.) P.I. |
| Uighur (2) . . . . . | Tashkent S.U. | — |
| | Leningrad S.U. | |
| Ukrainian (25) . . . | Kiev S.U. | Drogobič (L'vov Obl., Ukrain S.S.R.) P.I. |
| | Dnepropetrovsk S.U. | Donec (Ukrain S.S.R.) P.I. |
| | Odessa S.U. | Žitomir (Ukrain S.S.R.) P.I. |
| | Černovcy S.U. | Zaporože (Ukrain S.S.R.) P.I. |
| | Užgorod S.U. | Kamenec-Podol'sk (Ukrain S.S.R.) P.I. |
| | Xarkov S.U. | Kiev P.I. |
| | | Kirovgrad (Ukrain S.S.R.) P.I. |
| | | Lugansk (Ukrain S.S.R.) P.I. |
| | | Luck (Ukrain S.S.R.) P.I. |
| | | Nežin (Ukrain S.S.R.) P.I. |
| | | Nikolaevsk (Ukrain S.S.R.) P.I. |
| | | Poltava P.I. |
| | | Rovno (Ukrain S.S.R.) P.I. |
| | | Stanislav (Ukrain S.S.R.) P.I. |
| | | Crimean (Simferopol', Ukrain S.S.R.) |
| | | Vinnica (Ukrain S.S.R.) P.I. |
| | | Šumy (Ukrain S.S.R.) P.I. |
| | | Xerson (Ukrain S.S.R.) P.I. |
| | | Čerkassy (Ukrain S.S.R.) P.I. |

[28] The only remaining 2-year teachers' institute.

*Table III (Continued)*

| Language | State University (S.U.) | Pedagogic Institute (P.I.) |
|---|---|---|
| Uzbek (11). . . . . | Tashkent S.U.<br>Samarkand S.U. | Tashkent P.I.<br>Adžikan (Uzbek S.S.R.) P.I.<br>Buxara (Uzbek S.S.R.) P.I.<br>Kara-Kalpak (Uzbek S.S.R.) P.I.<br>Kokanda (Uzbek S.S.R.) P.I.<br>Karši (Uzbek S.S.R.) P.I.<br>Namangan (Uzbek S.S.R.) P.I.<br>Fergan (Uzbek S.S.R.) P.I.<br>Xorezm (Uzbek S.S.R.) P.I. |
| Vietnamese (1) . . . | Leningrad S.U. | — |
| Xakasian (1) . . . . | — | Abakan P.I. |

The following State Universities teach English and German, and also, where indicated by (F), French.[29]

Vil'nius S.U. (F)
Voronež S.U. (F)
Dagestan S.U.
Dal'nevostočnyj (Far Eastern) S.U. (English only)
Erevan S.U. (F)
Kabardino-Balkar S.U.
Kiev S.U. (F)
Latvian S.U.
Leningrad S.U. (F)
L'vov S.U. (F)
Mordvinian S.U.
Moscow S.U. (F)
Odessa S.U. (F)
Perm' S.U. (F)
Samarkand S.U.
Tartu S.U. (F)
Tbilisi S.U. (F)
Turkmen S.U.
Xar'kov S.U. (F)
Černovcy S.U.

The following Pedagogic Institutes teach English, German, and/or French. Russian is also taught in most if not all of the Pedagogic Institutes.[30]

Arxangelsk P.I.
Astraxan P.I.
Barnaul P.I.
Batumi P.I.
Adygej P.I., Majkop
Arzamas P.I.
Bel'gorod (RSFSR) P.I.
Blagoveščensk (Amur Obl., RSFSR) P.I.
Bel'cy (Moldavian S.S.R.) P.I.

[29] *Spravočnik*, pp. 31-40.
[30] *Spravočnik*, pp. 108-24.

Birsk (Bashkir A.S.S.R., RSFSR) P.I.
Burjat P.I., Ulan Ude
Buxara (Uzbek S.S.R.) P.I.
Vil'nius P. I.
Daugavpilis (Latvian S.S.R.) P.I.
Drogobič (L'vov Obl., Ukrain S.S.R.) P.I.
Elabuž (Tatar A.S.S.R., RSFSR) P.I.
Ivanovo (RSFSR) P.I.
Kaliningrad P.I.
Kaluga (RSFSR) P.I.
Kara-Kalpak (Uzbek S.S.R.) P.I.
Kirgiz P.I., Frunze
Kirovgrad (Ukraine S.S.R.) P.I.
Kirov (RSFSR) P.I.
Komi (Sytyvkar, RSFSR) P.I.
Krasnodar P.I.
Krasnojarsk (RSFSR) P.I.
Kujbyšev P.I.
Kursk P.I.
Magnitogorsk P.I.
Kutajsi (Georgian S.S.R.) P.I.
Leningrad P.I. imeni Gercen
Melekess (RSFSR) P.I.
Moscow Regional (Oblastnoj) P.I. imeni N.K. Krupskaja
Nežin (Ukrain S.S.R.) P.I.
Nižnyj Tagil' (RSFSR) P.I.
Novgorod P.I.
Novozybkov (RSFSR) P.I.
Novokuzneck (RSFSR) P.I.
Novosibirsk P.I.
Omsk P.I.
Orexovo-Zuevo (RSFSR) P.I.
Orenburg P.I.
Orel P.I.
Orsk (RSFSR) P.I.
Oš (Kirgiz S.S.R.) P.I.
Perm' P.I.
Prževal'sk (Kirgiz S.S.R.) P.I.
Pskov P.I.
Rostov-na-donu P.I.
Rjazan' P.I.
Saratov P.I.
Sverdlovsk P.I.
North Ossetian (Ordžonokidze, RSFSR) P.I.
Smolensk P.I.
Vladimir (RSFSR) P.I.
Volgograd P.I.
Vologda (RSFSR) P.I.
Vinnica (Ukraine S.S.R.) P.I.
Voronež P.I.
Vlazov (Udmurt ASSR, RSFSR) P.I.
Šumy (Ukraine S.S.R.) P.I.
Suxumi (Georgian S.S.R.) P.I.
Taganrog P.I.
Tallin (Estonian S.S.R.) P.I.
Tambov P.I.
Tobol'sk (RSFSR) P.I.
Tomsk P.I.
Tula P.I.
Turkmen State P.I.
Tjumen' P.I.
Udmurt (Udmurt S.S.R.) P.I.
Ul'janovsk P.I.
Ussurijsk (RSFSR) P.I.
Xabarovsk P.I.
Čerepovec (RSFSR) P.I.
Čerkassy (Ukrain S.S.R.) P.I.
Čita (RSFSR) P.I.
Čuvaš (Čeboksary, RSFSR) P.I.
Šadrin (RSFSR) P.I.
Šauljaj (Lithuanian S.S.R.) P.I.
Jaroslavl' P.I.

It is interesting to note that Karelian is not offered at Petrozavodsk State University. Perhaps this means that the Soviets do not intend to promote its development but will favor Great Russian.

*Training at Pedagogic Institutes and Other Vuz'es*

While, as we have noted above, considerable language instruction is carried on in the State Universities both for majors and non-majors, the Institutes, a fairly unique part of the Russian educational system, deserve some special commentary. These establishments, with their 5-6 years of intensive training for language specialists, have during the recent preoccupation with the Soviet educational system following Sputnik I, been the subject of considerable attention – most of it superficial – in the Western press, with exaggerated statements made about their achievements.

It should, however, be stressed that the Institutes are merely part of the teacher training network, supplying mostly the needs of secondary schools, although interpreters, translators, and personnel for work in multilingual newspapers also are prepared in them. Some pedagogic institutes, listed above, teach languages as one of the specialties, while eleven of them are devoted exclusively to foreign tongues.

By and large, *vuz* language teachers receive their training at such leading universities as Moscow State University imeni Lomonosov and Leningrad State University, with emphasis on the philological and literary approach.

According to the *Spravočnik*, the following are exclusively devoted to foreign language instruction:[31]

Azerbajdžan Pedagogic Institute of Foreign Languages, Baku
  English, German, French, Azerbajdžani
Armenian Pedagogic Institute of Russian and Foreign Languages, Erevan
  English, German, French
Gor'kij Pedagogic Institute of Foreign Languages, Gor'kij
  English, German, French
Gorlovka Pedagogic Institute of Foreign Languages, Gorlovka (Ukrainian S.S.R.)
  English, French
Irkutsk Pedagogic Institute of Foreign Languages, Irkutsk
  English, German, French, Spanish
Kiev Pedagogic Institute of Foreign Languages, Kiev
  English, German, French
First Moscow State Pedagogic Institute of Foreign Languages, Moscow
  English, German, French, Spanish, Italian; and also has "Translator-Interpreter Faculty" (in Pedagogičeskij Fakul'tet)
Minsk Pedagogic Institute of Foreign Languages, Minsk
  English, German, French
Pjatigorsk Pedagogic Institute of Foreign Languages, Pjatigorsk
  English, German, French, Spanish
Taškent Pedagogic Institute of Foreign Languages, Taškent
  English, German, French, Spanish, Uzbek

[31] From the 1962 Spravočnik, previously cited, pp. 124-25.

TABLE IV

*Curriculum for Pedagogic Institutes**

| Subjects | Hours per week by school year and by semester | | | | | | | | | | No. of hrs. Total |
|---|---|---|---|---|---|---|---|---|---|---|---|
| | 1 | | 2 | | 3 | | 4 | | 5 | | |
| | 1 (19 weeks) | 2 (16 weeks) | 3 (19 weeks) | 4 (16 weeks) | 5 (19 weeks) | 6 (13 weeks) | 7 (13 weeks) | 8 (16 weeks) | 9 (19 weeks) | 10 | |
| 1 | 2 | 3 | 4 | 5 | 6 | 7 | 8 | 9 | 10 | 11 | 12 |
| 1. History of the C.P.S.U. | 3/R | 4/E | 3/R | 4/E | — | — | — | — | — | — | 224 |
| 2. Political economy | — | — | — | — | 2/R | 3/E | 2/R | 3/E | — | — | 140 |
| 3. Dialectical and historical materialism | — | — | — | — | — | — | 2/R | 3/E | 4/E | 4 | 140 |
| 4. Psychology | 2 | 3/E | — | — | — | — | — | — | — | — | 84 |
| 5. Pedagogy | — | — | 4 | 3/RE | — | — | — | — | — | — | 120 |
| 6. History of pedagogy | — | — | — | — | 2 | 3/E | — | — | — | — | 72 |
| 7. School hygiene | — | — | — | — | — | — | 2/R | — | — | — | 36 |
| 8. Introduction to linguistics | 2 | 2/E | — | — | — | — | — | — | — | — | 80 |
| 9. Latin language | 2 | 1/R | — | — | — | — | — | — | — | — | 60 |
| 10. Methods of teaching foreign languages | — | — | — | — | 2 | 2/R | 2 | 2/R | –/E | — | 120 |
| 11. Phonetics of foreign languages | 6/E | 6/R | 4/E | 4/R | 2/E | 2/R | 2/E | — | — | — | 438 |
| 12. Grammar of foreign language | 6/R | 6/E | 6/R | 6/E | 4/R | 2/R | 2/R | 2/E | — | — | 578 |
| 13. Practical training in spoken (foreign) language | 7/RE | 6/RE | 4/RE | 4/RE | 6/RE | 6/RE | 5 | 5 | 8 | 8 | 854 |
| 14. Analysis of texts and written practice | 4 | 4 | 4 | 4 | 4 | 2 | 2/R | 2/RE | 2/RE | 2 | 476 |
| 15. Translation | — | — | — | — | — | — | — | 2/R | 2/R | 2 | 70 |
| 16. Lexicology | — | — | — | — | 2/R | 2/E | — | — | — | — | 64 |
| 17. History of language | — | — | — | — | — | — | 2 | 3/RE | — | — | 72 |
| 18. Literature in the foreign language studied | — | — | — | 2 | 2/R | 2/E | — | — | — | — | 96 |
| 19. Second foreign language | — | — | 4/R | 5/E | 6/E | 8/R | 8/E | 8/R | 10/RE | 10 | 800 |
| 20. Recent history of the country speaking the language studied | — | — | — | — | — | — | 3/R | — | — | — | 36 |
| 21. Special training | — | — | 3/R | — | — | — | — | — | — | — | 48 |
| 22. Physical education | –/R | –/R | 2/R | 2/R | — | — | — | — | — | — | 140 |
| 23. Practical training in audio-visual techniques | 2 | — | — | — | — | — | — | — | 4/R | 4 | 76 |
| Total hours | 34 | 34 | 34 | 34 | 32 | 32 | 32 | 30 | 30 | 30 | 4824 |

"R" after the number of hours per week in a semester column and separated by a diagonal (/) indicates a *report* required in that semester; for example, 3/R. This report is an oral test taken by the student in the presence of the instructor in charge. – "E", similarly placed, indicates an *examination* required in that semester.

| | Number of exams, reports, and projects by semester | | | | | | | | | |
|---|---|---|---|---|---|---|---|---|---|---|
| | 1 | | 2 | | 3 | | 4 | | 5 | |
| | 1 | 2 | 3 | 4 | 5 | 6 | 7 | 8 | 9 | 10 |
| 1 | 2 | 3 | 4 | 5 | 6 | 7 | 8 | 9 | 10 | 11 |
| Exams (33) | 2 | 5 | 2 | 5 | 3 | 5 | 2 | 5 | 4 | — |
| Reports (43) | 4 | 4 | 6 | 4 | 5 | 5 | 6 | 5 | 4 | — |
| Projects (3) | — | — | — | — | — | — | 1 | 1 | 1 | — |

TEACHER TRAINING (19 wks.)

1. In Pioneer camps (3 wks. in the 6th semester)
2. In schools (6 wks. in the 7th semester and 10 wks. in the 9th semester)

OPTIONAL COURSES (fakul'tativnye discipliny)

1. Practical training in extracurricular and out-of-school activities (100 hrs.)
2. History of the country speaking the language studied (20 hrs.)
3. History of the culture of the country speaking the language studied (40 hrs.)
4. Geography of the country speaking the language studied (40 hrs.)
5. Russian language (120 hrs.)
6. Literary style (40 hrs.)
7. Special course in philology (120 hrs.)
8. Special seminar in philology (120 hrs.)
9. Foreign literature (40 hrs.)
10. Improving sports skills (420 hrs.)
11. Logic (70 hrs.)
12. Choral singing (250 hrs.)
13. Individual instruction in playing musical instruments (250 hrs.)

* From Abraham Kreusler, "Soviet Foreign Language Teacher Training Schools", *Modern Language Journal*, XLVI (Jan. 1962), pp. 26-27.

Tbilisi Pedagogic Institute of Foreign Languages, Tbilisi
English, German, French

For translators, 6-year courses are offered at the First Moscow and the First Leningrad Pedagogic Institute of Foreign Languages, and at the Moscow Institute of Oriental Studies, connected with Moscow State University imeni Lomonosov.

As of 1955, there were some 18,000 students enrolled in the pedagogic institutes of foreign languages.

Table IV shows the latest approved curriculum for foreign language majors at pedagogic institutes.

The most complete first-hand report available to us is the already cited one by Fairbanks, who visited four foreign language pedagogic institutes, and again found considerable variation in performance. Work at the First Moscow Pedagogic Institute of Foreign Languages, another showplace displayed to many Western tourists, impressed the Cornell professor very favorably. By contrast, at the Pushkin Pedagogic Institute at Tbilisi procedures appeared to him quite traditional, with emphasis on reading and grammar.[32]

A visit by Fairbanks to English classes at the Moscow State University imeni Lomonosov and at the Leningrad State University Philological faculties revealed emphasis on reading and on the philological approach.[33] This is pretty much confirmed by Symond Yavener, who attended Moscow State University as an American exchange student enrolled in the philological faculty in 1959-60.[34]

It will be noted that the student actually has a major and a minor language of specialization, with these accounting for about 60 percent of the total course hours taken. In this connection, De Witt comments:

> The strong subject matter orientation of Soviet education is reflected in the pedagogical institute programs, and is the most outstanding feature of teaching education in the U.S.S.R.[35]

The table on pages 160-161 indicates the current prescribed curriculum for foreign language specialties in pedagogic institutes.

For some first-hand impressions of language specialist training, we rely upon Professor Gordon H. Fairbanks, professor of Russian and Linguistics at Cornell University, who visited the schools discussed immediately below.

*First Moscow Pedagogic Institute of Foreign Languages*

This is the showpiece of all the institutes, and it has been widely commented upon in the Western press.[36] About 5,000 students attend this school, devoted to English,

[32] Fairbanks, *op. cit.*, pp. 12-17.
[33] *Op. cit.*, p. 18.
[34] Yavener, "Observations of Language Teaching in the Soviet Union."
[35] De Witt, *Education and Professional Employment*, p. 297.
[36] E.g. William Jorden's glowing report of his visit to the Institute, in the September 22, 1956, *New York Times*.

French, and German. The course is a 5-year one, except for the 6-year interpreter curriculum. The students take about 800 hours of language a year, and the student-teacher ratio is about 1 to 7. Those planning to become teachers get one day a week of practice teaching in the fourth year and one semester in the fifth year. In addition, as in all the institutes, they must take certain required non-language courses, such as dialectical materialism and some "area" courses.

To qualify as an interpreter, a student must be able to translate 500 words an hour from Russian to English and 800 an hour from English to Russian. Standards and performance are, according to all first-hand observers, very high, and graduates are often assigned to high-level interpreting jobs, such as work with Soviet delegations visiting America and other lands, as well as international conference work.[37]

*Tashkent Pedagogic Institute of Foreign Languages*

There were about 1,400 students, 530 in English, 490 in German, and 300 in French. It was a 5-year course, with students required to take 4 years of a second tongue. Those with a major in either German or French had to take English as the second language, but those with an English major could select French or German as a minor. Both Russian and Uzbek students had to take some Uzbek as well as the foreign languages. There was an extensive correspondence course in connection with the institute, involving 1,200 students and 33 teachers.[38]

From all indications, there is a vast difference in the accomplishments of the institutes and *vuz*'*es* devoted to producing language specialists, and courses taught to non-language majors in the *vuz*'*es*. More will be said about the quality of Soviet language teaching in the following section.

*Leningrad Pedagogical Institute imeni Gercen*

This is a general pedagogic institute. About 250 students specialize in English, 150 in French and German respectively. Spanish is also available, according to the *Spravočnik*.[39] Classes consisted of groups of 8-10. Teachers and students generally handled English well, and many of the guide interpreters for tourists in Leningrad are graduates. There is also a Faculty of Northern Languages in this Institute, dealing with the languages of the North-east of the RSFSR, with some 400 students. This reportedly trains specialists for teaching Russian and other subjects to 22 nationalities of this region, in their native tongues.[40] The Institute conducts research in English, French, and German syntax.[41]

[37] Fairbanks, *op. cit.*, pp. 12-13.
[38] *Op. cit.*, p. 19.
[39] *Spravočnik*, p. 116.
[40] Deineko, *Forty Years of Public Education in the U.S.S.R.*, p. 113.
[41] Fairbanks, *op. cit.*, pp. 15-16.

*Moscow State Pedagogical Institute imeni Lenin*

This is also a general pedagogic institute. French, German, and Spanish are offered.[42] They had 250 students in English and 245 in French and German altogether. An English class observed by Fairbanks revealed poor performance both by a girl from Korea and one by a Great Russian student. In a conversation with the teacher, the Cornell educator was told that this was neither a good nor a typical class, because most of the students were from Siberia and were not well prepared on their entry to the school. He observes: "This may well indicate that the proficiency of the teachers and the achievement of the students outside the major cities is not nearly so good as in the major cities".[43]

*Tbilisi Pedagogical Institute imeni Pushkin*

This is a general pedagogic institute. At this institute there was a staff of 15 teachers of English, French, and German. Teachers of foreign languages were not prepared. Their faculties included one for Armenian language and literature; Azerbajdžani language and literature; and Russian for Russian schools. There were some teachers of Georgian, although the emphasis was on Russian, since there were seven other pedagogical institutes in the republic which also prepared teachers of Georgian.

Procedures appeared traditional, with emphasis on reading. Students registered in all faculties were required to take 2 years of a foreign language at the rate of 2 hours a week.[44]

*Moscow State University imeni Lomonosov*

The philological faculty trains language teachers and interpreters. The university differed from the institutes principally in emphasizing theoretical rather than practical studies. This was reflected by the short length of time – only one and a half months – devoted to practice teaching for prospective teachers, as compared with the much longer periods in the institutes. A total of 270 hours of Latin was also required of all students in this faculty.

An English class visited by Fairbanks was devoted largely to reading, followed by questions on the text. Pronunciation was weak.[45]

*Leningrad State University*

There was a faculty for English, French, and German, with 600 students of English and 300-400 of German, and a little less of French. Beginning in 1957, learners were

[42] See *Spravočnik*, p. 117.
[43] Fairbanks, *op. cit.*, pp. 11-12.
[44] *Op. cit.*, pp. 16-17.
[45] *Op. cit.*, pp. 14-15.

to have 14 hours of language weekly for the first 2 years. The remaining time was to be devoted to philology, phonetics, literature, and pedagogy. In the fifth year students were to write their diploma paper.[46]

### *Training in Eastern and African Languages*

Not only are the experimental elementary schools introducing such Eastern languages as Chinese and Arabic to 8-year-olds in the second grade, but a significant expansion is also taking place of Eastern and African studies at the *vuz* level. Newspaper reports have in the past few years played up the supposed prowess of Soviet overseas personnel in these languages. While it is clear that most diplomats generally receive thorough grounding in the languages of the lands to which they are accredited, this is definitely not true of all their foreign representatives. A Department of State study on this subject published in 1958 comments:

> Technical assistance personnel serving abroad usually have not had language and area training, but propaganda has exploited exceptional instances in order to create an impression that the U.S.S.R. has large numbers of language-trained technicians available.[47]

Moreover, in certain languages it is a fact that at present we have more universities offering them than do the Russians. For example, by now at least six American universities offer Swahili, compared with one in the Soviet; 28 teach Japanese, contrasting with 2 in Soviet Russia. Of course, these comparisons do not take into consideration teaching done under the various Soviet government ministries. On the other hand, there is no detailed information on the numbers involved in language training programs in government agencies. Kenneth Mildenberger, Marjorie Johnston, and Gordon H. Fairbanks, in an article on their 1960 trip to the U.S.S.R., note that: "Soviet institutions offer fewer programs in Asian and African languages than American universities, that their classes are generally smaller, and that language teaching is highly conservative but changing".[48]

In general, little detailed information is available on the Soviet African language area effort. One of the best sources is already 5 years old. It is Rodger Swearingen's "Asian Studies in the Soviet Union", appearing in the May 1958 issue of *The Journal of Asian Studies*.[49]

It is worth noting that in Oriental studies, the Soviet trend is away from the historical approach to the contemporary one. Swearingen notes that "A reorganization of the Academy of Sciences Oriental Institute in 1950 may be taken as the point of departure for a reorientation of the field along several lines". According to him, no less a personage than Anastas Mikoyan told the Twentieth Party Congress in 1956:

[46] *Ibid.*
[47] U.S. Department of State, *Soviet Language and Area Programs for Asia and Africa*, p. 1.
[48] Mildenberger, Johnston, & Fairbanks, "Foreign Languages in Soviet Schools."
[49] Swearingen, "Asian Studies in the Soviet Union."

But whom do we have, after all to engage in a serious study of these questions? ... The Academy of Sciences does have an institute that studies the problems of the East, but all that can be said of it is that although in one day the whole East has awakened that institute is still dozing.[50]

Although in the United States teaching and research on Asia and Africa is conducted much of it with the aid of National Defense Education Act funds, it is carried on by a number of higher institutions and organizations scattered throughout the country. In the U.S.S.R. it is limited to relatively few centers with Moscow and Leningrad Universities and the Academy of Sciences dominating the field, with Tashkent possibly being groomed as a third major center. Swearingen points out, however, that work in the Middle East, Central Asia, and the Far East is being conducted at Kazan, Kyzyl, Alma Ata, Baku, Ulan Bator, Ulan Ude, and Vladivostok, while significant research is pursued by such specialized institutes as the Institute of History, the Institute of Economics, the Institute of Ethnography, and the like, as well as by the Foreign Ministry, the Red Army, and other Government agencies.[51]

According to Swearingen, judging by the proportion of the Soviet Asian effort about 5 years ago, the priority went to China, followed by India, Japan and Korea, Central Asia and Mongolia, and the Middle East came next, all at about the same level, while Africa and Indonesia "... appear to be developing very rapidly from almost nothing two years ago". Finally, the American Orientalist feels that Indochina, Tibet, Burma, Cambodia, Laos, Thailand, and the Philippines, at least on the academic side, are "about as poorly represented in the Soviet Union as they are in the United States".[52]

As for African studies, as has been suggested, these were poorly developed until recently. Christopher Bird, an authority on Russian African studies, in an article published not long ago, tells that when in 1959 Haile Selassie visited the Soviet Union, from the time he left his plane in Moscow to his very departure, several guides were available to him who could speak his native Amharic, and he remarks: "No doubt the Negus was impressed".[53]

According to Bird, a special African section was established at the Oriental Institute of Leningrad State University as early as 1929. In 1934—35 it organized two cycles of study, one in Bantu, including Swahili, Zulu, and other tongues; the other in Hausa, Arabic, and Amharic, as well as a general course in African linguistics. The first Africanists to graduate under this program in 1939 consisted of three men and two women who completed the Bantu, and one man and one woman who completed the Hamitic cycle.[54]

[50] *Op. cit.*, p. 516.
[51] *Ibid.*
[52] *Op. cit.*, pp. 517-518.
[53] Bird, "Scholarship and Propaganda," p. 32.
[54] *Op. cit.*, p. 34.

Due to the proximity of Eastern lands, however, and the demands of foreign policy, Oriental studies always received far more attention than did African ones.

As we have noted, scant information is available on both Eastern and African studies, and it is only possible to repeat the details appearing in a few sources. The main centers for such subjects are apparently the following:

*Moscow State University imeni Lomonosov, Institute of Eastern Languages*

This was established in 1956, and according to the State Department study, it has moved toward an emphasis on the spoken language and in the direction of American-type integrated area studies. Students may choose either the history or the philology curriculum. There is a plan which calls for 40 students to be enrolled yearly in the 6-year program. In the latter event, they are required to study two Eastern and one Western tongue. In his major oriental tongue the student receives 16 hours of instruction for the first 2 years, and from 10 to 14 hours weekly thereafter. In addition to his major language, he must study 820 hours of either English or French. A minimum of 200 hours of some linguistically or geographically related third tongue is also required, as well as literature, philology, and "area" courses.[55]

According to Seymour Rosen, Specialist in Comparative Education for Eastern Europe in the Office of Education, African language and area subjects were not introduced until 1958 or 1959. Most of the students involved in the African program study Amharic, the official tongue of Ethiopia, and Hausa, spoken in northern Nigeria. Instead of these, they may also elect another African tongue. All of them also pursue Arabic, in which tongue they may also major.[56]

The tenth and eleventh semesters, or the latter half of the fifth year and the first half of the sixth year are devoted mostly to "practical work". Students may satisfy their thesis requirement by spending this time in the foreign country itself.[57]

In 1957, the second year of its existence, the Institute had some 80 students, in addition to a number who had transferred with advanced standing from the elements of other faculties which were combined to form the Institute. Most of the students are specializing in China and India. Judging by the size of the staff, the departments are, in order of importance: Chinese, Indian, Arabic, Indonesian, Japanese, Turkish, Iranian, Vietnamese, and Korean. Apparently Eastern students enrolled in other faculties are available as native speakers, and to provide conversational practice in an informal manner.[58]

Table V gives the curriculum of the Institute.

[55] See Fairbanks, "Foreign Language Teaching," pp. 15-16; Dept. of State, *Soviet Language and Area Programs*, pp. 4-6; Swearingen, "Asian Studies," pp. 521-522.
[56] Rosen, "Soviet Training Programs for Africa," p. 3.
[57] *Ibid.*
[58] Swearingen, *op. cit.*, pp. 518-521, and Dept. of State, *op. cit.*, p. 5.

TABLE V

*Curriculum for Institute of Eastern Languages (Attached to Moscow State University)*
*Specialty Eastern Languages and Literature*

*(Study in one of ten areas of Language and Literature: Chinese, Japanese, Korean, Indian, Arabic, Persian, Turkic, Indonesian, Vietnamese or African)**
*Length of Studies: 6 years*

| Subjects | Number of Hours: Total | including: Lectures | including: Laboratory Work | including: Seminars and Practical Training | 1st Year: 1st Semester 18 Weeks | 1st Year: 2nd Semester 16 Weeks | 2nd Year: 3rd Semester 18 Weeks | 2nd Year: 4th Semester 16 Weeks | 3rd Year: 5th Semester 16 Weeks | 3rd Year: 6th Semester 16 Weeks | 4th Year: 7th Semester 18 Weeks | 4th Year: 8th Semester 16 Weeks | 5th Year: 9th Semester 18 Weeks | 5th Year: 10th Semester 16 Weeks | 6th Year: 11th Semester 18 Weeks | 6th Year: 12th Semester 16 Weeks |
|---|---|---|---|---|---|---|---|---|---|---|---|---|---|---|---|---|
| Political Economy . . . . . . . . . . | 150 | 80 | — | 70 | 2 | 2 | 2 | 3 | — | — | — | — | — | — | — | — |
| Dialectical and Historical Materialism. | 140 | 70 | — | 70 | — | — | — | — | 2 | 2 | 2 | 3 | — | — | — | — |
| History of Communist Party of Soviet Union . . . . . . . . . . . . . . | 220 | 120 | — | 100 | — | — | — | — | 2 | 4 | 4 | 3 | — | — | — | — |
| History of Philosophy . . . . . . . . | 70 | 70 | — | — | — | — | — | — | — | — | — | — | 4 | — | — | — |
| Introduction to Linguistics . . . . . | 72 | 72 | — | — | 4 | — | — | — | — | — | — | — | — | — | — | — |
| Basic Language . . . . . . . . . . . | 2592 | 172 | 2420 | — | 16 | 16 | 16 | 16 | 16 | 14 | 12 | 12 | 10 | 10 | 10 | 4 |
| Theory of Grammar, Lexicology and History of Basic Language . . . . | 104 | 104 | — | — | — | — | — | — | — | 2 | 2 | — | 2 | — | — | — |
| Introduction to Special Philology. . . | 32 | 32 | — | — | — | — | — | — | 2 | — | — | — | — | — | — | — |
| Additional Eastern Language . . . . | 204 | — | — | 204 | — | — | — | — | — | 3 | 2 | 3 | 4 | — | — | — |

* From Seymour M. Rosen, "Report on Soviet Educational Reform Source Book", U.S. Dept. of Health Education and Welfare, Office of Education, International Educational Relations, (OE-14034-47), Oct. 1960, p. 12. This is based on: *Curriculums for University, Economic and Juridical Specialties* (Moscow, 1959), issued by the Ministry of Higher and Secondary Education of the U.S.S.R.

*Leningrad State University, Oriental Faculty*

The Eastern Faculty of Leningrad State University is more traditional in its approach than its counterpart at Moscow State University, paying more attention to literary and historical problems. According to our State Department study, in 1958 enrollments were as follows: Chinese 20, Korean 20, Japanese 15, Mongolian 10, Indian, Tibetan, and Indonesian, 25 in all; Arabic 10, Persian 10, African 10. By and large, the programs are 5 years in length.[59]

Fairbanks, writing in 1960, reported that Swahili, Hausa, Amharic, and Bantu were then being given. He noted also that there were some 200 students in all majoring in Eastern and African tongues. They take approximately 12 hours of their major tongue weekly plus 4 to 6 hours of a second language. Beginning in 1961 students were to take 14 hours in their major for the first 2 years, and the course, which included area subjects, was to be of 5½ years duration.[60]

The Oriental Faculty publishes several periodicals devoted to the East.

*Central Asian State University, Tashkent*

This is the third major center for Eastern tongues. In 1956 more than 150 students, at least half of them Uzbeks, were enrolled in the 5-year program. There were altogether four departments. The Chinese-Uighur department offered two Uighur dialects and Mandarin Chinese. The Irano-Afghan department taught Persian and Pashto, with Arabic as a compulsory minor. The Indian department provided courses in Hindi-Urdu and Bengali. The history department organized courses in international relations. The orientation appeared to be historical and traditional, although there have been demands that a more practical trend be followed and that increasing use be made of audio-visual aids.[61]

*Azerbajdžan State University*

In 1958 Persian, Turkish, and Arabic were taught here, with about 12 students in Arabic.[62]

*Kazan' State University*

Arabic is offered here.[63]

*Tadžik State University*

A faculty of Arabic and Persian languages was scheduled to be established here in

[59] Dept. of State, *op. cit.*, pp. 6-7.
[60] Fairbanks, *op. cit.*, pp. 16-17.
[61] Dept. of State, *op. cit.*, p. 8.
[62] *Ibid.*, and Swearingen, *op. cit.*, pp. 523-524.
[63] Dept. of State, *op. cit.*, p. 8.

1958.[64] The 1962 *Spravočnik dlja postupajuščix v vysšie učebnye zavedenija* does not list them.

*Research Centers*

Unlike the United States, where Asian and African research is carried on at a number of universities and institutes, in Russia this is mostly concentrated in several centers functioning under the Soviet Academy of Sciences. These centers also train graduate students.

*Institute of Oriental Studies of the Academy of Sciences, Moscow and Leningrad*[65]

In 1950 the Leningrad Eastern Institute and its Moscow branch were fused with the Institute of Pacific Studies in Moscow to form a single entity, directed by Gafurov, a member of the Central Committee and former secretary of the Tadžik Communist Party. Since that time the Moscow branch staff has quadrupled, with some 400 members and about 100 graduate students, as of 1958. The Leningrad branch is much smaller, with only about 50 staff members, engaged mostly in historical research.

The Institute issues four periodicals as well as a series of monographs. Somewhat over 100 titles were planned for publication in 1958.[66]

*Institute of Chinese Studies of the Academy of Sciences, Moscow*

This was set up in Moscow in 1956 by separating and expanding the Chinese Department of the Institute of Oriental Studies. The Institute in 1958 had some 80 specialists committed to study all things bearing on modern China including such area subjects as history, politics, language and literature, and culture. Ancient manuscripts as well as modern Chinese books of importance are being translated into Russian. As of 1958 a multi-volume work on Russo-Chinese relations was being prepared jointly with the Chinese Academy of Sciences.[67]

*Institute of Ethnography of the Academy of Sciences, Leningrad and Moscow*

Both branches conduct research on the Orient and Africa. At the Leningrad branch, the emphasis in African Studies is on language and history, while at the Moscow branch it is contemporary, mostly concerned with political and economic social developments. At the Leningrad branch, there are in preparation Hausa-Russian and Swahili-Russian dictionaries, and a series of linguistic and folklore studies.[68]

[64] *Ibid.*

[65] Apparently this Institute, or a part of it, has recently been renamed, the Institute of the Peoples of the East.

[66] Swearingen, *op. cit.*, pp. 524-525.

[67] *Op. cit.*, pp. 523-524.

[68] Rosen, *op. cit.*, p. 3.

*African Institute, Moscow*

This came into existence in October 1959 for African research and publication on African studies. It also publishes journals and studies on Africa.[69]

*Other Institutes*

An Institute of Eastern Studies functions in connection with the Uzbek and Azerbajdžan Academy of Sciences respectively.[70] Likewise, there have been indications that other union republic academies may create similar institutes.

In Eastern Europe oriental centers, apparently of modest proportions, are to be found in Czechoslavakia, Rumania, and Hungary. In Poland orientology appears to follow a more traditional pattern than is the case in other East European countries, where the contemporary phases are being emphasized.[71] It has recently been announced that an Oriental Study Center is being set up in the Yugoslav city of Zagreb, capital of Croatia.

## *Latin American Studies*

Of late the Soviets have been emphasizing the expansion of Latin American studies, which heretofore had received little attention. A few years ago, educational authorities announced that some Spanish would be taught in the secondary school, but from all indications few schools at this point do so. Only a small number of state universities and pedagogic institutes offer Spanish, and none, as far as the writer could determine, offers Portuguese. In the 1961 Council of Ministers statement, "Concerning the Improvement of Foreign Language Study", the need for Latin American along with Oriental and African studies was stressed.

The *Washington Post* of September 10, 1962, quotes a United Press International report that the Academy of Sciences has just established a Latin American Institute, for the training of experts on this area. According to this newspaper, "The new Moscow Institute apparently will seek to turn out linguists familiar with Latin American history, background, and social problems, as well as experts on a higher level".[72] Moreover, the Post informs us that in Prague there exists a Training Center for Latin American studies, numbering some 800 full-time students. Raul Castro, Fidel Castro's brother, it adds, is understood to be a graduate of this school.

[69] Bird, "Scholarship and Propaganda," p. 35. This article contains a large number of useful bibliographical references on African studies in Russia.

[70] As noted, according to N. DeRochefort, in a letter to the editor of the *Washington Post and Times-Herald* of Oct. 6, 1962, an Institute of Kurdish Studies has just been set up by the Armenian Academy of Sciences in Erevan.

[71] Dept. of State, *op. cit.*, pp. 14-16.

[72] *Washington Post*, September 10, 1962.

*Teaching of Russian to Foreign Students*

In the current "struggle for men's minds", the Soviet Union obviously places great importance upon winning over the students and youths of foreign lands. As of 1956-57 there were, according to Rosen, a total of 12,565 foreign students studying in the U.S.S.R., about 90 percent of them from Communist lands.[73] The regime has demonstrated increasing interest in developing the latter's control of Russian, and making available remedial instruction to those unprepared for college-level study.

A Ministry of Higher Education order, dated December 24, 1954, to directors of *vuz'es* was aimed at improving Russian-language teaching, by means of special measures to be taken through Russian departments, the preparation of special text materials, and the like. The Foreign Languages Publishing House has also undertaken the compilation of Russian texts for Arabic, Vietnamese, Greek, Pashto, and Hindi speakers, as well as other nationalities.

An effort to centralize the foreign student training program may be seen in the founding in 1960 of the Patrice Lumumba Friendship University. Located in Moscow, this institution apparently provides cost-free education to students from Asia, Africa, and Latin America. A Tass report of May 1961 declared that 700 students would be admitted for the 1961-62 academic year, but apparently the university intends to increase this to 3,000 to 4,000 each year eventually. Students are allowed to take examinations in English, French, Spanish, or any other native tongue.

According to our main source, Asian, African, and Latin American students spend most of the first academic year (890 hours) studying Russian. Russian students, on the other hand, pursue English, French, or Spanish, with a majority electing English. Instruction is intensive, with four hours a day, 6 days a week, spent in language classes. Students are expected to spend at least one hour daily in laboratory work and in informal conversational practice.

The widely different linguistic backgrounds of the student body motivates the school to make extensive use of audio-visual services, including radio, telephone, a movie, and slide projectors. Mr. Rosen recently visited the university, observing that:

> The language laboratory ... was well equipped with about 25 partitioned desks for student recording and listening, and with individual recorders and earphones. Supervisors in front of the classroom direct the students individually by a switchboard control and collectively by a loudspeaker.[74]

Soviet comment on the university appears occasionally. A brief article entitled, "The First Academic Year of the University for the Friendship of Peoples", appeared in a 1961 issue of the *Vestnik Vysšej Školy*, written by Dr. S. V. Rumjancev, its director. The latter largely approved the method of instruction followed, but called for the

[73] Rosen, *The People's Friendship University in the U.S.S.R.*, p. 13.
[74] *Op. cit.*, p. 10.

preparation of special texts on different subjects for students who have not yet fully mastered Russian, terming this "... one of our most urgent tasks".[75]

There have been stories in the Western press of incidents caused by friction between Russian and African students.

Reportedly, also, the Soviets may be teaching English as a second language to personnel bound for overseas assignments even in non-English-speaking lands. Apparently, this mostly refers to the training of missions of the technical assistance type.

It is a fact that the Russians in their technical contacts with Chinese and other Asian peoples often resort to English as a medium of communication.[76] Albert Parry of Colgate University tells that when Ju. Kazovskij, a prominent engineer specializing in electric power, was sent to Red China, he admitted that he had been obliged to lecture to many audiences in English. The Colgate professor also notes that some 70 percent of older Chinese technical personnel can read Russian in their own fields.[77] Despite this, English, even in the bloc lands, continues to be the most widely used inter-language – a fact which Xruščev himself lamented in 1955 when he told an audience of Indians that it was too bad that this tongue had to be employed between the Indian hosts and the Russian guests.

### *Government and Military Schools*

Scant information is available on the language teaching programs in the government and military services. According to our State Department study, the Ministry of Foreign Affairs conducts an Institute of International Relations, with a total enrollment of more than a thousand students, many of them from bloc lands. The course is a 6-year one, with supposedly 10 hours a week of the major and 6 hours of the minor language studied each week, in addition to courses in Marxism-Leninism and other subjects. It is not certain just how many languages are taught there, but apparently the program includes French, English, German, Spanish, Chinese, Japanese, Persian, Arabic, and African tongues.

The Military Institute of Foreign Languages in Moscow supposedly has an enrollment of about a thousand. It teaches military subjects, and European tongues. In addition, the Institute supposedly has a College of Eastern Languages, with an average enrollment of about 3,000 students in its 5-year course. Chinese, Japanese, Arabic, and Hindi are apparently the largest departments. Approximately 20 hours weekly are devoted to the major language, and 8 hours to the minor one.[78]

During recent years occasional criticism has appeared of inadequate language

[75] The citation is from the translation appearing in *Soviet Education* 4.62 (1961). This is a digest of Soviet educational articles.

[76] According to the Oct. 3, 1962 *New York Times*, when Soviet Foreign Minister Gromyko exchanged greetings with Cuban president Dr. Dorticós in New York, they employed English.

[77] Parry, "Moscow's Drive for a Common Tongue with Asia."

[78] Dept. of State, *op. cit.*, pp. 9-10.

knowledge on the part of service personnel. An article, for example, in the September 9, 1956, issue of the Navy Journal, *Sovetskij Flot*, complained that although many Russian naval personnel knew languages well, there is need for measures to improve over-all proficiency in this area. It added:

> ... one cannot close one's eyes to the fact that a considerable part of the officers either have a meager command of foreign languages or do not know them at all. The gap in the training of many of our officers is felt particularly strongly during friendship visits by Soviet ships, making more difficult close contact with the population.[79]

There is need for a study on governmental and armed services language teaching – undoubtedly the least known area of our entire subject.

## PART II

### THE REFORM OF SOVIET LANGUAGE TEACHING

Soviet language teaching, as a result of the calls for reform and measures taken to effect it, has been in a state of transition for the past 10 years. This makes our topic all the more difficult to discuss, and gives it an elusive fluidity which renders generalization almost impossible.

While there is no question about the vastness of the Soviet commitment to language study, particularly at the secondary school level, and in scientific and technological collegiate curricula, the results achieved apparently vary from poor to excellent. By and large, American and British visitors to Soviet classrooms have been well impressed by observation of what apparently constitutes their best teaching efforts. At the same time, the consensus is that most of the teaching is not of superior quality. Overly large classes, teachers with poor control of the foreign tongue, and a large proportion of class time devoted to grammatical analysis were repeatedly reported.[80]

A delegation headed by the then U.S. Commissioner of Education L. G. Derthick expressed admiration for the experimental schools but concluded that "The instruction that we observed in the Soviet secondary schools was not very different from foreign language instruction in American high schools".[81]

Kenneth W. Mildenberger, Marjorie C. Johnston of the U.S. Office of Education, and Gordon H. Fairbanks of Cornell University wrote as follows:

[79] *Sovetskij Flot*, September 9, 1956.

[80] See the following: Mildenberger, Johnston, & Fairbanks, "Foreign Languages in Soviet Schools;" Kaulfers, "The Russians Teach Languages Too;" Kaulfers, "Beginning French in Leningrad;" Dewey, "Learning English as a Foreign Language in Soviet Ten Year Schools;" Abell, "Language Teaching in the Soviet Union;" Parker, "The Teaching of English in a Soviet Middle School;" Ornstein, "Foreign Language Training in the Soviet Union – A Qualitative View." A British view, largely favorable, is given by Cartledge, "English in Russian Schools," published in London by the British Council.

[81] U.S. Department of Health, Education and Welfare, *Soviet Commitment to Education*, p. 34.

If in many instances the Soviets were deliberately showing us teachers they considered superior, then their best is of a very high order. We saw alert young women leading their classes in a very authentic if formal English, young women of warm personality and good humor, faithfully adhering to their orders to get pupils to speak English. When we had conversation with them, they easily understood us and responded readily.[82]

In the section on foreign language of the book, *The Changing Soviet School*, edited by Bereday, Brickman and Read and based on observations by a large team of American educators, W. W. Brickman, editor of *School and Society*, comes to the conclusion that by and large the samples of language teaching observed reflected inefficiency and poor results, considering the time allotted.[83]

It is, however, the Soviets themselves who are the harshest judges of their own efforts.[84] Officially the objectives of language study are those of learning to read, write, and speak a foreign language within the limits of the prescribed curriculum content, and lists of basic vocabulary and grammar have been compiled for this purpose.

Nevertheless, in actual practice, at both the secondary and *vuz* level, much of the time is spent in "analitičeskoe čtenie" or "analytical reading". This consists of a very minute grammatical analysis of sentences of brief reading portions. Although not without merit, this procedure leaves little time for drill and active reproduction of the language. In many ways, it is reminiscent of the parsing of sentences in traditional English classes of our country.

Particularly in the past decade has the chorus of criticism of this emphasis on grammatical analysis so grown that Soviet educators have moved to do somethign about it. In particular do the pages of *Inostrannye jazyki v škole*, organ of Soviet language teachers, abound in criticism of the grammar-translation approach. As a matter of fact, such statements can be culled at random almost anywhere in Soviet educational literature. Typical of the sort of thing one may read is the following, by a Soviet teacher:

It is necessary to point out that although in the written descriptions of the foreign language program it is asserted that grammar is not an end in itself, but as a means of teaching reading and so forth, in practice, due to the large number of rules which have to be mastered, it actually does become the main objective and occupies most of the time allotted to foreign language instruction.[85]

Three language instructors of the Krivoj Rog Mining Institute in a joint letter complained of the state of preparation of the 517 graduates who had completed 10-year schools in various parts of the U.S.S.R., and applied for admission to that school in

[82] Mildenberger, Johnston, & Fairbanks, *op. cit.*

[83] Bereday, Brickman, & Read, eds., *The Changing Soviet School*, pp. 227-239. The team which observed the language classes was headed by W. W. Brickman, former editor of the *Modern Language Journal* and present editor of *School and Society*.

[84] It must, of course, also be taken into consideration that the Soviet system itself, with its emphasis on "samokritika" or "self-criticism" encourages this sort of thing.

[85] Goxlerner, "O meste inostrannogo jazyka v srednej škole," pp. 99-100.

1952. Most of them read poorly and slowly, while not a single one was able to conduct the simplest conversation in French, English, or German.

It needs to be borne in mind that this emphasis on grammatical analysis is partly a result of doctrinal thinking about language teaching. By and large, it was L. V. Ščerba and his disciple I. V. Raxmanov, both members of the Academy of Pedagogic Sciences, who have dominated the language teaching scene, and whose preference for the grammatical approach has been reflected in both textbooks and methods.[86]

Through his writings, Raxmanov elaborated what was called the "conscious-comparative" method of teaching modern languages, regarded by its adherents as a truly "Soviet" approach. The basic idea of this method is that comprehension of a foreign text is possibly only through minute grammatical analysis.

Certain methodologists, such as V. E. Vejs even tried to demonstrate that this represented a great achievement of Soviet methodology, being superior to bourgeois pedagogic procedures. The direct method, or "prjamizm", was attacked and along with it the entire idea of learning a foreign tongue for practical purposes. Quotations from Marx and Lenin's wife Krupskaja were even taken out of context to "support" the conscious-comparative method. Kreusler observes that "The results of the conscious method were disastrous" and he notes:

> In practice this method reinforced the grammar-translation method, changing the foreign language lesson into endless theorizing in Russian on the foreign language and reducing conversation in the foreign language to negligible proportions.[87]

The denigration of Stalin was also reflected in the field of foreign language methodology, and he was blamed for much that had ailed both Soviet language teaching and linguistic. Observers of the Soviet foreign language scene largely agree that the Stalin period, with its atmosphere of suspicion regarding any pronounced interest in things foreign – including languages – was not conducive to study of other tongues. In 1954 a revolt was initiated against Raxmanov's conscious-comparative method – the official doctrine. The opposition movement was joined by such influential elements as the staff of *Inostrannye jazyki v škole*, official organ of language teachers. The most influential of the young Turks was Aničkov, supported by I. N. Gorelov and R. P. Nedjalkov, who blamed what they considered the failure of Soviet language teaching on the current passive translation method. They suggested that Soviet teachers should study Western methodologists, while Aničkov himself evolved something which he termed the neo-direct Soviet method, which combined features from both the direct and the grammar-translation approaches with stress on oral-aural work in the beginning phases. In so doing, Aničkov appealed to the works of Marx, Lenin, and Pavlov to "prove" that they had indicated an oral approach.

[86] Zališina, Fadeeva, & Stoletnjaja, "O preemstvennosti obučenija inostrannym jazykam v srednej škole i vuze," pp. 16-17.

[87] Kreusler, "The Soviet Modern Language Reform Movement," p. 162. This article constitutes one of the best statements regarding the post-Stalin revolt in language teaching, and contains a useful bibliography. See also: Turkevich, "Soviet Education," p. 115.

The orthodox supporters of Raxmanov's concepts naturally employed every possible argument to defend their views and current practices. They made much of the argument that without use of the student's native language, a great deal of confusion would result, and emphasized that without grammar there is too much danger of misinterpreting meanings in the target tongue.

All this ferment brought foreign language teaching problems to the forefront of attention in the educational area. The journal, *Inostrannye jazyki v škole*, although regarding the direct method as unsuitable for the Soviet school, came out for an eclectic approach, with much oral work and little translation. In February of 1958 a meeting of some 350 educational leaders was called in Moscow by the Ministry of Education and the Academy of Pedagogic Sciences to discuss the subject. This resulted in a project for reform which was submitted to a number of prominent language specialists throughout the U.S.S.R. and finally adopted, with some modifications. More will be said about this later.

It should be noted that the chorus of criticism of language teaching reached such huge proportions that two major reform attempts have been made since Stalin's death. On the basis of a resolution adopted at the 19th Party Congress, calling for major changes in the secondary school system, the Ministry of Education elaborated a new program, announced in 1954, and which was to go into effect in the 1955-56 school year. The changes called for were mild ones indeed, largely aimed at reducing the amount of content in favor of better mastery of it. Word lists were reduced to 2,500 for French and 2,600 for English and German, and the order of presentation of grammatical points was supposedly improved. Four weekly hours of instruction were prescribed for grades V and VI, and three weekly hours for grades VII through X.

By and large, the accomplishment expected after the six years of the new programs was, and still is, modest enough. This is evidenced by O. A. Kosova in an article in which she discusses the type of examinations appropriate for 10-year graduates applying for admission to a *vuz*. The student is expected to answer some simple questions in the foreign tongue. Then, following a favorite procedure dating to Czarist days, he is given a "bilet" consisting of two parts. The first asks him to translate a 65-word passage of "moderate" difficulty from a foreign language to Russian. Samples of the passages appear quite simple and suggest that the achievement has been a humble one for a total commitment of six years. Part two of the "bilet" asks the student to explain some grammatical rule.[88] Objective-type tests, so popular in America, scarcely seem to be used at all in the Soviet language classroom.

Much criticism has been leveled at textbooks. In December of 1954 the RSFSR Ministry of Education sponsored a special conference on textbook problems. The main criticism voiced at this conference regarding language manuals were that they included too much material, that many of the reading selections were dull, that there were too many brusque transitions in the presentation, and that the exercises were

[88] Kosova, "Programma srednej školy po inostrannym jazykam na 1956-57 učebnyj god," pp. 3-7. Also see: Benson, "The New Soviet Foreign Language Program," pp. 173-174.

often abstract and verbose. A schedule for new and improved text production was set up, according to which new texts were to be prepared for Grade 5 in 1956, for grades 6 and 7 in 1956-57, and for grades 8, 9, and 10 in 1957-58.

From the standpoint of American structural linguists committed to the "new key" or the "audio-lingual approach", Soviet texts are quite traditional and in some ways old-fashioned. They are all produced under the aegis of the Academy of Pedagogical Sciences. The best analysis of Soviet language texts is to be found in an article by Morton Benson, who examined 25 English texts for the *vuz* which differ little in format from those at other levels. He found the texts somewhat skimpy on exercises for oral-aural drill and too heavy on grammar and translation – a defect apparently endemic in Soviet language teaching practice. The highly tendentious nature of the reading matter was also noted. But he concludes:

Although in need of improvement, the textbooks examined are generally as well adaptable to oral work as many American textbooks. The success of conversational drill is dependent on the instructor, no matter how suitable a book may be.[89]

The problems of textbook construction continue to preoccupy the profession. For instance, in a lengthy article appearing in a 1961 issue of *Inostrannye jazyki v škole*, a university instructor complains that new texts are needed for *vuz'es* not engaged in training language specialists. According to him, existing ones are oriented to grammar and reading, rather than to furnishing abundant practice in the language.[90]

One thing which strikes the American student of Russian language teaching is the small extent to which audio devices are used. On the other hand, Soviet teachers appear to make considerable use of simple visual devices such as pictures, charts, cards, and flannel strips or "flannelograms". Although phonograph records are used here and there, the Soviets are definitely behind us in the use of electronic tape recorders and the building and use of language laboratories. R. M. Adler and I. V. Vol'nina, in an article published a few years ago recommended that Soviet teachers ought to borrow more extensively from U.S.A. and Western European practice in this regard.[91] It is significant that it was not until January 23-25, 1955, that audio-visual aids for languages were considered important enough to merit a special conference at the Lenin Pedagogical Institute in Moscow. There is a definite trend now to extend such facilities, particularly in the pedagogic institutes, although the movement is also involving secondary and other types of schools.

Although the secondary school has been the principal target of criticism as regards language training, the *vuz* has also been receiving its share. Belov, an *Učitel'skaja Gazeta* correspondent, reported in the July 17, 1957, issue of that paper that he had been shocked by his visit to a language class at a Moscow University. Although proficient in grammar, he observed that "When they attempted to use the language

89 Benson, "Soviet College Textbooks of English."
90 "Za korennoe ulučšenie izučenija inostrannyx jazykov," p. 18.
91 Adler & Vol'nina, "Upotreblenie texničeskix posobij v prepodavanii inostrannyx jazykov," p. 22f.

itself, if they attempted it at all, they could speak only in halting and muddled phraseology".

Even the Institutes have come under severe attack by reform-minded Russian educators. Abraham Kreusler, a former Russian school administrator, attributes much of the problem to the compartmentalization of *vuz* level instruction. Different instructors teach phonetics, grammar, lexicology, and the analysis of texts. One-third of instructional time is devoted to these descriptive aspects of a language, and only one-sixth of it to oral practice.[92]

Professor Kreusler tells how individual institutions, impatient with the slowness of improvement, have proceeded on their own initiative. The faculty at the Gor'kij Pedagogic Institute of Foreign Languages, held several stormy sessions, and decided to go about taking corrective measures, pretty much ignoring the official curriculum. An oral-aural approach was adopted, a modern laboratory installed, and a number of re-training courses held for secondary teachers of the area. The Institute has turned into a methodological center, where many conferences are held, and its methods have gained a great deal of approbation from the Ministry of Education. A similar face-lifting occurred at the Riga Pedagogic Institute, where oral skills are receiving top priority, and where research projects, language clubs and tables have vastly expanded language practice outside the classroom. Impressed by the new language laboratory at the Riga Institute, Secondary School No. 13 was able to obtain funds to construct a similar installation.[93]

It would be incorrect to affirm that traditional methods and texts are to blame for all that ails Soviet language teaching. As everywhere, the role of the teacher and his own preparation play a major role in the performance of students. First-hand observations by Western scholars bear out that there is no scarcity in the U.S.S.R. of both mediocre and excellent instructors. One point is noteworthy, however, and it is that there appears to be little attempt on their part to relate the implications of linguistics to the classroom. Fairbanks, in his unpublished report, "Linguistics in the U.S.S.R.", has this to say:

> In the Soviet Union, it is not generally realized that linguistics has any particular application to foreign language teaching. Whenever I asked about this at the schools, institutes or universities, I either received a definite "no" as an answer or they were puzzled and wondered what I was talking about.[94]

At the same time, it should be noted that there appears to be a growing interest in what American linguists are doing. Reflective of this interest is such an article as the one published last year by Ju. D. Apresjan and titled "What Is Structural Linguistics Like", which significantly enough appeared in *Inostrannye jazyki v škole*. This largely favorable statement concludes in the following way:

[92] Kreusler, "Soviet Foreign Language Teacher Training Schools," p. 23.
[93] *Op. cit.*, pp. 24-25.
[94] Fairbanks, "Linguistics in the U.S.S.R." I am indebted to Dr. Fairbanks and the U.S. Office of Education for permitting me to utilize this informative report.

Very often one can hear it said that structural linguistics offers nothing new to linguistic science, and only creates confusion by the introduction of terminological innovations. We have tried to demonstrate that this is not so. The basic significance of structural linguistics lies in the fact that through its development linguistics is changing from an empirical and descriptive discipline into an exact science.[95]

Regarding the general caliber of Soviet language teachers, it is difficult to generalize. Certainly they labor under a special obstacle, imposed by the Iron Curtain, and an inability to travel. Most of them have literally never heard their foreign tongue spoken by a native, a lack which could be only partially offset by the use of tapes and phonograph discs. That there may be something of a trend to provide some facilities for foreign travel may be reflected by an article in the *Vestnik vysšej školy*, which describes the 5-week sojourns of students and teachers of the Gor'kij Pedagogic Institute to England, France, and the German Democratic Republic.[96] Incidentally, it was considered that the French group had derived most benefit from their stay.

The Soviet educational authorities are indeed concerned about the inability of many instructors to speak the languages which they profess to teach, and the 1961 reform, to which we will refer shortly, recommends in-service training and "sabbatical" study for improvement. Some members of the profession are themselves trying to do something about their limitations. In the autumn of 1959 the Kuibyšev Advanced Teacher Training Institute organized a conversation club at the request of English language teachers in the Kirov district. This met weekly for a total of 110 hours a year, discussing everyday topics as well as English and American literature.[97]

At the Third Inter-Vuz Conference on the Methodology of Teaching Foreign Languages, which was also attended by the foreign language faculties of pedagogic institutes, and which was held at the Moscow State Pedagogic Institute imeni Lenin on January 30—February 1, 1961, a resolution was adopted calling upon the Ministry of Education to perform needed research in teaching methods, to designate one pedagogic institute as a methodological coordinating center, to prepare new texts and audio-visual aids, and to found a periodical concerned with teaching at this level.

At a similar meeting, the Third Republic (RSFSR) Conference of Foreign Language Teachers in Non-Language Faculties of Pedagogic Vuz'es, held at the same place in February of 1961, similar sentiments were expressed. In addition, most of the participants condemned present requirements at their institutions as inadequate, and urged that methodology courses be made compulsory for the entire five years. Sharp criticism was also voiced of the Teachers' Pedagogic Publishing House (Učitel'skoe Pedagogičeskoe Izdatel'stvo or "Učedpgiz") for preparing materials mostly for the secondary level and neglecting the pedagogic institutes.[98]

95 Apresjan, "Čto takoe struktural'naja lingvistika?", p. 96.

96 Jarnatovskaja, "Buduščie lingvisty usoveršenstvujut znanija zagranicej."

97 Pokrovskij, "Povyšsenie kvalifikacij učitelej anglijskogo jazyka."

98 Missjura & Smirnova, "Tret'ja mežvuzovskaja konferencija po metodike prepodovanija inostrannyx jazykov," and Kuxarčik, "Tret'ja respublikanskaja konferencija prepodovatelej inostrannyx jazykov nejazykovyx fakul'tetov pedvuzov."

Naturally the Institutes for the Improvement of Teachers' Qualifications are supposed to play a major role in raising instructor competence. The Burjat Institute, for example, had by 1961 trained 87 teachers in summer classes alone, not to mention others in three-month courses, year-long courses, and various types of seminars, as well as through self-study guided by "circuit-riding" staff members. In most of the above cases, the work consisted of language improvement, methodology, ideological training, and familiarization with Soviet scientific-technical achievements.[99]

David Burg in his chapter in *The Politics of Soviet Education* paints a rather unflattering picture of the position enjoyed by the language teachers. According to him, these constitute a profession low in prestige, which is avoided by the gifted. He remarks:

> The most able graduates of higher foreign language institutes become research workers, translators, editors and journalists; they work in military intelligence and in the censorship office. Only the average graduates, whose qualifications do not meet the requirements of more highly paid and more esteemed work, become teachers. This is why teachers of foreign languages are scarce, and why their work is poor.[100]

This generalization may be somewhat overdrawn, since visiting American teachers noted some very well qualified teachers in Soviet classrooms. Moreover, teaching at the *vuz* level does have prestige, and such appointments, filled in part by competitive examination, are much coveted and well rewarded.

Discussion could be carried on indefinitely regarding the specific problems faced by Soviet language training – many of which are, by no means, confined to the U.S.S.R. The important thing to remember, however, is that in the Soviet Union as in many parts of the world, the needs of communication in the jet and space age have brought about widespread dissatisfaction with achievements in this area and a striving for improvement. Since Sputnik I, the movement to overhaul language instruction has gained momentum, and it is now in a genuine state of flux.

During 1958 a great many conferences were devoted to the subject of foreign language study, the most important of these being the one called that year by the Ministry of Education and the Academy of Pedagogic Sciences. From these there resulted new programs of instruction based on the project drafted by V. D. Arakin, published in July of 1959 and submitted to widespread discussion. On March 3, 1960, the Ministry of Education of the RSFSR approved the new curriculum in a somewhat modified form.

Contrary to previous practice, the new curriculum emphasizes the spoken rather than the reading objective, although the aims of language instruction were stated as a reading and speaking knowledge of the foreign tongue. In the eight-year school, four hours a week were to be devoted to the subject in grade five or the first year, and three hours weekly thereafter. Altogether a total of 800 words were to be mastered by the

[99] Buljaev, "Povyšenie kvalifikacij učitelej inostrannyx jazykov."
[100] Bereday & Pennar, eds., *Politics of Soviet Education*, p. 127. See pp. 117-131, which are devoted to our topic.

end of grade 8, by which time the pupil will have studied the subject for four years. In the upper secondary, two class hours are to be devoted to language a week in grades 9 and 10, and three in grade 11. At least 700 additional words were to be learned. Altogether the vocabulary to be mastered was 1,500 words, in contrast with the approximately 2,500 previously required. Total instructional time in the eight-year school and in the three-year school with production training is 726 hours, or 66 hours more than in the pre-reform ten-year school. This, however, is spread out over 7 rather than 6 years.[101]

The 1960 reform finally succeeded in reversing the order of priorities, establishing speaking and understanding as the principal aim, and reading as the secondary objective, with writing a minor consideration. The introduction to the new official curriculum emphasizes the role of foreign language study in world affairs, and frankly announces that it is to be regarded as yet another means to Soviet patriotism and internationalism.

Graduates of the eight-year school are expected to be able to make brief statements in the target language and carry on conversations on the everyday topics indicated in the curriculum. The teacher should conduct the lesson in the foreign language and provide abundant drill, making use of the latest audio-visual devices.

As regards reading, pupils are expected to be able to understand without a dictionary selected materials employing familiar lexical items. Reading material is to be based on both classical and "progressive" writers, and should give information about Soviet life as well as the culture of the speakers of the foreign tongue. Texts for analytical reading (i.e., which serve as a basis of discussion of prominent grammatical features) should contain no more than 8 to 10 percent of new cognates, while those for synthetic reading (i.e., serving as a basis of non-grammatical discussion) are to have no more than 4 to 6 percent of recognizable cognates. Writing has the lowest priority and is to include copying, dictation, translations into the foreign language, summaries, and letters. Work in grades 9-11 is merely an extension of the above requirements. In all the grades the greatest possible use is to be made of extracurricular activity to develop speaking skills, including foreign language circles, playing of games, organization of foreign language evenings and performances, and "pen pal" correspondence with other countries. Homework is to consist of the independent reading of recommended literature, written assignments, and the memorizing of texts, and is not to exceed 30 minutes (sic!).

It is obvious that the new program, at least on paper, is an eclectic one. On one hand it retains both grammatical analysis and translation, two key elements of the conscious-comparative approach. On the other hand, it stresses speaking and understanding as the principal aim, thus satisfying advocates of the direct method and other theories concentrating on oral-aural emphasis. Perhaps this very flexibility may turn

[101] "Za korennoe ulučšenie prepodavanija inostrannyx jazykov v strane," and Kreusler, "The New Foreign Language Training Curriculum." Consult also: Arakin, "Proekt novoj programmy po inostrannym jazykam," and "Novaja programma po inostrannym jazykam dlja vos'miletnej školy."

out to be a doubtful blessing, since it could permit instructors to find justification in it for whatever procedures they personally prefer.

Since not all schools have yet been converted from the 10-year type, part of the reform measures still remain on paper. Desiring to emphasize the importance of language training at the highest level, the Council of Ministers on June 4, 1961, issued a special decree titled, "Concerning the Improvement of Foreign Language Study," and which was carried in *Pravda, Izvestija, Komsomol'skaja Pravda*, and other periodicals. The decree stated that:

A knowledge of foreign languages by specialists in different branches of science, technology and culture, as well as by the broad masses of the workers of our land has enormous significance for the broad development of international relations and the mutual exchange of cultural and scientific-technical developments.[102]

Although admitting that some amelioration had occurred in the past few years, it minced no words in criticizing the meager accomplishments of students completing language courses:

The overwhelming majority of students graduating from secondary school, special secondary school, or a university are in poor command of a foreign language. Their limited vocabulary and their formal knowledge of grammar do not permit them to translate a foreign text without the dictionary. They are especially poor in the vernacular and colloquial speech.[103]

The decree recommends the following specific measures for improvement:

1. Classes with more than 25 students are to be divided into two groups wherever possible.
2. More attention should be paid to early introduction of children to language study, with parents' consent, in the kindergartens, and elementary grades. The network of experimental schools with teaching of some subjects in a foreign language is to be expanded by 700 during 1961-65.
3. Teachers' qualifications are to be improved. Two-year courses for the preparation of teachers at the *vuz* level are to be set up. Teachers are to receive support and released time to attend training programs at universities. Special training should be set up for teachers intending to work in the experimental schools.
4. Attention is to be paid to providing supplementary practice in foreign tongues through extra-curricular activities, such as language circles.
5. An increased amount of teaching texts are to be produced, including dictionaries and readers, drawing upon the best contemporary classical writings of English, German, French, and Spanish literature, both in the original and in adapted form. Texts are to be prepared for *vuz'es* not engaged in training language specialists. Tapes, films, and audio-visual aids are to be prepared, and more language laboratories built.

[102] Council of Ministers of the USSR, "Ob ulučšenii izučenija inostrannyx jazykov," *Komsomol'skaja Pravda*, June 4, 1961.
[103] *Ibid.*

6. The range of languages offered is to be increased, to include Eastern, Latin American, and other tongues. More attention is to be paid to the selection of languages, since "... existing school practices have produced an unrational correlation of foreign languages to be studied. The peculiarities of the union republics are not sufficiently taken into consideration when the selection of languages to be offered in schools and universities is made."

7. Language training for adults is to be expanded, both through regular day and evening classes and through correspondence courses.

Widespread discontent still exists at this very writing over the slowness with which improvements are being made on the language front. An article in a recent issue of *Učitel'skaja Gazeta* complains that although a year has passed since the Council of Ministers' decree was announced, the reform of language teaching is progressing "exceedingly slowly". The writer tells how a group of Voronež secondary-school teachers, with assistance from instructors at the local university, took action to improve things. Utilizing the new experimental textbooks of A. P. Star'kova and G. E. Vedel', they shifted from the grammar-translation to the oral-aural approach. Paralleling American structuralist procedure, students were not allowed to see the writing system for three whole weeks. Practice with phrases and sentences, rather than memorizing of word lists, was made the core of the learning process. Results, according to the writer, were excellent.[104]

Testimonials like the above appear frequently enough to point up the eagerness with which many Soviet language teachers are endeavoring to sweep away the cobwebs of outdated procedures and materials. Despite the ambitious wording of the 1961 Council of Ministers' decree, it is obvious that Soviet language teaching has far to go in implementing even a modest portion of the aims, particularly in view of the tenacious hold which the grammar-translation approach has on an influential segment of the profession.

Now that the highest levels of government have come out in favor of a practical command of the spoken language rather than a mere reading knowledge, more and more language teachers are openly and vigorously demanding a hearing, and attacking the traditionalists. An article in the June 5, 1962 *Učitel'skaja Gazeta* takes as its title the Russian saying, "A voz i nyne tam", which might be rendered freely as, "Things haven't changed yet". The writer calls upon the Ministry of Education and other responsible organs to overhaul language teaching and urges new blood in the profession. Here are his words:

It is necessary to strengthen the cadres of the methodological organs. Creatively minded persons need to be drawn into their staffs, free from the taint of previous errors and prejudices. We can no longer accept a situation in which a group of methodologists, who occupy leading positions in the foreign language sectors of the Academy of Pedagogical Sciences, and in the Scientific Committee of the Ministry of Education of the RSFSR, as well as on the editorial board of the journal *Inostrannye jazyki v škole*, in a monopolistic

104 "Voronežcy podnimajut celinu," *Učitel'skaja Gazeta*, May 24, 1962.

fashion make decisions on all questions of foreign language teaching in the secondary school and *vuz*.[105]

From all indications, the clamor for improvement of language instruction is bound to continue, and may reach even greater proportions than has been the case thus far. From the standpoint of comparative education, Soviet language teaching, through its agitation and measures for improvement, is taking part in a world-wide movement for the reform of instruction in this subject.

## SOME CONCLUDING REMARKS

The writer must again come to largely the same conclusions as he did in his study, "Foreign Language Training in the Soviet Union; A Qualitative View", completed at Harvard University's Russian Research Center in 1958.[106] About the only major difference is that during the past four or five years, criticism of existing procedures has reached even greater proportions, and the reform movement is causing more and more Soviet language teachers to break free of the traditional grammar-translation method, both at the secondary and the *vuz* levels. Moreover, the expansion of the experimental schools is a further indication of the intention to introduce foreign language at an earlier age and to increase the intensity of the exposure.

It is not surprising, therefore, that, with only a few omissions and changes, one may repeat here the "trial balance" with which the 1958 article concluded. On the negative side, the following points still obtain today:

1. Overemphasis on grammatical analysis at all teaching levels, at the expense of reading practice and the spoken language;
2. Vacillation and lack of clarity in the statement of objectives, particularly at the secondary level;
3. Lack of texts specifically intended for oral-aural emphasis.
4. Failure to make widespread use of audio-visual aids;
5. Lack of anything resembling uniform written tests (such as College Board Examinations), which results in wide variation in standards;
6. Lack of opportunity for Soviet instructors to perfect themselves *sur place* in their specialty by foreign study, due to Iron Curtain travel restrictions.

On the credit side, the following points may be reiterated:

1. A universal belief in the value of foreign languages, and particularly in the post-Stalin period, the widespread desire among educational authorities to improve their teaching;
2. The vast numbers of students exposed to language instruction at both the secondary and the *vuz* levels partly through universal requirements;
3. A growing move to introduce language from the very beginning of schooling;

105 "A voz i nyne tam," *Učitel'skaja Gazeta*, June 5, 1962.
106 Ornstein, "Foreign Language Training," pp. 391-392.

4. Broad opportunities for language specialization in the quasi-intensive foreign language pedagogic institutes, of five-year duration, and at the state universities. These serve as a pool for the nation's language needs, and superior students are encouraged to attend them.

One may add to the above the drive to expand the range of languages taught, to include Oriental, African, and Latin American tongues.

As has been said several times before, it is dangerous to generalize too freely, in view of the fluid state of foreign language teaching today. At the same time, despite the ambitious aims of the 1961 reform, it is obvious that much time will be required before even a modest part of the program will be achieved.

The point which is most striking, however, in the entire picture is the magnitude of the Soviet commitment to foreign language study. This contrasts sharply with the situation in the United States, where language study is to a very large extent optional. At the secondary level, until 1959 less than 30 percent of our students were enrolled in a modern tongue while, by requirement, some 95 percent of Russian youngsters take this subject. Neither here, nor in most other lands, do we find schools paralleling the Soviet pedagogic institutes, with their five to six year language training programs. As far as intensive courses go, our lengthiest are apparently the intensive two-year programs in Chinese, Japanese, and Korean offered by the Army Language School and the Department of State's Foreign Service Institute.

The quality of Soviet language instruction is, of course, a multi-faceted question, with much excellent, a great deal of adequate, and considerable inferior instruction existing. This is by no means an exclusively Soviet phenomenon. Students of comparative education are well aware that throughout the world the reform and improvement of language instruction is a common objective. In France, Germany, and other parts of Western Europe, for example, language laboratories are becoming part of the scene. In many lands there is increasing clamor for stress on the spoken aspect of language – a direct consequence of the revolution in communication and transportation which has taken place in recent years, and the increased international contacts.

American experimentation with the application of linguistics in the classroom is being followed with interest in many countries. Recently, a rather favorable article on American structural linguistics even appeared in the Soviet language teacher's quarterly, *Inostrannye jazyki v škole*.[107]

From all indications, America is ahead as far as the development of integrated "language and area" studies is concerned, particularly on the graduate level. There is evidence that the Soviets are to some extent utilizing our experience here in this regard, especially with respect to the structure of such programs. It is noteworthy that, just as the Soviets' language instruction finds it hard to shake off its heavily grammar-translation orientation, their area studies appear to find it difficult to move

[107] See Apresjan, *op. cit.*

away from the compartmentalization of courses and their relative lack of articulation.

While the Soviets are doing more in experimenting with the introduction of Western and Eastern languages at the elementary school level, thanks in large part to the National Defense Education Act, the United States is conducting more over-all experimentation in language learning and teaching than any other nation, not excluding the U.S.S.R. Moreover, NDEA funds are also making possible the preparation and publication of structural analyses, texts, and dictionaries in a large number of heretofore neglected Eastern and African tongues. At the same time, Soviet textbook production, under the auspices of the Academy of Pedagogic Sciences and the Foreign Languages Publishing House, is being considerably stepped up.

The United States is far ahead in the use of audio equipment, particularly the tape recorder, and in some aspects of visual devices, such as film strips. Both at the secondary and collegiate levels, our schools have vastly more language laboratories than do the Soviets, and a recent survey indicated that there are now more than 2,500 of these in our high schools, as well as 600 in colleges.

As regards the preparation of language specialists, as has been noted, few if any countries offer programs of such long duration (5-6 years) as the Soviet pedagogic institutes and state universities. By and large, such training is much more subject-matter oriented than is the case with American curricula for language majors.

The problem of providing spoken practice in depth outside the classroom is one which is endemic to students of foreign tongues the world over. However, due to Iron Curtain restrictions, the Soviet learner of foreign tongues is at a greater disadvantage as far as opportunities to practice his language abroad is concerned. At the same time, most Soviet diplomatic personnel (far less so, technical personnel) assigned abroad reveal such a high state of both language and area preparation, that it has evoked the admiration even of other polyglot Europeans.

By and large, then, although the quality of foreign language teaching varies greatly in the U.S.S.R., quantitatively the proportions of the Soviet involvement in this study is a gigantic one – apparently the largest in the world. However, there is good reason for regarding U.S. language teaching, although lagging in many respects, and involving too few students, as often superior in technique. This is particularly true as it applies to our growing attention to oral-aural work, the influence of applied linguistics in the classroom, and current experimentation in second language learning. A goodly proportion of the American schoolmen who have visited Soviet language classes have felt that our best has somewhat of an edge over its Russian counterpart.

Everything considered, however, the fact remains that foreign language instruction in the Soviet Union, just as in many other lands, is in a state of ferment. Changes are being effected at the present moment, and further reform is in the offing.

## BIBLIOGRAPHY


Abell, M. A., "Foreign Language Teaching in the USSR", *MLJ* 43.72-78 (1959).

Abramson, I. A., "O nekotoryx voprosax prepodavanija anglijskogo jazyka v srednej škole", *IJaŠ* 1.102-104 (1956).

Adler, R. M., and Vol'nina, I. V., "Upotreblenie texničeskix posobij v prepodavanii inostrannyx jazykov b SŠA, Anglii i Francii", *IJaŠ* 3.22 (1959).

Ambler, E., "The Soviet Boarding School", *ASEER* 20.237-252 (1962).

Aničkov, I. E., "Osnovnaja pričina nedostatočnogo vysokogo urovnja prepodavanija inostrannyx jazykov v sovetskoj škole", *IJaŠ* 2.58-70 (1957).

Apresjan, Ju. D., "Čto takoe struktural'naja lingvistika", *IJaŠ* 3.82-96 (1961).

Arakin, V. D., *Metodika prepodavanija anglijskogo jazyka v VIII-X klassax* (Moscow, 1958).

——, "Proekt novoj programmy po inostrannym jazykam", *IJaŠ* 4.28-50 (1958).

"A voz i nyne tam", *Učitel'skaja Gazeta*, June 5, 1962.

Benson, M., "Soviet College Textbooks of English", *MLJ* 43.233-236 (1959).

——, "The New Soviet Foreign Language Program", *MLJ* 40.173-174 (1956).

Bereday, G. Z., Brickman, W. W., and Read, G. H. (eds.), *The Changing Soviet School* (Boston, 1960).

——, and Pennar, J. (eds.), *The Politics of Soviet Education* (New York, 1960).

Bird, C., "Scholarship and Propaganda", *Problems of Communism* 11.32-37 (March-April 1962).

Buljaev, D. D., "Povyšenie kvalifikacij učitelej inostrannyx jazykov", *IJaS* 3.121-124 (1961).

Burg, D., "Notes on Foreign Language Teaching in the U.S.S.R.", in Bereday and Pennar (eds.), *The Politics of Soviet Education*, pp. 117-131 (New York, 1959).

Cartledge, H. A., "English in Russian Schools", *English Language Teaching* 13.143-149 (July-September, 1959).

Childers, J. W., "Foreign Language Offerings and Enrollments in Public Secondary Schools, Fall 1959", in *Reports of Surveys and Studies in the Teaching of Modern Languages* (New York, PMLA, 1959-61).

Conant, J. B., *The American High School Today* (New York, 1959).

Counts, G. S., *The Challenge of Soviet Education* (New York, 1957).

Deineko, M., *Forty Years of Public Education in the USSR* (Moscow, Foreign Languages Publishing House, 1957).

Dewey, H. W., "Learning English as a Foreign Language in Soviet Ten-Year Schools", *LL* 9.57-66 (1959).

De Witt, N., *Soviet Professional Manpower, Its Education, Training and Supply* (Washington, National Science Foundation, 1955).

——, *Education and Professional Employment in the USSR* (Washington, 1961).

Fairbanks, G. H., "Linguistics in the USSR" (unpublished typescript, 1960).

——, "Foreign Language Teaching in the USSR" (unpublished typescript, 1960).

Galperin, I., "The Teaching of Foreign Languages", *University of Toronto Quarterly* 28.3-11 (1958).

Goxlerner, M. M., "O meste inostrannogo jazyka v srednej škole", *IJaŠ* 6.99-100 (1956).

Hechinger, F. M., *The Big Red Schoolhouse* (New York, 1959).

Jarnatovskaja, V. E., "Buduščie lingvisty usoveršenstvujut znanija zagranicej", *Vestnik Vysšej Školy* 5.74-75 (1960).

Karpov, I. V., *Sostojanie metodiki prepodavanija inostrannyx jazykov v srednej obščeobrazovatel'noj škole i zadači ee dal'nejšego razvitija* (Moscow, 1957).

——, and Miroljubov, A. A., "Sorok let sovetskoj metodiki prepodavanija inostrannyx jazykov", *IJaŠ* 2.107-108 (1956).

Kaulfers, W. V., "The Russians Teach Languages Too", *MLJ* 43. 113-115 (1959).

——, "A German Class in the Soviet Ukraine", *MLJ* 45 (May 1961).

Korol, A. G., *Soviet Education for Science and Technology* (Cambridge-New York, 1957).

Kosova, O. A., "Programma srednej školy po inostrannym jazykam na 1956-57 učebnyj god", *IJaŠ* 3.3-7 (1955).

Kreusler, A., "The New Soviet Foreign Language Curriculum", *SEEJ* 5.352-360 (1961).

——, "Modernization of the Russian Secondary School System", *SEEJ* 16.130-143 (1958).

——, "Soviet Foreign Language Teacher Training Schools", *MLJ* 46.22-28 (1962).

——, "Foreign Language Teaching in Prerevolutionary Russia", *ASEER* 20.109-113 (1961).

——, "Modernization of the Russian Secondary School System", *SEEJ* 16.130-144 (1958).

——, "The Soviet Modern Language Reform Movement", *SEEJ* 17.160-170 (1959).

——, "Language Study in Soviet Schools; the Story of a Search", *School Review* 68.335-367 (1960).

——, "The Drive for Quality in the Teaching of Modern Languages in the Soviet Union", *School Review* 69.276-285 (1961).

Kuxarčik, V. A., "Tret'ja respublikanskaja konferencija prepodavatelej inostrannyx jazykov nejazykovyx fakul'tetov pedvuzov", *IJaŠ* 5.127-128 (1961).

Medlin, W. K., Lindquist, C., and Schmitt, M. L., *Soviet Education Programs*, OE-14037 (= Bulletin No. 17. U.S. Department of Health, Education and Welfare, Office of Education) (Washington, 1960).

Mildenberger, K. W., Johnston, M. C., and Fairbanks, G. H., "Foreign Languages in Soviet Schools", *School Life* (October, 1960).

Missjura, N., and Smirnova, N., "Tret'ja mežvuzovskaja konferencija po metodike prepodavanija inostrannyx jazykov", *IJaŠ* 3.119-120 (1961).

*Narodnoe Xozjajstvo SSSR v 1960-m godu* (Moscow, Gosstatizdat, 1961).

"Novaja programma po inostrannym jazykam dlja vos'miletnej školy", *IJaŠ* 3.9-18 (1960).

Ornstein, J., "Foreign Language Training in the Soviet Union – A Qualitative View", *MLJ* 42.382-392 (1958).

——, "Soviet Language Policy: Theory and Practice", *SEEJ* 17.1-24 (1959).

Parker, F., "The New Curriculum in Soviet Schools", *SEEJ* 15.211-219 (1957).

——, "The Teaching of English in a Soviet Middle School", *MLJ* 41.229-233 (1957).

Parry, A., "Moscow's Drive for a Common Tongue with Asia", *Queen's Quarterly* (Toronto) 65.65-75 (1948).

*Pedagogičeskij Slovar'*, 2 vols. (Moscow, Izdatel'stvo Pedagogičeskix Nauk, 1960).

Pokrovskij, I. N., "Povyšenie kvalifikacii učitelej anglijskogo jazyka", *IJaŠ* 4.90-96 (1961).

"Rasširenie seti škol s prepodavaniem rjada disciplin na inostrannom jazyke", *IJaŠ* 1.23 (1960).

Raxmanov, I. V., *Metodika obučenija jazyku v staršix klassax* (Moscow, 1956).

——, *Osnovnye voprosy metodiki prepodavanija inostrannyx jazykov v srednej škole* (Moscow, 1948).

Rosen, S. M., "The Preparation and Education of Foreign Students in the USSR", (OE-14034-44) U.S. Department of Health, Education and Welfare, Office of Education (Washington, 1960). (In the series: *Information on Education Around the World.*)

——, "The Peoples' Friendship University in the USSR", U.S. Department of Health, Education and Welfare, Office of Education. (Washington, 1962). (In the series: *Studies in Comparative Education.*)

——, "Soviet Training Programs for Africa" (mimeographed). U.S. Department of Health, Education and Welfare, Office of Education, Division of International Education (Washington, 1962).

Snowden, F. M., Jr., "Observations on Some Soviet Textbooks for English Language Instruction", *Educational Record*, pp. 1-13 (April 1960).

Sovetkin, F. F., *Nacional'nye školy SSSR za poslednye 40 let* (Moscow, Izdatel'stvo Akademij Pedagogičeskix Nauk, 1958).

*Spravočnik dlja postupajuščix v vyssie učebnye zavedenija, 1962* (Moscow, Gosizdat, 1962).

Swearingen, R., "Asian Studies in the Soviet Union", *Journal of Asian Studies* 17.515-518 (1958).

Turkevich, L. B., "Soviet Education", *MLJ* 44.113-117 (1960).

——, "Status of Spanish Studies in the Soviet Union", *Hispania* 41.485-490.

"Ulučšit' prepodavanie inostrannyx jazykov" (editorial), *IJaŠ* 5.3-12 (1956).

U.S. Department of Health, Education and Welfare, Office of Education, *Soviet Commitment to Education* (OE-14062) (Washington, 1959).

——, "Textbooks for Russian Schools", (= *Information on Education Around the World*, No. 3) (Washington, 1960).

U.S. Department of State, Office of Intelligence Research, *Soviet Language and Area Programs for Asia and Africa* (= *Intelligence Report* No. 7783) (Washington, 1958).

U.S. House of Representatives, Committee on Education and Labor, 87th Congress, 2nd Session, *Higher Education in the Soviet Union*. (Washington, Government Printing Office, 1962).

U.S.S.R. Council of Ministers, "Ob ulučšenii izučenija inostrannyx jazykov", *Komsomol'skaja Pravda*, June 4, 1961.

Vamos, M., Margulis, H., and White, F. "Modern Foreign Language Enrollments in Four-Year Accredited Colleges and Universities", in *Reports of Surveys and Studies in the Teaching of Modern Foreign Languages*. (New York, PMLA, 1959-61).

Van Eerde, J., "Language Teaching in the Soviet Union", *MLJ* 38 (December 1954).

"Voronežcy podnimajut celinu", *Učitel'skaja Gazeta*, May 24, 1962.

Yavener, S., "Observations of Language Teaching in the Soviet Union", *SEEJ* 5.33-40 (1961).

"Za korennoe ulučšenie sistemy izučenija inostrannyx jazykov v strane", *IJaŠ* 4.11-19 (1961).

Zališina, N. G., Fadeeva, I. E., and Stoletnjaja, M., "O preemstvennosti obučenija inostrannym jazykam v srednej škole i vuze", *IJaŠ* 2.16-17 (1956).

# METRICS

KIRIL TARANOVSKI

In the U.S.S.R. in the forties and fifties there were heard more and more often statements concerning the necessity for investigating literary form. Many monographs and articles were devoted to studies of the language and style of several writers. There appeared also some new studies on versification. At first, in the forties and the early fifties, these were primarily studies on the verse of individual poets.

In 1941, for the centenary of Lermontov's death, there were prepared two volumes of *Literaturnoe nasledstvo* (43-44 and 45-46). The first volume, which was published during the war (Moscow, 1941), contains, among other articles devoted to Lermontov's life and work, four studies on his verse: "Narodno-poetičeskie tradicii v tvorčestve Lermontova [Folklore Traditions in Lermontov's Work]" by M. P. Štokmar; "Proizvedenija Lermontova v narodnopoetičeskom obixode [Lermontov's Poems in Folklore Usage]" by G. Vinogradov; "Stixovaja reč' Lermontova [The Poetic Language of Lermontov]" by L. Pumpjanskij, and "Lermontov v istorii russkogo stixa [Lermontov in the History of Russian Verse]" by I. N. Rozanov. The second of Lermontov volumes (*Literaturnoe nasledstvo*, 45-46) appeared only after the war (1948); it contains an article dealing with the problem of how and where Lermontov could have acquired his mastery of verse: "Stixovedčeskaja škola Lermontova [Lermontov's Education in Metrics]" by L. Grossman. All these articles, and especially that written by Rozanov, are of primary importance for the study of Lermontov's metrics. This applies even more to Rozanov's book *Lermontov – master stixa* [Lermontov – a Master of Verse] (Moscow, 1942), which abounds with fine observations on the development of the poet's verse technique.

In connection with the commemoration of the hundred and fiftieth anniversary of Griboedov's birth, there appeared an excellent study by B. V. Tomaševskij, "Stixotvornaja sistema *Gorja ot uma* [The Metric System of *Woe from Wit*]", first in *A. S. Griboedov, 1795-1829, Sbornik statej* (Moscow, 1946), and later, under a slightly modified title, "Stix *Gorja ot uma* [The Verse of *Woe from Wit*]" in *Russkie klassiki* (Leningrad-Moscow, 1947). The appearance of this study should be considered a very important event in Soviet scholarship. From 1916 on through the twenties Tomaševskij was one of the most distinguished scholars in the field of poetics, and especially metrics. His studies of Puškin's verse structure, later collected in a volume with the title *O stixe* (Leningrad, 1929), were of the utmost importance for the theory of verse' because of the statistical method of investigation, a method which he put on a scientific basis. On the theoretical level, this method allowed him to formulate the concept of the rhythmic inertia of verse and to determine certain regularities of its formation in Russian verse. On the practical level, it allowed him to date certain texts or to establish their authorship. Since 1930, after the condemnation of formalistic methods in Soviet literary scholarship, Tomaševskij has abandoned his original research on poetic form and confined himself almost completely to editorial work on Russian classics, especially Puškin, contributing brilliant introductions and excellent explanatory notes to the new editions. In his recent study of Griboedov's verse, Tomaševskij approaches the problems of verse in a new way. Here he no longer describes and analyzes the structure of the "abstract" rhythm; he investigates the verse in connection with the style and the general conception of the comedy. The problem of the declamatory style of Griboedov's verse, which is broached in this study, might also have general theoretical significance.

After World War II, the attention of scholars (and also, unfortunately, of dilettantes) was most often attracted by the verse technique of Majakovskij. There were many articles and many passionate polemics on this subject, both in scholarly publications and literary journals, and even in newspapers. The quality of all these writings was very uneven. Thus, for example, the book by I. Gutorov, *Poetičeskoe masterstvo Majakovskogo* [The Poetic Mastery of Majakovskij] (Moscow, 1950), was correctly qualified by V. Nikonov as a bad joke ("pechal'nyj anekdot"), *Voprosy literatury*, 7 (1958), p. 91. The article by V. Nazarenko, "Ob odnom rasprostranennom zabluždenii [On one Widespread Delusion]", *Zvezda*, 8 (1952), provoked the sharp criticism of V. Kotov, in the same journal under the title "Protiv psevdonaučnyx izmyšlenij [Against Pseudoscholarly Fabrications]", *Zvezda*, 1 (1953). The flimsiness of Nazarenko's concepts was also demonstrated by L. I. Timofeev in the article, "Ob izučenii stixa Majakovskogo [On the Study of Majakovskij's Verse]", *Literatura v škole*, 3 (1953).

A collection of articles, printed in Moscow in 1952 under the title *Tvorčestvo Majakovskogo* [The Creative Work of Majakovskij], was a serious attempt to expand the study of Majakovskij's poetic form. Two of the three articles dealing with Majakovskij's verse, one by A. Abramov, "Ritmika poemy *Vladimir Il'ič Lenin* [The Rhythm of the Long Poem *Vladimir Il'ič Lenin*]", and another by L. I. Timofeev, "Iz nabljudenij nad poetikoj Majakovskogo [From Observations on Majakovskij's Poetics]" may be recognized, at least partially, as positive achievements. The third article, by M. P. Štokmar, "O stixovoj sisteme Majakovskogo [On the Verse System of Majakovskij]", denying the organizational role of word-stress in Majakovskij's verse, should be qualified as a complete failure. However, the editors of the volume published Štokmar's article with reservations, as a highly controversial work, and it was rejected (or completely neglected) by later investigators. Of somewhat greater value is Štokmar's book, *Rifma Majakovskogo* [Majakovskij's Rhyme] (Moscow, 1958), which contains a good amount of material, unfortunately not always properly systematized and analyzed.

Among the recent works on Majakovskij's metrics, the following articles deserve attention: "Ritmika Majakovskogo [Majakovskij's Rhythm]" by V. Nikonov, *Voprosy literatury*, 7 (1958); "Ritmika poem Majakovskogo [The Rhythm of Majakovskij's Long Poems]" by A. N. Kolmogorov and A. M. Kondratov, *VJa*, vol. 11/3 (1962); and "Evoljucija ritmiki V. V. Majakovskogo [The Evolution of Majakovskij's Rhythm]" by A. M. Kondratov, *VJa*, vol. 11/5 (1962). In all three articles a statistical method of investigation was applied and it gave concrete and very important results. The article written by Kolmogorov together with Kondratov should be given special attention, because of its great methodological significance. Later we will return once more to Kolmogorov's research in metrics.

Several works which appeared after World War II dealt with Puškin's versification. Tomaševskij, who dedicated almost the whole of his life to the investigation of Puškin's poetic work, made in his last years a very thorough study of the structure of Puškin's strophes. The article on that subject, "Strofika Puškina" ["Puškin's strophes"] in *Puškin, Issledovanija i materialy*, vol. 2 (Moscow-Leningrad, 1958), was printed after the author's death. This study by Tomaševskij does not offer merely a more profound conception of the poet's verse technique; it has also great theoretical significance for all inquiry into rhythmic-syntactic verse structure. If we apply to his observations (which he made primarily while analyzing the stanza of *Evgenij Onegin*) the phonological theory of phrase intonation as a system of significant signals, the role of phrase intonation as a rhythmic factor in verse structure becomes totally clear. Such an approach enables us to distinguish versification ("stixosloženije", "Verslehre") from recitation ("stixoproiznesenie", "Versvortragslehre") on the syntactic and intonational levels too. – Many valuable observations on Puškin's syntax are contained in a book by N. S. Pospelov, *Sintaksičeskij stroj stixotvornyx proizvedenij Puškina* [The Syntactic Structure of Puškin's Poetic Works] (Moscow, 1960), although it is more controversial and less stimulating than Tomaševskij's study. – Puškin's verse is also the subject of a book by S. V. Šervinskij, published under the high-sounding title *Ritm i smysl* [Rhythm and Sense] (Moscow, 1961). As a matter of fact, this book belongs entirely to the sphere of recitation and does not have any connection with versification as such. This book testifies, however, to a good understanding by its author both of Puškin's poetry and of the art of recitation; beyond all doubt Šervinskij himself is a very good reciter. The book might be helpful for reciters and actors, especially for beginners, but none of its theoretical premises can withstand criticism. We will later return to them in another connection.

Among works with more general themes, the following three should be given first mention: 1. Tomaševskij's study, "K istorii russkoj rifmy [A Contribution to the History of Russian Rhyme]" in *Trudy Otdela novoj russkoj literatury*, vol. 1 (Moscow-Leningrad, 1948), which is a further step in the investigation of the problem after the fundamental work by V. Žirmunskij, *Rifma, ee istorija i teorija* [The Rhyme, its History and Theory] (Petersburg, 1923); 2. a book by M. P. Štokmar, *Issledovanija v oblasti russkogo narodnogo stixosloženija* [Investigations in the Field of Russian Folk

Versification] (Moscow, 1952); 3. a book by L. I. Timofeev, *Očerki teorii i istorii russkogo stixa* [Essays on the Theory and History of Russian Verse] (Moscow, 1958).

Štokmar's book gives a thorough review of the literature on Russian folk verse. Unfortunately, the lack of a chronological ordering and an attempt to place all the works noted within the artificial frames of abstract theories diminish the value of this review. His book also contains many interesting examples of Russian folk verse. In short, Štokmar's book can be helpful to future investigators by virtue of its materials. But his basic idea, that Russian folk verse merely reflects the "dynamic structure" of folk speech, which was supposedly also reflected in the Old Russian written language and was later modified in literary Russian under the influence of the Church Slavonic element, simply does not withstand any criticism. As I have shown in my detailed review of his book in *Južnoslovenski filolog*, 21 (1955-56), none of his arguments remain valid. For all his great conversance with the literature on the problem, Štokmar was not familiar with Trubeckoj's hypothesis on the formation of Russian folk epic verse (the verse of the *byliny*), put forth long ago, in an article published in Polish, "W sprawie wiersza byliny rosyjskiej [On the Problem of the Verse of Russian Epic Songs]", in the Festschrift *Prace ofiarowane K. Wóycickiemu* (Wilno, 1937). The remarkable study by R. Jakobson, "Studies in Comparative Slavic Metrics", *Oxford Slavonic Papers*, 3 (1952), which laid the foundation for Slavic comparative historical metrics, appeared at the same time as Štokmar's book. If Štokmar had known those two studies, he would have been forced to revise his own hypotheses. The problem of the origin of Slavic folk verse cannot be solved within the limits of a single language; as for Štokmar, he studied Russian folk verse without even comparing it to Ukrainian or Belorussian verse, as if it were a completely isolated phenomenon.

As a matter of fact, in his recent book on versification, L. I. Timofeev summarizes his earlier works – the books, *Problemy stixovedenija*, *Materialy k sociologii stixa* [Problems of Versification, Materials for the Sociology of Verse] (Moscow, 1931) and *Teorija stixa* [A Theory of Verse] (Moscow, 1939); and the article, "Puškin – reformator russkogo stixa [Puškin – the Reformer of Russian Verse]" in *A. S. Puškin, 1799-1949, Materialy jubilejnyx toržestv* (Moscow-Leningrad, 1951) – repeating all their merits and many of their defects. The book is divided into two parts: a theoretical one, "Stix kak sistema reči [Verse as a Speech System]" and a historical one, "Očerk istorii razvitija russkogo stixa do načala XIX veka [Essay on the Historical Evolution of Russian Verse up to the Beginning of the 19th Century]". In this review we must limit ourselves to several objections to Timofeev's general conclusions.

Aside from the fact that one cannot agree with Timofeev's definition of poetic language as an emotional speech type, one cannot accept his thesis that "the artistic function of verse is the representation of the emotional sides of a human character" (p. 106) and that verse in general "as a speech system" could be defined "in the first instance as a type of affective speech" (p. 18). In order to maintain this thesis Timofeev restricts the sphere of the usage of verse to purely literary genres, primarily lyric and lyric-epic ones. Therefore "the versified grammars and similar kinds of applied verse," according to Timofeev, "are not verse at all" (p. 41). As to epic folk verse, Timofeev considers it a completely separate verse system, and assumes that "the character of its rhythm is an essentially different one" (p. 104). Timofeev considers the difference between "song verse" (the verse of ritual, work and lyric songs) and "recitative verse" (the verse of epic songs and laments) to be immaterial. The doubtful statement that the earliest system of verse was "musical versification, connected with oral and primarily choral performance" (p. 203) was necessary to allow him to attribute spoken verse only to literature. It is obvious that Timofeev completely abandons the sphere of song and recitative verse to musicology. As to spoken folk verse, he reduces it to mere "buffoon verse" ("skomorošij stix") and alleges that it is also directly connected with the tradition of popular "musical versification" (p. 196). Timofeev does not pay any attention to the other varieties of spoken folk verse: the verse of the best man's speeches, of incantations, of oaths and other formulas of common law. Obviously, he is not familiar with R. Jakobson's studies in comparative Slavic metrics, which show that spoken verse can also be traced to a Common Slavic source.

Timofeev does not even mention the role which nonliterary verse plays in human life, beginning with so-called children's folklore (the counting-out rhymes, skip-rope rhymes, jeering songs, children's nonsense poetry, etc.) and ending with cheer-leaders' rhymes in sports and games and with the verse of modern advertising and political slogans. Modern metrics, as an independent scholarly discipline, must study all rhythmical verbal structures in all their manifestations and in all their functions, – aesthetic, mnemonic, stimulative, suggestive, propagandistic, etc., taking into account that these functions do not operate separately. Modern metrics cannot leave the study of folk verse to musicology: it is the aim of linguists to give an analysis of the linguistic structure both of song and of recitative verse as well.

The historical part of Timofeev's book is valuable because of the rich material he quotes and because of some interesting analyses of several examples. But one cannot agree with his conclusions. His hypothesis concerning "a process of spontaneous generation" of verse in Old Russian prose seems to be very shaky. Obviously, in this case, one has to do with the opposite phenomenon: the penetration of spoken folk verse into written prose (a phenomenon also found, for example, in Old Serbian literature). Speaking about Russian syllabic verse of the 17th century, Timofeev evidently attempts to deemphasize the importance of the Polish influence (p. 235-236). This, however, would hardly be worth mentioning if Timofeev did not in addition completely deny the influence of German in the formation of Russian syllabic-accentual (syllabic-tonic) verse. His assertion that "the clear-cut iambic cadence of 13-syllable verse, together with other shorter and, therefore, even more 'tonicized' meters, created a traditional basis for the creation of iambic verse in syllabic-tonic versification" (p. 327) is not based on one single example. While we do find a "trocheized" 13-syllable verse in Trediakovskij's work, "iambized" 13-syllable verse simply does not occur anywhere in the entire vast body of Russian syllabic poetry.

Mentioning that Lomonosov in 1739 *created* the "Ode on the Seizure of Khotin" (p. 313), in which iambic verse (iambic tetrameter) was introduced into Russian poetry, Timofeev passes over in silence the fact that an ode by Johann Christian Günther ("Auf den zwischen Ihro Röm. Kayserl. Majestät und der Pforte 1718 geschlossenen Frienden") served Lomonosov as a model. Lomonosov took from Günther not only the meter and the ten-line stanza with its rhyme pattern and syntactical and intonational structure; he was also influenced by the rhythmic inertia of the German verse, with its strong down beats at the beginning and end of the line (on the second and eighth syllable), and repeated it in his Russian verse. The first example of the six foot iambic verse in Lomonosov's writings is a translation of a German work – Juncker's ode on the coronation of Elisaveta Petrovna (April 29, 1742). These two iambic patterns became the most popular meters in the Russian poetry throughout the 18th century. To sum up, Timofeev gives a distorted picture of the evolution of Russian verse because he studies it in complete isolation from European poetry.

The history of Russian verse of the 17th and early 18th centuries has attracted the attention of two investigators, L. S. Šeptaev and A. V. Pozdneev. Šeptaev's article is devoted to Russian "buffoon verse" of the 17th century, "Russkij raešnik XVII veka", *Učenye zapiski Leningradskogo Gosudarstvennogo Pedagogičeskogo Instituta im. Gercena*, vol. 89 (Leningrad, 1949). Pozdneev's articles deal with the verse of lyric songs: "Rukopisnye pesenniki XVII-XVIII vekov [The Handwritten Song Collections of the 17th-18th Centuries]", *Učenye zapiski Moskovskogo gosudarstvennogo zaočnogo pedagogičeskogo instituta*, vol. 1 (Moscow, 1958) and "Rannie liričeskie knižnye pesni petrovskogo vremeni [The Early Lyric Literary Songs of Peter's Time]", *Naučnye doklady vysšej školy, Filologičeskie nauki*, No. 2 (1958); cf. also his German article, "Die tonischen Elemente im russischen syllabischen Vers", *Zeitschrift fur slavische Philologie*, 28 (1960). The material cited by Pozdneev is very interesting, but it requires a thorough description and a detailed statistical analysis. Operating only with specially chosen quotations, one can come to premature generalizations. The idea of "the tonicization" (or, more exactly, of "trocheization") of so-called syllabic verse was put forth by earlier writers (e.g., V. N. Peretc in 1901) and it is obviously correct. But this in no way diminishes Lomonosov's role in the reshaping of Russian verse in the forties of the 18th century: the introduction of iambic verse into Russian poetry was a revolutionary step.

Among critical articles devoted to the verse of Soviet poets one should be pointed out, "O ritmičeskom novatorstve sovetskoj poezii [On Rhythmic Innovations in Soviet Poetry]" by E. Ermilova in *Voprosy literatury*, 2 (1961).

The attentive reader may already have noticed that the number of books and articles on metrics increases greatly in the late fifties. And just at this time B. V. Tomaševskij dies suddenly (Aug. 24, 1957), in his late sixties, still full of creative power. His death occurred at a moment when the science of metrics was again flourishing in the U.S.S.R.; it was therefore an immense loss for Soviet scholarship. His two books dealing with versification were edited posthumously by his disciples and friends. The first one, *Stix i jazyk* [Verse and Language] (Moscow-Leningrad, 1959), is a collection of his last studies; in its first half were included a paper, prepared for the Fourth Congress of Slavicists in Moscow, from which the entire book takes its title, and his studies on the history of Russian rhyme, on Griboedov's verse and on Puškin's strophes. The second book, *Stilistika i stixosloženije* [Stylistics and Versification] (Leningrad, 1959), is a set of lectures given in one of his courses at the University of Leningrad.

A harmful development in Soviet scholarship must be seen in the attempt to revive a rhythmic theory which was given up long ago and which might mislead younger investigators. It is the so-called "musical bar theory", which is about a hundred years old. In Germany a distinguished representative of this theory was R. Westphal, who also wrote on Russian verse and exerted a great influence in Russia (on Ju. N. Mel'gunov, S. Šafranov, D. G. Gincburg, etc.). When in the twenties this theory laid the foundations of the poetics of the constructivist movement, it was already a theoretical anachronism. The theory was set forth by A. Kvjatkovskij, in the article, "Taktometr [Bar-meter]", *Biznes* [Business], *Sbornik literaturnogo centra konstruktivistov* (Moscow, 1929), and later was developed in a second article, "Metrika russkogo narodnogo stixa [The Metrics of Russian Folk Verse]", in *Literaturnyj kritik*, 5-6 (1940). Recently Kvjatkovskij published a new article, "Russkoe stixosloženie [Russian Versification]", *Russkaja literatura*, 1 (1960). There he divided all verse forms into dis-metrical (e.g. *vers libre*) and metrical (e.g. syllabic-accentual verse). Starting from the mistaken assumption that the experience of time in spoken verse is not a subjective, but an objective one (as in music), he attempts to fit all the "metrical" forms of Russian verse into his "bar-metrical periods", and if they do not fit in, he lengthens syllables into two units of measure or introduces "structural pauses" (if necessary, two or three in succession and sometimes even inside a word-unit). As a result of these manipulations the line disappears as a basic unit of verse: the "bar-metrical periods" do not coincide with the line limits. The absurdity of such a "method" is self-evident. The same shortcomings (the confusion of the problems of versification and recitation, the attempt to establish the objective time in spoken verse) mark the "theory of time compensations" advocated by S. V. Šervinskij and set forth for the first time in the article, "Vremennýe kompensacii v stixe [Time Compensations in Verse]", *IzvAN*, vol. 19, No. 6 (1960). This article, slightly reworked, was included as the second chapter of his book *Ritm i smysl*. Šervinskij takes as an axiom the assertion that in the Russian language stressed syllables are *always* longer than unstressed ones. Speaking about Russian stress, he quotes primarily Lomonosov. He obviously is not familiar with the remarkable study by N. I. Žinkin, "Vosprijatie udarenija v slovax russkogo jazyka [The Perception of the Stress in the Words of Russian]", *Izvestija Akademii pedagogičeskix nauk RSFSR*, 54 (1954), where Russian stress is described in all its complexity. If, for example, in an iambic line, one stress is lacking, in that case, according to Šervinskij, there occurs a series of phenomena, which together amount to "a compensation for the time decrease" (d. 30). Various "lengthenings" and "accelerations", "pauses" and even "groups of consonants", etc., function as such compensations. The author declares: "Moreover, it is difficult to foresee all the variants of conceivable time compensations" (p. 31). In the long run, Šervinskij's theory goes back to Westphal, to whom the author refers as to a high authority (p. 25). It is sufficient to listen to the records of the best Russian reciters to realize that none of Šervinskij's "compensations" is obligatory for anyone, even in recitation.

The "musical bar theory" is also reflected in the most recent book on versification, *Studija stixa* [Verse Study] (Moscow, 1962), by Il'ja Sel'vinskij, a gifted poet and teacher, at one time the head of the constructivist movement. Sel'vinskij, as a man much more sensitive to rhythm of verse than Kvjatkovskij, does not go to the extremes of the latter. Sel'vinskij only attempts to prove that there exists in modern Russian poetry, besides syllabic-accentual verse, "dol'niks" and purely accentual verse, a fourth type of verse, the "taktovik" (bar verse), which has, according to Sel'vinskij, a great future in Soviet poetry. A small grain of truth present in this statement has been developed to unusually enormous proportions in the theoretical part of his book. – Sel'-vinskij's work has a very curious "prehistory". In 1958 the first draft of his book, entitled *Stixija russkogo stixa* [The Nature of Russian Verse], was strongly criticized at a meeting of the Learned Council of the Gorkij Literary Institute, and later in the pages of the literary journal, *Literatura i žizn'* (July 23 and Aug. 27). Strange as it may seem, one of his most violent opponents in this discussion was his former friend Kvjatkovskij. Sel'vinskij tried once more to propagate his ideas in an article in *Literaturnaja gazeta* (Jan. 8, 1959), but again was criticized, this time by V. Druzin in an article appearing in the same issue of that periodical. A year later, in a pamphlet by A. Kovalenkov, *Praktika sovremennogo stixosloženija* [The Practice of Modern Versification] (Moscow, 1960), an entire chapter was devoted to the criticism of Sel'vinskij's unpublished book. From a comparison of the quotations in Kovalenkov with Sel'vinskij's printed book one can see that he thoroughly reworked the text, changed the titles both of the whole book and, probably, of its theoretical part; the latter is now entitled "My Poetics", stressing the subjective character of the author's theory. As a whole, Sel'vinskij's book is a remarkable piece of work, primarily as a poet's prose on poetry. It is written with verve and makes fascinating reading. It deserves to be discussed *sine ira.*

Among textbooks on Russian versification for college students or for beginning poets three works should be pointed out. The most important is B. V. Tomaševskij's *Stilistika i stixosloženie*, which was already mentioned. A book by V. E. Xolševnikov, *Osnovy russkogo stixosloženija* [Fundamentals of Russian Versification] (Leningrad, 1958, 2nd ed. 1959), is shorter than the chapter on metrics in Tomaševskij's book, but it is also very clearly written, although with some, sometimes unavoidable, simplifications. At any rate, it can be recommended as an introduction to the problems of Russian classical and modern verse. Considerably enlarged and with a modified title, *Osnovy stixovedenija, Russkoe stixosloženie* [Fundamentals of Metrics, Russian Versification], Xolševnikov's textbook appeared again in 1962 (in Leningrad). Among other additions to the book (on the stanzas and the sound pattern of Russian verse), the author also included, as the third chapter, a revised version of his article on intonation "O tipax intonacii russkogo klassičeskogo stixa [On Intonational Types of Russian Classical Verse]", formerly published in *Učenye zapiski Leningradskogo gosudarstvennogo universiteta*, No. 295 (1960). This third chapter, "Intonacija stixotvornoj reči [The Intonation of Versified Speech]", should be qualified as a failure, although it contains many correct statements. The author has confused the concept of the tonality of verse texts (melodical, rhetorical, colloquial, etc.) with the concept of phrase intonation as a system of significant phonemic signals. He identifies the intonational signals (cadences, anticadences, demicadences) with "stronger and weaker pauses", "conditionally" equating them with punctuation marks (period. semicolon, comma, p. 103). But we must not be too harsh on him for this error, since, for example, Timofeev in his *Očerki* (p. 70) identifies punctuation and intonation without any reservation.

The third book, G. A. Šengeli's *Texnika stixa* [Verse Technique] is intended for "beginning poets, young literary historians or teachers." It was published for the first time in 1940; the second posthumous edition appeared in 1960 (in Moscow), with a warm foreword by L. I. Timofeev. Unfortunately, the author did not complete the revision of the text; it was edited and partially abbreviated by Timofeev. In this book Šengeli gives in a popular form the results of his earlier studies on Russian verse; therefore this book shares all the merits and defects of his theories. Those theories in many ways made our knowledge of the structure of Russian syllabic-accentual verse and Russian prose more exact, but they have brought about a great confusion in the analysis of free verse (dol'niks, purely accentual verse and *vers libre*). However, there are in this second edition some valuable new observations. For example, attention should be paid to Šengeli's attempt at a new classification of sound-repetitions in verse (the so-called "instrumentation").

The most important event in Soviet scholarship in the sixties is the appearance of a whole group of scholars, mathematicians and linguists, interested in verse studies, primarily in the analysis of verse structure by means of mathematical methods. This group, attached to the Department of the Theory of Probability at the Moscow State University, is headed by an outstanding mathematician, A. N. Kolmogorov, and collaborates very closely with a number of gifted young Moscow linguists, in particular Vjačeslav Ivanov. Kolmogorov's group first appeared publicly at "the meeting devoted to the application of mathematical methods to the investigation of the language of literary works," which took place in Gorkij, Sept. 23-27, 1961. "The hosts" at this meeting were the members of another group primarily interested in the application of mathematical methods to the study of the language and style of Russian fiction and headed by B. N. Golovin, the chairman of the Russian Language Department at Gorkij State University. At the meeting there were also present scholars from other centers, e.g. from Leningrad. The meeting was opened with a lecture given by Kolmogorov: "The Theory of Combinations, Statistics and the Theory of Probability in Metrics." The papers delivered at the meeting showed the vast scope of the plans for the study of verse in Kolmogorov's group, both in the application of new methods and in the quality and quantity of material employed. At the end of the meeting Kolmogorov spoke about the significance of the investigation of poetry by mathematical methods for cybernetics. "The meeting adopted a resolution, stressing the importance of statistical works in the field of poetics and linguistics, the necessity of publishing the literature on these problems (particularly of reprinting old works by B. V. Tomaševskij and other authors) and the desirability of a constant interchange of the results of statistical investigations."[1]

One can only regret that the members of Kolmogorov's group do not hasten to publish their studies, some of which are already completely finished (e.g. by M. L. Gasparov on "dol'niks"). Those interested in metrics await their publications impatiently. This impatience became even greater when V. Šklovskij's brilliant interview with Kolmogorov was published in *Literaturnaja gazeta*, No. 57 (1962) under the title, "On the Vorobyev Hills". From this interview, we know even more about the vast scope of Kolmogorov's ideas.

Without any exaggeration, one can state that the study of verse in the Soviet Union is once again definitely on the upswing.

[1] See two thorough and competent reports on the meeting in Gorkij by I. I. Revzin in *VJa*, vol. 11/1 (1962), and in *Strukturno-tipologičeskie issledovanija, Sbornik statej* (Moscow, 1962), and a less competent report by E. Ermilova in *Voprosy literatury*, 3 (1962).

*LANGUAGES, LANGUAGE FAMILIES, AND AREAL GROUPINGS*

# INDO-EUROPEAN

WERNER WINTER

For its success, work in comparative linguistics in the traditional sense depends to a great extent on the existence of a secondary school system of the traditional European type: if a student leaving high school has been thoroughly trained in Latin and Greek and in one or two living European languages apart from his own, his advantages over the normal American high school graduate with just a couple of years of a Romance or Germanic language are obvious. It is not a matter of chance that a good number of the practicing Indo-Europeanists in this country are European-trained (which does of course not preclude that some scholars of American extraction are also doing excellent work in the Indo-European field), and it is also not surprising that the vast majority of our promising young students is attracted much more by the fields of linguistic theory or of exotic languages: to spend year upon year just acquainting oneself with essentially well-known languages and with an ever-growing mass of secondary literature must seem wasteful when so much satisfaction and so much excitement is readily to be had from fresh discoveries in little-explored areas.

There is much similarity between the professional situation in this country and that found in the Soviet Union: in spite of what has been said in praise of Soviet efforts in foreign language teaching, it has to be noted that there is no current Russian equivalent of the Swiss or German Gymnasium. While one may well question the usefulness of this type of school in a modern world, the fact remains that for the particular field of linguistic endeavor that is under consideration here, a school with a heavy emphasis on the classical languages and on foreign languages in general offers the best preparation. Again, as in the case of this country, we can expect a few scholars to overcome the handicaps and to become productive in the field of Indo-European, but we must also expect that on the whole the quantity of work published in this area will be small.

To assess the relative importance of comparative work in Indo-European our survey must consider two dimensions of the problem: our assessment must appraise both the quantity and the quality of the work. Of the two questions, the first requires a count of the material published and a projection of the results against a frame of reference; the second calls for evaluation and for the expression of preferences and can therefore be approached in a more eclectic manner than the first.

We will try to determine the role of comparative Indo-European studies by an analysis of the work done in non-Slavic Indo-European languages during a specific period. This period comprises the years 1950 through 1959. There is obviously little point in beginning a survey at a date earlier than the rejection of Marrism; while individual scholars of course produced good work during the preceding years, the predominant tendencies do not deserve to be considered in a context where Linguistics is held to be a science. That only a decade should be the period to be used for our analysis has its very practical reasons: 1959 is the last year covered at the time of this writing by the *Linguistic bibliography*, and this, together with books such as *Bibliografičeskij ukazatel' literatury po jazykoznaniju izdannoj v SSSR s 1918 po 1957 god* (vypusk 1, AN SSSR, Institut jazykoznanija; Izdatel'stvo AN SSSR, Moscow, 1958; 368 pages), remains the most practical source for the purpose of assembling a representative, if not complete, bibliography of Soviet publications, although a comparison with Soviet bibliographical lists shows that the coverage is at times uneven (additions for the last year of our decade, 1959, are to be expected in the next issue of *LB*).

In addition to 32 dictionaries, a total of 837 titles from the field of Indo-European languages (excluding the Slavic ones) was extracted from the sources available. These 837 titles comprised 50,134 pages. Of the total, 21 items with 4,724 pages were translations of publications that had previously appeared outside the Soviet Union; among the authors translated during our period are Bally, Benveniste, Chantraine, Ernout, Friedrich, Iordan, Krause, Lane, Lewis/Pedersen, Meillet, Prokosch, and Schuchardt. The total count of original publications then amounts to 816 titles with 45,410 pages.

A breakdown of these figures according to a number of different criteria follows:

1. *Languages and groups of languages treated*

| | | |
|---|---|---|
| A. Original studies | | |
| General Indo-European | 33 | |
| Anatolian | 8 | |
| Indo-Iranian | 152 | |
| Indic | | 29 |
| Iranian | | 120 |
| Tocharian | 5 | |
| Armenian | 44 | |
| Greek | 39 | |
| Pelasgian | 1 | |
| Albanian | 4 | |
| Italic, Latin, Romance | 205 | |
| Latin | | 10 |
| General Romance | | 7 |
| Spanish | | 13 |
| Portuguese | | 1 |

| | | |
|---|---|---|
| French | | 84 |
| Italian | | 5 |
| Rumanian (Moldavian) | | 84 |
| Germanic | 243 | |
| Gothic | | 6 |
| Scandinavian | | 16 |
| German | | 85 |
| Dutch, Afrikaans | | 3 |
| English | | 110 |
| Baltic (General Balto-Slavic) | 82 | |
| Old Prussian | | 1 |
| Lithuanian | | 18 |
| Latvian | | 46 |
| | 816 | |
| **B. Translations** | | |
| General Indo-European | 5 | |
| Anatolian | 1 | |
| Tocharian | 5 | |
| Greek | 1 | |
| Italic, Latin, Romance | 4 | |
| Latin | | 1 |
| General Romance | | 1 |
| French | | 1 |
| Rumanian | | 1 |
| Germanic | 4 | |
| German | | 1 |
| English | | 1 |
| Celtic | 1 | |
| | 21 | |
| **C. Dictionaries** | | |
| Indo-Iranian | 14 | |
| Indic | | 4 |
| Iranian | | 10 |
| Armenian | 1 | |
| Greek | 1 | |
| Albanian | 4 | |
| Romance | 6 | |
| Portuguese | | 1 |
| French | | 2 |
| Rumanian (Moldavian) | | 3 |

| | | |
|---|---|---|
| Germanic | 3 | |
| Danish | | 1 |
| German | | 1 |
| Dutch | | 1 |
| Baltic | 3 | |
| Lithuanian | | 2 |
| Latvian | | 1 |
| | 32 | |

2. *Fields of linguistic study treated*

| Field | Titles | Pages |
|---|---|---|
| Theory and general problems | 191 | 10,779 |
| Grammars, manuals | 62 | 12,002 |
| Phonology | 75 | 4,188 |
| Morphology | 86 | 3,878 |
| Syntax | 231 | 7,348 |
| Style | 20 | 860 |
| Lexicology | 66 | 1,994 |
| Etymology | 36 | 1,754 |
| Semasiology | 10 | 108 |
| Dialectology | 52 | 3,959 |
| Edition of texts | 22 | 3,214 |

3. *Fields of concentration in individual languages or language groups (only fields with five titles or more are listed)*

| | |
|---|---|
| A. English (total: 111) | |
| Syntax | 64 |
| Morphology | 14 |
| Phonology | 12 |
| Lexicology | 10 |
| B. Iranian (total: 130) | |
| Theory and general problems | 24 |
| Syntax | 19 |
| Grammar | 17 |
| Phonology | 14 |
| Dialectology | 13 |
| Dictionaries | 13 |
| Texts | 12 |
| Morphology | 9 |
| Lexicology | 8 |
| Etymology | 5 |

| | |
|---|---|
| C. Greek (total: 41) | |
| General problems | 10 |
| Etymology | 8 |
| Lexicology | 5 |
| D. Latin (total: 11) | |
| General problems | 5 |

4. *Participation of scholars in the study of individual languages or groups of languages*

| | |
|---|---|
| A. English | |
| Total number | 73 |
| Individuals with 1 contribution | 51 |
| 2 contributions | 10 |
| 3 contributions | 7 |
| 4 contributions | 2 |
| 5 contributions | 2 |
| 6 contributions | 1 |
| B. Iranian | |
| Total number | 65 |
| Individuals with 1 contribution | 38 |
| 2 contributions | 11 |
| 3 contributions | 5 |
| 4 contributions | 5 |
| 5 contributions | 0 |
| 6 contributions | 3 |
| 9 contributions | 1 |
| 11 contributions | 1 |
| 14 contributions | 1 |
| C. Greek | |
| Total number | 18 |
| Individuals with 1 contribution | 13 |
| 2 contributions | 1 |
| 4 contributions | 1 |
| 6 contributions | 2 |
| 8 contributions | 1 |
| D. Latin | |
| Total number | 12 |
| Individuals with 1 contribution | 11 |
| 4 contributions | 1 |

5. *Participation of scholars in the study of the general Indo-European field (translations excluded)*

| | |
|---|---|
| Total number | 21 |

| | | |
|---|---|---|
| Individuals with | 1 contribution | 14 |
| | 2 contributions | 2 |
| | 3 contributions | 2 |
| | 4 contributions | 1 |
| | 5 contributions | 1 |
| | 7 contributions | 1 |

6. *Fields of concentration in the study of general Indo-European (only fields with five or more titles are listed)*

| | |
|---|---|
| Total number of contributions | 33 |
| Theory and general problems | 23 |
| Phonology | 5 |

The tables given provide some interesting information about focal and marginal areas in the work of Soviet scholars:

From tables 1A and 1C, it is immediately obvious that the quantity of work concerned with problems of the entire Indo-European group and not just with the study of individual languages (albeit perhaps in their general Indo-European context) is by no means impressive. The number of titles is small, and so is the number of scholars concentrating in this area, as indicated by the figures in table 5: most prominent are B. V. Gornung, V. V. Ivanov, and A. V. Desnickaja, with 7, 5, and 4 titles respectively. As to be expected, there is a considerable number of contributors to this field whose main interest lies in specific subareas of Indo-European or in other language groups: we find, for instance, the names of V. Ī. Abaev, M. M. Guxman, S. Ja. Lur'e, B. A. Serebrennikov with one title each to their credit, names that are well known from the fields of Iranian, Germanic, Mycenean Greek, and Finno-Ugric. As is evident from table 6, problems of a general nature attract by far the greatest interest: the share of general works is slightly higher than 20% in the overall count (cf. table 2), but for general Indo-European it almost reaches 70% of all titles.

Returning to the figures given in table 1A, we note two broad areas of concentration: the study of non-Slavic languages of the Soviet Union and of territories immediately adjacent, and the study of the traditional "international" languages of Europe, English, German, and French. Thus we find two languages of the Romance group accorded preferential treatment – French and Rumanian (Moldavian), the one obviously for its international status, the other because of its areal interest. Work on the "national" languages of the Soviet Union is largely carried on in the respective republics and regions, and quality and quantity produced depends to a considerable extent on the linguistic tradition that can be found there: the relative prominence of work on Latvian appears to reflect the influence of one scholar of international stature, Janis Endzelīns, and the general productivity of Armenian scholars may be viewed as the result of the continuing vigorous interest of Armenians in all aspects of their cultural heritage, including their language.

In contrast to the focal areas we notice that some of the "classical" Indo-European languages and language groups attract at best very little attention: Italic and Latin are represented by only twelve titles, and Celtic by just one lonely item, a translation at that; and even the relative strength of Indic is essentially due to work in modern languages (Hindi, Urdu, Bengali) and not in Sanskrit or Middle Indic.

Both the emphasis and the deemphasis found indicate a utilitarian approach to the overall field of Indo-European languages: concentration takes place in areas that are significant for practical reasons. Where pure research is pursued (and recent years have indeed produced some impressive developments in this direction), a preference is noticeable for the less traditional, less explored fields of study: in the general context of international scholarship and international publications the Soviet contributions (to be sure still in terms of mere numbers) are not negligible in Anatolian or Tocharian as they are negligible, for instance, in Latin or Greek (with the significant exception of Mycenean Greek, again a new field).

Within the general context of purpose-oriented research interesting variations can be observed. The comparison of tables 4A and 4B yields some useful insights. While the total number of authors in the fields of English and of Iranian languages is roughly comparable (73:65), a striking difference appears once we consider again the number of individuals with more than a very few contributions. Suppose we take again into account only authors with four or more titles to their credit. In English, only five out of the total of 73 fall into this group, and the maximum reached is six titles (A. I. Smirnickij). In the Iranian field, on the other hand, we find 11 scholars (out of 65) providing four or more contributions, with maxima of 14, 11, and nine titles achieved by V. I. Abaev, V. S. Rastorgueva, and A. A. Frejman, respectively. In Iranian, the top group accounts for 72 titles, in English, for only 24.

Offhand we would conclude that the Iranian field is the center of a broader and deeper research interest than the field of English. We pursue this matter further by an inspection of the tables 3A and 3B.

Again the totals for English and Iranian are similar enough to be comparable (111 and 130 titles, respectively). The emphasis on specific fields of linguistic study, however, varies greatly: While Iranian shows the characteristics of an area broadly investigated in all its linguistic aspects, a curious lopsidedness appears in English. For all languages combined except English (cf. table 2), syntactic studies amount to 23% of all titles; for English, the ratio is 57.7%. The figures for morphology, phonology, and lexicology are rather similar in 3A and 3B; the most conspicuous further discrepancy between the values for English and Iranian is the complete lack of emphasis on the treatment of general problems in the English field (only two titles, one of them a translation, were recorded here as against 24 in Iranian). The difference can be interpreted as indicating again that much more work of a broad scope is carried on in Iranian than in English; but what does the numerically strong position of syntactic research in English mean?

A breakdown of the total number of syntactic studies according to principles similar to those utilized in compiling the tables under 4 is helpful in answering this question:

| | |
|---|---|
| Total number of contributions | 64 |
| Titles by authors with an overall total of | |
| 1 contribution | 29 |
| 2 contributions | 10 |
| 3 contributions | 15 |
| 4 contributions | 4 |
| 5 contributions | 5 |
| 6 contributions | 1 |

Only ten of the 64 titles, then, are by the "productive" group of authors referred to before. Syntax is the field most prominent among those treated by one-title authors: out of a total of 51 isolated contributions, 29 concern syntax as against six each from phonology and morphology and even fewer from other fields. The apparent strength of English studies in the field of syntax thus turns out to be highly questionable: syntax is the topic par excellence for the beginner, and the fact that the first try is not followed up by further scholarly contributions indicates that at least as a rule the first try itself was of little or no consequence. This, in turn, means that the large volume of titles from English syntax does not point to particular achievements in this field, at least not on a broad scale.

Before attempting a general assessment, we return to table 2 for some further deliberations. We have seen that the strength of syntax is only apparent (the field of English syntax constitutes a rather typical case). We find then that the focus of interest is to be found in the field of general problems and theory. However, before we consider this to be an indication of particular strength, we have to be aware that much that is included under this classification is not comparable with Western discussions of theory. Thus we note, upon further inspection of our materials, that matters of theory were the subject of the absolutely highest percentage of titles published during the years 1951 through 1953: 1951: 12 out of 41 titles; 1952: 31 out of 90; 1953: 16 out of 61. When we look at the titles themselves, we find that a large percentage would seem to qualify better for a heading Ideology in linguistics than for the general heading Theory: it is the title of the type "The problem X in the light of the linguistic teachings of I. V. Stalin" that accounts for the numerically strong position of "theory" during these years.

It is instructive to devote some attention also to the weak fields in table 2. Stylistics, a field by no means neglected in the study of Russian (witness the work of V. V. Vinogradov), has received very little attention for non-Slavic languages; a considerable number of the titles counted belong to the single-try category. One is tempted to conclude that this situation reflects the general status of stylistics in the total field of linguistics rather than deliberate neglect on the part of Soviet linguists. As for the most weakly represented field of linguistic endeavor, that of the study of meaning, one is led to think that here the break with the continental tradition and, in an oblique fashion, the fact that current Soviet linguistics owes much to American linguistic theory of the past decades manifest themselves.

At this point, we will try to sum up our findings about Soviet work in non-Slavic Indo-European languages during the years 1950-1959. The interest in comparative work encompassing the entire family of languages is severely limited. A concern with the study of less well known languages and language groups is indicated by the fact that a number of outstanding contributions by Western scholars were translated into Russian, thus allowing dissemination of information outside the major research centers with adequate library facilities. A concentration of effort is noticeable in what might be called "critical" languages: both the major languages of Western Europe (and of the United States) and the non-Slavic languages of the Soviet Union and adjacent regions are the subject of a great many publications. In fields promoted as well as in fields generally neglected we find evidence of the continuing research effort of a few outstanding scholars of the older generation (the names of Endzelīns and Frejman may stand for a number of others) and evidence for the rise of a generation of highly respectable young scholars, small in number but very productive (an example, chosen somewhat at random, would be V. V. Ivanov). If one were asked to single out a field in which the achievement was particularly impressive, a likely choice would be the field of Iranian; if the opposite was called for, one would be inclined to point out Latin where only one man, I. M. Tronskij, stands out with more than one publication to his credit.

To conclude this paper a few selected publications, in particular from years later than the period covered in our survey, will be discussed individually.

Iranian was just singled out as a field of special accomplishments. A publication just received provides a most convenient survey of Russian and Soviet research activity in this field (although the title sounds very comprehensive, Western work is not adequately covered): *Očerki po istorii izučenija iranskix jazykov*, a publication of the Institut vostokovedenija of the Union Academy of Sciences (Izdatel'stvo AN SSSR, Moskva, 1962; 148 pages) under the editorship of V. S. Rastorgueva. Particularly welcome are references to work undertaken in regional research centers, both published and unpublished, and to contributions written in the national languages. The publication is a team effort involving almost all prominent scholars in the Iranian field; thus a competent coverage is assured, the only negative feature being that the all-inclusive community effort tends to eliminate incisive criticism.

Perhaps the most important contribution from the point of view of a general Indo-Europeanist that is to be found among Soviet publications in the Iranian field is V. I. Abaev's monumental *Istoriko-ètimologičeskij slovar' osetinskogo jazyka*, the first volume of which, covering words beginning with the letters A through K', appeared in 1958 (AN SSSR, Institut jazykoznanija; Izdatel'stvo AN SSSR, Moskva-Leningrad; 656 pages). The work is competent in its coverage of both Western and

Russian sources; the author, being a native Ossetian, is a past master of the language material before him. One of the book's most valuable points is the generous inclusion of ethnological and folkloristic information – a reflection of Abaev's extralinguistic interests. A certain looseness with regard to phonological consistency can be observed in the treatment of suspected loans from Caucasian languages; it would seem that a great deal of more work will be required in this area before one can operate on safe ground. It is with great anticipation that we await the completion of Abaev's dictionary.

In general Indo-European studies we note repeated endeavors to analyze critically the work done in Western countries. This may be done again in teamwork or by individual authors. A contribution of the first type is the book *Voprosy metodiki sravnitel'no-istoričeskogo izučenija indoevropejskix jazykov* (AN SSSR, Institut jazykoznanija; Izdatel'stvo AN SSSR, Moscow, 1956; Editors: A. V. Desnickaja and B. A. Serebrennikov; 324 pages). The contributors are some of the most prominent Soviet linguists of the day: V. I. Abaev, R. I. Avanesov, O. S. Axmanova, B. V. Gornung, M. M. Guxman, P. S. Kuznecov, in addition to the editors. The book is an attempt to survey the entire field of Indo-European, with due attention paid to important Western publications. The strong interest in trying to gain an understanding of recent developments is manifested in a small but rather substantial chapter on laryngeal theory (by Gornung), a field which subsequently attracted the attention of several of the younger Indo-Europeanists of the Soviet Union. The book contains a selective bibliography of this lively field of work in Indo-European, but for an American reader it holds only limited interest in view of the much more comprehensive listings in Jaan Puhvel's *Laryngeals and the Indo-European verb* (= *University of California Publications in Linguistics*, 21, Berkeley-Los Angeles, 1960).

Similarly ambitious are some survey publications by individual authors. A recent one may be singled out for specific comment. T. A. Degtereva, in the second volume of her study entitled *Puti razvitija sovremennoj lingvistiki* (Akademija obščestvennyx nauk pri CK KPSS; Izdatel'stvo VPŠ i AON pri CK KPSS, Moscow, 1962; 215 pages) concerns herself with "ethnohistoric problems of Indo-European glottogony", trying to cover as diversified topics as "The linguistic controversies on the nature of the Armenian language", "The place of Greek within Indo-European", "The Tocharian languages and the theoretical implications of work on the determination of relative chronology", "Secrets of the Scythian world" and a few more of a similar order of complexity. Although the first and foremost interest of the author is to report on recent work, there can be no doubt that she overestimates her potential as a critic; she has to accept by far too much on faith, and she certainly is too lenient on some of her compatriots: when she, for instance, praisingly refers to the late V. S. Vorob'ev-Desjatovskij's presentation of a Sanskrit-Tocharian bilingual text (*Učenye zapiski Instituta vostokovedenija* 16.304-308 (1958), she obviously is unaware of the exceedingly poor quality of this publication.

A much more encyclopedic grasp of the total Indo-European field is found in the works of a Bulgarian scholar whose contributions have appeared at various times in the Soviet Union, namely, of Vladimir Georgiev. One cannot help being both impressed and irritated by Georgiev's scholarship; his studies are always extremely rich in detail often of the most inaccessible kind; his perception and imagination is admirable. At the same time, Georgiev weakens the impact of his scholarship by a failure to assess the probability of his suggestions; side by side one finds straightforward, simple, absolutely persuasive hypotheses and others that have not the faintest chance of appearing acceptable to fellow scholars. The almost tragic consequence is that this interweaving of the obviously solid and the obviously improbable leads with necessity to quick rejection by other scholars of many valuable contributions by this very productive investigator; it seems that the identification of an Indo-European pre-Greek language in Hellas, whether one wants to call it Pelasgian or not, remains a major contribution to Indo-European scholarship regardless of the many flaws in point of detail that can be detected with no great effort in Georgiev's discussions. A recent compendium of Georgiev's views on problems from the Indo-European field is his book *Issledovanija po sravnitel'no-istoričeskomu jazykoznaniju* (*Rodstvennye otnošenija indoevropejskix jazykov*) (Izdatel'stvo inostrannoj literatury, Moscow, 1958; 318 pages). It offers a welcome survey of data and interpretations of data from some of the least accessible fields of Indo-European that have consistently attracted Georgiev's attention; it shows his imaginativeness that lets him posit strikingly new approaches to old problems; it also demonstrates his persistent weakness – his failure to notice when he has left firm ground and is beginning to lose his foothold in the quicksand and quagmire of the unprovable.

Two titles may be mentioned in conclusion that illustrate the interest of the younger generation of Soviet scholars in the less developed fields of Indo-European studies.

In 1959, V. V. Ivanov published a book entitled *Toxarskie jazyki* (Izdatel'stvo inostrannoj literatury, Moscow; 223 pages), which consisted for the most part of translations of noteworthy Western contributions to Tocharian studies (among others by Benveniste, Krause, and Lane). Ivanov's own contribution consists of notes and a very perceptive introductory chapter ("The Tocharian languages and their importance for comparative-historical work in Indo-European languages"). The author frequently overreaches himself in trying to place certain Tocharian phenomena in a general Indo-European context; it also is obvious that he relies too heavily on secondary sources for some of his generalizations. Nevertheless, his brief paper is a worthwhile and certainly most stimulating contribution to Tocharian studies. The other original article in the volume, I. A. Mel'čuk's outline of Tocharian morphology, is of little lasting interest since it is merely a restatement of data in earlier treatments of Tocharian grammar.

In 1961, a joint publication of the Institut narodov Azii of the Akademija nauk SSSR and the Institut jazykoznanija Akademii nauk Gruzinskoj SSR appeared under the title *Peredneaziatskij sbornik. Voprosy xettologii i xurritologii* (Izdatel'stvo vostočnoj literatury, Moscow; 606 pages). From an Indo-European point of view, the contributions by T. V. Gamkrelidze, V. V. Ivanov, and I. M. D'jakonov are of special interest. Gamkrelidze attempts to interpret Hittite graphic data as indicating the existence of a Hittite soundshift; as postulated, his theory does not seem persuasive. Ivanov deals with questions of etymology and lexicology of Hittite; D'jakonov restudies the intricate problems of the relationship of Hittite, Armenian and Phrygian; he insists, as it would seem, rightly on the non-Anatolian character of Armenian, but his suggestions concerning the age-old question of Phrygian-Armenian ties suffer, like those of his fellow investigators, from the paralyzing paucity of data. A quick survey of the conclusions presented in this book is facilitated by the addition of an English summary of the articles included.

Soviet studies in the comparative Indo-European field are still relatively few in number; they do not grow from an unbroken tradition, which leaves them exposed to the danger of reckless experimentation, but also frees them from the bonds of antiquated theory. As greater freedom of research seems to make the intellectual climate quite different from that of the days of Marrism and of Stalin's guidance, we can look forward to not many, but internationally competitive publications during the years to come.

# BELORUSSIAN AND UKRAINIAN

GEORGE Y. SHEVELOV

*Author's note*: Bibliographical data on books and monographs are to be found in the text of the survey. Names of Ukrainian and Belorussian authors who also published their works in Russian are cited in their Ukrainian, resp. Belorussian forms. Place names, except those well established in English, are also given in their Ukrainian and Belorussian forms. The following abbreviations are used for cities: K. = Kiev, L. = Lviv, Od. = Odessa, X. = Kharkov. In Belorussian publications no indication of the place of publication means that it was published in Minsk. In references to periodicals the year is indicated by the last two figures.

## I. THE UKRAINE

Before 1917 Ukrainian linguistics could boast the work of several distinguished scholars. Suffice it to mention the names of A. Potebnja, K. Myxal'čuk, and P. Žytec'kyj. But as a rule it was kept apart from the universities and, consequently, was unable to found schools and build trends of any permanency. The revolution of 1917 and the foundation of the Ukrainian independent and, later, autonomous state changed the situation radically. Universities opened their doors to Ukrainian linguistics. The Ukrainian Academy of Sciences, in existence since 1918, became an important center of research. The 1920s were a time of breathtaking developments in the field.

Naturally, in a young nation foremost attention was given to practical problems of standardization of the language, compilation of dictionaries and a thesaurus, and elaboration of terminology. An archaisizing romantic trend, represented by Je. Tymčenko, S. Smerečyns'kyj, O. Kurylo (till 1925) and others, was in competition with the more sober and moderate approach of O. Synjavs'kyj, M. Sulyma, O. Kurylo (after 1925) and others. In the Synjavs'kyj's book *Normy ukrajins'koji literaturnoji movy* (1931) the research and the discussions of the time were summarized and scholarly foundations of the standardized Ukrainian language laid with poise and sense of responsibility.

Along with practically oriented work, research into history and dialectology of Ukrainian was developing broadly. V. Hancov and Kurylo proceeded from an accumulation of dialectal material to a daring concept of the origin of Ukrainian dialects and the Ukrainian language. P. Buzuk and Tymčenko published the first attempts at synthetic presentation of the history of Ukrainian, and Sulyma gave the first significant outline of the history of the literary language. Under the editorship of Tymčenko the first volume of an historical dictionary of Ukrainian was published (1930-32).

In method, philological and neo-grammarian approaches prevailed, tinged now sociologically in the spirit of A. Meillet, now philosophically in the vein of W. Humboldt or K. Vossler, but the methods of linguistic geography and of structuralism as represented by the Prague school were also introduced. In the western part of the Ukraine, then under Poland, the more conservative trend going back to Miklosich was predominant, but from the early 1930s an outspoken representative of Prague structuralism, V. Simovyč, contributed much to the spread of this trend. I. Zilyns'kyj's school outside of the Ukraine, in Kraków, put main emphasis on thorough phonetic methods and methods of linguistic geography.

The upsurge of the 1920s was halted, in the Soviet Ukraine, with the change of political atmosphere in the country and the rise of Stalin. The activities of the 1920s were characterized as bourgeois nationalist. By 1938 none of the linguists mentioned above was active. Of the outstanding linguists only two survived the crisis as scholars: L. Bulaxovs'kyj in Kharkov and M. Hruns'kyj in Kiev. The Institute of Linguistics founded in 1931 in the framework of the thoroughly purged Ukrainian Academy of Sciences was manned by young people, and the main task assigned to them was "unmasking" the "enemies of the people" in the field. Even a superficial glance at the publication of the new Institute's *Movoznavstvo* (begun 1934) shows the situation adequately. The pages of this publication were filled with denunciatory lampoons and only as a matter of exception did a piece of research find its place there. As to Marrism, it never was influential in the Ukraine, perhaps because positive research was lacking in general.

The campaign of political pamphleteering subsided by 1940. In 1941 Bulaxovs'kyj was appointed the editor of *Movoznavstvo*, which acquired the subtitle *Naukovi zapysky* and began anew with volume one. But with almost no qualified specialists and the tradition discontinued, without any contact with the West, with limited encouragement and financing, little could be done. This great deadlock in Ukrainian linguistics lasted approximately till 1953. After the occupation of the Western Ukraine, in 1939, it spread there, too. It is against this background that the situation thereafter may be properly understood.

A new generation of linguists had grown up by that time. Quantitatively, Ukrainian linguistics reached an unprecedented peak. Several conferences of linguists were organized by universities and the numbers of papers read are imposing: at the Conference on the history of Ukrainian held on December 15-19, 1959, in Kharkov, thirty papers were presented; at the Conference on applied linguistics on September 22-28, 1960, in Černivci, eighty; at the Conference on Slavistics, in Kharkov, December 23-27, 1960, sixty.[1] Publications in linguistics mushroomed. The Academy of Sciences in Kiev and the Institute of Social Sciences in Lviv, seven universities (Kiev,

[1] *Ukrajins'ka mova v školi*, 1960, 2, p. 83; 1961, 1, p. 90; 1961, 2, p. 90.

Kharkov, Lviv, Dnipropetrovsk, Odessa, Černivci, Užhorod) and thirty-one pedagogic institutes each have publications in this field and some of them two or more series.[2] Several occasional symposia and monographs also came out.

The quality of the materials published, however, in most cases does not stand up to the requirements of the time. Many articles only fill pages without bringing anything new. Competent editors are rare, and the level of publications reflects this fact faithfully. The whole research lacks planning and organization. Often subjects are repeated and authors duplicate each other. There is no comprehensive bibliography (But see UMŠ 58, 1 and 60, 6). Furthermore, there is no journal in linguistics. A bimonthly *Ukrajins'ka mova v školi* (from 1951) is devoted to problems of teaching and popularization. *Movoznavstvo* still is published on a non-periodical basis, roughly a book every two years. It is supplemented by two more non-periodical series of the Academy: *Leksykohrafičnyj bjuleten'* (from 1951) and *Dialektolohičnyj bjuleten'* (from 1949). Even typographically the publications are not on the proper level. After twenty-seven years of publication, *Movoznavstvo* still has no symbols to denote brevity, so that *ŏ* has to be printed as *o* with a *v* over it in a blank line (See M 16, p. 52); *ů* is replaced by *u* with an italic *o* over it, again in a blank line (see the monograph of L. Humec'ka discussed in section 2 of this survey, p. 224), minor but telling details!

As a rule only the publications of the Academy of Sciences and the University of Lviv are available in the West, and occasionally publications of other leading universities. Only exceptionally are publications of pedagogic institutes (which in general are printed in a very low number of copies, usually 300 to 500) sent abroad. Therefore, no comprehensive survey of the output of Soviet Ukrainian linguists can be given. The choice of items which are at the disposal of this surveyor is rather haphazard. Still, it may be reasonably assumed that what reaches him is rather representative publications, and highlights sufficient to give a general idea of the state of affairs. It is on this assumption that the present survey is based. The author apologizes

[2] For more detailed bibliography see the very conscientious survey by O. Horbatsch, "Pisljavojenni publikaciji z ukrajins'koji movy v URSR", *Sučasnist'* (Munich), 1961, 12 and 1962, 1, available also as an off-print. The bibliography in *Doslidžennja z movoznavstva v Ukrajins'kij RSR za sorok rokiv* (K., Akademija Nauk UkRSR, 1959) is far from being complete for the time before the World War II. The scholars who emigrated during the war as well as those who were not rehabilitated by that time are passed over in silence. But for the period of immediate interest in this survey, i.e. after 1953 no such gaps have been noticed. Cf. also Institut Jazykoznanija Akademii Nauk SSSR. I. Beloded, V. Borkovskij, P. Goreckij, *Izučenie ukrainskogo i belorusskogo jazykov* (Moscow, 1958) (Cyclostyle), where some Belorussian bibliography is also included.

Although in the text of the survey occasional remarks were made concerning availability or not of some publications it is appropriate to indicate here systematically which volumes of series incompletely or possibly incompletely covered have been encompassed in the article: DB, 5-8; DML, 1954 and 1957 (=ISN, 3, 4); KDU, 13,2 (1954), 14,2 (1955), 15,7 (1956); LB, 3-7; LPI, 12, 16 (1959-60); ODU, 3 (1953), 5-9 (1955-59), *Praci*, 148 (1958), 150 (1960); PIM, 1, 3-8; PSF, 1 (1960); PSM, 5-6 (1958); SM, 1-2 (1958); V, 1956-60.

for all the gaps, unavoidable as they are, and raises no claim to exhaustiveness.

The material will be presented according to fields of research within linguistics. Articles which were later published in a book by the same author will not be mentioned and all references will be given to these books alone. Abstracts of dissertations (*avtoreferaty*) are not covered at all in this survey.

### 1. *Phonetics and phonemics. Accentology*

Research in descriptive phonetics was hampered by the absence of laboratories. The first and only phonetic laboratory was founded as late as 1960, at the Institute of Linguistics. *Movoznavstvo* (16, p. 126) calls it "prerequisite for work in the new direction in Ukrainian linguistics". We are not told what the equipment of this laboratory is and to what extent it is satisfactory. The only research article in the field is L. Prokopova's (SH) on the articulation of Ukranian [l]. The observations are interesting but by necessity preliminary. As much as could be done on the basis of subjective perception, the most detailed and most reliable presentation of phonetics and phonemics of Modern Ukrainian is found in the chapter on this subject written by M. Nakonečnyj for the collective *Kurs sučasnoji ukrajins'koji literaturnoji movy*, ed. by L. Bulaxovs'kyj, two volumes (Kiev, 1951; further referred to as *Kurs*). What is found later is based on the conscientious work of Nakonečnyj: chapters on phonetics written by M. Žovtobrjux in *Kurs sučasnoji ukrajins'koji literaturnoji movy* by Žovtobrjux and B. Kulyk (K., 1959), in *Sučasna ukrajins'ka literaturna mova* by M. Ivčenko (K., 1960), in *Ukrajins'ka mova* by V. Vaščenko (X., 1961, second edition), and in *Sučasna ukrajins'ka literaturna mova* by Žovtobrjux (K., 1961), with only minor deviations. In all these presentations, distinctive features are not characterized systematically and acoustic and spectrographic analysis is not even referred to.

One point in Nakonečnyj's outline gave rise to a minor discussion: palatalization vs. non-palatalization of dental consonants before *i* which developed from Common Slavic *o* (*nosъ* > *nis* 'nose'). While Nakonečnyj admitted both pronunciations, P. Prystupa (DB 5, 1955), I. Petlyčnyj (PUM 1, 1956), and Žovtobrjux (M 16, 1961) stated that now the non-palatalized pronunciation is in retreat and required that the standard pronunciation should be palatalized. The argument in this discussion was the spread of the palatalized variant. None of the authors drew conclusions of a phonemic character: suppression of the distinction in palatalization before *i* means that *i* loses its phonemic status in Ukrainian and becomes an allophone of *y* (or vice versa). This means that the system of vocalic phonemes in Ukrainian becomes identical with Russian, a development which is natural under conditions of a *Sprachbund* and widespread bilingualism but which hardly follows from the internal tendencies of the Ukrainian phonemic system. Such a *désintéressement* in phonemics is typical of the Ukrainian linguists of today. Although the term *phoneme* is broadly used, it hardly means anything other than a speech sound in the traditional sense, partly on a phonetic, partly even on a graphic plane.

General outlines of the historical phonology of Ukrainian were published by F. Medvedjev (*Istoryčna hramatyka ukrajins'koji movy*, X., 1955) and M. Žovtobrjux (in *Istoryčna hramatyka ukrajins'koji movy* by O. Bezpal'ko, M. Bojčuk et al., K., 1957). Both are derivative, devoid of any innovations and abound in elementary mistakes. In factual material and methods they hardly go beyond *Lekcii po istorii russkogo jazyka* by A. Sobolevskij, last published in 1907. In Medvedjev's book up to half the text is devoted to quotations from Stalin and interpretations thereof. On quite a different level is L. Bulaxovs'kyj's *Pytannja poxodžennja ukrajins'koji movy* (K., 1956). This book also covers problems of morphology and vocabulary but its principal part is on phonology. Although cautious and occasionally perhaps deliberately vague in formulations, the book honestly and without distortions presents the views of the author who was first of all a Slavist with wide horizons. In defiance of official tenets the author shows Ukrainian phonetic features in the texts of the Old Rus' period. This material is, however, not new. It goes back to Sobolevskij, Šaxmatov and Durnovo. In some problems the book summarizes individual research by Bulaxovs'kyj. The most important of these points are the hypotheses that *i*-reflexes in pleophonic groups (*moróz* 'frost' with *o* vs. *holív* 'head', gen. pl., with *i*) are due to the new rising pitch, and that *e* changed into *i* only before a weak *ь*, but not before *ъ*. Both assumptions need further qualifications, the second should involve a complete revision of the traditional theory of how *o* and *e* allegedly lengthened before a syllable with *jers* to be lost, but the second is certainly here to stay in Slavic linguistics, and both are stimulating. Methodologically, the book of Bulaxovs'kyj is a solid study in the neo-grammariam vein, as is the whole work of this scholar of great integrity and broad knowledge, who died in 1961.

Studies in specific problems of the historical phonology of Ukrainian, Slavic, and Indo-European were but few. M. Peščak (DUM) investigated the development of the groups *ky*, *gy* > *hy*, *xy* in Ukrainian, I. Kovalyk (VSJa 3) clusters of the type stop + nasal consonant in Slavic, I. Svjencic'kyj (VSJa 4) the function of *jers* in the Smolensk charter of 1229, V. Martynov (ODU 6) the movable *s* in Slavic and Germanic. These are minor contributions, the material is mostly second-hand (except the unpublished data collected for the Ukrainian dialectological atlas as used by Peščak) and atomistically presented, and the exposition rather confused. A purported preservation of the Old Kievan pronouncing tradition in Moscow throughout the eighteenth century, a thesis promulgated by Šaxmatov, is buttressed by A. Hens'ors'kyj (PSM 5). In reality one has rather to reckon with the influence of the Ukrainian high clergy in seventeenth and eighteenth century Russia.

It was in 1956 that I. Kovalyk (PUM 1) ventured into an outline of what he calls "the history of the system of vocalic phonemes" in Ukrainian, the first attempt to re-introduce a phonemic approach, not practiced after the death of V. Simovyč (1944). But the author gives no real phonemic analysis, taking for granted that a letter in old texts denoted a phoneme. He has no doubts, for example, that nasal vowels *ǫ* and *ę* were independent phonemes. Kovalyk is unaware of the complexity of the phonemic status of Ukrainian *y* as discussed by K. Dejna, J. Šerech, and P. Zwoliński. The author establishes a tendency in the history of Ukrainian toward a reduction in the number of vocalic phonemes but, even so, he shows no reason for it, except to remark that those vowels were dropped which had lower frequency of use. Symptomatic in its re-born interest in phonemics, Kovalyk's article is limited in performance.

The most stimulating are the articles by O. Mel'nyčuk, published in Russian. In one of them (PSM 5) he attempts a new interpretation of the third palatalization of velars in Common Slavic as a morphological extension of the second palatalization. In another article (VJa 60, 3) he seeks traces of an Indo-European laryngeal stop in the glottal stop (*Stosston*) of Latvian and falling pitch on monophthongs in Slavic, bringing parallels from Hittite. Although the conclusions of Mel'nyčuk in both cases are hardly acceptable his approach is fresh, and the material is his own. He also is the only author, in questions of phonology, who is acquainted with Western publications and whose bibliography is up to date. To most of his colleagues these publications seem to be unknown or, at best, limited to Polish and German pre-war books and periodicals (Kovalyk). Less satisfactory is the phonetic part of Mel'nyčuk's article devoted to the origin of the Ukrainian and Belorussian past tense forms in -*v* (type *znav*) (SM 1). His attempt to attribute all cases of *l* > *u̯* in Ukrainian and Belorussian to the fourteenth century or later is far-fetched and cannot stand. A sportive kick against Simovyč and structural approach in general (P. 97) is unjustified, the less so because on p. 157 Mel'nyčuk is forced to accept Simovyč's views. Fortunately, the article is convincing in its main thesis, viz. that -*v* forms of the past tense are not the result of a phonetic change *l* > *u̯* (Simovyč proved this in 1937 but on much more limited material). Ï. Petlyčnyj brings data concerning phonetic features of the language of Samovydec' chronicle (VSJa 4).

Problems of Slavic accentology were indefatigably and systematically studied by L. Bulaxovs'kyj. His project was to present a series of what he called "accentological commentaries" on all the Slavic languages and so to approach a synthetic presentation of Slavic accentology. Of these "commentaries" he published *Akcentologičeskij kommentarij k pol'skomu jazyku* (K., 1950), *Akcentologičeskij kommentarij k češskomu jazyku*, I (K., 1953); II-III (K., 1956), and "Bolgarskij jazyk kak istočnik dlja rekonstrukcii drevnejšej slavjanskoj akcentologičeskoj sistemy" (In Akademija Nauk SSSR, *Issledovanija po slavjanskomu jazykoznaniju*, Moscow, 1961). Ukrainian stress is characterized by Bulaxovs'kyj in the corresponding chapter of *Kurs*, I. Besides that he produced every year several articles on partial questions of Slavic accentology, primarily Ukrainian and Russian, in Ukrainian, Russian and Bulgarian series and periodicals. In these works copious data are collected and interpreted, all of them first hand and indispensable for researchers. Undoubtedly Bulaxovs'kyj also had a general conception of the rise and development of pitch in Slavic accentual system(s). Yet he never came to a synthetic work. It seems that it was not only the question of lack of time but also of pressure of too many minor facts. In a systematic work the audacity of a surgeon is necessary to cut away what is unimportant or superfluous. This audacity was hardly a feature of Bulaxovs'kyj as a scholar. Perhaps he was too conscientious for that.

Bulaxovs'kyj left no successor in this field, which was his favorite. Works in accentology are not represented in Ukrainian linguistics of today, except an article by Z. Veselovs'ka on stress in the Belorussian "Didactic Gospel" of 1616 (FZ) of a purely descriptive character, and a booklet by A. Biloštan, *Naholos člennyx prykmetnykiv u sučasnij ukrajins'kij literaturnij movi* (K., 1958), whose historico-comparative commentary is scarce and second hand, and the synchronic presentation often inaccurate, particularly as he does not distinguish present day doublets from the changed forms which arose during the last three centuries and from the forms introduced from Russian by language planning institutions but not assimilated to the accentual system of Ukrainian. M. Pohribnyj published a useful *Slovnyk naholosiv ukrajins'koji literaturnoji movy* (K., 1959), a work on standardization.

## 2. *Word derivation*

An old tradition is followed in general courses of Ukrainian to characterize word derivation by listing suffixes broken down by broad semantic groups (persons, tools, place-names, etc.) with several haphazard examples of each suffix and with indications about the productivity of the suffix and the place of the stress. This tradition is followed in descriptive grammar by B. Kulyk (in Žovtobrjux and Kulyk's course) and, with numerous errors, in historical grammar, by I. Taranenko for substantives and less systematically by S. Samijlenko for adjectives (in the historical grammar by Bezpal'ko et al.). S. Bevzenko in his *Istoryčna morfolohija ukrajins'koji movy* (Užhorod, 1960) makes his lists more detailed and supplies each item with numerous examples from Middle Ukrainian texts; occasionally he also indulges in brief etymological explanations, but these are often dubious. The substantival suffix *-ač* is derived by him from *-ak* + *i* (108), whereas it goes back to **ak* + *jos*. He confuses the suffixes *-ar* (< *-arь*) and *-jar*, probably of another origin (107), not noticing interesting problems of the rise of the latter suffix in Western Slavic and the possible ties in this regard between Ukrainian and Western Slavic.

The same approach marks studies by I. Kovalyk, who in a series of articles characterizes one group of Ukrainian suffixes after another (substantives denoting persons, derived from adjectives and other substantives – PUM 2; substantives denoting things – PUM 3; substantives in *-tel'* – PUM 4; names of persons according to their nationality or religion – PSM 5; collective and single substantives – PSM 6; place names – SM 2). Kovalyk brings in parallels from other Slavic languages, thus establishing areas of each suffix, occasionally cites some historical or etymological data. Each of his assiduously written articles is introduced by a heavy barrage of quotations ranging from Pāṇini through Engels and Stalin to Vinogradov, of the type: "The forms of any existence are space and time; existence beyond time is as nonsensical as beyond space" (Engels), this to introduce a list of suffixes which denote place (SM 2, p. 6). Observations on substantives denoting persons, single and collective, are summarized by Kovalyk in his *Pytannja imennykovoho slovotvoru v sxidnoslovjans'kyx movax u porivnjanni z inšymy slovjans'kymy movamy*, I (L., 1958). Elementary mistakes are not rare in Kovalyk's works, e.g., the suffixes *-an* and *-jan* are confused (PSM 5, p. 148), *bratija* and *kavalerija* are said to have the same suffix (PSM 6, p. 34) as well as *pustynja* and *vysočynja* (SM 2, p. 11).

The articles of T. Voznyj on verbal suffixes (*-uva-*, PUM 2; *-nu-* PUM 3; *-y-*, PUM 4) follow the same pattern, only the semantic categories are smaller and the number of mistakes higher. Other articles are virtually collections of excerpts from various texts, as lists of "dialectal" (i.e. practically not used in the present day standard language) substantive suffix formations in Franko's short novel *Boryslav smijet'sja* by A. Burjačok (M 15), of Old Czech diminutives by R. Kravčuk (SM 2), of appositionally connected substantives by A. Martynenko (DLM), of derived substantives in Z. Kopystens'kyj's *Palinodija* by T. Molodid (DLM). P. Docenko has collected data concerning the use of suffixes in A. Malyško's poems, especially in his coinings (LB 4). G. Miževskaja studies the use of suffixes *-ik* and *-nik* in personal names in Eighteenth Century Russian (ODU 8), A. Smol'skaja the use of affective suffixes by M. Gor'kij (ODU 8). This is also the character of a somewhat larger collection of random excerpts published as a separate booklet: *Nekotorye osobennosti slovoobrazovanija v jazyke russkix povestej vtoroj poloviny XVII veka* by A. Danevič (K., 1958).

Other authors do not limit themselves to the presentation of their excerpts but draw some more general conclusions from them: N. Romanova defends the thesis that the suffix *-ka* to denote actions arose from "a tendency to structural derivation" (M 15, p. 75) and is not identical with the diminutive *-ka*. For the suffixes *-nie* and *-tie* in Russian, she shows that originally (the sixteenth century) these derivations preserved verbal aspect, but not if based on verbs in *-it'* (SM 2). N. Gromova poses the problem of homonymy in suffixes (LPI 12). L. Galenko presents materials on compound participles in Eighteenth Century Russian and accreted substantive pairs of the type *fabrika-kuxnja* in modern Russian (VRJa 4). T. Lukinova screens Slavic features from those due to imitation of German in Czech compounds (SM 1). None of these articles claims to be exhaustive, none even hints at the problem of distribution of various derivational types. Only two articles by K. Trofymovyč on Old Czech compounds (PSM 6, PSF 1) have a more formal approach and bring a statistical count.

Of the three monographs devoted to the problems of derivation one (V. Il'jin, *Prefiksy v sučasnij ukrajins'kij movi*, K., 1953) is basically a list of prefixes with subsequent lists of their "meanings" and numerous examples. The other, *Narys slovotvorčoji systemy ukrajins'koji aktovoji movy XIV-XV st.* (K., 1958) by L. Humec'ka basically shares its approach with the articles mentioned above. But it is exhaustive and occasionally adds some etymological considerations which, however, stop short where the Slavic data are insufficient and the Indo-European or non-Indo-European material is needed. The classification is still vaguely semantic, and formal points are mostly ignored. The author adheres to the theory, hardly defendable, that at its rise every suffix had a strictly delimited meaning which then is inevitably obscured as the suffix used with various stems becomes polysemic. The development is said to end in a purely structural function of the suffix. The main value of the book is in its data which, however, are hard to use because of the lack of indices (as a matter of fact no Ukrainian publication in linguistics has them!). Parallels from other Slavic languages are occasionally cited but the vital question of the relations between Middle Ukrainian word derivation, of the fourteenth-fifteenth century, and the Old Ukrainian one, of the eleventh-thirteenth century, on the one hand, and contemporary Belorussian word derivation (It was the time of the common Ukrainian-Belorussian literary language), on the other, is not even raised. Like some of her colleagues Humec'ka occasionally lapses into mistakes in the elementary breakdown of words into morphemes. She sees, for example, a suffix *-ovka* in *moskovka* (88), as Taranenko found a suffix *-ar* in *mylovar* (220)! L. Jurčuk's monograph *Pytannja sufiksal'noho slovotvorennja dijesliv u sučasnij ukrajins'kij movi* (K., 1959) is strictly synchronic. Derived verbs are classified according to their underlying forms. Little is said about frequency of various types and precise rules of distribution. Otherwise the analysis is conscientious and occasionally penetrating.

Instructors at the University of Odessa prepared a series of articles to characterize various types of suffixation in the Old Rus' language: adjectives by N. Bukatevič, fem. substantives by G. Miževskaja, verbs by S. Savickaja, and compounds denoting persons by A. Smol'skaja (ODU 9).

No authors treat problems of morphophonemics and none mentions works of Trubetzkoy or of any representative of American descriptive linguistics.

The only article on methods in studies of word derivation is by I. Kovalyk (FZ). Its main point is that word derivation must be characterized not by affixes alone, but by derivational types, a complex notion which encompasses the meaning (semantic category) of the word, the type of the stem and the affix. These recommendations are not followed consistently in any article available to me, the studies of Kovalyk included.

### 3. *Word inflection*

A comprehensive presentation of word inflection in the standard Ukrainian language is written by Il'jin for *Kurs*, by Ivčenko and Vaščenko in their courses, by M. Žovtobrjux and B. Kulyk in their course and by M. Volyns'kyj, S. Samijlenko and T. Bajmut for the collective *Porivnjal'na hramatyka ukrajins'koji i rosijs'koji mov*, 2nd edition (K., 1961[3]). The five presentations resemble each other and are devoid of originality. They are basically synchronic but with the traditional admixture of historical com-

[3] T. Bajmut's *Korotkyj narys porivnjal'noji hramatyky rosijs'koji ta ukrajins'koji mov* (K., 1954) was not available to me.

mentary. In the *Porivnjal'na hramatyka* not only Russian but also Belorussian is used for systematic comparison with Ukrainian. Stress is as a rule ignored, the spoken language not always distinguished from the orthography and factual errors occur, in particular in *Porivnjal'na hramatyka.*

The number of errors in historical morphology of Ukrainian grows high in F. Medvedjev's *Istoryčna hramatyka ukrajins'koji movy* (X., 1955) and in O. Bezpal'ko *et al.*'s *Istoryčna hramatyka ukrajins'koji movy* (K., 1957) in which the chapters on morphology are written by I. Taranenko, O. Bezpal'ko and S. Samijlenko. E.g., Samijlenko explains the preservation of "soft" adjectives, after the change of ь through *i* into *y* before *j* by influence of the pronouns *mij*, *tvij*, *svij* (p. 279) forgetting that, first, the declension of these pronouns is not "soft" and, second, that their *i* arose earliest in the sixteenth century. Spellings like *mokrij* in Galician texts of the sixteenth century he identifies with spread of *-ij* endings in the *-n-* adjectives in the dialects of Poltava area (280), whereas these spelling only reveal the general confusion of letters *i* and *y* due to the coalescence of /i/ and /y/ in Ukrainian of the time. More detailed and more reliable in its factual material is *Istoryčna morfolohija ukrajins'koji movy* by S. Bevzenko (Užhorod, 1960[4]), but explanations are often avoided and, if not, little convincing. The book which is primarily a result of assiduousness often indulges in clichés, shuns conjectures and constitutes a collection of data from various periods rather than a coherent history of Ukrainian inflexion. The author's authorities are for Common Slavic Meillet, for Old Church Slavonic Vaillant, for Ukrainian Sobolevskij, Hruns'kyj and Koval'ov, and Kuznecov, whose interpretations are often simply pieced together.

Among the articles two treat problems of distribution. Although somewhat impressionistic, they contain interesting observations: I. Varčenko's on the choice of the forms in *-sja* and *-s'* in reflexive verbs (UMŠ 58, 3) and M. Pylyns'kyj's on the choice of the infinitive forms in *-ty* and *t'* (UMŠ 61, 6). I. Kučerenko (KDU 14) classifies Ukrainian adverbs and characterizes them as an attributive part of speech.

The predominant type of article on problems of word inflection is that consisting of excerpts from various sources pasted together with a minimum of commentary. Thus, A. Matvijenko publishes her excerpts concerning vacillations in gender in Ukrainian substantives (DUM); in the endings of the genitive and vocative singular, dative, locative, and instrumental pl. in the Ukrainian substantive declension (SM 2); and tries to show how in general analogy operates in the substantive declension (M 16), but does not succeed in anything more than piling up heterogeneous examples. The material is broader, comes from all Slavic languages, and is much better organized in the article by L. Bulaxovs'kyj (SM 1) in which he shows which cases and numbers influenced each other in Slavic substantives. But essentially this is also but a collection of (very interesting) case-histories and does not grow into a generalization. I.

[4] It is an enlarged and thoroughly re-written variant of his *Narysy z istoryčnoji hramatyky ukrajins'koji movy* (K., 1953). The latter was not available to me.

Kernyc'kyj (DMUM 2, 3) presents rich excerpts of Ukrainian substantival declension from texts of the sixteenth century, M. Paraxina (LPI 12) on the declension of *-o*-stems in the First Novgorod Chronicle, L. Giglan (VRJa 4) on the declension of foreign place names in *Xoženie* by Af. Nikitin, Z. Rozova brings data on Serbo-Croatian substantives of common gender (VRJa 4), O. Šelepina tries to elucidate with random data, dialectal and historical, the history of consonantal stems in Russian (VRJa 3) and more specifically of the words *mat'* and *doč'* (VRJa 4), G. Miževskaja on the forms of the nominative and locative pl. of substantives in Radiščev (ODU 5), M. Pavljuk makes public his excerpts of pronominal forms in Polish of the fourteenth century (ODU 4). The comparative method is used in Z. Rozova's article (VRJa 3) on Russian and Serbo-Croatian masculine personal names with the endings *-o*, *-e*, and *-a*. The study sheds some new light on the old discussion of this problem. S. Savickaja (ODU 7) collects some random examples of numerals in Slavic. I. Macenko (DLM) proves that the ending *-am* superseded *-om* in the dative pl. masc. in the Novgorod area at least a century sooner than in Moscow, a contribution to historical dialectology of Russian; no reasons for this difference are suggested. K. Trofymovyč shows that in its treatment of animate and personal subgenders Sorbian is closer to Polish than to Czech (PSF 1).

V. Frančuk (M 16) outlines a period of spread in Ukrainian of adverbs in *-sko* (17-18th century). In a booklet *Narečija, obrazovannye ot imen prilagatel'nyx v russkom literaturnom jazyke XVIII v.* (K., 1961) she shows which adverbs were lost or arose in the eighteenth century Russian, with parallels from Ukrainian and modern Russian. L. Batjuk picks up some peculiarities of morphology in the Chronicle by Samovydec' (DUM), and so does I. Petlyčnyj (PUM 1).

In verbs, E. Širokorad (XDU 6) treats reflexive verbs in Lomonosov as compared with modern Russian; L. Bykova bases her characterization of pairless imperfective verbs in Russian on the naive semantic approach, which in reality reflects only the distribution of forms in modern Russian and makes the way of thinking completely circular (XDU 6). I. Kernyc'kyj (DML 3) presents interesting statistics to prove that the loss of the aorist and imperfect in Ukrainian resulted from the loss of the auxiliary verb in the perfect past tense, and traces the change in functions of these verbal forms through the sixteenth century. L. Kolomijec' studies the development of gerunds in Ukrainian (XDU 6), M. Šatux characterizes nominal forms of participles in the Old Rus' texts of the eleventh-twelfth century (ODU 8) and of the thirteenth-fourteenth century (ODU 9) to show their transformation into gerunds.

Two monographs are each devoted to one part of speech in Ukrainian: numerals and adverbs. *Čyslivnyky ukrajins'koji movy* by M. Ivčenko (K., 1955) reveals nothing but an insufficient preparation of the author. He ventures into a complicated subject without any knowledge of the basic literature (e.g. A. Belić's and A. Dostál's works on dual) and with manifestly inadequate training in linguistics. He speaks, e.g., of the Sorbian language in general, without specifying which, and the character of his judgment may be illustrated by a quotation: "At the time when men only started learning to speak and use fire they knew only two numerals: one and two" (p. 6).

The book by I. Čaplja, *Pryslivnyky v ukrajins'kij movi* (X., 1960), suffers some shortcomings, too. The author unnecessarily misuses Marxist clichés in his terminology and indulges in problems of glottogony. His innocence in Western linguistics is almost pathetic. After not finding much on the adverb in Miklosich and Meillet, he discards Western linguistics in general. A glance in, say, H. Paul's *Prinzipien der Sprachgeschichte*, section 258 (published in 1960 in Russian translation for Čaplja's convenience) would disclose to him not only that the adverb has been treated in the West but he would even find there some of the discoveries he made in his book. The final chapter, on "stylistics of the adverb" is superfluous, because it treats general problems of vocabulary, simply illustrated by examples with adverbs. But in general the book brings not only well selected first-hand examples but also a penetrating analysis on synchronical level with attention to the origin of adverbs, inasmuch as it still is a fact of today's language. The analysis of adverbialization and what are the varieties of what is usually covered by the term inflexibility is done in the good tradition of Potebnja's philosophical linguistic school. Purely formal features of adverb are not neglected (the author properly emphasizes transformation of endings of other parts of speech into suffixes in adverb, a view I suggested in 1951), but his main point of view is rather philosophical and psychological.

The book by I. Kučerenko, *Teoretyčni pytannja hramatyky ukrajins'koji movy, Morfolohija*, 1 (K., 1961), which also includes the text of two booklets he published previously: *Hramatyčni značennja i hramatyčni katehoriji v ukrajins'kij movi* (K., 1959) and *Katehorija vidminka v sučasnij ukrajins'kij movi* (L., 1961), seems to be the only contribution to the theory of morphology. Obviously dissatisfied with the deadlock which prevails in the treatment of morphology in Ukrainian linguistics Kučerenko begins with an attempt to revise what to him is the basic notion in this branch of linguistics: grammatical category. With consistently critical re-evaluations of the views that exist in Soviet linguistics he traces differences in the structure of referential and grammatical meanings and arrives at the conclusion that grammatical categories are to be sought not in the material components of the language and not in parts of speech but in the oppositions of grammatical meanings (p. 40). As the author's thinking here revolves within the triangle Potebnja – Šaxmatov – Peškovskij (plus some Soviet-Marxist terminology) he is to be congratulated for breaking this triangle and arriving at the foundations of a structural approach. In the following analysis of the parts of speech, cases and persons, Kučerenko often exaggerates "meaning" to the deterioration of grammar as such and his treatment of gender borders on naïveté. But he is justified in his criticism of the standard Soviet grammatical approach; he obviously feels the eclecticism of the latter: based on formal grammar as fostered in Russia in the twenties it underwent a radical switch to logical criteria in the thirties but many unmotivated traces of the preceding period were automatically incorporated into the "new" logical grammar. What Kučerenko does in the second part of his book is to mop up the debris of the formal approach in favor of a consistent logical grammar. But, as the consistent logical approach is incompatible with the very nature of language he cannot and does not succeed in his endeavors. Still the inquisitive mind of Kučerenko not willing to comply with a rehash of traditional half-truths is an asset, and more important results may be expected when he makes himself better acquainted with world linguistics and more attentive to the phenomena of language as such.

### 4. *Syntax. Parts of speech*

Syntax seems to be the most favored field of Soviet Ukrainian linguists. More is written in this field than in any other. In this survey the subject is broken into two parts: syntax of parts of speech and syntax of the sentence.

Only few studies are devoted to syntax of nouns. The most important is the article by O. Mel'nyčuk on history of the use of the dative without prepositions (DSUM). It wins one over by the wealth of its data, and its precision in analysis and elegance in presentation. While basically descriptive it opens broader vistas by linking the decline of some functions of this dative with the decline of the active participle in Ukrainian, unexpectedly but convincingly. A. Finkel' (XDU 6) tries to prove that the instrumental of cause is still alive in Russian. He has collected copious examples but did not take into consideration that even what originally was the instrumental of cause, with the destruction of the core of this function, could have been re-assigned to other functions of the instrumental, an operation easy with the wide range of functions typical of this case and lack of precise delimitations among many of them. The article is interesting in that it reveals some ties with the formalist school of the twenties, a trend with which Finkel' partly had associated himself, otherwise hardly discoverable in the Soviet Ukrainian linguistics of our days. Namely, Finkel' tries to establish a connection between the spread of the instrumental of cause and the vicissitudes of the classical style in Russian literature. O. Zarudnjak traces the use of the locative in Ukrainian (UMŠ 58, 6). T. Tulina classifies with many minutiae the functions of the genitive in Radiščev's *Putešestvie* (ODU 7, 8, 148, 150).

I. Matvijas depicts peculiarities in the use of various pronouns in the Ukrainian literature of the first half of the nineteenth century (DSUM, M 15) mostly developing the statements of the *Kurs*. B. Kobyljans'kyj (M 12) objects to the characterization of the nominal form after *dva*, *tri* and *četyre* in Russian as the genitive sg and proposes to see in it a special form of plural. I. Kanšin follows the details of syntactic and phraseological use of Russian *skol'ko*, *stol'ko* and similar words (LPI 12) and of Russian *odin* (LPI 16). D. Hrynčyšyn (PUM 2, DMUM 2, ISN) presents copious materials on substantivized adjectives from Old and Modern Ukrainian, A. Barzilovič treats the same subject for Russian (KDU 13), in DMUM 3 Hrynčyšyn describes substantivized numerals in modern Ukrainian, J. Bahmut (M 12) treats the use of participles in Ukrainian, as does F. Smahlenko (ODU 6). A. Kolodjažnyj in a monograph *Pryjmennyk* (X., 1960) describes in detail but without much originality prepositional constructions of modern Ukrainian, with some parallels from Old Ukrainian and other Slavic languages. The morphological structure of prepositions is left aside. N. Bukatevič devotes several articles to the preposition in the Old Rus' language and in Russian (ODU 4, 5, 6, 8). L. Humec'ka studies functions of prepositions in the Ukrainian documents of the fourteenth and fifteenth centuries (DMUM 3), M. Koval's'ka of prepositions which take the genitive in the Ukrainian chronicles of the seventeenth century (ODU 148).

More attention has been paid to the functions of verbal forms. Besides several articles three monographs are at hand. Problems of tense, aspect and voice are treated, mostly historically, in V. Rusanivs'kyj's *Značennja i vzajemozvjazok hramatyčnyx katehorij vydu i času v ukrajins'kij movi XVI-XVII st.* (K., 1959). The most convincing is his analysis of the use of future tense forms with *budu* and *imu*. In examining the past tense his endeavors to distinguish between aoristivity and perfectivity are futile because for the time under scrutiny these categories were extra-grammatical. In establishing "empty" prefixes of verbs he follows the known principle of opposition within the prefixed forms (*obohatyty* : *obohaščaty*) but it seems from his data that the principle is not applicable straightforward for the sixteenth century. In general, the merit of the book is in its material; in methodology it lacks rigidity and precision.

The analysis is much subtler in *Značennja form mynuloho času v halyc'ko-volyns'komu litopysu* by A. Hens'ors'kyj (K., 1957). The author arrives at the interesting conclusion that in the Chronicle of Halyč and Volynia the use of past tense forms did not reflect the spoken language but was rather strictly regulated by a set of artificial rules. This is a point of great importance for those who confuse the literary and spoken languages of the Old Ukrainian period, namely most present day linguists. The book is supplemented by an article of Hens'ors'kyj and I. Kernyc'kyj (DML 4) on the functions of the aorist and the imperfect in Old Ukrainian and the time of their decline. Kernyc'kyj also published an useful article on the history of the pluperfect in Ukrainian, in its three forms: with the imperfect, the aorist, and the perfect of the auxiliary verb (DMUM 1). P. Kryvoručko studies tense relations between the verbs of the principal and relative subordinate clause in modern Russian (FZ).

In DMUM 3 and ISN L. Koc' describes functions of the gerund in modern Ukrainian, while O. Mel'nyčuk (SM 1) publishes a study on the use, in the Old Rus' language, of *-vъ(ši)* participles as absolute predicates, deriving from this the modern Ukrainian and Belorussian past tense forms in *-v* (*-w*), of the type *znav* ~ *znaw*. Certain repercussions of the school of Z. Klemensiewicz in syntax are worth noting in Koc' article. G. Zelinskaja (ODU 148) has collected rich material on the use of gerunds in *-a* and *-uči* in Deržavin. I. Švec' classifies syntactic functions of the infinitive (ODU 150).

Reflexive verbs in the literary language of Old Rus' are studied in N. Zarickij's *Formy i funkcii vozvratnyx glagolov* (K., 1961). This book illustrates once more the dangers of insularity. Like many of his colleagues Zarickij refers only to books published in the U.S.S.R. and ignores anything that came out abroad. He obviously is unaware of R. Jakobson's views on reflexive verbs. Moreover, he is not acquainted with B. Havránek's *Genera verbi v slovanských jazycích*, whose first volume (Prague, 1928) treats the same problems as he and includes some Old Rus' material. As a matter of fact some examples are even identical ("Padesja pod nim' kon'" – Zarickij, p. 121; Havránek, p. 133; etc.). No wonder that many statements of Zarickij are anticipated by Havránek. If the work of Zarickij is not quite in vain this is so because his approach is mostly semantic and syntactic whereas Havránek was primarily morphologically oriented. There is abundant material in Zarickij, as well as a microscopic analysis, which make the book not useless. But the analysis is uneven, now penetrating, now subjective, and always impressionistic. For instance, Zarickij establishes degrees of transformation of the subject as shown by reflexive verbs. According to him this degree is higher in *mytisja* "wash oneself" than in *preobrazitisja* "transform" (into a dragon). Were the Slavs of the time so dirty? Belief in "advance" in language development (p. 5), references to how the people of the twelfth century "felt" linguistic facts (p. 11), and naïve semantic analysis are but other manifestations of the lack of any consistent and rigid method.

### 5. *Syntax of the sentence*

The most comprehensive survey of the sentence in standard Ukrainian of today is given in the *Kurs*, 2, by G. Shevelov (simple sentence, published without the name of the author), and O. Veržbyc'kyj (complex sentence), according to the traditional lines of the "Russian" school in syntax as established by Potebnja, A. Peškovskij, Šaxmatov, Bulaxovs'kyj et al., a compromise between psychological, logical and formal approaches. The main lines of this presentation constituted the foundation of M. Žovtobrjux's syntax in the collective *Porivnjal'na hramatyka ukrajins'koji i rosijs'koji mov*, with Russian and Belorussian parallels added. In the last years of his life Bulaxovs'kyj began writing a new version of the syntax of simple sentences for the planned second edition of the *Kurs*. The introductory section is published in DSUM. It is marked by greater flexibility in definitions and some concessions to logical grammar (e.g. it is stated that the subject can be used in the dative), but otherwise is based on the same principles.

Historical courses follow the same scheme, only the bulk of their examples is from the old texts. In O. Bespal'ko's *Narysy z istoryčnoho syntaksysu ukrajins'koji movy* (K., 1960; this is a slightly revised version of the corresponding chapter written by Bezpal'ko in the collective *Istoryčna hramatyka ukrajins'koji movy* by Bespal'ko, M. Bojčuk *et al.*) virtually no attention is paid to historical dialectology and not much to shifts in time, except for the officially required distinction of the Old Rus' and "Old Ukrainian" periods. Problems of interlingual relations are ignored so that Ukrainian syntax is taken, together with Russian and Belorussian, in an artificial isolation. In Ja. Sprinčak's *Očerk russkogo istoričeskogo sintaksisa, Prostoe predloženie* (K., 1960) there are more details; occasionally problems of loans are discussed, though with extreme caution; in a few instances dialectal distinctions are mentioned, but otherwise the same method of piling up examples without too much theorizing and generalizing is applied. As a result neither of the two books even tries to render syntactic development as a process. Both remain basically agglomerations of atomistically presented historical examples on the phenomena of the modern Ukrainian and Russian languages, just to say that some of these phenomena changed during the last nine centuries and others did not. Two booklets of A. Moskalenko, *Syntaksys prostoho rečennja davn'orus'koji i ukrajins'koji movy* and *Syntaksys skladnoho rečennja davn'orus'koji i ukrajins'koji movy* (both Od., 1959) do not claim to be anything more than elementary textbooks.

The petrified scheme in treatment of syntax allows production of a host of articles which only fill the cells of the same combs with new examples drawn from a specific text, or author, or texts of a period. What depends on the researcher is only the degree of detailing. And in this no limits are set because, with the lack of any rigid method, syntax easily drowns in the vast sea of phraseology and vocabulary. This genre of articles not only prevails but is almost the only one used in the Soviet Ukraine. Such are, in synchronic subjects, articles by H. Piskun on the copula in Ukrainian (LPl 16) and by G. Grudneva on the compound predicate in Russian (VRJa 3); by P. Dudyk on incomplete sentences (DSUM); by I. Petlyčnyj on sentences with generalized subject, with predicate in *-no*, *-to*, and with infinitive as predicate in I. Franko's work (PUM 2, 3, 4); by T. Malina on impersonal verbs and sentences (KDU 13); by E. Vojnova on interchangeability of adjectival and substantival possessive constructions (PSM 6); by V. Kolomijec' on functions of Czech coordinative conjunctions (SM 1, 2; PSM 5), and on word order as to subject and predicate in Czech of the nineteenth century (VSJa 3); by M. Karans'ka on functions of the conjunction *ščob* in Ukrainian (M 15); by A. Akišina on types of periods in modern Russian (VRJa 3, 4); by M. Pljušč-Vysokopojasnaja on comparative constructions in Gor'kij (DLM). The booklet by N. Hretčenko *Syntaksyčni osoblyvosti romana A. Holovka "Burjan"* (K., 1958) neither in size nor in approach exceeds an article. Random observations on word order, incomplete sentences and direct speech are pieced together.

This type of article is found in historical syntax as well, e.g., in O. Tkačenko's studies on conjunctions of objective clause in Polish of the sixteenth century (SM 1, 2, with an attempt to penetrate into the interplay of the competitive conjunctions); O. Petrenko's on the same in the Chronicle of S. Velyčko (M 12); I. Kovalyk's on negative sentences in B. Xmel'nyc'kyj's documents (VSJa 4). It is joined by the monograph of U. Jedlins'ka *Pytannja istoryčnoho syntaksysu ukrajins'koji movy* (K., 1961) in which she studies the letters of B. Xmel'nyc'kyj's chancellery to the Tsar Aleksej. The articles of V. Besedina-Nevzorova on constructions *imamь* and *xoštǫ* + infinitive in Old Church Slavonic (XDU 6) and of M. Kopylenko on hypotaxis in the Slavic translation of I. Malalas' chronicle are to be credited for their reference to Greek, otherwise unattested among Soviet Ukrainian linguists, but they are handicapped by lack of acquaintance with recent works in the same domain by Czech and German scholars.

In a few articles the composition is a little more complicated. They trace a certain category or construction through the whole history of the language or some periods. Such are the articles of O. Skoropada on the place of the relative clause (PUM 1, 2); of I. Slyn'ko on possessive constructions (PID); of O. Mel'nyčuk on interrogative, imperative, optative and conditional sentences in Ukrainian (SM 2), the latter also with some etymological suggestions concerning the conjunctions discussed.

All these studies are just bricks for a house to be built later. Yet the usefulness of great many of them is marred by their impressionistic character, haphazard material and vagueness of the method, which makes even some statistics not quite reliable (e.g. in Slyn'ko, Petlyčnyj). Against the background of this stagnation in method the book by I. Kučerenko *Porivnjal'ni konstrukciji movy v svitli hramatyky* (K., 1959) is interesting. Not that it breaks with the traditional approach (which he calls, p. 67, logical, although often it is rather illogical). But he is the only author who explicitly says that this is *an* approach and that it has its drawbacks. He still chooses it, and the great part of his book is devoted to discussions which look rather futile for anyone who does not work within the framework of the approach, e.g., that the clauses which fulfill the function of a modifier of manner are to be considered attributive and not adverbial. Kučerenko is also one of the few researchers who challenges some of the definitions of the *Kurs* (p. 13), although basically he remains within the same framework. If one disregards these manifestations of a more critical mind and, at the same time, unwillingness to liberate himself from the tradition, the book of Kučerenko appears as one more in the same file: it multiplies examples and adds details to the *Kurs*.

Discussion of syntactic problems on a theoretical level is limited and proceeds within the same framework. To an outsider it does not appear engrossing. Occasionally a contradiction or shortcoming within the traditional method is uncovered, only to be patched by an equally unsatisfactory pseudo-solution. L. Korobčinskaja (VRJa 4) presents one more re-hash on the subject of the predicatives in Russian (*kategorija sostojanija*, as launched by V. Vinogradov) without saying anything new. This topic is also taken up by T. Malina (KDU 14). P. Kostruba re-classifies the types of utterances (PUM 3) and of incomplete sentences (PUM 4). Je. Krotevyč revises definitions of governing, concord, and joining (VSJa 3), adding the notion of encircling, though it is on a quite different level; of word groups (*slovosočetanija* – VSJa 4); he discusses the types of complex sentences (VSJa 3) and relations of word, part of speech, and member of sentence (VRJa 4). These articles develop the ideas of his *Predloženie i ego priznaki* (L., 1954). V. Besedina-Nevzorova scrutinizes the ties between the word order and structure of the language (FZ) without adding anything to our knowledge. It is interesting to note that no study in syntax deals with the spoken standard language and all data are from literary and, rarely, scholarly texts. That has become so usual that when B. Zadorožnyj (and he alone!) raises the question of intonation in utterances (VSJa 3) he advises one to study it from records of folk songs and operatic recitatives!

### 6. *Vocabulary*

Here the very nature of the subject prompts the student to an atomistic treatment. No wonder that this treatment is found in the work of Soviet Ukrainian linguists. No attempts at any broader generalizations or systematization of linguistic character are to be reported. (Occasionally such generalizations are made on a political level: "advancement" in vocabulary and "perfection" attained after 1917.)

A rather futile type of article is those which present synonyms in the work of a writer: Franko (L. Poljuha for 'speak' and 'look', DMUM 2, for some other verbs and adjectives, DMUM 3, ISN; I. Oščypko, for random notions, PUM 1, 4; V. Morenec' for attributes, KDU 15; and A. Koval' for phraseology, KDU 15), Ševčenko (V. Il'jin, LB 5), Kocjubyns'kyj (L. Palamarčuk for adjectives and adverbs, LB 5), or in the language in general (synonyms of 'to see' in Ukrainian, by S. Kryvoručko, PUM 4). These are at best materials to be kept in files and used for dictionaries. For practical use they should be organized in the form of a synonymic dictionary. The first attempt in this direction is P. Derkač's *Korotkyj slovnyk synonimiv ukrajins'koji movy* (K., 1960). A more detailed but also more loosely arranged collection of synonyms, presented simply by excerpts from writers, without any characterizations of its own, was published in small installments in *Vitčyzna*, from No. 2, 1959. It is compiled by A. Bahmet, and by the end of 1961 reached the word *nastačaty*. (In No. 7, 1962, publication was interrupted, on the word *neščadno*.) I. Svjencic'kyj's remarks on vocabulary in particular groups of Ukrainian documents of the 14th and 15th centuries (PUM 2) are supposed to be a contribution to Ukrainian historical dialectology.

A little more creative are presentations of words in semantic groups, such as M. Xudaš does in his *Leksyka ukrajins'kyx dilovyx dokumentiv kincja XVI – počatku XVII st.* (K., 1961), on the basis of the documents of *Stavropihija* Brotherhood of Lviv, Je. Černov for some names of coins (LB 7) and N. Rjadčenko for the same (ODU 6, 150), Je. Rehuševs'kyj for grammatical terms in Franko (LB 7), M. Šarleman' for zoologic terms in P. Berynda (M 15), I. Oščypko for every day vocabulary in the same source (PUM 4), V. Ickovič for "modal words" in Russian (VRJa 3, 4), N. Kalamova for some random adverbs in Russian (VRJa 4), Ju. Bol'šova for pronominalized words in Russian (VRJa 4), V. Andel for abstract words in Czech of the thirteenth century (SF 1) and, quite unsystematically, A. Kyryčenko for color names in Eastern Slavic (PUM 4). The study of Xudaš is nearly duplicated by F. Tkač who characterizes the vocabulary of Ukrainian acts of the seventeenth century according to the same lines, only basing it primarily on the documents issued by the chancellery of B. Xmel'nyc'kyj (ODU 8, 9).

L. Kolomijec' collected some petrified idioms in the Ukrainian legal terminology of the fourteenth and fifteenth centuries (NĖF), which could lead to an interesting investigation on the continuity between the Middle Ukrainian official language as compared to Old Ukrainian (XI-XIII century), but she only made a passing remark on this. The method of accumulating dictionary items without almost any commentary is brought to its logical end by M. Puškar, who presents Czech vocabulary in long lists according to such categories as borrowings, archaisms, folk etymologies, etc. (VSJa 4, PSM 5), by I. Bilodid who gives a list of phraseological idioms current in modern Ukrainian, including Soviet newspaper clichés, incomplete and unsystematic, as it is expected to be (M 12), and by L. Batjuk, with some excerpts from Samovydec' Chronicle (DMUM 1). A collection of constructions consisting of *delat'* + a substantive denoting acts of thought, in modern Russian, is presented by V. Koz'menko (XDU 6). L. Humec'ka studies the relation between the terms coined by affixation and by syntactic combinations in modern Polish (LB 4). Differences in vocabulary between Ukrainian and Russian (Moscow) documents of the fourteenth and fifteenth centuries are characterized by Ja. Sprinčak (VJa 56, 6).

In some of these word collections facts from the history of the words treated are occasionally cited. This is the special subject of such articles as history of the word *sorok* in Eastern Slavic by Ju. Karpenko (PID) and some terms of Polish legal terminology by I. Kil'čevs'kyj (SM 2). Two monographs have also been published in this field. A. Burjačok's *Nazvy sporidnenosti i svojactva v ukrajins'kij movi* (K., 1961) brings some new facts concerning dialectal distribution of kinship and family terminology. Its historical data are haphazard and its etymologies all second hand or naive, as e.g. derivation of *bat'ko* "father" from IE *pətē(r) by accepting interchange of unvoiced and voiced consonants with reference to such pairs as Ukr. *tanec'* "dance" vs. Ukr. dial. *dánec'*, in reality the first borrowed from German, the second from Rumanian. *Narys istoriji ukrajins'koji hramatyčnoji terminolohiji* by N. Moskalenko (K., 1959) treats the subject which could be discussed against the background of various linguistic trends or of general "styles of life" (Romanticism, Positivism, etc.). Neither is done, so that the book is only a collection of data about who invented or used certain terms and when. In addition, Byzantine and Western contacts and influences are thoroughly ignored so that from ancient Rome and Greece the author immediately proceeds to *Adel'fotes* or Meletij Smotryc'kyj or, in the best case, Maksim Grek.

Several authors have worked on problems of borrowings. Je. Opel'baum presents Western Slavic borrowings in German (SM 1) and Common Slavic in Germanic (M 12), the latter fairly much along lines of wishful thinking. This applies also to V. Martynov's article on the same subject in ODU 7. I. Čerdenyčenko gives a list of Slavic words in Hungarian (PID), without much motivation. The author euphemistically avoids the word "borrowing". Instead, he speaks of "lexical convergences" and "fruitful influence". M. Onyškevyč (VSJa 4) speaks of supposedly Eastern Slavic words in Polish, M. Puškar (SF) and V. Kolomijec' (LB 4, M 12) present lists of Soviet clichés in Czech, Je. Mart'janova follows penetration of Sovietisms in the language of French Communist writers. She calls it "enrichment of French vocabulary by the Russian language". V. Akulenko (XDU 6) undertook an attempt to buttress linguistically what is currently called in the U.S.S.R. internationalisms. His article justly aroused serious objections and a subsequent discussion in *Voprosy jazykoznanija* (M. Makovskij, 1960, 1). The same problem is treated by A. Bilec'kyj (KDU 14).

Borrowings from Russian, real and alleged, into other languages and particularly into Ukrainian are constantly emphasized by many authors. H. Jižakevyč who devoted to the problem a biased, fact-distorting and superficial monograph *Pytannja rosijs'ko-ukrajins'kyx movnyx zvjazkiv* (K., 1954) in a later article on "creative ties" between Russian and Ukrainian (M 16) decided to seek criteria of "fruitfulness" in borrowings. She suggests as such a criterion "presence of certain additional semantic and/or stylistic nuances" in the loanwords. If consistently applied this would mean complete adaptation of the semantic structure of one language to the other. H. Hnatjuk in the booklet *Rosijs'ko-ukrajins'ki literaturno-movni zvjazky v druhij polovyni XVIII – peršij čverti XIX st.* (K., 1957) collected facts more conscientiously, and some of them were introduced to circulation for the first time. But she only presents scattered facts without showing general processes which stood behind them and which were of crucial importance, viz. that in the middle eighteenth century the Ukrainian intelligentsia voluntarily made an attempt to switch to Russian as the literary language of the Ukraine but by the end of the period under scrutiny, discarded this idea and started re-creating standard Ukrainian on the basis of the South Eastern Ukrainian dialects. I. Bilodid and O. Mel'nyčuk outline how Russian-Ukrainian language relations are programmatically slated for future (M 15; also VJa 59, 5).

The opposite direction of borrowings, into Russian and Ukrainian, seems to be taboo for most authors. They carefully shun it or try to minimize foreign influences. Only Xudaš in his book, as well as in a special article (DMUM 3), breaks with this attitude, albeit with many reservations and points to German and Polish loanwords in Ukrainian (which otherwise are generally known), as does partly F. Tkač (ODU 7).

A few articles on the history of Slavic lexicography (Czech lexicography by H. Lastovec'ka in VSJa 4, PSM 5 and SF 1; Ukrainian-Russian dictionaries before 1830 by H. Hnatjuk in LB 7 and P. Horec'kyj in LB 6; early Slavo-Romanian lexicography by M. Stanivs'kyj in PID) remind one of some well known facts and are hardly based on first hand studies. Of informative interest, on how dictionaries are compiled in the Soviet Ukraine, are the articles of S. Levčenko on the principles of a synonymic dictionary (LB 5), of N. Rodzevyč on the principles of a technological dictionary (LB 6. Published in K., 1961: *Rosijs'ko-ukrajins'kyj texničnyj slovnyk*, ed. by A. Vasylenko, N. Rodzevyč, M. Matijko), of M. Bojko on the principles of the dictionary of Ševčenko's language (LB 6 and ZPNK 6), and of B. Larin on the principles of Ukrainian regional dictionaries, with a survey of what has been done so far (DB 6). LB 3 is entirely devoted to discussion of *Russko-ukrainskij slovar'* (Moscow, 1948) (articles by L. Bulaxovs'kyj, I. Kryčenko, M. Pylyns'kyj, I. Kryvec'kyj, L. Dovhan', O. Kundzič).

Etymology seems to be the most neglected field. Except the articles of Bulaxovs'kyj on the origin of mythological names in the *Igor Tale* (M 15) and de-etymologization in modern Russian (VSJa 3) and V. Martynov's objections to evaluation of blended forms in etymology as made by Bulaxovs'kyj (ODU 4) there is only a note by M. Onyškevyč on the origin of Ukr. dial. (Bojkian) *pony* "up to" (SF 1). The etymologies of some pottery terms in the article by M. Kryvčans'ka (DB 7) and some plant names in the article by Ju. Karpenko (PID) are mere citations from etymological dictionaries and if there is anything new it concerns the history of the words in Ukrainian but not their etymology proper. The more so it is in the popularization of the known etymologies of plant names by J. Dzendzelivs'kyj (UMŠ 58, 2) and in the etymological notes by O. Tkačenko (UMŠ 58, 4; 59, 2) and R. Kravčuk (UMŠ 60, 6).

A general outline of Ukrainian lexicology is given by M. Žovtobrjux according to traditional lines (synonyms, archaisms, neologisms, etc.) in his and B. Kulyk's *Kurs* and for the second time in his own *Sučasna ukrajins'ka literaturna mova* as well as by M. Ivčenko in his book with the corresponding title.

### 7. *Stylistics. History of the literary language*

In the thirties at the time of the deepest crisis in Ukrainian linguistics, a genre of linguo-stylistic essays on the language of a particular writer or a work spread widely. These essays in most instances were impressionistic in approach and circular in analysis (for example: the word "sad" is used because the mood is sad; and one knows that the mood was sad because the word "sad" was used). Essays of this type are still quite numerous although some decrease in their number bears witness to growing maturity of Soviet Ukrainian linguistics. In the decade under survey linguo-stylistic peculiarities of the following writers were treated by the Ukrainian linguists: T. Ševčenko (by V. Il'jin, DSUM, PKD; V. Morenec', DLM; V. Vaščenko, and P. Petrova, ZPNK 7, 8; I. Mahura, ZPNK 4; and with more interesting details by Ja. Dzyra, UMŠ 61, 5), L. Hlibov (by V. Marynyčenko, LB 7, DUM), I. Franko (by Ja. Zakrevs'ka, DMUM 1, DUM; N. Kornijenko, M 13; Z. Franko, PKD), Lesja Ukrajinka (by S. Pljamovata and Ju. Sidun, PUM 4), M. Kocjubyns'kyj (by L. Palamarčuk, M 13 and O. Pyvovarov, DUM), M. Čeremšyna (by I. Petlyčnyj, VSJa 3), L. Martovyč (by A. Hryhoruk, ODU 8, 148), A. Teslenko (by S. Kryvoručko, VSJa 4, PUM 1, 2, 3), M. Bažan (by V. Karpova, DML 3, DMUM 1), Ja. Halan (by S. Didyk, LPI 16); I. Gončarov (by V. Brodskaja, VSJa 4), M. Saltykov-Ščedrin (by I. Iščenko, LPI 16), M. Gor'kij (by V. Sirotina, KDU 14, S. Savickaja, ODU 6, 8), A. N. Tolstoj (by V. Verbickaja, VRJa 3), L. Leonov (by Ė. Vojnova, VRJa 4), A. Fadeev (by S. Calenčuk, LPI 12), M. Šoloxov (by N. Rudjakov, ODU 6, 8, 148), and V. Majakovskij (by M. Il'jaš, ODU 8, 148, 150). A. Hens'ors'kyj's notes on stylistics of the Chronicle of Halyč and Volynia (DMUM 1; also in his *Halyc'ko-volyns'kyj litopys*, K., 1958) are to be added as well as random remarks of S. Savickaja on the language and style of the epistles of Ivan the Terrible (ODU 4).

The number of monographs in linguo-stylistics was higher than in any other part of linguistics. To three of them, *Osoblyvosti movy i stylju ukrajins'koji radjans'koji xudožn'o-istoryčnoji prozy* by L. Skrypnyk (K., 1958), *Ševčenkove slovo ta poetyčnyj kontekst* by P. Petrova (X., 1960), on stylistics of pronouns in Ševčenko's poetry, and A. Nazarevskij's *O literaturnoj storone gramot i drugix dokumentov Moskovskoj Rusi načala XVII veka* (K., 1961) applies what was said above about the articles in this field. I. Bilodid's *Pytannja rozvytku movy ukrajins'koji xudožn'oji prozy* (K., 1955), *Mova i styl' romana "Veršnyky" Ju. Janovs'koho* (K., 1955) and in particular *Mova tvoriv Oleksandra Dovženka, Zbirnyk "Začarovana Desna"* (K., 1959) reveal some good insights and sense of style. Some traces of acquaintance with Formalism and some Western studies may be discovered. But basically his books lean heavily to political propaganda, blasting against "bourgeois nationalists" and collecting and praising what the author calls "the use of scientific and publicist constructions" (p. 267), i.e. of political clichés. While speaking of Janovs'kyj's artistry Bilodid is right in showing its ties with Gogol' and Tyčyna, but he is silent about the connections of the writer with Hemingway from whom Janovs'kyj learned many devices. D. Barannyk and H. Haj in their *Dramatyčnyj dialoh* (K., 1961) analyze dialogue in Ukrainian realist plays of the nineteenth century, from psychological and syntactic points of view. *Mova ta styl' xudožnix tvoriv Panasa Myrnoho* by I. Hrycjutenko (K., 1959) was not available to me.

Two books on stylistics in general supplement each other. V. Vaščenko's *Stylistyčni javyšča v ukrajins'kij movi*, I (X., 1958) treats stylistical possibilities inherent in Ukrainian phonology, morphology and syntax; A. Koval's *Praktyčna stylistyka sučasnoji ukrajins'koji movy*, I (K., 1960) deals with vocabulary. Neither is systematic, exhaustive or scholarly, both present separate observations, samples, advice but are primarily collections of examples from fiction, folklore (particularly Vaščenko) and journalism. The booklet by A. Koval' *Pro kul'turu ukrajins'koji movy* (K., 1961) is even more subjective and impressiontic. It is interesting rather as a manifestation of purism being re-introduced, after decades of suppression, into Ukrainian linguistics albeit with constant bows to the Russian language and heavily influenced by the pattern of Soviet Russian purism.

History of the literary language, a field of research virtually introduced by the Formalists and very popular in the Soviet Ukraine (though no longer following the method of the founders) consists basically of two heterogeneous parts: external history of the standard language, and diachronical linguo-stylistics. Two outlines of the history of literary Ukrainian published both in Kiev in 1958 but written independently show how far uniformity in the field extends: P. Pljušč, *Narysy z istoriji ukrajins'koji literaturnoji movy*, and a collective work edited by I. Bilodid, *Kurs istoriji ukrajins'koji literaturnoji movy*, I. The book by Pljušč is more concise and for the period after Ševčenko becomes rather a brief synopsis. The collective volume is rich in details and puts particular emphasis on the nineteenth century (It covers the period up to 1917). Both follow the same periodization in Old Rus' (11-14th century), Old Ukrainian (15th – mid 17th century), the period of formation of a bourgeois nation (mid 17th century – 1917) and the period of a socialist nation (after 1917), which reflects in a rather inconsistent terminology the actual division in Old, Middle and Modern Ukrainian. Attaching the breakdown of the history of the language to political events this periodization is in striking contradiction to facts in establishing the boundary between Middle and Modern Ukrainian in the mid-seventeenth century. It is not the unification with Russia, in 1654, which brought about the end of Middle Ukrainian but the crucial defeat of Ukrainian autonomism in the battle of Poltava, in 1709. Bilodid is obviously aware of this discrepancy without overtly admitting it: he presents the status before and after 1709 in separate chapters. Pljušč passes the problem with silence.[5] Both books avoid any mention of the switch to Russian typical of the eighteenth-century Ukraine. Both in general do not discuss things undesirable or debatable. Outside of references to the general historical situation they avoid generalizations. Conflicts and changes of styles are not presented. Little is said about stylistic trends and schools, dynamics of their co-existence, clashes and ends. Instead, for each period writers are divided in those who were for people and those who were against. Essentially, this is an antihistorical approach, and when Bilodid's work concludes with an atomistic presentation of profiles of individual writers, this is only logical. Differences between the two books are rather technical. Pljušč, as stated, is shorter and uses more of a barrage of quotations, Bilodid more detailed. Pljušč's article on Middle Ukrainian (NĖF) adds some more materials but clings tenaciously to the old approach.

The second volume of the collective *Kurs istoriji ukrajins'koji literaturnoji movy* (K., 1961) is written by Z. Franko, H. Jižakevyč, M. Žovtobrjux and I. Bilodid, and edited by the latter. It covers the Soviet period which is divided into three subperiods: the twenties, the thirties, and the forties and fifties, with further breakdown in each period according to genres. Compared to the first volume this one sticks more to facts and sources; omissions are fewer (but some are still conspicuous: Zerov among the writers, Synjavs'kyj, N. Kahanovyč among the linguists, A. Xvylja among the political leaders, etc.). The overtones of political propaganda and slips into retelling of the works analyzed are not rare but less outspoken than previously. If to a great extent the history of the vocabulary is reduced to registration of various series of clichés superseded by others this very much reflects the state of affairs in the otherwise greatly uniform literature beginning in the thirties. Occasionally the authors even raise timidly their voices against too many clichés (e.g., p. 154). In the twenties there still were trends in literature, but they are greatly obliterated in the presentation by artificial grouping of writers. The development in syntax is basically devoted to penetration of Russian peculiarities, without saying so explicitly. The problem of penetration of some language elements from the Western Ukraine, and dialectal elements in general is fairly much subdued. To sum it up, the second volume of the *Kurs istoriji* is marked by more objectivity and maturity than its predecessor, but it still has far to go in this direction. If the volume remains basically a-historical, though, the compilers are only partially to be blamed for that.

The third book in the field, *Istorija russkogo literaturnogo jazyka*, I by V. Brodskaja

[5] Periodization of the history of standard Ukrainian became the subject of a discussion on pages of UMŠ: P. Tymošenko, 1958, 6; M. Žovtobrjux, 1959, 2; M. Bojčuk, 1959, 4; I. Hrycjutenko. 1959, 6. The discussion brought about no original points of view and ended virtually in nothing.

and S. Calenčuk (L., 1957) hardly deserves mentioning. It is an agglomeration of known facts and theories pieced together without any critical sense. This also refers to the writings of prolific I. Svjencic'kyj on the Old Ukrainian period (VSJa 3, 4; PSM 5, PUM 3). They are confused in presentation, amateurish and unreliable in rendering the facts. Other articles are either brief surveys as M. Stanivs'kyj's (PID) on literary Ukrainian in Moldavia and Bukovyna and U. Jedlins'ka's on the status of Ukrainian in the Transcarpathian Ukraine under Czecho-Slovakia in 1919-38 (FZ). Or they limit themselves to presentation of some data: the rise of philosophical terminology in Russian of the eighteenth century (A. Čičerin, VSJa 3), and in Ukrainian of the late nineteenth century (D. Kyryk, PUM 3), views on language by I. Kotljarevs'kyj (M. Pavljuk, ODU 8), P. Hrabovs'kyj (F. Smahlenko, ODU 8), L. Martovyč (V. Lesyk, VSJa 3) and L. Tolstoj (G. Skljarevskij, XDU 6). M. Bojko's pamphlet *Do pytannja pro rozvytok ukrajins'koji literaturnoji movy za roky radjans'koji vlady* (K., 1957) is manifestly intended to be a piece of propaganda.

There are no descriptions of all linguistic or linguo-stylistic aspects of old texts, except random notes by L. Batjuk on some peculiarities in the language of the chronicle of Xmil'nyk (DML 4) and U. Jedlins'ka's description of an unpublished book of records held in the office of the Bishop of Mukačiv in the second half of the eighteenth century (DMUM 3). M. Pavljuk collected materials concerning the attitude of contemporaries toward language and writing in the Old Rus' period but did not produce anything original (ODU 9). No full dictionaries of a writer's language were published but two useful word indices came out: to seven plays of Lesja Ukrajinka (M. Bojko, *Slovopokažčyk dramatyčnyx tvoriv Lesi Ukrajinky*, K., 1961) and V. Vaščenko, F. Medvedjev and P. Petrova's *Leksyka "Enejidy" I. P. Kotljarevs'koho* (X., 1955). P. Tymošenko prepared *Xrestomatija materialiv z istoriji ukrajins'koji literaturnoji movy*, 1-2 (K., 1959, 1961). It brings fragments from characterizations of the language of separate periods or writers made by scholars, pronouncements of writers on the language, materials of linguistic discussions, with the exclusions of anything that could be interpreted as hostile to the use of Russian in the Ukraine.

The publications in the field did not supersede the best presentations of the history of literary Ukrainian by M. Sulyma (1928) and H. Levčenko (1946), which took into account existence and conflicts of styles.

## 8. *Dialectology*

Broad work in collecting dialectal data was initiated by the Institute of Linguistics in Kiev, aiming at preparation of an atlas. The questionnaire was elaborated by F. Žylko, V. Il'jin, and P. Lysenko under guidance of B. Larin. *Prohrama dlja zbyrannja materialiv do dialektolohičnoho atlasa ukrajins'koji movy* published in 1948 and with some improvements anew in 1949 (K) contains 464 questions of which 262 refer to vocabulary and syntax. In scope and elaboration it cannot be compared with the best specimens of the genre (as, e.g., A. Zaręba's elaborate *Kwestionariusz do atlasu językovego Śląska*, Katowice, 1961), nor with the prerevolutionary questionnaires for Ukrainian by K. Myxal'čuk and Je. Tymčenko (1909) or by K. Myxal'čuk and A. Kryms'kyj (1910). But collecting materials with such detail is hardly feasible for the large area of the Ukraine and the new questionnaire is, generally, a fortunate compromise between the requirements of thoroughness and precision, on the one hand, and practical applicability, on the other. *Instrukcija dlja skladannja kart do atlasa ukrajins'koji movy* compiled by I. Matvijas is published as a supplement to DB 8.

The atlas is conceived of as a series of eight volumes. The territory of the country is divided in six "squares" and a volume is to be devoted to each square. Two additional volumes are planned for the presentation of summary isoglosses. Numerous materials have been collected for the atlas. The main source of these materials is the records made on the spot by four to five member groups consisting of one *aspirant* or instructor and three or four students of universities or pedagogical institutes. A six day residence in each settlement is considered sufficient to make reliable records. Mistakes in the work of these teams are criticized by I. Varčenko (DB 8).

Besides this centralized collecting work many linguists undertook field work in specific areas to prepare regional dialect descriptions. As a result of both types of endeavors a plethora of articles and monographs were published, with main concentration on Central and Western dialects.

For the central area, of basically descriptive character are P. Lysenko's description of phonetics and morphology of four villages in Dymer *rajon*, oblast Kiev (PKD), and of morphology of the dialect of Stavyšče *rajon*, same oblast (DB 6); V. Braxnov's of phonetics of three villages in Perejaslav *rajon* (PKD), of their morphology (DB 7) and syntax, with an interesting analysis of utterance intonation (DB 6, 7, SH); and P. Lysenko's of morphology in Čerkasy *rajon* (SH). The same topic in a more confused form is presented by A. Mohyla (SH). A. Očeretnyj on the basis of their consonantism establishes that the dialects of Uman' belong to the South-Western and not the Central type (SH). I. Matvijas re-tells the make-up of five unpublished maps of Kiev area (SH). Mere publication of the maps would be more rewarding. Collections of lexical data for the area are published by P. Lysenko (Stavyšče) according to semantic groups (DB 5), M. Kryvčans'ka (terms of ceramic handicraft in Poltava region, PKD), V. Matvjejeva (terms of embroidery in the same area, LB 7) and D. Tarasenko (fishing terms in the Middle Dnieper area, DB 8). On alphabetical principle is based P. Lysenko's dictionary of specific vocabulary of Čerkasy region (LB 6). On the borderline between linguistics and anthropology is V. Xomenko's attempt to delineate the geographic distribution of some fairy tale formulas with particular attention to differences between the Kiev and Poltava areas (DB 7). Of unusual interest are I. Varčenko's data on phonology of the West Poltava dialects: *y* ~ *i* distribution (DB 5), reflexes of strong *ъ* (DB 6), distribution of *e* ~ *y* (DB 7) and *o* ~ *i* (PKD), palatal and palatalized consonants (SH). The value of Varčenko's observations lies primarily in that he shows variability in the dialects and affords an insight in the current developments. It proves to be that many examples usually treated as a distortion of some peculiarities of the language of the educated actually reveal dialectal changes in progress, though often hampered by the influence of the standard language. The author in most cases is not aware of this situation. The data on irregularities in the alternation *o*, *e* : *i* are supplemented by A. Matvijenko (DB 8).

A mixed impression is made by B. Vaščenko's extensive monograph *Poltavs'ki hovory* (X., 1957). Based on records made in 133 settlements in the Eastern part of Poltava oblast, the greater part of Sumy oblast and north of Dnipropetrovsk oblast, compared where available with older records beginning from the seventeenth century, the book succeeds in presenting variability in the present day dialects of the area; in establishing tripartition of these dialects and South-Western foundation of the Eastern Poltava dialect; and in showing the scope of Russian influence (which contrary to expectations is rather limited). But its positive results are marred by repetitious composition, careless presentation, slipshod choice of examples, and a preconceived thesis, to be proved at any price, that the area was not re-settled in the sixteenth and seventeenth centuries but has preserved continuity of its Eastern Slavic population from the time immemorable. To this thesis I shall come back later while discussing the work by F. Žylko. The book is supplemented by Vaščenko's article (SH) on dynamics in the treatment of parallel forms in Poltava area today.

The South Western dialects are discussed in the articles by I. Hrycjutenko (Černjatyn, oblast Vinnycja. ODU 5), D. Bandrivs'kyj (morphology of the dialect of Turka, oblast Lviv. DMUM 2; phonology of Drohobyč dialects. DMUM 3; phonology and morphology of Lemkian settlers in Lypivec', *rajon* Drohobyč. DB 8), H. Šylo (South Western part of Rovno oblast. LPI 16), Ja. Pura (syntax of West Drohobyč dialects. PUM 4), I. Prystupa (palatalized consonants in South Western dialects. DMUM 1), M. Leonova (important data on the dialects of Northern Bukovyna. PID), L. Bova-Korol'čuk (summary characterization of the South Volynian dialects. PKD), and M. Peretjat'ko (morphology of Dubno dialects. DB 7); V. Nimčuk (numerals in Boržava dialects, Transcarpathia, DB 8). Basically the same area happened to be covered by two researchers: V. Černjak described vowels in fourteen settlements in the Bojkian area (PUM 4), D. Bandrivs'kyj vowels and consonants in seven settlements (DMUM 1). It is noteworthy that the results are occasionally not identical. Lexical materials were published by L. Palamarčuk (South Eastern dialects of Žytomyr oblast. LB 6), I. Kolisnyk (agricultural terms in Bukovyna, DB 8), Ju. Karpenko (names of cultured plants in Bukovyna. PID), V. Prokopenko (terms of kinship in Bukovyna. PID), J. Dzendzelivs'kyj (milling terms in Transcarpathia, DB 8), and Ja. Zakrevs'ka (names of the woodpecker in the Western Ukraine. DMUM 3). M. Onyškevyč who prepares a dictionary of Bojkian discusses the composition of the book in SF 1.

Of several monographs published in the field two were not available to me: H. Šylo's *Pivdenno-zaxidni hovory URSR na pivnič vid Dnistra* (L., 1957), and Ja. Pura's *Hovory zaxidnoji Drohobyččyny*, I (L., 1958). Two other monographs of descriptive character, P. Prystupa's *Hovirky Brjuxovyc'koho rajonu L'vivs'koji oblasti* (K., 1957) and D. Bandrivs'kyj's *Hovirky Pidbuz'koho rajonu L'vivs'koji oblasti* (K., 1960) are twins in many respects. Both are composed according to the same plan, both bring some new partial observations, and both present their data in a confused and inaccurate manner, with numerous errors which reveal insufficiency of linguistic training (like derivation of *bodnar* "cooper" from *dno* "bottom", Prystupa p. 35!). Record breaking in this respect is B. Kobyljans'kyj's *Dialekt i literaturna mova* (K., 1960) which is, however, not descriptive. It is devoted to the problem of how the Hucul and Pokuttja dialects arose. The main idea that these dialects to some extent continue the dialects of what originally was southern Eastern Slavs identified in the Primary Chronicle as *Uliči* and *Tiverci* is not new. But the identification of the Huculs directly with the *Uliči* and Pokutians with *Tiverci* is on the author's responsibility and so is the fantastic derivation of the name *Hucul* from *Uliči* (as well as *Moldava* from Sl. **mold-* "young", p. 156, and many other). The advantage of the author, that he has read much in German and Romanian, turns into a drawback because of his lack of linguistic training and critical sense. He piles up data of archeology, anthropology, history of literature, but he mixes the reliable and the fantastic, and makes the composition of his book chaotic. He shows no acquaintance with the studies which treat Balkan colonization and influences in the Carpathians in the fifteenth through the seventeenth centuries, which results in ascribing many relatively new developments to an old epoch. The book may be useful, if at all, in its incomplete but basically reliable survey of Ukrainian-Romanian linguistic interrelations.[6]

J. Dzendzelivs'kyj, who published in 1958 *Praktyčnyj slovnyk semantyčnyx dialektyzmiv Zakarpattja* (Užhorod; not available to me), undertook the publication of *Linhvistyčnyj atlas ukrajins'kyx narodnyx hovoriv Zakarpats'koji oblasti URSR*, I (Užhorod, 1958); II (Užhorod, 1960). Devoted exclusively to vocabulary and, in the first issue, not even marking regular phonetic differences, this work is serious and valuable, although poorly executed typographically. It presents first rate and first hand data recorded in 212 settlements and even has indices, an unusual procedure in Soviet Ukrainian publications. The two volumes comprise 270 maps of general distribution and 28 maps with summary isoglosses, and cover a vast range of lexical items, including even some personal names, with matter of fact concise commentaries.

Northern Ukrainian dialects are treated in the articles by F. Žylko (five villages in South Černihiv area, DB 5), I. Pryjmak (consonants in the north western dialects of Sumy oblast, DB 7[7]), S. Dorošenko (southern influences in the north western dialects of Sumy oblast, SH). P. Lysenko published *Slovnyk dialektnoji leksyky Seredn'oho i Sxidnoho Polissja* (K., 1961). T. Nazarova studies hypercorrect forms on the boundary of the Ukraine and Belorussia (*rajon* Čornobyl', obl. Kiev. DB 8).

[6] On a higher level is another book devoted to history of some South Western dialects: I. Pan'kevyč, *Narys istoriji ukrajins'kyx zakarpats'kyx hovoriv*, I: *Fonetyka* (Prague, 1958). As it was published outside the Uk.S.S.R. it does not fall into the scope of this survey.

[7] His regional dictionary *Do osoblyvostej miscevoji leksyky pivničnozaxidnyx rajoniv Sums'koji oblasti* (Nova Kaxovka, 1957) was not available to me.

Little attention was paid to studies in the dialects of the Eastern and Southern Ukraine and nothing was published on the Ukrainian dialects outside of the Ukrainian S.S.R. On the eastern dialects there is an article of B. Šarpylo on dialects of Starobil's'k (DB 7), an interesting subject because of the double graft of more western dialects in this area and many hypercorrect forms which resulted from these crossings. In the South relatively more attention was paid to the dialects in the lower reaches of the Dniester and the Danube: A. Mukan described the phonetics of the dialects along the Lower Danube, inadequately because he ignores the ties with Bulgarian and Romanian (DB 7), as did V. Drozdovs'kyj (ODU 150). J. Dzendzelivs'kyj studied the syntax of dialects near the lower Dniester (DB 5) and their vocabulary (LB 6). A special dictionary *Leksyka rybal'stva ukrajins'kyx hovoriv Nyžn'oho Podnistrovja* was published by A. Berlizov with introductory notes in which the make-up of the population and characterization of fishing methods are sketched (Černihiv, 1959; Deržavnyj Pedahohičnyj Instytut, *Naukovi zapysky*, IV, 4). A. Moskalenko's *Slovnyk dialektyzmiv ukrajins'kyx hovirok Odes'koji oblasti* (Od., 1958) was not available to me. S. Samijlenko picks up some phonetic peculiarities in the dialects of Zaporižžja oblast (DB 6), L. Tereško of *rajon* Kryvyj Rih, oblast Mykolajiv (DB 6). He also brings material about the spread of new agricultural terms in these dialects (ODU 5) and about the use of the vocative in the dialects of Odessa oblast (ODU 6). Together with I. Hrycjutenko he discusses how a dialectal dictionary of the Odessa oblast is to be compiled (ODU 9). Some morphological and syntactic features of the dialects around Pervomajs'k, obl. Mykolajiv, are summarily presented by H. Pelyx (ODU 150).

Russian dialects in the Ukraine were described by M. Tixomirova (Bol'šoe Ploskoe, obl. Odessa, VRJa 4), L. Buznik (Lipcy, obl. Kharkov, XDU 6) and V. Stolbunova (Belaja Krinica and Lipovany, obl. Černivci, PID). L. Loseva published her notes on syntax in dialects of Kursk oblast, outside of the Ukranian S.S.R. (PID).

Historical records as a basis for comparison with the modern dialects are used for the Poltava region by S. Samijlenko (PKD) and much more thoroughly and reliably, with the use of some unpublished documents, by O. Maštabej (SH); and for Transcarpathian dialects by I. Čerednyčenko (PID). S. Samijlenko made a summary of what forms of adjectives are used in various Ukrainian dialects (type *nova* vs. *navaja*. SH).

The imposing output of studies in dialectology is not so imposing if judged by its quality and findings. As a rule the works are uniform in their method: vowels are presented in alphabetical order, consonants according to their articulatory groups, morphology in parts of speech. The term phoneme is broadly used but just as a more "scientific" term for speech sound. There is not a single attempt at a phonemic or structural approach (but there are some kicks against it, e.g. in Kobyljans'kyj's monograph, p. 4). Historical considerations are unsystematically intermingled with descriptive ones. In most studies precision in formulations is lacking.

In terms of fact finding, and this is the tenor of Soviet Ukrainian dialectology, nothing was discovered to introduce basic changes into the generally accepted classification of the Ukrainian dialects. The main results were certain shifts in the previously established dialect boundaries and some insight in the dialectal developments of recent times. Some findings can have bearing on the history of Ukrainian. For instance, ǯ as the reflex of *dj outside of verbal forms which had been considered a Carpathian phenomenon was uncovered farther East; of the two types of dispalatalization of [r'], the Northern into [r] and the Western into [rj], some "northern" reflexes were found in the West and vice versa. But no conclusions from these observations have been drawn so far.

A synthetic presentation of the Ukrainian dialects, their classification, and their origin was undertaken by F. Žylko. His *Narysy z dialektolohiji ukrajins'koji movy* (K., 1955) was basically a survey of peculiarities typical of separate dialects and their groups as well as methods applied for collecting data. His second book *Hovory ukrajins'koji movy* (K., 1958) is intended to be a more popular survey of the same. Yet in many respects this book is more mature and original. Underlying it is an historical conception of changing relations between the dialects and the standard language; its formulations are preciser, its bibliography (which may be recommended to the readers of this survey) more complete, its critical sense more developed. Basically, however, both books primarily fill with data the classification launched as early as 1877 by K. Myxal'čuk, and rightly so because his views have withstood the vicissitudes of time and the flood of new data. Certain qualifications in the dialect boundaries are the subject of Žylko's article in FZ. In another article (DB 8) he makes a plea for phonemic approach in dialectology, although what he suggests is a far cry from real phonemics in the field.

The growing maturity of Žylko's approach is manifest also in his gradual revision of his original conception of the origin of the main Ukrainian dialects. This conception was expounded in PKD. In defiance of V. Hancov and O. Kurylo's assumption that Ukrainian arose from a merger of two originally different dialectal groups, Northern and South–Western, and that the South-Eastern dialects are the product of the new settlement in their area, where the Northern and South Western elements met (XV-XVII century) Žylko insisted that the South Eastern dialects were equally old and that the core of their area, South Kiev and Poltava areas, was never depopulated. (This theory possibly arose from an exaggerated need to buttress Stalin's statement that the "national" Ukrainian language is based on the dialects of Poltava and Kiev regions.) This view is still defended by Žylko in his article on diphthongs in Černihiv area (DB 6). He polemicizes here against T. Lehr-Spławiński and W. Kuraszkiewicz (actually with Hancov and Kurylo) about one or two ways of phonetic development in the Northern and South-Western dialects, thus defending his own conception. But in his article in FZ (1958) Žylko eliminated the Eastern Poltava dialect from what he insisted to be the third aboriginal Ukrainian dialectal unit. In a still later article (SH, 1960), under the pressure of facts, he let his third allegedly aboriginal dialectal group shrink to only South Kievan dialects. One may hope that the time is not far when Žylko who is conscientious toward facts will continue in the same direction, which eventually will lead to a re-habilitation of the two underlying dialect conception.

### 9. *Onomastics*

No monographs were published in this field. *Slovnyk vlasnyx imen ljudej* edited by S. Levčenko (K., 1961; first edition K., 1954) is normalizing and encompasses only few names in a form deviating from the standard. *Kataloh ričok Ukrajiny* by H. Švec', N. Drozd and S. Levčenko, ed. by V. Mokljak (K., 1957) is of even lesser research value. Not only is it normalizing, but most river names are taken from Russian, Polish, Hungarian, and Romanian maps and official lists with no attention paid to their Ukrainian names as used on the spot. *Rosijs'ko-ukrajins'kyj slovnyk heohrafičnyx nazv* by A. Kara-Mosko and M. Tokars'kyj (K., 1953), not available to me, is characterized as a failure by its Soviet Ukrainian reviewers (See *Doslidžennja*, p. 117).

Studies in person (family) names are represented by articles of O. Tkačenko on the origin of Ukrainian last names in *-enko* (SM 2) and of Ju. Red'ko on family names derived from proper personal names (LPI 12), from profession names (DMUM 1), on types of Ukrainian family names as a whole, with list of the suffixes used, statistics, and geography of separate types (FZ), and on ties between family names and toponyms (PSM 5). Red'ko's studies are based on a broad material (10,000 to 30,000 names) collected by the author. They have descriptive character and depend in their method on Polish works by Bystroń and Rospond. Tkačenko ventures into some genetic and etymological problems, but does not use recent publications, his newest reference being to Meillet's *Le slave commun.*

Toponymics attracted a few more researchers. Many articles have a descriptive character. Place-names are pigeonholed according to their derivational types (place-names derived from personal names in South Volynia by H. Šylo, LPI 12; place-names with prefixes and those derived from foreign names, and place-names derived from personal names in Lviv oblast, by Je. Černjaxivs'ka, M 14, PUM 4), or according to the meaning of the underlying stems (I. Kovalyk on Ukrainian place-names in *-ycja*, PUM 4), or both (O. Ripec'ka on place-names in the basins of the Vistula and the Odra, PSM 6; K. Cilujko on place-names of the *rajon* Pokrovs'ke, Dnipropetrovsk oblast, M 14). Examples of folk etymology in Western Slavic and German place-names, all second hand, are collected by O. Ripec'ka (SM 2). An etymological approach is attempted in Ju. Vynohrads'kyj's examination of random toponyms in Černihiv oblast (M 14, with the use of some archival materials), V. Braxnov's on river, settlement and microtoponymic names in the area of Perejaslav (M 14), and partly in K. Cilujko's survey of place-names in the Poltava oblast aimed at establishing the continuity of population in the area according to Žylko's 1954 views (PKD). In all these attempts the authors only use Slavic, mostly Eastern Slavic data and try to explain the names treated out of this material, as farfetched as it may be. The only article in which the author uses comparison with other languages, viz. Romanian, Turkic, and Finno-Ugric is O. Mel'nyčuk's study on place names in the Kodyma *rajon*, of Odessa oblast (M 14). With some interesting suggestions, the article is limited by not using works of M. Vasmer on the Eastern Slavic river names. In a special article Cilujko proves the need and discusses the principles of a toponymic dictionary based on local forms of geographic names (DB 6).

## 10. *Miscellanea*

Several articles elucidate problems in history of Slavic linguistics. A. Bahmut (SM 2) has collected materials on the views of Russian and Ukrainian scholars on the language of the Kiev and Prague Fragments, including an unpublished letter of Lamanskij. This article can contribute to a better understanding of the complex nature of Old Church Slavonic, which is still often considered in the Soviet Ukraine as "Old Bulgarian". F. Šolom (FZ) attempts to show the influence of Maksim Grek on Ivan Fedorov and the philologists of the Ukraine in the late sixteenth and seventeenth centuries. He succeeds in that for L. Zizanij and P. Berynda, but not for M. Smotryc'kyj. In the latter case Šolom's only proof, viz., that in Moscow edition of Smotryc'kyj's grammar (1648) articles by Maksim Grek were added, is of no value: as is well-known, this edition appeared some fifteen years after the author's death and his name was eliminated as an Uniate's. Šolom uses much unpublished material from the libraries of Kiev and Moscow. O. Tysovs'kyj (DML 4) characterizes the first grammar of modern Ukrainian by A. Pavlovskij, conscientiously but without much insight. N. Bukatevič and G. Miževskaja survey studies of Russian at the University of Odessa, M. Pavljuk does the same for the studies of other Slavic languages. To this Bukatevič adds a survey of the studies of Common Slavic in Russia and the U.S.S.R. (All in ODU 7). M. Kopylenko characterizes the theory of the complex sentence in Eastern Slavic linguistics before the nineteenth century (ODU 6). M. Pavljuk shows the achievements of F. Korš in the field of Ukrainian linguistics (with bibliography, ODU 6). On the occasion of his seventieth anniversary L. Bulaxovs'kyj was honored by a thin leaflet which contains an article by I. Bilodid and Bulaxovs'kyj's slightly purged bibliography compiled by N. Hretčenko (Akademija Nauk Ukrajins'koji RSR, Instytut movoznavstva. *Leonid Arsenijovyč Bulaxovs'kyj*, K., 1958). E. Voronec'kyj (FZ) describes the manuscript of A. Osiński's huge unpublished dictionary of Polish compiled in the first half of the nineteenth century as a classicist, normalizing work, in opposition to B. S. Linde's positivist approach. With more detail Voronec'kyj presents the same material in *Poradnik językowy* (59, 3-4, 5). Highlights from the history of Slavic linguistics are elucidated in R. Kravčuk's *Z istoriji slovjans'koho movoznavstva* (*Vydatni slavisty-movoznavci*) (K., 1961). For discussion of this book see section 11 of this chapter.

In the history of Ukrainian spelling V. Karpova (DMUM 2) recalls the developments in Galicia between 1917-39, in journalistic style but with many facts and dates useful to know.

In the publication of old texts for linguistic analysis, besides the new edition of P. Berynda's *Leksikon* characterized above, only two Bukovyna charters (1445 and 1453) were made available by M. Stanivs'kyj (UMŠ 60, 3), although archives and museums of the U.S.S.R. are full of unpublished materials priceless for the history of Ukrainian (E.g., see SH, p. 185). There were no publications of classics of Ukrainian linguistics. K. Myxal'čuk's articles, for instance, never came out in book form and are scattered in rare editions; A. Potebnja's works on Ukrainian subjects are bibliographical rarities and presumably some are still unpublished. Examples may be easily multiplied.

Je. Krotevyč and N. Rodzevyč published *Slovnyk linhvistyčnyx terminiv* (K., 1957), a book which might be useful in the Ukrainian S.S.R., where there were no books of that type at the time, before J. Marouzeau's dictionary came out in Russian translation, in 1960, but the Ukrainian book lacks originality and too often follows hackneyed but still hardly correct definitions. Two articles fall into the field of general linguistics: S. Kohan criticizes the view that language is a system of signs, mainly by quoting Lenin and Stalin (ODU 4); S. Savickaja makes some inconclusive remarks on the importance of language in fiction (ODU 5).

K. Trofymovyč's *Praktykum z porivnjal'noji hramatyky slovjans'kyx mov* (L., 1960) presents its subject in short formulas and exercises. No originality is aimed at in this book, either.

The only article in applied and mathematical linguistics is Ju. Karpenko's popular explanation of what mathematical linguistics is (UMŠ 62, 1). It is based on Russian sources exclusively, but is the only one among all the publications of the decade, along with Šolom's article in FZ, which gives reference to an American source. The lucky American authors are H. Josselson with his *The Russian Word Count* in the case of Karpenko, and R. Jakobson with his *Ivan Fedorov's Primer*, in the case of Šolom.

There were during the decade some publications outside Slavic and general linguistics, primarily in Germanic but also in Latin and French fields, e.g. in DLM. B. Zadorožnyj produced *Porivnjal'na fonetyka i morfolohija hots'koji movy* (L., 1960). It is beyond my competence to assess these publications. (Up to 1957 they are recorded in *Doslidžennja*, pp. 235-54).

## 11. *Concluding remarks*

The attainments and drawbacks of linguistic research in the Ukrainian S.S.R. are obvious from the preceding survey. Much has been done in collecting facts, and the future researcher who will undertake a synthetic work will be indebted to the fact-finders of today's generation. Presentation of data is the tenor of all serious work inasmuch as it is not affected by topical requirements. (Many studies are marred by these requirements. Yet some scholars manage to ignore these ever-changing requirements completely.) As to the interpretation of the facts found it is either absent or insufficient. One reason for this is lack of interest in theoretical questions and, in most cases, absence of acquaintance with the modern trends in the West, in the People's Democracies and even in Russia. Another reason and probably the most important is the insufficient preparation and lack of broader view. The background of facts, the parallels, the associations are absent so that when a subject is studied the scholar seldom is able to see it in a broader connection. It is not fortuitous that in historical studies researchers usually compare their findings only with the modern state of affairs: they have no other associations. This also accounts for neglect of such fields as etymology or etymologically minded onomastics, fields where broader comparisons and associations constitute the very essence of research.

The lack of preparation and adequate training is felt in many studies even in a more elementary way. When an author speaks of *nominum* (sic!) *agentis* (M 15, p. 74) and another considers Sumerian as an Indo-European language (Rusanivs'kyj, p. 6), these are hardly accidental slips of the pen, and more of such blunders may be easily found. As shown at the beginning of this survey, the insufficient training in linguistics and maybe not only in linguistics results from the stalemate in which linguistics (and cultural life in general) found itself since the thirties. With the old generation virtually obliterated, with many positions occupied since the "no-man's period" by mediocrities, youth often had no teachers in the real sense of the word. They had to be self-taught linguists, self-educated intelligentsia in general. What was achieved under these circumstances commands respect, but the damage inflicted is not yet entirely removed.

If one assesses the results of the decade's work as performed by Soviet Ukrainian linguists against an international standard, little can pass the test: some works by Bulaxovs'kyj, Mel'nyčuk, possibly Žylko, Hens'ors'kyj. Promising but still heavily handicapped are studies by Kučerenko, Čaplja. This is not much. But it is not quite just to judge the Soviet Ukrainian linguistics of the period by these criteria. What matters first of all is the direction of the development, its tempo and impetus. From this point of view the linguistics of the Soviet Ukraine proved that it is viable. It will be seen whether the next decade brings more significant achievements capable of standing evaluation from a universal standpoint.

This general characterization sheds light also on the question of trends in modern Soviet Ukrainian linguistics. There are virtually no clear-cut trends in it. Researchers work in a "good old manner" typical of linguistics, say, at the beginning of our century, which is basically Neogrammarian, with some streaks of sociological, occasionally psychological approach. (The admixture of politically tinged phraseology like *narodnist'* as opposed to *nacija*, etc., may be harmlessly discarded.) Interest in other approaches is almost nil. A few passing attacks against structuralism (e.g. in Kobyljans'kyj, N. Moskalenko, etc.) are made without any first-hand knowledge of the trend[8] and only show reluctance to anything new as such. In certain authors a weakly represented inheritance of some older trends may be discovered: few odds and ends of the Formalism in the studies of Finkel' or, say, Bilodid, of Polish linguistic schools in Humec'ka or Kovalyk, clearer in onomastics where W. Taszycki is the main model of imitation. But these marks of distinction are apparently rather subconscious and certainly too deformed to become a foundation for any programmatic and clearly shaped trends. Variety of trends in Soviet Ukrainian linguistics is to come if recovery proceeds successfully and smoothly further. Perhaps the "hypersemantic" studies by Kučerenko mark the birth of a trend in syntax.

In this conjunction it is worth while to return to R. Kravčuk's *Z istoriji slovjans'koho movoznavstva* published in 1961. This is a series of portraits of outstanding Slavists, varying from 15 pages to several lines, with basic bibliography. Some important names are lacking: among the Ukrainian Slavists V. Hancov, O. Kurylo, V. Simovyč, I. Zilyns'kyj, P. Buzuk; among foreign scholars, N. Trubetzkoy, Z. Stieber, R. Jakobson, *et al.* Characterizations of those included in the gallery of portraits are not quite free from hagiographic polish. But the very fact that a whole book is devoted to predecessors and contemporaries, about a third of it to those from the West is highly significant. It means that young researchers start feeling that gaps in their training must be filled and the insularity and isolation became unbearable. One might hope that Kravčuk's book is a harbinger of changes to come in Soviet Ukrainian linguistics.

## II. BELORUSSIA

The two main centers of linguistic research in BelSSR are the Institute of Linguistics at the Academy of Sciences of BelSSR, with its non-periodical *Pracy* since 1954 (actually published as an annual), and the Belorussian State University in Minsk, whose chairs of Belorussian and Russian publish jointly *Dasledavanni pa belaruskaj i ruskaj movax*, also non-periodical. Publications of the pedagogical institutes as well as abstracts of dissertations were not available for this survey. The available publications will be presented according to basically the same plan as for the Ukrainian ones.

[8] This refers also to N. Rodzevyč's lampoon *Reakcijna sut' sučasnyx buržuaznyx teorij u movoznavstvi* (K., 1954). It is typical that O. Mel'nyčuk who in 1949 wrote in the same genre an article ("Reakcijna sut' buržuaznoji fonolohiji", M 8) in 1957 had to admit: "Up to now the Ukrainian linguists made even no attempt to understand the essence of various trends of linguistic structuralism" (*Doslidžennja*, p. 260). In the point of fact, the first attempt at a diachronic phonemic approach falls into the time after the surveyed period. In 1962 F. Žylko ventured into a comprehensive phonemic interpretation of how *i* arose in Ukrainian in the newly closed syllables (UMŠ, 3). In an endeavor to graft on the old Sobolevskij's theory the views of Bulaxovs'kyj on the affects of the new rising pitch and of Myxal'čuk on *e*-alternations as modeling *o*-alternations he inevitably failed. But as a sign of an awakening interest in a synthetic phonemic explanation of historical developments the article may be a portent of significant shifts.

### 1. *Phonetics and phonemics. Accentology*

A general synchronic characterization of the phonetics and phonemics of Belorussian has been written by M. Biryla for *Kurs sučasnaj belaruskaj litaraturnaj movy* (further called *Kurs*), *Fanetyka, arfahrafija, leksikalohija* prepared by the Institute of Linguistics 1961[9]. Sounds of Standard Belorussian are described from an articulatory point of view. Simplified X-ray pictures are taken chiefly from *Fonetika sovremennogo russkogo literaturnogo jazyka* by R. Avanesov and *Obrazy rentgenograficzne głosek rosyjskich* by H. Koneczna and W. Zawadowski, without many scruples about possible distinctions between Belorussian and Russian. Much space is given to alternations of sounds. The productive alternations are characterized synchronically, the unproductive ones rather historically. The phonemic system is also presented broadly, with some remarks on distribution and morphophonemics. The author follows faithfully Avanesov's system, to whom he gives credit himself (p. 56). Not only there is the same general approach and terminology but even the selection of problems is the same. E.g., if from Avanesov one cannot find out what the phonetic nature of Russian stress is, falling, rising, or other, the same applies to Biryla. Long consonants are denied phonemic status in Belorussian apparently because they do not have it in Russian, in Avanesov's opinion. Occasionally Biryla ascribes phenomena of spelling to pronunciation (e.g. in his description of Belorussian *akan'e* in posttonic syllables) without really proving the identity. Biryla's chapters are supplemented by P. Šuba's outline of Belorussian writing and spelling. P. Jurhelevič's *Narys sučasnaj belaruskaj movy z histaryčnymi kamentaryjami* (1961; the first edition of 1958 was not available to me) follows the main lines of the collective *Kurs*. His phonemic analysis depends heavily on Avanesov's; the presentation is more popular, but he dwells more on some details (e.g., deviations from the normal type of *akan'e*), and the space devoted to historical commentaries is larger. Here occasionally he ventures into statements unusual in Soviet linguistics, e.g., about the prehistorical origin of *akan'e* and the change $g > h$; but more often his original views are merely erroneous, as derivation of the river names *Ut*, *Ucinka* from the tribal name *Antes* (9) or explanation of *i* in *cvice* 'blooms', *svitae* 'dawns' from *ě* (60).

N. Loban (PIM 4) presented a characterization of today's accentuation in the affixless substantives, aiming at completeness. Useful as a collection of materials, it is insufficient in its disregard of the developments in progress, too shy in singling out Russianisms and naïve in seeking direct links between stress types and semantic categories. The relation between Belorussian spelling and orthoepy is discussed by Biryla (V 58,3) and, from a normative standpoint, in F. Jankowski's *Belaruskae litaraturnae vymawlenne* (1960).

V. Martynaw and M. Karneeva-Petrulan work in historical phonology of Slavic. Martynaw (PIM 8) attempts to relegate the rise of *x* from Common Slavic to Indo-

[9] This course, in three parts (not numbered) was preceded by a collective one volume *Kurs sučasnaj belaruskaj litaraturnaj movy* (1957) not available to me.

European, which in his opinion had palatalizational development of *k* to *k'*, further yielding *x* or *s*. This gives him the possibility to unite a series of reflexes of *k*, *k'*, and *s*. Together with the acceptance of a free exchange of formants in Persson's style and with Benveniste's theory of roots, this opens possibilities of innumerable etymological combinations to him. Undoubtedly the basic point of Martynaw is incorrect and, consequently, so are his etymologies but his boldness and broadness in approach may impress one. This also applies to his article on the alleged borrowings from Slavic into West Germanic and by the same token, Common Germanic (VJa 60, 3). Martynaw's method may be linked with the new "Moscow school" of Indo-European and Slavic comparative studies as represented, for example, by V. Illič-Svityč, and traced, in the long run, to G. Il'inskij with his unrestricted *Lautschieberei.*

Karneeva-Petrulan (PIM 5) reconsiders the reasons for de Saussure and Fortunatov's law (which she takes for granted without referring to the iconoclastic theories of J. Kuryłowicz or Chr. Stang) on an arbitrary premise that all sound changes must be semantically motivated. After contending that verbs with final stress in 1 sg. (type *pišú*) have this because they emphasize the acting of a skilled person while those which preserve the root stress (type *mážu*) refer to actions which require no training, and without explaining whether the same action in other persons (*píšeš'*, *píšet*, etc.) presupposed no skill and training, she proceeds to metatony and seeks in the chaotically intermingled use of the letters *o* and *ъ*, *e*, *ь* and *ě* in the Smolensk charter of 1229 the traces of the new rising pitch in Belorussian. As proofs she cites Serbo-Croatian forms although Serbo-Croatian is exactly the language which does not have new rising pitch on brevities! It is hard to take these concepts too seriously, and so probably was the attitude of the printers who as a kind of practical joke printed an article on accent with the stress marks omitted in most examples!

In another article (BDU 58) Karneeva-Petrulan examines the charter of 1229 in more detail, to find there not only two sorts of *o* due to the assumed original difference in the pitch but also the beginnings of Belorussian *cekan'e* and *dzekan'e* and hardening or *r* (although hardening of *r* is not typical of North Eastern Belorussian anyway![10]). She develops the same arbitrary conception in the historical phonology of Belorussian in the collective *Narysy pa historyi belaruskaj movy* (1957; further referred to as *Narysy*). For this chapter she wrote sections on intonations and *akan'e* while M. Żydovič covered the rest of the field. Here Karneeva-Petrulan depicts a coherent history from the loss of phonemic pitch in Proto-Belorussian through *akan'e* of the Obojan' type, then *akan'e* of the Žizdra type to, finally, strong *akan'e* as links in one process toward constantly growing accentual unity of word. The theory is original but essentially a mere speculation. There are no traces of Obojan' type *akan'e* in

[10] Particular caution is recommended in drawing any conclusions from the charter of 1229 because there is a great possibility that it was written not by a native but by a German. Serious arguments in favor of this are given by V. Kiparsky in *Neuphilologische Mitteilungen*, XL (1939), pp. 84-87, and again more recently, LXI (1960), pp. 244-52.

Belorussian. Žydovič's part, on the contrary, is devoid of any originality, second hand and, in its Common Slavic sections, not always reliable.

Among the articles that of Žydovič (PIM 1) concerns historical phonology of Belorussian. The author describes phonetic peculiarities of the sixteenth century Suprasl' Chronicle. V. Aničėnka (V 60, 1) characterizes Belorussian phonetic features in the *Kurnicki* copy of *Alexandria*, of the sixteenth-seventeenth century.

No author mentions works of P. Buzuk on historical phonology of Belorussian and especially on the Old Belorussian charters (*Pracy* BDU 16, 1927) and, strangely enough, no one uses *Al-Kitab*, a peculiar and precious record of Belorussian in the sixteenth century, nearly phonetic in rendition of Belorussian sounds in the Arabic script, if properly deciphered by J. Stankevič (*Slavia* 12, 1933-34).

## 2. *Word derivation*

In the center of attention of Belorussian linguists in the field of word derivation, is characterization of functions of separate affixes or derivational procedures. Such are the descriptions of the substantival suffixes *-stvo* (in collective substantives) and its accreted variants by M. Pawlenka (BDU 60, PIM 8), *-izna* by M. Bulaxaw (PIM 8) and a very detailed and rich in material characterization of the suffix *-osc'* by M. Pawlenka (BDU 58); of verbal suffixes, *-yva-*, *-iva-* by Bulaxaw (PIM 3) and again of the same suffixes as well as *-ova-*, *-eva-* by A. Janovič (V 58,2; 60, 1,2); of the verbal prefix *iz-* by A. Birala (BDU 60) and *pa-* and *na-* as secondary prefixes by I. Hajdukevič (PIM 8). Types of word composition are studied in the same vein by Z. Krawčanka (substantive + substantive, PIM 7, 8) and B. Kasowski (compound adjectives, BDU 58). P. Kljusaw discusses doublet suffixes in the modern Belorussian terminology (V 60,3).

In other cases a semantic category is taken as a point of departure and the affixes which serve it are listed, with more or less numerous examples: plant names, by A. Kisjalewski (PIM 8), masc. persons by V. Xackevič (BDU 58), gradation of feature in adjectives by I. Karaban' (BDU 58). Or a grammatical category is characterized in the variety of its affixes: substantives neuter, by A. Jurėvič (PIM 7), adjectives in Middle Belorussian chronicles by B. Kasowski (BDU 60), and in general in Middle Belorussian, by M. Bulaxaw (PIM 7). In still other cases the material is classified according to the grammatical categories of underlying words (stems). So Bulaxaw shows which other parts of speech may be derived from adjectives and how (PIM 6) and P. Šuba does the same for adverbs (PIM 7). A. Birala (BDU 58) shows how verbs are derived from substantives, Šuba the formation of adverbs from verbs. A. Bordovič classifies, for Russian, modal words according to their origin (V 57,2).

Most of these studies combine Middle Belorussian data and those from the modern standard language. Some add dialectal material. Only Birala (in BDU 60) went farther back, to Old Belorussian. The historical data are presented by mere citation. They are not screened so that Polish, Church Slavonic and Ukrainian elements in

Belorussian are not separated from real Belorussian. Birala went so far that he included the Ukrainian dictionary by P. Berynda, of 1627, without any reservations, in the body of his evidence. He raised the problem of Polonisms in Middle Belorussian (BDU 58), but only to say that all those words which bear no phonetic earmarks of Polish are genuine Belorussian. The researchers mostly shun discussing and even mentioning problems of historical and theoretical character which follow from their data. Occasionally they mention some differences between Belorussian and Russian but do not go into them as if they wanted to play them down, so that the originality of some Belorussian developments remains unexplained. Instead they often readily indulge in minute semantic pigeonholing which is not justified grammatically. The only exceptions are P. Šuba's theoretical considerations on word derivation and homonymy and synonymy as applied to derivational types (PIM 5); and Bulaxaw's discussion on how the suffixes *-yva-*, *-iva-* in Belorussian verbs lost their first vowel (PIM 3). Otherwise the tenor of the whole work is a collection of raw data and their preliminary classification.

A comprehensive presentation of the word derivational system in modern Belorussian is found in the second part of *Kurs, Marfalohija* (1957). M. Žydovič presents the derivation of substantives, according to semantic categories. Adjectival declension is characterized more formally, according to various procedures used in it, by Bulaxaw. Adverbial derivation is presented chiefly etymologically, by Šuba. In the verb, Bulaxaw limited himself to a simple enumeration of prefixes and suffixes. In these varying approaches one is common to all authors: no attempts are made to find any more or less strict rules of distribution for various affixes, the authors operate with possibilities the language has, not with its laws.

### 3. *Word inflection*

Synchronically, with a few historical digressions, a comprehensive survey of the inflectional system of standard Belorussian is offered by A. Bazylenka, A. Birala, M. Bulaxaw, Ju. Mackevič, E. Ramanovič, P. Šuba, A. Žurawski, and M. Žydovič in the *Kurs, Marfalohija*. It is a fair presentation of the important facts, with paradigms and main deviations. Syntax of parts of speech is also elucidated. In its method (and lack of precision in characterization of vacilforms) it reminds one of the survey *Grammatika russkogo jazyka* of the Academy of Sciences of the U.S.S.R., vol. I (Moscow, 1952). Like the latter, the Belorussian book in treating the uninflected parts of speech substitutes syntax and etymology for morphology, according to a rather old tradition.

Outside of this book, Bulaxaw discusses in a separate article areas of fluidity in modern standard Belorussian (PIM 1) while Šuba delineates vacillations in the conjugation of standard Belorussian and shows how the productive types gradually supersede some forms of unproductive types.

More of a popular genre is the historical presentation of certain grammatical categories, often with a following description of the present day situation. Thus, A. Arašonkava publishes data on endings of present tense in the sixteenth century (PIM 5), and specifically *-mo* in 1 pl. (V 58, 2), A. Žurawski the forms of the imperative in Old, Middle, and Modern Belorussian (PIM 4), A. Hruco the forms of perfective aspect as used in the future tense in Middle Belorussian (PIM 7), the future tense formed with *budu* + infinitive (V 57, 4) and *budu* + *l*-participle (V 58,1), A. Janovič those aspectal forms of Middle Belorussian which differ from modern usage (PIM 7), U. Aničėnka the forms of the imperfect as a feature of the written language in the Middle Belorussian period (PIM 7), use of the copula in the perfect (PIM 6), and the use of the perfect in general (BDU 58). Substantives are studied by Ja. Jurėvič (vacillations in gender in Middle Belorussian and now, PIM 6; semantic groups within substantives masc., V 59,1; relations between gender and sex in substantives, V 59,3), E. Blinava (dual, BDU 60) and I. Ščarbakova (the interplay of the nom. and acc. in pl. in Middle Belorussian, BDU 58, with an extension to the situation in the dialects, BDU 60), while M. Žydovič (PIM 3) offers an outline of the general development of Belorussian substantival declension. M. Birala (PIM 1) published some excerpts from Middle Belorussian texts on the use of nominal and pronominal forms of adjectives and formation of the comparative, A. Kryvicki (V 57, 1) his observations on the third person pronouns in Middle Belorussian.

These studies resemble each other in some substantial features. They take for granted that the forms found in Belorussian texts are Belorussian and make no or little discrimination between the Belorussian forms and the Polish ones, not even collating translations of the seventeenth century novels made, often literally, from Polish, with their originals. In general Polish influence is denied or minimized. Nowhere was an attempt made to trace a borderline between Ukrainian and Belorussian elements in the common written language of the middle period. The analysis, if any, is functional and semantic, and conjectures are shunned. The only article of a theoretical character is B. Balin's on aspect in Slavic and Germanic, but it presents nothing new. Under these conditions, the articles surveyed are mainly collections of examples. They bring no basically new conclusions if compared with what had been established by Sobolevskij, Šaxmatov and Karskij but many more examples and a few supplemental details.

To a great extent this refers to the comprehensive presentation of Belorussian historical morphology in the collective *Narysy* as compiled by A. Birala, M. Bulaxaw, B. Lapaw, Ju. Mackevič and M. Žydovič. Here, too, Polish influences are played down and relations with Ukrainian not touched on at all. Each part of speech is presented in three chronological slices: the situation in the Old Rus' language is presented synchronically as the point of departure (references to Common Slavic are rather rare), then changes which occurred in Middle Belorussian are shown and finally the changes in Modern Belorussian. The presentation is strictly factual and rather dogmatic, avoiding controversial views and not indulging in one's own theories. As errors are rather few the book brings much useful reference material, but this is primarily raw data. One part of the book, however, differs from the rest. This is the principal sections of the chapter on verb. They are written by M. Karneeva-Petrulan and they are bold and original in approach. As in phonology, the author seeks direct connections and dependence between language changes and contended changes in mentality of speakers. Sometimes these speculations are tempting, though always in need of verification. Such is the analysis of changes in future tense forms as conditioned by the switch from thinking on two temporal planes, past and present, where future was but continuation of the present, to thinking in three temporal planes with a separate notion of the future. In other cases these speculations are completely unfounded, as ascribing the *-e*-verbs (Leskien's first three classes) "activity" and *-i*-verbs "inactivity" of the subject (by which rather lack of deliberation in behavior is understood) and deducing from this retention of ending *-c'* in 3 sg of *-i*-verbs and its loss in *-e*-verbs.

## 4. *Syntax*

The most popular type of studies in syntax are descriptions of functions of some types of syntactic pairs in the modern standard language. So A. Narkevič describes adnominal use of oblique cases, except the locative (PIM 7) while A. Šydlowski supplements him in describing the functions of the latter case (PIM 7). Non-prepositional constructions are also characterized by Šydlowski in V 59, 3. Several studies are devoted to the prepositional constructions in Belorussian (Narkevič, PIM 6, with rudimentary elements of transformational analysis, I. Zjanevič, V 58, 3, on *za* + instrumental) or in Belorussian as compared to Russian (M. Jawnevič, PIM 6; V 60, 4). A. Narkevič points to some complications in concord of adjectives with substantives (BDU 58), while M. Bulaxaw (PIM 5) gives a comprehensive picture of adjectives which govern substantives. In verbs, A. Žurawski describes functions of the imperative (PIM 6) in terms of the traditional theory of substitutions in verbal modes while A. Hruco writes about the functions of the constructions *maju* + infinitive (PIM 6). Ju. Mackevič in her monograph *Marfalohija dzejaslova w belaruskaj move* (1959) devotes several sections (lacking originality) to functions of person and tense forms. A. Bazylenka (BDU 58) classifies modal words according to their meaning and their formal structure. A. Narkevič (PIM 8) studies the pairs in which adverb modifies substantive while P. Šuba traces the transformation of adverbs into prepositions (PIM 6). Belorussian conjunctions are under scrutiny in the articles by L. Burak (*i*, *a*, PIM 6; in supplementing clauses, PIM 7, 8; *ažna*, V 59, 4) and the Russian ones by T. Pleščenko (in supplementing clauses, BDU 58, 60). M. Bazylenka (PIM 3) describes syntactic structure (as well as literary functions) of comparison in Ja. Kolas, L. Burak (V 56, 4; 58, 1; PIM 5) examines the types of clauses transitional between hypotactic and paratactic. B. Lapaw classifies syntactic pairs in which words with the same root are used (PIM 7). Word order in asynthetically connected clauses is sketched by N. Samojla (V 59, 3). M. Cikocki's *Nekatoryja vypadki stylistyčnaha vykarystannja sintaksičnyx srodkaw belaruskaj movy* (1958) pursues practical purposes in its selection of "difficult" syntactic constructions.

All these articles are preparatory or extending studies for a general course in syntax of modern Belorussian. Such a course was compiled and published in 1959 by a group of linguists: M. Bulaxaw, L. Burak, B. Lapaw, A. Narkevič, and P. Šuba (Akadėmija navuk Belaruskaj SSR, Instytut movaznawstva imja Ja. Kolasa, *Kurs sučasnaj belaruskaj litaraturnaj movy. Sintaksis*). In this book the approach slightly varies from one author to another. E.g., Burak gives a formal definition of parataxis (§ 106) while Lapaw sticks to the traditional logical definition (§ 123). But in general the presentation is kept within the traditional lines of logical grammar with emphasis on description, not on stylistics. At first glance, there are some innovations as compared with the usual pattern of these grammars: characterization of syntagms, analysis of comparative constructions, large sections on word order. In fact, however, most of these innovations follow the composition of *Grammatika russkogo jazyka* published by the Academy of Sciences of the U.S.S.R., vol. 2 (Moscow, 1954), on which the book is closely patterned. Intonation is ignored in the Belorussian book and all the data are from written texts.

Historical syntax has been rather neglected. One only finds several articles by I. Kramko based on the unpublished documents of the sixteenth century from Slonim (paratactic constructions, PIM 6; relative clauses, V 59, 4; objective clauses, V 60, 1) and the general presentation in the collective *Narysy*, where syntax is elaborated by M. Bulaxaw, B. Lapaw, and A. Žurawski. This is basically a synchronic presentation of the Middle Belorussian syntax, with some parallels drawn from "Old Russian" and modern Belorussian. Such a presentation in synchronic slices is greatly motivated by the situation of the sources: the sources for Old Belorussian are very scarce and hardly begin before the thirteenth century; between Middle Belorussian and modern Belorussian there is a gap of a century or so with virtually no texts. The authors' approach is purely descriptive, modeled mostly on S. Obnorskij and V. Borkovskij, so that the book is primarily a collection of examples with the minimum of explanations and almost no conjectures.

## 5. *Vocabulary*

The vocabulary of modern Belorussian is described in the traditional way (homonyms and synonyms, archaisms and neologisms, etc.) by M. Bulaxaw in the first part of the *Kurs* (*Fanetyka, arfahrafija, leksikalohija*, 1961). Unusual is a large section on loan word grouped according to source languages, without minimizing the importance of borrowings. Bulaxaw gives as a supplement a survey of Belorussian lexicography. In this he had a predecessor: M. Sudnik (PIM 4) had characterized Middle Belorussian glosses, especially in the Bible of Skaryna, and the dictionaries by L. Zizanij (1596) and P. Berynda (1627), whose relation to Ukrainian is left without much clarification. A concise survey of Belorussian lexicology in P. Jurhelevič's *Narys* does not claim any originality.

Several articles are devoted to Middle Belorussian vocabulary. H. Papova (BDU 58, 60) explains some prefixed verbs used as legal terms; V. Krywčyk (BDU 58) minimizes the role of Polonisms in the novels collected in the manuscript of Poznań, the sixteenth century; E. Mjacel'skaja (BDU 58) publishes her excerpts of Church Slavonic elements in the Suprasl' chronicle, without discriminating heterogeneous parts of the text. For modern Belorussian B. Lapaw presents the meanings of the word *katory* (PIM 6). In his book *Leksika belaruskix prykazak XIX stahoddzja w suvjazi z ahul'naj prablemaj frazealohii* (1958) A. Aksamitaw, after characterizing some semantic categories as represented in the vocabulary of Belorussian proverbs tries to show how idiomatic expressions rise from proverbs.

The monograph of N. Krukowski *Ruski leksičny wplyw na sučasnuju belaruskuju litaraturnuju movu* (1958) is marked by its attention to problems of method and endeavors for precision. The author analyzes direct borrowings, which in his opinion constitute up to 20% of Belorussian vocabulary, and loan translations, establishes lists of both, and shows Russian mediation in borrowing of Church Slavonic and Western words and affixes (in this he underestimates the part played by Polish). Much attention is paid to specific earmarks of borrowings from a closely related languages. Krukowski's study shows that its subject does not have to have character of a propaganda lampoon, nor use journalistic style, but can be a piece of serious and fruitful, albeit not definitive scholarly research.

While Krukowski's approach is basically synchronical and methodical Bulaxaw in his paper for the IVth International Congress of Slavists published as a pamphlet (Akadėmija navuk BSSR, Belaruski kamitėt slavistaw, M. Bulaxaw, *Razviccë belaruskaj litaraturnaj movy w XIX-XX st. st. va wzaemaadnosinax z inšymi slavjanskimi movami*, 1958) traces Russian loan words and loan constructions in Belorussian historically, as he also does with Polish borrowings (fairly objectively!) and, more impressionistically, Ukrainian. Of basically propagandistic character is V. Ljawdanski's article (V 56, 1) on how translations from Marx and Lenin have "enriched" Belorussian.

Etymological topics are rare. A. Vjaržbowski's attempt to prove the Baltic origin of Br *zubr* "aurochs" (V 60, 3) may be mentioned. It was preceded by his article on how to identify Baltisms in Belorussian (V 59, 2). Less important are M. Bulaxaw's etymology of Br *holtaj*, *hultjaj* "rascal" (V 58, 1) and P. Krapivin's attempt to derive the word *Rus'* from an Indo-European root denoting "water" (V 56, 3).

### 6. *Stylistics. History of literary language*

Circular "stylistic analysis" of works of writers so typical of some Ukrainian linguists is not widespread in Soviet Belorussian linguistics. It is, in Belorussia, practiced more by researchers of Russian than Belorussian. Here one may mention K. Kovaleva's inquiry into idiomatics of Sumarokov's fables and his use of vulgarisms and diminutives (BDU 58, 60); L. Ševčenko's characterization of phraseology and humoristic devices in Čexov (BDU 58, 60; V 60, 4); N. Možejko's classification of dialectal and standard language idioms in Šoloxov's novels (BDU 60); and A. Virkowskaja's remarks on the vocabulary of Lenin's *What are we to do?* (PIM 7). On the Belorussian side, M. Žyrkevič presents some observations on stylistic peculiarities of J. Kupala's poem "Bandarowna" (BDU 60) and on variants of his "Pawlinka" (BDU 58). Close to this genre is U. Jurėvič's *Slova i vobraz* (1961). It is in most part marshaled samples of what to the author is efficient or inefficient use of language by the contemporary Belorussian writers in choice of words, rhythmic organization, and phonic structure. The book does not claim to be a piece of research or to bear objective character.

In the field of the history of literary Belorussian most important contributions are L. Šakun's. His article on Church Slavonic components in Middle Belorussian (BDU 58) is factual, objective, and shows how and why there were changes in the attitude of the speakers and writers toward Church Slavonicisms. It is criticized but actually rather supplemented by considerations of A. Žurawski (PIM 8) on shifts in linguistic genres between early Middle Belorussian (which in the author's opinion did not differ in this respect from Old Belorussian) and later Middle Belorussian. Žurawski's paper for the IVth Congress of Slavists on Church Slavonicisms in Skaryna and Cjapinski (MMZ) is more limited in scope. Another article by Šakun, on the make-up of literary Belorussian of the middle period (BDU 60), is welcome in pointing to necessity of studies of relations between Belorussian proper and its Church Slavonic, Ukrainian and Polish components but too general and inconclusive. Šakun's *Narysy historyi belaruskaj litaraturnaj movy* (1960) is sketchy in its characterization of modern Belorussian, but generally reliable and penetrating in the main part of the study devoted to Old and Middle Belorussian (125 pages out of 221) in its genres and areal peculiarities.

Factually, observations of Šakun are supported by A. Žurawski's publication and commentary of V. Cjapinski's glosses to his translation of the Gospel (PIM 7) and by M. Karneeva-Petrulan on the interplay of colloquial and bookish elements in the seventeenth-century Chronicle of Barkulabava (PIM 3). V. Aničėnka's article on the grammar of L. Zizanij (V 56, 4) is basically limited to re-telling of the book's contents. *Xrėstatamatyja pa historyi belaruskaj movy* (Part 1, 1961; Part 2, 1962) compiled by U. Aničėnka, P. Vjarxow, A. Žurawski and Ja. Ramanovič, and edited by R. Avanesov although designed to be a book for instruction deserves special mention. It is based on manuscripts or hardly available first printings and brings quite a few so far unpublished texts reproduced scrupulously and conscientiously. Consequently, the anthology may be rightly considered not only a book for teachers and their students but also as a useful tool for researchers.

History of the modern standard Belorussian language is studied by N. Vajtovič, from the point of view of its dialectal background. After a preliminary characterization in VJa 54, 4, she elaborated the subject anew in her paper for the Fourth Congress of Slavists: N. Vajtovič, *Da pytannja ab farmiravanni nacyjanal'naj litaraturnaj belaruskaj movy* (*Ab suadnosinax litaraturnaj movy i dyjalektaw*) (1958). Vajtovič begins with a characterization of the dialectal basis in the work of important pre-revolutionary writers, shows first attempts at standardization and seeks the justification for a peculiar combination of various dialectal features in standard Belorussian in what she calls Central Belorussian dialects. While the last part is debatable, in general Vajtovič's paper sheds light on the formation of the modern standard Belorussian.

## 7. *Dialectology*

Dialectology is a field in which Belorussian linguists worked more than in any other and seem to achieve the most tangible results. This is due to collection of data for a dialectological atlas of the B.S.S.R. that was begun on large scale in 1948 and carried on the basis of *Prahrama pa vyvučennju belaruskix havorak i zbirannu zvestak dlja skladannja Dyjalektalahičnaha atlasa belaruskaj movy* (1950). The program contains 64 groups of questions on phonology, 58 on morphology, 30 on syntax, and 149 questions on vocabulary. On the basis of a draft by P. Rastarhuew (1947) it was fundamentally re-made by N. Biryla, Ju. Mackevič, and M. Žydovič. Groups of two or three, mostly students of pedagogic institutes are supposed to collect material as foreseen by the program, and record coherent speech utterances. About 1027 settlements have been investigated. Many publications contain (first drafts of?) maps designed for the atlas. *Xrėstamatyja pa belaruskaj dyjalektalohii*, ed. by R. Avanesov and M. Biryla (1962) consists primarily of numerous records made for the atlas.

Studies in dialectology as carried out in Belorussia are of various types. The simplest is the description of a local dialect, in a village or a little group of villages. These descriptions range from an impressionistic presentation of the most striking peculiarities of a dialect, through a thorough examination of a feature or aspect of a dialect, to a comprehensive characterization of a dialect as a whole. The first approach is represented by the articles of N. Kascjan on the dialect of Kirava, obl. Babrujsk (PIM 1), of I. Zen'ko on the (fundamentally Ukrainian) dialect of Pružany, obl. Brėst, in its phonology, with some elements of phonemics, and morphology (PIM 3), of E. Ramanovič on phonetic earmarks of the dialect of Uzda, obl. Minsk (PIM 5), of A. Kryvicki on the dialect of seven villages including and around Awcjuki, obl. Homel' (PIM 6), and of A. Manaenkova on the Russian dialect of Hrubno, obl. Černivci (BDU 60).

Concentration on a special problem as represented in a dialect characterizes the articles by A. Kryvicki who describes *akan'e* in the dialect of Lahojsk, obl. Minsk (PIM 3), Ja. Ramanovič who concentrates on some peculiarities in the syntactic use of parts of speech in the dialect of Uzda (PIM 6), P. Stėcko who makes the same for the dialect of Zel'va, obl. Hrodna (PIM 8), and F. Jankowski, for the dialect of Hlusk, obl. Minsk (V 56, 1). Russian dialects on Belorussian basis in Brjansk oblast are characterized by A. Pjan'kowski from the point of view of how they introduce historically unmotivated *a* instead of *o* in iterative verbs (PIM 5). More complete descriptions of a local dialect as a whole are represented by the work of N. Biryla devoted to the dialect of Čyrvonają Slabada, former Vyzna, obl. Minsk, based on his own observations and records made for the atlas. The detailed albeit by no means exhaustive presentation of the dialect in its phonology, morphology and partly syntax (PIM 1, 4) is patterned in method on R. Avanesov. It results in the breakdown of the South Western dialectal group in three subgroups, those of Hrodna, Brėst - Pinsk, and Sluck - Mazyr.

The vocabulary of a dialect is represented by F. Jankowski's *Dyjalektny slownik* (1959; part II, 1960), a differential dictionary of words and proverbs peculiar to the Hlusk *rajon*, obl. Minsk. The basic approach is rather anthropological and when, in the introduction, the compiler ventures in the field of etymology the results are frightful.

Larger dialects or groups of dialects are treated in the studies of Ju. Mackevič on the North Eastern dialects (*akan'e*, morphological peculiarities, predicative use of gerund. PIM 3) and A. Baxan'kow, on relative and objective clauses in the South Western dialects (V 60, 4; PIM 8).

Cross-sections of the whole or nearly the whole Belorussian area in reference to a special phonological phenomenon or morphological category are a substitute for dialectological maps, but they yield more than maps because they not only delineate the areas of certain phenomena but also discuss the problems of origin and spread of the phenomena. Here the thorough and richly detailed studies in phonology by N. Biryla are to be mentioned, as a rule with maps: on hardening of labials in various positions (PIM 3), on diphthongized or narrowed reflexes of *o*, *e*, and *ě* (PIM 6; some materials to that also in D. Celjancjuk, PIM 1), on reflexes of *t*' and *d*' (PIM 7) as well as N. Vajtovič's on vowels in the pretonic syllables in the dialects with *akan'e* (PIM 5) and on reflexes of *y* (PIM 7). In morphology A. Muraška published several articles on the forms of adjective: the forms of the locative sg, masc and neut (PIM 3), on adjectival declension as a whole (PIM 5), on nominal forms of adjectives (V 58, 2), and on degrees of comparison (PIM 8). Ju. Mackevič concentrated on morphology of verbs in its dialectal varieties. After an article in PIM 1, she published a monograph *Marfalohija dzejaslova w belaruskaj move* (1959). Along with some syntactic problems concerning predominantly standard Belorussian (See section 4 of this survey) Mackevič presents at length areal distribution of verbal forms. The book is saturated with facts, all of them first hand, many for the first time introduced into Slavic studies. In method the book is less interesting. It depends, in this respect, on R. Avanesov and S. Obnorskij. Western research is never mentioned except a few Polish books, and the author draws her comparison only from Russian and Ukrainian.

In vocabulary cross section presentations are rare and hardly bring more than a simple map would. Such are the brief articles by A. Arašonkava on dialectal words for 'lightning', A. Muraška for 'cattle', and A. Čabjaruk for 'battledore', all in PIM 7.

Accumulation of copious data on Belorussian dialects made it possible to revise the classification of the latter. N. Vajtovič suggested that along with the traditionally accepted South Western and North Eastern dialectal groups a Central group is to be delimited (VJA 54, 4). P. Hapanovič and Ju. Mackevič agreeing with the idea in principle objected limitation of this group to the region of Minsk-Maladečna alone and extended it farther South East (PIM 6 and VJa 59, 6). In the same article they denied the transitional character of these dialects. Yet they could not find any peculiarities specific of this group alone and not shared with South West or North East, except the endings of the 3rd sg in the present tense of verbs. Another attempt of Mackevič to buttress this view (PIM 8) resulted in a useful breakdown of the Central group into minor sub-groups but failed again to prove its primordiality. Historically, Belorussian still goes back to two and not three dialectal units. Useful and convincing in the first article by Hapanovič and Mackevič was the subdivision of the South Western dialectal group into three sub-groups and North Eastern into two. Regrettably, establishing of links with Northern Ukrainian dialects for the South Western Belorussian dialects and with Russian dialects for the North Eastern Belorussian dialects was not attempted. This is a general handicap of Soviet Belorussian dialectology of our days (as well as Soviet Ukrainian) that it identifies the administrative boundaries with the linguistic ones. Despite resistance to the facts Ukrainian dialects of Belorussia are treated as Belorussian while Belorussian dialects of the Ukraine as Ukrainian, to no advantage for a correct understanding of facts.

The article of I. Hajdukevič on changes in Belorussian dialects during the last decades (PIM 6) distinguishes itself by its objectivity. Contrary to theoretical expectations the author shows that in their phonology and morphology Belorussian dialects proved to be conservative and underwent almost no changes in recent time. In vocabulary, they accepted a lot of new items from Russian but very few from standard Belorussian.

Theoretical problems of dialectology did not attract the attention of Belorussian scholars, except for N. Biryla's article on how to compile dialectal dictionaries. He plans eight regional dictionaries to cover the whole country (PIM 5). These principles became the foundation of *Instrukcyja pa zbirannju materyjalaw dlja skladannja ablasnyx slownikaw belaruskaj movy* published in two issues by the Belorussian Academy of Sciences (1959, 1960).

## 8. *Miscellanea*

There are only very few works in onomastics. M. Hrynblat compiled a useful (but incomplete and overloaded with extraneous items) bibliography of Belorussian toponymics (PIM 7). In his paper at the Fourth International Congress of Slavists (MMZ) he gave a preliminary classification of formal and semantic types in Belorussian toponyms, with some special digressions. V. Žučkevič's *Proisxoždenie geografičeskix nazvanij* (*toponimika*) *Belorussii* (1961) linguistically is amateurish. The author is not acquainted with works of M. Vasmer, J. Rozwadowski, W. Taszycki or any other linguist in the field. His etymologies are arbitrary and often ludicrous: *Neman* he derives from *nem* "dumb", *Svisloč* from *Visla* because it leads to the Vistula (although it does not), *Buda* from *budka* "cabin", while in reality the meaning of the word still in the eighteenth century was "potassium factory", etc. Nor does he go to historical sources. Still in some respects this book is not useless: for the first time the names of Belorussian rivers, lakes and settlements are collected, broken down in semantic groups, characterized statistically and areally (with some maps). The count is inaccurate because of the wrong etymologies but it gives a general idea of the presence and distribution of at least some toponymic types. Fortunately, the author not too often ventures into etymologies and prefers to classify as unclear most names whose make-up is not obvious from modern Belorussian or Russian.

History of research in Belorussian linguistics is presented for the nineteenth and twentieth centuries by M. Sudnik (PIM 6). It is primarily a bibliographic enumeration without characterization of trends, but it is fairly complete in presenting high-lights of the development. It may be especially recommended to the reader of this survey for supplementing its bibliography by *avtoreferaty* of dissertations and articles published by pedagogical institutes in their series. Ja. Ramanovič and A. Jurėvič compiled a complete bibliography of E. Karskij's publications, introduced by an article of V. Borkovskij (PIM 8).

Of practical questions M. Krukowski discusses how to transliterate English family names in Belorussian (PIM 6) and B. Barkowski does the same for German proper names (PIM 8).

There are no studies of other Slavic languages, besides Belorussian and Russian, and only few on some Western European languages. To judge the latter this writer is not competent.

Theoretical linguistics is limited to a derivative article of N. Pelevina and Z. Levit (V 56, 1) on relations between word and notion, sentence and judgment.

## 9. *Concluding remarks*

Linguistic studies in Belorussia even more than in the Ukraine are concentrated on the accumulation of data, on fact finding, with indifference to the problems of method and new trends. Broad generalizations are mostly avoided. The range of the subjects is quite narrow: there are no studies in Western and South Slavic and only few in Russian field. The entire emphasis lies on Belorussian, its dialectology and history.

One of the reasons for these limitations is that the linguistic tradition in Belorussia plays an even smaller part than in the Ukraine. Before 1921 the country had no university. In the twenties there was only one outstanding linguist in Minsk, P. Buzuk, but he had to cease his activity before he could create any school of his own. It was only in 1952 that an Institute of Linguistics as an autonomous body within the framework of the Academy of Sciences was formed.[11]

And yet, in a sense, the absence of tradition was more favorable than the suppression of it. At least in part the new generation of linguists was trained in the spirit of Avanesov's Moscow school, which secured solid philological methods in history of language and a certain type of phonemic approach in phonology and dialectology, particularly obvious in the case of N. Biryla, but tangible in many authors, too. It is hard to say whether a higher degree of responsibility in treatment of facts and, hence, of reliability in results, which characterizes many Belorussian linguists of our day as compared with their Ukrainian colleagues also goes back to the training the Belorussians obtained outside of their country. Whatever caused this difference it is true that it does exist. It suffices to compare, e.g., Krukowski's study on Russian influence upon Belorussian with its counterpart for Ukrainian, by Jižakevyč; or the collective *Narysy pa historyi belaruskaj movy* with also collective *Istoryčna hramatyka ukrajins'koji movy* by Bezpal'ko and others; or Šakun's history of literary Belorussian with Pljušč's history of literary Ukrainian; or Hajdukevič's article on recent changes in Belorussian dialects with the corresponding article by Tereško on Ukrainian dialects, to see how much more free from propaganda requirements and more faithful to truth the Belorussian works are.

Other limitations in Belorussia seem to be the same or similar to those in the Ukraine. To Belorussian scholars, Western literature is hardly available or at least its knowledge is seldom revealed. Outside of Eastern Slavic too often they feel helpless and it is perhaps rather typical that one of the authors speaks about such Slavic languages as Dalmatian and Bosnian, referring to a source of 1842 (PIM 7, p. 132)!

Under these conditions it is hardly possible to speak about any clearcut trends in present day Soviet Belorussian linguistics. Nearly all scholars work in the traditions of Russian linguistic schools of Sobolevskij and Šaxmatov, with occasionally a tinge of Avanesov's phonemic approach. Karneeva-Petrulan stands apart with her attempts at semantic interpretation of phonetic changes, original but completely unfounded. The merit of linguistic research in Belorussia during the last decade is in the collection of new facts. And, in this, the materials gathered and classified are indispensable.

[11] V. Kuprėvič, *Akadėmija Navuk Belaruskaj SSR*, 1958, p. 18.

# LATVIAN

VALDIS J. ZEPS

## BACKGROUND

The end of World War II left the ranks of linguists in Latvia virtually empty. Of established linguists, Jānis Kauliņš died in 1940; Alvils Augstkalns committed suicide upon the occupation of Latvia by the Red Army in 1940; Juris Plāķis was deported to Russia, where he died in 1942; Anna Ābele, Ludis Bērziņš, Ernests Blese, Kārlis Draviņš, Edīte Hauzenberga-Šturma, Leonards Latkovskis, Velta Rūķe-Draviņa, and Jānis Zaube,[1] to mention just a few names in Baltic linguistics, left Latvia for Germany or Sweden, some subsequently for the United States of America. Along with the above were dispersed a number of less well established linguists and students, many of whom have since attained full professional status. Only the grand old man of Latvian linguistics – the late Jānis Endzelīns, and a few of his students remained in Latvia, where they were joined by at least one repatriate linguist from the U.S.S.R. proper – Jānis Loja.

Under the conditions, resumption of normal work was out of the question. A few works, begun well before the upheaval, were brought to completion, notably the monumental dictionary *Latviešu valodas vārdnīca*,[2] and Endzelīns' monograph on Baltic phonology and morphology.[3] A few immediate needs were attended to – a few hastily reworked textbooks, and some dictionaries of modest size[4] were published.

In addition to the lack of qualified personnel, virtually all overt activity ceased in the wake of a bitter in-fighting that arose between proponents of Marrism and those who declined to accept it.[5] The formal victory of Marrists was established in a series of "debates" among the members of the Institute of Language and Literature of the

[1] This paper has been limited to linguistics in Latvia only. The achievements of the exiles, which are by no means negligible, have been surveyed by Jēgers, "Latviešu valodniecība trimdā", and more recently, but less exhaustively, by Hauzenberga-Šturma in the article "Zinātne emigrācijā". The tasks of Latvian linguistics in Latvia and abroad have been surveyed by Rūķe-Draviņa, "Turpmākie uzdevumi latviešu valodas pētīšanā".

[2] Endzelīns & Mülenbachs, *Latviešu valodas vārdnīca*; Endzelīns & Hauzenberga, *Papildinājumi and labojumi K. Mülenbacha Latviešu valodas vārdnīcai*.

[3] Endzelīns, *Baltu valodu skaņas un formas*.

[4] E.g., *Latviešu valodas gramatika*: *Vidusskolu kurss*, or Loja, *Latyšsko-russkij slovar'*.

[5] Pelše, "Latviešu valodniecības stāvoklis un republikas valodnieku uzdevumi".

Latvian Academy of Sciences and the Faculty of Philology of the Latvian State University, whereby reactionary bourgeois tendencies of a formalistic nature were discovered in the Language Section of the Institute; whereupon it was undertaken to reconstruct the activities of the Institute in accordance with the teachings of Marr.[6]

In the summer of 1949, the guiding hand of the Party caught up with the Terminology Committee of the Academy of Sciences, whose bulletins constituted one of the few traces of linguistic activity in the period of Marrist domination. The Committee was instructed to adopt a materialistic and party-line approach to linguistic questions.

The same year saw the appearance of Meščaninov's *Obščee jazykoznanie* in a Latvian translation, providing local would-be Marrists with an easily accessible vademecum.[7]

Then the curtain fell on the Marrist heresy. Stalin's "Otnositel'no marksizma v jazykoznanii" and the subsequent related articles and letters appeared in Latvian, starting with the June 1950 issue of the Bulletin of the Academy of Sciences of the Latvian SSR.[8]

While the rout of the Marrists was complete and irreversible, the prestige of the Latvian Communist Party was deeply committed on the side of the Marrists, and a facile about-face was virtually impossible. The embarassment of the local Party was compounded by the fact that the staunchly anti-Marrist faction of the Institute of Language and Literature – Endzelīns and others – could by no stretch of imagination be considered Marxist in orientation. The denouement was protracted over several sessions; the purpose whereof was to demonstrate how the non-Marxist anti-Marrists, while victorious, were in the wrong, and how the prestige of the Party had not been compromised.

The final official view was not available until early 1952, when the following version of the events was proposed: Ever since the vulgar proclamations of Marr were adopted by the Latvian Academy of Sciences as orthodox Marxism, Latvian linguists deviated from true Marxism in two ways. Some were proponents of the Marrist heresy, while the specialists of the old bourgeois school were engaged in an objectivistic maiming of the discipline of linguistics. A number of instructors were discredited, Jānis Loja was singled out as having made the re-orientation from Marrism to Marxism in a fashion too obvious and unconvincing, and Endzelīns along with his students was reprimanded for a persistent refusal to accept criticism.[9]

Among the casualties of the re-orientation was the Head of the Institute – the writer Andrejs Upītis, who resigned in Nov. 1951 for reasons of ill health, and was succeeded by Ēvalds Svimpulis-Sokols.

The seven-year balance (1945-1951) was extremely dismal. Except for the work of

[6] Peive, "Osnovnye itogi naučno-issledovatel'skoj raboty Akademii nauk Latvijskoj SSR za 1948 god".

[7] Meščaninov, *Vispārīgā valodas zinātne*: *Par stadialitātes problēmu vārdā un teikumā*, translated from his *Obščee jazykoznanie*: *K probleme stadial'nosti v razvitii slova i predloženija* (Leningrad, 1940).

[8] Stalin, "Par marksismu valodniecībā". The original appeared in *Pravda*, June 20, 1950.

[9] Pelše, *op. cit.*, pp. 20-32.

Endzelīns, who had revised his *Lettische Grammatik* for a Latvian edition which appeared in 1951, once the Marrist regime was abolished, no scientific output to speak of appeared in print. In 1947 M. Saule-Sleine had published a 16 page article on the language of Andrejs Upītis in his mediocre novel *Zaļā zeme*; in 1948 I. Celmiņa had published a 5 page article on the adjective endings *-īgs* and *-isks*; in 1949 A. Ozols wrote a 5 page article on the teaching of declension via syntax; in 1951 J. Ozols wrote 8 pages on the same mediocre novel by Upītis; and N. Bogoļubova in a 9 page article compared the perfective and imperfective aspects in Latvian and Russian.[10]

This dearth of publications corresponded with a comparable lack of qualified personnel within the profession. Thus, in 1952, from among the 12 staff members of the Institute, only two held a degree, and none attained one during the period in question. Worse yet – only three had full control of Russian – a grave lack of qualification, considering the conditions.[11]

After the demise of Marrism, it again became possible to write a good linguistic article, provided one observed certain amenities. Except in the case of Endzelīns, who observed no strictures, the linguistic article had to begin with a two page accolade of Stalin and his works in linguistics; had to be niggardly in the praise allotted to bourgeois accomplishments; and could make no reference to the work of those Latvian linguists who had fled to the West.

As time wore on, however, the above strictures became increasingly relaxed. Thus, after Stalin's death, his praise could be restricted to a footnote, or, following de-Stalinization, omitted entirely. A discrete reference to Marx, although not necessary, is still in good taste; the more cautious author may also invoke reputable Russian linguists, prior to settling down to the real subject matter of the publication. Undoubtedly, some restraint in the praise of linguistic works from the period of Latvian independence or of those written by Latvian exiles, is still in order. Likewise, the prudent young Latvian linguist will chose a politically acceptable or neutral subject for his analysis, rather than risk complications. Nevertheless, such controls as remain are not severe enough to damage the vitality of the discipline, nor do they require the injection of massive doses of ideology in linguistic writing.

## RESEARCH

The institutions and publications relevant to current linguistis research in Latvia are the following: the Latvian Academy of Sciences (Latvijas PSR Zinātņu akadēmija)

[10] Endzelīns, *Latviešu valodas gramatika*, a revised edition of his *Lettische Grammatik*; Saule-Sleine, "Andreja Upīša valoda romānā *Zaļā zeme*"; Celmiņa, "Adjektīvi ar izskaņu *-īgs* un *-isks*"; Ozols, "Sintaktiskā pieeja locījumu mācībai" and "Vārdu bagātība A. Upīša *Zaļajā zemē*; Bogoļubova, "Darbības vārda un darbības vārda formu pabeigtais un nepabeigtais veids krievu valodā, salīdzinājumā ar latviešu valodu".

[11] Pelše, *op. cit.*, pp. 24-32.

and its Bulletin (Vēstis);[12] the Institute of Language and Literature of the Latvian Academy of Sciences (Latvijas PSR Zinātņu akadēmijas Valodas un literatūras institūts) and its Memoirs (Raksti);[13] the Latvian State University (Pētera Stučkas Latvijas Valsts universitāte) and its Memoirs (Zinātniskie raksti);[14] the former Rīga Pedagogical Institute (Rīgas Pedagoģiskais institūts) and its Memoirs (Raksti);[15] and the Daugavpils Pedagogical Institute (Daugavpils Pedagoģiskais institūts) and its Memoirs (Raksti).[16]

The bulk of linguistic research in Latvia[17] is connected directly with the activities of the Institute of Language and Linguistics. The Institute, in turn, has placed its main emphasis on the description of contemporary standard Latvian, concretely leading to the publication of two major reference works – a grammar of contemporary standard Latvian – and a dictionary of contemporary standard Latvian. Most of the scholarly output of the Institute is in one way or another directly related to these two major undertakings.

The first volume of the Academy Grammar[18] covering phonetics and morphology appeared in 1959. Written by an authors' collective, it is a huge uninspired tome, haphazardly eclectic in its theoretical orientation, and hopelessly confused as to what are the synchronic grammatical processes of Latvian, and what belongs properly to the history of the language. The importance of the Grammar should not, nevertheless, be underestimated. It is the first comprehensive grammar of contemporary standard Latvian in more than 50 years, is not misleading concerning facts, incorporates a considerable amount of new research, and is carefully documented.

The section on phonology has been written by A. Ahero, A. Bergmane, R. Grabis, M. Lepika, and T. Porīte. Apart from the Academy Grammar, Latvian phonology has been the subject matter of a monograph by Alīse Laua,[19] and articles by E. Liepa.[20] Sentence intonation has been discussed in an article by L. Ceplītis.[21]

Concerning Latvian morphology, A. Ahero has written about compound nouns

[12] *Latvijas PSR Zinātņu Akadēmijas Vēstis* (Riga, 1947?-). 12 per year, separately paginated (LZAV).

[13] *Latvijas PSR Zinātņu akadēmijas Valodas un literatūras institūta raksti*, Riga, 1(1952)-13(1961)-. Irregular. (RVLI).

[14] *Pētera Stučkas Latvijas valsts universitātes zinātniskie raksti*, Riga, 1(?)-9(1956)-43(1961)-. See also bibliographical note. (LUZR).

[15] *Rigas Pedagoģiskā institūta raksti*, Riga, 1(1955)-11(1958). (RRPI).

[16] *Daugavpils Pedagoģiskā institūta raksti*. Known to me only from the review by Semjonova, Juriks, & Brusočkina, "Učenye zapiski Daugavpilsskogo pedagogičeskogo instituta".

[17] I have utilized, a.o., the following bibliographical sources: Barbare, "Bibliografija. Publicējumi par valodniecības jautājumiem, kas nākuši klajā Latvijas PSR no 1945. līdz 1956 g.", and her "Bibliografija" (RVLI). Also Egle & Paeglis, "Prof. Dr. J. Endzelīna darbu bibliografija".

[18] Svimpulis-Sokols, ed., *Mūsdienu latviešu literārās valodas gramatika I: Fonētika un morfoloģija.*

[19] Laua, *Mūsdienu latviešu literārās valodas fonētikas jautājumi*; cf. her *Fonetičeski-fonologičeskaja sistema sovremennogo latyšskogo literaturnogo jazyka.*

[20] Liepa, "Daži mūsdienu latviešu literārās valodas fonēmu pareizrunas jautājumi" and "Sonantu izruna starp nebalsīgiem troksneņiem" (cf. her *Nekotorye voprosy proiznošenija fonem sovremennogo latyšskogo literaturnogo jazyka*).

[21] Ceplītis, "Daži vērojumi par runas intonāciju".

and adjectives,[22] and, jointly with A. Blinkena, on the adjective in general. A. Bergmane has written about derivation in general, the derivation of nouns, the category of number in nouns, the dative, the instrumental, the locative, the category of mood, the infinitive, and participles in general; as well as an article on the adjectivization of participles.[23] A. Blinkena, in addition to her work on the adjective, has written on verbal prefixes and interjections.[24] R. Grabis, in addition to co-ordinating all of the work for the Academy Grammar, has written the prefatory material to some of the sections of the Grammar, as well as the sections on numerals and prepositions. M. Lepika has written on the categories of gender and case, the nominative, the genitive, the accusative, the pronoun, verbal categories, and the conjugation. R. Melbikse has worked on derivation, and declension. A. Miķelsone has likewise worked on derivation, and written the sections on the adverb and the conjunction. M. Saule-Sleine has likewise contributed to the description of derivation in the Grammar, as well as written some articles on the same subject.[25] Apart from the Grammar, a number of other authors have dealt with topics from Latvian morphology. Thus, I. Celmiņa has written on adjectives in *-īgs* and *-isks*, I. Freidenfelds on participles and adjectives, V. Staltmane on verbal aspect,[26] and so on.

A large number of syntactical studies can be viewed as part of the preparatory work for the second volume of the Academy Grammar. These include articles by Dz. Barbare, A. Blinkena, A. Feldhūns, I. Freidenfelds, K. Gailums, J. Kārkliņš, V. Knospe, M. Lepika, I. Niselovičs, R. Melbikse, A. Ozols, T. Porīte, and J. Rozenbergs.[27]

[22] In the Academy Grammar, and in her "Galvenie salikto īpašības vārdu veidi" (cf. her *Složnye prilagatel'nye*).

[23] Bergmane, "Par latviešu valodas divdabju adjektivēšanos".

[24] Blinkena, "Izsauksmes vārdi un to lietošana".

[25] Saule-Sleine, "Par substantīvu un adjektīvu atvasinājumiem ar *-iņš*, *-iņa*" and "Par dažiem adjektīviem".

[26] Celmiņa, "Adjektivi ar izskanu *-īgs* un *-isks*"; Freidenfelds, "Īpašības vārdu noteiktās un nenoteiktās galotnes"; Staltman, "Perfektīvā un imperfektīva veida verbu gramatiskais raksturojums", "Verbu veidi" (RVLI), "Verbu veidi" (LZAV), and "Divu verbu veidu korrelācijas iespējas" (cf. her *O vidax glagola*).

[27] Barbare, "Paplašināts salikts teikums citu saliktu teikumu vidū", "Par paplašinātu saliktu teikumu", and "Par saliktu teikumu latviešu valodas gramatikā"; Blinkena, "Īstie un retoriskie pamudinājuma teikumi", "Jautājuma modalitāte un tās izteikšanas veidi", and "Pamudinājuma teikumi" (cf. her *Voprositel'nye i pobuditel'nye predloženija*); Feldhūns, "Par prievārda funkcijā lietotām divdabja formām"; Freidenfelds, "Relatīvais pakārtojums saliktos teikumos" and "Divdabja teiciens"; Gailums, *Obosoblennoe opredelenie*; Kārkliņš, "Par pienomenu papildanātāju" and *Glavnye tipy odnosostavnyx predloženij*; Knospe, "K voprosu o konversii"; Lepika, "Par ģenitīva vai akuzatīva objektu pie noliegta pārejoša verba", "Par objektu pie noliegta transitīva verba", "Par atributīvo ģenitīvu", and "Par konstrukciju ar noliegtu pārejošu verbu" (cf. her *Padež dopolnenija pri perexodnyx glagolax*); Niselovičs, "Dažas piezīmes par tā saucamo noģiedamo runu" and "Vienlīdzīgie teikuma locekļi no loģikas un stilistikas viedokļa"; Melbikse, "Daži saliktu bezsaikļu teikumo tipi"; Ozols, "Sintaktiskā pieeja locījumu mācībai" and "Vārds datīvā kā teikuma loceklis"; Porīte, "Par vārdu kārtu vienkāršajā teikumā" and "Vārdu kārta vienkāršajā teikumā" (cf. her *Porjadok slov v prostom predloženii*); Rozenbergs, "Objekta ģenitīva raksturs substantīvās vārdkopās un tā sintaktiskā funkcija" and "O nekotoryx konstrukcijax neodinočnogo opredelenija" (cf. his *Roditel'nyj bezpredložnyj padež v roli opredelenija*).

The history of the genesis of contemporary standard Latvian, has occupied A. Bojāte (use of cases), R. Grīsle and R. Grabis (17th century grammars), I. Freidenfelds (participles), M. Saule-Sleine (adjectives in *-isk-*), and E. Soida (phrase structure).[28] Note also I. Niselovičs' article on the first Latvian primers,[29] and K. Ancītis' article on the occasion of the centennial anniversary of the polemics between Juris Alunāns and Rudolf Schulz on the possibility of using Latvian as a literary language.[30]

The field of metrics has been totally vacant, although a very thorough investigation of the syntax of Latvian folksongs has been completed by Artūrs Ozols.[31] K. Arājs has written on the problem of textual criticism in the folksong collection *Latvju Dainas.*[32] Otherwise, folklore has remained unexamined from the linguistic point of view.

The collecting of folklore, lexical and toponymic materials, on the other hand, has made very significant progress. Numerous field-trips by the Folklore Section of the Institute of Language and Literature (formerly part of the Institute of Folklore and Ethnography) have considerably increased the holdings of the Archives of the Institute.[33] The first field-trips were very inadequately staffed, and were conducted under severe ideological constraints.[34] However, the situation has steadily improved, and materials of the highest quality have been collected in the more recent expeditions. None of the materials collected seem to have found their way into print, although some no doubt will be utilized in the long-promised Latvian Dialectological Atlas.[35] Such dialectological studies as have appeared all seem to be the results of the initiative of individual scholars, who did their own gathering of data. To be noted are contributions by E. Ādamsons (Tamian dialects in Vidzeme), Z. Birzniece (the dialect of Džūkste), M. Brence (Augstroze), V. Dambe (accentology), J. Endzelīns (dialects in Vidzeme), M. Graudiņa (Laidze, Kandava), A. Jankevics (Aizupe), J. Kušķis

[28] Bojāte, "Datīva locījuma nozīmes tiešajā verbālajā pārvaldījumā" and "Akuzatīva locījuma nozīmes tiešajā verbālajā pārvaldījumā"; Freidenfelds, "Divdabja formas rakstu krājumā *Sēta, daba* (*un*) *pasaule*"; Grīsle, "Konjugācija Adolfi gramatikā" and "17. gadsimta gramatikas kā latviešu valodas vēstures avots" (cf. her *Grammatiki XVII veka kak istočnik istorii latyšskogo jazyka*); Grabis, "Pārskats par 17. gs. latviešu valodas gramatikām"; Saule-Sleine, "Adjektīvi ar sufiksu *-isk-* dažos latviešu rakstu sākumperioda tekstos un XVII, XVIII un XIX gs. valodnieciskajos darbos"; Soida, *Slovosočetanija v publicistike "mladolatyšej"*.

[29] Niselovičs, "Pirmās latviešu ābeces".

[30] Ancītis, "Kādas valodnieciskas polemikas simtgadu piemiņai".

[31] See bibliographic listings under Ozols for names of his numerous articles on this subject. Many are included in his *Latviešu tautasdziesmu valoda.*

[32] Arājs, "Par Kr. Barona Latvju Dainās iespiesto tautasdziesmu tekstu saskaņu ar oriģināliem".

[33] Cf. e.g., Asare, "Pārskats par latgaliešu tautasdziesmu vākšanu un publicēšanu".

[34] Thus, during the 1949 field trip of the Folklore Institute, the following "folksong" was "collected" among the Latvians at Aizkraukle:

Da spasibo tebe, Stalin,
Da spasibo dvesti raz,
I eščë tebe spasibo
Za sovetskuju, za vlast'.

[35] *Latviešu valodas dialektoloģijas atlanta materiālu vākšanas programma*; Karulis, "Top dialektoloģijas atlants".

(Grostona, Meirāni), Mirdza Plūme (Rauna), S. Raǵe (Ērǵēme, Lugaži, Valka), M. Rudzīte (Braslava, Vecate, Bauņi, Vilzēni), and E. Šmite (Dauguļi).[36] Totally lacking are works on Latgalian dialects – already severely underrepresented in Latvian dialectology. Nor have any dialect dictionaries appeared, although the materials for at least three such works have been collated since some 20 years ago.[37] In general, dialectology in Latvia is only recently again coming into its own – all but a few of the articles cited above are from 1958 or later.

Latvian toponymy has received a very considerable impetus with Endzelīns' *Latvijas PSR vietvārdi*.[38] Of the 4 volumes planned, the second was published posthumously in 1961. Since most of the ms. for the remainder is in finished or nearly finished condition, it is unthinkable that this work should not be completed. Despite some damaging normalizations, the place names here published have an enormous value for further toponymic research. A very thorough study is V. Dambe's work on the place names of the county of Blīdiene.[39] Note also Semjonova's article on Latgalian toponymy.[40]

The other overriding committment of the Institute – a dictionary of contemporary standard Latvian[41] – is reflected in a large number of works on lexicography, the history of Latvian lexicography, practical dictionaries of special terms, articles on the linguistic aspects of literature, guides to spelling of foreign place and personal names, and, somewhat peripheral to the proper work of the Institute and more in the realm of politics, orthographic reform.

To comment on the last point briefly – in 1946 an orthographic reform was adopted,[42] although none was in fact needed. In particular, the marking of length in recent loanwords was abolished, as was the letter *ŗ*. In 1957, the marking of length was restored, but on a basis different from the previous one, and the letter combination *ch* was replaced by *h*.[43] The total effects of both of these reforms are trivial, and only partially for the better.

[36] Ādamsons, "Vārdu sarukšana Vidzemes lībiskajās izloksnēs"; Birzniece, "Džūkstes un dažu apkārtējo izloksņu fonētika"; Brence, "Piedēkļu un gala zilbju vokālisms Augstrozes izloksnē"; Dambe, "Zemgalisko izlokšņu intonācijas"; Endzelīns, "Latviešu valoda Vidzemē"; Graudiņa, "Laidzes un Kandavas izloksne", "Dazas seklo tāmnieku izlokšņu īpatnības" and "Dažas rak-sturīgākās iezīmes Kandavas un Laidzes izloksnes leksikā (cf. her *Lajdzenskij i kandavskij govory)*; Jankevics, "Aizupes izloksne"; Kuškix, "Intonācijas Grostonas un Meirānu izloksnē" and "Diftongi-zācija un monoftongizācija un Meirānu izloksnē"; Plūme, "Raunas izloksne"; Raǧe, *Opisanie trex pograničnyx govorov Severnoj Vidzeme*; Rudzīte, "Ziemeļvidzemes izloksnes Braslavā, Vecatē, Bauņos un Vilzēnos" (cf. her *Govory severnoj časti Vidzeme*); Šmite, "Latviešu dialektoloģija un tās turpmakie uzdevumi" and "Vidus un lībisko izlokšņu saskare Dauguļos" (cf. her *Vzaimodejstvie srednix i livonskix govorov v Dauguli*).

[37] Rūķe, "Turpmakie uzdevumi latviešu valodas pētīšanā".

[38] Endzelīns, *Latvijas PSR vietvārdi*.

[39] Dambe, "Blīdienes vietvārdi kā pagātnes liecinieki"; cf. her survey article "Vietvārdu vākšana un pētīšana Latvijas PSR".

[40] Semjonova, "Iz toponomiki Latgale".

[41] See, e.g., Pūķe, "Top mūsdienu latviešu literārās valodas vārdnīca".

[42] See bibliography under "Latvijas ... pareizrakstību".

[43] See bibliography under "Latvijas ... grozīšanu".

In addition to conventional orthographic guides,[44] a series in the Latvian spelling of foreign place and proper names has been instituted.[45] The format of the series (language by language) makes the individual booklets published therein useful for specialized work (e.g. cartography) but quite awkward for general reference.

Dictionaries of special terms[46] and lists of proposed terminology[47] have been appearing in considerable numbers, the latter mostly as supplements to the Bulletin of the Academy of Sciences. The lists can be evalued only in terms of their relationship to the forthcoming Academy Dictionary, since, individually, their reference value is minimal.

Other lexicographical and lexicological activity involves the sustained and thorough work in the history of Latvian lexicography by Daina Zemzare, especially her monograph on Latvian dictionaries up to 1900.[48] Vol. 13 of the Memoirs of the Institute of Language and Literature is devoted to lexicology and lexicography,[49] including articles by A. Feldhūns (orthography of loanwords), L. Roze (history of Latvian lexicography), V. Staltmane (principles of glossing), and others.[50] Curiously ill-conceived is the diminutive selective thesaurus by J. Ozols.[51]

The lexicon and style of individual authors has been the subject matter of more than a dozen investigations. Here in the choice of materials, political acceptability has more often than not outweighed literary merit. A. Blinkena and B. Šīra write about novels by Vilis Lācis; M. Mauriņa, J. Upītis, J. Ozols, and M. Saule-Sleine about Andrejs Upītis; M. Pūķe, M. Stengrevic, E. Svimpulis-Sokols, and D. Zemzare about Jānis Rainis; and D. Zemzare about J. Sudrabkalns.[52]

[44] *Latviešu valodas pareizrakstības vārdnīca*, and Bendiks, *Svešvārdu pareizrakstības vārdnīca.*

[45] The series appears under the overall title *Norādījumi par citvalodu īpašvārdu pareizrakstību un pareizrunu latviešu literārajā valodā.* Listed in the bibliography under individual authors.

[46] E.g., Latvijas PSR Zinātņu akadēmijas terminoloģijas komisija, *Terminoloģiskā vārdnīca 1: Metalu tehnoloģija un mašīnu elementi* (Riga, 1958).

[47] The lists appear under the overall title *Latvijas PSR Zinātnu akadēmijas Latviešu valodas terminoloģijas komisijas* [No.] *biļetens.*

[48] Zemzare, "Jaunlatviešu darbs leksikas izveidē", "Latyšskaja leksikografija", "XVIII gs. leksikografa J. Langes atzīmes", "Par kādu XVII gs. latviešu vārdnīcas manuskriptu", "Piezīmes par dažām latviešu un lietuviešu vārdnīcām", "Kāds XVIII gs. krievu-vācu-latviešu-igauņu salīdzināmās vārdnīcas manuskripts", and *Latviešu vārdnīcas* (*līdz 1900. gadam*) (cf. her *Xarakternye osobennosti razvitija latyšskoj leksikografii do 1900 g.*).

[49] Svimpulis-Sokols, ed., *Leksikoloģijas un leksikogrāfijas jautājumi.*

[50] Feldhūns, "Daži sengrieķu īpašvārdu rakstības jautājumi"; Roze, "Pēterburgas Avīžu sabiedriski politiskā leksika" and "Pirmā latviešu svešvārdu vārdnīca"; Staltmane, "Par dažiem priedēkļa verbu skaidrojuma principiem".

[51] Ozols, *Daži latviešu leksikas materiāli.*

[52] Blinkena, "Par leksiku Viļa Lāča romānā *Uz jauno krastu*"; Mauriņa, "Par dažām valodas un stila īpatnībām Adreja Upīša novelistikā"; Ozols, "Vārdu bagātība A. Upīša *Zaļajā zemē*"; Pūķe, "Daži vērojumi par J. Raiņa leksikas stilistisko izmantojumu" and "Daži vērojumi par neitrālās leksikas izmantojumo J. Raiņa dzejā"; Saule-Sleine, "Andreja Upīša valoda romānā *Zaļā zeme*" and "Daži vērojumi par valodu un stilu Andreja Upīša romānā *Plaisa mākoņos*"; Šīra, "Valodas meistarības jautājumi V. Lāča romānā *Vētra*"; Stengrevic, *Izpol'zovanie stilističeskix plastov leksiki v lirike Ja. Rajnisa*; Svimpulis-Sokols, "Raiņa cīņa par latviešu literārās valodas attīstību" and "Raiņa cīņa

Second only to the description of contemporary standard Latvian, is the linguistic work done on Russian, especially the teaching of Russian. Not a primary concern of the Institute of Language and Literature, Russian studies have been carried out by the Faculty of Russian of the Latvian State University and its counterparts in the Rīga and Daugavpils Pedagogical Institutes.

Predominantly syntactic problems of contemporary standard Russian have been discussed by E. Celma, N. Donec, V. Juriks, R. Kalnbērziņš, and Z. Tolmačeva.[53] Linguistic aspects of Chekhov's works have been studied by T. Pabauskaja, and of Paustovskij's works by N. Razdorova.[54] The language of Russian mss. from the 13th and 14th centuries in the city archives of Rīga, has been discussed by N. Bogoļubova and L. Taubenberga, and by E. Smirnova.[55] Other points in the history of Russian have been investigated by T. Jakubaite,[56] L. Taubenberga, M. Semjonova, and T. Sobanskaja.

Russian dialects in Latvia have been dealt with in articles by M. Novgorodov and M. Semjonova,[57] and in the anthology *Kratkij obzor russkix govorov Latvijskoj SSR*, which appeared as vol. 12 of the Memoirs of the Institute of Language and Literature.

---

par jauno literatūras valodu"; Upītis, "Andreja Upīša cīņa par latviešu literāro valodu"; Zemzare, "Tautas dzejnieka J. Sudrabkalna meistarības kalve"; Zemzare & Pūķe, "Par dažiem Raiņa valodas un stila pētīšanas jautājumiem". Of the above writers, Rainis is deservedly a classic; Sudrabkalns is a first rate poet, but has not produced anything of consequence since about 1940; and Upītis and Lācis are proven novelists who, nevertheless, cannot help producing only mediocre work under the conditions imposed upon them.

53 Celma, "K voprosu o sootnešenii predloženij s deeprastnymi oborotami i sinonimičeskix konstrukcij"; Donec, "Frazeologičeskie sočetanija v roli prostogo glagol'nogo skazuemogo", "K voprosu o granicax i tipax skazuemogo", "Parallel'noe upotreblenie obeix sinonemičeskix konstrukcij s imenitel'nym i predikativnym imeni suščestvitel'nogo", "Vozmožnost' upotreblenija tol'ko imenitel'-no predikativnogo imeni suščestvitel'nogo", Juriks, "K voprosu o sostave i funkcionirovanii form soslagatel'nogo naklonenija glagola"; Kalnbērziņš, "Sootnositel'noe upotrebenie predložnopadežnyx konstrukcij s prinčinnym vidom otnošenij (po materialami Gor'kogo)", "Pričinnye konstrukcii s zavisimoj čast'ju vyražennoj datel'nym padežom suščestvitel'nogo s predlogom *po*", "Vyraženie pričinnyx otnošenij slovosočitanijami s predlogom *ot*", "Sintaktičeskaja sinonomija predložnyx slovosočetanij s prinčinnymi otnošenijami"; Tolmačeva, "K voprosu ob oproščenii osnov"; Tolmačeva, "Ob obrazovanii i raspade grupp slov so svjazannymi osnovami".

54 Pabauskaja, "O rabote Čexova nad jazykom proizvedenij v 90-x – načale 900-x godov", "Rabota Čexova nad jazykom rasskaza *Krivoe zerkalo*", "Rabota Čexova nad jazykom", "Pis'ma latyšskix korrespondentov Čexovu", "K voprosu o rabote Čexova nad jazykom (*Krivoe zerkalo*)", "Mesto prostorečnoj leksiki v proizvedenijax Čexova", "Inojazyčnaja leksika i frazeoloģija v jazyke Čexova"; Razdorova, "Vzgljady Paustovskogo na jazyk xudožestvennyx proizvedenij", "Metaforičeskoe upotreblenie suščestvitel'nyx", and "Special'naja leksika v *Povest' o lesax i Roždenie morja*".

55 Bogoļubova & Taubenberga, "Nabljudenija nad jazykom XIII-XIV vv." and "O drevnerusskix pamjatnikax XIII-XIV vv."; Smirnova, "Morfologičeskie zametki".

56 Jakubaite, "Iz istorii imennogo sklonenija", "O nekotoryx osobennostjax russkoj poètičeskoj reči", and "O jazyke ody Lomonosova *Na den' voššestvija na prestol Elizavety Petrovny*"; Taubenberga, "O nekotoryx osobennostjax upravlenija v pamjatnikax russkogo jazyka"; Semjonova, "K voprosu o sočetanijax *dl, tl*"; Sobanskaja, "Vopros o produktivnosti tipov složnyx prilagatel'nyx".

57 Novgorodov, "Iz nabljudenij nad fonetikoj i morfologiej Dagdskogo rajona" and "Iz nabljudenij nad sintaksisom Dagdskogo rajona"; Semjonova, "Par vienu Latgales krievu izlokšņu īpatnību", "Po povodu dvux fonetičeskix javlenij", and "Obrazcy tekstov".

Teaching of Russian and studies contrasting Latvian with Russian, has been the subject of articles by N. Bogoļubova, M. Bykovskij, V. Juriks, G. Rumjanceva, M. Semjonova, and S. Važanova,[58] as well as that of the anthology *Slovarnaja rabota po russkomu jazyku i literature v latyšskix školax* (Rīga, 1958). One should also mention, in this connection, the two-volume, ca. 84,000-word, *Krievu-latviešu vārdnīca* (Rīga, 1959).

English as a subject matter of linguistic inquiry, ranks a poor third after Latvian and Russian. T. Babčina discusses a few international words in XVth and XVIth-century English, V. Beitāne reviews the oldest translation of Shakespeare into Latvian, S. Danengirša compares the categories "definite" and "indefinite" as between Latvian and English, G. Ginsburga compares the perfect tenses of English and Latvian, A. Grīnblats is interested in word clusters, and the problem of glossing, and M. Vecozola deals with the problems of a contrastive phonology of English and Latvian.[59]

The work done on Baltic and historical linguistics is almost coextensive with that done by Endzelīns prior to his death in 1961.[60] With his death, comparative and historical linguistics in Latvia has come to an end.

General linguistics has been the exclusive province of the repatriate Jānis Loja, who has written *inter alia* a textbook of Introduction to Linguistics and a textbook of History of Linguistics.[61] Textbooks of this kind have previously not been available in Latvian, hence Loja's contribution is very welcome, which is not to say that his treatment of every subject is satisfactory (that, after all, would be unreasonable to expect).

[58] Bogoļubova, "Darbības vārda un darbības vārda formu pabeigtais un napabeigtais veids krievu valodā", "Krievu prievārdi un tiem atbilstošo latviešu prievārdu lietošana un nozīme", "K voprosu ob ètimologii", and "K sravneniju predložnyx konstrukcij" (cf. her *Roditel'nyj-otložitel'nyj v russkom jazyke v sravnenii s roditel'nym-otložitel'nym v latyšskom jazyke*); Bykovskij, "Zvuk *y* i priemy ego izučenija", "Russkie glasnye", and "Nekotorye priemy izučenija soglasnyx zvukov"; Juriks, "Obščaja sistema zalogov predikativnyx form glagolov", and "Opyt strukturnogo analiza semantičeskogo polja cveta" and "Kategorija čisla imën suščestvitel'nyx" (cf. his *Formy i značenija predpoložitel'nogo naklonenija glagolov*); Rumjanceva, "Principy otbora russkix slov i vyrazenij" and "Leksičeskaja rabota"; Semjonova, "O prošedšem vremeni", "Nelokāmie lietvārdi", "Sopostavitel'naja grammatika", and "Voprosy russkoj fonetiki" (cf. her *K voprosu o formax prošedšix vremën glagola*); Važanova, "Nekotorye značenie poluznamenatel'nyx poluslužebnyx slov".

[59] Babčina, "Iz istorii nekotoryx internacionalizmov v anglijskom jazyke"; Beitāne, "Pirmie Šekspira traģēdiju tulkojumi"; Danengirša, "Par noteiktības un nenoteiktības kategoriju"; Ginsburga, "Angļu un latviešu valodas perfektīvo laiku analize, savstarpēji salīdzinot"; Grinblats, "Angļu-latviešu tulkojošo vārdnīcu frazeoloģijas izlases", "Postpozīta kopas homonīmija", and "Kopa *verbs ar postpositu*"; Vecozola, "Latviešu un angļu literārās valodas līdzskaņu fonēmu sistēmas sastatījums" and "Latviešu un angļu valodas patskaņu fonēmu sistēmas salīdzinājums" (cf. her *Sravnitel'nyj analiz sistem glasnyx fonem*).

[60] For Endzelīns' late work, see bibliography cited in footnote 17, or Jēgers' bibliography in *In honorem Endzelini*. Also see Bogoļubova & Jakubaite, "Istorija razrabotki voprosa o balto-slavjanskix jazykovyx otnošenijax".

[61] Loja, *Valodniecības pamatjautājumi* and *Valodniecības vēsture*.

SUMMARY

Since the fall of the Marrist regime, the recovery of linguistics in Latvia has been rapid, and the prognosis is very good. Research gains in the field of contemporary standard Latvian have been solid; other subject matters traditionally in the province of Latvian linguistics have fared less well. In particular, 1961 saw the demise of comparative and historical linguistics, in the person of Jānis Endzelīns. The next few years should see the fruits of much of the lexicographic research, the completion of Endzelīns' work on toponymy, the first installments of the dialectological atlas, and a continuation of the Academy Grammar. The current stress on the Russification of minorities is bound to produce additional scholarship in the field of Russian as well.

While a steady and fruitful linguistic research seems assured within the limits of Latvia, one must not forget that the Latvian State University is now *de facto* a provincial university, and that persons interested in research of more than local significance must look for it in Moscow or Leningrad. This circumstance, while not necessarily impairing the quality of work that one may expect from Rīga, nevertheless seriously limits the field of inquiry in which one can await significant contributions.

BIBLIOGRAPHY

Ādamsons, E., "Vārdu sarukšana Vidzemes lībiskajās izloksnēs", in *Rakstu krājums... Endzelīnam*, pp. 267-268 (Riga, 1959).

Ahero, A., "Galvenie salikto īpašības vārdu veidi mūsdienu latviešu valodā", *RVLI* 5.37-85 (1955).

——, *Složnye prilagatel'nye v sovremennom latyšskom jazyke* (Riga, 1956). (dissertation abstract)

——, *Norādījumi par citvalodu īpašvārdu pareizrakstību un pareizrunu latviešu literārajā valodā VI: Angļu valodas īpašvārdi* (Riga, 1961).

Ancītis, K., "Kādas valodnieciskas polemikas simtgadu piemiņai", *Rakstu krājums... Endzelīnam*, pp. 269-303 (Riga, 1959).

Arājs, K., "Par Kr. Barona Latvju Dainās iespiesto tautasdziesmu tekstu saskaņu ar oriģināliem", *RVLI* 11.301-324 (1959).

Asare, M., "Pārskats par latgaliešu tautasdziesmu vākšanu un publicēšanu", *RVLI* 11.325-337 (1959).

Babčina, T., "Iz istorii nekotoryx internacionalizmov v anglijskom jazyke", *LUZR* 25.239-258 (1958).

Barbare, Dz., "Bibliografija. Publicējumi par valodniecības jautājumiem, kas nākuši klajā Latvijas PSR no 1945. līdz 1956. g.", *RVLI* 7.257-267 (1958).

——, "Par paplašinātu saliktu teikumu mūsdienu latviešu literārajā valodā", *RVLI.* 10.5-79 (1959).

——, "Bibliografija", *RVLI* 10.239-246 (1959). (Monographs and articles on linguistics and language published in Latvia in 1957 and 1958)
——, "Par saliktu teikumu latviešu valodas gramatikā", *LZAV* 11.19-28 (1959).
——, "Paplašināts salikts teikums citu saliktu teikumu vidū", *LZAV* 1.17-28 (1960).
Beitāne, V., "Pirmie V. Šekspīra traģēdiji tulkojumi latviešu valodā", *LUZR* 30.93-121 (1959).
Bendiks, H., *Svešvārdu pareizrakstības vārdnīca* (Riga, 1958).
Bergmane, A., "Par latviešu valodas divdabju adjektivēšanos", *RVLI* 5.23-36 (1955).
Birzniece, Z., "Džūkstes un dažu apkārtējo izlokšņu fonētika", *Rakstu krājums ... Endzelīnam*, pp. 305-330 (Riga, 1959).
Blinkena, A., "Par ļeksiku Viļa Lāča romānā *Uz jauno krastu*", *Padomju Jaunatne* 189 (1954).
——, "Izsauksmes vārdi un to lietošana mūsdienu latviešu valodā", *RVLI* 5.5-22 (1955).
——, "Īstie un retoriskie pamudinājuma teikumi mūsdienu latviešu literārajā valodā", *LZAV* 2.47-58 (1958).
——, *Voprositel'nye i pobuditel'nye predloženija v sovremennom latyšskom jazyke.* (Riga, 1958). (dissertation abstract)
——, "Jautājuma modalitāte un tās izteikšanas veidi latviešu valodā", *RVLI* 7.159-207 (1958).
——, "Pamudinājuma teikumi mūsdienu latviešu literārajā valodā", *RVLI* 10.81-145 (1959).
Bogoļubova, N., "Darbības vārda un darbības vārda formu pabeigtais un nepabeigtais veids krievu valodā, salīdzinājumā ar latviešu valodu", *Padomju Latvijas Skola* 9.55-63 (1951).
——, "Krievu prievārdi un tiem atbilstošo latviešu prievārdu lietošana un nozīme", *Padomju Latvijas Skola* 2.63-73 (1952).
——, *Roditel'nyj – otložitel'nyj pri predlogax "iz," "iz-za," "iz-pod," "ot," "s" v russkom jazyke v sravnenii s roditel'nym – otložitel'nym pri predloge "no" (= nuo) v latyšskom jazyke* (Riga, 1955) (dissertation abstract).
——, "K voprosu ob ètimologii i istoričeskom analize formy predlogov *iz*, *ot*, *s* v russkom jazyke i predloga *no* (*nuo*) v latyšskom jazyke", *LZAV* 8.45-58 (1956).
——, "K sravneniju predložnyx kunstrukcij russkogo i latyšskogo jazykov", *LZAV* 6.25-32 (1957).
——, and Jakubaite, T., "Istorija razrabotki voprosa o balto-slavjanskix jazykovyx otnošenijax", *Rakstu krājums ... Endzelīnam*, pp. 331-375 (Riga, 1959).
——, and Taubenberga, L., "Nabljudenija nad jazykom XIII-XIV vv. Rižskogo gosudarstvennogo gorodskogo arxiva", *LUZR* 43.7-26 (1961).
——, and ——, "O drevnerusskix pamjatnikax XIII-XIV v.v. Rižskogo gorodskogo arxiva", *LUZR* 36.7-22 (1960).
Bojāte, A., "Datīva locījuma nozīmes tiešajā verbālajā pārvaldījumā jaunstrāvnieku publicistiskajos darbos (Dienas Lapā)", *LUZR* 25.91-114 (1958).

——, "Akuzatīva locījuma nozīmes tiešajā verbālajā pārvaldījumā jaunstrāvnieku publicistiskajos rakstos (Dienas Lapā)", *LUZR* 30.55-67 (1959).

Brence, M., "Piedēkļu un gala zilbju vokālisms Augstrozes izloksnē", *Rakstu krājums ... Endzelīnam*, pp. 377-390 (Riga, 1959).

Bykovskij, M., "Zvuk *y* i priemy ego izučenija v latyšskoj škole", *RRPI* 2 (1959).

——, "Russkie glasnye i nekotorye priemy ix izučenija v latyšskoj škole", *Učenye zapiski Daugavpilsskogo pedagogičeskogo instituta* 2 (1959).

——, "Nekotorye priemy izučenija soglasnyx z vukov russkogo jazyka v latyšskoj škole", *Učenye zapiski Daugavpilsskogo pedagogičeskogo instituta.*

Celma, E., "K voprosu o sootnešenii predloženij s deeprastnymi oborotami i sinonimičeskix konstrukcij", *LUZR* 43.99-112 (1961).

Celmiņa, I., "Adjektivi ar izskaņu *-īgs* un *-isks*", *LZAV* 7.85-89 (1948).

Ceplītis, L., "Daži vērojumi par runas intonāciju latviešu valodā", *RVLI* 7.129-157 (1958).

——, *Norādījumi par citvalodu īpašvārdu pareizrakstību un pareizrunu latviešu literārajā valodā VII: Spāņu valodas īpašvārdi* (Riga, 1961).

Dambe, V., "Vietvārdu vākšana un pētīšana Latvijas PSR", *RVLI* 3.175-187 (1954).

——, "Blīdienes vietvārdi kā pagātnes liecinieki", *Rakstu krājums ... Endzelīnam*, pp. 391-452 (Riga, 1959).

——, "Zemgalisko izlokšņu intonācijas", *LZAV* 12.29-38 (1960).

Danengirša, S., "Par noteiktības un nenoteiktības kategoriju angļu un latviešu valodā", *RRPI* 5.451-473 (1957).

*Daugavpils Pedagoģiskā institūta raksti.* Known to the author only from the review by Semjonova *et al.* (reviewed under the alternate title of the series, namely, *Učenye zapiski Daugavpilsskogo pedagogičeskogo instituta*).

Donec, N., "Vozmožnost' upotreblenija tol'ko imenitel'no predikativnogo imeni suščestvitel'nogo v sovremennom russkom literaturnom jazyke", *RRPI* 5.87-108 (1957).

——, "Parellel'noe upotreblenie obeix sinonimičeskix konstrukcij s imenitel'nym i predikativnym imeni suščestvitel'nogo v sovremennom russkom jazyke", *RRPI* 5.109-125 (1957).

——, "K voprosu o granicax i tipax skazuemogo", *LUZR* 36.57-76 (1960).

——, "Frazeologičeskie sočetanija v roli prostogo glagol'nogo skazuemogo", *LUZR* 43.75-97 (1961).

Egle, K. and Paeglis, J., "Prof. Dr. J. Endzelīna darbu bibliografija", *Rakstu krājums ... Endzelīnam*, pp. 653-730 (Riga, 1959).

Endzelīns, J., *Baltu valodu skaņas un formas* (Riga, 1948).

——, *Latviešu valodas gramatika* (a revised and enlarged translation of his *Lettische Grammatik*, with unchanged paragraphing) (Riga, 1951).

——, *Baltų kalbų garsai ir formos* (a Lithuanian translation of Endzelīns 1948) (Vilnius, 1957).

——, "Latviešu valoda Vidzemē", *RVLI* 3.125-136 (1954).

——, *Latvijas PSR vietvārdi*, Part I: Vol. 1, A-J; Vol. 2, K-O (Riga, 1956-61).

——, and Mülenbachs, K., *Latviešu valodas vārdnīca*, 4 vols. (Riga, 1923-32).

——, and Hauzenberga, E., *Papildinājumi un labojumi K. Mülenbacha Latviešu valodas vārdnīcai*, 2 vols. (Riga, 1934-46).

Feldhūns, A., "Par prievārda funkcijā lietotām divdabja formām", *Skolotāju Avīze* 51 (1958).

——, "Daži sengrieķu īpašvārdu rakstības jautājumi", *Leksikoloģijas un leksikografijas jautājumi. RVLI* 13.245-251 (1961).

Freidenfelds, I., "Īpašības vārdu noteiktās un nenoteiktās galotnes", *Literatūra un Māksla* 27 (1958).

——, "Relatīvais pakārtojums saliktos teikumos", *Literatūra un Māksla* 31 (1958).

——, "Divdabja formas rakstu krājumā *Sēta, daba (un) pasaule*", *LUZR* 25.115-134 (1958).

——, "Divdabja teiciens", *Rakstu krājums ... Endzelīnam*, pp. 453-477 (Riga, 1959).

Gailums, K., *Obosoblennoe opredelenie v sovremennom latyšskom literaturnom jazyke* (Riga, 1956). (dissertation abstract)

Ginsburga, G., "Angļu un latviešu valodas perfektīvo laiku analize, savstarpēji salīdzinot", *RRPI* 5.431-449 (1959).

Grabis, R., Review of Loja, Latyšsko-russkij slovar', in *Literatura un Māksla* 17 (1948).

——, "Pārskats par 17. gs. latviešu valodas gramatikām", *RVLI* 5.205-266 (1955).

Graudiņa, M., "Laidzes un Kandavas izloksne", *RVLI* 6.257-296 (1958).

——, "Dažas seklo tāmnieku izlokšņu īpatnības", *LZAV* 10.57-66 (1958).

——, "Dažas raksturīgākās iezīmes Kandavas un Laidzes izloksnes leksikā", *LZAV* 11.71-78 (1958).

——, *Lajdzenskij i kandavskij govory* (Riga, 1958). (dissertation abstract)

Grīnblats, A., "Angļu-latviešu tulkojošo vārdnīcu frazeoloģijas izlases, izkārtojuma un izklāsta problēmas," *LUZR* 16.133-150 (1957).

——, "Postpozīta kopas homonīmija mūsdienu angļu valodā", *LUZR* 30.123-137 (1959).

——, "Kopa *verbs ar postpozitu* mūsdienu angļu valodā", *LUZR* 25.259-315 (1958).

Grīsle, R., "Konjugācija Adolfi gramatikā", *RRPI* 5.39-59 (1957).

——, "17. gadsimta gramatikas kā latviešu valodas vēstures avots", *RVLI* 7.245-255 (1958).

——, *Grammatiki XVII veka kak istočnik istorii latyšskogo jazyka* (Riga, 1958). (dissertation abstract)

——, "Rēhehūzena gramatika un pret to vērstais Einhorna raksts", in *Rakstu krājums ... Endzelīnam*, pp. 479-526 (Riga, 1959).

Hauzenberga-Šturma, E., et al., "Zinātne emigrācijā", in *Latvju enciklopēdija: Papildinājumi*, pp. 212-213 (Stockholm, 1962).

Jankevics, A., "Aizupes izloksne", *RVLI* 6.297-317 (1958).

Jakubaite, T., "Iz istorii imennogo sklonenija v slavjanskix jazykax", *LZAV* 1.33-40 (1957).
——, "O nekotoryx osobennostjax russkoj poètičeskoj reči XVIII – načala XIX v.", *RRPI* 5.7-23 (1957).
——, "O jazyke ody M. V. Lomonosova *Na den' voššestvija na prestol Elizavety Petrovny*", *LUZR* 30.199-219 (1959).
Jēgers, B. "Latviešu valodniecība trimdā", *Klēts* 4.28-33 (1960).
Juriks, V., *Formy i značenija predpoložitel'nogo naklonenija glagolov latyšskogo i russkogo jazykov v sopostavitel'nom osveščenii* (Riga, 1955). (dissertation abstract)
——, "Obščaja sistema zalogov predikativnyx form glagolov russkogo i latyšskogo jazykov v sopostavitel'nom plane", *RRPI* 5.83-94 (1957).
——, "Opyt strukturnogo analiza semantičeskogo polja cveta v russkom i latyšskom jazykax", *LUZR* 25.185-198 (1958).
——, "K voprosu o sostave i funkcionirovanii form soslagatel'nogo naklonenija glagola v sovremennom russkom literaturnom jazyke", *LUZR* 30.159-170 (1959).
——, "Kategorija čisla imen suščestvitel'nyx v russkom i latyšskom jazykax", *LUZR* 43.197-205 (1961).
Kalnbērziņš, R., "Sootnositel'noe upotreblenie predložno-padežnyx konstrukcij s pričinnym vidom otnošenij v sovremennom russkom literaturnom jazyke (po materialam Polnogo sobiranija A. M. Gor'kogo"), *LZAV* 11.51-70 (1958).
——, "Pričinnye konstrukcii sovremennogo russkogo literaturnogo jazyka s zavisimoj čast'ju, vyražennoj datel'nym padežom suščestvitel'nogo s predlogom *po* (na materiale Polnogo sobranija sočinenij A. M. Gor'kogo)", *LZAV* 7.23-34 (1958).
——, "Vyraženie pričinnyx otnošenij slovosočetanijami s predlogom *ot* i roditel'nym padežom suščestvitel'nogo v sovremennom russkom jazyke (na materiale Polnogo sobiranija sočinenij A. M. Gor'kogo)", *LZAV* 11.49-56 (1956).
——, "Sintaktičeskaja sinonimija predložnyx slovosočetanij sovremennogo russkogo literaturnogo jazyka s pričinnymi otnošenijami (na materiale Polnogo sobranija sočinenij A. M. Gor'kogo)", *LZAV* 3.48-64 (1959).
Kārkliņš, T., "Par pienomenu papildinātāju", *LUZR* 25.69-89 (1958).
——, *Glavnye tipy odnosostavnyx predloženij v sovremennom latyšskom literaturnom jazyke* (Riga, 1952). (dissertation abstract)
Karulis, K., "Top dialektoloģijas atlants", *Literatūra un Māksla* 18 (1958).
Knospe, V., "K voprosu o konversii v latyšskom jazyke", *Latvijas Valsts universitātes studentu zinātniskie darbi* 2.5-14 (1957).
*Kratkij obzor russkix govorov Latvijskoj SSR*. Trudy Instituta jazyka i literatury Akademii nauk Latvijskoj SSR 12 (1960).
*Krievu-latviešu vārdnīca*, 2 vols. (Riga, 1959).
Kušķis, J., "Diftongizācija un monoftongizācija Grostonas un Meirānu izloksnē", *LUZR* 25.135-157 (1958).
——, "Intonācijas Grostonas un Meirānu iziokenē", *LUZR* 30.69-82 (1959).
*Latviešu valodas dialektoloģijas atlanta materialu vākšanas programma* (Riga, 1954).

*Latviešu valodas pareizrakstības vārdnīca* (Riga, 1951).

"Latvijas PSR Ministru Padomes lēmums Nr. 480 1946. g. 5. VI. Noteikumi par latviešu valodas pareizrakstību", *Padomju Latvijas Skola* 7.109 (1946). Also published in *Cīņa* 1946/132.

"Latvijas PSR Ministru Padomes lēmums Nr. 602, Riga, 1957. gada 26. decembrī. Par Latvijas PSR Ministru Padomes 1946. gada 5. jūnija lēmuma Nr. 480 daļēju grozīšanu", *Cīņa* 1957/306. Also in *Padomju Jaunatne* 1957/255.

*Latvijas PSR Zinātņu akadēmijas Latviešu valodas terminoloģijas komisijas biļetens*, Riga, 1 (1949) – 25 (1960-). Irregular supplement to *Latvijas PSR Zinātņu Akadēmijas Vēstis*. Individual issues appear with the issue number incorporated into the title, and with a subtitle. E.g., *Latvijas PSR Zinātņu akadēmijas Latviešu valodas terminoloģijas komisijas 25. biļetens: Hidromeliorācijas terminu projekti*. Supplement to *Latvijas PSR Zinātņu Akadēmijas Vēstis* 1960/11.

Latvijas PSR Zinātņu akadēmijas Terminoloģijas komisija. *Terminoloģiskā vārdnīca* 1: *Metalu tehnoloģija un mašīnu elementi* (Riga, 1958).

*Latvijas PSR Zinātņu akadēmijas Valodas un literatūras institūta raksti* Riga, 1 (1952)-13 (1961-). (Abbreviation: RVLI)

*Latvijas Zinātņu Akadēmijas Vēstis* (Riga, ?1947-). Appears 12 times a year. (Abbreviation: LZAV)

*Latviešu valodas gramatika: Vidusskolu kurss* (Riga, 1945).

*Latvijas Valsts universitates zinātniekie raksti. Vēstures un filoloģijas zinātnes.* See *Pētera Stučkas Latvijas Valsts universitātes zinātniskie raksti.*

Laua, A., *Fonetičeski-fonologičeskaja sistema sovremennogo latyšskogo literaturnogo jazyka* (Riga, 1954). (dissertation abstract)

——, *Mūsdienu latviešu literārās valodas fonētikas jautājumi* (Riga, 1961).

Lepika, M., "Par ģenitiva vai akuzativa objektu pie noliegta pārejoša verba latviešu literarajā valodā", *LZAV* 9.13-30 (1953).

——, "Par objektu pie noliegta transitiva verba latviešu literarajā valodā", *RVLI* 3.5-45 (1954).

——, "Par atributīvo ģenitīvu mūsdienu latviešu valodā", *RVLI* 3.47-76 (1954).

——, *Padež doplnenija pri perexodnyx glagolax s otricaniem v latyšskom literaturnom jazyke* (Riga, 1955). (dissertation abstract)

——, "Par konstrukciju ar noliegtu pārejošu verbu latviešu literārās valodas sākumos", *Rakstu krājums ... Endzelīnam*, pp. 527-554 (Riga, 1959).

Liepa, E., "Daži mūsdienu latviešu literārās valodas fonēmu pareizrunas jautājumi", *RRPI* 5.147-161 (1957).

——, "Sonantu izruna starp nebalsīgiem troksneņiem mūsdienu latviešu literārājā valodā", *RRPI* 5.163-176 (1957).

——, *Nekotorye voprosy proiznošenija fonem sovremennogo latyšskogo literaturnogo jazyka* (Riga, 1958). (dissertation abstract)

Loja, J., *Latyšsko-russkij slovar'* (Moscow, 1946). (A reprint of the same, issued in

1942, about 40,000 words, 252 pp. Review by R. Grabis, in *Literatūra un Māksla* 7 (1948).)

——, *Valodniecības pamatjautājumi* (Riga, 1958).

——, *Valodniecības vēsture* (Riga, 1961).

Mackovs, G., *Norādījumi par citvalodu īpašvārdu pareizrakstību un pareizrunu latviešu literārajā valodā II: Čehu un slovaku valodas īpašvārdi* (Riga, 1961).

Mauriņa, M., "Par dažām valodas un stila īpatnībām Andreja Upīša novelistikā", *LZAV* 12.25-34 (1957).

Melbikse, R., "Daži saliktu bezsaikļa teikumu tipi mūsdienu latviešu literārajā valodā", *RVLI* 7.210-243 (1958).

Meščaninov, I., *Vispārīgā valodas zinātne. Par stadialitātes problēmu vārda un teikuma attīstībā* (Riga, 1949). [Translated from *Obščee jazykoznanie: K probleme stadial'nosti v razvitii slova i predloženije* (Leningrad, 1940).]

Niselovičs, I., "Dažas piezīmes par tā saucamo noģiedamo runu", *Padomju Latvijas Skola* 5.83-89 (1952).

——, "Vienlīdzīgie teikuma locekļi no loģikas un stilistikas viedokļa", *Padomju Latvijas Skola* 8.39-45 (1955).

——, "Pirmās latviešu ābeces", *Padomju Latvijas Skola* 12.56-65 (1958).

Novgorodov, M., "Iz nabljudenij nad sintaksisom govora russkogo starožil'českogo naselenija Dagdskogo rajona Latvijskoj SSR", *Učenye zapiski Daugavpilsskogo pedagogičeskogo instituta.* Vol., date and pagination not available.

——, "Iz nabljudenij nad fonetikoj i morfologiej govora russkogo starožil'českogo naselenija Dagdskogo rajona Latvijakoj SSR", *Učenye zapiski Daugavpilsskogo pedagogičeskogo instituta.* Vol., date, and pagination not available.

Ozols, A., "Sintaktiskā pieeja locījumu mācībal", *Padomju Latvijas Skola* 2.83-87 (1949).

——, "Par dažām stilistikas problemām un latviešu klasisko tautasdziesmu valodas stilistikas jautājumiem", *LZAV* 10.13-29 (1955).

——, "Par dažiem vārdkopu sintakses jautājumiem latviešu klasiskajās tautasdziesmās", *LUZR* 11.171-213 (1956).

——, "Vārds datīvā kā teikuma loceklis", *LUZR* 16.7-62 (1957).

——, "Tautoloģija latviešu klasiskajās tautasdziesmās", *LUZR* 16.63-81 (1957).

——, "Pielikums, apzīmētājs un apzīmējums latviešu klasiskajās tautasdziesmās", *LUZR* 25.9-67 (1958).

——, "Latviešu klasisko tautasdziesmu teikumu modalitātes problēma sakarā ar partikulām", *LUZR* 7.99-128 (1958).

——, "Atonālā uzruna latviešu klasiskajās tautasdziesmās", *LZAV* 6.15-26 (1958).

——, "Adverbializācijas problēma un verbālās vārdkopas ar atkarīgiem adverbiem", *LZAV* 12.47-56 (1958).

——, "Latviešu tautasdziesmu frazeoloģijas pamatjautājumi", *RVLI* 10.201-238 (1959).

——, "Nominālo un adverbiālo predikatīvo attieksmju tipi latviešu klasiskajās tautasdziesmās", *RVLI* 10.147-200 (1959).

——, "Raksturīgākās latviešu tautasdziesmu nominālās vārdkopas", *RVLI* 30.7-54 (1959).

——, "Salīdzinājumi latviešu klasiskajās tautasdziesmās", *RVLI* 11.263-300 (1959).

——, "Verbālo predikātīvo attieksmju tipi latviešu klasiskajās tautasdziesmās", in *Rakstu krājums ... Endzelīnam*, pp. 567-594 (Riga, 1959).

——, "Latviešu tautasdziesmu izsauksmes vārdi kā leksikogramatiska un leksikostilistiska kategorija", *Leksikoloģijas un leksikogrāfijas jautājumi. RVLI* 13.7-85 (1961).

——, *Latviešu tautasdziesmu valoda* (Riga, 1961).

Ozols, J., "Vārdu bagātība A. Upīša *Zaļajā zemē*", *Karogs* 8.747-751 (1951).

——, *Daži latviešu leksikas materiāli* (Riga, 1958).

Pabauskaja, T., "O rabote A. P. Čexova nad jazykom proizvedenij v 90-x – načale 900-x godov", *LUZR* 11.235-262 (1956).

——, "Rabota A. P. Čexova nad jazykom rasskaza *Krivoe zerkalo*", *LUZR* 16.7-62. (1957).

——, "Rabota A. P. Čexova nad jazykom", *LUZR* 30.187-198 (1959).

——, "Pis'ma latyšskix korrespondentov A. P. Čexovu", *LUZR* 36.99-103 (1960).

——, "K voprosu o rabote A. P. Čexova nad jazykom (varianty rasskaza *Krivoe zerkalo*)", *LUZR* 36.91-97 (1960).

——, "Mesto prostorečnoj leksiki v proizvedenijax A. P. Čexova", *LUZR* 43.125-152 (1961).

——, "Inojazyčnaja leksika i frazeologija v jazyke A. P. Čexova", *LUZR* 43.113-123 (1961).

Peive, J., "Osnovnye itogi naučno-issledovatel'skoj raboty Akademii nauk Latvijskoj SSR za 1948 god", *LZAV* 3.5-36 (1949).

Pelše, A., "Latviešu valodniecības stāvoklis un republikas valodnieku uzdevumi", *LZAV*. Same, in Russian, in *Trudy Instituta jazykoznanija i literatury Akademii nauk Latvijskoj SSR* 2.5-22 (1953).

*Pētera Stučkas Latvijas Valsts universitātes zinātniskie raksti. Filoloģijas zinātnes.* See *Pētera Stučkas Latvijas Valsts universitātes zinātniskie raksti.*

*Pētera Stučkas Latvijas Valsts universitātes zinātniskie raksti*, Riga, 1 (?)-11 (1956)-43 (1961-). Formerly *Latvijas Valsts universitātes zinātniskie raksti.* Linguistic articles appear in the subseries *Filoloģijas zinātnes*, previously part of the subseries *Vēstures un filoloģijas zinātnes.* (Abbreviation: LUZR)

Plūme, M., "Raunas izloksne", *RVLI* 3.137-174 (1954).

Porīte, T., "Par vārdu kārtu latviešu literārās valodas vienkāršā teikumā", *RVLI* 3.77-112 (1954).

——, *Porjadok slov v prostom predloženii sovremennogo latyšskogo literaturnogo jazyka* (Riga, 1954). (dissertation abstract).

——, "Vārdu kārta mūsdienu latviešu literārās valodas vienkāršajā teikumā", *RVLI* 5.117-204 (1955).

Pūķe, M., "Daži vērojumi par neitrālās leksikas izmantojumu J. Raiņa dzejā", *LZAV* 2.31-56 (1957).

——, "Top mūsdienu latviešu literārās valodas vārdnīca", *Literatūra un Māksla* 8 (1958).

——, "Daži vērojumi par J. Raina leksikas stilistisko izmantojumu", *RVLI* 7.49-98 (1958).

Raģe, S., *Opisanie trex pograničnyx govorov Severnoj Vidzeme* (*Èrgeme, Lugaži, Valka*) (Riga, 1955). (dissertation abstract)

*Rakstu krājums ... Endzelīnam* see Svimpulis-Sokols, ed., *Rakstu krājums. Veltījums akadēmiķim profesoram Dr. Jānim Endzelīnam viņa 85 dzīves un 65 darba gadu atcerei.*

Razdorova, N., "Vzgljady K. G. Paustovskogo na jazyk xudožestvennyx proizvedenij", *LUZR* 30.171-185 (1959).

*Rīgas Pedagoģiskā institūta raksti.* Riga, 1 (1955-) – 11 (1958). (Abbreviation: RRPI)

——, "Metaforičeskoe upotreblenie suščestvitel'nyx", *LUZR* 36.77-89 (1960).

——, "Special'naja leksika v proizvedenijax K. G. Paustovskogo *Povest' o lesax i Roždenie morja*", *LUZR* 25.221-238 (1958).

Roze, L., "Pēterburgas Avīžu sabiedriski polītiskā leksika", *Leksikoloģijas un leksikografijas jautājumi. RVLI* 13.133-191 (1961).

——, "Pirmā latviešu svešvārdu vārdnīca", *Leksikoloģijas un leksikografijas jautājumi. RVLI* 13.273-299 (1961).

Rozenbergs, J., "Objekta ģenitīva raksturs substantīvās vārdkopās un tā sintaktiskā funkcija", *RRPI* 2.169-179 (1956).

——, *Roditel'nyj bezpredložnyj padež v roli opredelenija v sovremennom latyšskom literaturnom jazyke* (*v sravnenii s russkimi konstrukcijami*) (Riga, 1956). (dissertation abstract)

——, "O nekotoryx konstrukcijax neodinočnogo opredelenija", *RRPI* 5.61-85 (1957).

Rudzite, M., *Govory severnoj časti Vidzeme* (*braslavskij, vecatskij, baun'skij, vilzenskij* (Riga, 1954). (dissertation abstract)

——, "Ziemeļvidzemes izloksnes Braslavā, Vecatē, Bauņos un Vilzēnos", *RVLI* 6.101-256 (1958).

Rūķe-Draviņa, V., "Turpmākie uzdevumi latviešu valodas pētīšanā", *Ceļi* 10.5-16 (1961).

Rumjanceva, G., "Principy otbora russkix slov i vyraženij, prednaznačennyx dlja aktivnogo usvoenija na praktičeskix zanjatijax po russkomu jazyku v latyšskix gruppax", *LUZR* 25.199-220 (1958).

——, "Leksičeskaja rabota na urokax russkogo jazyka", in *Russkij jazyk v latyšskoj škole.* Riga, 1958. Pagination, editor of the anthology, and other data not available.

Saule-Sleine, M., "Andreja Upīša valoda romanā *Zaļā zeme*", *LZAV* 5.41-56 (1947).

——, "Daži vērojumi par valodu un stilu Andreja Upīša romanā *Plaisa mākoņos*", in *Tautas rakstnieka A. Upīša 75 gadi*, pp. 407-439 (Riga, 1952).

——, "Par substantivu un adjektivu atvasinājumiem ar *-iņš*, *-iņa* mūsdienu latviešu literarajā valodā", *RVLI* 5.87-116 (1955).

——, "Par dažiem adjektīviem", *Literatūra un Māksla* 37 (1958).

——, "Adjektīvi ar sufiksu *-isk-* dažos latviešu rakstu sākumperioda tekstos un XVII, XVIII un XIX gs. valodnieciskajos darbos", *Leksikoloģijas un leksikogrāfijas jautājumi. RVLI* 13.87-118 (1961).

Semjonova, M., *K voprosu o formax prošedšix vremen glagola v latyšskom jazyke* (*sravnitel'no s russkim*) (Riga, 1954) (dissertation abstract).

——, "Iz toponimiki Latgale", *LUZR* 11.215-233 (1956).

——, "O prošedšem vremeni v latyšskom jazyke sravnitel'no s russkim", *LUZR* 16.95-104 (1957).

——, "Voprosy russkoj fonetiki v latyšskoj škole", in *Russkij jazyk v latyšskoj škole* (Riga, 1958). Pagination, editor of the anthology, and other data not available.

——, "Par vienu Latgales krievu izlokšņu īpatnību", *RVLI* 6.319-323 (1958).

——, "Po povodu dvux fonetičeskix javlenij russkix i latyšskix govorov Latgale", *Rakstu krājums ... Endzelīnam*, pp. 595-606 (Riga, 1959).

——, "K voprosu o sočetanijax *dl, tl*", *LUZR* 30.83-92 (1959).

——, "Obrazcy tekstov nekotoryx russkix govorov Latvijskoj SSR", *RVLI* 36.53-56 (1960).

——, "Sopostavitel'naja grammatika russkogo i slatyšskogo jazykov", *LUZR* 43.153-196 (1961).

——, "Nelokāmie lietvārdi krievu un latviešu valodā", *LZAV* 1.43-50 (1962).

——, Juriks, V., and Brusočkina, V., "Učenye zapiski Daugavpilsskogo pedagogičeskogo instituta (Review)", *LZAV* 10.173-175 (1958).

Šīra, B., "Valodas meistarības jautājumi V. Lāča romānā *Vētra*", *LZAV* 9.47-58 (1957).

*Slovarnaja rabota po russkomu jazyku i literature v latyšskix školax* (*Materialy pedagogičeskix čtenij*) (Riga, 1958). Editor and contents of the anthology not available.

Smirnova, E., "Morfologičeskie zametki o novgorodskix gramotax XIII-XIV vv. xranjaščixsja v Rižskom gosudarstvennom gorodskom arxive", *LUZR* 43.27-41 (1961).

Smite, E., "Latviešu dialektoloģija un tās turpmākie uzdevumi", *RVLI* 3.113-123 (1954).

——, *Vzaimodejstvie srednix i livonskix govorov v Dauguli* (Riga, 1954) (dissertation abstract).

——, "Vidus un lībisko izlokšņu saskare Dauguļos", *RVLI* 6.5-99 (1958).

Sobanskaja, T., "Vopros o produktivnosti tipov složnyx prilagatel'nyx v istorii russkogo jazyka (na materiala XI-XVIII vv.)", *Učenye zapiski Daugavpilsskogo pedagogičeskogo instituta.* Known to me only from the review by Semjonova *et al.*

Soida, E., *Slovosočetanija v publicistike "mladolatyšej" (po gazete "Peterburgas Avizes").* (dissertation abstract).

Stalin, J., "Par marksismu valodniecībā", *LZAV* 6.5-18 (1950). Translated from his "Otnositel'no marksizma v jazykoznanii", *Pravda*, June 20, 1950.

——, *Marksisms un valodniecības jautājumi* (Riga, 1950). Translated from Russian.

Staltmane, V., "Perfektīvā un imperfektīvā veida verbu gramatiskais raksturojums mūsdienu latviešu literārajā valodā", *LZAV* 6.27-36 (1958).

——, "Verbu veidi mūsdienu latviešu literārajā valodā", *LZAV* 7.13-22 (1958).

——, "Verbu veidi mūsdienu latviešu literārajā valodā", *RVLI* 7.5-47 (1958).

——, *O vidax glagola v sovremennom latyšskom literaturnom jazyke* (Riga, 1958) (dissertation abstract).

——, "Divu verbu veidu (perfektīvā un imperfektīvā) korelācijas iespējas mūsdienu latviešu valodā", *Rakstu krājums ... Endzelīnam*, pp. 607-631 (Riga, 1959).

——, "Par dažiem priedēkļa verbu skaidrojuma principiem Latviešu literārās valodas vārdnīcā", *Leksikoloģijas un leksikogrāfijas jautājumi. RVLI* 13.193-208 (1961).

——, *Norādījumi par citvalodu īpašvārdu pareizrakstību un pareizrunu latviešu literārajā valodā V: Poļu valodas īpašvārdi* (Riga, 1961).

Stengrevica, M., *Izpol'zovanie stilističeskix plastov leksiki v lirike Ja. Rajnisa* (Riga, 1958) (dissertation abstract).

Svimpulis-Sokols, E., "Raiņa cīņa par jauno literatūras valodu", *LZAV* 3.361-376 (1951).

——, "Raiņa cīņa par latviešu literarās valodas attīstību", *RVLI* 3.203-227 (1954).

——, ed., *Mūsdienu latviešu literārās valodas gramatika I: Fonētika un morfoloģija* (Riga, 1959).

——, ed., *Rakstu krājums. Veltījums akadēmiķim profesoram Dr. Jānim Endzelīnam viņa 85 dzīves un 65 darba gadu atcerei* (Riga, 1959).

——, ed., *Leksikoloģijas un leksikogrāfijas jautājumi, RVLI* 13 (Riga, 1961).

Taubenberga, L., "O nekotoryx osobennostjax upravlenija v pamjatnikax russkogo jazyka konca XVII – načala XVIII veka", *RRPI* 5.25-38 (1957).

Tolmačeva, "K voprosu ob oproščenii osnov (oproščenie meždu pristavkoj i kornem v imenax suščestvitel'nyx s glagol'noj osnovoj, ne osložnennyx suffiksami)", *RRPI* 5.127-146 (1957).

——, "Ob obrazovanii i raspade grupp slov so svjazannymi oxnovami", *LUZR* 30.139-157 (1959).

*Trudy Instituta jazykoznanija i literatury Akademii nauk Latvijskoj SSR.* Alternate title of *Latvijas PSR Zinātņu akadēmijas Valodas un literatūras institūta raksti.*

*Učenye zapiski Daugavpilsskogo pedagogičeskogo instituta.* See *Daugavpils Pedagoģiskā institūta raksti.*

Upītis, J., "Andreja Upīša cīņa par latviešu literaro valodu", *Karogs* 5.498-505 (1952).

Važanova, S., "Nekotorye značenija poluznamenatel'nyx poluslužebnyx slov v russkom i latyšskom jazykax", *LUZR* 25.159-184 (1958).
Vecozola, M., "Latviešu un angļu literarās valodas līdzskaņu fonemu sistemas sastatījums", *RRPI* 2.181-218 (1956).
——, "Latviešu un angļu valodas patskaņu fonēmu sistēmas salīdzinājums un metodiski norādījumi angļu patskaņu pareizas izrunas ieviešanai latviešu skolās", *RRPI* 5.177-191 (1957).
——, *Sravnitel'nyj analiz sistem glasnyx fonem latyšskogo i anglijskogo jazykov* (Riga, 1954) (dissertation abstract).
Zemzare, D., "Jaunlatviešu darbs leksikas izveidē", *LZAV* 5.15-24 (1956).
——, "Latyšskaja leksikografija (do 1900 g.)", *LZAV* 9.45-62 (1956).
——, "XVIII gs. leksikografa J. Langes stzīmes par latviešu toponīmiku", *LZAV* 1.23-32 (1957).
——, "Par kādu XVII gs. latviešu vārdnīcas manuskriptu", *LZAV* 1.153-158 (1959).
——, "Piezīmes par dažām latviešu un lietuviešu vārdnīcām", in *Rakstu krājums ... Endzelīnam*, pp. 633-651 (Riga, 1961).
——, "Kāds XVIII gs. krievu-vācu-latviešu-igauņu salīdzināmās vārdnīcas manuskripts", *Leksikoloģijas un leksikografijas jautājumi. RVLI* 13.301-319 (1961).
——, *Latviešu vārdnīcas* (*līdz 1900. gadam*) (Riga, 1961).
——, "Tautas dzejnieka J. Sudrabkalna meistarības kalve", *Padomju Jaunatne* 128 (1954).
——, *Xarakternye osobennosti razvitija latyšskoj leksikografii* (*do 1900 g.*) (Riga, 1956) (dissertation abstract).
——, and Pūķe, M., "Par dažiem Raiņa valodas un stila pētīšanas jautājumiem", *LZAV* 9.27-50 (1954).

# LITHUANIAN

WILLIAM R. SCHMALSTIEG

0. In his article about the achievements of Lithuanian linguistics in the Soviet period, Jonas Palionis says that during the first post World War II years the rate of development of Soviet linguistics was retarded by the lack of trained scientific personnel and the harmful influence of N. Ja. Marr's anti-scientific theory of linguistics.[1] To be sure, some of the most well-known Lithuanian linguists such as Pranas Skardžius, Anthony (Antanas) Salys and Petras Jonikas had left Lithuania, but there still remained some older scholars such as Juozas Balčikonis who had received their training in pre-war years and most of the younger Lithuanian linguists such as E. Mikalauskaitė, Juozas Senkus, Kazys Ulvydas and Jonas Kruopas had training under Salys and Skardžius. The number of linguistic scholars in Lithuania has increased, although it cannot be attributed solely to Soviet auspices, since to a certain extent the Lithuanians are now reaping the fruit of the training of scientific personnel during the years of independence (1918-1940).

But the pernicious influence of Marr's theory is not to be doubted as we can see from the case of Jonas Kruopas who had written his dissertation in accordance with Marr's teaching. When Marr's theory lost favor Kruopas' candidate's degree was revoked; fortunately for Kruopas his degree was restored after he revised his dissertation "according to the demands of Stalinist science".[2] In fact Kazys Ulvydas had even written a book explaining Marr's approach to linguistics, but the book was withdrawn from circulation at the time of the Marrist controversy and to the best of my knowledge no copies are available in the Western world.

Nevertheless Palionis is certainly right in noting the considerable increase in linguistic activity in the decade of the fifties. This activity has been concentrated chiefly in the areas of (1) Lithuanian lexicography, (2) Lithuanian dialectology and (3) descriptive studies of Lithuanian; (4) historical linguistics is less well represented and (5) the number of scientific studies of foreign languages is relatively small.

1. Although in the United States we may consider lexicography to be on the border-

* Here I wish to express my thanks to Dr. Anthony Salys and Dr. Kostas Ostrauskas of the University of Pennsylvania, both of whom gave me much valuable information and lent me books from their personal libraries.

[1] Palionis, "Lietuvių kalbotyros laimėjimai tarybinės santvarkos metais".

[2] *Lithuanian Encyclopedia*, Vol. 13, p. 235 (Boston, 1958).

line of linguistics, the Lithuanians themselves believe that in this area they have done some of their most significant linguistic work. The history of the *Lietuvių kalbos žodynas* (planned as a thesaurus of Lithuanian) is too long and complicated to be recounted here, but it turned out that volume 1 (1941) and 2 (1947) contained some "ideological and factual errors".[3] As a result Juozas Balčikonis was relieved of his post as chief editor and a new set of instructions was prepared. In order that subsequent volumes might be more in line with Soviet practice, Boris Larin, a Russianized Ukrainian with some interest in Baltic languages, was assigned the task of overseeing the dictionary. Although the dictionary is supposed to cover both the spoken and the written language from the 16th century to the present,[4] the more recent volumes seem to stress the contemporary Soviet vocabulary at the expense of the archaic words. By 1960 volume 3 (G-H; 1956), 4 (I-J; 1957) and 5 (K-Klausinys) had been published, volume 6 had been prepared for publication, and volumes 7 and 8 were being written. The card file at that time contained about three million cards.

Some technical and orthographic and a number of bilingual dictionaries have also appeared. Worthy of mention is the long article by Antanas Lyberis and Kazys Ulvydas about the change in Lithuanian vocabulary during the Soviet period.[5] During this time, according to these authors, the Lithuanian language has changed in three directions: 1) many new words and idioms have appeared; 2) many bourgeois words are now only in the passive vocabulary; 3) many words have gained new meanings. Even a new method of word formation has appeared. For example, we now find *vietkomas* as an abbreviation for *vietinis komitetas* "local committee", *partorgas* for *partinis organizatorius* "party organizer". These contractions, of course, are on the pattern of Russ. *mestkom* "local committee", etc.

In general the lexicographic work is good, but it is not distinguished by any particular new theoretical approach.

2. As early as 1950 a start was made on collecting material for the Lithuanian Dialect Atlas, but systematic work was not begun until 1951.[6] The work is being administered by the dialectological specialists of the Institute of Lithuanian Language and Literature of the Lithuanian Academy of Sciences. This organization along with

[3] Ulvydas, chief ed., *Lietuvių kalbos žodynas*, Vol. 3, p. III. There were two versions of volume 2, with two different sets of editors. The second version has deleted the explanations of the abbreviations of the names of emigre scholars and authors, although the abbreviations themselves occur in the text. Place names such as Laz(d)ūnai and Gervėčiai located in White Russian territory are not further identified in order to avoid the chance that Lithuanians might claim territory outside of the borders established by the Soviet state. The text had been almost ready for publication in 1944, although the second volume did not appear until 1947. Upon the publication of this volume the Institute of Lithuanian Language and Literature was severely criticized by A. Sniečkus, the first secretary of the Lithuanian Communist Party.

[4] Kruopas, "Tarybinės lietuvių kalbotyros laimėjimai", *Mokslas Tarybų Lietuvoje*, p. 119.

[5] Lyberis & Ulvydas, "Lietuvių literatūrinės kalbos leksikos praturtėjimas tarybinės santvarkos metais".

[6] Palionis, *op. cit.*, p. 8.

the University of Vilna, the Vilna Pedagogical Institute and other pedagogical institutes, pedagogical schools and teachers' institutes are taking part in the preparation of the atlas. Even in the beginning courses students of Lithuanistics at the University of Vilna begin to gather material about their native dialects.

Plans were originally made to investigate 706 inhabited areas separated from each other by a distance of about 12 kilometers. In 1960 E. Grinaveckienė reported that more than 500 areas in Lithuania and several isolated dialects in White Russian territory had already been investigated.[7] In 1959 alone, dialect material was gathered from 85 points.

In 1954 Juozas Senkus prepared some instructions to aid those taking part in the preparation of the atlas.[8] According to Senkus, linguistic geography, which occupies an important position in the field of dialectology, is to be divided into two parts, viz. (1) the mapping of linguistic phenomena and (2) an explanation of the maps and the phenomena described thereon. A linguistic atlas then is a collection of linguistic maps with various appended commentaries. Senkus criticizes the "bourgeois" linguists of Western Europe, one group of which thought that material could be valuable only if gathered by specialists, whereas another group held exactly the opposite opinion, i.e. that basic material can be gathered by sending questionnaires not to specialists, but to people who know the dialect practically. Senkus finds that neither the first nor the second "extreme" is acceptable to Soviet science. The method of questionnaires is not to be rejected completely, but one should not limit oneself to this, because non-specialists can make grave errors. In Lithuania the gathering of materials is done chiefly by expeditions using well-prepared student linguists.

In dialect studies there are two separate areas of activity, says Senkus, (1) the description of dialects in monographs and (2) a systematic description of the entire Lithuanian language area.

In Senkus' opinion in dialect investigation one may aim at recording and investigating a single dialect or one might try to establish the relationships of dialects among each other, their territorial spread and classification. The Soviet dialectologist must first show the historical basis of the dialect, secondly he must describe the dialect's phonetic system and grammatical norm and thirdly he should show those changes which are currently taking place in the dialect.

According to Senkus, earlier dialectologists either compared the dialects with the literary language or cast about for left-overs of more ancient types of speech. But a comparison with the literary language without a study of the system of the entire dialect may miss many interesting facts and the study of a dialect from the historical point of view alone does not show the differences between productive linguistic procedures and those which are in the process of disappearing. Soviet dialectologists should use a synthesis of these methods.

The transcription used for the atlas has 54 basic signs (16 vowels, 13 diphthongs and

[7] Grinaveckienė, "Tarmių medžiagos rinkimas lietuvių kalbos atlasui".
[8] Senkus, *Lietuvių kalbos atlaso medžiagos rinkimo instrukcija.*

25 consonants) and 15 other signs to denote such items as length, hardness, softness, aspiration, syllabification, stress and pitch. It is based on the Latin alphabet (as used for standard Lithuanian), but also includes a few Greek and Russian letters and some diacritical marks.

The gathering of materials and the preparation of the first volume will be completed during the current seven-year plan.[9] There will be several hundred maps with commentaries and notes.

In spite of the constant references to Soviet science as opposed to "bourgeois" science there is essentially no theoretical approach that might not be found in American or Western European literature on the subject of dialectology.

In addition all Soviet publications omit the fact that Anthony Salys had begun work on a projected dialect atlas and that in 1940 questionnaires had been sent out to get information about the dialects. It was only 10 years later after the rejection of Marr's theory that the work was begun anew. The transcription to be used in the Soviet Lithuanian Dialect Atlas is less accurate than the transcription suggested by the Copenhagen Congress of 1925; before the Soviet occupation this latter transcription had been in common use for scientific work and was to be used in the Lithuanian dialect atlas.

Many dissertations have been written in the field of dialectology and more than forty articles based on (or extracted from) these dissertations have been published in various journals. For example, Vladas Grinaveckis wrote a dissertation about the north-western *dūnininkai* dialects and their phonetic development; Senkus worked on the north-western Kapsai dialect; E. Grinaveckienė did a dialect study of the Mituva river basin and Marija Kindurytė-Sivickienė wrote a dissertation about an isolated Lithuanian dialect in White Russian territory.[10]

Although Senkus talks of the necessity of describing the "system" of the language, these dialect studies do not attain this goal in the structural linguistic sense. Thus the various phonetic (generally the term *phoneme* is not used) and morphological phenomena are regarded as deviations from the norm of the standard language. Let us take, for example, the short article by J. Aleksandravičius in which he discusses the stress and intonation of the dialect of Kretinga (a coastal *dounininkai* dialect).[11] In this article we learn that there are five types of "intonation" in this dialect, viz. short, circumflex, broken, medium and acute, and five types of stress, viz. a basic retracted, a secondary stress, a secondary retracted, a basic stress and a forward shifted stress. I have no reason to doubt the phonetic accuracy of what Aleksandravičius says, but it seems likely that a phonemic analysis would simplify the picture at least to some degree. According to Aleksandravičius the "shifted" stress occurs when after the basic stress there is an originally long syllable or a long syllable which results from the loss of a short vowel in the following syllable (p. 99). From the

[9] Kruopas, *op. cit.*, p. 121.
[10] Palionis, *op. cit.*, p. 9.
[11] Aleksandravičius, "Kirtis ir priegaidė Kretingos tarmėje".

description it appears that the occurrence of the shifted stress can be determined in relationship to that of the basic stress. Therefore it is an allophonic, not a phonemic feature. Likewise the fact that a long syllable may result from the loss of a vowel in the following syllable is interesting historical information, but it is not essential for a descriptive study.

Similar criticism can be made of E. Grinaveckienė's long article on the dialect of the Mituva river basin.[12] In this dialect (p. 130) the vowels are listed as *a, ą, e, ę, ė, i, y, į, o, u, ū, ų*, and we are told that they differ little from the corresponding vowels of standard Lithuanian. In structuralist terms such technique is objectionable because *ū* and *ų* (and *y* and *į* respectively) are merely two different orthographic representations of the same phoneme in standard Lithuanian; the diacritical mark under the *ų* and *į* reflects an etymological nasalization which has been lost in the standard language. Grinaveckienė goes on to say that (1) the vowels *a, e, o* in this dialect can be long or half-long, (2) the vowels corresponding to standard Lithuanian *ą, ę, į, ų* can be either long or short, (3) the vowels *i* or *u* can be either short or half-long, (4) the vowels *ė, y, ū* are always long. In this analysis the dialect form *senis* "old man" contains an *-e-* (from group 1 above) which is phonemically the same as the *-ę-* in *gręšt* "to drill" (group 2 above), but the *-e-* and *-ę-* are listed separately because they have different historical origins. Grinaveckienė is probably right in stating that phonetically there are three degrees of length: long, half-long and short. Although the lack of crucial distributional information would make it difficult to prove, it seems likely that phonemically there are only two degrees of length.

I have given examples of only two articles, but these are typical and it would not be difficult to find deficiencies from the structural point of view in every article on Lithuanian dialectology. In defense of the work one must say that it appears careful and there is much valuable information in all the articles. Thus J. Kardelytė gives a careful analysis of the alternate imperative (the imperative without a cognate form in the standard language) of Eastern Lithuanian dialects.[13] It has been reported that the *u*-stem nom. plur. ending *-aus* actually exists (e.g. *sūnaus* "sons"), although doubt had been cast on the authenticity of this form previously.[14] In the Debeikiai dialect a masc. dat. sing. *vyrai* has been noted (as opposed to standard Lith. *vyrui* "to the husband").[15] In a personal conversation with the author of this article Prof. Anthony Salys said that he thought the *-a-* of the ending *-ai* was a reduced vowel which was probably the regular phonological result of the development of *-u-* of the diphthong *-ui* in this dialect, cf. Georg Gerullis, *Litauische Dialektstudien* (Leipzig, 1930), p. 83. Athematic verbs have been found in many dialects.[16] In the dialect of Laz(d)ūnai the four locative cases, the inessive, illative, adessive and allative have been retained.[17]

12 Grinaveckienė, "Mituvos upyno tarmės fonetika".
13 Kardelytė, "Liepiamosios nuosakos dvejopos formos ir jų vartojimas rytų Lietuvos tarmėse".
14 Sedelskytė, "Debeikių tarmės daiktavardžių linksniavimas".
15 *Op. cit.*, pp. 198-199.
16 Senkus, "Issledovanije litovskix dialektov".
17 Senkus, "Kai kurie Lazūnų tarmės ypatumai".

In the north-western Kapsai dialect an accusative may be used instead of the genitive as the direct object of a negated verb.[18] But, of course, all of this information would be even more valuable if it were analyzed in terms of the dialects concerned.

4. The Lithuanian Academy of Sciences is also preparing a three-volume *Grammar of the Contemporary Lithuanian Literary Language* which is supposed to be finished by 1965.[19] The first two volumes, to be published before 1965, will cover phonetics and morphology. In connection with the eventual publication of this grammar many articles of a descriptive linguistic nature have appeared.

For example, there have been several articles on the "phonemic" system of Lithuanian. In her article on the consonantal phonemes of Lithuanian, V. Vaitkevičiūtė says (I translate): "In contemporary linguistic literature the phoneme is considered to be the phonetic unit which separates the meanings of words and morphemes."[20] One could find fault with this definition, but I doubt that there exists a definition with which everybody is satisfied. The theoretical practice is not original, however, but is chiefly based on the work of the noted Russian scholar, L. V. Ščerba, whose work is constantly quoted. Either Vaitkevičiūtė is unaware of other linguistic approaches or she does not consider them worth mentioning.

In any case Vaitkevičiūtė finds that there are three types of consonants in Lithuanian, soft (*minkštas*), softened (*suminkštintas*) and hard (*kietas*). Both the soft and the hard consonants may occur before non-front vowels, but front vowels may be preceded only by softened consonants; in word final position only hard consonants are found. The degree of palatalization of the softened consonants depends upon the height of the following vowel, i.e. the higher the following vowel the greater the degree of palatalization. In Vaitkevičiūtė's opinion the degree of palatalization is an assimilatory phenomenon; therefore she reasons that the softened consonants are to be classed phonemically with the hard consonants. In doing this she claims to follow Ščerba, who in his analysis of Russian consonants before front vowels finds that the degree of palatalization before the vowel *-e-* is greater than would be necessary for a native speaker of Russian. A Russian could (and does in certain circumstances) pronounce *tè*, *dè*, etc. Therefore in Russian the palatalization of consonants before *-e-* is not of an assimilatory nature and hence phonemic. If I understand Vaitkevičiūtė correctly, her reasoning is thus: in Russian the palatalization of consonants before front vowels is not of an assimilatory nature and is phonemic; in Lithuanian the palatalization of consonants before front vowels is of an assimilatory nature and hence non-phonemic. From this it somehow follows that the consonants before front vowels are to be classed phonemically with the hard consonants. Apparently no regard is taken of the principle of phonetic likeness, a principle used by many American structuralists in determining the phonemes of a language.

[18] Senkus, "Kai kurie ryškesnieji̇̃ linksnių vartojimo atvejai pazanavykio kapsų tarmėje".
[19] Kruopas, *op. cit.*, p. 121.
[20] Vaitkevičiūtė, "Lietuvių literatūrinės kalbos priebalsinių fonemų sudėtis", p. 5.

Vaitkevičiūtė says (p. 8) that before her article there had been no investigation of the question of palatalization from the phonemic point of view. But Trubetzkoy uses Lithuanian (among other languages) to illustrate some of his theories of phonemics. He finds, for example, that the contrast between palatalized (soft) and unpalatalized (hard) consonants is neutralized before front vowels.[21]

Although the term *phoneme* occurs extensively in Vaitkevičiūtė's work, in general her articles appear to be oriented more towards phonetics than what I would call phonemics. Thus her article on the consonantal phonemes is filled with palatograms, photographs of the mouth and profile drawings of the tongue to accompany the description of each phoneme. In her article on Lithuanian vocalic quantity she gives elaborate tables illustrating the features conditioning vocalic length.[22] For example, she finds that vowels in open syllables are longer than those in closed syllables; vowels with the rising "intonation" are longer than those with the falling "intonation", etc. But she calls all diphthongs phonemes; there is a heading "phoneme *-ei-*", although this diphthong can easily be analyzed as two phonemes. Compare the following words: (nom. plur.) *geniaĩ* /ǵeńeĩ/ "wood-peckers", (nom. plur.) *geiniaĩ* /ǵeińeĩ/ "devices to aid bee-keepers climb trees" (cf. Russ. *žen'*) and *gineĩ* /ǵińeĩ/ "you (sing.) chased". Therefore I would consider it incorrect, at least in some cases, to label all Lithuanian diphthongs as single phonemes.

Likewise Vaitkevičiūtė uses the term *morpheme*, but not in the same sense that Americans would use it. In the words *kurpė* "shoe" and *kurpius* "shoe-maker" she talks of the morpheme *kur*, but on descriptive grounds there seems to be no reason for making such a morphemic cut in these words; the root morpheme is *kurp-*.[23]

An important contribution to Lithuanian phonology is Adelė Laigonaitė's article about Lithuanian pitch and stress.[24] She has tried to show experimentally that relative musical pitch does not furnish the basis for distinguishing the so-called circumflex and acute "intonations" of Lithuanian. Rather it is the relative amplitude of the first part of the syllable (for the acute) or of the second part of the syllable (for the circumflex). Unfortunately the work is difficult to evaluate because it was done in a motion picture studio rather than in a phonetics laboratory. Laigonaitė has also published a book of normative nature about the accentuation of Lithuanian.[25] Contrary to the teaching of many of the grammars of the "bourgeois period" she recommends that the masc. nom. sing. and plur. of the present active participle be end-stressed in all verbs (p. 81). It might be noted, however, that even some of the grammarians of the "bourgeois period" (e.g. in P. Klimas' school reader) recommend the same thing. A. Senn discusses the problem of this participle in his *Kleine litauische Sprachlehre* (Heidelberg, 1929), p. 206.

[21] *Principes de phonologie*, p. 249, i.e. Cantineau's translation of *Grundzüge der Phonologie* = *TCLP* 8.

[22] Vaitkevičiūtė, "Lietuvių kalbos balsių ir dvibalsių ilgumas arba kiekybė".

[23] "Lietuvių literatūrinės kalbos priebalsinių...", p. 7.

[24] Laigonaitė, "Dėl lietuvių kalbos kirčio ir priegaidės supratimo".

[25] *Literatūrinės lietuvių kalbos kirčiavimas.*

In connection with the projected grammar a book of normative articles about Lithuanian has recently been published.[26] Lithuanian morphology is represented by an article on the gender of Lithuanian nouns and one on nominal composition. Jonas Paulauskas in an article based on his dissertation on the verbal prefixes of Lithuanian finds that each verbal prefix has one, two or three primary meanings, which, for the most part, correspond in meaning to the cognate preposition.[27] Generally there are more secondary meanings than primary and several prefixes may have the same secondary meaning. A. Valeckienė has written on the formation and the use of adjectives in Lithuanian.[28] Adelė Laigonaitė has published a semantic classification of the various uses of the inessive and the illative cases in Lithuanian.[29] An article by Tamara Buchienė on the use of the Lithuanian preterit has appeared[30] and Leonardas Drotvinas has written about some characteristics of the Lithuanian conditional constructions.[31] Mention should also be made of J. Žukauskaitė's article about the conjunction *jog* "that" in Lithuanian.[32]

If stylistics is to be included as a linguistic discipline, then the name of J. Pikčilingis, author of a number of articles in this field, must be included.[33] In Pikčilingis' opinion brevity (among other things) is a stylistic characteristic to be sought after and he concludes one article with a Lithuanian translation of Hamlet's soliloquy, in the words of Pikčilingis "a masterful example of brevity".[34]

In 1961 a new journal, *Kalbos kultura* "Language culture", was initiated by the Lithuanian Academy of Sciences; the aim of this journal is to publish notes and articles of a normative nature.[35] From 1933 to 1940 the journal *Gimtoji kalba* "Native language" had performed a similar function, but its publication ceased after the Soviet occupation.

5. Characteristic of historical linguistic studies in Lithuania is concentration in the field of Balto-Slavic linguistics. Vincas Mykolaitis edited a volume entitled *Senoji lietuviška knyga* (on the occasion of the 400th anniversary of the first printed book in Lithuanian); this contains articles by various authors on literary and linguistic aspects of Mažvydas' Catechism (1547).[36] Daniel Klein's *Grammatica Litvanica* (1653) and his *Compendium Litvanico-Germanicum* (1654) have been published with an introduc-

[26] Kazlauskas, Laigonaitė, & Urbutis, eds., *Dabartinė lietuvių kalba.*
[27] Paulauskas, "Veiksmažodžių priešdėlių funkcijos dabartinėje literatūrinėje lietuvių kalboje".
[28] Valeckienė, "Kai kurie lietuvių kalbos būdvardžių darybos klausimai", and "Dabartinės lietuvių kalbos įvardžiuotinių būdvardžių vartojimas".
[29] Laigonaitė, *Vietininkų reikšmė ir vartosena dabartinėje lietuvių kalboje.*
[30] Buchienė, "Būtojo kartinio laiko vartojimas lietuvių literatūrinėje kalboje".
[31] Drotvinas, "Kai kurios lietuvių kalbos sąlygos konstrukcijų ypatybės".
[32] Žukauskaitė, "Lietuvių literatūrinės kalbos jungtukas *jog*".
[33] Pikčilingis, "Žodžio ir vaizdo ryšių klausimu".
[34] "Kalbos glaustumas", *Dabartinė lietuvių kalba*, p. 63.
[35] Ulvydas, chief ed., *Kalbos kultura* 1.3-4 (1961).
[36] *Senoji lietuviška knyga* (Vilna, 1947).

tion (by Tamara Buchienė and Jonas Palionis), a Lithuanian translation (by K. Eigminas) and an explanation of Klein's terminology and several indices.[37]

A Lithuanian translation of Jan Endzelin's book, *The Sounds and Forms of the Baltic Languages* was published in 1957.[38] At the end of the Latvian original there are some remarks by Boris Larin apologizing for Endzelin's adherence to the "laws of classical Indo-European linguistics", but these remarks are missing from the Lithuanian translation.[39] In the Latvian original Endzelin was being censured for not believing in Marr's theories, but by the time the Lithuanian translation was made Marr's theories had been rejected and Larin's criticism was no longer considered necessary.

Selected works of Kazimieras Būga and Jonas Jablonskis have been republished.[40] Many of the republished articles had been out of print for years. The work of Antanas Baranauskas and Kazimieras Jaunius is also being investigated.[41]

Zigmas Zinkevičius' history of the definite adjective in Lithuanian is a valuable collection of facts.[42] In the back of the book one finds statistics on the frequency of occurrence of the definite adjective in the works of several old and one modern Lithuanian author. Because of the relative independence of the position of the pronoun and various features of accentuation Zinkevičius comes to the conclusion that in Common Baltic the union of the pronoun with the adjective (to form the definite adjective) had not yet been completed. Rather it took place separately in the various Baltic languages.

A monograph on K. Širvydas' *Dictionarium trium linguarum* is being prepared for publication,[43] and one on Juška's Lithuanian dictionary (*Litovskij slovar' A. Juškeviča s tolkovaniem slov na russkom i pol'skom jazykax*) has been published.[44]

As in other fields dissertations have furnished the basis of many articles. Jonas Kazlauskas, whose dissertation was a study of the simplification of the Lithuanian declensional system, has written a number of articles on this subject, cf. for example, his article on the transfer of *i*-stem nouns into the *i̯o*-stem class.[45] The dative and instrumental "absolute" constructions in Lithuanian writings of the 16th and 17th centuries have been the subject of a number of articles by Vytautas Ambrazas.[46] A competent contemporary expert in the etymology of Lithuanian plant names is Albinas Sabaliauskas, who has published a large number of articles about this, the subject of his dissertation.[47] Kazys Ulvydas in articles from his dissertation about the

[37] Balčikonis, Larin, & Kruopas, eds., *Pirmoji lietuvių kalbos gramatika*.
[38] *Baltų kalbų garsai ir formos*. W. R. Schmalstieg and A. Salys are currently preparing an annotated English translation of this book.
[39] *Baltu valodu skaņas un formas*, p. 256C (Riga, 1948).
[40] Būga, *Rinktiniai raštai*, 3 vols; Jablonskis, *Rinktiniai raštai*, 2 vols.
[41] Kruopas, *op. cit.*, p. 123.
[42] Zinkevičius, *Lietuvių kalbos įvardžiuotinių būdvardžių istorijos bruožai.*
[43] Kruopas, *op. cit.*, p. 120.
[44] Tolutienė, "Antanas Juška leksikografas".
[45] Kazlauskas, "*I*-linksniavimo daiktavardžių perėjimas į *io*-linksniavimą". For other articles see bibliography.
[46] Cf. bibliography under Ambrazas.
[47] Cf. bibliography under Sabaliauskas.

adverbs of contemporary Lithuanian, has shown that constructions in the instrumental case passed to adverbs most easily, whereas the nominative and the accusative show the least tendency in that direction.[48]

Most of the younger Lithuanian scholars have received their degrees at the University of Vilna, but Vytautas Mažiulis received his at the University of Moscow, where he wrote his dissertation on the relationship of the Baltic numerals to the numerals of the other Indo-European languages. In the article based on his dissertation Mažiulis concludes (1) that there is no single archetype for the numeral "one" in the Indo-European languages, (2) that the decades (20-90) were only compound words, the initial components of which were 2-9 and the final component of which was **dek̑m̥t-* and (3) that the word for "hundred" was originally **dek̑m̥ dek̑m̥t*(*e*)*ə*$_2$, i.e. "ten tens".[49] To avoid alliterative repetition it was replaced by a single word (nomen collectivum) **dek̑m̥teə*$_2$ which underwent the following changes: **dek̑m̥tā* > **dk̑m̥tā* > **tk̑m̥tā* > **k̑m̥tā*. This latter form was used in the numbers 200, 300, etc. where the *-ā* was analyzed as a neuter nominative plural and hence the singular was reformed as **k̑m̥tom*.

In Mažiulis' recent contribution to the IVth International Congress of Slavists in Moscow he proposes several interesting solutions to the problem of the apparently aberrent root vocalism of Baltic and Slavic **dōtei* "to give" and **dētei* "to put".[50] He also discusses the reflexive particle *-si-*, the numerals and the genitive ending *-ā*. At the very end (p. 20) he rejects the necessity of establishing a Balto-Slavic proto-language or any special type of Balto-Slavic unity. It is difficult to see how the substance of his paper either supports (or for that matter refutes) his conclusion. This view of Mažiulis (and A. Senn, Antoine Meillet, etc.) is unpopular in the Soviet Union, because he was the only one to defend this opinion at the Congress.[51]

The work of the Sanskritist, Ričardas Mironas, is mentioned here only because he is one of the few to tackle problems of Indo-European phonology.[52] Mironas is familiar with the "laryngeal theory" and the work of Benveniste and Kuryłowicz, but I doubt that he has understood any of this very well. Mironas believes in the primordiality of a three vowel system (viz. *a*, *i*, *u*) which we find in Akkadian and (in his opinion) in Sanskrit. In fairness to Mironas I should point out that he realizes that Skt. *a* represents Indo-European **e*, **o*, **a*; but then he does not explain the status of Skt. *e* < **ai* or *o* < **au*. As we know, the laryngeal theory states that the Indo-European vowel **e* was split into *e*, *o* and *a* with the concomitant loss of a neighboring laryngeal. In the light of the primordiality of the system *a*, *i*, *u*, Mironas asks how there could have been an original Indo-European *e*? Passing to the consonantal system Mironas finds that the easiest sounds to pronounce are *b*, *d*, *g*;

[48] Palionis, *op. cit.*, p. 10; Ulvydas, "Vienaskaitos naudininko prieveiksmėjimas ir prieveiksmiai su formantais -(*i*)*ui*, *-i* lietuvių kalboje", *Kai kurie lietuvių kalbos gramatikos klausimai*, pp. 115-169.

[49] Mažiulis, "Indoevropejskaja decimal'naja sistema čislitel'nyx".

[50] Mažiulis, *Zametki k voprosu o drevenejšix otnošenijax baltijskix i slavjanskix jazykov*.

[51] Illič-Svityč, "Balto-slavjanskaja problematika na IV meždunarodnom s"ezde slavistov".

[52] Mironas, "Pastabos indoeuropiečių fonologinės sistemos kilmės klausimu".

hence these furnish the basis for the system of explosive consonants. He then says (p. 237; I translate): "Since primitive man had good health it was not at all difficult for him to pronounce the corresponding voiceless consonants which require a stronger air stream". Structural linguists are uneasy about defining "primitive man" and his speech habits. In addition Mironas misunderstands the phonemic (rather than the phonetic) nature of the symbol *e* used in various works on Indo-European phonology. On the other hand Mironas' statement that the *Lautverschiebung* of the Germanic languages did not basically touch the Indo-European consonantal system (p. 238) could be interpreted as a structural statement. Likewise Mironas' conclusion (p. 239) that the human articulatory organs must determine the phonological system of the language is true (at least in some sense), although perhaps banal.

In this section it is possibly appropriate to mention that the Lithuanian Academy of Sciences has undertaken the study of onomastics and material on personal and place names is now being gathered and checked.[53] Before the war a dictionary of names was prepared and after the war it was announced that this collection would be published, but for unknown reasons it never materialized.

6. Articles on the teaching of foreign languages are common, but scientific articles in this field are rare. I have seen a few scientific articles on French, German and English; this latter language is given more consideration than any other Western European language.[54] In the articles on English with one or two exceptions there are no references to British or American scholarly publications. Mostly the authors of these articles rely on various dictionaries and examples of usage from such Soviet favorites as Charles Dickens, A. J. Cronin, Theodore Dreiser, etc. to support their conclusions. A good contrastive study of (British) English and Lithuanian consonantal phonemes was prepared for Lithuanian students studying English, although it could be used to advantage by English-speaking students studying Lithuanian.[55] But I wonder whether an Englishman would hear the Lithuanian unaspirated /p/ as an English /b/, as the author states (p. 174). As a native speaker of American English, I never hear a Lithuanian /p/ as an English /b/.

7. Conclusion: Although a great deal of work has been done in linguistics in Lithuania, it has rather a parochial aspect. Interest is centered on problems of Lithuanian linguistics; inasmuch as a theoretical approach is necessary it is borrowed from the Russians. But I have not seen a single scholarly publication devoted to such

[53] Kruopas, *op. cit.*, p. 124.

[54] Meiksinaitė, "Die attributive Funktion des Infinitivs im Neuhochdeutschen"; Kameneckaitė, "Paprastų (nemetaforinių) veiksmažodinių frazeologinių junginių sinonimika dabartinėje anglų kalboje"; Levinaitė-Vengerova, "Priklausomiejī dalyviniai junginiai dabartinėje anglų kalboje"; Širvinskaite, "Veiksmažodinių frazeologinių tipo *to make & daiktavardas* junginių ir vienažodinio veiksmažodžio semantiniai santykiai"; Pareigytė, "Priesagos *-ment* anglų kalboje atsiradimo klausimu". All of vol. 9 of the *Mokslo darbai* of the Vilna Pedagogical Institute (1960) is devoted to articles (15 in all) which are semi-scientific, semi-pedagogical in nature.

[55] Aprijaskytė-Valdšteinienė, "Anglų ir lietuvių kalbų priebalsių lyginimas".

general linguistic topics as phonemics, morphemics or syntax. Perhaps the short article by B. Piesarskas about grammatical categories is an exception; but such weak conclusions as: "Grammatical categories are a union of grammatical meaning and grammatical form" (p. 13) would lead me to class this as a pedagogical rather than a scientific article.[56]

Although some Lithuanian scholars talk of the "system" of the language, they do not understand this system in the same way that any American structuralist would. By American standards most of the work would be found deficient and would have to be reanalyzed in terms of minimal contrastive units and the automatic occurrence of various entities. But, using the current standards of Soviet Lithuania, one must judge the work to be of good quality.

## LITHUANIAN BIBLIOGRAPHY

Aleksandravičius, J., "Kirtis ir priegaidė Kretingos tarmėje", *LKK* 1.97-107 (1957).

Ambrazas, Vytautas, "Absoliutinis naudininkas su dalyviu XVI-XVII aa. lietuvių kalbos paminkluose", *LMAD Serija A* 2/5.147-164 (1958).

——, "Dėl absoliutinio naudininko ir atitinkamų šalutinių sakinių vartosenos XVI-XVII aa. lietuvių kalbos paminkluose", *LMAD Serija A* 1/6.217-232 (1959).

——, "Dėl vadinamojo 'absoliutinio inagininko' XVI-XVII a. lietuvių kalbos paminkluose", *LKK* 2.47-53 (1959).

Aprijaskytė-Valdšteinienė, R., "Anglų ir lietuvių kalbų priebalsių lyginimas", *Kalbotyra* 2.167-185 (1960).

Balčikonis, Juozas, chief ed., *Lietuvių kalbos žodynas*. Vol. 1 (Vilna, 1941). Cf. Kazys Ulvydas and fn. 4 of this article.

——, Boris Larin and Jonas Kruopas (eds.), *Pirmoji lietuvių kalbos gramatika* (Vilna, 1957).

Buchienė, T., "Būtojo kartinio laiko vartojimas lietuvių literatūrinėje kalboje", *LMAD Serija A*. 2/3.219-228 (1957).

Būga, Kazimieras, *Rinktiniai raštai*, 3 vols. (Vilna, 1958).

Drotvinas, Leonardas, "Kai kurios lietuviu kalbos sąlygos konstrukcijų ypatybės", *Kalbotyra* 2.53-58 (1960).

Endzelins, Janis, *Baltu valodu skaņas un formas* (Riga, 1948). The Lithuanian translation is entitled *Baltų kalbų garsai ir formos* (Vilna, 1957).

Grinaveckienė, E., "Tarmių medžiagos rinkimas lietuvių kalbos atlasui", *LKK* 3.191-205 (1960).

——, "Mituvos upyno tarmės fonetika", *LKK* 1.119-180 (1957).

Illič-Svityč, V. M., "Balto-slavjanskaja problematika na IV meždunarodnom s"ezde slavistov", *VJa* 8/1.139-141 (1959).

[56] Piesarskas, "Apie gramatines kategorijas".

Kardelytė, J., "Liepiamosios nuosakos dvejopos formos ir jų vartojimas rytų Lietuvos tarmėse", *LKK* 1.181-188 (1957).

Jablonskis, Jonas, *Rinktiniai raštai*, 2 vols. (Vilna, 1957).

Kameneckaitė, N., "Paprastų (nemetaforinių) veiksmažodinių frazeologinių junginių sinonimika dabartinėje anglų kalboje", *Kalbotyra* 1.185-202 (1958).

Kazlauskas, Jonas, "*I*-linksniavimo daiktavardžių perėjimas į *io*-linksniavimą". *Kalbotyra* 1.33-50 (1958).

——, "Iš priebalsinio linksniavimo istorijos", *Kalbotyra* 3.61-71 (1961).

——, "Lietuvių kalbos *i*-kamieno daiktavardžių vienaskaitos įnagininko ir vietininko formų kilmės klausimu", *Kalbotyra* 1.51-69 (1958).

——, "Šakninių vardažodžių nykimas", *Kalbotyra* 3.73-78 (1961).

——, Adelė Laigonaitė and Vincas Urbutis (eds.), *Dabartinė lietuvių kalba* (Vilna, 1961).

Kruopas, Jonas, "Tarybinės lietuvių kalbotyros laimėjimai", *Mokslas Tarybų Lietuvoje*, pp. 118-126 (Vilna, 1961).

Laigonaitė, Adelė, *Vietininkų reikšmė ir vartosena dabartinėje lietuvių kalboje* (Vilna, 1957).

——, "Dėl lietuvių kalbos kirčio ir priegaidės supratimo", *Kalbotyra* 1.71-100 (1958).

——, *Literatūrinės lietuvių kalbos kirčiavimas* (Vilna, 1959).

Levinaitė-Vengerova, S., "Priklausomieji dalyviniai junginiai dabartinėje anglų kalboje", *Kalbotyra* 1.203-214 (1958).

Lyberis, Antanas and Kazys Ulvydas, "Lietuvių literatūrinės kalbos leksikos praturtėjimas tarybinės santvarkos metais", *LK* 3.31-110 (1958).

Mažiulis, Vytautas, "Indoevropejskaja decimal'naja sistema čislitel'nyx", *VJa* 5/4.53-59 (1956).

——, *Zametki k voprosu o drevnejšix otnošenijax baltijskix i slavjanskix jazykov* (Vilna, 1958).

Meikšinaitė, I., "Die attributive Funktion des Infinitivs im Neuhochdeutschen", *Kalbotyra* 3.191-205 (1961).

Mironas, R., "Pastabos indoeuropiečių fonologinės sistemos kilmės", *Kalbotyra* 3.191-205 (1961).

Mykolaitis, V. (ed.), *Senoji lietuviška knyga* (Vilna, 1947).

Paulauskas, Jonas, "Veiksmažodžių priešdėlių funkcijos dabartinėje literatūrinėje lietuvių kalboje", *LK* 3.301-453 (1958).

Palionis, Jonas, "Lietuvių kalbotyros laimėjimai tarybinės santvarkos metais", *Kalbotyra* 1.5-20 (1958).

Pareigytė, J., "Priesagos *-ment* anglų kalboje atsiradimo klausimu", *Kalbotyra* 2.157-166 (1960).

Piesarskas, B., "Apie gramatines kategorijas", *Vilniaus valstybinis pedagoginis institutas, Mokslo darbai* 9.5-15 (1960).

Pikčilingis, Juozas, "Kalbos glaustumas", *Dabartinė lietuvių kalba*, pp. 23-64 (Vilna, 1961).

——, "Žodžio ir vaizdo ryšių klausimu", *Pergalė* 10.99-103 (1956).

Sabaliauskas, Albinas, "Baltų kalbų žemės ūkio augalų pavadinimų kilmės klausimu", *LK* 3.454-461 (1958).

——, "Dėl kai kurių baltų kalbų augalų pavadinimų kilmės", *LKK* 2.65-74 (1959).

——, "Dėl kai kurių baltų kalbų žemės ūkio pavadinimų kilmės", *LKK* 3.257-268 (1960).

——, "Dėl kanapės pavadinimo", *LMAD Serija A* 2/3.199-210 (1957).

Sedelskytė, O., "Debeikių tarmės daiktavardžių linksiavimas", *LMAD Serija A* 1/4.195-208 (1958).

Senkus, Juozas, "Issledovanije litovskix dialektov", *VJa* 6/5.98-100 (1957).

——, "Kai kurie Lazūnų tarmės ypatumai", *LMAD Serija A* 1/4.183-194 (1958).

——, "Kai kurie ryškesnieji linksnių vartojimo atvejai pazanavykio kapsų tarmėje", *LMAD Serija A*, 2/7.177-189 (1959).

——, *Lietuvių kalbos atlaso medžiagos rinkimo instrukcija* (Vilna, 1954).

Skardžius, Pranas, "Kalbotyrinis darbas Lietuvoje", *Aidai* 3.111-116; 4.156-162 (1962).

——, "Tarybinė kalbotyra Lietuvoje", *Aidai* 10.444-451 (1958).

Širvinskaitė, D., "Veiksmažodinių frazeologinių tipo *to make* & daiktavardis junginių ir vienažodinio veiksmažodžio semantiniai santykiai", *Kalbotyra* 3.220-234 (1961).

Tolutienė, Birutė, "Antanas Juška leksikografas", *LK* 5.87-377 (1961).

Ulvydas, Kazys (ed.), *Kalbos kultūra* 1.3-4 (1961).

——, chief ed., *Lietuvių kalbos žodynas*, Vol. 2 (1947); Vol. 3 (1956); Vol. 4 (1957). Cf. Balčikonis, Juozas.

——, "Vienaskaitos naudininko prieveiksmėjimas ir prieveiksmiai su formantais -(*i*)*ui*, -*i* lietuvių kalboje", *Kai kurie lietuvių kalbos gramatikos klausimai*, pp. 115-169 (Vilna, 1957).

Vaitkevičiūtė, V., "Lietuvių kalbos balsių ir dvibalsių ilgumas arba kiekybė", *LKK* 3.207-217 (1960).

——, "Lietuvių literatūrinės kalbos priebalsinių fonemų sudėtis", *LKK* 1.5-66 (1957).

Valeckienė, A., "Dabartinės lietuvių kalbos įvardžiuotinių būdvardžių vartojimas", *LK* 2.161-328 (1957).

——, "Kai kurie lietuvių kalbos būdvardžių darybos klausimai", *LK Serija A* 2/5.179-182 (1958).

Zinkevičius, Zigmas, *Lietuvių kalbos įvardžiuotinių būdvardžių istorijos bruožai* (Vilna, 1957).

Žukauskaite, J., "Lietuvių literatūrinės kalbos jungtukas *jog*", *Kalbotyra* 2.33-52 (1960).

# ALTAIC

NICHOLAS POPPE

## 1

Altaic linguistics in the Soviet Union have a long tradition going back to the middle of the 19th century which produced such great Russian scholars as Böhtlingk and Radloff in the field of Turcology, and Bobrovnikov and Pozdneev in the field of Mongolian studies. During the Soviet period, Altaic linguistics have been developing along the same lines as Soviet linguistics in general. Prior to 1950, Altaic linguistics were influenced by Marr's theories, and Altaicists either based their research completely on the principles of his so-called "New Theory of Language" or at least paid lip-service to it.[1] When Marr's theories were denounced by Stalin, whose statements on the nature of speech and the tasks of linguistics became the official blueprint for linguistic research,[2] some former adherents to Marr's theories were publicly condemned,[3] others recanted, not waiting for criticism by other persons.[4] After that, a new period began, the period of Stalin's linguistics: the Altaicists, among them the former Marrists, started exalting Stalin's linguistic genius. Thus, the Mongolist Sanžeev published an article on the interrelationship of language and dialect on the basis of Stalin's doctrine,[5] another article on Mongolian languages and dialects,[6] a general survey of Mongolian linguistics in the USSR,[7] etc. Other Altaicists were much more moderate in showing their attitudes towards the change in the linguistic field and confined themselves to saying a few words of praise of Stalin in the prefaces to their

[1] Discussion of these principles would lead the readers too far away from the subject of this article. A good analysis of Marr's theories is found in Thomas, *The Linguistic Theories of N. Ya. Marr*. As examples of works on Altaic languages based on Marr's linguistics the author may quote: Sanžeev, *Grammatika burjat-mongol'skogo jazyka*; Avrorin, *Očerki po sintaksisu nanajskogo jazyka, prjamoe dopolnenie*; Sunik, *Očerki po sintaksisu tungusoman'čžurskix jazykov, Possessivnyj stroj predloženija.*

[2] Stalin, *Marksizm i voprosy jazykoznanija*; Serebrennikov, *Trudy I. V. Stalina po voprosam jazykoznanija i ix značenie*; *Materialy ob"edinennoj naučnoj sessii, posvjaščennoj trudam I. V. Stalina po jazykoznaniju*, etc.

[3] E.g. Meščaninov, cf. *Materialy ob"edinennoj naučnoj sessii*, p. 156.

[4] E.g. Avrorin, *Ob ošibkax v osveščenii nekotoryx voprosov grammatičeskogo stroja nanajskogo jazyka*, p. 107 f.

[5] Sanžeev, "Jazyk i dialect v svete trudov I. V. Stalina".

[6] Sanžeev, "Mongol'skie jazyki i dialekty". See the critical review by the author of these lines in *HJAS* 17.295-304 (1954).

[7] Sanžeev, "Mongol'skoe jazykoznanie v SSSR".

works, otherwise dealing with their material in their own traditional way. Thus, in the preface to his work on the Karakalpak language, Baskakov repeated what Stalin had said about the nature of dialects,[8] but it is hard to discover any influence of Stalin's utterances in the work itself. The same can be said about Todaeva's Mongolian grammar which, although it contains high praise of Stalin's theories and some statements directed against Marr,[9] otherwise represents a typical old-fashioned grammar of Khalkha-Mongolian.

When the present period of de-Stalinization began, nothing particular happened except that Stalin's name was no longer mentioned. Otherwise, works on Altaic linguistics remained more or less the same as those of authors who had confined themselves to a few words about the importance of Marr's or Stalin's theories, depending on the political situation at the time in question.

To conclude this section, the author of these lines would like to underscore that praise of Marr or Stalin had never been obligatory, and refraining from it had never been punishable. It was up to the authors to express their devotion to Marr or Stalin, depending on the period concerned. A large number of scholars took refuge in this method of self-protection by demonstrating their loyalty; on the other hand, one could quote many authors who never even mentioned Marr or Stalin in their works,[10] and, nevertheless, preserving their scholarly dignity and decency, were never arrested or deported.

## 2

Proceeding to the subject of this article, the author of these lines will commence with problems of phonetics and phonology.

Russian linguists have been familiar with the concept of the phoneme for a long time, namely, since Baudouin de Courtenay. Works on the Altaic languages are not different in this aspect from works on other languages. There has been for a long time a tendency to discuss phonemes and not just "sounds" of the languages in question, and all Altaicists use the term "phoneme". However, it should be pointed out that some authors do not know what a phoneme is. Thus, Sanžeev speaks of phonemes but in rather confusing terms. In his work on Khalkha-Mongolian, he says that the vowels are classified into back, middle, and front vowels, this being a physiological classification. From the phonemic point of view, however, these vowels should be divided, as he says, into male, female, and neutral vowels, as they are classified from

[8] Baskakov, *Karakalpakskij jazyk*, I, p. 3.

[9] Todaeva, *Grammatika sovremennogo mongol'skogo jazyka*, p. 1.

[10] Here is a random selection of titles of books which appeared between 1929 and 1951: Vladimircov, *Sravnitel'naja grammatika mongol'skogo pis'mennogo jazyka i xalxaskogo narečija* (1929), published at the peak of Marr's philippics against the "bourgeois" comparative method; Burdukov, *Russko-mongol'skij slovar' razgovornogo jazyka* (1935); Dyrenkova, *Grammatika ojrotskogo jazyka* (1940); Dmitriev, *Grammatika baškirskogo jazyka* (1948); Dmitriev, Axmerov, Baišev, eds., *Russko-baškirskij slovar'* (1948); Malov, *Pamjatniki drevnetjurkskoj pišmennosti* (1951).

the point of view of vowel-harmony.[11] It should be remarked that such a classification is by no means a phonemic one, since phonemics has nothing to do with vowel-harmony, which is a morpho-phonemic feature. Phonemically speaking, /i/ is simply not in the opposition of front *versus* back, whereas all the other vowels belong to two contrastive series of back vowel-phonemes *versus* front vowel-phonemes.

Sanžeev's pupil Todaeva has as vague an idea about phonemes as her teacher. Speaking about Khalkha-Mongolian phonemes, she mentions 14 vowel-phonemes, one of which is ы /ï/.[12] In reality, ы is used in official orthography to render the long vowel [ī] which does not palatalize the preceding consonant. This long [ī] originates from the suffix-vowel /ii/ added either to the stem-final consonant or to a stem-final vowel other than /i/: гарыг /gariig/: /gar/ "hand" + /-iig/ accusative-suffix; олзыг [olʒīg]: /olʒo/ "profit" + /-iig/ accusative-suffix.[13] It is by no means a phoneme but a graphical element rendering an allophone, and ы is phonemically unjustified. By the way, Todaeva should have paid attention to the fact that ы never occurs initially or in the first syllable of a word and appears only there where a suffix-vowel joins a stem.

Speaking about phonemes, Todaeva and some other authors do not make a clear distinction between phonemes and allophones. Thus, in her most recent work on the "Tung-hsiang language", i.e. Santa, Todaeva does not even use the term *phoneme* and speaks only about "sounds", making no distinction between phonemes and allophones. To give only one example, quote her statement that [f] occurs initially and only before [u], whereas in other positions only initial [x] and [h] occur.[14] It is obvious that there is a phoneme /h/ which in some positions is realized as [x] and in other positions as [f]. In another work of hers, Todaeva does speak about phonemes,[15] but when she arrives at the Santa language she changes again to the term "sounds" and regards [f, x, h] as three different and independent consonants,[16] which is correct if we regard them as three allophones but incorrect when phonemes are under discussion.

How far misconceptions about phonemes go is demonstrated in Amogolonov's Buriat grammar in which reproductions of "palatograms of phonemes /n, l, r/", etc., are given.[17] It is obvious that Amogolonov meant palatograms showing the articulations of certain allophones of the phonemes concerned.

Recent Soviet works on Turkic languages are much superior to those on Mongolian, the reason being that there are linguistically trained Turcologists. Of course, there are some exceptions, but in general, Turkic languages are studied in a more

[11] Sanžeev, *Sovremennyj mongol'skij jazyk*. The terms "male", "female", and "neutral" (lit. "hermaphrodite") are ancient Mongolian terms. "Male" is a back vowel, "female" is a front vowel, and /i/ is a "hermaphrodite".
[12] *Op. cit.*, p. 13.
[13] Austin states correctly that there is no reason for using ы: Austin, *Mongol Reader*, p. 2.
[14] Todaeva, *Dunsjanskij jazyk*, pp. 12-13.
[15] Todaeva, *Mongol'skie jazyki i dialekty Kitaja*, p. 23.
[16] *Op. cit.*, p. 90.
[17] Amogolonov, *Sovremennyj burjatskij jazyk*, p. 33 f.

satisfactory manner. To mention first a book which leaves much to be desired, the "Turkish Phonetics" by Sevortjan should be quoted.[18] Although Sevortjan sometimes uses the term *phoneme* (e.g., p. 9) and Chapter II of his work bears the title "Phonemes and their pronunciation", his approach is neither phonemic nor phonetic. When discussing individual phonemes (or allophones) he gives only such definitions as "the vowel *a* is close to Russian *a*"; "the vowel *e* under stress is close to Russian э"; "the consonants *b, d, f, j, m, n, s, š, v, z* are, in general, pronounced as the Russian б, д, ф, ж, м, н, с, ш, в, з respectively".[19] Consequently, this book is not a phonemic or phonetic description but an instruction with regard to how to read Turkish words and what sounds of the Russian language are to be substituted for what is rendered by this or that letter of the Turkish Romanized alphabet.

However, there are descriptions both phonological and phonetic. Thus Baskakov speaks about Karakalpak phonemes and gives his definition of a phoneme as a meaningful unit of speech, i.e., a unit whose function is semantical differentiation, which is part of the system of language sounds in their mutual oppositions and correlations.[20] Leaving aside the question of whether this definition is correct and exhaustive, and whether it is what is called a phoneme by different schools of thought in American linguistics, the author wishes to point out that a serious objection can be made to Baskakov's division of the vowel phonemes into "basic" and "those which appeared at a later time", because the establishment of phonemes existing in a language has nothing to do with the history of a language. These "more recent" vowel phonemes include [ii] and [uu].[21] In reality these represent /iy/ and /uw/ respectively, although /iy/ is a substitute for Russian /i/, and /uw/ is a substitute for Russian /u/. Therefore, there is no reason to establish the phonemes /ii, uu/. It should be also remarked that Baskakov does not use a phonemic transcription but the official Cyrillic alphabet with all its oddities such as гъ for /G/, нъ for /ŋ/, ю for /ü/, etc.

A very confusing book is the Tatar grammar of Gazizov, in which phonemes are confused with their allophones and even with Russian letters[22] and in which a "long vowel" ый is mentioned,[23] which is not a vowel phoneme at all, but the combination of phonemes /ïy/ [ə̂y], i.e., /ï/ + semi-vowel /y/. If ый were a phoneme, ай, ой, etc., should be also regarded as phonemes, although they are not. Gazizov was obviously influenced by the orthography and the Russian alphabet which is unsuitable for the rendition of phonemes of Turkic languages or any language in general.

However, there are good phonological descriptions of Turkic languages, e.g., Kononov's description of Turkish[24] and Uzbek[25] phonemes. An excellent phonemic

[18] Sevortjan, *Fonetika tureckogo literaturnogo jazyka.*
[19] *Op. cit.*, pp. 23-25.
[20] Baskakov, *op. cit.*, II, p. 25.
[21] *Op. cit.*, p. 49.
[22] Gazizov, *Sopostavitel'naja grammatika tatarskogo i russkogo jazykov.*
[23] *Op. cit.*, p. 18.
[24] Kononov, *Grammatika sovremennogo tureckogo literaturnogo jazyka.*
[25] Kononov, *Grammatika sovremennogo uzbekskogo literaturnogo jazyka.*

description of Uzbek is found in Rešetov's book in which phonemes and their allophones are strictly distinguished between and in which a phonemic transcription is used side by side with the official alphabet.[26]

A good phonemic description of the Nanai (Goldi) language is also found in Avrorin's book. His definition of the phoneme as a sound which is a class of sounds in complementary distribution is correct.[27] He has also correctly found that Nanai has six vowel phonemes, but he is mistaken when he regards the nasalized vowels as phonemes[28] because they are found only in word-final position, e.g., [xotõ] or, as he writes it, [xoto$^{n}$] "city". When a suffix is added the nasalized vowel is replaced by an oral vowel + [n], e.g., [xotondu] "in the city". Therefore, it would be more correct to strike out all the nasalized vowel phonemes and, instead, introduce two allophones of the phoneme /n/: an alveolar voiced nasal consonant in initial, intervocalic, and syllable-final position, and a weak nasalization of the preceding vowel in word-final position, i.e., /xotondu/ [xotondu]: /xoton/ [xotõ] or [xoto$^{n}$]. Speaking of phonetic descriptions of Altaic languages, one should mention Novikova's description of one of the Even (Lamut) dialects, which is good.[29]

To summarize, it can be remarked that the general trend in Soviet Altaic studies is to give phonemic analyses of languages, although most authors have a somewhat vague idea of what a phoneme is, hence, a frequent confusion of phonemes and allophones and introduction of such phonemes which are only allophones of certain phonemes.

## 3

Problems of morphology are, in general, still treated in accordance with traditional grammar based on the patterns of Russian grammar. A complete analysis of grammars of Altaic languages would lead one too far afield. Therefore, the author will confine himself to a few key problems.

Speaking of parts of speech, one may note that Soviet authors seem not to be aware of the fact that a group of words, in order to be regarded as a separate part of speech, must possess certain characteristic features which make them different from other categories of words. Thus, Soviet authors still treat numerals as a separate part of speech.[30] In reality, the numerals do not constitute a separate part of speech but their basic forms function in the same manner as what the authors of the grammars in question call adjectives. Some forms of numerals are substantives, other forms are

[26] Rešetov, *Uzbekskij jazyk*, I.

[27] Avrorin, *Grammatika nanajskogo jazyka*, I, p. 16. He says literally: "A phoneme is a sound around which a number of positional shades are grouped."

[28] *Op. cit.*, p. 29.

[29] Novikova, *Očerki dialektov èvenskogo jazyka, Ol'skij dialekt*, I.

[30] Kononov, *Grammatika tureckogo jazyka*, p. 58; Kononov, *Grammatika uzbekskogo jazyka*, p. 64; Amogolonov, *op. cit.*, p. 125; Rišes & Cincius, *Kratkij očerk grammatiki èvenskogo (lamutskogo) jazyka: Russko-èvenskij slovar'*, p. 707; Todaeva, *Dunsjanskij jazyk*, p. 34.

adverbs. Thus, the distributive numerals in Turkish are adverbs, whereas in Uzbek the collective numerals in /-Aw/ are substantives, but the ordinals function as adjectives and adverbs, and are also substantivized. Buriat numerals in /-tE/ are adverbs,[31] but diminutive, distributive, possessive, and ordinal numerals are adjectives.[32]

The group of pronouns, as treated in Soviet grammars, is also diffuse in that it includes words which are by no means pronouns. Actually only the personal and demonstrative pronouns should be regarded as pronouns, because they differ from other declinable parts of speech in that they have a nominative form distinct from the stem, the nominative form never functioning as a direct object, whereas the substantives do not have a nominative but a subject-object (direct object) form. In spite of this, Kononov includes also the reflexive noun /kendi/ "self", the interrogative nouns /kim/ "who" and /ne/ "what", etc.,[33] the reflexive noun /üz/ "self",[34] etc., although they do not differ in inflection from other substantives.

Much better is the classification of the parts of speech in Baskakov's book on the Karakalpak language. He establishes only three main parts of speech, namely nouns, verbs, and "auxiliary words".[35] The same classification is also found in Sanžeev's analysis of Khalkha,[36] in Vasilevič's Evenki (Tungus) grammar,[37] and in Novikova's survey of the Lamut dialects.[38]

The greatest confusion reigns, however, in the grammars of some Altaic languages as far as the verbs are concerned. It is verb-aspect which causes much headache. Bogorodickij was probably the first to speak about aspects in Turkic languages,[39] and his statements were repeated by Borovkov who believed that he had found two distinct aspects in Uighur, namely, the perfective and imperfective aspect.[40] It can be assumed that the theory about the aspects in Turkic originated as a result of an uncritical application of data of Russian grammar to that of the Turkic languages. As a matter of fact, the Turkic languages possess means to render the Russian aspects by using certain syntactic constructions. However, the Russian verb-aspect is a morphological category, whereas their *semantic* equivalents in Turkic are syntactic constructions. The confusion with regard to aspect is the direct result of not distinguishing between forms and meanings.

This confusion has reigned for almost thirty years. Baskakov established in Karakalpak three ways of expressing aspects: a syntactic way, suffixation, and using special auxiliary words. Thus, he says, a frequentative verb may be formed by using

[31] Poppe, *Buriat Grammar*, p. 104.
[32] Poppe, *op. cit.*, p. 94.
[33] Kononov, *Grammatika tureckogo jazyka*, p. 175, 177.
[34] Kononov, *Grammatika uzbekskogo jazyka*, p. 179.
[35] Baskakov, *op. cit.*, p. 161.
[36] Sanžeev, *Sovremennyj mongol'skij jazyk*, p. 45.
[37] Vasilevič, *Èvenkijsko-russkij slovar'*, p. 670.
[38] Novikova, *op. cit.*, p. 114.
[39] Bogorodickij, *Vvedenie v tatarskoe jazykoznanie v svjazi s drugimi tjurkskimi jazykami.*
[40] Borovkov, *Učebnik ujgurskogo jazyka*, p. 176 f.

the word /köp/ "much": /köp al-/ "to take, get", lit., "to take much".[41] However, /köp al-/ is not an aspect but a phrase consisting of a verb and a direct object. If this is aspect, English *to come often* would also be a special aspect (let us say, frequentative) but of course it is not. The same confusion is found in Juldašev's book on the Bashkir verb in which it is said that perfective verbs are formed by adding the verb /böt-/ "to finish, end" to a gerund, e.g., /əsəp böt-/ "to finish drinking".[42] This is another phrase but not an aspect-form, just as English "I finished drinking" is not a perfective aspect. Juldašev would have been right if he had said that such phrases correspond *in meaning* to or translate such Russian forms of the perfective aspect as я выпил чай "I drank the tea" or я напился чаю "I had enough tea". Axmerov's sketch of Bashkir grammar[43] is not different in that it gives information on all possible ways and means of translating the Russian verbs of the perfective and imperfective aspect: /atlay bašla-/ "to start pacing" (Russ. зашагать), /yoqlap al-/ "to take a nap" (Russ. задремать), etc. Again only syntactic constructions are given. The same can be said about Xaritonov's book on the aspects in the Yakut language.[44] This mistake is, however not repeated by Kononov who does not speak of the perfective and imperfective aspect. He even avoids the Russian term *vid* (aspect) and uses the word *aspekt* to denote the positive and negative verb-stems, but he too, regards the constructions of the type /yaza bilmek/ "to know to write" as the "aspect of possibility".[45] After this, one is not surprised to learn that combinations of gerunds with auxiliary or modal verbs are regarded as aspect-forms in Mongolian grammar too, cf. /saaǰ duusav/ "finished milking" (perfective aspect) and /ineeǰ suuv/ "sat laughing" (imperfective aspect). This interpretation is found both in Khalkha[46] and Buriat[47] grammar.

Side by side with this school of thought, there is another much sounder one which refuses to recognize the category of aspect in the Altaic verb. Thus, Sanžeev is absolutely right when he says that there is no evidence whatsoever that Turkic languages have aspects. He stated this in his speech on a conference convoked for the purpose of discussing controversial problems of Turkic grammar.[48] A special paper on aspects in Turkic languages was read there by Serebrennikov who concluded his paper by stating correctly that the Turkic languages do not have aspects.[49] The category of aspect is alien to the Turkic verb, and Mamanov was right when he said that those authors who label combinations of words (i.e., phrases) as aspects are

[41] Baskakov, *op. cit.*, p. 361.
[42] Juldašev, *Sistema slovoobrazovanija i sprjaženija glagola v baškirskom jazyke*, p. 75.
[43] Axmerov, *Kratkij očerk grammatiki baškirskogo jazyka*: *Baškirsko-russkij slovar'*, p. 777.
[44] Xaritonov, *Formy glagol'nogo vida v jakutskom jazyke*.
[45] Kononov, *Grammatika tureckogo jazyka*, p. 191; cf. his *Grammatika uzbekskogo jazyka*, pp. 200-201.
[46] Todaeva, *Grammatika sov. mongol'skogo jazyka*, pp. 117-119. However, Todaeva has noticed that the simple verb stem is neutral as far as aspect is concerned, cf. p. 113.
[47] Amogolonov, *op. cit.*, p. 203.
[48] *Voprosy grammatiki tjurkskix jazykov*, p. 60.
[49] *Op. cit.*, p. 30. Cf. Poppe, "Tempus und Aspekt...", p. 556.

prisoners of Russian grammar, trying to apply to Turkic languages and impose on them rules of Russian grammar.[50]

Thus it can be stated that there is a group of Soviet linguists who demand that expressions which translate the meanings of certain forms of the Russian verb should not be identified with the latter.

In concluding this section it should be remarked that the statements made above do not mean that none of the Altaic languages has aspects, because Tungus does have a perfective and imperfective aspect, cf. /tęgęčęę/ "he sat down" (Russ. сел), and /tęgęǰęčęę/ "he was sitting" (Russ. сидел).[51]

## 4

Proceeding to problems of syntax, it should be stated that there is still great confusion with regard to compound clauses and, in particular, subordinate clauses. Here again phrases translating certain Russian constructions are identified with the latter. Although such scholars as Dmitriev correctly treat clauses like /ul minəŋ äytkänəmdə itmäθ/ "he will not do what I say" (lit., "he will not do my said") as simple clauses,[52] there are still numerous authors who would regard English clauses of the type *he saw her come* as compound clauses and *her come* as a subordinate clause. Thus, in the Bashkir grammar by Axmerov, which is appended to the Bashkir-Russian dictionary, one finds that /öyö barðïŋ köyö bar/ "the one who has a house has his own order" is regarded as a compound clause, the portion /öyö barðïŋ/ being a subordinate clause, although /öyö barðïŋ/ is only an attribute of /köyö/ "his order". The verbatim translation of the whole is "the order is of the a-house-having-one".[53] There is no subordinate clause.

A similar mistake is made with regard to Oyrot by Baskakov. He finds subordinate clauses where there are gerundial phrases of the type /sen uyuktap ǰatkanča, men kïrga čïgïp oyto tüžüp keldim/ "while you were sleeping I climbed the mountain and [even] descended [back]".[54] He is also mistaken when he believes that Nogai /ol zaman ne zat alyaGïn oylandï/ "at that time he thought what thing he should take" is a compound clause, because it translates the Russian clause в то время он подумал о том, что ему следовало взять, but in reality this is not a compound clause, its verbatim translation being "at that time what-thing-future-taking he thought" ("future-taking" being in Nogai an accusative form, i.e., a direct object).[55] The clause /men on eki yašïma kelgende atam öldü/ "at my reaching the age of twelve my father died"[56] is not a compound clause either, nor is its English literal translation a

50 *Op. cit.*, p. 31.
51 Poppe, *op. cit.*, p. 557.
52 Dmitriev, *Grammatika baškirskogo jazyka*, p. 244.
53 *Baškirsko-russkij slovar'*, p. 802.
54 Baskakov & Toščakova, *Ojrotsko-russkij slovar'*, p. 302.
55 Baskakov, *Nogajskij jazyk i ego dialekty*, p. 124.
56 *Op. cit.*, p. 125.

compound clause, and it should not worry Baskakov that its Russian translation когда я достиг двенадцатилетнего возраста, мой отец умер is a compound clause. By the way, a far better Russian translation would be при моем достижении двенадцатилетнего возраста мой отец умер.

The same mistakes appear in Baskakov's more recent works. Thus, in his Khakas grammar (1953) he gives the following example of a compound clause with a subordinate clause: /ol maGa közït-pirgen, anïŋ üčün min ol kirektï čaxsï pïlčem/ "he showed to me, therefore I know this business well".[57] There are actually two clauses: /ol maGa közït-pirgen/ "he showed to me" and /anïŋ üčün min ol kirektï čaxsï pïlčem/ "therefore I know this business well".

It is also incorrect to regard /üydiŋ išinde ot söndi de ol qaraŋGï bolGanïn kördi/ (Karakalpak) "the light also went out in the house and he saw the past-becoming dark" (i.e., "that it had become dark") as a compound clause with subordination.[58]

The same confusion is also found in Xangildin's Tatar grammar in which clauses like /mohtar öyənä kaytkanda, ində yartï tönnär čamasï idə/ "at Mohtar's return to his home, it was already almost midnight" are regarded as compound clauses,[59] although /öyənä kaytkanda/ is only an adverbial complement, here a phrase ("at the return to his home") which lacks the characteristics of a clause.

To cut this discussion short, it should be remarked that participle-phrases (with a participle in an oblique case form) are regarded as subordinate clauses also by Nadžip,[60] whereas gerund-phrases are regarded as subordinate clauses by the investigators of Tungus languages, Rišes, Cincius,[61] and Vasilevič.[62]

Soviet Mongolists, however, do not make this mistake. Thus Sanžeev correctly states that Khalkha does not have subordinate clauses but only participle- and gerund-phrases.[63] Amogolonov distinguishes in Buriat between participle- and gerund-phrases on the one hand, and subordinate clauses on the other.[64] Buriat, indeed, has clause subordination.

The confusion reigning in Turkic linguistics with regard to such problems as aspect and compound clauses necessitated the convocation of a special conference which was held in 1956 in Alma-Ata, Kazakhstan, where a paper on compound clauses was read by Širaliev.[65] He demonstrated quite correctly that participial and gerundial phrases should not be considered as subordinated clauses.[66] He was supported by Serebrennikov who is a serious linguist, by the Mongolist Bertagaev,[67] the investigator

[57] Baskakov & Inkižekova-Grekul, *Xakassko-russkij slovar'*, p. 478.
[58] Baskakov, ed., *Karakalpaksko-russkij slovar'*, p. 866.
[59] Xangil'din, *Tatar tele grammatikasy*, p. 548.
[60] Nadžip, *Sovremennyj Ujgurskij jazyk*, p. 125.
[61] Cincius & Rišes, *Russko-èvenskij slovar'*, p. 777.
[62] Vasilevič, *Èvenkijsko-russkij slovar'*, p. 742.
[63] Sanžeev, *Sovremennyj mongol'skij jazyk*, p. 91.
[64] Amogolonov, *op. cit.*, p. 282, 283, 289.
[65] Širaliev, "Problema složnopodčinennogo predloženija", *Voprosy grammatiki tjurkskix jazykov*, p.79.
[66] *Op. cit.*, pp. 82-83.
[67] *Op. cit.*, p. 194.

of Tungus, Kolesnikova,[68] Baskakov,[69] Hussein-Zade,[70] and some other scholars. On the other hand, Gadžieva[71] and Sauranbaev[72] insisted, in their papers, on the recognition of participle- and gerund-phrases as subordinate clauses. Consequently, the conference did not succeed in replacing the misconceptions with regard to what clause subordination is with a sounder approach, and the confusion still remains in the heads of some Turcologists, mostly those who, surprisingly enough, are Turks in origin, such as Gadžieva, Sauranbaev,[73] Amanžolov, Balakaev, and some others. But it is encouraging that at least some Turcologists are freeing themselves from the strait-jacket of Russian grammar and refuse to regard as subordinate clauses everything which translates Russian subordinate clauses. This new approach is found in the article of Axmerov on adverbial phrases in Bashkir.[74] From this point of view the Turkish[75] and Uzbek[76] grammars by Kononov are also good.

In conclusion of this section, it can be stated that most Soviet Altaicists have become familiar with the thesis of modern linguistics that a member of a clause may be a word or a phrase, the latter not being, however, a dependent clause.

## 5

Comparative studies in the USSR occupy a modest place among works on Altaic languages. There is a symposium on Turkic languages edited by Dmitriev,[77] but it is not a comparative grammar of Turkic languages. It contains a number of articles such as "General description of the Turkic vocalism", "Alternations of back and front vowels in individual Turkic languages", "Uighur vocalism", "Vowel harmony", "Long vowels in Turkic languages", etc. Some of the articles do not contain anything new, e.g., Dmitriev's articles on the correspondences /l/ = /š/, /r/ = /z/, or his article on assimilations and dissimilations of consonants in Bashkir. The articles on morphologic features do not advance knowledge either. Thus, Sevortjan's article "The category of the case" surprises one by giving such vague definitions as "in some languages of the south-western group".[78]

68 *Op. cit.*, p. 200.
69 *Op. cit.*, p. 232.
70 *Op. cit.*, p. 236.
71 Gadžieva, "Kriterii vydelenija pridatočnyx predloženij v tjurkskix jazykax", *Op. cit.*, p. 91 f.
72 Sauranbaev, "Osnovnye sposoby svjazi sostavnyx častej v složnopodčinennom predloženii", *Op. cit.*, p. 109 f.
73 Cf. his statements with regard to the "subordinate clause" of this kind: /yegin bïyïl žaqsï šïqqanGa kolxozšïlar qattï kuanuda/ "the collective farmers are very happy about the good outcome of crops this year" (p. 119), with the "subordinate clause" being /yegin bïyïl žaqsï šïqqanGa/ "to-the-crops-this-year-well-having-come-out".
74 Axmerov, "Obstojatel'stvennye oboroty v grammatičeskoj sisteme baškirskogo jazyka", *Voprosy baškirskoj filologii*, p. 24 (1959).
75 Kononov, *Grammatika tureckogo jazyka.*
76 Kononov, *Grammatika uzbekskogo jazyka.*
77 Dmitriev, ed., *Issledovanija po sravnitel'noj grammatike tjurkskix jazykov*, I, II, III.
78 *Op. cit.*, II, p. 52.

Consequently, no comparative grammars of Turkic languages have yet been created. This explains why a translation of Räsänen's "Zur Lautgeschichte der türkischen Sprachen" (*Studia Orientalia*, XV, Helsinki, 1949) was made,[79] because it remains the only modern comparative study of Turkic languages.[80]

Mongolian comparative studies are still in a very primitive stage. Sanžeev's comparative grammar[81] was written at the time of domination of Stalin's linguistic theories and all too manifestly reflects Sanžeev's abrupt change from Marrism to Stalinist linguistics and must be now rather embarrassing to its author. Not giving anything new, his book is abundantly interspersed with quotations from and praise of Stalin.

The best Soviet comparative work in the Altaic field is so far Cincius' comparative phonology of the Manchu-Tungus languages[82] which is a serious scholarly work on a high level.

There are no Soviet works in which all or several Altaic languages are treated along the lines of comparative linguistics, and this may be responsible for the fact that Ramstedt's *Einführung in die altaische Sprachwissenschaft*[83] was translated into Russian.[84]

An interesting and rather good work is Baskakov's survey of Turkic languages.[85] The introduction deserves special attention, because it gives also Baskakov's view of the theory of genetic affinity of the Altaic languages. The author accepts the theory that Mongolian and Turkic languages had a common ancestor.[86] His etymologies and comparisons contain, however, mistakes. Thus /s/ cannot be regarded as a correspondence to /r/[87] but only /z/ = /r/. Nevertheless, his introduction deserves attention inasmuch as it is the first statement on the affinity of the Turkic and Mongolian languages made in the USSR since Vladimircov (1929).[88]

[79] Rjasjanen, *Materialy po istoričeskoj fonetike tjurkskix jazykov.*

[80] Much better than the volumes mentioned in footnote 79 is the interesting study on the development of the Turkic word stock: Ubrjatova, ed., *Istoričeskoe razvitie leksiki tjurkskix jazykov.* It contains a number of valuable articles.

[81] Sanžeev, *Sravnitel'naja grammatika mongol'skix jazykov*, I.

[82] Cincius, *Sravnitel'naja fonetika tunguso-man'čžurskix jazykov.*

[83] Ramstedt, *Einführung in die altaische Sprachwissenschaft.*

[84] So far only volume II (1957): Ramstedt, *Vvedenie v altajskoe jazykoznanie.* The notes contain mistakes resulting from inadequate knowledge of German. Thus, in note 188 Ramstedt's translation "Medizin" is corrected to "drug" although German *Medizin* means both "medical science" and "drug". Likewise, Ramstedt translates /tülеši/ correctly as "Brennstoff" i.e., fuel, and Sanžeev's criticism that /tüleši/ is not gasoline is out of place, since *Brennstoff* is fuel in general (any fuel) and gasoline is in German *Treibstoff* but never *Brennstoff.* Ramstedt is also right when he translates Mongolian /miqaši/ "to become fleshy", and Sanžeev's "correction" "to like meat, to become a meat-eater" is wrong, because /miqasa-/ is "to like meat". Thus the notes, additions, and "corrections" made by the Russian translators should be dismissed without attention, because they contain a large number of grotesque mistakes.

[85] Baskakov, *Tjurkskie jazyki.*

[86] *Op. cit.*, p. 32.

[87] *Op. cit.*, p. 36.

[88] Vladimircov, *op. cit.*, vide note 10.

## 6

In conclusion of this article, the author wishes to make a few summarizing remarks.

There is no doubt that the Soviet Altaicists make efforts to use modern linguistic methods in their research. Most of them do not speak any more about "sounds" but try to establish phonologic systems of the languages in question. Grammatical analysis is gradually being freed from the errors of traditional grammar, and grammatical forms are no longer viewed through the prism of Russian grammar. Some progress has also been made in research on syntax, and all Altaicists do not identify the Altaic constructions with their semantic correspondences in Russian translations.

It is true that there still occur errors with regard to individual problems, and comparative studies are still almost non-extant, but there is marked progress especially as far as numerous grammars and dictionaries are concerned which cover most of the Altaic languages, whereas there were no dictionaries and grammars of any kind for most of them as recently as twenty or twenty-five years ago.

## BIBLIOGRAPHY


Amogolonov, D. D., *Sovremennyj burjatskij jazyk* (Ulan Ude, 1958).

Avrorin, V. A., *Grammatika nanajskogo jazyka*, I (Moscow-Leningrad, 1959).

——, *Očerki po sintaksisu nanajskogo jazyka, Prjamoe dopolnenie*. Učpedgiz (Leningrad, 1948).

——, *Ob ošibkax v osveščenii nekotoryx voprosov grammatičeskogo stroja nanajskogo jazyka i ego istorii*, DSIJa 5(1953).

Austin, William M., Gombojab Hangin, Urgunge Onon, *Mongol Reader* (Washington, 1956).

Axmerov, K. Z., *Kratkij očerk grammatiki baškirskogo jazyka: Baškirsko-russkij slovar'* (Moscow, 1958).

——, *Obstojatel'stvennye oboroty v grammatičeskoj sisteme baškirskogo jazyka, Voprosy baškirskoj filologii* (Moscow, 1959).

Baskakov, N. A. and Toščakova, T. M., *Ojrotsko-russkij slovar'* (Moscow, 1947).

Baskakov, N. A., *Karakalpakskij jazyk*, I; *Materialy po dialektologii* (Moscow, 1951).

——, *Nogajskij jazyk i ego dialekty* (Moscow-Leningrad, 1940).

——, ed., *Karakalpaksko-russkij slovar'* (Moscow, 1958).

——, *Tjurkskie jazyki* (Moscow, 1960).

Bogorodickij, V. A., *Vvedenie v tatarskoe jazykoznanie v svjazi s drugimi tjurkskimi jazykami* (Kazan, 1934).

Borovkov, A. K., *Učebnik ujgurskogo jazyka* (Leningrad, 1935).

Burdukov, A. V., *Russko-mongol'skij slovar' razgovornogo jazyka* (Leningrad, 1935).

Cincius, V. I., *Sravnitel'naja fonetika tunguso-man'čžurskix jazykov* (Leningrad, 1949).

Cincius, V. I. and Rišes, L. D., *Russko-èvenskij slovar'* (Moscow, 1952).

Dmitriev, N. K., ed., *Issledovanija po sravnitel'noj grammatike tjurkskix jazykov*, I: *Fonetika*; II: *Morfologija*; III: *Sintaksis* (Moscow, 1955-56-61).
Dmitriev, N. K., Axmerov, K. Z., and Baišev, T. T., eds., *Russko-baškirskij slovar'* (Moscow, 1948).
Dmitriev, N. K., *Grammatika baškirskogo jazyka* (Moscow-Leningrad, 1948).
Dyrenkova, N. P., *Grammatika ojrotskogo jazyka* (Moscow-Leningrad, 1940).
Gazizov, S., *Sopostavitel'naja grammatika tatarskogo i russkogo jazykov* (Kazan, 1959).
Inkižekova-Grekul, A. I. and Baskakov, N. A., *Xakassko-russkij slovar'* (Moscow, 1953).
*Istoričeskoe razvitie leksiki tjurkskix jazykov* (Moscow, 1961).
Juldašev, A. A., *Sistema slovoobrazovanija i sprjaženija glagola v baškirskom jazyke* (Moscow, 1958).
Kononov, A. N., *Grammatika sovremennogo uzbekskogo literaturnogo jazyka* (Moscow-Leningrad, 1960).
——, *Grammatika sovremennogo tureckogo literaturnogo jazyka* (Moscow-Leningrad, 1956).
*Materialy ob" edinennoj naučnoj sessii, posvjaščennoj trudam I. V. Stalina po jazykoznaniju.* Izd. Akademii Pedagogičeskix Nauk RSFSR (Moscow, 1951).
Malov, S. E., *Pamjatniki drevnetjurkskoj pis'mennosti, Teksty i issledovanija* (Moscow-Leningrad, 1951).
Nadžip, E. N., *Sovremennyj ujgurskij jazyk* (Moscow, 1960).
Novikova, K. L., *Očerki dialektov èvenskogo jazyka I, Ol'skij dialekt* (Moscow-Leningrad, 1960).
Poppe, N., *Buriat Grammar.* Indiana University Publications, Vol. 2 of the Uralic and Altaic Series (Bloomington, 1960).
Poppe, N., "Tempus und Aspekt in den altaischen Sprachen", *Studium Generale* 8/9.556 (1955).
Ramstedt, G. J., *Vvedenie v altajskoe jazykoznanie*, perevod s nemeckogo L. S. Slonima, pod redakciej i s predisloviem N. A. Baskakova, Primečanija Baskakova i Sanžeeva (Moscow, 1957).
——, *Einführung in die altaische Sprachwissenschaft*, Bearbeitet und herausgegeben von Pentti Aalto. I: Lautlehre (Helsinki, 1957); II (Helsinki, 1952).
Rešetov, V. V., *Uzbekskij jazyk*, I: *Vvedenie i fonetika* (Tashkent, 1959).
Rjasjanen, M., *Materialy po istoričeskoj fonetike tjurkskix jazykov*, perevod c nemeckogo A. A. Juldaševa (Moscow, 1955).
Sanžeev, G. D., *Grammatika burjat-mongol'skogo jazyka* (Moscow-Leningrad, 1941).
——, "Jazyk i dialekt v svete trudov I. V. Stalina", *UZIV* 3.1-31 (1951).
——, "Mongol'skie jazyki i dialekty", *UZIV* 4.30-125 (1952).
——, "Mongol'skoe jazykoznanie v SSSR", *Lingua Poznaniensis* 4.154f. (1953).
——, *Sovremennyj mongol'skij jazyk* (Moscow, 1959).
——, *Sravnitel'naja grammatika mongol'skix jazykov*, I (Moscow, 1953).

Serebrennikov, B. A., *Trudy I. V. Stalina po voprosam jazykoznanija i ix značenie.* Goskul'tprosvetizdat (Moscow, 1951).

Sevortjan, E. V., *Fonetika tureckogo literaturnogo jazyka* (Moscow, 1955).

Širaliev, M. Š., *Problema složnopodčinennogo predloženija, Voprosy grammatiki tjurkskix jazykov* (Alma-Ata, 1958).

Stalin, I., *Marksizm i voprosy jazykoznanija*, izd. "Pravda" (Moscow, 1950).

Sunik, O. P., *Očerki po sintaksisu tunguso-man'čžurskix jazykov, Possessivnyj stroj predloženija.* Učpedgiz (Leningrad, 1947).

Thomas, Lawrence L., "The Linguistic Theories of N. Ya. Marr", *University of California Publications in Linguistics 14* (Berkeley and Los Angeles, 1957).

Todaeva, B. X., *Dunsjanskij jazyk* (Moscow, 1961).

——, *Grammatika sovremennogo mongol'skogo jazyka, Fonetika i morfologija* (Moscow, 1951).

——, *Mongol'skie jazyki i dialekty Kitaja* (Moscow, 1960).

Vasilevič, G. M., *Evenkijsko-russkij slovar', Grammatičeskij očerk èvenkijskogo jazyka* (Moscow, 1958).

Vladimircov, B. Ja., *Sravnitel'naja grammatika mongol'skogo pis'mennogo jazyka i xalxaskogo narečija, Vvedenie i fonetika* (Leningrad, 1929).

*Voprosy grammatiki tjurkskix jazykov* (Alma-Ata, 1958).

Xangil'din, V. N., *Tatar tele grammatikasy* (Kazan, 1959).

Xaritonov, L. N., *Formy glagol'nogo vida v jakutskom jazyke* (Moscow-Leningrad, 1960).

# CAUCASIAN*

AERT H. KUIPERS

**1.** The term "Caucasian languages" is applied to ca. 35 languages spoken in the Caucasus and NE Anatolia (also by emigrant groups in Turkey, Syria, Jordan and Iran), and unrelated to any of the large known language-families. They fall into a S (or Kartvelian), a NW and a NE group. The existence of a genetic relationship between NW and NE Cauc. is probable; the relations of S Cauc. to this N group so far remain unclear,[1] though many Soviet linguists take a genetic relationship for granted, or at least start from it as a working hypothesis. In the USSR, the term "Japhetic languages" was in use besides "Caucasian", especially among the followers of Marr. At present, the name "Ibero-Caucasian" is often used, "Iberian" being equivalent to S Cauc. or Kartvelian, and "Caucasian" to N Cauc.

**2.** These languages are here summed up according to the latest information from a variety of Soviet sources. The major dialects are included in parentheses.[2] Where necessary, Russian designations are added in italics.

NW CAUC. *abxazo-adygskie jazyki*: 1. Abxazo-Abaza (dial. Bzyb, Abžuj*, Samurzakan, Ašxar, Tapanta*, the latter two combinedly called *abazinskij jazyk*, though Tapanta stands apart from the first four dialects); 2. Ubyx (no longer spoken in the

* References to literature are made by name of author, year of publication, where necessary, part of the title, and page. For the period after 1950 an attempt has been made to mention all books, all articles of a comparative nature, and all descriptive articles dealing with languages as a whole or with phonology. Descriptive articles treating other parts of individual language-systems are mentioned only in exceptional cases. Of publications before 1950, and especially before 1945, only some of the most important ones are mentioned. In the case of Georgian books with an added Russian title-page, and of articles with a summary in Russian, the Russian title is quoted. Georgian titles are provided with an English translation. Some of the literature quoted was inaccessible to the author at the time of writing this article.

For older surveys of Caucasian linguistics cf. Polák, 1950; E. Bokarev, 1954; Dešeriev, 1958; Bokarev and Dešeriev, 1959, 202-283: Čikobava, 1959. Bibliographies: Kačarava and Topuria, 1958; *Bibliografija jazykovedčeskix rabot*, 1958; Čxubianišvili, 1961.

[1] This appraisal of the possible genetic relationships between the three groups is based on the number of reasonable etymologies that have been proposed, cf. especially N. S. Trubetzkoy, "Nordkaukasische Wortgleichungen", *WZKM* 37.76ff.(1930). For a different view based on typological considerations cf. Klimov, *A Contribution* 1960 and section 21.

[2] The indication "dial." means that the language is divided up into the dialects mentioned, "with dial." means that one dialects bears the name by which the language is known, one or more other dialects being known by the additional names quoted. Dialects on which literary languages are based are marked with an asterisk.

Caucasus and dying out in Turkey); 3. Circassian *adygskie jazyki* comprising 3a. Kjax or W Circassian *adygejskij* (dial. Natuxaj, Šapsug with sub-dial. Xakuči, Bžedux, Abadzex, Temirgoj*) and 3b. Kabardian or E Circassian (*kabardino*)*čerkesskij* (dial. Greater Kabardian*, Baksan, Lesser Kabardian, Malka, Mozdok, Kuban, Čerkes, Beslenej; the latter stands apart as a transitional dialect between 1 and 2).

NE Cauc. *čečeno-dagestanskie jazyki*, subdivided into four groups:

I. Vejnax *naxskie*, *kistinskie jazyki*: 1. Čečen (dial. Greater Čečen*, Itumkala, Čeberloj, Galančog; the Akka or Aux dialect stands between 1 and 2); 2. Inguš; 3. Bac *bacbijskij*, which stands apart from 1 and 2.

II. Avaro-Andi-Dido: 1. Avar (dial. A. Northern, subdivided into NW or Salatav, N Central or Xunzax*, and NE; B. Southern: Hid, Andalal, Karax, Ancux, Batlux, Zakataly or Čar; C. Transitional: Keleb, Bacadin, Untib, Šulanin, Kaxib); 2. Andi-group, comprising 2a. Andi proper (with dial. Munin, Rikvani, Kvanxidatl, Gagatl, Zilo); 2b. Botlix; 2c. Godoberi; 2d. Karata (with dial. Tokita,987nčix); 2e. Tindi; 2f. Bagulal or Kvanada (with dial Tlisi); 2g. Čamalal (dial. Gakvari-Gadyri, Gigatl); 2h. Axvax (with dial. Kaxib); 3. Dido- or Cez-group, comprising 3a. Dido or Cez; 3b. Xvarši (with dial. Inxokvari); 3c. Ginux; 3d. Bežita or Kapuča; 3e. Gunzib.

III. Lak-Dargwa: 1. Lak (dial. Vicxin, Kumux*, Vixlin, Aštikulin, Balxar-Calakkan); 2. Dargwa (dial. Cudaxar, Uraxa-Axuša*, Urkarax, Kajtak or Xajdak, Kubači, Dejbuk, Xarbuk, Muirin, Sirxin).

IV. Lezghian group: 1. Lezghian proper (dial. Kjuri*, Axty, Kuba, Gjunej, Garkin; sub-dial. Anyx, Stal'); 2. Agul (with dial. Keren, Košan, Gekxun); 3. Rutul (with dial. Šina, Ixreko-Muxrek, Borč); 4. Caxur (with dial. Kirmico-Lek, Mikik, Mišleš); 5. Tabasaran (dial. S* and N Tabasaran); 6. Budux; 7. Kryc or Džek (dial. Kryc, Džek, Xaput); 8. Udi (dial. Vartašen, Nidž); 9. Xinalug; 10. Arči.

S Cauc. *kartvel'skie*, *iberijskie jazyki*: 1. Georgian *gruzinskij* (dial. A. Eastern: Kartlian*, Kaxetian, Ingilo, Tuš, Xevsur, Moxev, Pšav, Mtiul, Ferejdan in Iran; B. Western: Imeretian, Rača, Lečxum, Gurian (including Adžar), Imerxev in Turkey); 2. Mingrelian *megrel'skij* (dial. Samurzakan-Zugdidi, Senaki); 3. Laz or Chan (dial. A. Eastern: Xopa, Čxala; B. Western: Vice-Arxava, Atina); 4. Svan (dial. Upper Bal, Lower Bal, Lašx, Lentex). Mingrelian and Laz are combinedly called Zan; Svan stands apart from the three others.

**3.** Soviet linguists now regard (a) Botlix and Godoberi, (b) Bežita and Gunzib, and (c) Mingrelian and Laz as dialects of the same languages. The inclusion of Arči and especially of Xinalug in the Lezghian group is tentative (cf. Bokarev *Vvedenie* 1961: 31f., Dešeriev 1959:207).

In many cases the "dialects" differ considerably from one another, and the tendency of Soviet linguists to work with larger units such as the ones just mentioned sometimes has the result that forms are quoted without a clear indication of the dialect to which they belong. In view of the great difficulties which are encountered in comparative work (cf. 14), it would seem preferable to distinguish a greater rather than a smaller number of "languages".

**4.** The following languages, being those with the largest numbers of speakers, have official status as "literary languages"[3] in the USSR: *Georgian* (2,700,000; Georgian SSR, cap. Tbilisi), *Abxaz* (65,000; Abxaz ASSR, cap. Suxumi), *Abaza* (20,000; Karačaevo-Čerkes AO, cap. Čerkessk), *W Circassian*, Russ. *adygejskij jazyk* (80,000; Adygej AO, cap. Majkop), *Kabardian* (204,000; Kabardino-Balkar ASSR, cap. Nal'čik; also in the Karačaevo-Čerkes AO), *Čečen* (419,000) and *Inguš* (106,000; both in the Čečeno-Inguš ASSR, cap. Groznyj), *Avar* (207,000), *Lak* (64,000), *Dargwa* (158,000), *Lezghian* (223,000) and *Tabasaran* (35,000; the latter five in the Dagestan ASSR, cap. Maxačkala). Of these, Georgian is the only language with an ancient literary tradition (5th cent.); it has a script of its own, the other languages now being written with Cyrillic characters.

**5.** The Cauc. languages (especially N Cauc.) are characterized by very rich consonant-systems. Ubiquitous are the buccal series *p*, *t*, *c*, *č*, *k*, *q* (with corresponding fricatives), to which N Cauc. frequently adds laterals (affricate *ƛ*, fricative *λ*) and glottals (*ʔ*, *h*), often also pharyngeal fricatives (vl. *ḫ*, vd. *ʕ*) and sometimes alveolopalatals (*ç*, *ş*). The plosives occur in triplets of the type *t*, *d*, *t'*, the fricatives usually in pairs *s*, *z*, though glottalic fricatives are found in a few languages. NW Cauc. opposes plain consonants to palatalized and labialized ones (*k*, *k'*, *k°*); in the Bzyb dialect of Abxaz the latter two features occur combined (*š*, *š'*, *š°*, *š'°*). Especially NE Cauc. opposes weak and strong (geminate) consonants (*t* versus *t:*, etc.).[4] Consonant-systems with over 50 members are no exception. The vowel-systems are maximally simple in NW Cauc. (only *a* and *ə*, and the latter is a juncture-feature); in the other languages they comprise at least five, and sometimes as many as twenty and more vowels (short and long, plain and nasal, plain and pharyngalized, in addition to distinctions of timbre).

Morphemes are short; especially in the case of the N Cauc. languages there is evidence that historically many if not all morphemes consisted of single consonants or of consonant-groups with homogenous glottal articulation (so-called "harmonic complexes").

While the NW Cauc. languages have simple case-systems and a rich, polypersonal conjugation, NE Cauc. has extensive, serial case-systems and mostly does not express person in the verb. The S Cauc. languages occupy in both respects an intermediate position. In many of the NE Cauc. languages morphology and syntax are dominated by a division of nouns into classes (rational, subdivided into male and female, and one or more non-rational classes). The verb contains class-indicators rather than person-

[3] This means that primers, school-grammars, etc., are published in these languages. Some of this material, especially in the case of the languages of the Dagestan ASSR, is very rare outside the republics of issue.

[4] Some W Circassian dialects oppose aspirated to unaspirated plosives and fricatives; the latter are also transcribed *p:*, *š:*, etc. In Russian terminology, the plosives of this type are called *poluabruptivy* or *preruptivy*.

affixes, e.g. Avar sing. rat. masc. *w*, fem. *j*, irrat. *b*; plur. *r*, *l* (all classes): *dun w-ač'una* "I (man) come", *dun j-ač'una* "I (woman) come", *ču b-ač'una* "the horse comes", *niž r-ač'una* "we come", *wac: roq:'o-w w-ugo* "brother at-home is", *jac: roq:'o-j j-igo* "sister id.", *t'ex: roq:'o-b b-ugo* "book in-the-house is", *roq:'o-r r-ugo* "they are at home". Lexical elements may contain petrified class-prefixes, cf. *wac:* "brother", *jac:* "sister", *rağ* "battle" (root *-ağ-*, cf. *b-ağ-ize*, etc. "to quarrel"), *roq:'* "house".

All the Cauc. languages have different cases for the subject of an intransitive and for the actor of a transitive verb (secondary modifications in S Cauc.); the trans. actor is expressed either by a special "ergative" case or by a general "oblique" case, the intrans. subject and the goal of a trans. verb being expressed by a casus rectus (also called "nominative" or "absolutive"), so that from a Caucasian point of view the latter two categories are one and the same.

**6.** At present, the study of the Caucasian languages in the USSR is carried on mainly in the following institutions (their serial publications are given in parentheses):

Tbilisi: Ak. Nauk Gruz. SSR (*Soobščenija*; *Izvestija*); Institut jazykoznanija (*Iberijsko-kavkazskoe jazykoznanie*; *Voprosy struktury kartvel'skix jazykov*); Tbilisskij gos. universitet (*Trudy kafedry obščego jazykoznanija*; *Trudy kafedry novogruzinskogo jazyka*; *Trudy kafedry drevnegruzinskogo jazyka*; *Trudy kafedry kavkazskix jazykov*; *Soobščenija*); Institut rukopisej (*Pamjatniki drevnegruzinskogo jazyka*).

Suxumi: Abxazskij institut jazyka, literatury i istorii (*Trudy*).

Majkop: Adygejskij naučno-issledovatel'skij institut (*Učenye zapiski*); Institut izučenija adygejskogo jazyka.

Čerkessk: Karačaevo-čerkesskij n.-i. institut (*Trudy*).

Nal'čik: Kabardino-balkarskij n.-i. institut (*Učenye zapiski*); Kabardino-balkarskij gos. universitet (*Učenye zapiski*).

Groznyj: Čečeno-ingušskij n.-i. institut (*Izvestija* discontinued, *Trudy*).

Maxačkala: Institut istorii, jazyka i literatury im. G. Cadasy (*Učenye zapiski*); Dagestanskij gos. universitet.

Moscow: AN SSSR, Institut jazykoznanija (*Voprosy jazykoznanija*; *Trudy*; *Doklady i soobščenija*; *Kratkie soobščenija*) Sektor kavkazskix jazykov, Sektor obščego jazykoznanija.

Mention must further be made of the pedagogical and teachers' institutes in Tbilisi, Kutaisi, Batumi, Gori, Cxinvali, Suxumi, Majkop, Nal'čik and Maxačkala, some of which publish their own series.

**7.** In the second half of the 19th century an excellent foundation for N Cauc. linguistics was laid by P. K. Uslar, whose amazingly accurate and complete descriptions of Abxaz, Čečen, Avar, Lak. Dargwa (*xjurkilinskij*) and Lezghian (*kjurinskij*) still remain standard reference works.[5] Georgian had a native grammatival tradition (Čubinašvili, Kipiani, Kutateladze, Žordania, Cagareli and others). The basic Geor-

[5] For bibliographical data on works mentioned in sections 7 and 8 cf. W. K. Matthews, *Languages of the USSR* (Cambridge 1951), pp. 145-148.

gian-Mingrelian sound-correspondences were formulated by Cagareli in 1880. Shortly before the first world war, Mingrelian was described by Kipšidze, and Laz by Marr. Much linguistic material was gathered in the *Sbornik materialov dlja opisanija mestnostej i plemen Kavkaza* (Tbilisi 1881-1915) by Lopatinskij, Dirr, Nižaradze and others. Uslar has been the first to voice the opinion that the Cauc. languages form one family.[6]

**8.** After the revolution, heavy stress was laid on the practical tasks of creating alphabets, school-grammars and practical dictionaries for the languages so far unwritten, and these tasks required a theoretical foundation. The phonemic principle, already evident in Uslar's work, was consistently applied by Jakovlev in his work on Circassian, while Žirkov published concise grammars of Avar and Dargwa, attempting to bring out the salient grammatical features. Mention must further be made of Marr's Abxaz-Russian dictionary and of Genko's work on Lezghian. The school-grammars and practical dictionaries which appeared in the twenties and thirties were often quite important as collections of new material, e.g., Maciev's Čečen-Russian and Žirkov's Avar-Russian dictionaries. It must be emphasized, however, that the value of such works for comparative purposes is limited, as the newly created literary languages were in many instances based on the phonetically simplest dialects, or even on a *koine* combining features of several dialects. In addition, the official orthography sometimes fails to render all the phonemic distinctions which exist in the literary dialects.

**9.** A much more serious obstacle in the way of comparative studies was the fact that from ca. 1930–1950 the school of Marr achieved a monopolist position in Soviet linguistics. This school regarded convergence of languages (rather than the divergence as observed by the comparatists) as the only legitimate object of study and imposed a "stadial" scheme of development on the history of language in general. It is not accidental that these theories were put forward by a Caucasologist, for due to the fact that historical data are in almost all cases unavailable, and also because of the phonetic structure of the languages themselves (see 14), the comparative method did not yield ready results in this field, while the Caucasus does provide instances of peculiarly "mixed" languages (e.g. Armenian). However, the Marrist school did not develop a methodology even for the study of convergence, while its so-called paleontological element-analysis, which aimed at reducing the roots of all languages to a small number of primeval elements, was characterized by a total absence of method, quite arbitrary sound-changes being postulated *ad hoc* in order to connect various disparate elements. Nevertheless, some important work was done during this period, especially in Georgia.

**10.** NW Cauc. – In Georgia, the school of A. Čikobava kept aloof from Marrism in so far as this was possible; to it we thank K. Lomtatidze's excellent description of the Tapanta dialect of Abxaz (1944), which includes extensive text-material from the

[6] P. K. Uslar, *Ètnografija Kavkaza. Jazykoznanie II: Čečenskij jazyk* (Tiflis, 1888), Otd. I-yj, p. 35.

different sub-dialects, a welcome feature in view of the scantity of texts published in the USSR even up to the present day. Other Abaza material was published by Serdjučenko (1947, 1949; about the former cf. Lomtatidze, 1949). A significant contribution was made by N. F. Jakovlev, who published grammars of the two literary Circassian languages (*adygejskij* 1941, *kabardinočerkesskij* 1948). These books contain interesting ideas besides many Marrist aberrations, but they are not on a level with Jakovlev's brilliant work of the twenties.

**11.** NE Cauc. – Žirkov followed up his grammars of languages described earlier by Uslar with his grammar of Lezghian (1941); in 1948 he published a Tabasaran grammar, interesting from the point of view of general linguistics because of his discussion of the comparative and structural-illustrative use made of this language by Dumézil and Hjelmslev respectively, but limited to the literary dialect, and with only two pages of texts. Important contributions of this period are further Šaumjan's Agul grammar with texts and vocabulary (1941), and Jakovlev's Čečen syntax (1940). After the war, the flow of publications increased. Cercvadze gave the first description of a Southern Avar dialect (1948), Uslar's earlier description being based on one of the Northern dialects (Xunzax) which is now the basis of the literary language. Other Avar dialects were discussed by Mikailov (1948, 1949). Axvax texts were published by Žirkov (1949). The Vixlin dialect of Lak was treated by Murkelinskij (1949), the Cudaxar dialect of Dargwa by Gaprindašvili (1948). In 1949, A. A. Bokarev's Avar syntax and Čamalal grammar were published posthumously.

**12.** S Cauc. – Linguistic work in Georgia during this period compares favorably – qualitatively as well as quantitatively – with that elsewhere in the USSR. On Svan, there appeared V. Topuria's description of the verb (1931) and a collection of texts by A. Šanidze and V. Topuria (1939); a Svan phonetics was published by S. Žgenti in 1949. On Laz there appeared a grammar with texts by Čikobava (1936); this book also contains a discussion of Georgian-Laz comparison. Additional texts were published by Žgenti (1938), who also gave a description of the Gurian dialect of Georgian (1939). Other material on Georgian dialects was published in the *Izvestija Instituta jazyka, istorii i material'noj kul'tury* which appeared in Tbilisi 1936-1941. A large number of articles on various problems of detail were published by I. Abuladze, G. Axvlediani, A. Čikobava, A. Šanidze, V. Topuria and many others. – In 1940 Rudenko published the only Georgian grammar written in Russian during the Soviet period.

A most important event in Kartvelian philology was the publication of a comparative Laz-Mingrelian-Georgian dictionary by Čikobava in 1938. In the introduction, the regular Georgian ~ Mingrelo-Laz sound-correspondences are stated: G. *e* ~ ML. *a*; G. *a* ~ ML. *o*; G. *c*, *ʒ*, *c'*, *s*, *z* ~ ML. *č*, *ǯ*, *č'*, *š* or *sk*, *ž*; G. *č*, *ǯ*, *č'*, *š* ~ ML. *čk*, *ǯg*, *č'k'*, *šk* or *sk* (e.g. G. *k'aci* ~ ML. *k'oči* "man"; G. *šeni* ~ ML. *skani* "your, sing."; G. *č'am-* ~ ML. *č'k'om-* "to eat"). Čikobava regards the ML. "harmonic groups" *šk*, etc., as secondary (< **š*, etc., cf. Čikobava, 1936, 18f.; 1938, 442, 447, 452). The question of the "sibilant correspondences" has given rise to much further discussion (cf. 20). Čikobava's dictionary, which contains 291 items and includes also a certain amount of Svan material, represents a milestone in Kartvelian comparative linguistics.

In 1948 Čikobava published the first volume of his series on the problem of the ergative construction in the Ibero-Caucasian languages, the second volume of which appeared in 1961. Whereas the latter deals with the general-linguistic problem of the ergative, the former is devoted to a detailed analysis of the possibilities of expression of the "real subject" by a nominative, ergative, dative or "indefinite" case in the Kartvelian languages, especially in Old Georgian. From the point of view of Caucasology the book is important in the first place as a systematic collection of material and in the second place because of the author's conclusion that the Kartvelian transitive verb originally knew only the ergative construction, which means that these languages at one time were typologically closer to NE and NW Cauc. than they are at present.

**13.** ALL-CAUC. – Another line of investigation must be mentioned here because of the great influence it has had – and to a certain extent still has – on the thinking of a number of Georgian linguists. In 1937 the great Georgian historian Ivane Džavaxišvili published the second volume of his "Introduction to the History of the Georgian People", sub-titled "The Original Structure and the Relationship of Georgian and the Caucasian Languages". Here an attempt is made to find remains of a noun-class division of the NE Cauc. type (see 5) in Kartvelian, and thus to furnish evidence for the relationship of S and N Cauc. This idea was taken up (in a different form) by Čikobava in his interesting book "The Oldest Structure of the Nominal Bases in the Kartvelian Languages" (1942; cf. also Čikobava 1948). The book gives a detailed analysis of the Kartvelian nominal bases into prefixes, roots, root-determinatives and suffixes. On the basis (1) of the distinction *vin* "who?" versus *ra* "what?" (animal or thing), and (2) of the distinction between the Georgian suffixes *-el-* versus *-ur-/-ul-* referring to persons and things respectively (e.g., *kartveli* "Georgian (person)", *kartuli* "Georgian (object)"), Čikobava concludes that the distinction of persons and things must be old in the Kartvelian languages: the Georgian dialects show that the differentiation of *-el-* and *-ur-/-ul-* in this function is a secondary phenomenon. Therefore – thus Čikobava reasons – it must have arisen as a compensation for the loss of another formal expression of this distinction. Čikobava finds this older formal expression in the prefixes *m-* "person" versus *s-*, *d-*, *n-*, *r-*, *l-*, *b-* "thing", cf. *m-tav-ar-i* "chief" (*tav-i* "head"), *m-did-ar-i* "rich" (*did-i* "large") but *šeša* "firewood" < **se-ša*, cf. Mingrelian *di-ška* "id." with another prefix, Georgien *rʒe* "milk" < *s-ʒe*, which is the Old Georgian form, cf. Svan *lə-ʒe* "id.". Furthermore, the Georgian active participle, likely to refer to persons, has *m-*, while the passive-necessitative participle has *s-*, e.g., *m-k'et-eb-el-i* "making" versus *sa-k'et-eb-el-i* "to be made" (root *k'et-*). The prefix *m-* is brought in connection with the NE Cauc. prefix *w-* "rational, male", and *d-* (cf. *di-ška* above) with NE Cauc. *d-* for one of the non-rational classes. This brief account must suffice for Čikobava's theory, which is not without speculative elements, as it lacks the support of a strict comparative-phonetic methodology. The book initiated a search for petrified class-prefixes in various Cauc. languages and the yield has been rich (cf. also

Rogava 1956) but it has not always been able to withstand sober comparative-phonetic and -morphological criticism.[7]

**14.** Towards the end of the forties there was a marked upswing in the work of Soviet Caucasologists, cf. the publications mentioned at the end of sections 10-12, to which may be added a comparative article by K. Lomtatidze (1949) establishing the intra-Abxaz sound-correspondence Tapanta *c*, *ʒ*, *c'* ~ Bzyb, etc., *f*, *v*, *f'*, both going back to **c*°, **ʒ*°, **c'*° (cf. also Lomtatidze, 1944, 31f., 224f.). Mention must further be made of G. Axvlediani's book on general phonetics (1949) which contains much Cauc. material.

At the scientific session dedicated to the menory of N. Ja. Marr, held in Moscow on Jan. 24-27, 1950, Čikobava and Axvlediani were sharply criticized for their open attacks against Marrist linguistics (cf. Simmons, 1951, 5). On May 9th of that year, the Pravda opened its famous "free discussion" on linguistics with an article by Čikobava which heralded a new period in Soviet linguistics.

The most urgent task in Caucasian linguistics remained the recording of facts: the description of the grammatical structure and the collection of lexical material of languages and dialects so far not or insufficiently studied. Two reasons made this task particularly urgent. In the first place, due to the prestige of the literary languages and of Russian, combined with changes in culture and increased mobility of the population, more and more dialect-material threatened to be irretrievably lost. In the second place, this task had to be fulfilled before comparative work could be undertaken with any chance of success. The N Cauc. languages – especially the NW group – put great obstacles in the way of phonetic comparison. This is due to the fact that the roots of these languages in general consist of a single consonant (or a harmonic complex); as a result, each morpheme tends to present a unique combination of features, so that it is difficult to find *series* of comparisons involving the same sound (in principle, this is possible only in the case of homonyms). Thus, objectively speaking, the material prescribes a very careful approach: comparative work can be succesful where closely similar languages or dialects are concerned. Furthermore, it is in general the non-literary dialects that are phonetically the most complex, i.e., these dialects preserve distinctions lost in the literary dialects. The non-literary dialects are therefore of the utmost importance for the reconstruction of the proto-forms of the various dialect-groups, and such a reconstruction is necessary before one can fruitfully start comparing one dialect-group with the next. It is clear, therefore, that the description of dialects *with a view to their importance for inter-dialect comparison* is an indispensable prerequisite for the further development of comparative Cauc. linguistics. Unfortunately, in this respect the 20-year Marrist period has had a double negative effect, which is wearing off only gradually. In the first place, it has stimulated the tendency –

[7] Cf. G. Deeters, "Gab es Nominalklassen in allen kaukasischen Sprachen?", *Corolla Linguistica* (Wiesbaden, 1955), pp. 26-33; K. H. Schmidt, *Studien zur Rekonstruktion des Lautstandes der südkaukasischen Grundsprache* (Wiesbaden 1962), particularly p. 18; A. H. Kuipers, "Proto-Circassian Phonology: An Essay in Reconstruction", *Studia Caucasica* 1.65-101 (1963), sect. 4.

which existed already before in Caucasology, Soviet as well as Western – to premature comparisons and large-scale speculation as to relationships. In the second place, it has failed to develop in a whole generation of linguists a strict phonetic-methodological discipline and an understanding of the basic tenets of the comparative method, or at least an appreciation of the necessity of applying them. As a result, part of the efforts of Soviet scholars has been diverted into speculative channels, while much indispensable spade-work remained to be done. At the same time, some of the descriptive work that has been done falls short of the exigencies stated above. Several dialect-descriptions contend themselves with a summing-up of the features of the dialect in question (usually in terms of deviations from the standard language), without singling out for fuller treatment those features which affect the comparative picture (say, a distinction between two sounds which have merged in the literary language). Sometimes a mere mentioning of such a distinction, with a few examples, in considered sufficient, and the distinction is not expressed in the transcription of the dialect except in the one section dealing with it specifically. The result is that such works have to be used with the greatest care, and that their value for comparative purposes is smaller than it might have been.

**15.** NW CAUC. (DESCRIPTIVE) – K. Lomtatidze continued her excellent descriptive work on Abxaz with her book on the Ašxar dialect (1954), which, like its companion-volume on Tapanta, is liberally provided with texts in the different sub-dialects (106 pages!). In 1955, Genko's Tapanta grammar, finished as early as 1934, was published posthumously by Lomtatidze and Serebrennikov; the work usefully supplements Lomtatidze's grammar of 1944. A short survey of the Bzyb dialect was published by Bgažba (1957, 1960), one of Abžuj by Cikolia (1958). In 1961, K. Šakryl published a book on affixation in Abxaz, a welcome contribution to the inventory of lexico-grammatical items of this language; in an appendix. Bzyb and Abžuj texts are given with Russian translations. Important for lexicology are Džanašia's Abxaz-Georgian dictionary (1954) and the Russian-Abaza (i.e., Tapanta) dictionary prepared by the *Čerkesskij n.-i. institut* under the editorship of Žirov and Èkba (1956).

Of W Circassian only the Šapsug dialect was described in some detail by Keraševa (1957); the book contains a 50-page listing of lexical items peculiar to Šapsug, unfortunately in a transcription which does not reflect all the phonemic distinctions existing in the dialect. The peculiarities of Abadzex were briefly treated by Z. Kumaxova (1960). The very important Bžedux dialect so far remains undescribed. The lexicology of W Circassian was greatly advanced by Vodoždokov's Russian-Adygej dictionary (1960) and especially by Xatanov and Keraševa's explanatory W Circassian dictionary (1960), supplied with Russian translations and with illustrations of items peculiar to Circassian material culture. – Of E Circassian, the archaic, phonetically rich Beslenej dialect was described by Balkarov (1959); the book includes over 30 pages of texts with interlinear translation and a list of some 150 lexical items peculiar to the dialect. Mamrešev published a monography on the Baksan dialect (1959). The other dialects of E Circassian were treated in a number of articles (Turčaninov,

1946; Kuaševa, 1957; Kumaxov, 1959, 1961, Šagirov, 1961). A new grammar of literary Kabardian (Abitov and others 1957) is less systematic than Jakovlev's description of 1948 but adds some morphological and syntactic details. Of considerable historical interest is the publication in 1956 (I) and 1959 (II) of the material of the 19th cent. native scholar Š. Nogma (1801-44) by the *Kabardinskij n.-i. institut*; the material consists of a grammar, texts and a dictionary of Kabardian. A Russian-Kabardian dictionary (Šogencukov, 1955) and a Kabardian-Russian counterpart (Kardanov, 1957) now provide extensive (though still incomplete) lexical material of the literary language.

Other descriptive articles on various matters of detail of NW Cauc. were published by Bgažba, Čkadua, Kvarčelia, Lekiašvili, Lomtatidze, Šinkuba (Abxaz) and by Bagov, Balkarov, Èl'berdov, Keraševa, Kumaxov, Rogava, Sakiev, Šagirov (Circassian).

**16.** NW CAUC. (COMPARATIVE). – The comparative study of the NW Cauc. languages is in a less advanced stage than that of NE and S Cauc. This is due to the exceptionally complex phonetic structure of the languages. A certain amount of intra-Abxaz comparison is contained in Lomtatidze's grammars of 1944 and 1954; her comparative article of 1949 was already mentioned in section 14. A systematic survey of the phonetic relations between Tapanta and the other Abxaz dialects is given in a posthumous article by Genko, written in 1935 and published in the *Trudy* of the Abxaz Institute (1957). This article contains a summing-up of the simplest roots (type CV) in both types of dialects, in so far as these roots occur in the contemporary language (roots established by historical-lexical analysis are excluded). – Some details of comparison between Circassian dialects were treated by Rogava (1955, 1958). Mention must further be made of Šagirov's book on the comparative lexicology of the Circassian languages (1962), which includes, among others, a summing-up of 80 Circassian-Abxaz etymologies proposed by Trubetzkoy, Dumézil, von Mészáros, Rogava, Lomtatidze,[8] and by the author; the book also contains a useful section on borrowings. However, intra-Circassian comparison as such was not materially advanced by these works beyond what is evident from N. F. Jakovlev's comparative tables published in 1930 in the journal *Caucasica*, IV (p. 1-19).

As long as the comparison of the Abxaz and that of the Circassian dialects have not been worked out in detail, comparisons between these two languages will probably remain incidental and doubtful (Lomtatidze, 1958, 1960). In 1953 Lomtatidze published an article in which an interesting attempt is made to identify Circassian *ş*, *ẓ*, *ş*' with the Abxaz series (Bzyb) *c'*, *ʒ'*, *c*'', *s'*, *z'* on the basis of phonetic-structural considerations: the Cauc. languages oppose in general triplets of plosives to pairs of fricatives, therefore the above Circassian series of fricatives may go back to a full series **ç*, **ʒ̧*, **ç*', **ş*, **ẓ* (with subsequent fricativization of the affricates, a common phenomenon in Circassian), and this full series is identified with the Abxaz series.

[8] Some of Lomtatidze's most interesting etymologies are not included, cf. 22 nos. 2 and 3.

Lomtatidze's article does not convince because in the end only three etymologies are given which involve only two of the five alleged Proto-NW Cauc. phonemes. But the article is interesting from a methodological point of view: normally, one *first* observes regular sound-correspondences between semantically comparable elements in different languages, and *then* one reconstructs the way in which the languages became differentiated. Lomtatidze, working on languages where the first step involves great difficulties, begins with the second stage and ends with the etymological material. This procedure constitutes and interesting innovation in the technique of comparative linguistics, called forth by the peculiar nature of the material. The introduction of diachronic-structural considerations in comparative work allows at least the setting up of working hypotheses; but the etymological material must in the end decide for or against accepting these.

In the footsteps of Čikobava (cf. 13), Rogava tried to identify petrified class-prefixes and root-determinatives in Circassian (1956). The work contains much interesting material, but in the absence of a strict phonetic methodology such attempts necessarily remain speculative and unconvincing. It is possible that some of Rogava's etymologies will prove to be correct (cf. 22), but this could be established only on the basis of a step by step comparison first of closely and later of more distantly related dialects and languages.

**17.** NE CAUC. (DESCRIPTIVE). – Of the *Vejnax* group, the Bac language was described in detail by Dešeriev (1953), who also published a Čečen phonetics (1960). The dialect of Aux was treated by Arsaxanov (1959); the book gives 16 pages of texts with Russian translation, and a detailed grammatical analysis of one of the texts. Jakovlev's Čečen morphology, finished in 1939, was published in 1960. A new Čečen-Russian dictionary was published by Maciev in 1961; the fact that Čečen orthography does not reflect all the phonemic distinctions is partly made up for by the indication of vowel-length by a macron.

*Avaro-Andi-Dido*. Descriptive work on Avar dialects was continued by Džaparidze (1959), È. Mikailov (1960) and especially by Š. Mikailov (1957, 1959), whose *Očerki* constitute a milestone in Avar dialectology: besides a clear survey of the dialects (in so far as they are spoken in the Dagestan ASSR), a large amount of new linguistic information is provided here. One regrets only the absence of texts and the sometimes inconsistent notation. A full and excellent description of Avar was published in 1962 by Čikobava and Cercvadze. This work is especially valuable because of the systematic attention paid to the dialects. Parallel texts are given in the Xunzax, Hid, Čox, Karax, Ancux and Čar dialects. A Russian-Avar dictionary was published by Saidov and Mikailov in 1951. – A survey of the Andi dialects was given by Cercvadze (1959), who also devoted a special study to Andi phonetics (1953). Other studies on the Andi group are Sulejmanov 1959 (Andi), Magomedbekova 1955 (Axvax), 1960 (Tokita), 1961 (Bagulal), and Gudava's detailed account of Tindi phonetics (1953). Most of these articles also contain information of a comparative nature. – As to the Dido group, a sketch of Kapuča-Gunzib was given by Lomtadze (1956), while Gunzib lexical material was published by E. Bokarev (1961). Madieva published a sketch of Bežita (1954), Šarafutdinova and Levina one of Xvarši (1961). Very important is Bokarev's book on the Dido (Cez) languages (1959), where Gunzib, Bežita, Ginux, Xvarši and Cez are discussed separately in some detail.

*Lak-Dargwa.* Žirkov's Lak grammar (1955) describes the literary dialect of Kumux (while Uslar's description was based on the Vicxin dialect). The peculiarities of the Vixlin dialect were treated by Murkelinskij (1949), those of Balxar by Xajdakov (1954). Lexical studies on Lak were written by Murkelinskij (1954) and by Xajdakov (1961); the latter contains information on the structure of words, word-formation, affixes, borrowings and onomastics, besides comparative data. A Russian-Lak dictionary was published by Murkelinskij in 1953, a Lak-Russian one by Xajdakov in 1962. On Dargwa there appeared a grammar by Abdullaev (1954), a classification and a phonetic study of the dialects by Gaprindašvili (1952; 1956), one on the Dejbuk and Xarbuk dialects by Gasanova (1957), a monography on noun-declension in the Urkarax dialect by Abakarova (1956) and a phonetic survey of Kubači by Magometov (1958). A Russian-Dargwa dictionary was published by Abdullaev in 1950.

*Lezghian group.* G. Topuria devoted a monography to the Lezghian verb (1959), based on the Kjuri and Axty dialects. Lezghian syntax was dealt with by Gadžiev (1954, 1956). Dialect-descriptions were given by Gajdarov 1955 (Axty), Mejlanova 1957 (Gjunej), 1958 (Gilijar), 1959 (Stal') and by Gadžiev 1957 (Anyx). A Russian-Lezghian dictionary was published by Gadžiev in 1950. As regards the other languages of this group, Tabasaran phonetics was treated by Magometov (1959), a lexical study of Kryc was written by Saadiev (1959); important is further Kaxadze's study on the Arči laterals (1958), correcting the earlier data of Uslar and Dirr. Džejranišvili gave an interesting description of pharyngalized vowels in Caxur-Rutul and Udi (1959), illustrated with X-ray pictures. Very important is the publication of a Xinalug grammar by Dešeriev (1959); this language, known so far by name only, approaches NW Cauc. by the complexity of its phoneme-system (59 consonants, 15 vowels). Dešeriev (p. 207) leaves open the question whether Xinalug is a deviating member of the Lezghian group, a separate subdivision of NE Cauc., or even a separate unit on a level with NW and NE Cauc., strongly influenced by Lezghian. – Šanidze (1960) discussed the language of the ancient Transcaucasian Albanians, known only from a few inscriptions and from quotations of names; it may have been connected with NE Cauc., in particular with Udi.

Other descriptive articles on various matters of detail concerning the NE Cauc. languages were published by Črelašvili, Dešeriev, Gagua, D. Imnaišvili (Vejnax), by Cercvadze, Čikobava, Gudava, Kikvidze, Magomedbekova (Avaro-Andi), by D. Imnaišvili, Lomtadze (Dido), by Gaprindašvili, Xajdakov (Lak), by Gaprindašvili, Magometov (Dargwa), by Džejranišvili (Lezghian group, Caxur, Rutul, Udi), by Gigineišvili, Pančvidze (Udi), by Magometov (Tabasaran), by Magometbekova (Axvax) and by G. Topuria (Kryc).

**18.** NE CAUC. (COMPARATIVE). – Considerable progress has been made in the comparative study of the NE Cauc. languages since 1950. The linguistic material is here more favorable to comparison than in the case of NW Cauc. Even though several languages and many dialects remain insufficiently described, there is a much larger number of languages as material for comparison. Furthermore, the originally uniconsonantal roots are often provided with identical affixes in a number of languages, which facilitates comparison.

Many of the descriptive works mentioned in section 17 contain comparative data. For the comparison of Avar dialects Mikailov's books (1958. 1959) contain precious data. Important comparative studies on the Avaro-Andi languages are Gudava's articles on the pharyngals[9] and on the affricates (1958; *Affrikaty*, 1959), in both, comparative sound-tables are given. In 1959 Gudava published a comparative analysis of the verbal bases in Avaro-Andi. In this book, 242 corresponding verbal bases are quoted in their Avar, Andi, Botlix, Čamalal, Tindi, Bagulal, Karata and Axvax forms. In an introductory chapter the makeup of the bases in terms of class-indicators, determinatives, thematic and other suffixes is discussed. Mention must further be made of Gudava's study on labialized consonants in Avaro-Andi (1956) and of Cercvadze's article on an Avaro-Andi vowel-correspondence (1958).

On the Dido languages there appeared, besides a few comparative articles treating problems of detail (Lomtadze, 1956; Imnaišvili, 1956), the solid work of Bokarev (1959) already mentioned in section 17 (cf. also Bokarev, 1955). The final chapter of this book (p. 222-284) gives a comparative-historical analysis of this group of languages. The book is distinguished by a strict phonetic methodology, and this prevents the author from attempting a systematic reconstruction of Proto-Dido forms, for which, in view of the difficulty of the material, more detailed studies will be necessary.

The Avaro-Andi-Dido group as a whole is considered in Cercvadze's article on the so-called "fifth lateral" (1952), which in literary Avar appears as *t*ʾ, while four other laterals (*λ*, *λ*:, *ƛ*:, *ƛ*:ʾ) are preserved here. The fifth lateral, non-geminate *ƛ*ʾ, is preserved in some Avar dialects, in some Andi dialects, in Karata and in Axvax. – Comparative sound-tables for this group of languages are given by Gudava, Imnaišvili, Lomtadze, Magomedbekova and Cercvadze in their joint report of 1952.

Sound-correspondences between Lak and Dargwa are treated *in extenso* by Gaprindašvili (1954). The Lak sounds corresponding to the Avar laterals are discussed by Cercvadze (1960); the correspondences are Avar *λ* ~ Lak *x*′/*š*, Avar *λ*:, *ƛ*: ~ Lak *x*:′/*š*:, Avar *ƛ*:ʾ ~ Lak *k*ʾ/*č*ʾ or *l*, Avar *t*ʾ (dial. *ƛ*ʾ) ~ Lak *k*ʾ/*č*ʾ. Comparative material is also included in Xajdakov's lexical study of Lak (1961).

The comparative study of the Lezghian languages is as yet in its infancy. A few articles by R. I. Gajdarov and B. B. Talibov which appeared in Maxačkala are known to me only from a reference in Bokarev, 1961, 52, 57. A reconstruction of the Proto-Lezghian case-system was attempted by Bokarev (1960). Mention must further

[9] This term is used by Georgian scholars for the *q*-series, in Western terminology "uvulars".

be made of Kaxadze's article of 1959 proposing new Lak correspondences for some of the Arči laterals.[10]

Several publications of E. Bokarev (1958, 1960, 1961) are concerned with the NE Cauc. languages as a whole or with the "Dagestan languages", which is NE Cauc. minus Vejnax. In 1958 Bokarev attempted a reconstruction of the Proto-NE Cauc. glottalic affricates. On the basis of sufficient material to be convincing, he arrives at the following NE Cauc. phonemes: **c*ʾ, **c*:ʾ, **c*:ʾ°, **č*ʾ, **č*:ʾ, *č:ʾ°, *ƛ*ʾ, *ƛ*:ʾ, (in addition: **ʒ*, **ǯ*, **k*ʾ°). In 1961 Bokarev published an "Introduction to the Comparative-Historical Study of the Dagestan Languages", containing a phonetic survey of each of the languages or language-groups (Avar, Andi group, Dido group, Lak, Dargwa, Lezghian, Tabasaran, other Lezghian languages), a reconstruction of the Proto-Dagestan consonant- and vowel-systems, with sound-tables of the contemporary languages (illustrated with examples), and brief statements of the fundamental phonetic processes which have lead to the present-day languages. In the sections on consonants and vowels, 191 and 37 words from the various languages are quoted respectively. The consonant-system as reconstructed by Bokarev (p. 58) is reproduced here, in a modified arrangement:

| | | PLOSIVES | | | FRICATIVES | | SONORANTS |
|---|---|---|---|---|---|---|---|
| | | voiceless | voiced | glottalic | voiceless | voiced | |
| Labial | | *p* | *b* | *p*ʾ | | | *m* |
| Dent. | Stop | *t* | *d* | *t*ʾ | | | |
| | Affric. | *c c*: | *ʒ* | *c*ʾ *c*:ʾ | *s s*: | *z* | *n, l, r* |
| Palatal | | *č č*: | *ǯ* | *č*ʾ *č*:ʾ | *š š*: | *ž* | |
| Lateral | | | *dl* | *ƛ*ʾ *ƛ*:ʾ | λ λ: | | |
| Velar | | *k k*: | *g* | *k*ʾ *k*:ʾ | *x x*: | *ĝ* | |
| Uvular | Stop | *q* | | *q*ʾ | | | |
| | Affric. | *q q*: | *G* | *q̌*ʾ *q̌*:ʾ | *x̌ x̌*: | *ǧ* | |

This system does not include the labialized consonants, which are presupposed by special vowel-correspondences. The Proto-Dagestan vowel-system knew, according to Bokarev, the timbres *i*, *e*, *æ*, *u*, (*o*), *a* and probably opposed plain to pharyngalized and nasal vowels. This first attempt at a large-scale reconstruction will in all likelihood have to be revised and extended as the detailed comparative study of the individual NE Cauc. groups progresses. There are as yet great differences of opinion even on fundamental points, e.g., on the history of the laterals, which according to some scholars do not go back to Proto-NE Cauc. (cf. Čikobava 1959:131, Kaxadze 1959).[11]

[10] Here, as in other cases, controversial questions simply cannot be settled because of insufficient data, cf. R. Lafon's discussion of Kaxadze's article in *BSL* 66:2.232-236(1961).

[11] Bokarev's book, printed in a very small edition (500 copies), contains a large number of printing errors; furthermore, the author uses for some languages his own phonemic transcription, for others the official one, so that the same signs sometimes stand for quite different sounds (cf. p. 58). A project

**19.** S CAUC. (DESCRIPTIVE). – Descriptive Georgian linguistics is in a much more advanced state than that of the N Cauc. languages, as is to be expected in the case of an ancient literary language, the speakers of which continue an old intellectual tradition. There are excellent recent standard works on Georgian phonetics (Žgenti 1956; for accentuation cf. also Žgenti *Osnovnye voprosy*, 1953) and on morphology (Šanidze, 1953, 1955). A definitive eight-volume Georgian explanatory dictionary is being published by the Tbilisi *Institut jazykoznanija* under the editorship of A. Čikobava (1950-; cf. Čikobava, 1957); so far, seven volumes have appeared. This great work is also of prime importance for the further study of Georgian grammar, particularly for that of the complex verb-system: are quoted all forms of the indicative (3d pers) of the present-tense group (which includes forms with "future" and/or "perfective" meaning), with and without version-vowels (which may modify the lexical meaning, the tense or aspect, or the syntactic valence of the verb), active as well as passive. In this way, there are separate entries of the type *c'ers* "he writes", *ac'ers* "he writes on it", etc.; *dac'ers* "he will write", *daac'ers* "id. on it", etc.; *ic'ereba* "he writes (intrans.)". "it is (being) written", *ec'ereba* "it is written for him (or: on it, etc.)"; *daic'ereba, daec'ereba* "id., perfective"; *sc'eria* "it is written (exists in writing)", *ac'eria* "id. on it", etc. With each verb-form, aorist and perfect are quoted. Where certain forms do not exist, this is indicated. For each meaning of each form, examples are quoted from Georgian literature. With this dictionary, Georgian lexicology has been raised to a high level of excellence. Mention must further be made of Saxokia's three-volume dictionary of idiomatic expressions (1955-) and of the three-volume Russian-Georgian dictionary published by the Georgian Academy of Sciences under the editorship of Axvlediani and others (1956-).

The study of the Georgian dialects has also made great progress, cf. the monographies on Kaxetian by Martirosov and Imnaišvili (1956), on Tuš by Uturgaidze (1960), on Xevsur by Čincarauli (1960), on the Okrib sub-dialect of Imeretian by Kaxadze (1954), on Adžar by Nižaradze (1961) and by Nogaideli (1960), and further the articles or *avtoreferaty* on the Boržomi sub-dialect of Kartlian by G. Imnaišvili (1956), on Kaxetian by Šalamberidze (1955), on Moxev by Každaja (1954), on Ingilo by Ǧambašidze (1948), on Imeretian by Cxadadze (1954) and by Gačečiladze (1956), on Rača by V. Topuria (1961). In Dzidziguri's "Studies on Georgian Dialectology" (1954) separate chapters are devoted to Mesx, Imeretian, Lečxum and Rača; the book also gives a bibliography of Georgian dialectology. An excellent comprehensive survey, with copious texts and vocabularies of all the dialects, is given by Gigineišvili, Topuria and Kavtaradze in the first volume of their "Georgian Dialectology" (1961); the second volume of this great work will deal with theoretical, methodological and historical questions.

Important for the study of Old Georgian are the text-publications of the Tbilisi

for a unified transcription for the Caucasian languages is under way (Klimov, *O proekte*, 1962). – Kaxadze's useful article on the Arči laterals (1958) was not taken into account by Bokarev; fortunately this does not affect the comparative-linguistic picture.

*Institut rukopisej* (*Pamjatniki drevnegruzinskogo jazyka*) and the *Trudy* of the *Kafedra drevnegruzinskogo jazyka* of Tbilisi University. In the latter series, I. I. Imnaišvili published his very thorough description of the declension and the functions of the cases in Old Georgian (1957). The history of Georgian conjunctions was treated in a book by Dzidziguri (1959). A number of fundamental articles of A. Šanidze were reissued in the first volume of his *Voprosy struktury i istorii gruzinskogo jazyka* (1957). Of historical interest is further the publication (1961) of N. Čubinašvili's Georgian dictionary compiled in 1812-25 and used as a source by the famous Georgian lexicographer D. Čubinašvili. An excellent Old Georgian-Russian dictionary to the four Gospels was published in 1962 by Serebrjakov; the book contains an index of Russian words and one of personal forms of verbs. Under each head, sentences and phrases are quoted as examples.

Every issue of the *Iberijsko-kavkazskoe jazykoznanie* and of the *Voprosy struktury kartvel'skix jazykov* contains articles on various porblems of Modern and Old Georgian by such authors as Abuladze, Čikobava, Čxubianišvili, Dzidzišvili, Gačečiladze, Gaprindašvili, Imnaišvili, Kaladze, Kavtaradze, Kaxadze, Kiziria, Ležava, Lomtatidze, Mačavariani, Mandžgaladze, Martirosov, Natadze, Nozadze, Osidze, Počxua, Rogava, Šalamberidze, V. Topuria, Zurabišvili.

*Mingrelo-Laz and Svan*. A book on Mingrelo-Laz phonetics was published by Žgenti in 1953 (*Fonetika*). The phonetics of the Samurzakan-Zugdidi dialect of Mingrelian was treated by Cikolia (1954). Asatiani published an *avtoreferat* on preverbs in Mingrelo-Laz (1953). – A companion-volume to Šanidze and Topuria's Svan (Upper Bal) texts was published by Davitiani, Kaldani and Topuria in 1957; this volume contains Lower Bal texts. Kaldani published furthermore a number of studies on Lower Bal (1955, 1956, 1958, 1959) and one on the Lentex dialect (1961). The Cxumar sub-dialect of Lower Bal was treated by Šaradzenidze (1958). In Šanidze's *Voprosy* (1957), mentioned in the paragraph on Georgian, his fundamental article on the Umlaut in Svan is reprinted (p. 323-376).

Other descriptive articles on various matters of detail were published by Kartozia (Mingrelian), Kaldani and Šaradzenidze (Svan).

**20.** S CAUC. (COMPARATIVE). – The Proto-Kartvelian sound-system can for a large part be reconstructed with confidence (cf. Klimov, *Opyt*, 1960). The dental and palatal affricates and fricatives cause difficulties. Leaving these apart, the system is structurally and etymologically almost identical with that of Old Georgian, the only exception being the possible presence of a voiced uvular plosive in Proto-Kartvelian: *p, b, p*'; *t, d, t*'; *k, g, k*'; *q* (> Mod. Georg. *x*), *G* (?), *q*', *x, ğ*; *m, n, l, r, j* (> Mod. Georg. *zero*); vowels *a, e, o, i, u*. More difficult is the question of the dentals and palatals. As was mentioned before (cf. 12), the Georgian *c*-series corresponds to the Zan and Svan *č*-series, while the Georgian *č*-series corresponds to the Zan *čk*- and Svan *šg*-series, with occasionally a hissing rather than a hushing fricative in the latter languages (*sk* besides *šk*, etc.). An interesting attempt at a further systematizing of these correspondences was made by the Georgian Hittitologist and Kartvelist Th.

Gamkrelidze (1959). With other Georgian scholars, Gamkrelidze assumes that Georgian has preserved the original *c*- and *č*-series, so that Zan *čk* < **č*; he attempts to show that the development *sk* rather than *šk* results from a following *w*, which in some cases was subsequently lost, so that Zan *sk*(*w*) < **šw*. Furthermore, besides the abovementioned correspondences, there are cases where all the Kartvelian languages have hissing sounds (Klimov *Opyt* 1960:26, Mačavariani 1960), so that an additional series must be postulated for Proto-Kartvelian:

| | | | |
|---|---|---|---|
| Proto-Kartv. *$c_1$ | Georgian *c* | Zan *c* | Svan *c* |
| ,, **c* | ,, *c* | ,, *č* | ,, *č* |
| ,, **č* | ,, *č* | ,, *čk* | ,, *šg* (< **čk*)[12] |

For problems of detail cf. Rogava (1949) on the correspondence Mingrelian *r* ~ Georgian *g*, V. Topuria (1956, 1960) on affricate-correspondences, Mačavariani (1956, 1958) on vowel-correspondences, Rogava (1959) on the correspondence Zan *ǯ* ~ Georgian *r*. In 1962 Rogava published a book on certain problems of the history of vowels in the Kartvelian languages. A series of fundamental issues in comparative Kartvelian philology are touched upon by Klimov (*Iz istorii*, 1961) who points out (p. 272) that the explanation of many deviations from the established sound-correspondences (sometimes attributed to the "sporadic" character of the Kartvelian sound-changes) will have to await a more detailed study of the fundamental questions of comparative Kartvelian phonetics. Of one such a deviating correspondence: Georg. *t* ~ Zan *t* ~ Svan *šd* (besides the correspondence *t* ~ *t* ~ *t*) Klimov (p. 26) gives an elegant solution by assuming a Proto-Kartvelian **st*, this group being absent from Georgian and Zan. – Žgenti's book on the structure of the syllable in Kartvelian (1960) involves genetic as well as typological comparison.

A reconstruction of the Proto-Kartvelian declension-system was carried out by Klimov in an article (*Opyt* 1961) and, more detailed, in his interesting, well-documented monography of 1962 (*Sklonenie*).

**21.** ALL-CAUC. (TYPOLOGICAL). – A few publications are concerned with the Cauc. languages as a whole without being historical-comparative in the strict sense of the word. They are grouped here under the heading "typological", though all of them also have historical implications.

The Polish linguist Milewski, pointing out (1955, 1961) that the Causacian languages show a strong numerical predominance of consonants over vowels in their phoneme-systems, draws some parallels between Caucasian and American Indian languanges; in particular he compares the phoneme-systems of Rutul and Lutuami, Georgian and Kechua, Arči and Coeur d'Alene, Ubyx and Coos. Milewski's conclusion that this similarity goes back to an old "Sprachbund" in Central Asia (1961,

[12] Other solutions were proposed by Polák (1955) and by K. H. Schmidt, *Studien zur Rekonstruktion des Lautstandes der südkaukasischen Grundsprache* (Wiesbaden, 1962), pp. 54-67. Schmidt regards *čk*, etc., as original and assumes Proto-Kartvelian **c*, **č*, **čk* for the three series. This solution has certain advantages; for objections cf. Klimov 1960, pp. 28-29.

83), like Jakovlev's idea of ancient linguistic ties between the Caucasus and America (1947), cannot be accepted on typological evidence alone.

In his paper presented at the XXVth International Congress of Orientalists (1960), Čikobava discussed the types of conjugation found in the Cauc. languages. Some have a conjugation by class only (Čečen, Inguš, Avaro-Andi-Dido, several Lezghian languages), others one by class and person (Abxaz, Bac, Lak, Dargwa, Tabasaran), others one by person only (Circassian, Udi, Kartvelian), while in some languages the verb is conjugated neither by class nor by person (Lezghian, Agul). Among the second group, there is a sharp distinction between the Abxaz type and the NE Cauc. type, of which Lak may serve as an example. Though both languages distinguish a rational male (I), a rat. female (II) and an irrational class (III), these distinctions are by no means maintained in parallel ways, cf. the conjugation of the verb "to be" in 1, 2, 3 sing.:

| Person | Class | Lak | Abxaz | |
|---|---|---|---|---|
| 1 | I | | *sə-q’awp’* | "I am" (m. sp.) |
| 1 | II | *ur-a* | | "I am" (w. sp.) |
| 2 | I | *d-ur-a* | *wə-q’awp’* | "you are" (m. addr.) |
| 2 | II | | *bə-q’awp’* | "you are" (w. addr.) |
| 3 | I | *ur-i* | | "he is" |
| 3 | II | *d-ur-i* | *də-q’awp’* | "she is" |
| 3 | III | *b-ur-i* | *q’awp’* | "it is" |

Lak distinguishes classes everywhere, Abxaz only in the 2nd and 3d pers., merging I and II in the latter. Lak has specific class-prefixes: I *zero*, II *d-*, III *b-*; Abxaz lacks them. On the other hand, Lak distinguishes only third (*-i*) and non-third person (*-a*), while Abxaz distinguishes all three. In the historical part of his report, Čikobava concludes (p. 9) that class-conjugation is historically primary, and conjugation by person an innovation, on the grounds that in "all the Ibero-Caucasian languages . . . prefixation . . . is older than suffixation". Apart from the fact that in Abxaz person, too, is expressed by prefixes, the typological part of Čikobava's report rather emphasizes the large gap which exists between the facts of Abxaz and of NE Cauc., and certainly does not contradict the view, held by some, that the distinction of classes in Abxaz is an innovation.

At the same congress, Klimov (1960) gave a typological survey of the three groups of Caucasian languages, with special emphasis on the typological position of S Cauc. Phonologically, the Kartvelian consonant-system represents that system which NW and NE Cauc. have in common, without either the development of palatalization- and labialization-oppositions characteristic of the former, or the gemination-correlation widespread in the latter. The vowel-system (minimally five) is richer than the NW Cauc. one, and is comparable to the simpler NE Cauc. types. Morphologically, S Cauc. has a richer case-system than NW Cauc. but lacks the rich seriality found in the NE Cauc. case-systems. The S Cauc. verb, like that in NW Cauc., has subject- and object-prefixes and a supplementary prefixation of "versional" type (cf. 19), but neither prefixation is as amply developed as in NW Cauc. On the other hand, like NE Cauc., S Cauc. admits the inclusion of only one subject/object-prefix (other than zero). Nominal prefixation is most richly developed in NW Cauc., less in S Cauc. and least of all in NE Cauc., where it is limited to class-prefixes. NE Cauc. stands apart by its characteristic system of noun-classes. Syntactically, agreement plays a role in NE Cauc. (class-prefixes) and to a lesser extent in S Cauc. (case suffixes); it is absent from NW Cauc. The latter also stands apart in employing compounding where the other two groups have attributive syntagms. Thus, S Cauc. shares some features with NW Cauc., others with NE Cauc.; it has few features which set it off from both (and these are innovations, cf. 12, end). Klimov concludes that the investigation of genetic relationships between the three groups must take into account the possibility of a "chain-relationship".

**22.** ALL-CAUC. (COMPARATIVE). – While descriptive and limited comparative work is being done at an increasing and impressive rate, sweeping generalizations and long-range comparisons are being attempted less and less. Comparisons exceeding the limits of one of the three Cauc. groups are put forward only occasionally. The conviction is gaining ground that the actual *proof* of suggested long-range comparisons can be supplied only on the basis of a step-by-step piecing together of the historical picture of each individual language-group.[13] It is possible that some of the proposed All-Caucasian etymologies will prove to be correct, either because they belong to a Proto-Cauc. language, or because they belong to a common substratum or represent ancient loans.

In an article published in 1953, Rogava attempted to bridge the gap between the person- and class-systems of NW and NE Cauc. (cf. 21) by assuming that old class-prefixes developed into person-indicators. In particular, he identifies the NW Cauc. element *w-* "2nd, pers. sing." and S Cauc. *v-* "1st sing. subj." with the NE Cauc. *w-* of the first (rational male) class. However, the NW Cauc. morphemes for 1 sing. *s-*, 2 sing. *w-* and 2 plur. W Circassian *ş*° (regularly corresponding to E Circ. *f-*), Abxaz *š*° are paralleled in several NE Cauc. languages by person- (and not class-) elements, cf. Čečen *suo* "I", *huo* "thou", *šu* "you", Tabasaran *izu*, *iwu*, *ič°u*, etc., so that it is difficult to accept Rogava's identification.[14]

Some interesting parallels between NW and S Cauc. were pointed out by Lomtatidze (*Nekotorye voprosy zvukovyx processov*, 1955), who suggests fourteen etymologies, seven of which concern Abxaz, Circassian and Kartvelian, the remaining seven being limited to Abxaz and Kartvelian. It is true, this (for Caucasian) rather large number is reached at the cost of exact phonetic parallelism, words with Abxaz *h'*°, *h*, *h*° being compared to Circ. *q'*°, *ğ*°, *j* and to Kartvelian *q'v* (*q'u*), *ğ*, *ğv*, *r*, *rv*. But

[13] Cf. Klimov's review of K. Bouda's "Südkaukasisch-nordkaukasische Etymologien", *RO* 25(1). 156-158.

[14] Cf. G. Deeters, "Gab es Nominalklassen in allen kaukasischen Sprachen?", *Corolla Linguistica* (Wiesbaden, 1955), pp. 28-30.

two of Lomtatidze's examples are exactly parallel: 1. Abxaz *h'°(-ba)*, Circassian *(t'-) q'°ə* "two", Georgian *(t'-)q'u(-č'i)* "twins", *(c'-)q'v(-ili)* "pair"; 2. Abxaz *(aa-)h'°(-t')* "was audible", Circassian *(da-)q'°a(-n)* "to hear", Georgian *q'u(-ri)* "ear". A third example, Abxaz *(a-ba-)h'°* "bone', Georgian *(ba-)q'v(-i)* "thighbone" has in Circassian *q:°* rather than *q'°* (the latter form, quoted by the author, occurs secondarily in Kabardian, where *q:°* > *q'°*), but one might assume that **q'°* and **q:°* coincided in Abxaz and Kartvelian, since only Circassian distinguishes the two. Lomtatidze quotes for Circassian, Kabardian *q'°ə(-pṣẖa)* "bone" (W Circ. *q:°əpṣẖa*); formally closer to the Abxaz and Kartvelian forms is Circ. (Kabardian) *baq'°a(-n)* "to step, stride" (for the meaning, cf. Proto-Slavic **kork* "bone" and Polish *krok* "step"; for other cognates cf. Rogava 1956, pp. 8, 16). This would yield, for all three languages, the protoforms **q'°* 1. "two", 2. "hearing" or "ear", **ba-q:°(a)* "bone" (the latter clearly bimorphemic, cf. also Laz *q'v(-ili)* "bone"). Undoubtedly, these parallels pointed out by Lomtatidze and Rogava are of the utmost importance: only rarely does one find *series* of exact correspondences between one Cauc. group and another. But to determine the historical status of the above words more detailed studies of the individual language-groups will be necessary, and especially the question whether *ba-* is a petrified class-prefix (Rogava) cannot be settled in the present state of our knowledge.

The question of the possible relationship of the Cauc. languages with Basque and/or the ancient Mediterranean and Asianic languages was discussed in the journal *Voprosy jazykoznanija* in the years 1954-56 (cf. Georgiev, 1954; D'jakonov, 1954; Dunaevskaja, 1954; Kakabadze, 1955; Lomtatidze, *Nekotorye voprosy ib.-kavk.*, 1955; Zycar', 1955; Čikobava, 1955; *K itogam*, 1956). The conclusion of the last of these articles is that for none of the suggested outside connections of the Cauc. languages sufficient evidence has been brought forward.

**23.** Work in Progress. *NW Cauc.* A collection of material peculiar to the Bzyb dialect of Abxaz is being prepered by X. S. Bgažba. A new W Circassain grammar will be published by G. V. Rogava. Autlev is preparing a monography on the Bžedux dialect of W Circassian. A new Kabardian grammar is being prepared by the Kabardian *n.-i. institut* (Nal'čik) in cooperation with the *Institut izučenija adygejskogo jazyka* in Majkop. In addition, the Kabardian institute is working on an explanatory dictionary of Kabardian. B. M. Kardanov will shortly publish a Kabardian-Russian phraseological dictionary. A monography on word-formation in Circassian by M. A. Kumaxov is in press.

*NE Cauc.* An Andi grammar is being prepared by I. I. Cercvadze, a Botlix grammer with texts and vocabulary by T. E. Gudava, a Ginux grammar by È. A. Lomtadze. A. A. Magometov is working on descriptions of Kubači, Tabasaran and Agul; he has also prepared for publication Uslar's manuscript on Tabasaran. A book on Lak dialectology by S. M. Xajdakov will appear in 1964. T. E. Gudava is preparing a comparative phonetics of the Avaro-Andi languages. S. M. Xajdakov will publish a comparative (*sravnitel'no-sopostavitel'nyj*) dictionary of the Dagestan languages.

*S Cauc.* The Tbilisi *Institut jazykoznanija* will start publishing a six-volume course of Georgian, the first volume of which will deal with the history of the study of the Georgian language. Subsequent volumes will treat the grammar, dialectology and the history of Georgian and the other Kartvelian languages. Other publications being prepared by the Institute are the 2nd volume of the "Georgian Dialectology" (cf. Gigineišvili 1961 and section 19), a one-volume Georgian explanatory dictionary, a one-volume Russian-Georgian dictionary and a three-volume Georgian-Russian dictionary. In addition, a Georgian etymological dictionary is being prepared under the editorship of A. Čikobava. At Tbilisi University, A. G. Šanidze will publish a two-volume dictionary of Old Georgian; S. M. Žgenti will shortly publish his book on "Rhythmics and Melodic Structure of the Georgian Language". A Svan-Georgian-Russian dictionary and a textbook of Svan will be published by V. T. Topuria. At the Tbilisi *Institut rukopisej* I. V. Abuladze is preparing for publication a new edition of the Georgian dictionary (*sit'q'vis k'ona*) of Sulxan-Saba Orbeliani (1658-1725). In 1963 a book by T. V. Gamkrelidze and G. I. Mačavariani will appear, entitled "The System of Sonants and the Ablaut in the Kartvelian Languages". G. A. Klimov has finished the manuscript of a Kartvelian historical-etymological dictionary (cf. Klimov, *Iz opyta*, 1962).

*University of Leiden*

## BIBLIOGRAPHY[15]

Abakarova, F. O., *Imennoe sklonenie v urkaraxskom dialekte darginskogo jazyka* (dissertation abstract) (Moscow, 1956).

Abdullaev, S. M., *Russko-darginskij slovar'* (Maxačkala, 1950).

—, *Grammatika darginskogo jazyka* (*fonetika i morfologija*) (Maxačkala, 1954).

Abitov, M. L., et al. (eds.), *Grammatika kabardinočerkesskogo literaturnogo jazyka* (Moscow, 1957).

Arsaxanov, I., *Akkinskij dialekt v sisteme čečeno-ingušskogo jazyka* (Groznyj, 1959).

Asatiani, I. S., *Preverby v zanskom* (*megrel'skočanskom*) *jazyke* (dissertation abstract) (Tbilisi, 1953).

Axvlediani, G. S., *Osnovy obščej fonetiki* (Tbilisi, 1949). [G]

—, et al. (eds.), *Russko-gruzinskij slovar'*, 3 vols (Tbilisi, 1956, 1958, 1959).

Balkarov, B. X., *Jazyk besleneevcev* (Nal'čik, 1959).

Bgažba, X. S., "Bzybskij dialekt abxazskogo jazyka", *TAI*, 28 (1957).

—, "Bzybskij dialekt abxazskogo jazyka i ego govory", *MKV* (1960).

"Bibliografija jazykovedčeskix rabot, vypolnennyx v naučnyx učreždenijax Gruzinskoj SSR", *IKJa* 9-10.377-495(1958).

Bokarev, A. A., *Očerk grammatiki čamalinskogo jazyka* (Moscow-Leningrad, 1949).

—, *Sintaksis avarskogo jazyka* (Moscow-Leningrad, 1949).

[15] For contents of the bibliography cf. footnote * on p. 315. Some publications to which the author never had access are not included. [G] = written in Georgian; [G; R.s.] = written in Georgian, with a summary in Russian. For other abbreviations see master list.

Bokarev, E. A., "Zadači sravnitel'no-istoričeskogo izučenija kavkazskix jazykov", *VJA* 3/3.41-53 (1954).
—, *Opyt sravnitel'no-istoričeskogo izučenija cezskix jazykov* (dissertation abstract) (Moscow, 1955).
—, "Smyčnogortannye affrikaty pradagestanskogo jazyka", *VJa* 7/4.3-11 (1958).
—, *Cezskie (didojskie) jazyki Dagestana* (Moscow, 1959).
—, "K rekonstrukcii padežnoj sistemy pralezginskogo jazyka", *Voprosy grammatiki*, pp. 43-50 (Moscow, 1960).
—, "Grundfragen der historischen Phonetik der daghestanischen Sprachen", *MKV* (1960).
—, "Materialy k slovarju gunzibskogo jazyka", *VIIKJa* (1961), pp. 147-182.
—, *Vvedenie v sravnitel'no-istoričeskoe izučenie dagestanskix jazykov* (Maxačkala, 1961).
—, (ed.), *Voprosy izučenija iberijsko-kavkazskix jazykov* (Moscow, 1961).
—, and Dešeriev, Ju. D. (eds.), *Mladopis'mennye jazyki narodov SSSR* (Moscow-Leningrad, 1959).
Cercvadze, I. I., "Ancuxskij dialekt avarskogo jazyka", *IKJa* 2.117-214(1948). [G; R.s.]
—, "Ob odnom lateral'nom soglasnom i sootvetstvujuščix emu refleksax v avaro-andijsko-didojskoj gruppe dagestanskix jazykov", *SANG* 13.433-439(1952). [G; R.s.]
—, "K voprosam fonetiki andijskogo jazyka", *IKJa* 5.265-316(1953). [G; R.s.]
—, "Govory andijskogo jazyka", *TTGU* 55.213-219(1954).
—, "K zvukovym izmenenijam v avaro-andijskix jazykax", *IKJa* 9-10.251-256(1958). [G; R.s.]
—, "Govory andijskogo jazyka", *TTGU* 55.213-219(1954).
—, "O lakskix sootvetstvijax avarskim lateral'nym soglasnym", *IKJa* 12.339-344 (1960).
Cikolia, M. M., "Fonetičeskij obzor samurzakano-zugdidskogo govora megrel'skogo dialekta", *TAI* 25.323-343(1954).
—, *Abžujskij dialekt abxazskogo jazyka* (Tbilisi, 1948).
Cxadadze, A., *Margvel'skij govor imerskogo dialekta gruzinskogo jazyka* (dissertation abstract) (Tbilisi, 1954).
Čikobava, A. S., *Grammatičeskij analiz čanskogo (lazskogo) dialekta (s tekstami)* (Tbilisi, 1936). [G; R.s.; French summary]
—, *Čansko-megrel'sko-gruzinskij sravnitel'nyj slovar'* (Tbilisi, 1938). [G; R.s.; French summary]
—, *Drevnejšaja struktura imennyx osnov v kartvel'skix jazykax* (Tbilisi, 1942). [G; R.s.; English summary]
—, "Kartvel'skie jazyki, ix istoričeskij sostav i drevnij lingvističeskij oblik", *IKJa* 2.255-275(1948).
—, *Problema èrgativnoj konstrukcii v iberijsko-kavkazskix jazykax*, 1-2 (Tbilisi, 1948, 1961). [G; R.s.]

—, "O dvux osnovnyx voprosax izučenija iberijsko-kavkazskix jazykov", *VJa* 4/6.66-92 1955).
—, "O principax sostavlenija Tolkovogo slovarja gruzinskogo jazyka", *Leksikografičeskij sbornik*, 1.58-67 (Moscow, 1957).
—, (Tschikobawa), "Die ibero-kaukasischen Gebirgssprachen und der heutige Stand ihrer Erforschung in Georgien", *AOH* 9.109-161(Budapest, 1959).
—, "Osnovnye tipy sprjaženija glagolov i ix istoričeskie vzaimootnošenija v iberijsko-kavkazskix jazykax", *MKV* (1960).
—, (ed.), *Tolkovyj slovar' gruzinskogo jazyka*, 1-7 (Tbilisi, 1950-1962) (vol. 8 still to appear).
—, and Cercvadze, I. I., *Avarskij jazyk* (Tbilisi, 1962). [G]
Č'inč'arauli, A., *Xevsurulis taviseburebani, t'ekst'ebita da indeksit* (Tbilisi, 1960). (The Peculiatiries of Xevsur, with Texts and an Index)
Čubinašvili, N., *Slovar' gruzinskogo jazyka s russkim perevodom* (ed. A. A. Glonti) (Tbilisi, 1961).
Čxubianišvili, D. Z., "Bibliografija opublikovannoj v 1959 godu literatury po kartvel'skim jazykam", *VSKJa* 2.261-280(1961).
Davitiani, A., Kaldani, M., and Topuria, V., *Svanskie prozaičeskie teksty*, 2: *nižnebal'skoe narečie* (Tbilisi, 1957).
Dešeriev, Ju. D., *Bacbijskij jazyk* (Moscow, 1953).
—, *Razvitie mladopis'mennyx jazykov narodov SSSR* (Moscow, 1958).
—, *Grammatika xinalugskogo jazyka* (Moscow, 1959).
—, *Sovremennyj čečenskij literaturnyj jazyk, 1; fonetika* (Groznyj, 1960).
—, Klimov, G. A., and Talibov, B. B., "Ob unifikacii naimenovanij nekotoryx jazykov Kavkaza", *VJa* 8/3.61-65(1959).
D'jakonov, I. M., "O jazykax drevnej Perednej Azii", *VJa* 3/5.43-65(1954).
Dunaevskaja, I. M., "O xaraktere i svjazjax jazykov drevnej Maloj Azii", *VJa* 3/6.62-80(1954).
Dzidziguri, Š., *Dziebani kartuli dialekt'ologiidan* (Tbilisi, 1954). (Researches in Georgian Dialectology.)
—, *Kartuli salit'erat'uro enis ist'oriisatvis* (*k'avširebi da sak'avširebeli sit'q'vebi*) (Tbilisi, 1959). (On the History of the Georgian Literary Language [Conjunctions and Conjunctional Words]).
Džanašia, B. P., *Abxazsko-gruzinskij slovar'* (Tbilisi, 1954).
Džaparidze, Z. N., *Osnovnye fonetičeskie i morfologičeskie osobennosti manasaul'sko-arkasskogo govora avarskogo jazyka* (dissertation abstract) (Moscow, 1959).
Džavaxišvili, I. A., *Vvedenie v istoriju gruzinskogo naroda, 2: Pervonačal'nyj stroj i rodstvo gruzinskogo i kavkazskix jazykov* (Tbilisi, 1937). [G]
Džejranišvili, E. F., "Faringalizovannye glasnye v caxursko-rutul'skom i udinskom jazykax", *IKJa* 11.339-359(1959). [G; R.s.]
Gačečiladze, P. L., "Xansko-zeganskij govor imerskogo dialekta gruzinskogo jazyka", *IKJa* 8.109-150(1956). [G; R.s.].

Gadžiev, M. M., *Russko-lezginskij slovar'* (Maxačkala, 1950).
—, *Sintaksis lezginskogo jazyka, 1: prostoe predloženie.* (Maxačkala, 1954).
—, "Složnopodčinennoe predloženie v lezginskom jazyke", *VJa* 5/1.99-107(1956).
—, *Sintaksis složnogo predloženija v lezginskom jazyke* (dissertation abstract) (Moscow-Leningrad, 1956).
—, "O nekotoryx osobennostjax anyxskogo govora lezginskogo jazyka", *UZIC* 2 (1957).
Gajdarov, R., *Axtynskij dialekt lezginskogo jazyka* (dissertation abstract) (Maxačkala, 1955).
Gambašidze, see Ǧambašidze.
Gamkrelidze, T. V., *Sibiljantnye sootvetstvija i nekotorye voprosy drevnejšej struktury kartvel'skix jazykov* (Tbilisi, 1959). [G; Preface in Russian and English].
Gaprindašvili, Š. G., "Fonetičeskie osobennosti cudaxarskogo dialekta darginskogo jazyka po dannym aula Xožal-Max'i", *JaD* 1.105-135(1948).
—, "K voprosu o klassifikacii dialektov i govorov darginskogo jazyka", *III (IX) naučnaja sessija Instituta jazykoznanija. Plan raboty i tezisy dokladov*, pp. 55-57. (Tbilisi, 1952).
—, "O laksko-darginskix zvukosootvetstvijax", *IKJa* 6.281-326(1954). [G; R.s.]
—, *Fonetika darginskogo jazyka po dannym dialektov* (dissertation abstract) (Tbilisi, 1956).
Gasanova, S., "Kratkie svedenija o dejbukskom i xarbukskom govorax darginskogo jazyka", *UZIC* 2.251-260(1957).
Genko, A. N., *Abazinskij jazyk* (*grammatičeskij očerk narečija tapanta*) (Mocsow, 1955).
—, "Fonetičeskie vzaimootnošenija abxazskogo i abazinskogo jazykov", *TAI* 28.177-225(1957).
Georgiev, V., "Voprosy rodstva sredizemnomorskix jazykov", *VJa* 3/4.42-76(1954).
Gigineišvili, I. M., Kavtaradze, I. I., and Topuria, V. T., *Gruzinskaja dialektologija, 1: Kratkij obzor dialektov gruzinskogo jazyka. Teksty. Slovar'* (Tbilisi, 1961).
Gudava, T. E., "Fonetičeskij obzor tindijskogo jazyka", *IKJa* 5.327-394(1953). [G; R.s.].
—, "K izmeneniju labializovannyx soglasnyx v avarskom i andijskix jazykax", *IKJa* 8.215-234(1956).
—, "K voprosu o faringal'nyx soglasnyx v avarskom i andijskix jazykax", *IKJa* 9-10.256-267(1958). [G; R.s.].
—, *Sravnitel'nyj analiz glagol'nyx osnov v avarskom i andijskix jazykax* (Maxačkala, 1959).
—, "Affrikaty v andijskix jazykax", *IKJa* 11.261-290(1959). [G; R.s.].
—, Imnaišvili, D. S., Lomtadze, È. A., Magomedbekova, Z. M. and Cercvadze, I. I., "O zvukovyx sootvetstvijax v jazykax avarsko-andijsko-didojskoj gruppy", *III (IX) naučnaja sessija Instituta jazykoznanija. Plan raboty i tezisy dokladov*, pp. 32-35 (Tbilisi, 1952).

Ǧambašidze, R. B., *Ingilojskij govor. Grammatičeskij obzor i slovar'* (dissertation abstract) (Tbilisi, 1948). [G].
—, "Ingilouri k'ilo, t'ekstebi", *TTGU* 30(1947). (The Ingilo Dialect, Texts.)
Imnaišvili, D. S., "Fonetičeskie izmenenija v didojskom jazyke v sravnenii s ginuxskim i xvaršinskim jazykami", *IKJa* 8.243-268(1956). [G; R.s.].
Imnaišvili, G. M., "Osobennosti kartlijskogo narečija boržomskogo uščel'ja", *IKJa* 8.83-107(1956). [G; R.s.].
Imnaišvili, I. V., *Sklonenie imen i funkcii padežej v drevnegruzinskom* (Tbilisi, 1957). [G].
*Izvestija Instituta jazyka, istorii i material'noj kul'tury im. akad. N. Ja. Marra* (Tbilisi, 1936-1941).
Jakovlev, N. F. *Sintaksis čečenskogo literaturnogo jazyka* (Moscow-Leningrad, 1940).
—, "Drevnie svjazi jazykov Kavkaza, Azii i Ameriki", *Trudy Instituta ètnografii im. N. N. Mikluxo-Maklaja, n. s., 2*, p. 169f (Moscow, 1947).
—, *Grammatika literaturnogo kabardinočerkesskogo jazyka* (Moscow-Leningrad, 1948).
—, *Morfologija čečenskogo jazyka* (Groznyj, 1960).
—, and Ašxamaf, D. A., *Grammatika adygejskogo literaturnogo jazyka* (Moscow-Leningrad, 1941).
Kačarava, G. N., and Topuria, G. V., *Bibliografija jazykovedčeskoj literatury ob iberijsko-kavkazskix jazykax, 1: Gorskie iberijsko-kavkazskie jazyki* (Tbilisi, 1958).
Kakabadze, S. S., "O tak nazyvaemyx 'xettsko-iberijskix' jazykax", *VJa* 4/4.65-73 (1955).
Kaldani, M. M., "Fonetičeskie osobennosti laxamul'skogo podnarečija svanskogo jazyka", *IKJa* 7.137-205(1955). [G; R.s.].
—, "Grammatičeskie osobennosti laxamul'skogo podnarečija svanskogo jazyka", *IKJa* 7.161-177(1956). [G; R.s.].
—, "Osobennosti èc̣erskogo govora nižnebal'skogo dialekta svanskogo jazyka", *IKJa* 9-10.201-219(1958). [G; R.s.].
—, "Fonetičeskie i morfologičeskie osobennosti čubexevskogo govora svanskogo jazyka", *IKJa* 11.213-234(1959). [G; R.s.].
—, "Nekotorye fonetičeskie osobennosti lentexskogo narečija svanskogo jazyka", *VSKJa* 2.167-184(1961). [G; R.s.].
Kardanov, B. M., *Kabardinsko-russkij slovar'* (Moscow, 1957).
Kaxadze, O. I., "Nekotorye osobennosti okribskogo govora", *IKJa* 6.163-180(1954). [G; R.s.].
—, "Lateral'nye soglasnye v arčinskom", *IKJa* 9-10.339-344(1958). [G; R.s.].
—, "Nekotorye zamečanija po povodu lateral'nyx soglasnyx", *IKJa* 11.303-312(1959). [G; R.s.].
Každaja, O., *Moxevskij dialekt gruzinskogo jazyka* (dissertation abstract) (Tbilisi, 1954).
Keraševa, Z. I., *Osobennosti šapsugskogo dialekta adygejskogo jazyka* (Majkop, 1957).

"K itogam diskussii o «xetto-iberijskom» jazykovom edinstve", *VJa* 5/1.68-73(1956).

Klimov, G. A., "A Contribution to the Typological Description of the Kartvelian Languages (in Comparison with other Caucasian Languages)", *MKV* (1960).

—, "Opyt rekonstrukcii fonemnogo sostava obščekartvel'skogo jazyka-osnovy", *IzvAN* 1960, pp. 22-31.

—, "Opyt sravnitel'no-istoričeskoj rekonstrukcii sistemy sklonenija obščekartvel'-skogo jazyka-osnovy", *VJa* 10/6.14-21(1961).

—, "Iz istorii zvukosootvetstvij v kartvel'skix jazykax", *VIIKJa* (1961), pp. 271-281.

—, "Iz opyta raboty nad sravnitel'no-istoričeskim slovarem kartvel'skix jazykov", *VJa* 11/3.151-153(1962).

—, *O proekte edinoj fonetičeskoj transkripcii dlja kavkazskix jazykov* (Moscow-Leningrad, 1962).

—, *Sklonenie v kartvel'skix jazykax v sravnitel'no-istoričeskom aspekte* (Moscow, 1962).

Kuaševa, T. X., "Terskie govory", *UZKI* 13.271-290(1957).

Kumaxov, M. A., "O leksičeskix osobennostjax kubanskogo dialekta kabardinočer-kesskogo jazyka", *UZIC* 14.171-181(1959).

—, "Fonetičeskie osobennosti kubanskogo dialekta kabardinočerkesskogo jazyka", *VIIKJa* (1961), pp. 23-34.

Kumaxova, Z. Ju., *Osobennosti abadzexskogo dialekta adygejskogo jazyka* (dissertation abstract) (Moscow, 1960).

Lomtadze, È. A., "Sootvetstvija meždu glasnymi v didojskoj gruppe dagestanskix jazykov (Kapučinsko-gunzibskij, xvaršinskij, ginuxskij, didojskij)", *SANG* 17.81-88 (1956).

—, "Analiz kapučino-gunzibskogo jazyka", *IKJa* 8.369-412(1956).

Lomtatidze, K. V., *Tapantskij dialekt abxazskogo jazyka* (*s tekstami*) (Tbilisi, 1944). [G; R.s.].

—, "Ob odnoj fonetičeskoj zakonomernosti v abxazo-abazinskix dialektax", *SANG* 3(8).861-868(1949).

—, "Nekotorye zamečanija na raboty prof. G. P. Serdjučenko po abazinskomu jazyku", *TAI* 23.165-178(1949).

—, "K genezisu odnogo rjada troečnyx spirantov v adygskix jazykax", *DSIJa* 4.91-98(1953).

—, *Ašxarskij dialekt i ego mesto sredi drugix abxazsko-abazinskix dialektov* (*s tekstami*) (Tbilisi, 1954). [G; R.s.].

—, "Nekotorye voprosy zvukovyx processov i zvukovyx sootvetstvij v iberijsko-kavkazskix jazykax (po dannym kartvel'skix i abxaszko-adygskix jazykov)", *SANG* 16.821-828(1955).

—, "Nekotorye voprosy iberijsko-kavkazskogo jazykoznanija", *VJa* 4/4.73-83(1955).

—, "*ğ* ~ *r* bgeratmimartebisatvis apxazur-adiğur enebši", *SANG* 21.623-626(1958). (On the Sound-Relation *ğ* ~ *r* in the Abxazo-Adyghe Languages.)

—, "Nekotorye voprosy istorii fonetičeskoj sistemy abxazo-adygskix jazykov", *MKV* (1960).

Maciev, A. G., *Čečensko-russkij slovar'* (Moscow, 1961).

Mačavariani, G. I., "Slučai labializacii glasnogo *a* v svanskom jazyke", *SANG* 17. 365-368(1956).

—, "Iz istorii glasnyx sootvetstvij v kartvel'skix jazykax", *TTGU* 69.265-276(1958).

—, "O trex rjadax sibiljantnyx spirantov i affrikat v kartvel'skix jazykax", *MKV* (1960).

Madieva, G. I., *Grammatičeskij očerk bežitinskogo jazyka* (dissertation abstract) (Moscow, 1954).

Magomedbekova, Z. M., "Voprosy fonetiki axvaxskogo jazyka", *IKJa* 7.289-309(1955).

—, "O fonetičeskix osobennostjax tokitinskogo dialekta karatinskogo jazyka", *IKJa* 12.357-366(1960).

—, "Bagvalinskij jazyk (predvaritel'noe soobščenie)", *VIIKJa* (1961), pp. 123-129.

Magometov, A. A., "Fonetičeskij obzor kubačinskogo dialekta darginskogo jazyka", *IKJa* 9-10.315-338(1958).

—, "Kratkij obzor fonetiki tabasaranskogo jazyka", *IKJa* 11.313-337(1959).

Mamrešev, K. T., *Osobennosti baksanskogo dialekta kabardinskogo jazyka* (Nal'čik, 1959).

Martirosov, A. G., and Imnaišvili, G. M., *Kaxetinskij dialekt gruzinskogo jazyka. Issledovanie i teksty so slovarem* (Tbilisi, 1956). [G].

Mejlanova, U. A., "Kratkaja xarakteristika gjunejskogo dialekta lezginskogo jazyka", *UZIC* 3.213-243(1957).

—, "Gilijarskij smešannyj dialekt i ego mesto v sisteme lezginskix dialektov", *UZIC* 5 (1958).

—, "Stal'skij govor lezginskogo jazyka", *UZIC*, (1959), pp. 307-330.

Mikailov, È. Š., "Govor aula Čuni", *UZIC* (1960).

Mikailov, Š. I., "Osnovnye fonetiko-morfologičeskie osobennosti čoxskogo govora avarskogo jazyka", *JaD* 1.41-72(1948).

—, "O nekotoryx fonetičeskix osobennostjax južnoavarskix dialektov", *Trudy 2-oj naučnoj sessii Dagestanskoj bazy AN SSSR* (Maxačkala, 1949).

—, "Sogratlinskij govor južnogo narečija avarskogo jazyka", *UZIC* (1957).

—, *Sravnitel'no-istoričeskaja fonetika avarskix dialektov* (Maxačkala, 1958).

—, *Očerki avarskoj dialektologii* (Moscow-Leningrad, 1959).

Milewski, T., "La comparaison des systèmes phonologiques des langues caucasiennes et américaines", *Lingua Posnaniensis* 5.136-165(1955).

—, "Jazykovye svjazi Azii i Ameriki (avtoreferat dvux rabot)", *Zarubežnoe vostokovedenie, 2: Soobščenija pol'skix orientalistov*, pp. 74-90 (Moscow, 1961).

Murkelinskij, G. B., "Kratkie svedenija o vixlinskom dialekte lakskogo jazyka", *JaSKD* 2.87-98(1949).

—, *Russko-lakskij slovar'* (Maxačkala, 1953).

—, "O slovarnom sostave lakskogo jazyka", *JaD* 2.209-226(1954).

Nižaradze, Š., *Verxneadžarskij dialekt gruzinskogo jazyka. Issledovanie i teksty so slovarem* (Batumi, 1961). [G].

Nogma, Š. B., *Filologičeskie trudy, 1-2* (Nal'čik, 1956, 1959).

Nog̃aideli, Dž., *Ač'aruli k'ilos taviseburebani* (Batumi, 1960). (The Peculiarities of the Adžar dialect.)

Polák, V., "L'état actuel des études linguistiques caucasiennes", *AO* 18.383-407(1950).

—, "Contributions à la grammaire historique des langues kartvéliennes", *AO* 23(1955).

—, "Notules kartvéliennes", *Le Muséon* 68.279-296 (Louvain, 1955).

Rogava, G. V., "Iz zvukosootvetstvij kartvel'skix jazykov: megr. *r* ~ gruz. *g*", *SANG* 10.499-503(1949).

—, "K voprosu o perexode klassnogo sprjaženija v ličnoe sprjaženie v iberijsko-kavkazskix jazykax", *SANG* 14.443ff.(1953).

—, "K istorii abruptivnogo smyčnogo *p*' v adyskix jazykax", *IKJa* 7.279-282(1955).

—, *K voprosu o strukture imennyx osnov i kategorijax grammatičeskix klassov v adygskix (čerkesskix) jazykax* (Tbilisi, 1956).

—, "Šišina sp'irant'ta istoriisatvis qabardoul enaši", *Izvestija AN Gruz. SSR* 10.615-620 (1958). (On the History of the Hushing Fricatives in Kabardian).

—, "Iz oblasti zvukosootvetstvij v kartvel'skix jazykax: *r* ~ *ǯ*", *VSKJa* 1.277-280 (1959).

—, *Voprosy istoričeskoj fonetiki kartvel'skix jazykov, 1: Nekotorye voprosy istorii glasnyx v kartvel'skix jazykax* (Tbilisi, 1962). [G; R.s.].

Rudenko, B. T., *Grammatika gruzinskogo jazyka* (Moscow-Leningrad, 1940).

Saadiev, Š. M., "Ob ustojčivyx èlementax slovarnogo sostava kryzskogo jazyka", *Izvestija AN Azerb. SSR, Serija obščestvennyx nauk*, 1959:1.111-119.

Saidov, S. M., and Mikailov, Š. I., *Russko-avarskij slovar'* (Maxačkala, 1951).

Saxok'ia, T., *Kartuli xat'ovani sit'qva-tkmani, 1-3* (Tbilisi, 1950, 1954, 1955). (Georgian Idiomatic Expressions).

Serdjučenko, G. P., "Abazinskaja fonetika. Abazinskie mestoimenija. Abazinskie teksty", *Učenye zapiski Rostovskogo na Donu gos. universiteta, 5, Trudy ist.-fil. fakul'teta* 2.55-101(Taganrog, 1947).

—, "Abazinskie skazki", *JaSKD* 2.61-86(1949).

Serebrjakov, S. B., *Drevnegruzinsko-russkij slovar'* (*po 2-m drevnim redakcijam četveroglava*) (Tbilisi, 1962).

Simmons, E. J. (ed.), *The Soviet Linguistic Controversy* (*Translated from the Soviet Press*) (New York, 1951).

Sulejmanov, Ju., "Nekotorye voprosy andijskogo jazyka (po dannym selenija Rikvani)", *UZIC* 6.331-368(1959).

Šagirov, A. K., "Fonetičeskie osobennosti malkinskogo govora kabardinočerkesskogo jazyka", *VIIKJ* (1961), pp. 14-22.

—, *Očerki po sravnitel'noj leksikologii adygskix jazykov* (Nal'čik, 1962).

Šakryl, K. S., *Affiksacija v abxazskom jazyke* (Suxumi, 1961).

Šalamberidze, G. E., "Osobennosti kaxetinskogo narečija gruzinskogo jazyka po dannym reči sel. Kvareli", *IKJa* 7.101-118(1955). [G; R.s.].

Šanidze, A. G., *Osnovy gruzinskoj grammatiki, 1: morfologija* (Tbilisi, 1953). [G].

—, *Grammatika gruzinskogo jazyka, 1: morfologija* (Tbilisi, 1955). [G].

—, *Voprosy struktury i istorii gruzinskogo jazyka*, 1 (Tbilisi, 1957).

—, "Jazyk i pis'mo kavkazskix albancev", *Vestnik otdelenija obščestvennyx nauk AN Gruz. SSR* 1.168-189(Tbilisi, 1960).

—, and Topuria, V. T., *Svanskie prozaičeskie teksty, 1: verxnebal'skoe narečie* (Tbilisi, 1939).

Šaradzenidze, T. S., "Osobennosti cxumarskogo podgovora svanskogo jazyka", *IKJa* 9-10.221-250(1958). [G; R.s.].

Šarafutdinova, R., and Levina, R., "Xvaršinskij jazyk (predvaritel'noe soobščenie)", *VIIKJ* (1961), pp. 89-122.

Šaumjan, R., *Grammatičeskij očerk agul'skogo jazyka* (*s tekstami i slovarem*) (Moscow-Leningrad, 1941).

Šogencukov, A. O. (ed.), *Russko-kabardinsko-čerkesskij slovar*" (Moscow 1955).

Topuria, G. V., *Osnovnye morfologičeskie kategorii lezginskogo glagola* (*po dannym kjurinskogo i axtynskogo dialektov*) (Tbilisi, 1959). [G; R.s.].

Topuria, V. T., *Svanuri ena, 1: zmna* (Tbilisi, 1931). (The Svan Language, 1: The Verb).

—, "Nekotorye voprosy izmenenija i sootvetstvij affrikat v kartvel'skix jazykax (predvaritel'noe soobščenie)", *XIII naučnaja sessija Instituta jazykoznanija AN Gruz. SSR* (Tbilisi, 1956).

—, "Nekotorye voprosy sravnitel'noj fonetiki kartvel'skix jazykov", *MKV* (1960).

—, "O govorax račinskogo dialekta gruzinskogo jazyka", *VSKJa* 2.235-248(1961). [G; R.s.].

Tschikobawa, see Čikobava.

Turčaninov, G. F., "Materialy po dialektu mozdokskix kabardincev", *UZKI* 1.203-239(1946).

Uturgaidze, F., *Tušinskij dialekt gruzinskogo jazyka* (Tbilisi, 1960). [G].

Vodoždokov, X. D. (ed.), *Russko-adygejskij slovar'* (Moscow, 1960).

Xajdakov, S. M., "Balxarskij dialekt lakskogo jazyka", *TIJa* 3.258-262(1954).

—, *Očerki po leksike lakskogo jazyka* (Moscow, 1961).

—, *Laksko-russkij slovar'* (Moscow, 1962).

Xatanov, A. A., and Keraševa, Z. I., *Tolkovyj slovar' adygejskogo jazyka* (Majkop, 1960).

Zycar', Ju. V., "O rodstve baskskogo jazyka s kavkazskimi", *VJa* 4/5.52-65(1955).

Žgenti, S. M., *Čanskie* (*lazskie*) *teksty. Arxavskij govor* (Tbilisi, 1938).

—, *Gurijskij dialekt. Issledovanie, teksty, slovar'* (Tbilisi, 1939). [G; R.s.].

—, *Osnovnye voprosy fonetiki svanskogo jazyka* (Tbilisi, 1949). [G; R.s.].

—, "Osnovnye voprosy akcentuacii gruzinskogo literaturnogo jazyka", *IKJa* 5.125-163(1953). [G; R.s.].

—, *Fonetika čansko-megrel'skogo jazyka* (Tbilisi, 1953). [G].

—, *Fonetika gruzinskogo jazyka* (Tbilisi, 1956). [G].
—, *Sravnitel'naja fonetika kartvel'skix jazykov, 1: Problema struktury sloga* (Tbilisi, 1960). G; R.s.; English summary].
Žirkov, L. I., *Grammatika lezginskogo jazyka* (Maxačkala, 1941).
—, *Tabasaranskij jazyk* (Moscow-Leningrad, 1948).
—, "Axvakskie skazki". *JaSKD* 2.109-126(1949).
—, *Lakskij jazyk (fonetika i morfologija)* (Moscow, 1955).
Žirov, X. D., and Èkba, N. B., (eds.) *Russko-abazinskij slovar'* (Moscow, 1956).

# PALEOSIBERIAN

DEAN WORTH

Paleosiberian languages, as the term is used in this bibliographical survey, include Chukchee, Koryak, and Kamchadal (these three languages forming the Chukchee or Luoravetlan group; cf. however Skorik's proposed reclassification below), Yukaghir, Gilyak, and Ket. Some linguists include Asiatic Eskimo and Ainu in the "Paleoasiatic" group, but these languages are not treated in the present discussion, in spite of the great interest, e.g., of Menovščikov's studies of Eskimo. For typological reasons, the Paleosiberian languages were of great interest to the Marr school linguists, although relatively little of value resulted from their investigations. With the dethroning of Meščaninov during the linguistic controversy of 1952, Paleosiberian studies went forward on a firmer factual basis. In recent years, Soviet scholars have published a number of excellent articles, and there have already appeared two basic monographs, Skorik's Chukchee grammar and Krejnovič's grammar of Yukaghir. Most studies have been of Chukchee, Koryak, Yukaghir and Gilyak; Ket has been the subject of but a single article, and Kamchadal has been entirely neglected.

In the following survey, general works will be given first, followed by works dealing with the individual languages. The reviewer has tried to extract the most interesting facts from the books and articles examined, although in the case of the longer works, obviously only a fraction of the linguistic material can even be mentioned, much less discussed in significant detail. Occasional repetitions reflect the fact that Soviet authors, like others, must at times re-use material which has already appeared in print (cf., for example, Skorik's 1948 and 1960 articles on voice in Chukchee). In this connection, it must be pointed out that the comments on several books and articles which appeared in 1957 and subsequent years have been taken (usually in revised and somewhat abridged form) from the "Paleosiberian Abstracts" prepared for the *International Journal of American Linguistics*, XXVII, 4 (1961) and XXIX, 1 (1963); material from these issues of *IJAL* is identified by an asterisk preceding the title.

## 1. GENERAL AND COMPARATIVE STUDIES

I. I. Meščaninov's general typological survey, "Paleoaziatskie jazyki", *IzvAN* 7/6.500-510 (1948), gives a brief and rather superficial outline of the history of Paleosiberian studies, points out the inaccuracy of the term "Paleoasiatic" introduced by Schrenck, and makes a series of broad typological comparisons among the Paleosiberian languages (e.g., of Chukchee with Asiatic Eskimo) and between these languages as a group and other groups such as the Caucasian. There are a few remarks on individual features of Yukaghir, Ket, Gilyak and Ainu. The article is schematic and completely devoid of factual material (in ten pages there is not a single example from any of the languages discussed), although the typological discussion of sentence types may be of some interest to those who are not interested in the languages themselves.

In a brief note on "Èksperimental'noe izučenie fonetiki severnyx jazykov [Experimental study of the phonetics of northern languages]", *IzvAN* 7/6.579-581 (1948), L. R. Zinder insists on the inseparability of phonetics and phonology, and points out certain of the general features of "northern" languages (i.e., Paleosiberian, Tungus, etc.), among which he notes especially the absence of "exotic" sounds (clicks, etc.) throughout Siberia. Most Siberian languages, according to Zinder, use roughly the same articulatory base as Turkic, Finno-Ugric, or Indo-European (e.g., they have almost no laryngeals, pharyngeals, etc.). The article ends with a very brief discussion of the individual features of certain Paleosiberian languages.

One is unhappily reminded of the sorry situation that prevailed in Soviet scholarship only a decade ago when reading P. Ja. Skorik's "Teorija stadial'nosti i inkorporacija v paleoaziatskix jazykax [The theory of stadialness and incorporation in the Paleosiberian languages]", which appeared together with many similar attacks on Marr and Meščaninov in the collective volume *Protiv vul'garizacii i izvraščenija marksizma v jazykoznanii* [Against vulgarization and corruption of Marxism in linguistics], Sbornik statej, part 2 (Moscow, 1952), pp. 136-156. Skorik attacks the "metaphysical essence" of stadial theories, describes incorporation in several Paleosiberian languages, and attacks Marr's and Meščaninov's views of incorporation, with an occasional *mea culpa* to demonstrate that he himself had seen the light. The only interesting fact in the whole distasteful procedure is Skorik's admission that his earlier statements to the effect that incorporation was dying out among the younger generation of more cultivated sedentary Chukchees were not true. The article closes with a dutiful bow to Stalin's *Marksizm i voprosy jazykoznanija. Plus ça changeait, plus ç'était la même chose*, and one can only rejoice at the giant steps that Soviet scholarship has taken in the past decade.

A collective volume published by scholars at the Leningrad Pedagogical Institute (Leningradskij gosudarstvennyj pedagogičeskij Institut imeni A. I. Gercena, *Učenye zapiski*, Tom 101, Fakul'tet Narodov Severa, Leningrad, 1954) contains three articles on Paleosiberian languages, together with over a dozen papers on other minor languages of the U.S.S.R. These are V.N. Savel'eva's study on Gilyak declensional forms ("Sklonenie imen suščestvitel'nyx v nivxskom jazyke", pp. 239-254), T. A. Moll's paper on auxiliary verbs in Chukchee ("K voprosu o vspomogatel'nyx glagolax v čukotskom jazyke", pp. 281-291), and A. N. Žukova's description of agreement and incorporation as two principal means of connecting modifiers with their modified words ("Dva osnovnyx sposoba svjazi opredelenija s opredeljaemym v korjakskom jazyke", pp. 293-304). These papers will be discussed under the individual language headings below.

In 1954 there appeared the first general survey of the history of Paleosiberian studies, I.S. Vdovin's *Istorija izučenija paleoaziatskix jazykov* [History of the study of Paleosiberian languages] (Moscow-Leningrad, 1954), 165 pp. Vdovin's book carries this topic only up to the 1917 revolution, and even within these limits it is heavily oriented toward the earlier periods; nonetheless, the book is rich in bibliographical information, and has for the first time made extensive use of 17th- and 18th-century archive materials.

A brief and highly political "Introduction" complains that bourgeois scholars have neglected the role of Russian investigators in the Paleosiberian field, especially that of V.N. Tatiščev, and then, after a brief castigation of Marr and encomium of Stalin as linguist (*de rigueur* in those days), outlines the geographical distribution of the Paleosiberian peoples. The following Chapter I sketches in the history of the earliest reports of the existence of Paleosiberian peoples and languages in the 17th century, and gives hitherto unpublished word lists (mostly numerals) from the archives of the Academy of Sciences. Most of this lexical material, however, is not from Paleosiberian languages, but from the other minor languages of Siberia (Ostyak, Tungus, Yakut, etc.).

Chapter II, "V. N. Tatiščev and the study of northern languages", pp. 17-39, contains a certain amount of extraneous material regarding Tatiščev's views on language and society, before passing to his role in organizing some of the earliest investigations of Paleosiberian languages. Tatiščev was instrumental in drawing up and distributing the earliest lexical lists, some of which were sent to the members of the first Kamchatka expedition in 1737, and was directly or indirectly responsible for much of the rapidly growing interest in Siberian languages and the ethnogenesis of Siberian peoples.

Chapter III, "The first Academic expedition and the study of northern languages", pp. 40-52, describes the dictionary work completed under the auspices of the Academy, and in particular the lexical results of the Kamchatka expedition, which did not become known until 1755, when Krašeninnikov's fundamental work *Opisanie zemli Kamčatki* [A description of Kamchatka] was published. The several brief dictionaries collected by Krašeninnikov (Kamchadal, Koryak, Ainu) are described in their manuscript form, as are some of Krašeninnikov's still unpublished materials.

The following three chapters describe, in increasing detail, the further study of Paleosiberian languages in the latter 18th century (pp. 53-67), characterized primarily by the lexical activity of Pallas and Catherine II, the early 19th century (pp. 68-82), during which most new information resulted from maritime expeditions, notably that of J. Billings through and near the Chukchee peninsula, and the mid and later 19th century (pp. 83-105), which saw a considerable expansion of linguistic activity in Siberia. Vdovin outlines the results of Veniaminov's labors among the Aleuts, the work of Argentov and Radloff on Chukchee, of Castrén on Ket, of Tjušov on Kamchadal, and of Schrenck on Gilyak. It was Schrenck who advanced for the first time the so-called "Paleosiberian hypothesis", according to which the Paleosiberian peoples were the aboriginal inhabitants of Siberia, but had been thrust out to the North and East by the advance of more highly developed Manchu-Tungus and Turkic peoples from the South.

It was only in the last decades of the 19th century that serious linguistic study of the Paleosiberian languages was undertaken in close connection with study of the non-linguistic culture of these peoples. This period, which carried over into the twentieth century, is connected above all with the names of two great ethnographer-linguists, V. G. Bogoraz and V. I. Jochelson. Both had been exiled by the Tsar's police for illegal political activity, and both turned their years of residence in Siberia into a laboratory period for the first genuinely deep and modern study of the languages of this area. Chapter VII of Vdovin's book, "The study of Paleosiberian languages in connection with the study of ethnography of North-East Asia", describes this period in separate sections, devoted to Chukchee – Koryak, to Yukaghir, to Aleut, to Asiatic Eskimo, and to Gilyak (pp. 106-149). The fruits of these men's labors, e.g. Bogoraz' *Chukchee* (actually a comparative grammar of Chukchee, Koryak and Kamchadal) or Jochelson's *The Koryak*, are well-known to science and even today are standard works in this field. Vdovin describes in some detail the scholarly activity of Bogoraz and Jochelson, making use of their unpublished correspondence and other manuscript materials, and discussing the evolution of their linguistic thought in connection with their continually deepening practical command of the languages they worked with. Jochelson and Bogoraz worked in the Northeast, among the Chukchee, Koryak, Kamchadal, Yukaghir, and Aleut; the Gilyak language to the South was investigated by yet another political exile, L. Ja. Šternberg, who also investigated the linguistic relations between Gilyak and the languages of the North American Indians. As Vdovin correctly notes in the last paragraph of his book, it was the work of these three men that laid the basis for all further study of Paleosiberian languages in the post-revolutionary period.

One of the most valuable features of Vdovin's book is the appendix, pp. 150-164, which lists many manuscript items of great interest from the 18th (pp. 150-159) and 19th-20th (pp. 160-164) centuries. In spite of the few weaknesses noted at the beginning of this comment, Vdovin's book remains a very valuable contribution to our knowledge of the history of the study of Paleosiberian languages. One looks forward to the day when it will be possible to tell the full story of the Soviet sequel to this work.

One of the few extensive comparisons between Paleosiberian and other language groups to appear in the Soviet Union since the war is E. A. Krejnovič's "Giljacko-Tungusoman'čžurskie jazykovye paralleli [Gilyak linguistic parallels with Tungus-Manchu]", *DSIJa* 8.135-167 (1955). Krejnovič, making extensive use both of published works and his own wide field experience, comes to the conclusion that the Gilyaks must in the past have lived somewhere well to the south of their present territory, and must have been in close contact with speakers of Korean. The parallels

Krejnovič finds between Gilyak and Korean are exclusively typological in nature. After moving north, the Gilyaks were subjected to a long and strong period of influence on the part of some Manchu-Tungus group, the linguistic results of which are apparent in the phonology, grammar and lexicon of Gilyak. The bulk of the article describes these correspondences in some detail. Krejnovič gives a good deal of supporting material on Gilyak itself in the course of his exposition, which lists all phonetic correspondences between Gilyak and various Manchu-Tungus languages, and establishes twenty-six sets of corresponding grammatical morphemes, of which the most striking are the collective plural suffixes. In his treatment of lexical borrowings, which were extensive and which go back to a great (but undefined) time depth, Krejnovič draws several interesting conclusions regarding the development of the material culture of the Gilyaks. The article ends with a dictionary of Gilyak borrowings from the Manchu-Tungus languages (app. 235 items) and a thorough bibliography of the subject.

The collectively authored volume **Mladopis'mennye jazyki narodov SSSR* [Newly literary languages of the *USSR*], edited by E. A. Bokarev and Ju. D. Dešeriev (Moscow-Leningrad, 1959), presents a survey of Turkic, Caucasian, Finno-Ugric, Iranian and Mongol languages within the confines of the Soviet Union, as well as an interesting general survey of the languages of the so-called "peoples of the North", which include the speakers of Eskimo and Aleut, Manchu-Tungus languages, and the Chukchee-Koryak-Kamchadal group. This last group is described on pp. 352-379 by P. Ja. Skorik, the Chukchee specialist, who outlines the study of these three languages both before and after the 1917 revulotion . The survey is followed by a brief typological comparison of these languages. The same facts are dealt with more fully in Skorik's 1958 articles in the *Izvestija* and *Voprosy jazykoznanija*. I. S. Vdovin's introductory survey in the same volume, "Obščie svedenija o sozdanii pis'mennosti na jazykax narodov severa [General information on the creation of literary languages among the peoples of the north]", *ibid.*, pp. 284-299, is oriented toward the history of Paleosiberian studies rather than toward the languages themselves, and forms a useful addendum to the same author's *Istorija izučenija paleoaziatskix jazykov*. For some reason, *Mladopis'mennye jazyki narodov severa* neglects to mention both Yukaghir and Gilyak.

B. O. Dolgix's basic work **Rodovoj i plemennoj sostav narodov Sibiri v XVII veke* [The tribal structure of Siberian peoples in the 17th century], which appeared as volume fifty of the new series of AN SSSR, Institut Ètnografii, *Trudy* (Moscow, 1960), 614 pp. + tables and maps, is one of the most important books on the Siberian peoples ever to appear. The work deals with the Chukchee, Koryak and Kamchadal on pp. 549-578, and although Dolgix's orientation is primarily ethnographic, this section contains a certain amount of linguistic material, the bulk of which is however taken from Krašeninnikov's *Opisanie zemli Kamčatki*, 1949 edition, and will serve to enlighten the ethnographer more than the linguist. A great merit of this book, however, is its detailed statistical treatment of population change. Dolgix also underlines the partially self-contradictory nature of some of Krašeninnikov's reports on the tribal adherence of the Kamchatka population in the early 18th century (were the Western Kamchadals really Koryaks? the Southern Kamchadals really Ainus?), which is particularly important since later investigators have too often tended to take Krašeninnikov's accounts at face value.

In 1960 a group of scholars in Leningrad and Moscow celebrated the seventy-fifth birthday of Academician I. I. Meščaninov with a substantial collective volume dealing with many problems of general linguistics. *Voprosy grammatiki. Sbornik statej k 75-letiju Akademika I. I. Meščaninov* [Problems of grammar. A collective volume on the occasion of the 75th birthday of Academician I. I. Meščaninov] (Moscow-Leningrad, 1960), pp. 472. Three of the articles in this volume deal with Paleosiberian languages: P. Ja. Skorik's "O kategorii zaloga v čukotskom jazyke [On the category of voice in Chukchee]", A. N. Žukova's "Tipy sklonenija suščestvitel'nyx v korjakskom jazyke [Types of noun declension in Koryak]", and V. Z. Panfilov's "O zaloge glagola v nivxskom jazyke [On verbal voice in Gilyak]". These articles are discussed in the individual language sections below.

I. I. Meščaninov himself makes extensive use of examples from Paleosiberian languages, especially Chukchee, in his general discussion of the nature of certain syntactic devices, "Aggljutinacija i inkorporirovanie [Agglutination and incorporation]", *VJa* 11(5).24-31 (1962). Meščaninov outlines the syntactic function of both word combinations and incorporating complexes, noting that the agglutinative affixes in Chukchee and Koryak enclose single words in free combinations, but entire complexes (of base and incorporated modifier) in the case of incorporation. There does not appear to be much information in Meščaninov's article that could not be gathered from the more detailed descriptions of individual languages by Skorik, Žukova, and Krejnovič, although as a general summary his remarks are adequate and interesting.

## 2. THE CHUKCHEE GROUP

P. Ja. Skorik proposes a new classification of the Chukchee-Koryak-Kamchadal group of languages in two articles appearing in 1958. The first, *"K voprosu o sravnitel'nom izučenii čukotsko-kamčatskix jazykov [On the comparative study of the Chukchee-Kamchatkan languages]", *IzvAN* 17/6.534-546 (1958), makes several revised statements concerning the origin and development of the NE Paleosiberian languages (Chukchee, Koryak, Kerek, Aljutor, Kamchadal). Ch(ukchee), Ko(ryak), Ke(rek) and Al(jutor) are much more closely related to each other than they are as a group to Kam(chadal), which has a voiced-voiceless opposition, a palatalized-non-palatalized opposition, fortis vs. lenis stops in addition to voiced-voiceless pairs, free clustering of consonants (Ch, Ko, Ke, Al permit a maximum of two consonants together), no incorporation, and does not express person in nouns and adjectives. Skorik establishes that the present degrees and types of synharmonism (regular in Ch, almost regular in Ko, sporadic in Kam, vestigial in Al, entirely absent from Ke) arose from an original double-step synharmonism of which the Kam alternations /i/ ~ /e/ ~ /a/ and /u/ ~ /a/ ~ /o/ are traces. In morphology, Skorik assumes that the three motion cases of Ko (ablative, dative and delative [Russian *prodol'nyj*]) and two of Ch (ablative, dative) developed from a single relative case. The Ko verb pre- and suffixes *ku/k-. . .n* can be identified with the Kam participles in *k'-. . .-in/en/an*. Transitive and intransitive verbs were probably not distinguished in proto-Chukchee-Kamchadal; originally, there was simply a suffix indicating "substantive involved in verbal action", which later split into the present actor-goal dichotomy.

Many linguistic facts of this group can be explained by substrata. Ch and Ko took over territories from the Shelagi, Anauly, and Chuvancy, as well as from the Yukaghir and the Eskimo. Al and Ke are particularly influenced by Eskimo (loss of synharmonism, no /e/ or /o/ in Ke, etc.). Al probably arose from Ch and Ke from Ko, but cross-influence of Ch on Ke and of Ko on Al compounded the influence of Esk on both to produce the present complicated situation. Kam separated very early from the general stock, and also underwent much stronger external influence than Ch, Ko, Ke, and Al. This influence, manifested in the different auxiliary verbs, different suffixes for 4/6 of cases, etc., is of unknown origin.

Skorik's second article on reclassification, *"K voprosu o klassifikacii čukotsko-kamčatskix jazykov [Toward a classification of the Chukchee-Kamchatkan languages] *VJa* 1.21-35 (1958), proposes to revise the traditional classification of the northeastern group of Paleosiberian languages, which include the languages usually called Chukchee, Koryak, and Kamchadal (Russ. Itel'men). The group name "Chukchee-Kamchatkan", based on the area inhabited by this group (the Chukchee and Kamchatka peninsulas), is suggested as a replacement for the cumbersome and inaccurate generically-oriented terms used in the past.

All languages of this group share many common traits in their phonemic systems (the post-velar consonants, absence of the palatalized : : non-palatalized opposition, etc.). Kamchadal has the most elaborate phonemic system, Kerek (formerly considered a Chukchee dialect, but treated here as a separate language) the simplest. All languages but Kerek are synharmonic. There are many regular sound correspondences among these languages, e.g. Ch(ukchee) /r/ – Ko(ryak) /j/, /r/, or /t/ – Kam(chadal) /z/ – Ke(rek) /r/ or /n/. In morphology, all show prefixal and suffixal agglutination, in all but Kam nouns express person, adjectives are declined not in case but only in person and number. Ch, Kam, and some Ko dialects express singular and plural, whereas Ke and other Ko dialects have the dual as well. Nominal suffixes are closely related in Ch, Ke, and Ko, as are derivative procedures; in both respects Kam stands somewhat apart, although Kam verb morphology is like that of the other languages. All but Kam show extensive incorporation, and all without exception have both nominative and ergative structures. Lexical differences are greater than grammatical, although there are marked similarities among pronouns and some kinship and body-part terms. Kam is opposed to Ch, Ko, and Ke, by most of its lexicon; Ke coincides partly with

Ch, partly with Ko, as in morphology. The general conclusion is that all (Ch, Ke, Ko, Kam) are genetically related, but that Kam is opposed to the other three taken together by many important features. This first half of Skorik's article partially repeats and partially reinforces his *Izvestija* article mentioned above.

The second half of the article deals with Koryak dialectology. Of the eight traditional Koryak dialects, two are of major importance (Čavčuvenskij and Aljutorskij). The differences between these two are treated in some detail; Skorik proposes to elevate Aljutor to the status of a separate language, which would include the Karaga and Palan dialects.

The final classification of northeast Paleosiberian, according to Skorik, is then: (1) Chukchee (with dialects Uellenskij, Pevekskij, Enmylinskij, Nunligranskij and Xatyrskij); (2) Kerek, (Majna-pil'ginskij and Xatyrskij dialects); (3) Koryak, (dialects of Čavčuvenskij, Apokinskij, Kamenskij, Parenskij and Itkanskij); (4) Aljutor, (Aljutorskij, Karaginskij and Palanskij dialects); (5) Kamchadal (Itel'men) (Sedanskij, Xajrjuzovskij, Napanskij and Sopočnovskij dialects).

## 3. CHUKCHEE

One of the earliest of the several studies on incorporation in the Paleosiberian languages was P. Ja. Skorik's article, "Inkorporacija v čukotskom jazyke kak sposob vyraženija sintaksičeskix otnošenij [Incorporation in Chukchee as a means of expressing syntactic relations]", *IzvAN* 6/6.520-532 (1947). Skorik notes that although incorporation is a phenomenon spread throughout North Asia and North America, it has never been adequately described, since American linguists such as Sapir were inclined to consider it a morphological rather than a syntactic phenomenon. Skorik points out as well that incorporation is less widespread in Chukchee than was formerly believed, and that ordinary word combinations play a considerable role in the structure of the Chukchee sentence.

The article outlines the principal types of incorporating complex (cf. the survey of these types in the abstract of his book *Očerki po sintaksisu čukotskogo jazyka, Inkorporacija*, below), and gives many examples of the difference between incorporating complexes and simple word combinations with the same bases, e.g. *vykvylgyn* "stone" : : *elg-y-vykvylgyn* "white-stone", *n-y-patkenat* "they are cooking" : : *ny-takečg-y-patkenat* "they are meat-cooking". Skorik then outlines the syntactic functions of these complexes (as subject, predicate, attribute, etc.). In its so-called "basic form" (= absolute case of nouns, conjugable forms of verbs), incorporation is facultative, i.e. one can have either the incorporating complex *ryngy-kora-t* "frighten-reindeer" or the free word combination *ny-ryngy-kinet* (adj.) *kora-t* (noun) "frightened reindeer". In the "indirect forms" (= oblique case forms of nouns, non-conjugable verb forms) incorporation is either obligatory (as for nouns) or nearly so (for verbs), since the modifying elements of such binary pairs, regardless of whether they are qualitative, substantival etc. in origin, cannot themselves take oblique case forms, and must therefore be incorporated into the complex headed by the base they modify.

The article closes with some Marristic meanderings concerning incorporation "as a less perfected form of expression of thought" than the more analytic expresssion, and makes the undocumented and undocumentable assertion that (a) at an older stage, Chukchee expressed syntactic relations by simple juxtaposition of bare roots and (b) incorporation represents an intermediary stage between such archaic syntactic juxtaposition and a later, more highly developed, agglutinating stage of the language. This is typical of the "stadial" nonsense required during the Marr period, but Skorik's article, which is rich in material and soberly concrete in most of its presentation, is of no less value for this unnecessary encrustation.

The same author reexamines the nature of the Chukchee word class formed by the suffix *-l(g)-*, considered by Bogoraz to be participles, in his article, "O pričastijax v čukotskom jazyke [On participles in Chukchee]", *IzvAN* 7/4.317-327 (1948). These *-l(g)-* forms in Chukchee can be declined like nouns (*vakotva-l(g)-ety* "sitting" [dative], cf. *kljavol-ety* "man" [dative]), can take possessive postfixes (*vakotva-l(g)-en* "of the sitting [person]", cf. *kljavol-en* "of the man"), and when used in the predicate can take markers of person (*vinrety-l(g)-igym* "helping-I", cf. *n'evysket-igym* "woman-I"); all these features join the *-l(g)* -forms to the Chukchee noun. Unlike the noun, however, the *-l(g)-* forms have a special negative form *e-. . .-ky-*, the latter formant of which is infixed between the root and the suffix *-l(g)-*, e.g. from *čejvy-l(g)-yn* "going, walking" > the negative *e-čejvy-ky-l(g)-yn* "not going"; both nouns and verbs are negated by the affixes *e-. . .-ke*, the latter formant of which comes in final position, e.g. from *kupre-n* "net" > *e-kupre-ke* "without a net", *kumeeri-k* "to be silly" > *e-kumeeri-ke* "not be silly". Semantically, the *-l(g)-* forms fall midway between noun and verb; the sentence *ynky čejvy-l(g)-yn* could be translated variously as "there walks (he)", "there a walking-one is," or "there is a walker". Although tense is not formally expressed in the *-l(g)-* words, they can be modified by temporal adverbs to form the equivalent of regular verbal sentences in present or past.

Forms in *-l(g)-* can be derived from substantival and qualitative stems as well as from verbs, e.g. from *evirŭ* "clothing" > *evirŭ-l(g)-yn* "having-clothes-he", i.e. "he has clothes", from *ilg*, the stem meaning "white" (cf. the adjective *n-ilg-y-kin* "white") > *ilg-y-l(g)-yn* "being or showing white", "has whiteness", "is white", etc. According to Skorik, forms in *-l(g)-* can be derived from every stem of the language, and all such derivatives have the identical morphological characteristics outlined above. He considers these *-l(g)-* forms to be a separate part of speech, neither noun nor verb, but also not simply an adjectivized verb as are, e.g. the Russian participles.

Part II of Skorik's article identifies the segment *-l(g)-* of the past tense verb affix *ge/ga. . .l(g)in/en* (vowel variants due to vocalic harmony) as derived from the verbal stem (initial) *lyn'-*, (medial) *-lg-*, and considers it identical to the formant *-l(g)-* of the "participles". In his opinion, all instances of modern Chukchee *-l(g)-* arose from the fusion of an originally independent verb *lyn'-/-l(g)-* (the meaning of which is not specified, but was presumably "be") into a derivative affix which now occurs both in the quasi-participial forms, and in the conjugation of the verb.

The problem of voice in Chukchee is taken up by P. Ja. Skorik in "Vyraženie sub"-ektno-ob"ektnyx otnošenij v čukotskom jazyke [The expression of subject-object relations in Chukchee]", *IzvAN* 7/6.568-578 (1948), although the term "voice" itself is not used (Russian *zalog*); cf. his later article, below. After recalling briefly the two principal types of sentence in Chukchee, namely the nominal sentence with intransitive verb and the ergative sentence with transitive verb and actor in the ergative or instrumental case, Skorik notes that the ergative structure has not yet been adequately described. He points out that Chukchee has two present tense forms, one used to express a single concrete instance of an action, with a definite, specific object (*gym-nan pojg-yg ty-pelja-rky- nat* "I [these specific) spears leave [at this specific moment]"), and the other used as a generalized present/past, with a generalized object (*morgynan n-ena-pelja-more korat* "We leave [at any time, present or past] [some unspecified] reindeer"). There are also two past tenses, one expressing either a semelfactive action or a series of actions coming one after the other, and the second expressing the result of an action occurring in the past, the result being unspecified as to time. Since the non-specific forms of the verb take the conjugational morphemes of the intransitive declension, Skorik separates them from the ergative constructions, and comes to the conclusion that there are four types of subject/object relation possible in Chukchee, viz.: (1) those in sentences "of absolute construction" (i.e., with the subject in the absolute case) with intransitive verb predicate; (2) those in sentences of ergative construction, with the definite object marked in number and person in the transitive verb predicate, and with the subject in ergative or instrumental case; (3) those in sentences of absolute construction with "potential-objective" verbs, e.g. *n-ena-pelja-more* above; (4) sentences of absolute construction with the direct object incorporated into the verbal complex. Skorik closes his article with some historical suppositions, e.g. that the absolute constructions preceded the ergative constructions in time. The "voice" aspect of these sentence types is worked out more fully in his later article, below.

One of the first post-war works of any size to deal with the Paleosiberian languages was the candidate's dissertation (= American Ph. D.) of P. Ja. Skorik, *Očerki po sintaksisu čukotskogo jazyka. Inkorporacija* [An outline of Chukchee syntax. Incorporation], edited by I. I. Meščaninov (Leningrad, 1948), 176 pp. Skorik gave his readers a brief survey of the history of Chukchee studies, emphasizing the major role played by W. Bogoraz, but pointing out that Bogoraz tended to overemphasize the importance of incorporation in Chukchee. According to Skorik, incorporation, although undoubtedly still a major feature of Chukchee syntax, nonetheless plays a less important role in sentence structure than the free combination of complete words into combinations and syntactic groups. Furthermore, incorporation appears to be losing ground, especially among the sedentary Chukchee of the younger generation. Skorik attributes this progressive decay of incorporation to the higher cultural level of the sedentary Chukchee, but it should be remembered that this dissertation was written during the Marrist period, and under the leading advocate of Marr's stadial theories, I. I. Meščaninov.

The book consists of three sections. Section I, "The distribution of incorporation in Chukchee and the forms in which it is manifested" (pp. 14-47) gives a brief phonetic and morphological outline of Chukchee, and then summarizes the general features of incorporating complexes, all of which consist of one base lexical morpheme (nominal, verbal, or adverbal) preceded by one or more modifying morphemes, incorporated as bare roots (or, rarely, as stems), without any of the class markers which distinguish the same morphemes used as modifiers in free syntactic word combinations.

Section II describes in considerable detail, with many examples, the types of nominal, verbal, and adverbal incorporating complex. Nominal base morphemes can incorporate adjective-base modifiers (*Min'-kri* RYNGY-KORA-*n'y nyvytretkin* "For frightened-reindeer is-seen"; cf. the same combination of morphemes in free syntactic word combination, *ny*-RYNGY-*kin* KORA-*n'y* "frightened reindeer"), other nominal bases (*Neme* GALGA-LEGLEGKAJ *min'ky nytvaken* "Also bird-egg where is"; cf. without incorporation GALG-*en* LIGLIGKEJ "bird's egg"), or verbs (TIPEJN'E-NE'VYSKET *ynky gatvalen* "Sing-woman there was"; cf. TIPEJN'E-*lŭyn* N'EVYSTEK "singing woman"). Pronominal and numeral morphemes can also be incorporated, but such complexes are less frequent than the above. Incorporating complexes can consist not only of two, but of three or more roots, e.g. *Kynver* VUE-RAMKI-VETGAV *valomnen* "Finally die-people-talk he-understood", i.e. "He finally understood the conversation of those who had died"; cf. the non-incorporating sequence of two adjectives and a noun, VUI-*lu-in* REMK-*in* VETGAV "having-died people's conversation". Skorik also describes the morphophonemics of the incorporating process in some detail.

Verbal complexes, like the nominal, can incorporate adjectival stems (*Yrytkuk ge*-TEN'-Y-GJULET-*linet* "To-shoot well-they-learned"; cf. without incorporation *ny*-TEN'-*ev ge*-GJULET-*linet* "well they-learned"), nominal stems (YNN-*y*-TKE-*rkyn* "fish-smells"; cf. YNN-*e* TYKE-*rkyn* "like-fish it-smells"), and secondary verbal stems (*Opopy yttoolagty amgymnan my*-GAGČAV-AKVAT-*gat* "Let-me only I-hurrying-shall-go"; cf. GAGČAVA, *m*-EKVET-*gek* "hurrying, I-shall-go"). Verbal incorporating complexes can also occur with more than one incorporated stem, e.g. *Opopy myn-jaa-melgar-račvin'-marav-myk* "Let-us we-from-afar-gun-contesting-shall-fight", i.e. "Let us do battle with guns at a distance from each other". Certain peculiarities in the flexion of these verbal incorporating complexes are described; these are distinct from the flexional features of the nominal complexes.

The third type of incorporating complex is the adverbal, which can include secondary nominal stems (*Vykvyl-gyn pirinin, n'aj-kaletly rintynnin jaa* "Stone he-took, mountain-down he-threw far", i.e. "He threw a stone a great distance down from the mountain top"; N.B. the bare stem *n'aj/n'ej* instead of the locative case *n'ej-yk* "on the mountain"), adjective stems (*Kynver tan'-ora nŭelgi* "Finally good-visible it-became"; N.B. the stem *ten'/tan'* instead of the full adjective *ny-ten'-kin* "good"), and secondary adverbal stems (*Amyn-ym gym telen-jen čavčyvajgym* "But-really I long-time-since reindeer-herder-I-was"). Adverbal complexes, as will have been noted, cannot contain secondary verbal stems, nor can adverb stems be incorporated into complexes with nominal or verbal bases; Skorik notes that adverbal-base complexes can very easily turn into simple compound words. It is also to be noted that no incorporating complexes can be formed on adjectival base morphemes. In Skorik's opinion, both the nominal and the verbal complexes arose when original free syntactic word combinations were fused together and lost their class markers; this explanation, it seems, is only partially satisfactory, since the incorporating complexes themselves are not fixed units (in this case, they would be indistinguishable from other compound words), but are in free combination – a combination, however, which is distinguished from free syntactic word combinations by the absence of any grammatical morphemes (e.g., adjective formants) in the incorporated elements.

The third section of *An outline of Chukchee syntax* describes the sentence functions of the various incorporating complexes (subject, verbal predicate, secondary modifiers, etc.). It appears that the secondary elements within the sentence, such as circumstantial modifiers of time and place, are more likely to appear in the form of incorporating complexes than are the principal elements of the sentence, such as absolute-case subjects, verb, etc., which can be either free syntactic combinations or incorporating complexes.

In general, Skorik's book is a sober and well-documented presentation. Its theoretical weaknesses, such as they are (e.g., over-reliance on Meščaninov's syntactic theories), are easily compensated for by the diligent presentation of original material connected with incorporation.

T. A. Moll studies the Chukchee auxiliary verb for the first time in "K voprosu o vspomogatel'nyx glagolax v čukotskom jazyke [On the auxiliary verb in Chukchee]", *UZLPedI* 101.281-291 (1954). The class of auxiliary verbs in Chukchee contains verbs which can occur either independently or as subordinate members of verbal complexes. There are three intransitive auxiliaries and three transitive: (1) *vak* "be, remain" (initial [anlaut] form *va-*, medial form *-tva-*), (2) *ityk* "be, seem" (stem variants *it, et*), (3) *nŭelyk* "become" (stem variants *nŭel, nŭal*); (4) *rytčyk* "make somebody or something into something" (initial form *rytčy-*, medial form *-tčy-*), (5) *lyn'yk* "consider as, use as" (initial form *lyn'-*, medial form *-lgy'-*), (6) *rytyk* "have as, in quality of, function of" (initial form *ryt-*, medial form *-nty-*). These auxiliaries are paired in forming transitive and intransitive compound verbs with the same base, e.g., *jetan' rytčyk* "to prepare (something)" : : *jetan' nŭelyk* "to prepare oneself".

Moll then studies the function of auxiliaries in different types of sentence. There are two principal types of sentence in Chukchee, the first of which has a subject in the absolute case and an intransitive verb agreeing with this subject (*gym t-ekvet-gŭek amnon'ety* "I set off into the tundra"), and the second of which a subject in the instrumental, a transitive verb agreeing with both subject and object, and an object in the absolute case (*gymnan ty-pelja-gŭan orgor emnun'ky* "I left the sleigh in the tundra").

The verbs occurring in such ergative sentences are called analytic by Moll, those in the intransitive (objectless) sentences synthetic. Auxiliary verbs, e.g. *rytčyk*, *lyn'yk*, can be used to render intransitives transitive; in the meaning "begin", *rytčyk* corresponds to the incorporated base *-mgo-* "begin" of intransitive verbs (*ajylgavymgok* "to begin to fear" : : *ajylgo rytčyk* "to begin to fear someone or something"). In some cases, the analytic and the synthetic forms of the verb have the same general meaning, but the analytic form serves as a marker of lexical emphasis, opposing the given verb to all other verbs of similar meaning, e.g. *imtik* (synthetic) "to carry on one's back" : : *imti-te rytyk* (analytic) "to carry on one's back, and not on a sleigh or in any other way".

Finally, Moll outlines briefly the role of the auxiliary verbs in the formation of an optative-like analytic construction meaning "order, ask, cause to do something" (*iljuleti jgut rytyk* "cause, ask to dance", *ejmiti jgut ityk* "ask to take"), in the formation of temporal adverbs derived from a numeral and a verb (from *k'ul/k'ol* "one" and *ityk* "to be", *k'ol itgŭi* "once"), and in several kinds of negative construction, in which the auxiliary takes the negative affixes *e/a . . . ke/ka* (*vejmen'u lyn'yk* "to respect", *vejmen'u e-lgy-ke rytyk* "not to respect", *vejmen'u rytčyk* "to begin to respect", *vejmen'u e-tčy-ke rytyk* "not to begin to respect"). The entire article, although only ten pages long, is very rich in concrete material, and provides an interesting survey of a hitherto unexplored segment of Chukchee syntax.

The **Čukotsko-russkij slovar'* [Chukchee-Russian dictionary], by T.A. Moll and P. I. Inènlikèj, edited by P. Ja. Skorik (Leningrad, 1957), of 8000 words, is designed for use in Chukchee schools rather than as a scholarly tool, but is nonetheless a most valuable addition to the meager lexical resources available in Paleosiberian. The dictionary contains a number of dialect words in addition to those from the literary language, and is also seeded with Russian borrowings. The dictionary proper is followed by a phonemic and grammatical sketch of Chukchee, and by a list of verbal stems which alternate morphophonemically in an- and inlaut position. The dictionary was unfortunately not provided with a Russian-Chukchee root list.

P. Ja. Skorik's article, *"K voprosu o sostave fonem čukotskogo jazyka [On the composition of Chukchee phonemes]", *DSIJa* 11.121-136 (1958), is the second on Chukchee phonology to appear since the war; the first was G. I. Mel'nikov's "Fonemy čukotskogo jazyka (po dannym predvaritel'nogo èksperimental'nogo issledovanija) [The phonemes of Chukchee (from the data of a preliminary experimental investigation)]" in *Jazyk i myšlenie* 11.208-209 (1948). Skorik first notes the great disparities in the descriptions of Chukchee phonology up to and including Mel'nikov: Bogoraz counted not only allophones, but even idiophones, as phonemic, and systems based on his transcriptions run as high as 13 vowel and 32 consonant phonemes. The practical orthography worked out in the Chukchee school system is based on 6 vowels and 16 consonants. Mel'nikov proposed a system of 13 vowels and 13 consonants. Skorik agrees with Mel'nikov that [v] and [w] are allophones of /w/ and that [ș] and [č] are allophones of /ś/, but disagrees strongly with Mel'nikov's opinion that Chukchee has no glottal stop, but instead a series of glottalized vowels parallel to the regular series /a i o u e ə/. Skorik adduces convincing flexional data in support of his position that /ʔ/ is an independent phoneme.

It has been customary since the days of Bogoraz to consider that Chukchee has five diphthongs /$i^w$, $e^w$, $a^w$, $u^w$, $o^w$/, but Skorik considers Bogoraz' interpretation incorrect, since these presumed diphthongs are always followed by the post-consonantal and not the post-vocalic allomorphs of desinences. Mel'nikov posited a diphthongoid $^e$i, the existence of which is denied by Skorik on the basis of the fact that this glide occurs only after /ʔ/, and that parallel glides are observed with all mid and high vowels: [$^a$e, $^o$u]. Skorik's system consists of six vowels /a i o u e ə/ and fourteen consonants /w g j k q l' m n ŋ p r t ś ʔ/. He notes in addition that the speech of women contains a voiceless dental affricate [c] which corresponds to both /r/ and /ś/ in the speech of men and which assimilates following /k/, e.g. (male) *reqəkən* "what-is-he-doing" = (female) *ceqəccən*. The article ends with a brief discussion of the problems of rendering this phonemic system accurately and conveniently in a practical alphabet.

P. Ja. Skorik subjects the category of voice in Chukchee to a detailed examination in "O kategorii zaloga v čukotskom jazyke [On the category of voice in Chukchee]", *Voprosy grammatiki. Sbornik statej k 75-letiju Akademika I. I. Meščaninova* (Moscow-Leningrad, 1960), pp. 129-150. Skorik defines voice as a strictly verbal category which expresses subjective/objective relations. As a part of morphology, voice is to be considered independent of syntax, and as a verbal category, independent of certain Chukchee nominal structures which also deal with both subject and object of an action. Furthermore, voice can be expressed only in the transitive verb, since the intransitive verb by definition cannot express objective relations. Skorik notes the interrelation of voice with the transitive and intransitive conjugation types, but insists on the independence of voice as a grammatical category of verb morphology. His approach is based on examination of contrasting minimal pairs, and is closer to that of certain Western structuralists than is the work of most Soviet specialists on Paleosiberian.

The formal means of expression of subjective-objective relations are described in some detail. There are five classes of verbal structure in which such relations are expressed: (1) "Concrete-objective" transitive verbs express person and number of the direct object as well as of the subject (*t-y-ret-y-rkyn-igyt* "I take you [sing.]" : : *t-y-ret-y-rkyn-ityk* "I take you [plur.]"); (2) "general-objective" verb forms are derived from intransitives by means of the suffix *ine/ena*, and mark the presence of an object, which is not specified in person and number, and need not be present lexically (*t-ine-gynrit-y-rkyn* "I am saving [something]"); (3) "potential-objective" verbs are similar to the general-objective category just mentioned, but only hint at the existence of what Skorik calls a "hidden object"; this group is formed with the suffix *-tku/-tko*, and remains somewhat less than crystal clear even after repeated readings; (4) incorporation forms what Skorik terms an "inclusive-objective" class, in which the direct object is incorporated directly into the verbal complex, becoming a single word together with its verbal base (*t-y-valja-mna-rkyn* "I knife-sharpen"). A number of related phenomena are investigated, but dismissed as not belonging to the voice system proper. The four types of verbs just listed form a closed system of subjective-objective relations, and are therefore voice-expressing forms. The meanings of the four voices can be summarized as: (1) the concrete-objective voice concentrates attention on both subject and object of an action, but primarily on the object; (2) the general-objective voice concentrates attention on the subject, but insists on the presence of an unnamed object; (3) the potential-objective voice concentrates attention more highly upon the subject and only indicates the presence of a "hidden" object; (4) the inclusive objective voice also concentrates attention on the subject, but the object forms an integral part of the verb itself, thus creating what Skorik terms a peculiar type of verb-internal transitivity (*vnutriglagol'naja perexodnost'*). The semantic classification of these four voice categories is less satisfactory than the formal classification, but the article is in general clear and well-illustrated. Cf. his earlier article, above.

F. N. Šemjakin's compact article *"K probleme slovesnyx i čuvstvennyx obobščenij (na materiale nazvanij cveta v čukotskom jazyke) [On the problem of verbal and sensory generalizations (from Chukchee material on color names)]", *Myšlenie i reč', Trudy Instituta psixologii* (= *Izvestija Akademii pedagogičeskix nauk RSFSR*, 113), 1960, pp. 72-75, tests two widespread psychological theories concerning color terms, first that such terms develop earlier for colors at the red end of the spectrum and later for colors at the blue end, and second that all names of colors are derived from names of objects. The first hypothesis is confirmed by the Chukchee material, but the second only partially so. The Chukchee terms for "white", "black" and "red" are primary, and unconnected with the names of any objects, whereas "green", "blue" and terms for neighboring colors are derived from animal, earth or bird names and are probably secondary. Color terms in Chukchee are in general far less precise than in Russian, although in Šemjakin's opinion the development of a Chukchee literary language is beginning to change this situation.

A major landmark in the postwar advance of Paleosiberian studies in the USSR is formed by P. Ja. Skorik's detailed grammar of Chukchee, **Grammatika čukotskogo jazyka. Čast' pervaja, Fonetika i morfologija imennyx častej reči* [Chukchee grammar. Part I, phonetics and noun morphology] (Moscow-Leningrad, 1961), pp. 448.

The Phonetics (pp. 15-76) lists the vocalic (/i u e ə o a/) and consonantal (/w g j k q [voiceless uvular stop] l' m n ŋ p r t ś [a voiceless dental continuant with secondary articulation similar to Polish ś and allophonically Russian č] ʔ/) phonemes, with detailed descriptions of their combinatory variants. Chukchee synharmonism has two series of vowel phonemes: high or "weak" vowels (e i u) and low or "strong" vowels (a e o – the fact that /e/ shows up in both sets is explained by the existence of two morphonemes: /e/ alternating with /i/ on the one hand and /e/ alternating with /a/ on the other). /ə/ is unaffected by, and does not affect, synharmonism. Whenever an intonational unit contains a low (strong) vowel, all vowels within the unit must become low, i.e. all original /e/ > /a/, /i/ > /e/, /u/ > /o/. It must be noted, however, that Chukchee is now undergoing a process of vowel reduction which tends to confuse the strong and weak series; ə seems to be a reduction of both /a/ and /e/. It is this process, in Skorik's opinion, that has partially destroyed the synharmonic structure of languages related to Chukchee (in Koryak, the phenomenon is less widespread than in Chukchee; in Kamchadal, it is seldom encountered, and in Kerek and Aljutor it has disappeared altogether). Further sections of the Phonetics describe assimilation and dissimilation, simplifications of consonant clusters, the syllabic structure of Chukchee (one vowel with one or two consonants on either side, maximally CCVCC), stress (bound to the base [final or penult, depending on affixal types] regardless of how many affixes are added), and the orthography of the present literary language.

The Morphology corrects Bogoraz' oversimplified view of the importance of incorporation in Chukchee. Skorik shows that agglutination and even analytic structures play an important role in sentence formation. The Chukchee sentence usually consists of a string of affixed and unaffixed words, among which there may but need not occur both incorporating and agglutinative formations.

Chukchee distinguishes singular and plural number, although not in all cases. There are nine cases: basic or nominative, used to name objects, to mark the subject in nominative sentences (either with verbs or not; in both cases opposed to ergative sentences), and to mark the direct object in ergative sentences; instrumental case forms mark the subject in ergative constructions, e.g. *riqukete genulin tykečʔyn* "by the fox(es) was-eaten the bait", as the object in nominative sentences, e.g. *tinenlʔetetyrkyn kimitje* "I-carry-away-by-means-of-the-axe", i.e. "I carry the axe away", and is used thirdly in the normal meaning of instrument, e.g. *tyvaŋerkyn titite* "I sew by-means-of-a-needle". The locative case expresses the place of an action (*memylte kuprek gakvalenat* "the-seals in-the-net got-stuck"), the object of an action in nominative constructions (*typiritkurkyn ŋilgyk* "I-seize concerning-the-net"), and the place or object with which something is compared (*ŋegny tynupyk ekvyŋ valʔyn* "the-mountain concerning-the-hill higher being", i.e. "the mountain is higher than the hill'). The ablative expresses the object from which or in connection with which an action begins or occurs (*qaat mrangyry gyntekvjet* "the-reindeer from-the-mosquitos ran-away", *vjaglyŋyn terkepy kykvatgʔe* "the-grass from-the-sun dried-out"). The dative names the object toward which, or for the benefit of which, an action occurs, and can also express the direct object of an action in nominative constructions. The determinative case expresses the object in regard to or in accordance with which an action is performed (*ŋinqegti nylqytqinet nylgylʔygʔet* "the children were-going orienting-themselves-according-to-the-smoke"). The comitative (Russ. *sovmestnyj*) case expresses a secondary participant, always in the singular, of an action performed by an actor expressed by a noun in the nominative or instrumental (*qynver iʔny geqepere enajʔogʔat qaagty* "finally the-wolf together-with-the-wolverine reached the-reindeer"). The subcomitative (R. *soprovoditel'nyj*) is identical in meaning with the comitative, except for the fact that the secondary actor is subordinated in importance to the primary actor; the participation in the action is likely to be incidental, since the noun in the subcomitative more or less accidentally happens to be in the same place as the principal noun (*milger gam amena nyjmetvaqen renmyk* "the-gun with-the-cartridges hangs on-the-wall"). Finally, the designative case is used to express the role or form in which the subject or object of an action appears (*ynqo l'uur notqen yʔttʔyn iʔgu qʔol'agʔe* "why that dog suddenly like-a-wolf howled?").

The Chukchee noun expresses person as well as case, e.g. *čavčyvajgym* "nomad-I", *čavčyvamore* "nomad-we", *čavčyvajgyt* "nomad-thou", *čavčyvatore* "nomad-you", cf. *čavčyv* "nomad-he" and *čavčyvat* "nomad-they". There are special possessive and relative forms of the noun, the possessive indicating an unalterable, inherent relation between objects (*veem-in pycʔyčʔyn* "of-the-river the-current") and the relative a temporary or accidental relation (*veemkin vykvylgyn* "of-the-river the-stones"). Each of these two forms has a full declensional system. Possession can also be expressed by incorporation of the possessing noun, cf. the possessive form *ŋevysqet-in evirʔyn* "of-a-woman clothing" and the incorporating form *ŋevysqet-evirʔyn* "woman('s)-clothing". There are also special negative forms, indicating that an object is absent in some situation, e.g. that the subject of a sentence acts without having some object in his possession. The Chukchee noun marks two other categories by prefixation: a category of limitation (*titit* "needles", *emtitit* "only-needles") and a category of separation (*em-qynŋevysqet* "each-woman", cf. *ŋevysqet* "woman"). There are also suffixal forms expressing subjective evaluations (augmentatives, diminutives, etc.).

Almost one hundred pages are devoted to derivational morphology. Of particular interest in Chukchee is the group of participle-nouns, which can be used either as attribute or as nouns, parallel to our participles and nouns respectively. These participle-nouns can be correlated with actions, objects, or qualities, e.g. *ryjulʔyn* "being-shepherd", "shepherd" (cf. *ryjuk* "to herd reindeer"), *yʔttʔylʔyn* "having-dogs", "dog-owner" (cf. *yʔttʔyn* "dog"); *gytiŋylʔyn* "being-handsome", "handsome man" (cf. *nygtiŋqin* "handsome"). Such noun-participles are declined in all cases. Cf. Skorik's article on Chukchee "participles", discussed earlier.

A few pages at the end of the book discuss the formation of certain case endings, e.g. of the *-(y)ŋ* component of the ablative, delative and dative cases from the verb *ep-yk* "go from or along" and *et-yk* "go towards". The entire volume has been carefully prepared, and is obviously the result of years of work by a first-hand connoisseur of Chukchee.

## 4. KORYAK

A. N. Žukova investigates the differences between incorporation and agreement as formal means of expressing the relation of modifier and modified in "Dva osnovnyx sposoba svjazi opredelenija s opredeljaemym v korjakskom jazyke [Two principal means of connecting modifier with modified in Koryak]", *UZLPedI* 101.293-304(1954). Žukova begins with a general outline of incorporating procedures in Koryak, and notes that the usual classification of incorporating bases is inconsistent, being founded partially on semantic criteria (qualitative, substantival, numeral bases) and partially on morphosyntactic (part-of-speech) criteria (verbal, adverbal, and pronominal bases). The modifying stem of the modifier-modified combination can be incorporated either as a bare root (more rarely, as a stem consisting of root plus derivational affix), or in a special "complex form". If the modifier is itself modified by a third stem, it can no longer be incorporated (i.e., only one degree of incorporative nesting is permitted); cf. *Yčgynan nakojavan'nav'* NALGYKIMITŬAV' "They wear of-skins-clothes" and *Yčgynan nakojavan'nav' k'ojanalgenav' kimitŭav'* "They wear of-reindeer-skins clothes".

In Žukova's opinion, the differences between incorporation and compounding can be summed up under three headings: (1) Whereas incorporating complexes are freely formed and freely dissolved, compounds are fixed in form (i.e., the former are syntactic, the latter morphological combinations); (2) compounds, as fixed vocabulary units, are not opposed in any way to free combinations of two words (modifier plus modified), whereas incorporating complexes, which can occur with the same roots as the free two-word combinations, are so opposed; (3) The meanings of the constituents in incorporating complexes are autonomous, and the meaning of the complex is always equal to the sum of the meanings of its constituents, whereas the constituent meanings in compounds are fused into a new and single meaning.

Žukova corrects in passing an oversimplification of earlier observers (e.g., S. N. Stebnickij, *Iz istorii padežnyx suffiksov korjakskogo i čukotskogo jazykov*, Leningrad, 1941) to the effect that each base in an incorporating complex modifies the immediately following base; Žukova demonstrates on convincing examples that in a complex of bases A+B+C, both A and B can modify C directly, e.g. *ketyk'ojanalgo* "frozen-reindeer-skins", < *kety-* "frozen", *k'oja* "reindeer", *nalgo* "skins". She also points out that compounds can sometimes occur within an incorporating complex (i.e., compounds act like simple roots in this respect), e.g. *umvilnalgu* "much-costing-skins", which consists of the compound *umvil* "expensive" (< *um* "broad, wide" + *vil* "price") incorporated into a complex on the base *nalgu* "skins".

The second part of the article describes some features of agreement in the free two-word combination of modifier and modified. It is noted that such agreement occurs primarily when the modified noun is in the absolute case; when this noun is in some oblique case, the modifier is almost always incorporated rather than preposed, although in exceptional cases the agreeing modifier may also take oblique-case endings (only in the instrumental and locative, however). Agreement is most frequently used when incorporation is impossible, e.g. when several modifiers modify one noun in an oblique case. It is interesting to note that agreement, rather than incorporation, is used whenever there is a particular emphasis on the modifier; agreement, that is, marks a reversal of the ordinary topic – comment relation within such a combination. Another noteworthy use of the agreement structure is to mark a quality (i.e., an adjective) when it is attached to an object (noun) for the first time; when the same modifier-modified combination occurs subsequently in the same utterance, the modifier is incorporated. Žukova considers this an "attributive-predicative" use of agreement; the construction has partial parallels in our distinction between indefinite and definite articles, and also with apposition vs. preposition of adjective modifiers. One draws the general conclusion that both incorporation and agreement are important features of Koryak syntax, and that agreement is a particular, marked form of the modifier-modified relationship.

E. A. Krejnovič takes issue with the traditional view of syllabic structure in Koryak in his article, *"Opyt issledovanija struktury sloga v koryakskom jazyke [An investigation of Koryak syllabic structure]", *DSIJa* 11.151-167 (1958). This traditional view held that Koryak tolerates no CCC clusters medially and no CC clusters in anlaut and auslaut positions; whenever such a cluster is caused morphologically, it is broken up by an inserted vowel [y]. Basing himself on earlier studies by T. A. Moll ("Fonemnyj sostav i osnovnye fonetičeskie zakonomernosti čavčuvenskogo dialekta korjakskogo jazyka [The phonemic composition and basic phonetic regularities of the Čavčuv dialect of Koryak]", *UZLPedI* 111, 1955; "Nekotorye voprosy fonetiki korjakskogo jazyka [Some problems of Koryak phonetics]", *V pomošč' učitelju škol Krajnego Severa*, 7, Leningrad, 1957), Krejnovič posits a phonemic system of eighteen consonants /p w (f) m v t n n' l l' č j k γ ŋ q ʁ ʔ/ and five vowels /a e i o u/. The Koryak syllable can have the structures V (*e-jek* "lamp"), VC (*eč-γi* "today"), CV (*wa-la* "knife"), CVC (*aj-kol* "bed"), CCV (*kla-ve* "ran"), CCVC (*tjan-mŋn* "I shall kill him"), C (*wa-n* "den") and CC (*mi-ml* "water"). Monosyllabic nouns, numerals, and verbs must begin with a CC sequence; this explains the frequently occurring phenomenon of reduplication, since a root with a single initial consonant cannot stand alone. Krejnovič's position is that the inserted [y], which although brief is a phonetic reality, is not a phoneme but a combinatory variant of a cluster in certain conditions: the root *wyt* "leaf", reduplicated *wytwyt*, keeps its [y], since the syllabic boundary falls between *t* and *w* (*wyt-wyt*), but in the verbal form *kowtp-ʁan* "the leaves turn yellow" the syllabic boundary falls between *w* and *t* (*kow-tp-ʁan*) and the [y] disappears. Krejnovič provides several other examples of the [y]-zero alternation. Furthermore, this [y] differs in several ways from the vocalic phoneme: it cannot be lengthened, it does not play any role in synharmonism, and it disappears in certain positions, which never occurs with /a e i o u/. [y] can occur only medially, whereas the phonemic vowels can occur in initial and final position as well. After a detailed discussion of the various syllabic types, Krejnovič notes that native speakers deny the presence of any vowel at all in such clusters as *kət-kət* "snowcrust", but have no trouble in identifying /i/ in *kit-kit* "a little". Krejnovič, like Skorik, denies the existence of glottalized vowels in Koryak.

In her article "Slova korjakskogo jazyka, oboznačajuščie kačestvennoe sostojanie [Koryak words signifying qualitative condition]", *DSIJa* 11.77-85 (1958), A. N. Žukova describes a series of words in Koryak which have usually been considered either adjectives or adverbs, and suggests that they be recognized as an intermediate category. These are the words formed on adjective roots by the affixes (*e-/a-*)*. . .-ke/-ka* (*e-/a-*

omitted before roots with vocalic anlaut), e.g. the pure adjective *ny-mel-qin* "good", the adverb *ny-mel-ŭew*' "well", and the intermediate *e-mel-ke* "good, all right, (it is) permissible". Most such words express physical or psychological conditions in man or his surroundings. They are largely but not completely indeclinable, and thus distinguished both from the declinable adjectives and the non-declinable adverbs. Syntactically they usually stand as head word of impersonal sentences, e.g. *umkyčyku igyke* "in-the-woods (it-is)-cool", *eppa ečgyka* "still (is-it)-light?", *ečgyka* "(it-is)-light". A problem is posed by the fact that the affixes which form this category of qualitative condition coincide exactly with those which express negation (this is true of Chukchee as well), e.g. *jylgu elilike koqajawlaŋ* "fingers without-mittens freeze" (*lilit* "mittens", *elilike* "without-mittens" ["not-mittens"]). In Miss Žukova's opinion these affixes are not simply homonymous, but are genetically identical. The original meaning of *e-/a-. . .-ke/-ka* was predicativity; negation was expressed by this predicativity marker together with special particles such as *kytyl, čemoč*, which dropped because of their redundancy; the words signifying qualitative condition grew from the same original affixes by loss of original copulative verbs.

Koryak morphology is the subject of A. N. Žukova's brief but incisive study, "Tipy sklonenija suščestvitel'nyx v korjakskom jazyke [Types of noun declension in Koryak]", *Voprosy grammatiki. Sbornik statej k 75-letiju Akademika I. I. Meščaninova* (Moscow-Leningrad, 1960), pp. 60-70. Žukova recapitulates briefly the Koryak case system as presented by Bogoraz (*Chukchee, Handbook of American Indian languages*, part 2, Washington, 1922), Korsakov ("Grammatičeskij očerk", *Nymylansko-russkij slovar*', Moscow, 1939), and Stebnickij (*Iz istorii padežnyx suffiksov v korjakskom i čukotskom jazykax*, Leningrad, 1941), and compares this system with that of Chukchee as given by Bogoraz ("Luoravetlanskij [čukotskij] jazyk", *Jazyki i pis'mennost' narodov severa*, III, Moscow-Leningrad, 1934; the same, "Kratkij očerk grammatiki luoravetlanskogo jazyka", *Luoravetlansko-russkij slovar*', Leningrad, 1937) and Skorik ("Kratkie svedenija po grammatike čukotskogo jazyka", *Russko-čukotskij slovar*', Leningrad, 1941), noting, however, that the two basic types of declension in Koryak have not yet been adequately characterized in the literature. The bulk of Žukova's article describes these two declension types with well-chosen examples.

Type I contains names of objects and of animals (= "non-intelligent beings" in Žukova's terminology), and Type II contains personal names, and the nicknames by which animals are called. Kinship terms, and in general names of people other than personal names, can be declined according to either Type I or Type II. Žukova outlines the formal differences between Types I and II (Type II nouns cannot form a comitative, but unlike those of Type I, they do distinguish between singular and plural in almost all cases), and points out that Type II forms are derived from those of Type I, plus a formant *-ne/na, -jk*. The meaning of Type II endings is that of Type I, plus an element of specificity, of definiteness (rather like the English article) which separates out the given noun from all others of the same class; this explains why kinship terms can be declined according to either of the two types (in Type I, with the general meaning, e.g., "an uncle", in Type II with the specific deictic meaning "my uncle"), as well as why personal and animal names are always declined in Type II. Of those kinship terms which can take endings of either type, the names for the closest relations are usually of Type II, since they are more specifically deictic ("mamma", "papa", etc.). The article explains this interesting system neatly and precisely.

## 5. YUKAGHIR

E. A. Krejnovič describes the morphological markers of emphasis ("comment" in Hockett's "topic"-"comment" dichotomy) in his paper, "Sistema morfologičeskogo vyraženija logičeskogo udarenija v jukagirskom jazyke [The system of morphological expression of logical emphasis in Yukaghir]", *DSIJa* 7.99-115 (1955). Emphasis is expressed purely morphologically in Yukaghir, and can be marked in either the subject or the predicate. The subject is emphasized by addition of the morpheme *l'* (etymologically a noun of being derived from the verb "to be"), e.g. *il'eŋ mekot'egej* "the reindeer ran away" : : *il'el'eŋ kot'egel* "the *reindeer* ran away". The verbal predicate is marked by the prefix *me-*, as in the first of the two examples just adduced; such an emphasized predicate is opposed to the negated predicate, e.g. *il'eŋ el'kot'ege* "the reindeer didn't run away'; the emphatic morphemes *l'* and *me* are mutually exclusive. In subjects containing an attribute as well as a noun, emphasis is marked by a different morpheme, *k*, which is also used to emphasize first and second person pronominal subjects e.g., *met merūjeŋ* "I was going" (< *met* "I", *ūl* "go") : : *metek ūl* "It was I who was going". The opposition of subject vs. predicate emphasis (i.e., of a topic-comment organization of the sentence coinciding with or contradicting the subject-predicate organization) obtains with qualitative (adjectival) predicates as well, e.g., *tetek qālul* "you (sing.) are powerful" : : *tet qālit'ek* "you are *powerful*". Several pages of the article are devoted to the morphological analysis of the flexional forms of emphasized sentence parts; Krejnovič comes to the conclusion that the similarities observed among nominal, verbal, and adjectival stems are due to the emphatic markers which have been added to originally disparate flexional types.

The role of logical emphasis in the transitive verb is somewhat more complicated, since not only the subject and the predicate, but also the object within the latter, can be emphatically marked. Cf. for example *met pun'* "I killed (something)" : : *met mepun'iŋ* "I *killed* (something)" : : *met il'eŋ-mepun'iŋ* "I killed a reindeer" : : *met il'el'-e-bun'meŋ* "I killed a *reindeer*"; cf. the negated transitive (which then takes the intransitive conjugation) *met el'bun'd'eg* "I did not kill", *met il'eŋ-el'bun'd'eŋ* "I did not kill a reindeer"; if, on the other hand, the negation is applied only to part of the predicate, the verb remains in its transitive form *met amat'ed-il'ek el'bun'meŋ* "It wasn't a *good* reindeer I killed". Krejnovič closes his article with the comment that the highly refined system of marking logical emphasis is one of the most striking features of the Yukaghir language. His article corroborates this statement in a clear and convincing manner.

Like the Chukchee grammar by Skorik (E. A. Krejnovič's **Jukagirskij jazyk* [The Yukaghir language] (Moscow-Leningrad, 1958), 288 pp., is a major accomplishment in the study of Paleosiberian languages, which provides us with the first really thorough description of Yukaghir. The book consists of a compact phonology (pp. 9-19), a detailed morphology (pp. 20-220), a comparative survey of the relations between Yukaghir and other languages of Siberia, Eastern Europe, and Central Asia (pp. 221-54), and an appendix (pp. 255-84) containing a seven-page Yukaghir text, the Russian translation thereof, and two short dictionaries of the Tundra and Kolyma dialects.

In the phonology, we learn that Yukaghir has six vocalic phonemes /i u e θ [a rarely encountered slightly rounded mid central vowel, the phonemic status of which is not quite clear] o a/ and twenty consonants, including four sets of palatalized – nonpalatalized dentals /p b m w, t t' d d' n n' s l l' r, j, k g ŋ, voiced uvular stop and continuant q h/. Sequential restrictions within the syllable and morphophonemic alternations (which include /s/ ~ /r/ and /d/ ~ /r/) are illustrated, as are the principal phonemic correspondences between the Tundra and Kolyma dialects.

The morphology begins with a description of the morphological structure of the word, in which Krejnovič distinguishes root, stem (= root + certain affixes) and affixes, the latter subdivided into prefixes, derivational suffixes, and flexional endings. Judging by the examples, both prefixes and suffixes play a role in flexion. The Yukaghir noun has eight case forms. The basic form is the bare stem, used both as subject and as object of transitive verbs (*ileŋ meket'egej* "the reindeer ran away", *met ileŋ mepun'iŋ* "I killed the reindeer"). Yukaghir also has an instrumental (*met ārilek meraiŋ* "I by-means-of-a-rifle shot"), which is used as well in cases where other languages might have a direct object (*ejele moim* "a bow he is holding"), a locative, a "delative" case (Russian *prodol'nyj*) and an ablative, both formed by combining the locative marker *ha* with other spatial markers *n* "beside" and *t* "from". There is also a dative, and a genitive expressing various internominal relations. Plurality is marked only in cases where it must be insisted upon; the neutral sentence contains no reference to either singularity or plurality.

A peculiarity of Yukaghir is its complicated system of deverbative nouns: one finds nouns of transitive action, intransitive action, quality, and quantity, all derived from the various verb classes, cf. *ūl* "walking" < *ūk* "go", *med'il* "taking" < *men'k* "take", *kijol* "two" < *kijon'* "to be two".

Yukaghir distinguishes transitive and intransitive verbs, each of which has its own conjugation; passive, reciprocal, and negative voices of transitive verbs take the intransitive conjugation. In addition to active and middle voices, Yukaghir has a factitive (*wiel* "do", *wiesel* "make somebody do something", passive, reflexive, and reciprocal (*ket'il* "bring", *meniket'inuŋi* "bring to each other" = "help each other"). The aspect system is also elaborate, containing aspects indicating that the speaker is ready to perform the action named in the verb root, that he is on his way to perform this action, or that the action is inchoative, habitual, non-durative, iterative, or semelfactive; each of these aspects has a clear morphological marker. Yukaghir distinguishes six moods: indicative, conditional, optative, assurative (the suffix *mori*, *mod'i* indicating that an action will really take place in the future, e.g. *n'an'ir lewmoriŋ* "there really will be some fat"), obligative (the suffix *moraw* "should"), imperative, and what might be called apparitive (Russian *očevidnoe naklonenie*) indicating that a given action, although not witnessed directly by the speaker, is so obvious that it can hardly be questioned. The apparitive suffix is *l'el*, deverbative of *l'e* "to be": *met-ama mārqan-n'awn'ikliek pull'elmele* "my father killed one polar fox" (I did not see it happen); the same sentence with *pun'mele* instead of *pull'elmele* will mean "and I saw him do it".

Krejnovič's "Comparative-historical study of Yukaghir" (pp. 221-254) leads him to certain tentative conclusions, viz.: Yukaghir and Kot (formerly spoken on the upper Jenissej near Krasnojarsk) have several morphological features in common, especially in conjugation. These features do not indicate genetic relationship, however, but only prolonged proximity. Krejnovič supposes that the Yukaghirs came to their present location from the Ural region. There are also some correspondences between Yukaghir and Ket, but these are purely typological in nature. Yukaghir and Samoyed, on the other hand, show extensive correspondences, including some 80 lexical equations. Again, however, Krejnovič attributes the similarity to borrowings due to proximity, and emphatically denies the validity of Collinder's thesis of Yukaghir-Altaic relationship. There are also some possible similarities between Yukaghir and both Turkic (Oirot) and Mongol (Burjat) groups, including approximately 20 lexical equations in each case. As to the Chukchee-Koryak-Kamchadal group, often considered related to Yukaghir, Krejnovič finds no evidence of close connection at all. The Tungus and Yakut languages, which came to the Far North several centuries after Yukaghir, have influenced the latter surprisingly little, in spite of long contact, in the case of Tungus at least. Finally, Russian influence on Yukaghir is evident in the vocabulary only: Krejnovič gives 76 lexical equations. The author's approach is careful and modest throughout, and his final conclusion is that the greatest influence on Yukaghir was exercised by Altaic and Samoyed languages.

## 6. GILYAK

K. A. Novikova and V. N. Savel'eva give an extensive but informal report of the 1949 Academy of Sciences expedition to Saxalin and the Amur Basin in "K voprosu o jazykax korennyx narodnostej Saxalina (Po materialam lingvističeskoj èkspedicii 1949 g.) [On the languages of the aboriginal inhabitants of Saxalin (From materials of the 1949 linguistic expedition)]", *UZLU* (Serija Fakul'teta Narodov Severa 2) 157.84-133 (1953). After an outline sketch of the development of Gilyak studies since the days of Šternberg, the authors describe the externals of their expedition, including the great joy they experienced at finding so many Gilyaks happily ensconced in kolkhozes, and then proceed to give samples of the linguistic materials they collected, not only from the Gilyak (from whom they acquired valuable indices of the differences between the Saxalin and Amur dialects), but also from the Evenki (a Tungus people) and in a fragmentary fashion from a few Ainu speakers. A good many texts were collected, although not on tape. Among the interesting dialect differences in Gilyak, one finds radically different pronominal systems, as well as a striking degree of divergence among basic vocabulary items (the words for man, woman, bear, squirrel, hatchet, fishhook, river, sand, snow, mud, tree, face, mouth, eyes, ears, teeth, belly, etc.); one wonders what a glottochronological study would have to say about the time of separation of these two dialects.

V. N. Savel'eva studies the case system of the Gilyak noun in her paper, "Sklonenie imen suščestvitel'nyx v nivxskom jazyke [The declension of nouns in Gilyak]", *UZLPedI* 101.239-254 (1954). Savel'eva finds earlier studies by Šternberg and Krejnovič to have been incomplete, and to have taken the Gilyak case system for a system of postfixes rather than of case endings. According to Savel'eva, case is marked both by special case suffixes, and by position within the sentence; within a given case, further distinctions can be achieved by the use of postfixes. There are nine cases in the system Savel'eva proposes for Gilyak. The ABSOLUTE CASE is distinguished by the absence of any endings at all; it is used to mark the subject (*Og'la n'ulidĭ* "The-child smiles"), predicate noun (*Nazgun – og'la* "Nazgun [is a] child"), and various types of nominal modifier (*Ymyk og'la-djudĭ* "The-mother washed-the-child"; *Nĭyn' og'la-yumydĭ* "We-heard a-child's-voice"); the circle of verbs with which absolute case forms can express indirect objects, possessives, etc., is quite restricted (verbs of motion, of helping, giving, saying). The DATIVE-ACCUSATIVE CASE, expressed by the suffix *-ax*, occurs only with the class of verbs called "causative transitives", which have the meaning of forcing, allowing, not hindering, etc., someone to do something (these verbs contain the suffix *-ku, -gu*). It marks the object or so-called logical subject with such verbs, e.g. *Og'lagu pŭn'afkkax pitg'y-urugudĭ* "The-children forced (their) comrade (to) read the-book", *Ymyk nanakax alo-tozgudĭ* "The-mother ordered sister (to) divide the berries". Another type of dative, the DATIVE-DIRECTIVE CASE, contains the suffix *-t(o)x, -r(o)x, -d(o)x*, and denotes the person toward whom an action develops (*Penĭguk pŭymykrox ittĭ* "Penguk [proper name] spoke to [his] mother"), the goal or designation of an object (*Atikrox matĭki-lakk-lyttĭg'u* "For-little-brother they-made-small-skis"), or the direction in which a motion occurs (*Tilvytn'an mer xotarox vinydĭ* "In-autumn we to-the-city go"). The LOCATIVE CASE, formed by the suffix *-uin* (sometimes shortened to *-un* after consonants and to *-in* after vowels), designates the place where an action occurs or an object is located (*Og'lagu klyin lerdĭg'u* "The-children play on-the-streets", *Nanak ena-voin x'umdĭ* "Sister lives in-another-village"), the person who has something (*Yknuin pila-gan jivdĭ* "Brother a-big-dog has"), or the time when some action or event accurs (*Nyyn' čuz-yruin* x'*umdĭ* "We live in-a-new-time"). The ABLATIVE CASE, containing the suffix *-ux* (after vowels, *-x*), indicates the point of origin of an action, the source of some item of knowledge, the whole of which something is a part, and similar meanings connected with origin (*Parf mer palux pŭudĭ* "In-evening we-came-out of-the-forest", *Atakux mer n'yzit-rajudĭ* "From grandfather we wrote-down-the-tale", *Nanakux mer ext vidĭ* "From-sister we went home", *Nĭykyn nŭn'afkkux meuču-ged'* "Brother from-a-friend bought-a-gun"), and can also indicate the time when some action begins (*Ni namk čazux oztŭadĭ* "At nine-o'clock I-get-up"). The DATIVE-DELIMITATIVE CASE, formed by means of the suffix *-tog'o*, *-rog'o*, *-dog'o* (in the Amur dialect, *-tŭyky*, *-ršyky*), denotes the space or object within which or up to which some activity (usually some action) occurs (*Matĭki-erirog'o vija*! "As-far-as-the-little-river go!"), as well as the time by which some action has been completed (*Parftog'o pŭog'laumgu-n'armadĭ* "Until-evening they-waited-for-their-daughter"). Gilyak, like many Siberian languages, has a type of DELATIVE CASE, formed with the suffix *-ug'e*, which is used to mark the place or object along which, down beside which, some motion takes place (*Nĭyn' pila-du-zyrug'e vinydĭ* "We shall-go along-the-edge-of-a-big-lake", *Matĭki-mu eriug'e lyrktĭ* "The-little-boat sails down-the-river"). The INSTRUMENTAL CASE is expressed by the suffix *-kir*, *-g'ir*, *-xir*, *-gir* (initial alternants conditioned by the stem-final phoneme preceding the suffix), and has the usual wide range of meanings of such a case, e.g. means of accomplishing an action (*Ni mur-djaskir mur-djadĭ* "I- struck the-horse with-the-whip"), means of travel (*Imn' čoln'ig'ir vidĭg'u* "They drove-off on-reindeer"), the material of which something is made (*Nanak čarbg'ir x'ontk-ottĭ* "Sister sewed a-tobacco-pouch of silk"), etc. Finally, Savel'eva terms a VOCATIVE CASE those forms with the suffix *-a* which are used in addressing people (*Ykyna*! "Brother!", etc.).

Savel'eva gives two pages of tables showing the allomorphic forms of these several case suffixes, and notes the presence in Gilyak of two special markers, which are not in her opinion to be considered cases; the first of these two is the suffix *-g'e*, *-ke*, *-xe*, *-ge*, which marks the COMITATIVE RELATION between two nouns (*Nanakxe atikxe als-pŭet vidĭg'u* "Sister-with little-brother-with looking-for-berries went"), and the second is the suffix *-yk*, attached to the noun to which another noun is compared, thus marking the COMPARATIVE RELATION (*Kka vytĭyk tekkadĭ* "Steel than-iron is-stronger").

All Gilyak nouns have the same declension, and even plural nouns are declined as singulars in *-n*. In the presence of this remarkable flexional unity, and given the complete absence of syncretic endings, one wonders if the distinction between postfixes on the one hand and declensional endings on the other is not somewhat specious. In any case, Savel'eva's article provides a good deal of interesting material on noun forms in Gilyak.

E. A. Krejnovič takes issue with V. Z. Panfilov's view of the status of incorporation in Gilyak ("K voprosu ob inkorporirovanii", *VJa* 3/6) in his article, "Ob inkorporirovanii v nivxskom jazyke [On incorporation in Gilyak]", *VJa* 7/6.21-33 (1958). Krejnovič shares the views of Skorik concerning incorporation, and derives his definition of this phenomenon from Franz Boas, who held that incorporation is a special type of syntactic compounding, most frequently consisting of a transitive verb plus its nominal or pronominal direct object. Gilyak, as Krejnovič points out, also has a nominal type of incorporating complex, consisting of a noun and its incorporated attribute. To the outsider, the data adduced by the one and the other scholar do not seem adequate to confirm either view absolutely, and one wonders if the continuing debate is not to a considerable extent terminological in nature.

As V. Z. Panfilov shows in *"Složnye suščestvitel'nye v nivxskom jazyke i ix otličie ot slovosočetanij (k probleme slova) [Compound nouns in Gilyak and how they differ from word-combinations (toward the problem of the word)]", *VJa* 7/1.105-111(1958), affixation is rather limited in Gilyak, whereas compounding is quite productive. Panfilov discusses the problem of distinguishing compound words from free word-combinations. Although compound words occasionally show morphonological distinctions from word-combinations (e.g., vowels drop out in the former,) they are more often than not devoid of any morphological indications of syntactic status, e.g. *utkuoγla* "boy" = *utku* "man" + *oγla* "child", a compound word, but *utku mu* "the-man's boat" is a word-combination. Panfilov comes to the conclusion that semantic criteria are decisive in distinguishing compounds from combinations: whenever the meaning of two conjoined items is more than the sum of the meanings of the individual items, one has to do with compounding. He thus differs from such scholars as Šternberg and Krejnovič, who saw no difference between the two types. Other criteria for distinguishing compounds from combinations are: (1) the components of compounds may not be used independently at all; (2) these components may be used independently, but in a different meaning. Panfilov gives a "syntactico-semantic" typology of Gilyak compound words. These are either (a) subordinating or (b) coordinating compounds, and the former are further divided into aa) determinative, in which "the semantic relation between the two components is attributive in nature", and ab) objective, in which the first component "makes concrete" the action expressed by the second. The article contains many illustrative examples, but approaches the problem from the semantic rather than from the formal side.

In *"Grammatičeskoe čislo suščestvitel'nyx v nivxskom jazyke [Grammatical number in the Gilyak noun]", *DSIJa* 11.46-61 (1958), V. Z. Panfilov illustrates the use of the plural suffix *-ku, -xu, -gu, -γu,* (Amur dialect), *-kun, -xun, -gun, -γun* (East Sakhalin) with unpublished archival materials. Gilyak nouns in the unmarked singular (= bare stem), can also express plurality in some cases. Panfilov distinguishes three grades of numbering: individuality (individual singular), collectivity (collective singular or unitary plurality), and distributive plurality. The plural suffixes can express only the latter two of these grades, the unmarked singular usually only the former two. Abstract nouns cannot take plural suffixes. In some cases the plural markers play a role in derivation, as in Russian and English (items : : types of item, e.g. beer : : beers). In some cases, Gilyak expresses plurality by means of reduplication instead of suffixation; in Panfilov's opinion, this was originally the only method of expressing plurality in Gilyak.

V. Z. Panfilov devotes a rather long article to the category of voice in Gilyak in "O zaloge glagola v nivxskom jazyke [On voice in the Gilyak verb]", *Voprosy gram-*

*matiki. Sbornik statej k 75-letiju Akademika I. I. Meščaninova* (Moscow-Leningrad, 1960), pp. 103-131. After a few pages of general theoretical remarks on voice as a grammatical category and the relation thereof to other linguistic or semi-linguistic categories such as subject, logical subject, actor, etc., Panfilov posits the existence of five voices in Gilyak, viz. (1) basic, (2) incitative (*pobuditel'nyj*), (3) reflexive, (4) incitative-reflexive, and (5) reciprocal. Since the category of voice is closely connected with that of transitivity, Panfilov lists three classes of verbs in which the five classes of voice are manifested: transitives, intransitives, and transitive-intransitives. The bulk of the article is given over to a detailed morphological analysis of these three transitivity classes and their many sub-classes, and it is only on the last three pages that Panfilov returns to the problem of voice and lists the transitivity types of verb in which each of the five Gilyak voices can be expressed. The article is somewhat loosely centered on the category of voice, although it does contain a good deal of interesting morphological data on the Gilyak verb.

The problem of a semantic system dealing with directional oppositions is the subject of E. A. Krejnovič's study, *"Vyraženie prostranstvennoj orientacii v nivxskom jazyke (K istorii orientacii v prostranstve) [The expression of spatial orientation in Gilyak (Toward a history of orientation in space)]", *VJa* 9/1.78-89 (1960). Krejnovič wishes to demonstrate how the expression of spatial orientation develops in primitive peoples, specifically among the Gilyaks of the lower Amur and Sakhalin, who in the nineteenth century were still living in a primitive hunting and fishing economy. It is Krejnovič's view that the vocabulary of spatial orientation developed gradually, and of course not in our north-east-south-west terms. The basic dimensions of Gilyak spatial orientation are organized in binary pairs. The roots *kʰe-* ~ *xe* and *a* ~ *ja* refer to directions upstream and downstream, or north and south along the seashore; the pair *he* ~ *je* and *qo* ~ *ʁʰo* mean "toward the interior" (from the shore); the root *tʰa* ~ *ša* means "toward the open sea" (from the shore) and its opposite *he* ~ *je* "toward the shore" (from the sea), cf. above. To these horizontal dimensions there are added paired roots *kʰi* ~ *xi* and *qo* ~ *ʁo* meaning "up" and "down" (from a mountain, a tree, or out of the interior toward the shore) respectively. Krejnovič analyzes many Gilyak forms built on these roots, and concludes that a thorough study of all case forms connected with spatial orientation will be necessary before this system can be completely understood.

An interesting although not conclusive attempt to use the techniques of experimental phonetics to solve the problem of whether or not Gilyak incorporation differs at all from simple apposition (see the several articles by Krejnovič, Panfilov et al. elsewhere in this report) is described by L. V. Bondarenko and L. R. Zinder in "Fonetičeskaja xarakteristika različnyx tipov sintaksičeskix sočetanij v nivxskom jazyke [Phonetic characteristics of various types of syntactic groups in Gilyak]", *VJa* 11/4.84-89 (1962). Using tapes of thirty sentences as spoken by five Gilyak natives, Bondarenko and Zinder establish that whereas a combination of independent words (e.g., *Aŋ xad'* "Who shot?") shows two peaks of loudness, the same stems as part of an incorporating complex (e.g., *If aŋ-q'ad'* "Whom did he shoot?") show only a single peak on the first component. The length of the vowel in the second component (*-q'ad'*) is also considerably reduced in the incorporating complex. These results were obtained for all such verb + object complexes. Nominal groups showed less conclusive results, but in most cases also contained only a single amplitude peak on the first of two conjoined elements; the free combination *Nivx lyγi-n'yŋd'* "The man whale-catches" has bursts on *Nivx* and on *lyγi-*, whereas the complex *lyγi-n'yŋ-nivx* "whale-catching-man" has a single burst on *lyγi-*. Bondarenko and Zinder consider Krejnovič's viewpoint (that Gilyak does indeed have incorporation distinct from simple apposition) to be correct, and Panfilov's view (that there is no incorporation at all in Gilyak) to be wrong. The results of this investigation appear less conclusive than the authors think, however, since it is not impossible that any endocentric combination, whether appositive or incorporated, have only a single amplitude peak on its chief term. The results of the phonetic investigation themselves, however, are interesting and valuable regardless of their bearing on the problem of incorporation.

## 7. KET

E. A. Krejnovič, whose investigations range among many Paleosiberian languages, turns his attention to Ket morphology in *"Imennye klassy i grammatičeskie sredstva ix vyraženija v ketskom jazyke [Nominal classes and the grammatical means of expressing them in Ket]", *VJa* 10/2.106-116 (1961), where he describes the various formal markers of gender in Ket. Gender is expressed not in nouns themselves, but in the various classes which combine with nouns: adjectives, verbs, and numerals. Gender of both subject and object can be expressed, in intransitive and transitive verbs. The categories of gender and number are mutually exclusive as in Russian; in both, gender is expressed only in the singular. There is also some evidence pointing to the existence of a category of whole, undivided organisms (entire fish, opposed to cut-up fish, etc.), of which masculine and feminine are sub-categories. The overwhelming majority of Ket words are neuter. Among the masculines are names of men and male animals, several series of fish, birds, insects and reptiles, some kinds of trees, and certain cosmic bodies. Feminines include names of women and female animals, other kinds of birds, fish, reptiles, cosmic bodies, and certain plants, geographical locations, parts of the body, skin diseases, and objects of material culture. The article includes several complete conjugations.

The foregoing survey has tried to cover most of Soviet scholarship in the Paleosiberian field since the end of the Second World War. A few articles which were unavailable for personal inspection have been mentioned only in passing, within the discussion of other works; otherwise, everything mentioned herein has been studied personally. No attempt has been made to cover the several elementary textbooks which have appeared during this period, although these are not devoid of interest. Since publications in the Paleosiberian field often appear in journals unavailable in the West, and since the reviewer's library resources are still somewhat limited, it is quite possible that a few items have escaped his attention. It can be hoped, however, that in spite of such gaps the survey offered here will have been adequate to demonstrate both the great progress which has been made in Soviet linguistic study of Paleosiberian languages, and the equally great gaps which still remain to be filled.

# SEMITIC

HAIM BLANC

## 1. OVERALL VIEW

1.1. Linguistic studies in the field of Semitics have traditionally been connected with, and ancillary to, historical and cultural investigations of the ancient and modern Near East. This is as true of the USSR and Eastern Europe as it is of the major centers of Semitic research further West, so that the singling out of works that are purely or even primarily of linguistic interest is not an easy task, and inevitably results in inconsistencies. In what follows I have nevertheless tried to draw the line between linguistic works and philological works concentrating on the former and excluding (or at best barely mentioning) most of the latter. I was not able to consult all of the materials listed, and do not feel competent to comment on much of the rest; fortunately, however, most of the relevant works were both available and included within the areas of Semitic linguistics with which I am most familiar.[1]

1.2. Semitic studies have reached an advanced level in the USSR and, to a lesser degree, in Czechoslovakia; there are individual scholars of note in Poland and Hungary, but I find little or nothing to report for Yugoslavia, Rumania and Bulgaria.[2]

[1] For expert guidance through the bibliographical maze, I am primarily indebted to H. J. Polotsky; I also owe many helpful hints to M. Altbauer, R. Cohen, R. Hetzron, S. Morag, Ch. Rabin and H. Tadmor. I have relied on a good many surveys and bibliographical compilations, principally the following, which the reader may consult for further details: for the USSR, I. Ju. Kračkovskij, *Očerki po istorii russkoj arabistiki* (Moscow, 1950), reprinted in the same author's *Izbrannye Sočinenija* 5.9-192 (1958), and available also in a German translation, *Die Russische Arabistik – Umriss ihrer Entwicklung* (Leipzig, 1957); idem, "Semitologija v universitetax SSSR", *VJa* 4/4.83-88 (1955); G. V. Cereteli, "Al-dirāsāt al-ʿarabīya fī al-ittiḥād al-sōvyētī", *Revue de l'Académie Arabe de Damas* 31.3-20 (1956); G. Š. Šarbatov, *Arabistika v SSSR* (*Filologija*) *1917-1959* (Moscow, 1959) and its up-dated Arabic translation *Al-Istiʿrāb fī al-Ittiḥād al-Sōvyētī* (*al-luġa wa-l-adab*) *1917-1961* (Moscow, 1961); A. N. Kononov, ed., *Vostokovedenie v Leningradskom Universitete, UZLU nr. 296, Serija Vostokovedčeskix Nauk* 13 (Leningrad, 1960); J. Jedlička and K. Petráček, "Die Semitologie in der Georgischen SSR – Bibliographische Übersicht", *AUC-Ph, Orientalia Pragensia* 1.83-95 (1960); J. Klima, "Zur Entwicklung der Sowjetischen Keilschriftlichen Studien", *AO* 21.448-466 (1953). On Czechoslovakia, K. Petráček, "Les études arabes et islamiques et la sémitologie en Tchécoslovaquie", *AO* 19.98-117 (1951); D. Zbavitel, *Die Orientalistik in der Tschechoslowakei* (Prague, 1959); J. Klima, "L'état actuel des études concernant l'Orient ancien en Tchécoslovaquie", *AOH* 5.25-27 (1955). On other countries, see next footnote.

[2] On Poland, cf. "Dix ans d'études orientales en Pologne populaire", *RO* 20.7-17 (1956); on Hungary, see section 4 of the present survey. In Yugoslavia, Rumania and Bulgaria (I have no information

In the USSR, these studies emanate from three main centers, viz. Leningrad State University, the J. V. Stalin State University at Tbilisi, Georgia, and Moscow University. Outside the USSR the main center is at Charles University, Prague. There are no journals devoted exclusively to Semitics, so that papers in this field are published in Orientalist periodicals or, more rarely, in general linguistics publications. The publication of articles in Western journals and/or in Western languages, which is the rule for Czech, Polish and Hungarian scholars, was abandoned by Soviet scholars in the thirties; there has recently been a very slight trend in favor of its renewal, but the bulk of Soviet output is in Russian or, in the case of the Georgian scholars, often in Georgian with Russian summaries.

1.3 Among languages studied and taught, Classical Arabic holds the first rank, Aramaic and Syriac the second followed by some of the Arabic dialects, Hebrew, Phoenician, Ugaritic and Akkadian in varying order of importance depending on the various centers; very little has been done in Ethiopic and South Arabic, and a few scholars have done significant work in general and comparative Semitics. Outside the USSR, East European Semitics has gravitated almost entirely around the ancient and medieval languages; in the USSR, a good deal of attention has been paid to living languages as well, chiefly modern literary Arabic. Field investigation of spoken languages is not highly developed, but has been given some impetus by the existence, within the Soviet Union, of two small Semitic-speaking minorities, the Arabs of Uzbekistan and the "Assyrians" (Aramaic-speaking Nestorians) of the Caucasus. Several developments of recent years may be attributed to the re-orientation of the post-Stalin era. More active Soviet interest in the Middle East has resulted in increased work in various aspects of Modern Arabic (chiefly, again, the literary idiom) and in an increased and improved production of teaching materials for that language. Some loosening-up may have taken place in the teaching and publication of Hebraic studies, though this is as yet hard to gauge. More cognizance is being taken of work done in the West, and there is a fresh desire, taking the shape of Western-language summaries of papers and the like, of being read abroad. With one or two minor exceptions, there is no trace of Marxian or Marrist ideology or phraseology in the works under review, regardless of their date of publication.

1.4. Few of the scholars involved consider themselves primarily linguists. Even among those who do, there has been little application or discussion of recent theoretical notions in vogue among American, European, or for that matter Soviet methodologists. In this, Eastern Semitists differ little from their Western colleagues. Taking the works under review as a whole, one finds little grammatical or phonological analysis, somewhat more work in lexicography, and a good deal of attention paid to

on Albania) even more than in Poland and Hungary, Oriental studies are largely devoted to Turcology and little or nothing has been done in Semitics; cf. J. Kabrda, "Les études orientales en Yougoslavie (L'activité de l'Institut Oriental à Sarajevo)", *AO* 25.147-155 (1957); M. Guboglu, "Contributions roumaines aux études orientales", *AO* 24.454-475 (1956); Xr. Gande and B. Nedko, "Vostokovedenie v Bolgarii", *SovV* 4.137-145 (1958).

the publication and translation of texts either for their own sake or as teaching aids. Detailed monographic work is rarer, overall surveying perhaps more common, than in the West. What analytical and descriptive work there is has tended, with some notable exceptions, to be mediocre to poor, and that of the lexicographical, philological and pedagogical work fair to good. Before entering into details, it may be useful to list the half-dozen or so studies of most lasting interest to the world of scholarship. These include J. Kuryłowicz's distinguished contribution to early Semitic history, *L'Apophonie en Sémitique* (see 4.1), Baranov's excellent Arabic-Russian dictionary (2.21), the studies on the Arabic dialects of Central Asia by G. V. Cereteli and I. N. Vinnikov (2.22) and the latter scholar's lexicographical work on epigraphic and Palestinian Aramaic (2.32); from a different viewpoint, one must include among the most important publications of recent years the six volumes of I. Ju. Kračkovskij's selected writings, which cover the author's working life span and deal with nearly all aspects of Arabic studies (2.21, 2.22, 2.23).

1.5. In what follows, I have organized the material by countries, dealing first with the USSR, then with Czechoslovakia, and finally with "other countries", principally Poland and Hungary. Within each country the discussion is arranged under the following headings: 1) General and comparative Semitics; 2) Arabic; 3) Northwest Semitic; 4) Akkadian; 5) Ethiopic and South-Arabic. Each of these is then subdivided whenever necessary.

## 2. THE USSR

### 2.1. *General and comparative Semitics*

Courses are given at Leningrad, Moscow and Tbilisi, but recent publications in this field are few. Before World War II, some interesting and original work on the Proto-Semitic consonantal system was done by Nikolaj Vladimirovič Jušmanov (1896-1946)[3] and Jakov Solomonovič Vilenčik (1902–1939);[4] neither lived long enough to see his ideas accepted and developed by Western specialists.[5] Also during that period, Aleksander Pavlovič Riftin (1900–1945) probed the origin and history of some grammatical categories.[6] More recently, Isaak Naumovič Vinnikov (b. 1897) used

[3] N. V. Jušmanov, "Théorie des consonnes emphatiques sémitiques", *DAN*, 1925, pp. 55-58; "La correspondence du Dād arabe au 'Ayn araméen", *DAN*, May-June 1926, pp. 41-44. On Jušmanov's life and works, see I. Ju. Kračkovskij, *Izbrannye Sočinenija* 5.448-452 (1958).

[4] J. Vilenčik, "Welchen Lautwert hatte *ḍ* im Ursemitischen?", *OLZ* 33.89-98 (1930); "Zum Ursemitischen Konsonantensystem", *OLZ* 34.505-506 (1931). Cf. the obituary notice on him by Kračkovskij, *SovV* 2.228-230 (1941) = *Izbrannye Sočinenija* 5.397-400 (1958).

[5] Cf. J. Cantineau, "Le consonantisme du sémitique", *Semitica* 4.79-94 (1951), and A. Martinet, "Remarques sur le consonantisme sémitique", *BSL* 49(1).78-89 (1953).

[6] A. P. Riftin, "K proisxoždeniju form naklonenij v arabskom i akkadskom jazykax", *TIV* 36.127-132 (1941); "Iz istorii množestvennogo čisla", *UZLU serija filologičeskix nauk* 10.37-56 (1946). On his life and works, cf. I. Ju. Kračkovskij, *Izb. Soč.* 5.435-439 (1958).

some of the Central Asian Arabic materials he collected to elucidate some lexical problems of Hebrew, Classical Arabic and Akkadian,[7] and confronted some Koranic expressions with parallels from Classical Hebrew.[8] Bencion Meerovič Grande, who wrote the article "Semitic languages" in the first edition of the *Bol'šaja Sovetskaja Enciklopedija* (in the second edition, the article is by I. M. Diakonov) gives a cursory treatment intended for lay consumption of some ways in which grammatical categories are expressed in Semitic,[9] and has promised an introduction to comparative Semitic grammar for 1963. Quite recently A. M. Gazov-Ginsberg, a young Leningrad Hebraist, presented some original and carefully worked out ideas as to the relation between some onomatopoetic Semitic morphemes and corresponding *n*-initial roots.[10] Cf. also Šanidze in 2.32 below.

## 2.2 *Arabic*

2.21. Arabic studies, chiefly philological and literary, have been pursued at Leningrad for over a century; they have produced many noteworthy results and several names of world renown. Similar studies were introduced at Moscow nearly as early, and at Tbilisi during the interwar period. The most distinguished name of the recent past is undoubtedly that of Ignatij Julianovič Kračkovskij (1883–1951), whose scholarly activity lasted over forty years and produced over 450 major and minor works. Most of these are now available in the six volumes of his *Selected Writings*,[11] and are primarily concerned with Arabic literature, both medieval and modern. Nevertheless, his philological and text-critical works as well as his translations are replete with remarks of linguistic import, and a small number of his papers are directly concerned with linguistic matters. Among works deserving mention here (their selection is bound to be somewhat arbitrary), we may include the early but excellent review of Graf's work on Christian Arabic,[12] and his comments on a work on Persian loanwords in Arabic;[13] his edition of the 11th century poet Abu al-ʿalāʾ al-Māʾarrī's *Risālat al-Malāʾika* contains a valuable glossary,[14] and much interesting material is to be found in his commentary on the *Kitāb al-Badiʿ* of Ibn al-Muʿtazz,[15] and in

[7] I. N. Vinnikov, "Iz oblasti semitskoj leksikografii", *PSb* 2.87-96 (1956).

[8] I. N. Vinnikov, "Koraničeskie zametki", *Sbornik v čest' Akademika I. A. Orbeli* (Moscow-Leningrad, 1960), pp. 309-312.

[9] B. M. Grande, "Morfologičeskie i leksičeskie vyraženija grammatičeskix kategorii v semitskix jazykax", *PV* 3.126-128 (1959).

[10] A. M. Gazov-Ginsberg, "Čeredovanie obščesemitskix kornej tipa plpl, ppl → n-pl", *PSb* 7.152-158 (1962).

[11] I. Ju. Kračkovskij, *Izbrannye Sočinenija* (Moscow-Leningrad: I, 1955; II, 1956; III, 1956; IV, 1957; V, 1958; VI, 1960). (= *Izb. Soč.*)

[12] I. Ju. Kračkovskij, rev. of G. Graf, *Der Sprachgebrauch der ältesten Christlich-Arabischen Literatur* (Leipzig, 1906), in *Izb. Soč.* 1.337-343 (1955), first published 1907.

[13] Rev. of A. Šēr, *Kitāb al-alfāẓ al-fārisīya al-muʿarraba* (Beirut, 1908), in *Izb. Soč.* 1.350-359 (1955), first published 1910.

[14] *TIV*, t. 3 (Leningrad, 1932).

[15] *Izb. Soč.* 6.97-333 (1960), first published 1917-1933.

his study of a 16th century Christian epistle from Syria.[16] His prefatory comments to Jušmanov's Arabic grammar and Baranov's dictionary are largely bibliographical.[17] Some of his work touches on vernacular Arabic and related questions (see 2.22, 2.23); he did some work on Ethiopic and South-Arabic (2.5) and he paid a good deal of attention to the history of Arabic studies in the USSR (see fn.1 above). Turning now to more strictly linguistic works on Classical Arabic, we note that N. V. Jušmanov's 1928 Arabic grammar[18] was the first and perhaps the most important of his major works and is still the only work of its kind in Russian, but is hard to come by. B. M. Grande's new grammar, said to be on comparative and historical lines, was scheduled to appear in 1962, but does not seem to have come out as of this writing.[19] Jušmanov subsequently also published a briefer sketch of Arabic structure,[20] now available in English translation,[21] which gives the essentials of Classical phonetics and grammar. This useful, highly condensed attempt to deal simultaneously with all forms of Arabic and to include data from disparate sources as well as hypotheses and conjectures naturally could not avoid disproportion and inaccuracies of detail; the proposed classification of all Arabic dialects into "urban" and "rural" dialects is not entirely baseless, but as it stands is unsatisfactory and smacks of Marrism. I have not yet seen Šarbatov's recent sketch of modern literary Arabic.[22] Jušmanov also devoted a paper to the "enigma" of the Arabic diptotes.[23] These works contain relatively little discussion of syntax and since little has been done on the syntax of the modern literary language by Western *or* Eastern Arabists, Semenov's book on this subject partly fills a double gap.[24] Although far from exhaustive, it analyzes most sentence types and some of the uses of verbal tenses and moods to be found in a selection of modern writings, chiefly Egyptian; all examples are quoted from these writings, but are referred to by name of author only, and are given in Arabic script and in transcription; the latter, though useful, often surprisingly bears witness to serious misreadings.[25] The phenomena thus analyzed are essentially the same as those found in older stages of the Classical language. A good deal more work is needed on specifically modern usage, and it is to the credit of the present generation of Soviet

[16] *Ibid.*, pp. 445-454 (esp. pp. 453-454), first published 1924.

[17] Preface to Jušmanov's Grammar (see fn. 18), *Izb. Soč.* 1.301-309 (1955), first published 1928; preface to Baranov's dictionary (see fn. 30), reprinted in 2nd ed., 1957, as well as in *Izb. Soč.* 1.319-336 (1955), first published 1940.

[18] *Grammatika literaturnogo arabskogo jazyka* (Leningrad, 1928).

[19] Cf. C. Harkavi, *Ha-Arec* (Tel Aviv, 13 July 1962). Grande has also published some grammatical tables, *Grammatičeskie tablicy arabskogo literaturnogo jazyka* (Moscow, 1950).

[20] *Stroj arabskogo jazyka* (Moscow-Leningrad, 1938).

[21] *The Structure of the Arabic Language*. Tr. M. Perlmann (Washington, 1961).

[22] G. Š. Šarbatov, *Sovremennyj arabskij jazyk* (Moscow, 1961).

[23] "Zagadka dvuxpadežnyx imen arabskogo klasičeskogo jazyka", *Trudy 2-oj sessii associacii arabistov* (Moscow-Leningrad, 1941), pp. 149-159.

[24] D. V. Semenov, *Sintaksis sovremennogo arabskogo literaturnogo jazyka. TIV* t. 43 (Moscow-Leningrad, 1941).

[25] I am indebted to H. J. Polotsky for lending me his copy of this rare book and for letting me consult his list of errata.

Arabists (and of their mentors) that a number of specific studies of modern syntactic problems have recently made their appearance. I know them only from the listing in Šarbatov's *Arabistika* (see fn. 1); they are mostly *kandidat* dissertations reproduced by *steklografija* as *avtoreferaty* (authors' summaries), though some have yielded published articles.[26] A number of articles on various morphological, lexical and semantic questions[27] and on word stress of modern literary Arabic[28] have appeared in the past two decades, especially in the fifties. A. S. Lekiašvili is the author of a number of papers (mostly in Georgian with Russian summaries) on the genesis of several Classical Arabic constructions.[29] The second edition of Xarlampij Karpovič Baranov's Arabic-Russian dictionary to the modern language[30] is an outstanding contribution to Arabic lexicography, and compares well with H. Wehr's Arabic-German (now also Arabic-English) dictionary. There is a small but serviceable Russian-Arabic dictionary,[31] and two larger ones are in preparation.[32] A number of university level textbooks have made their appearance recently, of which the one by Aleksander

[26] V. M. Borisov, *Modal'nye slova v sovremennom arabskom jazyke* (Moscow, 1956); S. A. Kuzmin, *Složnopodčinennoe predloženie s pridatočnym dopolnitel'nom v literaturnom arabskom jazyke* (Moscow, 1955); A. A. Mamedov, *O prostom predloženii v sovremennom arabskom literaturnom jazyke* (Moscow, 1953); V. E. Šagal', *Strukturno-semantičeskaja xarakteristika substantivnyx slovosočitanij v arabskom literaturnom jazyke* (Moscow, 1958); S. A. Timofeev, *Složnopodčinennye predloženija s pridatočnymi opredelitel'nymi v sovremennom arabskom literaturnom jazyke* (Moscow, 1954); all these are listed as authors' summaries of *kandidat* dissertations; Timofeev also published two articles on the subject of his thesis in two military organs, one in *Trudy Voennogo Instituta Inostrannyx Jazykov* 7.68-81 (1955), and the other in *Sbornik trudov po jazykoznaniju Voennoj Akademii Sovetskoj Armii* 1.191-215 (1957).

[27] X. K. Baranov, "O sposobax vyraženija narečija v sovremennom literaturnom arabskom jazyke", *Trudy moskovskogo Instituta vostokovedenija*, 3.240-247 (1941); D. A. Baširov, *Vyraženie kategorii opredelennosti v sovremennom literaturnom arabskom jazyke* (Moscow, 1953); V. M. Belkin, *Tipy rasširennyx glagol'nyx osnov v sovremennom arabskom literaturnom jazyke* (Moscow, 1956); A. A. Kovalev, *Vyraženie kategorii vremeni v sovremennom arabskom literaturnom jazyke* (Moscow, 1951). The last three are authors' summaries of *kandidat* dissertations; Kovalev also published an article on his thesis subject in the *Trudy Voennogo Instituta inostrannyx jazykov* 1.72-85 (1952).

[28] N. S. Kamenskij, "Udarenie v sovremennom arabskom literaturnom jazyke", *Učenye zapiski Voennogo Instituta inostrannyx jazykov* 2(3).17-27 (1946); X. K. Baranov, "K stat'e ob udarenii v sovremennom arabskom jazyke", *ibid.*, 16; G. Š. Šarbatov, "Ob otnositel'noj podvižnosti udarenija v sovremennom arabskom literaturnom jazyke", *ibid.*, 5.89-96 (1954).

[29] "Iz istorii kornej v arabskom", *Soobščenija Akademii nauk gruzinskogo SSR* 17.1.69-72 (1955); "Polnoe otricanie v arabskom jazyke", *ibid.*, 25.6.787-798 (1960); "K obrazovaniju form lomannogo množestvennogo v arabskom", *Doklady delegacii SSSR* (Moscow, 25th International Congress of Orientalists, 1955; mimeogr.). Other papers (in Georgian with Russian summaries) on Arabic roots, vocative constructions, elative constructions, etc., are listed in Jedlička-Petráček, 1960 (with German translation of titles) and in the Arabic translation of Šarbatov's *Arabistika*, 1961 (with Arabic translation of titles).

[30] *Arabsko-Russkij Slovar', pod redakcii i s predisloviem I. Ju. Kračkovskogo* (Moscow, 1940-1946; 2nd ed. 1957). Cf. its review and comparison with Wehr by V. P. Starinin in *PV* 2.217-219 (1959).

[31] T. A. Il-Farxi and V. N. Krasnovskij, *Karmannyj russko-arabskij slovar'* (Moscow, 1959). Cf. its review by V. P. Starinin, *PV* 5.251-252 (1959).

[32] A limited pre-publication edition of the *Russko-arabskij slovar'* by X. K. Baranov, K. V. Ode-Vasil'eva, A. F. Sultanov *et al.* is available in two fascicules, *A* to *E* (Moscow, 1955) and *Ž* to *I* (Moscow, 1957). G. V. Cereteli is working on a large Russian-Arabic dictionary, cf. *VJa* 7/5.147 (1958), and has published an Arabic-Georgian dictionary, *Arabul-Kart'uli Lek'sikoni* (Tbilisi, 1951).

Aleksandrovič Kovalev and Grigorij Šamil'evič Šarbatov[33] is as good an introduction to the modern language as anything available in the West. A few textbooks are available in Azerbaidžani and in Tadžik.[34] There are a number of collections of prose texts for students, some only in mimeographed form; the most well-known of the printed works is K. V. Ode-Vasil'eva's readings in early modern literature, then the first such in Europe, with its valuable prefatory survey by Kračkovskij;[35] she has also published a collection of more recent authors.[36]

2.22. Until the discovery of the Central Asian dialects, Arabic dialect studies were not very numerous. Before World War II they concentrated largely about the Syrian area; in recent years there has been some interest in the Egyptian and Iraqi dialects. During the interwar period, the chief worker in the field was Ja. S. Vilenčik who, despite the fact that he did not live beyond the age of 37 and that he was completely deaf, produced a number of interesting articles, dealing mainly with phonology,[37] and has left a monumental dictionary of Syrian Arabic which has, except for a posthumous sample, remained unpublished.[38] In 1926, Kračkovskij tried his hand, with indifferent success, at transcribing and translating two texts from Nazareth, which remain the only ones available in that dialect to this day.[39] In 1929, Semenov published a chrestomathy of texts from the Syrian area, consisting largely of previously

[33] A. A. Kovalev and G. Š. Šarbatov, *Učebnik arabskogo jazyka* (Moscow, 1960). V. M. Segal's briefer and more recent *Načal'nyj kurs arabskogo jazyka* (Moscow, 1962) also seems quite adequate. Among earlier manuals, mention may be made of X. K. Baranov, *Učebnik arabskogo jazyka* (Moscow, 1947); N. S. Kamenskij, *Vvodnyj kurs sovremennogo arabskogo literaturnogo jazyka* (Moscow, 1952) and *Kratkij vvodnyj kurs fonetiki arabskogo literaturnogo jazyka* (Moscow, 1952); and K. V. Ode-Vasil'eva, *Učebnik arabskogo jazyka* (Leningrad, 1936), which tried to incorporate notions of both classical and colloquial usage.

[34] S. Ağazadə, Ə. Jusifi and M. Əfəndiev, *Azərbajjan məktablərinin IV sinfi učun ərəb dili dərsliji* (Baku, 1958); M. Əfəndizadə, *Ərəb dilinin ačary* (Baku, 1947); Ə. Č. Məmmədov, *Ərəb dili* (Baku, 1958), cf. rev. by G. Š. Šarbatov, *SovV* 6.108-110 (1958); I. Alizoda and V. Dimidčik, *Kitob-ul-madrasi, kitobi darsī baroi omūxtani zaboni arabī dar sinfhoi III-IV maktabi ibtidoī* (Stalinabad, 1958).

[35] K. V. Ode-Vasil'eva, *Obrazcy novoarabskoj literatury, 1889-1925* (Leningrad: I, 1928; II, 1929).

[36] K. V. Ode-Vasil'eva, *Obrazcy novoarabskoj literatury, 1889-1947* (Moscow, 1949); also, in a "steklographed" edition, *Obrazcy sovremennoj arabskoj literatury* (Moscow, 1956). A more specialized reader of diplomatic correspondence, by the same author and in a similarly limited edition, is her *Xrestomatija diplomatičeskoj perepiski* (Moscow, 1949), and she also published a *Xrestomatija dlja domašnego čtenija* (Moscow, 1956). Among other readers, cf. X. K. Baranov, *Arabskaja xrestomatija* (Moscow, 1937); D. A. Baširov, *Xrestomatija ekonomičeskix tekstov na arabskom jazyke* (Moscow, 1955, steklogr.); and G. V. Cereteli, *Arabskaja xrestomatija so slovarem* (with Arabic-Georgian glossary, Tbilisi, 1937), and *Arabskaja xrestomatija* (Tbilisi, 1949).

[37] Vilenčik, J. "Studien zur historischen Fonetik der Vulgärarabischen Dialekte", *DAN* 12.261-264 (1928), 12.219-222 (1929), 17.328-329 (1929); "Syro-arabische Studien", *DAN* 6.105-108 (1939); "Sistema glasnyx v narodno-arabskom jazyke gorožan Sirii i Palestiny", *ZIV* 6.133-140 (1936); cf. also his review of M. Feghali, *Syntaxe des parlers arabes actuels du Liban* (Paris, 1928) in *Der Islam* 18.275-282 (1929); and a briefer comment on Semenov's chrestomathy (see fn. 40 below) *ibid.* 19.41-42 (1930).

[38] Ja. S. Vilenčik, "O rabote po slovar'ju narodno-arabskix dialektov perednego vostoka", *SovV* 2.228-251 (1941). The task of preparing the dictionary for publication was begun in 1957 (cf. Šarbatov, *Arabistika*, 1959, p. 17).

[39] I. Ju. Kračkovskij, "Dve arabskie skazki iz Nazareta", *Soobščenija rossijskogo palestinskogo obščestva* 29.28-41 (1926).

published materials.[40] The 17th-century Egyptian manuscript of which a fragment was published by Kračkovskij should prove of considerable interest for the historical study of Egyptian Arabic.[41] On the eve of World War II, G. V Cereteli (b. 1904) and I. N. Vinnikov both began their studies of the Arabic dialects of Central Asia; these were to yield, in the forties and fifties, numerous publications containing the only reliable information on these dialects. These are, for the most part, texts in transcription, with translations and some commentary, though some are descriptive or attempts at characterization.[42] Cereteli's transcription is somewhat more explicit than Vinnikov's, but neither is phonetically very sophisticated and no attempt is made at phonemic analysis; nevertheless, the material thus made available is of the highest interest. Cereteli's 1956 volume of texts deals with the Bukhara dialect, and is announced as the first of a series of four, of which the second is to be devoted to texts in the Qašqadarya dialect, while the third and fourth are to deal respectively with the lexicon and grammar of both dialects. Vinnikov's 1949 texts are accompanied by an excellent glossary, which also sets forth much grammatical detail, and the 1957 article (part II) contains valuable historical and dialectological comments. His long-awaited *Slovar' dialekta buxarskix arabov PSb*, 10, 1962) appeared as this article was being printed. Cereteli's papers give useful analyses of specific points, describe some of the Iranian and Turkic influences which these dialects have so markedly undergone, and attempt to outline their general characteristics. Cereteli points out their apparent relation to the dialects of the Mesopotamian area, a matter which has also been discussed by other scholars and deserves detailed investigation.[43] These

[40] D. V. Semenov, *Xrestomatija razgovornogo arabskogo jazyka, sirijskoe narečie* (Leningrad, 1929).

[41] I. Ju. Kračkovskij, "Jūsuf al-Maġribī i ego slovar'", *IAN* serija VI, 20.277-300 (1926), now also in *Izb. Soč.* 1.368-385 (1955).

[42] G. V. Cereteli, "The Arabic dialects of Central Asia (preliminary sketch)" (in Georgian), *Izvestija Instituta istorii, jazyka i material'noj kul'tury gruzinskogo filiala AN SSSR* 1.295-307 (1937); "Materialy dlja izučenija arabskix dialektov Srednej Azii: Arabskaja skazka iz kišlaka Džågarȳ gidžduvanskogo rajona Uzbekskoj SSR", *ZIV* 7.254-283 (1939); "K xaraketeristike jazyka sredneaziatskix arabov (predvoritel'noe sočinenie)", *Trudy 2-oj sessii associacii arabistov*, pp. 133-148 (1941); "On the formation of some basic verbal forms in the Arabic dialect of Bukhara" (in Georgian), *Trudy Tbiliskogo gosudarstvennogo universiteta* 30.1.6.461-470 (1947); "Arabic Dialects in Central Asia", *Papers of the Soviet Delegation to the 24th International Congress of Orientalists* (in English and Russian) (Moscow, 1954); "K izučeniju jazyka sredneaziatskix arabov: Obrazcy reči ķašķadar'inskix arabov", *TIJa, serija vostočnyx jazykov* 1.251-272 (1954); *Arabskie dialekty Srednej Azii, Tom I*: *Buxarskij arabskij dialekt* (Tbilisi, 1956). I. N. Vinnikov, *Araby v SSSR* (*Etnografija, folklor i jazyk*). *Tezisy doktorskoj dissertacii* (Leningrad, 1941); the dissertation itself does not seem to have been published, but the following articles no doubt form part of it: "Materialy po jazyku i folkloru buxarskix arabov", *SovV* 5.120-145 (1949); "Folklor buxarskix arabov", *AOH* 6.181-206 (1956); "Obrazcy folklora buxarskix arabov", *AO* 25.173-189 (1957), 25.426-451 (1957). Cf. also next footnote.

[43] Cf. e.g. G. V. Cereteli, "K xarakteristike", 1941, p. 147. Similar general observations on some similarities between Central Asian and Mesopotamian Arabic were made by H. S. Nyberg in *Le Monde Oriental* 24.121-126 (1930) and by N. V. Jušmanov "Arabskoe narečie sovetskogo vostoka", *Kul'tura i pismennost' vostoka* 10.76-84 (1935); both are based on the first and rather inadequate published account of the Central Asian dialects, N. N. Burykina and M. M. Izmailova, "Nekotorye dannye po jazyku arabov kišlaka Džugary buxarskogo okruga i kišlaka Džejnau kaškadar'inskogo

dialects, whose speakers have been isolated from the Arab world for generations, perhaps centuries, offer to Arabic dialectology an entirely new and unique field of investigation, and the attention they have received so far is wholly deserved. On the other hand, recent work on the dialects of the *zarubežnyj vostok*, the "non-Soviet East", is meager. G. Š. Šarbatov's *kandidat* dissertation on Egyptian Arabic and his Egyptian reader, which I have not seen, were followed by an article on Egyptian Arabic negative and interrogative sentences.[44] In the latter, the discussion of negative sentences is very summary indeed and might as well have been left out; the more extensive section on interrogative sentences is more satisfactory. The sentences analyzed are taken from published materials (including literary productions in the vernacular, a source largely ignored in the West) and Egyptian usage is compared with that of Classical Arabic and of some other dialects; two pages are given over to text taken from a standard English handbook and translated into Russian. The facts thus made available to the Russian reader include little that has not been published previously in the West. I have not seen Šarbatov's paper on the "analytical" character of the Arabic dialects in general;[45] his brief characterization of the Iraqi dialect[46] is admittedly "preliminary", and appears to be a first attempt at actual field work. It contains some accurate observations as well as some serious misunderstandings. In Georgia, V. G. Axvlediani did a *kandidat* dissertation and several papers on the reflexes of the pharyngeals in the Arabic dialects.[47]

2.23. Various aspects of the Arabic *questione della lingua* have been considered by Soviet scholars. The colloquial vs. classical controversy was briefly taken up by Kračkovskij in the twenties, and discussed at somewhat greater length by Vilenčik and Semenov in the thirties.[48] In the post-Stalin era this controversy and some related

---

okruga uzbekskoj SSR", *Zapiski Kollegii Vostokovedov* 5.527-549 (1930). The problem was taken up at the 25th International Congress of Orientalists (Moscow, 1960) by W. Fischer, whose paper is not available to me; the same author also published a detailed description of the Central Asian dialects, based on most of the published literature, viz. "Die Sprache der Arabischen Sprachinsel in Uzbekistan", *Der Islam* 36.232-263 (1961).

[44] G. Š. Šarbatov, *Xrestomatija po egipetskomu dialektu* (steklogr., Moscow, 1952); *Leksiko-grammatičeskaja xarakteristika sovremennogo egipetskogo dialekta* (author's summary of *kandidat* dissertation, Moscow, 1955); "O voprositel'nyx i otricatel'nyx predloženijax v sovremennom egipetskom dialekte arabskogo jazyka", *KSIV* 29.52-58 (1959).

[45] *Ob analitičnosti stroja sovremennyx arabskix dialektov* (Moscow, 1960).

[46] "Nekotorye osobennosti irakskogo dialekta, arabskogo jazyka", *KSIV* 40.80-86 (1960).

[47] "Refleksy faringal'nyx soglasnyx v sovremennyx arabskix dialektax (avtoreferat kandidatskoj dissertacii)", *Naučnaja sessija tbiliskogo gosudarstvennogo universiteta*, Sbornik dokladov (Tbilisi, 1953). For his Georgian articles on the alternation of pharyngeals (1954) and on their articulation (1957), see Jedlička-Petráček, *Semitologie*, 1960 (fns. 13 and 17), with German translation of titles, or Šarbatov, *Isti'rāb*, 1961 (p. 135), with Arabic translation of titles.

[48] I. Ju. Kračkovskij, "O rabotax Marūna Ġuṣna 'Al-luġa al-'āmmīya' i 'Fī mitlu hal-kitāb'", *Zapiski Kollegii Vostokovedov* 3.186-191 (1928). (= *Izbr. Soč.* 1.386-390, 1955); J. Vilenčik, "Zur Genesis der Arabischen Zweisprachigkeit", *OLZ* 38.721-727 (1935); rev. of J. Lecerf, *Litérature dialectale et renaissance arabe moderne* (Damascus, 1932), in *Bibliografija Vostoka* 8-9.121-123 (1936); rev. of Yaḥyā Nāmiq, "Luġat al-iḏā'a bayn al-'arabīya wa-l-'āmmīya", in *Bibliografija Vostoka* 10.197-198 (1937); D. V. Semenov, "Vzgljady francuzskix učenyx na sovremennoe položenie arabskogo jazyka i ego buduščee", *ibid.* pp. 17-50.

matters have again been taken up by A. F. Sultanov in three articles reporting and interpreting current Arab opinions.[49] The first two (1953 and 1955) are very nearly identical and deal with the relations between the literary and vernacular idioms; the gleanings from the Arab press are welcome, the descriptive and historical statements need straightening out and the fierce "Marxian" interpretations add nothing of value. Sultanov's third article is, happily, almost free of excess baggage and largely reports on more recent Arab views regarding language problems, especially the question of lexical expansion to meet the needs of modernization. A far better account of these matters is given by V. M. Belkin in a single, succinct and admirably clear-headed paper.[50] Belkin has also published a good survey of recent Arabic works on linguistic subjects.[51] In 1958, V. A. Zvegincev published his 1942 *kandidat* dissertation surveying, largely from secondary sources, the history of medieval Arabic philology.[52]

## 2.3. *Northwest Semitic*

### 2.31. *Aramaic*

The ancient varieties have been studied mostly at Leningrad, the modern dialects, largely at Tbilisi. In the former category, I. N. Vinnikov has begun publishing in installments a dictionary of epigraphic Aramaic,[53] and has published a sample of his dictionary and concordance of the Jerusalem Talmud;[54] both represent solid achievements of many years' scholarly activity. V. V. Pigulevskaja has for some time been editing unpublished Syriac manuscripts.[55] Vinnikov has also published several papers on the interpretation of recently discovered Aramaic inscriptions.[56] The Neo-Aramaic (Neo-Syriac) dialect spoken by the Nestorians now residing in some of the Soviet republics of the Caucasus is that of Urmia in Iran, whence it was imported a few

[49] A. F. Sultanov, "Nacional'nyj jazyk i reforma pis'mennosti v stranax arabskogo vostoka", in *Akademiku V. A. Gordlevskomu k ego semidesjatiletju*, pp. 253-275 (Moscow, 1953); "Problema formirovanija nacional'nogo jazyka v Egipte", *VJa* 4/6.32-47 (1955); "O literaturnoj norme i naučnoj terminologii v arabskom jazyke", *UZIV* 19.113-124 (1959). Cf. also A. Sultanov and V. Ušakov, rev. of Ḥasan ʿAwn, *Al-luġa al-ʿarabiya wa-qawāʿiduhā* (Alexandria, 1956), *ibid.*, pp. 125-130.

[50] V. M. Belkin, "Obsuždenie problem nacional'nogo jazyka v arabskoj pečati", *VJa* 2.122-127 (1959).

[51] V. M. Belkin, "Arabskoe jazykoznanie poslednix let", *VJa* 6/6.95-100 (1957).

[52] V. A. Zvegincev, *Istorija arabskogo jazykoznanija – kratkij očerk* (Moscow, 1958); cf. rev. by G. Š. Šarbatov, *PV* 3.184-186 (1959).

[53] I. N. Vinnikov, "Slovar' aramejskix nadpisej", *PSb* 3.171-216 (1958), 4.196-240 (1959), 7.192-237 (1962), up to and including the letter *h* of the Hebrew alphabet.

[54] I. N. Vinnikov, "Opyt slovarja i konkordancii Palestinskoj tradicionnoj literatury (Bukva *gimel*)", *PSb* 5.151-229 (1960).

[55] Among the most recent of her many publications in this field are the trilingual fragments of the Psalter published under the title "Greko-Siro-Arabskaja rukopis' 9-ogo veka", *PSb* 1.59-90 (1954), and the *Katalog sirijskix rukopisej Leningrada* to which vol. 6 of the *Palestinskij Sbornik* (1960) is entirely devoted.

[56] I. N. Vinnikov, "O jazyke pismennyx pamjatnikov iz Nisy (Južnyj Turkmenistan)", *VDI* 2.115-128 (1954); "Novaja interpretacija nadpisi Zakara carja Xamata i Lu'aša", *Epigrafika Vostoka* 5.84-94 (1955).

generations ago; both literary materials in the dialect and studies based on that material, as well as on the spoken idiom have appeared in the USSR and elsewhere.[57] In the thirties, N. V. Jušmanov devoted three articles to the dialect, in which he "admirably dealt with" the problem of phonetic synharmonism and found an "ingenious explanation" for a puzzling feature of the imperative.[58] Two decades later, Neo-Aramaic is again being studied by K. G. Cereteli whose 1955 doctoral dissertation was published in 1958 and is a first attempt at a comparative phonetics of all modern dialects on which he had material.[59] This forms the background to a number of papers on the synchronic and diachronic phonetics of the Urmi dialect, as well as to a number of articles on grammatical problems in the same dialect.[60] K. G. Cereteli has also published a chrestomathy of Neo-Aramaic literary texts, including Bible translations.[61]

2.32. *Hebrew, Phoenician, Ugaritic.*

Though several varieties of Hebrew, including the modern language (called *Ivrit*

[57] For a discussion of pre-World War II Soviet materials on and in Neo-Aramaic, see H. J. Polotsky, "Studies in Modern Syriac", *JSS* 6.1-32 (1961). Cf. also J. Friedrich, "Neusyrisches in Lateinschrift aus der Sowjetunion", *ZDMG* 109.50-81 (1959), and the same author's *Zwei Russische Novellen in Neusyrischer Übersetzung und Lateinschrift* (= *Abhandlungen für die Kunde des Morgenlandes* XXXIX, 4) (Wiesbaden, 1960) and rev. by H. J. Polotsky, *Orientalia* 31.273-283 (1962).

[58] N. V. Jušmanov, "Assirijskij jazyk i ego pis'mo", *Pis'mennost' i Revoljucija* 1.112-128 (1933); "Zagadočnoe -m- novosirijskogo imperativa", *Jazyk i myšlenie* 5.93-96 (1935); "Singarmonizm Urmijskogo narečija", *Pamjati Akademika N. Ja. Marra* (Moscow-Leningrad, 1938), pp. 295-314. The brief evaluations are quoted from H. J. Polotsky, "Studies", 1960 (see previous footnote), pp. 28 and 8 respectively.

[59] K. G. Cereteli, *Očerk sravnitel'noj fonetiki sovremennyx assirijskix dialektov* (in Georgian with Russian summary, Tbilisi, 1958); a slightly abridged translation of the Russian summary has been published by N. Reiter under the title "Abriss der Vergleichenden Phonetik der modernen Assyrischen Dialekte" in F. Altheim, *Geschichte der Hunnen*, 3.218-266 (Berlin, 1961), and a longish account of the same Russian summary is to be found, also in German, in S. Segert, "Semitistische Marginalien", *AO* 29.96-115 (1961). Cf. also the paper he delivered at the 25th International Congress of Orientalists, "K sravnitel'no-istoričeskomu izučeniju fonetičeskix osobennostej sovremennyx vostočnoaramejskix dialektov" (13 pp., mimeogr., Moscow, 1960) available also in a German version, "Zur Phonetik der Ostaramäischen Dialekte der Gegenwart (ein historisch-vergleichender Beitrag)" (18 pp., mimeogr., Moscow, 1960).

[60] All are in Georgian with Russian summaries; the Georgian titles, with brief comments on some of the papers, may be found in Jedlička-Petráček, *Semitologie*, 1960; most of them are also listed in Šarbatov, *Arabistika*, 1959, and *Isti'rāb*, 1961. K. G. Cereteli, "Cases of palatalization in the Urmi dialect of Aramaic", *Soobščenija AN gruzinskogo SSR* 9.507-531 (1948); "The possessive pronouns in the Urmi dialect of Aramaic", *ibid.* 13.491-494 (1952); "On gemination in the Urmi dialect of Aramaic", *ibid.* pp. 569-72; "The formation of epenthetic vowels in the Urmi dialect", *ibid.* 14.47-54 (1953); "Urmi synharmony: general characteristics", *ibid.* 5.493-499 (1946); "The principles of Urmi synharmony", *ibid.* 7.663-670 (1946); "Traces of the causative in ša/sa in the Urmi dialect of modern Assyrian", *ibid.* 19.17-24 (1957); "Long vowels in the Urmi dialect of Aramaic", *Trudy tbiliskogo gosudarstvennogo Universiteta* 47.91-110 (1952); "Cases of consonantal assimilation in the Urmi dialect of Aramaic", *TIJa, serija vostočnyx jazykov* 1.283-323 (1954); "The conjugation system of the modern Assyrian (East Aramaic) dialects", *ibid.* 2.125-156 (1957).

[61] K. G. Cereteli, *Xrestomatija sovremennogo assirijskogo jazyka, so slovarem, pod redakcii i s predisloviem Pr. G. V. Cereteli. Trudy kafedry semitologii tbiliskogo gosudarstvennogo Universiteta 4.* (Tbilisi, 1958). Rev. by S. Segert, *AO* 27.702-703 (1959).

by Soviet scholars) are taught at the three main centers of Semitic learning, little or nothing has been published. Works in comparative Semitics and the other Northwest Semitic languages, especially Vinnikov's papers, often rely on or contribute to, Hebrew scholarship. A modern Hebrew-Russian dictionary was begun by Feliks L'vovič Šapiro, who died in 1961 without completing it; it is now being prepared for publication by B. M. Grande, together with a grammatical sketch.[62] In the only *kandidat* dissertation on ancient Hebrew mentioned in bibliographical surveys, M. A. Šanidze discusses the Hebrew velar spirants and is said to demonstrate the existence of the voiceless velar spirant [ġ] in proto-Semitic,[63] a matter that had aroused violent feelings in some East European quarters (cf. 3.1 below). Several scholars have been working on the rich collection of medieval Hebrew manuscripts of the Leningrad Public and State Library and publishing hitherto unknown works of medieval authors;[64] the USSR has also had its share (relatively not very large) of writers on the Dead Sea Scrolls.[65] Finally, Vinnikov has published a number of linguistic comments on Phoenician and Ugaritic inscriptions.[66]

### 2.4. *Akkadian*

Cuneiform studies in their historical and sociological aspects are fairly numerous and, I gather, fairly advanced in the USSR;[67] specifically linguistic studies in the domain of Akkadian are few. Their chief bearer was, until 1945, A. P. Riftin (cf. 2.1 above), who wrote a paper on the complex sentence and another on the conditional

[62] F. L. Šapiro, *Ivrit-russkij slovar', pod redakcii i s predisloviem B. M. Grande* (to appear); cf. Hebrew translation of the introduction published by C. Harkavi in *Ha-Arec* (Tel Aviv), 13 August 1962.

[63] "On the question of the existence of back spirants in Ancient Hebrew" (in Georgian with Russian summary), *TIJa, serija vostočnyx jazykov* 1.42-72 (1954); cf. Jedlička-Petráček, *Semitologie*, 1960, p. 92, and Šarbatov, *Arabistika*, 1959, pp. 52, 59.

[64] On an 11th-century Hebrew grammar written in Judeo-Arabic, cf. M. N. Zislin, "K voprosu o značenii grammatičeskogo sočinenija Abū-l-Faradž Harūn 'Al-Kāfī'", *PV* 3.208-211 (1962), and "Glava iz grammatičeskogo sočinenija 'Al-Kāfī' Abū-l-Faradža Harūn ibn al-Faradža", *PSb* 7.178-184 (1962). To mention only K. B. Starkova's most recent publications, cf. e.g. "Iz materialov 2-oj sobranija Firkoviča gosudarstvennoj publičnoj biblioteki imeni Saltykova-Ščedrina (iz fragmentov Divana Jehuda Halevi)", *Sbornik v čest' Akademika I. A. Orbeli* (Moscow-Leningrad, 1960), pp. 445-450; and the paper she delivered at the 25th International Congress of Orientalists (Moscow, 1960), "Redakcija Divana Jehuda Halevi soglasno leningradskim fragmentam" (mimeogr., 10 pp.); also given at the same congress: G. M. Gluskina, "Neizdannye rukopisi sočinenija al-Ḥarizi 'Taḥkemoni' v gosudarstvennoj publičnoj biblioteke v Leningrade" (mimeogr., 22 pp.).

[65] K. B. Starkova, "Rukopisi iz okrestnostej mertvogo morja", *VDI* 1.87-102 (1956). I. D. Amusin, *Rukopisi mertvogo morja* (Moscow, 1960).

[66] I. N. Vinnikov, "Novye feničeskie nadpisi iz Kilikii", *VDI* 3.86-97 (1950); "Vnov' najdennye feničeskie nadpisi", *Epigrafika vostoka* 5.121-133 (1951); "Nekotorye nabljudenija nad jazykom ugaritskoj povesti o Kerete", *Doklady 25-ogo meždunarodnogo kongressa vostokovedov* (Moscow, 1960) mimeogr., 15 pp.

[67] Cf. the survey by J. Klima quoted in fn. 1 above, and also V. I. Avdiev, *Sovetskaja nauka o drevnem vostoke za sorok let* (Moscow, 1958), and I. M. Diakonoff, "Ancient Near East in Soviet Research", *AO* 27.143-148 (1959).

clause.[68] At present the main brunt of Akkadian linguistics is being carried by L. A. Lipin, who teaches in Leningrad and has recently published a two volume textbook, of which the first is a chrestomathy and the second a glossary.[69] He has also published papers on some aspects of Akkadian morphology and semantics.[70]

### 2.5. *Ethiopic and South Arabic*

Since Jušmanov's days, Ethiopic studies are handled only by his student T. L. Tjutrjumova, who gives Geez and Amharic courses at the Department of African Studies in Leningrad.[71] Jušmanov wrote a structural sketch of Amharic in 1936, which was to form a sort of trilogy with his "Structure of Hausa" (1937), his "Structure of Arabic" (1938),[72] and some surveys of the languages of Ethiopia.[73] Kračkovskij's posthumous "Introduction to Ethiopic Philology" is a survey, largely bibliographical, of the status of the field, and carries little linguistic information and no linguistic analysis.[74] On South Arabic, Kračkovskij published an early article on some points of epigraphy,[75] and Jušmanov devoted an article to an analysis of data on Eḥkili (Šxawri), a modern South-Arabic dialect.[76]

## 3. CZECHOSLOVAKIA

### 3.1. *General and Comparative Semitics*

A good deal of interest in comparative and general studies has, in the last decade or so, been manifested by Karel Petráček (b. 1926) who mostly specializes in Arabic and Ethiopic, and, at least in the area of Northwest Semitic, by Stanislav Segert. They are heirs to a tradition established at Prague largely by Rudolf Růžička

[68] A. P. Riftin, "O dvux putjax razvitija složnogo predloženija v akkadskom jazyke", *SJa* 3.59-67 (1937); "K uslovnym predloženijam v epoxu pervogo vavilonskoj dinastii", *SovV* 4.129-134 (1947); cf. also fn. 6 above.

[69] L. A. Lipin, *Akkadskij (vavilono-assirijskij) jazyk*, 2 vols. (Leningrad, 1957).

[70] L. A. Lipin, "Značenie sojuza *ú* v zakonax Xamurabi", *Sbornik v čest' Akademika I. A. Orbeli* (Moscow-Leningrad, 1960), pp. 374-378; "Elementy aggljutinacii v akkadskom jazyke po materialam ličnyx mestoimenij", *25-yj meždunarodnyj kongress vostokovedov, doklady delegacii SSSR* (Moscow, 1960), mimeogr., 13 pp.

[71] Cf. *Vostokovedenie v leningradskom Universitete*, 1960, p. 199.

[72] N. V. Jušmanov, *Stroj amxarskogo jazyka* (Leningrad, 1936).

[73] N. V. Jušmanov, "Jazyki Abissinii", in *Abissinija* (Moscow-Leningrad, 1936), pp. 259-291; "O jazykax Efiopii", *SovEtn* 1.40-44 (1936).

[74] I. Ju. Kračkovskij, *Vvedenie v efiopskuju filologiju pod redakcii D. A. Olderogge* (Leningrad, 1955). Cf. rev. by K. Petráček, *AO* 24.652-655 (1956); S. Strelcyn, *SovV* 2.179-191 (1957); and by the same in *RO* 22.157-161 (1957).

[75] I. Ju. Kračkovskij, "Dve južno-arabskie nadpisi v Leningrade", *Izb. Soč.* 1.396-414 (1955), first published 1931.

[76] N. V. Jušmanov, "Dannye *Fresnel*-ja o južno-arabskom narečii eḥkili", *Zapiski kollegii vostokovedov* 5.375-391 (1930).

(1878-1957); most of his works on Semitic phonology and morphology antedate 1920 and are left out of account here.[77] Overshadowing his scholarly, administrative and pedagogical contributions to Czech Oriental studies, his pet theory as to the non-existence of a proto-Semitic voiced velar spirant [ġ] occupied him for many years, produced much sterile controversy and became an *idée fixe*; it has been rejected or ignored by competent specialists.[78] Petráček twice touched on the question, with special reference to the [ġ] of Classical Arabic (see fn. 78) but his main work on comparative Semitics has taken the form of an ambitious and long-winded monograph on the "internal flection" of Semitic, which has been appearing in installments.[79] Despite needless disquisitions and some dubious statements, it has the merit of drawing together vast quantities of material from the whole field of Hamito-Semitic. Both Petráček and Segert do much of their work in the form of reviews and review articles in the *Archiv Orientální*; they have given their critical appraisal of the Semitological portions of the *Handbuch der Orientalistik*,[80] and have discussed, together with other scholars meeting in the "Semitic Circle", current literature and on-going work.[81] Segert, who has been working on a comparative dictionary of Northwest Semitic, has considered the problem of a unified transcription,[82] and reviewed the available lexicographical material;[83] among his other review articles, we may mention his discussion of the West Semitic alphabet in opposition to the views of I. J. Gelb,[84] and discusses, in yet another review article, Garbini's *Semitico di Nordovest*.[85]

### 3.2. *Arabic*

The literary language has been taught at Prague for many years, and philological endeavors have borne some fruit, but linguistic research in the area is just beginning to make some strides, largely through the work of K. Petráček. Besides a Czech

77 On R. Růžička's life and works, cf. K. Petráček, *AO* 22.23-28 (1954), 26.177-178 (1957), and Zbavitel, *Orientalistik*, 1959, p. 28.

78 Cf. his lengthy, final and somewhat poignant summing up of the controversy, "La question de l'existence du ġ dans les langues sémitiques en général et dans la langue ugaritienne en particulier", *AO* 22.176-237 (1954). Cf. also K. Petráček, "Der doppelte Charakter des Ghain im Klassischen Arabisch", *AO* 21.240-262 (1953), and "Die Struktur der Semitischen Wurzelmorpheme und der Übergang 'Ain → Ghain und Ghain → R im Arabischen", *AO* 23.475-480 (1955).

79 K. Petráček, "Die innere Flexion in den Semitischen Sprachen", *AO* 28.547-560 (1960), 29.513-545 (1961), to be continued.

80 K. Petráček and S. Segert, "Bemerkungen zur Semitistik", *AO* 22.588-596 (1954), 24.476-483 (1956).

81 *AO* 24.622-634 (1956), 28.657-680 (1956).

82 S. Segert, "A Transcription of Semitic Alphabets for the Purpose of Comparative Linguistics", *AO* 28.480-487 (1960).

83 S. Segert, "Considerations on Semitic Comparative Lexicography", *AO* 28.470-480 (1960); "Semitistische Marginalien", *AO* 29.80-96 (1961).

84 S. Segert, "Charakter des Westsemitischen Alphabets", *AO* 26.243-247 (1958), and "Noch zum Charakter des Westsemitischen Alphabets", *AO* 26.657-659 (1958).

85 S. Segert, "Semitistische Marginalien", *AO* 29.115-118 (1961).

textbook for beginners,[86] he has published a study of the language of an early Islamic poet, a welcome beginning in the much needed monographic re-examination of literary usage on the basis of actual texts.[87] The Islamic historian Felix Tauer (b. 1893) has published a number of philological observations[88] and a translation of the "Thousand and One Nights".[89] The Slovak philologist Jan Bakoš (b. 1890) has published a study of the psychology of Ibn Sīnā.[90] The many distinguished works of A. R. Nykl on Hispano-Arabic poetry and related subjects, though not strictly linguistic and done, for the most part, outside of Czechoslovakia, deserve mention here, as does his translation of the Koran into Czech.[91] As for Arabic dialect studies, they are even less advanced. To the explorer and geographer Alois Musil (1868-1944) we owe a large number of texts in the Beduin dialects of the Syrian desert and Southern Palestine and Transjordan; these can be and have been used by linguists to advantage, but Musil's talents and interests lay in other domains.[92] More recently, there is little to report beyond Petráček's not very enlightening discussion of Coptic influences in Egyptian Arabic.[93]

### 3.3. *Northwest Semitic*

Segert's general and comparative work on the basis of Northwest Semitic has already been mentioned in 3.1 above. Segert, who has written a good many reviews and review articles on Hebrew and especially Aramaic problems, largely connected with linguistic aspects of Biblical research,[94] has also written on problems of Hebrew and Canaanite phonetics.[95] He collaborated with O. Klima on a grammar of Biblical

[86] K. Petráček, *Učebnice arabštiny* (Prague, 1957).

[87] K. Petráček, "Material zum Altarabischen Dialekt von Al-Madīna", *AO* 22.460-466 (1954); "Morphologisches aus dem Diwan des Al-Aḥwas al-Anṣārī", *AO* 28.67-71 (1960); "Syntaktisches aus dem Diwan des Al-Aḥwas Al-Anṣārī", *AO* 28.147-180 (1960).

[88] F. Tauer, "Annotations critiques au texte du Tuḥfat al-Albāb d'Abū Ḥāmid al-Māzinī par G. Ferrand", *AO* 18.298-316 (1950).

[89] Cf. K. Petráček, *AO* 19.101 (1951).

[90] J. Bakoš, "Introduction d'Avicenne à sa Psychologie: extrait de l'ouvrage Aš-Šifā", *AO* 17.27-30 (1949); *La psychologie d'Ibn Sīnā* (*Avicenne*) *d'après son ouvrage Aš-Šifā*, 2 vols. (Prague, 1956). On Bakoš's life and works, cf. Zbavitel, *Orientalistik*, 1959, p. 41, and S. Segert, *AO* 28.1-4 (1960).

[91] For a partial bibliography, cf. K. Petráček, *AO* 19.103-104 and fn. 10 (1951).

[92] On his controversy with G. Bergsträsser with regard to the latter's *Sprachatlas von Syrien und Palästina* (Leipzig, 1915), cf. G. Bergsträsser, "In Sachen meines Sprachatlas", *Zeitschrift für Semitistik* 1.218-226 (1922). Musil's most important collections of texts are to be found in his *Arabia Petraea*, vol. III (Vienna, 1908) and *The Manners and Customs of the Ruwala Beduins* (New York, 1928). On his life and works, cf. J. Rypka, *AO* 10.1-34 (1938), 15.i-viii (1946).

[93] K. Petráček, "Zum Arabischen Dialekt von Ägypten: zum Koptischen Einfluss", *AO* 24.291-294 (1956).

[94] S. Segert, "Neue Aramäische Texte aus Ägypten", *AO* 24.284-291 (1956); "Aramäische Studien", *AO* 24.383-403 (1956), 25.21-37 (1957), 26.551-584 (1958); "Textkritische Erwägungen in Margine des Kommentars zu den Chronikbüchern von W. Rudolph", *AO* 25.671-675 (1957); "New Books on the Dead Sea Scrolls", *AO* 27.447-462 (1959).

[95] S. Segert, "Zu einigen assimilierenden Verba im Hebräischen", *AO* 23.183 (1955) and the ensuing discussion by Petráček and Segert *AO* 24.131-134 (1956); "Zum Übergang ā → ō in den Kanaanäischen Dialekten", *AO* 23.478 (1955).

Hebrew and Biblical Aramaic,[96] and cogently summed up all that has been written on the language of the famous "Moabite stone".[97] On the latter he concludes that it was written by an Israelite captive and that its language is a dialect of Hebrew and not true Moabite. His summary of K. G. Cereteli's work on comparative Neo-Aramaic phonetics has already been mentioned (fn. 59). The area of Syriac philology is Jan Bakoš's main interest, and a number of important texts have been published by him with translation and commentary.[98]

### 3.4. *Akkadian*

As in the USSR, research into ancient Mesopotamia has concentrated on history and sociology,[99] and little has been done in Akkadian linguistics. Recently Lubor Matouš has, in addition to his historical and philological works, published some comments on an edition of Akkadian texts from Rās Šamra,[100] and, together with Petráček, some comments on Akkadian phonetics.[101] His elements of Akkadian grammar (introductory notes on phonology and morphology) are available only in mimeographed form.[102]

### 3.5. *Ethiopic and South-Arabic*

The only work done recently in these languages seems to be that of Petráček, which has been epigraphic (notes on some South-Arabic inscriptions[103]) and philological (e.g. review of Kračkovskij's *Vvedenie*[104]) rather than linguistic.

## 4. OTHER COUNTRIES

### 4.1. *General and comparative Semitics*

The most original and most sophisticated work to come out of Eastern Europe in recent years emanates neither from the Soviet Union nor from Czechoslovakia and

[96] O. Klima and S. Segert, *Mluvnice hebrejštiny a aramejštiny* (Prague, 1956).
[97] S. Segert, "Die Sprache der Moabitischen Königsinschrift", *AO* 29.197-267 (1961).
[98] J. Bakoš, *Psychologie de Grégoire Abu al-Faradj dit Bar-Hebraeus* (Leiden, 1948). For earlier publications on this and related subjects, cf. S. Segert, *AO* 28.1-4 (1960).
[99] Cf. J. Klima, "L'état actuel des études concernant l'Orient ancien en Tchécoslovaquie", *AOH* 5.25-27 (1955).
[100] L. Matouš, "Les textes akkadiens d'Ugarit", *AO* 24.375-382 (1956).
[101] L. Matouš and K. Petráček, "Beiträge zur Akkadischen Grammatik I – Die Liquiden in ihrem Verhältniss zum Vokal im Assyrischen", *AO* 24.1-14 (1956).
[102] L. Matouš, *Základy akkadskí gramatiky* (Prague, 1952; mimeogr.).
[103] K. Petráček, "Annotations aux inscriptions sud-arabes RY 603-614 du Dār al-Ḍiyāfa à Ṣan'ā", *AO* 29.444-447 (1961).
[104] Cf. fn. 74 above; Petráček also discusses much Ethiopic material in his "Innere Flexion", cf. fn. 79 above.

is not from the pen of a Semitist. While working out problems of apophony (*Ablaut*) in Indo-European,[105] Jerzy Kuryłowicz published a number of articles dealing with proto-Semitic and ancient Semitic morphophonemics;[106] he has now refurbished and expanded them into an impressive volume on Semitic apophony[107] which it will take a long while to digest and evaluate properly. This book is also, so far as I can see, the only one in the area of general Semitics to come out of Poland or, for that matter, the rest of Eastern Europe outside of the USSR and Czechoslovakia.

### 4.2. *Arabic*

In Poland, Arabic studies before World War II were a secondary interest of the man with whose name they are mostly associated, Tadeusz Kowalski (1890-1948), who has left a few works in the realm of Arabic philology and literary history.[108] Nowadays Józef Bielawski has published a longish paper, interesting but still preliminary, on the problem of lexical innovations (especially in technical domains) in both medieval and modern literary Arabic.[109] In the realm of dialectology, a single modest work by Andrzej Czapkiewicz[110] has come to my attention. It presents a tape-recorded text, with translation and comments, in the dialect of Mādaba in Jordan; the transcription and observations are amateurish and sometimes erroneous, and the translation is not flawless, but the booklet does throw some light on a hitherto unknown area. In Hungary, a number of fine papers in the realm of Arabic philology and literary history have been contributed by J. Somogyi (now in the United States);[111] Abdul Karim Julius Germanus did a lengthy review of Wehr's Arabic-German dictionary, suggesting many additional items, and devoted an article to the modern *questione della lingua*.[112] In his review of Oriental studies in Yugoslavia (see fn. 2) J. Kabrda lists a paper on the triconsonantal root in Arabic (T. Muftić) and one on the syntactic functions of the Arabic preposition (Ś. Sikirić).

[105] J. Kuryłowicz, *L'apophonie en indo-européen* (Wrocław, 1956).

[106] J. Kuryłowicz, "Le système verbal du sémitique", *BSL* 45.47-56 (1949); "La mimation et l'article en arabe", *AO* 18.323-328 (1950); "T. zw. dyptotyzm deklinacji arabskiej a konstrukcja liczebników", *BPTJ* 11.164-180 (1952); "Le degré long en sémitique", *RO* 17.138-145 (1954); "La genèse de certaines alternances quantitatives en sémitique", *BPTJ* 13.109-116 (1954); "Esquisse d'une théorie de l'apophonie en sémitique", *BSL* 53.1-38 (1957/8).

[107] J. Kuryłowicz, *L'apophonie en sémitique* (Wrocław-Warszawa-Kraków, 1961).

[108] Cf. A. Zajączkowski, "Tadeusz Kowalski i jego prace orientalistyczne", *RO* 17.ix-xvi (1951/2), and W. Zajączkowski, "Bibliografia Tadeusza Kowalskiego", *RO* 17.xvii-xxxvi (1951/2).

[109] J. Bielawski, "Deux périodes dans la formation de la terminologie scientifique arabe: la période classique et la période moderne", *RO* 20.263-320 (1956).

[110] A. Czapkiewicz, *Sprachproben aus Mādabā* (= *Prace monograficzne nr. 2, Polska Akademia Nauk, oddział w Krakowie, komisja orientalistyczna*) (Kraków, 1960).

[111] Cf. e.g. J. Somogyi, "Ibn al-Jawzī's School of Historiography", *AOH* 6.207-214 (1956) and some of his reviews, e.g. *AOH* 6.290-292, 4.318-321 (1954).

[112] J. Germanus, rev. of H. Wehr, *Arabisches Wörterbuch für die Schriftsprache der Gegenwart* (Leipzig, 1952), *AOH* 3.313-322 (1953); "Ibn Rūmī's Dichtkunst", *AOH* 6.215-226 (1956); "Linguistic Foundation of the Unity of the Arabic-speaking Peoples", *The Islamic Review* 38.3.21-24 (1950).

### 4.3. *Northwest Semitic*

The most significant work in this area is that of the Hungarian scholar Jozsef Aistleitner (1883-1960)[113] on Ugaritic; he has published a number of annotated texts, but also straight linguistic studies of the phonetics, morphology and lexicon.[114] Károly Czeglédy has written a study of the voiced velar spirant of Ugaritic and a number of reviews of works on Northwest Semitic.[115] Alexander Scheiber has been publishing, also in Hungary, Hebrew manuscripts from the Kaufmann Geniza, with only occasional notes of linguistic interest.[116] In Poland, a recent attempt by Władisław Tubielewicz to characterize modern Hebrew, with special reference to foreign influences, is only partly successful and contains a good many errors.[117] Jan Szeruda's work on the Dead Sea scrolls includes linguistic observations.[118] For Romania, Guboglu's survey (see fn. 2) reports a few Hebrew and Old Testament studies.

### 4.4. *Akkadian*

No studies in this field outside the USSR and Czechoslovakia have come to my attention.

### 4.5. *Ethiopic and South Arabic*

A single name stands out, that of the Polish Ethiopist Stefan Strelcyn. His work is largely philological, yet some of his writings are of linguistic interest, e.g. his review of E. Ullendorf's *The Semitic Languages of Ethiopia – A Comparative Phonology* (London, 1955) and one of his reviews of Kračkovskij's *Vvedenie*.[119] I do not list his many text editions, which are largely concerned with liturgy and magic.

[113] Cf. K. Czeglédy, "Joseph Aistleitner (1883-1960)", *AOH* 10.299-300 (1960).

[114] J. Aistleitner, "Untersuchungen zum Mitlautbestand des Ugaritisch-Semitischen", *Goldziher Memorial Volume* 1.209-224 (Budapest, 1948); *Untersuchungen zur Grammatik des Ugaritischen, Berichte über die Verhandlungen der Sächsischen Akademie der Wissenschaften zu Leipzig, Philologisch-Historische Klasse, Band 100, Heft 6* (Berlin, 1954); "Studien zur Frage der Sprachverwandtschaft des Ugaritischen", *AOH* 7.251-307 (1957), 8.51-98 (1958); "Lexikalisches zu den Ugaritischen Texten", *AOH* 11.29-34 (1960). For other works, mostly publications of Ugaritic texts, cf. the obituary notice by Czeglédy in previous footnote.

[115] K. Czeglédy, *A zöngés veláris spiráns az ugariti sémi feliratokban* (Budapest, 1940).

[116] For various Hebrew fragments published by him, cf. e.g. *Goldziher Memorial Volume* II (Budapest, 1958), pp. 55-58 of Hebrew section; *AOH* 3.107-133 (1953), 7.27-63 (1957), 8.189-199 (1958), 10.90-95 (1960), 14.231-239 (1962); and for several Judeo-Arabic fragments from the same collection published in collaboration with S. Hahn, cf. *AOH* 5.231-247 (1955), 8.99-107 (1958), 9.97-107 (1959).

[117] W. Tubielewicz, "Vom Einfluss Europäischer Sprachen auf die Gestaltung des Modernen Hebräisch", *RO* 20.337-351 (1956).

[118] Cf. e.g. *RO* 16.144-163 (1954).

[119] S. Strelcyn, rev. of Ullendorf, *RO* 22(1).161-164 (1958); rev. of several works on Ethiopic lexicography, *ibid.* 164-168; on a paper on Ethiopian alphabet reform, *ibid.* 168-170; cf. also his "Matériaux éthiopiens pour servir à l'étude de la prononciation arabisée du copte", *ibid.* 7-54. For his reviews of Kračkovskij's *Vvedenie*, see fn. 74 above.

# URALIC

GÜNTER J. STIPA*

## ORGANIZATION OF LINGUISTIC WORK

*Private Initiative.* – In the first and second decades after the Revolution concern for and study of the native languages of Finno-Ugric nationalities in the Soviet Union lay almost entirely in the hands of educators, writers, and some patriotically-minded linguists. It was these who accomplished the pioneer task of establishing the literary language. They worked on systems of writing, of orthography, on normative grammars and dictionaries, organized expeditions for dialect investigation, held linguistic conferences, etc. The impetus for this and the enthusiasm in connection with it were doubtless connected with the founding of the autonomous republics and national districts.

The advantage of the new regime was that speakers of Finno-Ugric languages could themselves make their native language the object of linguistic work. A disadvantage was that, owing to the borders of republics (and districts), an isolation of linguistic investigation became evident to a certain degree, and that the linguists of different nationalities had no contact with one another and did not even aspire to Finno-Ugric studies as a subject.

Before the Revolution there were beginnings of Finno-Ugric studies at the University of Kazan. Two Estonian researchers held posts there in Finno-Ugric linguistics: M. Veske (1887-1890), who even made research trips to the Cheremis, and N. Anderson (1894-1904). Most impressive of all was the fact that the famous Slavicist A. A. Šaxmatov (died 1920 in Leningrad) devoted himself to Mordvin in Kazan.[1] At the University of St. Petersburg Finnish scholars (A. Sjögren, M. A. Castrén, F. J. Wiedemann) had been lecturing, even at the beginning of this century (e.g., O. Kallas). Moreover, the Russian scholar S. Patkanov had directed the interest of scholars to the Ostyaks.[2]

In the first years after the Revolution the connections between Finno-Ugric studies

* The English translation was made by Ernst A. Scemann; the text has been edited and condensed by the Assistant Editor with the kind help of Felix J. Oinas.

[1] He collected ethnographic and linguistic material for his voluminous work *Mordovskij ètnografičeskij sbornik* (St. Petersburg, 1910) among the Mordvins.

[2] He reported on this in his article "Zur Rechtfertigung", *Finnisch-ugrische Forschungen*, 7(1-3). 41-44 (Helsingfors, 1907).

and linguistics of the USSR were broken off. Kazan had become the center of the Tatar Autonomous Republic and the Volgaic groups established as a substitute for it their own pedagogical institutes in their republics. Today there is a state university in one of the republics (the Mordvin).

The fact that Finno-Ugric linguistics had been pursued at the University of Kazan before the Revolution, had decisive significance for the beginnings of native linguistic work among the Mordvin, Cheremis, and Votyaks. It was a stroke of fortune that in that moment, when men were needed who were suitable to be founders of linguistic studies, outstanding students of Veske and Anderson were to be found among each of these nationalities, and actually played a leading role in the development of linguistics. We shall hear more about them later. Zyryan linguists received their education at Moscow and Leningrad, the most outstanding of them in Finland and Hungary as well (at the end of the 1920's).

*Research Institutes.* – Linguistic conferences in the several republics soon revealed the necessity of establishing permanent committees and institutions to execute linguistic tasks. In the 1930's scientific research institutes for language and literature subject to the state administrative departments were founded in the capitals of the various republics and districts, respectively. They took over the tasks which hitherto had been up to private initiative, organized them in the form of plans according to definite programs and annual plans, published books and continuously published small scholarly investigations in the scientific series of these institutes (the so-called zapiski, trudy, or sborniki). In the course of years the staff of collaborators was increased and through the establishment of such positions as *aspirant* they built up a scholarly generation to succeed themselves.

The Pedagogical Institutes which had been founded in those cities and in which there were lectureships of the language and literature for that country rendered great service to the linguistic institutes. For the Ob-Ugrics and Samoyeds, the Institute for the Peoples of the North in Leningrad and the Pedagogical Institute there had great significance.

*Chairs at Universities.* – A chair for Finno-Ugric linguistics was founded at Leningrad University in 1925. Dmitrij Vladimirovič Bubrix (1890-1949) became the occupant of the chair. He had originally been a Slavist, a pupil of Šaxmatov, and had been directed by him towards the study of Finno-Ugric languages. Bubrix's significance lies in two fields. He was the great organizer for Finno-Ugric peoples in the USSR who personally took part in dialect expeditions, edited the first sizeable dictionaries of various languages, saw to the setting up of *aspirant* positions at the Universities of Leningrad and Moscow, and schooled students from the various republics and districts of Finno-Ugric peoples in linguistics. Under his direction a great number of dissertations were written. Almost all the present-day members of scientific research institutes were students of Bubrix. Moreover, he supported the research institutes through his contributions to their scholarly series.

Even more significant than his organizational accomplishment is his research work in the linguistic field. His specialties in Finno-Ugric studies were Mordvin, Zyryan, Votyak, and Karelian. Particularly worth mentioning are his books on historical phonetics of Erza, Udmurt, and Finnish, as well as his grammars of the Mordvin, Komi, and Karelian literary languages. He also wrote a series of articles on general linguistic questions in the field of Finno-Ugristics. All told, he authored approximately 100 linguistic papers.[3] In 1946 he became a corresponding member of the Academy of Sciences.

His scholarly accomplishments were considerably impaired in their quality by the pressures exerted on the entire field of linguistics in the Soviet Union until 1950 by N. Ja. Marr. Under this influence, he refrained in his historical grammars, for instance, from comparing the linguistic phenomena under discussion with their equivalents in related languages, and he also refrained from tracing their development back to a common source, namely, Proto-Finno-Ugric, which he did not recognize.

In order to use a comparative historical method in spite of the persecutions of the Marrists, he invented a theory which did not seem to be contrary to the theses of Marr, namely, the "contact theory", which he first developed in 1940. It is based on the assumption that related languages receive their similarities and identical features by being in contact with one another, thereby developing by reciprocal assimilation. Differences arose through contacts with dialects or languages of different types. According to Bubrix, the investigation of the similarities and dissimilarities therefore allows historical conclusions. The Marrists attacked his contact theory vigorously, as is shown among other things by the polemics between D. V. Bubrix and the historian N. N. Čeboksarov.[4] It can actually be proven that this theory, at some points, led him to incorrect conclusions.[5]

The historical-comparative method of Bubrix restricts itself to comparing the dialects of one language or language group. Nevertheless he should be given great credit for maintaining this traditional method of Finno-Ugric studies in the USSR in the years before 1950, even if only clandestinely.

Leningrad was the real center of Finno-Ugric studies until 1950. The instruction in Finno-Ugric linguistics has been continued to this very day by the instructor Z. M. Dubrovina, who specializes in Balto-Finnic languages. Professor A. J. Popov is concerned with the toponymics of the Nordic and Finno-Ugric peoples.

As early as Bubrix's time provision had already been made for *aspirant* positions in Finno-Ugric studies at Moscow University. There, the Zyryan V. I. Lytkin received

[3] A short biography in Russian is contained in *Voprosy finno-ugorskogo jazykoznanija*, pp. 5-8 (Moscow-Leningrad, 1962) published on the occasion of his 70th birthday. M. M. Hämäläinen reports on his life, including a bibliography, in *Pribaltijsko-finskoe jazykoznanie* (= *Trudy Karel'skogo Filiala AN SSSR*, 23.3-15) (Moscow-Leningrad, 1960-1).

[4] N. N. Čeboksarov, "Nekotorye voprosy izučenija finnougorskix narodov v SSSR", *SovÈtn*, 3.176-185 (1948) and D. V. Bubrix, "O sovetskom finnougrovedenii", *SovÈtn*, 2.189-196 (1949); N. N. Čeboksarov, "Eščë raz o nekotoryx voprosax izučenija finnougorskix narodov", *SovÈtn*, 2.197-204 (1949).

[5] Cf. the statements by Gornung, Levin, and Sidorov in *VJa*, 1.41-64 (1952) and of Fokos-Fuchs, "Učenye Zapiski", *ALH* 2(1-2).228ff. (1952).

the degree of Doctor of Philosophy in Permic languages. Finno-Ugric languages are also taught in the Institute of National Schools of the Pedagogic Academy of the RFSFR in Moscow. For the Hungarian minority of the USSR living in the Carpathian Mountains of the Ukraine, the chair of Hungarian language at the University of Ushgorod is of importance. Outposts are being maintained by the research scholar A. K. Matveev at the University of Sverdlovsk, who specializes in the loanword relationships between Ob-Ugric (more generally: Finno-Ugric) languages and Russian; and by the lecturer M. P. Čhaydze, in Tbilisi (Tiflis) in Georgia.

For Balto-Finnic languages there are, aside from Leningrad, chairs at the University of the Karelian ASSR in Petrozavodsk, and naturally also in Estonia at Tartu University, where Professor A. Kask is currently professor of Estonian. Since 1945 P. Ariste has held the chair of Finno-Ugric languages. This with the accompanying lectureships, is the largest chair of Finno-Ugric studies in the USSR. It is worthy of note that some Mordvins, Cheremis, and Votyaks have already studied there.

*Institutes at Academies.* – Early in the '50's a division of Finno-Ugric linguistics was established in the Department of Linguistics of the Academy of Sciences of the USSR in Moscow, consisting originally of three scholarly staff members. By 1958 this division had seven staff members from all branches of Finno-Ugric peoples. Several *aspirants* were guided in their seminar work, simultaneously with their university studies, by V. I. Lytkin, and given special instruction in Hungarian by K. E. Majtinskaja. Credit for this progress is due in large degree to the present president of the Institute of Linguistics, Boris A. Serebrennikov, a member of the Academy. In the '50's he received his Ph. D. in Permic and Volgaic languages at Moscow University with a dissertation on "The Category of Tense and Aspect in the Finno-Ugric languages of the Permic and Volgaic groups". His interest in various language families (Turkic among others) and a broad general linguistic basis of linguistic knowledge[6] gave him the broad view that, along with investigation of the individual Finno-Ugric languages, comparative linguistics too should be developed by correspondingly skilled forces. It is particularly fortunate that the secretary of the Department of Linguistics of the Moscow Academy, Ju. S. Eliseev, and a specialist in Balto-Finnic languages, is also a Finno-Ugric scholar.

The Academy of Sciences of the USSR established branches, the so-called *filiali*, in two autonomous republics of Finno-Ugric peoples, namely, the "Komi filial AN SSSR" in Syktyvkar in 1944 which replaced the previous scientific research institute, and the "Karelskij filial AN SSSR" in Petrozavodsk in 1949. Both were provided with openings for *aspirants* to educate young scholars. In Syktyvkar, the linguistic department under its head N. A. Kolegova has been expanded by sections for linguistics (which includes a young scholar, E. S. Guljaev, specially selected for comparative Finno-Ugric studies), literature, and folklore and folk music (20 scholarly staff members).

[6] Cf. the thorough bibliography which he compiled. About his research in Permian grammar see G. Stipa, "Funktionen der Nominalformen des Verbs in den permischen Sprachen", *MSFOu*, 121 (Helsinki, 1960).

Independently there also exists the Academy of Sciences in Estonia, "Eesti NSV Teaduste Akadeemia" (now located in Tallinn), with institutes for the investigation of Estonian language and literature. Quite recently, also a division of Finno-Ugric languages has been established there.

*Congresses in Finno-Ugric Linguistics.* – The climax of Bubrix's organizing activities was the arranging of the first scholarly congress in 1947 in Leningrad on problems of Finno-Ugric linguistics, which lasted two weeks. Numerous representatives of Finno-Ugric peoples and delegates of various universities participated. Fifty-four papers on linguistic, folkloristic, and ethnological topics were on the program. Some of them have been published in the two volumes *Soviet Studies in Finno-Ugristics* (Vol. 1: Leningrad, 1948; Vol. 2: Saransk, 1948). The importance of this congress lay above all in the contacts between scholars of various Finno-Ugric peoples, the creation of organs to co-ordinate research, and in the distribution of research fields and tasks.

The second congress for Finno-Ugric linguistics in the USSR was held in 1954 in Moscow under the guidance of the Department of Linguistics of the Academy. Since the Marr doctrine had by now been condemned as erroneous, new concepts for methods and tasks of Finno-Ugric linguistics were created. Special emphasis was given to the tasks of scientific and historical research. More than 80 scholars, lecturers, and *aspirants* participated.

The third congress for Finno-Ugric linguistics in the USSR was held in 1959, again in Moscow. The main topic was *Questions of Historical Grammar and Historical Dialectology of the Finno-Ugric Languages.* The Department of Linguistics of the Academy published synopses of the papers that were read. (See "Soveščanie po voprosam . . . .", Moscow, 1959.)

The fourth congress for Finno-Ugric linguistics was held in 1961 in Petrozavodsk. The numerous papers on individual morphological and semantic problems in Finno-Ugric studies have been published as synopses or in so-called "theses". (See "Vsesojuznoe Soveščanie po voprosam . . .", Petrozavodsk, 1961.)

Conferences and congresses revealed the necessity to publish journals devoted to Finno-Ugric research. Until then, scholarly serials had been published only by scientific research institutes of individual autonomous republics. A few articles, though, had been printed in journals of more general character, as, for instance, *Voprosy Jazykoznanija* and *Izvestija Akademii nauk SSSR.* Yet, except for the proceedings of the congresses, there was no serial publication in which the work of all Finno-Ugrists of the entire Soviet Union was united. An organ for Finno-Ugric linguistics in the USSR was lacking.

Therefore, the Linguistic Department of the Academy published a complete review of Finno-Ugric studies, the first book of which was entitled *Problems in Finno-Ugric Linguistics* (Moscow-Leningrad, 1962). The editor-in-charge was Serebrennikov, with Lytkin and Majtinskaja as co-editors. The book is divided into three parts: Part 1 treats general problems of Finno-Ugristics; part 2 contains investigations of individual Finno-Ugric languages; and part 3 honors the research work of Finno-Ugricists of merit (E. Beke, on his 70th birthday; D. R. Fokos-Fuchs on his 75th birthday; and Paasonen's accomplishments in Mordvin research). The appendix contains sample texts of a few Finno-Ugric dialects in phonetic transcription and Russian translation.

*Methods and Tasks.* – In the development of linguistic research among the Finno-Ugric peoples of the USSR, several periods can be distinguished. After the first 1½ decades of free initiative, simultaneously with the introduction of the Russian alphabet in place of the temporary Latin alphabet in the 30's and the founding of the scientific research institutes attached to the Councils of Ministers of various republics, there began the period of planned scholarly work on the basis of resolutions, directives, and partly of party programs from the viewpoint of Marxist-Leninist linguistics in the Soviet Union. The few researchers of the older generation, of whom a portion were more folklorists and ethnologists than linguists, remained true to the comparative-historical method of their teachers. Yet even before 1930 the Japhetic theory of Marr began to take effect on Finno-Ugric peoples. Contributing to this was the fact that Marr studied these languages himself: Mordvin in 1927, Cheremis (research expedition) in 1930, Votyak in 1931. Since ideology replaced the investigation of linguistic facts, and since the inner regularity of languages could not even be mentioned, investigation into language relationships and the study of the history of languages ceased. Even in descriptive treatment of dialects it became impossible to analyze phonemic differences and phonetic systems. This did immeasurable harm to Finno-Ugric linguistics. Scholarly work was possible for the members of research institutes mainly in one field: the drafting of a normative grammar of the written language which was coming into being. Nevertheless, they laid the proper groundwork, even in the days of the supremacy of Marr's "new doctrine". However, not until after 1950, after the fall of the "Arakščeev Regime" could Finno-Ugric linguistics in the USSR fully develop.

Now it was again permissable to use the comparative-historical method. Naturally not in the sense of the "young grammarians", whose one-sided opinion of structural laws of a language had been out-dated for some time, but only according to the methods of the leading Slavists in the Soviet Union, particularly those of V. V. Vinogradov. Least well developed in Uralic linguistics in the USSR were the methods of phonetics. Only in the mid-50's did some young researchers acquire phonetic training at Leningrad University under L. P. Zinder, and at the University of Tartu under P. Ariste. They also found guidance from the phonetician of the Linguistic Department of the Academy of Sciences in Moscow.

During the 4th congress of Finno-Ugrists of the USSR in Petrozavodsk in 1961, Serebrennikov emphasized that Finno-Ugrists would have to learn to use the methods of structural linguistics, after the fashion in which, in his opinion, for instance, the Norwegian Lappologist Knut Bergsland practises them.

In October 1962 there was a linguistic conference for the entire USSR held in Alma-Ata concerned with the problems of the development of the literary languages of the various nationalities within the territories of the USSR. A Finno-Ugric section was formed which presented papers "on the present status and the future development of the recent literary languages of the Finno-Ugric peoples". In preparation for this the major tasks of the contemporary Soviet Russian linguistics had been enumerated in 30 points in *VJa*, 4.1-8(1962).[7]

The authority for these 30 points is the resolutions of the 22nd Congress of the Communist Party of the USSR. The article cited states the major problem of the young literary languages to be the role of Russian as the carrier of culture and the means of communication between members of various nationalities. This is a recurring problem in various aspects of Soviet Russian linguistics. Some of these aspects are: the study of the regularity of the creation of a common lexicographic stock for the languages of the peoples of the USSR; the study of the social functions of Russian and its influence on the development of national languages; investigation of the origin and the development of various types of bilingualism in the USSR; investigation of the results of the influence of Russian on the languages of the peoples of the USSR; the study of the interrelationship of the social functions between the national literary languages and the supranational means of communications in the USSR. The necessity of adopting Russian works into the national languages has been particularly emphasized in the terminology of social life, of natural sciences, and of technology.[8]

For the national languages, the mapping-out of theories of grammar and of "functional" stylistics, of principles of structural and simultaneously historical typology, and of structural linguistics in the meaning of a general theory of language has been recommended, together with a detailed study of the structure of these languages and the writing of comparative-historical grammars for related groups of languages.

Linguistic literature in the USSR is written chiefly in Russian. In the following, we shall cite the titles of those papers in translation and shall indicate when a paper was written in a language other than Russian.

## MORDVIN LINGUISTICS

### 1. *Before 1950*

*Early Researchers.* – The beginnings of Mordvin linguistics are tied to the names of two important persons. As the first, one must name the Slavist A. A. Šaxmatov (1864-1920), whose *Ethnographic Collection of Mordvin* (St. Petersburg, 1910), contains valuable linguistic material as well as a linguistic investigation of morphologic and phonetic peculiarities of two dialects spoken in the Saratov *gouvernement*.

[7] "K izučeniju sostojanija i razvitija nacional'nyx literaturnyx jazykov narodov Sovetskogo Sojuza", *VJa*, 4.1-8 (1962).

[8] In this respect it is instructive to study the Communist theories on the development from "national" languages to "zonal" languages, and finally, to one single universal language after the victory of socialism. See Avanesov, *Voprosy razvitija jazyka i dialektov v svete I. V. Stalina po jazykoznaniju* (Moscow, 1951).

His pupil, the Mordvin M. E. Evsevjev (1864-1931), a native of the Mordvin village of Malye Karmaly in the Simbirsk *gouvernement*, was a folklorist, ethnologist, and linguist.[9] His folkloristic collections, which he started in the 80's of the last century, have great value for the Finno-Ugrist as linguistic material. His most important folkloristic book *The Marriage Customs of the Mordvins* (1931), the basis of which are the faithfully transcribed stories of his mother, contains also 3500 stanzas of lamentations with variants from a variety of dialects. His activity as a collector is best represented by the fact that he personally took notes in more than 450 Mordvin villages in the most varied regions. Preparations are under way for a complete edition of his works ("Izbrannye trudy"). Vol. 1, *Folksongs of the Mordvins*, was published recently (Saransk, 1961) containing 112 folk songs of historical and legendary content of family life, social life, and military life, with highly valuable historical and ethnographical annotations by the author. Four more volumes are to follow.

Due to his linguistic training at the University of Kazan and due to his excellent knowledge of Mordvin dialects, Evsevjev was able to undertake with outstanding success a task invaluable for Finno-Ugric linguistics, that of editing a dictionary of the Erza dialect (with Russian translation) under the Mordvin title *Èrźań-ruzoń valks* (Moscow, 1931). Unfortunately, it did not progress beyond the letter K, as his sudden death interrupted the work. Of particular value are the explanations of words by means of proverbs, song fragments, idioms, etc., specifying also the meaning in each individual dialect.

Evsevjev's importance for Finno-Ugristics is particularly strong in the field of grammar. His *Basic Outline of Mordvin Grammar* (Moscow, 1928-29) is still valuable today. Of fundamental importance is the description of the sounds and sound patterns of Erza. Especially the morphological part, with its appendix on Mokša, offers the Finno-Ugrist many new insights, for instance, the fact that there is a second preterite in Mordvin.

Evsevjev was the leading personality in all questions of the national linguistic movement. He decided, for instance, that the Kozlov dialect was the suitable basis for the Erza literary language. His sudden death was a great loss to Mordvin linguistics, because after his death the feuding parties could not come to an agreement on the problems of normalizing the grammar.

*Drafting the Bases of the Literary Language*. – During the first conference on problems of Mordvin language and literature in Saransk in 1933 and during the conferences in the two following years, it became evident how difficult it would be to reach an agreement on the alphabet, orthography, paradigms of declension and conjugation, etc. Even after the Scientific Research Institute of Language and Literature in Saransk had been founded in 1933, it was impossible to pave the way for clarifying the individual structure of both literary languages, Erza and Mokša. Then came a deci-

9 An exhaustive biography was written by V. I. Bezzubov, "M. E. Evsevjev – Ètnograf mordovskogo naroda", *SovÈtn* 2.134-137 (1949). Even more exhaustive is the biography in the preface of the first volume *M. E. Evsevjev, Izbrannye Trudy I. Narodnye pesni mordvy*, pp. 5-39 (Saransk, 1961).

sion from the "linguistic conference on problems of orthography, morphology, and grammatical terminology of the Mordvin literary languages" in Saransk in 1938. As related by M. N. Koljadenkov, a leading personality in Mordvin linguistics, in his report "Thirty Years of Mordvin linguistics",[10] the problems were solved in the following fashion.

For the writing system, the idea of Latinization of the alphabet was rejected with finality. The palatal sounds of Russian could serve as well to describe the palatal sounds of Mordvin. The morphological principle of Russian orthography was radically carried out (only in Mokša were there a few exceptions).

The standardization of the grammar was effected according to the principle that everything which Erza or Mokša had in common with Russian grammar (and with the other Mordvin language) became a norm for the written language. The grammar written according to these decisions[11] was forced into the structural pattern of Russian grammar. The syntax had not been discussed at that time, but became a special task of the members of the Scientific Research Institute. Koljadenkov emphasized that the living colloquial language, literature and folklore should serve as research material for this purpose. This syntax was adopted at the conference in 1940, so that the normative grammar of Mordvin was conclusively established for both languages.[12]

In the 1940s the first normative dictionaries for both literary languages also appeared.

*Individual Scholarly Investigations.* – In 1940 it was decided to publish a scientific journal of the Institute (zapiski). In the course of the following years a number of short scholarly papers appeared in it, among others by Bubrix, Koljadenkov, Cyganov, Pigin, and Potapkin.

The monographs by Bubrix in the field of phonetics and morphology of this period demand special attention. His first phonetic investigation of the Kozlov dialect, *Sounds and Forms of Spoken Erza* (Moscow, 1930), is remarkable because he had already found the generally accepted division into three parts of the Erza dialect through the method of progressive or regressive assimilation. In his article "The Mordvin System of Morphemes" (*Zapiski*, Saransk, 1941) and even more in the phonetic part of his posthumously published *Historical Grammar of Erza* (Saransk, 1953), he discusses origin and evolution of the sounds, but was content to use only Erza and Mokša dialects for his comparisons without citing related languages. In spite of the labors of Bubrix and a few other Mordvin scholars, A. P. Feoktistov[13] has concluded that the phonetic structure of the Mordvin languages is insufficiently investigated. Bubrix's chief topics in the field of Mordvin morphology are: the "inner locative case" of the declension, which he tries to explain as arising from postpositions

[10] M. N. Koljadenkov, "Mordovskoe jazykoznanie za 30 let", *Trudy mordovskogo NIJaLIE* 20, Serija filologičeskaja, pp. 3-22 (Saransk, 1960).

[11] M. N. Koljadenkov & S. G. Potapkin, *Morfologija, orfografija i grammatičeskaja terminologija èrzanskogo i mokšanskogo jazykov* (Rešenija 4-oj jazykovoj konferencii 1938 goda, Saransk, 1938).

[12] M. N. Koljadenkov, *Sintaksis i punktuacija mordovskix* (*èrzanskogo i mokšanskogo*) *jazykov* (Rešenija naučnoj sessii 1940 goda po voprosam sintaksisa).

[13] "Mordovskie jazyki", *Mladopis'mennye jazyki narodov SSSR*, p. 430 (1959).

with later suffixation (in two articles: Petrozavodsk, 1947, Moscow-Leningrad, 1948; and in his *Historical Grammar*, Chapter II, pp. 39-85 and Chapter IV, pp. 190-213);[14] the differences between "definite" and "indefinite" declensions, which are characteristic of Mordvin (in his *Historical Grammar*, p. 97 ff.) are new and discerning observations; the origin of verbal conjugation (with charts reconstructing original forms, in *Historical Grammar*, pp. 143-145); and many others.

His *Historical Grammar of Erza* remains unfinished. One methodological weakness is the limitation of the comparative material to Erza and Mokša alone, and the absence of etymologies for the suffixes, for which reason his historical conclusions are often incorrect.

## 2. *After 1950*

*The Present Generation of Scholars.* As early as the first congress for Finno-Ugric linguistics in Leningrad in 1947, a remarkably large number of young Mordvin scholars demonstrated their ability. Vol. II of the proceedings of the congress, entitled *Soviet Finno-Ugristics* (Saransk, 1948) comprising 10 papers, is wholly dedicated to Mordvin topics. The activity of the members of the Scientific Research Institute in Saransk is especially demonstrated by the fact that up to 1960, mainly in the 50's, 16 *kandidats* in Philosophy and one Doctor of Philosophy defended their dissertations. These dissertations appeared entirely or in part in print.

The senior member and Head of the Institute is Professor M. N. Koljadenkov. One of the older leading members was N. F. Cyganov, now professor of Mordvin languages at the Mordvin State University. The lecturer for Mordvin at the same university is F. I. Peterburgskij.

*Continuation of Establishing the Written Language.* – During the Scientific Conference on Problems of Mordvin Linguistics in Saransk, 1952, the normative grammar was once more accurately compiled. The result was published under the title *Materialy*, II . . . (Saransk, 1955), a morphology and syntax (including rules of orthography and punctuation) of Erza and Mokša. The resolutions of the conference and the preceding decree of the Ministry were also concerned with two problems of the development of the literary language:

1. The fact that there are two literary languages of Mordvin in the one republic. These are allowed to exist under the given circumstances, yet the viewpoint of "linguists of the republic who are working towards an artificial division of the Mokša and Erza literary language" is to be condemned. On the contrary, it is necessary "for the linguists of the republic to make all possible efforts to concentrate on emphasizing the common traits of Erza and Mokša".[15]

2. The role of Russian in the development of the literary languages. The fact was

[14] *Materialy naučnoj sessii po voprosam mordovskogo jazykoznanija II* (Saransk, 1955).
[15] *Op. cit.*, p. 7, in the section "Rešenie naučnoj sessii po voprosam mordovskogo jazykoznanija".

acknowledged that the major expansion of the Mordvin vocabulary occurs by means of loanwords from Russian, namely in connection with the changes in social structure, industrial development, culture, science, etc. Therefore, it is the duty of linguists to study the problem of Russian loan-words for inclusion into the Mordvin language system. This directive sounds more comprehensive than the guide-lines presently given (1962) for the nationalities of the USSR, which speak much more vaguely of adoption of Russian vocabulary into "the terminology of social life, natural sciences, and technology".

Lexicologically noteworthy are new editions of normative dictionaries, particularly the *Russian-Mokša Dictionary* by S. G. Potapkin and A. K. Imjarekov (40,000 words, Saransk, 1951).

*Individual Scholarly Investigations.* There are only a few articles on Mordvin phonetics apart from descriptions of the phonetic forms and systems in various dialects. Worth mentioning is Cyganov's article "On the Vocalism of the non-initial syllable of the dialects of the progressive assimilating type in Erza-Mordvin" (*Zapiski*, Saransk, 1955).

A greater number of articles and some dissertations are available on morphology. The analyses of case formation, started by Bubrix, are being continued by A. I. Bočkaeva in her article "Semantics of the Inner Locative Case in Erza-Mordvin" (*Zapiski*, Saransk, 1953). In this article the author establishes a great number of extended (non-locative) functions of these cases, for instance, more than ten meanings for the elative. In connection with these cases, she investigates postpositions in the following article: "The use of postpositions with the inner locative case in Erza-Mordvin" (*Trudy AN SSSR*, 3, Moscow, 1954).

A number of larger articles are devoted to certain word classes. R. A. Zavodova wrote her dissertation on *The Adjectives in Mordvin Languages* (Moscow, 1952). Later she discussed portions of these problems in individual articles. She also investigated "The System of the Parts of Speech in Mordvin Languages" (*Materialy* . . . Part 1, Lectures, Saransk, 1955).

O. I. Čudaeva investigated the *nomina actionis* in her dissertation *The Nomina actionis in -m in Mokša-Mordvin* (Moscow, 1952). The forms of expressions using these *nomina actionis*, particularly of the adverbial type, are treated by the author in a few later articles (*Zapiski*, Saransk, 1953, and *Trudy AN SSSR*, 3, Moscow, 1954). These articles resulted above all in conclusions as to the type of words with which this *nomen actionis* is connected in its various functions. In the study published in the Zapiski the author also compares the use of the *nomen actionis* in -m in Mokša with the one in other Finno-Ugric languages, particularly in Cheremis, and arrives at the conclusion that Mokša has retained a feature of quite basic origin.

The verb offers a wide field of inquiry. Very significant is a monograph on the verbal derivational suffixes, which was presented as a dissertation by the Estonian A. P. Hallap in Tartu, 1955, under the title *Suffixes of Verb Formation in Mordvin Languages* (Common-Mordvin suffixes). Here we can see how the historical-comparative method was correctly used with the help of a wealth of linguistic material from various related languages and with the knowledge of their etymology. The author was able to prove conclusively which of the present day verbal derivational suffixes of Mordvin go back to pre-Mordvin times.

Young scholars concern themselves with forms which can be interpreted in various ways, namely the *genera*, *modi* or *tempora* of the verb. M. I. Pigin undertakes in his dissertation the investigation of the problem of *Genus of the Verb in Erza-Mordvin* (in manuscript), which for the time being must be considered unresolved. More tangible are his studies on the *modi*. In his article "The Origin of the Subjunctive in Mordvin Languages" (*Učenye Zapiski*, 4:1, Petrozavodsk, 1954) he maintains that these modal forms in Erza were not formed by fusion of the auxiliary verb with the stem, as was commonly assumed, but by a reflexive-passive suffix.

To explain particular tenses by a derivational suffix is the undertaking of the young Estonian scholar V. Pall in his dissertation *Tempora and Modi in Mordvin* (Tartu, 1955). He derives the second preterite from a frequentative suffix.

The complicated problem of the mode of action in connection with derivational suffixes is discussed in the dissertation of the Mordvin È. S. Ippolitova, *Formation of Direction-Action Verbs in Mordvin Languages* (Saransk, 1954). The author establishes an iterative suffix which, in her opinion, expresses the "grammatical category of mode of action" (in the sense of the Russian *vid*). Other suffixes for expressing modes of action were limited to small groups of verbs. Almost simultaneously the Finno-Ugrist Serebrennikov, mentioned earlier, investigated in his doctoral dissertation *The Categories of Tense and Aspect* (*vid*) *in the Finno-Ugric Languages of the Permic and Volgaic Groups* (Avtoreferat, Moscow, 1956; edition of the Academy, Moscow, 1960). He arrives at the conclusion that the respective iterative suffix can be connected only with 70 to 80% of the verbs and therefore cannot be linked to the mode of action (in the sense of the Russian *vid*). He also makes the interesting observation that this suffix in its diminutive meaning can denote a less intensive action. In the comprehensive study by Serebrennikov one also finds several other novel conclusions, for instance, on aspect meaning of verb pairs, of which the second member is the auxiliary *to do*. Subsequently he specifically discusses the respective derivational suffixes of Mokša. His material was taken mainly from the *Erza-Russian Dictionary* (1949) and from works in the newly developing Mordvin literature (including translations).

In the field of syntax N. M. Koljadenkov has been writing ever better and longer studies throughout the last two decades. He devoted his special attention to the predicate and particularly to the word groups formed by it. Yielding to the need for a normative syntax of the written language, he published a grammar of Mordvin (Erza-Mokša) languages, Part II: *Syntax* (Saransk, 1954). Those constructions which he treated in this study only in a descriptive manner have been considerably expanded in his doctoral dissertation *The Structure of the Simple Sentence in Mordvin Languages* (the sentence and its primary parts, Saransk, 1959).

Part I thoroughly analyzes the modes of expression to designate syntactical relationships between subject and predicate, particularly word fusions of coordinating and sub-ordinating type. He divides the types of sentences according to the principle of whether individual parts of the sentence are expressed by one word or a number of words. In Part II he studies the predicate. His treatment of the non-verbal predicate (formed by flexion of the nomina) is of particular value. The Finno-Ugrist finds here important analyses of samples of this predicative flexion (unique for Mordvin and Samoyed) which the author combines with declension. This study is also important for the problem of Finno-Ugric nominal sentences. He devotes an entire separate chapter (the last) of his book to case syntax, of which the identification of the object must be emphasized. He finds conformity to a large degree with Finnish (total and partial object).

There recently appeared the long awaited *Grammar of Mordvin* (*Mokša and Erza*) *languages* (Saransk, 1962), a very important book, printed unfortunately in so small a number of copies as to be scarcely available in the book trade. It gives a scientific presentation of the phonemes (from the pen of the late Bubrix) and of the morphology, of which the first chapter, on word formation, was composed by Koljadenkov (pp. 36-61). Among the suffixations he also mentions the predicativing personal suffixes (including the tense character) for forming nominal predicates, a unique feature of Mordvin, which is unfortunately mentioned neither under nouns nor verbs in the later chapters of the book. In such a matter, as in many points of paragraph arrangement, are the deficiences of collective authorship, which is not always completely coordinated, to be seen. The tenses, which return to true inflection, crop up in the midst of the modes. Apart from these small flaws the work is distinguished by a clear and thorough depiction, especially in the treatment of the case forms and of their carefully spelled out functions (pp. 79-164). The chapter on the "secondary declension" (pp. 165-166) too deserves special attention. F. P. Markov and N. F. Cyganov shared authorship of the treatment of substantives. R. A. Zavodova composed the theoretical portion on word classes, as well as the chapters on adjectives, numerals and the finite forms of the verb. The non-finite verb forms (nomina actionis, infinitive, participles and verbal adverbs), as well as the pronouns and adverbs are treated by O. I. Čudaeva. Capping this detailed morphology are sections on postpositions, conjunctions particles and caritive words as presented by A. K. Imjarekov. This grammar will no doubt remain the basic reference work for the study of Mordvin for the next decade.

In the field of lexicology, N. F. Cyganov has distinguished himself by a series of investigations, particularly in his dissertation *Problems of Vocabulary and Lexicography in Mordvin Languages* (Moscow, 1952). In this dissertation he discusses the principles of compiling bilingual dictionaries and the need for separate consideration of the differing linguistic systems.

A very important study is expected in the very near future: the publication of the oldest Mordvin dictionary, which was completed in manuscript in 1785 by Bishop

Damaskin. The editor is a member of the Department of Linguistics at the Academy in Moscow, the Mokša-Mordvin A. P. Feoktistov.

Dialectology is still in its beginnings. Nevertheless, since 1958, a staff of trained workers has been in the process of systematically recording with modern methods (tape recordings, etc.) and evaluating the material of various dialects. Until very recently not a single monograph on any individual dialect existed, but now the carefully planned work is beginning to bear fruit. A short while ago (1961) the first volume of a series of monographs on Mordvin dialects appeared. This *Basic Outline* (*Očerki*) *of Mordvin Dialects* (Vol, 1. Saransk, 1961) describes four Erza dialects: F. P. Markov on "The Dialect of Alatyr" (Alatyr is a river in northeast Mordva ASSR and the northwest Chuvash ASSR); V. D. Ob"jedkin, "The Dialect of Starye Turdaki" (Tašto-Murza in the Kočkurov Kraj in the Mordva ASSR); A. P. Jakuškin, "The Dialect of Drakino" (the population comes from the Teńgušev kraj in the Mordva ASSR); D. V. Cygankin, "The Dialect of Šugurovo" (in the middle reaches of the Sura). In each case the phonetic and morphological traits of each dialect are discussed in the grammatical section. This was done very systematically in more than fifty pages per dialect. Text samples of folkloristic material (also some fifty pages each), personally collected by the researchers, follows in phonetic transcription and Russian translation. The value of these texts is increased by the fact that the collectors knew the respective dialects thoroughly. V. D. Ob"jedkin for instance investigates the dialect of his own native region, which he speaks himself.

## CHEREMIS LINGUISTICS

### *1. Before 1950*

*Early Researches.* – For more than a decade the study of Cheremis was exclusively in the hands of educators and patriotically inclined linguists, of whom two deserve particular mention: V. M. Vasiljev and G. G. Karmazin. The more important of the two is Vasiljev, who was born in 1883 in Susadi Èbalák (Bashkir A. R.). He studied in Kazan and became a teacher at the Pedagogical Seminary there. Since 1907 he has published a popular calendar in Cheremis language entitled *Marla Kalendaŕ*. In this calendar he included folkloristic items such as Cheremis songs, riddles, etc. As early as 1911 he edited a Cheremis-Russian dictionary of Meadow and Eastern Cheremis. A Cheremis first reader for grade school children folllowed – all of this in Czarist Russia. When the Revolution made it possible to use this language freely in schools and in literature, V. M. Vasiljev had already prepared the first Cheremis grammar: *Grammatical Sketches of the Mari Peoples*: *Materials for Etymology and Syntax* (Kazan, 1918). Since these beginnings of Cheremis linguistics he has consistently occupied an important position. His research work extends up to the present and spans more than half a century. All told he has published more then 25 linguistic and approximately

20 folkloristic and ethnographic papers. *Materials for a Cheremis Grammar*, his last work, was written in 1958, when he was almost blind. He died in 1962.

Vasiljev's most important work for the Finno-Ugrist was written quite early, the comparative dictionary of Cheremis dialects *Marij Mutèr* (Moscow, 1926-28). In this work the word-forms of all important dialects with their specific meanings are represented in a scholarly manner which is an achievement unparalleled in this country to this day. Yet even the title, in which he uses a neologism, namely *mut* "word" with the suffix *-er* for collective terms (meaning approximately "collection of words"), instead of the Russian *slovar'*, placed him under suspicion of being a nationalist. Indeed, a pause in his work actually occurred in the 30's. When he resumed publishing in the 40's, the "Marr Doctrine" was dominant. Except for his dissertation *Course of a Scientific Grammar of the Cheremis Language* (manuscript, Joškar-Ola, 1946), his linguistic articles did not start flowing more freely until the 50's. His friend, the educator and linguist Karmazin, wrote especially in the 30's on problems of the case system, orthography, and other points of importance for a normative grammar.

One of most important results of Vasilyev's grammatical investigation is the fact that he was the first correctly to analyze the past tenses in the very confusing Cheremis conjugations. This he accomplished by making a distinction unknown until this time between "apparency" of the action, Russ. *očevidnost'* (about which the speaker reports, so to speak, as an "eye-witness") and the "non-apparency" of the action, Russ. *neočevidnost'* (about which the speaker reports in the words of the third person or in the form of conjecture), and this distinction he applied to the respective past tenses. This terminology has since been adopted not only in the Cheremis grammars but also in the grammars of related Volga-Finnic and Permic languages. He also was the first to correctly define the number of verbal adverbs in Cheremis.

*Delineating the Bases of the Written Language*. – One particular difficulty in creating a Cheremis literary language was found in the division of the people into three dialect groups. Until the establishment of the Cheremis Autonomous Republic, newspapers and books appeared in different dialects. Thereafter the headquarters of the publication authorities in Moscow decreed that it was permissible to publish only in two main branches of the Cheremis language: Meadow and Hill Cheremis. From that time on the two literary languages began to develop. The east Cheremis started in 1938 gradually to change over to the written language of the Meadow Cheremis, which was closest to their own language. The fact that the Hill Cheremis have a written language gave Cheremis linguists much trouble. In contrast to Mordvin, in which Erza and Mokša are recognized as equal written languages, bilingualism in Cheremis is to a certain degree suffered only as a necessary evil. No agreement can be reached on the question of whether Hill Cheremis should be considered an individual language or not. This has been a point of debate among linguists in discussions held for that very purpose as early as 1926 and later during the first linguistic conference of the Mari in 1937. Yet the debate was still going on in the 50's. Later we shall return to the present state of the problem.

One fact admitted by all Cheremis linguists, apart from the differences in phonetics and a number of grammatical forms, is the existence of more than a thousand common words in Hill Cheremis, which are not understood by the Meadow and Eastern Cheremis. The differences are sufficiently great so that students from the Hill Cheremis territory need one year at the Pedagogical Academy in Joškar-Ola to learn the local language in order to be able to use it tolerably well in speaking and writing.

In the beginning they continued to use the Russian alphabet as a writing system in the form as applied by the Russian missionaries to the three main dialects in the 19th century. There were strong trends in the 30's to latinize the alphabet, a process also evident among various other peoples of the USSR at this time. But public opinion was against it, as it were, and in 1938 a final reform of the alphabet on the basis of the Russian writing system was effected. Orthography was one of the most pressing tasks for linguists. This was unified in the aforementioned conference and during the same year normative orthographical dictionaries appeared. The new editions of 1948 contained only minor changes.

*Individual Scholarly Investigations.* – A number of articles by Vasiljev and Karmazin on Cheremis phonetics appeared, which concerned themselves mainly with the stress system. P. A. Bogorodickij attempted to give characteristics of the sound system (*IzvAN*, 3, Moscow, 1944). A definite progress in research was his conclusion that the so-called "vowel harmony" occurred in Hill Cheremis according to the principle of palatalization, in Meadow and in Eastern Cheremis, on the other hand, according to the principle of labialization. The greatest vagueness seemed to be in the study of the quantity of vowels for which the author found seven gradations. One can not yet speak of true scholarly phonetic studies. Yet a fine description of the existing sounds in all dialects was furnished by N. T. Pengitov "On the phonetic composition of present day Cheremis" (*Učenye Zapiski*, Joškar-Ola, 1948).

Apart from the above mentioned basic morphological work of Vasiljev and Karmazin three main problems were investigated separately: the case system (M. P. Čhaidze in *Trudy*, Kozmodem'jansk, 1940), the tenses of the verb (Čhaidze, Moscow-Leningrad, 1939), and the modes of action (Russ. *vid*) of the verb (Vasiljev in the collection of articles *Nekotorye voprosy* . . . Joškar-Ola, 1948). The analysis of periphrastic means of expression for completion or non-completion of an action, as well as the characterization of the momentary and iterative mode of action in Vasiljev's investigations became the bases for all subsequent discussions.

## 2. *After 1950*

*The Present Generation of Scholars.* – In the Scientific Research Institute for Language, Literature and History of the Marij Autonomous Republic founded in 1930, young researchers were gradually groomed to be future scientific workers. More than a dozen young Cheremis linguists defended their dissertations in the 50's, namely in Moscow, Leningrad, and even in Tartu. The resultant upsurge in Cheremis linguistics can be seen in the numerous contributions to scholarly journals of the research institute *Trudy* (6-13) and *Učenye Zapiski* (4-6) and of the State Pedagogical Institute *Učenye Zapiski* (9, 16, 21, 23). The names of most of these collaborators can be found in a recently published normative grammar of a new type: *The Present-day Marij Language. Phonetics* (1960), *Morphology* (1960), *Syntax* (1961). Members of the editorial staff are I. D. Galkin, N. I. Isanbaev, N. T. Pengitov, Z. F. Barceva.

*Continuating the delineation of the written language.* – Before we devote ourselves to this important new appearance in connection with the written language, we have to sketch in the present situation of the two Cheremis written languages. Of major importance was the linguistic conference of 1953 on development of the Marij literary language in Joškar-Ola (*Naučnaja sessija* . . . Tezisy dokladov; See A. A. Asylbaev's report "Scholarly meeting on problems of the development of the Marij literary language December 27-29, 1953" in *Učenye Zapiski* . . . 6.217-227, Joškar-Ola, 1954).

According to reports most speakers advocated the creation of a common literary language for all Cheremis-speaking people on the basis of Meadow-Eastern Cheremis, because 80% of all Cheremis people read and write this dialect. Concrete modes of action were resolved to make it possible to reach this goal. Therefore, rules for a new orthography were designed which approximate the orthography of the Hill Cheremis to the Meadow-Eastern. Accordingly, A. Asylbaev and Z. Učaev wrote a *Mari Orthographical Dictionary* (Joškar-Ola, 1954). This has not yet solved the problem.

Some time later, a separate orthographical dictionary of Hill Cheremis appeared, written by A. A. Savatkova (Joškar-Ola, 1956). Today, all publications in literary Hill Cheremis are limited to local newspapers, high school texts, and the literary products of local authors and poets (N. Ignatjev, P. Peršut, N. Il'jakov, and others). It no longer plays a role in the public life of the republic, that is, in radio broadcasts, theatrical performances, etc. Officially one speaks only of a Mari literary language which is based on Meadow Cheremis, and which has absorbed a few elements of Eastern Cheremis. At the same time there is a secondary "literary norm" for Hill Cheremis.[16]

The comparative dictionary of Meadow and Hill Cheremis idioms by P. G. Rybakova and Z. V. Učaev (86 pp.; Joškar-Ola, 1955) serves to bring these two literary norms closer together.

The 1953 conference stressed the role of Russian for the development of the literary languages here as well as in other republics of the Finno-Ugric nationalities. Lately, the lexicological and phraseological wealth of the dialects has been recommended more than in earlier days as a source for formation of words for the literary language.

The new normative grammar of the Cheremis language contains a section on phonetics on pp. 32-57 of Volume I. The author, L. P. Gruzov, stressed in his introduction that he had received instruction and guidance from the phoneticians from Leningrad University, especially from Professor L. R. Zinder.[17] The subject of his descrip-

[16] See *Sovremennyj marijskij jazyk. Fonetika*, p. 30 (Joškar-Ola, 1960).

[17] Zinder, *Voprosy fonetiki* (Leningrad, 1948); "Èksperimental'noe naučenie fonetika severnyx jazykov", *IzvAN*, 7 (6).579-581 (1948); see also his later works.

tions are not all the sounds found in the various dialects, but only the phonemes of the Meadow-Eastern Cheremis literary language. Of the two phonemes which are unique to Hill Cheremis, one is not mentioned at all, and the other (a variant of the reduced vowel) is barely touched upon. Also, two phonemes characteristic for the dialect of Joškar-Ola have not been accepted into the phonemic inventory of the literary language. Those four phonemes which were excluded from the literary language are listed by the author in the vowel chart in parentheses. This suits the purpose of the book, which is to give teachers and students of universities a descriptive explanation of the "Hochlautung" (standardized pronounciation). For pedagogical reasons the comparison with Russian is made, but a phonetic transcription and comparison to other Finno-Ugric languages is lacking. Only sporadically does the author make short excurses into the historical phonology of the Finno-Ugric languages. He establishes the important fact that even the shortest vowel in one-syllable words can become half-long. A number of charts containing the results of experimental phonetic measurements explain the quantitative proportions. The articulation of each individual phoneme is described exhaustively and illustrated by roentgengrams, palatograms, and kymograms.

The most important part of the grammar *The Present Day Cheremis Language* is the small volume entitled *Morfologija* (1961), for which N. T. Pengitov signs as editor in charge. All told, more than 10 collaborators have participated in the writing of the individual chapters. The word categories which are organized according to the scheme of Indo-European and Slavic grammars, are treated from the viewpoint of word formation and word mutation. Only very few indications referring to inherited material of the Finno-Ugric languages can be found, because the treatment of the material is strictly descriptive. Meadow Cheremis is to be sure placed in the foreground, but divergent forms of Eastern or Hill Cheremis are explained and examples given in the form of annotations. Therefore, the book encompasses the morphology of all three major forms of Cheremis, even if only in the literary languages. Consequently, the only quotations are from recent Cheremis literature, a restriction which appears methodologically one-sided.

A positive aspect of its methodology lies in the simultaneous treatment of word form and word meaning, which conforms to the predominant trend in present-day Soviet Russian linguistics. In the paradigms and in the form analyses the original phonetic value is given in Cyrillic letters, and the differing orthographic spelling is given in parentheses alongside. The increased knowledge of the development of languages in our days can be seen in the usually etymologically correct division of the elements of the stem and the suffixes. The divergences can be found in the formation of suffixes which have not been cleared up etymologically, as, for instance, in the case of the very difficult 7th case of the (absolute) declension, and so-called adverbial case, which might be more properly called lative. As the analysis of case usage shows, this 7th case stands between inessive and illative; in Hill Cheremis it also serves for the dative (allative). This example shows the great value of the aforementioned simultaneous treatment of form and meaning to the Finno-Ugrist. In many places in this grammar the linguist finds extremely important explanations of the use of certain forms with words of particular classes of meaning. It is only now becoming possible to establish such facts in a Cheremis grammar when native Cheremis begin to analyze the indubitably correct meanings of forms and word-groups which are in use. This morphology is, at the moment, the best and most important.

The grammar is extremely instructive in dealing with the verb, with its 6 past tenses, 4 modes, and 4 "genera", and last, but not least, with the formation of "verb-pairs" by means of 31 auxiliary verbs to express widely different modalities and aspects of verbal action. The conciseness and lucidity of the grammar is remarkable, considering such complexity.

As Part 3 of *The Present Day Cheremis Language*, the *Syntax of the Compound Sentence*, was published in 1961. V. T. Timofeeva, the author of the major part, calls it "a first essay on the syntax of the sentence in Cheremis". Unfortunately, major emphasis is given to the subjunctive subordinate clauses, which come into the written language due to the influence of Russian, while participial or gerundial constructions are not given their due. N. I. Isanbaev describes, in the appendix on direct-speech and indirect-speech in subordinate clauses, the pertinent groups of verbs and the constructions of subordinate clauses. Actually this syntax belongs to the field of stylistics.

A tremendous step forward in the creation of the literary language is the normative dictionary entitled *Mari-Russian Dictionary* (*Marijsko-Russkij Slovar'*, 21,000 words, Moscow, 1956). B. A. Serebrennikov is the editor-in-charge. The authors of the short grammar given in the appendix are A. A. Savatkova and Z. V. Učaev. The vocabulary is not limited to Meadow Cheremis, but also contains differing varieties of Eastern and Hill Cheremis. Dialect words and expressions from the spoken language are also included and the word meaning is explained where necessary by idiomatic phrases.

*Individual Scholarly Investigations.* – L. P. Gruzov, the above-mentioned expert, wrote a series of papers on phonetics, for instance his dissertation *Vowels and Consonants of Cheremis* (*Meadow dialect*) *in the light of experimental data.* His article "Modifications of Cheremis Phonemes" (*Trudy*, Joškar-Ola, 1957) and "The Quantity of Cheremis Vowels" (*Trudy*, Joškar-Ola, 1958) deal with experimental phonetics. As a phonetician, he is presently investigating various dialects.

Very little investigation has been conducted into the morphology of nouns. One of the more sizeable works is the dissertation by M. F. Družinina *The Locative Cases in Cheremis* (Moscow, 1951). The author arrives at the conclusion that only three locative cases are to be included in the paradigm. Consequently, only 7 cases belong to the declension proper, a simplification incorporated immediately into textbooks. Unclear, though, remains the so-called "adverbial case" (lative).

The main interest of research was directed toward the verb, especially the tenses and modes of action or aspects (Russian *vid*). Not forms, but their meanings, are the concern, in which tense and mode of action are closely related. V. M. Vasiljev from his first to his very last work concerned himself over and over again with these problems, and produced, as was mentioned above, completely new viewpoints of analyses. One should also mention the monograph on tense by L. P. Vasikova *The Past Tense of the Verb in Cheremis* (Tartu, 1955), a dissertation. She considers the durative and resultative modes of action characteristic basic meanings of the past tenses. However, Russ. "neočevidnost' " can also be contained in them. In opposition to this, L. R. Anisimova emphasized that the tense only characterizes the mode of action (in her pedagogical work *Evaluation of the Grammar of the Mother Tongue in Studying the Russian Verb in Cheremis Schools* (Moscow, 1955); see also her article "On the Question of the Verb Tenses in Hill dialect of Cheremis" (*Trudy*, Joškar-Ola, 1956).

Serebrennikov participated in the discussion with his aforementioned doctoral dissertation *The Categories of Tense and Aspect in the Finno-Ugric languages of the Permic and Volgaic Groups*. He is to be given credit for distinguishing in the past forms between the two categories of the tense and mode as having different lexical meaning. By comparing with related languages he establishes a number of forms of the "absentive" (Modus obliquus) which are formally identical with the tenses.

Concerning the question of modes of action, he opposed the prevalent opinion that in Cheremis individual modes of action and aspects identified through verbal suffixes and periphrastic forms existed similarly as in the Russian verb. He proves that these forms are possible only with a very limited number of verbs, and that one therefore can speak only of *vidovye klassy*, that is, aspective verbal groups. His investigation also shows that the system of modes of action in Cheremis became disordered and retrogressive under the influence of Turkic languages through new means of expressing modality and the aspect of action.

Finally, V. M. Vasiljev states in his last publication *Materialy po grammatike ...* (Joškar-Ola, 1958) on the problem of the Russian *vid* in Cheremis that there are no phonetic facts in Cheremis verbs which indicate the conclusion of an action, and that the past forms can express either the conclusion or the non-conclusion of action.

Yet the discussion goes on concerning the question of analytical ways of expression for modality and aspect. This way of expression exists in the characteristically Cheremis combination of two verbs into a pair, whereby periphrastic forms are created. M. P. Čhaidze recently devoted to this combination his article "Paired Verbs in Cheremis" (Joškar-Ola, 1960). The author attempts to replace the old imprecise terms with the term "paired verbs", which he invented. He exhaustively investigates the interrelationship of the verbs which were combined into pairs. He establishes 4 types of association or subordination of verb partners. With only two of them does the second component, the so-called auxiliary verb (modifier), express aspect of action. His understanding of aspect is the expression of the course of action in time. From the Turkologist A. N. Kononov he adopts the term for an action aimed at a definite goal: "teleological action". The author finds the term "teleological action" realized in two types of Cheremis verbal composition. A chart shows the comparison with the Turkic languages which Cheremis exceeds in number and function of the so-called modifiers, the auxiliary verbs in the verbal composition, by far.

V. M. Vasiljev writes on the old literary language in his article "Literary Monuments in Cheremis of the end of the 18th and the first half of the 19th centuries" (*Učenye Zapiski*, Joškar-Ola, 1953). A very positive evaluation of the translation of the New Testament of 1874 had been given earlier by S. I. Èman in the first issue of *Trudy* (Kozmodem'jansk, 1939-40).

Theoretical contributions to lexicology were made by G. S. Patrušev *Main Approaches to Enrichment of the Vocabulary of the Cheremis Language* (by application of the inner possibilities and laws of the language and by borrowing words – dissertation, Leningrad, 1955); I. S. Galkin, "On the History of the Common Finno-Ugric Vocabulary in Cheremis" (*Trudy*, Joškar-Ola, 1958); and A. A. Savatkova *Russian Loan Words in Hill Cheremis* (dissertation, Moscow, 1953).

## THE PERMIAN GROUP

### A. VOTYAK (UDMURT) LINGUISTICS

#### 1. *Before 1950*

*Ear.y Researchers.* – Directly after the Revolution the founders of Votyak linguistic were educators and writers. They were members of the generation who had studied under the Czarist regime in Kazan or Leningrad. Of these, one should name the following:

I. V. Jakovlev, whose *Udmurt kyl rad'jan* (an elementary grammar written in Votyak, Iževsk, 1927) had three editions in a very short period of time. The Kazan school shows in his early work *Comparative Dictionary of Votyak Dialects* (Kazan, 1920).

P. P. Glezdenev and M. I. Iljin emphasized in articles and drafts of dictionaries the relationship of Votyak to the adjoining Finno-Ugric languages. At this time A. P. Emeljanov made his scholarly investigation of Votyak, his *Grammar of the Votyak Language* (Leningrad, 1927) is an attempt to write a historical grammar. Its main value lies in the fact that the author bases his work on the research of leading Finno-Ugrists outside the USSR, who investigated Votyak, and in the carefully selected examples of not previously published forms, which are investigated morphologically. Very active in lexicological and especially morphological research was S. P. Žujkov. He even appeared before the Academy in Moscow in 1932 with a lecture on Votyak case-suffixes (*Trudy* I, Iževsk, 1935). He also read papers at the first linguistic congress in Iževsk in 1937 on "The Bases of the Grammar of the Votyak Language" (*Tezisy* . . . Iževsk, 1937).

*Delineating the Bases of the Literary Language.* – The Votyaks did not have any particular problem in the creation of an alphabet, as they were able to continue the alphabet in current use in the 19th century, which was Cyrillic. Nevertheless, the Latinization of the alphabet was also discussed by the Votyaks after 1928. S. P.

Žujkov advocated the so-called "unification" of the writing, on which Bubrix commented in *Kul'tura i piś'mennost' Vostoka*, 10 (Moscow, 1931).

Votyak was in a particularly favorable situation as regards the standardization of its grammar and vocabulary. The literary language was based on the central dialects of the Udmurt Republic and accepted without difficulty lesser known words or forms from other dialects. Moreover, dialect differences in Votyak are generally small. An important step towards standardization of the literary language was the linguistic conference of 1937 in Iževsk, which resulted in the first rule book of orthography and a book in Votyak entitled *Materials for the Grammar of the Udmurt Language* (Iževsk, 1937), published by the Scientific Research Institute of the Council of Ministers of the Udmurt Autonomous Republic (founded in 1936).

Of basic importance as a normative dictionary was the *Udmurt-Russian Dictionary* (Iževsk, 1948), with a short grammatical treatise by P. M. Perevoščikov (76 pp.).

*Individual Scholarly Investigations.* – Apart from the aforementioned *Grammar of the Votyak Language* by A. J. Emeljanov, only one larger research work needs to be mentioned, namely D. V. Bubrix's *Historical Phonetics of the Udmurt Language* (Iževsk, 1948). The aim of the work is to analyze the Votyak phonetic system on a historical basis. Bubrix sets up 33 phonemes. According to Bubrix, of all the vowels, 7 different vowels occur in non-initial syllables. He treats consonant changes by dialects, consonant mutation or loss according to the position in the word. Bubrix also attempts a reconstruction of the original Permic phonetic system, using only Permic material. As he does not use Finno-Ugric etymologies, his attempt at reconstruction must needs lead to erroneous conclusions. In the field of dialectology, two of the earliest collections are T. K. Borisov's *South Votyak Songs* (Iževsk, 1929) and the *Udmurt-Russian Explanatory Dictionary* (Iževsk, 1932).

## 2. *Since 1950*

*The Present-Day Generation of Researchers.* – During the last decade six young Votyak linguists have defended their dissertations. The oldest member of the Scientific Institute, P. N. Perevoščikov, earned the degree of Doctor of Philosophy. A number of linguists are lecturers at pedagogical universities. The linguistic research institute is left to its own devices, and has a relatively small number of staff members. There are no branches of the Academy in the Udmurt Autonomous Republic, as is the case in the Komi Autonomous Republic. Particularly lacking are suitable experts for the investigation of dialects.

*Continuation of the Delineation of the Literary Language.* – This work concentrates, as with all the other new literary languages of the USSR, on normative grammar. Lately, the *Grammar of the Present Day Udmurt Language*, Phonetics and Morphology (Iževsk, 1962) was finally published. It is a collective enterprise by a number of authors. Editor-in-charge is P. N. Perevoščikov, members of the editorial staff are the lecturers of the Pedagogical University in Iževsk I. P. Alatyrev, and A. A. Pozdeeva, as well as the candidates V. M. Vahrušev‎ and I. V. Tarakanov. Among the authors of individual parts of the grammar are members of the Linguistic Research Institute, lecturers of pedagogical institutes in Iževsk and Glazov, editors of the Udmurt Book Publishing House, and a member of the editorial staff of a newspaper. The linguistic department of the Academy in Moscow is represented by its head, Academy member B. A. Serebrennikov, by Professor V. I. Lytkin, and his wife, a native Votyak, T. I. Tepljašina.

The latter two authored the voluminous first part of the grammar, *Phonetics*, pp. 7-55. In this part a precise description of the Votyak phonetic system is given for the first time. It distinguishes itself by showing up the differences between the dialects with pertinent examples, which is not the case in the morphological part. It is in keeping with the pedagogical purpose of this grammar that the pronunciation of the vowels is illustrated. Oscillograms show the influence of stress on vowel length. Statistics covering the percentual proportion of vowels and consonants show that there are approximately 129 consonants for 100 vowels. Very instructive is the distinctly differing pronunciation of affricates in the individual dialects.

For the Finno-Ugrist, the paradigms of the conjugation and the declension are of great informational value. They show, according to the present day linguistic feeling of the Votyak, what belongs to this "common language". It is important to see that the approximative in *-lań* be considered one of the 15 cases of the substantive which, according to recent opinions, had been counted among the adverbs. On the other hand, secondary forms, as for instance the adessive and allative, which developed out of postpositions, were left out of the paradigm with justification. This could have given cause for treating the important problem of the postpositions in case functions. However, normative grammar is too schematic in this regard. In the treatment of the so-called possessive declension, it is commendable that the use of certain possessive suffixes was explained in connection with certain groups of meanings of the substantives.

Excurses into the history of language (V. I. Alatyrev) and the analysis of word structure (with occasional etymologies) complete the impression of the scholarly nature of this work, which signifies great progress in Votyak linguistics.

It seems odd but justified that two classes of conjugations are distinguished (according to the vowel between stem and ending), as the difference between the respective endings can be seen in the various tenses and modes. Evidently a new development of linguistic feeling is in the offing.

The development of the vocabulary of the written language will be fostered by the new edition of a large *Russian-Udmurt Dictionary* (Moscow, 1956). The editor-in-chief is V. M. Vahrušev‎. It contains 40,000 words of Russian with Votyak translation. It was designed on the basis of the guidelines which were laid down by the *State Publishing House For Foreign and National Dictionaries* (*Slovnik dlja russko-nacional'nyx slovarej* (Moscow, 1951). It was planned for translators of Russian works into Votyak, for writers, teachers, and persons who wish to learn Votyak through the medium of

Russian. In many cases the Russian word as a loanword is placed first in the Votyak translation, but Votyak words with the same meaning are also cited. Thus, one nevertheless gets an insight into the wealth of the Votyak language, and particularly in the case of phrases which are generally translated by specifically Votyak expressions.

Similar to the above mentioned Udmurt dictionary, this dictionary has as an appendix, a *Short Grammatical Sketch of the Udmurt Language* by P. N. Perevoščikov.

*Individual Scholarly Investigations*. – Votyak linguistics is still in its infancy as far as questions of phonetics are concerned. First attempts can be found in the investigation of dialects (I. V. Tarakanov) and in Ü. Bajčura's "On the Character of the Accent in Udmurt" (Tallinn, 1959).

In morphology most of the attention of researchers is given to the verb, in particular the nominal forms. This is the specialty of P. N. Perevoščikov. Apart from individual investigations, as for instance on the verbal adverb in *-sa* (*Tezisy dokladov na soveščanii* . . ., Moscow, 1954) he distinguished himself with a voluminous monograph entitled *Verbal Adverbs and Verbal Adverbial Constructions in the Udmurt Language* (328 pp., Iževsk, 1959).

In the first chapter, he discusses the morphological markers of 5 adverbial forms (divided into two groups according to the possibility or impossibiliy of combination with possessive suffixes). This shows up the methodological difficult of discussing the verbal adverbs by themselves, separately from the verbal nouns. The pattern of Indo-European and Slavic grammars induces the scholar to divide the nominal forms of the Votyak verb into word classes which has a particularly disadvantageous effect on the respective chapters on the *Grammar of the Present-Day Udmurt Language*, pp. 255-259. The particular value of the work can be found in the analysis of the functions of the verbal adverbs in the third part of the monograph. Here the Finno-Ugrist finds genuinely interpretative material for comparative and syntactic studies (for instance on the question of the Nominative absolute).

A collection of articles of varied content is offered by V. I. Alatyrev in the volume edited by him entitled *Problems of Udmurt Philology*, Vol. I (Iževsk, 1959). It contains problems of the development of the Udmurt vocabulary (pp. 5-39), word investigations (comparative and etymological, pp. 40-72), an able and exhaustive investigation of the "Verbs of Fictive Action" (pp. 73-139), which the author considers a grammatical category by itself, on the history of the suffix *-ći* in Votyak (pp. 140-163), on several expressions of mode of action in Votyak (pp. 164-203 – this article was evidently written before the appearance of newer investigations and is therefore out of date), on phonetic transcription and on the treatment of various sentence components in teaching.

A leading contributor to the field of lexicology was V. M. Vahrušev. His main topic is the role of Russian in the development of the Votyak literary language. His dissertation *The Socio-Political Vocabulary in Udmurt* (Moscow, 1955) is devoted to the latest loan-words.

During the "Scientific Conference on Problems of Udmurt Language and Literature" in Iževsk in 1952, P. M. Jašin emphasized the importance of dialect study for the enrichment of the literary language. P. N. Perevoščikov underscored the importance of the structural idiosyncracies of Udmurt, which should be retained even in in adopting Russian idioms (*Naučnoje soveščanije po voprosam udmurtskogo jazyka i pis'mennosti*, *Tezisy dokladov*, Iževsk, 1952).

The first scholarly investigation of a Votyak dialect is a dissertation of a staff member at the Linguistic Academy in Moscow, T. I. Tepljašina, *The Tylovaj Dialect of Udmurt* (Moscow, 1955), in which she discusses with extreme thoroughness and knowledge of the material phonetic and morphologic traits as well as geographical borders of the dialect. On the phonetic characteristics of the same dialect the author published an article (*Zapiski* 18, Iževsk, 1957).

In 1956-1957, I. V. Tarakanov undertook an expedition (with the assistance of the University of Tartu) to the Votyaks in the Tatar Autonomous Republic, in particular to the district of Bavlini. He wrote an article on the phonetic features of this dialect (*TRÜT*, 77, Tartu, 1959) and a dissertation entitled *Phonetic Features of the Bavlini Dialect of Udmurt in the Light of Experimental Data* (Tartu, 1959). Ů. Bajčura discusses the stress relationships in two-syllable words on the basis of kymograms in his "The Character of the Accent in Udmurt", *ESA*, 5.294-307 (Tallinn, 1959).

Sample Votyak texts from various dialects were recently published by T. I. Tepljašina in the above mentioned *Problems in Finno-Ugric Linguistics* (Moscow-Leningrad, 1962).

Folkloristic language material is offered in the book *Proverbs and Sayings of the Votyak People* – Poslovicy i pogovorki udmurtskogo naroda (Iževsk, 1960), 208 pp.

## B. KOMI LINGUISTICS

### I. *Komi-Zyryan*

#### 1. *Before 1950*

*Early Researchers.* – Two names should be written in glowing letters over the first chapter of Zyryan linguistics after the Revolution: A. S. Sidorov and V. I. Lytkin.

The native Zyryan A. S. Sidorov (1892-1953) was basically a folklorist, ethnographer, and archeologist, but also won great merit in the field of linguistics. During his scholarly career of forty years, he travelled through the entire Zyryan country, on foot and by boat. He must have travelled 10,000 km. in order to collect the monuments of the intellectual culture of his people, and also to collect linguistic material from story-tellers of various dialects. The result of his work is on the one hand the discovery of important linguistic documents, on the other hand valuable collections and editions of Zyryan dialect material.

Among his discoveries belong lost monuments of the old Zyryan literary language, for instance a few lines of the lost Permic Script and liturgical texts with chants in the translation language of St. Stephan, the Apostle of the Zyryans who died in 1396. This is a copy in Cyrillic letters. This discovery was made in 1919, and published in *Problems in Finno-Ugric Linguistics* (1962).

Of great importance for literature as well as history of language was his discovery of literary works by the first important Zyryan poet, A. I. Kuratov (1839-1875), in the poet's own handwriting. It contained not only poetic works, but also linguistic papers by Kuratov on the grammar and vocabulary of mid-19th Century Zyryan. This made it possible to issue the collected works of Kuratov on the occasion of the poet's 100th birthday in 1939 in Syktyvkar, with an introduction by P. Doronin. Volume II contains the linguistic papers.

Systematic dialect collections were made by Sidorov and Lytkin, mostly in the years from 1928 to 1932, and they were published in a collection (Sbornik) I (Syktyvkar, 1930). Together with Lytkin, he worked on a large dictionary of the Komi dialects.

Vasilij Iljič Lytkin, nowadays the leading Zyryan linguist and well-known Finno-Ugrist in the Soviet Union, was born in 1895 in Syktyvkar. He finished his studies at Moscow University in 1925 and subsequently studied Finno-Ugric philology in Finland and Hungary. From 1928 to 1932, he organized the collecting of Zyryan dialect material with such great success that in the first decades more was achieved in the Komi Republic than among any other Finno-Ugric people of the USSR. The results of the work of "The Commission for Collecting the Vocabulary and the Study of the Dialects of the Komi Language" were published in the *Sbornik I* (Syktyvkar, 1930), and the *Sbornik II* (Moscow, 1931).

At the same time, together with Sidorov, he finished editing the manuscript of a large comparative dictionary of the Komi dialects. Suddenly this dialect research was interrupted, the commission was dissolved in 1933, and the manuscript of the dialect dictionary was subsequently lost. Lytkin spent the following years in Moscow as lecturer and scientific collaborator and earned a Ph. D. in Permic Languages. From 1939 to 1959 he was Professor of Russian at various pedagogical universities of the USSR (Čkalov, Moscow, Rjazan). In the 50's he became senior staff member of the division of Finno-Ugric languages at the Linguistic Department of the Academy of Sciences of the USSR in Moscow, where he presently is engaged in research work, and supervises the graduate work of a number of young scholars (Zyryans, Permiacs, Mordvins, etc.). His more important publication in his special fields appeared mostly in the 50's. It should be noted that he is also a poet well received and well liked by the Zyryans. His poems were published under the pseudonym Il'ja Vaś.

*Delineation of the Bases of the Written Language.* – The task of creating a suitable Zyryan alphabet was rather complicated because the modest literary tradition of the 19th and early 20th centuries varied in the different dialects. The Zyryan alphabet has been changed three times since the Revolution. The first alphabet was based on Cyrillic and Latin characters, compiled by Molodcov in 1918. It was not yet fully suitable to reproduce Zyryan sounds in a generally understandable fashion. As in many other national republics of the USSR, the Latin alphabet was also introduced into the Autonomous Komi Republic in 1929, following the resolution of a linguistic conference in Syktyvkar. This "New Alphabet", or NA for short, was abolished in 1936, following the example of other republics, because it was allegedly based on bourgeois influences. In its stead, a third alphabet was adopted which consisted solely of Cyrillic letters plus the Latin *ö*. The ostensible differences from the Votyak alphabet are actually only a different way of denoting the affricates and non-palatalized *i*. There is no difference in the normative pronunciation between those two related languages.

The standardization of orthography since 1936, since the introduction of the third alphabet, is one of the specific tasks of the Department for Language and Literature at the Scientific Research Institute of the Komi Republic, which was founded in 1932 in Syktyvkar. The ad hoc "Committee for Orthography" issued the orthographical dictionary of the Komi language in 1939. There were a number of revisions and reprints: 1942, 1953[18] and 1959.

Normative grammars were first created for the high schools. Lytkin and Sidorov edited the first these of in 1928 and 1929, which were followed by others (1934). The Scientific Research Institute has been in charge of such publications since 1939. The 1948 edition already offers a rather exhaustive description of Zyryan phonetics and morphology. A branch of the Academy of Sciences of the USSR was established in Syktyvkar in 1944, the so-called "Komi Filial AN SSSR". The existing research institute was associated with it and permanently enlarged.

*Individual Scholarly Investigations.* – D. V. Bubrix's *Grammar of the Komi-Zyryan Literary Language* (Leningrad, 1949) deserves special mention. This excellent work, which was not drawn up on the pattern of Slavic grammars, is the result of Bubrix's stay in Syktyvkar, 1941-44. In this book the author offers, besides phonetics, exhaustive morphological analyses of the forms of the declensions and conjugations and discusses especially the use of verbal nouns and verbal adverbs. The present head of the Department of Language and Literature, N. A. Kolegova, wrote her dissertation on *The Adverbs of the Komi Language* (Syktyvkar, 1947).

## 2. *Since 1950*

*The Present-Day Generation of Scholars.* – During the last decade more than ten young scholars have defended their dissertations on Zyryan language (and literature). Three doctoral dissertations on Permic languages must also be mentioned, namely those by V. I. Lytkin, A. S. Sidorov, and B. A. Serebrennikov. A few *aspirants* of Zyryan and Permic extraction are preparing their dissertations at this time. The department gained new specialists, particularly in the field of literature, folklore, and even folk music. Besides this, a young scholar by the name of E. S. Guljaev works in

[18] See A. I. Podorova, "Voprosy orfografii komi jazyka", *Trudy Komi Filial AN SSSR*, 1 (Syktyvkar, 1953).

the field of Finno-Ugric languages. All told, there are twenty staff members in the department.

*Continuating the Delineation of the Literary Language.* – After Marr's "new doctrine" had been condemned, there was in the Komi Republic, similar to other autonomous republics, a conference on problems of study of the Komi language under the guidance of the Academy in Syktyvkar in 1952.[19] The main problem was the role of Russian in the development of the new literary language. The senior scholar of Zyryan linguistics, A. S. Sidorov, who was one of the speakers, advocated utilizing the wealth of the colloquial language and the creative use of the dialects for new word formations. He was supported also by his Votyak colleagues. He was sharply attacked by one of the speakers, who claimed that he intended to nullify the role of Russian in the creation of the new literary language. Even Serebrennikov was censured in spite of the fact that he spoke against substituting new Zyryan words for the customary Russian terms of scientific, social, and political life, and warned against the spread of "dialectisms".[20] It is quite evident that Russian terminology was used in the 50's even for expressions of cultural life. It is therefore understandable that during a conference of writers and linguists in March, 1960 in Syktyvkar the opinion was again expressed that writers, above all, should study the living language of the people, and the wealth of the dialects, in order to use them creatively in their artistic language. Nobody disagreed with these opinions, and it seems that the situation is going to improve now.

Very beneficial for the literary language was the publication of the modern normative grammar *The Present-Day Komi Language: Textbook for secondary schools, Part I: Phonetics, vocabulary, morphology*, edited by V. I. Lytkin, 312 pp. (Syktyvkar, 1955). Nine Zyryan linguists collaborated on this book. This descriptive grammar does not limit itself exclusively to the Zyryan written language and a short excursus in the dialects of the Komi ASSR but offers in many cases parallels from Komi-Permic and Jazva-Komi and even linguistic historical discussions referring to old Zyryan literary relics, and to Votyak.

The introduction gives a broad view of the three major forms of Komi. The voluminous phonetics part (pp. 13-78), written by Lytkin, treats the characteristic phonetic phenomena in the field of consonantism, among others assimilation. Thirty-three phonemes are described and we learn that the phonetic principle generally determines orthography. The chapter on vocabulary contains notes on chronological strata, archaisms, neologisms, and discussions of dictionaries.

The largest part is the morphology (pp. 111-299). The extensive section on word formation is followed by the section on categories of word classes. Sixteen cases have been incorporated in the paradigm of the literary language, but excluding the Preclusive in *-śa*, which is usually counted as a case by Finno-Ugrists.

[19] A. S. Sidorov, "Soveščanie po voprosam izučenija komi jazyka", *VJa* 4.144 (1953).

[20] One can see the actual practice in the article by N. A. Kolegova, "O nekotoryx voprosax istorii komi pis'mennosti", *Istoriko-filologičeskij sbornik* 3.52 (Syktyvkar, 1956).

Of even greater importance to the literary language is the recently published *Komi-Russian Dictionary* (Moscow, 1961, 923 pp.), edited by Professor Lytkin. It contains approximately 25,000 Komi-Zyryan words (more than all earlier Zyryan dictionaries) and represents the vocabulary of the more recent Zyryan language. It is interesting that a considerable proportion of the words were derived from the dialects, especially from the Syktyvkar region. This shows how much the literary language is based on the colloquial language and how writers have refined these words and adapted them to more sophisticated uses, enlarging their scope of meanings for the communication of more complicated ideas and sentiments. The enriching of the literary language is effected through the vocabulary of the dialects. At the same time a movement to renovate the language can be discerned. Obsolete and colloquial words are given figurative meanings and new derivatives and compounds are created. Simultaneously, there are naturally a great number of Russian loanwords. The very fine grammatical sketch written in Russian which is included in the book cites some examples of the work of the linguistic renovators. Very useful is the list of Zyryan suffixes and the list of Zyryan place names. In the articles on words, which are arranged in alphabetical order, idioms are given to explain word meanings, sayings, and proverbs. All these have been translated, not only in their present but also in their original meaning, and a literal translation is given. This is very valuable.

*Individual Scholarly Investigations.* – V. J. Lytkin has competently written on Zyryan phonetics. In his treatise "On Problems of Vocalism in Permic Languages" (*TIJa*, I, Moscow, 1952), he proves by the now acceptable method of comparative and historical linguistics that the Finno-Ugric palatal vowels have become velar in Permic languages. As far as Finno-Ugric vocalism is concerned, he goes too far, though, in reducing all proto-Permic narrow vowels to Finno-Ugric reduced vowels.[21]

His latest treatise, "Some Problems of Vocalism in Finno-Ugric Languages", was published in *Voprosy Finno-Ugorskogo Jazykoznanija* (Moscow-Leningrad, 1962). Lytkin shows, following an introduction on the present state of this heavily debated problem, that the only successful method is to investigate primarily the system of phonemes of the individual languages and their dialects in great detail. This treatise is supposed to initiate such investigations. He chose three archaic dialects of the Komi-Zyryan, the Jažva-Komi and Votyak, in order to trace the development of the Permic [o]. With the help of Finno-Ugric etymology, he finds three type-variants of the etymological Permic [o] of the initial syllable in sounds of the Jažva and Votyak dialect. These triple variants have exact parallel in the variation of reflexes which have been left over in the inherited Permic words by the corresponding Finno-Ugric palatal vowels in opposition to the Finno-Ugric velar vowels. The treatise shows a high scholarly level in its method and in the caution with which conclusions are drawn.

An important contribution to the phonetics of the Permic languages is the first part of the *Historical Grammar of the Komi Language* (Syktyvkar, 1957).

[21] Cf. E. Itkonen, "Zur Geschichte des Vokalismus der ersten Silbe im Tscheremissischen und in den permischen Sprachen", *Finnisch-Ugrische Forschungen*, 31(3).335 (Helsinki, 1953-5).

A number of *kandidat* dissertations are devoted to topics of morphology: E. G. Žiževa, *The Category of Grammatical Numbers in the Komi Language* (Leningrad, 1950; cf. also "On the Importance of the Suffix *-öś*", *Lingvističeskij Sbornik*, Syktyvkar, 1952); M. A. Saharova, *The Adjective in the Komi Language* (Syktyvkar, 1953; cf. also "On the Problem of Substantivation of Adjectives and Adjectivization of Substantives", *Istoriko-filologičeskij sbornik* 3, Syktyvkar, 1956); A. I. Podorova, *The Particles in the Komi Language* (Moscow, 1954); E. S. Guljaev, *The Cases with the Suffix -ś in the Komi Language* (Moscow, 1958). A number of articles on the origin and the function of some cases were published by the latter author: On the Egressive (*Soveščanie*, Moscow, 1959), the Elative and other *s*'-endings (*Istoriko-filologičeskij sbornik*, 4-5, Syktyvkar, 1958-60). As a pupil of Lytkin, he used the methods of comparative and historical linguistics. The most recent investigation of the cases is by Serebrennikov in his article, "On the History of the Case System of the Permic Languages" (*Voprosy* . . ., Moscow-Leningrad, 1962), in which he adopts a viewpoint different from that of Guljaev. His articles on the flexion of nouns (*Istoriko-filologičeskij sbornik*, 4, Syktyvkar, 1958) and on the endings of the declensions (*Istoriko-filologičeskij sbornik*, 5, Syktyvkar, 1960) should be used for comparison.

Serebrennikov treats the verb in the previously mentioned esssay *The Categories of Tense and Aspect in the Finno-Ugric languages of the Permic and Volgaic Groups* in a fashion considerably different from that of Sidorov. In the treatment of the tenses of Zyryan, Serebrennikov evokes interest by emphasizing that the preterite can occasionally have the meaning of the present perfect and past perfect. In the present perfect, which is formally identical with the perfect participle, he divides from the temporal meaning the modal meaning of "non-obviousness" which occurs in certain definite contexts, and that is, that the speaker relates an action with the word s o others (not as an eye-witness) or as a mere conjecture. The second part of his *Historical Grammar of the Komi Language, Part II: Morphology*, by this author, is to be expected in the near future.

The major emphasis of Zyryan linguistics of the last century is in the field of Old Zyryan and in the field of dialectology. There are early records of Zyryan, some of which go back to the beginning of the 15th century. They appear, even if only somewhat more recent copies, in the times of the Apostle and first "bishop of the Permians", St. Stephan, who died in 1396. Some of the oldest documents are inscriptions on ikons and entries of glosses in old codices using the so-called Permic script, which was introduced by St. Stephan. By virtue of his translations of the Greek Orthodox liturgy and various Bible texts, etc., St. Stephan became the creater of the Old Zyryan literary language. Since these texts as well as the Permic script have been lost except for a few remnants, the interest of the scholar has been directed for more than 200 years to those written records of this epoch.

After the Revolution Sidorov and Lytkin, above all others, searched vigorously for such written records, and also investigated the Old Zyryan language. Their work could not be published until after 1950.

Lytkin's fundamental work *The Old Permic Language*, texts, grammar, dictionary (*AN SSSR*, Moscow, 1952) deserves widest attention. In the first part of the work, Lytkin shows initially the preserved records of the "Old Permic alphabet" in photographic copies, All told there are 12, most of which have been unknown until now. They are followed (also in photographic copies) by the three oldest written records in Permic Script, with a reconstruction of the text, the reading, a translation, and linguistic apparatus. In the third section we find the old Zyryan texts in Russian script in two variants (Lepechin-Evgenij). Aside from the easily readable reconstruction of the text, there are 22 plates with photographic copies. This is followed by Russian texts in Permic script, which was used by some scribes as a form of secret writing. The fifth part offers a linguistic evaluation in its "grammar of the Old Permic language". An alphabetic index of words and an appendix containing Lepechin's dictionary complete this carefully executed work. For the study of the signs of Permic script there is a chart of the names of the letters from the preserved alphabet and a table with illustrations of these signs arranged by documents. For the sake of comparison, Cyrillic and Greek letters are added.[22] Lytkin traces the majority of the Permic script back to the Greek minuscle, while Sidorov sees more similarities to the Old Church Slavic cursive.

Supplementing Lytkin's research on Old Zyryan records are the finds made by Sidorov. Some of them have been published by Lytkin in his introduction to *Historical Grammar of the Komi Language* (Syktyvkar, 1957), but they have now been published in their entirety under Sidorov's name entitled "New Records of Old Zyryan literature" with commentary, notes, and a postface by Lytkin in *Voprosy finno-ugroskogo jazykoznanija* (AN SSR, 1962). In 1930 Sidorov found two glosses written in Permic script in a codex, (a) A short Obituary to a Deceased Reader of the Book, and (b) a prayer. More important, though, is the copy of the liturgy (with chants in Old Zyryan, but Old Church Slavic script), which Sidorov found as early as 1919. This was copied in the second half of the 17th century from a text in Permic script. In many respects it has to be considered equal to Evgenij's text. Particular interest evoke the clearly marked word stresses, which according to Lytkin, show that the stress in Permic languages is not necessarily on the first syllable.

Research work in dialectology was taken up again with increasing intensity shortly after the establishment of the Komi filial AN SSSR. Extensive collections of material resulting from expeditions in remote dialect areas can be found as manuscripts in the archives of this branch of the Academy (by T. I. Žilina, N. A. Kolegova, M. A. Saharova, and V. A. Sorvačeva).

This research work resulted in *The Comparative Dictionary of Komi-Zyryan Dialects* (491 pp., Syktuvkar, 1961). It contains material from eleven Zyryan dialects of various

[22] Cf., however, G. Stipa, "Der Ursprung der permischen Schrift", *ZDMG*, 110(2).342-364 (Neue Folge, Band 35, Wiesbaden, 1961) and Lytkin's investigation on the Iranian loan-word *ńebög* in *Virittäjä*, pp. 58-61 (1963).

regions of the Komi Autonomous Republic. The dictionary was edited by V. A. Sorvačeva who also authored the extremely instructive grammatical sketch in the appendix. The book contains 25,000 words.

A. S. Sidorov published interesting investigations in the field of dialectology, as for instance on the syntactical structure of the Ižma dialect and its lyric-epic songs (in *Lingvističeskij sbornik*, 2, Syktyvkar, 1952).

Lytkin's dialectological works were published collectively in a chrestomathy entitled *Dialectical Chrestomathy of the Permic Languages*, Part 1, 126 pp. (AN, Institut jazykoznanija, Moscow, 1955). This part discusses the three major forms of the Komi language (Komi-Zyryan, Komi-Permiac, and Jažva-Komi). Votyak (Udmurt) is to be discussed in a subsequent volume, but a characterization of it with the chief differences from Komi is offered in the introduction.

The introduction offers an excellent characterization of the three major forms of Komi with all sub-dialects, from phonetic and morphological viewpoints, and there are three maps of the three different territories. In the main part (pp. 37-87) there are 50 samples of 23 different dialects (fairy tales, narrations of every-day-life, folksongs, proverbs, riddles, etc.). Most of the text samples have been collected by Lytkin himself. These texts are an excellent introduction for the student. The scholar may take exception to the incomplete and obsolete transcription. No glossary of the words occurring in the texts is given. On the other hand, it is advantageous that there are Russian translations of the texts. Besides, the chrestomathy has an appendix entitled "Materials for a Dialect Dictionary of the Komi Language" (pp. 91-126). This constitutes the salvaged remains of the lost manuscripts for the dialect dictionary of the Komi language which was authored by Lytkin, Sidorov, and other collaborators, from 1928 to 1932.

The publications from the Jažva dialect are the first samples of a large investigation by Lytkin, which will be mentioned in connection with Permic.

Only a few theoretical works need to be mentioned in the field of lexicology. More important investigations are concerned with the investigation of loan-words.

First one has to mention Lytkin's general remarks on the various groups of loan-words in the corresponding languages, which can be found in his essays on *The Present-Day Komi Language* and the *Historical Grammar of the Komi Language*.

The following essays on individual groups of loan-words should be mentioned: The article "On some Iranian loan-words in Permic languages" (*IzvAN*, 4.385ff., 1951), "Vepsic-Karelian Loan-words in Komi-Zyryan" (collection of articles in honor of Academician V. V. Vinogradov on the occasion of his 70th birthday, Moscow, 1956). Especially numerous are the articles on Russian-Zyryan loan-word relationships: "Phonetics of the North Russian Dialects and Borrowings from Russian into Komi" (*Materials and investigations on dialectology* 2, Moscow-Leningrad, 1949); "North Russian Dialects in the light of Russian-Komi loan-words' (*Učenye Zapiski*, 3, Chkalov, 1949); on the change of Russian *e* into *o* in the Russian loan-words of the Komi Language (*Doklady* . . . , 2, Moscow, 1952), "On the History of some

Russian words which have been taken over into Finno-Ugric languages" (*Učenye Zapiski* . . . , 10, Rjazan, 1955) etc.

On the influence of Russian on the development of present-day Komi A. S. Sidorov wrote considering certain phonetic phenomena and grammatical structure (in *Tezisy dokladov* on the occasion of the Scientific Conference in Syktyvkar in 1952, and in *VJa*, [4], Moscow, 1953). S. A. Šamaxov reported on Russian loan-words in the language of Komi hunters (in *Učenye Zapiski* of the Pedagogical Institute 4. Syktyvkar, 1953).

## II. *Komi-Permiac*

### 1. *Before 1950*

The first Permiac scholars worked on the bases of the literary language using Komi-Zyryan linguistics as a model. Of the early authors of Permiac textbooks and grammars, A. N. Zubov (1889-1945) deserves first mention. He received his education as a teacher in Syktyvkar and later taught Permiac in Kudymkar schools, in his home town. He graduated from the University in Perm in 1926 and subsequently became member of the staff of the Scientific Research Bureau of the Komi-Permiac National District in Kudymkar. In this position he did important work for linguistic science in editing Permiac grammars: *Bases of the Grammar of the Permiac Dialect of the Komi Language* (Moscow, 1931). At the same time he was a poet and writer, writing under the pseudonym Pitju Önjö. The Permiac educator and poet N. P. Lihačev (1901 to 1945) worked in a similar fashion on the bases of the literary language. He edited a dozen high school grammars, collected folkloristic material, and he excelled in an exemplary style in his own literary creations. In all problems of the written language, as for instance, alphabet, orthography, etc., the Permiac speech area follows the model of Komi-Zyryan.

Since the only differences between Komi-Zyryan and Komi-Permiac are dialectal, we can restrict ourselves to those lexicographic works which have particular dialectological value when considering works published prior to 1950. The vocabulary of the Permiac literary language (based on the Kudymkar dialect) is supposed to be represented in the *Russian-Komi-Permiac Dictionary* by P. S. Kuznecov and A. M. Sporova (387 pp., Kudymkar, 1946). Its major shortcoming lies in the citation forms, which have been taken from Russian dictionaries, and that includes some which are absolutely unintelligible to the Permiac. Therefore, it gives an incorrect impression of the Permiac literary language. Far better in this respect is the *Komi-Permiac Orthographical Dictionary* by S. F. Gribanov (Kudymkar, 1945), which was re-issued in 1955. It contains approximately 9000 commonly used Komi-Permiac words.

Real dialect dictionaries are: N. A. Šahov, *Komi-Russian Dictionary* (Ust'sysol'sk, 1924; in this book the Permiac dialect of Iǹva is represented beside other Komi dialects); an article by G. Nečaev in the dialect collection *Sbornik komissii*, 2 (Moscow, 1931), 14-32, contains 400 words of the Kočevo dialect.

2. *Since 1950*

A small group of Permiac scholars was formed during the last decade. Lecturers in pedagogical institutes of various cities (Perm, Syktyvkar), staff members of the Komi filial AN SSR in Syktyvkar, (Lj. S. Gribova) and a lady *aspirant* in the Finno-Ugric division of the Linguistic Department of the Academy in Moscow (R. M. Batalova) made up this group.

They deserve credit for editing the recently published normative grammar *The Komi-Permiac Language: Introduction, Phonetics, Vocabulary, and Morphology* (Kudymkar, 1962). The editor-in-charge is V.I. Lytkin, who also authored large parts of the book. Similar to the already mentioned new normative grammars of Cheremis, Udmurt, and Komi, this book also contains general linguistic explanations for the student and comparisons with Russian. It intentionally deviates in certain points from Russian grammar, for instance, in discussing the participles in the section on adjectives, for which specific reasons are offered.

Scholarly articles on noun suffixes with specific meanings have been published (E.V. Boteva, *Tezisy dokladov . . . Soveščanie . . .*, Moscow, 1959, and in *Voprosy finno-ugorskogo jazykoznanija*, pp. 229-235, Moscow-Leningrad, 1962), on the categories of the adjectives (A. S. Gantman, *Sbornik v pomošč učitelju*, Kudymkar, 1956), on the categories of the animate and inanimate and the functions of the accusative ending *-ös* in the Komi language (Syktyvkar, 1959), and on dialectology (P. S. Kuznecov "Permiac Studies", *TIJa*, 4, Moscow, 1954; A. S. Krivoščekova-Gantman, "On the change of *l* to *v* and the loss of *v* in theIńva dialect of Komi-Permiac", *Voprosy finno-ugorskogo jazykoznanija* pp. 212-228; R. M. Batalova, "Phonetics of the Oni dialect of the Komi-Permiac language", *Istoriko-filologičeskij sbornik*, 7 (Syktyvkar, 1961). One should mention that A. S. Gantman-Krivoščekova has written her dissertation on the vocabulary and word formation of the Ińva dialect of Komi-Permiac (Leningrad, 1951).

V. I. Lytkin describes most lucidly the Permiac dialects with text samples in the above mentioned *Dialectological Chrestomathy of the Permic Languages* (Moscow, 1955).

A major achievement in the field of Permiac dialectology is V.I. Lytkin's most recent book *The Komi-Jaźva Dialect* (Moscow, 1961), a comprehensive monograph of 227 pages. A precise description of the territory and of the speakers of the dialect of Jaźva (called East-Permiac by earlier scholars) can be found, also detailed phonetics and morphology (60 pages), a dictionary (120 pp.), and texts in phonetic transcriptions with Russian translation (more than 20 pp.). This part, the phonetic part, and the dictionary, are the most important items of the valuable research work in a field which Lytkin was first to investigate thoroughly.

## KARELIAN-VEPSIAN GROUP

### 1. *Before 1950*

D. V. Bubrix was the leading scholar in the Karelian speech area inside the USSR.

He was very close to this region because he held the chair for Finno-Ugristics in Leningrad. As early as 1930 he organized the first expedition for dialect research to Karelia. He studied Finnish, Karelian, Vepsic, and other Balto-Finnic languages. He initiated an edition of the Finnish epic *Kalevala* in 1933. His *Grammar of the Karelian Language* was published in Petrozavodsk in 1937. At the same time he published a program for a material collection for a dialectological atlas of Karelian (189 pp.). He contributed an article to the *Liber saecularis* of the *Litterarum Societas Esthonica 1838-1938*. In connection with his work on the Karelian dialect atlas which he could not finish before his death, he wrote interesting articles on the history of the Karelian language. He was particularly interested in problems of historical phonology.

In connection with his studies of Karelian languages one finds his *Historical Phonetics of Suomi-Finnish* (Petrozavodsk, 1948). Of the Balto-Finnic topics one should above all mention his paper at the Finno-Ugric conference in Leningrad in 1947 on the origin of the nouns in *-inen*. Posthumously published was his *Historical Morphology of the Finnish Language* with a lengthy commentary by V. I. Lytkin (Moscow-Leningrad, 1955).

In the late 40's A. I. Popov, whose specialty had originally been Old Russian and Russian dialectology, began his toponymic studies with the article "On the toponymics of Karelia" (1949).

## 2. *Since 1950*

Since Bubrix's death, Leningrad is no longer the center of Finno-Ugristics, and not even the center for Karelian-Vepsian linguistics. In the capital of the Karelian ASSR in Petrozavodsk a university with four faculties was founded in 1940. The Scientific Research Institute of the republic was transformed into a branch of the Academy of Sciences, the so-called Karel'skij filial AN SSSR, in 1949.

N. I. Bogdanov (1905-1959) was made head of the linguistic division. His specialty was Vepsian. In this field he defended in 1952 his dissertation *History of the Development of the Vocabulary of the Vepsian language* at Leningrad University.

In the scholarly publication series of the linguistic department of the Karel'skij filial *Pribaltijsko-Finskoe jazykoznanie* he published a series of articles, e.g. "The Vepsian language in its present-day state of development" (Petrozavodsk, 1958). In the field of Finnish studies he contributed the part "Phonetics" to the *Grammar of the Finnish Language, Phonetics and Morphology* (Moscow-Leningrad, 1958). His most important work was his participation in the *Dialectological Atlas of the Karelian Language* as editor and author of commentary. He also lectured at the university in Petrozavodsk, where there is a Finno-Ugric department.

A. A. Beljakov has devoted himself particularly to dialectology. Aside from his collaboration on the dialect atlas, he published numerous articles, among others "Linguistic phenomena on the border of the dialects of the Karelian language in the Karelian ASSR" (Petrozavodsk, 1958), and on the Karelian of the region of Kalinin

(Tver): on phonetics (in *SovF* 5, Petrozavodsk, 1949), and on morphology (*Trudy Karel'skogo filiala AN SSSR*, 1, Petrozavodsk, 1954). Another of his specialities is the Russian loan-words in Karelian.

V. E. Zlobina wrote a number of articles on the Balto-Fennic vocabulary, semantics and word formation.

Very productive is M. M. Hämäläinen with a series of articles on case problems of the north-eastern group of Balto-Finnic, on other problems of Vepsian, and also on grammatical problems of Finnish. He also wrote on the cases in the northeastern group of Balto-Finnic languages.

Two young scholars defended their dissertations in 1955: V. M. Ollikainen, *Verbal suffixes with gender meaning in the present-day Finnish literary language* (Moscow, 1955; a synopsis was published in *Pribaltijsko-finskoe jazykoznanie*, Petrozavodsk, 1961) and G. N. Makarov, *Nominal (substantive) attributive word compounds in Finnish* (Moscow, 1955). Makarov concerns himself above all with the problem of the dividing line between word compounds and word combinations in Finnish (see *Pribaltijsko-finskoe jazykoznanie*, Petrozavodsk, 1958 and 1961).

The literary language of the Karelians in the Karelian ASSR is Finnish. Therefore the younger scholars especially concentrate their attention on research in Finnish with reference to the literary language. G. M. Kert can be considered leading in this group of younger scholars. He wrote his dissertation on the *Infinitive in -m in the Finnish literary language* (the so-called third infinitive, Petrozavodsk, 1953).

*Lapp in the Karelian Autonomous Republic.* – Kert is above all a Lappologist and contributes important scholarly work by collecting and investigating Lapp language material which is hardly accessible anymore and will be completely unavailable before long. Aside from papers at the conferences in Tartu in 1958 and in Moscow in 1959 he has now written a number of lengthy articles on the chief differences and similarities of the Lapp dialects of the Kola peninsula. He reports that there are 1800 Lapps living in the Soviet Union.

Research in Lapp in the Soviet Union began in the 30's. The first primer in Lapp language for the Lapps of the Kola peninsula by Z. E. Černjakov was published in 1933. In the anthology *Languages and Literature of the Peoples of the North, Part* 1: *Language and Literature of the Lapp and Finno-Ugric peoples* (Moscow-Leningrad, 1937), this author describes the geographical distribution of the Lapps, and A. G. Èndjukovskij offers a lengthy article on "The Saame (Lapp) language" (pp. 125-162). This is a descriptive grammar (phonetics, morphology, syntax, dictionary) of Kildin Lapp for practical attempts at a written language. It is therefore relatively sketchy.

In the aforementioned article, Kert describes all Lapp dialects of the Kola peninsula and has much new material to offer, especially in his monograph about Kola Lapp.

This work is based on the material of the linguistic expedition of 1954 to 1956, in which students of the university of Petrozavodsk, and Lapp students of the Leningrad Pedagogical Institute participated. The part on phonetics contains among other material an exact compilation of the consonant combinations and the corresponding vowels and consonants of the various dealects. In the part on morphology, we find the forms of the nouns with nine cases, the forms of postpositions and prepositions, adjectives (comparison), possessive suffixes, pronouns, numbers, deverbal nouns of action, the conjugation of the verb with various stems, and the participle.

Phonetic and morphological comparisons of the Kola-Lapp dialects have also been published by V. V. Senkevič-Gudkova (*UZ Karel'skogo Pedinstituta* 6, Petrozavodsk, 1959). She also compares these to the Paleosiberian languages (*UZ* 9, 1959-60).

*Finnish Studies in Leningrad and Moscow.* – D. V. Bubrix's chair at the University of Leningrad is now held by the lecturer Z. M. Dubrovina. Her specialty is Finno-Ugric languages. She wrote her dissertation on *Postpositions and prepositions in the contemporary Finnish literary language* (Leningrad, 1952). She devoted some research to the secondary cases of Balto-Finnic which developed out of postpositions (*Vestnik LGU* 11:14, 1956) and *Tezisy dokladov na soveščanii . . .*, Moscow, 1954).

One of the oldest written records of the Balto-Finnic languages found, old Russian documents written on birch bark, were unearthed in Novgorod in 1951: an inscription on birch bark in a Balto-Finnic language. Ju. S. Eliseev, the secretary of the linguistic department of the Academy of Sciences in Moscow, whose specialty is Balto-Finnic languages, was able to reconstruct the enigmatic text three lines long, and to interpret its meaning convincingly (*IzvAN*, 18:1, 1959, and *Virittäjä*, 1961).

On the basis of linguistic evidence, he determined that the inscription dated back to the beginning of the 13th century. According to his explanation, it was a formula of popular magic very widespread among the Balto-Finns for protection against the danger of lightning. The linguistic form has certain Karelian implications. This birch bark record is the oldest Balto-Finnic written record with a connected text.

Eliseev had already chosen a topic on Finnish syntax for his dissertation: *Forms of expressing the direct object in the contemporary Finnish written language* (Moscow, 1953). He also discusses one problem of Finnish syntax in his monograph *Chief Types of Syntactical Word Combinations in Contemporary Finnish Language* (124 pp., Moscow, 1959).

## ESTONIAN

### 1. *Before 1950*

When Estonia became a Soviet Republic in 1940, the two existing chairs for Estonian language and Balto-Finnic (A. Saareste and J. Mägiste), the chair for Uralic linguistics (J. Mark), and lectureship for Estonian (P. Ariste) at the University of Tartu remained intact for the time being. The subsequent war disturbances interrupted all teaching and research activities from 1941 to 1944. Since the three first named scholars emigrated, P. Ariste was the only one to remain. He was able to combine the phonetics laboratory of the university with his department. Since 1946, the chairs for Estonian and for Finno-Ugristics again exist separately. P. Ariste has retained the chair for Finno-Ugristics.

The old Estonian Academy of Sciences was reorganized along the lines of the Academy of Sciences of the USSR, and was moved with all its research institutes to Tallinn. It nevertheless remained independent. On account of the fact that the institute for language and literature of the academy took along a part of the linguistic collections there now existed two linguistic archives. This was a disadvantage for scholarly work because neither of the archives was complete. The Society for Advancement of the Mother Language (Emakeele Selts) was incorporated into the Academy together with its archive collections. The esteemed scholar J. V. Veski, who deserves great credit for his work in the Estonian literary language, collaborated at the Academy as expert on the Estonian literary language and lexicology.

A fresh development in Estonian linguistics in the second half of the 40's could not be brought about, since Marr's new doctrine spread its domination also into Estonia. Even the study of the literary language which was supposed to be investigated according to the viewpoint of the class struggle, the study of etymologies for which the merely similar connotations with apparent homonymity of the words were to be considered decisive, and the compilation of scientific dictionaries into which no "bourgeois" words were to be included, became impossible. During all the time until 1950 only one dissertation in the field of Finno-Ugric linguistics was defended (K. Aben, *Estonian and Livonian loan-words in Latvian*, Tartu, 1947).

Only J. V. Veski and P. Ariste were able to publish scholarly papers in these times (Veski on the relationships between the literary language and the dialects, and Ariste on phonetics of Estonian in 1946, and grammar of the Vote language in 1948). On the occasion of the conference in Leningrad in 1947, there were the first contacts of Estonian scholars with scholars of other Finno-Ugric peoples in the USSR. They were assigned the specific tasks of investigating Livonian and Vote.

## 2. *Since 1950*

The more liberal approach in the methods of linguistics led to a strong upsurge of Finno-Ugric studies at the University of Tartu. Noteworthy is the rapid education of young scholars and the contact with other Finno-Ugric peoples. The young *aspirants* were sent on expeditions to the Mordvins, Cheremis (Mari), and even to the Hungarians in the Carpathian Mountains in the Ukraine. Votyaks and Cheremis nationals came to study at Tartu University.

A remarkably large number of dissertations was finished in the 50's. There are eight in Finno-Ugric languages, and more than 14 if one includes Estonian. Some of the candidates are Cheremis, Votyaks, and Karelians. Since 1952, 11 *aspirants* finished their studies with their dissertations under Professor Ariste. All told, the number of *aspirants* whose education is either completed or in progress in the Finno-Ugric departments was 21 up to 1961. Two lecturers participate in teaching: E. Vääri, whose specialty is lexicology and Livonian, and P. Palmeos, who includes Hungarian, Finnish, and Karelian among her specialties.

Professor A. Kask holds the professorship for Estonian language.

Of the individual scholarly works one has to mention foremost of all those of P. Ariste. The following details of his life should be mentioned. He was born in Torma in 1905, became *Magister phil.* in Estonian in 1931, Ph. D. in 1939. From 1940 to 1944 he was a lecturer of Estonian. Since 1945 he has been professor of Finno-Ugric languages. He is a member of the Academy of Sciences. His earliest papers are on phonetic investigation of Estonian dialects. Phonetics seems to be his forte. Simultaneously as linguist and folklorist, he did work of considerable importance in the investigation of a number of Balto-Finnic languages, of which there are only few speech islands left. In his article "The development of the Vote language" (Tartu, 1947), he maintains that this language developed out of a North Estonian dialect, which was spoken east of the River Narva. Of the Ingermanlandian language, an eastern Finnish dialect, whose area of spread borders southwest Karelia, Ariste expresses a peculiar opinion. In his article "On the Ingermanlandian language" (Tartu, 1956), he takes the view that this was an independent Balto-Finnic language. Of importance is his article "On the problem of the development of the Livonian language" (*TIJa* 4, Moscow, 1954).

He discusses an important problem of the study of Balto-Finnic cases in his article "On the formation of the inner locative case in Balto-Finnic languages" (Tallinn, 1954). His paper entitled "The development of the Balto-Finnic languages and the earlier period of development" (in the symposium *Eesti rahva etnilisest ajaloost*, pp. 5-23, Tallinn, 1956), was even awarded a prize in Estonia.

His foremost linguistic achievements are in the field of Estonian phonetics. Aside from individual studies, he offered his phonetic investigation descriptively in its final version in the book *Phonetics of the Estonian language* (132 pp., Tallinn, 1953).

The field of loan-word research interested him in the 50's, in particular in view of the Russian loan-word relationships. Under the influence of certain theories of Russian prehistorians and archeologists, he places the beginnings of Slavo-Finnic loan-words into a much earlier period then was customary up to now in the linguistic chronology of loan-words ("On the earliest contacts between Slavs and Balto-Finns", *Looming*, 6.698-706, Tallinn, 1952).

As editor of the yearbook *Emakeele Seltsi aastaraamat* (since 1955), he has strongly encouraged publications in the field of Finno-Ugric linguistics. Some of these were also published in the journal of the Linguistic Department of the Academy, *Keele ja kirjanduse instituudi uurimised*. On account of most of the research work in the USSR being done in scientific institutes rather than at universities, it is of major importance that a division of Finno-Ugric linguistics was founded in 1957 in the institute for language and literature of the Estonian Academy of Sciences. Not counting the head of the division, there now are four senior and five junior scholars, and eight *aspirants*. Some of the most important tasks of the institute are now linguistic research expeditions (formerly initiated by the University of Tartu), publication of texts, expecially samples, from the dialects (the most important ones are from Ingermanlandian, Vote, and Valdai-Karelian of the region of Novgorod), history of language, study of the vocabulary and of the role of Russian in the development of the Estonian literary language.

Articles on individual topics of Finno-Ugric linguistics were written, among others, by the following persons: H. K. Rätsep, *Infinitive Verb Forms in Finno-Ugric languages* (dissertation, Tartu, 1954), V. Pall on tense and mode in Mordvin (dissertation, Tartu, 1955), and on the problems of Mordvin conjugation (*ESA* 1-3, 5-6), E. Päll on the infinitive in Estonian (*KKIU* 1, Tartu, 1956), V. Hallap on verbal derivational suffixes in Mordvin (dissertation, Tartu, 1956).

On lexicological problems of the Estonian language J. V. Veski wrote "Inadequacies in the Vocabulary of the Estonian literary language" (*Teaduste Akadeemia Toimetised*, 5,2, Tallinn, 1956). He also wrote on other problems of language development and language improvement in its phonetic and morphological aspects. He participated to a large degree in the two orthographic dictionaries, *Suur ôigekeelsussônaraamat* (Tallinn, 1951— ....) and *Väike ôigekeelsuse sônaraamat* (Tallinn, 1953). A. Kask wrote numerous papers on the literary language, its history, and its relationship to the dialects. One should mention *The Development of the Estonian Literary language against the background of the dialects* (139 pp., Tartu, 1962). Very important scholarly work of collecting and investigating was done in this field by the Kirjandusmuuseum in Tartu (which is named after Fr. R. Kreutzwald).

Russian loan-words in Estonian have been thoroughly investigated by M. Must in his dissertation (Tartu, 1954) and in various individual articles.

## OB-UGRIC GROUP

### VOGUL (MANSI) AND OSTYAK (HANTY) LINGUISTICS

#### 1. *Before 1950*

After the establishment of elementary schools for Voguls and Ostyaks with instruction in their own language (in the primary grades) linguistic work toward the founding of literary languages for both branches began. This is organized by the "Institute of the Peoples of the North". A scientific research committee for instruction in literature also has charge of Vogul and Ostyak and edits a scholarly publication series (*Učenye Zapiski*).

The first scholar to concern himself with these languages was the ethnologist and archeologist V. N. Černecov, a native Vogul. In the early 30's he designed an alphabet for Vogul, based on the Latin alphabet.[23]

[23] V. N. Černicov reports on this in "Mansijskij (vogul'skij) jazyk", *Jazyki i pis'mennost' narodov Severa*, 1.168-170 (Leningrad, 1937).

Černecov's first Vogul primer was published in 1933, entitled *The New Path* (*Ilpi lonhh*, Leningrad, 1933). A collection of Vogul fairy tales was published in 1935 by I. Ja. Černecova (*Mansi mojt*, Leningrad, 1935). These two scholars edited collectively a Vogul dictionary *Concise Vogul-Russian Dictionary* (Moscow-Leningrad, 1936). It is of immense practical and scholarly value to the linguist, even though it contains only 3000 words, because it is the basis of the nascent literature, and its introduction and grammatical sketch (phonetics, morphology, syntax) is valuable. The first epoch of Vogul linguistics came to end in 1936 with the abolition of the Latinized alphabet. In this regard V. N. Černecov's "Mansi (Vogul) language" (*Trudy po lingvistike*, 1, Moscow-Leningrad, 1937) is worth reading.

With the introduction of the Russian alphabet in 1937 translations of literature from Russian begin. The basis of the literary language becomes the northern dialect.

An alphabet on the basis of Latin was created for Ostyak in the same way as for Vogul. The first Ostyak primer was published in 1931 by P. Je. Xatanzejev, *Hanti Knjiga* (Moscow, 1931).

It was extremely difficult to create a unified system of writing and a unified literary language for Ostyak because the differences between the individual dialects are so great that they render communication impossible in many cases. The first Latinized alphabet was based on the dialect of Obdorsk. The changeover to the Russian occurred in 1937, and the dialect of Kazym became the basis of the written language.

The necessity to choose a transitional dialect between north and south Ostyak for the basis of the literary language became apparent. A commission for the drafting of the Ostyak literary language in Hanti-Mansijsk decided on the dialect of the middle reaches of the Ob River. Following the guidelines of this committee, P. K. Životnikov published a grammatical sketch of Ostyak (Hanti-Mansijsk, 1942). Yet this attempt too was ill-fated, because the majority of the still-existing Ostyaks speak the eastern dialect and do not understand the Obdorsk written language.

One should mention that the Finno-Ugrist Wolfgang Steinitz lived a number of years with the Ostyaks and worked especially in the "Institute of the Peoples of the North", where he published an article on Ostyak ("Hanti (Ostyak) language" in *Trudy po lingvistike*, 1, Moscow-Leningrad, 1937).

### 2. *Since 1950*

A. N. Balandin has earned special merits in his work for the founding of the literary language and the investigation of Vogul. It is of great importance that he edited, in collaboration with M. P. Vahruševa, a textbook for the students of the Pedagogical Institute in Leningrad, in which Vogul and Ostyak teachers are being trained: *The Vogul Language* (275 pp., Leningrad, 1957). Even more important for the literary language is the *Vogul-Russian Dictionary*, with comparisons of the vocabulary of the southern Vogul (Konda-) dialect (227 pp., Leningrad, 1958), edited by the same authors.

A member of the younger generation of Vogul scholars is a native Vogul, E. I. Rombandeeva, who comes from the region of the river Sigva in the district of Berjezov. She wrote the *Russian-Vogul Dictionary* (492 pp. Leningrad, 1954) for Vogul schools. It contains approximately 10,800 words, with charts of conjugations, orthographic rules, and a postface by A. N. Balandin. The early loan-words from Russian which have been included can be easily distinguished from the recent. The scholar finds in this dictionary a wealth of Vogul words which were up to now unknown in the literature. One severe shortcoming which can be attributed to the orthography influenced by Russian lies in the fact that the spelling does not distinguish between long and short vowels even though this is phonemic.

A scholarly study on Vogul verbs is E. I. Rombandeeva's article "Causative verbs in active and passive constructions in the Vogul language" (in *Voprosy finno-ugorskogo jazykoznanija*, Moscow-Leningrad, 1962). More recently A. N. Balandin published a Vogul grammar for self-study entitled *Vogul self-taught* (Leningrad, 1960).

At the conference for the languages of the peoples of the North in Leningrad in 1952, the necessity of using the eastern dialects as the basis for the development of the Ostyak literary language was emphasized. The best-known scholars are Ju. N. Russkaja and N. I. Tereškin.

Ju. N. Russkaja's phonetic training which she acquired in Leningrad is obvious. At the Finno-Ugric conference in Tartu in 1958 she read a paper on "The consonants of the Kazym dialect of Ostyak according to experimental data". Her most recent article "On some features of the case system of the Uralic dialects of Ostyak" was published in the above mentioned *Voprosy Finno-ugorskogo jazykoznanija*.

N. I. Tereškin wrote an excellent monograph on the Vah dialect of Ostyak: *Sketch of the Dialects of Ostyak, Part I: the Vah dialect* (Moscow-Leningrad, 1961). The first chapter, on phonetics, gives a lucid description of the phonemes according to quality and quantity, and on various phonetic features, such as vowel harmony, vowel alternation, gemination (as glides), etc. In the main section, on morphology (pp. 29-97), the number of cases of the noun, namely 8, evokes particular interest. In the section on the verbs, similar to the section on the nouns, the derivational syllables are treated first. After the analysis of the tenses follow the forms of flexion of the subjective and objective conjugations, the passive, the infinitive, the participles, and the verbal adverbs.

The third part consists of texts with Russian translation (pp. 99-123). These are the first publications of Vah dialect texts, in three variations. The texts are phonemically transcribed. There also is a dictionary of approximately 80 pages.

## SAMOYED LINGUISTICS[24]

The beginnings of Samoyed linguistics in the USSR are linked to the name of the gifted, but unfortunately prematurely deceased linguist G. N. Prokofjev. Being a

[24] See also Hajdú, P., *Finn-ugor népek és nyelvek*, pp. 332-385 (Budapest, 1962) and N. M. Tereščenko, "Samodijskie jazyki", in *Mladopis'mennye jazyki narodov SSSR*, pp. 380-399 (Moscow, 1959).

native Samoyed, he founded the first school with instruction in Selkup-Samoyed language in 1925 in Janov-Stan in the vicinity of the Turuhan River. Simultaneously, while being the principal of the school, he published research papers on "The Ostyak-Samoyeds of the Turuhan country" (*SovÈtn*, 2, Moscow-Leningrad, 1928), "Ethnology of the peoples of the Ob-Yenisei valley" (*SovÈtn*, 1943), primers and grammars: *Short grammar of the Samoyed* (*Nenec-Samoyed*) *language* (duplicated manuscript, Leningrad, 1934), a Nenec-Samoyed primer for the first and second grades (using the earlier Latinized orthography, Moscow-Leningrad, 1935), a Selkup (Ostyak-Samoyed) grammar (1935), a textbook for self-study of the Nenec language (1936), drafts for the orthographical system and the teaching of the Nenec, Ènec, Selkup, and Nganasan Samoyed languages (using the Latinized alphabet). The latter can be found in the symposium *Jazyki i pis'mennost' narodov Severa*, I, (Leningrad, 1937).

In the 30's schools with instruction in Samoyed languages were created in various districts inhabited by Samoyeds, and on this basis two Samoyed written languages were created: the Nenec (Yurak) and the Selkup (Ostyak) Samoyed literary languages. In 1939 the Cyrillic alphabet was introduced.

The linguistic achievements of Prokofjev can be found mainly in the description of the grammatical structure of these Samoyed languages.

Among his individual articles are "On the problem of the transitive in the Samoyed languages" (Moscow-Leningrad, 1937), "Numerals in Samoyed languages" (Leningrad, 1939). Prokofjev also added a Nenec-Russian glossary to his *Nenec self-taught* (pp. 166-171, Moscow-Leningrad, 1936).

*Continuing the Delineation of the Literary Languages.* – This demands a planned scholarly collecting of language material in time-consuming field work. The linguistic institute of the peoples of the North in Leningrad undertook to organize this task.

The promising Samoyed Anton P. Pyrerka, a staff member of this institute, wrote jointly with N. M. Tereščenko the *Russian-Samoyed dictionary* (approximately 15,000 words, Moscow, 1948).

In the work of the research institute, and especially on field trips, Samoyed students of the Herzen Institute in Leningrad also participated, especially the assistant of the corresponding faculty of this institute, A. M. Ščerbakova. She published articles in the scholarly publication series of the institute, e.g. "Forms of negation in the Nenec language" (*Učenye Zapiski*, 101, Leningrad, 1954, a short synopsis of her dissertation) and "The future tense in the Nenec language" (*Učenye Zapiski*, 111, 1955).

Three other dissertations must be listed: L. A. Varkovickaja, *Verbal word formation in Selkup-Samoyed* (1954), K. E. Čuprova, *Modes of expressing the indirect object in Nenec* (1956); a résumé is given in the symposium, *V pomošč učitelju škol Krajnego Severa*, 8, Leningrad, 1958), and G. D. Verbov, *The dialect of the forest Yuraks* (preserved in the archives of the Academy in Leningrad).

The leader in Samoyed research is N. M. Tereščenko. On the basis of experimental phonetics, N. M. Tereščenko and A. I. Rožin found two laryngeal occlusives (Kehlkopfverschlusslaute) in word-final position, which are phonemic in Nenec-Samoyed

(*Materialy i issledovanija po jazyku nencev*, 1956). Tereščenko distinguishes between productive and non-productive grammatical categories in contemporary Nenec (*Voprosy teorii i istorii jazyka*, Moscow, 1952). In his article "On the problem of the origin of the postpositions" (*DSIJa*, 11, Moscow-Leningrad, 1958) he shows that these postpositions developed from independent words. He also wrote "On the mode of expression of the possessive relationships in Samoyed" (in *Voprosy finno-ugorskogo jazykoznanija*, 1962).

Of basic importance is the symposium edited by N. M. Tereščenko with the collaboration of A. I. Rožin *Materials and research of the language of the Nencev* (Moscow-Leningrad, 1956). It contains in part 1 individual studies of phonetics (laryngeal occlusives), and of morphology (pp. 13-181). Of the morphological problems, of special interest is the expression of number, the genitive, which occurs in the presence of a laryngeal occlusive (pp. 55f.), the verbal classes arranged by stems (with conjugation examples), the variation of the forms of transitive and intransitive verbs, and of attributive (adjectives).

The second part of the book offers a precise analysis of the chief dialects of the Nenec language (Tundra and Forest-Yurak) especially the dialect of the Jamal Peninsula in the form of a dialectology.

In an appendix of 30 pages there are three lengthy texts of each of the dialect groups discussed in phonemic transcription with Russian translation and commentary. This work of sterling quality assures Samoyed linguistics in the USSR a place in Finno-Ugristics.

The *Nenec-Russian dictionary* (approximately 8000 words, Leningrad, 1955) written by N. M. Tereščenko is progressive in so far as it gives the basic meanings as well as the figurative meanings of the words. Furthermore, illuminating sample sentences illustrate the meaning and the use of words.

The dialect research of the 50's (see the reports by N. M. Tereščenko and L. V. Homič in *DSIJa*, 7, Moscow, 1953, and A. I. Vyučejskaja in *Učenye Zapiski*, 101, Leningrad, 1954) furnish new results on the dialects of the island of Kolgujev, and the peninsulas of Kanin, Jamal, and Taz.

## BIBLIOGRAPHY

In compiling this Bibliography, I have found very useful the work of mag. phil. Martti Kahla, *Bibliografinen luettelo Nuevostoliitossa vuosina 1918-1959 julkaistusta suomalais-ugrilaisesta kielitieteellisestä kirjallisuudesta*. Osa 1: "Tieteelliset tutkimukset ja artikkelit", *Journal de la Société Finno-ougrienne*, 62 (Helsinki, 1960).

Part Two is now in press and will appear in the same Journal, 63. Magister Kahla has very kindly placed the proofs at my disposal. For this, as well as for much useful information and bibliographical assistance, I here express my best thanks to him.

Aben, K., "Eesti ja liivi laene läti sõnavaras", *ESA*, 3.199-216 (1957).
Ahven, E., "Akadeemik J. V. Veski 85-aastane", *Rahva hääl*, 27, No. 6 (1958).

—, "Eesti kirjakeele arenemine a. 1900-1917", *ETAT*, 2(3).343-356 (1953).
—, *Eesti kirjakeele arenemine aastail 1900-1917*, *KKIU*, 4 (Tallinn, 1958).
—, "Eesti kirjakeele arendamise põhimõtteist käesoleva sajandi algul", *Looming*, 4.481-489 (1954).
—, "1905.-1907. a. revolutsiooni mõjust eesti kirjakeele sõnavarasse", *ESA*, 2.23-31 (1956).
Ahven, H., "Akadeemilise Emakeele Seltsi murdekorrespondentide tööst", *ETAT*, 1(2).124-126 (1952).
—, "Aruanne Emakeele Seltsi tööst aastal 1957", *ESA*, 4.312-318 (1958/59).
—, "Dialektoloogia-alane koordineerimis-nõupidamine", *ETAT*, 4(1).155-157 (1955).
—, "Emakeele Selts", in *Kümme aastat Eesti NSV Teaduste Akadeemiat* (*1946-1956*), pp. 209-212 (1956).
—, "Emakeele Seltsi korrespondentide murdetekstidest", *ETAT*, 3(4).608-618 (1954).
—, "Emakeele Seltsi tegevusest sõjajärgseil aastail (1945-1954)", *ESA*, 1.5-26 (1955).
—, "Emakeele Seltsi tööst aastal 1955", *ESA*, 2.252-258 (1956).
—, "Emakeele Seltsi tööst aastal 1956", *ESA*, 3.231-236 (1957).
—, "Märkmeid kirjakeelse sõnavara ulatusest F. J. Wiedemanni eesti-saksa sõnaraamatu esimeses trükis", *ESA*, 4.28-47 (1958/9).
—, "Märkmeid murdematerjalide kogumise võistluse tulemustest", *KK*, 2(2).126-128 (1959).
Alatyrev, V. I., "Glagoly pritvornogo dejstvija v udmurtskom jazyke", *VJa*, 8(1). 90-95 (1959).
—, "Imena s affiksom *-os* v udmurtskom jazyke", *Zapiski. Udmurtskij NIIIÈLJa*, 19.113-148 (Iževsk, 1959).
—, "Kačestvennye imena na *-ly* v udmurtskom jazyke", *Zapiski. Udmurtskij NIIIÈLJa*, 18.145-159 (Iževsk, 1957).
—, "Pilk udmurdi keele uurimisele", *KK*, 2(8).480-484 (1959).
—, "Suščestvuet li zvuk *c* v udmurtskom jazyke?", *Zapiski. Udmurtskij NIIIÈLJa*, 17.177-192 (Iževsk, 1955).
—, *Voprosy udmurtskogo jazykoznanija*, Tom 1 (Iževsk, 1959), 215 pp.
Alla, H., *Ainsuse osastav eesti keeles* (Diplomitöö). TRÜ (Tartu, 1954).
Alvre, P., "Kehaosi märkivate nimetuste nuumerusest", *KK*, 5.97-104, 5.160-167 (1962).
*A magyar helyesirás szabályai. Az Ukrán SzSzK magyar tannyelvü iskoláinak használatára* (Kyjiv-Užsgorod, 1956), 318 pp.
Ambus, A., "Lôuna-eesti kohanimesid Pihkva kroonikais", *KK*, 3.736-743 (1960).
—, *Refleksiivne verb läänemeresoome keelte põhjarühmas* (Diploomitöö). TRÜ (Tartu, 1955).
Anepajo, J., *Allatiiv eesti murdeis* (Diplomitöö). TRÜ (Tartu, 1952).
Anisimova, L. R., *Glagol v gorno-marijskom jazyke i metodika ego prepodavanija v škole* (dissertation abstract). Akademija pedag. nauk RSFSR, Institut metodov obučenii (Moscow, 1951), 24 pp.

—, *Ispol'zovanie grammatiki rodnogo jazyka pri izučenii russkogo glagola v marijs koj škole* (Moscow, 1955), 124 pp.
—, "K voprosu o vremenax glogola v gornom dialekte marijskogo jazyka", *Trudy. Marijskij NIIJaLI*, 8.47-67 (Joškar-Ola, 1956).
—, "K voprosu o glagol'nyx vidax v gornom dialekte marijskogo jazyka", in *Rodnoj i russkij jazyki v školax narodov finno-ugorskoj gruppy* (Moscow, 1956).
Ariste, P., "Adverbide arenemisest läänemere keeltes", in *Teaduslikud tööd pühendatud Tartu riikliku ülikooli 150. aastapäevale*, pp. 99-124 (1952).
—, "Eesti asesõnade 'me', 'te' ja 'meie', 'teie' suhteist", *KKIU*, 1.53-59 (1956).
—, *Eesti foneetika* (Tartu, 1946); *Eesti keele foneetika* (Tallinn, 1953), 132 pp.
—, "Eesti sõnade etümoloogiaid", *ESA*, 2.146-149 (1956).
—, "Ekstsessiivist läänemere keeltes", *ESA*, 6.145-161 (1960).
—, "Foneem eesti keeles", *ETAT*, 2.(3).357-367 (1953).
—, *Foneetilisi probleeme eesti keele alalt*, Nõukogude soome-ugri teadused (TRÜT Filoloogilised teadused) 6 (Tartu, 1947).
—, "Isuri keelenäiteid", *KKIU*, 5.7-68 (1960).
—, "Isuri keelest", *ESA*, 2.32-52 (1956).
—, "K voprosu o razvitii livskogo jazyka", *TIJa*, 4.254-307 (1954).
—, "Liivi keele palatalisatsiooni olemusest", *ESA*, 4.256-262 (1958/9).
—, "Läänemere keelte kujunemine ja vanem arenemisjärk", in *Eesti rahva etnilisest ajaloost*, pp. 5-23 (1956).
—, "Läänemere keelte sõnasiseste üksiksulghäälikute olemusest", *ETAT*, 8(4).425-431 (1959).
—, "Maakeel ja eesti keel", *ETAT*, 5(2).117-127 (1956).
—, "Metanalüüsi osa keele arengus", *KK*, 1(11).681-688 (1958).
—, "Miks on lõuna-eesti murdes 'lapse' asemel 'lats'?", *ETAT*, 4(2).317-320 (1955).
—, "Minevikust ja lähemast tulevikust" (TRÜ soome-ugri keelte kateedrist), *TRÜ*, 30, No. 1 (1959).
—, "Mõningaid märkmeid komi keele foneetika alalt", *ESA*, 5.253-256 (1959).
—, "O nekotoryx grammatičeskix voprosax finskogo jazyka", *Trudy Karel'skogo filiala AN SSSR*, 1.26-34 (Petrozavodsk, 1954).
—, "'Pandivere', 'Pandja' ja 'Pandju'", *ESA*, 3.130-133 (1957).
—, "Sisekohakäänete kujunemisest läänemere keeltes", *ETAT*, 3(1).41-50 (1954).
—, "Slaavlaste ja läänemerelaste vanimaist keelelisist kokkupuuteist", *Looming* 6.698-706 (1952).
—, "Soome-ugri keelte uurimise Eesti NSV-s", *Kodumaale tagasipöördumise eest*, pp. 32-88 (1957).
—, "Soome-ugri keelte uurimise minevikust ja tänapäevast", *ETAT*, 6(2).208-209 (1957).
—, "Soome-ugri keelte viljakas uurimistöö" (dialektoloogilised ekspeditsioonid), *Kodumaa*, 1959:5 (10).
—, "S-ovyj illativ v pribaltijskofinskix jazykax", *DSIJa*, 7.22-31 (1955).

—, "Vanimast läänemerelaste põllundusest keeleliste andmete põhjal", *TRÜT*, 38.193-203 (1955).
—, "Vene laensõnadest vanemas eesti kirjakeeles", *KK*, 1(1).25-33 (1958).
—, "Über die früheste Entwicklungsstufe der ostseefinnischen Sprachen", *ETAT*, 10(3).260-268 (1961).
—, "Ühest eesti keele astmevahelduse küsimusest", *ETAT*, 3(4).529-537 (1954).
—, "Ühest keelekontakti juhust", *KK*, 5(9).550-556 (1962).
—, "Ühest küsimusest fennougristika valdkonnas", *Edasi*, 1, VII (1958).
—, "Ületaotlusest (eriti vadja keeles)", *ESA*, 7.3-10 (1961).
—, *Vadjalaste laule* (Tallinn, 1960).
—, *Vadja muinasjutte* (Tallinn, 1962).
—, "Õueraha. Vana eestikeelne sõna", *KK*, 1(2).103-104 (1958).
Asylbaev, A. A., "Kratkie itogi èkspedicii Marijskogo Naučnogo issledovatel'skogo instituta 1952 goda (po jazyku, fol'kloru i arxeologii)", *UZ Marijskogo issledovatel'skogo instituta* 5, 273-283 (Joškar-Ola, 1953).
—, "Naučnaja sessija po voprosam razvitija marijskogo literaturnogo jazyka (27-29 dekabrja 1953 g.)", *UZ. Mariiskij NIIJaLI*, 6.217-227 (Joškar-Ola, 1954).
—, "Voprosy razvitii marijskogo literaturnogo jazyka", *Naučnaja sessija po voprosam razvitija marijskogo literaturnogo jazyka, 27-30 dekabrja 1953* g. (*tezisy dokladov*), pp. 3-9 (Joškar-Ola, 1953).
—, and Učaev, Z., *Marij orfografičeskij slovaŕ* (Joškar-Ola, 1954), 94 pp.
Avrovin, V. A., "Literaturnye jazyki narodov Severa i mestnye dialekty", *VJa*, 2(2).7-24 (1953).
—, "Novye issledovanija po jazykam narodnostej Severa", *IzvAN*, 16(5).469-477 (1957).
—, "Sostojanie i bližajšie izučenija jazykov narodov Severa", in *Protiv vul'garizacii i izvraščenija marksizma v jazykoznanii*, pp. 409-428 (Moscow, 1952).
Baxman, K. I., "O nekotoryx tipologičeskix osobennostjax russkix leksičeskix zaimstvovanij v èstonskom jazyke", *TRÜT*, 78.258-268 (Tartu, 1959).
—, *Issledovanie russkix leksičeskix zaimstvovanij v èstonskom jazyke* (*po materialam publicistiki i leksikografii vtoroj poloviny XIX i načala XX vv.*) (dissertation abstract) (Leningrad, 1956), 15 pp.
Baitšura, Ü., "Sõnarõhu iseloomust udmurdi keeles (kümograafi abil saadud andmete põhjal", *ESA*, 5.294-307 (1959).
Balakin, P. G., "Ablativ (otnošitel'nyj padež) mordovskogo sklonenija", *Zapiski. NIJaLIE Mordovskoj ASSR*, 12.105-131 (Saransk, 1951).
Balandin, A. N., "Mansijsko-xantyjskie sootvetsvija složnopodčinennym predloženijam russkogo jazyka", in *V pomošč učitelju škol Krajnego Severa*, pp. 111-121 (Leningrad, 1956).
—, "O jazykax i dialektax xanty", in *V pomošč učitelju škol Krajnego Severa*, pp. 75-90 (Leningrad, 1955).
—, and Vaxruševa, M. P., *Mansijskij jazyk* (Leningrad, 1957), 275 pp.

—, and —, *Mansijsko-russkij slovar'. S leksičeskimi paralleljami iz južno-mansijskogo (kondinskogo) dialekta* (Leningrad, 1958), 227 pp.

Beljakov, A. A., "Fonetika karel'skogo dialekta s. Tolmači Kalininskoj oblasti", *SovF*, 5.67-98 (Petrozavodsk, 1949).

—, "Jazykovye javlenija, opredeljajuščie granicy dialektov i govorov karel'skogo jazyka v Karel'skoj ASSR", *Pribaltijsko-finskoe jazykoznanie* (= *Trudy Karel'skogo filiala AN SSSR*, 12.49-62) (Petrozavodsk, 1958).

—, "Morfologičeskaja sistema sobstvenno-karel'skogo dialekta (kalininskoe narečie)", *Trudy Karelo-finskogo filiala AN SSSR*, 1.68-97 (Petrozavodsk, 1954).

Bereczki, Gábor, "Etümoloogilisi märkmeid mari keelest", *ESA*, 5.288-293 (1959).

—, *Finno-ugorskie èlementy v leksike marijskogo jazyka* (dissertation abstract) (Leningrad, 1957).

Bezzubov, V. I., *Dokumenty o žizni i naučnoj dejatel'nosti M. E. Evsevjeva* (Saransk, 1950), 160 pp.

—, "Pervaja mordovskaja grammatika (Iz istorii sozdanija grammatiki P. Ornotovym)", *Literaturnaja Mordovija*, 17.229-233 (Saransk, 1959).

Bibikov, K., *Magyar-orosz szótár az Ukrán SzSzK magyar tannyelvü iskoláinak használatára* (Kijav-Uzsgorod, 1959), 380 pp.

Bočkaeva, A. I., *Mestnye padeži v mordovskom jazyke* (dissertation abstract, AN SSSR) (Moscow, 1952), 13 pp.

—, "Semantika vnutrenno-mestnyx padežej v èrzja-mordovskom jazyke", *Zapiski. NIIJaLIE Mordovskoj ASSR*, 14.75-95 (Saransk, 1953).

—, "Upotreblenie poslelogov s vnutrenno-mestnymi padežami èrzja-mordovskogo jazyka", *TIJa*, 3.174-180 (1954).

Bogdanov, N. I., *Istorija razvitija leksiki vepsskogo jazyka* (dissertation abstract) (Leningrad, 1952), 22 pp.

—, "Narodnost' vepsy i ix jazyk", in *Pribaltijsko-finskoe jazykoznanie* (= *Trudy Karel'skogo filiala AN SSSR*, 12.63-75) (1958).

—, "O nekotoryx osobennostjax vostočnovepsskix govorov – kujskogo i pondal'iskogo", in *Pribaltijsko-finskoe jazykoznanie* (= *Trudy Karelskogo filiala AN SSSR* 32.33-41) (1960).

—, "Vepsskij jazyk na sovremennom ètape razvitija", in *Pribaltijsko-finskoe jazykoznanie* (= *Trudy Karel'skogo filiala AN SSSR* 12.76-82) (1958).

Bogorodickij, V. A., "Xarakteristika zvukovoj sistemy marijskogo (čeremisskogo) jazyka", *IzvAN*, 3(6).251-263 (1944).

Boteva, E. V., "Suffiksy sub"ektivnoj ocenki suščestvitel'nyx sovremennogo komi-permjackogo jazyka", in *Voprosy finno-ugorskogo jazykoznanija*, pp. 129-235 (Moscow-Leningrad, 1962).

Bubrix, D. V., "Drevnejšie čislovye i padežnye formy imeni v finnougorskix jazykax", *Jazyk i myšlenie*, 11.69-90 (1948).

—, *Èrzja-mordovskaja grammatika minimum* (Saransk, 1947).

—, "Èrzja-mordovskij jazyk i uralo-altajskie postroenija", *SJa*, 1.69-92 (1935).

—, "Eščë o 'singarmonizme' glasnyx v mordovskix jazykax", *Izvestija. NIJaLIE Mordovskoj ASSR*, 1 (Saransk, 1935).

—, *Grammatika karel'skogo jazyka* (Petrozavodsk, 1937), 29 pp.

—, *Grammatika literaturnogo komi jazyka. SovF*, 14 (Leningrad, 1949).

—, *Istoričeskaja fonetika finskogo-suomi jazyka. SovF*, 8 (Petrozavodsk, 1948).

—, "K voprosu o zvukoperexode *ti* > *si* v finskom jazyke", *SovF* 5.123-313 (Petrozavodsk, 1949).

—, *Istoričeskaja fonetika udmurtskogo jazyka* (*sravnitel'no s komi jazykom*) (Iževsk, 1948), 112 pp.

—, *Istoričeskaja grammatika èrzjanskogo jazyka*. Eds. M. N. Koljadënkova and N. F. Cyganova (Saransk, 1953), 272 pp.

—, *Istoričeskaja morfologija finskogo jazyka* (Moscow-Leningrad, 1955), 186 pp. Priloženie: *Primečanija V. I. Lytkina k knige D. V. Bubrixa* "Istoričeskaja morfologija finskogo jazyka" (Leningrad, 1956). 17 pp.

—, "Istoričeskoe prošloe karel'skogo naroda v svete lingvističeskix dannyx", *Izvestija Karelo-finskoj naučno-issledovatel'skoj bazy AN SSSR*, 3. 42-50 (Petrozavodsk,1948).

—, "Iz istorii mordovskogo vokalizma. (Po povodu odnoj stat'i P. Ravila: "Über eine doppelte vertretung des urfinnisch-wolgaischen *a* der nichtersten silbe im mordwinischen", *FUF*, 20)", *SJa*, 3.69-91 (1937).

—, *Karely i karel'skij jazyk* (Moscow, 1932).

—, "K voprosu ob otnošenijax meždu samoedskimi i finnougorskimi jazykami", *IzvAN*, 7(6).511-117 (1948).

—, "K voprosu o čeredovanijax finsk. a (ä) v nepervom sloge slova", *Jazyk i literatura*, 3.232-240 (1929).

—, "Mordovskaja sistema fonem", *Zapiski. NIJaLIE Mordovskoj ASSR*, 2.51-78 (Saransk, 1941).

—, "Mordovskoe sklonenie", *Zapiski. NIJaLIE Mordovskoj ASSR*, 2.79-102 (Sarnask 1941).

—, "Mordovskoe sprjaženie", *Zapiski. NIJaLIE Mordovskoj ASSR*, 4.3-53 (Saransk, 1941).

—, "O bylom èrzjanskom udarenii", *Zapiski. NIJaLIE Mordovskoj ASSR*, 12.83-87 (Saransk, 1951).

—, "O drevnej pribaltijsko-finskoj reči", *Izvestija Karelo-finskoj naučno-issledovatel'skoj bazy AN SSSR*, 1.47-56 (1949).

—, "O proisxoždenii finskogo translativa", *SovF*. 1.182-192 (Leningrad, 1948).

—, "O sovetskom finnougrovedenii" (Otvet N. N. Čeboksarovu), *SovEtn*, 2.189-196 (1949).

—, "Osnovnye linii istorii mordovskix form iz"javitel'nogo naklonenija v bezob"ektnom i ob"ektnyx rjadax", *UZ. Institut ètničeskix i nacional'nyx kul'tur narodov Vostoka*, 1.115-144 (Moscow, 1930).

—, "O stadijax razvitija glagol'nogo predloženija, preimuščestvenno po finnougorskim dannym", *UZ Karelo-finskogo gosudarstvennogo universiteta*, 2(1).125-154 (Petrozavodsk, 1948).

—, "Otnošenie mordovskix jazykov k drugim finnougorskim", *Zapiski. NIJaLIE Mordovskoj ASSR*, 5.23-49 (Saransk, 1946).

—, "O vzaimootnošenijax russkogo i finskogo jazykov", *Bjulleten'*. Leningradskoe obščestvo issledovalej kul'tury finnougorskix narodnostej (= LOIKFN), 2 (Leningrad, 1929).

—, *Programma po sobiraniju materiala dlja dialektologičeskogo atlasa karel'skogo jazyka*, 2-e. izd., dopoln. pri učastii N. A. Anisimova, E. N. Simadovoj, N. I. Bogdanova. Ed. V. I. Alatyreva (Petrozavodsk, 1946), 175 pp.

—, "Proisxoždenie imen na *-inen* s osnovoj na *-ise* v pribaltijsko-finskix jazykax", *SovF*, 5.4-32 (Petrozavodsk, 1949).

—, "Proisxoždenie *s*-ovyx vnutrenno-mestnyx padežej v zapadnyx gruppirovkax finnougorskix jazykov", *UZ Karelo-finskogo gosudarstvennogo universiteta*, 1.23-45 (1947).

—, "Sravnitel'naja grammatika finno-ugorskix jazykov v SSSR", *SovF*, 1.47-80 (Leningrad, 1948).

—, "Sravnitel'noe izučenie mordovskogo jazyka v SSSR", in *Sbornik. LOIKFN*, 1.161-177 (Leningrad, 1929).

—, "Svistjaščie i šipjaščie soglasnye v karel'skix dialektax. K voprosu ob ètničeskix èlementax v sostave karel'skogo naroda", *SovF*, 1.129-159 (Leningrad, 1948).

—, "'Unifikatory' v mirovom masštabe" (Po povodu stat'i S. P. Žujkova 'Latinizacija ili unifikacija' v sbornike k voprosu o reforme udmurtskogo pis'ma)", *Kultura i pis'mennost' Vostoka*, 10.61-64 (1931).

—, "Vokalizm pervogo sloga slova v permskix jazykax", *Naučnaja sessija LU:a 1945 g. Tezisy dokladov po sekcii vostokovedenija*, pp. 33-35 (Leningrad, 1945).

—, *Zvuki i formy èrzjanskoj reči* (*Po govoru s. Kozlovki*) (Moscow, 1930), 66 pp.

Cygankin, D. V., "Fonetika šugurovskogo dialekta èrzja-mordovskogo jazyka", *Zapiski. NIJaLIE Mordovskoj ASSR*, 18.154-159 (Saransk, 1958).

—, "Nekotorye fonetičeskie izmenenija v zaimstvovannyx slovax iz russkogo jazyka (na jazykovyx materialax šugurovskogo dialekta)", *Trudy. Mordovskij NIJaLIE Mordovskoj ASSR* 20.42-47 (Saransk, 1960).

—, *Šugurovskij dialekt èrzja-mordovskogo jazyka* (dissertation abstract) (Moscow, 1958), 23 pp.

Cyganov, N. F., "Iz istorii mordovskoj leksikografii", *Zapiski. NIJaLIE Mordovskoj ASSR*, 14.107-136 (Saransk, 1953).

—, "Izučenie mordovskix (mokša i èrzja) jazykov za 20 let dejatel'nosti instituta", *Zapiski. NIJaLIE Mordovskoj ASSR*, 14.3-27 (Saransk, 1953).

—, "Izučenie mordovskix jazykov i jazykovoe stroitel'stvo v Mordovii", *Zapiski. NIJaLIE Mordovskoj ASSR*, 10.3-18 (Saransk, 1948).

—, "K voprosu ob osnovnom slovarnom fonde mordovskix jazykov", *Zapiski. NIJaLIE Mordovskoj ASSR*, 12.19-41 (Saransk, 1951).

—, "O vokalizme ne-pervogo sloga progressivno-assimiljatornogo tipa govorov èrzjan-mordovskogo jazyka", *Zapiski. NIJaLIE Mordovskoj ASSR*, 16.112-124 (Saransk, 1955).

—, "Puti razvitija slovarnogo sostava mordovskix jazykov", *Materialy naučnoj sessii po voprosam mordovskogo jazykoznanija I*, pp. 88-130 (Saransk, 1955).

—, "Suščestvuet li v mokšanskom jazyke suffiks vidovoj napravlennosti *pn*?", *Zapiski. NIJaLIE Mordovskoj ASSR*, 16.108-111 (Saransk, 1955).

—, *Voprosy leksiki i leksikografii mordovskix jazykov* (dissertation abstract) (Moscow, 1952), 24 pp.

Čeboksarov, N. N., "K voprosu o proisxoždenii narodov ugrofinskoj jazykovoj gruppy", *SovÈtn*, 1.39-50 (1952).

Černecov, V. N., "Mansijskij (vogul'skij) jazyk", in *Trudy po lingvistike*, N.-i assoc. Institut narodov Severa I, pp. 163-192 (Moscow-Leningrad, 1937).

—, and I. Ja. Černecova, *Kratkij mansijsko-russkij slovar' s priloženiem grammatičeskogo očerka* (Moscow-Leningrad, 1936), 115 pp.

Četkarev, K. A., "Plemennye nazvanija marijcev", *UZ. Marijskij NIJaLI*, 5.107-132 (Joškar-Ola, 1953).

Čxaidze, M. P., *Sparennye glagoly v marijskom jazyke* (Joškar-Ola, 1960), 106 pp.

Čudaeva, O. I., "Leksiko-semantičeskie osobennosti m-ovyx imen dejstvija v mokšamordovskom jazyke", *TIJa*, 3.181-187 (1954).

—, *M-ovye imena dejstvija v mokšamordovskom jazyke* (dissertation abstract) (Moscow, 1952).

—, "Rukopisi po mokša-mordovskomu jazyku konca XIX veka", *Trudy. NIJaLIE Mordovskoj ASSR*, 20.55-61 (Saransk, 1960).

—, "Udarenie i reducirovanie v mokša-mordovskom jazyke", *Zapiski. NIJaLIE Mordovskoj ASSR*, 18.217-229 (Saransk, 1958).

—, "Vyraženie glagol'nosti m-ovymi im enami dejstvija v mokša-mordovskom jazyke", *Zapiski. NIJaLIE Mordovskoj ASSR*, 14.51-74 (Saransk, 1953).

Čuprova, K. E., *Sposoby vyraženija kosvennogo dopolnenija v neneckom jazyke* (dissertation abstract) (Leningrad, 1956), 18 pp.

Dokučaeva, T. A., "Fonetičeskie osobennosti russkoj reči mordvy-èrzi", *UZ Goŕkogo universiteta*, 44.91-113 (1957).

Dolgix, B. O., "Mifologičeskie skazki i istoričeskie predanija èncev", *Trudy instituta ètnografii*, 66 (Moscow, 1961).

Dolja, T. G., "O nekotoryx osobennostjax bespredložnogo i predložnogo upravlenija v govorax Zaonežskogo rajona Karel'skoj ASSR", *UZ Petrozavodskogo gosudarstvennogo universiteta*, 7(1).247-260 (1957).

Družinina, M. F., *Prostranstvenno-mestnye padeži v marijskom jazyke* (dissertation). Rukopiś v IJa AN SSSR (Moscow, 1951), 200 + VI pp. (Same, dissertation abstract, Moscow, 1952, 20 pp.).

Dubrovina, Z. M., "Ob obrazovanii vtoričnyx padežej iz posleložnyx konstrukcij v pribaltijskofinskix jazykax", *VLU*, 11(14).69-86 (1956).

—, "Dmitrij Vladimirovič Bubrix kak issledovatel' finno-ugorskix jazykov", *Finno-ugorskaja filologija = UZLU*, 314(63).5-18 (1962).

—, "Ob odnom tipe slov s častičnoj paradigmoj sklonenija v finskom jazyke", *Finno-ugorskaja filologija = UZLU*, 314(63).38-55 (1962).

—, *Poslelogi i predlogi v sovremennom finskom literaturnom jazyke* (dissertation abstract) (Leningrad, 1952).

Efremov, V. A., "Poslelogi kak sredstvo vyraženija grammatičeskix otnošenij v marijskom jazyke", *Trudy. Marijskij NIJaLI*, 7.134-171 (Joškar-Ola, 1955).

—, "Poslolegi v marijskom jazyke", *Trudy Marijskij NIJaLI*, 9.59-85 (Joškar-Ola, 1956).

Eliseev, Ju. S., "Drevnejšij pis'mennyj pamjatnik odnogo iz pribaltijsko-finskix jazykov", *IzvAN*, 18.(1)65-72 (1959).

—, "Kratkij grammatičeskij očerk finskogo jazyka", in *Finsko-russkij slovar'*, pp. 607-672 (Moscow, 1955).

—, *Osnovnye tipy sintaksičeskix slovosočetanij v sovremennom finskom jazyke* (Moscow, 1959), 124 pp.

—, *Suomalais-venäläinen taskusanakirja* (Moscow, 1962), 323 pp.

—, *Vyraženie prjamogo dopolnenija v sovremennom literaturnom finskom jazyke* (dissertation abstract) (Moscow 1953), 17 pp.

Emeljanov, A. I., *Grammatika votjackogo jazyka* (Leningrad, 1927), 160 pp.

Èndjukovskij, A. G., "Saamskij (loparskij) jazyk", in *Jazyki i piśmennosť narodov Severa. I: Jazyki i piśmennosť samoedskix i finno-ugorskix narodov*, pp. 125-162 (Moscow, Leningrad, 1937).

Ernits, V. J., "O nekotoryx indo-ural'skix suffiksax, preimuščestvenno v russkom i èstonskom jazykax", *TRÜT*, 78.212-228 (Tartu, 1959).

Evseev, V. Ja., "Termin 'viro' v karelo-finskix runax" (K voprosu o russko-karelo-èstonskix svjazjax), *Izvestija Karelo-finskogo filiala AN SSSR*, 1.103-115 (Petrozavodsk, 1950).

Evsevjev, M. E., *Èrzjań-ruzoń valks I: A–K* (Moscow, 1931), 227 pp.

—, *Izbrannye trudy. Tom I: Narodnye pesni mordvy* (Saransk, 1961). 384 pp.

—, *Osnovy mordovskoj grammatiki. S priloženiem obrazcov mokšanskix sklonenij i sprjaženij* (Moscow, 1928), 446 + 21 pp.

Feoktistov, A. ,"Esimene mordva sõnastik", *ESA*, 5.268-287 (1959).

—, *Lično-pritjažateľnye suffiksy imen suščetviteľnyx v mordovskix jazykax* (dissertation abstract) (Moscow, 1955), 16 pp.

—, "Mokša-mordovskij jazyk", in *Voprosy finno-ugorskogo jazykoznanija*, pp. 304-316.

—, "Mordovskie jazyki", in *Mladopiśmennye jazyki narodov SSSR*, pp. 424-438 (Moscow-Leningrad, 1959).

—, "O trudax H. Paasonena po mordovskim jazykam", in *Voprosy finno-ugorskogo jazykoznanija*, pp. 275-281.

—, "O vsesojuznom soveščanii po finno-ugorskomu jazykoznaniju", *Trudy. Mordovskij NIJaLIE Mordovskoj ASSR*, 20.62-69 (Saransk, 1960).

*Finsko-russkij slovaŕ*. Pod. red. Ol'gi Viktorovny Kukkonen, Hel'mi Juganovny Lehmus i Ir'i Avgustovny Lindroos. 40,000 words, 672 pp. Priloženie: Ju. S. Eliseev: "Kratkij grammatičeskij očerk finskogo jazyka" (Moscow, 1955).

Frolova, T. I., "Imennye kategorii verxne-vymskix govorov severnogo dialekta komi jazyka" (dissertation abstract), *Lingvističeskij sbornik*, 2.49-61 (Syktyvkar, 1952).

Galkin, I. S., "Iz istorij obščefinno-ugorskoj leksiki v marijskom jazyke", *Trudy Marijskij NIJaLI*, 12.121-136 (Joškar-Ola, 1958).

—, "K voprosu o priosxoždenii složnyx glagoloobrazovatel'nyx suffiksov marijskogo jazyka", *UZ. Marijskij NIJaLI*, 16.61-76 (Joškar-Ola, 1958).

—, "K voprosu o vozniknovenii dvux tipov sprjaženija v marijskom jazyke", in *Voprosy finno-ugorskoj jazykoznanija*, pp. 165-177 (Moscow-Leningrad, 1962).

—, "K istorii nekotoryx glagoloobrazovatel'nyx suffiksov marijskogo jazyka" (iz dissertacii), *Trudy Marijskogo NIJaLI*, 10.90-107 (Joškar-Ola, 1957).

—, "Mari keele sufiksi *an* päritolust", *ESA*, 6.220-222 (1960).

—, "Märkmeid verbi tuletussufiksite vokalismist mari keeles", *ESA*, 3.224-230 (1957).

—, "Mitmuse 1. ja 2. isiku personaalpronoomeni genitiivi ja akusatiivi vormi ajaloost mari keeles", *ESA*, 7.201-205 (1961).

—, and Gruzov, L. P., "Nekotorye itogi dialektologičeskoj èkspedicii MarNII 1958 goda", *Trudy Marijskogo NIJaLI*, 13.189-207. (Joškar-Ola, 1959/60).

—, "Obščefinno-ugorskie suffiksy s *l*-ovym èlementom v sovremennom marijskom jazyke", *TRÜT*, 51.67-80 (Tartu, 1957).

—, *Suffiksal'noe obrazovanie glagolov v sovremennom marijskom jazyke* (dissertation abstract) (Tartu, 1956), 20 pp.

—, *Zalogi v marijskom jazyke* (Joškar-Ola, 1958), 52 pp.

Galuškina, È. S., "Tendencija k parnosti mordovskix glagolov s vidovymi značenijami", *Trudy. NIJaLIE Mordovskoj ASSR*, 20.48-54 (Saransk, 1960).

Gordeev, F. I., "Fonetičeskoe osvoenie tatarskix zaimstvovanij v marijskom literaturnom jazyke", *Trudy Marijskogo NIJaLI*, 13.153-163 (Joškar-Ola, 1959/60).

—, *Kosvennye naklonenija v marijskom jazyke* (dissertation).

—, "O laskatel'noj forme glagolov sovremennogo marijskogo jazyka" (Iz dissertacii Kosvennye naklonenija v marijskom jazyke), *Trudy Marijskogo NIJaLI*, 12.180-188 (Joškar-Ola, 1958).

—, "O sposobe vyraženija neproizvol'nogo želanija v sovremennom marijskom jazyke", *UZ Marijskij NIJaLI*, 21.112-121 (Joškar-Ola, 1958).

—, "Povelitel'noe naklonenie v sovremennom marijskom jazyke", *Trudy Marijskogo NIJaLI*, 13.101-120 (Joškar-Ola, 1959/60).

—, "Tegevuse mittetäielikkust väljendav vorm kaasaegses mari keeles", *ESA*, 7.206-209 (1961).

*Grammatika finskogo jazyka. Fonetika i morfologija* (Moscow-Leningrad, 1958), 296 pp.

*Grammatika mordovskix (mokšankogo i èrzjanskogo) jazykov. Časť 1. Fonetika i morfologija. NIJaLI* Mordovskoj ASSR. M. N. Koljadenkov and R. A. Zavodova, Eds. (Saransk, 1962), 376 pp.

*Grammatika sovremennogo udmurtskogo jazyka. Fonetika i morfologija.* P. N. Perevoščikov, ed. (Iževsk ,1962), 376 pp.

Gruzov, L. P., "Dlitel'nost' marijskix glasnyx", *Trudy Marijskogo NIJaLI*, 12.137-158 (Joškar-Ola, 1958).

—, *Glasnye i soglasnye marijskogo jazyka (lugovoj dialekt) v svete èksperimentaľnyx dannyx* (dissertation abstract) (Leningrad, 1957), 17 pp.

—, "K voprosu o sostave i sisteme soglasnyx fonem lugovogo dialekta marijskogo jazyka", *UZ Marijskij gos. pedagogičeskij institut*, 16.45-59 (Joškar-Ola, 1958).

—, "O sostave fonem sardajal'sko-arborskogo govora marijskogo jazyka". Po materialam dialektologičeskoj èkspedicii MarNII 1957 g. *Trudy Marijskogo NIJaLI*, 13.145-152 (Joškar-Ola, 1959/60).

—, "Vidoizmenenie (modifikacija) fonem marijskogo jazyka", *Trudy Marijskogo NIJaLI*, 10.135-162 (Joškar-Ola, 1957).

Guljaev, E. S., "Funkcii isxodnogo padeža v komi jazyke", *Istoriko-filologičeskij sbornik*. Komi filial AN SSSR, 4.197-212 (Syktyvkar, 1958).

—, "K voprosu o proisxoždenii ègressiva v permskix jazykax" (Tezisy), *Soveščanie po voprosam istoričeskoj grammatiki i istoričeskoj dialektologii finno-ugorskix jazykov (Tezisy dokladov)*, pp. 5-12 (Moscow, 1959).

—, "Proisxoždenie padežej s èlementom ś v komi jazyke", *Istoriko-filologičeskij sbornik*. Komi filial AN SSSR, 5.131-163 (Syktyvkar, 1960).

—, *ś-ovye padeži v komi jazyke* (dissertation).

Haas, È. S., *Russko-vengerskij slovař*. K. E. Majtinskoj, ed., 2nd ed. (Moscow, 1951), 25,000 words, 607 pp.

Hallap, V., "Lõuna-eesti verbaaltuletussufiksist *-se, -sa, -sä*", *ETAT*, 6(1).56-64 (1957).

—, "Mordva keele verbaaltuletussufiksite vasteid lähemates sugulaskeeltes", *ESA*, 1.171-181 (1955).

—, "Mordva keelte deskriptiivseid verbe tuletavate sufiksite vasteid läänemere keeltes", *ESA* 2.92-105 (1956).

—, "Soome-ugri transkriptsioon ja fonoloogine transkriptsioon", *KKIU*, 6.217-237 (1961).

—, *Valdai karjala murde ajalooline foneetika* (Diplomitöö). TRÜ (1952).

—, *Verbaaltuletussufiksid mordva keeltes* (Kandidaadiväitekiri). Eesti NSV Teaduste Akadeemia, *KK* (1956).

Hämäläinen, N. N., "Dmitrij Vladimirovič Bubrix", in *Pribaltijsko-finskoe jazykoznanie (= Trudy Kareľskogo filiala AN SSSR* 23.3-15) (1960).

—, "K voprosu o čeredovanii stupenej soglasnyx v prošlom vepsskogo jazyka", *Trudy Karelo-finskogo filiala AN SSSR*, 1.98-108 (1954).

—, "O leksike karel'skix run", in *Trudy jubilejnoj naučnoj sessii, posvjaščennoj 100-letiju polnogo izdanija 'Kalevaly'*", pp. 152-165 (Petrozavodsk, 1950).

—, "Ob aggljutinatax v vepsskom jazyke v južnokarel'skix govorax karel'skogo jazyka", in *Pribaltijsko-finskoe jazykoznanie* (= *Trudy Karel'skogo filiala AN SSSR* 12.83-94) (1958).

—, "O razvitii vnutrenne-mestnyx padežej v severo-vostočnoj gruppe pribaltijsko-finskix jazykov", *Pribaltijsko-finskoe jazykoznanie* (= *Trudy Karel'skogo filiala AN SSSR* 23.84-109) (1960).

—, "Problemy grammatiki finskogo jazyka", *Trudy Karelo-finskogo filiala AN SSSR*, 1.35-43 (1954.)

—, "Vnešnie-mestnye padeži v severo-vostočnoj gruppe pribaltijsko-finskix jazykov", in *Voprosu finno-ugorskogo jazykoznanija*, pp. 109-126 (Moscow-Leningrad, 1962).

Hiedel, E., *Vepsa keele käänded* (Diplomitöö). *TRÜ* (1954).

Hiio, V., *Viru rannamurde ja eesti rahvalaulu-keele morfoloogiline suhe* (Diplomitöö). *TRÜ* (1952).

Ibius, O., and Univere, A., "Tartu voorimeeste tsunfti määrus 1684. aastast", *KK*, 1.46-52 (1960).

Imjarekov, A. K., Potapkin, S. G., and Šiškanov, P. S., *Mokšeń orfografičeskij slovaŕ* (Saransk, 1957), 229 pp.

Ippolitova, E. S., *Obrazovanie glagolov vidovoj napravlennosti v mordovskix jazykax* (dissertation abstract) (Moscow, 1954), 23 pp.

Isanbaev, N. J., *Deepričastija v marijskom jazyke* (Joškar-Ola, 1961), 149 pp.

—, "K voprosu o proisxoždenii suffiksa *eške* v marijskom jazyke", *Trudy. Marijskij NIJaLI* 13.65-71 (Joškar-Ola, 1959/60).

—, *N-ovye deepričastija v marijskom jazyke* (dissertation abstract) (Moscow, 1955), 14 pp.

—, "Sintaksičeskie funkcii deepričastija na *-n* v sovremennom marijskom jazyke", *UZ Marijskij gosudarstvennyj pedagogičeskij institut* 16.84-99 (Joškar-Ola, 1958).

—, "Sostavnye glagoly v sovremennom marijskom jazyke", *Trudy Marijskogo NIJaLI*, 13.13-63 (Joškar-Ola, 1959/60).

Ivanov, V. S., *Porjadok slov v opredelitel'nyx slovosočetanijax v vengerskom jazyke* (dissertation abstract) (Moscow, 1953), 14 pp.

—, "Sredstva vyraženija i klassifikacija obstojateĺstv v vengerskom jazyke", *Voprosy lingvistiki i metodiki prepodavanija inostrannyx jazykov* (= *Učenye zapiski kafedr inostrannyx jazykov Zapadnogo fakul'teta* 1.113-129) (Moscow, 1958).

Ivaško, L. A., "Zaimstvovannye slova v pečorskix govorax", *UZLU* (Serija filol. nauk 42) 243.84-103 (1958).

Jaakson, E., *Kalanimetusi läänemere keeltes* (Diplomitöö). *TRÜ* (1952).

Jakubinskaja, È. Ja., "K voprosu o vyraženii prjamogo dopolnenija v èrzja-mordovskom jazyke", *Soveščanie po voprosam istoričeskoj grammatiki i istoričeskoj dialektologii finno-ugorskix jazykov* (Tezisy dokladov, No. 74) (Moscow, 1959).

Jakubinskaja-Lemberg, È. A., "Finno-ugorskaja leksika v russkix professional'nyx dialektax", *Finno-ugorskaja filologija* 314 (63).56-59 (1962).

—, "K voprosu o vyraženii prjamogo dopolnenija v èrzja-mordovskom jazyke", *Finno-ugorskaja filologija* = *UZLU* 314 (63),75-84 (1962).

Jakuškin, A. V., *Drakinskij dialekt èrzja-mordovskogo jazyka* (dissertation abstract) (Moscow, 1959), 24 pp.

—, "Osobennosti vokalizma i konsonantizma drakinskogo dialekta èrzja-mordovskogo jazyka", *Zapiski. NIJaLIE Mordovskoj ASSR*, 18.196-216 (Saransk, 1958).

—, *Osobennosti morfologii drakinskogo dialekta èrzja-mordovskogo jazyka* (Saransk, 1959), 59 pp.

*K voprosu o reforme udmurtskogo pis'ma* (sbornik statej) (Iževsk, 1931), 59 pp.

Kalašinkova, V. G., "K voprosu o vidax glagola v udmurtskom jazyke", *UZ Glazovskij gos. pedagogičeskij institut* 1.54-68 (Iževsk, 1954).

Karelson, R., "Läänemere keelte *mi-* ja *mū-* tüvelised sidesõnad", *KK*, 1 (12).738-746 (1958).

—, "Pronoomenitüvedest *e-*, *ja-* ja *jo-* tulenevaid sidesõnu läänemeresoome keeltes", *TRÜT* 77.3-44 (1959).

—, "Pronoomenitüvedest *ko-* ja *ku-* pärinevad sidesõnad läänemeresoome keeltes", *ESA*, 5.151-189 (1959).

—, "Pronoomenitüvest *se-* tulenevad sidesônad läänemeresoome keeltes", *ESA*, 7.122-141 (1961).

—, *Sidesônad läänemeresoome keeltes* (dissertation) (Tallinn, 1959).

Karmazin, G. G., *Materialy k izučeniju marijskogo jazyka* (Krasnokokšajsk, 1925), 152 pp.

—, "O proisxoždenii slovoobrazovatel'nyx suffiksov glagolov v marijskom jazyke" (Doloženo 18.II. 1931 g. na pervoj sessii MarNII) (Joškar-Ola, 1931), 12 pp.

—, "O sklonenii imen suščestvitel'nyx i ob ustanovlenii količestva padežej v marijskom jazyke", *Marijskaja Avtonomnaja Oblast'* 1934 n:o 10/12. 75-114 (Joškar-Ola, 1934).

—, "Padeži v marijskom jazyke", *Marijskaja Avtonomnaja Oblast'* 1935 n:o 10/12 (Joškar-Ola, 1935).

—, *Sbornik statej po marijskomu jazyku* (Joškar-Ola, 1936), 56 pp.

Kartina, A. I., "Slovosloženie imen v mansijskom jazyke", *V pomošč učitelju škol Krajnego Severa* 8.280-295 (Leningrad, 1958).

—, *Imennoe slovoobrazovanie v sovremennom mansijskom jazyke* (dissertation abstract). (Leningrad, 1955), 16 pp.

—, "Suffiksal'noe slovoobrazovanie imen v sovremennom mansijskom jazyke", *Trudy*. 13.79-99 (Joškar-Ola, 1959/60).

Kask, A., "Eesti keele lauseliigendusest ja lauseliikmeist", *KK*, 3.237-243 (1960).

—, *Eesti kirjakeele murdelise tausta kujunemisest* (Tartu, 1962), 139 pp.

—, "Eesti murrete kujunemisest ja rühmitumisest", in *Eesti rahva etnilisest ajaloost*, pp. 24-40 (1956).

—, "J. C. Clare eesti keele grammatikast", *KKIU*, 2.53-62 (1958).

—, "K. A. Hermanni 'Eesti keele grammatikast'", *ESA*, 5.3-17 (1959).

—, "Môningaid jooni eesti rahvuskeele kujunemisest", in *Teaduslikud tööd pühendatud*

*Tartu riikliku ülikooli 150. aastapäevale*, pp. 26-42 (Tallinn, 1952).
—, "Môningaid täiendavaid andmeid eesti väldete käsitluse ajaloost", *TRÜT*, 51.3-14 (1957).
—, "15 aastat Nôukogude Eesti keeleteadust", *ESA*, 2.3-22 (1956).
—, *Vôitlus vana ja uue kirjaviisi vahel XIX sajandi eesti kirjakeeles*. Kandidaadiväitekiri, kaitstud 1955 a. Tartu ülikoolis (1955). Emakeele seltsi toimetised 2 (Tallinn, 1958), 215 pp.
—, "K voprosu ob obrazovanii i gruppirovke èstonskix dialektov", in *Voprosy ètničeskoj istorii èstonskogo naroda*, pp. 28-48 (Tallinn, 1956).
—, "Ülevaade eesti leksikograafiast 1917 aastani", *KKIU*, 1.140-176 (1956).
Kents, J., "Eesti 'kôrve' - nimelised kohad – ürgse maastiku ja asustusloo ilmendajad", *TRÜT*, Geoloogia ja geograafia, 2 (1947), 87 pp.
Kerik, H., *Môisa- ja taluelu kujutav sônavara feodalismiaegses eesti keeles* (Diplomitöö). (Tartu, 1950), 287 pp.
Kert, G. M., "Imennaja i glogol'naja osnovy v kil'dinskom dialekte saamskogo jazyka", *VJa*, 1962, pp. 143-153.
—, *M-ovye infinitivnye formy v finskom literaturnom jazyke* (*t.n. III-j infinitiv*) (dissertation abstract) (Petrozavodsk, 1953), 20 pp.
—, "M-ovye infinitivnye formy v finskom jazyke", *Izvestija Karel'skogo i Kol'skogo filialov AN SSSR* 4.156-165 (Petrozavodsk, 1958).
—, "Osnovnye sxodstva i različija v saamskix dialektax Kol'skogo poluostrova", in *Pribaltijsko-finskoe jazykoznanie* (= *Trudy Karel'skogo filiala AN SSSR* 23.110-134) (1960).
—, "Značenie saamskogo jazyka dlja finno-ugorsko jazykoznanija", in *Pribaltijsko-finskoe jazykoznanie* (= *Trudy Karel'skogo filiala AN SSSR* 12.104-117) (Petrozavodsk, 1958).
—, and Matusevič, M. I., "K voprosu o sostave soglasnyx fonem v voron'inskom govore Kil'dinskogo dialekta saamskogo jazyka", *Finno-ugorskaja filologija* (= *UZLU* 314(63). 19-37) (1962).
Klindok, A., *Murdeline sônavara Ed. Vilde loomingus*. Kandidaadiväitekiri, kaitstud 1954 a. Tartu ülikoolis (Tartu, 1954).
Kinks, L., *n-lised käänded ja nende funktsioonid soome-ugri keeltes* (Diplomitöö) (Tartu, 1950), 149 pp.
Klepko, V. I., *K voprosu o vyraženii opredelennosti i neopredelennosti imeni suščestvitel'nogo v vengerskom jazyke* (dissertation abstract) (Moscow, 1953), 16 pp.
Koff, E., *Eesti vôôrsônade ja vôôrnimede ortograafia kujunemisest* (Diplomitöö)- (Tartu, 1950), 177 pp.
Koit, È., *Istoričeskij očerk grammatiki govora Kixelkona* (dissertation abstract) (Tartu, 1959), 19 pp.
—, "Jooni kihelkonna murraku sônavarast", *TRÜT*, 51.35-51 (1957).
—, "Jooni kihelkonna murrakust", *ESA* 4.127-144 (1958).
—, *Kihelkonna murraku keele-ajalooline ülevaade* (dissertation) (Tartu, 1959).

Kokla, P. "Mari possessiivsufiksite *-em*, *-et* ajaloost ja esinemusest", *ESA*, 7.210-219 (1961).

—, "Mônedest vepsa keele derivatsioonisufikseist", *TRÜT*, 42.48-56 (1957).

—, *Noomeni ja verbi tuletussufiksid vepsa keeles* (Diplomitöö) (Tartu, 1955), 211 pp.

Kolegova, N. A., "O nekotoryx voprosax istorii komi piśmennosti", *Istoriko-filologičeskij sbornik*, 3.48-56 (Syktyvkar, 1956).

—, *Stroiteľstvo komi literaturnogo jazyka* (manuscript) (Syktyvkar, 1950).

Koljadenkov, M. N., "Glagol'noe skazuemoe v mordovskix jazykax", *Zapiski. NIJaLIE Mordovskoj ASSR*, 4.93-126 (Saransk, 1941).

—, "Glagol'noe slovoobrazovanie v mordovskix jazykax", *Zapiski. NIJaLIE Mordovskoj ASSR*, 16.91-107 (Saransk, 1955).

—, *Grammatika mordovskix (èrzjanskogo i mokšanskogo) jazykov. II: Sintaksis.* (Saransk, 1954), 326 pp.

—, "K voprosu o zaimstvovanijax v mordovskix jazykax", *Zapiski. NIJaLIE Mordovskoj ASSR*, 5.68-75 (Saransk, 1946).

—, "K voprosu o proisxoždenii glagolov ot imennyx osnov v mordovskix jazykax", *Zapiski. NIJaLIE Mordovskoj ASSR*, 14.28-31 (Saransk, 1953).

—, "Mordovskoe jazykoznanie za 30 let", *Trudy. NIJaLIE Mordovskoj ASSR* 20. 3-22 (Saransk, 1960).

—, "Obrazovanie i puti razvitija mokšanskogo i èrzjanskogo literaturnyx jazykov", in *Materialy naučnoj sessii po voprosam mordovskogo jazykoznanija I*, pp. 59-87 (Saransk, 1955).

—, "Podležaščee kak sredstvo vyraženija sub"ekta v mordovskix jazykax", *Zapiski. NIJaLIE Mordovskoj ASSR*, 12.88-104 (Saransk, 1951).

—, "Skazuemoe v mordovskix jazykax", *SovF*, 2.76-167 (Saransk, 1948).

—, "Sovremennyj mordovskij literaturnyj jazyk", *Literaturnaja Mordovija*, 2.148-167 (Saransk, 1949).

—, *Struktura prostogo predloženija v mordovskix jazykax. Predloženie i ego glavnye členy* (Saransk, 1959), 291, pp. Dissertation abstract (Moscow, 1956), 27 pp.

—, "Učenie I. V. Stalina o jazyke i zadači po izučeniju mordovskix jazykov". *Zapiski. NIJaLIE Mordovskoj ASSR*, 12.3-18 (Saransk, 1951).

—, and Balakin, P. G., *Èrzjań keleń orfografičeskij slovaŕ* (Saransk, 1955), 337 pp.

—, and Potapkin, S. G., *Morfologia orfografija i grammatičeskaja terminologija èrzjanskogo i mokšanskogo jazykov* (Saransk, 1938/39), 154 pp.

—, —, and Tarasov, L. P., *Sintaksis i punktuacija mordovskix (èrzjanskogo i mokšanskogo) jazykov* (Saransk, 1940), 144 pp.

*Komi-permjackij jazyk (fonetika, leksika i morfologija, učebnik dlja vysšix učebnyx zavedenij).* V. I. Lytkin, ed. (Kudymkar, 1962), 340 pp.

*Komi orfografičeskij slovaŕ* (Syktyvkar, 1959), 224 pp.

*Komi-russkij slovaŕ*: V. I. Lytkin, ed. (Moscow, 1961), 25.000 words, 923 pp.

Kont, I., "Eesti nominaalsufiksi *-sk* päritolust ja semantikast", *ESA*, 3.104-115 (1957).

—, *Isikut märkivad sufiksilised nimisônad eesti keeles*. Kandidaadiväitekiri, kaitstud 1955 a. Tartu ülikoolis (1955).

—, "Eriarenguist totaal- ja partsiaalobjekti kasutamises läänemeresoome keeltes", *ESA*, 5.132-150 (1959).

—, *Genitiivsuse väljendamine soome-ugri keeltes* (Diplomitöö) (Tartu, 1950), 133 pp.

—, "Lause eitavast sisust sôltuv objekt läänemeresoome keeltes", *ESA*, 4.233-248 (1958).

Kont, K., "Liikumist tähistavate verbide objektist läänemeresoome keeltes", *KK* 2 (5).283-294 (1959).

—, "Läänemeresoome keelte objekti probleeme", *KK* 1(3).155-163 (1958).

—, "Läänemeresoome partitiivist, mordva ablatiivist ja baltislaavi genitiivist", *KKIU*, 6.190-199 (1961).

—, *Päritolu ja omandilise kuuluvuse väljendamine soome-ugri keeltes* (Diplomitöö) (Tartu, 1953), 134 pp.

—, "Substantiivide atributiivsest seosest soome-ugri keeltes. Nominatiivse ja genitiivse atribuudi seos pôhisônaga", *KK*, 1.105-126 (1956).

—, "Translatiivist läänemeresoome keeltes ja mordva ning lapi keeles", *ESA*, 1.163-170 (1955).

Korjus, I., *Tingiv kôneviis eesti murretes* (Diplomitöö) (Tartu, 1952), 139 pp.

Kovedjaeva, E. I., "Kratkaja sravnitel'naja xarakteristika zvukovux sistem russkogo i marijskogo jazykov", in *Rodnoj i russkij jazyki v školax narodov finnougorskoj gruppy*, pp. 12-49 (Moscow, 1956).

—, "Marijskij jazyk", in *Voprosy finno-ugorskogo jazykoznanija*, pp. 317-328 (Moscow-Leningrad, 1962).

Kristian, M., *Verb kesk- vepsa murdes*. (Diplomitöö) (Tartu, 1954), 80 pp.

Krivoščekova-Gantman, A. S., "K voprosu o kategorii imën čislitel'nyx v komi-permjackom jazyke", in *V pomošč učitelju* (Kudymkar, 1956).

—, *Slovarnyj sostav i slovoizmenenie ińvenskogo dialekta komi-permjackogo jazyka* (dissertation abstract) (Leningrad, 1951), 18 pp.

—, "K voprosu o kategorii imën prilagatel'nyx v komi-permjackom jazyke", in *V pomošč učitelju* (Kudymkar, 1950).

—, "O nekotoryx osobennostjax ińvenskogo dialekta komi-permjackogo jazyka", *UZ. Permskij gos. pedagogičeskij institut* 17.123-140 (Perm, 1958).

—, "O perexode *l* v *v* i čeredovanii *v* s nulem zvuka v ińvenskom dialekte komi-permjackogo jazyka", in *Voprosy finnougorskogo jazykoznanija*, pp. 212-228 (Moscow-Leningrad, 1962).

Kullemägi, H., *Väliskohakäänded ja nende tähenduslikud funktsioonid läänemeresoome keelis* (Diplomitöö) (Tartu, 1950), 160 pp.

Kuprijanova, Z. N., "K xarakteristike neneckogo èposa", *UZLPedI*, 132.181-240 (1957).

—, *Neneckij folklor* (*učebnoe sposobie dlja pedagogičeskix učilišč*) (Leningrad, 1960).

—, *Osnovnye žanry neneckogo* (*jurako-samoedskogo*) *folklora* (dissertation abstract). *VLU*, 2(7).93-95 (1947).

—, "Sobiranie i izučenie ustnogo tvorčestva nencev za 25 let" (Kratkij obzor), in *V pomošč učitelju škol Krajnego Severa* 6.54-67 (Leningrad, 1956).
—, "Terminologija rodstva v ustnom narodnom tvorčestve nencev", *Učenye zapiski. Leningradskij gosudarstvennyj pedagogičeskij institut imeni A. I. Gercena* 101.159-179 (1954).
—, Xomič, L. V. and Ščerbakova, A. M., *Neneckij jazyk* (*učebnoe posobie dlja pedagogičeskix učilišč*) (Leningrad, 1957), 255 pp.
Kure, K., "Tegusôna 'olema' funksioonidest ja tähendustest", *ESA*, 2.124-137 (1956).
Kuum, J., *Valik soo- ja maaparandusalaseid oskussônu ning môisteid* (Tallinn, 1954), 40 pp.
Kuus, A., *Objekt eesti murretes* (Diplomitöö) (Tartu, 1951), 252 pp.
Kuusinen, M. È., "K voprosu ob aktivnyx pričastijax nezakončennogo dejstvija v finskom jazyke", *Trudy Karelo-finskogo filiala AN SSSR*, 1.44-59 (Petrozavodsk, 1954).
—, *Pričastija v finskom jazyke* (dissertation abstract) (Petrozavodsk, 1954), 16 pp.
Kuzakova, E. A., "Služebnye časti reči južno-mansijskogo dialekta", *V pomošč učitelju škol Krajnego Severa*, 8.307-318 (Leningrad, 1958).
Kuznecov, P. S., "Komi-permjackie ètjudy", *TIJa*, 4.308-323 (1954).
—, Reformackij, A. A., and Serebrennikov, B. A., "O metode ustanovlenija jazykovogo rodstva" in *Tezisy dokladov naučnyx sotrudnikov Instituta jazykoznanija na ob"edinennoj sessii Inst. ètnografii, Inst. istorii material'noj kul'tury, Inst. istorii i Inst. jazykoznanija AN SSSR* (Moscow, 1951).
Kuznecova, Z. I., "Obzor pamjatnikov komi piśmennosti XVIII v.", *Istoriko-filologičeskij sbornik* 4.213-240 (Syktyvkar, 1958).
Laanest, A., *Adverbidest vepsa keeles* (Diplomitöö) (Tartu, 1955), 112 pp.
—, "Ees- ja tagasônadest vepsa keeles", *TRÜT*, 41.157-170 (1956).
—, "Isuri keele oredeži murdest", *ESA*, 6.179-195 (1960).
—, "Isuri murrete rühmitamisest", *KKIU*, 6.200-216 (1961).
—, "Liiki ja laadi väljendavast genitiivatribuudist läänemeresoome keeltes ja tema vahekorrast genitiivi muude tähendusfunktsioonidega", *ETAT* 7(4).276-291 (1958).
—, "Nekotorye voprosy izučenija ižorskogo jazyka" (Tekst doklada, pročitannogo na soveščanii po voprosam istoričeskoj grammatiki 1959), *ETAT* 9(3).263-267 (1960).
—, "Partitiivi abil väljendatud substantiivsest atribuudist läänemeresoome keeltes", *ESA* 4.214-232 (1958).
—, "Sisekohakäänete vormis esinevatest nimisônalistest atribuutidest läänemeresoome keeltes", *KKIU*, 5.69-87 (1960).
Laanpere, H., *Adjektiiv vepsa keeles* (Diplomitöö) (Tarty, 1955), 115 pp.
Laugaste, Ed., "Arhailised jooned eesti rahvalaulude keeles", *TRÜT*, 38.95-144 (1955).
—, "Môningaid sônatähenduslikke küsimusi seoses Kreutzwaldi 'Kalevipojaga'", *ESA*, 3.116-129 (1957).
Laugaste, G., "Konsonantide palatalisatsioon eesti keeles", *TRÜT*, 43.74-88 (1956).
Lehari, V., *Sôna ja sônaliigid eesti keeles* (Diplomitöö) (Tartu, 1955), 134 pp.

—, "Sônaliikide küsimus eesti keeles", *TRÜT*, 47.34-47 (1957).

Leppik, Ed., *Liivi keele üldsoome-ugriline sônavara* (Diplomitöö) (Tartu, 1952), 107 pp.

—, "Subjekti ja predikaadi kongruentsist karjala valdai murdes", *ESA*, 6.196-209 (1960).

Leppik, J., *Inessiiv eesti keeles* (Diplomitöö) (Tartu, 1952), 108 pp.

Liiv, G., "Acoustical Features of Estonian Vowels Pronounced in Isolation and in Three Phonological Degrees of Length", *ETAT*, 11(1).63-97 (1962).

—, "Eesti keele kolme vältusastme vokaalide kestus ja meloodiatüübid", *KK*, 4.412-424 and 480-490 (1961).

—, "On Qualitative Features of Estonian Stressed Monophthongs of Three Phonological Degrees of Length", *ETAT*, 10(1).43-66 and 10(2).113-131 (1961).

—, "Pronoomenist *iťš'e* ~ *itše* vepsa keeles", *TRÜT*, 47.17-33 (1957).

Lytkin, V. I., "Časti reči v finno-ugorskix jazykax", in *Tezisy dokladov na otkrytom rasširennom zasedanii Učenogo soveta, posvjaščennom diskussii o probleme častej reči v jazykax raznyx tipov*, 28-30 *julja* 1954, pp. 29-31 (Moscow, 1945).

—, "Dialekt Kobry", *Sbornik Komissii po sobiraniju slovarja i izučeniju dialektov komi jazyka* 1.29-47 (Syktyvkar, 1930).

—, *Dialektologičeskaja xrestomatija po permskim jazykam I* (*s obzorom dialektov i dialektologičeskim slovarem*) (Moscow, 1955), 128 pp.

—, *Drevnepermskij jazyk. Čtenie tekstov, grammatika, slovar'* (Moscow, 1952), 174 pp.

—, "Drevnerusskie *š, ž* – zyrjanskie *ś, ź*", *DAN*, V, 14.298-301 (1928).

—, "D. R. Fokoš-Fuks. (K 75- letiju so dnja roždenija)", in *Voprosy finno-ugorskogo jazykoznanija*, pp. 270-274 (Moscow-Leningrad, 1962).

—, "Fonetika severnovelikorusskix govorov i zaimstvovanija iz russkogo jazyka v komijskij", *Materialy i issledovanija po russkoj dialektologii* 2.128-201 (Moscow-Leningrad, 1949).

—, "Iz istorii nekotoryx russkix slov, zaimstvovannyx finnougorskimi jazykami", *UZ Rjazanskogo pedagogičeskogo instituta*, 10.115-134 (Rjazan, 1955).

—, "Iz istorii slovarnogo sostava permskix jazykov", *VJa*, 2(5).48-69 (1953).

—, "Izučenie dialektov komi jazyka", *VJa*, 6(5).108-110 (1957).

—, *Istoričeskaja grammatika komi jazyka. I, Vvedenie, fonetika* (*učebnoe posobie dlja vysšix učebnyx zavedenij*) (Syktyvkar, 1957), 135 pp.

—, "K voprosu o vokalizme permskix jazykax", *TIJa*, 1.58-106 (1952).

—, "K voprosu o deètimologizacii slov v permskix jazykax", *DSIJa*, 7.5-21 (1955).

—, "K istorii komi piśmennosti", *Kuľtura i piśmennosť Vostoka*, 7/8.173-188 (Moscow, 1931).

—, *Komi-Jaźvinskij dialekt* (Moscow, 1961), 225 pp.

—, "Kratkij obzor dialektov komi jazyka", *Zapiski obsčestva izučenii Komi kraja* 5.31-40 (Syktyvkar, 1930).

—, "Nekotorye voprosy vokalizma finno-ugorskix jazykov (Tezisy)", *Soveščanie po voprosam istoričeskoj grammatiki i istoričeskoj dialektologii finno-ugorskix jazykov* (*Tezisy dokladov*), pp. 15-22 (Moscow, 1959).

—, "Nekotorye voprosy vokalizma finno-ugorskix jazykov", in *Voprosy finno-ugorskogo jazykoznanija*, pp. 33-64 (Moscow-Leningrad, 1962).
—, "O govore drevne-komi plemen", *Sbornik Komissii po sobiraniju slovarja i izučeniju dialektov komi jazyka* 2.32-50 (Moscow, 1931).
—, "O nekotoryx iranskix zaimstvovanijax v permskix jazykax", *IzvAN*, 10(4).385-392 (1951).
—, "O nekotoryx ètimologijax N. Ja. Marra po ugrofinskim jazykam", in *Protiv vul'garizacii i izvraščenija marksizma v jazykoznanii* II, pp. 492-500 (Moscow, 1952).
—, "Ob udarenii v komi-permjackom jazyke", *TIJa*, 1.107-119 (1952).
—, "Otraženie perexoda drevnerusskogo *e* v *o* v russkix zaimstvovanijax jazyka komi", *DSIJa*, 2.72-82 (1952).
—, "Očerednye zadači stroitel'stva komi literaturnogo jazyka", *Sbornik Komissii po sobiraniju slovarja i izučeniju dialektov komi jazyka*, 2.5-14 (Moscow, 1931).
—, "o-hääliku ajaloo küsimusest komi keeles", *ESA*, 7.220-231 (1961).
—, "Permskie jazyki", in *Mladopiśmennye jazyki narodov SSSR*, pp. 411-423 (Moscow-Leningrad, 1959).
—, "Ponuditel'nyi zalog v permskix jazykax", *Zapiski. NIIELJa Udmurtskoj ASSR*, 18.93-113 (Iževsk, 1957).
—, "Severno-russkie dialekty v svete komi-russkix zaimstvovanij", in *Naučnaja konferencija po voprosam finnougorskoj filologii, 23 janvarja – 4 fevralja 1947 g.* (*Tezisy dokladov*) (Leningrad, 1947).
—, "Vepssko-karel'skie zaimstvovanija v komi-zyrjanskix dialektax", in *Akademiku Viktoru Vladimiroviču Vinogradovu k ego šestidesjatiletiju*, pp. 779-189 (Moscow, 1956).
—, "V. G. Orlova. Istorija affrikat v russkom jazyke v svjazi s obrazovaniem russkix narodnyx govorov", *IzvAN*, 20(1).79-86 (1961).
—, "Voprosy istorii permskix jazykov", *Naučnoe soveščanie po voprosam udmurtskogo jazyka i piśmennosti, 1-4 ijulja 1952 g.* (*Tezisy dokladov*), pp. 11-20 (Iževsk, 1952).
—, and Majtinskaja, K. E., "Dmitrij Vladimirovič Bubrix", in *Voprosy finno-ugorskogo jazykoznanija*, pp. 5-8 (Moscow-Leningrad, 1962).
—, and Popov, S. A., "Jaźvinskie komi", *SovÈtn*, 4.194-199 (1950).
—, and Teplašina, T. I., "Nekotorye osobennosti glazovskogo dialekta", *Zapiski. NIIELJa Udmurtskoj. ASSR*, 19.218-227 (Iževsk, 1959).
*Magyar-orosz társalgó* (Moscow, 1956), 128 pp.
Majtinskaja, K. E., "È. Beke. (K 75-letiju so dnja roždenija)", in *Voprosy finno-ugorskogo jazykoznanija*, pp. 265-269 (Moscow-Leningrad, 1962).
Majtinskaja, K. E., "Funkcija mestoimennogo suffiksa *-n* v ličnyx i voprositel'nyx mestoimenijax finno-ugorskix jazykov", in *Voprosy finno-ugorskogo jazykoznanija* pp. 65-80 (Moscow-Leningrad, 1962).
—, *Vengerskij jazyk. I: Vvedenie, fonetika, morfologija* (Moscow, 1955), 304 pp; *II: Grammatičeskoe slovoobrazovanie* (Moscow, 1959), 226 pp.

—, "K voprosu o kategorii padeža (Na materiale finno-ugorskix jazykov)", in *Voprosy grammatičeskogo stroja*, pp. 226-249 (Moscow, 1955).

—, "Neopredelennyj padež i absoljutnaja forma v vengerskom jazyke", *UZ Voennogo instituta inostrannyx jazykov*, 6.67-77 (1948).

—, "Obščie svedenija o finno-ugorskix jazykax", in *Mladopiśmennye jazyki narodov SSSR*, pp. 400-410 (Moscow-Leningrad, 1959).

—, "Otraženie različij grammatičeskogo stroja v dvujazyčnyx slovarjax (Na materiale finno-ugorskix jazykov s privlečeniem tjurkskix)", *Leksikografičeskij sbornik* 1.160-171 (Moscow, 1957).

—, *Razvitie sistemy padežej v vengerskom jazyke* (dissertation). 554 pp. Dissertation Abstract (Mowcow, 1950), 34 pp.

—, "Soome-ugri keelte kirjeldavate grammatikate koostamise printsiibid", *KKIU*, 1.26-52 (1956).

—, "Značenie različij v grammatičeskoj strukture jazykov dlja postroenija dvujazyčnyx slovarej (Na materialax finno-ugorskix i tjurkskix jazykov)", *Soveščanie po voprosam opisateľnoj grammatiki, leksikografii i dialektologii* (*Tezisy dokladov*), pp. 14-20 (Moscow, 1953).

Majšev, I. I., *Poslelogi v permskix jazykax* (manuscript).

—, *Razvitie suffiksa komi öś, udmurtskogo èś* (*eś*) (manuscript).

Makarov, G. N., *Imennye* (*substantivnye*) *opredeliteľnye slovosočetanija v finskom jazyke* (dissertation abstract) (Moscow, 1955), 23 pp.

—, "K voprosu ob otgraničenii složnogo slova ot slovosočetanija v literaturnom finskom jazyke", *Pribaltijsko-finskoe jazykoznanie* = *Trudy Kareľskogo filiala AN SSSR* 12.25-48 (Petrozavodsk, 1958).

—, "Substantivnye slovosočetanija tipa "imja suščestvitel'noe + imja suščestvitel'noe v kosvennyx padežax" v finskom jazyke", *Pribaltijsko-finskoe jazykoznanie* (= *Trudy Kareľskogo filiala AN SSSR* 23.63-77) (1960).

*Marij literaturnyj jylmyn orfografijže* (= *Orfografija marijskogo literaturnogo jazyka*) (Joškar-Ola, 1954), 19 pp.

*Marijsko-russkij slovar'* (*s priloženiem kratkogo grammatičeskogo očerka marijskogo jazyka*) (Moscow, 1956), 863 pp.

*Marij literaturnyj jylmyn orfografijžy* (= *Orfografija marijskogo literaturnogo jazyka* – Hill Cheremis) (Koźmodemjansk, 1954), 20 pp.

Markov, F. P., "O zvukovom sostave i fonetičeskix javlenijax prialatyrskogo dialekta èrzjanskogo jazyka (na materiale govorov ss. Nizovka, Čukaly, Kučenjaevo, Pikejasy, Djurki i Llovo Mordovskoj ASSR)", *KKIU*, 5.154-176 (1960).

—, *Prialatyrskij dialekt èrzja-mordovskogo jazyka* (dissertation abstract) (Saransk, 1959), 20 pp.

—, *Sistema slovoizmeniteľnyx form prialatyrskogo dialekta èrzja-mordovskogo jazyka* (Saransk, 1959), 47 pp.

—, "Želatel'noe naklonenie v mordovskix jazykax", *Trudy. NIJaLIE Mordovskoj ASSR* 20.23-41 (Saransk, 1960).

Maskaev, A. I., "O principax perevoda s russkogo na mordovskie (èrzja i mokša) jazyki", *Materialy naučnoj sessii po voprosam mordovskogo jazykoznanija*, 1.158-179 (Saransk, 1955).

Masing, U., "Ühest võimalikust akadi laensõnast", *ESA*, 2.160-181 (1956).

Mašezerskij, V. I., "Naučno-issledovatel'skaja rabota instituta jazyka, literatury i istorii Karel'skogo filiala AN SSSR za gody Sovetskoj vlasti", *Izvestija Karel'skogo i Kol'skogo filialov AN SSSR* 1.26-34 (Petrozavodsk, 1957).

*Materialy naučnoj sessii po voprosam mordovskogo jazykoznanija II. Normy mordovskix (mokša i èrzja) literaturnyx jazykov* (Saransk, 1955), 240 pp.

Matveev, A. K., "Finno-ugorskie zaimstvovanija v russkix govorax Severnogo Urala", *UZ Sverdlovskogo pedagogičeskogo instituta* 16.201-215 (Sverdlovsk, 1958). *UZ Ural'skogo gos. universiteta im. A. M. Gor'kogo* 32 (Sverdlovsk, 1959), 123 pp. Dissertation abstract (Leningrad, 1959), 16 pp.

—, "Mansijskie zaimstvovanija v russkix govorax po reke Pelymu", *UZ Ural'skogo gos. universiteta* 20.71-85 (Sverdlovsk, 1958).

—, "Novye dannye o finno-ugorskix zaimstvovanijax v russkix govorax Urala i Zapadnoj Sibiri", in *Voprosy finno-ugorskogo jazykoznanija*, pp. 127-142 (Moscow-Leningrad, 1962).

Mäger, M., "Eesti linnunimetuste alused", *ESA*, 7.54-73 (1961).

Mälksoo, T., *Kesk-vepsamurde foneetika* (Diplomitöö) (Tartu, 1955), 133 pp.

Männik, E., *Mitmuse genitiiv eesti murdeis* (Diplomitöö) (Tartu, 1954), 154 pp.

Meščerskij, N. A., "Russko-karel'skie slovarnye zapisi XVII-načala XVIII v.", in *Pribaltijsko-finskoe jazykoznanie = Trudy Karel'skogo filiala AN SSSR*, 23.16-32 (1960).

Mičurina, N. P., "Složnye slova s padežno-neoformlennym pervym komponentom v finskom jazyke", *SovF*, 1.193-198 (Leningrad, 1948).

Mihkla, K., "Probleeme seoses eesti keele teadusliku süntaksiga", *KKIU*, 6.61-80 (1961).

Mikušev, A. K., *Pesennoe tvorčestvo naroda komi v sovetskuju èpoxu* (dissertation, 1953), 124 pp.

—, "Iz istorii russkoj nauki o komi narodnoj poèzii", *Russkij fol'klor*, 4.230-234 (Moscow-Leningrad, 1959).

Mokań, A. A., "Važnejšie fonetičeskie i morfologičeskie osobennosti vengerskix zaimstvovanij v ukrainskom ukajuščem dialekte Tjačeskogo rajona Zakarpatskoj oblasti", *Finno-ugorskaja filologija = UZLU*, 314 (63).60-74 (1962).

Mordinov, A., and Sanžeev, G., "Nekotorye voprosy mladopiśmennyx jazykov narodov SSSR", *Bol'ševik*, 8.38-48 (1951).

Morozova, A. G., "Traktovka sintaksičeskoj kategorii skazuemogo i obstojatel'stva v finskom jazyke", *UZ Karelo-finskogo gos. universiteta*, 5(1).161-167 (Petrozavodsk, 1955).

—, *Upravlenie glagolov v finskom jazyke* (dissertation) (Petrozavodsk, 1952).

Možarskij, Ja. G., "Obsko-ugorskie jazyki", in *Mladopiśmennye jazyki narodov SSSR*, pp. 455-461 (Moscow-Leningrad, 1959).

Muhel, V., *Väike vene-eesti sônaraamat* (Tallinn, 1960), 14,000 words.

Mullonen, M. I., "Bezličnye predloženija v sovremennom finskom jazyke", *UZ Petrozavodskogo gos. universiteta* 5 (1).161-167 (Petrozavodsk, 1957).

Must, M., "Haruldasi sônu kirde-eesti rannikumurdest", *ESA*, 6.132-141 (1960).

—, "Môningaid vene laensõnu eesti murretes", *ESA*, 4.157-163 (1958).

—, "Murdetekst Juuru Kain murrakust", *ESA* 7. 11-121 (1961).

—, "Pôhja-eesti keskmurde läänepiirist", *KKIU* 2.86-95 (1958).

—, *Vene laensônad setu murdes* (Diplomitöö) (Tartu, 1946), 314 pp.

—, "Vene laensônade laenamisel ja kodunemisel valitsevatest seaduspärasustest eesti keeles", *ETAT*, 5(2).128-142 (1956).

—, *Vene-Eesti suhete kajastumine lôunaeesti murrete sônavaras.* Kandidaadiväitekiri, kaitstud 1954 a. Tartu ülikoolis (Tartu, 1954).

Nassar, H., *Verb liivi keeles* (Diplomitöö) (Tartu, 1952), 83 pp.

Nečaev, G. A., "Funkcii formanta *-ös* vinitel'nogo padeža v komi jazyke (Tezisy)", *Soveščanie po voprosam istoričeskoj grammatiki i istoričeskoj dialektologii finno-ugorskix jazykov*, pp. 64-67 (Moscow, 1959).

—, "K voprosu o grammatičeskoj kategorii oduševlennosti i neoduševlennosti v komi jazyke", *UZ Komi gos. pedagogičeskij institut*, 7.177-200 (Syktyvkar, 1959).

Nigol, S., "Afrikaadid hargla murrakus", *ESA*, 3.82-103 (1957).

—, "h-häälik hargla murrakus", *KKIU*, 2.118-147 (1958).

—, *Häälikulooline ülevaade Hargla murrakust* (dissertation manuscript) (Tartu, 1959).

—, *Istoričeskaja fonetika govora Xargla, Konsonantizm* (dissertation abstract). (Tartu, 1959), 26 pp.

Noorkôiv, V., *Käänetest kujunenud adverbe läänemeresoome keeltes* (Diplomitöö). (Tartu, 1951), 223 pp.

Norvik, M., "Isuri ja vadja keele sufiksi *-zikko* päritolust", *ESA*, 5.244-250 (1959).

Nurm, E., "Deklineerimise üksikküsimusi", *ESA*, 3.36-48 (1957).

—, "Ôigekeelsuse sônaraamatute koostamise pôhimôtteist ja nende rakendamisest", *ETAT*, 4(2).204-216.

—, Raiet, E., and Kindlam, M., *Ôigekeelsuse sônaraamat* (Tallinn, 1960), 872 pp.

Nurmekund, P., "Sôna *sada* päritolust", *ESA*, 4.173-183 (1958).

Ob"edkin, V. D., "Fonetika staro-turdakovskogo dialekta èrzja-mordovskogo jazyka", *Zapiski. NIJaLIE Mordovskoj ASSR*, 18.114-153 (Saransk, 1958).

—, *Staro-turdakovskij dialekt èrzjamordovskogo jazyka* (dissertation abstract) (Moscow, 1958), 19 pp.

*Očerki mordovskix dialektov.* Tom I. Saransk, 1961. 396 pp. Authors: Markov, F. P., (Prialatyrskij dialekt); Ob"edkin, V. D. (Staro-turdakovskij dialekt); Jakuškin, A. V. (Drakinskij dialekt); Cygankin, D. V. (Šugurovskij dialekt).

Oldal, G., and Geiger, B., *Magyar-orosz zsebszótár* (Moscow, 1960), 9,000 words.

Ollikainen, V. M., *Glagolnye suffiksy s zalogovym značeniem v sovremennom finskom literaturnom jazyke* (dissertation abstract) (Moscow, 1955), 21 pp.

—, "O glagol'nyx suffiksax s zalogovoj napravlennost'ju v sovremennom finskom literaturnom jazyke", in *Pribaltijsko-finskoe jazykoznanie* (= *Trudy Karelskogo filiala AN SSSR* 23.42-62) (1960).

Osipov, I., *Višerskie pesni i skazki* (Syktyvkar, 1941), 341 pp.

Paabo, O., *Mitmuse osastav eesti vanemas kirjakeeles* (Diplomitöö) (Tartu, 1955), 175 pp.

Pajusalu, E., "Adessiivi funktsioonid eesti murretes ja lähemates sugulaskeeltes", *KK*, 1(4/5).246-258 (1958).

—, *Läänemere keelte väliskohakäänded* (Käänete funktsioonid). Kandidaadiväitekiri (Tallinn, 1957).

—, "Läänemere keelte allatiivi funktsioonid", *KKIU*, 5.68-116 (1960).

—, "Soome-ugri *l*-käänetest", *ESA*, 3.159-172 (1957).

—, "Ülevaade läänemere keelte ablatiivi funktsioonidest", *ETAT*, 6(2).133-153 (1957).

Paljak, J., "Supletiivsusest eesti keeles", *ESA*, 7.17-30 (1961).

Pall, V., *Ajad ja kôneviisid mordva keeles*. Kandidaadiväitekiri, kaitstud 1955. a. Tartu ülikoolis (Tartu, 1955).

—, *Ajakategooria tunnused läänemere keeltes* (Diplomitöö) (Tartu, 1952), 139 pp.

—, "Liitsônalistest kohanimedest pôhisônaga *saar*", *ESA*, 6.39-47 (1960).

—, "Märkmeid mordva keele konjunktiivi kujunemisest", *ESA*, 1.182-187 (1955).

—, "Märkmeid mordva keelte konjugatsioonist", *ESA*, 5.261-267 (1959).

—, "Kohanimedest ja nende uurimisest", *KK*, 4.217-223 (1961).

—, "Negatsioonist mordva keeles", *ESA*, 3.217-223 (1957).

—, "Ob izučenii èstonskoj toponomiki", in *Voprosy finno-ugorskoj jazykoznanija*, pp. 154-160 (Moscow-Leningrad, 1962).

—, "Veekogude nimedest endisel Pôhja-Tartumaal", *ESA*, 7.74-85 (1961).

Palli, H., "Eesti isikunimedest Harju- ja Järvamaal XVI sajandil", *KK*, 2.595-608 (1959).

Palmeos, P., "Eesti keele pronoomenist 'enese ~ enda'", *ESA*, 2.106-123 (1956).

—, "Eesti keele sônavara pôhifondi soome-ugrilisest osast, mis on ühine ungari keelega", in *Teaduslikud tööd pühendatud Tartu riikliku ülikooli 150. aastapäevale*, pp. 125-157 (Tallinn, 1952).

—, "Eesti koduloomede nimedest", *ESA*, 1.97-117 (1955).

—, "Karjala valdai murret uurimas", *KK*, 1(4/5).293-298 (1958).

—, "Märkmeid karjala valdai murdest", *ESA*, 3.180-198 (1957).

Patrušev, G. S., "Iz istorii izučenii marijskogo jazyka", *UZ Marijskogo gos. pedagogičeskogo instituta* 16.3-28 (Joškar-Ola, 1958).

—, *Osnovnye puti obogaščenija slovarnogo sostava marijskogo jazyka* (dissertation abstract) (Leningrad, 1955), 16 pp.

—, "Puti obogaščenija slovarnogo sostava marijskogo jazyka", *Učenye zapiski. Marijskij NIJaLI* 6.23-39 (Joškar-Ola, 1954).

—, "V. M. Vasil'ev kak leksikograf", *Trudy Marijskogo NIJaLI* 13.165-176 (Joškar-Ola, 1959/60).

Päll, E., "Infinitiiv alusena ja öeldisena eesti keeles", *KKIU*, 1.60-75 (1956).

—, "Infinitiiv eesti keele fraseoloogia allikana", *ESA*, 2.138-145 (1956).

—, "NLKP XXII kongress ja eesti nôukogude filoloogia ülesanded", *KK*, 5:6, 321-328 (1962).

Peegel, J., "*Eesti regivärsilise rahvalaulu keelest* (Tartu, 1961), 107 pp.

—, *Eesti vanade rahvalaulude keele morfoloogia.* Kandidaadiväitekiri, kaitstud 1954 a. Tartu ülikoolis (Tartu, 1954).

—, "Häälikuloolisi ääremärkusi rahvalaulude keelest", *ESA* 2.53-61 (1956).

—, *Lôuna-eesti rahvalaulu- ja murdekeele suhe morfoloogia alal.* (Diplomitöö) (Tartu, 1945).

—, "Mônede 'Kalevipojas' esinevate morfoloogiliste nähtuste ning vormide taustast", *TRÜT*, 53.145-162 (1957).

—, "Mônedest arhailistest ja omapärastest vormidest rahvalaulude keeles", *ESA*, 1.88-96 (1955).

—, "O jazyke staryx èstonskix narodnyx pesen", in *Voprosy finno-ugorskoj jazykoznanija*, pp. 161-164 (Moscow-Leningrad, 1962).

—, "Tingiva kôneviisi tähenduslikest funktsioonidest ja kohast eesti kôneviiside süsteemis", *ESA*, 3.49-71 (1957).

Pengitov, N. T., "Formy čisla imen i osobennosti ix upotreblenija v marijskom jazyke", *Trudy Marijskogo NIJaLI*, 10.77-89 (Joškar-Ola, 1957).

—, "Itogi marijskoj dialektologičeskoj èkspedicii MarNII 1957 goda", *Trudy Marijskogo NIJaLI*, 13.177-188 (Joškar-Ola, 1959/60).

—, "K voprosu o sčetnyx birkax u marijcev", *Trudy Marijskogo NIJaLI*, 14.151-157 (Joškar-Ola, 1959).

—, "Nekotorye voprosy grammatiki marijskogo jazyka", *Trudy Marijskogo NIJaLI*, 7.81-96 (Joškar-Ola, 1955).

—, "O nekotoryx osobennostjax narečij v marijskom jazyke", *Trudy. Marijskij gos. pedagogičeskij institut imeni N. K. Krupskoj*, 5.69-82 (Kozmodemjansk, 1946).

—, "O padežax v marijskom jazyke", *Trudy Marijskogo NIJaLI*, 9.37-57 (Joškar-Ola, 1956).

—, *Pričastija v marijskom jazyke* = *UZ. Marijskij gos. pedagogičeskij institut* 9.116-132 (Joškar-Ola, 1955). Dissertation Abstract (Joškar-Ola, 1951), 16 pp.

—, *Sopostavitel'naja grammatika russkogo i marijskogo jazykov. I: Vvedenie, fonetika, morfologija* (Joškar-Ola, 1958), 175 pp.

—, "Sostojanie i zadači marijskogo jazykoznanija", *Trudy Marijskogo NIJaLI*, 13.3-12 (Joškar-Ola, 1959).

Perevoščikov, P. N., *Deepričastija i deepričastnye konstrukcii v udmurtskom jazyke* (Iževsk, 1959), 328 pp.

—, "Deepričastija na *-sa* v udmurtskom jazyke", in *Tezisy dokladov na soveščanii* *po voprosam finno-ugorskogo jazykoznanija, 9-12 marta 1954* g., pp. 16-18 (Moscow, 1954).

—, "Funkcii i proisxoždenie podčinitel'nogo sojuza *bere* v udmurtskom jazyke", *SovF*, 4.3-19 (Iževsk, 1949).

—, "K voprosu obosoblenija členov predloženija v udmurtskom jazyke, vyražennyx deepričastnymi oborotami", *Zapiski. NIIELJa Udmurtskoj ASSR*, 19.102-112 (Iževsk, 1959).

—, "O nekotoryx sintaksičeskix konstrukcijax v udmurtskom jazyke", *VJa*, 1(6).103-119 (1952).

—, "Prjamaja i kosvennaja reč' v udmurtskom jazyke", *Zapiski. NIIELJa Udmurtskoj ASSR*, 15.155-192 (Iževsk, 1951).

—, "Pritjažatel'nye formy svjazi imen v opredelitel'nyx slovosočetanijax udmurtskogo jazyka", *Zapiski. NIIELJa Udmurtskoj ASSR*, 18.71-92 (Iževsk, 1957).

Pervik, A., *Vene keele mõjustusi vepsa keele süntaksis* (Diplomitöö) (Tartu, 1955), 145 pp.

Peterburgskij, F. I., "O tak nazyvaemom pritjažatel'nom sklonenii v mordovskix jazykax", *UZ. Mordovskij ped. institut imeni A. I. Poležaeva*, 6.170-204 (Saransk, 1957).

Plesovskij, F. V., "K voprosu o razvitii sem'i u komi i udmurtov (po terminam rodstva)", *Istoriko-filologičeskij sbornik*. Komi filial AN SSSR 6.105 -129 (Syktyvkar, 1960).

Pigin, M. I., "Proisxoždenie soslagatel'nogo naklonenija v mordovskix jazykax", *UZ Karelo-finskogo gos. universiteta* 4(1).66-83 (Petrozavodsk, 1954).

—, *Zalogi v èrzja-mordovskom jazyke* (dissertation), 309 pp.

Pihel, K., *Ainsuse 3. isiku tarvitamine mitmuse 3. isiku asemel soome keeles* (Diplomitöö) (Tartu, 1954), 69 pp.

Pikamäe, A., "Eesti keele vältesüsteemist", *ESA*, 4.101-109 (1958).

—, *Tüveline astmevaheldus läänemerekeeltes* (Diplomitöö) (Tartu, 1953), 157 pp.

—, *Tüveline astmevaheldus läänemeresoome keeltes ja lapi keeles*. Kandidaadiväitekiri = *TRÜT* 50 (Tartu, 1957), 50 pp.

Ploom, H., *Kaassõnad eesti murdeis* (Diplomitöö) (Tartu, 1955), 219 pp.

Podorova, A. I., "Časticy v komi jazyke", *Istoriko-filologičeskij sbornik* 3.119-130 (Syktyvkar, 1956).

—, *Časticy v komi jazyke* (manuscript). 384 pp. Institut jazykoznanija. Dissertation abstract, 19 pp. Komi filial (Moscow, 1954).

*Poslovicy i pogovorki udmurtskogo naroda* (Iževsk, 1960), 208 pp.

Popov, A. I., "Pribaltijsko-finskie ličnye imena v novgorodskix berestjanyx gramotax", *Pribaltijsko-finskoe jazykoznanie* (= *Trudy Karel'skogo filiala AN SSSR* 12.95-100) (Petrozavodsk, 1958).

Poppe, N. N., "K voprosu ob otnošenii altajskix jazykov k ural'skim", *Izvestija Obščestva obsledovanija i izučenija Azerbajdžana* 3.99-106 (Baku, 1926).

—, *Lingvističeskie problemy Vostočnoj Sibiri* ("Jazyki neneckoj gruppy") (Moscow-Irkutsk, 1933), 54 pp.

—, "O desjatkax v finno-ugorskix jazykax", *Jazykovednye problemy po čisliteľnym* 1.120-126 (Leningrad, 1927).

—, "O čisliteľnom "voseḿ" v ugorskix jazykax", *Jazykovednye problemy po čisliteľnym*, 1.127-129 (Leningrad, 1927).

—, "Sovremennoe položenie izučenija finno-ugorskix jazykov i bližajšie zadači ego", *Jafetičeskij sbornik*, 7.141-155 (Leningrad, 1932).

—, "Uralo-altajskaja teorija v svete Sovetskogo jazykoznanija", *IzvAN*, 3.79-88 (1940).

Potapkin, S. G., and Imjarekov, A. K., *Mokšansko-russkij slovaŕ* (Moscow, 1949), 17,000 words, 359 pp.

—, and —, *Russko-mokšanskij slovar'* (Moscow, 1951), 40,000 words, 688 pp.

Pozdeeva, A. A., *Sintaksičeskie funkcii imennoj formy na ėz i ys v permskix jazykax* (dissertation abstract). (Leningrad), 6 pp.

Pôld, E., "Jooni lääne-nigula murraku konsonantismist", *TRÜT*, 41.127-140 (1956).

—, *Lääne-nigula murrak* (Diplomitöö) (Tartu, 1955), 217 pp.

*Pravila udmurtskoj orfografii i punktuacii* (Iževsk, 1958), 81 pp.

Prokofjev, G. N., "Ėneckij (jenisejsko-samoedskij) dialekt", *Trudy po lingvistike, Institut narodov Severa I*, pp. 75-90 (= *Jazyki i piśmennosť narodov Severa 1.*) (Moscow-Leningrad, 1937).

—, *Kratkaja grammatika samoedskogo (neneckogo) jazyka* (stekl.) (Leningrad, 1934).

—, "Neneckij (jurako-samoedskij) jazyk", *Trudy po lingvistike, Institut narodov Severa. Tom 1*, pp. 5-52 (Moscow-Leningrad, 1937).

—, "Nganasanskij (tavgijskij) dialekt", *Trudy po lingvistike, Institut narodov Severa* 1.53-74 (Moscow-Leningrad, 1937) (= *Jazyki i piśmennosť narodov Severa*, I).

—, "*Seľkupskaja (ostjako-samoedskaja) grammatika*", *Trudy po lingvistike, Institut narodov Severa*, Tom 4:1 (Leningrad, 1935). 131 + 5 pp.

—, "Sel'kupskij (ostjako-samoedskij) jazyk", *Trudy po lingvistike, Institut narodov Severa*, Tom 1. pp. 91-124 (Moscow-Leningrad, 1937) (= *Jazyki i piśmennosť narodov Severa*, I).

Pyrerka, V., "Čelovek iz roda Pyrerka. (O neneckom filologe A. P. Pyrerka. Očerk)", *Neva*, 7.177-184 (Moscow-Leningrad, 1959).

Pyrerka, A. P., *Olenevodčeskaja terminologija v neneckom jazyke* (manuscript). Rukopiś v Arxive AN SSSR v Leningrade.

—, and Tereščenko, N. M., *Russko-neneckij slovaŕ*. I. I. Meščaninova, ed. = *SovF*, 15 (Moscow, 1948). 15,000 words, 405 pp.

Raiet, E., "Inglise laensônade kujust tänapäeva eesti kirjakeeles", *KKIU*, 5.154-189 (1961).

—, "Küsimusi eesti liitverbi alalt", *KKIU*, 1.76-87 (1956).

Randmaa, M., *Umbisikulise tegumoe olevik eesti murretes* (Diplomitöö) (Tartu, 1955), 162 pp.

Rannut, L. "Ajamäärus eesti keeles", *ESA*, 6.71-112 (1960).

—, *Obstojateľstvo vremeni v èstonskom jazyke* (dissertation abstract) (Tallinn, 1960), 37 pp.

—, "Seesütlev ja alalütlev ajamääruse käänetena", *ESA*, 5.55-77 (1959).

Rätsep, H., "Aspektikategooriast eesti keeles", *ESA*, 3.72-81 (1957).

—, *Infiniitsed verbivormid soome-ugri keeltes* (Kandidaadiväitekiri) (Tartu, 1954).

—, "i-sufiksilistest verbidest eesti keeles", *ESA*, 2.74-91 (1956).

—, "Liivi fraseoloogiat", *ESA*, 5.226-242 (1959).

—, "Läänemeresoome keelte *t*-lise infinitiivi päritoluga seoses olevaid probleeme", *ESA*, 1.152-162 (1955).

—, "*n*-ilistest infiniitsetest verbivormidest soome-ugri keeltes", *TRÜT*, 43.100-113 —(1956).

, "Ob istoričeskom issledovanii frazeologii pribaltijsko-finskix jazykov (na materiale èstonskogo jazyka)", in *Voprosy finno-ugorskogo jazykoznanija*, pp. 101-108 (Moscow-Leningrad, 1962).

—, *Ühisest fraseoloogiast läänemere keeltes* (Diplomitöö) (Tartu, 1951), 89 pp.

—, "Vadja fraseoloogiat", *ESA*, 6.162-178 (1960).

Remmel, N., "Eesti keele sônajärjestuse küsimusi", *KK*, 1(9).543-555 and 1(10). 610-619 (1958).

Riikoja, È., *Eesti keele nimisônade nominatiivse liitumise reeglite rahvakeelne alus* (dissertation manuscript). 386 pp. (Tallinn, 1960).

—, "Kahest nominatiivse liitumise rühmast", *KKIU*, 2.7-23 (1958).

—, "Kehaliiget ja abinôu märkivate sônade liitumisest", *KK*, 1(4/5).280-289 (1958).

—, "*môte*-tüüpi täiendsôna liitumisest", *KK*, 5(4).222-228 (1962).

—, "Nimisônade nominatiivset ja genetiivset liitumist môjustavaid tegureid", *KK*, 5:10.612-622 (1962).

—, *Narodnojazykovaja osnova pravil nominativnogo složenija suščestviteľnyx v èstonskom jazyke* (dissertation abstract) (Tallinn, 1960), 31 pp.

—, "Olulist asukohta vôi esinemisaega märkiva täiendsôna liitumine", *KK*, 2(3). 157-165 and 2(4).209-217 (1959).

Rombandeeva, E. I., "Kauzativnye glagoly v aktivnyx i passivnyx sintaksičeskix konstrukcijax mansijskogo jazyka", in *Voprosy finno-ugorskogo jazykoznanija*, pp. 236-256 (Moscow-Leningrad, 1962).

—, *Russko-mansijskij slovar̕ dlja mansijskoj školy* (Leningrad, 1954), 10,800 words, 392 pp.

Rot, A. M., "K voprosu o sklonenii imen v finno-ugorskix jazykax", *Naučnye zapiski. Užgorodskij gos. universitet*, 13.115-131 (Lvov, 1955).

Russkaja, Ju. N., "O nekotoryx osobennostjax padežnoj sistemy priural'skogo govora xantyjskogo jazyka", in *Voprosy finno-ugorskogo jazykoznanija* pp. 257-264 (Moscow-Leningrad, 1962).

—, "Soglasnye kazymskogo dialekta xantyjskogo jazyka po èksperimental'nym dannym", in *Soome-ugri keelte dialektoloogia alane nôupidamine* (Ettekannete teesid), pp. 26-30 (Tartu, 1958).

*Russko-udmurtskoj slovar'* (= Russko-udmurtskij slovar') (Moscow, 1956). 40,000 words, 1,360 pp.

Rybakova, P. G., and Učaev, Z. V., *Kuryk marij den olyk marij mut-vlakym tangastaryme slovar'* (= Sravnitel'nyj slovar' na lugovom i gorno-marijskom narečijax) (Joškar-Ola, 1955), 86 pp.

Saar, J., *Läänemeresoome ja volga keelte sisekohakäänete funktsioonid* (Diplomitöö) (Tartu, 1950).

Sabo, L., "Upotreblenie pritjažatel'nyx suffiksov i sposoby ix zameščenija v sovremennom vodskom jazyke", *Finno-ugorskaja filologija* = *UZLU* 314(63).85-100 (1962).

Santo, E. A., "Formal'noe vyraženie povelitel'nogo naklonenija v sovremennom vengerskom jazyke", *TIJa*, 3.155-173 (1954).

—, *Povelitel'noe naklonenie v sovremennom vengerskom jazyke* (dissertation abstract) (Moscow, 1952), 15 pp.

Sarv, I., "Eesti kõnekäändude liikidest ja funktsioonidest", *KK*, 1(4/5).231-245 (1958).

Saxarova, M. A., *Bezličnye predloženija v komi jazyke* (manuscript), 1956.

—, *Imja prilagatel'noe v komi jazyke* (dissertation) (Syktyvkar, 1953), 168 + 19 pp. Komi filial AN SSSR. Dissertation abstract (Syktyvkar, 1953), 16 pp.

—, "K voprosu o substantivizacii imen prilagatel'nyx i ad"ektivizacii imen suščestvitel'nyx", *Istoriko- filologičeskij sbornik*, 3.70-78 (Syktyvkar, 1956).

—, "Problema naučnoj i političeskoj termonologii v komi jazyke", *Trudy Komi filiala AN SSSR*, 1:105-108 (Syktyvkar, 1953).

—, and Sel'kov, N. N., "Nekotorye osobennosti govora kol'skix komi", *Istoriko-filologičeskij sbornik*. Komi filial AN SSSR 6.130-151 (Syktyvkar, 1960).

Savatkova, A. A., *Marij orfografičeskij slovar'* (Hill Cheremis) (Joškar-Ola, 1956), 156 pp.

—, *Russkie zaimstvovanija v gornom narečii marijskogo jazyka* (dissertation manuscript, Institut jazykoznanija) (Moscow, 1953), 239 pp. Dissertation abstract (Moscow, 1953), 16 p.

Senkevič-Gudkova, V. V., "D. V. Bubrix kak issledovatel' finno-ugorskix jazykov", *IzvAN*, 9(3).186-195 (1950).

—, "K voprosu o fonetičeskix i nekotoryx morfologičeskix obščnostjax Kol'skosaamskix dialektov s samodijskimi jazykami", *Tezisy. Soveščanie po voprosam istoričeskoj grammatiki i istoričeskoj dialektologii finno-ugorskix jazykov*, pp. 35-39 (Moscow, 1959).

—, "K voprosu o fonetičeskix i nekotoryx morfologičeskix sxodstvax i različijax kol'sko-saamskix dialektov s samodijskimi jazykami", *UZ Karel'skogo pedagogičeskogo instituta*, 6.139-167 (Petrozavodsk, 1959).

—, "K voprosu ob obščnosti saamskogo jazyka (kol'sko-saamskix dialektov) s paleoaziatskimi jazykami", *UZ Karel'skogo pedagogičeskogo instituta* 9.67-84 (Petrozavodsk, 1959).

—, "U saami (Iz bloknota dialektologa)". *Na rubeže*, 1.135-147 (Petrozavodsk, 1957).

Serebrennikov, B. A., "Dva spornyx voprosa sravnitel'noj grammatiki finno-ugorskix

jazykov. 1. O proisxoždenii èlementa *l* v okončanijax tak nazyvaemyx vnešnemestnyx padežej. 2. Suščestvoval li v marijskom jazyke perexod zvukosočetanij *šn* > *št*?", *VJa*, 8(4). 79-85 (1959).
—, "Iz istorii obrazovanija glagol'nyx vremen v komi jazyke", *Istoriko-filologičeskij sbornik*, 3.57-69 (Syktyvkar, 1956).
—, "Iz istorii obrazovanija form otricatel'nogo glagola v jazyke komi", *Istoriko-filologičeskij sbornik*. Komi filial AN SSSR 6.178-183 (Syktyvkar, 1960).
—, "Iz istorii padežnoj sistemy permskix jazykov", in *Voprosy finno-ugorskogo jazykoznanija*, pp. 9-32 (Moscow-Leningrad, 1962).
—, "Iz istorii sklonenija imen suščestvitel'nyx i ličnyx mestoimenij v permskix jazykax", *Tezisy. Soveščanie po voprosam istoričeskoj grammatiki i istoričeskoj dialektologii finno-ugorskix jazykov*, pp. 40-43 (Moscow, 1959).
—, "Izoglossnye javlenija čuvašskogo i marijskogo jazykov", in *Akademiku Vladimiru Aleksandroviču Gordlevskomu k ego semidesjatipjatiletiju*, pp. 231-242 (1953).
—, "K kritike nekotoryx metodov tipologičeskix issledovanij", *VJa*, 7(5).24-33 (1958).
—, "K probleme svjazi javlenij jazyka s istoriej obščestva", *VJa*, 2(1).34-51 (1953).
—, "K probleme tipov leksičeskoj i grammatičeskoj abstrakcii", in *Voprosy grammatičeskogo stroja*, pp. 54-73 (Moscow, 1955).
—, *Kategorii vremeni i vida v finno-ugorskix jazykax permskoj i volžskoj grupp* (dissertation abstract) (Moscow, 1956), 31 pp.
—, *Kategorii vremeni i vida v finno-ugorskix jazykax permskoj i volžskoj grupp* (Moscow, 1960), 300 pp.
—, "Kategorii vremeni v pribaltijsko-finskix jazykax", in *Eesti keele süntaksi küsimusi*. (Eesti keele ja kirjanduse instituut, Tallinn, 1963), pp. 426-513.
—, "O dejstvitel'nom količestve glagol'nyx vremen v udmurtskom jazyke", *Zapiski. NIIELJa Udmurtskoj ASSR*, 19.93-101 (Iževsk, 1959).
—, "O finno-ugorskix ètimologijax v 'etimologičeskom slovare russkogo jazyka' M. Vasmera", *Leksikografičeskij sbornik*, 4 (Moscow, 1962), pp. 30-35.
—, "O metodax izučenija toponimičeskix nazvanij", *VJa*, 8.636-50 (1959).
—, "O nekotoryx sledax vlijanija finno-ugorskogo jazykovogo substrata v jazyke kazanskix tatar", in *Akademiku Viktoru Vladimiroviču Vinogradovu*, pp. 214-224 (1956).
—, "O nekotoryx voprosax istoričeskoj grammatiki komi jazyka", *Istoriko-filologičeskij sbornik*. Komi filial AN SSSR 5.119-130 (Syktyvkar, 1960).
—, "O prirode prošedšego neočevidnogo vremeni v permskix i marijskom jazykax", *Tezisy dokladov na soveščanii po voprosam finno-ugorskogo jazykoznanija, 9-12 marta 1954 g.*, pp. 37-42 (1954).
—, "O redkix slučajax sočetanija v odnoj glagol'noj forme dvux modal'nyx značenij v nekotoryx finno-ugorskix jazykax", in *Voprosy grammatiki* (*Sbornik statej k 75-letiju Akademika I. I. Meščaninova*), pp. 103-121 (Moscow-Leningrad, 1960).
—, "O vidovyx značenijax prošedšego očevidnogo i neočevidnogo vremeni v lugovostočnom marijskom jazyke", *DSIJa*, 2.91-96 (1952).

—, "O vzaimodejstvii jazykov (Problema substrata)", *VJa,* 4(1).7-25 (1955).

—, "Pluskvamperfekti ja perfekti päritolu probleemist läänemeresoome keeltes", *ESA,* 4.249-255 (1957).

—, "Problema substrata", *DSIJa* 9.33-56 (1956).

—, "Problemy sravnitel'no-istoričeskogo metoda i proisxoždenie jazykovyx semej", *Doklady i soobščenija, pročitannye na naučnoj konferencii po jazykoznaniju (Ijun', 1951 g.,)* pp. 202-224 (Moscow, 1952).

—, "Sravnitel'no-istoričeskij metod i kritika tak nazyvaemogo četyrexèlementnogo analiza N. Ja. Marra", in *Voprosy jazykoznanija v svete trudov I. V. Stalina,* pp. 145-170 (1950).

—, "Trud I. V. Stalina "Marksizm i voprosy jazykoznanija" i zadači izučenia mordovskix (èrzja i mokša) jazykov", *Materialy naučnoj sessii po voprosam mordovskogo jazykoznanija* 1.9-32 (Saransk, 1955).

—, "Volgo-okskaja toponimika na territorii Evropejskoj časti SSSR", *VJa,* 4(6).19-31 (1955).

—, "Volgo-okskaja toponimika na territorii Evropejskoj časti Sovetskogo Sojuza", *DSIJa,* 8.120-134 (1955).

—, "Voprosy razvitija osnovnogo slovarnogo fonda", *Trudy.* Institut jazyka i literatury AN Latvijskoj SSR 2.83-105 (Riga, 1953).

—, "Zadači v oblasti izučenija i razvitija marijskogo jazyka", *Marijskij NIJaLI,* 6.3-22 (Joškar-Ola, 1954).

—, "Zaključitel'noe slovo (na zasedanii Učenogo soveta Instituta jazykoznanija AN SSSR, posvjaščennom diskussii o teorii substrata. Fevr., 1955 g.)", *DSIJa,* 9.158-164 (1956).

—, "Zametki po istorii komi jazyka", *Istoriko-filologičeskij sbornik* 4.189-196 (Syktyvkar, 1958).

Sidorov, A. S., *Analiz dialektov komi jazyka* (manuscript). Rukopisnyj fond Komi filiala AN SSSR.

—, "Bytovye liriko-èpičeskie ižemskie pesni", *Lingvističeskij sbornik,* 2 (1952).

—, "Naučnoe soveščanie po voprosam jazykoznanija (Syktyvkar, 29.I.-1.II. 1952 g.)", *Trudy Komi filiala AN SSSR,* 1.119-124 (Syktyvkar, 1953).

—, "Nekotorye osobennosti sintaksičeskogo stroja severnogo (ižemskogo) dialekta komi jazyka", *Lingvističeskij sbornik,* 2.68-81 (Syktyvkar, 1952).

—, "Novye pamjatniki drevnekomi piśmennosti (S kommentarijami, podstročnymi, primečanijami i zaključeniem V. I. Lytkina)", in *Voprosy finno-ugorskogo jazykoznanija,* pp. 178-211 (Moscow-Leningrad, 1962).

—, "Otricatel'nye predloženija i otricatel'nye oboroty v komi jazyke", *DSIJa,* 7.55-67 (1955).

—, *Pis'mennost' èpoxi rannego feodalizma* (manuscript).

—, "Porjadok slov v komi predloženii", *Naučnaja konferencija po voprosam finno-ugorskoj filologii, Jan. 23 – Feb. 4 1947 g. (Tezisy dokladov),* pp. 54-55 (Leningrad, 1947) = *SovF* 4.20-32 (Iževsk, 1949).

—, *Porjadok slov v predloženii komi jazyka* (dissertation manuscript). (Syktyvkar, 1953), 104 pp. (Syktyvkar, 1945), AN SSSR, Baza v Komi ASSR, 13 + 369 pp.
—, *Prinadležnostno-ukazatel'nye ličnye suffiksy v komi jazyke* (dissertation manuscript). Syktyvkar, AN SSSR, Baza v Komi ASSR.
—, "Priroda sintaksičeskoj svjazi meždu opredeljajuščim i opredeljaemym slovami v jazyke komi", *Zapiski Obščestva izučenija Komi kraja* 5.41-50 (Syktyvkar, 1930).
—, "Puti razvitija komi literaturnogo jazyka", in *Naučnoe soveščanie po voprosam jazykoznanija v g. Syktyvkare, 28-31 janvarja 1952 g.* (*Tezisy dokladov*), pp. 8-14 (Moscow, 1952).
—, *Sintaksis komi jazyka* (manuscript). Komi filial AN SSSR (Syktyvkar, 1952).
—, "Sintaksičeskie i leksiko-semantičeskie formy vyraženija glagol'nogo vida v komi jazyke", *Lingvističeskij sbornik*, 2.8-28 (Syktyvkar, 1952).
—, "Soveščanie po voprosam izučenija komi jazyka", *VJa*, 2(4).144-148 (1953).
—, "Terminy rodstva u komi", *Lingvističeskij sbornik*, 2.62-67 (Syktyvkar, 1952).
—, "Xarakteristika udorskogo (važskogo) dialekta", *Sbornik Komissii po sobiraniju slovarja i izučeniju dialektov komi jazyka* 1.49-56 (Syktyvkar, 1930).
—, "Vlijanie russkogo jazyka na grammatičeskij stroj komi jazyka", *Naučnoe soveščanie po voprosam jazykoznanija v gorode Syktyvkare, 28-31 janvarja 1952 g.*, pp. 15-20 (Moscow, 1952).
Simka, R., *Tähendusmuutusi tööd ja töölist kujutavas sônavaras seoses ühiskondlikkude formatsioonide vaheldumisega* (Diplomitöö). (Tartu, 1950), 224 pp.
Smirnova-Bubrix, V. D., "Iz oblasti mordovskogo vokalizma ne-pervyx slogov slova. (Sočetanija glasnyj pljus *j* v ne-pervyx slogax slova v mordovskix jazykax)", *SovF*, 2.42-75 (Saransk, 1948).
Sokolov, V. T., *Marij grammatik. Sintaksis* (= *Grammatika marijskogo jazyka*) (Moscow, 1935), 80 pp.
Sokolova, K. A., *Složnye slova v sovremennom literaturnom finskom jazyke* (dissertation abstract) (Leningrad, 1956), 14 pp.
Soosaar, S., *Ilmaütlev kääne eesti keeles* (Diplomitöö). (Tartu, 1954), 97 pp.
Sorvačeva, V. A., *Materialy dialektologičeskoj èkspedicii za 2948, 1949, 1951-1953 gg.* (manuscript), 1955.
—, *Naučnye otčety po udorskomu i nižnevyčegodskomu dialektam i višerskomu govoru verxnevyčegodskogo dialekta* (manuscript) (Syktyvkar, 1953).
—, "Nekotorye fonetičeskie i morfologičeskie osobennosti verxne-vašskogo govora udorskogo dialekta", *Lingvističeskij sbornik* 2.37-48 (Syktyvkar, 1952).
—, "Neneckie i xantyjskie zaimstvovanija v govore zaural'skix komi", *Istoriko-filologičeskij sbornik*. Komi filial AN SSSR 6.171-177 (Syktyvkar, 1960).
Sovetkin, F. F., "Metodika obučenija gramote na rodnom jazyke v mordovskoj (èrzja) škole", in *Rodnoj i russkij jazyki v nacional'noj škole*, pp. 111-148 (Moscow, 1953).
*Sovremennyj komi jazyk. Učebnik dlja vysšix učebnyx zavedenij. 1: Fonetika, leksika, morfologija* (Syktyvkar, 1955), 312 pp.
*Sovremennyj marijskij jazyk. Fonetika.* (Joškar-Ola, 1960), 162 pp.

*Sovremennyj marijskij jazyk. Sintaksis složnogo predloženija.* Galkin, I. S., ed. (Joškar-Ola, 1961), 151 pp.

*Sovremennyj marijskij jazyk. Morfologija.* Pengitov, N. T., ed. (Joškar-Ola, 1961), 324 pp.

Sorvačeva, V. A. *Morfologičeskie osobennosti verxne-vašskogo govora* (dissertation manuscript) (Syktyvkar, 1950), Komi filial AN SSSR, 184 pp. Dissertation abstract (Syktyvkar, 1950), 13 pp.

Steinitz, V. K., "Xantyjskij (ostjackij) jazyk", in *Trudy po lingvistike, Institut narodov Severa*, Tom 1 (Moscow-Leningrad, 1937).

Suxanova, V. S., *Deepričastnye narečija v komi jazyke* (dissertation abstract) (Petrozavodsk, 1951), 26 pp.

—, "O pritjažatel'nyx formax v finno-ugorskix jazykax", *UZ Karelo-finskogo gos. universiteta* 4:1.112-120 (Petrozavodsk, 1954).

—, "O semantike pritjažatel'nyx suffiksov v pribaltijsko-finskix i permskix jazykax" (Suffiks 1-go lica edinstvennogo čisla)", *UZ Petrozavodskogo gos. universiteta* 7:1.285-292 (Petrozavodsk, 1957).

—, "Verxne-pečorskij dialekt komi jazyka. (Materialy èkspedicii 1948 goda)", *Tret'ja naučnaja sessija Karelo-finskogo gos. universiteta, 19-22 nojabrja 1948 g.* Tezisy dokladov 17. (Petrozavodsk, 1948), 2 pp.

*Suur ôigekeelsus-sônaraamat.* Eesti NSV Teaduste Akadeemia (Tartu, 1948; Tallinn, 1951—. . .).

Šamaxov, S. A., "O russkoj zaimstvovannoj leksike v komi jazyke, xarakterizujuščej oxoty", *UZ. Komi gos. pedagogičeskij institut* 4.41-54 (Syktyvkar, 1953).

Šestakova, A. E., *Obrazovanie suščestvitel'nyx i prilagatel'nyx ot imennyx osnov v mordovskix jazykax* (dissertation abstract), (Moscow, 1952), 15 pp.

Ščerbakova, A. M., "Buduščee vremja v neneckom jazyke", *UZLPedI*, 111.159-161 (1955).

—, "Formy otricanija v neneckom jazyke", *UZLPedI* 101.181-231 (1954). Dissertation abstract (Leningrad, 1951), 18 pp.

—, *Nenècja vadako* (= Neneckie skazki) (Leningrad, 1960).

—, "Vyraženie soveršennogo i nesoveršennogo vida russkogo glagola sredstvami neneckogo jazyka", *V pomošč učitelju škol Krajnego Severa* 7.99-114 (Leningrad, 1957).

Šemjakin, F. N., "K voprosu ob istoričeskom razvitii nazvanij cveta (Nazvanija cveta v neneckom (jurako-samoedskom) jazyke)", *Voprosy psixologii* 5(4).16-29 (Moscow, 1959). Summary: F. N. Shemiakin, "Color names in Nenetz."

Šestakova, A. E., "Suffiksy sub"ektivnoj ocenki imën suščestvitel'nyx v èrzja-mordovskom jazyke", *Zapiski. NIJaLIE Mordovskoj ASSR*, 14.96-106 (Saransk, 1953).

Šiškanov, P. S., "O poslelogax v mokšanskom jazyke", *UZ. Mordovskij pedagogičeskij institut*, 6.162-169 (Saransk, 1957).

Šmeljov, D., "Andmeid eesti laensônade kohta vanavene allikates", *KK*, 2(11).674-675 (1959).

—, "Läänemeresoome laensônu vanavene allikates", *KK*, 3.430-431 (1960).
—, "Läänemeresoome laensônu vana-vene allikais", *KK*, 4.353-355 (1961).
Šmit, È. Ja., *Vzaimodejstvie srednix i livons-(livskix) govorov v Lauguli* (dissertation abstract) (Riga, 1954), 25 pp.
Tael, E., "Imperfekti pluurali 3. pööre Rammu saare murrakus", *ESA*, 4.152-156 (1958).
—, *Rammu saare murrak* (Diplomitöö) (Tartu, 1951), 163 pp.
Tamm, J., *Eesti-vene sônaraamat*. Toimetanud B. Pravdin (Tallinn, 1955), 822 pp.
Tanning, S., "Mulgi murde ja liivi keele suhetest", *KKIU*, 2.105-117 (1958).
—, *Mulgi murdetekstid. ETAT, KK*. Eesti murdeid 1. (Tallinn, 1961), 186 pp.
Tarabukin, I. I., *Kratkij komi-russkij frazeologičeskij slovaŕ* (Syktyvkar, 1959), 147 pp.
Tarakanov, I., "Lühike ülevaade udmurdi murrete uurimise ajaloost", *ESA*, 4.299-311 (1958).
—, "Nekotorye javlenija assimiljacii, èlizii i vstavki zvukov v udmurtskom jazyke. (Iz materiale bavlinskogo dialekta)", *KKIU*, 5.117-153 (Tallinn, 1960).
Telliskivi, V., *Imperatiiv läänemeresoome keeltes* (Diplomitöö) (Tartu, 1952), 122 pp.
Tepljašina, T. I., "Fonetičeskaja xarakteristika Tylovajskogo govora", *Zapiski. NIIELIJa Udmurtskoj ASSR*, 18.114-140 (Iževsk, 1957).
—, *Tylovajskij dialekt udmurtskogo jazyka* (dissertation manuscript) (Moscow, 1955), Institut jazykoznanija AN ASSR 215 pp. Dissertation abstract (Moscow, 1955), 20 pp.
—, "Udmurtskij jazyk", in *Voprosy finno-ugorskogo jazykoznanija*, pp. 282-303 (Moscow-Leningrad, 1962).
Tereščenko, N. M., "Imennoj predikat v neneckom jazyke", in *Naučnaja konferencija po voprosam finnougorskoj filologii, 23 janvarja-4 fevralja 1947 g*. (*Tezisy dokladov*), pp. 73-75 (Leningrad, 1947).
—, "Imennoe skazuemoe v neneckom jazyke", *Sovetskoe finnougrovedenie* 1.316-329 (Leningrad, 1948).
—, "K voprosu o vzaimootnošenii samodijskix jazykov s jazykami drugix grupp", *VJa*, 6(5).101-103 (1957).
—, "K voprosu o nenecko-xantyjskix jazykovyx svjazjax", *VJa* 8(2).96-103 (1959).
—, "K voprosu o proisxoždenii poslelogov (na materiale neneckogo jazyka)", *DSIJa* 11.62-76 (1958).
—, *Materialy i issledovanija po jazyku nencev* (Moscow-Leningrad, 1956), 282 pp.
—, *Nenecko-russkij slovaŕ*. S kratkim očerkom grammatiki i leksiki neneckogo jazyka (Leningrad, 1955), 315 pp., 8,000 words.
—, *Očerk grammatiki neneckogo (jurak-samoedskogo) jazyka 1: Fonetika i morfologija* (Leningrad, 1947), 271 pp.
—, "O kategorii zaloga v samodijskix jazykax", in *Voprosy grammatiki. Sbornik statej k 75-letiju Akademika I. I. Meščaninova*, pp. 178-193 (Moscow-Leningrad, 1960).
—, "O nekotoryx osobennostjax grammatičeskogo stroja neneckogo jazyka. (Kategorii perexodnosti i neperexodnosti)", *Naučnaja sessija Leningradskogo gosudar-*

*stvennogo pedagogičeskogo instituta im. A. I. Gercena, 1951-1952 g. Tezisy dokladov po sekcii fakuľteta narodov Severa*, pp. 18-21 (Leningrad, 1952).
—, Kolesnikova, V. D. and Menovščikov, G. A., "O progressivnom vlijanii russkogo jazyka na jazyki narodnostej Severa", *Soveščanie po jazykam narodov Severa (Tezisy dokladov)*, pp. 13-19. (Moscow-Leningrad, 1952).
—, "O razvitii grammatičeskix kategorij neneckogo jazyka (Na primer kategorii pričastija", in *Voprosy teorii i istorii jazyka v svete trudov I. V. Stalina po jazykoznaniju*, pp. 368-386 (Moscow, 1952).
—, "O russkix vlijanijax na neneckij jazyk (po materialam leksiki)", in *V pomošč* učitelju škol Krajnego Severa 3.64-89 (Moscow-Leningrad, 1952 (= *Jazyki i istorija narodnostej Krajnego Severa SSSR*, pp. 60-83 (Leningrad, 1953).
—, "O vyraženii possessivnyx otnošenij v samodijskix jazykax", in *Soveščanie po voprosam istoričeskoj grammatiki i istoričeskoj dialektologii finno-ugorskix jazykov (Tezisy dokladov)*, pp. 44-50 (Moscow, 1959).
—, "O vyraženii possessivnyx otnošenij v samodijskix jazykax", in *Voprosy finno-ugorskogo jazykoznanija*, pp. 81-93 (Moscow-Leningrad, 1962).
—, "Pričastie v neneckom jazyke", *Naučnaja sessija Leningradskogo universiteta 1946 g.* (*Tezisy dokladov po sekcii vostokovedenija*), pp. 66-70 (Leningrad, 1946).
—, "Samodijskie jazyki", in *Mladopiśmennye jazyki narodov SSSR*, pp. 380-399 (Moscow-Leningrad, 1959).
—, *V pomošč samostojateľno izučajuščim neneckij jazyk. Opyt sopostaviteľnoj grammatiki neneckogo i russkogo jazykov* (Leningrad, 1959), 148 pp.
—, and Xomič, L. V., "Otčet o rabote lingvističeskoj èkspedicii Instituta jazykoznanija AN SSSR v Jamalo-Neneckij okrug Tjumenskoj oblasti letom 1953 g.", *DSIJa*, 7.147-165 (1955).
Tereškin, N. I., *Očerki dialektov xantyjskogo jazyka*, I (Moscow-Leningrad, 1961), 204 pp.
—, "O nekotoryx osobennostjax vaxovskogo, surgutskogo i kazymskogo dialektov xantyjskogo jazyka", *V pomošč učitelju škol Krajnego Severa*, 8.319-330 (Leningrad, 1958).
—, *Vaxovskij dialekt xantyjskogo jazyka* (manuscript).
Tikk, E., *Essiiv eesti kirjakeeeles* (Diplomitöö) (Tartu, 1953), 122 pp.
Timmo, V., *Meremäe murrak* (Diplomitöö) (Tartu, 1951), 321 pp.
Timofeeva, V. T., "Dopolniteľnye pridatočnye predloženija v marijskom jazyke", *Trudy Marijskogo NIJaLI*, 12.167-172 (Joškar-Ola, 1958).
—, "Pridatočnye predloženija vremeni v marijskom jazyke", *Trudy Marijskogo NIJaLI* 13.137-143 (Joškar-Ola, 1959/1960).
—, *Složnosočinennye predloženija v marijskom jazyke* (dissertation).
—, "Složnosočinenye predloženija s protiviteľnymi sojuzami v marijskom jazyke", *UZ. Udmurtskij gos. pedagogičeskij institut*, 16.110-128 (Joškar-Ola, 1958).
—, "Složnosočinennye predloženija s razdeliteľnymi sojuzami v marijskom jazyke", *Trudy Marijskogo NIJaLI*, 10.130-134 (Joškar-Ola, 1957).

—, "Složnosočinennye predloženija s soedinitel'nymi sojuzami v marijskom jazyke", *Trudy Marijskogo NIJaLI*, 10.108-129 (Joškar-Ola, 1957).

Timušev, D. A., "O starom denežnom sčete komi i istorii komi denežnego termina 'ur'", *Trudy Komi filiala AN SSSR*, 2.171-178 (Syktyvkar, 1954).

Tolmačeva, V. D., *Nekotorye xantyjskie sootvetstvija russkim prefiksal'no-osložnennym glagolam dviženija* (dissertation abstract) (Leningrad, 1951), 21 pp.

Toomsalu, C., *tud-kesksôna esinemus eesti murretes* (Tartu, 1955), 219 pp.

Trefilov, A., "O drevnosti udmurtov", *Zapiski. NIIELJa Udmurtskoj ASSR*, 15.55-77 (Iževsk, 1951).

Tret'jakov, P. N., "Volgo-okskaja toponimika i nekotorye voprosy ètnogeneza finno-ugorskix narodov Povolž'ja", *SovÈtn*, 4.9-17 (1958).

Tultaev, I. G., "Reducirovannye glasnye v mokšanskom jazyke, istorija ix proisxoždenija i pravila pravopisanija", *Sbornik studenčeskix naučnyx rabot. Mordovskij pedagogičeskij institut*, 1.68-78 (Saransk, 1954).

Turu, E., *Imperfekti esinemus eesti keeles* (Diplomitöö) (Tartu, 1954), 160 pp.

—, "Kahesilbiliste e-tüveliste verbide imperfektist eesti murretes", *ESA*, 5.78-98 (1959).

—, "Ühesilbiliste vokaaltüveliste verbide imperfektist", *KK*, 3.36-45 (1960).

Tuuksam, L. *Alaltütlev kääne eesti keeles* (Diplomitöö) (Tartu, 1955), 152 pp.

Učaev, Z. V., "Bezličnye predloženija v marijskom jazyke", *Trudy Marijskogo NIJaLI*, 8.68-94 (Joškar-Ola, 1956).

—, "Infinitivnye predloženija v marijskom jazyke", *Trudy Marijskogo NIJaLI*, 13.121-135 (Joškar-Ola, 1959/1960).

—, "Kratkie itogi èkspedicii MarNII 1953 g.", *UZ. Marijskij NIJaLI*, 6.229-236 (Joškar-Ola, 1954).

—, "O skazuemostnom upotreblenii pričastij buduščevo vremeni v marijskom jazyke", *Trudy Marijskogo NIJaLI*, 12.159-166 (Joškar-Ola, 1958).

*Udmurt orfografičeskoj slovar'* (= Udmurtskij orfografičeskij slovar) (Iževsk, 1959). 216 pp.

*Udmurtsko-russkij slovar'*. S priloženiem grammatičeskogo očerka udmurtskogo jazyka. (Moscow, 1948), 15,000 words, 447 pp.

"Ugro-finskie narodnosti perexodjat na latinizirovannyj alfavit", *Kul'tura i pis'mennost' Vostoka*, 7-8.212 (Moscow, 1931).

Univere, A., "*a-listest mitmuse vormidest eesti murdeis*", *ESA*, 1.118-127 (1955).

—, "Eesti rahvakeele sônaraamatust", *KKIU*, 6.46-60 (1961).

—, "Issledovanie dialektov v Èstonii i dialektologičeskie materialy Arxiva èstonskogo i finno-ugorskix jazykov", *SovF*, 3.101-114 (Tartu, 1947).

—, "Ühesilbiliste vokaaltüvede pluurali genitiivist", *KKIU*, 2.96-104 (Tartu, 1958).

Uuspôld, E., *Mitmuse osastav XIX sajandi kirjakeeles* (Diplomitöö). (Tartu, 1953), 166 pp.

Valdre, E., *Vene laensônad valdai karjala keeles* (Diplomitöö) (Tartu, 1953), 373 pp.

Valmet, A., *Mitmuse osastav eesti vanemas kirjakeeles (1524-1857)*. Kandidaadiväitekiri (Tartu, 1956).
—, *Sugulusmôisteid märkivat sônavara eesti keeles* (Diplomitöö) (Tartu, 1952), 169 pp.
Vals, H., *Kaasaütlev kääne eesti keeles* (Diplomitöö). (Tartu, 1953), 161 pp.
Vasikova, L., "Imperfekt ja perfekt mari keeles", *ESA*, 4.286-198 (1958).
—, *Prošedšee vremja glagola v marijskom jazyke* (dissertation abstract). (Tartu, 1955), 17 pp.
Vasiljev, V. M., *Čeremissko-russkij slovar'* (Kazan, 1911).
—, "Funkcional'naja semantika v marijskom jazyke", *UZ. Marijskij NIJaLI*, 1.35-53 (Joškar-Ola, 1948).
—, "Idiomy-, inoskazatel'nye narečenija, slova-perežitki v marijskom jazyke", *UZ. Marijskij NIJaLI*, 1:1.107-129 (Joškar-Ola, 1948).
—, *Marij mutèr* (= Sravnitel'nyj slovar narečij marijskogo jazyka – in Cheremis Languages) (Moscow, 1926, 1928), 347 pp.
—, *Materialy po grammatike marijskogo jazyka* (Joškar-Ola, 1958), 88 pp.
—, "Naklonenija i nekotoryc otglagol'nye formy v marijskom jazyke", *Trudy Marijskogo NIJaLI* 7.97-133 (Joškar-Ola, 1955).
—, *Nekotorye voprosy marijskogo jazykoznanija.* Sbornik statej (Kozmodem'jansk, 1948), 120 pp.
—, "O vnutrennyx zakonax razvitija marijskogo jazyka", *Učenye zapiski. Marijskij NIJaLI*, 5.71-108 (Joškar-Ola, 1953).
—, "Pis'mennye pamjatniki na marijskom jazyke konca XVIII i pervoj poloviny XIX v. (O perevodax i rabotax po marijskomu jazykoznaniju)", *Učenye zapiski. Marijskij NIJaLI*, 5.255-271 (Joškar-Ola, 1953).
—, "Prošedšee vremja v marijskom jazyke", *Učenye zapiski. Marijskij NIJaLI*, 2.67-84 (Joškar-Ola, 1941).
—, *Zapiski po grammatike jazyka naroda mari* (Kazan, 1918), 80 pp.
Vaxrušev, V. M., "K voprosu razvitija leksiki udmurtskogo jazyka", *Zapiski. NIJELJa Udmurtskoj ASSR*, 19.167-217 (Iževsk, 1959).
—, "Ob osobennostjax govorov severnogo dialekta udmurtskogo jazyka", *Zapiski. NIIELJa Udmurtskoj ASSR*, 19.228-241 (Iževsk, 1959).
—, *Obščestvenno-političeskaja leksika v udmurtskom jazyke* (dissertation). Rukopis' v Institute jazykoznanija AN SSSR. Moscow, 1955. 292 pp. Dissertation abstract (Moscow, 1955), 21 pp.
Vääri, E., "Kaukaasia eestlaste keelest", *KK*, 3.425-429 (1960).
—, "Liivi keele uurimise ajaloost", *ESA*, 5.190-225 (1959).
—, "Soomeugriline sônavara eesti sugulasnimedes", *ESA*, 2.150- 159 (1956).
—, *Sugulusalane sônavara läänemeresoome keeltes.* Kandidaadiväitekiri (Tartu, 1953).
—, *Vene laensônad vadja keeles* (Diplomitöö) (Tartu, 1950). 438 pp.
*Väike ôigekeelsuse sônaraamat* (Tallinn, 1953), 352 pp.
Vdovin, I. S., and N. M. Tereščenko, *Očerki istorii izučenija paleoaziatskix i samodijskix jazykov.* (= *Istorija otečestvennogo jazykoznanija*", 3) (Leningrad, 1959), 117 pp.

Verbov, G. D., *Dialekt lesnyx nencev* (dissertation manuscript). v arxive Instituta ètnografii AN SSSR v Leningrade fond n:o 2. opiś 1.
Veski, J. V., "Arenemise sihtjooni eesti kirjakeele foneetikas ja morfoloogias", *ETAT*, 4(2).192-203 (1955).
—, "Ääremärkusi nimisônade liitmise kohta eesti kirjakeeles", *ESA*, 3.21-35 (1957).
—, "Ebakohti eesti kirjakeele sônavaras", *ETAT*, 5(2).103-116 (1956).
—, "Voprosy èstonskoj terminologii", *Trudy Instituta jazyka i literatury AN latvijskoj SSR* 2.159-169 (Riga, 1953).
Veskis, S., *h-häälik eesti keeles* (Diplomitöö) (Tartu, 1955), 219 pp.
Vežev, A. A., *I. A. Kuratov: Lingvističeskie raboty*, Tom 2, pp. 3-26 (Syktyvkar, 1939).
Vihma, H., *Muhu murraku häälikuline ja morfoloogiline ülevaade* (Diplomitöö) (Tartu, 1957).
Viires, H., "Adjektiivse täiendsônaga liitsônadest eesti murretes", *KKIU*, 2.63-85 (1958).
—, "Eesti püttsepise terminoloogiast", *ESA*, 2.182-194 (1956).
—, "Eesti murrete uurimisest Eesti NSV Teaduste Akadeemia Keele ja kirjanduse instituudis", *KKIU*, 1.175-195 (1956).
—, "Kalevi sônapere", *KK*, 4.668-676 (1961).
—, "*ne*-omadussônade tähendusrühmad eesti murretes", *ESA*, 6.48-70 (1960).
—, "*se* ~ *tse* vaheldus eesti *ne*-adjektiivides", *ESA*, 7.31-53 (1961).
Viitso, T. R., "Vadja keele Luutsa- Liivtšülä murraku fonoloogia", *ESA*, 7.142-174 (1961).
Vilbaste, G., "Kaukaasia eestlaste keelest ja rahvaluulest", *ESA*, 6.121-131 (1960).
—, "Rahvapäraste taimenimede kogumise katseid möödunud sajanditel", *ESA*, 2.195-216 (1956).
—, "Taimenimed 'Kalevipojas'", *TRÜT*, 53.163-194 (1957).
—, "Vadja taimenimesid", *ESA*, 3.173-179 (1957).
Villup, A., *Viisiadverb ja selle arenemine eesti keeles*. Kandidaadiväitekiri (Tartu, 1954).
Vinogradov, V. V., and B. A. Serebrennikov, "O zadačax sovetskogo jazykoznanija v oblasti istoričeskogo i sravnitel'nogo izučenija jazykov", *VJa*, 5(2).3-17 (1956).
Voronin, I. D., "K voprosu o proisxoždenii nazvanij "burtasy", "mordva", "meščera", *Literaturnaja Mordovija*, 14.208-226 (Saransk, 1957/8).
Vyučejskaja, A. I., "Nekotorye fonetičeskie osobennosti kolguevskogo govora neneckogo jazyka", *UZLPedI*, 101.321-327 (1954).
Xomič, L. V., "Imja prilagatel'noe v neneckom jazyke", *DSIJa*, 12.148-158 (1959).
—, *Nenecko-russkij slovaŕ* (*dlja neneckoj načaľnoj školy*) (Leningrad, 1954), 4,500 words, 123 pp.
Xozjainova, È. E., "Fonetičeskaja sistema komi jazyka", in *Rodnoj i russkij jazyki v školax narodov finno-ugorskoj grupp* (sbornik statej), pp. 118-145 (Moscow, 1956).
Xvataj-Muxa, K. F., *Funkcii mestno-tvoriteľnogo padeža v sredneobskom dialekte jazyka severnyx xanty* (dissertation abstract) (Leningrad, 1954), 20 pp.

—, "Mestno-tvoritel'nyj padež v značenii sovmestnosti v jazyke severnyx xanty (sredneobskoj i kazymskij dialekty)", *UZMPedI*, 101.233-238 (1954).

—, and Obatin, A. M., *Pouročnye razrabotki k bukvarju na jazyke kazymskix xanty* (Leningrad, 1959), 187 pp.

Zaitseva, M., "Vepsa keele verbaaltuletussufikseist -sku ja skōt'ta) (-škōt'ta)", *ESA*, 7.193-196 (1961).

Zaxarov, V. N., "Sravnitel'naja xarakteristika glasnyx zvukov russkogo i udmurtskogo jazykov", *UZ. Udmurtskij gos. pedagogičeskij institut*, 10.153-169 (Iževsk, 1956).

—, "Sravitel'naja xarakteristika zvukovyx sistem russkogo i udmurtskogo jazykov", in *Rodnoj i russkij jazyki v školax narodov finno-ugorskoj gruppy*, pp. 83-117 (Moscow, 1956).

Zavodova, R. A., *Imja prilagatel'noe v mordovskix jazykax* (dissertation abstract) (Moscow, 1952), 11 pp.

—, "K voprosu o substantivizacii prilagatel'nyx", *Zapiski. NIJaLIE Mordovskoj ASSR*, 16.125-132 (Saransk, 1955).

—, "Proizvodnye prilagatel'nye v mordovskix jazykax", *Zapiski. NIJaLIE Mordovskoj ASSR*, 14.32-50 (Saransk, 1953).

—, "Sistema častej reči v mordovskix jazykax", *Materilay naučnoj sessii po voprosam mordovskogo jazykoznanija* 1.131-157 (Saransk, 1955).

Zlobina, V. E., "Iz istorii slov, vyražajuščix sostojanie, v pribaltijsko-finskix jazykax", in *Voprosy finno-ugorskogo jazykoznanija*, pp. 94-100 (Moscow-Leningrad, 1962).

—, "K voprosu o pričinax perexoda slov iz odnoj časti reči v druguju v finskom jazyke", in *Pribaltijsko-finskoe jazykoznanie* (= *Trudy Karel'skogo filiala AN ASSR* 23.78-83) (1960).

—, "O slovax, vyražajuščix sostojanie v sovremennom finskom jazyke", *UZP etrozavodskogo gos. universiteta*, 7.261-270 (Petrozavodsk, 1957).

—, "Ob osobennostjax istoričeskogo razvitija slovarnogo sostava finskogo jazyka", *UZ Karelo-finskogo gos. universiteta*, 4(1).121-131 (Petrozavodsk, 1954).

Žilina, T. I., *Imennye kategorii verxne-vymskix govorov severnogo dialekta komi jazyka* (manuscript). Komi Filial AN SSSR (Syktyvkar).

—, *Materialy dialektologičeskix issledovanij za 1948, 1949, 1951, 1952, 1953 gg.* (manuscript). Komi Filial AN SSSR (Syktyvkar).

—, *Naučnoe otčety po vymskomu, verxnesysol'skomu i luzsko-letskomu dialektam* (manuscript) komi Filial AN SSSR (Syktyvkar).

—, "O govore sela Sludka", *Istoriko-filologičeskij sbornik*. Komi filial AN SSSR, 3.79-86 (Syktyvkar, 1956).

—, *Otčet ob èkspedicii v Kojgorodskij rajon* (manuscript). V fonde Komi filiala AN SSSR (Syktyvkar).

—, and Kolegova, N. A., "Nekotorye osobennosti govora Obskix komi (ss. Muži i Šuryškary)", *Istoriko-filologičeskij sbornik*. Komi filial AN SSSR 6.152-170 (Syktyvkar, 1960).

—, Saxarova, M. A., and Sorvačeva, V. A., *Sraviteľnyj slovař komi-zyrjanskix dialektov* (Syktyvkar, 1961). 25,000 words, 489 pp.

Živòtikov, P. K., *Očerk grammatiki xantyjskogo jazyka* (*Sredne-obskyj dialekt*). Ju. N. Russkoj, ed. (Xanti-Mansijsk, 1942), 122 pp.

Žiževa, E. G., *Kategorija grammatičeskogo čisla v komi jazyke* (dissertation manuscript). v IJa AN SSSR. (Leningrad, 1950), 122 pp. Dissertation abstract (Leningrad, 1950), 11 pp.

—, "O značenii suffiksa *-öś*", *Lingvističeskij sbornik*. Komi filial AN SSSR, 2.29-36 (Syktyvkar, 1952).

Žujkov, S. P., *Osnovy grammatiki udmurtskogo jazyka* (Tezisy k pervoj respublikanskoj jazykovoj konferencii.) (Iževsk, 1937), 47 pp.

—, "Udmurtskie padežnye okončanija", *Doklad, sdelan v Akademii Nauk SSSR 27. 1. 1932 g. Trudy*. Udmurtskij naučno-issledovatel'skij institut, 1 (Iževsk, 1935), pp. 23-31.

# PART TWO

## *LINGUISTICS IN EASTERN EUROPE*

# BULGARIA

ZBIGNIEW GOŁĄB

It is understandable that in a country like Bulgaria linguistic studies show a tendency to be limited to problems of Bulgarian. And indeed, the overwhelming majority of linguistic publications in that country are concerned with Bulgarian and Old Church Slavonic or other Slavic languages which to some extent represent historical sources or parallels to Bulgarian. Nevertheless, problems of Indo-European treated from a comparative historical standpoint, especially those of Pre-Hellenic Indo-European languages in the eastern part of the Mediterranean, and those of ancient Indo-European languages of the Balkan Peninsula, have been studied too. Only general theoretical problems have found a weak response among Bulgarian linguists except for some articles caused by Stalin's famous enunciation about Marxism in linguistics in 1951.

I will organize my review according to the following topics:

1. General linguistics,
2. Indo-European linguistics,
3. Slavic linguistics,
4. Bulgarian language,
   a. historical grammar and history of language,
   b. dialectology,
   c. descriptive grammar of contemporary Standard Bulgarian,
   d. Bulgarian and other Balkan languages,
   e. lexicology and etymology.

1. In the field of general linguistics, first of all, the following positions are worth mentioning:

I. Lekov, "Za dialektikata na ezikovata sistema", *GodSU*, 44, no. 2 (1947-48), 33 pp., and the collection of articles *Vəprosi na ezikoznanieto v Stalinsko osvetlenie* (Sofia, 1951), 200 pp., published by the Institute of Bulgarian Languages at the Bulgarian Academy of Sciences. The collection contains these articles: S. Stojkov, "Ezik i obštestvo" (p. 5-20); L. Andrejčin, "Kəm vəprosa za otnošenieto meždu ezik i mislene" (p. 21-34); K. Mirčev, "Razvoj na ezika" (p. 35-48); I. Lekov, "Vətrešnite zakoni na ezika" (p. 49-68); V. Georgiev, "Sravnitelno-istoričeskijat metod i Marovijat četirielementen analiz" (p. 79-138); S. Mladenov, "Morfologičeska i genealogičeska klassifikacija na ezicite s ogled kəm indoevropejskite i uraloaltajskite ezici" (p. 139-150); S. Romanski, "Krəstosvane na ezicite" (p. 157-162); C. Todorov, "Problemət za etničnite i lingvistični edinstva" (p. 163-200). As is generally known, such collections of general linguistic articles appeared in all socialist countries immediately after Stalin's authoritative statement about the correct Marxist approach to language. They represented the usual "tribute" paid by scholars to the official state ideology, but on the other hand, they compelled these scholars to make precise their general theoretical views and to express them in a more popular form. The positive result of the whole phenomenon was an awakening, to some extent, of general linguistic interests among scholars who traditionally were concerned with concrete historical and descriptive problems of their own languages.

As a continuation of the collection mentioned above we can quote: V. Georgiev, *Stalinskoto učenie za ezika i zadačite na bəlgarskoto ezikoznanie* (Sofia, 1951), 96 pp.; L. Andrejčin, "Gramatikata kato nauka i nejnoto značenie v svetlinata na Stalinovite trudove za ezikoznanieto" *EzLit*, 6 (1951), p. 145-150; the same, "Leksikologijata v svetlina na Stalinskoto ezikoznanic", *BəlEz*, 3 (1953), p. 202-208; the same, "Vəprosət za nacionalnata samobitnost na ezika", *IzvIBE*, 2 (1952), p. 29-54, which treats the problem with special reference to Bulgarian.

Very interesting and rich with general linguistic problems is the article by M. Minkov, "Za analitizma v anglijski i bəlgarski ezik", *Ezikovedski izsledvanija v čest na akad. S. Mladenov* (Sofia, 1957), p. 503-514. The author compares the historical development of English and Bulgarian from the primary synthetic type to the secondary analytic one, states the resemblances and differences, quotes similar facts from other Germanic languages when endeavoring to establish some general rules of linguistic development. There are in the article also interesting remarks on linguistic typology, e.g. English and Bulgarian are classified as verbal languages in opposition to Russian which is determined as nominal language. A serious lack in the article is a rather unprecise and confusing definition of "analyticism". Worth mentioning is also a new handbook of general linguistics, namely: V. Georgiev and I. Duridanov, *Uvod v ezikoznanieto. Učebnik za učitelskite instituti* (Sofia, 1958), 172 pp. (the older one is by S. Mladenov, *Uvod vəv vseobštoto ezikoznanie*, Sofia, 1943).

2. Much more interest is concentrated on Indo-European comparative linguistics. Almost all works in this field are connected with the name of Vladimir Georgiev who devoted himself first of all to problems of Prehellenic ("Pelasgian") and ancient Indo-European languages of the Balkans. This direction of scientific investigation is clearly expressed in his early book *Vorgriechische Sprachwissenschaft* (Sofia, 1941). A kind of synthetic review of his numerous publications and the results of his investigations are given in his book *Issledovanija po sravnitel'no-istoričeskomu jazykoznaniju* (*Rodstvennye otnošenija indoevropejskix jazykov*) (Moscow, 1958), 317 pp. Before we pass to some remarks on this important work let us quote at least the titles of earlier publications by the same author: *Die sprachliche Zugehörigkeit der Etrusker*

(Sofia, 1943); *Le déchiffrement des inscriptions minoennes* (Sofia, 1948-49); *Contribution à l'étude de la toponymie grecque: noms de lieux prétendus préhelléniques* (Sofia, 1948); *Nynešnee sostojanie tolkovanija krito-mikenskix nadpisej* (Sofia, 1954); *Le déchiffrement des inscriptions crétoises en linéaire A* (Sofia, 1957); *Problemy minojskogo jazyka* (Sofia, 1953); *Slovar' krito-mikenskix nadpisej* (Sofia, 1955); and *Dopolnenie k slovarju krito-mikenskix nadpisej* (Sofia, 1955); *La position du dialecte crétois des inscriptions en linéaire A* (Sofia, 1957); *Trakijskijat ezik* (Sofia, 1957); "Koncepcija ob indoevropejskix guttural'nyx soglasnyx i eë ograničenie na etimologii slavjanskix slov", *Beogradski međunarodni slavistički sastanak* (Belgrad, 1957); *Etudes mycéniennes* (Paris, 1956); *Die altgriechischen Flussnamen* (Sofia, 1958); "Baltoslavjanskij i toxarskij", *Voprosy jazykoznanija*, 1958, 6; "Baltoslavjansko-germanskoto ezikovo edinstvo", *IzvSS*, 8-9 (1948); "Kəm vəprosa za balto-slavjanskata ezikova obštnost", *BəlEz*, 8 (1958).

The book *Issledovanija* ... in its basic scope represents a course of lectures given by V. Georgiev during his visit to the University of Moscow in September and October 1956. It comprises the following chapters: 1. "Tretij period v razvitii indoevropejskogo sravnitel'no-istoričeskogo jazykoznanija"; 2. "Vopros ob indoevropejskix guttural'nyx i teorija centum-satəm"; 3. "Drevnejšee jazyki južnoj časti Balkanskogo poluostrova i ix značenie dlja sravnitel'no-istoričeskogo jazykoznanija"; 4. "Trakijskij jazyk"; 5. "Drevnie indoevropejskie jazyki Maloj Azii"; 6. "Voprosy rodstva sredizemnomorskix jazykov (baskskij jazyk, ètruskij jazyk ... jazyk lemnoskix nadpisej, xattskij, xurritskij i urartskij; šumerskij, èlamskij i kassitskij)"; 7. "Baltoslavjanskij, germanskij i indoiranskij"; 8. "Problema vozniknovenija i prarodiny indoevropejskix jazykov". The book has also an index of words and authors.

Among the many topics discussed in the book, the problem of Proto-Indo-European "gutturals" and the *centum-satəm* theory represent probably the most important ones, as the author himself emphasizes in the introduction. The basic view of V. Georgiev is that in Proto-Indo-European there existed only two sets of guttural stops; the velars of the type *k* etc. and the labio-velars of the type $k^w$ etc. In this respect the author continues the views of J. Schmidt and H. Hirt opposing the traditional and very popular theory of three sets of "gutturals": *k'*, *k*, $k^w$. The crucial point of Georgiev's view is an explanation of the origin of the palatal *k'* set and its further change in affricates and sibilants respectively in the so-called *satəm* languages. This explanation operates with two rules: the rule of palatalization and the rule of unification of split roots. The palatalization of the primary *k* into *k'* took place before primary front vowels (also in the clusters *kle*, *kre*, *kwe*, etc.) resulting in a phonetic splitting of word roots because before back vowels the primary velar *k* was maintained, e.g. **kosā* : **k'eseti* > Slavic *kosa*: Sanskr. *śasati* etc. The processes of the palatalization of the primary velar stops happened in a very old epoch independently of each other in different Proto-Indo-European dialects which have been grouped by traditional comparative grammar under the common label "*satəm* languages". For example in Indo-Iranian that "first" palatalization (and assibilation) of the primary velars (*ke* >)

*k'e* > *će* > *śe*) took place before the change $k^{w}e$ > *k'e* > *ce* > *ca*, probably in the first half of the 3rd millenium or earlier before Christ (cf. *loc. cit.*, 38). Those remote processes of the palatalization and assibilation of the primary velar stops having resulted in the phonetic splitting of word roots were secondarily obscured by the so-called "unification of split root" which is simply morphological analogy acting in different directions. The processes of that "unification of split root" took place to a large extent in the so-called "*satəm* languages" producing the sequences of the type *k'o* etc., that is the palatal stop + back vowel. This in its turn brought about the replacement of the phonemic opposition $k{:}k^{w}$ by the opposition *k'* (later on *ć/č*, *ś/š* etc.): *k*, thus the primary labio-velars lost their labialization. The main result of this theory is the removal of the traditional bipartition of Proto-Indo-European dialects respectively Indo-European languages into two groups *satəm* and *centum*. Although there are many uncertain items concerning the "unification of split root", which was stressed by the Polish scholar Kuryłowicz in his *L'apophonie* ..., p. 357, the hypothesis of V. Georgiev can quote for its justification numerous parallels from historic Indo-European languages, e.g. the changes of *satəm* type we observe in French in comparison with Classic Latin or archaic Sardinian (*centum/kentum*: *quis/*$k^{w}$*is/*>*cent/sã/*:*qui/ki/*); the items of analogy bringing about "the unification of split root" we can find in many Slavic languages (Proto-Slavic and Old Church Slavonic *pekǫ*, *pečeši* etc. is replaced in Bulgarian by *peča*, *pečeš* etc.). Nevertheless, there are some theoretical difficulties which do not permit a clear explanation of the phonemization of the *k'*, *g'*, *g'h* caused by the alleged palatalization of the primary velars and the replacement of the primary opposition $k{:}k^{w}$ by the secondary *k'*:*k*. Therefore J. Kuryłowicz in the book mentioned above opposes the view represented by V. Georgiev and accepts for Proto-Indo-European as the starting point the binary system of the *satəm* type (*k'*:*k*) treating the *centum* type ($k{:}k^{w}$) as a secondary one.

A great part of the linguistic investigations in the field of the so-called "Prehellenic linguistics" consists of toponomastic researches. The same is true about the ancient Indo-European languages of the Balkans. The importance of toponomastics for the solution of the prehellenic and ancient linguistic situation of the Balkan Peninsula is clearly expressed in the works by V. Georgiev as can be seen from some of the titles quoted above. A recent book in this field synthesizing previous investigations is V. Georgiev's *La toponymie ancienne de la péninsule Balkanique et la thèse méditerranéenne. Publié à l'occasion du VIIe Congres International des Sciences Onomastiques à Florence-Pise du 4 au 8 Avril 1961* (Sofia, 1961), 62 pp. (in the series *Linguistique Balkanique*, III, Fasc. 1), published by Bulgarian Academy of Sciences. The book contains the following chapters: 1. "Les unités ethniques anciennes de la péninsule Balkanique" (the author established 7 ethnic regions: dacomysienne, thrace, préhellénique/pélasgique/, protohellénique, macédonienne, protophrygienne, illyrienne)"; 2. "La situation ethnique ancienne de la péninsule Balkanique et la thèse méditerranéenne". There is a map and an index of proper names added at the end. Among the general conclusions drawn by the author one especially is worth quoting, namely:

La toponymie ancienne de la péninsule Balkanique ne donne aucune preuve sûre pour l'existence d'une population pré-indoeuropéenne. S'il y a eu dans l'antiquité des infiltrations de tribus non-indoeuropéennes, elles ont été peu nombreuses: le fait qu'elles n'ont pas laissé de traces dans la toponymie en est preuve suffisante. Toutfois, pendant l'epoque de la societé esclavagiste, qui a commencé dans l'Egéide de très bonne heure (au moins dès le IIe millénaire) on a importé la un nombre considérable d'esclaves provenant de régions diverses: ces esclaves ont été plus tard successivement assimilés par la population indigène. (*loc. cit.*, 52.)

We can also add here: V. Georgiev, "Die Herkunft der Namen der grössten Flüsse der Balkanhalbinsel und ihre Bedeutung zur Ethnogenese der Balkanvölker", *Balkansko ezikoznanie – Linguistique Balkanique*, I (Sofia, 1959), p. 5-17, Anhang; "Die altgriechischen Flussnamen, II", *ibid.*, p. 17-27; "Albanisch, Dakisch-Mysisch und Rumänisch", *ibid.*, II (Sofia, 1960), p. 1-19 (the article contains some important data about the genetic relationship between Daco-Mysian and Albanian which permit a treatment of Albanian as the descendant of the former and establish its primary country in the North of the central part of the Balkan peninsula (the contemporary region of *Niš-Sofia-Skopje*).

Another scholar who has been working for a long time in the field of ancient Indo-European languages of the Balkans is D. Dečev. I will mention here his two recent books: *Xarakteristika na trakijskija ezik* (Sofia, 1952), 134 pp. (with a parallel text in German; the 2nd edition (after the death of the author) with some alterations prepared by himself appeared in German as "Charakteristik der thrakischen Sprache", *Balkansko ezikoznanie – Linguistique Balkanique*, II, Sofia, 1960, p. 145-213), and *Die thrakischen Sprachreste* (Vienna, 1957), IX + 584 pp., published by the Austrian Academy of Sciences (the book contains the complete material of Thracian language). The attention paid just to Thracian is not a casual phenomenon. The primary South Slavic tribes, who later acquired the secondary name "Bulgarian" from a little Turkish tribe, settled just that territory which in the ancient epoch was occupied by the Thracians. This historical fact stimulated the scientific imagination of many linguists (e.g. F. Miklosich) in the 19th century who wanted to find a common prehistorical source for the explanation of the so-called "Balkanisms" in Bulgarian, Rumanian and Albanian: hence the hypothesis of "Thracian linguistic-substratum". This hypothesis, although deprived of any linguistic base (we do not know the grammatical structure of Thracian) and even from a purely historical point of view unacceptable because in the time of the Slavic invasion in the Balkans the majority of the ancient Thracians were already romanized or hellenicized, seems to be maintained to date by some scholars.

3. Now we pass to comparative Slavic linguistics. Most publications in this field are connected with the name of I. Lekov. Here can be quoted the following positions: "Fonologičnata stojnost na udəlženite i udvoeni səglasni zvukove v slavjanskite ezici", *GodSU*, 36, No. 4 (1940), 110 pp.; "Projavi na fonologična svərxstaratelnost [hypercorrectness] v razvoja na bəlgarskija, polskija i češkija ezik", *SpBAN* 58 (1939),

p. 85-106 (according to the opinion of K. Mirčev the Bulgarian items are not well chosen and do not represent examples of hypercorrectness), "Xarakteristika na obštite čerti v bəlgarski i istočno-slavjanski", *SborBAN*, 37 (1942), p. 1-100, "Iz slavjanskata leksika. Abstraktni səštestvitelni imena v osnovnija rečnikov fond na bəlgarski ezik v sravnenie s leksikata na drugite slavjanski ezici", *IzvIBE*, 2 (1954), p. 11-60; a similar subject is treated also in the book *Edinstvo i nacionalno svoeobrazie na slavjanskite ezici v texnija osnoven rečnikov fond* (Sofia, 1955), 108 pp. As it can be seen from the titles quoted above, the investigations of I. Lekov are more concerned with historical similarities and differences between Slavic languages than with problems of prehistoric (Proto-Slavic) linguistic processes which are the object of traditional comparative grammar. This leads the author towards purely synchronic comparison and classification of Slavic languages: *Slovoobrazovatelni sklonnosti na slavjanskite ezici* (Sofia, 1958), 78 pp. (the problem of prefixation and suffixation) and *Obštnost i mnogoobrazie v gramatičnija stroj na slavjanskite ezici* (Sofia, 1958), 126 pp. The same problems are synthetically treated in the article: "Značenie na gramatičeskite, slovoobrazovatelni i leksikalni danni za klasifikacijata na slavjanskite ezici ot səvremenno gledište", *Slavjanskaja Filologija*, II (Moscow, 1958), p. 64-76. Here can be added "Razprostranenieto na edin smesen vid na slovoobrazuvane v slavjanskite ezici", *Slavističen Sbornik*, I (1958), p. 1-12. Among many articles by I. Lekov, devoted to different subjects of comparative Slavic linguistics and published mainly in *Bəlgarski Ezik* and *Ezik i Literatura* the two following are worth mentioning: "Projekt za plan na kratka sravnitelna i səpostavitelna istorija na slavjanskite literaturni ezici", *BəlEz*, 5 (1955), p. 316-318, and "Kəm vəprosa za məžkoličnija rod v slavjanskite ezici", *ibid.*, 6 (1956), p. 317-327. Interesting are also the articles "Otklonenija ot flektivnija stroež na slavjanskite ezici", *Beogradski međunarodni slavistički sastanak* (Belgrad, 1957), p. 551-558 (the same in *Voprosy Jazykoznanija*, 1956, 2, p. 18-26) and "Kəm vəprosa za ustrojstvoto na padežnata sistema v slavjanskite ezici", *Ezikovedsko-etnografski izsledvanija v pamet na akad. S. Romanski* (Sofia, 1960), p. 53-65.

In the field of comparative Slavic linguistics there are also some works treating especially the relationship between Bulgarian and Russian, e.g. G. Tagamlicka, "Nekotorye nabljudenija v svjazi s bolgarskim predlogom "sreštu" i ego russkimi paralleljami", *GodSU*, 46, no. 3 (1949), 75 pp.; "K voprosu o predložnom upravlenii v russkom i bolgarskom jazykax"; *Ibid.*, 51, no. 4 (1955), 173 pp.; "Iz istorii predložnyx konstrukcij v russkom i bolgarskom jazykax"; *Godišnik na Visšeto učilište za teatralno izkustvo*, 1 (1956), p. 175-244; "Zamečanija ob otnositel'nyx prilagatel'nyx s sufiksom -šń-, -šn- v russkom i bolgarskom jazykax", *Slavističen Sbornik*, I (Sofia, 1958), p. 79-90; "O razvitii nekotoryx značenij datel'nogo padeža v russkom i bolgarskom jazykax", *Ezikovedsko-etnografski izsledvanija v pamet na akad. S. Romanski* (Sofia, 1960), p. 145-167; S. Čukalov, "Leksikalnoto rodstvo meždu ruskija i bəlgarskija ezik"; *Slavističen Sbornik*, I (Sofia, 1958), p. 133-144; "Rusko-bəlgarska omonimika", *Ezikovedsko-etnografiski izsledvanija v pamet na akad. S. Romanski* (Sofia, 1960),

p. 109-131; P. Filkova, "Iz istorijata na rusko-bəlgarskite ezikovi vrəzki", *Izvestija na Viššata škola "Stanko Dimitrov" pri CK na BKP*, vol. II (1958), p. 403-430 (in the article the author treats exhaustively the so-called "slavonisms" in Russian). Early Old Russian phonemics is the concern of an article by J. Elenski, "Kəm istorijata na erovite glasni v staroruski ezik (vərxu material ot Svetoslavovija sbornik, 1073 g.)", *Ezikovedsko-etnografski izsledvanija v pamet na akad. S. Romanski* (Sofia, 1960), p. 169-193.

4a. The problems connected with the historical development of Bulgarian represent probably the most attractive subject of linguistics in Bulgaria. This fact is understandable. Bulgarian (together with Macedonian which from a historical point of view may be treated as secondarily separated from Bulgarian) is the only Slavic language that in the course of its history underwent deep structural changes having resulted in a linguistic type different from all other Slavic languages. The investigation of the mechanism of those changes and their causes has been attracting the interest of Bulgarian linguists for three generations. The subject involves the complicated problems of the Balkan linguistic league (its historical "making") and inevitably some general questions of linguistic development as such. To some extent it involves also the national feelings of those scholars who would like to demonstrate the originality and independence of their own language.

Let us begin with synthetic presentations of the history of Bulgarian. After the works of B. Conev and S. Mladenov, the former of which was not systematic and the latter oriented rather towards the demonstration of Common Slavic elements being continued in Bulgarian, the philological public got two systematic and synthetic books by K. Mirčev, *Istoričeska gramatika na bəlgarskija ezik* (Sofia, 1953) (the second unchanged edition 1953, and the third, largely amplified, 275 pp., Sofia, 1958). The book represents the history of Bulgarian "sensu stricto", that means after the period of Old Church Slavonic ("*starobəlgarski*") and with special reference to the transitional period of Middle Bulgarian (12th, 13th, 14th centuries) from which many data are quoted for the first time. It is conceived primarily as a handbook for students of Bulgarian philology, but it is, none the less, also in many respects a new scientific contribution to knowledge of the historical development of Bulgarian. One of its chapters treats a very important external linguistic problem, namely the historical relations of Bulgarian with other languages (pp. 59-86), among them, first of all, those of Bulgarian with Balkan languages. The views of the author upon the causes of the so-called "Balkanisms" in Bulgarian (which incidently speaking represent the most striking structural changes in its history) are rather cautious, but in comparison with those of the older school (L. Miletič, S. Mladenov) who in principle did not like to accept any foreign influences – they are reasonable. The following statement is characteristic for K. Mirčev:

Много слаб успех в науката имат опитите да се установят взаимни влияния между балканските езици във връзка с възникването на най-важните техни прилики. Все по-дълбокото и по-подробно историческо изследване на тия прилики установява вън от всяко съмнение, че създалите се вследствие на продължително общуване общи развойни тенденции са се осъществявали във всеки отделен балкански език със собствени средства и най-често по напълно различен път. Това найдобре се установява, като се проследи историческият развой на българската и румунската членна форма, чиято постпозиция най-лесно подвеждаше наблюдателите да предполагат взаимни влияния (*loc. cit.*, 59).

Of course the mysterious notion "obšti razvojni tendencii" (common evolutionary tendencies) which refers to the results of historical development of a language rather than to its causes – should be discussed more precisely in connection with the fact of "prodəlžitelno obštuvane" (long symbiosis) between the languages in question. Such a discussion would bring us inevitably to the fundamental socio-linguistic fact of "bilingualism", the only one that may render understandable the structural interference between Balkan languages and their "common evolutionary tendencies".

As in the field of comparative Slavic linguistics the name of I. Lekov represents a whole chapter, the same is true about K. Mirčev in the field of the history of Bulgarian. The best evidence of that are the following publications: "Bəlgarskijat ezik prez vekovete", *EzLit*, 11 (1956), p. 420-432; "Za periodizacijata na istorijata na bəlgarskija ezik", *IzvIBE*, 2 (1952), p. 194-202 (in connection with the discussion caused by S. B. Bernštejn, viz. below); "Kəm razčitaneto na bəlgarskija tekst v Danilovija četiriezičnik", *MakPr*, 12 (1940), 3, p. 36-42 (the object of the analysis is a West Macedonian dialect from the end of the 18th century used in the famous *Didaskalija* by Daniel from Moskopole); "Upotrebata na vəzvratnoto pritežatelno mestoimenie svoj v staro- i novobəlgarski", *GodSU*, 42, no. 6 (1946), 59 pp.; "Ima li glagol MъČATI v Suprasəlskija sbornik", *BəlEz*, 8 (1958), p. 50-51 (according to the author the form *mъčimi* in that monument is to be read *məčimi* and represents the pres. pass. participle of the OChSl *mǫčiti* = Greek βασανίζω: thus the evidence of a very early-XI century passage, at least in some Bulgarian dialects, of the primary *ǫ* > ъ(ə)!); "Analitični formi za sravnitelna stepen v dva srednobəlgarski pametnika ot XIV v.", *BəlEz*, 1 (1951), p. 215-217; "Po vəprosa za naj-rannite primeri ot analitičen datelen padež v bəlgarskite pametnici", *Ezikovedski izsledvanija v čest na akad. S. Mladenov* (Sofia, 1957), p. 37-46 (viz. the remarks below!); "Koga vəznikva člennata forma v bəlgarskija ezik", *BəlEz*, 3 (1953), p. 45-50; "Za člennite formi v Dobrejšovo evangelie, srednobəlgarski pametnik ot XIII v.", *BəlEz*, 6 (1956), p. 226-228; "Glagolnite formi be i beše v razvoja na bəlgarskija ezik", *MakPr*, 12, 2 (1940), p. 63-70; "Za smesvaneto na okončanijata v minato svəršeno i minalo nesvəršeno vreme na glagolite v bəlgarski ezik", *BəlEz*, 2 (1952), p. 36-45; "Ot MATI do majka", *BəlEz*, 7 (1957), p. 262-265 (the development of Common Slavic *mati* in Bulgarian: the form *majka* appears for the first time in the *Dobrejšovo evangelie* in the 13th century).

The most discussable problems in the history of Bulgarian are: its periodization, the disappearance of nominal declension and the origin of postpositive article. The discussion about the periodization started with the article by the Russian scholar

S. B. Bernštejn, "K voprosu o periodizacii istorii bolgarskogo jazyka", *Izvestija Akad. Nauk, Otdel. literatury i jazyka*, 9, 2 (1950), p. 108-118. The author opposes the traditional division of the history of Bulgarian into three epochs: Old Bulgarian (9th-11th centuries), Middle Bulgarian (11th-15th centuries) and New Bulgarian (since the 15th century) and proposes a bipartition: the first period would comprise the formation of Bulgarian as a separate South Slavic language between the 9th and the 19th centuries, the second period would comprise the time after the formation of Standard Bulgarian in the second half of the 19th century up to date. This conception is based upon the view that Old Church Slavonic ("Old Bulgarian") does not represent the actual folk language spoken by the Bulgarians and therefore can not be taken into account as the first stage in the development of Bulgarian. The real folk language which underwent a deep structural influence of Thracian substratum (sic!) could not be expressed in Old Church Slavonic monuments detached from the living spoken language and only gradually, during the so-called second Bulgarian Tsardom (the 13th century) did it begin to leave traces in written monuments. Another conception of historical bipartition of Bulgarian was proposed by V. Georgiev in the articles: "Opit za periodizacija na istorijata na bəlgarskija ezik", *IzvIBE*, 2 (1952), p. 71-116, and "Problema periodizacii istorii jazyka i periodizacija istorii bolgarskogo jazyka", *Slavističen Sbornik*, I (Sofia, 1958), p. 165-183. V. Georgiev distinguishes the Old Bulgarian period since the 6th century until the 14th century and the New Bulgarian period starting from the 15th century. The basic principle of that division is the passage of Bulgarian from the synthetic linguistic type to the analytic one which happened in the transitional period of Middle Bulgarian deprived in that new (Georgiev's) periodization of independent historical status. The views of V. Georgiev were criticized by K. Mirčev in the article quoted above and by S. Stojanov in: "Po vəprosa za periodizacijata na istorijata na bəlgarskija ezik", *IzvIBE*, 2 (1952), p. 207-212. K. Mirčev decisevely defends the traditional "tripartition" of the history of Bulgarian and consequently applies it in his book quoted above. For the majority of Bulgarian linguists there is no doubt that Old Church Slavonic, usually called by them "Old Bulgarian" (*starobəlgarski*, *Altbulgarisch*) represents the earliest attested stage in the development of their national language. Therefore the works treating OChSl are usually viewed as belonging to the history of Bulgarian. This approach seems to be justified whatever we could say about the artificial and bookish character of OChSl. But another question arises which also plays a significant role in Bulgarian dialectology, namely: the historical relationship between Macedonian and Bulgarian and subsequently between Old Macedonian and Old Church Slavonic ("Old Bulgarian"). As is known, the Macedonians claim OChSl to be the oldest attested stage of their own national language and therefore the most adequate name for it would be "Old Macedonian". Leaving aside national feelings involved in the discussion we can state some objective facts which seem to solve the question from a scientific point of view. The appearance of Macedonian as a separate national language is a recent socio-cultural phenomenon (Standard Macedonian was not formed until after the

Second World War) connected with political conditions in Macedonia in the second part of the 19th and in the 20th century. From a linguistic point of view the majority of characteristic features distinguishing Macedonian from Bulgarian are of relatively young origin; the archaic Macedonian dialects indicate that in the epoch when OChSl was born there were only very slight dialectal differences between Macedonian and Bulgarian and therefore the Macedonian and Bulgarian territory in the 9th century should be treated as one linguistic whole. The language used by Cyril and Methodius for religious purpose represents in its fundamentals a South East Macedonian dialect whose continuation (e.g. *Suxo* and *Visoka* vernaculars) in the 20th century show in some respects typical East Bulgarian features. Thus OChSl can be claimed with equal right by both the Bulgarians and the Macedonians as the oldest historical stage in their national languages.

Among recent Bulgarian works refering to OChSl the following are worth quotation: I. Gošev, *Rilski glagoličeski listove* (Sofia, 1958), 149 pp. + 10 tables (the parallel texts in OChSl – Cyrillic transcription – and Greek, paleographic and linguistic analysis, word register); K. Mirčev, *Starobəlgarski ezik za učitelskite instituti*, 1st edition (Sofia, 1954), 2nd edition (Sofia, 1956); among the OChSl anthologies *Starobəlgarski ezik. Tekstove i rečnik* (Sofia, 1956), 196 pp. and tables by M. Janakiev and S. Stojanov is to be mentioned thanks to its dictionary and valuable text remarks. More detailed problems of OChSl are treated in the following publications: B. Gerov, "Die Form der griechischen und semitischen Nomina auf -i(s) im Altbulgarischen", *StSer*, 2 (1940), pp. 99-117; "Die Griechischen, semitischen und lateinischen Nomina im Altbulgarischen", *GodSU*, 39, no. 11 (1943), 38 pp.; "Zastəpvane na dvojnite glasni i səglasni pri čuždite imena i dumi v starobəlgarski", *IzvDS*, I (1942), p. 57-72; F. Aleksandrov, "O značenijax i funkcijax mestoimenij kotoryj, iže, kyj v osnovnyx pamjatnikax drevnebolgarskogo jazyka", *Slavističen Sbornik*, I (Sofia, 1958), p. 145-163; I. Duridanov, "Beležki vərxu starobəlgarskija prevod na evangelieto", *Ezikovedski izsledvanija v čest na akad. S. Mladenov* (Sofia, 1957), p. 225-233 (the author shows on the one hand the influence of the Greek original upon the syntax of OChSl translation, but on the other hand some divergences between the Greek original and the OChSl translation are underlined which indicates the very beginning of analytic tendencies in OChSl); Z. Vitox, "Za složnoto səstavno izrečenie v Suprasəlskija sbornik"; *SpBAN*, 34 (1950), p. 28-44.

As we mentioned above, the main problems of the historical development of Bulgarian are the disappearance of the nominal declension and the origin of the postpositive article. The most important work referring to the first problem is I. Duridanov's "Kəm problemata za razvoja na bəlgarskija ezik ot sintetizəm kəm analitizəm", *GodSU*, 51 (1955), p. 87-272. The author collected a large material of case forms and prepositional constructions from Middle Bulgarian sources which differ from OChSl usage and therefore may throw the light upon the gradual decline of the synthetic OChSl declension type and its replacement by an analytic one. Among many topics the New Bulgarian prepositional construction with *na* "on" and noun replacing the old Dative case in both its "purely dative" and possessive functions is one that evokes the more interest. I. Duridanov's views in this respect are criticized by K. Mirčev (see below). I. Duridanov endeavours also to discover some general forces steering the evolution of Bulgarian from synthetic declension towards analytic one He finds them in the conflict of two opposite tendencies (synthetic: analytic) which appeared in the history of the language. The same author published an article "Edin slučaj na ranna upotreba na predloga "na" za izrazjavane na datelno otnošenie", *BəlEz*, 3 (1953), p. 58-60, which aims to demonstrate that in one place of Dobrejšovo evangelie, a Middle Bulgarian text from the 13th century, the oldest example of the analytic *na*-construction in dative function appears. The problem of the oldest examples of the analytic Dative in Bulgarian was critically reviewed by K. Mirčev in the article published in *Ezikovedski izsledvanija v čest na S. Mladenov* (Sofia, 1957) we mentioned above. The author analyzed all previously published material supplementing it with some new items from *Bolonski psaltir*. The results of the study he summarizes in the following words:

От критичния анализ, който направихме на публикувания досега материал, а така също и от новия материал, който за първ път се изнася в тази статия, се вижда, че доста сигурни следи от аналатично предаване на дателния падеж се срещат в българските паметници още от XII–XIII в. Примерите са действително оскъдни, както е оскъдно всичко ново, проникнало в среднобългарските паметници. Те не могат да се изтълкуват като доказателства, че в посоченото време аналитизмът е бил вече настанен в българския език. Но те са несъмнени показатели, че най-съществената черта в развоя на българския език – загубването на падежната флексия – се е намирала в процес на бърз развой (*loc. cit.*, 46).

We have stopped at this subject because it seems to be one of the crucial problems in the historical morphology of Bulgarian and the precise analysis by K. Mirčev may be representative of his philological-linguistic method. But may we be allowed to make one additional remark. Among the OChSl constructions with *na* + Accusative the author quotes the type with the meaning "*pravi nešto sreštu njakogo*" (to make/do something in the face of somebody"), e.g. *da uže ubo otъvêtъ sъtvoriti na nь* (Supr. 152, 29, cf. *loc. cit.*, 43), then among the constructions with *na* + Locative he quotes the type with the meaning "*za,kəm, v interesa na, za blagoto na*" ("for, on behalf of") e.g. *razumêjǫtъ vêrnii milosti gĩę, byvъšǫǫ na člověcě* (Bol. psalt. CVI, 43, cf. *loc. cit.*, 44). It seems to be very essential that just these analytic constructions, admissible already in OChSl and functionally very close to the Dative, provided a "domestic, indigenous" model for the further development of the "analytic" Dative which being supported by foreign "Balkanic" influences substituted the old synthetic Dative. This aspect of the problem has not been stressed in the article by K. Mirčev.

The second most discussed problem of Bulgarian historical morphology is the postpositive article. A fresh air into the discussion has been brought by I. Gələbov's article "Za člena v bəlgarski ezik", *Izvestija na Narodnija muzej v Burgas*, I (1951), p. 171-227. This study represents very important progress in comparison with the older works by L. Miletič. I. Gələbov's fundamental idea is that the Bulgarian article continues a weakly stressed demonstrative pronoun which subsequently became enclitic. The author investigates and analyzes the use of such a "weakened" post-positive demonstrative pronoun in OChSl texts with special reference to their Greek original, insisting upon those cases where in Greek the noun is not accompanied by an article and demonstrative pronoun or where there are differences in word order, namely the "weakened" demonstrative pronoun in OChSl stands after the first word of a nominal group. There are only a few such cases. But they exhibit clearly the germs of the postpositive article born from the "weakened" demonstrative pronoun becoming a kind of "determinative". Unfortunately the author denies any foreign influence on the part of other Balkan languages upon the further development of the article. This reluctance towards foreign influences characteristic for the older school (L. Miletič, S. Mladenov) is criticized by K. Mirčev (cf. his review of Bulgarian linguistics in *Zeitschrift für Slavische Philologie*, XXVIII 1, p. 180). But it may be – to some extent – understandable when we consider the fact that the majority of Bulgarian linguists (I. Gələbov included) do not distinguish in the whole phenomenon the "substantial" aspect from the functional one: the crucial point is that OChSl did not have the article as a functional grammatical category while Middle Bulgarian, especially later Middle Bulgarian, did. The origin of the Bulgarian article as a functional grammatical category can not be explained without the Balkan linguistic background.

Although the Bulgarian verbal system underwent very profound changes in the course of its history it does not evoke so much interest among Bulgarian scholars as the two former problems do. We can quote only – besides the two articles by K. Mirčev mentioned above – I. Duridanov, "Iz istorijata na pričastijata v bəlgarski ezik", *BəlEz*, 6 (1956), p. 148-152; D. Ivanova, "Kəm vəprosa za razvoja na pričastnite konstrukcii v bəlgarskija ezik", *IzvIBE*, 2 (1952), p. 212-217; L. Vankov, "Kəm istorijata na glagolnija sufiks -iram v bəlgarski", *Ezikovedski izsledvanija v čest na akad. S. Mladenov* (Sofia, 1957), p. 141-155; X. Pərvev, "Iz 'preistorijata' na problemata za preizkaznoto naklonenie", *BəlEz*, 8 (1958), p. 434-441.

In the other fields of historical morphology the following publications are worth mentioning: I. Gələbov, "Kəm istorijata na otnositelnite mestoimenija v bəlgarski ezik", *Ezikovedski izsledvanija v čest na S. Mladenov*, p. 65-72 (the author points out very early – already in the language of Joan Ekzarx – the use of the particle *-to* in the relative function before the disappearance of the primary pronouns *iže* etc.).

In the field of historical syntax we can quote: I. Gələbov, "Zur Frage der bulgarischen Enklitika", *Zeitschrift für Slavische Philologie*, XX, p. 417-438 (the article opposes the views of the Polish scholar F. Sławski expressed in his book *Miejsce enklityki odmiennej w dziejach języka bułgarskiego*, Krakow, 1946; I. Gələbov maintains the conception of the principal mobility of Bulgarian enclitics); the same "Pet, pettjax, petima, petmina", *BəlEz*, 4 (1954), p. 250-257 (the article treats first of all the constructions of the type *dva, tri, četiri učenika* with the so-called New Bulgarian "countable" plural ending with *-a* whose origin the author explains as the result of a replacement of primary Nom. -Acc. Dual. by Gen. Sing.; the form *petima*, an old Instrumental, was taken over from passive constructions where the agent stood primarily in Instr.). Of course the problems connected with the disappearance of the primary synthetic nominal declension belong also to a great extent to syntax. With them are in some respect related the problems of prepositions which are treated in A. Minčeva's, "Kəm istorijata na predlozite v bəlgarskija ezik", *BəlEz*, 11 (1961), p. 209-223.

In the field of historical phonology there are only a few contributions: I. Gələbov, "Kəm razvoja na y v imenitelen padež na složnite prilagatelni v bəlgarski ezik", *IzvIBE*, 1 (1952), p. 168-180 (on the basis of the dialects of Salonika region the author indicates that in some of them *-yj* (≦ *-ъjь*) of determinate adjectives did not develop in *-y*, but was maintained as *-ъj* etc. which may explain the frequent OChSl spelling *ЪU* not *ЪI*), and I. Kočev, "Zastəpnici na mekata erova glasna v bəlgarskija ezik", *SMBD*, 9 (1959), p. 51-90 (a historical study with reference to dialects). We can also quote here as an exception the article by the German scholar E. Košmider (Koschmieder) published in *IzvIBE*, 7 (1961), p. 81-93, "Grupite tъrt// trъt itn. v bəlgarski ezik".

4b. Dialectology takes a very important place in linguistic research in Bulgaria, and is usually connected with the history of language. After World War II a special department of dialectology at the Institute of Bulgarian Language in the framework of Bulgarian Academy of Sciences was organized under the direction of S. Stojkov. This fact makes it possible to undertake new collective investigations "in the field" according to a strictly determined scientific program which was published by S. Stojkov as *Kratək osvedomitelen vəprosnik za proučvane na bəlgarskite mestni govori*, 1st edition (Sofia, 1947), 2nd edition (Sofia, 1950), 3rd edition (Sofia, 1954). In connection with the above remains "Pravilata za fonetično zapisvane na bəlgarski dialektni tekstove", *BəlEz*, 3 (1953), p. 72-73 established by the same scholar.

There are two main tasks of contemporary Bulgarian dialectological research: the dialectological atlas and the dialectological dictionary of Bulgarian. The first task is being prepared by the department of dialectology at the Institute of Bulgarian Language under the direction of S. Stojkov in close collaboration with the Institute of Slavic Studies (*Institut Slavjanovedenija*) at the Soviet Academy of Sciences under the direction of S. B. Bernštejn. The second task is being prepared solely by the Bulgarian department of dialectology mentioned above. The close collaboration with the Russians in the preparation of the dialectological atlas is due to the initiative of the Russian slavicist S. B. Bernštejn who in 1948 published the article "Bolgarskij lingvističeskij atlas", *Vestnik Akademii Nauk SSSR*, Nr. 2, p. 119-122, beginning a discussion which ended with *Programa za səbirane na materiali za bəlgarski dialekten atlas* (Sofia, 1955). Based on this program, some dialectological expeditions were undertaken whose reports have been published in the following articles: S. Stojkov and S. B. Bernštejn, "Rezultati ot pərvata ekspedicija za səbirane na materiali za bəlgarski dialekten atlas", *BəlEz*, 7 (1957), p. 181-186; S. Stojkov, "Vtorata bəlgarsko-səvetska ekspedicija za səbirane na materiali za bəlgarski dialekten atlas", *BəlEz*, 7 (1957), p. 478-480; "Bəlgarski dialekten atlas", *EzLit*, 12 (1957), p. 285-291; E. V. Češko (a Russian scholar), "Sovmestnaja rabota bolgarskix i sovetskix filologov", *Vestnik Akad. Nauk SSSR*, 1957, Nr. 1, p. 81-82. Of course the results of those dialectological expeditions are stored in the department of the Institute of Bulgarian Language mentioned above and are being prepared for publication. In connection with the dialectological investigations performed in Bulgaria, research on Bulgarian dialects spoken in the southern part of Soviet Union was done. Here also the initiative was on the part of S. B. Bernštejn who directed the whole enterprise in the framework of the department of Slavic linguistics at the Institute of Slavic Studies (*Institut Slavjanovedenija*) of the Soviet Academy of Sciences. The program of the work was drawn by S. B. Bernštejn in the following articles: "Lingvističeskij atlas bolgarskix govorov SSSR", *IzvAN SSSR*, 8 (1948), p. 245-253, and "Atlas bolgarskix govorov SSSR", *Doklady i soobščenija Inst. jazykoznanija AN*, 1952, p. 135-141. In the years 1948-1950 collective expeditions "in the field" were organized and in 1958 the work was finished with the publication *Atlas bolgarskix govorov v SSSR* (Moscow, 1958), 109 maps and a supplement entitled *Atlas bolgarskix govorov v SSSR. Vstupitel'nye stat'i, kommentarii k kartam* (Moscow, 1958), 84 pp. As the authors quoted: S. B. Bernštejn, E. V. Češko and E. I. Zelenina.

As usual, the majority of the maps present phonetic phenomena (45 items); the second place is taken by lexical phenomena (38 items); morphological questions are presented by the smallest number of the maps (20 items). The atlas, although it is an achievement of the Russian school of dialectology, should be mentioned here because it will undoubtedly influence the ways of investigation and the ultimate shape of the dialectological atlas being prepared in Bulgaria. On the margin of those Russian investigations some monographic works devoted to different problems of the Bulgarian dialects spoken in the Soviet Union were published in the special series *Stat'i i materialy po bolgarskoj dialektologii SSSR* (abbreviation: *SMBD*); the first volume published in 1950 was included in *Učenye zapiski Instituta Slavjanovedenija*, II, p. 219-308, others appeared separately. A critical review of the first seven volumes was made by S. Stojkov, "Novi proučvanija na bəlgarskite govori v Səvetskija səjuz", *IzvIBE*, 4 (1956), p. 427-482.

As for the investigations of dialectal vocabulary in Bulgaria they are oriented according to the "Programa za səbirane na rečnikovi materiali ot bəlgarskite narodni govori", *EzLit*, 10 (1955), p. 445-449, established by S. Stojkov. The department of dialectology at the Institute of Bulgarian Language already possesses over 80,000 lexical items prepared for a Bulgarian dialectal dictionary.

Passing on to individual publications in the field of Bulgarian dialectology, we should mention at the very beginning some synthetic and pedagogical works. Here again publications by S. Stojkov take the first place, *Bəlgarska dialektologija*, 1st edition (Sofia, 1949), 132 pp., 2nd revised edition (Sofia, 1954), 240 pp., 3rd edition

(Sofia, 1956), 226 pp.; *Xristomatija po bəlgarska dialektologija* (Sofia, 1950), 102 pp. (a dictionary added); "Dialektologijata i nejnoto značenie za cjalostnoto proučvane na ezika", *BəlEz*, 5 (1955), p. 10-18; "Literaturen ezik i dialekti", *IvzIBE*, 2 (1952), p. 129-171; "Postiženija i zadači na bəlgarskata dialektologija", *BəlEz*, 9 (1959), p. 340-346. Problems on the borderline between the history of language and dialectology are treated in the article by B. Velčeva, "Kəm ustanovjavaneto na vzaimootnešenijata i dialektnata osnova na novobəlgarskite damaskini", *BəlEz*, 11 (1961), p. 402-417 (the author classifies the "damaskins" according to their dialectal features).

Besides collective research aiming at the dialectological atlas and the dialectal dictionary of Bulgarian, dialectological investigations are usually concerned with monographic description of a single dialect. In this field quite a few publications appeared in the post war period. Since K. Mirčev in his review of Bulgarian linguistics in *Zeitschrift für Slavische Philologie*, XXIX (1961), p. 173-182 gave an exhaustive account of all publications between 1935 and 1958, I will here limit myself to some more important positions and additional data concerning the publications appearing after 1958. K. Popov, "Govorət na S. Gabare, Beloslatinsko", *IzvIBE*, 4 (1956), p. 103-176; the collective work of the students of the University of Sofia, "Govorət na s. Govedarci, Samokovsko", *IzvIBE*, 4 (1956), p. 255-338; R. Angelova, "Selo Raduil, Samokovsko", *IzvSS*, 8-9 (1948), p. 47-130 (includes ethnographical material); I. Umlenski, "Fonetični i morfologični osobenosti na kjustendilskija govor", *BəlEz*, 11 (1961), p. 444-457. All the above publications concern the West Bulgarian, especially the North West Bulgarian dialects. The South East Bulgarian dialects which before the war were very little known are treated e.g. in the following works: S. Kabasanov, "Govorət na s. Momčilovci", *IzvIBE*, 4 (1955), p. 5-101; G. Xristov, "Govorət na s. Nadežda, Xaskovsko", *ibid.*, p. 177-253; S. Stojkov, "Strandžanskijat govor", *BəlEz*, 7 (1957), p. 205-215.

Another trend in monographic dialectological investigations is oriented towards the description of the specific dialectal features of a given dialect. In connection with that we can quote, e.g. B. Simeonov, "Člennata forma v prexodnite govori", *Ezikovedsko-etnografski izsledvanija v pamet na akad. S. Romanski* (Sofia, 1960), p. 379-391 (the author treats especially the forms with inflected article of the type *vəlkatóga*//*vəlkáta* (Gen.-Acc.) etc. used in some North West Bulgarian dialects; in connection with that he discusses again the problem of the origin of the Bulgarian postpositive article); S. Stojkov, "Edna nova promjana na səglasnata *l* v bəlgarski ezik. Prexod na səglasnata *l* v *u̯* i *v* v govora na s. Korovo, Velingradsko", *BəlEz*, 6 (1956), p. 239-244; "Edno novo fonetično javlenie v zapadnite bəlgarski govori (zamjana na palatalno *l s j*)", *IzvIBE*, 1 (1952); M. Vəglenov, "Za formite miti i piti v bəlgarskite govori", *Sbornik v čest na A. Teodorov-Balan* (Sofia, 1956), p. 185-186. Here can be also mentioned numerous contributions to the knowledge of Bulgarian dialectal vocabulary quoted by K. Mirčev in his review (cf. *op. cit.*, pp. 178-179).

In the field of social dialects ("argots") the following publications are worth mentioning: S. Stojkov, "Bəlgarski socialni govori", *EzLit*, 2 (1947), p. 1-14, and

"Social'nye dialekty", *Voprosy Jazykoznanija*, 1957, 1, p. 78-84 (general characteristics of the phenomenon); "Sofijskijat učeničeski govor. Prinos kəm bəlgarskata socialna dialektologija", *GodSU*, 42, 73 pp.; K. Kostov, "Italijanski dumi v profesionalnija govor na bəlgarskite obuštari", *BəlEz*, 3 (1953), p. 256-258; "Ciganski elementi v bəlgarskite tajni govori", *IzvIBE*, 4 (1955), p. 411-425; I. Kənčev, "Taen zidarski govor v s. Smolsko, Pirdopsko", *ibid.*, p. 369-410.

To the field of the history of literary Macedonian belongs "Ezikət na "Bəlgarski narodni pesni" ot bratja Miladinovi", *BəlEz*, 11 (1961), p. 385-401 by V. Georgiev.

4c. The problems of purely descriptive (synchronic) grammar seem to play a rather secondary role in Bulgarian linguistics as compared with those of historical grammar and dialectology. The best proof of such a situation is the review by K. Mirčev quoted above in which the descriptive grammar of Bulgarian has not been included at all. Besides that the subjects of descriptive grammar are usually oriented along the same lines as the historical problems we have presented above, namely: analytic tendencies in morphology and syntax, the article, the new verbal categories. The number of publications is rather significant. The first place among them is taken by the works and articles of L. Andrejčin. We can quote the following: L. Andrejčin, *Osnovna bəlgarska gramatika* (Sofia, 1944), 559 pp.; the same in the collaboration with M. Ivanov, K. Popov, *Səvremenen bəlgarski ezik*, vol. I (Sofia, 1954), 256 pp., vol. II (Sofia, 1957), 409 pp. (these are the fundamental descriptions of Contemporary Standard Bulgarian). The same character we find in *Nova bəlgarska gramatika* (Sofia, 1940), 487 pp. by A. Teodorov-Balan (it was revised and published in two volumes with the title *Nova bəlgarska gramatika za vsjakogo*, Sofia, 1954-1958, 276 pp. and 276-409 pp.). Among the publications treating more general problems are to be mentioned: L. Andrejčin, "Vəprosət na nacionalnata samobitnost na ezika", *IzvIBE*, 2 (1952), p. 29-54, and A. Teodorov-Balan, *Səstojanie na bəlgarskata gramatika. Kritična studija* (Sofia, 1948), VI + 240 pp. (it is a collection of articles published earlier in different journals).

Passing to the special sections of descriptive grammar we list first of all articles:

a) Phonology (phonemics and phonetics): L. Andrejčin, "Za mekite səglasni v bəlgarski ezik", *EzLit*, 5 (1950), p. 333-334; "Za mekostta na bəlgarskija ezik", *BəlEz*, 7 (1957), p. 489-498; "Po vəprosa za upodobjavaneto na bezzvučnite səglasni pred zvučni v bəlgarski ezik", *BəlEz*, 8 (1958), p. 266-268; V. Georgiev, "Po vəprosa za upodobjavaneto na səglasnite v bəlgarski", *BəlEz*, 8 (1958), p. 52-56. Problems of accent are treated in the following articles by M. Georgieva: "Udarenieto na dvusričnite səštestvitelni imena ot məžki rod s predstavka v bəlgarski ezik", *BəlEz*, 7 (1957), p. 19-30; "Udarenieto na səštestvitelnite imena v səvremennija bəlgarski literaturen i sceničen govor", *Godišnik na Visšija institut za teatralno izkustvo "Krəst'o Sarafov"*, I (Sofia, 1956), p. 247-324; "Udarenieto na ličnite sobstveni imena v səvremennija literaturen ezik", *BəlEz*, 10 (1960), p. 332-349; "Udarenieto v glagolnata sistema na səvremennija bəlgarski literaturen i sceničen izgovor", *BəlEz*, 9 (1959), p. 391-402;

I. Lekov, "Opit za fonologična xarakteristika na bəlgarskija ezik", *GodSU*, 37 (Sofia, 1940-41), p. 1-37; S. Stojkov, "Bəlgarski knižoven izgovor. Opitno izsledvanie", *SborBAN*, 37 (Sofia, 1942), p. 281-416 (the author distinguishes 29 consonantic and 6 vocalic phonemes, includes in the publication palatograms and linguograms, and determines the Bulgarian accent to be a dynamic one). S. Stojkov wrote a number of articles devoted to different phonemic and phonetic problems of contemporary Bulgarian. The book *Uvod v bəlgarskata fonetika* (Sofia, 1955), 174 pp. (2nd revised edition, Sofia, 1961, 204 pp.) may be treated as a kind of theoretical synthesis of his earlier investigations. Besides that his article "Jatovijat vəpros v novobəlgarskija knižoven ezik", *GodSU*, 44 (1948), p. 1-145 is worth mentioning. The article treats the *'á* : *é* pronunciation of the primary *ě* in Standard Bulgarian, showing and explaining the "exceptions" from the rule; it contains, of course, historical data too as the material from the 19th century has been taken into account.

b) Morphology. Here we can quote: L. Andrejčin, "Za vəprosite i praktikata na členuvaneto v bəlgarskija knižoven ezik", *BəlEz*, 8 (1958), p. 3-10; "Kəm vəprosa za analitičnija xarakter na səvremennija bəlgarski ezik", *BəlEz*, 2 (1952), p. 20-35 (the author – among other topics – quotes the remnants of cases in contemporary Bulgarian and tries to define the terms "analytic", "synthetic" and "case"); "Mjastoto na ostatəcite na infinitiv v bəlgarskoto sprežеnie", *BəlEz*, 3 (1953), p. 65; "Glagolnite vremena v bəlgarskoto stradatelno spreženie", *Sbornik v čest na A. Teodorov-Balan* (Sofia, 1955), p. 69-76; "Kəm morfologičnata xarakteristika na vidovata sistema v səvremennija bəlgarski ezik", *Slavističen Sbornik*, I (Sofia, 1958), p. 257-262; "Kəm xarakteristikata na perfekta (minalo neopredeleno vreme) v bəlgarski ezik", *Ezikovedski izsledvanija v čest na akad. S. Mladenov* (Sofia, 1957), p. 57-64; "Zalogət v bəlgarskata glagolna sistema", *BəlEz*, 6 (1956), p. 106-120; "Ošte po vəprosa za preizkaznoto naklonenie", *BəlEz*, 12 (1962), p. 91-99. As we can see, first of all, problems of the Bulgarian verbal system have been attracting the scientific interest of L. Andrejčin, the main representative of Bulgarian synchronic linguistics. The phenomenon is obviously caused by the well known intricateness of that system.

The most discussed problems of Contemporary Bulgarian are: the article and "articled" nominal forms, nominal declension (if such a term is at all justified in Bulgarian grammar) and the verbal category often determined as "*preizkazno naklonenie*". Leaving aside other less central problems let us pay attention to the publications concerned with those key topics. Besides the above quoted articles by L. Andrejčin we can list the following: S. Ivančev, "Nabljudenija vərxu upotrebata na člena v bəlgarski ezik", *BəlEz*, 7 (1957), p. 499-524; S. Stojanov, "Kəm vəprosa za upotrebata i značenieto na opredelitelnija člen v səvremennija bəlgarski knižoven ezik", *BəlEz*, 8 (1958), p. 248-257, and *EzLit*, 6 (1958), p. 414-426, the same also in *Ezikovedsko-etnografski izsledvanija v pamet na akad S. Romanski* (Sofia, 1960), p. 259-270; S. Stojkov, "Členuvane na imenata ot məžki rod, edinstveno čislo v bəlgarski knižoven ezik", *GodSU*, 46 (1950), p. 1-46. As in the post-war years a close collaboration and mutual theoretical influence between Bulgarian and Russian scholars in the field of linguistics, especially dialectology, appeared, it is sometimes indispensable to mention the works by Russian linguists treating Bulgarian and published in Bulgaria. In connection with that the article by V. Borodič, "Ob obščix principax upotreblenija člennyx form i glagol'nyx vremen v bolgarskom jazyke", *IzvIBE*, 7 (1961), p. 49-80 is worth mentioning. The author introduces the opposition of "concrete": "abstract" which cuts through both the nominal and verbal system of Bulgarian being expressed within the nouns by "articled" form versus "unarticled" form and within the verbs by "*prjako vreme*" (denoting a witnessed action) versus "*preizkazno vreme*" (denoting an unwitnessed action).

Very interesting discussion was held about the problem of the existence and non-existence, respectively, of nominal cases in Bulgarian. It was initiated by A. Teodorov-Balan in his article "Bəlgarsko sklonenie", *BəlEz*, 4 (1954), p. 40-61. In that article the author accepts the existence of nominal cases in contemporary Bulgarian starting from a definition of case as a purely logical-syntactic relationship between the noun and other words in sentence and disregarding the form which serves to express that relationship. Of course, such a definition of casc provoked a series of articles, namely: N. M. Dilevski, "Səštestvuvat li padeži v səvremennija bəlgarski ezik?", *BəlEz*, 5 (1955), p. 31-38; I. Duridanov, "Ponjatieto padež i vəprosət na bəlgarskoto 'sklonenie'", *BəlEz*, 4 (1954), p. 145-150; I. Xadžov, "Kəm vəprosa za sklonenieto v dnešnija knižoven bəlgarski ezik", *BəlEz*, 4 (1954), p. 158-167; G. Mixajlov, "Kəm vəprosa za səštestvuvaneto na padeži v bəlgarski ezik", *BəlEz*, 5 (1955), p. 336-342; K. Mirčev, "Po vəprosa za sklonenieto v bəlgarski ezik", *BəlEz*, 4 (1954), p. 61-64.

The majority of Bulgarian linguists deny the existence of nominal cases in contemporary Bulgarian. A clear theoretical justification of this negative attitude is given in the article by I. Duridanov quoted in the above list.

As to the problem of the so-called "*preizkazni vremena*" (other terms for it are: the tenses of reported speech, auditive, imperceptive) besides the articles by L. Andrejčin and V. Borodič mentioned above we can quote the following publications: another Russian scholar J. S. Maslov, "K voprosu o sisteme form pereskazyvatel'nogo naklonenija", *Sbornik v čest na A. Teodorov-Balan* (Sofia, 1956), p. 311-318; A. Teodorov-Balan, "Četvərto naklonenie", *BəlEz*, 7 (1957), p. 303-317 (the author treats the "auditive" forms as the 4th verbal mood of Bulgarian conjugation); T. Ponželarkov, "Po vəprosa za preizkaznoto naklonenie", *BəlEz*, 12 (1962), p. 84-91. Among other publications devoted to the special problems of the Bulgarian verbal system worth mentioning are the following: V. Georgiev, "Vəznikvane na novi složni glagolni formi səs spomagatelen glagol 'imam' ", *IzvIBE*, 5 (1957), p. 31-59 (the author treats the "new perfect" of the type *imam kupena knigata* "I have bought the book" which is spreading in contemporary spoken Bulgarian and which represents a common Balkan construction accepted by Literary Macedonian in the form *ja imam kupeno knigata*); D. X. Mateev, "Semantikata na glagolnite predstavki i nejnoto otnošenie kəm vidovoto značenie na glagolite", *IzvIBE*, 1 (1952), p. 65-91; R. Mutafčief, "Smjana na glagolnite vremena v razkaz na minali səbitija", *BəlEz*, 11

(1961), p. 308-321; in connection with that V. Borodič, "Za funkciite na minalo predvaritelno vreme v səvremennija bəlgarski ezik", *BəlEz*, 7 (1957), p. 430-451; S. Stojkov, "Obrazuvane na bədešte vreme (futurum) v səvremennija bəlgarski ezik", *Ezikovedsko-etnografski izsledvanija v pamet na akad. S. Romanski* (Sofia, 1960), p. 239-257 (the author quotes a rich dialectal material including in the article a synthetic map); P. Pašov, "Formite bidox, bide v bəlgarskija knižoven ezik"; *BəlEz*, 8 (1958), p. 385-400; X. Pərčev, "Ustanovjavane na deepričastieto v səvremennija knižoven bəlgarski ezik", *BəlEz*, 8 (1958), p. 122-139; J. Simeonov, "Za vida na glagolite ot čužd proizxod na -iram, -uvam (-ovam)", *BəlEz*, 9 (1959), p. 160-164; S. Stojkov, "Glagolnoto okončanie -me v bəlgarskija knižoven ezik (Upotreba na okončanieto -me za l lice množ. čislo seg. vreme pri glagolite ot I i II sprežėnie)", *Sbornik v čest na A. Teodorov-Balan* (Sofia, 1956), p. 365-374; B. Velčeva, "Kəm vəprosa za imperativno značenie na formite za otricatelno bədešte vreme v bəlgarski ezik", *BəlEz*, 10 (1960), p. 47-51; G. K. Venediktov, "Otnosno nastavkite za imperfektivizacija v səvremennija bəlgarski literaturen ezik", *BəlEz*, 10 (1960), p. 116-129; A. Teodorov-Balan, "Vidovo prevraštenie u naši glagoli", *BəlEz*, 2 (1952), p. 218-226; "Sklonenie i sprežėnie v bəlgarskata gramatika", *Ezikovedski izsledvanija v čest na akad. S. Mladenov* (Sofia, 1957), p. 29-36.

Besides the problems concerning the "declension" and conjugation of contemporary Bulgarian, relatively much attention has been paid to word formation. As examples we can quote: M. Dimitrova, "Umalitelnite imena v knižnija bəlgarski ezik", *IzvIBE*, 6 (1959), p. 263-319; E. Georgieva, "Imenata na -'o, -jo v bəlgarski ezik", *BəlEz*, 6 (1956), p. 27-35; G. Ivanov, "Kolektivnite imena v bəlgarski ezik", *Ezikovedski izsledvanija v čest na S. Mladenov*, p. 85-91; K. Ivanova, "Vərxu imenata na -tel, -telen s ogled na vidovata im osnova i vidovoto im značenie", *BəlEz*, 9 (1959), p. 220-235; S. Radeva (a Bulgarian scholar working in Poland), "Budowa i znaczenie wyrazów złożonych w języku bułgarskim", *Studia z Filologii Polskiej i Slowiańskiej*, 1 (Warsaw, 1955), p. 384-417, and "Složni imena v bəlgarski ezik", *EzLit*, 3 (1948), p. 275-283.

In the field of syntax there are some important positions to be mentioned: I. Baseva, "Sintaktična upotreba na deepričastijata", *BəlEz*, 12 (1962), p. 71-83; S. Bojadžiev, "Upotreba na predloga *na* v bəlgarskija knižoven ezik", *BəlEz*, 1 (1952), p. 93-120; E. V. Češko (a Russian scholar), "K izučeniju bezpredložnyx sočetanij v sovremennom bolgarskom jazyke", *Sbornik v čest na A. Teodorov-Balan* (Sofia, 1956), p. 425-436; "Datel'nyj padež v sovremennom bolgarskom jazyke i sinonimičnye predložnye konstrukcii", *Ezikovedski izsledvanija v čest na S. Mladenov*, p. 47-56. It is clear that in connection with the disappearance of nominal declension in New Bulgarian the problem of prepositional constructions plays a key role in the analysis of syntactic structures involving nouns. Cf. here also the article by J. Zaimov, "Upotreba na predloga *za* v bəlgarskija ezik"; *IzvIBE*, 6 (1959), p. 321-372. Among other syntactic articles the following are worth mentioning: M. Moskov, "Kəm vəprosa za obstojatelstvenite izrečenija v bəlgarski ezik", *BəlEz*, 9 (1959), p. 246-251;

"Səstavno skazuemo i podčineno dopəlnitelno izrečenie", *BəlEz*, 8 (1958), p. 183-184; "Za upotrebata na otglagolno səštestvitelno v stroeža na izrečenieto", *BəlEz*, 6 (1956), p. 121-129; J. Penčev, "Prisəedinjavaneto kato sintaktično javlenie", *BəlEz*, 12 (1962), p. 57-70.

4d. For a deeper understanding of the structure and history of Bulgarian a knowledge of adjacent Balkan languages seems to be indispensable. Unfortunately, traditional Bulgarian linguistics did not pay enough attention to the relationship between Bulgarian and other Balkan languages (Rumanian, Modern Greek, Albanian). Some change in that attitude may be observed after the last world war. The obvious symptom of that change is the historical grammar of Bulgarian by K. Mirčev which in comparison with the old book by S. Mladenov (*Geschichte der bulgarischen Sprache*) treats to a large extent the relationship between Bulgarian and the Balkan languages, liberated from the narrow "nationalist" standpoint of the old school. Nevertheless the majority of works in this field are devoted to lexical problems which seem to be rather secondary in comparison with purely grammatical ones. In connection with that we can quote: A. Milev, "Grəckite səštestvitelni imena v bəlgarski ezik", *BəlEz*, 5 (1955), p. 127-147; K. Mirčev, "Nešto za grəckite zaemki v bəlgarski ezik", *EzLit*, 2 (1947), p. 23-27 (a general treatment of the problem); P. Skorčev, "Grəcko-vizantijskite dumi v našija naroden govor", *Bəlgarska misəl*, 1943, 18, p. 181-186; "Grəckata duma v našija naroden govor", *ibid.*, p. 241-248; "Bəlgari i gərci v minaloto. Sledi ot obštuvaneto im v našija naroden govor", *ibid.*, p. 30-35; B. Simeonov, "Za njakoi rumənski dumi v bəlgarskite narodni govori", *Omagiu lui I. Iordan* (Bucharest, 1958), p. 799-804. Here can also be mentioned the article by I. Gələbov, "Stari bəlgarski ezikovi areali na dakorumənskata ezikova teritorija", *EzLit*, 1961, p. 39-48, which provides some historical-geographical data about the relationship between the languages in question.

The best evidence of a growing interest in the adjacent Balkan languages are also the following dictionaries published in recent years: V. Georgiev and M. Filipova, *Novogrəcko-bəlgarski rečnik* (Sofia, Bəlgarska Akademija na Naukite, 1957), 588 pp.; V. Arnaudov and L. Mišu, *Rumənsko-bəlgarski rečnik* (Sofia, 1954), 918 pp.; T. Kacori etc., *Bəlgarsko-albanski rečnik* (Sofia, Bəlgarska Akademija na Naukite, 1959), 871 pp. Although Turkish does not belong to the Balkan languages in the linguistic sense of this term its role in the history of Bulgarian vocabulary was so significant that it should be considered when speaking about a more intimate relationship between Bulgarian and the adjacent languages of the Balkans. In this field worth mentioning are the following publications: K. Mirčev, "Za sədbata na turcizmite v bəlgarski ezik", *IzvIBE*, 2 (1952), p. 117-127; C. Vranska, "Turskite naimenovanija na otvlečeni ponjatija v ezika na bəlgarskija folklor", *IzvIBE*, 2 (1952), 220-222; G. Klasov and S. Nikolov, *Bəlgarsko-turski rečnik* (Sofia, 1957), 592 pp.; N. Vančev, J. Kerimov, G. Klasov, S. Nikolov, T. Popov under the direction of S. Romanski, S. Ilčev, T. Deliorman, *Bəlgarsko-turski rečnik* (Sofia, 1961), XVI + 1249 pp.;

V. Vančev, G. Gələbov and G. Klasov, *Tursko-bəlgarski rečnik* (Sofia, Bəlgarska Akademija na Naukite, 1956).

The dictionaries lead us to the problems of lexicology (4e). This field of linguistic research is developing widely in Bulgaria. Since K. Mirčev in his review of Bulgarian linguistics mentioned above gave an exhaustive list of the works in question, I will only underline the most important positions and add the recent ones which could not be quoted by K. Mirčev.

It is beyond any doubt that the central problem of lexicology, at least from a traditional standpoint, consists in etymology. The basic work in this domain is S. Mladenov's, *Etimologičeski i pravopisen rečnik na bəlgarskija knižoven ezik* (Sofia, 1941), 704 pp. But it does not satisfy the requirements of the contemporary etymology while operating too often with bare "Wurzeletymologie". The need for a new etymological dictionary became obvious in Bulgaria. The general program of research in this field has been drafted by V. Georgiev, "Po vəprosa za etimologijata na slavjanskite dumi i nedostatəcite na sravnitelno-istoričeskija metod", *BəlEz*, 2 (1952), p. 248-252. The same author published the book *Vəprosi na bəlgarskata etimologija* (Sofia, Bəlgarska Akademija na Naukite, 1958), 158 pp. Since the book is rich in many historical problems and very characteristic of the preoccupations and methods of the author it is worth mentioning what special topics are treated in it. In the first part of that book different morphologically isolated words have been etymologized according to the following groups: a) Slavic element, b) Balkan substratum (Thracian, Balkan-Latin, Proto-Bulgarian), c) later loanwords, loanwords from adjacent languages, international words. In the second part of the book there are the three following chapters: "Najstarite slavjanski mestni imena na Balkanskija poluostrov i tjaxnoto značenie za našija ezik i našata istorija" (p. 67-88) – the same was published in *BəlEz*, 8 (1958), p. 321-342 –, "Trakijci, mizijci, dakijci i predslavjanskijat proizxod na jatovata granica" (p. 89-120), "Koncepcijata za indoevropejskite gutarali i nejnoto otraženie vərxu etimologijata na slavjanskite dumi" (p. 121-129) – the same was published in Russian in *Beogradski međunarodni slavistički sastanak* (Belgrad, 1957), p. 511-517 (cf. above). The collective work on a Bulgarian etymological dictionary undertaken under the direction of V. Georgiev has already yielded its first result: *Bəlgarski etimologičen rečnik. Səstavili*: V. Georgiev, I. Gələbov, J. Zaimov, S. Ilčev (Sofia, 1962), fasc. 1 *a-bronz*, 80 pp. In connection with etymological dictionary there usually remains a dictionary of foreign words. The recent Bulgarian dictionary of foreign words is a collective work of three authors: A. Milev, J. Bratkov and B. Nikolov, *Rečnik na čuždite dumi v bəlgarski ezik* (Sofia, 1958), XII + 744 pp. Among other lexicological studies in recent years the following are worth mentioning: N. M. Dilevski, "Glavnejšie osobennosti obščeslavjanskoj leksiki sovremennogo bolgarskogo jazyka (v sopostavlenii s obščeslavjanskoj leksikoj russkogo jazyka)", *Slavističen Sbornik*, I (Sofia, 1958), p. 91-132; "Osnovni osobenosti na rečnikovija səstav na səvremennija bəlgarski knižoven ezik (səpostavitelno s ruskija ezik)",

*BəlEz*, 9 (1959), p. 201-219; I. Lekov, "Besonderheiten des Grundwortbestandes der bulgarischen Sprache", *Vorträge auf der Berliner Slavistentagung (11-13 November 1954)* (Berlin, 1956), p. 80-83; M. Milov, "Iz semantičnata istorija na glagolnata predstavka po- v bəlgarskija ezik", *BəlEz*, 11 (1961), p. 418-435 (the problem belongs rather to word formation); K. Mirčev, "Kəm bəlgarskata istoričeska leksikologija", *BəlEz*, 11 (1961), p. 247-250; "Za novobəlgarskoto narečie *veče*", *BəlEz*, 11 (1961), p. 39-41; S. Spasova-Mixajlova, "Leksiko-semantični različija pri səštestvitelnite imena v bəlgarskija knižoven ezik s ogled kəm kategorijata čislo". *IzvIBE*, 7 (1961), p. 225-306.

For reasons of space I do not review onomastics at all although this branch of linguistic investigations plays a significant role in Bulgarian linguistics. Those who are interested in that field will find a comprehensive review of the investigations in question in the Polish journal *Onomastica*, namely the two articles by I. Duridanov, "Razvoj na bəlgarskata onomastika. I Antroponimija", *Onomastica*, 2 (Krakow, 1956), p. 365-379, and "II Toponimija", *ibid.*, 3 (Krakow, 1957), p. 227-251.

# CZECHOSLOVAKIA

PAUL L. GARVIN

Czechoslovakia is linguistically a very active country. At each of its four major universities (Prague, Brno, Bratislava, Olomouc), as well as in the Czechoslovak Academy of Science, a variety of linguistic specialties is represented. The chairs, departments and institutes are staffed by many distinguished scholars, a number of them world-renowned. Linguistic publishing activity is extensive, both in journals and serials, and in separate books. Although the bulk of the material is published in Czech, it is most often accompanied by summaries in one of the Western languages, and one journal – *Philologica Pragensia* – is in its entirety written in Western languages. It is interesting to note the large circulation of Czech-language linguistic publications. A recent monograph, for instance, was printed in 1500 copies, which is the equivalent of 18,000 copies for a U.S. publication (calculated in terms of the relative populations of the two countries, not the relative sizes of the Czech and English speech communities). Czechoslovak linguists publish regularly in the country's press – occasionally in dailies and often in intellectual magazines; they conduct educational radio and television programs. Furthermore, they play a very definite and significant part in the educational system, where they have had an influence in matters of language curricula and textbooks in primary, and especially secondary, schools, as well as a part in the compilation of normative language aids for both Czech and Slovak (grammars and dictionaries). Thus, a conspicuous feature of linguistics in Czechoslovakia is the strong impact that the profession has had on the overall development of intellectual life. At the same time, Czech linguistics has produced an original tradition – the Prague School – which, as is well known, has contributed to the development of modern structural linguistics on a world-wide scale.

What has happened to the Prague tradition since the thirties? This is the question to which we here address ourselves. The present paper therefore does not propose to give a comprehensive coverage of recent linguistic activities. Extensive areas of interest in which a great deal of important work has been done, such as Slavic studies or dialectology, have been ignored in order to concentrate on our major aim: to evaluate the present status of a major school of thought in contemporary structural linguistics. This evaluation will attempt to answer two questions: (1) What are the essential features of the Prague tradition in linguistics; (2) What is the present status of that tradition. To answer the first question, we must consider not only the theoretical position of the Prague linguists, but also the place of linguistics in Czech society. A survey of these points will allow us to answer the second question.

To most American linguists, the term Prague School evokes the names of Troubetzkoy and Jakobson, and denotes a particular approach to phonemics, as represented for instance in Troubetzkoy's *Grundzüge der Phonologie*. While this indeed constitutes a major achievement of the Prague School, it is not sufficient to account for the strong impact which linguistics has had in Czechoslovakia on intellectual life in general. In this reviewer's opinion, two major factors can serve to explain this impact: first, the fact the Czech linguists have had a conception of structuralism which is broad and not limited to linguistics; second, their willingness to engage themselves in problem areas which, in addition to their linguistic interest, also have social significance – primarily, problems of standard language and language planning (not, of course, to the exclusion of more esoteric matters).

The following quotation exemplifies the Prague School conception of structuralism:

> Structuralism is neither a theory nor a method, it is an epistemological point of view. It starts out from the observation that every concept in a given system is determined by all other concepts of that system and has no significance by itself alone; it does not become unequivocal until it is integrated into the system, the structure, of which it forms part and in which it has a definite fixed place. The scientific work of the structuralist is thus a synthesis of the science of romanticism – which achieved new cognition by deduction from its philosophic system by which it a posteriori classified and evaluated the facts, and of the empirical, positivist view – which, on the contrary, constructs its philosophy from the facts which it has ascertained empirically. For the structuralist, there is an interrelation between the data (facts) and the philosophic assumptions, not a unilateral dependence. From this follows that there is no search for the one and only right method; on the contrary, "new material usually also entails a change in scientific procedure".[1] Just as no concept is unequivocal until it is integrated into its proper structure, so are facts by themselves not unequivocal; this is why the structuralist attempts to integrate the facts into the kind of relationships in which their unequivocality can come to the fore, as well as their superordination and subordination, in one word, the entire structure, which is more than a mechanical summary of the properties of its components, since it gives rise to new qualities.[2]

The participation of the Prague School linguists in the intellectual life of the Czech nation can best be illustrated by the following passages from B. Havránek's editorial in *Slovo a Slovesnost* of 1960:

> *Slovo a Slovesnost* into its Third Decade
>
> With this volume, *Slovo a slovesnost* enters into its third decade. Our journal was founded in 1935; it took as its aim the propagation of a new attitude towards the study of contemporary language, particularly the standard language, and the promotion of the program set forth in the compendium "Standard Czech and the Cultivation of Good Language" of 1932, in which a group of young linguists not only launched an attack on the unclear and hence often authoritarian attitude towards questions of the standard language held by their predecessors in linguistics, but also proposed a program of their own.

[1] J. Mukařovský, *Kapitoly z české poetiky* [Chapters from Czech Poetics], I (Prague, 1948), p. 15.
[2] Josef Hrabák, *SaS*, 7.203 (1942).

*Slovo a slovesnost* was inaugurated with the words: "What can the science of language, linguistics, give to the standard language? Must it limit itself to proclaiming conservative laws and prohibitions, or can it make a positive contribution to its development? It depends on the kind of linguistics we have in mind." Our answer at that time was that of course it had a contribution to make. The problem area of standard language was not the only subject matter area of the journal, but it was a fundamental one; the journal was conceived broadly, from general theory to the solution of concrete questions and to practical requirements, from spoken language to artistic and poetic language. And this problem area has remained fundamental for the journal all along – in spite of changes in method and ideology...

The first decade was marked not only by a fighting and critical spirit, but also by a relative methodological unity, proclaiming and developing Prague structuralism; this first period ends with Vol. IX, which was the last before the suppression of the journal under the German occupation. The results achieved by our work on the standard language and its norms are summed up in my article "The Principles of the Linguistic Circle of Prague and the New Codification of Standard Czech" in Vol. X of *Slovo a Slovesnost* (pp. 13ff.), 1947, when after the liberation the publication of our journal was resumed.

The second decade, which began after the liberation with this tenth volume, was marked by methodological ferment, the search of new paths ...

In its forthcoming third decade our journal rests on foundations that are different from the first decade during which it constituted primarily the critical opposition in linguistics; it is now changing into a journal which is at the center of the broadly organized new linguistic work in our country; on the other hand, by clarifying and unifying its methodological direction, our journal wishes to continue the tradition of basic methodological unity of its first decade, albeit a new and critically re-valued unity...[3]

Havránek's editorial also has bearing on our second question, namely, the present status of the Prague tradition. It strongly suggests that the Prague School has preserved its identity and maintained continuity in its theoretical outlook and interests.

In our opinion, the constant throughout the development of the Prague School from its beginnings to the present has been the stress on function – where the concept of function is not used in the mathematical sense but has to do with aim and purpose.[4] Thus, in the analysis of linguistic structure the emphasis has often been placed on the function of the elements, in addition to their structural relations (hence the term "functional linguistics" used by many of them). Function has also governed the Prague linguists' view of language planning; their major concern here is with the function of language in society, and with the function of the linguist in the intellectual life of the nation. This dual interest is best expressed in their work on the standard language.

The term "functional linguistics" and the emphasis on function that it implies are closely linked to the name of Vilém Mathesius, just as the problem area of standard language is associated with the name of Bohuslav Havránek. Havránek, now an academy member, is still active in the leadership of Czech linguistic affairs. The passing of Mathesius in 1945 did not cause a break in the school of thought which he

[3] Havránek (1960).

[4] Cf. Roman Jakobson's discussion of the "means-ends model", presented to the IX International Congress of Linguists, Cambridge, Mass., 27-31 August, 1962.

originated: he has a sizeable and productive following of students and students' students.

These two areas have been chosen to illustrate the present status of the Prague tradition in some detail.

One of the best examples of the development of the functional approach to language by Mathesius and his followers is their work on "functional sentence perspective".[5]

This concept was developed against the background of the Prague School view of the functions of language.[6] The functioning of the speech sign is related to the three basic components of the speech situation: the speaker, the hearer, and the objects and states of fact referred to. In each instance of speech, the speech signs of which the utterance is composed vary with each of these three components, and each co-variance constitutes a particular function of language.[7] The co-variance of sign with speaker constitutes the expressive function, that of sign with hearer the appeal function, that of sign with the objects and states of fact the communicative function. The latter is considered to be the primary function of language. The pattern of relaxed speech, in which the communicative function predominates and is little if at all affected by the other functions, is the basic mode of speech communication. The formal characteristic of relaxed speech is the absence of special prosodic features such as contrastive stress or non-neutral intonation patterns (or their written equivalents, such as special type fonts or punctuation marks).

The basic mode is altered in excited speech, where the communicative function is strongly affected by the expressive and appeal functions. The formal characteristic of excited speech is the presence of the special prosodic features named above (or their written equivalents).

The functions of language manifest themselves through particular utterances, and they can be studied through these manifestations. Since the communicative function is the primary function of language, it will be the primary object of such a study. The conceptual framework for this approach is provided by that of functional sentence perspective. It is based on the assumption that the aim of the communicative function in particular utterances (and hence the purpose of communicative utterances)[8]

[5] This is the English term now used by the Prague linguists themselves. The original Czech term "aktuální členění větné", which I translate by "information-bearing structure of the sentence", still predominates in their Czech-language writings.

[6] The presentation of the functions of language by Karl Bühler, *Sprachtheorie*, (Jena, 1934), pp. 28-30, was fairly generally accepted by the Prague School linguists of the thirties.

[7] Note that Roman Jakobson has now extended the number of functions to six, cf. his "Closing Statement: Linguistics and Poetics", in *Style in Language*, edited by Thomas A. Sebeok (New York-London, 1960), pp. 355-7.

[8] The concept of the "purpose of an utterance" as distinst from the "functions of language" is discussed by Bohuslav Havránek in "Úkoly spisovného jazyka a jeho kultura" [The Functions of the Standard Language and its Cultivation], *Spisovná čeština a jazyková kultura* [*Standard Czech and the Cultivation of Good Language*], edited by Bohuslav Havránek and Miloš Weingart, (Prague, 1932), p. 41, translated in "The Functional Differentiation of the Standard Language", *A Prague School Reader on Esthetics, Literary Structure, and Style*, Selected and Translated from the Original Czech by Paul L. Garvin (Washington, 1955), p. 1.

is to impart new information. This is the criterion for singling out, within the content of an utterance, two basic types of information: (1) old information, setting the stage for the purposeful content of the utterance, which is (2) the new information. The fundamental question then is: by what means do the elements of the utterance become the carriers of the two basic types of information. Or, more concretely: given a certain syntactic structure, what are the devices available for differentiating between old and new information?

In Mathesius' own words: "The information-bearing structure of the sentence[9] should be considered in opposition to its formal structure. Whereas the formal structure concerns the way in which a sentence is composed of grammatical elements, the information-bearing structure concerns the way in which a sentence is integrated into the factual situation during which it was produced. The basic elements of the formal structure of the sentence are the grammatical subject and the grammatical predicate, the basic elements of the information-bearing structure are the foundation of the utterance – whatever in a given situation is known or at least obvious and thus forms a point of departure for the speaker – and the core of the utterance, that is, whatever the speaker affirms about the foundation of the utterance or in terms of it."[10] (The terms "foundation" and "core" are in the present English writings of the Prague linguists replaced by the classical terms "theme" and "rheme" respectively.)[11]

The technique used by Mathesius and his followers for the study of functional sentence perspective is that of analytic comparison. This technique consists in comparing different modes of expression of the same content in two structurally different languages: the aim is to hold the content as nearly constant as possible, in order to permit the study of differences in expression. In practice, this is achieved by comparing a text in one language with its translation into another language. A cross-check is achieved by alternating the two languages as original languages and translation languages respectively.

As a technique, analytic comparison is reminiscent of the recent efforts in contrastive analysis for language teaching purposes, but its aim is to characterize particular linguistic structures. This is similar to Whorf's well-known comparison of Standard Average European to Hopi.[12]

[9] I.e., the functional sentence perspective. For the terminology, see fn. 5.

[10] Vilém Mathesius, "O tak zvaném aktuálním členění věty" [On the So-Called Information-Bearing Structure of the Sentence], *SaS*, 5.171 (1939); reprinted in Vilém Mathesius, *Čeština a obecný jazykozpyt* [The Czech Language and General Linguistics] (Prague, 1948), p. 234.

[11] Theme and rheme are further developments of the traditional 19th-century concepts of "psychological subject" and "psychological predicate". The Czechs ascertain theme and rheme in a given utterance impressionistically, but it is possible to formulate behavioral tests for thematic and rhematic function. A suggested approach would be the formulation of the question to which the utterance under investigation would be an appropriate answer. It might then turn out that the theme is that portion of the utterance which is held in common by both question and answer, and the rheme is the portion of the utterance which constitutes the actual answer to the question.

[12] Cf. particularly Benjamin Lee Whorf, "The Relation of Habitual Thought and Behavior to Language", *Language, Culture and Personality, Essays in Memory of Edward Sapir*, edited by Leslie

The two languages most often selected for analytic comparison are Czech and English; the comparison deals with English originals and their Czech translations, as well as with Czech originals and their English translations. Their well-known grammatical differences (for instance, with respect to the inflectional patterns or the syntactic function of word order) made these two languages particularly well suited for analytic comparison.

The analytic comparison of Czech and English has highlighted the role of word order in the achievement of functional sentence perspective. As stated by Mathesius, word order – in this connection, the relative order of theme and rheme – is the primary formal expression of functional sentence perspective. The order of theme and rheme varies with the modes of speech communication discussed further above. In the basic mode, i.e. relaxed speech, the theme – all other things being alike – precedes the rheme. This is by Mathesius called "objective order".[13] In the mode characterized by special prosodic features, e.i. excited speech, the rheme – all other things being alike – precedes the theme. This is by Mathesius called "subjective order".[14]

An example of objective order would be the utterance "Mary didn't come" with ordinary declarative intonation and no contrastive stress (theme: "Mary"', rheme: "didn't come"), as for instance in answer to the question "What happened to Mary?" Subjective order is illustrated by the same utterance, but with contrastive stress on "Mary" (hence, theme: "didn't come", rheme: "Mary"), as for instance in answer to the question "Who else didn't come?"

As shown by analytic comparison, the grammatical differences between Czech and English have crucial bearing on the devices by which functional sentence perspective is implemented.

In Czech (and languages like Czech from the standpoint of word order), the order of clause members can be varied to achieve the desired functional sentence perspective. Thus, in an ordinary declarative sentence in Czech, either the subject may precede the predicate or the predicate may precede the subject. Thanks to the flexible order of clause members permitted by the grammar, different functional sentence perspectives can be achieved while retaining the objective order of theme preceding rheme. The following are the two basic alternatives: When subject precedes predicate, subject will be theme and predicate will be rheme, as in: *nikdo nepřišel*, "nobody came". When predicate precedes subject, predicate will be theme and subject will be rheme, as in: *nepřišel nikdo*, "nobody, but nobody came" (for the difference in English translations, see below).

No such simple utilization of word order as a device of functional sentence perspective is possible in English (and languages like English from the standpoint of word order). When word order is an essential recognition criterion of clause function it can not be

Spier (Menasha, Wis., 1941), pp. 75-93, reprinted in *Language, Thought, and Reality. Selected Writings of Benjamin Lee Whorf*, edited by John B. Carroll (New York-London, 1956), pp. 134-159.

[13] *Op. cit.* in fn. 10, p. 174.

[14] *Ibid.*

freely manipulated for purposes of functional sentence perspective. A given syntactic pattern will – all other things being alike – permit only one functional sentence perspective. Thus, in an ordinary active declarative sentence such as the one cited above, "nobody came", the fixed order of subject preceding predicate and object allows only one functional sentence perspective in objective order: subject is theme, predicate or object is rheme.[15]

Since the free manipulation of word order is not permitted, by what formal means can different functional sentence perspectives of the same message be achieved in a language such as English?[16] More specifically: how can the message be modified in such a way that the subject changes from theme to rheme and the predicate of object changes from rheme to theme, while no other changes are introduced in the content of the message.

The devices for achieving functional sentence perspective in English which the Prague School has observed can be arranged in an ascending order of complexity: from phonological to syntactic to semantic.

The device which is simplest in this sense is the use of special prosodic features by means of which a shift from "objective" to "subjective" order is achieved (see above). Contrastive stress will impart the rhematic function to an utterance element in spite of its initial position, as is shown by the change effected by the use of this prosodic feature in the functional sentence perspective of the previously cited example: thus, in "*nobody* came", "subjective" order prevails and the subject is rheme, the predicate theme. Mathesius and others have pointed out that subjective order can be reinforced by periphrastic devices, as shown by a further modification of our example: "nobody, but nobody came".

Special prosodic features are restricted in usefulness, for two main reasons. They are often difficult or even impossible to render in writing (and hence restricted to spoken language). They are in addition not acceptable in all functional dialects of the language (most conspicuously not in technical parlance). The more complex devices for functional sentence perspective, the syntactic and semantic, are therefore essential for a language like English. The principle involved in these devices is not the shift from objective to subjective order, but the appropriate manipulation of message elements while retaining the objective order of theme followed by rheme.

The syntactic device for varying functional sentence perspective is a change in syntactic construction. The most conspicuous instance is the change from an active to a passive construction; this use of the passive is one of the main reasons given by Mathesius and his followers to explain the significantly greater frequency of passive constructions in English as compared to Czech.

[15] Czech linguists, who are fond of dialectic terminology, refer to this situation as a "conflict" between the word order requirements of syntactic structure (which requires fixed order) and those of functional sentence perspective (which requires flexible order).

[16] Or, to use the Czechs' dialectic terminology, how is the "conflict" mentioned in the preceding footnote "resolved?"

The change of funtional sentence perspective takes place as follows: the active subject, as is well known, becomes the agent object of the passive sentence, thereby changing from the initial, thematic position to the final, rhematic position; the active object, on other hand, becomes the subject of the passive sentence, changing from the rhematic to the thematic position. The message element which in the active sentence was rheme, becomes the theme of the corresponding passive sentence, and conversely, the theme of the active sentence becomes the rheme of the corresponding passive sentence.[17]

Other instances of the effect of changes in construction on functional sentence perspective are cited in the rather extencive analytic work on English that has come out of Czechoslovakia since Mathesius.

The most complex device of functional sentence perspective is semantic. It consists in the utilization of the differential semantic content of individual words, as pointed out in the work of Jan Firbas: words with more specific meanings are more likely to function as rhemes, words with more general meanings as themes. The capacity of a word for assuming thc rhematic function by virtue of its semantic specificity is by him called "communicative dynamism". It is viewed as a matter of degree: the elements of an utterance are no longer simply classed as theme or rheme, but are considered to have a given degree of thematic or rhematic function, or to represent a given degree of transition.[18]

Firbas uses this concept to compare verbs and nouns in Czech and English in terms of communicative dynamism. He concludes that verbs in Czech have greater dynamism than verbs in English. This is shown by the frequent use in English of semantically vague verbs in construction with a more precise noun, where in Czech a single precise verb might be used. An example would be English "comes to a conclusion" as compared to Czech *končí* (lit.: "ends"). In Firbas' opinion, this difference accounts for the much greater frequency of nominal constructions in English as compared to Czech.[19]

The important and very complex question of the interrelations between the various devices for functional sentence perspective has not yet been treated by the Prague School. Perhaps this will be their next field of study.[20]

[17] By way of illustration, let us compare the two sentences "Mathesius and his students did a great deal of work on English" and "A great deal of work on English was done by Mathesius and his students". Using the behavioral test suggested in fn. 11, we may propose that the most likely question answered by the active sentence is: "What did Mathesius and his students work on?" If we accept this, "Mathesius and his students" becomes the message element shared by both question and answer, hence, the theme, and "a great deal of work on English" is the actual answer to the question, hence, the rheme. On the other hand, the most likely question answered by the passive sentence might be: "By whom was a great deal of work done on English?" "A great deal of work on English" then is theme, and "Mathesius and his students" is rheme.

[18] Firbas (1959, 1961).

[19] Firbas (1961), pp. 95-96.

[20] On the other hand, the role of functional sentence perspective in the interpretation of style has received a great deal of attention. As has been shown, functional sentence perspective allows the

To make the conceptual framework of functional sentence perspective stand out more clearly, we should like to compare a recent Czech study of a problem in German to an equally recent American study of the same question.

The Czech sample study is Eduard Beneš, "Die Verbstellung im Deutschen, von der Mitteilungsperspektive her betrachtet".[21] Its American counterpart is Emmon Bach, "The Order of Elements in a Transformational Grammar of German".[22] Both studies are reactions – Beneš's in its entirety, Bach's in part – to a major work: Karl Boost, *Neue Untersuchungen zum Wesen und zur Struktur des deutschen Satzes: der Satz als Spannungsfeld*.[23] As is apparent from the titles of the papers, the Czech treatment is slanted towards functional sentence perspective, the American treatment follows transformational analysis.

Both authors accept Boost's major factual assertion: that the finite verb in a German sentence has three basic order positions: first, second, or last. Both authors then ask the questions that are typical of their respective approaches.

Beneš's concern is:

"For each of the three basic positions of the finite verb, we must ascertain:

1. To what extent the fixed position of the verb in German agrees with the requirements of functional sentence perspective, and to what extent it contradicts them.
2. How the contradictions between functional sentence persepctive and the fixed position of the verb can be resolved within the system of the German language."[24]

Note that the questions than Beneš asks about German are essentially similar to those asked about English, as was discussed further above. The answers that Beneš arrives at are likewise similar to the answers which the Prague School gives for English, namely, that the conflict between functional sentence perspective and fixed word order is resolved by the use of "compensatory" changes in structure.[25]

Bach, on the other hand, formulates the problem as follows:

"Unless we wish to treat the three contrasting orders as completely unrelated constructions (ignoring the parallelism that otherwise exists and repeating numerous rules of co-occurrence and government several times), we must set up the verb phrase in one order and derive the other orders from this one by shifts of the finite verb, also following the general technique, mentioned above, of deriving discontinuous constructions from continuous sequences."[26]

Unlike Beneš, Bach's major interest lies in establishing a hierarchy of derivation of one syntactic structure from another.

presentation of the same message content in a variety of ways – the study of the use of functional sentence perspective can then become the basis for the study of style. Cf. Vilém Mathesius, "Řeč a sloh" [Speech and Style], *Čtení o jazyce a poesii* [*Readings on Language and Poetry*], edited by Bohuslav Havránek and Jan Mukařovský (Prague, 1942), pp. 11-102.

21 Beneš (1962).

22 *Language*, 38.263-9 (1962).

23 Berlin 1956.

24 Beneš (1962), p. 7. Note the dialectic terminology, cf. fnsn. 14, 15.

25 *Ibid.*, p. 19.

26 *Op. cit.* in fn. 21, p. 266.

The difference between the two approaches is highlighted by a comparison of the two authors' responses to Boost's concept of the "Thema".

Beneš attempts to relate Boost's work to the Mathesius tradition. He accepts the earlier opinions in Czech linguistic literature that Boost's concepts of "Thema" and "Rhema" are not the same as the "theme" and "rheme" of functional sentence perspective.[27] From this he concludes that Boost's "Thema" constitutes an additional element of functional sentence perspective, the "basis", separate from both theme and rheme, and introductory to them. It allows him to redefine Boost's concept and relate it to the "communicative tension" which is Boost's analog of functional sentence perspective: "By basis we here understand the sentence opening which, serving as a point of departure for the communication, is directly linked to the context, produces the [communicative] tension (expectation), and points the communication in a previously determined direction."[28]

Boost's "Thema" thus gives Beneš ground to expand the two-term schema (theme-rheme) of functional sentence perspective into a three-term schema (basis-theme-rheme), which is comparable to the addition of the concept of "transition" by Firbas (see above).

Bach, on the other hand, is content to include the "Thema" (which he calls "topic") as simply another transformation, namely, the optional transformation of topic-shift.

He says about it: "This rule permits the shift of any element, including the finite verb, to front position. . . . Many shifts are the result of preceding context where the first element represents a 'topic' from the preceding sentence. It may be possible to reformulate this rule as a two-sentence transformation in which only the second of a pair of sentences undergoes any change."[29]

Thus, Bach treats as incidental the problem which to Beneš is central, namely, the relation of a particular feature of word order to the manifestation of the communicative function of language.

Another area of functional linguistics has been the study of the standard language as an aspect of the functional stratification of language. The Havránek editorial cited further above[30] shows that this was important to the Prague School both for reasons of professional interest and as an opportunity to participate in the intellectual life of the nation.

The major principles of the Prague School approach to the question were formulated in the early thirties.[31] These principles can be summed up as follows:[32] A standard

[27] For this earlier discussion, see Firbas (1958), and Beneš (1959).
[28] Beneš (1962), p. 6.
[29] *Op. cit.* in fn. 22, p. 268.
[30] See p. 000.
[31] See fn. 30 and *op. cit.* in fn. 8.
[32] This summary is taken from Paul L. Garvin and Madeleine Mathiot, "The Urbanization of the Guaraní Language – A Problem in Language and Culture", *Selected Papers of the 5th International Congress of Anthropological and Ethnological Sciences, Philadelphia, September 1-9, 1956*, edited under the chairmanship of Anthony F. C. Wallace (Philadelphia, 1960), pp. 783-90.

language can tentatively be defined as "a codified form of language, accepted by and serving as a model to, a larger speech community".[33] The two basic properties which the Prague School attributes to a standard language are flexible stability[34] and intellectualization.[35] The former is a goal to be achieved, "an ideal property: a standard language, in order to function efficiently, must be stabilized by appropriate codification; it must at the same time be flexible enough in its codification to allow for modification in line with culture change".[36] Intellectualization can be characterized as "a tendency towards increasingly more definite and accurate expression", or, more specifically, as "a tendency towards greater relational systematization and explicitness of statement",[37] the former involving the grammar, the latter the lexicon.

The present theoretical emphasis of the Prague School is on the further functional stratification of language. In addition to the literary standard as outlined above, attention has turned to the so-called Bohemian colloquial standard (*obecná čeština*) which, though not literary, nevertheless represents a form of language standardization. This question, which in the earlier days of the Prague School was given only occasional attention,[38] has in the past ten years stimulated their interest. The American Slavicist Henry Kučera[39] has likewise dealt with the problem. This gives us another opportunity to compare a Prague School and an American treatment of the same data.

A significant characteristic of the Bohemian colloquial standard is that in the conversational speech of educated Czechs[40] it is mixed with forms of Standard Czech. Kučera is concerned with the description of this situation. He treats it as a case of coexisting paterns[41] following the well-known paper by Pike and Fries.[42] His major interest is in the proportions of the mixture, and his most original contribution is a statistical analysis of these proportions in samples of live Czech speech as well as literary text.[43]

[33] *Ibid.*, p. 783.

[34] Vilém Mathesius, "O požadavku stability ve spisovném jazyce" [The Requirement of Stability for a Standard Language], *op. cit.* in fn. 8, pp. 14-31.

[35] Bohuslav Havránek, "Úkoly spisovného jazyka a jeho kultura" [The Purposes of a Standard Language and its Cultivation], *op. cit.* in fn. 8, pp. 32-84.

[36] *Op. cit.* in fn. 32, p. 784.

[37] *Ibid.*, p. 785.

[38] Havránek in 1932 calls it a "form of folk speech " and defines it in a footnote as "an overall dialect, that is, a dialect used over a larger area in which otherwise local dialects are used, for instance, the Bohemian colloquial standard" . . . , but does not deal with it in further detail. *Op. cit.* in fn. 8, p. 42; translated in *op. cit.* in fn. 8, p. 2.

[39] Most recently in *The Phonology of Czech* ('s-Gravenhage, 1961), particularly pp. 11-20 and 86-107. Kučera's term for standard Czech is "literary language" (p. 13), his term for the Bohemian colloquial standard is "the Czech Common Language" (pp. 14 ff.).

[40] Kučera calls it "colloquial Czech", *op. cit.*, p. 16 ff.

[41] *Op. cit.*, pp. 86 ff. See also the earlier discussion in Henry Kučera, "Inquiry into Coexistent Phonemic Systems in Slavic Languages", *American Contributions to the Fourth International Congress of Slavicists* ('s-Gravenhage, 1958), pp. 169-89, especially pp. 182 ff.

[42] Charles C. Fries and Kenneth L. Pike, "Coexistent Phonemic Systems", *Language*, 25.29-50 (1949).

[43] *Op. cit.* in fn. 39, pp. 94 ff.

In Prague, on the other hand, a lively debate has recently developed which is concerned with a rather different aspect of the question: the place of the colloquial standard in the development of present-day Czech society, its relation to the literary standard, and the effect that it can be expected to have (or that it should be encouraged to have) on the literary standard . It was provoked by an article by the young linguist Petr Sgall in Voprosy jazykoznanija.[44] It includes to date: the initial critique of Sgall's paper by Bělič, Havránek, Jedlička and Trávníček,[45] Sgall's reply,[46] and Bělič, Havránek and Jedlička's retort to the reply,[47] as well as two additional papers that are contributions to the discussion rather than polemics,[48] with more to follow, no doubt.

In the debate, one of Sgall's main assertions is that the literary standard will be strongly affected by the colloquial standard because of the democratization of Czech society. His opponents take issue with him on the grounds that, on the contrary, the conversational form of the literary standard can be expected to have an increased influence, because of the spread of education and culture under the present conditions of mass access to educational and cultural facilities. As before, we have a conflict of functions.[49] But unlike the case of functional sentence perspective which involved the communicative function, we now deal with two conflicting social functions: the democratizing function of the colloquial standard, and the educational-cultural function of the literary standard.

It is typical that the non-polemic contributions to the debate point out that the democratizing and educational-cultural functions are not mutually exclusive.

Again, the major concern of the Prague School is with a functional interpretation of a given aspect of language, while the corresponding American contribution is centered on a rigorous statement (for instance, statistical), of the situation, without hazarding an interpretation.

The interest of the Prague School in problems of standard language has not been restricted to the theoretical study of the functional aspects of standardization. It has included extensive practical work on both Standard Czech and Standard Slovak, stemming from their conviction that it is the linguistic scientist's responsibility to society to take an active part in the codification of the standard language, in order to insure a sound scientific basis for it. In addition to participation in the creation of normative grammars, this has led to a strong concentration on practical lexicography and problems of lexical meaning.

Here also, a good portion of the general theoretical orientation goes back to Mathe-

[44] Petr Sgall, "Obixodno-razgovornyj češskij jazyk" [The Colloquial Standard Czech Language], *VJa*, 9.11-20 (1960).
[45] Bělič et al. (1961).
[46] Sgall (1962).
[47] Bělič et al. (1962).
[48] Hausenblas (1962); Skalička (1962).
[49] Cf. fns. 15 and 16.

sius, as shown in K. Horálek's summary discussion of the problem.[50] The aspect of Mathesius' thinking most relevant in this connection is his attempt to develop a field of onomatology,[51] that is, the study of the naming patterns used in a particular language, as separate from the study of the grammatical patterns. Lexicography, in the Mathesius tradition, then becomes a practical implementation of the results of onomatological study.

Examples of detailed treatments of onomatology are the monograph series on word formation in Czech, of which the first volume by Dokulil has appeared,[52] and the recent monograph on synonyms by Filipec.[53] The most significant linguistic contribution in the field of monolingual lexicography is the participation of both the older (e.g., Havránek) and the younger (e.g., Daneš) generation of linguists in the compilation of the Dictionary of the Czechoslovak Academy and in the compilation and maintenance of the permanent lexical file on which that dictionary is based.[54]

In the last few years, two additional areas of interest have emerged in Czechoslovak structural linguistics: the description of exotic languages, and the mathematical modeling of languages.

The work on exotic languages is centered in the Oriental Institute of the Czechoslovak Academy of Sciences, and particularly the younger workers have been strongly influenced by the field-work approach practiced in the study of American Indian languages. An interesting example is the attempt by K. Zvelebil to use Pike's tagmemic approach[55] in the description of Tamil.[56] This descriptive interest is a continuation of the empirical tradition in Czechoslovak linguistics. It resumes the ties which the Prague School of the thirties had established with Sapir and Bloomfield.

The modeling approach, on the other hand, is a new departure. In Czechoslovakia, it is closely tied to machine translation.[57] Although both are as yet in their beginnings, interest in this new approach has been strongly stimulated by current trends in the Soviet Union as well as in the United States, and the number of model-oriented papers has been on the increase. Whether this indicates a change in the fundamental emphasis of structural linguistics in Czechoslovakia, or whether it is merely an attempt to keep abreast of recent developments abroad, only the future will tell.

[50] Cf. Karel Horálek, "K theorii pojmenování" [On the Theory of Naming], *Lexikografický sborník* (Bratislava, 1953), pp. 9-19.
[51] Cf. Vilém Mathesius, "On Some Problems of the Systematic Analysis of Grammar," *Travaux du Cercle Linguistique de Prague* 6.95-107 (1936).
[52] Dokulil (1962).
[53] Filipec (1961).
[54] Cf. Filipec (1958).
[55] Cf. Kenneth L. Pike, *Language in Relation to a Unified Theory of the Structure of Human Behavior*, 3 vols. (Glendale, Calif., 1954, 1955, 1960).
[56] Cf. Zvelebil (1962).
[57] Cf. Novák (1962).

## LITERATURE

### *1. Bibliographies and Surveys*

Tyl, Z., *Bibliografie české linguistiky za léta 1945-50. Jazykověda obecná, indoevropská, slovanská a česká.* Nakladatelstvi ČSAV (Prague, 1955), 360 pp.

—, Bibliografie české linguistiky za léta 1951-1955. Jazykověda obecná, indoevorpská, slovanská a česká. Nakladatelství ČSAV. (Prague, 1957), 539 pp.

—, "Česká jazykověda v roce 1956 (mimo bohemistiku)", *SaS*, 18.184-192 (1957).

—, "Česká jazykověda v roce 1956. Část druhá: Práce bohemistické", *SaS*, 18.236-252 (1957).

—, "Bohemistické práce v roce 1957", *SaS*, 19.164-176 (1958).

—, "Česká jazykověda v roce 1957 (mimo bohemistiku)", *SaS*, 19.235-247 (1958).

—, "Česká jazykověda v roce 1958. Část první: Lingvistika obecná, srovnávací indoevropská a slovanská", *SaS*, 20.217-336 (1959).

—, "Česká jazykověda v roce 1958, Část druhá: Práce bohemistické", *SaS*, 20.972-316 (1959).

—, "Česká jazykověda v roce 1959. Část první: Lingvistika obecná, srovnávací indoevropská a slovanská", *SaS*, 21.226-238 (1960).

—, "Česká jazykověda v roce 1959. Část druhá: Práce bohemistické", *SaS*, 21.296-314 (1960).

—, and Tylová, M., "Česká jazykověda v roce 1960. Část první: Lingvistika obecná, srovnávací indoevropská a slovanská", *SaS*, 22.222-237 (1961).

—, and —, "Česká jazykověda v roce 1960. Část druhá: Prace bohemistické", *SaS*, 22.298-318 (1961).

Mattušová, M., ed., *Bibliografie československé moderní filologie za rok 1958* (Prague, 1959), 101 pp. (For internal distribution).

Kejzlar, R. and Povejšil, R., eds., *Bibliografie československé moderní filologie za rok 1959.* Kruh moderních filologů při ČSAV. Kabinet pro moderní filologii ČSAV. (Prague, 1961), 52 pp.

Ladislav, D., *Bibliografia slovenskej jazykovedy za roky 1948-52.* Matica slovenská. Turčiansky Sv. Martin, 1957. 234 pp.

—, *Bibliografia slovenskej jazykovedy za roky 1953-56.* Matica slovenská. Turčiansky Sv. Martin, 1958. 339 pp.

Doležel, L., "Bohemistika 15 let po sovobození ČSR", *SaS*, 21.81-86 (1960).

Fried, V., *Die tschechoslowakische Anglistik.* Kruh moderních filologů při ČSAV. Kabinet pro moderní filologii ČSAV. (Prague, 1959), 14 pp.

Hampejs, Zd., and Hořejší, V., eds., *Les études romanes en Tchécoslovaquie.* Kruh moderních filologu při ČSAV. Kabinet pro moderní filologii ČSAV. (Prague, 1960), 24 pp.

Oriental Instutite, Prague, "Activities of the Linguistic Group", *AO*, 30.143-155 (1962).

## 2. *Selected Publications in Structural Linguistics, 1958-1962*

The aim of this selection is not to be comprehensive, but to serve as an illustration of the argument presented in the body of the "Appraisal."

English translations of the original Czech titles indicate summaries in other languages.

Baganec, L. "Pokus o vymedzenie verbálnej prefixácie v nemčine v porovnaní so švédčinou" (Attempt at a Delimitation of Verbal Prefixation in German as Compared to Swedish), *ČMF*, 40.209-214 (1958). German summary, p. 215.

—, "K fonologickej funkcii prízvuku vo švédčine" (To the Phonemic Function of Stress in Swedish), *ČMF*, 43.235-237 (1961). German summary, p. 237.

—, "Strukturní rozbor staroislandské deklinace substantiva" (Structural Analysis of Old Icelandic Noun Declension), *ČMF*, 44.90-99 (1962). German summary, p. 99.

Bartoš, L., "Observations sur les réalisations phonétiques dans le langage d'un enfant de deux ans", *SFFB*, A7.5-19 (1959).

Bauer, J., "Russkie sojuzy v sopostavlenii s češskimi", *SFFB* A5.8-24 (1957).

—, *Vývoj českého souvětí* (Development of the Czech Compound Sentence). Studie a práce lingvistické IV, Nakladatelství ČSAV. (Prague, 1960), 401 pp. Russian summary, pp. 363-372.

Bečka, J. V., "Stylistika a rozvíjení myšlenkové linie", *SaS*, 18.197-216 (1957).

Bělič, J., "Vznik hovorové češtiny a její poměr k čestině spisovné", *Československý komitét slavistů*, 1958, pp. 59-71.

—, "Stav a úkoly české dialektologie (Situační zpráva)", Československý komitét slavistů, 1958, pp. 197-208.

—, Havránek, B., and Jedlička, A., "Problematika obecné češtiny a jejího poměru k jazyku spisovnému" (The Problem Area of the Bohemian Colloquial Standard and its Relation to Standard Czech), *SaS*, 23.108-126 (1962). Russian summary, pp 25-26.

—, —, —, and Trávníček, F., "K otázce obecné češtiny a jejího poměru k češtině spisovné" (To the Question of the Bohemian Colloquial Standard and its Relation to Standard Czech), *SaS*, 22.98-107 (1961). French summary, pp. 106-107.

Beneš, E., "Začátek německé věty z hlediska aktuálního členění výpovědi" (Sentence Beginning in German from the Standpoint of Functional Sentence Perspective), *ČMF*, 41.205-216 (1959). German summary: p. 217.

—, "Terminologická poznámka k pojmům 'norma' a 'kodifikace' (Příspěvek k diskusi)", with a note by B. Havránek, *SaS*, 22.273-277 (1961).

—, "Die Verbstellung im Deutschen, von der Mitteilungsperspektive her betrachtet", *PP*, 5.6-19 (1962).

Berka, K., "O některých aplikacích moderní formální logiky v jazy kovědě", *SaS*, 22.198-208 (1961).

Blanár, V., "K problémom porovnávacej lexikológie slovanských jazykov", Československý komitét slavistů, 1958, pp. 159-168.

—, "K základným otázkam lexikológie", in Dostál, 1958, pp. 195-197.

Borovičková, B., "K otázce spektrální analýzy mluvené řeči", *SaS*, 22.268-268 (1961).

—, and Novotná, J., "K použití strojů na děrné štítky pro výběr slovních tabulek při zkouškách srozumitelnosti", *SaS*, 21.265-270 (1960).

—, and Maláč, V., "Fonetická problematika měření indexu poznatelnosti", *SaS*, 22. 41-48 (1961).

Brčáková, D., "O vyjadřování kategorie osoby v ruštině" (On the Expression of the Category of Person in Russian), *Slavica Pragensia II*. AUC-Ph, 3.171-180 (1961). Russian summary, pp. 179-180; French summary, p. 180.

Československý komitét slavistů, *Československé přednášky pro IV, Mezinárodní sjezd slavistů v Moskvě*. Nakladatelství ČSAV. (Prague, 1958), 429 pp.

Daneš, F., "Intonace a verš" (Intonation and Verse), *SaS*, 19.103-124 (1958). Russian summary, pp. 122-124.

—, "K otázce pořádku slov v slovanských jazycích" (To the Qestion of Word Order in the Slavic Languages), *SaS*, 20.1-10 (1959). Russian summary, pp. 9-10.

Dokulil, M., "K otázce morfologických protikladů. Kritika předpokladu binárních korelací v morfologii češtiny" (On the Qestion of Morphological Oppositions. Critique of the Assumption of Binary Correlations in the Morphology of Czech), *SaS*, 19.81-103 (1958). Rusian sumary, pp. 100-103.

—, "K záklakním otázkám tvoření slov", in Dostál, 1958, pp. 154-169.

—, *Teorie odvozováni slov. Tvořeni slov v češtině* (The Theory of Word Derivation. Word Formation in Czech), vol. I. Nakladatelství ČSAV (Prague, 1962), 263 pp. English summary, pp. 220-250.

—, and Daneš, F., "K t. zv. významové a mluvnické výstavbě věty", in Dostăl, 1958, pp. 231-246.

Dostál, A., ed., *O vědeckém poznání soudobých jazyků*. Nakladatelství ČSAV. (Prague, 1958), 302 pp.

Dubský, J., "Atténuation de la valeur aspectuelle de la périphrase du verbe *venir de* suivi de l'infinitif", *SFFB*, A5.101-104 (1957).

—, "L'aspect du verbe et l'action verbale en français et en espagnol", *SFFB*, A9.457-161 (1961).

Ducháček, O., "Od pojmemování ke změně významu" (From Naming to Meaning Change), *SFFB*, A3.78-94 (1955). French summary, p. 94.

—, "K zobecňování odborných slov ve francouzštině" (The Generalization of Technical Terms in French), *SFFB*, A4.66-76 (1956). French translation, pp. 75-76.

—, "K otázce systému ve významosloví se zvlášním zřetelem k romanistickému materiálu" (To the Qestion of the Semantic System, with Particular Attention to Romance Material), *SFFB*, A5.105-117 (1957). French summary, p. 107.

—, "Les champs linguistiques", *PP*, 3.22-35 (1960).

—, "Různé kategorie synonym" (Various Categories of Synonyms), *ČMF*, 42.157-166 (1960). French summary, pp. 166-167.

Dvořáková, E., "Poznámky k postavení příslovečného určení situačního v angličtině a češtině z hlediska aktuálního členění větného" (Notes on the Situational Adverbs in English and Czech from the Point of View of Functional Sentence Perspective), *SFFB*, A9.141-151 (1961). English summary, pp. 149-150.

Filipec, J., "Akademický příruční slovník jazyka českého dokončen", *SaS*, 19.211-224 (1959).

—, *Česká synonyma z hlediska stylistiky a lexikologie* (Czech Synonyms from the Standpoint of Stylistics and Lexicology). Studie a práce lingvistické V. Nakladatelství ČSAV. (Prague, 1961), 384 pp. German summary, pp. 326-338.

—, "Lexikálně sémantická výstavba hesla – ústřední otázka lexikografické práce (na materiále jednojazyčných slovníků)", *SaS*, 18.129-150 (1957). See also Havránek and Filipec, 1958.

Firbas, J., "Poznámky k problematice anglického slovního pořádku s hlediska aktuálního členění větného" (Some Notes on the Problem of English Word Order from the Point of View of Actual Sentence Analysis), *SFFB*, A4.93-107 (1956). English summary, pp. 106-107.

—, "Some Thoughts on the Function of Word-Order in Old English and Modern English", *SFFB*, A5.72-100 (1957).

—, "Thoughts on the Communicative Function of the Verb in English, German and Czech", *Brno Studies in English*, 1.39-63 (1959).

—, "More Thoughts on the Communicative Function of the English Verb", *SFFB*, A7.74-98 (1959).

—, "Ještě k postavení příslovečného určení v angličtineě a češtině z hlediska aktuálního členění větného. Dovětek k článku E. Dvořákové" (Another Note on the Position of the Situational Adverb in English and Czech from the Point of View of Functional Sentence Perspective. An Afterthought to E. Dvořáková's article), *SFFB*, A9.153-156 (1961). English summary, p. 155.

—, "On the Communicative Value of the Modern English Finite Verb", *Brno Studies in English*, 3.79-104 (1961).

—, "Ze srovnávacích studií slovosledných" (From Comparative Word Order Studies), *SaS*, 23.161-174 (1962). English summary, pp. 173-174.

Grepl, M., "Vývoj spisovné češtiny za obrození a jazyková theorie" (The Development of Standard Czech During the National Revival Period and the Theory of Language), *SFFB*, A6.74-93 (1958). German summary, p. 93.

—, and Lamprecht, A., "K otázce syntaktické klasifikace slovních druhů" (To the Qestion of the Syntactic Classification of Word Classes), *SFFB*, A7.31-36 (1959). German summary, p.p 35-36.

Hála, B., *Nature acoustique des voyelles*. AUC-Ph, Vol. V (1956), 119 pp.

Hampejs, Z., "Poznámky ke skladbě portugalského infinitivu časovaného" (Remarks to the Syntax of the Inflected Infinitive in Portuguese), *ČMF*, 41.142-156 (1959). German summary, pp. 156-157.

Hausenblas, K., "Syntaktická závislost, způsoby a prostředky jejího vyjadřování", *Bull. Vysoké školy ruského jazyka a literatury*, 2.3-31 (1958).

—, *Vývoj předmětového genetivu v češtině* (The Development of the Objective Genetive in Czech). Studie a práce linguistické III. Nakladatelství ČSAV. (Prague, 1958). 230 pp. Russian summary, pp. 201-206; German summary, pp. 207-212.

—, "Styly jazykových projevů a rozvrstvení jazyka. K diskusi o obecné a hovorové češtině" (Styles of Utterances and the Stratification of Language. Discussion of the Colloquial Standard and Conversational Czech), *SaS*, 23.189-201 (1962). Russian summary, pp. 200-201.

Havránek, B., "K obecným vývojovým zákonitostem spisovných jazyků slovanských. Vývoj spisovného jazyka českého ve vztahu k vývoji národního společenství", *Československý komitét slavistů*, 1958, pp. 47-57.

—, "Slovo a Slovesnost do třetí desítky", *SaS*, 21.1-3 (1960).

—, and Filipec, J., "Lexikálně sémantická výstavba hesla – ústřední otázka lexikografické práce (Na materiále jednojazyčných slovníků českých)", in Dostál, 1958, pp. 177-190. See also Filipec, 1957.

Hladký, J., "Remarks on Complex Condensation Phenomena in Some English and Czech Contexts", *Brno Studies in English*, 3.105-118 (1961).

Horálek, K., *Počátky novočeského verše* (The Beginnings of the Modern Czech Verse), AUC-Ph, Vol. IV (1956), 107 pp. Russian summary, pp. 103-104; French summary, pp. 105-106.

—, "O poměru jazykovědy k vědám příbuzným", *SaS*, 18.10-16 (1957).

—, "Možnosti a úkoly popisné jazykovědy", in Dostál, 1958, pp. 13-17.

—, "Zásady a úkoly vědeckého studia slovanských jazyků", Československý komitét slavistů, 1958, pp. 7-11.

—, "K otácze tzv, vedlejších jazykových funkcí" (To the Qestion of the So-Called Secondary Functions of Language), *SaS*, 21.4-7 (1960). German summary, p. 7.

—, *Úvod do studia slovanských jazyků*. Nakladatelství ČSAV. (Prague, 1962), 535 pp.

Horecký, J., "Otázka medzinárodnej slovanskej terminológie, jej súčasný stav a historický vývoj", Československý komitét slavistů, 1958, pp. 97-107.

Hořejší, V., "Analyse structurale de l'orthographe française", *PP*, 5.225-236 (1962).

Hrabě, V., "Poznámka k řešení jedné sporné otázky ruskéskladby metodou transformačního rozboru" (Some Remarks on the Possibility of Solving a Very Knotty Problem of Russian Syntax by Means of Transformational Analysis). *Slavica Pragensia III*. AUC-Ph, 3.165-170 (1961). Russian summary, p. 169; English summary, p. 169-170.

Chloupek, J., "Some Notes on the Study of Dialectal Syntax", *SFFB*, A6.35-42 (1958).

Isačenko, A. V., "Slovo a veta", in Dostál, 1958, pp. 87-92.

Jančák, P., *Zvuková stránka českého pozdravu*. Rozpravy Československé adakemie věd, Řada společenských věd, vol. 67, No. 5. Nakladatelství ČSAV. (Prague, 1957), 112 pp.

Janota, P., "K výzkumu individuálního hlasového timbru v češtině" (On Individual Vocal Timbre in Czech). *Slavica Pragensia III*. AUC-Ph, 3.89-99 (1961). Russian summary, p. 98; English summary, pp. 98-99.

Jelínek, J., Bečka, J. V., and Těšitelová, M., *Frekvence slov, slovních druhů a tvarů v českém jazyce*. Státní pedagogické nakladatelství (Prague, 1961), 587 pp.

Jiráček, J., "Přípona *-tor* v ruštině a češtině" (The Suffix *-tor* in Russian and Czech), *SFFB*, A9.61-69 (1961). English summary, p. 69.

Kalousková, J., "Le problème du mot chinois dans les travaux de Lu Chih-wei", *AO*, 28.488-493 (1960).

—, "De l'autonomie de certaines unités linguistiques dans la langue chinoise moderne", *AO*, 29.626-651 (1961).

—, "Les constructions verbales contenant les morphèmes "*shih*" et "*ti*" dans le langue chinoise moderne", *AO*, 20.1-26 (1962).

Konečná, D., "K jazykové situaci v malém východomoravském městě" (The Language Situation in a Small Town in Eastern Moravia). *Slavica Pragensia III*. AUC-Ph, 3.119-126 (1961). Russian summary, p. 125; German summary, p. 126.

—, "Ukázka použití statistického zkoumání při příparvě strojové syntézy českého jednoduchého slovesného tvaru indikativiního" (An Example of the Use of Statistical Research in the Preparation of the Machine Synthesis of the Simple Indicative Verb Forms of Czech,) *SaS*, 22.268-273 (1961).

Kopeckij, L. V., "Aktuální otázky dvojjazyčného slovníku", in Dostál, 1958, pp. 191-194.

—, "Zásady zpracování dvoujazyčných slovníků slovanských jazyků" (Principles for the Compilation of Bilingual Dictionaries of the Slavic Languages), Československý komitét slavistů, 1958, pp. 181-195.

Kopečný, F., "Základní pojmy souvztažnosti syntaktické", in Dostál, 1958, pp. 213-224.

Krámský, J., "Teorie sdělné promluvy", *SaS*, 20.55-66 (1959).

Kratochvíl, P., "Concepts and the Actuality of Some Basic Units in Modern Chinese", *AO*, 30.27-48 (1962).

—, Novotná, Z., Šťovíčková, D., and Zgusta, L., "Some Problems of a Czech-Chinese Dictionary", *AO*, 30.258-313 (1962).

Krupa, V., and Altmann, G., "Semantic Analysis of the System of Personal Pronouns in the Indonesian Language", *AO*, 29.620-625 (1961).

Latt, M., "The Prague Method Romanization of Burmese", *AO*, 26.145-167 (1958).

—, "A Contribution Towards the Identification of the Word and the Parts of Speech in Modern Burmese", *AO*, 27.318-335 (1959).

—, "First Report on Studies in Burmese Grammar", *AO*, 30.49-115 (1962).

Levý, J., ed., *České theorie překladu*. Státní nakladatelství krásné literatury, hudby a umění (Prague, 1957), 947 pp.

—, "Izochronie taktů a izosylabismus jako činitelé básnichéko rytmu" (Isochrony of Rhythm Units and Isosyllabism as Factors in Poetic Rhythm), *SaS*, 23.1-8, 83-94 (1962). Russian summary, pp. 93-94.

Macháček, J., "K otázce predikačních vztahů v moderní angličtině" (Notes on Some

Predicational Relations in Modern English), *ČMF*, 40.159-163, 219-224 (1958). English summary, p. 225.

—, "A Contribution to the Problem of the So-Called Copulas in Modern English", *PP*, 2.14-20 (1959).

Mathesius, V. (J. Vachek, ed.), *Obsahový rozbor současné angličtiny na základě obecně lingvistickém* (*A Functional Analysis of Present-Day English on a General Linguistic Basis*). Nakladatelství ČSAV (Prague, 1961), 279 pp. English summary, pp. 230-239.

Michl, J. B., "K problémům dvou spisovných jazyků v Norsku" (To the Problem of Two Standard Languages in Norway), *SFFB*, A3.49-62 (1955). German summary, pp. 61-62.

Moravec, J., "K otázkám jazykových vztahů na základě bilingvismu" (On Questions of Linguistic Relations on the Basis of Bilingualism), *SaS*, 21.161-173 (1960). Russian summary, pp. 172-173.

Mrázek, R., "Příspěvek k teorii jmenného přísudku", *SaS*, 18.16-29 (1957).

—, "Problema skazuemogo i ego klassifikacii" (The Problem of the Predicate and its Classification), *SFFB*, A6.10-34 (1958). German summary, pp. 33-34.

—, "Sintaksičeskie otnošenija i člены predloženija" (Syntactic Relations and Sentence Elements), *SFFB*, A9.47-60 (1961). German summary, p. 60.

—, "K otázce českých větných schémat a typů, zvlášě neslovesných" (To the Question of Sentence Patterns and Sentence Types, Particularly Verbless, in Czech), *SaS*, 23.21-36 (1962). Russian summary, pp. 35-36.

Nebeský, L., and Sgall, P., "Vztah formy a funkce v jazyce. Pokus o axiomatizaci" (The Relation of Form and Function in Language. An Attempt at Axiomatization), *SaS*, 23.174-189 (1962). Russian summary, p. 189.

Neústupný, J. V., "Accent in Japanese and Russian – A Typological Study", *AO*, 27.122-142 (1959).

Nosek, J., "Několik poznámek k polovětným vazbám v angličtině XVII. století" Some Remarks Concerning 'Semi-Sentence' Constructions in 17th Century English), *Acta Universitatis Carolinae, Philologica et Historia*, 1954, pp. 23-36. Russian summary, p. 35; English summary, pp. 35-36.

—, "Adverbial Subclauses in Modern English", *PP*, 1.10-15, 41-49 (1958).

—, "Plusquamperfektum v moderní angličtině" (The Pluperfect in Modern English), *ČMF*, 40.193-208 (1958). English summary, p. 209.

—, "Studies in Post-Shakespearian English: Adverbial Clauses", *Prague Studies in English VIII*. AUC-Ph, 2.3-72 (1959).

—, "Relative Clauses in Modern English", *PP* 3.85-104 (1960).

Novák, M., "Euphonie im Haiku", *AO*, 30.192-210 (1962).

Novák, P., "K otázce obecného významu grammatických jednotek" (On the Question of the General Meaning of Grammatical Units), *SaS*, 20.81-88 (1959). Russian summary, pp. 87-88.

—, "Některé otázky syntaktické analýzy z hlediska strojového překladu (Some Questions of Syntactic Analysis From the Standpoint of Machine Translation)", *SaS*, 23.9-20 (1962). Russian summary, p. 20.

Novotná, Z., "Some Remarks on the Analysis of Compound Types of Chinese Characters", *AO*, 30.597-623 (1962).

Ohnesorg, K., *Druhá fonetická studie o dětské řeči*. Spisy filos. fakulty university v Brně, vol. 57. Státní pedagodické nakladatelství. (Prague, 1959), 164 pp.

—, "Růst slovní zásoby v dětské řeči" (The Growth of the Vocabulary in Children's Language), *AUC-Ph*, 1.85-105 (1955). Russian summary, pp. 102-103. French summary, pp. 104-105.

Pačesová, J., "Contribution à l'étude de la phonétique du langage enfantin", *SFFB*, A7.20-30 (1959).

Palek, B., "Nekotorye lingvističeskie voprosy informacionnogo jazyka" (Some Linguistic Problems of Language for Information Storage and Retrieval). *Slavica Pragensia III*. AUC-Ph, 3.197-208 (1961). English summary, pp. 207-208.

Pauliny, E., "Kultúrnohistorické podmienky a spoločenské funkcie bilingvizmu v dejinách spisovnej slovenčiny", Československý komitét slavistů, 1958, pp. 37-45.

—, "Systém v jazyku", in Dostál, 1958, pp. 18-28.

Petráček, K., "Die innere Flexion in den semitischen Sprachen. Entstehung und Entwicklung des Systems", *AO*. 28.547-606 (1960), 29.513-545 (1961), 30.361-408 (1962).

Plachý, Z., "Využití protikladu časů *imperfecto* a *pretérito indefinido* v souvislém vyprávěni ve španělštině" (The Opposition Between the Pretérito Indefinido and the Pretérito Imperfecto in Spanish Narrative Style), *ČMF*, 41.22-28 (1959). English summary, p. 28.

—, "The Prepositional Complementations of the Spanish Verb", *PP*, 5.108-111 (1962).

Poldauf, I., "Vyjadřování kvantity v češtině", *SaS*, 18.71-85 (1957).

—, "Tvoření slov", in Dostál, 1958, pp. 143-153.

—, "Děj v infinitivu" (The Action in the Infinitive), *SaS*, 20.183-202 (1959). German summary, pp. 201-202.

Porák, J., "Dvojčlenné infinitivní věty v češtině" (Infinitival Sentences with Two Members in Czech). *Slavica Pragensia III*. AUC-Ph, 3.137-150 (1961). Russian summary, pp. 149-150. German summary, p. 150.

Renský, M., "Funkce slabiky v jazykovém systému" (The Function of the Syllable in the System of Language), *SaS*, 21.86-95 (1960). Russian summary, pp. 94-95.

Romportl, M., *Zvuková stránka souvislé řeči v nářečích na Těšínsku. Fonetická studie*. Publikace Slezského studijního ústavu v Opavě, vol. 23. Krajské nakladatelství v Ostravě. (Ostrava, 1958), 125 pp.

—, "K otázce spisovnosti větně fonetických prvků, zejména intonace" (The Extent to which Sentence Phonetic Elements, Particularly Intonation, are Part of the Standard Language), *SS*, 22.1-8 (1961). Russian summary, p. 8.

—, "K ruskému vokalickému systému" (To the Russian Vowel System). *Slavica Pragensia III*. AUC-Ph, 3.101-117 (1961). Russian summary, pp. 115-116; German summary, pp. 116-117.

Růžička, K. F., "Locative Formations in Bantu Languages", *AO*, 27.208-250, 604-669 (1959), 28.181-219 (1960).

Sgall, P., "Nové otázky matematických metod v jazykovědě", *SaS*, 20.44-55 (1959).

—, Znovu o obecné češtině" (More on the Bohemian Colloquial Standard), *SaS*, 23.37-46 (1962). Russian summary, p. 46.

—, Panevová, J., Piťha, P., and Pala, K., "Ze syntaktické analýzy češtiny. Přípravné práce ke strojovému překladu", (Syntactic Analysis of the Czech Language Preparatory to Machine Translation). *Slavica Pragensia III*. AUC-Ph, 3.181-196 (1961). Russian summary, p. 195; English summary, pp. 195-196.

Skalička, V., "O konkretnosti a abstraktnosti při tvoření slov" (Concreteness and Abstractness in Word Formation), *AUC-Ph*, 1.75-84 (1955). Russian summary, p. 84.

—, "O fonémech základních a zvláštních" (The Fundamental and the Special Phonemes), *AUC-Ph*, 2.41-53 (1956). Russian summary, p. 52. English summary, pp. 52-53.

—, "Vztah morfologie a syntaxe", *SaS*, 18.65-71 (1957).

—, "O současném stavu typologie", *SaS*, 19.224-232 (1958).

—, "Syntax promluvy (enunciace)" (The Syntax of the Utterance), *SaS*, 21.241-249 (1960). German summary, p. 249.

—, "Text, Kontext, Subtext", *Slavica Pragensia III*. AUC-Ph, 3.73-78 (1961).

—, "Poznámsky o obecné češtině" (Notes on the Bohemian Colloquial Standard), *SaS*, 23.201-205 (1962). Russian summary, p. 205.

Skaličková, A., "K otázce větného přízvuku v češtině" (The Problem of Stress in Czech Sentences), *AUC-Ph*, 2.55-66 (1956). Russian summary, pp. 64-65; English summary, pp. 65-66.

Slavíčková, E., "Metoda morfémové analýzy založená na aplikaci teorie pravděpodobnosti" (A Method of Morphemic Analysis Based on the Application of Probability Theory), *SaS*, 23.94-107 (1962). Russian summary, p. 107.

Stuchlík, J., "K fenomenologii patologických jazykových novotvarů" (Phenomenology of the Pathological Neoformations of Language), *SaS*, 21.257-265 (1960). English summary, pp. 264-265.

Svoboda, K. F., "Mluvnická povaha infinitivu v součesné češtině" (The Grammatical Nature of the Infinitive in Contemporary Standard Czech), *SaS*, 20.161-183 (1959). German summary, pp. 182-183.

—, "Determinace platnosti sdělení v souvětích" (Determination of the Validity of the Communication in Compound Sentences). *Slavica Pragensia III*. AUC-Ph, 3.127-136 (1961). Russian summary, p. 136; German summary, p. 136.

Štindlová, J., "Stroje na zpracování informací a jejich význam pro jazykovědu", *SaS*, 22.208-215 (1961).

Těšitelová, M., "K statistickému výzkumu slovní zásoby" (The Statistical Investigation of the Lexicon), *SaS*, 22.171-181 (1961). Russian summary, pp. 180-181.

Trávníček, F., "Zásady monografického popisu jednotlivých slovanských lidových dialektů", Československý komitét slavistů, 1958, pp. 209-214.

Trnka, B., "Určování fonému" (Determining the Phoneme), *Acta Universitatis Caro-*

*linae, Philologica et Historica*, 1954, pp. 16-22. Russian summary, pp. 20-21; English summary, pp. 21-22.
—, "Morfologické protiklady", in Dostál, 1958, pp. 92-104.
—, "O morfonologické analogii" (On Morphonological Analogy), *ČMF*, 43.65-73 (1961). English summary,. p 73.
—, "'Principles of Morphological Analysis", *PP*, 4.129-137 (1961).
—, "O nynějším studiu anglických jmen místních" (On the Present-Day Study of English Place-Names), *ČMF*, 44.7-21 (1962). English summary, p. 21.
—, Vachek, J., et el., "Prague Structural Linguistics", *PP*, 1.33-40 (1958).
Trost, P., "K dnešní situaci historickě fonologie" (On the Present State of Historical Phonology), *SaS*, 21.7-9 (1960). German summary, p. 9.
Vachek, J., "Some Thoughts on the So-Called Complex Condensation in Modern English", *SFFB*, A3.63-77 (1955).
—, "Phonemic Remarks on the 'Short Mixed Vowel' of Modern English", *SFFB*, A4.81-92 (1956).
—, "Notes on the Development of Language Seen as a System of Systems", *SFFB*, A6.94-106 (1958).
—, "Význam historického studia jazyků pro vědecký výklad současných jazyků, se zvláštním zřetelem k materiálu anglickému", in Dostál, 1958, pp. 58-63.
—, "Two Chapters on Written English", *Brno Studies in English*, 1.8-38 (1959).
—, "On Social Differentiation of English Speech Habits", *PP*, 3.222-227 (1960).
—, "A propos de la terminologie linguistique et du système de concepts linguistiques de l'Ecole de Prague", *PP*, 4.65-78 (1961).
—, "Some Less Familiar Aspects of the Analytical Trend of English", *Brno Studies in English*, 3.9-78 (1961).
—, "Some Thoughts on the Phonology of Cockney English", *PP*, 5.159-66 (1962).
Zima, J., "K problému expresivity slova", in Dostál, 1958, pp. 201-206.
—, "O expresivitě substantivních deminutiv v češtině" (On the Expressivity of Substantival Diminutives in Czech), *SaS* 19.254-260 (1958). Russian summary, pp. 259-260.
—, *Expresivita slova v současné češtině. Studie lexikologická a stylistická.* Rozpravy Československé akademie věd, Řada společenských věd, vol. 71, No. 16. Nakladatelství ČSAV. (Prague, 1961), 139 pp.
Zima, P., "K otázce klasifikace mluvního tempa" (On the Question of the Classification of the Tempo of Speech), *SaS*, 20.96-117 (1959). German summary, pp. 115-117.
Zvelebil, K., "I*n*iyavaina*r*patu, A study in Late Old Tamil Philology", *AO*, 26.385-426 (1958).
—, "Dialects of Tamil I", *AO*, 27.272-317 (1959).
—, "Dialects of Tamil II", *AO*, 27.572-603 (1959), 28.220-224 (1960).
—, "Dialects of Tamil III, Madurai, Interpretation and Descriptive Statement", *AO*, 28.414-456 (1960).
—, "How to Handle the Structure of Tamil", *AO*, 30.116-142 (1962).

Žaža, S., "K voprosu o xaraktere russkoj i češskoj punktuacii", (On the Question of the Nature of Russian and Czech Puntuation), *SFFB*, A6.5673 (1958). German summary, p. 73.

# HUNGARY

GYULA DÉCSY

The development of linguistic research in Hungary since 1945 has been determined by three factors: 1) the tradition of this important field of science in Hungary; 2) the ideological pressure on linguists by the Communist Party; 3) the great financial help granted by the government.

Scientific research on languages in Hungary has a tradition of more than one and a half centuries. Hungarian scholars are fond of the fact that in their country the principles of the historical-comparative method in linguistics were used by the Hungarian scholars Sajnovics (1733-1785) and Gyarmathi (1751-1830) at the end of the 18th century, several decades before the publication of works by Bopp, Grimm and Rask. Important names of Hungarian linguists in the 19th century and in the beginning of the 20th century are: József Budenz (1836-92), József Szinnyei (1857-1943), Zsigmond Simonyi (1853-1919) and Zoltán Gombocz (1877-1935). The achievement of these linguists and their generation was an elaboration of the method of modern Finno-Ugric language comparison, in addition to scientific studies of the history and grammar of the Hungarian language.

The demands of the Communist Party on linguists since 1945, particularly since 1948 (the year the Communists came to power in Hungary), have been of an ideological nature. The acceptance of dialectical materialism and of a materialistic conception of life was the condition for all scientific work. Between 1949 and 1951 attempts were made to find new followers among linguists for the so-called "new doctrine of language" by Marr. But since 1951 these attempts have stopped and linguists have been able to continue their researches in the traditional Hungarian way.

During the last ten years, the government in Hungary has been extremely generous with regard to subsidies for linguistic studies. Several new departments of linguistics were established in addition to those at the Universities of Budapest, Debrecen and Szeged. In 1950 the Linguistic Institute of the Hungarian Academy was founded, and in 1960 it employed about sixty collaborators.

The old well-known journals for Hungarian Linguistics (*Nyelvtudományi Közlemények*, *Magyar Nyelv*, *Magyar Nyelvőr*) were able to enlarge their size. New journals were founded, of which *Acta Linguistica*, *Acta Orientalia* and *Studia Slavica* with their articles and book-reviews in English, German, French and Russian soon became well-known even beyond the borders of Hungary. It is obvious that the years from

1945 to 1951 in Hungary were a time of vegetation for linguistics and that the years since 1951 are years of revival and rise.

## HUNGARIAN PHILOLOGY

Among all areas of philology, most has been done in the field of Hungarian philology. We mention the following books and programs:

1. "Explanatory Dictionary of the Hungarian Language", directed by G. Bárczi, L. Országh and J. Balázs in the Linguistic Institute of the Hungarian Academy. This dictionary will present the vocabulary of modern Hungarian literature. It will contain about 60,000 word-articles, to which examples from many works by Hungarian authors will be added. Up to now four volumes have come out; it is expected that by the end of 1962 all six volumes will be finished.

2. "The Great Dictionary of the Hungarian Language". This dictionary as well originated from a group project of the Linguistic Institute of the Hungarian Academy under the direction of L. Gáldi. It is supposed to contain the entire vocabulary of the Hungarian language since the end of the 18th century, which means about 800,000 word-articles. It cannot be said at the moment at what date this work will be completed and published.

3. "Atlas of Hungarian Dialects". This is another group project of the Linguistic Institute of the Hungarian Academy, directed by G. Bárczi. The team working on this atlas consists of the best scientists of Hungarian dialect-research (J. Végh, B. Kálmán, L. Papp, L. Bunko, M. Kázmér). The way of preparing this atlas and the method of illustrating the linguistic details on maps has even interested foreign countries. The atlas will be printed by next year.

4. A descriptive grammar of the Hungarian language is being prepared under the direction of J. Tompa and D. Pais in the Linguistic Institute of the Academy. The first volume came out in 1961 (Introduction, Phonetics, Syntax). More than ten collaborators were necessary for the composition of the first volume of this grammar.

Other important projects accomplished by the Linguistic Institute of the Hungarian Academy are: a new historical dictionary of the Hungarian language, a new etymological dictionary and a new dictionary of the Hungarian dialects. The implementation of all these projects will extend over several years. One department of the institute is occupied with all questions concerning the culture of the language; its articles are mainly published in *Magyar Nyelvőr*. It is an important fact that extreme purism in the care of language has diminished since 1945.

Apart from these projects several extensive individual works on Hungarian philology have been published in Hungary in the last ten years. We mention the following works: 1) G. Bárczi: "Charter of Foundation of Tihany Abbey from 1055" (1951); 2) I. Kniezsa: "History of Hungarian Orthography in the Middle Ages" (1952); 3) Kiss-Keresztes: "Vocabulary of the dialect of Ormányság" (1952); 4) S. Károly:

"The System of The Hungarian Verbal Nouns in the Codices of the 15th century" (1956); 5) S. Bálint: "Vocabulary of the Dialect of Szeged" (1957); 6) L. Gáldi: "The Hungarian Lexicography in the Renaissance and Reform Period" (19th century) (1957); 7) J. Balázs: "Johann Sylvester and his Epoch", a brilliant monograph on the famous Hungarian humanist in the 16th century (1958); 8) J. Végh: "The Areal Dialect Atlas of Őrség and Hetés" (1959); 9) L. Benkő: "The Language of Hungarian Literature in the Renaissance Period" (19th century) (1960).

A number of greater and smaller essays and reviews on descriptive grammar, history of language, history of word, history of idioms, history of dialects etc. was published in *Magyar Nyelv*, *Magyar Nyelvőr*, *Acta Linguistica* and *Nyelvtudományi Közlemények*.

We also refer to the articles of D. Pais, G. Bárczi, S. Károly, L. Benkő, B. Zolnai, G. O. Nagy, M. Kovalovszky, J. Balázs, E. Ruzsiczky, B. E. Lőrinczy, S. Imre, L. Deme, L. Antal, F. Szilágyi, L. Lőrincze, Gy. Szépe, J. Tompa etc. B. Zolnai, I. Szatmári and J. Balázs wrote on problems of Hungarian style. It is a pity that the interest in place-names compared with the time before 1945 had diminished.

The Nestor of all Hungarian linguists is D. Pais, professor emeritus of Budapest University, since 1925 editor of *Magyar Nyelv*. On the occasion of his seventieth birthday in 1956, a grand anniversary publication was published in Budapest.

In the series *Egyetemi Magyar Nyelvészeti Füzetek*, famous linguists published extracts from several fields of Hungarian philology. The series *Nyelvtudományi Értekezések* published important essays on Hungarian philology and the yearbook *Magyar Nyelvjárások* under the direction of B. Kálmán in Debrecen is mainly connected with research on Hungarian dialects.

## URALIC PHILOLOGY

The Linguistic Institute of the Hungarian Academy has recently established a department for Finno-Ugric languages under the direction of Gy. Lakó; Gy. Lakó holds since 1956 a chair for Finno-Ugric philology at the Budapest University. For more than ten years this department has investigated the Uralic and Finno-Ugric, respectively, parts of the Hungarian vocabulary, a work which is hindered by the fact that the editor uses the most complicated phonetic transcription of Karjalainen and Kannisto.

The close relations with the Soviet Union sometimes enable specialists in Finno-Ugric and Samoyed languages to go on educational trips to the Soviet Union. Since 1953, for instance, Lakó, Hajdú, Kálmán, Erdődi, Bereczki and Radanovics stayed for a shorter or longer time in the Soviet Union. There they were able to collect dialectical material from Vogul, Ostyak, Cheremis, Yurak and other informants and to publish their results later in one of the Hungarian special periodicals: *Acta Linguistica* and *Nyelvtudományi Közlemények*.

Uralic philology profited by the fact that in the 1950's a second chair for Finno-Ugric languages was founded in Budapest, a third in Debrecen and a fourth in Szeged. The second chair in Budapest is held by Ö. Beke, the one in Debrecen by B. Kálmán and that in Szeged by P. Hajdú. After 1956 Hungarian-Finnish cultural relations became enlivened, which even brought about a cultural agreement between Finland and Hungary. By this agreement many Hungarian philologists were enabled to travel to Finland.

J. Papp, Professor at Debrecen University, did very much for the Finnish language in Hungary during the time mentioned above. He published a descriptive grammar of the Finnish language, a Finnish Compendium and a Finnish Chrestomathy. Ö. Lavotha wrote a fair textbook of the Estonian language in Hungarian.

The most important publications in the field of Uralic philology since 1945 are: Zsirai's publication of Ostyak Heroic Songs from Reguly's materials, Kálmán's publication of Vogulic Bear songs from Munkácsi's materials, Fokos-Fuchs' collection of Zyryan dialectal texts and his large Zyryan-German dictionary, the Cheremis dialectal texts by Ö. Beke, a Mokša-Mordvin word index by J. Juhász and J. Erdélyi and Kálmán's book on Russian loanwords in the Vogul language. Besides this, Uralic linguists are engaged in the question of the Uralic and Finno-Ugric homeland; they take part in the discussions on the history of the origin of the Hungarian people, a discussion which arose from a book by the Marxistic historian E. Molnár. In this connection P. Hajdú published a well founded modern summary of the investigations of the Uralic (Finno-Ugric) homeland. In several voluminous essays E. Moór reported on new conceptions of the origin history of the Hungarians.

Smaller studies on Finno-Ugric and Samoyed languages came out in *Nyelvtudományi Közlemények* and *Acta Linguistica.* The majority of these studies dealt with detailed questions of phonetics, morphology and lexicology. Gy. Lakó, B. Kálmán, J. Gulya, K. Radanovics, E. K. Sal and E. Vértes examined the Ob-ugric language, Gy. Lakó and D. R. Fokos-Fuchs the Permian languages, Ö. Beke, J. Erdődi and G. Bereczki studied the questions of the Volga languages (Mordvin and Cheremis) and J. N. Sebestyén those of the Proto-Lappic language. J. N. Sebestyén and P. Hajdú investigated the Samoyed languages, F. Kovács dealt with some remarks on Uralic numeralia. *Nyelvtudományi Közlemények* has been published yearly since 1953; of great value are the book reviews that include in addition to those works published in Hungary and Finland, works that come out in Russia as well.

## SLAVONIC LANGUAGES

The close relations after 1945 between Hungary, Russia and the Slavonic countries (Czechoslovakia, Poland, Yugoslavia, Bulgaria) caused increased interest in Slavonic languages and their investigation; a great number of young specialists were educated for the various Slavonic languages. Following the tradition of linguists in Hungary great attention was paid to Hungarian-Slavonic linguistic relations. J. Kniezsa, since 1941 Professor for Slavonic languages at Budapest University, published in 1955 the first part of his great work on Slavonic loanwords in the Hungarian language. Other linguists performed research on the Hungarian loanwords in the Slavonic languages. We call special attention to the studies of F. Baleczky and L. Dezső on Ukrainian-Hungarian linguistic relations.

Great interest was paid to investigations of the Slovak, Serbo-Croatian and Slovenian languages, as certain dialects of these languages have their home in Hungary. The Linguistic Institute plans the publication of an "Atlas of Slavonic Dialects in Hungary"; at various places in the country statements were collected for this work. I. Kniezsa, L. Hadrovics, E. Baleczky and P. Király are directing the preparations for a catalogue of the old Slavonic codices and manuscripts in the public collections of Hungary. In the course of this work several – up to this date unknown – documents of the Slovak and Slovenian language were discovered. Parts of them have been already published.

In the years 1948-49 Hungarian scholars of Slavonic languages edited together with Romance specialists the *Études Slaves et Roumaines*. Since 1955 the Hungarian scholars of Slavonic languages possess a periodical of their own, *Studia Slavica*, edited by I. Kniezsa. Besides articles in German, French and English, this magazine also prints essays in the Slavonic languages (Russian, Slovak, Czech, Polish, Serbo-Croatian etc.). Many essays deal with the grammar and history of individual Slavonic languages.

The extraordinary interest in Hungary for the Russian language after 1945 was bound up with the practical learning of this language. A series of Russian-Hungarian and Hungarian-Russian dictionaries as well as grammars and textbooks for practical lessons therefore came into being. Besides this, I. Fodor, J. Juhász and M. Péter dealt with certain questions of Russian grammar, pretending to be scientific.

Among greater publications in the field of Slavonic languages are worth mentioning: a collection of Czech documents from the 15th and 16th century edited by I. Kniezsa and P. Király; a book on the printed monuments of East Slovak dialects from the 18th and 19th century by P. Király; a book on a medical manuscript written in Czech with Middle Slovak elements by Gy. Décsy, and J. Sipos' work on a mixed dialect of Slovak Czech Polish from the Bükk-Mountain district of North East-Hungary. L. Dobossy edited a large Czech-Hungarian dictionary and another team of specialists edited a Polish-Hungarian dictionary.

## MODERN AND INDO-GERMANIC PHILOLOGY

Before 1945 the interest in modern languages (English, French, German, Italian) and Indogermanic philology was traditional in Hungary. From 1945-48 the studies of English and French were furthermore supported, whereas German lessons were reduced for political reasons. After 1948 the Russian language gained an exceptional position at the expense of English, French and German as foreign languages at school. Only a limited number of students in English, French, Italian and German (4-5 per year in each subject) were granted at the universities.

In spite of this fact large dictionaries for English, French, German and Italian have been published during the years of 1950-60: L. Országh's dictionaries in English-Hungarian, S. Eckhardt's French-Hungarian and E. Halász's German-Hungarian dictionaries have been accomodated to the development of the Hungarian vocabulary after 1945. On the other hand one can notice that the authors of these works are no longer familiar with the modern use of English, French, German and Italian. In the field of English and French philology study reports came out only sporadically in book form in Hungary. The chair for English Philology and Literature at Debrecen University was abolished after 1948, the Professor for English language and literature in Budapest, M. Szenci, had to resign and the well-known Romance specialist at Budapest University, S. Eckhardt, attended to investigations in the history of Hungarian literature. The young scholars F. Bakos, J. Herman and I. Fónagy studied individual problems of the history of the French language, style and phonetics. Gy. Herczeg published several essays on stylistic problems in the Italian language. L. Tamás, L. Gáldi and Gy. Herczeg paid attention to Rumanian linguistic problems.

After the restoration of relations between Hungary and East Germany in 1949, interest for German language and literature enlivened again. At Budapest University the chair for German language and literature mentioned above was founded; a few young German scholars were enabled to continue the tradition of Hungarian Germanistics, however in a modest way. K. Mollay dealt with the problem of German-Hungarian place-names in Western Hungary, and in 1960 he published the German Law-Book of Ofen in the Middle Ages. K. Hutterer investigated the dialects of isolated German districts in Hungary.

After the end of the war a chair for Indogermanic philology was founded at Budapest University which was held by O. Szemerényi until 1948. At the moment I. Harmatta is Professor for Indo-Germanic languages at the Budapest University. He works mainly in the field of Greek and Iranian. I. Trencsényi-Waldapfel, J. Horváth and J. Borzsák worked on classical philology. Zs. Telegdy published some essays on Middle and New Persian linguistic problems. Ö. Schütz published contributions on the Armenian language. J. Vekerdy dealt with some special questions concerning Sanskrit and the Gipsy language. A small Albanian-Hungarian dictionary published by L. Tamás is only one proof for the political dependent interest in Hungary.

## ORIENTAL STUDIES

Before 1945 Altaic philology, with special respect to the Turkish languages and their relations to the Hungarian language, was the classical field of activity for Orientalism in Hungary. Altaic linguistics therefore were at the service of the history of the Hungarian people. After 1945 and 1948, respectively, the circle of the Hungarian orientalists increased in an imposing way. J. Németh, the Turkologist, and L. Ligeti, Mongolist and Sinologist, are the leading personalities of Altaic philology in Hungary. In 1950 Hungarian orientalists received a new scientific periodical: *Acta Orientalia*. In this periodical essays and book-reviews are published in English, German, French and Russian. It is a continuation of the former Hungarian orientalist reviews *Keleti Szemle* and *Kőrősi Csoma Archivum*.

In the field of Turkish philology J. Németh and his students G. Hazai and Mrs. S. Kakuk submitted valuable contributions on Turkish dialects on the Balkan peninsula (Bulgaria and Albania). M. K. Palló traced the problem of the Chuvash-Hungarian linguistic relations from the VII-IX centuries. L. Rásonyi studied the nomenclaturial questions of the Turkish language. K. Czeglédy submitted essays on Turkish and Arabic philology to investigate the early history of the Hungarians and steppe-people in Southern Russia. The works of the young scholars around L. Ligeti who are engaged in Mongolistics, Tungusology, Sinology and Tibetology have turned out to be extremely rich. It is worth stressing the homogeneous way of work in this group that is combined with a strong discipline in the diachronic method of consideration of languages and dialects that are studied. Ligeti himself has mainly studied questions of Mongolology and Tungusology (including Manchu). Among the younger linguists K. Kőhalmi, G. Kara, L. Bese and V. Diószegi have worked together in the same field. In Sinology B. Csongor systematically interpreted the Chinese loanwords in the Uigur language to reconstruct the Middle Chinese pronounciation. In the field of Tibetology G. Uray and A. Róna Tas published remarkable linguistic contributions. W. Wessetzky wrote essays on Egyptology and A. Schreiber on the Hebrew language.

Most remarkable book-reviews were published in the *Acta Orientalia*. The editors were fortunate in finding foreign contributors in eastern countries (Rintschen, Baičura) as well as in western (Minorsky, Vajda, von Gabain).

## GENERAL LINGUISTICS AND PHONETICS

After 1948 the field of general linguistics in Hungary was more than anywhere else exposed to ideological interventions by the Communist Party. Julius Laziczius, professor for general linguistics and phonetics at the Budapest University was pensioned off by force in 1949 because he had refused Marxist ideology. After that general linguistics in Hungary no longer had a leading personality. Representatives of the special linguistic disciplines worked from now on general linguistic problems and that sometimes according to the opinions of the Party that were valid or had often changed.

In 1953 G. Bárczi, Professor for Hungarian Linguistics at the Budapest University published "An Introduction to Linguistics". It is an excellent, short and critical description of the development and the method of general linguistics with regards to results and needs in Hungary. Bárczi found out that a special linguistic tendency had developed in Hungary, based on the theories of the young grammarians, by the works of Simonyi, Szinnyei and Gombocz. One could call this tendency the "Budapest School", which is characterised by "linguistic realism". By their method the Budapest School overcame the stiffness of the young grammarians (neogrammarians). They broke the scope of positivism, even if not being able to get free from the extreme psychological neogrammarians' point of view.[1] Bárczi gives in his book only a summary of the prevailing theories of Hungarian linguistics of that time; he did not develop any new theory of language.

Since 1948 efforts were made to acquaint Hungarian linguists with theories of Soviet linguists. Therefore a hectographed magazine was published (*A Nyelvtudományi Intézet Közleményei*). In this magazine chiefly articles by Russian linguists on general linguistic problems were printed. From 1945-1951 only a few insignificant representatives of Hungarian philology based their theories on Marr. Well-known professors from the universities, e.g., M. Zsirai, sometimes opposed in a heroic way Marr's doctrine and that partly in an official way in the Hungarian Linguistic Society. The unproductive discussion in Hungary of no purpose on the works of Marr absorbed vim and interest in questions of general linguistics. A serious posing of the problem was impossible because of the compulsory use and repetition of the thesis spread out by the Communist Party. After 1953 and even more after 1956 the ideological pressure on general linguistics finally grew less. In that time some scholars tried to tackle single problems of general linguistics under a certain self-sufficiency, often however, disguised in the terminology ordered by the Party.

The so-called "phonological discussion" in Hungary from 1955-57 is remarkable.[2] They developed independent thoughts on the distinctive trends of the language. The works on general linguistics were mostly published in the *Nyelvtudományi Közlemények* and *Acta Linguistica*. Phonetics in Hungary was closely connected with general linguistics. Besides Laziczius, L. Hegedűs and J. Fónagy were its most remarkable representatives. They examined mostly experimental phonetical problems; however they rarely could use their results for philology. It is worth stressing the statistical studies on the phonetic structure of the Hungarian language from E. Vértes. We mention the most useful indices of content, subject and word by J. Juhász for *Nyelvtudományi Közlemények* I-L and *Magyar Nyelv* XXV-L.

Before 1945 Hungarian linguistics tended mostly towards the languages of the Western countries (Germany, France). After 1945, however, also linguistics in the neighboring countries, especially the ones of the Slavonic languages, were observed as far as possible. But we hope that the earlier traditional connections between the Hungarian and the western philology will remain and that the former tendency towards

1 Cf. Bárczi, *Bevezetés a nyelvtudományba*, p. 137.
2 Cf. *Ural-Altaische Jahrbücher*, 1960, p. 266.

western philology mentioned above will not be replaced by a new and different one.

During the past ten years publishing activity in philology has been striking. It is a pity that quantity sometimes overcame quality. To blame is the habit of the editors of some linguistic reviews to publish most works twice: once in Hungarian in the *Nyelvtudományi Közlemények* or in *Magyar Nyelv* and later on once again in German, French, English or Russian in the *Acta Linguistica*, *Acta Orientalia* or in the *Studia Slavica*. The fact of second publishing is often not stated. The reader often wastes time until he finds out that this is the same article he read before. In the second printing the place of the first should always be named.

It is a pity that the style of the essays often is unnecessarily prolix and the language now and then is sometimes neglected. These symptoms are due to the endeavors of mass-production. They were unknown in Hungarian linguistics before 1945.

## BIBLIOGRAPHY OF BOOKS

*A Magyar Nyelv Értelmező Szótára*: 1. *A-D*; 2. *E-Gy*; 3. *H-K* (Budapest, 1959-60).
Balázs, János, *Sylvester János és kora* (Budapest, 1958).
Bálint, Sándor, *Szegedi szótár: I-II* (Budapest, 1957).
Bárczi, Géza, *Bevezetés a nyelvtudományba*, EMNyF. (Budapest, 1953).
——, *Magyar Hangtörténet*. EMNyF. (Budapest, 1958).
——, *A Magyar Szókincs Eredete*. EMNyF. (Budapest, 1958).
——, *A Magyar Nyelvatlasz munkamódszere* (Budapest, 1955). (red.)
——, *A Tihanyi Apátság alapítólevele mint nyelvi emlék* (Budapest, 1951).
Bartha, Katalin D., *A Magyar Szóképzés Története*, Magyar Történeti Szóalaktan II. EMNyF. (Budapest, 1958).
Beke, Ödön, *Tscheremissische Texte* (Budapest, 1957).
——, *Volksdichtungen und Gebräuche der Tscheremissen* (*Maris*) (Budapest, 1951).
Benkő, Loránd, *Magyar Nyelvjárástörténet*. EMNyF. (Budapest, 1957).
——, *A magyar irodalmi írásbeliség a felvilágosodás korának első szakaszában* (Budapest, 1960).
Bẹrrár, Jolán, *Magyar Történeti Mondattan*. EMNyF. (Budapest, 1957).
Borzsák, István, *Budai Ézsaiás és klasszika filológiánk kezdetei* (Budapest, 1956).
Décsy, Gyula, *Eine slowakische medizinische Handschrift aus dem 17. Jahrhundert. Monographische Bearbeitung eines Sprachdenkmals* (Budapest, 1956).
Deme, László, *Nyelvatlaszunk funkciója és további problémái* (Budapest, 1956).
Eckhardt, Sándor, *Francia-magyar szótár* (Budapest, 1953).
——, *Magyar-francia szótár* (Budapest, 1960).
Dobossy, László, *Cseh-magyar szótár* (Budapest, 1960).
*Emlékkönyv Pais Dezső hetvenedik születésnapjára* (Budapest, 1956).
Fábián, Pál, Szathmári, István, Terestyéni, Ferenc, *A Magyar Stilisztika Vázlata*. EMNyF. (Budapest, 1958).

Fokos-Fuchs, D. Rafael, *Syrjänisches Wörterbuch*. In zwei Bänden (Budapest, 1959).
——, *Volksdichtung der Komi* (*Syrjänen*) (Budapest, 1951).
Gáldi, László, *A magyar szótárirodalom a felvilágosodás korában és a reformkorban* (Budapest, 1957).
Hadrovics, László, and Gáldi, László, *Orosz-magyar szótár* (Budapest, 1951).
——, *Magyar-orosz szótár* (Budapest, 1952).
Hajdú, Péter, *A magyarság kialakulásának előzményei*, Nyelvtudományi Értekezések (Budapest, 1953).
Halász, Előd, *Magyar-német szótár* (Budapest, 1957).
——, *Német-magyar szótár* (Budapest, 1952).
Herczeg, Gyula, *Olasz-magyar szótár* (Budapest, 1952).
Horváth, János, *Árpád-kori latinnyelvű irodalmunk stílusproblémái* (Budapest, 1954).
Imre, Samu, *A "Szabács viadala"*. Nyelvészeti tanulmányok (Budapest, 1958).
Kálmán, Béla, *A Mai Magyar Nyelvjárások*, EMNyF. (Budapest, 1951).
——, *Manysi Nyelvkönyv*, EMNyF. (Budapest, 1955).
——, *Die russischen Lehnwörter im Wogulischen* (Budapest, 1961).
Károly, Sándor, *Igenévrendszerünk a kódexirodalom első szakaszában*, Nyelvtudományi értekezések, 10 (Budapest, 1956).
Király, Péter, *A keletszlovák nyelvjárás nyomtatott emlékei* (Budapest, 1953).
Kiss, Géza, and Keresztes, Kálmán (eds.), *Ormánysági szótár* (Budapest, 1952).
Kniezsa, István, *A Magyar Helyesírás Története*, EMNyF. (Budapest, 1952).
——, *Helyesírásunk története a könyvnyomtatás koráig*, Nyelvészeti tanulmányok 2 (Budapest, 1952).
——, *A magyar nyelv szláv jövevényszavai*, 1-2 (Budapest, 1955).
Lavotha, Ödön, *Észt Nyelvkönyv* (Budapest, 1960).
*Lengyel-magyar szótár* (Budapest, 1959).
Lőrinczy, Éva B., *A Königsbergi Töredék és Szalagjai mint nyelvi emlék*. Nyelvészeti tanulmányok (Budapest, 1953).
Munkácsi, Bernát, Kálmán, Béla, *Manysi* (*vogul*) *népköltési gyűjtemény* (Budapest, 1952).
Mikesy, Sándor (ed.), *Névtudományi vizsgálatok* (Budapest, 1960).
Országh, László, *Magyar-angol szótár* (Budapest, 1953).
——, *Angol-magyar szótár* (Budapest, 1960).
Papp, István, *Finn Nyelvtan* (Budapest, 1956).
Sipos, István, *Geschichte der slowakischen Mundarten der Huta- und Hámor-Gemeinden des Bükk-Gebirges* (Budapest, 1958).
*Stredoveké české listiny* (Budapest, 1951).
Szabó, Dénes, *A Magyar Nyelvemlékek*, EMNyF. (Budapest, 1952).
Végh, József, *Őrségi és Hetési Nyelvatlasz* (Budapest, 1959).
Zsirai, Miklós, *A Finnugorság Ismertetése*. EMNyF. (Budapest, 1952).
——, *Osztják* (*chanti*) *hősénekek* (Budapest, 1951).

## BIBLIOGRAPHY OF ARTICLES

Aistleitner, Joseph, "Studien zur Sprachverwandtschaft des Ugaritischen I", *AOH*, 1957, 251-307.

Baičura, U. S., "Experimentell-phonetische Beiträge zur Kenntnis des Kasan-Tatarischen", *ALH*, 1958, 173-247.

Bakos, Ferenc, "Contributions a l'étude des formules des politesse en ancien français", *ALH*, 1955, 295-367.

Baleczky, Emil, "Pamjatnik ukrainskogo delovogo jazyka XVII veka", *SSlav*, 1956, 373-381.

——, "O jazykovoj prinadležnosti i zaselenii sela Komlóška", *SSlav*, 1956, 345-363.

——, "Vengerskoe kert v zakarpatskix ukrainskix govorax", *SSlav*, 1960, 247-265.

Bárczi, Géza, "Les travaux de l'Atlas linguistique de la Hongrie", *ALH*, 1957, 1-52.

Beke, Ödön, "Neuere finnisch-ugrische morphologische Untersuchungen", *ALH*, 1954, 95-131.

——, "Zur Geschichte einiger permischer Nominalbildungssuffixe", *ALH*, 1953, 317-353.

Benda, Kálmán, and Hadrovics, László, "Kroatisches Freiheitsgedicht aus dem Jahre 1794", *SSlav*, 1956, 381-387.

Bese, Lajos, "Einige Bemerkungen zur partikulären Reduplikation im Mongolischen", *AOH*, 1960, 43-50.

——, "Zwillingswörter im Mongolischen", *AOH*, 1957, 199-211.

Csongor, Barna, "Chinese in the Uighur Script of the T'ang-period", *AOH*, 1952, 73-122.

——, "Remarks on a problem of Negation in Middle Chinese", *AOH*, 1960, 69-74.

——, "Some Chinese Texts in Tibetan Script from Tun-Huang", *AOH*, 1960, 94-140.

——, "Some more Chinese Glosses in Uighur Script", *AOH*, 1955, 251-258.

Czeglédy, Károly, "Khazar Raids in Transcaucasia in A.D. 762-764", *AOH*, 1960, 75-88.

——, "Bahrām Čōbīn and the Persian Apocalyptic Literature", *AOH*, 1958, 21-44.

Deme, László, "Disputed Aspects of Phonetics", *ALH*, 1961, 99-156.

——, "On the Inherent Laws Governing the Development of Language", *ALH*, 1957, 107-143.

Dezső, László, "Urbarial'nye zapisi s Maramoroškoj Verxoviny", *SSlav*, 1957, 235-260.

——, "K voprosu o vengerskix zaimstvovanijax v zakarpatskix pamjatnikax XVI-XVII vekov", *SSlav*, 1958, 71-96; 1961, 139-176.

Fodor, István, "Sintaksčeskie javlenija Zadonščiny", *SSlav*, 1955, 137-178.

Fokos-Fuchs, D. R., "Aus dem Gebiete der Lehnbeziehungen", *ALH*, 1953, 211-289.

——, "Aus der Syntax der ural-ataischen Sprachen", *ALH*, 1960, 423-456.

——, "Umstandsbestimmungen des Masses und der Menge in den finnisch-ugrischen Sprachen", *ALH*, 1955, 35-66.

——, "Die Verbaladverbien der permischen Sprachen", *ALH*, 1958, 273-342.
Fónagy, Iván, "Über die Schallfülle der ungarischen Vokale", *ALH*, 1954, 383-425.
——, "Über den Verlauf des Lautwandels", *ALH*, 1957, 173-278.
Gaál, László, "Zur Interpretation der awestischen Gathas", *AOH*, 1952, 173-181.
Gáldi, László, "Contributions hongroises a la découverte de la langue roumaine", *ALH*, 1958, 1-39.
Hadrovics, László, "Adverbien als Verbalpräfixe in der Schriftsprache der ungarländischen Kroaten", *SSlav*, 1958, 211-249.
——, "Bruchstück eines unbekannten kroatischen kirchlichen Dramas", *SSlav*, 1956, 395-396.
——, "Ein Bubgedicht der ungarländischen Slowenen aus dem 17. Jh", *SSlav*, 1956, 388-394.
——, "Gebete und Gesänge einer slowenischen Rosenkranzbruderschaft", *SSlav*, 1957, 379-401.
——, "Der südslawische Trojaroman und seine ungarische Vorlage", *SSlav*, 1955, 49-135.
Hajdú, Péter, "The Form of the Object in the Forest Yurak", *ALH*, 1960, 95-115.
——, "Noch einmal über den Stimmbandverschlusslaut im Jurakischen", *ALH*, 1958, 245-272.
——, "Die sekundären anlautenden Nasale (ŋ, ń-) im Samojedischen", *ALH*, 1954, 17-67.
Harmatta, János, "Elamica", *ALH*, 1954, 287-311.
——, "Studies in the Language of the Iranian tribes in South Russia", *AOH*, 1951, 261-314.
Hazai, Georg, "Les dialectes turcs du Rhodope", *AOH*, 1959, 205-229.
——, "Monuments linguistiques osmanlisturcs", *AOH*, 1960, 221-234.
——, "Textes turcs du Rhodope", *AOH*, 1960, 184-229.
Hegedűs, Lajos, "Experimental Phonetics in the Service of the Linguistic Atlas. I-II", *ALH*, 1955, 185-217, 369-413.
——, "On the problem of the Pause of Speech", *ALH*, 1953, 1-36.
Herczeg, Gyula, "La syntaxe du participe passé dans la langue littéraire roumaine", *ALH*, 1953, 211-223.
——, "Stile nominale nella italiana contemporanea", *ALH*, 1954, 171-192.
Herman, József, "Les changements analogiques", *ALH*, 1951, 119-170.
——, "Recherches sur l'ordre des mots dans les plus anciens textes français en prose (I-II)", *ALH*, 1954, 69-94, 351-382.
Juhász, József, "Atributivnye konstrukcii s prostoj formoj sravnitel'noj stepeni prilagatelńyx v roli opredelenija", *SSlav*, 1957, 299-326.
Kakuk, Suzanne, "Constructions hypotactiques dans le dialecte turc de la Bulgarie Occidentale", *AOH*, 1960, 249-258.
——, "Le dialecte turc de Kazanlyk", *AOH*, 1958, 169-188.
Kara, Georg, "Sur le colophon de l'Altan gerel oïrat", *AOH*, 1960, 255-262.

——, "Notes sur les dialectes oïrat de la Mongolie Occidentale", *AOH*, 1958, 111-168.

——, "Un Texte mongol en écriture soyombo", *AOH*, 1959, 1-38.

Király, Péter, "Das Budapester glagolitische Fragment", *SSlav*, 1955, 311-322.

——, "Geschichte des ungarischen Wortes paraszt 'Bauer'", *ALH*, 1953, 63-123.

——, "Latsny Adamus: Dictionarum saec. XVIII", *SSlav*, 1957, 59-111.

Kniezsa, Stefan, "Chronologie der slowakischen Orstnamentypen", *SSlav*, 1959, 173-180.

——, "Slawische Bestandteile der ungarischen staatlichen und juridischen Terminologie", *SSlav*, 1955, 363-370.

——, "Die Sprache der alten Slawen Transdanubiens", *SSlav*, 1955, 29-48.

Kovács, Ferenc, "A propos d'une loi sémantique", *ALH*, 1961, 405-413.

——, "Some Remarks on Uralic Numerals", *ALH*, 1960, 117-129.

——, "Ist das ungarische Zahlwort Húsz 'viginti' eine Zusammensetzung?", *ALH*, 1958, 343-360.

——, "The Verb pońat' (ponimat') 'begreifen, verstehen' and Some of its Synonyms in Russian", *SSlav*, 1957, 207-221.

Lakó, György, "Nordmansische Sprachstudien", *ALH*, 1957, 347-423.

——, "Present Situation and Future Tasks of Finno-Ugric Linguistics in Hungary", *ALH*, 1959, 7-33.

Ligeti, Louis, "Les ancien éléments mongols dans le mandchou", *AOH*, 1960, 231-248.

——, "Un épisode d'origine chinoise du 'Geser-qan'", *AOH*, 1951, 339-357.

——, "A propos des éléments 'altaiques' de la langue hongroise", *ALH*, 1961, 15-42.

——, "A propos de l'écriture mandchoue", *AOH*, 1952, 235-301.

——, "Le Po kia sing en écriture "phags-pa", *AOH*, 1956, 1-52.

——, "Note Préliminaire sur le déchiffrement des 'petits caracteres' Joutchen", *AOH*, 1953, 211-228.

——, "Un vocabulaire mongol d'Istanboul", *AOH*, 1962, 3-100.

Mollay, Károly, "Zur Chronologie deutscher Ortsnamentypen im mittelalterlichen Westungarn", *ALH*, 1961, 67-98.

——, "Das älteste deutsche Lehngut der ungarischen Sprache", *ALH*, 1951, 373-418.

Moór, Elemér, "Die Ausbildung des urungarischen Volkes im Lichte der Laut- und Wortgeschichte, I", *ALH*, 1957, 279-341.

Németh, Julius, "Traces of the Turkish language in Albania", *AOH*, 1961, 9-30.

Országh, László, "Problems and Principles of the New Dictionary of the Hungarian Language", *ALH*, 1960, 211-273.

Pais, Dezső, "Survivances slavo-hongroises du castellum romain", *ALH*, 1954, 269-286.

Palló, Margarete K., "Zur Frage der tschuwaschischen v-Prothese", *AOH*, 1961, 33-44.

Péter, Mihály, "Melodika voprositel'nogo predloženija v russkom jazyke", *SSlav*, 1955, 245-259.

Rásonyi, László, "Les noms de nombre dans l'anthroponymie turque", *AOH*, 1961, 45-72.

——, "Les noms toponymiques comans du Kiskunság", *ALH*, 1958, 73-146.
——, "Zu den Namen der ersten türkischen Herren von Jerusalem", *AOH*, 1961, 89-94.
——, "L'origine du nom Székely (sicule)", *ALH*, 1961, 175-188.
——, "Sur quelques catégories de noms de personnes en turc", *ALH*, 1953, 323-351.
Róna Tas, András, "Remarks on the Phonology of the Monguor Language", *AOH*, 1960, 263-268.
——, "Tally-stick and Divination-dice in the Iconography of Lha-mo", *AOH*, 1956, 163-180.
——, "Social Terms in the List of Grants of the Tibetan Tun-Huang Chronicle", *AOH*, 1955, 249-270.
Scheiber, Alexander, "An Old Polemic Work from the Kaufmann Geniza", *AOH*, 1957, 27-63.
——, "Isaac Ibn Chalfon's Panegyric Poem", *AOH*, 1960, 91-95.
——, "Die hebräische Handschrift Cod. Hebr. XXXII. in der Kgl. Bibliothek von Kopenhagen", *AOH*, 1961, 134-45.
Schütz, Ödön, "Armenian *Xašar*", *AOH*, 1958, 17-20.
——, "An Armeno-Kipchak Print from Lvov", *AOH*, 1961, 123-130.
——, "Nicholas Misztótfalusi Kis and the Armenian Book Printing", *AOH*, 1959, 63-73.
Sebestyén, Irene N., "Attributive Konstruktionen im Samojedischen", *ALH*, 1959, 35-115.
——, "Zur Frage der determinierenden Deklination im Juraksamojedischen", *ALH*, 1960, 55-93.
——, "Die possessiven Fügungen im Samojedischen und das Problem des uralischen Genitivs (I-II.)", *ALH*, 1958, 41-71, 273-340.
——, "Zur Frage des alten Wohngebietes der uralischen Völker", *ALH*, 1951, 273-346.
——, "A. Sprogis' Wörterverzeichnis und grammatikalische Aufzeichnungen aus der Kanin-Mundart des Jurak-Samojedischen", *ALH*, 1953, 97-188.
Sipos, Štefan, "Zo skúseností výskumu slovenských nárečí v Mad'arsku", *SSlav*, 1955, 389-408.
Sulán, Béla, "Zu der Streitfrage über den Ursprung der mittel- bzw. südosteuropäischen Wörter hajdú ~ hajduk ~ hajdut usw.", *SSlav*, 1961, 177-186.
Tamás, Lajos, "Zur Frage der slawische-rumänischen und ungarisch-rumänischen sprachlichen Beziehungen", *SSlav*, 1958, 385-394.
——, "Zum ungarisch-slawisch-deutschen Wortgut des Rumänischen", *ALH*, 1959, 241-260.
Tarnóczy, Tamás, "Die akustische Struktur der stimmlosen Engelaute", *ALH*, 1954, 313-349.
Telegdi, Zsigmond, "Beiträge zur historischen Grammatik des Neupersischen", *ALH*, 1955, 67-183.

Tompa, József, "Über die Vorbereitungsarbeiten zur Grammatik der heutigen ungarischen Sprache", *ALH*, 1957, 441-447.

Trencsényi-Waldapfel, Imre, "Die orientalische Verwandtschaft des Prooimions der hesiodischen Theogenia", *AOH*, 1955, 46-74.

Uray, Géza, "Duplication, Gemination and Triplication in Tibetan", *AOH*, 1955, 177-244.

——, "Some problems of the Ancient Tibetan Verbal Morphology", *ALH*, 1953, 37-62.

——, "A Tibetan diminutive suffix", *AOH*, 1952, 183-220.

——, "On the Tibetan Letters Ba and Wa", *AOH*, 1955, 101-122.

Vekerdi, József, "Gypsy Fragments from the Early 18th Century", *AOH*, 1962, 123-130.

——, "Gypsy Texts", *AOH*, 1961, 305-323.

——, "On Past Tense and Verbal Aspects in the Rgveda", *AOH*, 1955, 75-100.

Vértes, Edit, "Statistische Untersuchungen über den phonetischen Aufbau der ungarischen Sprache", *ALH*, 1953, 125-158, 411-430; 1954, 193-224.

Wessetzky, Vilmos, "Die Wirkung des Altägyptischen in einem koptischen Zauberspruch", *AOH*, 1950, 26-30.

# POLAND

## EDWARD STANKIEWICZ

After World War II, Polish linguistics devoted itself even more than before to the many-sided investigation of the Polish language. It also continued, though on a scale not equal to that of Polish, the study of other Slavic languages. The works published in these two areas constitute the bulk of linguistic production. Many of the Slavic linguistic studies have addressed themselves to general linguistic problems, which are, however, treated explicitly in journals devoted specifically to general linguistics (e.g. the *Biuletyn polskiego towarzystwa językoznawczego*, published since 1927). Some Polish linguists (e.g. J. Kuryłowicz, L. Zawadowski, T. Milewski, A. Heinz, Z. Rysiewicz) have been active primarily in the field of general linguistics, even if their illustrative material is often drawn from Polish and from other Slavic languages.

The following discussion, which has no claim to exhaustiveness, limits itself only to a survey of post-war linguistic research in Poland, devoted to Polish and to other Slavic languages.

The strong tradition of pre-war Polish linguistics, represented by the illustrious names of Baudouin de Courtenay, Kruszewski, Rozwadowski, Gawroński and Nitsch, saved Polish scholarship the embarrassments of a meandering course due to political factors and pressures. As Polish scholarship between the two wars was able to avoid nationalism in treating the sensitive questions of border-dialects, it managed right after the war to steer away from Marrism, and not to swallow uncritically the linguistic "discoveries" of Stalin. Polish linguistics has, in fact, continued on its own course to a point that it did not immediately respond to the various trends of Western linguistics: linguistic "neo-idealism", Italian "areal linguistics", and Prague or Copenhagen structuralism found few adherents in the immediate post-war years. This phenomenon explains (with some notable exceptions) the dearth of phonological studies, the dominant historical orientation, and the central themes of Polish linguistic research. The impact of Baudouin de Courtenay is only now gaining the upper hand over that of Nitsch or Łoś, and structuralism is beginning to shape more and more decisively the physiognomy of present-day linguistics in Poland. The preponderant interest in historical research impresses, however, anyone who follows the Polish linguistic scene, with its projects, discussions and controversies, and who compares the output in diachronic studies with that of synchronic descriptions.

It is noteworthy that so far there is no single authoritative and exhaustive grammar of the contemporary standard language. The book of Doroszewski,[1] which is the only new work in this area, does not methodologically surpass the pre-war grammars of Szober, Lehr-Spławiński and Klemensiewicz,[2] although it enlarges on them in its treatment of morphophonemics and derivation.

The study of Polish sounds has been the subject of a few monographs and of various articles. Among the former, we find the more traditional treatments of Benni and Dłuska,[3] X-ray studies of Polish consonants and vowels carried out by Koneczna and Zawadowski, and the acoustic investigation of Skorupka.[4] Experimental analyses of Polish sounds have also been published by Jassem,[5] who signals discrepancies of his findings with those of American scholars concerning the acoustic correlates of some distinctive features. The same author has also tried to show in a recent monograph[6] that tone differences, rather than those of intensity, are the characteristic feature of Polish accent. Modern Polish stress has been the subject of several investigations, the most important one by Dłuska (*Prozodia języka polskiego*, Cracow, 1947). In a series of articles, Mańczak tried to discard the traditional distinction between atonic and orthotonic words based on the difference between "full words" and unaccented enclitics and proclitics. His arguments are persuasively refuted by Dłuska.[7]

Polish consonantal clusters have been tackled in an historically oriented study by Ułaszyn, and exhaustively analyzed by Bargiełówna; the latter's synchronic description served as the basis for Kuryłowicz' discussion of the rules of syllable-division and of structuring of consonantal groups.[8] A statistical study of the Polish sounds is that by Steffen.[9] An interesting discussion evolved around the subject of Polish "potential" phonemes, the status of which was first raised by Milewski.[10] Z. Stieber

[1] Doroszewski, W., *Podstawy gramatyki polskiej* (Warsaw, 1952), I, 320 pp.

[2] Klemensiewicz, Z., *Gramatyka współczesnej polszczyzny kulturalnej w zarysie* (Wrocław, 1947[3]), 179 pp.; Lehr-Spławiński, T., *Gramatyka języka polskiego* (Wrocław, 1957[7]), 208 pp.; Szober, S., *Gramatyka języka polskiego* (Warsaw, 1959[5]), xvi + 389 pp.

[3] Benni T., *Fonetyka opisowa języka polskiego. Z obrazami głosek polskich podług M. Abińskiego* (Wrocław, 1959), 92 pp.; Dłuska, M., *Fonetyka polska* (Cracow, 1950), 144 pp.

[4] Koneczna,H., Zawadowski, W., *Przekroje rentgenograficzne głosek polskich* (Warsaw, 1951), 16 pp. + 14 plates; Skorupka, S., *Studia nad budową akustyczną samogłosek polskich* (Wrocław, 1955), 197 pp.

[5] Jassem, W., Suwalski, J., "Klanganalysen der polnischer Vokale", *ZPAS* 12.125-235 (1961); Jassem, W., "The Formants of Sustained Polish Vowels. A Preliminary Study", in *Study of Sounds. Articles Contributed in Commemoration of the 30th Anniversary of the Founding of the Phonetic Society of Japan* (Tokyo, 1957), pp. 335-349; Jassem, W., Suwalski, J., "Analiza akustyczna polskich spółgłosek szumiących", *Przegląd Telekomunikacyjny* 1.5ff. (1957).

[6] Jassem, W., *Akcent języka polskiego* (Wrocław-Warsaw-Cracow, 1962), 116 pp.

[7] Mańczak, W., "O akcentuacji grup dwuwyrazowych", *JP* 32.15-24 (1952); idem, "Enklityki i proklityki w języku polskim", *JP* 32.145-156 (1952); idem, "O akcentuacji grup ponaddwuwyrazowych", *JP* 32.145-156 (1952); Dłuska, M., "Akcent i atona w języku polskim", *SFPSł* 2.92-121 (1957).

[8] Ułaszyn, H., *Z studiów nad grupami spółgłoskowymi w języku polskim* (Wrocław, 1956), 74 pp.; Bargiełówna, M., "Grupy fonemów społgłoskowych współczesnej polszczyzny kulturalnej", *BPTJ* 10.1-25 (1950); Kuryłowicz, J., "Uwagi o polskich grupach spółgłoskowych", *BPTJ* 11.54-69 (1952).

[9] Steffen, M., "Częstość występowania głosek polskich", *BPTJ* 16.145-164 (1957).

[10] Milewski, T., "Derywacja fonologiczna", *BPTJ* 9.43-57 (1949); Stieber, Z., "Na marginesie *derywacji fonologicznej*", *BPTJ* 10 (1950); Zwoliński, P., "Dokoła fonemów potencjalnych", *LPos* 3 (1951).

has devoted several studies to questions of Polish phonology, dealing with the relations of some individual phonemes, with the question of phonemic equilibrium and with Polish junctural features.[11]

The literature on Polish synchronic morphology is not vast; the primary emphasis is here given to problems of derivation, to which Doroszewski devoted a series of articles before the war. The largest study on Polish inflection is that of Tokarski, which gives a popularizing survey of the syntactic function of Polish verbs, of their meanings and stem-alternations, followed by a dictionary and tables of paradigms.[12] The variant forms of the gen. sing. masc. (-a/-u) have engendered a great many commentaries (some of them rather amusing or trivial).[13] A classification of Polish possessive adjectives, from a formal and semantic point of view, is found in a monograph of Szlifersztejnowa.[14] The question of transitiveness of the verb has received attention in two recent studies which set up various subcategories within the transitive and intransitive verbs, depending on their syntactic function and lexical meanings.[15] Derivation of adjectives has been discussed in a synchronically not quite consistent monograph of Kurkowska, who has also devoted a separate article to this problem; compound-formation is spotlighted by J. Klemensiewicz, while Wesołowska considers the order of components in compound adjectives.[16] Z. Klemensiewicz has pointed out that the principal function of verbal prefixes is that of aspect and gender, whereas Skulina has dealt in detail with the back-formation of some Polish augmentative substantives.[17] Other studies have gone into the question of adverbial derivation, and into individual suffixes of substantives.[18]

[11] Stieber, Z., "Dwa problemy z polskiej fonologii. 1. Fonologiczna funkcja samogłosek nosowych. 2. Fonologiczne sposoby oznaczania granicy słowa i morfemu", *BPTJ* 8.56-78 (1948); idem, "O zaburzeniach równowagi fonologicznej", *BPTJ* 9 (1949); idem, "Über das gegenseitige Verhältnis der heutigen polnischen Phoneme *s-š* und *z-ž*", *WSl* 6.121-124 (1961).

[12] Tokarski, J., *Czasowniki polskie; formy, typy, wyjątki* (Warsaw, 1951), 288 pp.

[13] Mańczak, W., "O repartycji końcówek depołniacza *-a* : *-u*", *JP* 33.70-84 (1953); Zwoliński, P., "Przyczynki do repartycji koncowek -a/-u w dopełnieniu l. poj. rodz. męsk.", *JP* 28.174-177 (1948); Słuszkiewicz, W., "O dopełniaczu na -a i na -u w nazwach części ciała", *JP* 30.120-123 (1950); Jodłowski, S., "O formach *budyniu, pasztetu//omleta, biszkopta*", *JP* 33.84-94 (1953).

[14] Szlifersztejnowa, S., *Przymiotniki dzierżawcze w języku polskim* (Wrocław, 1960), 193 pp.

[15] Stamirowska, Z., "O wpływie przechodniosci i nieprzechodniości czasownika na jego znaczenie indywidualne", *JP* 35.247-267 (1955); Wesołowska, D., "Przechodniość i nieprzechodniość tego samego czasownika w zależności od znaczenia", *JP* 41.19-30 (1961).

[16] Kurkowska, H., *Budowa słowotwórcza przymiotników polskich* (Wrocław, 1954), 175 pp.; idem, "Uwagi o żywotnych typach słowotwórczych przymiotników", *Por. Jęz.*, 1950, pp. 4-10 and 1951, pp. 3-7; Klemensiewicz, I., *Wyrazy złożone nowszej polszczyzny kulturalnej, Próba systematyki* (Cracow, 1948), 96 pp.; Wesołowska, D., "Kolejność członów w przymiotnikach złożonych", *JP* 39.264-275 (1959).

[17] Klemensiewicz, Z., "Próba charakterystyki dwu naczelnych funkcji przedrostka w polskim czasowniku", *SAU*, 52 (1951); Skulina, T., "Rzeczowniki augmentatywne wstecznie derywowane", *JP* 39.190-202 (1959).

[18] Śmiech, W., "O polskich przysłówkach odprzymiotnikowych na *-o, -e*", *Rozp ŁTN* 5.61-76 (1957) + table; Majewska-Grzegorczykowa, R., "Z zagadnień słowotwórstwa przysłówków. Typ: *chyłkiem, z wolna,*" *Por. Jęz.*, 1957, pp. 193-205. Zołotowa, W., "Rzeczowniki osobowe z sufiksem *-ec* (*-owiec*) we współczesnym języku polskim", *Por. Jęz.*, 1957, pp. 359-367, 397-410; Kreja, B., "Funkcje sufiksu *-/i/dło*", *JP* 37.268-272 (1957).

The chief contributions to Polish syntax come from the pen of Z. Klemensiewicz. They include his "Outline of Polish Syntax", which is pedagogical in scope, and a variety of studies which reveal a psychological orientation.[19] Word-order and its stylistic functions have recently been discussed by Jodłowski, whereas Koneczna devoted an interesting article to impersonal constructions.[20] The role of the participle in expressing aspect and time, the use of the infinitive, and the oscillations in the use of the genitive or accusative, have been taken up in the most recent syntactic studies.[21]

Of a purely synchronic and normative nature are the several works devoted to Polish orthoepy, punctuation and orthography.[22]

The diachronic investigation of the Polish language is the fundamental theme of contemporary Polsih linguistics. Even such fields as dialectology and stylistics are ultimately viewed as sources for that history, specifically for the history of the literary language. The historical evolution of the language is generally conceived broadly with relation to the history of culture and as a reflection of that culture. The broad, "external" approach was typical for Brückner's "Story of the Polish Language", which was reprinted after the war.[23] The books of Słoński and Lehr-Spławiński are inspired by the same principle.[24] The most exhaustive historical grammar, tracing the internal development of Polish, is that of Klemensiewicz, Lehr-Spławiński and Urbańczyk. But although it incorporates the results of post-war investigations, it does not differ methodologically from pre-war traditional works such as the monumental historical grammar of Łoś.[25] To the book of the three authors, there has recently been added Volume I of Klemensiewicz' history of the language, dealing with the period up to the 16th century.[26] This work contributes little to our knowledge of the language; its chief merit is probably the detailed discussion of various views concerning the history of the literary language and the question of "mazurzenie".

[19] Klemensiewicz, Z., *Zarys składnii polskiej* (Warsaw, 1953), 74 pp.; 1957², 133 pp.; idem, *Skupienia, czyli syntaktyczne grupe wyrazowe* (Cracow, 1948), 96 pp.; idem, "O syntaktycznym stosunku nawiązania," *Slavia*, 19, no. 1/2 (1944).

[20] Jodłowski, X., "Zasady polskiego szyku wyrazów", *Dziesięciolecie Wyższej Szkoły Pedagogicznej w Krakowie 1946-1956* (Cracow, 1957), pp. 309-329; Koneczna, H., "Od zdań podmiotowych do bezpodmiotowych", *Por. Jęz.*, 1955, pp. 281-292.

[21] Klimonow, W., "Aspekt i czas w konstrukcjach imiesłowowobiernych w języku polskim", *Por. Jęz.*, 1959, pp. 132-147; idem, "Konstrukcje imiesłowowo-bierne z imiesłowem niedokonanym w języku polskim", *Por. Jęz.*, 1960, pp. 207-217; Harrer-Pisarkowa, K., "Przypadek dopełnienia w polskim zdaniu zaprzeczonym", *JP* 39.9-32 (1959); Misz. H., "O pewnym rodzaju użycia bezokolicznika w dzisiejszym języku polskim", *Zeszyty Naukowe Uniw. M. Kopernika w Toruniu, Nauki Hum-społ. 3, Filologia Polska* 2.37-51 (1960).

[22] Doroszewski, W., *Kryteria poprawności językowej* (Cracow, 1950), 123 pp.; Słoński, S., *Słownik polskich błędów językowych* (Warsaw, 1947), 282 pp.; Szober, S., *Słownik poprawnej polszczyzny* (Warsaw, 1948).

[23] Brückner, A., *Dzieje języka polskiego* (Lwow, 1906), 186 pp. (1913²; 1925³; 1960⁴), 204 pp.

[24] Słoński, S., *Historia języka polskiego w zarysie* (Lwów, 1934), 176 pp. (Warsaw, 1953³), 145 pp.; Lehr-Spławiński, T., *Język polski: pochodzenie, powstanie, rozwój* (Warsaw, 1947), 482 pp. + 2 maps (1951²), 513 pp.

[25] Klemensiewicz, Z., Lehr-Spławinski, T., Urbańczyk, S., *Gramatyka historyczna języka polskiego* (Warsaw, 1955), 596 pp.

[26] Klemensiewicz, Z., *Historia języka polskiego*, I: *Doba staropolska* (Warsaw, 1961), 232 pp.

Methodologically new is Stieber's "Phonological development of the Polish language". Although its treatment of the oldest period does not surpass the still excellent study of Rozwadowski,[27] it gives a lucid description of the phonemic inventories of Polish at various phases of its evolution; it provides, in addition, a phonemic survey of various Polish dialects and a sketch of the phonemic development of Kashubian.

Various problems of Polish historical phonetics and phonology have been taken up in various articles and monographs. The history of Polish prosodic features has received special attention. The stabilization of Polish stress has been given a new interpretation by Turska, who established four stages in the development of the Polish accent[28] The force of her arguments is not always persuasive . The evolution of Polish accent since the XVI century has been described and documented most exhaustively by Topolińska.[29] The loss of Old Polish quantity and the subsequent disappearance of the narrow vowels has been discussed by Stieber, Cyran, Bajerowa and Zieniukowa.[30] The development of Polish vocalism has heen studied against a general Slavic background by Furdal.[31] Some changes in Polish consonantism have been investigated by Kuraszkiewicz and Zwoliński, while the question of vowel-contraction has been taken up by Winklerówna.[32] The history of consonant-clusters, of assimilation and dissimilation within and across word-boundaries has attracted new attention.[33] Some of these changes are interpreted phonologically by Stieber.[34] Rospond has also investigated the Northern Polish loss of palatalization in labial consonants.[35]

The central topic in the history of Polish consonantism remains, however, the

[27] Rozwadowski, J. M., "Historyczna fonetyka, czyli głosownia języka polskiego", *Gramatyka języka polskiego* (Cracow, 1915), pp. 289-422, 1923[2], pp. 57-206. Reprinted: *Wybór pism.*, 1 (Warsaw 1959), pp. 73-224; Stieber, Z., *Rozwój fonologiczny języka polskiego* (Warsaw, 1952), 95 pp., 1958[2], 96 pp.

[28] Turska, H., "Zagadnienie miejsca akcentu w języku polskim", *Pam. lit.* 41.434-468 (1950).

[29] Topolińska, Z., *Z historii akcentu polskiego od wieku XVI do dziś* (Cracow, 1961), 288 pp.

[30] Stieber, Z., "Czas i przyczyny zaniku polskiego iloczasu", *SAU* 46.103-106 (1945); Cyran, W., "Ślady iloczasu w głównych zabytkach języka polskiego XIV-XVI wieku", *BPTJ* 11.1-21 (1952); Bajerowa, I., "W sprawie zaniku samogłosek pochylonych w języku polskim", *JP* 38.325-339 (1958); Zieniukowa, J., "Uwagi o zaniku *a* pochylonego w polskim języku literackim", *Por. Jęz.*, 1959, pp. 346-348.

[31] Furdal, A., "O podobieństwie w rozwoju polskiego i ogólnosłowiańskiego wokalizmu", *Rozp. Kom. Jęz. WTN* 3.139-149 (1961).

[32] Kuraszkiewicz, W., "Najdawniejszy przejaw zbieżności wymowy *rz* i *ż* u pisarza pyzdrskiego lat 1410-1418", *JP* 33.381-386 (1953); Zwoliński, P., "Przejście *ł* > *u̯* w języku polskim", *BPTJ* 9.81-96 (1959); Winklerówna, I., "Ściągnięte i nie ściągnięte formy słów *stać* i *bać*", *JP* 31.29-32 (1951).

[33] Klemensiewicz-Bajerowa, I., "Z historii polskich grup spółgłoskowych", *BPTJ* 12.129-147 (1953); Karaś, M., "Ze studiów nad polskimi grupami spółgłoskowymi", *BPTJ* 16.115-144 (1957) + map; Śmiech, W., *Rozwój historyczny polskich grup spółgłoskowych *sŕ, *zŕ, *žŕ* (Łódź, 1953), 164 pp. + map; Brajerski, T., "Staropolskie *ćwi(e)rdzić* i *twi(e)rdzić*", *Por. Jęz.*, 1956, pp. 61-66; Śmiech, W., "O fonetyce międzywyrazowej w języku polskim na tle ogólnosłowiańskim", *JP* 41.95-103 (1961).

[34] Stieber, Z., "Dlaczego mówimy *tszy kszywe kszaki* a nie *dży gżywe gżaki*?", *JP* 26.76-78 (1946); idem, "Skąd się wzięła wymowa *tfoja śfica*?", *JP* 26.107-109 (1946).

[35] Rospond, S., "Z badań nad przeszłością języka polskiego literackiego, II, Palatalność spółgłosek wargowych", *JP* 33.19-25 (1953).

phenomenon of "mazurzenie". This phenomenon refers to the change of the consonants *č*, *ǯ*, *š*, *ž*, into *c ʒ*, *s*, *z* in the dialects of Małopolska and Mazovia. It involves, however, a number of important questions: the cause of the change, its chronology, its territorial origin, and its relation to other changes, especially to the development of the nasal consonants and to the change of *-x* into *-k*. The controversy on the origin of "mazurzenie" and on its relationship to the genesis of the Polish literary language, dates back to the beginning of our century, when it was unleashed by A. Brückner and K. Nitsch; since then it has been the focal point of Polish linguistic research, the inspiration of dialectal and philological studies, and the source of endless speculation. As to the causes of "mazurzenie", Polish linguists are of two opposing views: according to one (presently held by Urbańczyk, Taszycki, Milewski and Lehr-Spławiński),[36] it is due to a foreign, Finnish, Prussian or Celtic substratum, whereas in the other view (held by Nitsch, Rudnicki, Koneczna, Brajerski, Kuryłowicz[37]), it is an independent, internal development. The chronology of "mazurzenie", which Nitsch had at one time connected with the prehistoric tribal divisions, is now generally believed( on grounds of relative chronology) to have occurred after the 11th or 12th century. But Taszycki[38] and Milewski place the change in the 15th-16th centuries, when the Polish literary language was already formed; consequently they reject the "Wielkopolska hypothesis" of the origin of the literary language, since "mazurzenie", which is absent from the literary language (as it is in Wielkopolska), should have been lacking also in 16th-century Cracow. More recently, the controversy has been centering around the definition of a literary language, and around the development of Standard Polish, which I discuss below.

The modern literary language agrees with the Wielkopolska development also in the split of the original nasal vowels into *ę*, *ǫ* and their subsequent change, in most environments, into vowel plus nasal consonant, But there is same doubt whether this development was very old in Wielkopolska. This question has recently been explored in a large number of studies.[39] Taszycki has also argued in favor of the late

[36] Urbańczyk, S., "Gwary polskie na substracie staropruskim i geneza mazurzenia", in *Księga pamiątkowa 75-lecia Tow. Naukowego w Toruniu* (Toruń, 1952), pp. 217-228; Taszycki, W., *Dawność tzw. mazurzenia w języku polskim* (Warsaw, 1948), 33 pp.; Milewski, T., "Stosunki językowe polsko-pruskie", *SO* 18.21-84 (1947); idem, "Chronologia i przyczyny mazurzenia", *ZIJFil* 2.5-57 (1956).

[37] Rudnicki, M., "Najnowsze prace o mazurzeniu i własne uwagi", *Por. Jęz.*, 1955, pp. 185-193; Koneczna, H., "Co to jest mazurzenie?", *Por. Jęz.*, 1.1-17 (1953); Brajerski, T., "Jak mogło powstać polskie mazurzenie?", *BPTJ* 13.1-7 (1954); Kuryłowicz, J., "Uwagi o mazurzeniu", *BPTJ* 13.9-19 (1954).

[38] Taszycki, W., *Dawność tzw. mazurzenia w języku polskim*, Warsaw, 1948, 33 pp.; idem, "Nowy argument za późnością mazurzenia", *BPTJ* 13.51-56 (1954).

[39] Taszycki, W., "Dlaczego w wyrazach rodzimych jednakowo oznaczamy samogłoski nosowe i co z tego wynika", *JP* 29.62-68 (1949); idem, "Pierwsze druki polskie rozróżniające samogłoski nosowe", *SFPSł* 3.129-134 (1958); Rospond, S., *JP* 32 (1952); Stieber, Z., "Przyczynki do historii polskich rymów. I. Rymy sandomierskie XVI i XVII wieku", *JP* 30.110-113 (1950); Kuraszkiewicz, W., "Znaczenie druków renesansowych w rozwoju polskich samogłosek nosowych", *JP* 33.245-254 (1953); Bargiełówna, M., "Samogłoski nosowe w rękopisach polskich pierwszej połowy XVI wieku", *Rosp. ŁTN* 2.159-192 (1955).

change of -*x*> -*k*,[40] believed to be (by Nitsch and others) of old Małopolska origin The question of its dialectal isogloss has recently been restudied by Dejna.[41] The "mazurzenie" controversy has also given rise to a more detailed philological examination of Old Polish texts, to the study of orthography, printing conventions and foreign influences concerning the literary monuments.[42]

There has been far less activity in the field of Polish historical morphology. The question of "mazurzenie" has had repercussions here too, inasmuch as it affected the flexional endings of the noun, as shown by Kuraszkiewicz and Moszyński.[43] 18th-century flexion has been discussed by Bajerowa,[44] while the changes in the plural desinences have been examined in a series of articles.[45] The changes in adjectives and pronouns have been investigated in their formal aspects, and with a view to phonological developments.[46] The fate of prepositions[47] and of the superlative prefixes in adjectives and adverbs[48] has been taken up by several scholars.

[40] Taszycki, W., "O małopolskich formach "grok" 'groch', "na nogak" 'na nogach', "robiłek" 'robiłech = robiłem'", *JP* 29.195-202 (1949); idem, "Południowo-zachodnia granica mazurzenia i przejścia -*ch* w -*k*", *SAU*, 51 (1950).

[41] Dejna, K., "Północnowschodnia izoglosa małopolskiego przejścia -*ch* w -*k*", *Sprawozdania ŁTN*, 16, fasc. 3.1-4 (1961).

[42] Rospond, S., *Druki mazurskie XVI w.* (Olsztyn, 1948), 126 pp.; idem, "Mazurzenie w oświetleniu filologicznym", *SAU*, 50 (1949); idem, *Dawność mazurzenia w świetle grafiki staropolskiej* (Wrocław, 1957), 503 pp. 16 tables; idem, "Czy mazurzyli Małopolanie na przełomie XV-XVI wieku?", *JP* 29.23-27 (1949); Taszycki, W., "Czas i miejsce powstania Psałterza puławskiego", *Por. Jęz.*, 10.8-17 (1954); Kuraszkiewicz, W., "Psałterz puławski nie pochodzi z drugiej połowy XV wieku", *Por. Jęz.* 1955, pp. 107-112; Zembatówna, M., "Analiza historyczno-dialektologiczna Psałterza puławskiego", *Zeszyty Naukowe Uniw. Wrocł. im. B. Bieruta.*, Ser. A., 5.41-63 (1957); Bobowska-Kowalska, M., "Przynależność dialektyczna Biblii królowej Zofii", *ZUJFil* 6.15-148 (1960), + tables.

[43] Kuraszkiewicz, W., *Oboczność -'ev//-'ov w dawnej polszczyźnie i w dzisiejszych gwarach* (Wrocław, 1951), 48 pp. + tables; Moszyński, L., *Wyrównania deklinacyjne w związku z mazurzeniem polskim, ruskim, połabskim* (Wrocław, 1960), 167 pp. + tables + 5 maps.

[44] Bajerowa, I., "Uwagi o rozwoju niektórych polskich form fleksyjnych w XVIII w.", in *Zeszyty Naukowe. Sekcja Językoznawstwa* (*Prace Katedry Języka Polskiego*) (Katowice, 1959), pp. 5-18.

[45] Turska, H., "Mianownik l. mn. typu *chłopy*, *draby* w języku ogólnopolskim", *JP* 33.129-155 (1953); Kuryłowicz, J., "Męski acc.-gen. i nom.-acc. w języku polskim", *SAU*, 48 (1947); Jankowska, B., Zawadzki, Z., "Narzędnik liczby mnogiej rzeczowników w historii języka polskiego", *Zeszyty Naukowe Uniw. M. Kopernika w Toruniu, Nauki Hum. – Społ. 3. Filologia Polska* 2.3-36 (1960) + tables; Lubaś, W., "Oboczność rzeczownikowej końcówki miejscownika l. mn. -*ach*//-*âch* w historii i dialektach języka polskiego", *ZUJFil* 6.149-183 (1960) + table.

[46] Lindertówna, B., "Końcówka gen.-dat.-loc. sg. -*e* i -*ej* w odmianie zaimkowo-przymiotnikowej rodzaju żeńskiego", *SFPSł* 2.139-180 (1957); Koneczna, H., Formy zaimków dzierżawczych w języku staropolskim", *SKJWar*, 1952; Lindert, B., "Forma genetivu i dativu singularis zaimka osobowego "mnie" obok "mienie" w języku staropolskim", *Rocz. Slaw.* 18.15-19 (1956).

[47] Karaś, M., "Historia i geografia prepozycji *ot*//*od* w języku polskim", *SFPSł* 1.59-110 (1955) + tables; Stieber, Z., "Uwagi o rozwoju polskich przyimków", *SAU* 47.308-310 (1946); Rospond, S., "Z badań nad przeszłością polskiego języka literackiego, I, Przyimkowe i prefiksalne *s*(*e*)//*z*(*e*)", *JP* 31.211-219 (1951); Klemensiewicz, Z., Bajerowa, I., "Polska oboczność e//ø w przyimkach i przedrostkach", *SFPSł* 1.162-202 (1955); Bajerowa, I., "Oboczność *k*//*ku* w języku polskim", in *Zeszyty Naukowe. Sekcja Językoznawstwa* (*Prace Katedry Języka Polskiego*) (Katowice, 1959), pp. 85-94.

[48] Jędrzejewska, M., Stieber, Z., "Przedrostki stopnia najwyższego *na* w dawnej polszczyźnie i dzisiejszych gwarach", *JP* 31.155-158 (1951); Koneczna, H., "Z historii przysłówków stopnia w języku polskim", *SKJWar*, 4 (1952).

Among the diachronic studies on Polish derivation, deserving of attention are the monographs and articles devoted to the formation of numerals, of prepositions,[49] of 16th-century expressive derivation and compound-formation.[50]

Polish historical syntax has so far received little elaboration.[51]

The investigation of the origin and subsequent development of the Polish literary language, which depends for its solutions on dialectology, stylistics, and literary history, has been viewed as the most urgent problem of modern Polish linguistics. The distinction of a "Kultursprache" and "Schriftsprache" (due to Brückner), and the awareness of various stylistic and social layers in the formation of a literary language, have partially dulled the edge of the controversy on the Wielkopolska vs. Małopolska origin of the Polish literary language. It has become clear that a strictly geographical approach oversimplifies the history of a literary or standard language. The champions of the "Wielkopolska hypothesis" are, however, of the opinion that medieval Polish, as represented by its literary monuments, was a fully developed, unified language,[52] while according to a more moderate view, it had a preponderance of Wielkopolska features with an admixture of other dialectal traits.[53] The adherents of the "Małopolska hypothesis" believe, on the other hand, that medieval Polish, with its narrow social (aristocratic and ecclesiastical) base and purely religious texts, can hold no claim to being a unified, national vehicle of culture.[54] Stieber has pointed out that

[49] Zwoliński, P., *Liczebniki zespołowe typu samotrzeć w języku polskim na tle słowiańskim i indoeuropejskim* (Wrocław, 1954), 91 pp.; Brodowska, M., "Historyczne procesy przekształceń polskiego celownika w formy przyimkowe", *SFPSł* 1.1-58 (1955).

[50] Zaleski, J., "Wyrazy zdrobniałe w polszczyźnie XVI wieku", *ZUJFil* 4.93-184 (1958); idem, "Geneza funkcji przymiotnikowego sufiksu *-awy* /typ *białawy, gorzkawy*/", *JP* 37.351-357 (1957); Ostrowska, E., "Z historii przymiotników złożonych typu *biało-czerwony* i *jasno-niebieski*", *JP* 28 (1948).

[51] Ostrowska, E., "Historyczna składnia komparatywu względnego w języku polskim", *SAU* 46.272-276 (1945); Rospond, S., *BPTJ*, 8 (1948); Brodowska, M., *BPTJ*, 14, (1953); Bartula, Cz., "Ze studiów nad składnią Kazań Świętokrzyskich", *SFPSł* 2.7-39 (1957).

[52] Lehr-Spławiński, T., "Jeszcze o pochodzeniu polskiego języka literackiego", *JP* 37.1-19 (1957); Urbańczyk, W., "W Sprawie polskiego języka literackiego", *JP* 30.79-109, 145-160 (1950); idem, "Dzisiejszy stan sporów o pochodzeniu polskiego języka literackiego", *Slavia* 20.1-39 (1950/1) + 2 maps; idem, "Głos w dyskusji o pochodzeniu języka literackiego", *Pam. lit.* 44.196-215 (1955). Reprinted in *Pochodzenie polskiego języka literackiego* (Wrocław, 1956), pp. 82-101; Rospond, S., "Problem genezy polskiego języka literackiego. Uwagi polemiczne do artykułów T. Milewskiego i W. Taszyckiego", *Pam. lit.* 44.512-547 (1954). Reprinted in *Pochodzenie polskiego języka literackiego* (Wrocław, 1956), p. 117-177; Rudnicki, M., "Najnowsze prace o pochodzeniu polskiego języka literackiego", *Przeg. zach.* 11.209-232 (1955); idem, "W sprawie pochodzenia polskiego języka literackiego. Pokłosie dyskusji", *Por. Jęz.* 1952 (5), pp. 1-12.

[53] Kuraszkiewicz, W., *Pochodzenie polskiego języka literackiego w świetle wyników dialektologii historycznej* (Wrocław, 1953), 121 pp. Reprinted in *Pochodzenie polskiego języka literackiego* (Wrocław, 1956), pp. 242-336; idem, "Tło społeczne rozwoju polskiego języka literackiego", *Z dziejów powstawania językow narodowych i literackich* (Warsaw, 1956), pp. 37-96; idem, "Z rozważań o pochodzeniu polskiego języka literackiego", *Pochodzenie polskiego języka literackiego* (Wrocław, 1956), pp. 18-29.

[54] Taszycki, W., "Powstanie i pochodzenie polskiego języka literackiego. Kraków kolebką literackiej polszczyzny", *Twórczość* 5.100-117 (1949); idem, "Geneza polskiego języka literackiego w świetle faktów historycznojęzykowych", *LP* 3.206-247 (1951). Reprinted in *Pochodzenie polskiego języka*

the early Polish literary language can best be considered a compromise-formula of various dialects, shaped simultaneously under the influence of other Slavic languages, notably Czech.[55] The functional varieties of the older and modern Polish literary languages have been re-examined by Klemensiewicz and Urbańczyk,[56] whereas the questions of literary languages and of their formation was on the agenda of a special linguistic conference.[57]

In order to gain a clearer picture of the social and literary status of 16th and 17th-century Polish, some linguists have investigated the attitudes towards the language, as expressed by contemporary writers and grammarians.[58] Various works have also probed into the growing importance of Polish since the 15th century as a vehicle of national unity and culture.[59] The relation of Polish to other Slavic languages, particularly to Czech, its older literary model, has been investigated in a number of important publications.[60] Recent studies have also shown the impact of Ukrainian

---

*literackiego* (Wrocław, 1956), pp. 30-59; Milewski, T., "Genealogia społeczna polskiego języka literackiego", *Wiedza i Życie* 19.261-271 (1950); idem, "Nowe prace o pochodzeniu polskiego języka literackiego", *Pam. lit.* 43.312-334 (1952); Taszycki, W., Milewski, T., "Polski język literacki powstał w Małopolsce?", *Pochodzenie polskiego języka literackiego* (Wrocław, 1956), pp. 364-436; Milewski, T., "Rola kościoła w kształtowaniu polskiego języka literackiego", *Znak* 4.408-425, 484-485 (1958); idem, "Le problème des origines du polonais littéraire", *IJSLP* 1/2.133-142 (1959); idem, "Główne etapy rozwoju polskiego języka literackiego", *Ruch literacki* 1/2.19-28 (1960).

55 Stieber, Z., "Głos w dyskusji o pochodzeniu polskiego języka literackiego", *Pam. lit.* 43.917-932 (1952). Reprinted in *Pochodzenie polskiego języka literackiego* (Wrocław, 1956), pp. 102-116; idem, "Rol' otdel'nyx dialektov v formirovanii pol'skogo literaturnogo jazyka", *VJa* 3.25-45 (1956).

56 Klemensiewicz, Z., *O różnych odmianach współczesnej polszczyzny. Próba charakterystyki odmian współczesnej polszczyzny z uwzględnieniem przypuszczalnych warunków ich początkowego rozwoju* (Warsaw, 1953), 96 pp. Reprinted in *Pochodzenie polskiego języka literackiego* (Wrocław, 1956), pp. 178-241; idem, *Czynniki sprawcze w rozwoju polszczyzny w dobie Odrodzenia* (Warsaw, 1954), 47 pp.; Urbańczyk, S., "Ogólne warunki powstawania słowiańskich języków narodowych i literackich we wczesnym średniowieczu (na przykładzie polskim)", *Z polskich studiów slawistycznych. Prace językoznawcze...* (Warsaw, 1958), pp. 7-23; idem, "Rola wielkich pisarzy złotego wieku na tle innych czynników kształtujących normy języka literackiego", *Odrodzenie w Polsce*, 3, *Historia języka*, pt. 1 (Warsaw, 1960), pp. 425-453 + table. Discussion, pp. 454-465.

57 *Z dziejów powstawania języków narodowych i literackich.* Materiały metodologiczne konferencji szkoleniowej PAN, Zakopane, marzec 1955. Edited by Z. Stieber (Warsaw, 1956), 153 pp.

58 Rospond, S., *Studia nad językiem polskim XVI wieku* (Wrocław, 1949), 534 pp.; Zwoliński, P., "Wypowiedzi gramatyków XVI i XVII wieku o dialektyzmach w ówczesnej polszczyźnie", *Pam. lit.* 43.375-407 (1952); idem, "Gramatyki języka polskiego z XVII wieku, jako źródło poznania ówczesnej polszczyzny", *Por. Jęz.* 7.251-260, 8.310-321, 9.356-369 (1956).

59 Taszycki, W., *Obrońcy języka polskiego, Wiek XV-XVIII* (Wrocław, 1953), lxxxix + 393 pp.; Mayenowa, M. R., *Walka o język w życiu i literaturze staropolskiej* (Warsaw, 1955²), 216 pp. + 4 tables; Mikulski, T., "Walka o język polski w czasach Oświecenia", *Pam. lit.* 42.796-815 (1951); Borecki, M., "Walka o język polski w dobie pierwszego bezkrólewia (1572-1573)", *SFPSl* 2.40-57 (1957); Taszycki, W., "Uprawa języka polskiego w dobie Odrodzenia", *ZNUJFil* 8.7-26 (1961); Zarębski, I., *Rola języka polskiego w nauczaniu szkolnym w Polsce w XVI w.* (Wrocław, 1955), 81 pp.

60 Urbańczyk, V., "Z dawnych stosunków językowych polsko-czeskich. l. Biblia królowej Zofii a staroczeskie przekłady Pisma św.", *RWF* 67(2).88-171 (1946); Lehr-Spławiński, T., "Dědičné kulturní svazky polsko-české", *ČČM* 116.26-37 (1947); Stieber, Z., "O czechizmach w kronice Galla", *Por. Jęz.* pp. 245-248 (1956); idem, Les éléments tchèques dans le polonais littéraire", *RÉS* 39.7-16 (1962); Siatkowski, J., "Czechizmy w języku Jana z Koszyczek", *IJSLP* 1/2.143-176 (1959).

(through the writers of the "Kresy") on the formation of 16th-17th-century Polish'.[61]

Polish dialectology, founded and developed by Nitsch, reached new heights in the post-war period. It is no longer the concern of a few individuals, but is centered in well-endowed institutes and pursued by teams of dialectologists. However, the objectives and methods of dialectology have remained essentially the same as they were for Nitsch: the main goal of dialect studies is viewed as retrospective, i.e. as a contribution to diachronic linguistics, and, in the first place, to the reconstruction of the history of the literary language. It is not surprising that some Polish linguists have proposed to include in the domain of historical dialectology even the philological study of texts; this expansionist position has met with the opposition of Nitsch himself.[62] The historical orientation continues, however, to pervade even descriptive studies of Polish dialects. Nitsch was, furthermore, indifferent to phonological theory (despite the closeness of Cracow to Prague); but he was an excellent phonetician with a strong intuitive grasp of phonemic realities. And it is noteworthy that there is not a single consistent and comprehensive phonological description of any Polish dialect. Problems of methodology have, nevertheless, come into the forefront of Polish dialectology, which is presently divided into two schools: one, with its centers in Cracow and in the II Dialectological Laboratory in Warsaw (directed by Stieber), focuses attention on the qualitative differences of sounds in order to establish the basic sound-patterns of each dialect; the other, with its center in the I Dialectological Laboratory in Warsaw (under the direction of Doroszewski), defends a quentitative approach intended to record the minutest variations in the sounds of a dialect. The first is, in other words, interested in "langue", whereas the second emphasizes the priority of "parole", as an index to prospective historical tendencies. [63] In the dialectal descriptions of this school the phonemic profiles of individual dialacts consequently appear blurred.

The only synthesis of the Polish dialects remains Nitsch's "The Dialects of the Polish Language". Urbańczyk's textbook enlarges on it only in its treatment of derivation and syntax.[64] The "Small Atlas of Polish Dialects", of which four volumes have so far appeared, is the most significant post-war contribution to Polish dialectology.[65]

Despite the new and concerted effort to describe dialectal areas which have been poorly investigated before the war, Wielkopolska has, as before, received little atten-

[61] Hrabec, S., *Elementy kresowe w języku niektórych pisarzy polskich XVI i XVII w.* (Toruń, 1949), 159 pp.

[62] Taszycki, W., "Co to jest dialektologia historyczna", *ZUJFil* 2.59-61 (1956); Kuraszkiewicz, W., *Pochodzenie polskiego języka literackiego w świetle wyników dialektologii historycznej* (Wrocław, 1953); Nitsch, K., "Co to jest dialektologia historyczna", *BPTJ* 8 (1948).

[63] Doroszewski, W., "Przedmiot i metody dialektologii", *Por. Jęz.* 1.1-8, 2.1-7, 3.2-10, 4.4-12 (1953); idem, "Strukturalizm a dialektologia", *SPAN* 1/2.26-34 (1958).

[64] Nitsch, K., "Dialekty języka polskiego", *Język polski i jego historia...*, 2.238-343 (1915). Reprinted in *Gramatyka języka polskiego* (Cracow, 1923), pp. 409-520 and in *Wybór*, 4.7-115. Separate publication (Wrocław, 1957), 122 pp. + 3 maps; Urbańczyk, S., *Zarys dialektologii polskiej* (Warsaw, 1953), 78 pp. + 2 maps.

[65] Nitsch, K., and Urbańczyk, S., *Mały atlas gwar polskich*, Vol. 1-4 (Wrocław, 1957-1960).

tion.[66] The largest number of monographs and articles has been written on the Silesian and Northern Polish dialects. The former have been described both from descriptive and historical points of view by Bąk, Dejna and P. Gołąb, whereas Rospond has provided valuable studies on the history of Polish and Polish documents in Silesia.[67] The study of Northern Polish dialects, directed by Doroszewski and Turska, has yielded a significant number of new publications.[68] Several studies (some of them prepared before the war) have also appeared on the dialects of Mazovia.[69] Dialects of other regions have been treated in several monographs and articles.[70]

Certain phonetic developments have been described by Taszycki from the standpoint of historical dialectology.[71] Questions of derivation have been raised by Chludzińska and Zaręba, who points our their neglect in available dialectological descriptions.[72]

Dialect lexicology, initiated scientifically by Nitsch,[73] has in the last few years witnessed a spectacular expansion. Here are to be noted the studies of Zaręba on the

[66] Lenart, P., and Zagórski, Z., *O mowie ludowej w Wielkopolsce* (Poznań, 1962), 26 pp., 2 maps; Ziętkówna, A., "Mazurzenie w południowej Wielkopolsce", *JP* 36.132-138 (1956) + map.

[67] Bąk, S., *Dialekty śląskie*, *Oblicze Ziem Odzyskanych*, 1, *Dolny Śląsk*, pt. 2 (Wrocław, 1948), p. 285-332; Bąk, S., *Gwary ludowe na Dolnym Śląsku*, pt. 1, Głosownia (Poznań, 1956), 129 pp.; idem, "Z historii badań nad gwarami dolnośląskimi", *Zesz. Nauk. U. Wrocł.*, Ser. A, 5.65-130 (1957) + map; Dejna, K., "Z najnowszej dialektologii śląskiej", *JP* 29.206-215 (1949); Gołąb, P., *Gwara Schodni i okolicy*, (Wrocław, 1955), 202 pp. + 3 maps; Rospond, S., *Zabytki języka polskiego na Śląsku* (Wrocław-Katowice), 1948, 264 pp.; *Z badań nad przeszłością dialektu śląskiego*. Edited by S. Rospond, vol. 1-3 (vol. 2 with J. Mayer); Rospond, S., *Dzieje polszczyzny śląskiej* (Katowice, 1959), 480 pp.

[68] Doroszewski, W., Koneczna, H., Pomianowska, W., "Gwary Warmii i Mazur", *Konferencja Pomorska* (Warsaw, 1956), pp. 113-148; Zduńska, H., "Spólgłoski wargowe i wargowo-zębowe palatalne w wygłosie na Warmii, Mazurach i Mazowszu", *Por. Jęz.* 1957, pp. 75-79 + 2 maps; *Studia fonetyczne z Warmii i Mazur*, 1. *Konsonantyzm*. (Wrocław, 1959), 237 pp. + 51 maps; Basara, A., Basara, J., Wójtowicz, J., Zduńska, H., *Studia fonetyczne z Warmii i Mazur*, I: *Konsonantyzm* (Wrocław, 1959), 237 pp. + 51 maps; Turska, H., "Dialekt ziemi chełmińskiej i jego ekspansja na dialekty sąsiednie", *Konferencja Pomorska*, pp. 87-112; Górnowicz, H., "Zmiany w dialekcie malborskim w ostatnim pięćdziesięcioleciu", *Rozp. ŁTN* 8.157-184 (1962).

[69] Friedrich, H., *Gwara kurpiowska, Fonetyka* (Warsaw, 1955), 132 pp.; Doroszewski, W., *Studia fonetyczne z kilku wsi mazowieckich* (Wrocław, 1955), 72 pp.; Furdal, A., *Mazowieckie dyspalatalizacje spółgłosek wargowych miękkich* (Wrocław, 1955), 64 pp. + 4 maps.

[70] Stieber, Z., *Problem językowej i etnicznej odrębności Podhala* (Łodz, 1947), 19 pp.; Gołąb, Z., "O zróżnicowaniu wewnętrznym gwary podhalańskiej", *JP* 34 (1954); Cyran, W., *Gwary polskie w okolicach Siedlec* (Łódź, 1960), 227 pp. + map; Pawłowski, E., *Gwara podegrodzka wraz z próbą wyznaczenia południowo-zachodniej granicy gwar sądeckich* (Wrocław, 1955), 304 pp. + 3 maps; Moszyński, L., "Szkic monograficzny gwary wsi Rudy, powiat Puławy", *SFPSł* 3.7-60 (1958); Sobierajski, Z., *Gwary Kujawskie* (Poznan, 1952), iv + 128 pp. + map; Lindertówna, B., "Gwara gminy Spiczyn w województwie lubelskim", *SFPSł* 1.203-222 (1955).

[71] Taszycki, W., "Dwa rozdziały z historycznej dialektologii polskiej. 1: Przejście połączenia *tart* w *tert*. 2: Przyrostki *-k*, *-c* i formy podobne", *SAU* 48.311-316 (1947); idem, "O gwarowych formach *mgleć, mgły, moglić się, moglitwa* itp. (Rozdział z historycznej dialektologii polskiej)", *SFPSł* 2.230-246.

[72] Chludzińska, J., "Przymiotniki w gwarach Warmii i Mazur. Uwagi słowotwórczo-semantyczne", *Por. Jęz.*, 1956, pp. 21-27; Zaręba, A., "Uwagi o geografii słowotwórczej", *BPTJ* 16.165-174 (1957).

[73] Nitsch, K., "Z geografii wyrazów polskich", *Rocz. Slaw.* 8.60-148 (1918). Reprinted in *Wybór* 2.20-85; idem, *Studia z historii polskiego słownictwa* (Cracow, 1948), xxii + 193 pp.

names of colors, by Bartnicka on the names of mushrooms (in Eastern dialects), and by Kaczmarek on the names of birds (in Wielkopolska).[74] A comparative dictionary of three Małopolska villages was prepared by Kucała.[75] The bulk of lexicological work deals, however, with Warmia and Mazury, covering a large variety of lexical fields.[76]

The exploration of dialects transitional between Polish and other Slavic languages has likewise received new impetus. Of special importance here are the studies devoted to the Polish-Czech and Polish-Ukrainian dialects.[77]

Social dialects have been dealt with in two important works: thief-argot was described exhaustively by Ułaszyn, and the argot of wandering merchants by Budziszewska. Remarks on party-slang are found in an article by Karaś.[78]

Polish linguistics counts new achievements in lexicography and lexicology. Of foremost importance in this area is the preparation and publication of dictionaries of the contemporary language and of various historical periods, as well as the theoretical studies which emanated from their research. The epochal dictionary of Linde and the so-called "Warsaw dictionary"[79] have long been superannuated. In addition to Doroszewski's dictionary of the contemporary language, there have now appeared several volumes of the new normative dictionary of the Polish language.[80] The history

[74] Zaręba, A., *Nazwy barw w dialektach i historii języka polskiego* (Wrocław, 1954), 204 pp. + 2 maps; idem, "Z geografii i historii synonimów koloru", *JP* 32 (1952); Bartnicka, B., "Nazwy grzybów w dialektach wschodnich Polski", *Por. Jęz.*, 1958, pp. 346-351; Kaczmarek, L., "Z geografii wielkopolskich nazw ptaków, wilga", *JP* 37.55-62 (1957) + map.

[75] Kucała, M., *Porównawczy słownik trzech wsi małopolskich* (Wrocław, 1957), 408 pp.

[76] Symoni-Sułkowska, J., *Słownictwo Warmii i Mazur. Transport i komunikacja* (Wrocław, 1958), 120 pp. + 17 maps; Horodyska, H., *Słownictwo Warmii i Mazur. Hodowla* (Wrocław, 1958), 108 pp., 35 maps; Jurkowski, E., Łapiński, I., Szymczak, M., *Słownictwo Warmii i Mazur. Stopnie pokrewieństwa, życie społeczne i zawody* (Wrocław, 1959), 99 pp.; Mocarska-Falińska, B., *Słownictwo Warmii i Mazur. Uprawa i obróbka lnu* (Wrocław, 1959), 219 pp.; Kupiszewski, W., Wegiełek-Januszewska, Z., *Słownictwo Warmii i Mazur. Astronomia ludowa, miary czasu i meteorologia* (Wrocław, 1959), 103 pp., 7 maps; Judycka, I., *Słownictwo z zakresu uprawy roli w gwarach Pomorza Mazowieckiego. Stan obecny, historia i związki z terenami przyległymi* (Wrocław-Warsaw-Cracow, 1961), 168 pp., 8 maps; Siatkowski, J., *Słownictwo Warmii i Mazur. Budownictwo i obróbka drewna* (Wrocław, 1958), 140 pp. + 64 maps.

[77] Dejna, K., *Polsko-laskie pogranicze językowe na terenie Polski*, vol. 1 (Łódź, 1951), Atlas, 408 pp. (includes 364 maps); vol. 2 (Łódź, 1952), 270 pp. + 16 maps; idem, "Z zagadnień polsko-czeskiego pogranicza językowego", *Česko-polský sborník vedeckých prací*, 2 (Prague, 1955), pp. 113-131; Topolińska, Z., "Stosunki akcentowe na pograniczu polsko-czeskim", *Slavia* 29.582-587 (1960); Urbańczyk, S., "Czesko-polska granica etniczna w średniowieczu w świetle nazw miejscowych", *SAU*, 47 (1946); Dejna, K., "Elementy polskie w gwarach zachodniomałoruskich", *JP* 28.72-79 (1948); Zdancewicz, T., "Z zagadnień gwar przejściowych pogranicza polsko-białoruskiego," in *Z polskich studiów slawistycznych. l. Prace językoznawcze*... (Warsaw, 1958), pp. 205-215.

[78] Ułaszyn, H., *Język złodziejski* (Łódź, 1951), 90 pp.; Budziszewska, W., *Żargon ochweśnicki* (Łódź, 1957), 108 pp. + map; Karaś, "Kika uwag o polskiej gwarze partyjnej przed pierwszą wojną światową", *JP* 21.15-23 (1951).

[79] Linde, S. B., *Słownik języka polskiego* (Warsaw, 1807-14), 6 vols. (1953[3]); Karłowicz, J., Kryński, A., Niedźwiedzki, W., *Słownik języka polskiego* (Warsaw, 1900-1927). Reprinted 1952-3[2].

[80] Doroszewski, W., *Słownik współczesnego języka polskiego* (Warsaw, 1951), xviii + 159 pp.; Doroszewski, W., Skorupka, S., Wieczorkiewicz, B., *Słownik języka polskiego*, vol. 1-3 (Warsaw, 1959-61).

of Polish lexicography and some general lexicological problems have been discussed by Doroszewski, whereas Skorupka has devoted a number of important essays to Polish idioms, phraseology, synonymy and their stylistic functions.[81] There is also a number of new special dictionaries, such as the dictionary of synonyms or of legal and military terminology.[82] Of a peculiar interest are the dictionaries recording terms of war, of concentration camps, of Polish uprisings and of drunkards.[83]

The greatest effort has been made in the field of Polish historical lexicology. The most significant works here are the dictionary of Old Polish up to the 16th century (prepared under the editorship of Urbańczyk), and the dictionary of 16th-century Polish of which there has so far appeared only a pilot study.[84] A Mickiewicz dictionary and a dictionary of 17th-century Polish are likewise in preparation. These monumental studies are not expected to be completed before another decade. Among the lexical works, one should also note the historical dictionary of nautical terms and the studies of Skorupka (on the genesis of some idiomatic expressions), and of Zaręba.[85]

Polish etymological research registers an important new contribution: the Polish etymological dictionary of Sławski, of which there have so far appeared seven fascicles. This dictionary surpasses the older work of Brückner in precision, in richness of quotations and of bibliographical references, and in its attention to linguistic geography. Of high value are the critical reviews of this dictionary by K. Moszyński.[86]

Closely related to the increased emphasis on lexicology is the progress of Polish onomastics, which found a solid foundation in the pre-war works of Rozwadowski, Kozierowski and Taszycki. Faced with the practical need for re-naming locations in the newly acquired Western and Northern Polish territories, the Poles have produced large dictionaries of place-names, many of which concealed under their previous

[81] Doroszewski, W., *Z zagadnień leksykografii polskiej* (Warsaw, 1954), 147 pp.; Skorupka, S., "Kompozycja grup frazeologicznych", *Por. Jęz.* 4.19-25 (1950); Skorupka, S., "Z zagadnień frazeologii", *Sprawozdania TNW* 4.147-180 (1952); idem, "Frazeologia a semantyka", *Por. Jęz.* 7.9-16, 8.17-25 (1952); idem, "Wyrazy bliskoznaczne i ich wartość stylistyczna", *Por. Jęz.* 4.8-15, 5.13-19 (1954); idem, "Frazeologia a stylistyka", *Por. Jęz.* 1960, pp. 97-111.

[82] Skorupka, S., *Słownik wyrazów bliskoznacznych* (Warsaw, 1957), 448 pp. (1958[2], 1959[3]); *Słownik terminów wojskowych* (Warsaw, 1958), 325 pp.; Wróblewski, B., *Język prawny i prawniczy* (Cracow, 1948), V + 184 pp.

[83] Ułaszyn, H., Wojna i język. "Słownictwo polskie z drugiej wojny światowej", *Rozp. ŁTN* 5.7-41 (1957); Kuraszkiewicz, W., *Język polski w obozie koncentracyjnym* (Lublin, 1947), 47 pp.; Milik, J. T., "Słownictwo powstańcze", *JP* 27.97-100 (1947); Tuwim, J., *Polski słownik pijacki i antologia bachiczna* (Warsaw, 1959), 354 pp. + table.

[84] *Słownik staropolski*, edited by K. Nitsch, Z. Klemensiewicz, S. Urbańczyk, J. Sarafewicz, Vol. 1-3 (Warsaw, 1953-1961); *Słownik polszczyzny XVI wieku. Zeszyt próbny*. Edited by S Bąk (Wrocław, 1956), lix 118 pp.

[85] Drapella, W. A., *Ster. Ze studiów nad kształtowaniem się pojęć morskich. Wiek XV-XX.* (Gdańsk, 1955), 95 pp.; Skorupka, S., "Idiomatyzmy frazeologiczne w języku polskim i ich geneza", *Slavjanskaja filologija* 3.124-155 (1958); Zaręba, A., "Z geografii i historii wyrazów ijpolskich", *SFPSł* 3.135-186 (1958).

[86] Brückner, A., *Słownik etymologiczny języka polskiego* (Cracow, 1927), xiv + 805 pp. (Warsaw, 1957[2]); Sławski, F., *Słownik etymologiczny języka polskiego* (Cracow, 1952-1961), Vol. I-II, fasc. 1-7. K. Moszyński's reviews in *JP*, 1953 ff.

German shapes, original Old Polish, and even Lichitic forms.[87] The most extensive toponymic studies have been written on the dialects of Mazovia and of Warmia-Mazury.[88] More and more emphasis in Polish toponomastics is being placed on the analysis of the derivational structure of Slavic and Polish place-names. This approach is exemplified in the monographs of Karaś, Bajerowa and Rospond, and in a number of recent articles.[89] It is presently being applied also in the field of Slavic and Polish hydronymy.

In addition to the reprinted work of Taszycki,[90] there have appeared impressive monographic studies on Polish proper names by Kozierowski and Rospond.[91] Zwoliński has traced the derivational transformation of the element *-sław*, whereas others have analyzed the foreing origin of proper names, their historical attestation and dialectal distribution.[92]

Child-language has been studied from the vantage point of both linguistics and psychology. The latter line of investigation is represented in the contributions of Szuman and Przetacznikowa, the former in those of Kaczmarek and Smoczyński, who operate with modern linguistic concepts. Geppertowa has tackled a syntactical problem of child-language.[93]

[87] Rospond, S., *Słownik nazw geograficznych Polski zachodniej i północnej* (Wrocław-Warsaw, 1951), 794 pp. + 3 maps; Hrabec, S., *Nazwy dzielnic i okolic Gdańska* (Poznań, 1949), 53 pp.; Dejna, K., "Terenowe nazwy śląskie", *Onom.* 1.103 ff. (1956); Rospond, S., *Śląskie studia toponomastyczne...*, pt. 1, *Topographica*, *Rozp. Kom. Jęz.* 2.31-64 (1959); Rudnicki, M., "Nazwy Odry i jej ważniejszych dopływów", in *Monografia Odry* (Poznań, 1948), pp. 19-69.

[88] Zierhoffer, K., *Nazwy miejscowe północnego Mazowsza* (Wrocław, 1957), 417 pp. + 6 maps; Wolff, A., "Nazwy miejscowe na Mazowszu", *Onom.* 1.60-116 (1955) + table, 2.69-94, 2.211-212 (1956); Zabrocki, L., *Nazewnictwo, Warmia i Mazury*, I (Poznań, 1953).

[89] Karaś, M., *Nazwy miejscowe typu Podgóra, Zalas w języku polskim i w innych językach słowiańskich* (Wrocław, 1955), 147 pp.; idem, "O staropolskich imionach dwuczłonowych zachowanych w nazwach miejscowych", *Onom.* 2.260-281, 2.431 (1956); Bajerowa, I., "Polskie nazwy miejscowe typu *Dębe, Orlo*", *Onom.* 3.1-42, 3.293-323 (1957), 12 maps; Safarewiczowa, H., *Nazwy miejscowe typu Mroczkowizna, Klimontowszczyzna* (Wrocław, 1956), 352 pp. + map; Karplukówna, M., "Polskie nazwy miejscowe od imion kobiecych", *SFPSl* 1.111-161 (1955); Pałucki, W., "Nazwy miejscowe typu *Białystok, Ponikłystok*", *Onom.* 7.45-81 (1961).

[90] Taszycki, W., *Rozprawy i studia polonistyczne*, I, *Onomastyka*, (Wrocław, 1958), 345 pp. + maps.

[91] Kozierowski, S., *Nazwiska, przezwiska, przydomki, imiona polskie niektórych typów słowiańskich* (Poznań, 1948), 1, xvi + 128 pp.; 2, pt. 1, xx + 85 pp.; Rospond, S., *Nazwiska Ślązaków* (Opole, 1960), 116 pp.

[92] Zwoliński, P., "Funkcja słowotwórcza elementu -sław w staropolskich imionach osobowych", *BPTJ* X (1950); Safarewicz, J., "Polskie imiona osobowe pochodzenia litewskiego", *JP* 30.113-119 (1950); Karplukówna, M., "Z badań nad polskim nazewnictwem osobowym XV i początku XVI wieku", *Onom.* 3.179-187 (1957) + table; 3.381-392, 3.569 (1957); Zaręba, A., "Polskie imiona ludowe. Problematyka zagadnienia", *Onom.* 3. 129-178, 3.419-446, 3.570-571 (1957); Natanson-Leski, J., "Nazwy plemienne w Polsce", *Onom.* 5.195-229, 5.415-449, 5.583-584 (1959).

[93] Szuman, S., "Rozwój imion własych i rzeczowników osobowych w mowie dziecka", *Dziesięciolecie WSP* (Cracow, 1957), pp. 81-118; Przetacznikowa, M., "Rozwój i rola przysłówków w mowie i myśleniu dziecka do lat trzech", *BPTJ* 15.139-193 (1956); Kaczmarek, L., *Kształtowanie się mowy dziecka* (Poznań, 1953), 91 pp.; Smoczyński, P., *Przyswajanie przez dziecko podstaw systemu językowego* (Łódź, 1955), 233 pp.; Geppertowa, L., *Rola spójników hipotaktycznych w ujmowaniu stosunków przez dzieci* (Cracow, 1959), 115 pp.

The language of Polish writers, from the Renaissance up to our time, has received special attention both as a source four the history of the literary language, and because of its relevance to an historical Polish stylistics. The spotlight has been directed in the first place on the Romantics, especially on Mickiewicz and on Słowacki. Of the Renaissance writers, Kochanowski has received the closest scrutiny, as a linguistic archaist and innovator, as a stylist and as a source for 16th century Polish. Methodologically innovating are the studies of Doroszewski (on the language of the 19th-century writer Jeż) and of Mayenowa (on the language of positivist lyrical poetry). The linguistic peculiarities of modern writers and poets have been examined in numerous articles. The list of publications given in this footnote is only a fraction of the available literature on the language of individual writers.[94]

Old Polish lexicon and syntax have been scrutinized with attention to their stylistic possibilities in a few important studies.[95] The synthetic outline of Polish stylistics by Kurkowska and Skorupka pursues a purely pedagogical goal.[96]

The geminal pre-war investigations in metrics, by Wóycicki, Siedlecki and Łoś, as well as the Polish contact with Russian formalism, have yielded a rich harvest in the post-war period. Zawodziński's "Studies in Polish Versification" is empressive in scope and richness of observation.[97] The trail-blazing contributions of Dłuska have covered all phases of Polish verse, from medieval syllabism up to modern free verse, establishing their constants, tendencies, internal relations and transformations.[98] Of a popularizing nature are the books on Polish meters by Furmanik.[99] Polish syllabotonic meters, the existence of which was challenged by Budzyk, provoked a number

[94] *O języku Adama Mickiewicza. Studia.* Collection of articles edited by Z. Klemensiewicz (Wrocław, 1959), 524 pp.; Klemensiewicz, Z., "Szkic gramatycznej charakterystyki poetyckiego języka Słowackiego", *JP* 31.1-14, 31.68-75 (1951); Słoński, S., *O języku Jana Kochanowskiego* (Warsaw, 1949), 104 pp.; Kuraszkiewicz, W., "Szkice o języku Mikołaja Reja," in *Odrodzenie w Polsce, Historia języka*, 1 (Warsaw, 1960), pp. 113-360 + tables and illustrations. Discussion pp. 376-395; Stieber, Z., "Uwagi o języku Wacława Potockiego", *Prace Pol.*, Ser. 5 (1947), pp. 9-32; Rzeuska, M., "*Chłopi*" *Reymonta* (Warsaw, 1950), 264 pp.; Sinielnikoff, R., "Narzędnik sposobu w poezji Juliana Tuwima", *Por. Jęz.*, 1959, pp. 393-408; Sinielnikoff, R., "Narzędnik tautologiczny w poezji Juliana Tuwima", *Por. Jęz.*, 1960, pp. 193-207; Sobierajski, Z., *Elementy gwarowe w utworach Kasprowicza* (Poznań, 1950), 26 pp.; Mayenowa, M. R., *Język liryki pozytywistycznej* (Wrocław, 1950/1951); Doroszewski, W., *Język Teodora Tomasza Jeża* (*Zygmunta mitkowskiego*). *Studium z dziejów języka polskiego XIX wieku* (Warsaw, 1949), 417 pp.

[95] Kuraszkiewicz, W., "Stylistyczne badanie słownictwa polskich tekstów XVI wieku", in *Z polskich studiów slawistycznych*, I, *Prace językoznawcze*... (Warsaw, 1958), pp. 240-257; W. Górny, "O stylistycznej interpretacji składni", *Pam. lit.* 51.475-500 (1960); Klemensiewicz, Z., "Historia składni języka poetyckiego", *Pam. lit.* 41.184-187 (1950); Wierzbicka, A., "Okres retoryczny a ogólne tendencje składni szesnastowiecznej", *Pam. lit.* 52.125-138 (1961).

[96] Kurkowska, H., Skorupka, S., *Stylistyka polska. Zarys.*, (Warsaw, 1959), 368 pp.

[97] Zawodziński, K. W., *Studia z wersyfikacji polskiej* (Wrocław, 1954), li + 476 pp. + 1 table.

[98] Dłuska, M., *Studia z historii i teorii wersyfikacji polskiej*, vol. 1 (Cracow, 1948), vi + 367 pp.; vol. 2 (1950), v + 379 pp.; idem, *O wersyfikacji Mickiewicza.* (*Próba syntezy*). pt. 1 (Warsaw, 1955), 166 pp., pt. 2, *Pam. lit.*, 47 (1956), p. 403-443; idem, *Próba teorii wiersza polskiego* (Warsaw, 1961), 310 pp.

[99] Furmanik, S., *Podstawy wersyfikacji polskiej.* (*Nauka o wierszu polskim*) (Warsaw, 1947), 324 pp.; idem, *Z zagadnień wersyfikacji polskiej* (Warsaw, 1956), 317 pp.

of studies clarifying their status within a phonemically "toneless" language.[100] The metrical and rhyming peculiarities of different periods, schools and poets have been explored in a number of analyses full of insight.[101] The most outstanding achievement in the field of versification is the *Encyclopedic Outline*, two volumes of which have so far dealt with Polish syllabic and syllabotonic meters from structural and historical points of view. [102] In addition to Polish, the same series includes also outlines of Czech Ukrainian, French, English and classical (Greek-Roman) versification systems. The Institute of Literary Research (IBL), which is responsible for the series, was also the host and organizer for an International Conference of Poetics (in August, 1960), the contributions to which have recently been published in a separate volume, *Poetics. Poetyka. Poetica* (1962).

The non-genetic relations of Polish to other languages have been considered from the viewpoint of lexical borrowing and typology. The lexical influences of Polish on other Slavic languages has been touched upon by Zaręba, while Russian loans in Polish have been described by Witkowski. Zajączkowski has investigated Oriental loanwords in Polish, and others have sketched the penetration of loanwords of Hungarian, Italian, Rumanian, and even Japanese and Indonesian provenience.[103] Polish-Macedonian parallelisms have been dicussed by Z. Gołąb and Topolińska whereas Kielski has made an attempt to compare the structural properties of Polish and French, without reaching any serious typological conclusions.[104]

Comparative Slavic linguistics of the post-war period has witnessed a deepening of

[100] Woronczak, J., "W sprawie polskiego sylabotonizmu", *Pam. lit.* 46.159-170 (1955) + tables; Budzyk, K., *Spór o polski sylabotonizm* (Warsaw, 1957), 302 pp.; Furmanik, S., "O sylabotoniźmie", *Pam. lit.* 47.448-460 (1956); Mayenowa, M. R., "Jeszcze w sprawie polskiego sylabotonizmu", *Pam. lit.* 46.469-482 (1955).

[101] Grzędzielska, M., "Wiersz wolny Jana Kasprowicza w ramach polskiej wersyfikacji nieregularnej", *Pam. lit.* 42.842-884 (1951) + tables; Woronczak, J., "Z badań nad wierszem Biernata z Lublina", *Pam. lit.* 49.97-118 (1958) + tables; Pszczołowska, L., "O wierszu dramatu Mickiewiczowskiego", *Pam. lit.* 50.517-574 (1959); Kopczyńska, Z., "Wiersz epiki Mickiewicza", *Pam. lit.* 51.105-148 (1960); idem, "O wierszu 'Beniowskiego'", *Pam. lit.* 52.139-152 (1961); Siatkowski, Z., "Wersyfikacja Tadeusza Różewicza wśród współczesnych metod kształtowania wiersza", *Pam. lit.* 49.119-150 (1958); Trzynadlowski, J., "Rymotwórcza funkcja akcentu w wierszu staropolskim," *Prace Pol.*, Ser. 12, 1955, pp. 71-95.

[102] *Poetyka. Zarys encyklopedyczny*, Wrocław, Section 3, *Wersyfikacja*, vol. 3, Kopczyńska, Z., Mayenowa, M. R., *Sylabizm*, 1956, 518 pp., vol. 4, Dłuska, M., Kuryś, T., *Sylabotonizm*, 1957, 374 pp.

[103] Zaręba, A., "Wpływy polszczyzny na słownictwo innych języków słowiańskich", *JP* 41.1-19 (1961); Witkowski, W., "Rusycyzmy we współczesnym języku polskim", *Jęz. Ros.* 2.73-77 (1957); Zajączkowski, A., *Studia orientalistyczne z dziejów słownictwa polskiego* (Wrocław, 1953), 126 pp.; Zaręba, A., "Włoskie zapożyczenia w współczesnej polszczyźnie", *JP* 27.16-21 (1947); idem, "Węgierskie zapożyczenia w polszczyźnie", *JP* 31.113-125 (1951); Kotański, W., "Japońskie wyrazy w języku polskim", *JP* 27.161-166 (1947); Stiller, R., "Indonezyjskie elementy leksykalne w języku polskim", *Rocz. Orient.* 22.113-143 (1957).

[104] Gołąb, Z., "Za nekoi sličnosti meģu polskite i makedonskite govori", *MJ* 8.129-135 (1957); Topolińska, Z., "Od polsko-makedonskite akcentski paraleli", *MJ* 10.13-18 (1959); Kielski, B., *Struktura języków francuskiego i polskiego w świetle analizy porównawczej* (Łódź, 1, 1957; 2, 1960, 247 pp.; idem, *Język francuski a polski, Przyczynek do typologii języków* (Łódź, 1957), p. 28.

its methodology and a concentration on some pivotal problems of comparative phonology and grammar. The investigation of other Slavic languages has at the same time been narrowed in scope, but intensified in a few select areas. One might say that the center of gravity has, because of the new geo-political situation, shifted from the East to the West: increased emphasis has been put on the study of the Lechitic dialects (Kashubian and Polabian), whereas the principal post-war works on Ukrainian were prepared before the war, and the investigation of Byelorussian has progressed at a snail's pace. Czech has continued to attract attention, but there have appeared few significant contributions on Lusatian and Slovak. Polish research in the South Slavic languages has never been interrupted, but the works of Sławski, Gołąb, Zwoliński and Topolińska are more limited in range and in scope than the pre-war investigations in this field. The typological study of the contemporary Slavic languages is, on the whole, neglected, and no scientific synthesis dealing with the structure or history of the Slavic languages has come forth.

Balto-Slavic linguistic relations are, as before, a focal point of comparative Slavic research. Polish linguists subscribe, on the whole, to the hypothesis of an original Balto-Slavic unity. The various arguments in its favor have been put forth by Otrębski, Safarewicz, Kuryłowicz and Lehr-Spławiński; the latter emphasizes, further, their common relation to a Celtic to and Finnish substratum, drawing far-reaching (and speculative) conclusions on the ethnogenesis of the Slavs.[105] The hypothesis of Balto-Slavic unity has received further support in the monumental study of Kuryłowicz on the Indo-European accents, which provides also the most radical revision of the traditional approaches to Proto-Slavic accentology. Kuryłowicz rejects as a fiction the existence of an acute on unaccented syllables and, consequently, the validity of de Saussure's law for Proto-Slavic; he also emphasizes the importance of morphological analogy, interpreted structurally, for the development of the Balto-Slavic movable paradigms, and for the rise of the so-called "neo-circumflex" in late Common Slavic.[106] Phonemic-morphological questions of Balto-Slavic have also been discussed in Kuryłowicz' book on I-E apophony.[107] The same author also approached from a new angle

[105] Otrębski, J., "O jedności językowej bałto-słowiańskiej", *BPTJ* 16.70-113 (1957); idem, "Slavjano-baltijskoe jazykovoe edinstvo", *VJa* 3(5).27-42 (1954); idem, "Rozwój wzajemnych stosunków między grupą językową bałtycką a słowiańską", in *Z polskich studiów slawistycznych*. I. *Prace jezykoznawcze...* (Warsaw, 1958), pp. 146-148; Safarewicz, J., "Bałtosłowiańska wspólnota językowa", in *Słownik Star. Słow.* (Warsaw, 1958), pp. 4-6; Kuryłowicz, J., "O jedności językowej bałto-słowianskiej", *BPTJ* 16.70-113 (1957); Lehr-Spławiński, T., "Wspólnota językowa bałtosłowiańska a problem etnogenezy Słowian", *Slavia Antiqua* 3.1-22 (1953); idem, "Podstawy indoeuropejskiej wspólnoty językowej bałto-słowiańskiej", in *Z polskich studiów slawistycznych, I, Prace językoznawcze...* (Warsaw, 1958), pp. 125-136; Lehr-Spławiński, T., "Kilka uwag o stosunkach językowych celtycko-prasłowiańskich", *Rocz. Slaw.* 18.1-10 (1956).

[106] Kuryłowicz, J., *L'accentuation des langues indo-européennes* (Cracow, 1952), 526 pp. ("Balto-Slavic accentology", pp. 191-422), (Wrocław-Cracow, 1958²), 434 pp.

[107] Kuryłowicz, J., *L'apophonie en indo-européen* (Wrocław-Cracow, 1956), 430 pp. ("Balto-Slavic and Common Slavic", pp. 209-308).

the chronology of Germanic loans in Proto-Slavic on the basis of accentual phenomena.[108]

Questions of Common Slavic with relation to the ethnogenesis of the Slavs were put to the fore right after the war by Polish ethnographers, anthropologists, archeologists and linguists. The so-called "autochthonic theory" has found champions in a series of major studies of Kostrzewski (1946), Jażdżewski (1947 and 1948), Nosek (1947), Tymieniecki (1951) and Czekanowski (1957), attempting to prove that the proto-Slavic habitat was located between the Vistula and the Oder. On the linguistic side, this theory received support in the works of Lehr-Spławiński, Rudnicki and Milewski.[109] Moszyński, the champion of the "Eastern theory" of the proto-Slavic habitat, has expressed distrust of any extra-linguistic evidence; in his most recent work he locates the original habitat further to the West, in the Dnepr basis.[110] A moderate position and critical review of the various theories from a linguistic point of view is represented in the book of Ułaszyn.[111] Of methodological importance are the attempts of Lehr-Spławiński to establish different stages in the history of Proto-Slavic on the basis of its grammatical and lexical evolution.[112] His ideas have been further developed in the articles of Gołąb and Polański and of Orłoś.[113] Connected with the periodization of Common Slavic are the studies of Lehr-Spławinski, Furdal and Mańczak[114] devoted to the problem of the breakdown of the Slavic unity and to the genealogical classification of the Slavic languages. The criteria of classification have been tackled in the collective survey of the Slavic languages, and elaborated in greater detail with respect to and within each of the three Slavic linguistic groups by Stieber, Kuraszkiewicz and Sławski.[115]

[108] Kuryłowicz, J., "Związki językowe słowiańsko-germańskie", *Przegląd Zachodni* 7.191-206 (1951).

[109] Lehr-Spławiński, T., *O pochodzeniu i praojczyźnie Słowian* (Poznań, 1946), p. 246; Rudnicki, M., *Prasłowiańszczyzna – Lechia – Polska*, I: *Wyłonienie się Słowian spośród ludów indoeuropejskich i ich pierwotne siedziby*, II: *Wspólnota słowiańska – wspólnota lechicka – Polska* (Poznań, 1, 1959), 281 pp., 2 (1961), 310 pp.; Milewski, T., "Dwa ujęcia problemu granic prasłowiańskiego obszaru językowego", *Rocz. Slaw.* 21.41-76 (1960).

[110] Moszyński, K., *Pierwotny zasięg języka prasłowiańskiego* (Wrocław-Cracow, 1957), 332 pp.

[111] Ułaszyn, H., *Praojczyzna Słowian* (Łódź, 1959), 106 pp.

[112] Lehr-Spławiński, T., (Ler-Splavinjski), "Nacrt na istorijata na praslovenskiot jazik", *MJ* 7.145-175 (1956); Lehr-Spławiński, T., "Szkic dziejów języka prasłowiańskiego", *SFPSl* 3.243-265 (1958).

[113] Gołąb, Z., Polański, K., "Z badań nad słownictwem prasłowiańskim", *Slavia* 29.525-540 (1960); Orłoś, T. Z., "Element prasłowiański w dzisiejszym słownictwie czeskim", *SFPSl* 3.209-283 (1958).

[114] Lehr-Spławiński, T., "Powstanie, rozrost i rozpad wspólnoty prasłowiańskiej", *Przegląd Zachodni* 1.350-378 (1951); Lehr-Spławiński, T., "Problem ugrupowania językow słowiańskich", *BPTJ* 14.112-121 (1955); Furdal, A., *Rozpad języka prasłowiańskiego w świetle rozwoju głosowego* (Wrocław, 1961), 114 pp.; Mańczak, W., "Problem klasyfikacji genealogicznej języków słowiańskich", in *Z polskich studió w slawistycznych.* I. *Prace jezykoznawcze*... (Warsaw, 1958), pp. 35-51.

[115] Lehr-Spławinski, T., Kuraszkiewicz, W., Sławski, F., *Przegląd i charakterystyka języków słowiańskich* (Warsaw, 1954), 161 pp.; Stieber, Z., "Wzajemne stosunki języków zachodnio-słowiańskich", *BPTJ* 14.73-93 (1955); Kuraszkiewicz, W., "Ugrupowania języków wschodnio-slowiańskich", *BPTJ* 14.94-102 (1955); Sławski, F., "Ugrupowanie języków południowo-słowiańskich", *BPTJ* 14.103-111 (1955).

A valuable source for the study of the Slavic languages are the collections of South, West and East Slavic texts published by Lehr-Spławiński.[116] Special problems of Slavic historical phonology have been treated by various authors.[117] Lehr-Spławiński has re-examined the chronology of the second palatalization, while Furdal has dealt with the feature of palatalization in the history of the Slavic languages, and Stieber with the fate of the phoneme *x*.[118] The latter author has also studied phenomena of convergence in the historical development of various Slavic dialects.[119]

Problems in Slavic lexicology and derivation have been investigated in connection with the Slavic linguistic Atlas (sponsored by an international committee of Slavicists).[120] Etymological observations on Slavic vocabulary were made by Sławski.[121] Slavic onomastics has been treated against a broad comparative framework in the pioneering work of Rozwadowski and in more recent theoretical and factual investigations of Lehr-Spławiński, Taszycki and Rospond, who emphasizes the importance of derivational criteria in the classification of Slavic toponyms and anthroponyms.[122]

Old Church Slavonic has received only limited attention on the part of Polish Slavists. In addition to the traditional grammar of Słoński (prepared before the war), it has been described with historical depth by Lehr-Spławiński.[123] The most detailed analysis of adjective derivation in OCS is that by Brodowska-Honowska, who treats the material descriptively and diachronically, establishing a "synthetic" (according to bases) and "analytic" (according to suffixes) classification of the derived adjectives.[124] Various articles (written by Małecki, Lehr-Spławiński and Sławski) have also dealt

[116] Lehr-Spławiński, T., *Chrestomatia słowiańska*, I: *Teksty południowo-słowiańskie* (Cracow, 1949). 236 pp.; II: *Teksty zachodnio-słowiańskie* (Cracow, 1950), 291 pp.

[117] Sławski, F., "Obocznosc *ǫ*: *u* w językach słowiańskich", *SO* 18.246-290, 539 (1947). Zwoliński, P., "Stosunek fenemu *y* do *i* w historii języków słowiańskich", in *Z polskich studiów slawistycznych*, 1: *Prace językoznawcze*... (Warsaw, 1958), pp. 52-60; Koneczna, H., "Z zagadnień wokalizmu słowiańskiego", *Por. Jęz.*, 1961, pp. 202-209.

[118] Lehr-Spławiński, T., "Próba datowania tzw. II. palatalizacji spółgłosek tylnojęzykowych w języku prasłowiańskim", *SFPSł* 1.375-383 (1955); Furdal, A., "Uwagi o rozwoju słowiańskiej kategorii palatalności", *Rozp. WTN* 2.175-186 (1959); Stieber, Z., "The Development of Primitive Slavic *x* in the Slavic Languages and Dialects", *IJSLP* 4.1-6 (1961).

[119] Stieber, Z., "O niektórych paralelach w rozwoju dialektów słowiańskich", *SO* 20.165-167 (1960).

[120] Grzegorczykowa, R., Puzynina, J., "Zagadnienia słowotwórcze w atlasie ogólnosłowiańskim", *Por. Jęz.* 1961, pp. 10-23; Pomianowska, W., "W sprawie atlasu języków słowiańskich", *Por. Jęz.* 1957, pp. 385-392.

[121] Sławski, F., "Uwagi o badaniach etymologicznych nad słownictwem słowiańskim", *SFPSł* 3.99-107 (1958).

[122] Rozwadowski, J., *Studia nad nazwami wód słowiańskich* (Cracow, 1948), 344 pp.; Lehr-Spławiński, T., "Rozmieszczenie geograficzne prasłowiańskich nazw wodnych", *Rocz. Slaw.* 21.5-22 (1960); Taszycki, W., *Słowiańskie nazwy miejscowe. Ustalenie podziału* (Cracow, 1946), 64 pp.; Rospond, S., "Onomastyka słowiańska", *Onom.* 2.217-248 (1956); Rospond, S., *Klasyfikacja strukturalno-gramatyczna słowiańskich nazw geograficznych* (Wrocław, 1957), 75 pp.

[123] Słoński, St., *Gramatyka języka starosłowiańskiego* (*starobułgarskiego*) (Warsaw, 1950), p. 172; Lehr-Spławiński, T., *Zarys gramatyki języka staro-cerkiewno-słowiańskiego na tle porównawczym* (Cracow, 1949), p. 110.

[124] Brodowska-Honowska, M., *Słowotwórstwo przymiotnika w języku staro-cerkiewno-słowiańskim* (Cracow-Wrocław-Warsaw, 1962), 276 pp.

with the role and development of OCS as a language of Slavic liturgy and culture.

A synthetic survey of the Southern Slavic languages and dialects, incorporating the results of recent research (without an attempt, however, at a modern interpretation of the data), is given in the new book of Sławski.[125] To the same author belongs also a very useful descriptive grammar of standard Bulgarian, and articles on the Bulgarian enclitics and infiinitive.[126] The syntactic function of particles in the South Slavic languages has been analyzed by Z. Gołąb,[127] whereas Zwoliński has contributed observations on Bulgarian toponomastics.[128]

From the pen of Gołąb come several studies on the youngest Slavic literary language, Macedonian. His analysis of the speech-sounds of some Macadonian dialects is phonological, and the grammatical parallelisms which hold between Macedonian and Arumanian are treated within a structural typological setting.[129]

With the exception of Kuryłowicz' article on the Slovenian accent, Slovene (the study of which in the 19th-century was most advanced by a Pole) has attracted no interest in post-war Poland.[130]

Frančić's descriptive grammar of Serbo-Croatian is a useful, though scientifically unsatisfactory textbook.[131] The same author has also written a work on the collective substantives in -ād. An interesting study on foreign suffixes in Serbo-Croatian was produced by Stachowski,[132] whereas Sławski described the infinitive in the modern language, in its history and dialects.[133]

The best survey of the Western Slavic dialects and languages is that by Stieber, which incorporates much of his own research in the field.[134] The first volume of his historical grammar of Czech, written jointly with Lehr-Spławiński, shows also a phonological approach to the history of the Czech sound-system and its dialects.

[125] Sławski, F., *Zarys dialektologii południowosłowiańskiej* (Warsaw, 1962), 252 pp. + 5 maps.

[126] Sławski, F., *Gramatyka języka bułgarskiego* (Warsaw, 1954), 176 pp.; idem, *Miejsce enklityki odmiennej w dziejach języka bułgarskiego* (Cracow, 1946), vii + 87 pp.; idem, "Podstawy staro-cerkiewno-słowiańskie zaniku infinitiwu w języku bułgarskim", *SAU* 46.265-269 (1945).

[127] Gołąb, Z., "Funkcja syntaktyczna partykuły *da* w językach pd. słowianskich (bułgarskim, macedońskim, serbochorwackim)", *BPTJ* 13.67-72 (1954).

[128] Zwoliński, P., "Studia nad toponomastyką Bułgarii. I. Nazwy z sufiksem -štica. 2. Słowiańskie nazwy miejscowe Bułgarii. 3. Nazwy miejscowe pamiątkowe w Bułgarii", *SAU* 49.261-264 (1949), 51.495-498, 51.673-676 (1950).

[129] Gołąb, Z., "Nekolku beleški za palatalizacijata na soglaskite vo makedonskiot jazik", *MJ* 8.165-171 (1957); idem, "Nowomacedoński typ perfektum ze słowem *imam* // sum", *ZUJFil* 8, pp. 321-325; idem, "Z fonologii gwar Bogdańska (na tle ogólno-makedońskim)", *SFPSł* 1.289-333 (1955); idem, "Some Arumanian-Macedonian Isogrammatisms and the Social Background of their Development", *Word* 15.415-435 (1959).

[130] Kuryłowicz, J., "L'intonation "néodouce" et l'accentuation en slovene", *IJSLP* 3.79-88 (1960).

[131] Frančić, V., *Gramatyka opisowa języka serbochorwackiego* (Warsaw, 1956), 293 pp. + map.

[132] Frančić, V., *Budowa słowotwórcza serbochorwackich kolektywów* (Cracow, 1961), 81 pp.; Stachowski, S., *Przyrostki obcego pochodzenia w języku serbochorwackim* (Cracow, 1961), 163 pp.

[133] Sławski, F., "Infinitivus w języku serbochorwackim", *SFPSł* 3.345-361 (1958).

[134] Stieber, Z., *Zarys dialektologii języków zachodnio-słowiańskich*, z wyborem tekstów gwarowych (Warsaw, 1956), 132 pp. + maps.

In addition to this grammar, there are also two textbooks of Lehr-Spławiński, of which one is historical and includes also the history of Czech flexion. [135] The grouping of modern Czech dialects has been connected by this author (not too convincingly) with medieval Czech tribal divisions. A recent monograph by Siatkowski describes in detail a Czech dialect, while Stieber and Dejna deal, in addition to the works mentioned above, with selected problems in Czech dialectology.[136]

Lusatian has been examined briefly in the context of Polish-Lusatian lexical and dialectal relations.[137]

A great amount of work has been done on Kashubian, which is genetically closely related to Polish ("plus polonais que le polonais même", according to Baudouin de Courtenay). The nature of this relationship, which figured prominently in the older literature on Kashubian, has again been recently spotlighted by Stieber, who views it as a transitional dialect between Polish and Western Lechitic.[138] Kashubian accentology has been discussed in several recent studies. As shown by Stieber (and contrary to older descriptions), Kashubian must have lost phonemic quantity around the turn of the century, while retaining phonemic stress in its Northern dialects. The question of Kashubian quantity and accent have also been taken up in studies of Popowska-Taborska, of Topolinska, and of Kuryłowicz.[139] Kuryłowicz has also described the accentual innovations of Slovincian with respect to the Common Slavic system.[140] Kashubian vocalic and consonantal developments have been surveyed in several recent works,[141] and the dialect-boundaries drawn up by Lorentz have been revised in connection with the preparation of the Kashubian linguistic atlas (directed by Stieber in

[135] Lehr-Spławiński, T., Stieber, Z., *Gramatyka historyczna języka czeskiego*, I: *Wstęp. Fonetyka historyczna. Dialektologia.* (with a map) (Warsaw, 1957), pp. 142; Lehr-Spławiński, T., *Gramatyka języka czeskiego* (Warsaw-Wrocław, 1950), p. 79; Lehr-Spławiński, T., *Zarys gramatyki historycznej języka czeskiego: głosownia i fleksja historyczna* (Cracow, 1953), p. 125 (Łódź, 1957²), p. 142.

[136] Lehr-Spławiński, T., "Tło historyczne ugrupowania gwar czeskich", *Rocz. Slaw.* 17.19-27 (1952/3); Siatkowski, J., *Dialekt czeski okolic Kudowy*, Cz. I: *Fonetyka – Słowotworstwo* (Wrocław-Warsaw-Cracow, 1962), 174 pp.; Dejna, K., "Gwara kurczowska na tle innych gwar czeskich", *Rozp. ŁTN* 3.6-30 (1955); Stieber, Z., "Kontynuanty dawnych czeskich sonantycznych r, l, w dzisiejszych gwarach języka czeskiego", *Rocz. Slaw.* 18.11-14 (1956).

[137] Gruchmanowa, M., "Związki językowe dialektu Kramsk z Łużycami", *JP* 37.241-252 (1957); Budziszewska, W., "Związki językowe polsko-łużyckie w zakresie terminologii przyrodniczej", *Rozp. ŁTN* 8.127-134 (1962).

[138] Stieber, Z., "Stosunek kaszubszczyzny do dialektów Polski lądowej", in *Konferencja Pomorska*, pp. 37-48; *Vorträge auf der Berliner Slawistentagung* (Berlin, 1954), pp. 57-67.

[139] Stieber, Z., "Elementy prozodii w dialektach kaszubskich (iloczas, intonacja wyrazowa, przycisk wyrazowy)", *Slavia* 26.362-364 (1957); Popowska-Taborska, H., "Isčeznovenie kašubskix dolgot", *VJa* 7(4).60-66 (1959); Topolińska, Z., "Aktualny stan akcentu kaszubskiego", *Slavia* 27.381-385 (1958). Kuryłowicz, J., "Uwagi o akcencie kaszubskim", *SO* 20.71-77 (1960).

[140] Kuryłowicz, J., "Akcentuacja słowińska (pomorska)", *Rocz. Slaw.* 17.1-18 (1952).

[141] Topolińska, Z., "Zu Fragen des kaschubischen Vocalismus (Das gegenseitige Verhältnis der alten langen *o*, *a*, und des hinteren Nasalvokals in den süd-kaschubischen Dialekten)", *ZSl* 5.161-170 (1960); Popowska-Taborska, H., "O samogłoskach nosowych w Borzę i Jastarni", *SO* 20.125-131 (1960); Smoczyński, P., "W Sprawie zmian k-g na Kaszubach i w zachodnich dialektach północno-polskich", *SFPSl* 3.61-79 (1958).

the II Dialectological Laboratory).[142] Several minor contributions have also been made to Kashubian onomastics,[143] and to Kashubian-German linguistic relations.[144] Lorentz' "Pomeranian Grammar" has been reprinted in Poland (in 1958-1959), and his Dictionary in East Berlin (in 1958). There has, in addition, appeared a small dictionary of the Kashubian language.[145]

The extinct Western Lechitic dialects have been briefly surveyed by Lehr-Spławiński;[146] their phonetic and grammatical features have been extensively treated, on the basis of written records, in a monograph by Jeżowa. Linguistically more dependable is Polański's study of German loanwords in Polabian, which provides in effect a new grammatical description of that language.[147] Kuryłowicz has attempted to demonstrate (against the older views of Lehr-Spławiński and Trubetzkoy) that the Polabian accent was initial.[148] Remarks on Polabian phonology are found in the articles of Polański and Kempf.[149] An etymological Polabian dictionary is presently being prepared in Krakow; in the meantime there have appeared several works devoted to the vocabulary of the Polabians and to their social life as reconstructed on its basis.[150]

The Eastern Slavic languages and dialects have received a synthetic treatment in a textbook of Kuraszkiewicz, who has remained also after the war the most active scholar in theis field.[151] From him comes also a highly informative work on the "Novgorod

[142] Topolińska, Z., "Aktualny zasięg zwartego obszaru dialektów kaszubskich", *Rocz. Gdański* 15/16.393-399 (1956-7) + map; Zieniukowa, J., "Typowe zasięgi zjawisk językowych na Kaszubach", *Por. Jęz.* 6.287-303 (1958).

[143] Mańczak, W., "Uwagi o nazwach miejscowych Pomorza gdańskiego", in *Konferencja Pomorska*, pp. 175-189; Sychta, B., "Etymologia ludowa kaszubskich nazw miejscowych", *Onom.* 7.285-287 (1958); idem, "Przezwiska u Kaszubów", *JP* 36.97-108 (1956); Kamińska-Rzetelska, E., "Z onomastyki kaszubskiej. Nazwiska na *-oc, -ec, -ic//-yc*", *Onom.* 8.177-193 (1959).

[144] Zabrocki, L., "Związki jezykowe niemiecko-pomorskie", in *Konferencja Pomorska.*

[145] Labuda, A., Popowska-Taborska, H., Topolińska, Z., *Słowniczek Kaszubski* (Warsaw, 1960), 116 pp.

[146] Lehr-Spławiński, T., "O dawnych narzeczach Słowian Pomorza Zachodniego i ziem przyległych", in *Konferencja Pomorska*, pp. 21-36.

[147] Jeżowa, M., *Dawne słowiańskie dialekty Meklemburgii* (Wrocław-Warsaw-Cracow, 1961); Polański, K., *Morfologia zapożyczeń niemieckich w języku połabskim* (Wrocław-Warsaw-Cracow, 1962), 198 pp.

[148] Kuryłowicz, J., "Akcentuacja połabska", *SFPSł* 1.394-374 (1955).

[149] Polański, K., "Polabica I. I-III", *ZUJFil* 2.109-137 (1956), 4.158-201 (1958), 6.53-64 (1960); Kempf, Z., "'Geneza połabskich *ö ü* w swietle średniowiecznych zapisów onomastycznych", *SIJUJ* 1.22-25 (1954).

[150] Lehr-Spławiński, T., Polański, K., "Z prac nad słownikiem etymologicznym języka połabskiego", *SPAN* 5.59-71 (1958); Szydłowska, B., "Semantyczna analiza połabskiego zasobu leksykalnego", in *Z polskich studiów slawistycznych. Prace językoznawcze...* (Warsaw, 1958), pp. 198-204; Szydłowska, B., "Życie Połabian w świetle szczątków ich języka", *Pam. Słow.* 3.58-105 (1952); idem, "Hodowla zwierząt domowych u Połabian w świetle języka połabskiego", *SFPSł* 1 (1955); idem, "Zdobywanie i przygotowywanie żywności u Połabian w świetle zabytków ich języka", *SFPSł* 2.414-440 (1957).

[151] Kuraszkiewicz, W., *Zarys dialektologii wschodnio-słowiańskiej z wyborem tekstów gwarowych* (Warsaw, 1954), 146 pp., 4 maps.

gramoty" and on some Ukrainian dialects.[152] Ossowski, who is primarily known from his pre-war investigations of Byelorussian, has traced the fate of the narrow vowel *o* in Russian manuscripts and in modern dialects.[153] Comparative studies of Russian and Polish have been carried out by Otrębski.[154] The Polish descriptive grammars of Russian are textbooks without scientific aspirations.[155] The best post-war description of Western Ukrainian dialects was written by Dejna, and Stieber published a monumental atlas on the Lemki dialect and observations on its historical phonology.[156] He and Hrabec have also contributed studies on Ukrainian toponomastics.[157]

The influence of Polish on the Byelorussian literary language has been surveyed by Żurawski.[158] A short outline of the linguistic and cultural history of the Ukrainian language was published in 1956.[159]

In conclusion, one may say that the chief effort of Slavic linguistics in Poland lies in building up a massive storehouse of data pertaining to the history of the Polish language and to its dialects. This is shown by the nature of the major collective enterprises which are in progress and which are expected to endure for many years to come: the various dictionaries of the Polish language, the Polish and Kashubian linguistic atlases, the lexical monographs of dialects, the toponomastic collections, the Encyclopedia of metrics. These ambitious undertakings, which require large funds and engage sizable teams of scholars are intended to provide a more detailed and many-sided knowledge of the Polish language, and to constitute the basis for future theoretical generalizations. In the meantime, they direct the sights of Polish linguists (and particularly of its younger cadres) to field-work and textual analysis. In practice, the majority of Polish linguists finds itself, therefore, on empirical grounds, pursuing its work as if inspired by the neo-grammarian credo: "zuerst sammeln, dann erklären".

Inasmuch as collective and large scale research can build most profitably on foundations prepared by previous investigators and by their methods, it comes as no surprise

[152] Kuraszkiewicz, W., *Gramoty nowogrodzkie na brzozowej korze* (1957). Zesz. A, Opracowanie językowe, Zesz. B, *Fotografie i przerysy*, 104 pp., 42 tables; idem, "Rozwój *'a* na tle dyftongow i palatalizacji w dawnych gwarach ruskiego Podlasia i Chełmszczyzny", *SFPSl* 3.211-241 (1958) + map.

[153] Ossowski, L., "O zwężonym lub dyftongicznym *o* w pewnych gwarach i zabytkach rosyjskich (ze studiów nad akcentem rosyjskim)", *BPTJ* 10.141-147 (1950).

[154] Otrębski, J., "Charakterystyka języka rosyjskiego w porównaniu z polskim", *Jęz. Ros.* 4.8-18 (1951); idem, "Właściwości charakterystyczne składni rosyjskiej w porównaniu z polską", *Jęz. Ros.* 4(5).10-21 (1951).

[155] Gałecki, W., Jakubowski, W., Lehr-Spławinski, T., *Gramatyka języka rosyjskiego* (Warsaw, 1950[1], 1953[4]), 258 pp.; Mirowicz, A., *Gramatyka opisowa języka rosyjskiego* (Warsaw, 1953), 80 pp.

[156] Dejna, K., *Gwary ukraińskie Tarnopolszczyzny* (1957), 164 pp., 9 maps; Stieber, Z., *Atlas językowy dawnej Łemkowszczyzny* (Łódź, 1956-1962), fasc. 1-6, 300 maps; idem, "Z fonetyki historycznej dialektu Łemków", *SFPSl* 3.363-381 (1958).

[157] Stieber, Z., *Toponomastyka Łemkowszczyzny*, I: *Nazwy miejscowosci*; II: *Nazwy terenowe* (Łódź, 1948-1949), p. 78, 113; Hrabec, St., *Nazwy geograficzne Huculszczyzny* (Cracow, 1950), p. 264.

[158] Żurawski, A., "Uwagi o pożyczkach polskich w języku piśmiennictwa białoruskiego XVI-XVII w.", *Slavia Orientalis* 10.37-55 (1961).

[159] Lehr-Spławiński, T., Zwoliński, P., Hrabec, S., *Dzieje języka ukraińskiego w zarysie* (Warsaw, 1956), 69 pp.

that Slavistics in Poland has achieved most in the traditional field of historical linguistics, and least in the synchronic and typological analysis of the Slavic languages. The most pioneering studies are, interestingly enough, not specifically in the field of Slavic linguistics, but in Indo-European (Kuryłowicz), in American Indian (Milewski), and in general linguistics (Kuryłowicz, Zawadowski). Structural linguistics is also the order of the day in Poland; but its impact has so far been greatest in diachronic phonology, and least on the levels of descriptive and historical morphology and syntax. In this respect, however, the development of Polish linguistics shows similarity to that of other countries.

## BIBLIOGRAPHY

Lehr-Spławiński, T., "Główne kierunki i wyniki badań nad językami słowiańskimi w dziesięcioleciu Polski Ludowej", *BPTJ* 14.24-34 (1955).

—, and Zaręba, A., "Polski dorobek badawczy w zakresie językoznawstwa słowiańskiego po drugiej wojnie światowej", *MSS* (Belgrade, 1957), pp. 389-410.

Doroszewski, W., *Materiały do bibliografii słowotwórstwa języków słowiańskich*, I (Warsaw, 1958), p. 69.

Karaś, M., "Prace dialektologiczne w dziesięcioleciu, 1944-1954", *JP* 1955, pp. 202-213, 300-308.

—, "O rabote nad slovarjami pol'skogo jazyka XVI i XVII vv.", *VJa* 7/4.148-149 (1958).

—, "Pol'skaja dialektologija posle vtoroj mirovoj vojny", *VJa* 9/2.111-120 (1960).

Klemensiewicz, Z., "Dorobek językoznawstwa polonistycznego w dziesięcioleciu Polski Ludowej", *BPTJ* 14.35-72 (1955).

Milewski, T., "Nowe prace o pochodzeniu polkiego języka literackiego", *Studia staropolskie* 3.60-81 (1956).

Rospond, S., "Stan i perspektywy onomastyki polskiej", *I Międzynarowdoa Slawistyczna Konferencja onomastyczna. Ksiega referatów* (Wrocław-Warsaw-Cracow, 1961), pp. 59-68.

Skorupka, S., "Stan i zadania leksykografii polskiej", *Por. Jęz.*, 9 (1952), pp. 1-9.

Stiber (= Stieber), Z., "Pol'skoe jazykoznaznie v 1945-1955 gg.", *VJa* 6/4.142-151 (1956).

Taszycki, W., Karaś, M., and Turasiewicz, A., *Bibliografia onomastyki polskiej do roku 1958 włącznie*, 1960, p. 336.

Zaręba, A., "Słowiańska geografia wyrazowa w polskiej literaturze językoznawczej", in *Z polskich studiów slawistycznych* (Warsaw, 1958), pp. 109-124.

Kamińska, E., and Pałkowska, J., *Z historii badań nad gwarami kaszubskimi* (Gdańsk, 1958).

Polański, K., "Prace powojenne dotyczące języka połabskich Drzewian", *Roczn. Slaw.*, 20.90-117 (1958).

# YUGOSLAVIA

HORACE G. LUNT

The multinational kingdom of Yugoslavia set up in 1918 might seem to have been potentially a marvelous field laboratory for the linguist. It contained not only a fantastic crazy-quilt of Slavic dialects belonging to at least three languages (Slovene, Serbo-Croatian, Bulgarian and/or Macedonian) and three major religions (Catholic, Orthodox, Moslem), but several other varieties of Indo-European (German, Italian, Arumanian, Judeo-Spanish, Gypsy, Albanian), beside some non-Indo-European (Hungarian, Turkish). Unfortunately, however, the linguistic diversity was only one manifestation of the ethnic and cultural potpourri; among the utterly heterogeneous ethnic, religious, and socio-economic groups there existed a multitude of major and minor differences that made for an uneasy life both on the local and national level, not to mention the several irredentisms that marred the international scene. Doubtless this all combined with the general economic backwardness of most of the country to deter outside linguists from coming to make many studies. The few native scholars had their hands full with the practical problems of education, although too many of them took the time to keep the local-national antagonisms hot. Nonetheless, a certain amount of descriptive work on the Slavic dialects was accomplished.

Yugoslavia simply disintegrated when the war finally came; the local loyalties proved to be strong enough to prevent united action in the face of outside enemies. It is difficult for Americans to imagine what Yugoslavs endured in the short period between the surprise bombing of Belgrade on Easter Sunday of 1941 and the final expulsion of the last German troops in the spring of 1945. The country was overrun by foreign troops and dismembered. What was not annexed outright by Germany, Italy, Hungary, Bulgaria or Italian-controlled Albania was divided into the pitiable rump state of Serbia, run by well-meaning but helpless quislings, and the incredibly-named Independent State of Croatia, whose titular rulers could only dance frantically to the tunes of their fascist Italian trainers and their Nazi German masters. Some local scores were at once settled by individual murder, and more complex problems were handled by mass murder and the slower quasi-judicial murder in prison and concentration camp. Civil war flared up, and the struggle against the foreign occupiers and their native puppets was complicated by internecine conflict between groups with differing socio-economic and ethnic views.

In 1945 a slightly different picture was emerging from the physical ruins. The

Germans, having eliminated most of the Gypsies and Jews, were themselves expelled, as were the overwhelming majority of Italians. The new government loudly proclaimed local autonomy and especially local option for language and culture. Most groups realized that even though life in Yugoslavia was not good, existence without it was impossible; willy nilly there came about the recognition of the absolute necessity for a degree of tolerance. The stage would seem to be set for a flowering of linguistic studies. It has not yet taken place.

The Federated Republic of Yugoslavia today consists of six republics wth a high degree of local responsibility. Slovenia and Macedonia have their own languages, while the others (Serbia, Croatia, Bosnia-Hercegovina, Montenegro) use Serbo-Croatian. All three languages are legally valid everywhere. Other national groups enjoy cultural autonomy, and especially the right to schools in their own language. The existence of newspapers and other publications depends on the size of the minority and its cultural demands, as well as, to some degree, on the economic viability of publications. For the most part, attention to the linguistic problems of the minorities has involved practical questions of standardization for schools and the press.

The largest minority group are the Albanians, called according to the local dialect Šiptars. They live mostly in the Serbian province of Kosovo-Metohija (Kosmet) or in Macedonia, and are on the whole peasants and shepherds, rural dwellers of low economic status. They have their own schools and the beginnings of a native intelligentsia, but post-war political conditions have completely sealed them off from what little scholarly development has been achieved in Albania. Priština, their political center, has recently acquired a university faculty, and it is probable that from here, and from the Albanian chairs in Belgrade and Skopje, serious linguistic works will eventually come. The bibliographies chronicle a series of publications on linguistic problems, mostly, insofar as I can judge, of a popular character and to be classed under the heading of applied linguistics. I am unable to comment on their quality. Henrik Barić (1888-1957), professor in Sarajevo, published many studies on the history of Albanian, on Illyrian and other pre-Slavic Balkan languages. From my little knowledge of the field, I can only say that I view his work somewhat skeptically, but Professor Eric Hamp has assured me that some of Barić's investigations into Albanian are valuable.

The miniscule Turkish minority has produced only a few schoolbooks, and the more serious Moslem scholars have been little interested in specifically linguistic questions. Hungarian has only recently begun to be taught on a university level, and there seems to be no linguistic production of note. Communications with Budapest have been intermittently good enough so that Yugoslav Hungarians are not isolated culturally. Yugoslav Romance scholars of various nationalities have turned out many philological studies, some of merit, but none of such linguistic significance as to be pertinent to this survey.

The primary fact of recent Yugoslav linguistics is that its direction remained until about 1950 firmly in the hands of men who had been the leading professors in old

Yugoslavia. Their chief training had been gained in the Austrian and German universities before 1918. Linguistics therefore was nearly synonymous with historical and comparative studies, while the point of view remained fairly orthodox Young Grammarian. Turkish and the cultural languages of Islam were scarcely mentioned, being associated with the painful centuries of subjection to the sultans of Istanbul. Linguistics indeed meant Indoeuropean, and especially of course Slavic. Descriptive work on dialects was conceived and carried out in this framework, sometimes with the added dimension of politico-ethnic polemics. The views of Meillet had some influence, and the name of De Saussure was mentioned from time to time, but the excitement of the new ideas being developed in Vienna and Prague, not to mention Copenhagen and America, did not penetrate Yugoslavia.

The broadest international reputation belongs to Aleksandar Belić (1876-1960), long professor in Belgrade and a leader of the Serbian Academy. His very early work on čakavski dialects became and remained a classic, particularly frequently cited in discussions of Slavic and Indo-European accentology. It is to him and some of his students that we owe a very large part of our exact knowledge of Serbo-Croatian dialectology. A prolific writer, he was essentially a Serbo-Croatist, but frequently dealt with broader Slavic problems. He founded and edited the most important linguistic – philological would perhaps be a more accurate term – journal, *Južnoslovenski filolog* (1912-), and directed the principal linguistic publications of the Serbian Academy (notably the *Dijalektološki zbornik*, 1905-). Unquestionably the greatest authority on the history of Serbo-Croatian, Belić repeatedly promised to write the definitive work, but constantly put it off. A number of versions of his university lectures on the subject appeared from time to time in lithographed and other avowedly preliminary forms. It is now clear that the four parts that have been printed since 1948 make up the most comprehensive historical grammar of Serbo-Croatian we are likely to have for some time. He treats the phonetics and accentology, word-formation, declension, and conjugation. To a large extent these publications appear to be relatively old versions of Belić's views, with little utilization of newer material gathered by his students and colleagues.

Belić's work on this magnum opus was held up partly by the perfectionist desire for completeness that has left many a study a mere torso of unorganized notes and partly by his increasing concern with wider problems of general linguistics. His major essay, "On the Nature and Development of Language" (*O jezičkoj prirodi i jezičkom razvitku*), came out just as the war began in 1941, so that any influence it may have exerted belongs to the post-war period. A second printing was issued in 1958 (331 pp.), and a second part (183 pp.) appeared in 1959. There are many interesting observations and some arresting thoughts in these pages, but nothing really new; certainly Belić did not manage to achieve a convincingly coherent view of linguistic phenomena. He quotes from Wundt and Hjelmslev and Marr and Whatmough, from Buyssens, Marcel Cohen and Meščaninov, from Meillet and Sapir, from Karlgren and Benveniste, yet he remains essentially a Young Grammarian with strong Indo-European orientation and a curious inability to comprehend the importance of form in language. For example in his discussions of "word" he is often talking about morphemes or even about purely semantic categories, so that much of what he says simply does not correspond to any of the languages he believes he is explaining. He outlined his principal views in "A Letter on Linguistics" (*For Roman Jakobson*, The Hague, 1956, pp. 31-33), but his book is much more meaningful than one might expect from that summary statement. It surely is capable of arousing in a student an interest in linguistics and stimulating him to read on.

This is perhaps the place to mention the only avowed introduction to general linguistics, *Uvod u opću lingvistiku* (Zagreb, 1958), by Sreten Živković, professor at the teachers college in Zagreb, and author of numerous small articles about Serbo-Croatian. It is a concise textbook (202 pp., plus indices) of a generalized frame of reference about the nature of language, extant language-families, phonetics, phonetic changes, grammatical categories, lexicology, the origin of language, and the history of linguistics. Phonemics and structuralism in general are given a modest place, yet one feels that the author prefers the approach of Meillet and Vendryes. There is abundant bibliography, though without a guide to tell the student where to start and how to proceed.

In Belgrade, Belić held almost undisputed reign, but in Zagreb and Ljubljana four other men were chiefly responsible for linguistic education and scholarly activity in both Yugoslavias.

Petar Skok (1881-1956), professor of Romance Philology at Zagreb, was surely the broadest in his interests as well as the most productive. He was chiefly concerned with Balkan Latin and its daughter dialects, and therefore in all Romance traces in toponyms, in curious Slavic dialect words, and whatever scraps of information any kind of written records could furnish. He studied Albanian and the "Balkanization" of the eastern South Slavic dialects, and the mutual influences of all sorts of speech types in effecting linguistic change. Among his most valuable works are the study of Romance and Slavic peoples and culture on the Adriatic islands (*Slavenstvo i romanstvona jadranskim otocima*, I-II, 1952) and – presumably – the Serbo-Croatian etymological dictionary, which was completed before his death but has yet to be published. Skok's etymologies are frequently controversial, but on the whole his evidence is reliable and his methods reasonably rigorous. He also turned up much new material himself and therefore was able to make fresh observations.

Stjepan Ivšić (1884-1961), university professor of Serbo-Croatian at Zagreb and leading member of the Yugoslav Academy, was primarily a Croatist. His post-war influence was much diminished because he was adjudged guilty of collaboration with the Germans during the occupation. It was his pupils, Mate Hraste and Josip Hamm (since 1961 Professor of Slavic at Vienna), who were in charge of Slavic and linguistics in Zagreb. Hraste is strictly a dialectologist, operating with traditional methods unmodified by a hint of phonemic or other structural theory. Hamm, after an unfortunate excursion into a theory of Gothic influence in South Slavic, did valuable dialectological and accentological studies, and more recently has been operating with phonemics. He was a leader in the Staroslovenski Institut and its efforts to classify and study the many Croatian Church Slavonic texts preserved in Yugoslavia and elsewhere.

In Ljubljana the elder statemen was Rajko Nahtigal (1877-1958), a Slavic linguist and philologist. His useful general handbook "The Slavic languages" (*Slovenski jeziki*, 2nd ed., 1952) has recently been translated into German (by J. Schütz, Wiesbaden, Harrassowitz, 1961) and Russian, although one should not forget that despite the publication date it was actually written in the late thirties. Fran Ramovš (1890-1952) was the chief dialectologist and historian of Slovenian, and the most active organizer of the Slovenian linguistic periodicals, the normalizing handbooks, and finally the Slovenian Academy itself.

Of all these men it must be said that their main importance lies in the materials they collected and published and in the journals and institutes they founded and built up. They increased our knowledge of Serbo-Croatian and Slovenian dialects and their history, but they made no special contribution to linguistic theory or methodology. Nor did they leave many active disciples to carry on their work. Most frequently the chairs have simply been occupied by slightly younger but less gifted men who in turn have neither inspired their students nor published works of high quality.

In Ljubljana the most promising students perished in accidents or the war. Both Ramovš and Nahtigal were too ill after 1945 to carry the many burdens that fell on them in coping with the appalling problems of reorganizing Slovene cultural life and educating a new generation. The young people have managed to carry on, but they have been forced to try to teach others while struggling to teach themselves. The search for new methods can be perceived in some of the published discussions in both the frankly popular and the semi-professional daily and periodical press, but the traditionalists remain in control. Serious attempts to look at Slovene from a phonology-slanted point of view can be discerned in the few articles so far published by Jože Toporišič (e.g. "Probleme der slovenischen Schriftsprache", *Scandoslavica* 6.53-74, Copenhagen, 1960).

In Zagreb one hears of a group of young people discussing the works of contemporary linguistics, but evidence of a change from the old and safe practices is so far lacking. Dalibor Brozović, at present teaching in Zadar and working principally in dialectology, shows promise of organizing in new and original ways the data he is assiduously collecting. Otherwise Zagreb has produced only a series of philological publications of older linguistic texts and dictionaries and some dialect descriptions in the traditional style.

Belić himself had few good students during his prime years, and his immediate successors at Belgrade University are narrow Serbists with few and undistinguished publications to their credit. But Belić took great pains with the young people, born in the 1920's, who came to him immediately after the war, and it is they who brighten the whole picture of Yugoslav linguistics.

The most prolific was the gifted but hasty and misguided Ivan Popović (1923-1961), who in his work resolutely rejected wherever possible both the teachings of Belić and the structuralism which was attracting his colleagues. This unfortunately left him without any firm theoretical principles and he impulsively jumped from one methodology to another. In his impatience to get down his own notions and communicate interesting details he felt he had discovered, he never took the time to think things through, to digest the myriad ideas which came with his omnivorous reading, nor even to check back on the accuracy and internal consistency of his own notes and statements. It will be very difficult to separate out his real contribution from the slap-dash mass of writing he produced. For a more detailed analysis of his "History of the Serbo-Croatian Language," see *Language* 37.424-433 (1961).

Very solid work is being done by Irina Grickat, who is concerned with problems of the Serbo-Croatian and Russian verb. Her dissertation on two competing forms of the perfect tense in Serbo-Croatian is particularly interesting for its attempt to discern the meaning and basis of usage of the forms, one of which is still largely of affective nature. Her time is mostly occupied with routine tasks for the Academy dictionary, but we can expect to have more significant observations from her in the future.

The most active Yugoslav linguists are Pavle Ivić and his wife Milka, both professors at Novi Sad. Pavle Ivić is primarily a Serbo-Croatist, with special emphasis on dialectology. Mrs. Ivić is more concerned with general linguistics, her chief interest being syntax. The material she works with comes primarily from Serbo-Croatian and then from other Slavic languages. Unlike their elder colleagues, the Ivićes utilize their practical knowledge of languages to read current scholarly literature; their ability to use English sets them apart from nearly all the older professors. Their desire to discover new and more effective ways to handle the problems they face in reinterpreting the work of their predecessors and handling the new data they are amassing again distinguishes them from their elders. Contact with all sorts of linguists in Europe – both west and east – and a year in New York have given them the opportunity to learn more about current theory and practice.

Pavle Ivić's initial major contribution is the first volume of "The Serbo-Croatian Dialects" (*Die serbokroatischen Dialekte*, I, The Hague, 1958), with a discussion of general problems and a close survey of the štokavian dialect. This is the first detailed attempt to put the facts of the various types of Serbo-Croatian systematically into one and the same framework and to see just what structures and structural relationships exist. Ivić's concern with the theory of dialects and the methodology of investigation and presentation of dialect materials has continued; see his papers for the General Dialectology Congress (Louvain, 1960, to appear in *Orbis*) and the Ninth International Congress of Linguists (Cambridge, Mass., 1962, in press in the *Proceedings*). The close examination of the dialects naturally brings observations of value for a full description of the standard language (e.g. the cases).

Milka Ivić is demonstrating how linguistic principles are to be tested first with limited linguistic data (SC), then with broader terms of comparison (other Slavic languages) which can lead to generalized questions of even broader validity. Thus she has moved, for example, from details observed in a comprehensive study of the SC instrumental case, to some syntactical comparisons of several languages, and then the statement of a principle of omissibility ~ non-omissibility that promises to be of great value in general syntax; cf. her paper for the Ninth International Congress of Linguists (Cambridge, Mass., 1962).

The courses given by the Ivić's at Novi Sad, and even more their lectures and their informal contacts with students and young teachers around the country supplement their publications and are of great importance in bringing an understanding of modern linguistics to Yugoslavia. Mrs. Ivić has been particularly active in discussing new ideas. Her book *Pravci u lingvistici* (ca. 170 pp. plus indices) now in press (Ljubljana, Državna Založba), is an effort to explain how different men and schools have viewed language and its study. The table of contents and some parts I have been able to read in typescript intimate that this is perhaps the most lucid, as well as the most concise, account of linguistics from Humboldt to Chomsky available in any language.

Macedonia, part of the Ottoman Empire until 1912 and the goal of political expansionists on all sides, was treated in old Yugoslavia as a Serbian province and during the war as a Bulgarian province. Since 1945 the Macedonian Slavs have been viewed officially as a separate nation, and the area, with its sizeable Albanian minority and smaller groups of Turks, Arumanians, and Gypsies, is a separate republic. The leader of the movement to establish the Macedonian language, indeed almost the embodiment of the language itself, is Blaže Koneski, professor at Skopje (born 1921). As a poet, publicist, and educator he has demonstrated by example the principles he set forth as a linguist and scholar. His descriptive "Macedonian Grammar" (*Gramatika na makedonskiot literaturen jazik*, I-II, 1952-4) is of necessity aimed at a broad native audience, and he makes little attempt to depart from the traditional framework of school grammars. Yet he keeps only the labels needed for real categories in the language and expounds the structure lucidly. Intensive efforts are being made to record and describe the Macedonian dialects. Leader in this work is Božo Vidoeski, who has produced a long series of useful articles.

In sum, Yugoslav linguists are on the whole still involved with carrying on the traditional tasks of educating the school children and a broader public to use an acceptable standardized form of the local language. The theoretical discussion and the resulting textbooks of, say, 1960, differ all too little from those of, say 1920 (excepting, of course in the socio-political ideology and concrete examples), and the aim is far more to prescribe than to describe. The compilation of linguistic data from dialects and older texts has continued, and much has been made available in useful form. Lexicography is in particularly good shape. The monumental Zagreb dictionary of Serbo-Croatian, started in 1880, seemed dead after 1935, but publication resumed in 1952 and has proceded apace, so that one can believe it will be completed, perhaps even by 1970. The Serbian Academy has at last brought out the first volume of its own dictionary, which will take at least twenty years to complete. The Macedonians have published the first half of a fairly comprehensive lexicon, with glosses in Serbo-Croatian, and the other volume will apparently be ready in a couple of years. The Slovenes alone are far behind here; they seem only to have discussed plans for starting a dictionary, but no concrete steps have yet been made.

Publication is not centralized or particularly well organized. The *Južnoslovenski filolog* (Belgrade, 1912-) continues to be the leading linguistic journal, but some articles of broader appeal have been printed in the *Slavistična revija* (Ljubljana, 1948-) and scattered in the serial publications of the academies and universities (e.g. the Ivićes regularly contribute to the Novi Sad Yearbook – *Godišnjak filozofskog fakulteta u Novom Sadu*, 1956-). The *Južnoslovenski filolog* is particularly valuable for its annotated running bibliography of all works on language and linguistics published in Yugoslavia. One hears with dismay that the extraordinarily helpful notes and resumés are now to be omitted, but nonetheless the complete listing will be useful. (A warning: *JF* does *not* list any works published abroad, even those by Yugoslav authors.) The contributions in the little journals devoted to the individual languages (e.g. *Makedonski jazik*, *Naš jezik* [Belgrade], *Jezik* [Zagreb], or the wider *Jezik in slovstvo* ([Ljubljana]) interest the Slavic specialist, but only rarely – at least so far, one adds hopefully – does one find new theories applied or even suggested.

As late as ten years ago, the narrow local isolationist traditions all over Yugoslavia were still so strong that the various centers had only the most tenuous contacts. Even the senior scholars knew each other chiefly through written discussions, often acrimonious, or from meeting abroad at international conferences, while the younger men often did not have any idea of the interests and work of their opposite numbers. As a part of the general effort to weld the provinces and localities into a real nation, communications between Yugoslav scholars has been officially encouraged of late. In Slavic studies this has taken the form of organized, indeed rather elaborate, biannual conferences with papers and seminars and open discussions. There has been a somewhat greater exchange of students and younger teachers, and more frequent appearance of guest lecturers in all the university centers. It seems safe to say that the chief result has been to prepare the ground for a revolution in the linguistic thought and practice. The young people, eager in any case to reject the past, have separately and collectively discovered exciting notions in the work of Czech, Polish, Russian, and even American linguists, and they are pressing to hear more about the new ideas precisely because of the reluctance, or even active opposition, of most of their professors. Yugoslav linguistics is – on the surface – still resolutely a solid fifty years behind America and the Soviet Union, but there is every reason to hope that there will be astonishing breakthroughs during the 1960's.

# BIOGRAPHICAL NOTES

ROBERT H. ABERNATHY (1924-) received degrees from University of Arizona and Harvard University, and is presently Associate Professor of Slavic Linguistics at the University of Washington in Seattle. His interests in mathematical linguistics and poetics are reflected in his published articles. He is now compiling a dictionary of Russian roots, and translating a work in Russian on speech mechanisms on a commission from the Committee for the Promotion of Advanced Slavic Cultural Studies.

HAIM BLANC (1926-) was born in Rumania and spent his childhood in Paris. He did undergraduate work at Harvard University and took his doctorate at Hebrew University in Jerusalem, where he has been teaching since 1955 with a two-year interruption on a research fellowship at Harvard Center for Middle Eastern Studies. His publications include a textbook for Spoken Israeli Hebrew and many works on Arabic dialects.

GYULA DÉCSY (1925-) belongs to the generation of Hungarian linguists that received the major portion of its training after the Second World War. After completing his studies at the University of Budapest in 1948 he joined the staff of the Hungarian Academy of Sciences. Since 1956 he has been living in Western Germany, teaches Finno-Ugric Philology at the University of Hamburg, and is currently Visiting Associate Professor in Uralic and Altaic Studies at Indiana University. He is a coeditor of the periodical *Ural-Altaische Jahrbücher*.

PAUL L. GARVIN (1919-) received his early schooling in Czechoslovakia, and completed graduate studies in linguistics at Indiana University. He has taught at the University of Oklahoma and Georgetown University, and done research at Columbia University and the Bureau of Social Science Research in Washington, D.C. Since 1960 he has been Manager of Linguistic Projects at Thompson Ramo Wooldridge Inc. and also teaches part-time at the University of California in Los Angeles.

ZBIGNIEW GOŁĄB (1923-), a native of Poland, completed his doctoral studies at the University of Krakow with a dissertation on Macedonian dialects, and has since broadened his specialty to include many areas of Comparative Slavic and Indo-

European. Before coming to the United States in 1961 he was on the staff of the Polish Academy of Sciences and Arts and taught at the Catholic University of Lublin. He is presently teaching Slavic linguistics as Visiting Associate Professor at the University of Chicago.

MORRIS HALLE (1923-) came to the United States from Latvia, studied at the City College of New York, the University of Chicago, Columbia University, and completed doctoral work at Harvard under Professor Roman Jakobson, with whom he collaborated on a number of important publications. He has held fellowships from the J. S. Guggenheim Memorial Foundation and the Center for Advanced Study in the Behavioral Sciences. In 1963 he was elected Fellow of the American Academy of Arts and Sciences. Since 1951 he has been on the faculty of the Massachusetts Institute of Technology where he is now Professor in the Department of Modern Languages. His list of publications reflects his interest in acoustic phonetics, the theoretical foundations of phonology, and the study of the Slavic languages.

KENNETH E. HARPER (1918-) received his doctorate at Columbia University, where he studied at the Russian Institute. His papers on research in machine translation have been widely read at national and international conferences, and he is personally acquainted with several Soviet researchers in the same field. Present research in automatic language analysis includes studies on combinatorial properties of Russian nouns, adjectives, and verbs, and distributional semantics. He is presently Associate Professor of Slavic Languages at the University of California in Los Angeles and Consultant to the Rand Corporation.

VALENTIN KIPARSKY (1904-) moved to Finland from St. Petersburg as a boy, and is a Finnish citizen. He studied at Helsinki University and the University of Prague, and did research in several Baltic countries and in Paris. His long and varied career encompasses thirty years of teaching and lecturing in most European countries and the United States, and government service during the war years. His books and articles are written in 10 different languages. Since 1958 he has been Director of the East European Institute at the Free University of West Berlin.

JOHN R. KRUEGER (1927-) took degrees at the George Washington University and the University of Washington. As Fulbright scholar to the Central Asian Institute, he studied Turko-Mongolian languages and history at the University of Copenhagen, and has written extensively in Altaic and American Indian areas. After teaching at the University of Washington, Reed College, and the University of California at Berkeley, he assumed his present position at Indiana University in the Uralic-Altaic Program where, among other projects, he is developing a teaching program in Turkish.

AERT H. KUIPERS (1919-) received his academic training in Holland and the U.S.A.

He taught at the University of British Columbia, Columbia University and, since 1960, at the University of Leiden, where he is Professor of Balto-Slavic and Caucasian languages. He is editor of *Studia Caucasica*.

HORACE G. LUNT (1918-) received his doctorate at Columbia University after studying at Harvard, the University of California at Berkeley, and Charles University in Prague. He has written books on Old Church Slavonic, Macedonian, and Russian, and articles on various Slavic topics, chiefly comparative and historical linguistics. He joined the Harvard faculty in 1949 and became Chairman of the Department of Slavic Languages and Literatures in 1959.

ROSE NASH (1923-), a native Chicagoan, earned degrees at Northwestern University and Middlebury College. After several years as supervisory linguist with the Indiana University Intensive Language Center, directing the teaching of Russian, she resumed graduate work toward a Ph.D. degree in Linguistics with a concentration in Altaic studies at the same university. During 1963-4, she will continue to study Turkish under an NDEA Title VI Fellowship at the University of California (Los Angeles).

JACOB ORNSTEIN (1915-) was one of the first native-born American scholars to work in the Slavic and East European field – an interest unusual in the 30's. Receiving his degrees at Ohio State University and the University of Wisconsin, he has taught at a number of schools and investigated Soviet language teaching at Harvard's Russian Research Center. He has also written many articles dealing with Eastern European language policies and reforms, and a monograph on the status of Slavic and East European studies in the Western Hemisphere for the Department of State. In 1941 he helped to found the American Association of Slavic and East European Languages. On the staff of *Modern Language Journal* until recently, he is now with the Graduate School of the U.S. Department of Agriculture, serving also on the Panel of Examiners for Polish for the U.S. Civil Service Commission.

NICHOLAS POPPE (1897-) was born in China and brought up in Russia. He lived in Leningrad until World War II, and his long academic career in the Soviet Union was closely tied to his professorship at Leningrad University, where he had studied Oriental languages. He taught also at the Leningrad Geography Institute, and was a member of the Academy of Sciences. He made numerous linguistic expeditions to Outer Mongolia and Eastern Siberia, publishing more than 300 books and articles on these areas. After leaving the USSR during the war he joined the faculty of the University of Berlin, and, since 1949, has been Professor at the Far Eastern and Russian Institute of the University of Washington.

WILLIAM R. SCHMALSTIEG (1929-) is Associate Professor of Russian at the University of Minnesota. He has served on the staffs of the *Kentucky Foreign Language Quarterly* and *General Linguistics* and is an associate bibliographer of the Modern Language Association. He has contributed articles and reviews on Baltic and Slavic linguistics to journals here and abroad, and is presently working on a practical grammar of Lithuanian.

THOMAS A. SEBEOK (1920-) is a native of Budapest who has lived in the United States since 1937. After studying literary criticism, anthropology, and linguistics at the University of Chicago, he earned his doctorate at Princeton University in Oriental languages and civilizations. He has been a member of the Indiana University faculty in Linguistics since 1943, and for the past eight years has served as Chairman of the University's Research Center in Anthropology, Folklore, and Linguistics. For many years he was also Chairman of Uralic and Altaic Studies, served as the first Director of the Uralic and Altaic Language and Area Center, and has continued, since 1960, as Editor of the *Uralic and Altaic Series*. He has held fellowships from the John Simon Guggenheim Memorial Foundation and the Center for Advanced Study in the Behavioral Sciences. He organized and, until 1963, was Chairman of the Committee on Linguistic Information. Currently he is also Director of the Linguistic Institute. His major research interest centers on the Uralic languages and peoples; his list of publications includes books on Hungarian and Finnish and a series of monographs on the Cheremis.

GEORGE Y. SHEVELOV (1908-) completed his studies at the University of Kharkov and remained to teach Slavic linguistics. In 1945 he moved to Munich, where he was on the faculty of the Ukrainian Free University, and subsequently carried out teaching assignments at the University of Lund in Sweden, Harvard University, and Columbia University, the post he has occupied since 1954. His many published books and articles deal with historical, comparative, and contemporary aspects of Slavic, in particular, the Eastern Slavic languages. He has been a Guggenheim Fellow and past President of the Ukrainian Academy of Arts and Sciences in the United States.

EDWARD STANKIEWICZ (1920-), a native of Poland, completed his doctoral work at Harvard University, taught for a number of years at Indiana University, and is now Professor of Slavic Linguistics at the University of Chicago. He has held grants from the Ford Foundation and the American Council of Learned Societies, and made field trips to Europe to do research in Slovenian dialectology and Serbo-Croatian linguistics. His publications include works on phonemic typology, kinship terminology, Slavic versification, poetic language, structural dialectology, and Slavic morphology and morphophonemics.

GÜNTER J. STIPA (1907-) was born in Upper Silesia and studied philosophy in Holland. While teaching in Estonia he began to study Balto-Finnic languages. After the incorporation of Estonia into the Soviet Union in 1940 he moved to Vienna, where he continued his theological studies at the University of Vienna. Serving for a time as pastor in Berlin, he earned a doctorate in Slavic and Finno-Ugric Philology at the University of Göttingen, where he is now lecturer, in addition to his instructorship in German at the University of Helsinki. His special interest is the Permic and Volgaic groups of Finno-Ugric languages. His discoveries on the origin of the Permic alphabet and the results of a research trip to the Komi Republic in 1961 have been accorded recognition in scientific circles.

KIRIL TARANOVSKI (1911-) was born in Estonia and moved to Yugoslavia in 1920. He studied law and Slavistics at the University of Belgrade, and spent some time at Charles University in Prague. After many years on the faculty of Belgrade University he came to the University of California at Los Angeles in 1959 and, since January 1963, has been Professor of Slavic Languages and Literatures at Harvard University.

CORNELIS H. VAN SCHOONEVELD (1921-) was born in The Netherlands, where he received his initial training in Slavic philology at the University of Leiden with N. van Wijk. He was Professor of Baltic and Slavic Languages at the same University from 1952 until 1959, when he was appointed Professor of Slavic Languages and Literatures at Stanford. During the years of his Leiden professorship he was the Dutch member of the International Committee of Slavists. His main research is in structural semantics, diachronic as well as synchronic. His publications include, in addition to articles, books on semantic analysis of the Old Russian finite preterite system and the sentence intonation of Contemporary Standard Russian. He is the editor of "Slavistic Printings and Reprintings", the monograph series "Janua Linguarum", and a coeditor of the *International Journal of Slavic Linguistics and Poetics*.

URIEL WEINREICH (1926-) is the Chairman of the Department of Linguistics and Professor of Yiddish Language, Literature, and Culture on the Atran Chair at Columbia University, where he received his academic training. He is editor of *The Field of Yiddish*, director of the Language and Culture Atlas of Ashkenazic Jewry, and principal investigator in a study of the semantic structure of natural languages.
WERNER WINTER (1923-) was born in Germany and educated in Germany, Switzerland, and the United States. His research centers around general linguistics, Indo-European, Tocharian, and Armenian, and he is presently preparing a monograph on stylistics of Russian and Czech. He is Professor of Germanic and Slavic Languages at the University of Texas.

DEAN S. WORTH (1927-) studied at the Phillips Exeter Academy, Dartmouth College, the School of Oriental Languages and the Sorbonne in Paris, and at Harvard University, where he took the doctorate in 1956. He has taught at Dartmouth, Harvard, and, since 1957, at the University of California in Los Angeles, where he is Associate Professor of Slavic Languages. He is active in several scholarly organizations and has taken part in international congresses here and abroad. His principal scholarly interests are the structural analysis of modern Russian, the comparative and historical analysis of Paleosiberian languages, especially Kamchadal, the older periods of Russian literature, and problems of general linguistics, especially syntactic theory.

VALDIS J. ZEPS (1932-), a native of Latvia, came to the United States in 1950. He earned degrees from Miami University (Ohio) and Indiana University, and now teaches at the University of Wisconsin. He did research as a Regular Post-doctoral Fellow of the National Science Foundation at the Center for Advanded Study in the Behavioral Sciences. He has also lectured on Old Church Slavonic at Georgetown University and worked with the Office of Geography of the U.S. Department of the Interior. He has written on linguistic convergences in Latvian and Finnic, and is currently working on a generative grammar of Latvian and on the morphophonemics of Latgalian.

# LINGUISTIC INDEX

To conform to the usage of some authors, the Index retains a few descriptive words (as Old, New, General, Ancient) as main entries cross-referring them to the language. Geographical and historical terms and dialects are listed under the head language.

# INDEX OF NAMES

Initial Ǝ comes after Z